THE STRUCTURE OF THE LEGAL ENVIRONMENT OF BUSINESS

 THIRD EDITION

Bill Shaw
University of Texas at Austin

Art Wolfe
Michigan State University

Steve Salbu
University of Texas at Austin

SOUTH-WESTERN College Publishing

An International Thomson Publishing Company

Publisher/Team Director: Valerie Ashton
Sponsoring Editor: Robert Dewey
Developmental Editor: Kurt Gerdenich
Production Editor: Sue Ellen Brown
Marketing Manager: Scott Person
Cover Designer: Joseph M. Devine
Production House: A. W. Kingston Publishing
Team Assistants: Ronda Faulkner, Cory Broadfoot, B. J. Parker

LE68CA
Copyright © 1996
by South-Western College Publishing
Cincinnati, Ohio

Library of Congress Cataloging-in-Publication Data

Shaw, Bill
   The structure of the legal environment of business / Bill M. Shaw,
Art D. Wolfe, Steve R. Salbu. — 3rd ed.
     p.   cm.
   Includes bibliographical refrences and index.
   ISBN 0-538-84428-0 (hard cover : acid-free paper)
   1. Industrial laws and legislation—United States. 2. Trade
regulation—United States. 3. Commercial law—United States.
4. Business ethics—United States. 5. Industry—Social aspects—
United States. I. Wolfe, Arthur D. II. Salbu, Steven R., 1957– .
III. Title
KF1600.S483 1996
346.73'07–dc20   95-31396
[347.3067]   CIP

I(T)P International Thomson Publishing
South-Western College Publishing is an ITP Company.
The ITP trademark is used under license.

♲ This book is printed on acid-free paper that meets Environmental Protection
Agency standards for recyled paper.

1 2 3 4 5 6 K 0 9 8 7 6 5
Printed in the United States of America

Brief Contents

Contents

TWO *Commercial Law: Traditional and Emerging Concepts   177*

8 *Contract Law*   302

FOUR *Classic and Emerging Issues in the Legal Environment of Business   569*

Preface

The third edition of *The Structure of the Legal Environment of Business* offers three new chapters—Chapter 5, Business Crimes, Chapter 6, Private Property, Law, and the Control of Economic Power, Chapter 14, Employment Law: Discrimination and Equal Opportunity—updated and timely new cases, and the addition of a new author, Steven Salbu, to our team. The basic premise of the book, however, remains unchanged. We provide a broad view of the complex legal issues and questions that affect business with the hope that students learn more than simply a set of rules to follow; rather, students learn how to perceive, discuss, and reflect upon the ambiguous nature of our legal environment. This understanding of not just legal rules, but the structure of the legal environment of business, including its legal rules, ethical principles, and business practices, is essential for success in business.

The Structure of the Legal Environment of Business contains a mixture of three types of material. First, we provide in our own textual material a discussion of the law as we see it. Second, we include excerpts from relevant court decisions, in the language of the court, in which judges define and apply the rules of our legal system. Third, we collect the best writings we know of addressing law and public policy. These include excerpts from law review articles, various opinion pieces from national journals (e.g., the Harvard Business Review), a classic parable from Kafka, and essays that address the problems of the structural biases in our legal system.

These sources are arranged to explore the three major themes of this text. First, we start the study of law with a discussion of the rules that form the basis of our legal system.

However, a list of rules to memorize is not sufficient. Students need to understand how these rules are applied. Thus, we provide an explicit treatment of the nature of our moral and ethical values and the methods of discourse that underpin and surround the application of these rules. Material on ethics is found in all chapters and in a variety of forms.

Finally, students must understand why these rules arise in the first place. Rules and ethical ideas are not created from, nor are they applied in, a social vacuum. We present a realistic picture of the legal environment of business and the circumstances to which these rules and ideas are a response. Some or these circumstances are identifiable as the underlying structures that shape our business society. The most powerful of these are the large business corporation and the federal government.

In short, we represent in this book our own view of legal education. We distinguish education from training, which is the process of narrowing one's perspective to accomplish a specific task. Rather, we show students the broad legal, ethical, and social structures in which business operates. We cannot provide obvious and easy solutions to the problems that these structures impose. Simply, there are none. In many areas we explain and then challenge the legal and commercial patterns often established by nothing more than the raw use of power or the conditioning of unthinking experience. Rather, we teach students how to become active and effective participants in the legal environment of business.

We thank the following reviewers of this edition, and of prior editions, for their helpful comments and suggestions:

Mark. A. Buchanan
St. Cloud State University

John Collins
Syracuse University

Daniel V. Davidson
Radford University

Murray Diamond
Hofstra University

William G. Elliott
Saginaw Valley State University

Ronald R. Glassman
Kent State University

Michael E. Howard
University of Iowa

Marianne M. Jennings
Arizona State University

Thomas M. Kerr
Carnegie-Mellon University

Elliot Klayman
Ohio State University

Janice Loutzenhiser
California State University, San Bernadino

Bradley J. McDonald
Northern Illinois University

Sharlene A. McEvoy
Fairfield University

Nancy R. Mansfield
Georgia State University

Gregory J. Naples
Marquette University

Elwood F. Oakley, III
Georgia State University

James Owens
California State University, Chico

Michael W. Pustay
Texas A&M University

Lawrence W. Ross
University of Oregon

Linda B. Samuels
George Mason University

S. Jay Sklar
Temple University

George Spiro
University of Massachusetts

William Vanderpool
Appalachian State University

Burke T. Ward
Villanova University

Wayne R. Wells
St. Cloud State University

Fran Zollers
Syracuse University

About the Authors

Bill Shaw holds a B.S. in business administration and an MBA from Louisiana Tech University, a J.D. from Tulane University, and an LL.M. from the University of Texas. He is currently Professor of Business Law at the University of Texas, Austin. Professor Shaw has served as President of the American Business Law Association (now the Academy of Legal Studies in Business).

Art Wolfe holds both a B.A. in history and a J.D. from the Ohio State University, as well as an M.A. in economics from the University of Illinois. He is currently Professor of Business Law and Public Policy at Michigan State University. Professor Wolfe has been a visiting scholar with both the Business Policy Group and the Public Policy Group at the University of California, Berkeley, as well as a visiting scholar with the Kellogg School of Management at Northwestern University.

Steve Salbu holds a B.A. in psychology and music from Hofstra University, a J.D. from the College of William and Mary, an M.A. in liberal studies from Dartmouth College, and an Ph.D. in organization and strategy from the Wharton School, University of Pennsylvania. He currently is Associate Professor of Business Law at the University of Texas, Austin, a position in which he has won four teaching awards. Professor Salbu is also a Senior Consultant with Strategic Management Group facilitating corporate education programs. Professor Salbu has been a visiting scholar at the Wharton School, University of Pennsylvania.

Dedications

BILL SHAW   To my students, my family, and my new grandson Willie.

ART WOLFE   To the memory of my father, Allen H. Wolfe.

STEVE SALBU   To my parents with love and thanks.

Introduction to the Study of the American Legal Environment

Part One examines the fundamentals of the U.S. legal system. Chapter 1 explains the nature of our legal rules and presents the major groupings of ideas that interpret those rules. The study of the philosophy of law and of legal rules is called jurisprudence, which literally means the study of legal wisdom or the wisdom of the law. Why do we have law? and Where is it taking us? are two questions that dominate this field.

In the first chapter, we also examine the nature of our American morality and some of the dominant ethical theories of today and the past, and discuss the process of "moral reasoning." We end the chapter with a parable from the Harvard Business Review that illustrates the nature of many moral dilemmas today: We are torn between our obligations to others and our commitments to make meaningful lives for ourselves.

Chapter 2 presents a detailed picture of the structure and operation of our legal system. We explain the contributions of the civil law and common law systems and find that ours is a unique blend of the two. We survey the types of rules and the various levels of courts in our legal system. Law and legal systems, however, are not without their problems. One such problem, illustrated by Franz Kafka, is that law breeds an elite of sorts: the class of professionals (lawyers) who interpret and apply the law for us. We describe the part that lawyers, judges, and the jury play in our legal system and then turn to the writing of Jerome Frank to provide insights that are often overlooked in introductory materials. Finally, a short story by B. Traven suggests that all legal and economic systems are systems of belief that often blind us to the patterns in other cultures.

The Social and Ethical Responsibility of Corporate Management, Chapter 3, develops a framework and preents applications of moral behavior. It explores corporate culture, corporate social responsibility, and closes by relating these concepts to the Johnson & Johnson Tylenol case.

A formal study of the law and legal rules begins with Chapter 4, the U.S. Constitution. We have presented cases, text, and readings on the basics of the Constitution, and on the important constitutional principles that apply in the legal environment of business.

CHAPTER 1

Introduction to the Study of the Legal Environment of Business

Justice, the protection of life, the sanctity of property, the direction of social control—these fundamentals are the business of the law. . . .

★ ★ ★

Only a limited degree of legal certainty can be attained. The current demand for exactness and predictability in law is incapable of satisfaction because a greater degree of legal finality is sought than is procurable, desirable or necessary. [Frank, J., *Law and the Modern Mind*, 3, 11 (1930)]

INTRODUCTION

If laws were unchanging and if human behavior were simple, then the study of law would be a matter of memorizing fixed rules and the situations they govern. You would merely commit to memory the constitutions and statute books of federal, state, and local governments, the rulings of administrative agencies, and the opinions of courts. But the study of law is not this simple. The legal system reflects the energy of life within society. The law has the complex vitality of a living organism. Do not think of the law as a social system characterized by the deadweight of inert and fixed rules. Think of it, instead, as an area of study characterized by action—by growth and change.

The materials in this book reflect our shared belief that a university-level explanation of the legal environment of business must focus on three major subjects. The first is an understanding of legal rules, but memorization is not an adequate way to deal with them. Rules are the written expression of public policy found in the constitutions, statute books, and court opinions of federal and state governments and in the rulings of administrative agencies. So it is convenient to begin this study with a statement of the most significant rules that we believe are applicable to the business environment.

A singular focus on rules presents a sterile and lifeless picture, however. There are reasons for rules. A study of these reasons reveals their moral content. That is, rules are neither created nor applied in a vacuum; rather, they are created and used time and again for a purpose. Rules are intended to accomplish some objective; they are intended to either move people in a certain direction assumed to be "good" or desirable or prohibit movement in a direction believed to be "bad" or undesirable. Thus, an explicit treatment of the moral basis of the rules found in the legal environment of business is the second major subject of focus.

What complicates the task significantly is that although one may understand the rules and the reasons for them, they are without value unless the rules can be applied to present-day events, to current commercial reality, in a way that is consistent with the reasons for the rules. In light of this, the third subject of focus in this book is a discussion of the events and societal structures that we believe constitute the current commercial reality. Because these events and societal structures are always moving and always changing, it is fitting to speak of commercial "life."

In sum, this book focuses on three themes: *(1) rules or statements of desired conduct, (2) the moral ideals that permeate these rules and that give them direction and meaning, and (3) the circumstances or "facts" of social and commercial life.* These three themes are the essential elements of our definition of law itself, which should be thought of as much more than a statement of rules. Law is best expressed as a statement of a rule, the circumstances in which it is applied, and the reasons that it is applied as it is.

THE NATURE OF LEGAL RULES: THE APPELLATE CASE AS TEXT

We could begin our study of the law with the recitation of rules from the rule or statute books, but this is an almost meaningless task because rules and statements alone are boring and lifeless. Unless rules are presented in a social context, they disappear from one's memory almost as quickly as they are read or memorized. Rules come to life when one sees their application to real-life situations.

Rule application takes place most prominently in the court system, which is a social setting established and controlled by the state and federal governments. The most basic or first level of this system is the trial courts. You probably already have a rather accurate view of how a trial court operates. Here, we present just a sketch of the trial court process; in the Appendix of Chapter 2, we present a detailed account of this process.

The plaintiff or the party bringing the case first introduces its evidence into a court presided over by a judge. The evidence is tested by the opposing party—the defendant—who objects if the evidence seems irrelevant or is so stimulating to a jury that they cannot objectively evaluate it. When the plaintiff (an individual, a business entity such as a corporation, or, in criminal cases, the state or federal government) is finished, the defendant (an individual or business entity) introduces its evidence. This evidence may be challenged by objections and the cross-examination of the plaintiff. After all of the evidence is in, the judge reads the appropriate rules to the jury. The members of the jury apply the rules to the facts as they believe them to be and thus decide the matters at issue. In some cases, the judge may sit without a jury (a "bench" trial) and decide the issues alone.

Once a judgment has been made, the case may be appealed to the next level in the court system, the appellate courts. In an appellate court, three or more judges review the evidence introduced in the trial court, listen to and read the legal arguments of the parties, and then make their decision. Such decisions are often printed and made available to the public. Because they carefully reproduce the happenings or the "stories" that unfolded in the trial court and because they carefully state the rules applied, appellate decisions integrate the sterile rules with the activity of everyday life and are thus rich with meaning.

Appellate decisions are a kind of real-life text of social existence. They not only demonstrate rules in action but also often unknowingly reveal individual and collective notions of morality as well. They are excellent examples of how beliefs and ideals are put into practice. Plainly stated, the law, and printed appellate cases in particular, are statements about the experiences of a society. So, in every meaning of the word, they are a text; they are the words, thoughts, and actions people reveal about how they should live with one another.

The law and appellate decisions are complex and often contain many layers of meaning. We demonstrate this point with the following excerpt from an old English appellate opinion. Read this decision and ask yourself how this case should be decided.

Regina v. *Dudley and Stephens*
Queens Bench Division, 1884
14 Q.B.D. 273

LORD COLERIDGE, CHIEF JUSTICE

[O]n July 5, 1884, the prisoners, Thomas Dudley and . . . Stephens, with one Brooks, all able-bodied English seamen, and the deceased also an English boy, between seventeen and eighteen years of age, the crew of an English yacht, . . . were cast away in a storm on the high seas 1,600 miles from the Cape of Good Hope, and were compelled to put into an open boat belonging to the said yacht. That in this boat they had no supply of water and no supply of food, except two 1 lb. tins of turnips, and for three days they had nothing else to subsist upon. That on the fourth day they caught a small turtle, upon which they subsisted for a few days, and this was the only food they had up to the twentieth day when the act now in question was committed. . . . That on the 24th of July, the day before the act now in question, the prisoner Dudley proposed to Stephens and Brooks that lots should be cast who should be put to death to save the rest. But Brooks refused to consent, and it was not put to the boy, and in point of fact there was no drawing of lots. That on the day the prisoners spoke of their families, and suggested it would be better to kill the boy that their lives should be saved, and Dudley proposed that if there was no vessel in sight by the morrow morning the boy should be killed. That next day, the 25th of July, no vessel appearing, Dudley told Brooks that he had better go and have a sleep, and made signs to Stephens and Brooks that the boy had better be killed. The prisoner Stephens agreed to the act, but Brooks dissented from it. That the boy was then lying at the bottom of the boat quite helpless and extremely weakened by famine and by drinking sea water, and unable to make any resistance, nor did he ever assent to his being killed. The prisoner Dudley offered a prayer asking forgiveness for them all if either of them should be tempted to commit a rash act, and that their souls might be saved. That Dudley, with the assent of Stephens, went to the boy, and telling him that his time was come, put a knife into his throat and killed him then and there; that the three men fed upon the body and blood of the boy for four days; that on the fourth day after the act had been committed the boat was picked up by a passing vessel, and the prisoners were rescued, still alive, but in the lowest state of prostration. That they were carried to the port of Falmouth, and committed for trial at Exeter. That if the men had not fed upon the body of the boy they would probably not have survived to be so picked up and rescued, but would within the four days have died of famine. That the boy, being in a much weaker condition, was likely to have died before them. That at the time of the act in question there was no sail in sight, nor any reasonable prospect of relief. That under these circumstances there appeared to the prisoners every probability that unless they then fed or very soon fed upon the boy or one of themselves they would die of starvation. That there was no appreciable chance of saving life except by killing some one for the others to eat. . . .

. . . [T]he real question in the case [is] whether killing under the circumstances set forth in the verdict be or be not murder. The contention that it could be anything else was, to the minds of us all, both new and strange. . . . First it is said that it follows from various definitions of murder in books of authority, which definitions imply, if they do not state, the doctrine, that in order to save your own life you may lawfully take away the life of another, when that other is neither attempting nor threatening yours, nor is guilty of any illegal act whatever towards you or any one else. But if these definitions be looked at they will not be found to sustain this contention. . . .

It is . . . clear . . . that the doctrine contended for receives no support from the great authority of Lord Hale. It is plain that in his view the necessity which justified homicide is that only which has always been and is now considered a justification. . . . Lord Hale regarded the private necessity which justified, and alone justified, the taking the life of another for the safeguard of one's own to be what is commonly called "self-defence." (Hale's Pleas of the Crown, i. 478)

But if this could be even doubtful upon Lord Hale's words, Lord Hale himself has made it clear. For in the chapter in which he deals with the exemption created by compulsion or necessity he thus expresses himself:—"If a man be desperately assaulted and in peril of death, and cannot otherwise escape unless, to satisfy his assailant's fury, he will kill an innocent person then present, the fear and actual force will not acquit him of the crime and punishment of murder, if he commit the fact, for he ought rather to die himself than kill an innocent; but if he cannot otherwise save his own life the law permits him in his own defence to kill the assailant. . . . "

⋆ ⋆ ⋆

. . . [W]e exclude from our consideration all the incidents of war. We are dealing with a case of private homicide, not one imposed upon men in the service of their Sovereign and in the defence of their country. Now it is admitted that the deliberate killing of this unoffending and unresisting boy was clearly murder, unless the killing can be justified by some well-recognized excuse admitted by the law. It is further admitted that there was in this case no such excuse, unless the killing was justified by what has been called "necessity." But the temptation to the act which existed here was not what the law has ever called necessity. Nor is this to be regretted. Though law and morality are not the same, and many things may be immoral which are not necessarily illegal, yet the absolute divorce of law from morality would be of fatal consequence; and such divorce would follow if the temptation to murder in this case were to be held by law an absolute defence of it. It is not so. To preserve one's life is generally speaking a duty, but it may be the plainest and the highest duty to sacrifice it. War is full of instances in which it is a man's duty not to live, but to die. . . . [T]hese duties impose on men the moral necessity, not of the preservation, but of the sacrifice of their lives for others. . . . It is not needful to point out the awful danger of admitting the principle which has been contended for. Who is to be the judge of this sort of necessity? By what measure is the comparative value of lives to be measured? Is it to be strength, or intellect, or what? It is plain that the principle leaves to him who is to profit by it to determine the necessity which will justify him in deliberately taking another's life to save his own. In this case the weakest, the youngest, the most unresisting, was chosen. Was it more necessary to kill him than one of the grown men? The answer must be "No"—

[I]t is quite plain that such a principle once admitted might be made the legal cloak for unbridled passion and atrocious crime. There is no safe path for judges to tread but to ascertain the law to the best of their ability and to declare it according to their judgment; and if in any case the law appears to be too severe on individuals, to leave it to the Sovereign to exercise that prerogative of mercy which the Constitution has intrusted to the hands fittest to dispense it.

It must not be supposed that in refusing to admit temptation to be an excuse for crime it is forgotten how terrible the temptation was; how awful the suffering; how hard in such trials to keep the judgment straight and the conduct pure. We are often compelled to set up standards we cannot reach ourselves, and to lay down rules which we could not ourselves satisfy. But a man has no right to declare temptation to be an excuse, though he might himself have yielded to it, nor allow compassion for the criminal to change or weaken in any manner the legal definition of the crime. It is therefore our duty to declare that the prisoners' act in this case was wilful murder, that the facts as stated in the verdict are no legal justification of the homicide; and to say that in our unanimous opinion the prisoners are upon this special verdict guilty of Murder.

The Court then proceeded to pass sentence of death upon the prisoners.

CASE FOLLOW-UP

This case, read as a text about society and about law, presents a very complex picture of issues of vital importance to any society.

At a rather simple level, assume a statute (usually a rule passed by some legislative authority) defined murder as follows: "Whoever willfully takes the life of another without justification is guilty of murder." Did these men willfully take the life of another? The answer is obviously "yes." Are they therefore guilty of murder? The issues in this case are not as simple as this cause-and-effect approach makes them seem.

At another level entirely, the case disturbs most people who read it. Why? The answer may be that people often define morality (what they believe is basically right and wrong) by how they believe they would act in a given situation. Many people believe they would act as the sailors did in this case. Indeed, until this case was heard, the custom of the high seas reflected this notion of morality. In England, no one had ever been prosecuted for cannibalism in such circumstances.[1] This lack of prosecution explains why the captain of the ship, Tom Dudley, dutifully wrote a full account of the act when he returned to port. He, the crew, and the public never expected a prosecution for murder in such a case.

How can this prosecution be explained? In the latter part of the nineteenth century, England was experiencing an era of commitment to notions of a "high-sounding" morality influenced by the court and government of Queen Victoria. The ruling class viewed itself as the pinnacle of civilization. Its agents were out conquering the subcontinent of India and large parts of Africa in the name of the British Empire. Cannibalism was something that happened in other parts of the world in which the "great civilization of The Empire" had not taken root. To the upper classes, cannibalism under any circumstances was unthinkable. One hallmark of this perceived "great" civilization was the abiding belief in law. The proponents of Victorian England preached that they were a society of laws, not of men and women. The unfortunate men of the sailing Yacht *Mignonette* (the ship in the *Dudley* case) re-

turned to this social climate in 1884. After Dudley filed his report and the prosecutors heard about the case of death and the word spread to members of the ruling class, the prosecutors arrested and charged the seamen with murder.

In the seagoing communities of England, the outcry was immediate and reflected the custom of the time. The popular sentiment was that it was manifestly unfair to prosecute these men. They were released on bail but were ultimately convicted of murder. The high moral tone of the ruling classes was satisfied; law had triumphed and civilization had moved forward. The public discontent in the sea towns, however, would not die down. Finally, the establishment relented and Sir William Harcourt, the Home Secretary in Queen Victoria's government, recommended to the Queen that the death penalty be commuted. She agreed and set punishment at six months' imprisonment.

The uproar over the case raises a key question about the law as a reflection of morality: Whose morality does the law reflect? Men who actually went to sea saw the acts of the convicted seamen as moral and not punishable. Members of the Victorian court saw the cannibalism as a heinous crime and sought the imposition of the full force of the law.

A lesson one can take from this case is that often the law reflects the general morality of society, but sometimes it does not. In some instances, a disagreement occurs because of differing social, historical, and economic perspectives. These various perspectives present significant tensions in the law. Abortion and the proper remedies for discrimination based on race, gender, national origin, age, and religion are a few examples in today's society.

This case also reveals much about the nature of legal rules. First, rules may appear to be absolute, permanent, and without exception. What more absolute rule is there than the prohibition against willfully taking another's life? But, as the reduction of the punishment to six months indicates, *rules are likely to have exceptions that can be justified under certain circumstances.* Rules will probably have exceptions because the rule makers are not sufficiently thoughtful and farsighted to anticipate all situations to which the rules will be applied.

Second, the ability of rule makers to write perfect rules is severely limited because their vocabularies (ultimately, their intellect) is too impoverished to penetrate and give voice to feelings and emotions. The case also demonstrates that law is both content and process. The content here is the rule; the process is the method of reasoning that the judge uses in the opinion. Legal reasoning is not a formal type of reasoning such as inductive or deductive reasoning. It is more informal and can be described as a process of reasoning by analogy.

In the opinion, the judge cited other justices and legal scholars and their opinions based on certain examples. By saying that this case is more like a particular example or not like the example, as the case may be, the judge reached a conclusion. Legal opinions, rule application, and the very process of judging are not done in a vacuum. Citing previous cases and arguments by noted judges and scholars is a hallmark of the legal process and legal reasoning.

Finally, this case illustrates a kind of tension between individuals and groups that is discussed in more detail later in this chapter. Were the Victorians wrong? A civilized nation needs certain rules to enhance the security and well-being of individuals. One of these rules is the prohibition against murder. In some instances, however, rules necessary to preserve the individual may seem plainly wrong when applied to a group such as those in the lifeboat.

But can the rules be said to be wrong from the point of view of Richard Parker, the victim? He was the subject of violent group action while helpless in the lifeboat, and like other individuals in society who threaten no harm, Parker deserved protection. If justice can be conceived as a balance or an equilibrium in the tension between individuals and groups, was the outcome of this case a fair one?

What should the objectives of rules and of the law be? Before we explore some of the possible answers to the question, we remind you that we do not always use the term *rules* and *law* interchangeably. Rules, as we have suggested, refer to the words in constitutions, state books, appellate court opinions, and the like that are short statements of desirable or undesirable human behavior. The word *law* refers to a broader idea. We use the word *law* to communicate the rule, along with the circumstances in which it will be applied. This statement will include the reasons and objectives of the rule.

In short, law is a composite of rules, circumstances, reasons, and objectives. It keys the behavior of those in charge of enforcement and explains when, why, and how they will act. We now return briefly to a discussion of the objectives and reasons for rules and the law.

SCHOOLS OF THOUGHT ABOUT RULES AND THE SCOPE OF LAW

The study of the functions and objectives of law is the study of jurisprudence. Although no single correct version of jurisprudence has emerged during the past 2,500 years of recorded history, some categories or schools of thought about the functions and objectives of law have developed.

What is interesting about these views of jurisprudence is that, even today, one can use one or more of the perspectives to understand and appreciate the law. Often, for example, the U.S. Supreme Court is divided in its opinion, and the justices may write as many as four or five separate opinions. Within these opinions, one can see the present-day refinement of the ideas in these schools of thought. Or, consider that your class may have as many as three or four views of the outcome of the *Dudley* case. Which view is correct? We cannot answer this question, but we can, at least, explore some of the possible answers. In the material that follows, we outline the basic distinguishing characteristics of these schools and present an excerpt from an article that brings into focus the practical implications of knowing these distinguishing characteristics.

THE NATURALIST SCHOOL

The Naturalist School is the oldest body of opinion about the nature of law and dates from before Aristotle. The essence of this school is the view that *law is an expression of an ideal for which humans search*. A branch of this body of thought advances the idea that a deity or a god knows the perfect law and that the function of humans is to try to find, recognize, or achieve this deity's knowledge of law.

For the present inquiry, though, we are more interested in the thought of Aristotle (384–322 B.C.) that was later developed by St. Thomas Aquinas (1224–1274). As scientist and biologist, Aristotle saw a purpose or function (a *telos*) for everything in life. The ultimate purpose of humans was happiness. Human happiness was characterized as a life of rational activity in accordance with virtue; that is, the real purpose of humans was to seek a kind of rational justice. Aristotle spoke of justice as a moral virtue—a character trait or habit of acting justly.

Justice was understood as an objective or unbiased force and, therefore, the same for everyone. This thought distinguished justice from other moral virtues, such as bravery and temperance, that dealt with emotions and passions. These moral virtues were subjective—that is, different for different people. For example, bravery was understood as the midpoint between the extremes of rashness and cowardice, and this point would be different for each person. *Law and justice, then, were ideals that humans could and should pursue through the use of their reasoning abilities.* Morality or "goodness" was part of this reasoning process and, therefore, part of law and justice. All law contained a moral component that would be agreed on through the process of reasoned judgment.

John Locke, an English philosopher who significantly influenced the framers of the U.S. Constitution, was another proponent of natural law. He advanced the view that reason, in itself, was sufficient to teach that men and women are free, autonomous beings. Further, he related that when people mix their labor with the natural resources of the environment (e.g., hunting, trapping, fishing, farming, cutting timber, mining ore), they produce private property that the law should protect. Locke supposed that as a precondition to the acquisition of private property in this manner, "enough" and "as good" would remain for others. Locke's concepts of private property ownership, of freedom to make contracts and to have contract rights respected by others, and of a form of limited representative government that is strong enough to keep peace and order in society and to keep the courts open to enforce contractual bargains are still valid.

THE LEGAL POSITIVISTS OR THE POSITIVE SCHOOL

Perhaps the dominant school for the past 200 years has been that of the legal positivists, which was a response to the naturalist school of thought. The proponents of this school believe that law is like a machine or a chemical—a process or an element that can be analyzed, classified, and studied scientifically. *According to some legal scholars, law lacks moral content and is, simply stated, nothing more than statements of the very word of the sovereign.* These statements include a sovereign's command that entails a purpose and exhibits a power to impose sanctions on those who disobey. *Much of the law that is taught in law schools and business schools today is presented in the positivist tradition.* Law, usually in the form of statutes, court opinions, and other rules generated by a person in authority, is studied and applied with little or no view to the moral content of the rules. These rules are merely classified and arranged in order of priority and applied to various circumstances.

LEGAL REALISM SCHOOL

Oliver Wendell Holmes (1841–1935) and the American "realists" took yet another view of law. "The life of the law has not been logic," said Holmes, "it has been experience." He also said, "The prophecies of what the court will do in fact, and nothing more pretentious, are what I mean by the law." Holmes and the more modern writers in this tradition—Karl Llewellyn and Jerome Frank—pulled away from the positivists and warned scholars against shuffling "paper rules" whether they were the apparent word of the sovereign or not. What counted for them was what officials do about disputes. Rules, by themselves, are very uninformative.

Llewellyn put his philosophy to good use. He was the chief drafter for Article 2 of the Uniform Commercial Code on the Law of Sales, which is a vital part of business law. To draft this code, Llewellyn made a valiant attempt to study the best and most desirable business practices of merchants and then to incorporate them into his code. He realized that the code itself would become static and rigid unless he provided judges with the potential to use their discretion to keep it flexible. He therefore intentionally used the word reasonable more than ninety times in the sales article. Reading that behavior must be "commercially reasonable" often drives students of law crazy because it lacks precision on the printed page; when a court is given the opportunity to decide between competing commercial claims, however, such a standard enables the judge to decide on the best alternative, given the real circumstances. Hence, this view of law is "realistic."

HISTORICAL SCHOOL

The historical school of thought about law and its objectives is mostly European in character and not as dominant in AngloAmerican legal thought as positivism. It was begun by a German scholar, Karl von Friedrich Savigny (1779–1861), and is of fairly recent origin. *The central idea of this school is that a nation's enforced customs are the best example of law and that the objective of legal scholars should be to uncover the historical reasons for the major legal traditions of a society.* The natural law approach and the positivist approach were rejected by historical scholars in favor of a study of custom and tradition peculiar to each state or sovereign. In this sense, law is "found" by scholars and not "made" by the sovereign. Law is rooted in national or folk traditions and not in some ideal that is located by applying reasoned judgment.

The school of thought begun by Henry Maine (1822–1888) in England is closely related to the historical school. In addition to the study of history, Maine emphasized the study of what today is called sociology. He maintained that law incorporates the opinions, beliefs, and superstitions produced by institutions and human nature as they affect one another. To Maine, law could not be divorced from history, but neither could it be divorced from the study of humans, their institutions, and how they interact.

MARXIST VIEWS

The most prominent theorists who provide a historical view of law are Karl Marx (1818–1883) and Friedrich Engels (1820-1895). Although they are not in the mainstream of the historical school, the hallmark of their analysis of society is certainly historical, and law plays an important part in it. Their view was influenced heavily by G.W.F. Hegel (1770–1831), a German philosopher who saw history in terms of a dialectic. A *dialectic* is a process of arriving at a truth by disclosing the contradictions in an opposing point of view. Thus, society evolved through a process of change characterized by the statement of one group of forces (a *thesis*) that became transformed into its opposite (an *antithesis*). These opposing forces were resolved or fulfilled by a combination of the two in a higher form of truth, the *synthesis*. Marx and Engels saw the opposing historical forces as actions by those who owned the means of production and actions by those who worked for the owners, the workers. Of course, they wrote specifically about capitalistic societies and in particular about England. Marx wrote that legislation in England from the end of the Middle Ages to the nineteenth century favored those who owned the means of production (the *bourgeoisie*) over the poor workers who had been driven from their land. According to Marx, the role of law is central to maintaining the power of owners over workers.

Many thoughtful writers have seen law as a reflection of various kinds of class struggles. The Marxist perspective of law and society is based on Marx's observations that access to the means of production through law is the chief characteristic of capitalism and that capitalism will ultimately fail and the workers will create their own government. Of course, Marx's predictions have not come true, but this does not diminish the importance of his observations that much of law is economically motivated and class oriented and that when this is the case, one group usually benefits economically at the expense of the other.

CRITICAL LEGAL STUDIES

Critical legal studies, (CLS) is the name given to a diverse group of legal scholars and educators trying to establish yet another view of law and legal education. Their movement offers not so much a positive new perspective of law as it does a disciplined (and critical) reflection on law and legal education. They assert that legal scholarship and training appear objective and neutral but are loaded with forces that bring about the subtle conditioning of students, practitioners, and ultimately the public. They see law as the structuring of mass consciousness, which in turn serves to reproduce many of the traditional values in society. Law as traditionally conceived masks power relationships in society and perpetuates the existing social order.

CLS scholars analyze law in an attempt to expose the assumptions about individuals and groups implicit in it. Legal doctrine, they say, is presented in law schools and to the public as natural, dependent on history, necessary, inevitable, and in large measure, just. This view, however, serves the interests of those entrenched in power, whether labor unions, school boards, management, or whoever. These interests often work against individual citizens and keep them from imagining a different and better legal order. Even the apparent logic of legal reasoning and scholarly articles in law journals is really a smoke screen for a system that is largely obscure. In short, people do not know as much about law and themselves as a society as the heavy and important-looking writings about law would lead one to believe.

FEMINIST LEGAL STUDIES

Although feminist legal studies (FLS) is no easier to capture in a few paragraphs than any of the above, it is probably fair to say that the essence of feminist studies is the exploration of "the women question." Katherine MacKinnon, a leading feminist scholar, sees FLS as a challenge to legal doctrines and methods on the ground that they disadvantage women. Because women are systematically disadvantaged by their gender, properly designed remedial measures can legitimately be framed by reference to sex, in MacKinnon's view. This "inequality approach"—an approach that uses sex as a proxy for gender—would allow separate standards for women and men so long as the remedy did not foster an underclass—that is, reduce males to the status of secondary citizenship.

The opposite end of the FLS spectrum is dominated by the work of psychologist, Carol Gilligan. *In a Different Voice*, her 1982 critique of Lawrence Kohlberg's *Stages of Moral Development*, portrays women as nurturers, defined by their relationships and focused on contextual thinking. Men are described as abstract thinkers and defined by individual achievement. Gilligan and numerous legal scholars who support her view urge a cultural transformation compatible with this voice—a transformation based on womanly values of responsibility, connection, selflessness, and caring, rather than on separation, autonomy, and hierarchy.

Clearly, much more can be said about FLS. These scholars are as diverse and intense in their work as those in other areas of the law. Although the impact of their work is felt in many areas of the law, you will be able to trace the implications of FLS most clearly in segments of our chapters on constitutional law, labor law, and employment discrimination.

This description of FLS is based principally on the work of Linda R. Hirshman, "The Book of 'A'," 70 *Texas L. Rev.* 971-1012 (1992); and Joan C. Williams, "Deconstructing Gender," in *Feminist Jurisprudence*, Patricia Smith, ed. (1993).

NONSTATE LEGAL SYSTEMS

Most writers of jurisprudence believe that law is defined primarily by the actions of courts and officials who have the authority to act in the name of the government. If one defines law as a system of organized principles and administered sanctions for violation of the principles, one must account for informal systems of behavior and justice in society. Some activity that appears lawlike is really not, or it is problematic when viewed through the norms of the formal, state-sponsored legal system. For example, in the Summer Olympics of 1988, the winner of the 100-meter dash, Ben Johnson, tested positive for steroid use. The Olympic Committee asked him to return the gold medal he had won and awarded it to Carl Lewis, the second-place finisher in the race. This activity by an organization certainly had a substantial impact on Ben Johnson, the other 100-meter participants, and much of organized sports, and it was accomplished outside the formal, state-sponsored legal system. In another case, the office of the commissioner of baseball conducted an investigation of Pete Rose, the manager of the Cincinnati Reds, who allegedly engaged in betting on his own team. Betting, if done in Las Vegas, is legal, yet Pete Rose was expelled from a professional role in baseball for the rest of his life. By what authority was Ben Johnson stripped of his medal and Pete Rose expelled?

Discipline is a process usually imposed by the formal legal system that is constructed to guarantee certain protections to those accused of illegal behavior. In the case cited here, the prosecuting agencies were beyond the formal legal system, so how can one be sure the accused men were given any form of fairness, or "due process?"

Is this activity law? Some legal scholars would say so or at least agree that the study of such informally imposed sanctions for the violation of a commonly understood rule of principle should be included when one studies law.

SCHOOLS OF THOUGHT: CONCLUSION

This brief introduction to centuries of thought about law leaves the crucial question: "What is law?" or "Which view of law is the most accurate?" The answer is that they are all accurate. Each defines a different dimension of legal thinking or the legal process. Each provides its own particular insights into society. Legal rules are to justice as religion is to truth. The meaning of legal rules is often as vague as the meaning of religion. Legal rules and religion are both human attempts at understanding and controlling life. Just as it is not possible to define a human being or a life in a few short sentences or even in a chapter of a book, it is likewise not possible to present a short, handy definition of the chief social system by which humans order the environment. Numerous views of what law is are better than one view.

For example, the public debate about abortion has pronounced naturalistic facets. When does life begin? What are the "natural" rights of a mother, a father, or a fetus? Certainly, these questions demand reasoned judgment about the greater forces that define life. And what of the Internal Revenue Code? Are there any natural tendencies in it? If there are, not many. In this instance, we can say for sure that it is a command of the sovereign, and like Article 2 of the Uniform Commercial Code on Sales, it must be logically consistent internally and can best be explained only after the study of the minute details that form it. This is certainly the positivist view of law. And what about the law of the future, such as a comprehensive law that deals with a firm's liability for its defective products? Any such law must be based on the "realistic" assessment of the general expectations and capabilities of producers of products, or else it will not work. And so on.

THE MORAL POINT OF VIEW AND MORAL REASONING

The rules in the American legal environment are centered on ideas of what is good, fair, and just. What are some of these ideas? A starting point for this discussion must be to distinguish among three terms used almost interchangeably to this point: values, morals, and ethics.

Values is the broadest term and denotes anything one person or group has a preference for or aversion to. If you like the color blue, then you will have a value for it. Similarly, you might prefer Buicks over Fords, Plymouths over Chevys, or whatever. *Values need not have a moral component, but they can.*

People attach value to things and to ideas that interest them. If a person is made to feel better by the openness and expanse of the blue sky, then that person may come to value the color blue so much that it becomes "my favorite color" in some internal ordering of colors. With regard to automobiles, perhaps the size of a particular model appeals to an inner need or interest that might even be below the level of consciousness. In any event, people attach top priority to things that respond satisfactorily to their needs. Hence, "Guess what. I just bought a big, blue Buick."

Morality or *morals* refers to human behavior that people find good and just. *Immorality* or *immoral* refers to conduct that people find evil, bad, or unjust. *Ethics* is the study of morals and morality; therefore, it is proper to refer to an ethical theory that helps define one's view of morality.

When we speak of the moral point of view, we are speaking of a mental process that precedes and accompanies an individual's conduct. This process does not compel a single outcome enthusiastically supported by all, nor should it be expected to. People are simply too different and too much shaped by a rich diversity of cultural conditions to somehow "naturally" all arrive at the same conclusion as to a moral point of view. However, *we believe not only that rational discourse on moral issues is possible but that it is compelled by today's business environment.*

This discourse may be made "rational" through the process of moral reasoning. Moral reasoning involves the process of moving from premise to conclusion as one seeks to determine the right course of action. This movement must be logical: Assumptions should be clear and explicit, and both the assumptions and premises or moral standards should be open to criticism. In addition, the factual evidence must be accurate, relevant, and complete, and the process of reaching a conclusion (reasoning) must be consistent in two ways. First, there must be no internal conflicts between or among premises (moral standards); second, there must be no "double standards." What is defined as good/bad or just/unjust must apply to both yourself and others. That is, you must be willing to accept the consequences if the situation were to be reversed and the action proposed for another were, in fact, imposed on you.

We are saying that people may differ in their moral points of view and that this difference should be respected, but the process of arriving at this point of view should in each instance be characterized by reasons proceeding from articulated premises to a conclusion. Without this process, all moral discourse is reduced to the proposition, "You have your opinion and I have mine." If this were the case, no agreement, no understanding, and no respect for other points of view would exist.

In the law, this kind of agreement can be illustrated by the concept of due process, which is explained in several chapters in this text. Due process has both substantive and procedural aspects. In its procedural mode, due process requires, at a minimum, reasonable notice and a hearing before an impartial tribunal before an individual can be deprived of life, liberty, or property. Not everyone will agree that the judgment or the verdict was the right one, but it is possible to agree that due process should be observed. It is illustrative of a rational, mature process, and it respects the rights of all parties involved. Over the long term, one can say with confidence that the legal and moral quality of society is advanced by adherence to these processes and that they should become internalized.

THE PROCESS OF MORAL REASONING

We have explained our belief that moral discourse is desirable in the business environment and that this discourse is possible if the process is rational (proceeds logically from premise to conclusion). In this section, we suggest that the process of moral reasoning should be preceded by a step we call *perception* and followed by two steps we call *coordination* and *implementation*. We define these terms and then give an illustration of how they work in an individual case.

Perception.   Perception involves recognizing and defining moral issues from the raw material of the environment. As one monitors the surroundings, events of moral significance are incorporated into the information net. For example, in the scenario below, a morally neutral or nonmoral event, such as the sale of real estate, should be noted along with the moral issue of how the sale was accomplished (e.g., with fraud or deception).

Reasoning.   Here is the process we described above. It is based on premises and proceeds to a conclusion. The premise or premises may be stated as a commitment to some fundamental ethical theory. For example, if a person is influenced by utilitarianism—an ethical theory that advances the course of action with the greatest proportion of good over bad—then he or she would weigh the good against the bad consequences of each alternative. Thus, fraud or deception in the sale of real estate could be counterbalanced by the positive consequences of having made the sale and having enough money from the commission on the sale to feed one's family. The moral point of view, however, demands that this outcome not involve a double standard; that is, if one favors fraud and deception, then one must be consistent and be willing to be defrauded or deceived by others.

Coordination.   Before one acts, when in a moral dilemma, one should attempt to reconcile or coordinate the proposed action with simple prudence or the practical consequences of the action. This step is not really separate from the reasoning process, but rather is part of it. The step should be taken, however, as one prepares for action. For example, in the following scenario, a woman is urged to engage in what some people would call deception to make a sale of real estate. If she does not make the sale she may lose her job. Certainly, the loss of the job is a consequence that must be considered in the process. She must coordinate (or reconcile) this outcome with the outcome suggested by reasoning.

Implementation.   The concluding step involves following through in such a manner that good intentions become a reality. The action may not be of the ideal or ivory-tower type, but the important thing is to arrive at a course of conduct that, despite its shortcomings, can be supported by the strongest reasons and can be applied to others as well as to oneself.

AN EXAMPLE OF MORAL REASONING: THE DILEMMA OF JEAN McGUIRE

Attempt to apply the process of moral reasoning to the scenario that follows. In your attempt to do this, you will find that moral reasoning and moral discourse are valuable.

In Wright's [the sales director's] view, the job of a land salesperson was "to help the prospect make the decision to buy." This didn't mean that salespeople should misrepresent a piece of property or in any way mislead people about what they were purchasing. "Law prohibits this," Wright pointed out, "and personally I find such behavior repugnant. What I'm talking about is helping them buy a lot they genuinely want and which you're convinced will be compatible with their needs and interests." In a word, for Wright Boazman, salespeople should serve as motivators, people who could provide whatever impulse was needed for prospects to close the deal.

In Wright's experience one of the most effective closing techniques was what he termed "the other party." It went something like this.

Suppose someone like Jean McGuire had a "hot" prospect, someone who was exhibiting a real interest in a lot but who was having trouble deciding. To motivate the prospect into buying, Jean ought to tell the person that she wasn't even sure the lot was still available, since there were a number of other salespeople showing the same lot, and they could already have closed a deal on it. As Wright put it, "This first play generally has the effect of increasing the prospect's interest in the property, and, more important to us, in closing the deal *pronto*."

Next Jean should say something like, "Why don't we go back to the office and I'll call headquarters to find out the status of the lot?" Wright indicated that such a suggestion ordinarily "whets their appetite" even more. In addition, it turns prospects away from wondering whether or not they should purchase the land and toward hoping that it's still available.

When they return to the office, Jean should make a call in the presence of the prospect. The call, of course, would not be to "headquarters" but to a private office only yards from where she and the prospect sit. Wright or someone else would receive the call, and Jean should fake a conversation about the property's availability, punctuating her comments with enough contagious excitement about its desirability. When she hangs up, she should breathe a sigh of relief that the lot's still available—but barely. At any minute, Jean should explain anxiously, the lot could be "green tagged," which means that headquarters is expecting a call from another salesperson who's about to close a deal and will remove the lot from open stock. (An effective variation of this, Wright had pointed out, would have Jean abruptly excuse herself upon hanging up and dart over to another sales representative with whom she'd engage in a heated, though staged, debate about the availability of the property, loud enough, of course, for the prospect to hear. The intended effect, according to Wright, would place the prospect in the "now or never" frame of mind.)

When Jean first heard about this and other closing techniques, she felt uneasy. Even though the property was everything it was represented to be, and the law allowed purchasers ten days to change their minds after closing a deal, she instinctively objected to the use of psychological manipulation. Nevertheless, Jean never expressed her reservations to anyone, primarily because she didn't want to endanger her job. She desperately needed it owing to the recent and unexpected death of her husband, which left her as the sole support of herself and three young children. Besides, Jean had convinced herself that she could deal with closures more respectably than Wright and other salespeople might. But the truth was that after six months of selling land for sunrise, Jean's sales lagged far behind those of the other sales representatives. Whether she liked it or not, Jean had to admit that she was losing a considerable number of sales because she couldn't close. And she couldn't close because, in Wright Boazman's words, she lacked technique. She wasn't employing the psychological closing devices that he and others had found so successful.

Now as she drove back to the office with two "hot prospects" in hand, she wondered what to do?[2]

Perception.   How would you define the moral issue or problem in this scenario? Obviously, Jean McGuire is bothered by the suggested sales technique. This technique may not be in violation of law because there is no misrepresentation of material fact. Failing to find a violation of law is often the case with "moral" problems. Clearly, though, Jean McGuire thinks that what she is being asked to do is not right. She evidently believes that the sales technique is deceptive. So, in general terms, the moral problem seems to be, Should Jean McGuire act against what she believes to be right conduct in order to achieve some other objective (the sale of the property) deemed desirable to her?

Reasoning.   As the data of perception inform the reasoning process, formulate a premise—a general moral standard or principle of action—and as you move logically to a conclusion, make certain that your factual evidence is accurate, relevant, and complete. The conclusion must be internally consistent; it must follow from the preceding steps and must be consistent in the sense that it can be applied to Jean as well as to everyone else.

First, question the facts that were given. Is it a fact that Jean may lose her job if she does not agree to engage in this kind of sales technique? Does her relatively poor sales record really result from her refusal to use this technique? If the answers to these and related questions all lead to a confrontation with the moral problem, then Jean should evaluate the principles of ethical theory. Basically, these theories present alternative modes of thought and action. Theories that focus only on the consequences of an action say that one should act to maximize the total good in society. In our example, if Jean wanted to act consistently with this principle, she would believe that everyone, or at least most people affected by her actions in this case, would be better off if she engaged in the sales technique. If this was her view, then she should go ahead with the sales technique. Alternatively, Jean may be influenced to act differently through exposure to other ethical concepts discussed in this chapter.

At this point, we note that no clearly right or wrong course of action may be evident in cases like this one. Our objective is to illustrate that, through reasoned discourse on moral issues, people may all be better off. In this case, Jean could confront her manager and ask whether, in his judgment, selling the property was more important than violating her commitment to principle—treating others as she would be willing to be treated.

Coordination.   Jean should explore what would really happen to her if she were to refuse to use the recommended sales technique. She should evaluate the consequences of having to search for another job. To do this, she should seek out friends and others who can give her objective, unemotional advice. She should also evaluate having to live with action that violated her commitment to a moral principle. If Jean believes that theories based on consequences would be the better to use here, then she might evaluate the long-run success of this business firm if all salespeople used such methods. Using this theory, she may conclude that if she went ahead with the sales technique, the results could be counterproductive. In the long run, purchasers might resent the high-pressure techniques that urged them to buy something they did not really want.

Implementation.   What should Jean do? The answer is not easy and may vary for each person. Jean may put her job security and the need of her family ahead of the commitment to principle and go ahead with the sales tactic. If she chooses this course of conduct one can say, at the least, she has been morally responsible and has thought through her action. If she chooses not to make the sale, she may have to suffer some rather harsh consequences, but she will be secure in the knowledge that she acted out of commitment to principle.

Perhaps the best that could be hoped for in this case is that if Jean believed in acting in a manner consistent with how she wanted to be treated, then she would raise the moral issue with her manager. In doing so, they both may discover that this sales technique offends other employees and that alternative, nondeceptive methods could be used instead. Who is to say that only tricky closing techniques will work?

To sharpen the focus on the study of moral issues, we explore certain basic ethical theories of Western culture.

ETHICAL THEORIES

In the study of moral issues today, certain ethical theories have been inherited from some of the most important philosophers in Western culture. You should view these theories, not as technical ideas, but as fundamental concepts that today pervade law, economics, and politics as well as philosophy. They are really alternative methods of thought. Some writers think these theories provide very different perspectives on life and result in different conclusions about all matters of public policy. We placed the treatment of these theories after the Jean McGuire example so that you may first have a context for understanding how they may be applied.

UTILITARIANISM: A CONSEQUENTIALIST THEORY

Utilitarianism means that the moral worth of an action is determined solely by its consequences.[3] It is a teleological theory because it is shaped by the goal or objective (*telos*) of maximizing the aggregate common good or public welfare. In the world of the utilitarian, there is no such idea as a basic commitment to principle that would override the focus on the consequences of an action. *This theory defines right or good conduct as that which provides the greatest possible balance of good over bad consequences.*

The first major utilitarian philosopher was David Hume (1711–1776). He was followed by Jeremy Bentham (1748–1832) and John Stuart Mill (1806–1873).

Bentham is perhaps the best philosopher to focus on because of his impact on the legal system. Bentham argued that the legal system should provide punishments that "fit" the crimes; that is, the state should punish up to, but should not exceed, the point at which the infliction of pain brings about the greatest benefits in deterrence of the crime. This method of thought required the definition or quantification of both *pain* and *benefit*. Today, *pain* and *bad* have been replaced in the business context by the concept of cost.

Utilitarianism inevitably depends on a weighing of various consequences, good and bad. In today's business world, the familiar idea of cost-benefit is a utilitarian method of operation because action is based on consequences alone. The briefest definition of utilitarianism is "the greatest good for the greatest number." We emphasize several components of this theory.

First, this principle is orientated toward maximizing the *good* even though utilitarians are not in exact agreement as to what the good is. Although each person is likely to have a different idea about what constitutes the public good or general welfare, most people will agree that efficient methods are the best way of producing it. As students of business, we can identify with this view. We cannot easily determine whether a new means of doing something (e.g., using some new technological device) is, in itself, good, but if it appears to do something in an efficient manner (e.g., using fewer resources than alternative methods while producing the same or a greater output), we tend to favor it.

Second, implicit in the concept of utilitarianism is that goods, services, and courses of action can indeed be measured and thus compared. Certainly, cost-benefit analysis is based on this principle. Whether the actor is an individual or the government, one assumes that one can measure the cost and benefits of an action.

At this point, you can see that utilitarianism, somewhat modified, is the dominant ethical theory in business today. When applied by individual business firms, the well-being or good of the firm is maximized, not the public good or general welfare.

It is not overstating the case to say that, in business, if an item or service sells, and especially if it sells well, this is the mark of a "good" product. The legal system has great difficulty dealing with instances in which items sell well but, in certain instances, produce adverse consequences. For example, several national "sensational" magazines sell well but almost always defame those about whom the stories are written, The fact that they sell well is, in itself, a statement that they are preferred and, therefore, good. Thus, on a utilitarian basis, if the good feelings of the readers of these magazines outweigh the negative consequences to the few subjects of the stories, then the selling of these magazines is good and should be allowed. Next, we offer some standard criticism of this theory.

A CRITIQUE OF UTILITARIANISM

Five main criticisms of teleological theories are typically advanced by those committed to some duty-based principle.

1. Teleological theories are helpful only after a commitment to principle has been made. The use of cost-benefit analysis, by itself, is meaningless unless it is understood to apply to some greater objective. For example, once a commitment is made to clean up the environment, it should be done in a manner that promotes the greatest good for the greatest number. But without this objective, cost-benefit analysis cannot be used.

2. In determining the greatest good for the greatest number, no single scale exists against which all choices can be measured. For example, in a business sense, it costs money to clean up the environment and to provide job safety and health. How does one compare the costs of these actions to the increased benefits that result from cleaning the environment and the improved health and safety conditions of employees?

3. A related idea is that the definition of what is good or a benefit and what is bad or a cost is almost necessarily subjective. What may be a benefit to a child of eight (candy) may be a cost (extra pounds) to an adult of forty.

4. In many cases, especially those instances involving business, it seems unfair to weigh bad consequences against the good of an action because the entire structure of business record keeping is focused on computing the bad consequences (costs) and not the public good or benefit. Almost every business can report on the cost of cleaning up the environment. But can they value and thus report on the benefits? People are used to keeping track of some data. When they are asked to weigh decisions that involve these data, the natural tendency is to favor the most concrete choice. The most concrete choice favors the alternative with the most data, and typically that means costs will outweigh benefits.

5. Finally, the weighing of good against bad does not usually involve a time scale. What may be good for today may be bad for tomorrow. In the Jean McGuire example, the sales technique proposed may sell the property in the short run. The technique could have adverse long-run consequences, however, if many of the people who bought property did not really want to buy it and, in the end, felt "hustled" into a decision. Ten years from now, that business may be unable to sell any property because of the ill-will in the community.

DEONTOLOGICAL OR DUTY-BASED THEORIES

Deontological ethical theories deny that the consequences of an action determine its worth. These theories are based on the notion that commitment to duty is independent of the consequences: "Let justice be done, though the heavens fall," or, "No matter what, never tell a lie."

An example of this kind of theory applied in a business context is the sanctity of contracts. This moral notion has been incorporated into the law of contracts in the following way: A person injured by a breach of promise embodied in a contract is entitled to a judgment for money damages that will compensate for the loss even though a greater number of people would benefit by a breach.

In a wider context, consider some of the basic duty-based notions that form or define Western culture. One of the most widely regarded deontological theories is the Golden Rule. In one of its earliest formulations, it reads, "Therefore all things whatsoever ye would that men should do to you, do ye even so to them: for this is the law of the prophets."[4]

One of the most noted deontologists was Immanuel Kant. He dealt with this concept in a different vein when he formulated basic moral rights and duties in terms of a categorical imperative or overriding moral principle. He advised, "Always act in such a way that you can will the maxim or basis for your action to become universal."[5] This principle means that you should live your life so that you would be willing to have your conduct serve as the standard for universal conduct.

This standard of universalizability embodies the concept of reversibility found in the Golden Rule; that is, if you apply Kant's first principle to other people, there will be a logical contradiction unless you are willing to apply it to yourself as well. This can be understood to mean that you should treat others as you want to be treated yourself.

A second principle advocated by Kant was as follows: "Always act in such a way that other people will be treated as ends rather than as mere means to an end."[6] This is understood to mean that other people should not be manipulated or exploited solely for one's own advantage. Kant's second categorical imperative is simply a reformulation and reinforcement of the first. For example, it would be wrong to lie to and defraud the purchaser of an automobile regarding some component of the brake mechanism or transmission in order to make a sale. That would be wrong because it would not be showing respect for the dignity or the worth of the buyer as a human being. It would be treating the buyer as a mere instrument or tool (means) to advance one's own selfish advantage (end).

We could illustrate the same point by using Kant's first principle. A rational person could not advocate fraudulent conduct as a universal rule to be applied to all people everywhere. The reason is that no rational person could willingly invite that kind of conduct to be imposed on him or her in return. In other words, if you don't want to be defrauded, cheated, or exploited, don't practice that conduct on other people.

To meet Kant's criterion of universality, a proposed rule that is to be applied to others must be "reversed" and applied to the "rule maker." This reversal sets up the test of "noncontradiction." To continue with our illustration, it would certainly contradict our sense of reason to say that a rational person could willingly invite others to defraud, cheat, or exploit him or her in return.

Keep in mind that this test has nothing to do with the bad consequences a utilitarian might attribute to fraud. This is purely a mental or intellectual test, so if a reasonable person could not say that he or she would be willing to be defrauded by others, then fraudulent conduct is immoral. One could apply this test to many other civil and criminal wrongs—for example, duress, undue influence, false imprisonment, battery, assault, defamation, and invasion of privacy.

In another rendition of Kant's position, but one that brings to that position the kind of mathematical certainty he was trying to give it, try this thought experiment. Could a rational person ever imagine that 2 + 2 will ever equal anything but 4? Even conceding that we may have some intellectual and imaginative shortcomings, the precision of mathematics will not tolerate any other answer. Kant believed that his moral system operated with exactly this precision. He argued that it was absolute and objective, that it was applicable to all people at all times and in every culture, and that, in this universal context, a rational person could no more advocate the principle of deception than he or she could advocate the principle that 2 + 2 equalled anything but 4.

A CRITIQUE OF KANT

Immanuel Kant is one of the monumental figures in the history of moral philosophy. In venturing a critique, it is undertaken with an enormous amount of respect for his many insightful contributions. Kant's great works were written toward the close of the eighteenth century in an age known as the Enlightenment. He drew inspiration from the French Revolution and from the marvelous liberating spirit—of individual freedom, dignity, and equality—that blazed across Western Europe. The message of the French Revolution, at least in part, was that common people were no longer to be ruled by the whims and dictates of divine right monarchs. The old order was swept away, and a new order, indeed a new age, began.

The new age was something that Kant welcomed, that he anticipated in his early writings, and that he helped shape for generations to come. It was abundantly clear to thoughtful people, however, that the chaos and bloodbath that followed the revolution could not and should not continue unabated. If the old order, the old notion of the "good," was dead, something had to govern the tempers and appetites of those who took up the banner of "Liberty, Equality, Fraternity."

Kant found that governing force in human reason. Kant believed that by probing the depths and expanding the insights of human reason, he could articulate certain fundamental and unimpeachable moral principles that would apply to all people in every part of the globe and for all time. Those principles were the categorical imperatives (absolute commands) discussed in the paragraphs above. He believed that if a principle could be universalized, the process of universalization itself gave that principle moral content and moral worth. Hence, universalization of something like the Golden Rule led him to claim that one should never treat other people with lack of respect for their freedom and dignity. It follows from this principle that others should never be exploited or manipulated (by deception or otherwise) as a means of advancing one's own selfish purposes. Sure, I can hire laborers at a fair wage to work for me—that's not exploitive—but I would not be morally justified in paying an unfair wage. What's fair, or a fair wage? Kant doesn't address that point. He had to leave something for us to do.

The process of universalizing a rule—a rule that passes the test of noncontradiction—does not necessarily give that rule moral force, content, or substance. For example, what about universalizing the rule that "Everyone ought to go out and have a good time on Monday evenings?" Trivial, but it doesn't sound like a bad idea, does it? Anything wrong with applying that rule to oneself as well as to other people?

The point, of course, is that universalizing a rule and applying it to other people and to oneself does not necessarily give that rule any moral dignity or substance or compelling force. Try another example. "Everybody ought to wave his or her hand to passing cars." Silly as it is, that rule can be universalized as well, and who could object to being waved to? Again, however, the rule is totally trivial and has not an ounce of moral content.

Where does that leave us? It leaves us with big questions about Kant's method of identifying universal moral principles. Clearly, there are problems with this approach, and he supplies no further guidance.

Additional problems crop up when rules that pass the universalization and noncontradiction test clash with one another. For example, one can universalize a rule "to always tell the truth" and a rule "to always protect innocent human life." How does one proceed, however, when the only way to protect innocent life is to lie to a would-be murderer? Confronted with that dilemma, a person would have to decide which "value"—telling the truth or protecting innocent human life—was more important, and then that person would have to have the moral courage to act on that choice.

Alternatively, one could compromise on middle ground by deciding to lie only when necessary to protect human life. Either way, however, one has to choose between or among competing values, and Kant offers no assistance on how to do that. Again, he has left us an important task. Before we criticize him for that, however, we should admit that we have no reason to expect him to do all the hard work for us.

W. D. Ross in *The Right and the Good* (1931), addressed this problem by arguing that everyone has certain prima facie moral duties and that everyone should act in accordance with those duties in the absence of a conflict between or among them. The duties that Ross believed to be prima facie were as follows:

Fidelity	Beneficence
Gratitude	Self-improvement
Justice	Non-injury

Ross understood *fidelity* to mean honesty and promisekeeping. *Gratitude*, or loyalty, honors the relationships among family members, friends, and business associates. *Justice* consists of the distribution of goods on the basis of merit. *Beneficence* means advancing the well-being of others; *self-improvement* relates to the full development of one's own potential; and *non-injury* simply forbids people from causing harm to others.

Assuming, without argument, that these are the foremost duties and that people are morally bound to honor them in the absence of conflict, how does one proceed when there is a conflict? In that case, Ross advises to follow the most obligatory duty—the one that embodies the greatest amount of rightness over wrongness. Although this approach extends somewhat beyond the point that Kant left off, it still requires people to make fine distinctions and tough judgments. No philosopher is ever going to be able to lift that burden from us.

SOCIAL CONTRACT

John Rawls: A Theory of Justice

From John Locke, an eighteenth-century philosopher with a concept of private property as a natural right, to Karl Marx, a nineteenth-century philosopher with a view of private property as theft, and on through the twentieth century, a number of philosophers have had a vision of a just society. One such person is John Rawls. Rawls asserts the central importance of justice in human society: "Justice is the first virtue of social institutions, as truth is of systems of thought."[7] His thrust is directed at all types of justice in society. Largely, however, he deals with the issue of distributive justice (how rights and goods are distributed or allocated throughout society and how fairly the members of a society share in the benefits and opportunities of social institutions). His emphasis is on how fundamental rights and duties are allocated and on economic opportunities and social conditions.

In his approach to justice, Rawls states that he is constructing his theory so as to avoid two flawed philosophical treatments of justice: intuitionism and utilitarianism.[8] The *intuitionist view* is that people know what is just but have no way of rationally and logically ordering these perceptions of justice. Although a person can know the just course of action, he or she has no way to get behind this knowledge and construct a logically consistent theory of justice. The reasoning behind intuitionism is that moral questions are simply too complex to submit to logical order. At times, a person "feels" that we know the right decision but is unable logically to articulate the reason for that choice. Principles conflict, and no system exists for bringing order (or priorities) into the process. Rawls believes he can construct a systematic and comprehensive theory of justice, so he rejects intuitionism, as he does utilitarianism.

Utilitarianism is, in fact, the central philosophical point of view that he wants to overcome in his theory. *Utilitarianism* maximizes the good, which is the aggregate satisfaction of the greatest number of people. Defining justice according to utilitarian principles is wrong, according to Rawls, because it does not necessarily limit the sorts of activities people might pursue to achieve satisfaction. Men might conceivably pursue satisfaction in ways that reasonable people would regard as unjust—war, repression, and slavery.

Rawls's other objection to a utilitarian concept of justice is that the important matter for utilitarians is the sum of satisfaction, not the fairness with which that satisfaction is parceled out to members of society. Thus, it would be possible in a utilitarian view to raise the general satisfaction level at the expense of the powerless members of society. Such a course of action would hardly seem just in the ordinary sense of the word.

We note, in fairness to utilitarianism, that there are ways to qualify this lack of concern for individual well-being. In one version of utilitarianism, the stipulation is made that no one may be made worse off in order that the general level of satisfaction is enhanced. *Pareto optimality* is the point that the general level of satisfaction cannot be improved without making someone worse off.

Rawls's theory is more of a deontological theory that places the rightness of any action prior to any consideration of the consequences of the action. Rawls acknowledges, however, that it is impossible to totally overlook consideration of goals and consequences.

To develop his theory of justice, Rawls turns to social contract theory. He begins by presupposing an environment in which rules of justice could be formulated. Next, he creates a hypothetical situation in which, before any government exists and before any social positions in society exist, people reason together about what is to be just. These people who reason together, he assumes, do not know their age, their gender, their race, or any of the other social or genetic benefits that one is born with. Nor do these people know the time when they were born. In this manner, Rawls prevents a person from setting up a society that would impoverish other segments of society or other generations to enhance the material worth of his or her own segment or generation.

The people sitting behind Rawls's "veil of ignorance," an environment with no government or other constraints, are in what he calls the *original position*. He endows the people in the original position with human qualities, however. They are self-interested rather than altruistic. Altruism, the inclination for self-sacrifice, is not necessary for justice to work, Rawls maintains. Another assumption he makes is that these people would prefer more primary social goods (income, wealth, authority) rather than less. In other words, rationality to Rawls means that the parties are able to know their best interests and to press for these interests. The reasoning process of the individuals in the original position and behind the veil of ignorance will be such that they must consider the well-being of even the least fortunate members because they may, in the future, find themselves in the least fortunate positions.

The above conditions are necessary to keep people from choosing a social structure that would suit their own particular philosophical or psychological makeup. If, for instance, a person knew that he or she would be a gambler by temperament with a high tolerance for risk, then they might choose a social structure tilted in favor of people in society being either big winners or big losers. Rawls withholds this information from those in the original position to keep them objective.

Further, persons in the original position do not know the particular circumstances of their own society (its economic or political situation or the level of civilization and culture it has been able to achieve). This condition prevents any distortion of justice in favor of a particular nation or civilization.

Having thus delineated the conditions in which the social contract is made, Rawls expounds two rules that would inevitably and unanimously be chosen in the original position. First, the *liberty principle* is that each person is to have an equal right to the most extensive basic liberty compatible with a similar liberty for others. Second, the *difference principle* is that social and economic inequalities are to be arranged so that they are both (1) to the greatest extent of benefit to the least advantaged persons and (2) attached to positions and offices open to all in fair equality of opportunity.

The liberty principle pertains to guaranteeing the liberty of the members of society. These liberties include political liberty (e.g., the right to vote and to be eligible for public office), together with freedom of speech and assembly, liberty of conscience and freedom of thought, freedom of the person along with the right to hold property, and freedom from arbitrary arrest and seizure as defined by the concept of the rule of law.

This first principle is directed toward liberty; the second principle deals with the equality with which wealth and position in society are distributed. Differences or inequalities of wealth and position are permitted only if the existence of these inequalities is of benefit to the least advantaged members of society and if everyone has equal opportunity for everyone to hold any position.

What sort of place does Rawls's thought have in the education of businesspeople? First, he has a wider audience in mind. His focus is not specifically on the operation of business firms. Second, Rawls's vision is structural or systemic. It builds from the bottom up, anchored in principles he regards as just; it is not in any measure dependent on utility or altruism.

For the individual and the business firm, this view does not mean that all dilemmas are resolved or that ethical problems will fade away. It does mean, however, that if these principles are followed, a person acting out of self-interest can press his or her claims with confidence that they will be mediated by just political and social institutions.

Rawls's ideas are noteworthy because they are rooted in a twentieth-century reality. Although human thought and action are still a significant part of the business climate, so are actions by business institutions (primarily corporations) and governments. His ideas are concerned with the structure of these institutions, as well as with individual thought. In short, these institutions should be structured so that they help achieve justice.

A CRITIQUE OF RAWLS

John Rawls is a contemporary moral philosopher who added powerful insights to those of a long and highly regarded line of social contractarians. The common thread that links this line of philosophers is that law and ethics rest on an agreement of some sort between the people and the state. The test, then, of whether something is legal or ethical depends on whether it is commanded or permitted by the agreement.

Having made that broad generalization, however, we proffer the qualification that it does not capture the thoughts of every contractarian. Contractarians are influenced by a variety of moral concepts (including some that are discussed in this chapter—utility, rights and duties, and virtue ethics), and they use these concepts in various ways to give body and substance to their contracts. So do not expect our initial description to hold up in every case. We merely claim that it's close enough for an initial approximation.

You may remember that Socrates, condemned to death by an Athenian jury, was given a chance to escape if he would allow his friends to bribe the guards. He declined to do that and tried to console his friends with the notion that the government was something like a parent that made and enforced rules for the benefit of family, and further that a family member should not expect to be supported and benefited by the family and, at the same time, escape punishment for breaking the rules. So, to his friends' sorrow, Socrates honored the contract and drank the hemlock. In the view of most accounts of the trial, Socrates became a victim of an unjust verdict and, in a sense, a victim of the "social contract."

One of Socrates' friends who witnessed this event was Plato. In later years, Plato advanced a visionary state, the *Republic*, that would be governed by philosopher-kings. Through the centuries many such proposals have been made.

John Hobbes's *Leviathan* is another example. In Hobbes's view, life before the creation of civil governments was life in a "state of nature," which entailed a war of every man against every other man. In this state of nature, men and women had an inalienable right of self-defense, but no other inalienable rights. The state of nature was governed by the law of nature, and the law of nature urged men and women to seek the peace, to relinquish all rights except the right of self-defense, and to obey the terms of the social covenant or social contract. Not until the formation of a civil government emerged could anything like justice exist. In a state of nature, justice is not a recognized concept. After the formation of a civil government, justice consisted of obedience to the terms of the contract.

Clearly, Rawls's social contract differs from that of Hobbes. Hobbes faced a different problem—that of the divine right of monarchs to govern without consent of the people—and the *Leviathan* was his response to it. Rawls dealt with the problem of distributive justice—the distribution of political rights and the distribution of material rights.

Rawls was in conflict with utilitarians and with intuitionists. He believed that certain fundamental principles of justice should be embodied in democratic institutions even though those principles may not serve the greatest good for the greatest number, and, contrary to the intuitionists, he believed there was a way to bring a rational, defensible structure to the distribution of goods.

Rawls chose a method that guarded against the formulation of rules that sanctioned personal bias. He did this by enclosing his rational, self-interested men and women in a veil of ignorance. They could formulate the rules inside the veil, but once they stepped outside, the rules would be applied to them. Hence, the rules were freed of the taint of favoritism on the basis of race, gender, age, or generation.

How well did Rawls succeed in projecting a blueprint for just institutions in a democratic society? Evidence suggests that he did an excellent job. Many critics have pointed out, however, that people are never behind such a veil, and that he is writing from some sort of Walt Disney fantasy world that has no relation to reality. His Harvard colleague Robert Nozick blasted him most severely. Nozick claimed that property is justly distributed if it has been justly acquired (meaning that historically wrongful acquisitions, such as theft, have to be rectified) and justly transferred. In Nozick's view, whatever comes out of the "end of the pipe" (unequal distribution of wealth) is just.

It is argued that Rawls left "risktakers" out of his deliberations and that some rational people are risktakers rather than adherents to his "maximin" hypotheses. Rawls's notion of rationality is limited to those who support his maximin hypotheses—the theory that rational people will always choose rules that will maximize the best outcomes and minimize the worst ones. Further, it is insisted, Rawls projected no notion of the good, or the virtues, and evidently believed that those things followed simply from obeying the rules.

This critique is not intended to pass judgment on Rawls's thoughtful and painstaking work. It is simply an observation that, like the philosophers before him, much else is yet to be done in shaping democratic institutions in such a way that people can be assured of justice in the distribution of political and social goods.

VIRTUE ETHICS

Our earlier discussion of natural law quickly brought us to the work of "the Philosopher," an accolade that St. Thomas Aquinas bestowed on Aristotle. Unlike Plato, his equally famous teacher, Aristotle did not believe that ideals of truth, knowledge, or beauty were to be found in absolute or eternal "forms," nor did he teach that, by comparison with these absolute forms, our earthly representations were poor and shabby copies. Instead of looking for an absolute form and then trying to model human institutions and human conduct on its ideal and perfect nature, Aristotle found his inspiration in natural, scientific, and distinctly more "worldly" institutions and pursuits.

Very little of the provocative and controversial Socrates is found in Aristotle's writings, or anything of Plato's poetry or imagination. By comparison, Aristotle does not come off as particularly exciting. It is as if he was born middle-aged, privileged, and more than a little condescending toward anything non-Athenian. Aristotle took for granted the traditions and institutions of his city, and he focused on the character of his fellow Athenians as the baseline of his ethics. From this level, he projected a vision of a good community with good laws. Central to this development was an elaboration of the virtues—defined as habits of character or propensities to excellence—that good citizens would need in order to participate in such a community and to enjoy a fulfilling and happy life.

Aristotle advanced the view that the good—the ultimate goal, or aim, or telos of humankind—is happiness. Happiness is the highest and greatest good because all men and women aim at that objective and because everything else they do—all the means that they employ and all the alternatives that they pursue—is focused on that end.

Happiness was something to be achieved over a lifetime by active participation in the life of the community. It was not to be mistaken for mere pleasure as the utilitarians would have it. Pleasure could be considered an ingredient of happiness, but not the whole thing. Happiness had a more enduring quality. Pleasure was far too transitory and fickle to fulfill that requirement.

In Aristotle's vision, happiness could be achieved only in a polis, that is, a community or city-state very much like Athens. Although Athens was in decline—well past the golden age of Solon and Pericles—it was still the cultural center of the Western world. Although Aristotle distinctly preferred a city governed by an aristocracy and was frequently disdainful of its democratic institutions, he took it as his working model and regarded non-Athenian efforts as primitive by comparison. He looked on the historical Athens as a diamond in the rough.

Women played a subordinate role in the Athens of Aristotle's day and in his ethics as well. Although the contributions of women as wives, mothers, and household managers were highly valued, women were not permitted to participate in the civic life of the community. For example, the normal roles of Athenian men were to (1) participate in the law courts as jurors who would interpret and apply the law, (2) serve in the Assembly to make the law, and (3) administer the law. In none of these roles was a distinction made between men of high or low station, wealth, or privilege; all were assumed to be competent for the task.

Women did not even enter into these calculations. It was as if the idea of women in public life was so far-fetched that it simply never entered into mainstream Greek thought and tradition.

Some, but not many, cultures today accept such a diminished role for women. None tolerate slavery. But in Aristotle's day, and in his ethics, slaves had a role. Some people, in his view, were "natural slaves." It would be "better for them as for all inferiors that they should be under the rule of a master" and "where there is a man of this sort, then he ought to be a slave." Slavery imposed by force or conquest, however, Aristotle condemned as unjust.

How could Aristotle possibly be relevant to students and young managers marching into the twenty-first century? To begin with, one has to understand that as marvelously wise and insightful as Aristotle was, he was also a product of his times. Aristotle did not begin with some innovative vision of the ideal society. Instead, he took the traditions and institutions of his age and tried to move them toward a social arrangement that would most likely produce the good, indeed, the best society, one driven by people of virtue. By the word *virtue*, Aristotle intended to convey the idea of excellence or, more properly, excellences in all of one's endeavors. A good society would be one in which justice was the first and principle virtue, but not the only one.

People of virtue—that is, those who from childhood were instructed by their parents, family, friends, and community to identify with and to advance the good of the whole—became virtuous by this lifelong conditioning to behave virtuously. But this sounds like circular reasoning! How do parents know what is good? That is a crucial question in virtue ethics. Parents and other members of the community have to know what is good so that they can aim at it, teach their children to aim at it, and shape their public institutions to aim at it.

In Aristotle's view, consistent with Greek tradition, it made sense to aim at happiness, and it further made sense to acknowledge that people could only be happy if they could "flourish" or reach the full development of their potential. The full development of achievement of one's natural talents could only take place in a good society with good laws, and the obligation of this society to set the stage upon which people could flourish both materially and psychologically is the closest Aristotle ever came to moral or social "rights." In fact, the concept of moral rights, which people take as more or less commonplace, did not begin to emerge until the thirteenth and fourteenth centuries.

Aristotle took this way of looking at things to be "natural." Naturalness, in this sense was essentially given or assumed, and the basis for this assumption was his own observation, experience, and version of the Greek tradition. In philosophy, there has to be a starting point (evidently), and this starting point—nature or natural—was not something to be questioned or critiqued (not by Aristotle, at least), it just *was!*

Further, the citizens of this good society were assumed to be "political animals" (social creatures by nature). Political animals who naturally recognize that their happiness is linked to good and just social institutions also naturally recognize that their fate (their lives, their happiness) is linked to active participation in that society through the development of good character.

A person of good character is a person who, among other things, has been trained to be just—that is, has developed the habit of acting virtuously. This person clearly observes bottom-line rules, but virtues in Aristotle's ethics were not rules. Virtues were not bottom line in any sense. Rules merely tell what is bottom line or minimally permissible. They are necessary but not sufficient for the moral life. Virtues are the very best in people, always striving to excel—never the minimum.

Justice in the sense that Aristotle intended was again a natural concept—the same all over the world regardless of race, culture, or other differences. Metaphorically, justice was a flame and the "fire burns both here and in Persia." In this sense, Aristotle was speaking of conduct that was bad in itself, *mala in se*—for example, deliberately taking an innocent human life without reason. Other wrongs—wrongs that may be forbidden in some cultures but not others—were *mala prohibit*, or bad only because they were prohibited by law or custom. For example, it would be wrong not to observe the conventional laws—paying taxes or doing one's civic jury duty—that advance the welfare of the community.

Aristotle was no capitalist, and maximization of wealth was not a good that he acknowledged. He did respect good household management, however, and because procreation and family were natural to all humankind, the kind of economics—home economics—that was natural to the family was clearly natural to the community and instrumentally to the chief good—happiness.

He generally held merchants and businesspeople in contempt because he saw them as constantly grasping, greedy, and acquisitive, totally absorbed in the pursuit of material goods. Because these people did not recognize and were not guided by the chief good, but endlessly pursued an unattainable and ignoble good, they were not virtuous and were deserving of all the contempt heaped on them.

Material goods played an important role in Aristotle's notion of the good life, however. A life characterized by poverty, hunger, and homelessness could no more be a happy life than one riveted on acquisitiveness and greed. An improvement in one's economic status through voluntary, deliberate, and uncoerced exchanges—for example, sales and barter transactions that were fair and equal in worth to the satisfaction of all parties—were not condemned. This was his concept of *communative* justice. After all, if it was natural for a household to sell or barter eggs for clothing, or farm animals for furniture, and if that transaction was voluntary, and if it could be fairly said that all parties were equally advantaged given the circumstances, how could one conclude that comparable transactions on a larger, commercial scale were not also natural and good?

Aristotle did not invent the law of supply and demand, but he clearly saw that the need and demand for the material goods of another person could lead to a fair commercial exchange. Virtuous persons recognized, however, that material goods obtained in this manner were not the chief good; they were merely instrumental goods, goods that fostered the principal and ultimate good, namely, happiness.

As you look forward to a business career in the closing years of the twentieth century, and well into the next, what does it make sense to hold on to in the ethics of this (by some accounts) pompous old aristocrat propped up in his comfortable middle and declining years by the Macedonian forces of his student, Alexander the Great? Shortly after Alexander's untimely death in Persia, Aristotle left the Lyceum—the school he had founded in Athens as a rival to Plato's Academy—returned to Macedonia, and within a year, at age 63, committed suicide.

Some things you can hold on to, but others you can put aside immediately—for example, Aristotle's notion of an ideal city-state governed by an elite, even priggish, aristocracy that relegated women to a secondary status, that condoned natural slavery, and that articulated a world view permeated with near-derision for other cultures. In an age in which your life and career will literally circle a globe of immense diversity in religious, ethnic, and material circumstance, and in an age in which it has become painfully apparent that people must cultivate every human and other resource to keep the peace, to provide basic necessities for an expanding population on an ecologically vulnerable planet, and to promise future generations some sense of a better life, Aristotle's ancient city-state is simply not an adequate model.

But there is much in Aristotle's vision beyond his time-bound and parochial Athens. His teleological concept—the concept that the natural aim and purpose of humankind is happiness in the sense of flourishing or developing one's full potential materially, intellectually, emotionally, and in all other ways—is a monumental contribution to philosophy. The same can be said of his emphasis on the virtues or the development of good character habits through training, discipline, and learning from the exemplary conduct of virtuous men and women. The virtues he espouses are not duties for the sake of duties, nor do they shape a life totally opposed to natural inclinations. Quite the contrary is true. Virtues are badges of civilization and good upbringing that give evidence of people's propensity to forge a middle way—a golden mean—between excess and deficit, between rashness and cowardice, between prodigality and selfishness, between lack of judgment and dithering, and so on.

Your business career is not the only aspect of your life that you have to tend to for years to come. You will have to find some means of weighing, balancing, and accommodating the interests of your spouse or companion, your close and extended family, your friends, your community, and your employer or business associates. A person with a clear vision of the good in the sense of happiness or flourishing, a person of good character who from years of training exemplifies the virtues of justice, courage, love, and practical wisdom (including the many kindred and related virtues), and a person who embraces the identity of the virtuous and the good and happy life is a person whom Aristotle has touched over the passage of twenty-four centuries.

A CRITIQUE OF VIRTUE ETHICS

Do not assume we have detailed the story of virtue ethics with the depth it deserves; that is equally true of our sketch of utilitarian, deontological, and contractarian theories as well. Each of these themes has many variations, and, of course, we carry into our descriptions all of the biases and presuppositions of

Western philosophy. Beyond that, you cannot have failed to notice that there is nothing here of the great moral content of the Talmud or the Koran or of Buddhism, Confucianism, or Taoism. Some of these things are simply beyond the scope of this book.

Regarding virtue ethics, some writers advance the position that virtue is no more than rule obedience or the propensity to adhere to rules—obedience to the Golden Rule, for example, or to the rule advancing the greatest good for the greatest number, or to one of the rules devised in Rawls's original position. In Aristotle's view, virtues could never be reduced to rules. How, after all, could a rule capture the richness of love or friendship, or the many faces of courage? As important as rules can be—for example, in the education and discipline of children or the enforcement of conventional laws—they have important shortcomings. Rules either mark the bare minimal behavior that is morally permissible or are so vague and abstract that they give no guidance at all. In any event, obedience to rules is very far from the excellences implicit in the virtues as Aristotle portrays them.

Aristotle's notion of happiness is open to a number of interpretations. Happiness, flourishing, and fulfillment can be given quite a different spin by a Nazi, a Ku Klux Klanner, or a religious fanatic like David Koresh. Aristotle, of course, would concede nothing to these or other representatives of the criminal world. After all, he did project a secondary status for women, held practically everything non-Athenian in contempt, and endorsed the notion of natural slavery. What other blind spots might one find? How is one to know what parts of Aristotle to hold on to and what to let go?

ETHICAL THEORIES AND JUSTICE

Teleological theories (including utilitarianism and virtue ethics) and duty-based (deontological) theories have been around for centuries. One can see manifestations of both in the law and in economic theories. For example, you have probably never read about an attempt to justify the cost of the freedoms protected by the First Amendment. Nor is it likely that you have ever heard anyone say that the First Amendment should be kept only if its benefits outweigh its costs. The idea of justifying the cost of principles of liberty and freedom is simply repugnant, but in the process of implementing these principles, courts do sometimes "balance" or weigh the costs against the benefits.[9]

Many other courses of action and commitments are made by a weighing of good against bad. Much of the environmental protection legislation includes a requirement of cost-benefit analysis. Industries are not required to clean up the environment to perfection, but rather to a level that the cost to industry does not exceed benefits to the nation. Questions of the common good and general welfare usually have no single right answers. After all, how clean is clean enough?

This line of thought brings up the following questions: Should cost-benefit procedures be applied to the commitment to justice? Do people cheapen or weaken the concept of justice by asking whether it is affordable? Certainly people should require justice in the legal system, but should the business institutions be just? Is justice merely the product of an efficient economic system?

WHAT IS JUSTICE?

If law is conceived as a justice-seeking process, particular laws must be evaluated on the basis of their contribution to this ideal. What, then, is justice? Is it purely contextual, meaning one thing in Russia, another in Hitler's Germany, and still something else in South Africa, El Salvador, and the United States? Or does it embody some immutable, objective content? We do not claim to have resolved this matter, but we do adhere to the notion that fairness, liberty, and equality are the chief components of justice. In political terms, it means at least this: Individuals within the public body are regarded as equally free and worthy of dignity and respect as human beings; they are, nevertheless, subject to reasonable and objective restraints that are fitting, appropriate, or proportionate to their behavior.

In an age-old dialogue recorded by Plato, Socrates elicited from Polemarches at least an entry-level definition of justice: giving people their "due."[10] We understand Plato's insight to mean that the substance of this concept pervades two interrelated levels: social and individual. We focus on the broad outlines of the types of justice and offer a way to think about this difficult-to-achieve ideal.

In U. S. society, there are two levels of justice: the social level and the individual level. Each of these has at least two components. On the *social level*, justice is viewed as distributive and retributive.

Distributive justice addresses the allocation of social goods and bads: wealth-poverty, income-unemployment, power-powerlessness, and so on. These issues are usually dealt with by Congress and state legislatures. Distributive justice is a principal concern of democratic institutions.

Retributive justice, or retribution, refers to public sanctions or penalties that are applied to those who engage in certain kinds of antisocial behavior—for example, murder, rape, and kidnapping. The criminal statutes of the federal, state, and local governments are examples of this type of justice.

On the *individual level*, justice is viewed as compensatory and commutative.

Compensatory justice means simply that a person who wrongfully inflicts harm on another person or that person's property must repay or repair the damage; that is, the one causing harm must try to place the injured party in as good a position as that person would have enjoyed had the wrong not been inflicted. Contract law, which gives a remedy for a breach of a promise, and tort law, which provides a remedy for intentional or negligent damage to our person or property, are examples of this type of justice.

Commutative justice entails fairness of a private bargain or exchange. Mutual satisfaction with regard to the substance of such an agreement presupposes full information, truthfulness, mental capacity, absence of coercion, and subjective satisfaction (as opposed to dollar-for-dollar equivalency) of the exchange. Some basic notions of contract law and other areas of law requiring "good faith" conduct are examples of this type of justice.

Learning the concepts of justice does not really deepen one's understanding of the nature of the subject matter. They are principally elaborations on the original theme of fairness or rendering to each person his or her due in a specific public or private setting. When, referring to a particular event or outcome, people say that "justice was served" or when they make a similar reference to the process or procedure (due process) of achieving that outcome, they are really talking about *right conduct*—right in the sense that it brings about or advances something that is essentially good, as opposed to evil, or that it maximizes the balance of good over evil.

So, one asks, where are we in this confusing blizzard of words—good and evil, justice and injustice, law and lawlessness? Although these terms cannot be defined to everyone's satisfaction, our point is that, like law, justice can be studied, analyzed, and discussed.

THE NATURE OF THE BUSINESS ENVIRONMENT

We mentioned in the introduction to this chapter that the third subject of this textbook was an examination of the nature of current commercial society. We believe that business-related circumstances have changed dramatically in the last fifty years. This change has profound implications for the legal system, for many business enterprises, and even for traditional notions of morality.

Briefly stated, the nature of this change is from a nineteenth-century society oriented toward individualism—individual thoughts and actions—to the current business society dominated by group thoughts and actions. To make this point clearer, consider for a moment the nature of business law at the turn of the century or shortly thereafter. The major emphasis was on contract law and the exchange of promises between autonomous and independent persons or individuals (business corporations were treated as persons). The law, in most cases, assumed that the parties to a contract were of roughly equal bargaining power; therefore, the enforcement of business-related promises was at the heart of business law. Now, look at the table of contents of this book. Describe the nature of the law you see outlined there. The major emphasis is on the law of products liability, employment discrimination, and employee safety and health; the law of federal securities; and the law that protects the environment. We have honored our past by including a single chapter on contract law and a few other chapters that reflect the very traditional law, but the dominant type of law is that passed by Congress and aimed at controlling and directing the behavior of large and medium-sized corporations.

Many of you will work for someone else after you graduate. In many cases, your employer will be a business corporation. Moreover, even if you establish your own business firm, you most probably will deal with others who work for medium-sized or large businesses. What is the impact of this changing reality? We do not pretend to supply you with a final answer, but we can convey to you an approach that may lead to an answer. When you go to work for a group of people in today's business environment, you will be exposed to a set of group values and group morals. You will carry with you your own set of individual values and moral beliefs, and this unique structure will both be reinforced by and, in some cases, conflict with those of the group. This process of reinforcement, tension, and conflict between individual notions of morality and those of the group help explain the recent interest in business ethics and corporate social responsibility. It may also help explain the sharply increased role of government in business affairs since the 1960s.

We can do no more than point to this change in the nature of the business environment. Bowen McCoy's article illustrates how this change is being felt by people in the business environment and explores some of the consequences or our ideas of law and morality in such a setting.

BOWEN H. MCCOY

The Parable of the Sadhu

[*Author's note*: Buzz McCoy, his friend Stephen, Pasang, their Sherpa guide, and porters were poised at the 15,500 foot mark and about to begin a 3:30 A.M. assault on an 18,000 foot Himalayan pass to Muklinath, an ancient Nepalese holy place, when a strange event began to unfold. An angry New Zealander from the party just ahead retraced his course with the almost naked, barefoot body of a sadhu, an Indian holy man, who was found lying on the ice and suffering badly of hypothermia. The New Zealander, having done his part, returned quickly to his group. Stephen and members of a Swiss party dressed the sadhu warmly in clothes of their own. Buzz then began his ascent with a small number of porters vaguely entertaining the notion that Stephen and Pasang would arrange with a party of Japanese, lower on the slope, to use their horse and transport the sadhu to the safety of a hut 1,000 feet below.

An hour after he had reached the pass, however, Buzz was joined by a distraught Stephen who glared at him and said: "How do you feel about contributing to the death of a fellow man?" Buzz did not fully comprehend what he meant. "Is the sadhu dead?" "No," replied Stephen, "but he surely will be!"

Neither the Japanese nor Pasang were cooperative about transporting the sadhu to the hut below. The time and energy consumed there would jeopardize their safety, it was argued. Due evidently to Stephen's persistence, the sadhu was taken 500 feet down, left in a sunny spot with food and water, and directed to make his way to the hut alone. We do not know if the sadhu lived or died.

For many of the following days and evenings Stephen and Buzz debated their behavior toward the sadhu. Stephen was a committed Quaker with deep moral vision.][11]

He said, "I feel that what happened with the sadhu is a good example of the breakdown between the individual ethic and the corporate ethic. No one person was willing to assume ultimate responsibility for the sadhu. Each was willing to do his bit just so long as it was not too inconvenient. When it got to be a bother, everyone just passed the buck to someone else and took off. . . . "

I defended the larger group, saying, "Look, we all cared. We all stopped and gave aid and comfort. Everyone did his bit. The New Zealander carried him down below the snow line. I took his pulse and suggested we treat him for hypothermia. You and the Swiss gave him clothing and got him warmed up. The Japanese gave him food and water. The Sherpas carried him down to the sun and pointed out the easy trail toward the hut. He was well enough to throw rocks at a dog. What more could we do?"

"You have just described the typical affluent Westerner's response to a problem. Throwing money—in this case food and sweaters—at it, but not solving the fundamentals!" Stephen retorted.

"What would satisfy you?" I said. "Here we are, a group of New Zealanders, Swiss, Americans, and Japanese who have never met before and who are at the apex of one of the most powerful experiences of our lives. Some years the pass is so bad no one gets over it. What right does an almost naked pilgrim who chooses the wrong trail have to disrupt our lives? Even the Sherpas had no interest in risking the trip to help him beyond a certain point."

Stephen calmly rebutted, "I wonder what the Sherpas would have done if the sadhu had been a well-dressed Nepali, or what the Japanese would have done if the sadhu had been a well-dressed Asian, or what you would have done, Buzz, if the sadhu had been a well-dressed Western woman?"

"Where, in your opinion," I asked instead, "is the limit of our responsibility in a situation like this? We had our own well-being to worry about. Our Sherpa guides were unwilling to jeopardize us or the porters for the sadhu. No one else on the mountain was willing to commit himself beyond certain self-imposed limits."

★ ★ ★

The Individual vs. the Group Ethic

Despite my arguments, I felt and continue to feel guilt about the sadhu. I had literally walked through a classic moral dilemma without fully thinking through the consequences. My excuses for my actions include a high adrenaline flow, a superordinate goal, and a once-in-a-lifetime opportunity—factors in the usual corporate situation, espe-

cially when one is under stress.

Real moral dilemmas are ambiguous, and many of us hike right through them, unaware that they exist. When, usually after the fact, someone makes an issue of them, we tend to resent his or her bringing it up. Often, when the full import of what we have done (or not done) falls on us, we dig into a defensive position from which it is very difficult to emerge. In rare circumstances we may contemplate what we have done from inside a prison.

Had we mountaineers been free of physical and mental stress caused by the effort and the high altitude, we might have treated the sadhu differently. Yet isn't stress the real test of personal and corporate values? The instant decisions executives make under pressure reveal the most about personal and corporate character.

Among the many questions that occur to me when pondering my experience are: What are the practical limits of moral imagination and vision? Is there a collective or institutional ethic beyond the ethics of the individual? At what level of effort or commitment can one discharge one's ethical responsibilities?

Not every ethical dilemma has a right solution. Reasonable people often disagree; otherwise there would be no dilemma. In a business context, however, it is essential that managers agree on a process for dealing with dilemmas.

★ ★ ★

One of our problems was that as a group we had no process for developing a consensus. We had no sense of purpose or plan. The difficulties of dealing with the sadhu were so complex that no one person could handle it. Because it did not have a set of preconditions that could guide its action to an acceptable resolution, the group reacted instinctively as individuals. The cross-cultural nature of the group added a further layer of complexity. We had no leader with whom we could all identify and in whose purpose we believed. Only Stephen was willing to take charge, but he could not gain adequate support to care for the sadhu.

* * *

For 20 years I have been exposed at senior levels to a variety of corporations and organizations. It is amazing how quickly an outsider can sense the tone and style of an organization and the degree of tolerated openness and freedom to challenge management.

Organizations that do not have a heritage of mutually accepted, shared values tend to become unhinged during stress, with each individual bailing out for himself. In the great takeover battles we have witnessed during past years, companies that had strong cultures drew the wagons around them and fought it out, while other companies saw executives, supported by their golden parachutes, bail out of the struggles.

Because corporations and their members are interdependent, for the corporation to be strong the members need to share a preconceived notion of what is correct behavior, a "business ethic," and think of it as a positive force, not a constraint.

* * *

The word "ethics" turns off many and confuses more. Yet the notions of shared values and agreed-on process for dealing with adversity and change—what many people mean when they talk about corporate culture—seem to be at the heart of the ethical issue. People who are in touch with their own core beliefs and the beliefs of others and are sustained by them can be more comfortable living on the cutting edge. At times, taking a tough line or a decisive stand in a muddle of ambiguity is the only ethical thing to do. If a manager is indecisive and

spends time trying to figure out the "good" thing to do, the enterprise may be lost.

Business ethics, then, has to do with the authenticity and integrity of the enterprise. To be ethical is to follow the business as well as the cultural goals of the corporation, its owners, its employees, and its customers. Those who cannot serve the corporate vision are not authentic business people and, therefore, are not ethical in the business sense.

* * *

What would have happened had Stephen and I carried the sadhu for two days back to the village and become involved with the villagers in his care? In four trips to Nepal my most interesting experiences occurred in 1975 when I lived in a Sherpa home in the Khumbu for five days recovering from altitude sickness. The high point of Stephen's trip was an invitation to participate in a family funeral ceremony in Manang. Neither experience had to do with climbing the high passes of the Himalayas. Why were we so reluctant to try the lower path, the ambiguous trail? Perhaps because we did not have a leader who could reveal the greater purpose of the trip to us.

Why didn't Stephen with his moral vision opt to take the sadhu under his personal care? The answer is because, in part, Stephen was hard-stressed physically himself, and because, in part, without some support system that involved our involuntary and episodic community on the mountain, it was beyond his individual capacity to do so.

I see the current interest in corporate culture and corporate value systems as a positive response to Stephen's pessimism about the decline of the role of the individual in large organizations. Individuals who operate from a thoughtful set of personal values provide the foundation for a corporate culture. A corporate tradition that encourages freedom of inquiry, supports personal values, and reinforces a focused sense of direction can fulfill the need for individuality along with the prosperity and success of the group. Without such corporate support, the individual is lost.

That is the lesson of the sadhu. In a complex corporate situation, the individual requires and deserves the support of the group. If people cannot find such support from their organization, they don't know how to act. If such support is forthcoming, a person has a stake in the success of the group, and can add much to the process of establishing and maintaining a corporate culture. It is management's challenge to be sensitive to individual needs, to shape them, and to direct and focus them for the benefit of the group as a whole

For each of us the sadhu lives. Should we stop what we are doing and comfort him; or should we keep trudging up toward the high pass? Should I pause to help the derelict I pass on the street each night as I walk by the Yale Club en route to Grand Central Station? Am I his brother? What is the nature of our responsibility if we consider ourselves to be ethical persons? Perhaps it is to change the values of the group so that it can, with all its resources, take the other road.

ARTICLE FOLLOW-UP

This parable is one man's account of the tension he felt when a conflict arose between the objectives of his group (the climbing unit) and the need of an individual who could have frustrated these objectives. Notice the tendency of the climbers to pass the sadhu on to the group with the apparent means to care for him. The New Zealanders thought the author's party was better able to handle him than they were; the Americans thought that the Japanese, with their horse, could better care for the sadhu than they. The pattern here is a common one today. People tend to pass their frustrations on to the group with the apparent resources to deal with the problem rather than attend to it themselves. This may be one result of the loss of individual power that people feel. At least this pattern may help explain why so many have looked to government for guidance and help.

The response of our students to this parable during the past several years has been diverse, but much of it has focused on the "guilt trip" that Stephen put on Buzz. "Under the circumstances, the climbers didn't do too bad a job," many of our students have related. "It is not the climbers' fault that a hungry and poorly clothed man fell into their midst. Beyond that, they didn't ignore him. They attended to his immediate needs and left him in 'decent' shape. Give me a break, Stephen," they add.

Perhaps even Buzz fails to give proper emphasis to what we consider, at least in hindsight, to be the crucial point: Buzz, in his own words, "literally walked through a classic moral dilemma without fully thinking through the consequences." In fact, it is unlikely that he even recognized the dilemma until after the fact—that is, until Stephen explained the problem. Buzz was so carried away with his own concerns, as we frequently are with ours, that he did not bring consciously to mind that someone could be dying. What should people do about something like that? They simply have to become sensitized to the well-being of the other person so that they recognize that there is a problem.

This essay introduces the idea of a corporate culture. A corporate culture focuses on the "shared values" that a group subscribes to, and it influences group behavior through an "agreed-on process" of dealing with adversity, ambiguity, and change. A corporate culture, shaped by strong moral leadership, brings coherence, purpose, and guidance to the group and a sense of personal worth to group members. Strong cultures do not just happen; they have to be built, nurtured, and reinforced. There was no corporate culture on the mountain pass, and that explains, in part, why Buzz and the other climbers did not act as a unit as well as they might have.

This parable can also inform about the law. Can you draft a rule that would have directed the author to the proper behavior in this story? We admit there may be some disagreement about the proper response of the author to the sadhu, but for purposes of argument, assume that the best response was for the author to take the responsibility for this sick man. How can such a rule be worded?

THE DUTY TO RESCUE

Several European countries have in their penal codes provisions imposing a duty to rescue. The Dutch Penal Code, Article 450, is typical: "One who, witnessing the danger of death with which another is suddenly threatened, neglects to give or furnish him such assistance as he can give or procure without reasonable fear of danger to himself or to others, is to be punished, if the death of the person in distress follows, by a detention of three months at most, and an amende of three hundred florins at most." [12]

In this section, you receive some, but very little, guidance about the formulation of rules that require you to help other people who are in distress. Rules, as we have said before, spell out minimal, bottom-line, merely permissible behaviors. They are not very effective in inspiring people to give their best efforts. When rules don't work, or when they are not working well in a particular situation, you might consider the advice of Buzz McCoy, and Aristotle as well. Focus on something good. Let yourself be guided by the highest and noblest values you can imagine. In a group (a climbing group or a corporate boardroom), these must be "shared values" if the effort is to be successful.

In high-tension, high-stakes corporate dramas, you are not likely to have much time to discuss which course of action will lead to the greatest good for the greatest number, or how to apply Kant's categorical imperative, or Rawls's liberty of difference principle. When confronted with situations such as this, people are most likely guided by the norms of the group or the community. As Buzz McCoy put it, officers and employees are guided by their corporate culture.

People react as they have been trained to react, and they have been trained in a corporate culture that fosters the virtues, they will react virtuously. They will advance the highest and noblest values. Depending on the circumstances, that could lead to a number of different outcomes. In the comfort of our classrooms, we must take care not to condemn Buzz's conduct too hastily, but as you reflect on this scenario, do you think that virtuous people would have reacted the same way Buzz did, or differently?

The Vermont legislature passed a statute providing "(a) A person who knows that another is exposed to grave physical harm shall, to the extent that the same can be rendered without danger or peril to himself or without interference with important duties owed to other, give reasonable assistance to the exposed person unless that violates subsection (a) of this section shall be fined not more than $100" (Vt. Stat. Ann. title 12, sec. 519(1973)).[13]

Do you gain from these statutes any insight into the problem of drafting one applicable to business associations? Should business efforts to "rescue" or contribute to community well-being be limited to those situations in which the "victim" is in danger of death or, more realistically, in which the local United Fund or other community group is about to become insolvent? What about a criminal statute that requires business firms to care for the hungry and homeless in the local community?

Law, at least as it has been traditionally thought of, has noticeable limits. It is very difficult, if not impossible, to describe and then compel desirable behavior. It is much easier to describe prohibited or undesirable behavior. From this, you should learn that, from the point where the law ends, you have only notions of morality to guide you.

CONCLUSION

If you are interested in the study of the social forces that direct and hold society together, the study of the law should fascinate you. It is incorrect to think of the law as numerous overlapping rules that are laid out, analyzed, shuffled and rearranged, and then studied. The study of law is not the memorization of rules and the technicalities of legal procedure in which the rules are applied; rather we believe the law is much more directly accessible to you, and we hope to persuade you of this viewpoint in this textbook.

The law is motion; it is, like life, activity. Law changes and grows and is shaped by the collective morality of society. As the *Regina* v. *Dudley* case illustrates, sometimes groups in society have differing moral views of events. These different views cause social tension, which can be seen in the activity of the law. An existing tension in social matters, however, does not mean that the matter is complex; rather, it means contending forces should be studied, understood, and appreciated. The law is filled with such tensions because our social life is filled with them.

Through the centuries, bodies of organized thought about the purposes and nature of law have been created. These schools of thought about the law are generally referred to as studies in jurisprudence. Jurisprudence is a study of law as an expression of collective morality and individual moral reasoning. In this chapter, we explored the notion of moral reasoning and suggested that we could gain from an understanding of it. We also suggested two often competing or clashing methods or procedures of moral reasoning (whether individual or collective). We can see both utilitarian and deontological processes in the everyday operation of government and in our own lives.

Most people proceed on the assumption that they all have good intentions. As the parable of the sadhu makes clear, however, sometimes good intentions are not enough. The nature of the business environment often narrowly channels social pressures and goals so that even the best people lose sight of their good intentions. When this happens, what is the proper approach? Is the law structured to make people good, or is it capable only of defining behavior that falls below a social minimum? This difficult question recurs throughout this book.

Professor Lon Fuller of the Harvard Law School (1939–1972) maintained that the law "as it is" cannot be divorced from the law "as it ought to be." We adopt Fuller's view. If one takes a discussion of morality out of the law (as the positivists urge people to do), what's left is a seemingly sterile device such as a wheelbarrow—an empty one at that. It can be pushed in almost any direction and has no real power to go anywhere on its own, Professor Fuller would maintain.[14] We believe, like Professor Fuller, that through reasoned discussion and arguments that embody a moral component, we will learn about the objectives and limits of rules and the law. After all, wheelbarrows are built for a purpose, and we should examine and evaluate both the purpose and how well the wheelbarrow (the law) fulfills that purpose.

REVIEW QUESTIONS AND PROBLEMS

1. In the case *Regina* v. *Dudley and Stephens*, why do you suppose that "self-defense" was not recognized by the court as a means of reversing the conviction? Explain.

2. Following World War II and the discovery of Nazi atrocities at concentration camps, the Nuremberg trials of high Nazi officials proceeded on the thesis that certain kinds of behavior are totally reprehensible and unjustifiable. We call these "crimes against humanity." Conventional warfare, however, has escaped such official condemnation. Peace-time prohibitions against killing are usually suspended during a war.

   Would it be appropriate in the *Dudley and Stephens* case to suspend the rules because the parties were so far removed from civilization and, in a sense at war with the elements?

3. Immanuel Kant was an eighteenth-century philosopher whose ethical writings displayed a commitment to principles that could be logically universalized and applied to everyone as well as reversed and applied to oneself. In this regard Kant condemned all lying, even lying to protect others. Utilitarians are more "flexible" on this subject. They will approve of lying if it fosters the public good or welfare to a greater extent than any other alternative.

   Which of these do you find to be embodied in commercial reality today?

4. According to the author of the sadhu parable, what is business ethics all about?

ENDNOTES

1. See the interesting account of the circumstances surrounding the prosecution and disposition of this case in Mallin, In Warm Blood: Some Historical and Procedural Aspects of *Regina* v. *Dudley and Stephens,* 34 *U. Chi. L. Rev.* 387 (1967). See also Simpson, *The Story of the Tragic Last Voyage of the Mignonette and the Strange Legal Proceedings to Which It Gave Rise* (1984).

2. From *Moral Issues in Business,* by Vincent E. Barry, © 1979 by Wadsworth, Inc. Reprinted by permission of Wadsworth Publishing Co.

3. These definitions are taken from Beauchamp and Bowie, *Ethical Theory and Business* 2-20 (1979).

4. Matthew 7:12.

5. Kant, *Groundwork for the Metaphysics of Morals* 70 (Paton trans. 1964).

6. *Id.* at 96.

7. Rawls, *A Theory of Justice* 3 (1971).

8. This section of the text is based, in part, on Smith, *Ethical Components of Price,* by Ronald N. Smith, University of Texas (1980).

9. In *United States* v. *Leon,* 104 S. Ct. 3405, 3416 (1984), the Supreme Court related that it would evaluate the costs and benefits of suppressing reliable physical evidence seized by officers reasonably relying on a warrant issued by a detached and neutral magistrate.

10. *The Republic of Plato,* I. 331E-336A (F. Cornford trans. 1945).

11. Mr. McCoy is managing director of Morgan Stanley & Co., Inc. and president of Morgan Stanley Realty, Inc. He is also an ordained ruling elder of the United Presbyterian Church. This piece is reprinted by permission of *Harvard Business Review,* Excerpt from "The Parable of the Sadhu" by Bowen H. McCoy, *Harvard Business Review* (September-October 1983), pp. 103-108. Copyright © 1983 by the President and Fellows of Harvard College; all rights reserved.

12. For other examples, see Rudzinski, The Duty to Rescue: A Comparative Analysis, in Ratcliffe, *The Good Samaritan and the Law* 91 (1966).

13. See Franklin, Vermont Requires Rescue: A Comment, 25 *Stan. L. Rev.* 51 (1972).

14. Summers, *Lon S. Fuller* 25 (1984).

CHAPTER 2

Foundations of the American Legal System

INTRODUCTION

Before we discuss the substantive parts of the legal environment of business, we must explain how American law is established. The basic ideas of the law are mostly historical in nature and come from cultures that existed centuries ago. In the first part of this chapter we examine these ideas that form the basis for the values (e.g., individual freedom) that dominate the legal system today. In the second part of this chapter, we present an overview of the present types of American law and examine briefly the American judicial system.

In a general way, we can detect two basic methods of establishing law that, as methods of thought or logic, characterize most of the legal system of Western civilization today. One is called the civil law system. The second method, not nearly as old as the civil law system, comes from England and is called the common law system.

THE CIVIL LAW SYSTEM

To scholars of law, *civil law* means a system of jurisprudence created and first administered in the Roman Empire, particularly by Justinian and his successors. This civil law was a comprehensive code of conduct imposed by the sovereign. It was administered first by the articulation of a general principle or rule of law and then by the application of this principle to various circumstances. The civil law system is a good example of the law as defined by positivists and discussed in Chapter 1.

The Twelve Tables of Rome (450 B.C.)[1] mark the beginning of the publication of civil law codes. They emerged in response to the increasing social stature of the plebeians, who literally demanded publication of the codes in the marketplace—a stark contrast with the oral tradition that kept law in the private realm of patrician priests.

The Civil Code of Justinian, published in A.D. 533, like the Code Napoleon (the French Civil Code of 1804), was really the work of distinguished scholars, principally Tribonian, rather than the emperor for whom it was named. A fifteen-person commission (including law professors from Beirut and Constantinople, as well as practitioners) organized and drafted the centerpiece of this undertaking, called the Digest, which was based on the authority of jurists writing between A.D. 100 and 250.

Generally, civil law codes and the works of eminent Roman jurists that preceded them adopted a logical process *that moves from general standards to particular cases.* Neither the Roman magistrates nor civil law judges since that time have been "bound" to the doctrine of precedent, (the practice of being guided or influenced by previously decided cases). Precedent has no official role in civil law jurisdictions such as France and Louisiana. In a broad sense, one could say that the civil law is built from the top down (from general standards to specific cases), whereas the common law, which is discussed in the next section, is built from the ground up (from cases into general theories).

Today, when Congress studies a problem (e.g., employee safety and health), and then adopts a comprehensive statutory scheme to deal with it (e.g., the Occupational Safety and Health Act), Congress is following a pattern of establishing law that is centuries old. The impact of the civil law system of the Romans has been described this way:

It is no exaggeration to say that, next to the bible, no book has left a deeper mark upon the history of mankind than the *Corpus Juris Civilis.* Much has been written about the impact of Rome upon Western Civilization. Much has been disputed about "the ghost of the Roman Empire" that still lurks far beyond the shores of the Mediterranean. The heritage of Roman law is not a ghost but a living reality. It is present in the court as well as in the marketplace. It lives on not only in the institutions but even in the language of all civilized nations.[2]

THE COMMON LAW SYSTEM

A more recently developed method of establishing law, but one that is still centuries old, is the common law system. Its impact on the method of developing law today is as great as that of the civil law system, with which it contrasts in the following principal way: *The common law system starts with a specific event or case and then builds a general idea or operating principle.* In this way, authority for a decision in a case can be obtained by relying on the general principle accrued from earlier cases presenting the same or comparable circumstances. This doctrine of precedent, or *stare decisis,* is the hallmark of the common law and is examined in greater detail in the following article by Berman and Greiner.

HAROLD F. BERMAN

WILLIAM R. GREINER

The Common Law System: Historical Development of the Doctrine of Precedent

If we go back to the early history of modern English law, we find that by the end of the 12th century, virtually as soon as records of court proceedings were kept, there developed an interest in judicial decisions as guides to what the law is. Bracton in his treatise on English law, written in the middle of the 13th century, referred to about 500 decided cases; he also wrote a Notebook containing digests of 2000 cases. The word "precedent," however, is entirely absent from Bracton's vocabulary; cases for him and for his contemporaries were not binding authorities but merely illustrations of legal principles.

In the 14th, 15th and early 16th centuries law students kept notes of oral arguments in court cases. These notes, preserved in the so-called Yearbooks, show that not only the students but also the courts were concerned with analogizing and distinguishing cases. Again, however, the decisions were not treated as authorities in any sense, and if a judge did not approve of a decision he would just say it was wrong.

In the 16th and 17th centuries we get the first systematic reports of cases and the first mention of precedent. Judges then began to say that they are bound by precedents in matters of procedure, and especially in matters of pleading, and the practice of citing previous cases became firmly established. It is interesting to note, however, that in the first known use of the word precedent, in 1557, it is stated that a decision was given

"notwithstanding two precedents." Indeed, the doctrine of precedent which developed in these centuries did not provide that a single decision was binding but rather that a line of decisions would not be overturned. Lord Mansfield could still say, in the latter part of the 18th century, "The reason and spirit of cases make law; not the letter of particular precedents."[3]

* * *

In the later 19th century for the first time there developed the rule that a holding by a court in a previous case is binding on the same court (or on an inferior court) in a similar case. The doctrine was called *stare decisis*—"to stand by the decisions." It was never absolute. The court is only bound "in the absence of weighty reasons." There is always the possibility of overruling the previous holding.

Not only is *stare decisis* not absolute but it also has no clear meaning [because the real reason for the decision] is never certain. Moreover, the doctrine of precedent has different values in different fields of law. In dealing with questions of property law or commercial law a court is reluctant to overturn the holdings of previous cases since the community relies upon the stability of court decisions in making property or business transaction; indeed the expression "rule of property" is sometimes used with reference to a doctrine laid down in previous decisions which the court will not overturn because business people rely upon it (whether or not the doctrine relates to property law as such). In dealing with questions of tort law [personal injury] on the other hand, courts have less reason to be reluctant to overrule precedent or to "distinguish away" past cases; presumably if a driver of a car proceeds carelessly through an intersection when another careless driver is approaching from the opposite direction, he or she does not do so in reliance upon the rule that the contributory negligence of the other driver will bar the latter's recovery. Nevertheless, predictability of judicial decision is a factor to be considered in tort cases as in any other, if only for the reason that the lawyers for the parties rely on past decisions in bringing suit or in defending.

In matters of constitutional law—to take a third example—the doctrine of precedent has still less value than in matters of tort law, since it is a function of the courts under our system of law to adapt the provisions of the Constitution to the changing needs of society. This does not mean that the Constitution has no fixed meaning and that the courts will overturn previous constitutional decisions whenever they disapprove of them; on the contrary, the Constitution has an extraordinary stability as a framework of our social, economic and political life over the centuries, and the Supreme Court of the United States, in interpreting it, is strongly influenced by its own past decisions. But the interpretation of the Constitution is bound to be more flexible than the interpretation, say, of a contract.

Finally, *stare decisis* is often given a rather different value in matters of statutory interpretation because of a theory that a prior judicial decision interpreting a statute is presumed to have the approval of the legislature unless the legislature has overruled the decision by amending the statute. Thus a kind of legislative "rule of property," so to speak, is sometimes introduced into the field of statutory interpretation.

In the heyday of the doctrine of *stare decisis*, that is in the last quarter of the 19th and the first quarter of the 20th century, belief was prevalent that certainty in law could be obtained by a scientific use of precedent. The legislature alone was thought to have the function of changing the law; the court's function was "merely" to apply the law, and to apply it in accordance with the holdings of previous decisions. The common law as an organically growing body of experience and doctrine was supposed, in effect, to have been superseded by a body of fixed rules which could be mechanically applied.

The idea that the common law is a body of fixed rules vanished in the second quarter of the 20th century, and perhaps earlier, in the face of overwhelming changes in social, economic and political life. The mathematical or mechanical jurisprudence of the late 19th century which denied that there is an ethical element in the analogizing and distinguishing of cases can seldom be found today among leaders of legal thought, at least in the United States. This does not mean, however, that the doctrine of precedent has been repudiated. It means, rather, that there has been a return to an older concept of precedent. Precedent is seen as a means of marshalling past experience, of providing a historical context, for making the choice at hand. . . .

ARTICLE FOLLOW-UP

It is not accurate to think of the civil law system as one in which rules are established exclusively by the sovereign; nor is it accurate to think of the common law system as one in which rules evolve only from specific instances, with *stare decisis* creating general principles. Each system bears some methodological kinship with the other, but the dominant characteristic of each is as set out above.

Today the legal system contains examples of both systems. Until the 1950s, almost all contract law and tort law outside Louisiana was judge-made or evolved as common law by stare decisis. Today, only tort law and some contract law—that involving the sale

of a service, as opposed to the sale of an object—is established by the common law process. The civil law process is exemplified by the fact that almost every year Congress and state legislatures pass major pieces of legislation that affect people's lives.

As the common law system developed in England, it established a very important distinction between legal and "equitable" principles. Today this distinction still exists in our legal system, so it is to this historical distinction that we now turn our attention.

The word *equity* is derived from the Latin word *aequitas*, meaning "equality or justice." Like much of the law, this body of rules comes from England. As the English sovereigns began to gather legislative power to themselves in the thirteenth and fourteenth centuries, some of the law became more and more the very word of the sovereign. The law became rigid and inflexible, and often a very literal application of the law had such severe repercussions that the effect of its application served to defeat the intent of the rule. What we are talking about here is a common circumstance even today—the assertion that one follows a rule just because it is a rule.

To create flexibility in the application of law, the English sovereign (beginning about 1350) allowed his immediate subordinate, the chancellor, to hear grievances arising because of the harsh application of the law or where no remedy existed in the sovereign's law. The chancellor would hear only those cases he believed to be worthy and would decide each case according to his conscience and sense of justice. In short, he was to provide equity when the literal application of the law failed in some respect.

Thus, *equity law became a supplementary set of rules or principles that operated only when the established legal system of the sovereign would not provide that which in good conscience should be done.* The Tudor and Stuart sovereigns and the Puritan Revolution somewhat confined the powers of the chancellor, but by the colonial period, two legal systems were discernible: that based on the word of the sovereign (by then the Parliament) and enforced in courts of law; and that based on principles of what was fair, given the circumstances, and enforced in "courts of equity."

During and after colonization, the American legal system continued to provide separate law and equity courts, but by the middle of the nineteenth century the two separate courts were made one and a single judge administered both bodies of rules. Today, the federal system and all of the states have only one system of courts, but the judges presiding may from time to time invoke certain "equitable" principles in those situations for which the remedies provided by the law, (or, today, the legislative and individual rules) are either inadequate to do "justice" or work an "injustice" by their direct application. These equitable rules are still applied at the discretion of the judge and remain supplementary in nature. Two examples of present-day equitable principles are the remedies of the issuance of an injunction (a court order prohibiting activity) and the decree of specific performance (a court order directing that certain activity take place). Both of these remedies are given to a party in a lawsuit when the traditional remedy at law of awarding money damages would be insufficient to compensate the injured party.

RULE CREATION IN THE LEGAL ENVIRONMENT OF BUSINESS

Today, the source of rules can be found in two processes: legislative and judicial rule creation. The *law*, as we use the term, is broader than what we mean by the term *rules*. The law starts with rules, and this is why we focus here on the rules alone.

The basic source of rules in American law is the Constitution of the United States. This document proclaims that it is the supreme law of the land and that any other law or legal activity that conflicts with it is unconstitutional or illegal.

LEGISLATIVE RULE CREATION—FEDERAL

The Constitution creates three coequal branches of government: the legislature, whose prime responsibility is to create rules; the executive, whose prime responsibility is to implement and enforce the rules; and the judiciary whose responsibility is to adjudicate—that is, to provide a framework for deciding whether a breach of a rule has occurred. Because the Constitution delegates to the Congress the duty to create rules, any rule passed by Congress that is consistent with the powers delegated to Congress by the Constitution is the supreme law of the land.

Congress, like state legislatures, may delegate some of its rule-making powers to other governmental units called *administrative agencies*. For example, the Sixteenth Amendment to the Constitution gives Congress the authority to levy a tax on incomes. After Congress passed income tax legislation, it delegated the authority to enforce the code to the secretary of the treasury. Congress further provided that the president, with the advice and consent of the Senate, should appoint a commissioner of internal revenue who "shall be in the Department of the Treasury" and that the secretary or his or her delegate (usually the commissioner) shall prescribe all necessary rules and regulations for the enforcement of the Internal Revenue Code. So, both the secretary of the treasury and the commissioner of Internal Revenue have substantial rule-making authority. Some of the numerous federal administrative agencies are "independent," such as the Federal Trade Commission; some are more directly controlled by Congress, such as the Internal Revenue Service; and some are controlled by the president, such as the Department of Labor. All of these administrative agencies make rules, formally called *regulations*, which are applied by the agency itself (see figure 2.1)

We have been discussing rules created by the legislature, but as you can see from figure 2.1, the federal government's rules are the result of all branches working together. Today, the Internal Revenue Code is a living body of rules created by Congress, the executive branch (through the secretary of the treasury), and the judicial branch. The judicial branch hears appeals in particular cases when the other two branches have made a final disposition of a case, and yet a taxpayer thinks a misapplication of law has occurred.

FIGURE 2.1   *Example of Legislative Delegation of Power to Create Rules*

**Rule-Making Authority from the U.S. Constitution
to Your Local IRS Agent**

Sixteenth Amendment to the U.S. Constitution
(authority to levy a tax on incomes)
↓
U.S. Congress
(the Internal Revenue Code)
↓
Secretary of the Treasury
appointed by the president
(Department of Treasury)
↓
Commissioner of Internal Revenue
appointed by the president
prescribes rules and regulations
↓
Rules and regulations for application
of the Internal Revenue Code
applied by IRS agents

LEGISLATIVE RULE CREATION—STATE

The Tenth Amendment to the Constitution provides that those powers not expressly given to the federal government are reserved to the states. The rule-creating power within each state follows the same general pattern as that of the federal government. Each state has a constitution that creates the basic rights, duties, and privileges of the residents of the state and organizes the state system of government. The legislature, one of three branches of state government, is the primary rule-making body, and any rules made by it that are consistent with the state constitution's fundamental guidelines are the supreme law of the state. State rules that are consistent with state constitutional provisions are valid unless they conflict with a federal rule made by Congress that is consistent with the Constitution; that is, if state-made rules or the official acts of a state agency conflict with a federal statute or the Constitution, those state rules or activities may be declared unconstitutional or illegal.

State legislatures may also create administrative agencies; state departments of welfare, taxation, and education that have rule-making authority are examples. Moreover, a state may also delegate some of its rule-making authority to local governments, such as county and city governments, which enact ordinances.

JUDICIAL RULE CREATION

The role of the judiciary (court system) in rule creation may be divided into two broad categories First, the judiciary, in interpreting and applying legislative rules, inevitably creates rules of its own. These rules, whether in the form of an exception to the legislation or not, become part of the meaning of the legislative rules.

Second, and more applicable to this section, the judiciary may create substantive rights and duties where none existed in the statutory law. Generally, the rules of tort law are made by the judiciary, as are the rules regarding agency law. In addition, many fundamental ideas in the law of contracts were created by the judiciary. Rule creation that is separate from legislative enactments and that derives its authority from custom as adopted and recognized by the courts is, as we have already explained, referred to as the common law. Today the common law of the United States is determined only after reading numerous past decisions in which judges have attempted to describe the substantive rules in areas in which the legislatures have not acted and in which rules are needed to govern activity. To bring some uniformity to common law, legal scholars have collected and codified what they believe to be the best judicially created rules on a subject. These scholars publish and, from time to time, revise these rules in volumes entitled *Restatements of the Law*. In this text, we cite these restatements as a source of common law rules.

TYPES OF RULES

The types of rules generated by the two primary sources discussed above (the legislature and the judiciary) may be divided into two broad categories: criminal and civil. Neither the judiciary nor private persons can create criminal rules. These are created only by the federal and state legislatures. The criminal law is distinguished from the civil law primarily by (1) who initiates the prosecution process after a violation, (2) the standard of proof, and (3) the potential punishment or remedy (see Figure 2.2).

When we discuss civil law in this section, we focus on a category of rule violations that are vindicated by a private person who is injured or by the state seeking a noncriminal remedy. We do not mean to imply a connection between this civil law rule category and the civil law system of France or of Louisiana.

CRIMINAL AND CIVIL RULES DISTINGUISHED

A *crime* is an illegal act defined by a statute, the prosecution of which is initiated by a federal, state, or county prosecutor; the person being tried for the crime (the *defendant*) is tried on behalf of and in the name of the federal or state government. The civil law is usually "enforced" by private persons or by a governmental unit suing for the breach of a civil rule. The "wrong" involved in a criminal prosecution is one that usually manifests an "evil" intent. It is the purpose of the criminal law to punish this evil intent. If the defendant does not plead guilty, punishment may be imposed only after a trial is held and the defendant is found guilty.

In a criminal case, the government has the burden of proving guilt beyond a reasonable doubt. This differs substantially from the standard of proof in a civil case. In the latter instance, the plaintiff (the party that files the law suit) must prove that it is more probable than not that the defendant (the party that answers the claim filed by the plaintiff) committed the act complained of. Obviously, this standard of proof is less than that required in criminal cases.

Finally, in the prosecution of a criminal case, the remedy sought (by the court and jury) is the imposition of a fine or imprisonment. In a civil case, the law seeks to compensate the injured party, not to punish the defendant. Thus, the plaintiff seeks money damages for compensation or an equitable remedy.

FIGURE 2.2 *Types of Rules Distinguished*

	Criminal Rules	Civil Rules
1. Who initiates the prosecution process	Only federal or state governmental agencies	Private persons and federal and state governmental agencies
2. Standard of proof	The elements of the crime exist beyond a reasonable doubt	It is more likely than not that the elements of the civil wrong exist (majority or preponderance of evidence)
3. Potential punishment or remedy	Imposition of a fine or imprisonment	Award of money damages or an equitable remedy.

The criminal law is usually subdivided into two more categories: felonies and misdemeanors. A *felony* is a crime of a serious nature and is defined by the federal and state legislatures as an offense, the punishment for which may be a penitentiary sentence of more than one year or, in some states, more than six months. A *misdemeanor*, a less serious crime, is usually punishable by fine or imprisonment for less than one year, or six months in some states. Because the state legislatures have the duty of creating rules for the health and welfare of the residents of the state, most of the commonly known criminal rules are created by state legislatures.

These distinctions between the criminal and the civil law are, for the most part, procedural in nature. There are differences, however, of a more substantive sort.

A NOTE ON THE SUBSTANCE OF CRIMINAL AND CIVIL RULES

In Chapter 1, we suggest that the nature of commercial reality or the circumstances of the legal environment of business today are very different from those of a few decades ago. This difference has been noted, for example, in the development of criminal law.

Numerous television programs would have viewers believe that a defendant cannot be convicted of murder unless the district attorney (D.A.) can find a victim, a body, a corpus delicti. This portrayal is not even close to the truth. The words *corpus delicti* mean literally "the body of the crime" (or wrong). In practice, this means that the D.A. must prove beyond a reasonable doubt the elements or components of the crime, not that he or she must have a victim's body. At the turn of the century, almost all crimes required the element of intent. The D.A. or prosecutor had to prove beyond a reasonable doubt that the defendant had the intent to do the illegal act.

Examine, for example, the elements of the crime of theft. It consists of taking from the possession or control of the owner personal property without the owner's consent and *with the intent to deprive the owner of its value.* If, then, you mistakenly walked off with your roommate's sunglasses, thinking they were yours, no theft would have occurred because the required element of *intent* was not present.

Today, when an individual is charged with one of the traditional crimes such as robbery, murder, or rape, individual intent is central to finding the person guilty. Proving intentional wrongdoing, however, is complicated when the actor is a large corporation. Proof of intent is substantially less important when a corporation is the defendant. The focus is more on the very act itself. For example, if a corporation violates a state or federal statute prohibiting the discharge of toxic chemicals into the environment, all the prosecutor need prove is the act of the discharge itself.

Because proving the element of intent is not always an accurate way to distinguish between civil and criminal law, another way to better understand the difference is to look at the *remedy sought.* If the remedy sought by a prosecutor is called a penalty or if the statute provides that individuals who are guilty may be sent to jail, then the proceeding is a criminal one. If the remedy, sought by the prosecuting agent is called damages or is an equitable remedy such as an injunction, then the proceeding is one of civil law.

Some commentators prefer to classify law as either public or private. *Public law* is made by the various legislatures of the states or the federal government or an administrative agency and may be either criminal or civil. *Private law* is the set of rules enforced by courts and invoked by private individual parties. If, for example, you sue your landlord over a breach of a lease agreement, many commentators would see this as "private law" (see figure 2.3).

FIGURE 2.3 *Major Classifications of American Law*

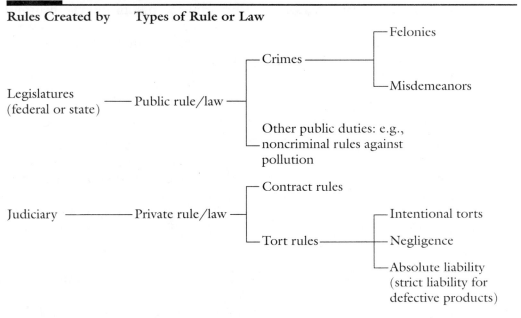

Rules Created by   Types of Rule or Law

Legislatures (federal or state) —— Public rule/law —┬— Crimes ——┬— Felonies
                                                     │   └— Misdemeanors
                                                     └— Other public duties: e.g., noncriminal rules against pollution

Judiciary —— Private rule/law —┬— Contract rules
                               └— Tort rules ——┬— Intentional torts
                                               ├— Negligence
                                               └— Absolute liability (strict liability for defective products)

Note: The legislatures create public rules and may create or refine some private rules, but courts do not usually create public rules. An exception would be an injunction requested by a private party and issued by a court to abate a public nuisance, such as a health or safety hazard not specifically covered by a statute.

THE AMERICAN JUDICIAL SYSTEM

Because the U.S. Constitution and all of the state constitutions create judicial systems for the redress of the breach of a rule, there are fifty-one different systems: one federal system and fifty state systems. The federal system is nationwide and is composed of three levels of courts. The courts on the initial level, the trial courts, are called the federal district courts. Each state is divided into districts, with as many federal district courts in each district as Congress deems necessary.

If a litigant in the federal system believes an error was committed at the trial stage, an appeal may be taken to the second level of the system, the federal circuit court of appeals. Currently, thirteen appellate circuits are in the federal system, plus a separate appellate circuit for the District of Columbia. An appeal from the circuit court level goes to the third level, the United States Supreme Court, composed of nine justices sitting in Washington, D.C. Usually, appeals will be heard by the Supreme Court if four justices vote to hear the case. Almost all appeals to the Supreme Court are heard at the discretion of the Court and very few appeals are heard as a matter of right. Those heard at the Court's discretion come before it on a *writ of certiorari*.

Generally, the various state systems are also of a three-level nature: an initial trial court, an appellate court level, and a final appellate court, usually called the supreme court of the state. This basic scheme may be varied by adding township, city, or small claims courts in which the amount in dispute may not exceed a given amount (usually $500) or by adding courts of special jurisdiction, such as those limited to probate, juvenile, or domestic relations. Nevertheless, the general scheme is similar to the federal scheme: one trial court level followed by two appellate levels.

THE FEDERAL COURT SYSTEM

The state and federal judicial systems are administered separately. The application of the criminal law provides the best example of the division of duties between the two systems. Prosecutions for the breach of the criminal rules created by Congress take place in the federal system. This is necessary to secure a uniform application of the federal criminal laws. The action must begin at the federal district court level and be prosecuted by a federal official, a U.S. attorney for the district, or the U.S. attorney's staff. These attorneys are agents of the U.S. Department of Justice under the U.S. attorney general. Any time a civil or criminal action is initiated in a federal court on the basis of the Constitution or some congressional enactment, it is said to be based on a *federal question*. That is one way of getting into a federal court. The other way is by diversity of citizenship and is discussed in a following section, "The Overlap Between the Two Court Systems."

THE STATE COURT SYSTEM

Most crimes, such as murder, assault and battery, and larceny, are defined by state legislatures. The prosecution of these crimes must begin at the trial court level in the state courts. These prosecutions are initiated by a state or, usually, a county prosecutor, who may be elected or, in some cases, appointed.

The judicial system selected by a *civil* litigant is determined by which legislative source, federal or state, created the rule that is the subject of the complaint. For example, if a violation of the Clayton Act is alleged and damages are sought, the suit must begin in the federal judiciary. If the failure to meet a rule created by the state legislature is the subject of the case, it usually begins in the state judicial system. The reason is, again, the necessity to preserve the uniformity of the federal rule application.

THE OVERLAP BETWEEN THE TWO COURT SYSTEMS

The two judicial systems overlap for at least two important reasons. The first is to alleviate the local prejudice that might be present when a citizen of one state is sues a citizen of another in the state court system (usually in the state of the defendant's citizenship). To this end, Congress created federal power (jurisdiction) to hear the case if the amount in controversy exceeds $50,000. In most cases based on this type of federal jurisdiction, called *diversity jurisdiction* because the parties in the case must be citizens of different states, the legal cause of action on which the suit proceeds is created by the state. It is assumed that local prejudice will be minimized in the federal district courts because the judges are appointed by the president, not by a local political body, and serve until they retire voluntarily or are impeached. They need not stand for election, as do some state or county judges. Moreover, the federal district is usually geographically larger than that of the state trial court; hence, jury members in the federal court are picked from a wider area, again minimizing the chance for local prejudice to influence the matter.

In summary, a private civil litigant with a state law claim may use the federal system if the parties to the case are from different states *and* the amount in controversy exceeds $50,000.

A second major reason for overlap of the federal and state judicial systems is to accommodate appeals from the state to the federal system. If either party in a state court case raises issues in which the state substantive or procedural law conflicts with the U.S. Constitution, the party may request an appeal to the United States Supreme Court—after appeals raising these same issues are taken through the highest state court that can hear the case. The Supreme Court has the final word on all interpretations of the Constitution, whether or not the case originated on the state or federal level.

We provide a rather detailed explanation of the civil trial process in the appendix at the end of this chapter. For now, we stop our explanation of rules and the processes in which they are used and ask you to reflect on the legal system as a whole. What are your feelings about this system? Whose interests are served? Is everyone, indeed, equal before the law?

You have probably lived within this major social system for at least twenty years and have many ideas about how it operates and how it affects you. The remaining material in this chapter is nontechnical in nature and is intended to broaden your perspective on the role of law in the environment of American business methods and institutions.

ALTERNATIVE DISPUTE RESOLUTION

Alternative dispute resolution (ADR) is a way of dealing with legal problems through a variety of means other than litigation. Although the name of the Chief Justice of the United States Supreme Court may not come readily to the mind of most business people, the name Judge Wapner is familiar to practically everyone. Under the laws of California, and those of a number of other states, if the parties agree to have their disputes resolved finally in a courtroom-like atmosphere, the decision of the rent-a-judge is unappealable, at least in the absence of fraud or other such conduct that would undermine the integrity of the process. Judge Wapner is simply the most notable of a large number of highly competent retired judges who render this valuable service. The phrase *rent-a-judge*, by the way, is by no means a derogatory one. It is simply a breezy way of referring to this particular ADR technique that has been picked up by the press and has become part of the business culture.

ADR offers many creative settlement techniques, but we do not claim too much for it. Given the nature and complexity of the legal problems involved and the range and immensity of the interests that hang in the balance, litigation may be the best alternative. We simply use this opportunity to explore different ways of "doing justice" not only between the parties but also for the business community and society as a whole.

Whether or not United States is really the "litigious society" that has become the popularly accepted cultural image is open to question. "Lies, damn lies, and statistics" seem to muddle rather than clarify the picture. One thing is clearer, however: Litigation is a very expensive process. U.S. firms pay something like $20 billion annually in litigation fees, and this does not count the indirect cost that takes a toll on the time and energy of business managers and the loss of a valued customer or supplier that almost always follows the dispute. According to Professor John Allison, writing for the *Harvard Business Review* (January—February 1990, pp. 166-177), "Long term business relationships can be as valuable to a company as long-term personal relationships. . . . [I]n either situation the resolution process itself can take a heavy toll on the participants if creative methods of resolving disputes are not given a chance." The ideal, of course, is to capture what is best about the legal process—fairness and finality—and to incorporate those virtues into an alternative process that remains as quick and simple as possible, that reduces direct and indirect costs of litigation, that is relatively private or at least not in the headlines, and that makes use of competent people who may be instrumental in preserving business relationships rather than destroying them.

Arbitration.   Arbitration may be agreed to by the parties before or after a dispute arises. Some contracts contain an arbitration clause, but the absence of such a clause does not prevent the parties from choosing an arbitrator, who may come from the ranks of the American Arbitration Association (or from one of several international associations), from the Better Business Bureau, or from the community at large. An arbitrator renders an award but normally does not write a legal opinion. After all, there is no requirement that the arbitrator be a lawyer or a judge. In the absence of conduct that reflects unfavorably on the integrity of the arbitration process, a court will enforce the award just as if it had been issued judicially.

Thirty-four states plus the District of Columbia have facilitated arbitration through the adoption of the Uniform Arbitration Act. It operates essentially as described above. Congress has fostered this process by passage of the Federal Arbitration Act which provides that arbitration under the terms of the contract related to interstate commerce shall be "valid, irrevocable, and enforceable." Under Articles of the Constitution, this act preempts all state laws to the extent that they are inconsistent with the federal statute. An agreement between a broker and client to arbitrate disputes that would otherwise require a judicial determination under the 1933 Securities Act and 1934 Securities and Exchange Act are arbitrable if the agreement is made prior to the dispute.

Mediation.   Unlike arbitration, mediation does not impose a solution on the parties. Instead, the role of a mediator is to facilitate the efforts of the disputants to work out their own solution. The virtues of a good mediator rival those of a diplomat. The parties, of course, have shown some disposition to settle the issues or they would not have sought the services of a mediator in the first place. Following this initial show of goodwill, however, the mediator must be skillful enough to focus the parties on the issues separating them and to convince them the only way to make progress is to recognize that all sides must be ready to "give a little." This process cannot be successful in the absence of willingness to compromise. A good mediator can show them the way but cannot dictate a solution.

Summary Jury Trial.   The parties may choose to proceed in a "moot court" by convening a panel of jurors that will hear the strongest arguments that both sides can make. The jurors will not be presented with the real evidence and will not render a final, enforceable verdict. The verdict can be very instructive to the parties, however, because they have heard the "best" case that can be developed by the disputants. If their verdict, then, is for the "other guy," that can be a pretty good indication that a compromise settlement is preferable to an actual trial. A variation on this theme is a *mini-trial,* in which the parties may stay within the bounds of traditional adjudication and agree to have one or more of the issues finally decided by a judge. This approach normally combines elements of arbitration and mediation with the conventional judicial process.

IMAGES OF LAW AND LEGAL SYSTEMS

In this section, we contrast two images of law and legal systems. We begin with one of the most basic American statements about the nature of humanity and the implied notion about the purposes of government and its laws. America's Declaration of Independence is one of the most forceful and uplifting public commitments to the greatness and freedom of human beings. It begins:

> We hold these truths to be self-evident, that all men are created equal, that they are endowed by their Creator with certain inalienable rights, that among these are life, liberty, and the pursuit of happiness. That to secure these rights, governments are instituted among men, deriving their just powers from the consent of the governed. That whenever any form of government becomes destructive of these ends, it is the right of the people to alter or to abolish it and to institute new government, laying its foundation on such principles and organizing its powers in such form as to them shall seem most likely to effect their safety and happiness.

Explicit in this statement is that all are created equal; that the "right" to life, liberty, and the pursuit of happiness should not be curtailed; and that the government and laws exist because the people give their consent that these should exist.

The language here is noble (as it should be for such a document), but one should not confuse the noble intent of this fundamental document with the reality of the legal process used to vindicate those rights. Hold in your mind the thoughts of the Declaration of Independence and contrast these thoughts with the feelings you experience in reading the following parable written by Franz Kafka.

Kafka was one of the most insightful modern writers about law and legal systems. He was born in Prague, Czechoslovakia, on July 3, 1883, and died of tuberculosis just before his forty-first birthday in 1924. Although he wrote very creatively, he worked most of his life as a lawyer deep in the bureaucracy of the semigovernmental Workers' Accident Insurance Institute in Prague.

FRANZ KAFKA

Before the Law

Before the Law stands a doorkeeper on guard. To this doorkeeper there comes a man from the country who begs for admittance to the Law. But the doorkeeper says that he cannot admit the man at the moment. The man, on reflection, asks, if he will be allowed, then to enter later. "It is possible," answers the doorkeeper, "but not at this moment." Since the door leading into the Law stands open as usual and the doorkeeper steps to one side, the man bends down to peer through the entrance. When the doorkeeper sees that, he laughs and says: "If you are so strangely tempted, try to get in without my permission. But note that I am powerful. And I am only the lowest doorkeeper. From hall to hall keepers stand at every door, one more powerful than the other. Even the third of these has an aspect that even I cannot bear to look at." These are difficulties which the man from the country has not expected to meet; the Law, he thinks, should be accessible to every man and at all times, but when he looks more closely at the doorkeeper in his furred robe, with his huge pointed nose and long, thin, Tartar beard, he decides that he had better wait until he gets permission to enter. The doorkeeper gives him a stool and lets him sit down at the side of the door. There he sits waiting for days and years. He makes many attempts to be allowed in and wearies the doorkeeper with his importunity. The doorkeeper often engages him in brief conversation, asking him about his home and about other matters, but the questions are put quite impersonally, as great men put questions, and always conclude with the statement that the man cannot be allowed to enter yet. The man, who has equipped himself with many things for his journey, parts with all he has, however valuable, in the hope of bribing the doorkeeper. The doorkeeper accepts it all, saying, however, as he takes each gift: "I take this only to keep you from feeling that you have left something undone." During all these long years the man watches the doorkeeper almost incessantly. He forgets about the other doorkeepers, and this one seems to him the only barrier between himself and the Law. In the first years he curses his evil fate aloud; later, as he grows old, he only mutters to himself. He grows childish, and since in his prolonged watch he has learned to know even the fleas in the doorkeeper's fur collar, he begs the very fleas to help him and to persuade the doorkeeper to change his mind. Finally his eyes grow dim and he does not know whether the world is really darkening around him or whether his eyes are only deceiving him. But in the darkness he can now perceive a radiance that streams immortally from the door of the Law. Now his life is drawing to a close. Before he dies, all that he has experienced during the whole time of his sojourn condenses in his mind into one question, which he has never yet put to the doorkeeper. He beckons the doorkeeper, since he can no longer raise his stiffening body. The doorkeeper has to bend far down to hear him, for the difference in size between them has increased very much to the man's disadvantage. "What do you want to know now?" Asks the doorkeeper, "you are insatiable." "Everyone strives to attain the Law," answers the man, "how does it come about, then that in all these years no one has come seeking admittance but me?" The doorkeeper perceives that the man is at the end of his strength and that his hearing is failing, so he bellows in his ear: "No one but you could gain admittance through this door, since this door was intended only for you. I am now going to shut it."[4]

PARABLE FOLLOW-UP

Parables are very efficient ways of communicating. They are short, they usually are in the form of a story that can be repeated and discussed, and they seem to raise issues that bear some relationship to truth, but no answers are provided.[5] Indeed, we cannot answer the issues Kafka raises, but we can try to provide some clarity by asking a few questions. Kafka is clearly writing about the legal system because he begins, "Before the Law stands a doorkeeper on guard." The law is behind the door. The other two actors in the parable are the doorkeeper and the countryman. Is their relationship a comfortable one? What is keeping the countryman from the law that he seeks? Does the doorkeeper bar his way? Is Kafka's view of the law and the legal system a pleasant one? Is it an accurate one? How does it contrast to the Declaration of Independence?

You are the only one who can answer these questions. The general notion addressed by Kafka is that each person probably does not have direct access to the law. People must seek it through various doorkeepers who may be the accepted practitioners of the legal system—lawyers, judges, and officials of one sort or another—whose function is to keep order. How do you feel about lawyers and judges? Are they friendly and accessible, or are they remote and interested in perpetuating a system that seems to benefit only their interests? Most people would admit to an uncomfortable feeling about the legal system and, more specifically, about lawyers, those persons charged with the responsibility of keeping the legal system meaningful. Even in a democracy, an elite or nobility of sort is necessary. The people cannot really take the law to themselves because if they do, there is no law; or, stated differently, if a group of people claim they are the new representatives of the people and have discharged the elite who administered the old laws, they are themselves the new elite. Perhaps the idea of a pure democracy and the necessity of having elites is contradictory; perhaps what the Declaration of Independence promises is not possible. Can everyone really be equal before the law? Very few people challenge the elites that stand before them. Like the countryman, they accept them.

LAWYERS AND THE LEGAL SYSTEM

One of the greatest commentators on the American political system was a Frenchman, Alexis de Tocqueville, who toured this country toward the middle of the nineteenth century and wrote *Democracy in America* (1840) about American life and institutions. In this classic book, he neatly pinpoints the place and value of lawyers in the American legal system:[6]

> The special information that lawyers derive from their studies ensures them a separate rank in society, and they constitute a sort of privileged body in the scale of intellect. This notion of their superiority perpetually recurs in them in the practice of their profession: They are the masters of a science which is necessary, but which is not very generally known; They serve as arbiters between the citizens; and the habit of directing to their purpose the blind passions of parties in litigation inspires them with certain contempt for the judgment of the multitude.

Do people criticize lawyers too harshly? Many legal commentators and writers in the popular press have made the point that lawyers seem to lack emotion and often appear arrogant and focused more on the legal system than on clients' feelings and needs. Lawyers respond that they are the mediators between a system of logic and reasoned judgments that attempt to be blind to the justice of an individual case. In short, lawyers are trained to see both sides of an issue and to press claims for their client, but they must also be guarded. They must warn their clients that their claim may appear "right" to them, but in the eyes of the system, many competing demands for justice must be reconciled. Thus, lawyers do often seem to be remote and, as a group, unemotional.

The lawyers' method of thinking is pressed on them almost every minute they are in law school. The following excerpt is from the book *One L* by Scott Turow, who wrote it during his first year at Harvard Law School. Turow and his fellow students could feel the changes in themselves as they sat through the first classes of the year.

> The deepest fear among us seemed to be . . . that, somehow, deep personal changes were being forced upon us by the process of legal education. More and more often as the year wore on, I would hear comments from classmates to the effect that we were being limited, harmed by the education, forced to substitute dry reason for emotion, to cultivate opinions that were "rational" but had no roots in the experience, the life we'd had before. We were being cut away from ourselves, we felt. And thus, more and more often I would scrutinize myself for the signs of those unwanted changes. On occasion I would find them.
>
> At home, for instance, my wife, Annette, told me that I had started to "lawyer" her when we quarreled, badgering and cross-examining her much as the professors did students in class. And there seemed to me other habits to be wary of. It was a grimly literal, linear, step-by-step process of thought that we were learning. The kind of highly structured problem-solving method taught in each class, that business of sorting through the initial details of a case and then moving outward toward the broadest implications, were an immensely useful technical skill, but I feared it would calcify my approach to other subjects. And besides rigidity, there was a sort of mood to legal thinking that I found plainly unattractive.

. . . "Legal thinking is nasty," I said . . . and I began to think later I'd hit on a substantial truth. Thinking like a lawyer involved being suspicious and distrustful. You re-evaluated statements, inferred from silences, looked for loopholes and ambiguities. You did everything but take a statement at face value.

So on one hand you believed nothing. And on the other, for the sake of logical consistency, and to preserve long-established rules, you would accept the most ridiculous fictions—that a corporation was a person, that an apartment tenant was renting land and not a dwelling.

. . . Eventually, I came to regard that kind of schooling not merely as objectionable, but even as inappropriate in light of the ultimate purpose of legal education—the fact that as future lawyers, my classmates and I were training to become the persons on whom this society rests the chief responsibility for making and doing justice.[7]

If the law and lawyers themselves sometimes appear remote, it is the result of an intentional process that begins early in legal education. The best law school faculties believe this process is the proper way to teach about the law, and their students, who become lawyers, adopt this perspective—the tendency to "substitute dry reason for emotion" and to "cultivate opinions that were rational but had no roots in experience" that Turow wrote about.

Lawyers are only one facet of the legal system. Another major facet involves the judging process.

JUDGES AND THE PROCESS OF JUDGING

Some commentators on law believe that if one can get the facts straight and then find the "right" legal principles, the result one gets from the legal system will be the product of simply applying the "right" principle to the facts. The positivist school would accept this scientific view of simply applying correct principles to facts. In reality, however, the process of law is much less scientific than this.

As we pointed out in Chapter 1, law is, above all, like life: It is activity, not theory, and life that is active is not always predictable. The following short article on judging by Jerome Frank (1889–1957)—a teacher, lawyer, and later judge—began to expose the realities of judicial process in *Law and the Modern Mind*. The book uncovered popular and professional myths about law and process, probed them psychoanalytically, and recommended changes that Frank thought would be helpful. His writing adds a vital link between law in theory and law in practice.

JEROME FRANK

The Judging Process and the Judge's Personality

As the word indicates, the judge in reaching a decision is making a judgment. And if we would understand what goes into the creating of that judgment, we must observe how ordinary men dealing with ordinary affairs arrive at their judgments.[8]

The process of judging, so the psychologists tell us, seldom begins with a premise from which a conclusion is subsequently worked out. Judging begins rather the other way around—with a conclusion more or less vaguely formed; a man ordinarily starts with such a conclusion and afterwards tries to find premises which will substantiate it.[9] If he cannot, to his satisfaction, find proper arguments to link up his conclusion with premises which he finds acceptable, he will, unless he is arbitrary or mad, reject the conclusion and seek another.

* * *

. . . In theory, the judge begins with some rule or principle of law as his premise, applies this premise to the facts, and thus arrives at his decision.

Now, since the judge is a human being and since no human being in his normal thinking processes arrives at decisions (except in dealing with a limited number of simple situations) by the route of any such syllogistic reasoning, it is fair to assume that the judge, merely by putting on the judicial ermine, will not acquire so artificial a method of reasoning. Judicial judgments, like other judgments, doubtless, in most cases are worked out backward from conclusions tentatively formulated.

* * *

But the conception that judges work back from conclusions to principles is so heretical that it seldom finds expression.[10] Daily, judges, in connection with their decisions, deliver so-called opinions in which they purport to set forth the bases of their conclusions. Yet you will study these opinions in vain to discover anything remotely resembling a statement of the actual judging process. They are written in conformity with the time-honored theory. They picture the judge applying rules and principles to the facts, that is, taking some rule or principle (usually derived from opinions in earlier cases) as his major premise, employing the facts of the case as the minor premise, and then coming to his judgment by processes of pure reasoning.

Now and again some judge, more clear-witted and outspoken than his fellows, describes (when off the bench) his methods in more homely terms: Recently Judge Hutchenson essayed such an honest report of the judicial process. He tells us that after canvassing all the available materials at his command and duly cogitating on it, he gives his imagination play.

. . . and brooding over the cause, waits for the feeling, the hunch—that intuitive flash of understanding that makes the jumpspark connection between question and decision and at the point where the path is darkest for the judicial feet, sets its light along the way. . . . In feeling or "hunching" out his decisions, the judge acts not differently from but precisely as the lawyers do in working on their cases, with only this exception, that the lawyer, in having a predetermined destination in view—to win the lawsuit for his client—looks for and regards only those hunches which keep him in the path that he has chosen, while the judge, being merely on his way with a roving commission to find the just solution, will follow his hunch wherever it leads him. . . .

And Judge Hutchenson adds:

. . . The vital motivating impulse for the decision is an intuitive sense of what is right or wrong in the particular case; and the astute judge, having so decided, enlists his every faculty and belabors his laggard mind, not only to justify that intuition to himself, but to make it pass muster with his critics. Accordingly, he passes in review all of the rules, principles, legal categories, and concepts which he may find useful, directly or by an analogy so as to select from them those which in his opinion will justify his desired result.

We may accept this as an approximately correct description of how all judges do their thinking. But see the consequences. If the law consists of the decisions of the judges and if those decisions are based on the judge's hunches, then the way in which the judge gets his hunches is the key to the judicial process. Whatever produces the judge's hunches makes the law.

What, then, are the hunch-producers? What are the stimuli which make a judge feel that he should try to justify one conclusion rather than another?

The rules and principles of law are one class of such stimuli. But there are many others, concealed or unrevealed, not frequently considered in discussions of the character or nature of law. To the infrequent extent that these other stimuli have been considered at all, they have been usually referred to as "the political, economic and moral prejudices" of the judge.[11] A moment's reflection would, indeed, induce any open-minded person to admit that factors of such character must be operating in the mind of the judge.

But are not those categories—political, economic and moral biases—too gross, too crude, too wide? Since judges are not a distinct race and since their judging processes must be substantially of like kind with those of other men, an analysis of the way in which judges reach their conclusions will be aided by answering the question, What are the hidden factors in the inferences and opinions of ordinary men? The answer surely is that those factors are multitudinous and complicated, depending often on peculiarly individual traits of the persons whose inferences and opinions are to be explained. These uniquely individual factors often are more important causes of judgments than anything which could be describes as political, economic, or moral biases.

In the first place, all other biases express themselves in connection with, and as modified by, these idiosyncratic biases. A man's political or economic prejudices are frequently cut across by his affection for or animosity to some particular individual or group, due to some unique experience he has had; or a racial antagonism which he entertains may be deflected in a particular case by a desire to be admired by someone who is devoid of such antagonism.

Second (and in the case of the judge more important), is the consideration that in learning the facts . . . the judge's sympathies and antipathies are likely to be active with respect to the persons of the witness, the attorneys and the parties to the suit. His own past may have created plus or minus reactions to women, or blonde women, or men with beards, or Southerners, or Italians, or Englishmen, or plumbers, or ministers, or college graduates, or Democrats. A certain twang or cough or gesture may start up memories painful or pleasant in the main. Those memories of the judge, while he is listening to a witness with such a twang or cough or gesture, may affect the judge's initial hearing of, or subsequent recollection of, what the witness said, or the weight or credibility which the judge will attach to the witness's testimony.

★ ★ ★

The courts have been alive to these grave possibilities of error and have therefore repeatedly declared that it is one of the most important functions of the trial judge, in determining the value and weight of the evidence, to consider the demeanor of the witness.

They have called attention, as of the gravest importance, to such facts as the tone of voice in which a witness's statement is made, the hesitation or readiness with which his answers are given, the look of the witness, his carriage, his evidences of surprise, his gesture, his zeal, his bearing, his expression, his yawns, the use of his eyes, his furtive or meaning glances, or his shrugs, the pitch of his voice, his self-possession or embarrassment, his air of candor or of seeming levity. It is because these circumstances can be manifest only to one who actually hears and sees the witnesses that upper courts have frequently stated that they are hesitant to overturn the decision of the trial judge in a case where the evidence has been based upon oral testimony; for the upper courts have recognized that they have before them only a stenographic or printed report of the testimony, and that such a black and white report cannot reproduce anything but the cold words of the witness. . . .

Strangely enough, it has been little observed that, while the witness is in this sense a judge, *the judge, in a like sense, is a witness.* He is a witness of what is occurring in his courtroom. He must determine what are the facts of the case from what he sees and hears; that is, from the words and gestures and other conduct of the witnesses. And like those who are testifying before him, the judge's determination of the facts is no mechanical art. If the witnesses are subject to lapses of memory or imaginative reconstruction of events, in the same manner the judge is subject to defects in his apprehension of the testimony, so that long before he has come to the point in the case where he must decide what is right or wrong, just or unjust, with reference to the facts of the case as a whole, the trial judge has been engaged in making numerous judgments or inferences as the testimony dribbles in. His beliefs as to what was said by the witnesses and with what truthfulness the witnesses said it, will determine what he believes to be the "facts of the case." If his final decision is based upon a hunch and that hunch is a function of the "facts," then of course what, as a fallible witness of what went on in his court-

room, he believes to be the "facts," will often be of controlling importance. So that the judge's innumerable unique traits, dispositions and habits often get in their work in shaping his decisions not only in his determination of what he thinks fair or just with reference to given sets of facts, but in the very processes by which he becomes convinced what those facts are. . . .

★ ★ ★

One bit of statistical evidence as to the differences between judges is available: A survey was made of the disposition of thousands of minor criminal cases by the several judges of the City Magistrate's Court in New York City during the years 1914 to 1916 with the express purpose of finding to what extent the "personal equation" entered into the administration of justice. It was disclosed that "the magistrates did differ to an amazing degree in their treatment of similar classes of cases." Thus of 546 persons charged with intoxication brought before one judge, he discharged only one and found the others (about 97%) guilty, whereas of the 673 arraigned before another judge, he found 531 (or 70%) not guilty. In disorderly conduct cases, one judge discharged only 18% and another discharged 54%. "In other words, one coming before Magistrate Simons had only 2 chances in 10 of getting off. If he had come before Judge Walsh he would have had more than 5 chances in 10 of getting off." . . . When it came to sentences, the same variations existed. One judge imposed fines on 84% of the persons he found guilty and gave suspended sentences to 7%, while one of his fellows fined 34% and gave suspended sentences to 50%. . . .

★ ★ ★

What we may hope some day to get from our judges are detailed autobiographies containing the sort of material that is recounted in the autobiographical novel; or opinions annotated, by the judge who writes them, with elaborate explorations of the background factors in his personal experience which swayed him in reaching his conclusions. For in the last push, a judge's decisions are the outcome of his entire life-history. Judges can take to heart the counsel Anatole France gave to the judges of literature:

> All those who deceive themselves into the belief that they put anything but their own personalities into their work are dupes of the most fallacious of illusions. The truth is that we can never get outside ourselves. . . . We are

shut up in our own personality as if in a perpetual prison. The best thing for us, it seems to me, is to admit this frightful condition with a good grace, and to confess that we speak of ourselves every time we have not strength enough to remain silent. . . .

. . . The judge's decision is determined by a hunch arrived at long after the event on the basis of his reaction to fallible testimony. It is, in every sense of the word, *ex post facto* [after the fact]. It is fantastic, then, to say that usually men can warrantably act in reliance upon "established law." Their inability to do so may be deplorable. But mature persons must face the truth, however unpleasant.

ARTICLE FOLLOW-UP

Is Jerome Frank being facetious? Probably not. Remember, his view of the operation of a judge's mind is just one view. Countering it is a substantial tradition, that for all practical purposes, dictates that judges must decide cases according to certain norms. One dominant norm is that judges should follow precedent and not decide a case contrary to the way a similar case has been decided, and this is especially true if the applicable legal principles were announced by the supreme court of the state in which the judge sits. In addition, a judicial pronouncement is almost always subject to an appeal if the judge's opinion varies too much from established traditions.

Frank does have a point, however. His central thesis is that the results of the judging process are much less certain than the results one gets when, in step one, you find the facts, and in step two, you apply the right legal principles to the facts. Many commentators make the law sound too technical, even scientific, in this respect, and in all probability, according to Frank, they are mistaken. Fortunately or unfortunately, the judge's personality, background, political position within the judicial hierarchy, and other so-called externalities determine some decisions.

THE JURY

A jury is used in many trials to perform two functions. First, it hears witnesses and sees evidence in an attempt to determine the facts of the case. Second, it listens to the judge recite the applicable law and then it retires to the jury room and applies the principles to the facts to determine the outcome of the case. What can be said about this process? One of the great judicial traditions is we do not inquire with any precision into the minds of the jurors in making their decisions. Very few empirical studies have been conducted on how juries decide cases. We imagine, though, that the mental process used by the jury in arriving at an assessment of the facts in a case and then applying the rule of law read to them by the judge is much like the process of judging described by Frank. Often, the conclusion will be set before the rationale for it is discovered.

We have been suggesting by the discussion of lawyers, judges, and the jury system that what goes on in the legal system is not as objective and certain as one usually imagines. Beacuse as the law deals with real life and beacuse law is made by individual lawyers, judges, and jurors, the emotional side of life finds its way into the legal system.

We do not present the legal system in its "ideal" form. We began this section with a reading from the Declaration of Independence, which is, no doubt, as ideal as one can get. But the Kafka parable is more accurate in describing a legal system because so many people do accept it as somehow "above" them and set there permanently. The everyday work of lawyers, judges, and jurors, however, is not that remote. Law is made by human beings, and it has all the variety, fairness, and unfairness of life itself.

SOCIAL SYSTEMS AS VALUE SYSTEMS

We are about ready to leave our introductory comments on the American legal system. Before we do, however, we want to emphasize that the two great social systems you have learned about at your university—law and economics (or business)—are not as objective and value-free as textbooks often portray them.

All social systems are erected on a group of values shared by members of a society. These shared values make possible a common vocabulary and ways of thinking and seeing social events. When the vocabulary and ways of thinking are entrenched enough—shared by enough people over a fairly long time—people tend to believe that they can build a "science" on the shared values. The word *capitalism*, for instance, refers to a collection of values about how business should be conducted. These values include freedom, private property, profit, efficiency, wealth, and the importance of the individual. Enough people believe in these values that they have been able to create a social system supported by complete disciplines, such as economics, marketing, and management.

Social science, however, is not the same as, say, the science of physics. Social science is based on assumptions about the nature of human beings; physics is based on assumptions about matter. There is a world of difference between the behavior of physical matter, such as steel, and the behavior of human beings. The point is that the legal and economic systems, both of which are usually referred to as *capitalistic*, are really systems of values adopted over the decades and centuries. They do not have the ironclad, immutable quality that our physical sciences have. It is very difficult to judge social systems or to compare them with the social systems of other countries because we are really talking about which values are best.

In U.S. schools, children are often taught that the American system of laws and government (and of business) is best. Indeed, as this edition of the text is being written, the countries of Eastern Europe have, it seems, succeeded in throwing off the old legal, political, and economic orders and have opted for many of the beliefs and values that help define America's chief social systems. Is the United States better off? Is Eastern Europe better off? In the following story, B. Traven contrasts one social system with another and, in the process, shows how ways of life are determined by beliefs over time. Which system is better? You be the judge.

B. TRAVEN

Assembly Line

Mr. E.L. Winthrop of New York was on vacation in the Republic of Mexico. It wasn't long before he realized that this strange and really wild country had not yet been fully and satisfactorily explored by Rotarians and Lions, who are forever conscious of their glorious mission on earth. Therefore, he considered it his duty as a good American citizen to do his part in correcting this oversight.

In search for opportunities to indulge in his new avocation, he left the beaten track and ventured into regions not especially mentioned, and hence not recommended, by travel agents to foreign tourists. So it happened that one day he found himself in a little, quaint Indian village somewhere in the State of Oaxaca.

Walking along the dusty main street of this pueblecito, which knew nothing of pavements, drainage, plumbing, or of any means of artificial light save candles or pine splinters, he met with an Indian squatting on the earthen-floor front porch of a palm hut, a so-called jacalito.

The Indian was busy making little baskets from bast and from all kinds of fibers gathered by him in the immense tropical bush which surrounded the village on all sides.

The material used had not only been well prepared for its purpose but was also richly colored with dyes that the basket-maker himself extracted from various native plants, barks, roots and from certain insects by a process known only to him and the members of his family.[12]

In spite of being by profession just a plain peasant, it was clearly seen from the small baskets he made that at heart he was an artist, a true and accomplished artist. Each basket looked as if covered all over with the most beautiful sometimes fantastic ornaments, flowers, butterflies, birds, squirrels, antelope, tigers, and a score of other animals of the wilds. Yet, the most amazing thing was that these decorations, all of them symphonies of color, were not painted on the baskets but were instead actually part of the baskets themselves. Bast and fibers dyed in dozens of different colors were so cleverly—one must actually say intrinsically—interwoven that those attractive designs appeared on the inner part of the basket as well as on the outside. Not by painting but by weaving were those highly artistic effects achieved. This performance he accomplished without ever looking at any sketch or pattern. While working on a basket these designs came to light as if by magic, and as long as the basket was not entirely finished one could not perceive what in this case or that the decoration would be like.

★ ★ ★

He had little if any knowledge of the outside world or he would have known that what happened to him was happening every hour of every day to every artist all over the world. That knowledge would perhaps have made him very proud, because he would have realized that he belonged to the little army which is the salt of the earth and which keeps culture, urbanity and beauty for their own sake from passing away.

Often it was not possible for him to sell all the baskets he had brought to market, for people here as elsewhere in the world preferred things made by the millions and each so much like the other that you were unable, even with the help of a magnifying glass, to tell which was which and where was the difference between two of the same kind.

Yet, he, this craftsman, had in his life made several hundreds of those exquisite baskets, but so far no two of them had he ever turned out alike in design. Each was an individual piece of art and as different from the other as was a Murillo from a Velasquez.

★ ★ ★

The Indian squatted on the earthen floor in the portico of his hut, attended to his work and showed no special interest in the curiosity of Mr. Winthrop watching him. He acted almost as if he ignored the presence of the American altogether.

"How much for the little basket, friend?" Mr. Winthrop asked when he felt that he at least had to say something as not to appear idiotic.

"Fifty centavitos, patroncito, my good little lordy, four reales," the Indian answered politely.

★ ★ ★

He had expected to hear a price of three or even four pesos. The moment he realized that he had judged the value six times too high, he saw right away what great business possibilities this miserable Indian village might offer to a dynamic promoter like himself. Without further delay he started exploring those possibilities. "Suppose, my good friend, I buy ten of these little baskets of yours which, as I might as well admit right here and now, have practically no real use whatsoever. Well, as I was saying if I buy ten, how much would you then charge me apiece?"

The Indian hesitated for a few seconds as if making calculations. Finally he said, "If you buy ten I can let you have them for forty-five centavos each, senorito gentleman."

"All right, amigo. And now, let's suppose I buy from you straight away one hundred of these absolutely useless baskets, how much will they cost me each?"

The Indian, never fully looking up to the American standing before him and hardly taking his eyes off his work, said politely and without the slightest trace of enthusiasm in his voice, "In such a case I might not be quite unwilling to sell each for forty centavitos."

Mr. Winthrop bought sixteen baskets, which was all the Indian had in stock.

After three weeks' stay in the Republic, Mr. Winthrop was convinced that he knew this country perfectly, that he had seen everything and knew all about the inhabitants, their character and their way of life, and that there was nothing left for him to explore. So he returned to good old Nooyorg and felt happy to be once more in a civilized country, as he expressed it to himself.

One day going out for lunch he passed a confectioner's and looking at the display in the window, he suddenly remembered the little basket he had bought in that faraway Indian village.

He hurried home and took all the baskets he still had left to one of the best-known candy-makers in the city.

"I can offer you here," Mr. Winthrop said to the confectioner, "one of the most artistic and at the same time the most original of boxes, if you wish to call them that. These little baskets would be just right for the most expensive chocolates meant for elegant and high-priced gifts. Just have a good look at them, sir, and let me listen."

He shrugged his shoulders and said, "Well, I don't know. If you asked me I'd say it isn't quite what I'm after. However, we might give it a try. It depends, of course, on the price. In our business the package mustn't cost more than what's in it."

"Do I hear an offer?" Mr. Winthrop asked.

"Why don't you tell me in round figures how much you want for them? I'm not good in guessing."

"Well, I'll tell you, Mr. Kemple: since I'm the smart guy who discovered these baskets and since I'm the only Jack who knows where to lay his hands on more, I'm selling to the highest bidder, on an exclusive basis, of course. I'm positive you can see it my way, Mr. Kemple."

"Quite so, and may the best man win," the confectioner said. "I'll talk the matter over with my partners. See me tomorrow same time, please, and I'll let you know how far we might be willing to go."

Next day when both gentlemen met again Mr. Kemple said, "Now, to be frank with you, I know art on seeing it, no getting around that. And these baskets are little works of art, they surely are. However, we are no art dealers, you realize that of course. We've no other use for these pretty little things except as fancy packing for our

French pralines made by us. We can't pay for them what we might pay considering them pieces of art. After all to us they're only wrapping. Fine wrappings, perhaps, but nevertheless wrappings. You'll see it our way I hope, Mr.—oh yes, Mr. Winthrop. So, here is our offer, take it or leave it; a dollar and a quarter apiece and not one cent more."

Mr. Winthrop made a gesture as if he had been struck over the head.

The confectioner, misunderstanding this involuntary gesture of Mr. Winthrop, added quickly, "All right, all right, no reason to get excited, no reason at all. Perhaps we can do a trifle better. Let's say one-fifty."

"Make it one-seventy-five," Mr. Winthrop snapped, swallowing his breath while wiping his forehead.

"Sold. One-seventy-five apiece free at port of New York. We pay the customs and you pay the shipping. Right?"

"Sold," Mr. Winthrop said also and the deal was closed.

"There is of course, one condition," the confectioner explained just when Mr. Winthrop was to leave. "One or two hundred won't do for us. It wouldn't pay the trouble and the advertising. I won't consider less that ten thousand, or one thousand dozens if that sounds better in your ears. And they must come in no less than twelve different patterns well assorted. How about that?"

"I can make it sixty different patterns or designs."

"So much the better. And you're sure you can deliver ten thousand let's say early October?"

"Absolutely," Mr. Winthrop avowed and signed the contract.

* * *

Practically all the way back to Mexico, Mr. Winthrop had a notebook in his left hand and a pencil in his right and he was writing figures, long rows of them, to find out exactly how much richer he would be when this business had been put through.

"Now, let's sum up the whole goddamn thing," he muttered to himself. "Damn it, where is that cursed pencil again? I had it right between my fingers. Ah, there it is. Ten thousand he ordered. Well, well, there we got a clean-cut profit of fifteen thousand four hundred and forty genuine dollars. Sweet smackers. Fifteen grand right into papa's pocket. Come to think of it, that Republic isn't so backward after all."

"Buenas tardes, mi amigo, how are you?" He greeted the Indian whom he found squatting in the porch of his jacalito as if he had never moved from his place since Mr. Winthrop had left for New York.

The Indian rose, took off his hat, bowed politely and said in his soft voice, "Be welcome, patroncito. Thank you, I feel fine, thank you. Muy buenas tardes. This house and all I have is at your kind disposal." He bowed once more, moved his right hand in a gesture of greeting and sat down again. But he excused himself for doing so by saying, "Perdoneme, patroncito, I have to take advantage of the daylight, soon it will be night."

"I've got big business for you, my friend," Mr. Winthrop began.

"Good to hear that, señor."

Mr. Winthrop said to himself, "Now, he'll jump up and go wild when he learns what I've got for him." And aloud he said; "Do you think you can make me one thousand of these little baskets?"

"Why not, patroncito? If I can make sixteen, I can make one thousand also."

"That's right, my good man. Can you also make five thousand?"

"Of course, señor, I can make five thousand if I can make one thousand."

"Good. Now, if I should ask you to make me ten thousand, what would you say? And what would be the price of each? You can make ten thousand, can't you?"

"Of course, I can señor. I can make as many as you wish. You see, I am an expert in this sort of work. No one else in the whole state can make them the way I do."

"That's what I thought and that's exactly why I came to you."

"Thank you for the honor, patroncito."

"Suppose I order you to make me ten thousand of these baskets, how much time do you think you would need to deliver them?"

The Indian, without interrupting his work, cocked his head to one side and then to the other as if he were counting the days or weeks it would cast him to make all these basket.

After a few minutes he said in a slow voice, "It will take a good long time to make so many baskets, patroncito. You see, the bast and the fibers must be very dry before they can be used properly. Then all during the time they are slowly drying, they must be worked and handled in a very special way so that while drying they won't lose their softness and their flexibility and their natural brilliance. Even when dry they must look fresh. They must never lose their natural properties or they will look just as lifeless and dull as straw. Then while they are drying up I got to get the plants and roots and barks and insects from which I brew the dyes. That takes much time also, believe me. The plants must be gathered when the moon is just right or they won't give the right color. The insects I pick from the plants must also be gathered at the right time and under the right conditions or else they produce no rich colors and are just like dust. But, of course, jefecito, I can make as many as these canastitas as you wish, even as many as three dozens if you want them. Only give me time.

"Three dozens? Three dozens?" Mr. Winthrop yelled, and threw up both arms in desperation. "Three dozens!" He repeated as if he had to say it many times in his own voice so as to understand the real meaning of it, because for a while he thought that he was dreaming. He had expected the Indian to go crazy on hearing that he was to sell ten thousand of his baskets. . . .

So the American took up the question of price again, by which he hoped to activate the Indian's ambition. "You told me that if I take one hundred baskets you will let me have them for forty centavos apiece. Is that right, my friend?"

"Quite right, jefecito."

"Now," Mr. Winthrop took a deep breath, "now, ten times one hundred baskets, how much will they cost me, each basket?"

That figure was too high for the Indian to grasp. He became slightly confused and for the first time since Mr. Winthrop had arrived he interrupted his work and tried to think it out.

Several times he shook his head and looked vaguely around as if for help. Finally he said, "Excuse me, jefecito, little chief, that is by far too much for me to count. Tomorrow, if you will do me the honor, come and see me again and I think I shall have my answer ready for you, patroncito."

When on the next morning Mr. Winthrop came to the hut he found the Indian as usual squatting on the floor under the overhanging palm roof working at his baskets.

"Have you got the price for ten thousand?" He asked the Indian the very moment he saw him, without taking the trouble to say "Good Morning!"

"Si, patroncito, I have the price ready. You may believe me when I say it has cost me much labor and worry to find out the exact price, because, you see, I do not wish to cheat you out of your honest money."

"Skip that, amigo. Come out with the salad. What's the price?" Mr. Winthrop asked nervously.

"The price is well calculated now without any mistake on my side. If I got to make one thousand canastitas each will cost three pesos. If I must make five thousand, each will cost nine pesos. And if I have to make ten thousand, in such a case I can't make them for less than fifteen pesos each." Immediately he returned to his work as if he were afraid of losing too much time with such idle talk.

Mr. Winthrop thought that perhaps it was his faulty knowledge of this foreign language that had played a trick on him.

"Did I hear you say fifteen pesos each if I eventually would buy ten thousand?"

"That's exactly and without any mistake what I've said, patroncito," the Indian answered in his soft courteous voice.

"But now, see here, my good man, you can't do this to me. I'm your friend and I want to help you get on your feet."

"Yes, patroncito, I know this and I don't doubt any of your words."

"Now, let's be patient and talk this over quietly as man to man. Didn't you tell me that if I would buy one hundred you would sell each for forty centavos?"

"Si, jefecito, that's what I said. If you buy one hundred you can have them for forty centavos apiece, provided that I have one hundred, which I don't."

"Yes, yes, I see that." Mr. Winthrop felt as if he would go insane any minute now. "Yes, so you said. Only what I can't comprehend is why you cannot sell at the same price if you make me ten thousand. I certainly don't wish to chisel on the price. I am not that kind. Only, well, let's see now, if you can sell for forty centavos at all, be it for twenty or fifty or a hundred. I can't quite get the idea why the price has to jump that high if I buy more than a hundred."

"Bueno, patroncito, what is there so difficult to understand? It's all very simple. One thousand canastitas cost me a hundred times more work than a dozen. Ten thousand cost me so much time and labor that I could never finish them, not even in a hundred years. For a thousand canastitas I need more bast than for a hundred, and I need more little red beetles and more plants and roots and bark for the dyes. It isn't that you just can walk into the bush and pick all the things you need at your heart's desire. One root with the true violet blue may cost me four or five days until I can find one in the jungle. And have you thought how much time it costs and how much hard work to prepare the bast and fibers? What is more, if I must make so many baskets, who then will look after my corn and my beans and my goats and chase for me occasionally a rabbit for meat on Sunday? If I have no corn, then I have no tortillas to eat, and if I grow no beans, where do I get my frijoles from?"

"But since you'll get so much money from me for your baskets you can buy all the corn and beans in the world and more than you need."

"That's what you think, señorito, little lordy. But you see it is only the corn I grow myself that I am sure of. Of the corn which others may or may not grow, I cannot be sure to feast upon."

"Haven't you got some relatives here in this village who might help you to make baskets for me?" Mr. Winthrop asked hopefully.

"Practically the whole village is related to me somehow or other. Fact is, I got lots of close relatives in this here place."

"Why then can't they cultivate your fields and look after your goats while you make baskets for me? Not only this, they might gather for you the fibers and the colors in the bush and lend you a hand here and there in preparing the material you need for the baskets."

"They might, patroncito, yes, they might. Possible. But then you see who would take care of their fields and cattle if they work for me? And if they help me with the baskets it turns out the same. No one would any longer work his fields properly. In such a case corn and beans would get up so high in price that none of us could buy any and we all would starve to death. Besides, as the price of everything would rise and rise higher still how could I make baskets at forty centavos apiece? A pinch of salt or one green chili would set me back more than I'd collect for one single basket. Now you'll understand, highly esteemed caballero and jefecito, why I can't make the baskets any cheaper than fifteen pesos each if I got to make that many."

Mr. Winthrop was hard-boiled, no wonder considering the city he came from. He refused to give up the more than fifteen thousand dollars which at that moment seemed to slip through his fingers like nothing. Being really desperate now, he talked and bargained with the Indian for almost two full hours, trying to make him understand how rich he, the Indian, would become if he would take this greatest opportunity of his life.

The Indian never ceased working on his baskets while he explained his points of view.

"You know, my good man," Mr. Winthrop said, "such a wonderful chance might never again knock on your door, do you realize that? Let me explain to you in ice-cold figures what fortune you might miss if you leave me flat on this deal."

He tore out leaf after leaf from his notebook, covered each with figures and still more figures, and while doing so told the peasant he would be the richest man in the whole district.

The Indian without answering watched with a genuine expression of awe as Mr. Winthrop wrote down these long figures, executing complicated multiplications and divisions and subtractions so rapidly that it seemed to him the greatest miracle he had ever seen.

The American, noting this growing interest in the Indian, misjudged the real significance of it. "There you are, my friend," he said. "That's exactly how rich you're going to be. You'll have a bankroll of exactly four thousand pesos. And to show you that I'm a real friend of yours, I'll throw in a bonus. I'll make it a round five thousand pesos, and all in silver."

The Indian, however, had not for one moment thought of four thousand pesos. Such an amount of money had no meaning to him. He had been interested solely in Mr. Winthrop's ability to write figures so rapidly.

"So what do you say now? Is it a deal or is it? Say yes and you'll get your advance this very minute."

"As I have explained before, patroncito, the price is fifteen pesos each."

"But, my good man," Mr. Winthrop shouted at the poor Indian in utter despair, "where have you been all this time? On the moon or where? You are still at the same price as before."

"Yes, I know that, jefecito, my little chief," the Indian answered, entirely unconcerned. "It must be the same price because I cannot make any other one. Besides, señor, there's still another thing which perhaps you don't know. You see, my good lordy and ca-ballero, I've to make these canastitas my own way and with my song in them and with bits of my soul woven into them. If I were to make them in great numbers there would no longer be my soul in each, or my songs. Each would look like the other with no difference whatever and such a thing would slowly eat up my heart. Each has to be another song which I hear in the morning when the sun rises and when the birds begin to chirp and butterflies come and sit down on my baskets so that I may see a new beauty, because, you see, the butterflies like my baskets and the pretty colors on them, that's why they come and sit down, and I can make my canastitas after them. And now, señor jefecito, if you will kindly excuse me, I have wasted much time already, although it was a pleasure and a great honor to hear the talk of such a distinguished caballero like you. But I'm afraid I've to attend to my work now, for day after tomorrow is market day in town and I got to take my baskets there. Thank you, señor, for your visit. Adios."

And in this way it happened that American garbage cans escaped the fate of being turned into receptacles for empty, torn, and crumpled canastitas into which an Indian of Mexico had woven dreams of his soul, throbs of his heart; his unsung poems.

STORY FOLLOW-UP

How is this story related to a discussion of the American legal system? American Rules and procedures are the result of American values, beliefs, and history. They are "valid" or have meaning only within this culture. Outside this system of beliefs are alternative and competing systems.

In this story, Traven highlighted the differences between two cultures. The American society is dominated by the capitalist paradigm: the collection of values, that undergrid a business-oriented society. In contrast, Mexico is much more dominated by rural interests.

Between cultures are tensions and sometimes outright conflicts between different ethical norms. In this story, one can see the profit motive conflict with the Indian's idea of beauty. He would not give up his ability to produce beauty for promised power and profit. The small baskets he made were his own expression of value. Moreover, the Indian, perhaps correctly, saw more. American notions of freedom and individualism carried to their logical limits in both the law and the economic fabric of society actually breed a kind of dependence. If the Indian were to enlist all of his relatives to help him produce the baskets, his little society would become more fragile than it already is. A kind of dependence would ultimately take away his ability to make beauty. Is his society worse than ours? It all depends on what you grow used to.

CONCLUSION

The basic structure of the American legal system is centuries old. Indeed, many of the ways laws are "created" have been around so long that it is easy to lose sight of their roots. There are, however, two basic methods of creating law. The method used today in civil law jurisdictions, such as in France and Louisiana, begins with a comprehensive statement of a rule intended to apply to a given set of circumstances. The law in this system proceeds from the top down.

An alternative method evolves from the bottom up. The common law system that originated in England after the Middle Ages begins with a case and the announcement of a rule to decide that case. Over the years, similar cases are decided in a way consistent with the first one. Of course, no case is exactly like a previous one, so the applicability of the rule announced in the first case grows to "fit" all cases of a similar type.

The legal system today incorporates both legal methods. The basic rules in the legal system come from two sources: federal or state legislatures and the judiciary. Taken together, these sources provide the legal system with a variety of ways to create rules.

In the study of law, it is easy to overemphasize the importance of rules. The emphasis on rules one finds in law schools and colleges of business produces a vision that really does not see the forest for the trees. Trees come and go, after all, and it is the forest—its condition and its operation as living, breathing being— that must be tended to. To be sure, to understand the legal environment, one needs both a knowledge of some of the rules and an appreciation of the system in which they are applied. To continue the metaphor, one must see and know the trees as well as the forest. This is why, in the last half of this chapter, we chose Kafka and Traven to force us to take your eyes off the technicalities of legal rules and processes and focus on the broad view: Who and what are the key elements in a legal system, and where are social systems taking you?

These questions bring into focus the study of values and morals, which we highlighted in Chapter 1. Values and moral points of view underlie all social systems. They define the essential individual and collective beliefs that give purpose and direction to dominant social systems and to people's everyday lives.

REVIEW QUESTIONS AND PROBLEMS

1. What is the basic difference in legal methodology between the civil law system and the common law system?

2. What is the role of *stare decisis* in the American legal system?

3. How did equity evolve as a separate system from courts of law? What specific illustrations can you give of the survival of equity in the judicial system today?

4. In what two different ways might one use the term *civil law*?

5. Under what circumstances may cases be brought into federal courts?

6. What appears to be the principal idea or purpose behind federal diversity of citizenship jurisdiction? How is this purpose implemented?

7. In what two important ways does the judiciary contribute to the process of rule creation?

ENDNOTES

1. The Twelve Tables were largely procedural, from which we can conclude that, even at this early stage, the law was already in the hands of "experts." One of them provided: If a man is summoned to appear in court and does not come, let witnesses be heard and then let the plaintiff seize him. If he resists or absconds, the plaintiff can use force. If he is ill or too old, let the plaintiff provide a beast to bring him in: but if he declines this offer, the plaintiff need not provided a carriage. . . . [I]f a man is killed while committing theft in the night, that killing is lawful. [Wolf, *Roman Law: An Historical Introduction* 54 (1951).]

2. d'Entreves, *Natural Law* 17 (1976).

3. From Berman, H., and Greiner, W., *The Nature and Functions of Law* 586-589 (4th ed., 1980). Copyright ©1980 by The Foundation Press, Inc. Reprinted by permission of The Foundation Press, Inc.

4. Reprinted from *The Trial, Definitive Edition* by Franz Kafka. Translated by Willa and Edwin Muir, revised & with additional material by E.M. Butler, by permission of Shocken Books, a division of Random House, Inc. Copyright © 1925, 1935, 1946 by Shocken Books, Inc. Copyright renewed 1952, 1963, 1974 by Shocken Books, Inc. Copyright 1937, 1956 by Alfred A. Knopf, Inc. Copyright renewed 1964 by Alfred A. Knopf, Inc.

5. Bonsignore, et al., *Before the Law* xvii (4th ed., 1989). We acknowledge the influence of Professor Bonsignore on our own thoughts about law and legal systems, some of which have found their way into the last half of this chapter.

6. From *Democracy in America*, Volume I, by Alexis de Tocqueville, translated by Henry Reeve, Francis Bowen, and Phillips Bradley. © 1945, renewed 1973 by Alfred A. Knopf, Inc. Quoted at length in Bonsignore, *Id.* at 246.

7. Excerpt from *One L* by Scott Turow. Copyright © 1977 by Scott Turow. Reprinted by permission of Farrar, Straus and Giroux, Inc.

8. Selections from *Law and the Modern Mind* by Jerome Frank, © 1930 by Bren-tano's, Inc. Copyright renewed in 1958 by Florence Frank. Selections from Anchor Book Edition, 1963. By permission of the estate of Barbara Frank Kristein. Some footnotes have been deleted.

9. A convenient analogy is the technique of the author of a detective story.

10. Years ago the writer, just after being admitted to the bar, was shocked when advised by S.S. Gregory, an ex-president of the American Bar Association—a man more than ordinarily aware of legal realities—that "the way to win a case is to make the judge want to decide in your favor and then, and then only, to cite precedents which will justify such a determination. You will almost always find plenty of cases to cite in your favor." All successful lawyers are more or less consciously aware of this technique. But they seldom avow it—even to themselves.

11. Most of the suggestions that law is a function of the undisclosed attitudes of judges stress the judges' "education," "race," "class," "economic, political and social influences" which "make up a complex environment" of which the judges are not wholly aware but which affect their decisions by influencing their views of "public policy," or "social advantage" or their "economic and social philosophies" or " their notions of fair play or what is right and just."

   It is to the economic determinists and to the members of the school of "sociological jurisprudence" that we owe much of the recognition of the influence of the economic and political background of judges upon decisions. For this much thanks. But their work has perhaps been done too well. Interested as were these writers in problems of labor law and "public policy" questions, they overstressed a few of the multitude of unconscious factors and over-simplified the problem.

12. "Assembly Line" from *The Night Visitor* by B. Traven. Copyright © 1966 by B. Traven. Reprinted by permission of Hill and Wang, a division of Farrar, Straus and Giroux, Inc.

An Explanation of the Civil Trial Process

Introduction

The judicial system, with its use of courts, deals with the interpretation, validity, declaration, and application of law to the factual situations confronting the court. In this process, law is made, indicating what is legal now and, therefore, as case precedent, what applies for the future. The court acts only on matters brought before it by parties that want judicial action. It has only the jurisdiction and powers given to it by federal or state statute.

★ ★ ★

The opinions of the courts in decided cases are often contained in reports of those cases; such reports are available in libraries in court buildings, law schools, and other public places. Reference to a court opinion is called a *case citation*. For example, *Vigil* v. *Lamm*, 190 Colo. 180, 544 P.2d 631 (1976) refers to a Colorado case report found in volume 190 of the Colorado Reports at page 180, which may also be found in the regional Pacific Reporter in volume 544 second series at page 631. The date of the case is 1976.

One important way law is made is by the published opinions of appellate courts. Most of the abbreviated court decisions in this text are edited versions of appellate court opinions. To understand how the parties to a legal dispute get to an appellate court to have their case heard, we offer here a brief overview of the civil trial process. The process described may vary slightly from state to state, but the definitions of the terms used are widely accepted.[1]

The Trial of a Civil Case

A civil suit is initiated by the **plaintiff,** who files several documents in a trial court of general jurisdiction (usually a county court located in the county government building). The document of greatest importance is called the **complaint,** which is filed by the plaintiff. The complaint must contain the following information:

1. the names of the parties to the case, the plaintiff(s) and defendants(s)

2. a statement sufficient to show that the court has jurisdiction to hear the matter;

3. a short and plain statement of the facts, indicating:

    a. the existence of a legal duty and

    b. the breach of this duty and

    c. a claim for relief in the form of a request for a given amount of money damages and/or a claim for equitable relief, such as a request for an injunction or an order for specific performance of a contract.

The complaint normally is filed together with a **summons,** which directs the server of the papers (usually a county sheriff if the case is filed in a county court, or a federal marshall if filed in a federal court) to the last known address of the **defendant.** Usually a copy of the complaint is included for the purpose of this *service.* When the server of the papers located the defendant(s) or, in some states, when the server locates the permanent residence of the defending party(ies), the papers are left with someone of suitable age and discretion residing therein. The server then files a sworn statement with the court, often called a *return*, in which the server swears that the defendant(s) was (were) served.

The defendant may file a document with the court responding to the complaint, called an *answer*, within a given time period, usually twenty to thirty days. A copy of the answer is given to the plaintiff. The answer may admit all, part, or none of the facts as alleged in the complaint, and may admit or deny any or all of the legal consequences. In addition, the answer may include a claim for relief against the plaintiff, called a **counterclaim**, if the grounds exist.

The general rule defining those persons who may be plaintiffs or defendants is that they must have a direct interest in the subject matter of the suit; that is, these persons must be directly affected by the outcome.

This rule has been expanded somewhat recently by permitting *class action* suits.

Class action suits were first widely used on the federal level, but gradually states have been adopting procedures which provide for this type of litigation. The class action procedural rules provide that one or more members of a class may sue or be sued as representatives of a class of persons if: (1) the class is so numerous that joinder of all members of the class is not practicable; (2) there are questions of law or fact that are common to all members of the class; (3) the claims or defenses of the parties representing the class are typical of the claims or defenses of the class; (4) the representatives of the class will fairly protect the interests of the class; and (5) all the members of the class must be identifiable (within reason). In addition to these prerequisites, the court must find that the class action is superior to other available methods for the fair and efficient adjudication of the controversy.

If a party is properly served with the complaint and fails to file an answer within the time period provided by law, then the plaintiff may ask the court to enter a *default* judgment. If such is entered, the court is making a judgment that the plaintiff is entitled to the relief claimed in the complaint.

As stated earlier, a defendant may *answer*, or the defendant may challenge the plaintiff's case by **motion** before the issue is formally tried. There are several motions the parties may use to challenge the legal arguments of the other party asserted through the **pleadings** filed with the court. The first such opportunity to present such a motion is presented by the defendant, who may make a motion to the court to dismiss the complaint for failure to state a claim upon which relief may be granted. In this case the motion is made by filing a document labeled "Motion" with the court.

The filing of the "Motion to Dismiss for

Failure to State a Claim" by the defendant requires the judge to rule on whether or not the plaintiff has stated the existence and breach of a legal duty. The judge must consider the complaint and the facts stated therein and resolve every inference created by the facts in favor of the plaintiff. When this is done, the court will grant or deny the motion to dismiss.

Discovery. If the defendant files an answer, then the litigation moves into a phase of the process generally called the *discovery* stage. Generally the objectives of this *pre-trial* procedure are to: (1) simplify the issues; (2) obtain admissions of fact to avoid unnecessary arguments and avoid surprise; (3) limit the number of expert witnesses; and (4) cover any other matters which would expedite the trial.

The following legal devices permit an adverse party to discover almost all information relevant to the trial of a civil suit. The best known discovery device is the **deposition.** A deposition is a sworn statement of any person, including a party to the action (the plaintiff or defendant) or any witness, which is made in response to questions from the attorneys for the opposing sides. The deposition is used to discover physical evidence, to discover what a witness will say at trial, or to discover any other matter relevant to the subject of the case. A deposition is taken under oath or affirmation, usually in front of attorneys for both parties, and is transcribed by the court reporter. The final copy is signed as a true statement by the one being deposed and is filed with the court. This signed statement may be used at the trial if the witness is unavailable, or it may be used at the trial to challenge the oral testimony of the deposing witness if such testimony varies from that in the deposition.

If the party or witness cannot be interviewed in person, then a series of written questions may be sent and must be answered under oath. These written questions are called **interrogatories.**

In addition to depositions and interrogatories, a party may ask the court to order another party, if good cause is shown, to produce documents and other items of evidence for inspection, copying, or photographing. The subject of this order may be books, papers, accounts, letters, photographs, objects or tangible things, or other items which constitute evidence relating to the subject of the suit. If the mental or physical condition of the party is in controversy, the court may order the party to submit to a physical or mental examination by a physician if good cause is shown. This latter method of discovery is used in many cases where personal injury is the subject of the case.

Courts in the various states adopted many of these discovery procedures in the 1960s so they are viewed as relatively new. This adoption has resulted in many more cases being settled out of court because the procedures allow a party to discover almost all of the relevant evidence of the opposing party. The only evidence which in not obtainable by the opposing party are those materials which are **privileged.** Generally, the materials include an attorney's work product (thoughts and research on a case) and communications between the client and his attorney or the patient and his doctor.

If the parties decide to *settle* the case out of court, the attorneys ask the permission of the judge to dismiss the case. If this dismissal is done *with prejudice*, it means that a party will be barred from filing the suit again. If the pretrial procedures do not result in settlement, then the parties usually ask the judge to rule on another series of motions challenging the legal assertions of the adverse parties. After the pleadings are all filed, either party may make a motion to dismiss the claims of an adverse party and enter judgment for the moving party by asking for a *judgment on the pleadings* or **summary judgment**. Some procedural systems make a distinction between these two motions but, in essence, they are the same. Like the initial motion to dismiss described above, these motions require the judge to consider the arguments made in all of the pleadings, resolve every reasonable inference against the moving party, and make a finding as to whether the arguments made and facts asserted warrant submission of the case to the jury in a trial on the facts. Generally, if the judge finds that the legal arguments and facts presented could lead to but one reasonable conclusion, and that is in favor of the moving party, then the motion must be granted. If there are issues of fact present which would lead reasonable minds to differ, then the motion should be overruled.

A matter may be tried before a jury or a judge alone. If a party in a civil suit desires a jury trial, it must be demanded, usually during the initial pleading phase. In federal courts, the U.S. Constitution guarantees a trial by jury in all civil actions at common law where the value of the controversy exceeds twenty dollars. The U.S. Constitution does not guarantee the right of a trial by jury in civil cases in state courts. However, the constitutions of the states usually provide that there is such a right in cases similar to those where the common law gave such a right at the time the constitution was adopted. Practically speaking, this means that almost all matters involving judgments of fact and requests for money damages may be tried before a jury. Usually negligence cases, and other personal injury cases, are tried before a jury. On the other hand, cases involving the equity powers of the court or those involving very complex issues such as antitrust suits or breaches on industrial contracts and other cases where evaluation of the evidence requires rigorous analysis and expertise are usually tried before the judge

alone. In very exceptional cases, the judge may appoint a *master* or *referee* to hear some of the evidence and make findings of fact.

The process of questioning prospective jurors to determine which of them will be permitted to sit on the jury is called **voir dire**. This phrase is French in origin and means "to speak the truth." The voir dire procedure allows the court and parties to reject a prospective juror if, after questioning, it is revealed that the person is barred by *statute* to serve in that case (e.g., wife of the plaintiff) or might be prejudiced or unable to render an impartial judgment. Usually each party is given three challenges to use for *any* reason—called *peremptory challenges*, and additional challenges can be made for sufficient cause (statutory cause)—called *challenge for cause*.

Trial. At the trial, the plaintiff, through the attorney representing the plaintiff's interests, presents its side of the **evidence.** After each witness is sworn and "directly" examined by the plaintiff's attorney, the defendant's attorney may "cross-examine" the witness on matter brought out on direct examination. It must be emphasized at this point that, since most of the cases which proceed to trial do involve disputes of fact, the process by which the facts are "found" is the process of *direct examination* of a witness by the attorney who initially uses the witness followed by *cross-examination* by the attorney for the other side. The jury or the judge, by watching the witnesses respond to the questions asked, must determine whether they are telling the truth or accurately recalling an event. The answers which are given by the witness are considered by the fact-finder (jury or judge) together with the witness's demeanor (facial expressions and hand movements).

Following the plaintiff's version of the facts in the case, the defendant presents the evidence relevant to its side.

During the trial itself, a party may challenge the entire case of an adverse party by moving for **directed verdict.** Either party may move this, and it requires the judge to rule on whether there are still issues of fact present which warrant the continuation of the trial. If reasonable minds could differ about the interpretation or existence of certain crucial facts, or the inferences to be drawn from the facts, then the court will overrule the motion and the trial will proceed.

At the close of the defendant's case, both sides make summary arguments emphasizing the aspects of the testimony and other evidence they believe most pertinent to their arguments. Before the jury retires to make its finding of fact, the judge instructs the jury on the appropriate rules of law which the jurors are to apply to the facts as determined by them. Below is an example of the type of "instruction" the judge may give to the jury in a negligence case:

Negligence is lack of ordinary care. It is a failure to exercise that degree of care which a reasonably prudent person would have exercised under the same circumstances. It may arise from doing an act which a reasonably prudent person would not have done under the same circumstances, or, on the other hand, from failing to do an act which a reasonably prudent person would have done under the circumstances.[2]

In applying this statement of the law, each juror must decide by using his or her own life experience as a guide whether or not the defendant acted as a "reasonably prudent person" would have, given the circumstances.

The judge gives the jury instructions on each matter of law argued in the case. After the instructions, the jury retires to the jury room, where it applies all the rules stated by the judge to the facts as presented to them at the trial by the parties, witnesses, attorneys, and other evidence and reaches a verdict both as to liability (was the defendant legally at fault for a breach of a rule?) and damages (if the defendant was liable, what is the appropriate amount of damages that will compensate the plaintiff for the breach of the rule?).

A motion for *judgment notwithstanding the verdict* may be made by an aggrieved party against whom the verdict has been announced after the trial of the issues. This motion requires the judge to rule on whether or not the jury could reasonably have reached the verdict it did, given the evidence and the court's instructions. This motion is granted only when the judge believes that the jury reached a verdict by ignoring the instructions, or where, after hearing and seeing all of the evidence, the jury could not logically have reached the verdict it did. This motion, like the one for summary judgment or the one for a directed verdict, essentially challenges the legal sufficiency of a party's case. It must not be confused with a motion for a new trial, which may be made after a verdict is reached but is granted only where substantial errors in the trial process occurred.

The Appellate Process

If either of the parties believes that there was an error during the trial and that this error caused an unfavorable verdict, the party may appeal. The error must be one in the process of introducing evidence or in the statement of the law or in the application of the rule to the facts. *Parties usually cannot appeal the finding of a fact.* For example, if the jury finds that, as a matter of fact, the defendant did *sign* an agreement in question on a given date, then this may not be appealed. However, a party may appeal the issue of whether signing the agreement did legally *bind* the party. This latter conclusion is one which is a mixture of fact-finding and law application and is appropriate for appeal. The reasons for this are that a party should get only one chance to introduce the evidence the party deems appropriate. Therefore, the trial courts are set up to take evidence; all the procedures at this level are adopted to ensure the fairness of the evidence-producing process. The right to cross-examination, the right to demand and examine other evidence, and the right to object to the introduction of irrelevant or excessively prejudicial evidence all exist at the trial level.

Appellate courts are not equipped to hear testimony or inspect evidence. Appellate courts are composed of three or more judges who hear the arguments of the appealing parties as to why the statements or the rules in the trial court were erroneous or why the process of rule application was erroneous.

An appeal may be initiated by either party. The one appealing is called the **appellant** or, in some courts, the *petitioner*. The one answering the appeal is the **appellee** or the *respondent*. At the trial stage, the case is given a name or "style" (in legal language); almost always this is done by putting the name of the plaintiff first, followed by the name of the defendant. However, on appeal, some courts, but not all, put the name of the appellant first when reporting the case. So if the defendant appeals, the defendant's name goes first in the official report. You should be cautioned that the appellate case's style does not reveal who is the plaintiff or defendant in the original trial of the matter. This may be determined only by reading the appellate opinion.

The appellant must file with the appellate court at least two documents. One is the transcribed version of what occurred in the trial. During the trial a court reporter took down all of the testimony, all objections and motions, and other relevant happenings in a special form of shorthand. This shorthand version of the trial is not transcribed into prose unless it is requested and paid for by one of the parties. Together with this transcript, the appellant files a legal brief which contains the appellant's legal arguments. The appellate court considers the trial transcript, the written legal arguments (briefs) of both parties, and in many cases allows attorneys for the parties to appear before it to orally answer questions asked by the appellate court and, in general, to argue the merits of the issues advanced. For the reasons stated above, the appellate court does not consider additional evidence, cannot call new or recall the old witnesses, or, generally, view the evidence again. The *facts* as found by the trial court must be taken as given.

The appellate court then takes the matter under consideration, does considerable legal research on the matter, votes, and writes its opinion. If some of the judges do not agree with the majority of the court, they may write dissenting opinions stating their reasons. This appellate opinion is usually published and is available to all persons.

If either party is still of the belief that a *substantial* error in the statement of the rule or in the application of the rule to the facts was made by either the trial or the intermediate appellate court, the party may appeal the case to the next higher level, the supreme court of the state or federal system, which is usually the highest level. Again, the party appealing this time is called the appellant or petitioner and the answering party is the appellee or respondent. The name of the appellant is usually placed first. The same general practice is followed in filing the appeals papers and hearing the arguments, except that additional arguments are made either supporting or attacking the decision of the first appellate court.

An appellate court (either intermediate or supreme court) may do one of three things with the case before it. It may *affirm* the holding of the court immediately below it and state its reasons for affirming the holding. If it affirms the decision, the same party who won the case in the court below wins again.

The appellate court may *reverse* the decision being appealed and enter its own judgment, giving the reasons. The third option is to order all or part of the case *tried again* using the interpretation of the law as stated by the appellate court. In this case, if the parties so desire, the case will be tried again. The same trial judge may preside again, but a new jury will be chosen. . . .

This concludes our presentation of material on the trial and appeal of a civil case. The terms defined and the processes outlined are helpful in understanding how to study law because the published opinions of appellate judges are the best source available to indicate how the law is applied. For this reason, we use excerpts of mostly appellate cases to illustrate the application of important legal principles discussed in this book. We edited the irrelevant portions out of these opinions and left in enough information so that you may discern the complete outlines of how the disputes developed and how the legal rules were applied to solve the disputes.

Briefing Appellate Cases

Some of the appellate cases excerpted in the text, especially the longer ones, are very complex and will require some effort on your part to fully understand them. We suggest you keep notes on these cases. These notes are called *briefs*. Briefs usually have the following components:

1. A statement of the "facts" of the case as found by the trial court and restated by the appellate court.

2. A statement of the "legal" arguments advanced by both the plaintiff and the defendant.

3. A precise statement of the legal issue or legal problem facing the court, which usually involves an application of a legal principle (rule) or principles (rules) to the facts.

4. A summary of the court's reasoning used to reach its conclusion; this is best accomplished by stating in your own words which facts the court finds are "legally operative" and then summarizing how the legal principle or rule applies to those facts.

Most commentators agree that the American civil trial process is inefficient, expansive, and time-consuming, particularly in the large commercial centers of the country. At the start of 1990, for example, 67,776 civil lawsuits seeking damages in excess of $15,000 were pending in Cook County (Chicago), Illinois. Over 20 percent of them were at least five years old. It was estimated that, for a civil suit filed in Cook County in 1990, the average wait for those who chose to pursue a trial will be six years.[3] For this reason, many law firms are exploring alternative means of resolving disputes.

Endnotes

1. From Arthur D. Wolfe, "Appendix A: An Explanation of the Civil Trial Process," in Joseph L. Frascona, Edward J. Conry, Terry L. Lantry, Bill M. Shaw, George J. Siedel, George W. Spiro and Arthur D. Wolfe, *Business Law: The Legal Environment, Text and Cases*, 3rd edition. Copyright © 1987 by Allyn and Bacon. Reprinted with permission.

2. Committee on Pattern Jury Instructions, Associations of Supreme Court Justices, *New York Pattern Jury Instructions—Civil*, vol. 1, 2nd ed., 126 (1974).

3. *Chicago Tribune*, March 26, 1990, p. 1, col. 3.

Social and Ethical Responsibility of Corporate Management

INTRODUCTION

This chapter is about the conduct of individuals in a business setting. Specifically, it examines the concept of moral responsibility as applied to individuals in business, to the managerial roles they occupy, and to the business firm itself. This chapter is built on the assumption that management's compliance with the law in most respects may not be sufficient for individuals to achieve the kind of business environment they want.

As individuals involved in the process of living our lives, we do much more than merely comply with the law. The law sets the floor; it defines a kind of social minimum below which we act at our peril. But many of the most important things in life, such as showing an appreciation and respect for one another and the natural environment, involve much more than the minimum the law requires. This chapter focuses on a set of ideas that raise the question of whether management has or should have responsibilities that go beyond the law.

The first section of this chapter focuses on the actions and thoughts of individual managers within the context of a large business corporation. What mental processes should a manager develop that will facilitate the identification and resolution of moral issues? There are ways to perceive and deal with moral issues in business, and the task of responsible management is to create a corporate culture in which such moral issues are always in the forefront. Our *model of morally responsible behavior*, adaptable to the role of the manager and to the role of the business firm, provides a sound basis on which to build this part of the chapter and to evaluate the materials in the second section.

The second part of the chapter explores a complex question: Can a collective such as a business corporation be held morally accountable? That is, what view of the corporate collective is helpful in understanding the moral obligations of the group? In addressing this question, we rely on readings from a Nobel laureate, from professors of theology, and from noted legal scholars and philosophers. The questions raised in either of these sections have no clear answers. We believe, however, that there are ways to approach moral problems and that the ones we advance will be instrumental in working through the moral issues you will confront in your career.

A MODEL OF MORALLY RESPONSIBLE BEHAVIOR

Our thinking and our approach to this chapter are shaped by a model of morally responsible behavior. We identify its principal components below; you will see them in action on the pages that follow.

1. *Identify issues.* Monitor the business environment for moral issues embodied in your firm's operations—issues that will produce good or harm for human welfare. This means being proactive, not waiting for disaster to strike. It also means rendering a full and accurate account of all facts that link the moral actor (the manager or the firm) in a causal relationship with the foreseen or anticipated outcome of that behavior.

2. *Establish a moral principle.* Stand for something and articulate those principles by formulating a corporate code of ethics that can serve as rational justification for the behavior you believe is appropriate for circumstances in which you or your firm may foreseeably be involved. Going public with this code is the best way to get objective, constructive feedback that will prevent "tunnel vision" or moral blindness to certain issues. The moral corporate code or credo begins with a resolve to identify moral issues and then deals with those issues through a process that is rational and sensitive to moral concerns.

3. *Follow through.* Do justice to the words of your credo by living up to those standards in letter and in spirit. Rewards and punishments must be distributed evenhandedly to firm managers, and the organization of the firm itself must be restructured so that moral conduct will be enhanced and wrong conduct diminished.

Nothing about this model is particularly original. In fact, its principal value consists of building into the firm a comprehensive network—a moral infrastructure—to identify these issues and then to resolve them in a manner compatible with the corporate mission.

If these issues are not recognized and dealt with properly, some of them could result in legal liability to the firm or a firm manager; that is one good reason to integrate this model into the firm's routine operations. As highly as we regard compliance with the law, however, it is not in itself a sufficient measure of responsible moral behavior. Legal compliance is a good starting point, but for the most part, the main task of the law is to prohibit and penalize people's worst conduct. It is not a very good instrument for inducing people to live up to their potential or to give their very best. In fact, if the law tried to compel people's best behavior instead of prohibiting their worst, they would lose an immense amount of the freedom they enjoy in this country today, which is not an appealing alternative.

Our model steers clear of that pitfall. It seeks to induce the very best behaviors from everyone—in particular, businesspeople. The model anchors our chapter, and as you apply it, you will find ways to improve its operation.

Every manager and every student who expects to step into one of these positions has the right to expect strong moral leadership from the top, and those at the top have an obligation to provide it. Corporate employees have the right to a corporate culture that internalizes moral values and to expect the firm to institutionalize a working process that will put these values into operation.

When we say that the firm must internalize or institutionalize ethical values, we mean the firm is expected to exhibit in all of its activities a concern for the welfare of the lives it affects and that concern must transcend purely material values. We elaborate on this further in later sections.

Finally, the demands we make on business firms are not revolutionary; nor are our standards for business managers unrealistic. On the contrary, these criteria are elementary and, for those who are serious about professionalizing the role of manager, long overdue.

RESPONSIBLE MANAGEMENT IN THE CORPORATE REALITY

The conventional wisdom is that students and teachers live in an ivory tower, whereas businesspeople live in a dog-eat-dog world where they must cover their bottom line before worrying about doing good. Ever wonder where this idea came from? Some people attribute it, erroneously, to Adam Smith, and they may have been led into this error by taking some of his observations out of context. The following illustrative passages must be read in Smith's historical setting in order to avoid wrong inferences:

> It is not from the benevolence of the butcher, the baker, and the brewer that we expect our dinner, but from their regard for their self-interest. We address ourselves not to their humanity, but to their self-love, and never talk to them of our own necessities, but of their advantages.[1]

* * *

> By directing [one's] industry in such a manner as its produce may be of the greatest value, [the individual] intends only his own gain, and he is in this, as in many other cases, led by an invisible hand to promote an end that was no part of his intention. . . . Pursuing his own interests he frequently promotes that of society more effectively than when he really intends to promote it.[2]

Adam Smith was a moral philosopher and a remarkably perceptive one. He never lost his passion for moral excellence, not even in his later years when he turned his thoughts to the economic problems of his day. In his famous work *The Wealth of Nations*, Smith was doing battle with economists known as *mercantilists*, who favored tight control of prices, wages, and production. Economic freedom and free trade were the points on which Adam Smith hammered away. He believed that free enterprise would promote the public good, and not by any far stretch of the imagination did he ever condone illegality, dishonesty, fraud, or any other market practice that would be harmful to society or bring an individual or business firm into moral disrepute. He recognized that the kind of conduct that inflicted harm on other people through intentional, careless, or reckless behavior was a deadly enemy to the operation of free markets.

The free market system has an implicit morality, and it can never operate to its full potential if this moral code is not maintained intact. Markets depend on a high level of trust and confidence among people who scarcely know one another. These people are vulnerable to one another's integrity and to their strength of character. Businesspeople must speak and act honestly if they expect to sustain this level of confidence. To lie is to exploit and manipulate people for one's own purposes, and it spells certain doom for any mutually advantageous relationship in years to come.

Businesspeople must keep their promises and live by the kind of loyalty these promises impose. They must act fairly and in good faith because the violation of these moral norms risks the imposition of unjustifiable harm on other human beings. To act otherwise is to invite that conduct on oneself and to bring about a disintegration of business relationships.

This is not a novel proposition. It is the crux of political systems, as well as family and interpersonal relationships. These principles are endorsed and acted on by rational people from all corners of the globe. Rational people internalize these moral norms and live by them because this is the kind of treatment that they expect in return, the kind of behavior that promises the greatest good for the greatest number, and the kind of conduct that embodies the virtues and fosters the good (happiness or fulfillment).

Responsible managers have to understand these moral norms, and they have to understand that the role of business in society is not a purely material one. Business is a social institution with the task of producing wealth, jobs, and goods and services, but not at any cost. It must adhere to the important social norms, and among those are law and morality. We turn our attention now to the role that managers play in creating a business environment—a corporate culture—in which moral considerations come to the forefront.

CORPORATE CULTURE

In Chapter 1, Bowen McCoy, author of "The Parable of the Sadhu," introduced the concept of a corporate culture. The setting of the parable was ethnically diverse and highly intense people on a mountain pass in Nepal. There, the lack of cohesion among the climbing groups, the lack of leadership, and the lack of sensitivity to any problems but their own all contributed to a tragedy, the death or near-death of the Sadhu (in fact, no one including the author ever learned of the Sadhu's fate). Reflecting on this event, McCoy was appalled that his moral consciousness and sensitivity to the needs of others were so diminished by his singleminded purpose of reaching the next peak that he never paused to consider the Sadhu's unspoken, though far more pressing, claim. Initially, he voiced some fairly evident excuses, particularly in response to his friend Stephen's stern indictment, but in the final accounting McCoy acknowledged that he "literally walked through a classic moral dilemma without fully thinking through the consequences."

As a monument to that experience, McCoy wrote of the importance of creating defenses against even the possibility of repeating comparable errors in a corporate setting. He equated corporate culture with the notion of "shared values and an agreed-on process of dealing with adversity and change." We believe a corporate culture should also include a process for dealing with ambiguity because so many choices that managers have to deal with are in the gray area of "moral ambiguity." We elaborate on the elements of a corporate culture and then discuss the process of dealing with adversity, ambiguity, and change.

ELEMENTS OF A CORPORATE CULTURE

Moral Leadership from the Top.   "Find an ethical boss" is likely the most common advice that experienced businesspeople offer students and young managers. There is simply no substitute for strong moral leadership from the top. The distinguishing moral character of the firm, its guiding beliefs, and its ethos will be set in motion by this person. The boss may be the near-legendary founder, a strong CEO, or a high-profile executive, or the moral tone may be created and kept alive by the corporate credos and even by corporate stories and tales of sacrifice and caring for one another during hard times. The point is that well-intentioned individuals can get lost—alienated from themselves, their families, and their coworkers—in the maze of large organizations. These people deserve strong moral guidance and a support system that will dignify and enhance their sense of personal worth and integrity. If they deserved to be hired at all, it makes sense to find ways of keeping them in the firm and making them feel a part of its traditions. This is an important way of strengthening the firm's culture and moral fabric, and it is entirely compatible with advancing the firm's economic interests.

Respect for Corporate Stakeholders.   It would be silly to suggest that a business firm should not keep its corporate eye on the bottom line, and we do not intend this. But it is simply not the case that every corporate decision based on moral principle is costly to the firm or that such decisions will put the firm at a competitive disadvantage. The example just given of the employee "lost" in the corporate maze is an excellent illustration of the potential for harmonizing a firm's moral culture with its market interests.

We do not suggest that "good ethics is good business" by every short-term economic measurement. Some tough moral choices, those characterized by adversity, ambiguity, and change, are bound to cost the firm money and to affect it competitively. But think about the areas where ethical and business interests might possibly coincide. The greatest potential involves the firm's dealings with customers and employees. A real interest in workplace and product safety, founded on the moral principle of respect for others and of doing no harm, has enormous possibilities in creating a loyal, productive workforce with high morale and a strong preference among members of the consuming public for quality products that are worth paying for.

Multiple Communication Channels.   In many large organizations, people at the top don't want to know what is going on down below. Some managers seem to develop a kind of a tunnel vision that sees only profit at the other end of their policies, objectives, goals, and timetables. They expect their subordinates to "get the job done," but they don't want to hear about the nitty-gritty. Beyond that, frequently a palace guard makes sure the boss doesn't hear the bad news, and a middle tier of management knows it would be upsetting to their career objectives if the boss ever learned how the targets were met.

These are not signs of strong moral leadership. The larger the organization, the greater the need for being creative in building in fail-safe communication channels that speed information throughout the firm. Information gaps and misinformation can close off even the possibility of recognizing moral hazards, just as they can foreclose a recognition of economic hazards. From both perspectives, the long-term interests of the firm demand that truthful and relevant information be brought to the attention of decision makers before it is too late to avoid harm or to turn a potentially harmful situation into a positive one.

A Decision Process That Embodies the Moral Point of View.   Institutionalizing a rational decision-making process that incorporates moral norms into the daily operations of the firm brings life and substance to the moral point of view. In the moral point of view, part of our elaboration of the model of morally responsible behavior, the emphasis is on a process that involves (1) perception or identification of moral issues, (2) articulation of moral standards that serve as moral decision criteria, (3) application of the standards to the relevant facts, and (4) implementation or follow-through.

This process does not commit the firm, its officers, or its employees to a particular moral standard or moral theory. A manager does not have to be a philosopher to recognize that the operations of the firm have the potential for doing good, as well as the potential for doing harm. Nor does a manager have to be a philosopher to use critical thought in gathering the relevant facts and in evaluating the issues on the basis of sound moral principles.

We emphasize here that we are not teaching outcomes. The appropriate course of action to be taken in morally ambiguous situations cannot be resolved prior to the event. We are, however, contending for a process—a moral point of view—and it is our belief that this process will have a positive effect on the quality of moral decision making.

THE MORAL POINT OF VIEW

Our expectations for responsible management are influenced by the Chapter 1 discussion of the moral point of view. A corporation that internalizes this concept gives meaning and substance to its moral culture. Beyond that, it reinforces the model of morally responsible behavior that we introduced earlier: (1) identify issues, (2) establish a moral principle, and (3) follow through. Following are the steps in the process we call the moral point of view.

1. *Perception.* The leadership of business corporations should gather all of the relevant facts by monitoring the corporate environment. This monitoring is done by creating channels of communication that will not allow sensitive information to escape management's attention. The leadership must also develop measures that will encourage employees to relay this information through proper channels to the appropriate authority. These channels must be secure, and employees must be assured that the "pipeline" is open for this purpose and can be used without fear of disfavor or retaliation.

2. *Moral standards.* When the issues and the relevant facts are identified, the leadership is obligated to trigger its decision-making structure before anyone comes to harm and before opportunities for positive action are lost. The articulation of its moral values—whether by example, credo, legend, or corporate codes of moral behavior—must already be in place. In addition, it must have available a participatory process that will give employees an important stake in resolving these issues.

3. *Application.* The leadership must exercise judgment and control in dealing with issues that are raised and must consider alternative ways of resolving these issues. A participatory process does not necessarily mean a majority vote. The more difficult the issue, the less likely it is that all constituencies will be completely satisfied. The decision process will, of course, recognize that the corporation is a for-profit operation, but it must be sensitive to the firm's potential for doing harm, as well as for doing good. With due consideration for the bottom line, it must not allow profit always to dictate the outcome.

4. *Implementation.* Finally, the leadership of the firm is obligated to "make good" on this process, to implement its judgment, and to not be satisfied with good intentions only. That could involve some tough choices. In fact, it could mark the demise of the firm or the end of your career with that firm.

These very concerns, we may assume, were on Bob's mind when he came to you for advice in a case we call *Lawnsaw, Inc.*, or more appropriately, "The Case of the Killer Blade."

Bob Adair's job is to oversee engineering reports on product development for his employer, Lawnsaw, Inc., and to filter these reports to his supervisor, Karen McClellan. Lawnsaw, a lawn mower manufacturer, has been in some financial difficulty lately. Within the last two years, Lawnsaw lost a sizeable percentage of its market share.

   While examining the test reports on a new product that the company is depending on for its recovery, Bob noticed that the engineers had discovered a defect which could render the product harmful to the user under normal conditions. Their report showed that failure occurred in 1.2% of the tests and could result in extremely serious injury or even death.

Bob told Karen of the defect and included it in his report to her. He recommended that releasing the product be delayed until the defect was corrected. Karen thanked him for his work and instructed him to tell no one else of the report. She then ordered him to meet with the engineers running the tests and "reevaluate" the data to eliminate the concern.

"My superior will write the final report, Bob. You just work up the data and draw the graphs. We just work here. Leave the rest to the boss."[3]

We used a case similar to this in Chapter 1: "The Dilemma of Jean McGuire." Our purpose on both occasions is (1) to have you identify the issues and (2) to have you involved in the process of working through case studies that embody some of the same issues, though not the same facts, that may realistically confront you early in your career. Do not lose sight of the fact that Lawnsaw, Inc., is in business for a profit, that the shareholders expect a return on their investment, and that you are not a totally free moral agent. You are a manager in a capitalist system, and you have responsibilities to diverse constituencies. Profits must count for something, but for how much?

We are not going to walk through this case with you or suggest a preferred outcome, but we are going to ask you to reflect, first, on the moral culture of Lawnsaw, Inc. What is your *perception?* Is it strong enough to sensitize its employees to recognize the moral issue or issues? And on the assumption that the issues are identified, has Lawnsaw, Inc., adopted a process to deal with such matters?

It is important to develop the habit of familiarizing yourself thoroughly with the known facts in a case. Many times, you will have to operate with the uncertainty of incomplete and distorted facts. You cannot afford to let up, however, because the facts will point to the moral issues—the foreseeable good or harm that will likely result from the conduct of Lawnsaw's employees.

Next, list the moral issues you believe are involved in this case. Compare and combine your list with that of a friend or of a study group, and for the sake of organizing your thoughts, put the issues in descending order of importance. You may find it useful at this stage to write down what you consider to be the appropriate *moral standard or standards* that will guide your resolution of the issues. Make sure these standards are consistent with one another. If the standards point in different directions, you need to reconcile them.

Now you are at the *application* stage. Apply the standards to the facts to determine which course of action is the morally appropriate one. There may be several alternatives, none of which will be ideal and some of which will be impractical or impossible.

Finally, make up your mind—*implementation.* Moral purity (waiting for the perfect answer) and moral indecisiveness (postponing a decision until it's too late to resolve the matter) are the twin perils of moral effectiveness and effective management. Only now do you have to make up your mind, but you frequently have to do it in less time than you would like. And you have to be sure that your decision is one for which you can articulate a rational justification—the moral reasons that will be satisfactory to a thoughtful and unbiased audience.

Moral Dilemma/Moral Justification.   As you noticed in "The Case of the Killer Blade," moral duties sometimes tug in different directions. We call these quandaries *moral dilemmas.* For example, we want to honor confidentiality and keep our promises, but that may involve us in a conflict of interest or in failing to comply with the law. Or an employee may be on the edge of whistle-blowing but is held back by a respect for loyalty to the firm or to some officer of the firm. Or you can imagine a situation in which the obligation to do no harm begs the question of harm to whom—to the employer, customer, supplier, or some other stakeholder?

Beyond our emphasis on the moral point of view, we think very little can be taught about how to resolve these situations. It comes down to a matter of self-examination. You need to ask, What is the most important value at stake here? What are my priorities? Why do I consider one moral value to be more important than another? Given my role, to what extent am I capable of making these moral values operative in the marketplace?

The Moral Minimum.   Obeying the law, telling the truth, keeping promises, being loyal, being fair, doing no harm, helping other people—people have been conditioned by these values all of their lives, and these are the basis for the moral minimum. We call these values *prima facie values.* They do not have to be explained or justified because they are intrinsically right and good. In fact, the things that do have to be explained are violations of the law, lies, broken promises, disloyalty, unfairness, doing harm, and failing to help people when they are in need.

The problem is sorting out which of these values should be given priority in a particular situation. In your hierarchy of values, which is the most important? Which value trumps the others? Many challenging and ambiguous business problems will not present you with clear moral choices. Managers are confronted with unsettled gray areas and are compelled to choose among alternative visions of good or among the lesser of evils.

The questions you will face are not questions that anyone can answer for you, but it can be immensely helpful to talk over such matters in confidence with a friend. That is why Bob Adair sought your advice in "The Case of the Killer Blade." Discussing these problems with someone else frequently relieves needless anxiety, adds to your clarity of thought, and keeps you from being trapped by tunnel vision. It gives you the freedom to explore alternatives and to get a reasoned, confidential response from someone with a different perspective. Face it, some of these decisions are so emotionally draining that they are just too much for one person. Even with the best advice, you may not feel entirely confident about the choice you have made.

Figure 3.1 gives an enumeration of moral duties particularly appropriate in a business setting. We do not present these duties with the thought that memorization of a list is any way to resolve moral problems, but rather in the hope that it will give you a starting point.

FIGURE 3.1   *Moral Duties in a Business Setting*

1. **Willingly Comply with the Law**
    This principle involves compliance with the substance of legal provisions. It goes beyond merely employing a cost-benefit analysis of the impact of likely legal sanctions to determine whether to comply with a given rule. Confronting an immoral law might, in certain instances, justify noncompliance, but valid civil disobedience should occur extremely infrequently in business transactions.

2. **Honor Confidentiality**
    Information is confidential when it is made available to another with the express or implied understanding that it is to be used only for certain purposes. A principle of confidentiality may also pertain to information identified as proprietary or confidential, obtained by means other than direct disclosure by the owner.

3. **Avoid the Appearance of a Conflict of Interest**
    A conflict of interest arises when someone has a personal interest that contrasts with a duty owed to another or when mutually exclusive duties are owed to two or more (some call this competing interests). Binding duties may arise out of contractual obligations, noncontractual promises, role relationships (e.g., agent or trustee), or the law. Potential conflicts of interest can be deflected from becoming actual conflicts by, among other things, full disclosure, having an independent party certify as to fairness, or abstention.

4. **Exercise Due Care**
    This principle incorporates a concept of professional competency. One who has special training or experience should perform to the level generally expected of those with equivalent qualifications. The principle may be viewed as an ethical standard in that others rely upon and are affected by the quality of work performed by the business people to whom it applies.

5. **Act in Good Faith**
    Good faith incorporates a number of attributes, including honoring promises, being fair, employing just procedures, and responding to the reasonable expectations held by others. The essence of the concept is to act so as to sustain a long-term relationship.

6. **Respect the Liberty and Rights of Others**
    Business people, particularly those in supervisory roles, often have the power to affect the ability of others to exercise basic rights. The affected parties have a right to be treated with respect and to be able, to the extent feasible, to exercise their basic rights as citizens and human beings.

7. **Respect Human Well-Being**
    A fundamental principle is to do no harm to others. Although "harm" is a relative concept that is complex and difficult to define, this principle generally overrides any of the other six when conflicts arise.

Source: Dunfee, Thomas W., The Case for Professional Norms of Business Ethics, 25 *Amer. Bus. Law J.* 385-406 (1987).

We want to make clear our position of this enumeration of a moral minimum. On the one hand, familiarity with such a list will not resolve moral problems for anyone. On the other hand, one has to start somewhere, and we think these criteria make an excellent place to begin. Earlier in the chapter, you read of the moral significance of truth telling and promise keeping and of the importance of fairness, loyalty, and doing no harm. These are the moral concepts that bind society together. They serve as the intellectual basis of the more down-to-earth guidance provided by the moral minimum. The formulation of moral duties is especially appropriate for inclusion here because it focuses on the kind of ethical behavior expected of people in a business setting. We think the moral culture of the firm, and the process we call the moral point of view, will be strengthened as business managers gain experience in the application of the moral minimum.

The situation presented in the following case study gives you the opportunity to exercise and extend your understanding of these moral concepts.

FRANCES A. ZOLLERS

Drug Testing at Business Systems

The firm for which you work, Business Systems, Inc., provides consulting services to industry and government. The contracts it performs put the firm's employees in touch with sensitive information from the client, including personnel data, trade secrets, and customers lists. As a control measure, and to engender feelings of security by the clients, Business Systems has undertaken a program of mandatory drug testing of its employees. The system is fairly new, so it is not clear what happens if an employee tests positive for drugs. So far, the policy statements announcing the program have promised that the results of the testing will be held confidential from anyone outside the firm and from any employees within the firm who have no compelling need for the information.

The test procedure calls for urinalysis to be performed on urine samples provided by employees, under the observation of a supervisory level employee. If the sample tests positive, a second test will be performed to diminish the possibility of a false positive reading. If the second sample also tests positive, a much more sophisticated and expensive gas chromatography test will be performed to ensure accuracy. The simple urinalysis tests for some twenty substances. The final test tests for one hundred substances and is able to detect subtle differences in chemical compounds. For example, the final test can detect the difference between poppy seeds and morphine, something the urinalysis can do only occasionally.

When the drug testing program was announced, some employees left the firm. Others stayed on, but were fairly vocal in their opposition to the new policy. A person you supervise, Walter Anderson, has come to you with the following problem. He objects to the drug testing program on philosophical and personal grounds. Walter has a history of depression, for which he has from time to time sought psychiatric help. In addition to counseling, he has been prescribed low-level doses of diazepam, a drug used to combat depression. He has not had a debilitating bout with depression in a very long time, due in part to his daily dosage of diazepam. His illness does not appear to affect his work and you have given him high performance ratings each time you have had to evaluate his job performance.

The drug test will reveal the diazepam. Walter fears the consequences that might obtain from the revelation of his history of mental illness. He will not go to the managers above you to object to the program, but he trusts you and wants you to know that he will refuse to submit to the test when the time comes and why. He also wants you to make the case for abandoning the drug program on his behalf, while preserving his anonymity.

While you value Walter as a member of your working group, you realize that you may be putting your own job on the line if you go to bat for him. Still, you sense that he is right about the adverse consequences that might follow from the revelation that he is on an antidepressant, even if it is by prescription. You are fairly certain that the Business Systems testing program is designed to discover who might be using illicit drugs and therefore who may be unreliable custodians of sensitive information. However, you know that mental illness is generally misunderstood and that the revelation of Walter's history would almost certainly end his career with the firm, or at least stop any chances of advancement.[4]

ARTICLE FOLLOW-UP

Review our model of morally responsible behavior, as well as the materials on corporate culture, the moral point of view, moral dilemmas, and the moral minimum. Then look at this hypothetical case again and enumerate the moral issues as you see them.

Did Business Systems have a strong moral culture? Would the moral issues you named have arisen if it did have such a culture? Did Business Systems show respect for its employees? Did it establish communication channels that intercepted potential problems before they developed into big ones? Did you see any evidence of a decision process that embodied the moral point of view?

You must decide what you will do with Walter's information and request. Set out the steps of moral reasoning, apply them to yourself in this situation, and reason to a decision about what course of action you will take. You may decide to advocate the abandonment or modification of the drug-testing program, not to go to bat for Walter, or to reveal the information Walter has given you before he is compelled to take the test. You have other options as well. The point of this exercise is to have you go through the process of moral reasoning on paper and reason to a conclusion.

Excusing Conditions. Both *knowledge* and *freedom* are the prerequisites of moral responsibility, and this holds true whether a person is acting individually or on behalf of a business firm. In the absence of knowledge that certain conduct will produce harm, we could not say that a person acted with intent, and we would excuse such conduct unless we also knew that a person willfully refused to gain that knowledge or acted recklessly or negligently in this regard. For example, marketing a defective product may produce strict legal liability, but we would not automatically attach moral blame to that conduct.

If a person has been deprived of freedom and has acted under the force of some threat that a reasonable person could not resist, we would not attach moral blame to that conduct either. For example, when people act under a sufficient degree of duress, we do not hold them morally responsible because they were not free to do otherwise.

It is important to understand the roles of knowledge and freedom because, in a business context, as in any other, there may be a basis for excusing the conduct of an individual or for saying that mitigating circumstances reduce or eliminate moral blame. Events that preclude or diminish one's freedom of action (organizational or functional channels that place a matter beyond one's reach) or preclude or diminish one's knowledge (communication channels that do not bring the information to one's attention) give us a rational basis for saying that the person who has engaged in some morally changed conduct is not as blameworthy as may have originally been thought.

MORAL STATUS OF CORPORATIONS

Many ethical problems involve actions within the context of large business corporations. These problems are made more difficult when the individuals responsible for them disappear into the corporate bureaucracy to escape accountability. When elusion occurs, is it acceptable to treat corporations as moral persons capable of moral blame? Does the analogy between individual personhood and corporate personhood hold up when one is assessing moral culpability? In this section of the chapter, we ask the question, How should one think about moral responsibility for corporate conduct?

In a legal sense, corporations are persons, and they are accorded many of the same rights given to natural persons. For example, corporate property is accorded constitutional due process and equal protection coverage, and corporate speech falls within the ambit of the First Amendment because, like the speech of natural persons, it has an "inherent capacity to inform." That does not resolve the moral status of corporations, however.

We hold the fairly traditional view that natural persons are the primary moral actors because they act with a particular mental state—for example, intent—and in doing so cause certain consequences. There is a unity of mental state and conduct. If the consequences are bad, we find the intentional actor to be morally blameworthy. If the consequences are good, we find the intentional actor to be morally praiseworthy. If either set of consequences is produced by an actor with a mental state characterized by negligence or recklessness, we make appropriate adjustments in this evaluation.[5]

The moral blameworthiness of those who cause bad consequences is the basis for the criminal code. The general public, operating through its democratic institutions, penalizes actors whose conduct is characterized by a mental process (intentional, or on occasion, reckless or negligent) that causes harmful consequences. This penalizing is done to promote the "greatest good for the greatest number" (a utilitarian justification), to "balance the scales of justice" (a natural law justification), or simply because people would not "consent" to a social mode of behavior unless others were required to comply with the same rules (a social contract justification). Blame and punishment are connected to moral responsibility through these moral principles.

Corporations do not display this unity of mind and action. Assume that in Corporation A-B, wholly owned by A and B, corporate president A originates a good idea and corporate vice-president B intentionally executes it in a morally blameworthy way. Even if, according to state law, Corporation A-B and vice-president B are criminally liable, is the corporation morally liable? We have no hesitation in saying that the corporation is not morally responsible. We stick with the traditional analysis that only B is morally to blame and that the situation is no different than if A and B were not incorporated.

This view is buttressed by the observation that the legal existence of the corporation—the articles of incorporation, the charter, the bylaws, and so on—are spelled out on lifeless pieces of paper detailing impersonal rules, organizational tables, and standard operating procedures. For these reasons, philosopher John Ladd argues, corporations can have no more moral status than programmable robots.[6] "By nature," robots have no freedom or knowledge, both preconditions of moral conduct. Like a programmable robot, an organization's purely formal goals or a corporations's economic goals make moral considerations extraneous and, therefore, automatically irrelevant to the decision-making process.

The traditional analysis does not seem to us to be entirely appropriate, however. It does not explain enough, so we look for a different paradigm. At issue here is the analogy between individual moral personhood and collective, group, or corporate moral personhood.[7] At what point along the spectrum, as the firm grows from the size of Corporation A-B to the size of General Motors and AT&T, does it make sense to say that a purely legal person has become a moral person as well?

People behave differently in groups than they do as individuals. Singly, they know they will be held accountable for their conduct. Within a group, they might be willing to do things that we would not do alone. Individuals might be inclined to take greater risks if they are operating within a group because it is possible to spread the blame or to dodge accountability by pointing to someone else. The phrase *risky shift* has been applied to this form of group behavior.[8] On other occasions, people may allow group norms to overwhelm their thought process in such a way that they forego any realistic appraisal of alternative courses of action; in a word, people allow themselves to be victimized by "groupthink."[9]

Individuals within corporations are surely motivated by corporate purposes; in fact, individual action is a necessary precondition to corporate action. But the structure of corporations (divided lines of authority and responsibility, separation into profit centers and functional divisions, committees of all descriptions) processes individual thoughts and actions to the point that they are virtually anonymous, or at least that the corporate outcome is scarcely ever attributable to a single individual. After being "worked over" by the corporate process, the end-of-the-pipe decision is the result of so many turns and twists that it would be foolish to describe it as the decision of a single person. This group or collective outcome is uniquely corporate; individual conduct was necessary to it, but only the totality of the process is necessary and sufficient to explain it.[10]

Some corporate conduct, then, is unique. With regard to that conduct, we can only observe that "the whole is greater than the sum of its parts." This observation leads us to insist that there *is* corporate moral responsibility—responsibility for those uniquely corporate actions. We continue to regard natural persons as the primary moral actors. With regard to the corporate decision process and its effects, we characterize it as qualified or secondary moral responsibility.

Corporate managers and employees certainly do have moral rights and responsibilities. When we use the phrase *corporate moral responsibility,* we associate it with corporate officers and employees operating in a business context. When things get so complex that we cannot find one or more individuals to hold accountable, we speak of corporate moral responsibility in our qualified or secondary sense.

The concept of corporate moral personhood with rights and duties comparable to natural persons is not only difficult to establish clearly, but also of doubtful value. The real issue is, What should corporations do? How should corporations act when it is known that their actions will have an impact, positive or negative, on the lives of real human beings? How corporations should act is the subject of the next section.

ALTERNATIVE VIEWS: THE ROLE OF THE RESPONSIBLE MANAGER

MILTON FRIEDMAN AND CORPORATE SOCIAL RESPONSIBILITY

Milton Friedman's view of corporate social responsibility can be reduced to a simple directive: Corporations should follow the law and ethical custom and, beyond that, use all their resources to increase their profits. His reasons for this view are more fully set out below; beneath these reasons, however, is a fundamental belief that, above all, freedom should be the guiding value. Friedman and Robert Nozick (an intellectual rival and contemporary of John Rawls at Harvard) base their libertarian views on the philosophy of John Locke. Locke believed that freedom is a natural right; that is, in a state of nature, all inhabitants would be equally free and governed only by moral principles imposed by a supreme being. Locke coupled this natural right to be free with the accompanying natural right to privately own any property that, by one's own labor, could be taken from nature. Locke's philosophy in many ways forms the bedrock of capitalistic society. He said that humans seek

> [a] *state of perfect freedom* to order their actions and dispose of their possessions and persons as they think fit, within the bounds of the law of nature, without asking leave, or depending upon the will of any other man. A *state* also *of equality,* wherein all the power and jurisdiction is reciprocal, no one having more than another . . . without subordination or subjection [to another]. . . . But . . . the *state of nature* has a law of nature to govern it, which obliges everyone: and reason, which is that law, teaches all mankind, who will but consult it, that being all equal and independent, no one ought to harm another in his life, health, liberty, or possessions.[11]

★ ★ ★

> Every man has a *property* in his own *person*: This nobody has a right to but himself. The *labor* of his body, and the *work* of his hands, we may say, are properly his. Whatsoever then he removes out of the state that nature has provided and left in it, he has mixed his *labor* with, and joined to it something that is his own, and thereby makes it his property. . . . [For] this *labor* being the unquestionable property of the laborer, no man but he can have a right to what that [labor] is once joined to, at least where there is enough, and as good, left in common for others.[12]

The view espoused by Locke, Friedman, and Nozick is that government is needed only to the extent necessary to protect life, liberty, and property. Government should only be strong enough to act effectively when attempting to protect the liberty and freedom of one citizen from another citizen or to protect the country from a foreign enemy.

In Friedman's view, profits are a form of natural property that, in the context of the corporation as an actor, accrue to the shareholders. Thus, the management of such a firm has the primary moral obligation to act in the best interests of the shareholders. As faithful agents, management must maximize profits and return these profits to the shareholders in the form of dividends. As a matter of principle and as a matter of consequences, political questions are raised when business firms become socially responsible, according to Friedman. With regard to political principle, taxing and spending are constitutional functions, and private sector intrusions (social responsibility expenditures) on these functions lack the checks and balances of the political system. Managers of business firms scarcely have the experience or training to perceive and advance the public interest.

> The discussion of the "social responsibilities of business" are notable for their analytical looseness and lack of rigor. What does it mean to say that "business" has responsibilities? Only people can have responsibilities. A corporation is an artificial person and in this sense may have artificial responsibilities, but "business" as a whole cannot be said to have responsibilities, even in this vague sense. The first step toward clarity to examining the doctrine of social responsibility of business is to ask precisely what it implies for whom.

★ ★ ★

In a free-enterprise, private-property system, a corporate executive is an employee of the owners of the business. He has direct responsibility to his employer. That responsibility is to conduct the business in accordance with their desires, which generally will be to make as much money as possible while conforming to the basic rules of the society, both those embodied in law and those embodied in ethical custom.[13]

MILTON FRIEDMAN
The Social Responsibility of Business

The view has been gaining widespread acceptance that corporate officials and labor leaders have a "social responsibility" that goes beyond serving the interest of their stockholders or their members. This view shows a fundamental misconception of the character and nature of a free economy. In such an economy, there is one and only one social responsibility of business—to use its resources and engage in activities designed to increase its profits so long as it stays within the rules of the game, which is to say, engages in open and free competition, without deception or fraud. Similarly, the "social responsibility" of labor leaders is to serve the interests of the members of their unions. It is the responsibility of the rest of us to establish a framework of law such that an individual in pursuing his own interest is, to quote Adam Smith again, "led by an invisible hand to promote an end which was no part of the intention. Nor is it always the worse for the society that it was no part of it. By pursuing his own interests, he frequently promotes that of the society more effectually than when he really intends to promote it. I have never known much good done by those who affected to trade for the public good."[14]

Few trends could so thoroughly undermine the very foundations of our free society as the acceptance by corporate officials of a social responsibility other than to make as much money for their stockholders as pos-

sible. This is a fundamentally subversive doctrine. If businessmen do have a social responsibility other than making maximum profits for stockholders, how are they to know what it is? Can self-selected private individuals decide what the social interest is? Can they decide how great a burden they are justified in placing on themselves or their stockholders to serve that social interest? Is it tolerable that these public functions of taxation, expenditure, and control be exercised by the people who happen at the moment to be in charge of particular enterprises, chosen for those posts by strictly private groups? If businessmen are civil servants rather than the employees of their stockholders then in a democracy they will, sooner or later, be chosen by the public techniques of election and appointment.

★ ★ ★

One topic in the area of social responsibility that I feel duty-bound to touch on, because it affects my own personal interests, has been the claim that business should contribute to the support of charitable activities and especially to universities. Such giving by corporations is an inappropriate use of corporate funds in a free-enterprise society.

The corporation is an instrument of the stockholders who own it. If the corporation makes a contribution, it prevents the individual stockholder from himself deciding how he should dispose of his funds. With the corporation tax and the deductibility of contributions, stockholders may of course want the corporation to make a gift on their behalf, since this would enable them to make a larger gift. The best solution would be the abolition of the corporate tax. But so long as there is a corporate tax there is no justification for permitting deductions for contributions to charitable and educational institutions. Such contributions should be made by the individuals who are the ultimate owners of property in our society.

People who urge extension of the deductibility of this kind of corporate contribution in the name of free enterprise are fundamentally working against their own interest. A major complaint made frequently against modern business is that it involves the separation of ownership and control-that the corporation has become a social institution that is a law unto itself, with irresponsible executives who do not serve the interests of their stockholders. This charge is not true. But the direction in which policy is now moving, of permitting corporations to make contributions for charitable purposes and allowing deductions for income tax, is a step in the direction of creating a true divorce between ownership and control and of undermining the basic nature and character of our society. It is a step away from an individualistic society and toward the corporate state.[15]

ARTICLE FOLLOW-UP

What does Friedman mean by the statement that corporate social responsibility "is a fundamentally subversive doctrine"? If shareholders do not protest or otherwise send corporate managers a negative message, in what way is it irresponsible for these managers to financially support universities, charitable activities, and other social projects?

Friedman is careful to distinguish corporate social obligations of humans. He does not deny that natural persons have moral responsibilities. But, he argues, people acting as managers of corporations should not exercise their personal views as to social responsibility. If they do so, they must make it clear that they are acting on their own behalf and spending their own money.

When Friedman writes of business persons and firms "conforming to the basic rules of society . . . embodied in law and ethical custom," how much clarity is he bringing to a dialogue that he perceives to be "notable for analytical looseness and lack of rigor"? Is there any reason to believe that Friedman would not be supportive of the moral minimum that has been suggested earlier in the chapter? If not, what could he possibly have meant by the phrase "ethical custom"?

To what extent would Friedman's argument suffer if one could show that, with regard to the largest 500 corporations, management is insulated from the shareholders and, in fact, is almost never voted out of office because shareholders are so geographically spread out and unorganized?

A REPLY TO FRIEDMAN

In a 1982 *Harvard Business Review* article, Professors Goodpaster and Matthews offered a reply to Milton Friedman within the context of a hypothetical situation:

James Weston is the president of Southern Steel Corporation (SSC) in a Southern state during the racially tense late-1960s. Under pressure from the federal government, SSC made great strides toward removing barriers to equal job opportunity in its several plants. Weston and other top corporate executives distinguished themselves in the community as individuals genuinely interested in promoting racial harmony. SSC, however, drew the line at using its substantial economic influence in the local area to advance the cause of civil rights by pressuring the more conservative institutions such as banks, suppliers, and the local government. Given this situation, Goodpaster and Matthews asked, What is the appropriate role of the corporation in advancing the cause of social justice in the community?

In addressing this issue, the authors recognized the same distinction that Friedman did. Thought and action by an individual are not the same things as thought and action by an agent for a corporation. When Weston confronts the issue directly, he advances the Friedman-like position as follows:

> As individuals we can exercise what influence we may have as citizens, . . . but for a corporation to attempt to exert any kind of economic compulsion to achieve a particular end in a social area seems to me to be quite beyond what a corporation should do and quite beyond what a corporation can do. I believe that while government may seek to compel social reforms, any attempt by a private organization like SSC to impose its views, its beliefs, and its will upon the community would be repugnant to our American constitutional concepts and that appropriate steps to correct this abuse of corporate power would be universally demanded by public opinion.[16]

Goodpaster and Matthews argued against this position, taking the social responsibility obligation one step farther than Friedman would. In doing so, they recognized explicitly the differences between individual and group thought and action. They advanced the argument that the only way one can know about group thought and action is to project moral concepts onto the group as if the group were an individual. This technique is called *moral projection*. To answer certain crucial questions (Does a corporation have a conscience? and What action, if any, should SSC take?), it is appropriate to project concepts of good and bad individual conduct onto corporations. "The principle of moral projection," the professors said, "not only helps us to conceptualize the kinds of demands that we might make of corporations and other organizations but also offers the prospect of harmonizing those demands with the demands that we make of ourselves." [17]

To arrive at a recommended course of action for SSC, Goodpaster and Matthews first had to answer critics of the technique of moral projection—critics, such as Friedman, who maintain that a corporation is not like a person, but rather is a mere organizational structure in which people should pursue profit legally and within the boundaries of ethical custom. The Goodpaster-Matthews position on moral projection is a valuable contribution to the corporate social responsibility debate: Are corporations to be thought of as individuals for purposes of the law and moral action, or are they to be thought of in some other way? The following article excerpt contains the authors' consideration of possible objections to analogizing corporations and persons and to the idea of moral projection.

KENNETH E. GOODPASTER
JOHN B. MATTHEWS, JR.

Can A Corporation Have A Conscience?

Objection 1 to the Analogy:

Corporations are not persons. They are artificial legal constructions, machines for mobilizing economic investments toward the efficient production of goods and services. We cannot hold a corporation responsible. We can only hold individuals responsible.

Reply:

Our frame of reference does not imply that corporations are persons in a literal sense. It simply means that in certain respects concepts and functions normally attributed to persons can also be attributed to organizations made up of persons. Goals, economic values, strategies, and other such personal attributes are often usefully projected to the corporate level by managers and researchers. Why should we not project the functions of conscience in the same way? As for holding corporations responsible, recent criminal prosecutions such as in the case of Ford Motor Company and its Pinto gas tanks suggest that society finds the idea both intelligible and useful.

Objection 2:

A corporations cannot be held responsible at the sacrifice of profit. Profitability and financial health have always been and should continue to be the "categorical imperatives" of a business operation.

Reply:

We must of course acknowledge the imperatives of survival, stability, and growth when we discuss corporations, as indeed we must acknowledge them when we discuss the life of an individual. Self-sacrifice has been identified with moral responsibility in only the most extreme cases. The pursuit of profit

and self-interest need not be pitted against the demands of moral responsibility. Moral demands are best viewed as containments—not replacements—for self interest.

This is not to say that profit maximization never conflicts with morality. But profit maximization contradicts with other managerial values as well. The point is to coordinate imperatives, not deny their validity.

Objection 3:

Corporate executives are not elected representatives of the people, nor are they anointed or appointed as social guardians. They therefore lack the social mandate that a democratic society rightly demands of those who would pursue ethically or socially motivated policies. By keeping corporate policies confined to economic motivations, we keep the power of corporate executives in its proper place.

Reply:

The objection betrays an oversimplified view of the relationship between the public and the private sector. Neither private individuals nor private corporations that guide their conduct by ethical or social values beyond the demands of law should be constrained merely because they are not elected to do so. The demands of moral responsibility are independent of the demands of political legitimacy and are in fact presupposed by them.

To be sure, the state and the political process will and must remain the primary mechanisms for protecting the public interest, but one might be forgiven the hope that the political process will not substitute for the moral judgment of the citizenry or other components of society such as corporations.

Objection 4:

Their system of law carefully defines the role of agent or fiduciary and makes corporate managers accountable to shareholders and investors for the use of their assets. Management cannot, in the name of corporate moral responsibility, arrogate to itself the right to manage these assets by partially noneconomic criteria.

Reply:

First, it is not so clear that investors insist on purely economic criteria in the management of their assets, especially if some of the shareholders' resolutions and board reforms of the last decade are any indication. For instance, companies doing business in South Africa have had stockholders question their activities, other companies have instituted audit committees for their boards before such auditing was mandated, and mutual funds for which "socially responsible behavior" is a major investment criterion now exist.

Second, the categories of "shareholder" and "investor" connote wider time span than do immediate or short-term returns. As a practical matter, considerations of stability and long-term return on investment enlarge the class of principals to which managers bear a fiduciary relationship.

Third, the trust that managers hold does not and never has extended to "any means available" to advance the interests of the principals. Both legal and moral constraints must be understood to qualify that trust—even, perhaps, in the name of a larger trust and a more basic fiduciary relationship to the members of society at large.

Objection 5:

The power, size, and scale of the modern corporation—domestic as well as international—are awesome. To unleash, even partially, such power from the discipline of the marketplace and the narrow or possibly nonexistent moral purpose implicit in that discipline would be socially dangerous. Had SSC acted in the community to further racial justice, its purposes might have been admirable, but those purposes could have led to a kind of moral imperialism or worse. Suppose SSC had thrown its power behind the Ku Klux Klan.

Reply:

This is a very real and important objection. What seems not to be appreciated is the fact that power affects when it is used as well as when it is not used. A decision by SSC not to exercise its economic influence according to "non-economic" criteria is inevitably a moral decision and just as inevitably affects the community. The issue in the end is not whether corporations (and other organizations) should be "unleashed" to exert moral force in our society but rather how critically and self-consciously they should choose to do so.

The degree of influence enjoyed by an agent, whether a person or an organization, is not so much a factor recommending moral disengagement as a factor demanding a high level of moral awareness. Imperialism is more to be feared when moral reasoning is absent than when it is present. Nor do we suggest that the "discipline of the marketplace" be diluted; rather, we call for it to be supplemented with the discipline of moral reflection.

Objection 6:

The idea of moral projection is a useful device for structuring corporate responsibility only if our understanding of moral responsibility at the level of the person is in some sense richer than our understanding of moral responsibility on the level of the organization as a whole. If we are not clear about individual responsibility, the projection is fruitless.

Reply:

The objection is well taken. The challenge offered by the idea of moral projection lies in our capacity to articulate criteria of frameworks of reasoning for the morally responsible person. And though such a challenge is formidable, it is not clear that it cannot be met, at least with sufficient consensus to be useful.

For centuries, the study and criticism of frameworks have gone on, carried forward by many disciplines, including psychology, the social sciences, and philosophy. And though it would be a mistake to suggest that any single framework (much less a decision mechanism) has emerged as the right one, it is true that recurrent patterns are discernible and well enough defined to structure moral discussion.

[Earlier in this article, we spoke of] rationality and respect as components of individual responsibility. Further analysis of these components would translate them into social costs and benefits, justice in the distribution of goods and services, basic rights and duties, and fidelity of contracts. The view that pluralism in our society has undercut all possibility of moral agreement is anything but self-evident. Sincere moral disagreement is, of course, inevitable and not clearly lamentable. But a process and a vocabulary of articulating such values as we share is no small step forward when compared with the alternatives. Perhaps in our exploration of the moral projection we might make some surprising and even reassuring discoveries about ourselves.

Objection 7:

Why is it necessary to project moral responsibility to the level of the organization? Isn't the task of defining corporate responsibility and business ethics sufficiently discharged if we clarify the responsibilities of men and women in business as individuals? Doesn't ethics finally rest on the honesty and integrity of the individual in the business world?

Reply:

Yes and no. Yes, in the sense that the control of large organizations does finally rest in the hands of managers, of men and women. No, in the sense that what is being controlled is a cooperative system for cooperative purpose. The projection of responsibility to the organization is simply an acknowledgment of the facts that the whole is more than the sum of its parts. Many intelligent people do not an intelligent organization make. Intelligence needs to be structured, organized, divided, and recombined in complex processes for complex purposes.

Studies of management have long shown that the attributes, successes, and failures of organizations are phenomena that emerge from the coordination of persons' attributes and that explanations of such phenomena require categories of analysis and description beyond the level of the individual. Moral responsibility is an attribute that can manifest itself in organizations as surely as competence or efficiency.

Objection 8:

Is the frame of reference here proposed intended to replace or undercut the relevance of the "invisible hand" and the "governed hand" views, which depend on external controls?

Reply:

No. Just as regulation and economic competition are not substitutes for corporate responsibility, so corporate responsibility is not a substitute for law and the market. The imperatives of ethics cannot be relied on—nor have they ever been relied on—without a context of external sanctions. And this is true as much for individuals as for organizations.

This frame of reference takes us beneath, but not beyond, the realm of external systems of rules and incentives and into the thought processes that interpret and respond to the corporation's environment. Morality is more than merely part of that environment. It aims at the projection of conscience, not the enthronement of it in either the state or the competitive process.

The rise of the modern large corporation and the concomitant rise of the professional manager demand a conceptual framework in which these phenomena can be accommodated to moral thought. The principle of moral projection furthers such accommodations by recognizing a new level of agency in society and thus a new level or responsibility.

Objection 9:

Corporations have always taken the interests of those outside the corporation into account in the sense that customer relations and public relations generally are an integral part of rational economic decision making. Market signals and social signals that filter through the market mechanism inevitably represent the interests of parties affected by the behavior of the company. What then, is the point of adding respect to rationality?

Reply:

Representing the affected parties solely as economic variables in the environment of the company is treating them as means or resources and not as ends in themselves. It implies that the only voice which affected parties should have in organizational decision making is that of potential buyers, sellers, regulators, or boycotters. Besides, many affected parties may not occupy such roles, and those who do may not be able to signal the organization with messages that effectively represent their stakes in its actions.

To be sure, classical economic theory would have us believe that perfect competition in free markets (with modest adjustments from the state) will result in all relevant signals being "heard," but the abstractions from reality implicit in such theory make it insufficient as a frame of reference for moral responsibility. In a world in which strict self-interest was congruent with the common good, moral responsibility might be unnecessary. We do not, alas, live in such a world.

The element of respect in our analysis of responsibility plays an essential role in ensuring the recognition of unrepresented or under represented voices in the decision making of organizations as agents. Showing respect for persons as ends and not mere means to organizational purposes is central to the concept of corporate moral responsibility.[18]

ARTICLE FOLLOW-UP

Goodpaster and Matthews believe that projecting onto corporations qualities of rationality and respect, derived from a model of human behavior, is a key to guiding corporate social responsibility. Is that model really sufficient in view of the fact that groups and collectives act in ways that individuals would never act alone?

Perhaps what lacks in the corporate social responsibility debate is a workable definition of corporate power. Economists measure power in a rather narrow way by such conventional signs as the percentage of sales in a relevant market. Goodpaster and Matthews believe that even the existence of corporate economic power has moral implications. "What seems not to be appreciated is the fact that power affects when it is used as well as when it is not used. A decision by SSC not to exercise its economic influence according to 'non-economic' criteria is inevitably a moral decision and just as inevitably affects the community." Do you believe the authors are correct when they imply that the presence of power creates moral obligations to act because not to act is also a form of moral commitment?

Goodpaster and Matthews were careful not to offer a detailed plan of action for SSC. They did, however, carry the social responsibility obligation farther than Friedman would. The Friedman position here would be that SSC should obey the law and, in addition, make steel of high quality at the least cost, maximize profits, and return those profits in the form of dividends to shareholders. Goodpaster and Matthews argued that, in addition, SSC has an obligation to act as a morally responsible individual would act: The firm should integrate into its decision-making process the two primary qualities of rationality and respect.

Acting rationally means acting with a lack of impulsiveness and with "care in mapping out alternatives and consequences, clarity about goals and purposes, (and) attention to details of implementation."[19] Respect means a "special awareness of and concern for the effects of one's decisions and policies on others, special in the sense that it goes beyond the kind of awareness and concern that would ordinarily be part of rationality, that is, beyond seeing others merely as instrumental to accomplishing one's own purposes."[20]

These authors suggested that the social obligation of SSC would be discharged if it acted rationally and with respect toward those seeking to gain and fully enjoy their civil rights. Thus, the management of SSC had the moral duty to discuss the possibility of taking action to pressure institutions around them to end employment discrimination. A deliberate and thoughtful evaluation of the alternatives is the core of responsible corporate policy, and SSC can fulfill its moral obligation even if it were to pursue a course of action different from the one you would choose. Honest, good-faith differences of opinion must be tolerated. After all, no one has *all* the right answers. Goodpaster and Matthews, then, would not require SSC to go beyond a thorough discussion of the matter and a full implementation of its decision, whatever that might be.

CHRISTOPHER STONE AND CORPORATE SOCIAL RESPONSIBILITY

Christopher Stone is a law professor at the University of Southern California and has written widely on the subject of corporate social responsibility. Even before Goodpaster and Matthews did so, Stone published widely on the idea of moral projection because he recognized the shortcomings of relying on the law to achieve all desirable social objectives.

Stone argues, first, that the inadequacies of the law in controlling certain aspects of human behavior are well recognized and that this is especially true when one attempts to apply law to corporations. But, he says, responsibility certainly involves more than following the law. It also involves a thoughtful, deliberate process. So far, this position does not go beyond the Goodpaster-Matthews position. He adds, however, that closely related to this process is giving adequate justification for what one is doing. Thus, in the example involving SSC, Stone would argue that the management has an obligation to explain the reason for its action.

CHRISTOPHER D. STONE

What "Corporate Responsibility" Might Really Mean

. . . [D]espite all the talk about corporations "being responsible," no one has ever made an attempt to carry the idea through seriously. If people are going to adopt the terminology of "responsibility" (with its allied concepts of corporate conscience) to suggest new, improved ways of dealing with corporations, then they ought to go back and examine in detail what "being responsible" entails—in the ordinary case of the responsible human being. Only after we have considered what being responsible calls for in general does it make sense to develop the notion of a corporation being responsible.

To begin with, for want of any real model of responsibility, the proponents of corporate responsibility all too often seem to identify it with corporate giving to charity—a sort of questionable cop-out, both theoretically and practically. But responsibility should not be confused with altruism. In the case of human beings it is to meet far more complex and subtle needs that responsibility is developed and nurtured.

We know that it is futile to hope that all socially undesirable behavior can be anticipated by legal rule-makers. We know that attempts to enforce all [socially desired things] by law would be more costly than it would be worth. We fear, too, that such attempts would unsatisfactorily enlarge the role of government while severely diminishing personal freedom. There are thus certain virtues, both to the individuals and to the society at large, of encouraging people to act in socially appropriate ways because they believe it the "right thing" to do, rather than because (and

thus, perhaps fully to the extent that) they are ordered to do so. Trusting to responsible behavior through some measure of self-control is often a preferable solution to some of the most difficult and perhaps otherwise unsolvable problems of social organization.

Why these observations are important is that when we look back now on the unsatisfactoriness of present measures for controlling corporations, we can identify the very sorts of problems that have led to the nurturing of responsibility in human beings.

- Many social-control mechanisms (short of law) are increasingly ineffective when brought to bear on corporations.
- In an increasingly complex society, there may be such widespread, legitimate failure of consensus as to what values ought to be pursued, that laws—with their mandatory, across-the-board solutions—may be neither feasible nor desirable in major problem areas.
- Even when societal values can be agreed upon, they often can be agreed upon only in the most general way, not adequately for translation into effective rules.
- Even to the extent legal control over corporations can be made effective, "federalist"-type values might lend us pause as to how far the government should assume control over their decisions.

★ ★ ★

- Some traditional legal sanctions developed to control human behavior are inapplicable where the corporation is the actor (imprisonment, the death penalty) or may be practically unavailable for other reasons (lack of effective jurisdiction over some operations of multinational corporations).

- Even where legal sanctions are theoretically available, both our counterorganizational strategies and the measures aimed at key personnel are less than perfect in bringing about the needed institutional responses.
- Corporations are so often moving ahead of the society that at no time will present legal rules (and even, perhaps, present moral rules) be adequate to provide them with satisfactory standards.

Thus, the functions for which we need responsibility in human beings have distinct counterparts in the realm of corporate behavior. But what does it mean to be responsible? What does being responsible involve?

Once we start to examine what responsibility consists of in an ordinary person, we can see more clearly why there is something so unsatisfactory about current discussions of corporate responsibility. . . .

The problem is that judgments of responsibility can be ascribed according to two schemes that are superficially distinct, if not in outright opposition. The first sense of responsibility, Responsibility 1, emphasizes following the law—abiding by the rules of one's social office: carrying out the authoritatively prescribed functions of a prosecutor, judge, soldier, or citizen. The second sense, Responsibility 2, emphasizes cognitive process, and, in a way almost diametrically opposed to Responsibility 1, puts a premium on autonomy, rather than rule obedience. Specifically, responsibility in the second sense emphasizes that a person's deliberations include the following elements:

- Viewed in its cognitive aspects, responsibility involves a degree of *repression*. The responsible person does not immediately implement his initial desires or impulses, his "gut reaction." It is in this sense that

one who, for example, simply vents his rage, is not being "responsible." Thus, reflection is always an ingredient of responsibility in this sense.

- Responsible behavior begins with perception. The responsible person observes phenomena the irresponsible person ignores; more than this, his perceptions are stamped with moral categories. The responsible person looks for certain morally significant features of his environment: other persons (and other creatures), harm, pain, benefit to the social group.
- A responsible person takes measure of the full range of his freedom. It is in this sense that a man is not responsible if he adopts the posture that his decision is predetermined by forces in his environment, institutional or physical. He acts with an awareness that he will be accountable for what happens.
- To be responsible in this sense emphasizes a person's taking into account the consequences and repercussions of his actions. Thus, a person who drops a lighted match in a forest would be deemed irresponsible not because he wanted to cause injury to others (in which case we would be more inclined to say that he was venal or malicious) but because he did not think of the repercussions of his actions.
- He must consider and weigh alternatives.
- Being responsible involves reflection in all the above senses, but reflection per se is not enough; the reflection must be structured by reference to the society's moral vocabulary—that is, by characterization in terms of "good," "bad," "just," and so forth, by thinking of "obligations," "rights," and "duties."
- One must have, in addition to a moral vocabulary, a moral inclination—a desire, probably as much internalized as conscious, to "do the right thing."

- Closely related is the fact that one must be prepared to give some justification for what he is doing. Overlooking for a moment the variation among traditional ethical theories, by and large they hold in common the view that to be responsible involves being prepared to explain, to give good reasons for one's actions; the responsible actor is willing to generalize the grounds for what he has done. This preparedness to justify, and especially the preparedness to do so in terms that admit of generalization (the Golden Rule, Kant's Categorical Imperative), is an important step toward the socialization of one's actions, inasmuch as it forces awareness of the social setting and the socially sanctified grounds of behavior.

* * *

Which of these two notions of responsibility—that which emphasizes following rules or that which emphasizes cognitive process, with some allowance for autonomy—would we ideally want to implant into corporations? The answer is both. For where it *is* feasible to design relatively unambiguous rules for corporate behavior—not to include nonskeletal meats in frankfurters—all we want is the responsibility of the rule-following, role-adhering sort. But as I have stressed throughout, there is also a large range of cases where rigid rules are increasingly ineffective, and perhaps even counterproductive, as instruments of corporate control. To meet the problems in those areas the responsibility that is needed—whether we are talking about corporations or persons—is a responsibility of the "mature" sort, emphasizing cognitive processes, rather than blind rule obedience.[21]

ARTICLE FOLLOW-UP

The excerpt was taken from Stone's book *Where the Law Ends: The Social Control of Corporate Behavior*. A reader or a critic will search its chapters in vain for the suggestion that corporate wealth should be squandered on trendy, purely public relations projects. To the contrary, responsible behavior is principally identified with good management, and good management involves integration of the long-term well-being of the firm with near-term quarterly profits. It involves the consideration of multiple corporate goals—such as stability, increased market share, innovation, and prestige—and not short-term profit alone.

Further, Stone identified "the corporation" with a wider spectrum of interests—shareholders, employees, consumers, the general public—than that of the managerial group that, for the time being, is vested with control. Not content merely to critique the antiresponsibility contingent, he developed ways and means of institutionalizing corporate responsibility—building it into the basic structure of the firm through laws affecting corporate structure.

To give one example only, Stone would have a certain number of publicly appointed members on corporate boards of major U.S. firms. The objective would be to offset insider control (control by corporate officers.) He sees the popular practice of bringing in "friendly outside directors" (representatives of law firms, banks, brokerage houses, suppliers, and others who have a vested interest in keeping the current officers in office) as not entirely in the best interests of the firm. Although the practice of using insiders and "friendlies" need not be forbidden, its "blind spots" could be overcome by a redefinition of what it means to be a director and by a public-director strategy that supports its appointees with a budget and a staff. This and other reforms suggested by Stone would ideally culminate in a new corporate culture that embodies the kinds of incentives needed to evoke the very best in managerial leadership. You might want to pursue a more detailed account of Stone's proposals in his book, but as you can tell from this brief illustration, his reforms move qualitatively away from simple rule following toward more mature and reflective measures designed to evoke the full potential of managers and of the institutions they control.

We understand the essence of Stone's position to be that if society wants corporations to be "responsible," society should build into corporations, through the law, structures that encourage reflection at the board and high-management levels. This reflection should be cast in moral terms, and ideally it would encourage a desire or moral inclination to do the right thing.

A critic would argue that here is where the Friedman argument has force. What gives large corporations the legitimacy to determine what the "right thing" is? In short, can there be agreement on the circumstances in which corporations should act when the action is not required by a legitimate political force—namely, the law? After all, lawmakers are accountable to the public, but corporate officers and directors are not.

WHEN CORPORATIONS SHOULD ACT: THE KEW GARDENS PRINCIPLE

Going to the Rescue. The rescue principle involves an extension of a business firm's responsibility into the life of the community. Beneficence, or the obligation individuals have to make life better for the people around them, is an important part of the "ethical custom." It is the kind of obligation that everyone experiences personally and one that prompts morally sensitive managers to commit corporate resources to community quality-of-life-projects that are not necessarily expected to produce any revenues for the firm.

The rescue principle, or the principle of beneficence, is binding on individuals even though they have not caused the problem they are trying to resolve. This obligation differentiates it from situations in which a direct causal link exists between, for example, Company X's false and deceptive advertising and the harm the advertising causes to consumers of X's product. The rescue principle involves corporations in social projects that are normally the function of the legislature or of private charitable institutions.

This obligation does not involve wasting corporate wealth on hopeless and poorly conceived projects, however. It involves the expenditure of corporate time, effort, money, and talent on programs that yield benefits that cannot be fully recovered by the firm. In one sense of the word, this is an exercise in corporate stewardship or corporate citizenship.

These ideas might bring to mind corporate sponsorship of programs supporting education, the arts and sciences, or other community and social endeavors.

This sponsorship does not amount to a mass giveaway, but rather to corporate support when rational people agree that (1) the need is sufficient, (2) the firm has the capacity to undertake such a task, (3) the need is at hand, proximate, or within the firm's sphere of influence, and (4) no one else is doing a job that needs to be done.

This principle is pursued in further detail in the following excerpt from *The Ethical Investor* by Simon, Powers, and Gunnemann.

J. G. SIMON
C. W. POWERS
J. P. GUNNEMANN

The Responsibilities of Corporations and Their Owners

For better or worse, the modern American business corporation is increasingly being asked to assume more responsibility for social problems and the public welfare. How corporate responsibility is understood, and whether it is perceived to be for better or worse, may depend in the last analysis on the beholder's emotional reaction to the corporation itself: one either extols the corporation as part of the creative process or condemns it as the work of the Devil. Thus, almost four centuries ago the English jurist Sir Edward Coke wrote of corporations that "they cannot commit treason nor be outlawed nor excommunicated for they have no souls," while more recently Justice Louis D. Brandeis characterized the corporation as the "master instrument of civilized life." . . .

Our analysis of the controversies surrounding the notion of corporate responsibility—and the suggestion that the university as an investor should be concerned with corporate responsibility—proceeds in large part from our approach to certain issues in the area of social responsibility and public morals. In particular, we (1) make a distinc-

tion between negative injunctions and affirmative duties; (2) assert that all men have the "moral minimum" obligation not to impose social injury; (3) delineate those conditions under which one is held responsible for social injury, even where it is not clear that the injury was self-caused; and (4) take a position in the argument between those who strive for moral purity and those who strive for moral effectiveness.

Negative Injunctions an Affirmative Duties
A distinction which informs much of our discussion differentiates between injunctions against activities that injure others and duties which require the affirmative pursuit of some good. The failure to make this distinction in debate on public ethics often results in false dichotomies. . . .

Our public discourse abounds with similar failures to distinguish between positive and perhaps lofty ideals and minimal requirements of social organization. During the election campaigns of the 1950's and the civil rights movement of the early 1960's, the slogan, "You can't legislate morality," was a popular cry on many fronts. Obviously, we have not succeeded in devising laws that create within our citizens a predisposition to love and kindness; but we can devise laws which will minimize the injury that one citizen must suffer at the hands of another. Although the virtue of love may be the possession of a few, justice—in the minimal sense of not injuring others—can be required of all.

The distinction between negative injunctions and affirmative duties is old, having roots in common law and equity jurisprudence. Here it is based on the premise that it is easier to specify and enjoin a civil wrong than to state what should be done. In the Ten Commandments, affirmative duties are spelled out only for one's relations with God and parents; for the more public relationships, we are given only the negative injunction "Thou shalt not . . ." Similarly, the Bill of Rights contains only negative injunctions.

Avoidance and Correction of Social Injury as a "Moral Minimum"

We do not mean to distinguish between negative injunctions and affirmative duties solely in the interests of analytical precision. The negative injunction to avoid and correct social injury threads its way through all morality. We call it a "moral minimum," implying that however one may choose to limit the concept of social responsibility, one cannot exclude this negative injunction. Although reasons may exist why certain persons or institutions cannot or should not be required to pursue moral or social good in all situations, there are many fewer reasons why one should be excused from the injunction against injuring others. . . .

In emphasizing the central role of the negative injunction, we do not suggest that affirmative duties are never important. A society where citizens go well beyond the requirement to avoid damage to others will surely be a better community. But we do recognize that individuals exhibit varying degrees of commitment to promote affirmatively the public welfare, whereas we expect everyone equally to refrain from injuring others.

* * *

. . . We know of no societies, from the literature of anthropology or comparative ethics, whose moral codes do not contain some injunction against harming others. The specific notion of *harm* or *social injury* may vary, as well as the mode of correction and restitution, but the injunctions are present.

* * *

In sum, we would affirm the . . . obligation of all citizens, both individual and institutional, to avoid and correct self-caused social injury. Much more in the way that affirmative acts may be expected of certain kinds of citizens, but none is exempt from this "moral minimum."

In some cases it may not be true—or at least it may not be clear—that one has caused or helped to cause social injury, and yet one may bear responsibility for correcting or averting the injury. We consider next the circumstances under which this responsibility may arise.

Need, Proximity, Capability, and the Last Resort (The Kew Gardens Principle)

Several years ago the public was shocked by the news accounts of the stabbing and agonizingly slow death of Kitty Genovese in the Kew Gardens section of New York City while thirty-eight people watched or heard and did nothing. What so deeply disturbed the public's moral sensibility was that in the face of a critical human need, people who were close to that need and had the power to do something about it failed to act.

The public's reaction suggests that, no matter how narrowly one may conceive of social responsibility, there are some situations in which a combination of circumstances thrusts upon us an obligation to respond. Life is fraught with emergency situations in which a failure to respond is a special form of violation of the negative injunction against causing social injury: a sin of omission becomes a sin of commission.

Legal responsibility for aiding someone in cases of grave distress or injury, even when caused by another, is recognized by many European civil codes and by the criminal laws of one of our states:

(A) A person who knows that another is exposed to grave physical harm shall, to the extent that the same can be rendered without danger or peril to himself or without interference with important duties owed to others, give reasonable assistance to the exposed person unless that assistance or care is being provided by others. . . .

(C) A person who wilfully violates subsection (A) of this section shall be fined not more than $100.00.

This Vermont statute recognizes that it is not reasonable in all cases to require a person to give assistance to someone who is endangered. If such aid imperils himself, or interferes with duties owed to others, or if there are others providing the aid, the person is excepted from the obligation. These conditions of responsibility give some shape to difficult cases and are in striking parallel with the conditions which existed at Kew Gardens. The salient features of the Kitty Genovese case are (1) critical need; (2) the proximity of the thirty-eight spectators; (3) the capability of the spectators to act helpfully (at least to telephone the police); and (4) the absence of other (including official) help; i.e., the thirty-eight were the last resort. There

would, we believe, be widespread agreement that a moral obligation to aid another arises when these four features are present. What we have called the "moral minimum" (the duty to avoid and correct self-caused social injury) is an obvious and easy example of fulfillment of these criteria—so obvious that there is little need to go through step-by-step analysis of these factors. Where the injury is not clearly self-caused, the application of these criteria aids in deciding responsibility. We have called this combination of features governing difficult cases the "Kew Gardens Principle." There follows a more detailed examination of each of the features:

Need. In cases where the other three criteria are constant, increased need increases responsibility. Just as there is no precise definition of social injury (one kind of need), there is no precise definition of need or way of measuring its extent.

Proximity. The thirty-eight witnesses of the Genovese slaying were geographically close to the deed. But proximity to a situation of need is not necessarily spatial. Proximity is largely a function of notice: we hold a person blameworthy if he knows of imperilment and does not do what he reasonably can do to remedy the situation. Thus, the thirty-eight at Kew Gardens were delinquent not because they were near but because nearness enabled them to know that someone was in need. A deaf person who could not hear the cries for help would not be considered blameworthy even if he were closer than those who could hear. So also, a man in Afghanistan is uniquely responsible for the serious illness of a man in Peoria, Illinois, if he has knowledge of the man's illness, if he can telephone a doctor about it, and if he alone has that notice. When we become aware of a wrongdoing or social injury, we take on obligations that we did not have while ignorant.

Notice does not exhaust the meaning of proximity, however. It is reasonable to maintain that the sick man's neighbors in Peoria were to some extent blameworthy if they made no effort to inquire into the man's welfare. Ignorance cannot always be helped, but we do expect certain persons and perhaps institutions to look harder for information about critical need. In this sense, proximity has to do with the network of social expectations that flow from notions of civic duty, duties to one's family, and so on. Thus, we expect a man to be more alert to the plight of his next-door neighbor than to the needs of a child in East Pakistan, just as we expect a man to be more alert to the situation of his own children than to the problems of the family down the block . . . .

Capability. Even if there is a need to which a person has proximity, that person is not usually held responsible unless there is something he can reasonably be expected to do to meet the need. . . . What one is reasonably capable of doing, of course, admits to some variety of interpretation. In the Kew Gardens incident, it might not have been reasonable to expect someone to place his body between the girl and the knife. It was surely reasonable to expect someone to call the police. So also it would not seem to be within the canons of reasonability for a university to sacrifice education for charity. . . . But if the university is able, by non-self-sacrificial means, to mitigate injury caused by a company of which it is an owner, it would not seem unreasonable to ask it to do so.

Last Resort. In the emergency situation we have been describing, one becomes more responsible the less likely it is that someone else will be able to aid. Physical proximity is a factor here, as is time. If the knife is drawn, one cannot wait for the policeman. It is important to note here that determination of last resort becomes more difficult the more complex the social situation or organization. The man on the road to Jericho, in spite of the presence of a few other travelers, probably had a fairly good notion that he was the only person who could help the man attacked by thieves. But on a street in New York City, there is always the hope that someone else will step forward to give aid. Surely this rationalization entered into the silence of each of the thirty-eight: there were, after all, thirty-seven others. Similarly, within large corporations it is difficult to know not only whether one alone has notice of a wrongdoing, but also whether there is anyone else who is able to respond. Because of this diffusion of responsibility in complex organizations and societies, the notion of last resort is less useful than the other Kew Gardens criteria in determining whether one ought to act in aid of someone in need or to avert or correct social injury. Failure to act because one hopes someone else will act—or because one is trying to find out who is the last resort—may frequently lead to a situation in which no one acts at all. This fact, we think, places more weight on the first three features of the Kew Gardens Principle in determining responsibility, and it creates a presumption in favor of taking action when those three conditions are present.[22]

ARTICLE FOLLOW-UP

There is a world of difference between articulating a principle and applying it. These authors forcefully address Friedman's objection to analytical looseness and lack of rigor and also propose a framework in which most people would agree action is desirable. They do not have the complete answer, however. For example, if we apply their Kew Gardens principle to the Southern Steel Corporation situation, is action required?

Again, several answers seem apparent depending on the facts. The heart of the suggestion made in the article above is that everyone is subject to a moral minimum duty to act to avoid injury and to correct self-caused injury. Did SSC cause the racial discrimination in its local environment? Or was racial discrimination simply an ugly fact of life that existed in the community long before SSC started its operations? Most businesspeople would argue that the social problems they confronted are "given" as part of the environment, rather than "caused" by their specific operations. This reply, then, takes us to the operation of the Kew Gardens principle: There is a moral obligation to act when there is a critical need, proximity of the actor to the need, the capability of the actor to be of help, and, of less importance according to the authors, the absence of other help. Unfortunately, we lack the information to apply this principle to SSC. Like most other important principles, application of Kew Gardens depends heavily on the facts. If, for example, SSC existed in an environment in which social discrimination had been particularly devastating, and if SSC were the only employer in a fairly large region of the South, and if its management believed it could indeed do something to counter the evils of discrimination, and if no other institutions were available to help with this problem, then one could argue that SSC had a moral obligation to act.

The Kew Gardens principle, like any other idea intended to inspire action, cannot be fully assessed as an instrument of corporate policy until someone decides to act. One of the most important ideas in U.S. law, the idea of due process, has evolved over the past 200 years because both government and private parties have contested its application and called on courts to breathe meaning into the principle. The same may be true of the Kew Gardens idea. Perhaps in the near future it will find its way into a litigated case and thereafter become a part of the common law or even find its way into statutory language. This latter possibility, however, seems unlikely because Americans have a tradition of not compelling action by statute.

ORGANIZATIONS AND THE LAW: THE PROBLEMS OF CIVIL AND CRIMINAL SANCTIONS

Reflecting on the collection of essays in this chapter, we believe that the writers have shared a number of important insights of value to business students. Milton Friedman acknowledges that businesspeople ought to operate within the parameters of the law and ethical custom while in the pursuit of profit. He does not specifically spell out what he means by "ethical custom," but at least it includes a prohibition against "deception and fraud." Much can be said in favor of Friedman's view, but we can support it only with the following modifications. Our position begins with the observation that all shareholders of the corporation are individuals with moral rights and responsibilities just like everyone else. If the moral responsibilities the shareholders have as individuals require, permit, or prohibit certain conduct, they cannot escape those responsibilities simply by purchasing stock in a corporation and authorizing a corporate agent or officer to act, or to refrain from acting, in a way that departs from those moral responsibilities. We subscribe to the view that ethical custom must also include a prohibition of harmful behaviors that are equal to or worse than deception and fraud. Our view is evidently shared by Simon, Powers, and Gunnemann in "The Responsibilities of Corporation and Their Owners," and we join them in the position that (under the conditions described in the Kew Gardens Principle) a corporation is morally obligated to go beyond the prohibition against doing harm and in some cases "go to the rescue."

Goodpaster and Matthews articulate a process—a moral point of view—consisting of rationality and respect for other people. We find linkages between that process and the concept of corporate culture that surfaced in "The Parable of the Sadhu," by Bowen McCoy: shared values and an agreed-on process for dealing with adversity, ambiguity, and change. Institutionalizing such a process is central to our view of corporate moral responsibility. The Goodpaster-Matthews theory of moral projection, extending Stone's groundbreaking work, "What 'Corporate Responsibility' Might Really Mean," onto a corporate "person," is intriguing, though we have real reservations whether a corporation should be spoken of as a person with moral rights and duties. We have no reservations, however, about Simon, Powers, and Gunnemann's thesis that, under certain circumstances, corporations are morally obligated to go to the rescue. Specifically, we mean that, under some circumstances, the obligation of beneficence attaches to the corporate body and that it is obliged to "do good" and to promote the community welfare even on occasions when that conduct will not necessarily be reflected in the corporation's bottom line.

Now we return to the way corporations actually operate in the marketplace and, given that make of operation, how it can best be understood and channeled toward the good. Because large corporations do not really act like natural persons and do not respond in the same way natural persons do to reward and punishment, how is one to deal with them in a legal regime? Increased criminal fines and civil damages levied on the corporate entity and longer prison sentences for corporate officers have, for the most part, marked the extent of penal creativity. But the more we learn about organizational behavior, the less fitting these approaches seem to be. Successful legal actions against the corporate entity can stigmatize innocent employees, and monetary penalties imposed on the firm are frequently passed along to the consuming public. Prosecution of individual officers is an alternative, but the nature of collective behavior makes it difficult to identify who is singularly responsible for the group effort.

The problems we encounter in applying legal and other sanctions to business corporations have to be tackled one step at a time. The first step is to go behind the scenes and try to understand what makes corporations and corporate people tick. Only then does it make sense to recommend ways of bringing corporate conduct into line with legal and ethical behavior. Our closing section, then, surveys widely held views of how corporations actually work and then focuses on the kind of individual character and corporate culture that fosters corporate performance—legal, ethical, economic performance—of the highest order.

BILL SHAW
FRANCES A. ZOLLERS

Models of Corporate Behavior

The literature of corporate organization and behavior proposes certain basic decision-making models. These models have been described as "conceptual lenses" through which past decisions may be analyzed and, more importantly, future decisions may be predicted. Furthermore, each model captures different "critical components" within its framework, and each of these components has an effect on the outcome of the decision making process. We present the models here in their simplest form, but acknowledge that in reality an organization may exhibit attributes of different models at various times in its history or in diverse circumstances.

The *rational actor model* is the most widely known of the models of corporate behavior. [N]eoclassical economics reifies the rational actor and the entire theory hinges on the predictable choices that he or she will make. Under this model, the behavior of decision makers is thought to be the result of a rational analysis which leads to the "value maximizing" choice.

It assumes that the actions taken are specifically chosen by a profit-maximizing actor in an effort to reach certain goals and objectives. The model presupposed that the actor makes these choices after considering the consequences of alternative courses of action and with the benefit of complete information. Thus, the rational actor model renders managerial decision-making "impersonal

and primarily economic." This process might also be described as self-interest, opportunistic, and egoistic.

Many writers have discussed the problems associated with this model. Among other things, the rational actor model does not recognize that decisions are often made by collectivities rather than individuals. Therefore, it ignores the organizational phenomena that affect corporate decisions. Herbert Simon observed that it "does not even remotely describe the processes that human beings use for making decisions in complex situations." Cyert and March argue that the model "has few of the characteristics we have come to identify with actual business firms . . . [it] has no complex organization, no problems of control, no standard operating procedure, no budget, no controller, and no aspiring middle management." In other words, the individual presupposed in the model does not translate well to the realities of an organizational setting.

The second model examined here is the *organizational process model*. This model assumes that behavior is not so much the deliberation of profit maximizing individuals as it is the "output" of large organizations that act according to a strict set of standard operating procedures (SOP's). It considers an organization to be made up of "loosely allied decision making units, each with a primary responsibility for a narrow range of problems." Decision making is routinized through the use of standard operating procedures that increase efficiency and standardization and decrease flexibility and individual choice. Here, "decisions are not made as much as they evolve from the policies, procedures, and rules which constitute the organization and its memory." For example, an engineering procedure would likely require that all design decisions be subject to a standardized cost-benefit analysis and achieve a certain "score" before being implemented.

According to this model, the way decisions are handled depends to a large extent on how well SOP's "fit" the problem. If SOP's are outdated or inefficient, results may be poor. Furthermore, organizations are slow to change their SOP's and, therefore, are likely to continue the same routines even after they cease being functional. In the example above, if the cost-benefit procedure was designed for a project that did not involve the cost of human suffering caused by an engineering defect, it would be unsurprising to have it applied to a project that did.

In sum, the organizational process model produces outcomes that are no less self-interested than those imagined by neoclassicists, but it relinquishes the pretense of an idealized "rational actor." Rational actors presumably fashion the SOP's and, depending on the circumstances, "shift gears" between SOP-1 and SOP-2. . . .

Third, the *bureaucratic politics model* assumes that events are the result of "bargaining games" among various political actors, each of which has his own power base agenda. Thus, this model focuses on the conflict which is inherent in organizations. Corporate action is not the choice of a rational actor, but rather the result of "games" played among actors, given their power and personality. Decision making that conforms to this model is likely to be a compromise if none of the players have the power necessary to determine the outcome.

It is probably fair to say that no other model typifies the full range of egoistic behavior as well as this one. Michael Maccoby's "jungle fighter" (a managerial type characterized by careerism and a willingness to exercise power ruthlessly) comes immediately to mind. . . .

This analysis of corporate structure brings your attention to focus on two widely held, but fallacious, assumptions about corporate behavior. The first is that men and women can always be depended on to make rational choices. This is designated the "rational person" model. Rational choices are defined as those that evaluate the alternatives and select the one that maximizes the self-interested preferences. It is a central tenant [*sic*] of this position that "all preferences are created equal" and, whatever those preferences may be, the only rational thing to do is to maximize them. The second fallacious assumption is that business corporations (for that matter, all bureaucratic organizations, large or small) act the same way that rational people do.

Supporters of the first proposition can only defend it by making themselves look ridiculous. Supporters of the second are discredited by a careful analysis of the way in which organizations actually behave. Your text, above, "Models of Corporate Behavior" from the *Business Ethics Quarterly* is ample evidence that the second assumption is unsupportable.

Defenders of the position that rational people always maximize self-interested preferences have to explain, and take full responsibility for, the following example. Suppose my preference is to get rich quickly and the easiest route to riches is to steal your car. Not only would that be defined as a rational decision, but, according to the above proposition, it would be on a moral par with that of Mother Teresa's decision to lead a life of caring and healing among the poorest people in her native land. Supporters of this view of rationality have "warped" it to such an extent that every choice, no matter what chosen, is rational just because it is chosen.

What about the assumption that all preferences are of equal moral worth and value? From the perspective of the rational actor model, preferences have to be on a moral par because every person is assumed to be a free and autonomous moral agent. Since everyone is free, and different from everyone else, you have to respect the choices of other people and they have to respect yours.

Does that mean that I can't be put in jail for stealing your car? No, it doesn't mean that because the law—the composite will of the majority or the sovereign—does not consider every choice to be of equal value. The law sets priorities, it makes judgments, and it may punish certain behavior even if it is rational by the above definition. Thieves beware! Your choices are still rational, but you had better count the cost of implementing them.

Mother Teresa's decision to live her life doing good works is at least legal. But, according to the rational actor model, it is neither different in quality, nor higher in value, than the choice of self-enrichment (the thief's decision to steal your car). Both choices are self-interested. Mother Teresa "feels good" about her choice, or she "feels better" about her choice than she would have felt about any other choice. So does the thief. Otherwise both of them would have made different choices. In fact, every choice that has ever been made since the beginning of time, and every choice that ever will be made until the end of time is self-interested. There is no example that escapes this description.

But then in "proving" their case, supporters of the rational actor position have proven too much. Their model of rational behavior has become a mere *truism*. This means that it is true only in the limited sense of being consistent with their assumptions, but of no possible value to anyone. This model or paradigm—commonly advanced in the legal arena by "law and economic" scholars, in philosophy by "ethical egoists," and in business schools by many teachers of economics and finance—has lost the power to do what theories are supposed to do.

Theories are supposed to explain and/or predict. A truism does neither. And this particular truism, the rational person truism, puts saints and sinners in the same bag. Mother Teresa is no less self-interested, and of no more moral worth, than a common thief. The rational person truism tells us only that we do what we prefer to do and that by doing what we prefer to do we are acting rationally. This truism would be equally comfortable with a Mother Teresa who stole from the church and a thief who donated 10% of the "loot" to charity. Whatever these people choose to do next—and the only clue that the rational person truism gives us is that it will be self-interested—it will qualify as rational simply just because they prefer to do it.

Our advice to you as business students and soon-to-be young managers and entrepreneurs is to put this loony-bin truism out of your mind completely. It teaches a warped version of what is rational, and it treats all preferences as equal. That kind of silliness has no place in a discussion among thoughtful adults.[23]

THE ROLE OF VIRTUE ETHICS IN CORPORATE CULTURE

We advance a view based on Aristotle's concept of virtue ethics and of happiness as the *telos* of humankind. We take from Aristotle the notion of happiness—happiness in the sense of flourishing or fulfillment over a lifetime of virtuous conduct and in a community of like-minded people—as the ultimate or chief good. Happiness in this sense does not necessarily follow from a social contract, from a collection of rules, or from trying to advance the greatest good for the greatest number. Virtue ethics is not entirely opposed to these concepts, however. It simply finds them to be inadequate to produce the chief or ultimate good. Rules that find support in other ethical theories might be considered necessary but not sufficient to produce the good.

The kind of culture—world culture, national culture, corporate culture—we are exploring on these pages, has plenty of room for thoughtful social contractarians like John Rawls and others, introspective geniuses like Immanuel Kant, and imaginative utilitarians like Jeremy Bentham and J. S. Mill. We are not advancing a culture that disregards and disrespects contracts and agreements, that disregards and disrespects the uniqueness and moral worth of other people, or that disregards and disrespects the conscientious efforts of those who would promote the public welfare.

What we are advancing is a culture that emphasizes the development of character habits—virtues—in a way that none of the other ethical theories do. Virtue ethics begins with certain bottom-line assumptions, such as treating other people with respect, and with obeying rules that are part of the basic fabric of government and society. Those assumptions are fundamental or foundational, and virtue ethics has always emphasized the importance of a community with good laws.

But of all these theories, only virtue ethics demands excellence in the way one lives one's life. Virtue ethics looks on the rules and agreements of other ethical theories as describing the very minimum—the moral minimum. Conduct is judged blameworthy if it falls below that minimum or that floor. It is required to meet a certain minimum, and it is permissible to be equal to or above that floor. The mission of virtue ethics, however, is to move people so far beyond that floor that they could not even conceive of falling below it.

Virtue ethics is riveted so singularly on what is good for humankind (happiness) and what is excellent in individual character (virtue) that, generally speaking, it is comfortable with leaving bottom-line legal and moral propositions to the rulemakers (utilitarians, contractarians, and deontologists). The resolution of ethical dilemmas or quandaries is not the main thrust of virtue ethics. With a clear vision of what is good and with the character habits or virtues that foster the good, men and women of virtue escape much of the dithering, the uncertainty, and the related anxiety that others encounter when confronted with tough choices. This is not a claim that "magic happens" and that every choice becomes an easy one, but, as we hope to make clear, virtuous people—people of character—simply are not plagued with the same kinds of doubts that others are.

VIRTUES AND THE ETHICS OF SCOUTING.

Consider the following example. Scouting is an experience shared by many Americans. It is an important component of popular culture, of the "American way of life." Maybe the first thing people hear about Boy Scouts and Girl Scouts and the thing they remember the longest is that the Scouts have been trained to assist elderly people safely across busy streets. (To avoid the bad jokes, we'll assume that the elderly person actually wants to cross the street.) Because of their training, Boy Scouts and Girl Scouts know that this is a good thing to do, and they have no hesitancy in doing so. No dithering, no uncertainty, no anxiety.

How does a Scout know, however, that helping an elderly person across a busy street is a good thing to do? The Scout has been told, the Scout has been trained, the Scout has seen good examples, and the Scout has been rewarded for following such examples and admonished and disciplined for not following those examples. How, then, do the Scout leaders know that helping elderly people across busy streets is a good thing to do and that young people should be trained to do it? The answer relates back to the history and tradition of Scouting and to the role that Scouting plays in the big picture in American society.

The practice of Scouting is defined, in part, by helping other people. Helping other people, even at some inconvenience or sacrifice to oneself, is identified with the "good." Hence, true to the integrity, the meaning, and the spirit of Scouting, each new generation of Cub Scouts and Brownies is taught to help other people. This training forms part of their character. This is the way Scouts acquire virtue. By extension of this example, this is the way everyone acquires virtue. Virtues are taught, not given.

VIRTUES AND THE ETHICS OF BUSINESS

Move this example into a modern, multinational business corporation, and you will get a variation on this theme. Business people, no less than others, have been trained in the view that the production of quality goods and services to be sold in a free and fair market at a price that will cover costs and return a profit to the owners is good. It is not the highest and noblest good—it is not happiness itself—but the production of such goods is instrumental to the achievement of the highest good.

Economic production is understood to be a necessary good, not a necessary evil. It is an essential precondition to the achievement of the highest good, but it takes more than economic goods to produce happiness. Happiness also requires spiritual goods, emotional goods, intellectual goods, and other goods beyond the range of this discussion.

How does one know that economic goods are good? Might they not be evil, or the root of all evil? We do not anchor our response in any immutable or absolute principle or ideal; we simply reply to the question of what is good in the same manner that Scout leaders reply: We consult our experience, our history, and our tradition of economic production and of free enterprise and ask, What is good about this?

Among other things, the economic system produces meaningful work, jobs for hands, and challenges for intellect. It produces roofs over heads, food for the table, children in school, money in the bank. Those things are good, and no one can deny it. We acknowledge that these goods are not as important as your religious beliefs, or your physical or emotional health, or your child's safety, but economic goods are nevertheless very important. They are supportive of and sometimes necessary to other and more important goods.

It follows, then, that if economic production is an essential instrumental good, economic or business virtues produce this good. What are these virtues? Without undertaking an exhaustive list, we supply a few examples. With regard to each of these, we are speaking of character habits—habits that, through long training and conditioning, have become second nature. Illustrative of these character habits are hard work, honesty, practical judgment, prudence, cooperativeness, friendship, and respect for others, including business rivals.

Our first observation about these and other virtues, however, is that they are not naturally given talents like great intellectual, artistic, or athletic potential. Virtues become second nature only as the result of good training, by good parents, in a good family, with good friends, and in a good community. Take away the support system, and what's left are vices instead of virtues, chaos instead of harmony, hatred instead of happiness. To the extent that many communities in the United States and throughout the world today are sunk in drugs, crime, and poverty and to the extent that many families are broken and many parents too selfish to nurture their children and give them love and proper instruction, virtue ethics cannot flourish and produce the goods that would otherwise be forthcoming.

As we examine the business virtues one at a time, you will see clearly that they are not exclusively limited to the practice of business or the production of economic goods. Hard work. The work ethic. It spills over into ministry, medicine, law, the arts and sciences, and many other disciplines as well. This virtue is cultivated in most, and probably every, corner of the globe.

The work ethic, like other business virtues, is a mean, or midway between two extremes (vices). On one extreme is laziness (not even in cultures where nature's gifts are bountiful is laziness respected); on the other extreme is "work-a-holicism" (a producer of neglected families and early heart attacks). The exercise of this virtue may "look different" in a farming community in the Middle East, compared with a fishing village in Chile or an investment bank in Bonn, but in all those cases, men and women with the work ethic will be diligently advancing their tasks day after day in the best way they know how.

Honesty. The midpoint between lying (deceit) and spilling-your-guts (blabbing) at the slightest provocation. This does not mean that a virtuous person would "never tell a lie"; it only means that it would be "out of character" for him or her to do so.

Practical judgment. The mean between dithering (unable to decide) and snap (arbitrary) decisions. This virtue entails fact-finding (gathering all of the relevant facts that the circumstances permit) and choosing the course of action most consistent with and most conducive of happiness.

Prudence.   The middle course between the vices of haste and shortsightedness, on the one hand, and overconcern about improbable events, on the other. Prudence in U.S. law today is frequently equated with reasonableness. It is not uncommon for a judge to ask a jury to return a verdict based on how a prudent person would act under the circumstances.

Cooperativeness.   The line between uncooperativeness and hostility, on one extreme, and collusion or complete submission to the will of another, at the opposite extreme. It presupposes that each group member may make different and uneven contributions and that no member will intentionally frustrate or obstruct the efforts of the group.

Friendship.   Love and affection for another human being, based on mutual well-being or shared concern for one another's well-being. It is to be distinguished from the vices of pretense and hypocrisy, on the one extreme, and an undifferentiated, mindless, and bleeding-heart attachment, on the other.

Respect.   High or special regard. The virtue of respect is modeled on that of friendship, but friendship presupposes that the parties at least know one another and/or share common values. Because it is not possible to have this kind of relationship with everyone in the world (except in the most abstract sense), the essential value and worth of other human lives can nevertheless be honored and their well-being supported in tangible and intangible ways.

For example, it would be impossible for the board of directors of a multinational firm to be friends with all of their customers, but they could show respect for those customers by selling them quality goods and services at a fair price. Respect for the well-being of others does not carry along with it the shared intimacy of close friends. In a business context, however, it translates into care and caring in one's relation with employees, customers, suppliers, and other members of the business community.

Could you spell out a rule commanding these virtues? How would you get a handle on friendship, for example, and compel judgment or cooperativeness, or any of the others? Virtues cannot be reduced to rules or to mere rule following—at least not in the sense that Aristotle wrote of the virtues and in the sense that we understand them to be applicable to the practice of business. Virtues are part of the human character, and character is not a quality that can be formulated or commanded by a rule.

Again, however, we emphasize that rules are important. Good rules are not to be disregarded any more than good laws are to be disregarded. Rules are especially valuable in training children in the virtues—for example, "Always hold hands and look both ways before crossing the street." What a marvelous rule! But there comes a time when children no longer need to be cautioned by such a rule. At some stage, they have internalized the wisdom of that rule and no longer need to be reminded. With patience and good training, individuals acquire the virtue of care and caring.

THE JOHNSON & JOHNSON CREDO: CARE AND CARING IN A BUSINESS CONTEXT

Without trying to recount the full story, we touch on some of the main aspects of Johnson & Johnson's Tylenol nightmare. J&J produced and distributed Tylenol, a headache remedy, which at the time of these events was the market leader. In various parts of the U.S., this product was criminally tampered with—taken from the shelf, laced with poison, and secretly returned to the shelf. This tampering resulted in the deaths of several innocent consumers.

The nation was stunned. Was this a deliberate act of sabotage by a J&J employee at the point of production? Was it some cruel and mindless prank? Or the act of a maniac? At the time of these events, nobody actually knew all the facts, but J&J disclosed to the public all facts that were available to it. Something had to be done. Consumers' lives were in danger. The reputation and the continued economic viability of the firm was in danger. And, frankly, everyone who consumed over-the-counter pharmaceutical, cosmetics, and foods was, if not in immediate danger, at least threatened by the prospect.

What had J&J done wrong? "Why me, Lord?" was the imagined plea. If J&J had caused such an outcome through its negligence—perhaps a failure in quality control or a failure to detect and screen out employees with such criminal propensities—it could be held liable to the victims, or rather their survivors, in a civil action for damages. Even in the absence of that scenario, if J&J could have reasonably foreseen or anticipated the criminal act of a maniac, and failed to take reasonable precautions to minimize the risk, it could again be held liable in a civil action.

What to do? No law compelled a recall, and under the powers delegated to it by Congress, the Food and Drug Administration declined to issue such an order.

J&J issued the recall. After collecting all the facts it could, the J&J board and senior management discussed their options and quickly decided on the one best alternative: Get Tylenol off the shelf immediately and at whatever cost. In the words of its board chairman and CEO, James Burke, there was never any question of J&J's willingness to do exactly that.

In its long history, J&J had prospered enormously, and that prosperity was, at least in part, attributed to an almost religious adherence to its credo. Now, in a sense, it was time to "pay the piper."

J&J CREDO

We believe our first responsibility is to the doctors, nurses and patients, to mothers and all others who use our products and services.

In meeting their need, everything we do must be of high quality.

We must constantly strive to reduce our costs in order to maintain reasonable prices.

Customers' orders must be serviced promptly and accurately.

Our suppliers and distributors must have an opportunity to make a fair profit.

We are responsible to our employees, the men and women who work with us throughout the world.

Everyone must be considered as an individual.

We must respect their sense of dignity and recognize their merit.

They must have a sense of security in their jobs.

Compensation must be fair and adequate, and working conditions clean, orderly and safe.

Employees must feel free to make suggestions and complaints.

There must be equal opportunity for employment, development and advancement for those qualified.

We must provide competent management, and their actions must be just and ethical.

We are responsible to the communities in which we live and work and to the world community as well.

We must be good citizens—support good works and charities and bear our fair share of taxes.

We must encourage civil improvements and better health and education.

We must maintain in good order the property we are privileged to use, protecting the environment and natural resources.

Our final responsibility is to our stockholder.

Business must make a sound profit.

We must experiment with new ideas.

Research must be carried on, innovative programs developed and mistakes paid for.

New equipment must be purchased, new facilities provided and new products launched.

Reserves must be created to provide for adverse times.

When we operate according to these principles, the stockholders should realize a fair return.

ETHICAL AND SOCIAL RESPONSIBILITY PERSPECTIVES ON THE RECALL.

How does one best understand Johnson & Johnson's decision? We consider first the work of Milton Friedman and second an interpretation of the combined work of Goodpaster/Matthews, Stone, and Simon/Powers/Gunnemann. For simplicity's sake, we refer to the first as the Friedman perspective, and because Christopher Stone is the elder and more widely known of the second group, we refer to the second as the Stone perspective.

The Friedman Perspective.   One way of looking at the Johnson & Johnson recall is from the view of Milton Friedman. Even though the law was silent and gave no immediate direction on what to do and even though profit maximization (long-run and short-run) looked bleak, ethical custom, vague as that phrase is, may be interpreted to mean that human life and economic profit are not commensurable goods and that priority must be placed on saving human life.

CHAPTER 3 · Social and Ethical Responsibility of Corporate Management   **129**

That is, to say the least, a generous interpretation of Friedman. Strictly speaking, he might not tolerate such an interpretation if the law did not compel a recall and if a recall would almost certainly jeopardize the solvency of the firm. Under the worse scenario, if one kills the firm—the goose that lays the golden egg—one also kills or substantially diminishes the investment of stockholders, the jobs of employees, the contracts of suppliers, the tax base of local communities, the benefits that J&J products bring to its consumers, and the research and social benefits that J&J may produce in the future.

Friedman's position, widely characterized as libertarian, is an amalgam of utilitarianism and social contract. Under either of the two interpretations that were offered above, free, rational human beings might plausibly enter a social contract under which every decision would be expected to advance the greatest good for the greatest number or, alternatively, to enter a social contract that would follow such a rule except when following the rule would almost certainly jeopardize innocent human life.

It is also possible to weave an interpretation of Immanuel Kant into this picture: "Always act in such a way as to advance the greatest good for the greatest number except in those situations in which it would almost certainly jeopardize innocent human life." That rule embodies both criteria for a categorical imperative. It can be universalized, and there is no inherent or logical contradiction in applying it to oneself, as well as to others.

The Stone Perspective.   How does one understand the Tylenol recall from the positions advanced by Goodpaster/Matthews, Stone, and Simon/Power/Gunnemann? Goodpaster/Matthews, you recall, try to imagine a corporation as a moral person and set about the task of building the moral qualities of a living, breathing human person into the structure of an artificial person. Stone's book *Where the Law Ends* was the model for the "moral projection" of Goodpaster/Matthews. In the brief segment of his book made available to you in this text, you see him busily describing the qualities of a moral person.

We believe that moral persons do sometimes place human life or health in jeopardy. It is one thing to say that the value of a human life is infinite, immeasurable, and of incalculable worth. It is another thing to live in a world of limited material, emotional, and intellectual resources and to know that people cannot always avoid choices that will jeopardize or end a human life.

At one level, people place human life or health in jeopardy every day in health care and insurance programs by denying coverage to those in need of life support systems and by denying assistance to those seeking untested or experimental medicines and procedures. At another level, people do it when they decide to produce pharmaceuticals, packaged foods, airplanes, trains, automobiles (together with their supporting infrastructures) that are "safe enough." People do it on the personal level when they purchase the lower-priced "economy model," rather than the safer but more expensive "deluxe model."

In fact, people do it every day and every time they pursue some good that comes into conflict with an incommensurable good such as human life. Have you ever exceeded the speed limit to get to class on time? If you have, you know exactly what we're talking about.

In our view, the Johnson & Johnson decision is best explained on a model supplied by the Stone perspective. It might even be valuable at this point for you to review Goodpaster/Matthews, "Can a Corporation Have a Conscience?" Stone, "What 'Corporate Responsibility' Might Really Mean," and Simon/Powers/Gunnemann, "The Responsibilities of Corporations and Their Owners."

You will find the Stone perspective to be in most ways consistent with McCoy's observations in "The Parable of the Sadhu," and with the text sections "Elements of a Corporate Culture" and "The Role of Virtue Ethics in Corporate Culture."

The Stone perspective envisions a corporation that internalizes the moral qualities of a natural person; these qualities are built into the structure of the firm. In a manner of speaking, the corporation is personified in the image of a responsible, moral person.

No one believes this can be done to perfection, but it is at least a start. The reason we emphasize that this is only a start is our conviction that bureaucracies frequently act irrationally, that they may be warped by internal political struggles, and that they sometimes conduct business on the basis of standard operating procedures that have little or no relevance to the problem at hand or that are not sophisticated enough to deal with the nuances of ethical problems.

With the image (albeit an imperfect image) of a corporation built on the model of a moral person, a corporation is morally obligated on some occasions, but not always, to go to the rescue of people in need. When it does undertake rescue measures, it should pursue them only with certain qualifications—qualifications roughly in accord with the suggestions provided by Simon/Power/Gunnemann in "The Responsibilities of Corporations and Their Owners."

How Johnson & Johnson's Decision Is Related to "The Parable of the Sadhu." This approach borrows from McCoy's "Parable of the Sadhu." As its credo makes clear, Johnson & Johnson plainly articulated its shared corporate values. Consumer health and welfare obviously occupied top priority; everything else was in second place. We don't know in detail the procedures the firm employed, but they served the firm marvelously well as it operated under conditions of adversity, ambiguity, and change.

How Johnson & Johnson's Decision Is Related to "Elements of a Corporate Culture." Reflect now on the text section "Elements of a Corporate Culture." The kind of corporate culture we are trying to foster must be led from the top, and there can be little question that strong moral leadership from the Chairperson of the board has always been a tradition at J&J. General Robert Johnson, who guided the firm through its early years, was the genius behind the original credo, but he didn't do it all himself. He put his indelible signature on the credo, of course, and his enthusiasm behind it, but the credo itself—with the principal focus on respect for the welfare of others, rather than on the corporate profits and stockholder interests—was the product of widely surveyed corporate constituents. Communication and participation were the hallmarks of the original credo, as was respect for the well-being of others.

The revised credo, the one that appears in this text, was initiated by James Burke, to the retired General Johnson's consternation. The general was fearful that the path charted out by his original work would be abandoned or somehow sidetracked. Burke, however, undertook the revision to see whether J&J's professed beliefs were firmly held and still relevant to a world market that was substantially different from the one that challenged the original credo. Again, the board chairperson played an instrumental role in the revision. He consulted widely and sought employee participation, as did his predecessor. And it must be clear by now that the revised credo displayed an immense amount of respect for the welfare of J&J customers.

In greatest likelihood, neither of these visionary leaders ever imagined that J&J would be confronted with the nightmare of a criminally contaminated product. With 20-20 hindsight, perhaps they should have anticipated it. But at least they were wise enough to see problems of significant magnitude down the road, and they took steps to ensure that the firm would be as prepared for those shocks as was humanly possible. The credo was their response.

Who could have foreseen at the time the recall decision was made that the enormous financial beating J&J took would be recovered many times over by the patronage of grateful customers who demonstrated their loyalty and their confidence in J&J's integrity. These customers returned in droves when the crisis was resolved and a tamper-proof Tylenol container was introduced. J&J also produced Tylenol exclusively in tablet form, instead of reintroducing the more easily contaminated capsule.

How Johnson & Johnson's Decision Is Related to "The Role of Virtue Ethics in Corporate Culture."   Finally, the conduct of J&J is most nearly in accord with virtue ethics than with any other moral theory. By articulating its values, J&J's credo defined the good for a multinational firm operating in a competitive, global market. In doing so, it created a 'corporate culture' that nourished the business virtues.

No question, J&J demonstrated the *virtue of honesty* by putting all its cards on the table. It was frank and forthright with its customers, employees, and with government regulators. Having made public all the facts that were available to it, and knowing that a decision had to be made, J&J did not dither; neither did it display haste or shortsightedness in its decision process. In other words, J&J displayed the *virtues of practical judgment and of prudence,* and though it hardly needs repeating, J&J clearly acted with the *virtue of respect for the welfare of others.*

CONCLUSION

Beginning with the model of morally responsible behavior, this chapter has focused on the importance of (1) establishing a corporate structure that internalizes moral norms; (2) identifying issues that affect human welfare in ways that can be described as good/bad and right/wrong; and (3) engaging in a rational, deliberative process that will lead to the implementation of sound moral values in every aspect of a firm's operations. The value of this effort is in spotting ethical problems early enough to be dealt with before harm is done—before organizational blindness, ineptness, carelessness, or greed explodes onto the scene as a social problem, and specifically a legal one.

None of this material involves memorizing moral theories, enumerating the elements of a strong corporate culture, or listing the moral minimum. It does however, involve building a corporation in such a way that the managerial roles you will be assuming are congruent with your moral values. The real worth of this chapter, then, ought to be gauged by how well it serves you during your business career in providing that kind of leadership.

REVIEW QUESTIONS AND PROBLEMS

1. What should a manager do when she believes that the employee about to be fired could have been rehabilitated if the company had not discontinued funding of its alcohol abuse program and put that money into a program for public television?

2. What kind of behavior is appropriate when a manager knows that a subordinate's lack of productivity stems from a divorce and that the divorce was caused, in part, by too many demands at work, too many hours, too little corporate support? Further, the manager knows that, unlike himself, the other two executives who took part in the evaluation have never experienced a divorce and believe that divorce is morally wrong.

3. What response should be made to an order to file suit against a customer that will surely be forced into bankruptcy despite a payment record that is scarcely worse than that of many others and despite a promise to that customer that it could have another sixty days to pay? Although no alternative or intermediate measures have been taken, the manager is told by his superior that other collections will be speeded up if get-tough legal steps are implemented and that, frankly, if something isn't done soon, the company itself may go under.

4. Suppose the service of a discontinued supplier (ConChip) has been declining. Also suppose a manager has some reason to believe the real reason for the termination is that the son of the division vice-president, who just happens to be the manager's boss, has been hired by Amtron, a competing supplier. The new employer of the Vice president's son has a questionable service reputation itself, but it has recently gained ConChip's discontinued contracts. If this information were to come to your attention as an employee of ConChip, what would be the morally appropriate course of action for you to follow?

5. Answer the following:

   a. Briefly relate Milton Friedman's view of corporate social responsibility.

   b. Describe the Goodpaster-Matthews concept of "moral projection."

   c. After reviewing the Kew Gardens Principle, explain the difference between what the authors label the "moral minimum" duty and the duty to "go to the rescue."

ENDNOTES

1. Smith, *An Inquiry into the Nature and Causes of the Wealth of Nations* 14 (1776).
2. *Id.* at 423.
3. From an unpublished case by Peter A. French, Lennox Distinguished Professor of Humanities and Professor of Philosophy, Trinity University, San Antonio, Texas. Used with permission.
4. Professor Frances E. Zollers, Law and Public Policy, School of Management, Syracuse University. Used with permission.
5. Velasquez, Why Corporations Are Not Morally Responsible for Anything They Do, 2 *Bus. & Prof. Ethics J.* 1-18 (1983).
6. Ladd, Morality and the Ideal of Rationality in Formal Organizations, 54 *Monist* 488-516 (1920).
7. Philosopher Peter French finds corporate moral personhood—a unity of corporate mind and action—in the Corporate Internal Decision structure, a system of policies, procedures, and lines of authority that subordinates and synthesizes the intentions and acts of natural persons into corporate decisions and actions. Corporate Moral Agency, in Beauchamp and Bowie, *Ethical Theory and Business,* 175-186 (1979). We see corporate action as derivative of the primary moral actions of natural persons, and when those primary actors are unidentified or unidentifiable or the action is a unique "group phenomenon," we find the corporation to have secondary moral responsibility.
8. Inesko and Shopler, *Experimental Social Psychology* 468 (1972).
9. Janis, Groupthink, in Staw, *Psychological Foundations of Organizational Behavior* 406 (1977).
10. Werhane, *Persons, Rights, and Corporations* 49-59 (1985).
11. Locke, *Two Treatises of Government* 309 (Laslett ed. 1963).
12. *Id.* at 328-329.
13. Friedman, The Social Responsibility of Business Is to Increase Its Profits, *New York Times*, September 13, 1970, at 36. Copyright © 1970 by the New York Times Company. Reprinted by permission.
14. From *Capitalism and Freedom* by Milton Friedman, pp. 133-136. Copyright © 1962 by the University of Chicago; all rights reserved. Reprinted by permission of the publisher.
15. "Adam Smith" *The Wealth of Nations* (1776) Bk. IV, Chapter ii (Cannon ed., London, 1930), p. 421.
16. Goodpaster and Matthews, Can a Corporation Have a Conscience? *Harvard Business Rev.* 132 (Jan.-Feb. 1982).
17. *Id.* at 138.
18. Reprinted by permission of *Harvard Business Review.* Excerpt from "Can a corporation have a conscience?" by Kenneth E. Goodpaster and John B. Matthews, Jr. (January-February 1982). Copyright © 1982 by the President and Fellows of Harvard College; all rights reserved.
19. *Id.* at 134.
20. *Id.*
21. Specified excerpt (pp. 111-116) from Chapter 12, "What Corporate Responsibility Might Really Mean," in *Where the Law Ends* by Christopher D. Stone. Copyright © 1975 by Christopher D. Stone. Reprinted by permission of Harper Collins Publishers, Inc.
22. From Simon, J.G., Powers, C.W., and Gunnemann, J.P., *The Ethical Investor: Universities and Corporate Responsibility* 15-25 (1972). Copyright © 1972 by Yale University. Reprinted by permission of Yale University Press.
23. Shaw and Zollers, Modes of Corporate Behavior, in Managers in the Moral Dimension: What Etzioni Might Mean to Corporate Managers, 3 *Business Ethics Quarterly* 153, 155-157 (1993).

CHAPTER 4

Constitutional Law

INTRODUCTION

Like all laws, the laws that affect business are circumscribed by the limitations and protections afforded by the U.S. Constitution. The Constitution is the supreme law of the land, and all state and federal laws are subject to constitutional requirements. In this chapter, we examine the constitutional provisions that affect business. Before we examine specific provisions in detail, it is helpful to explore briefly the history of the Constitution, as well as the most essential provisions.

In 1787, fifty-five delegates of the newly independent states met in Philadelphia to create a new government and a new political unity—the United States of America. The creation of such a government involved much compromise. The Virginia Plan called for separated powers, an institutionalized balance of powers among an executive, a judiciary, and a national legislature composed of an upper and a lower chamber, each in proportion to state population. William Paterson of New Jersey, later to serve on the Supreme Court, countered with a proposal favored by smaller states: Each state would be given an equal voice in Congress. Roger Sherman broke the deadlock with the Connecticut Compromise, under which the Senate became the states' chamber, with equal representation, and the House became the people's chamber, with representation apportioned on the basis of state population.

This arrangement marks the U.S. system of government as a *federalist republic*. *Federalism* designates a two-tiered system comprised of a central or federal level and a state or local level. Today, issues of federalism involve the balance of power between federal and state governments. This balance of power is a never-ending political issue. The word *republic* signifies that the people's voice is made known, not directly, but through representatives as would be the case in a New England town meeting.

ARTICLES OF THE CONSTITUTION

Article I.   The powers of Congress, one of three coequal branches, are enumerated in Article I, Section 8. By expressly delegating limited powers to the legislative and subsequently to the executive (Art. II) and the judicial (Art. III) branches, the framers of the Constitution were attempting to avoid the kind of arbitrary governmental action they had revolted against; to this end, a system of checks and balances among the three branches was sought. Congress was expressly authorized to control commerce in addition to eighteen other areas, including taxation and national defense. Beyond that, Congress was empowered to make all laws *necessary and proper* to implement its expressed powers. This meant that as long as congressional legislation was within its delegated powers, it could, within the bounds of other constitutional provisions, extend its control into unspecified areas as well. For example, Article I, Section 8 says nothing about Congress' power to control air pollution or to prohibit racial discrimination. But if either of these affects commerce between states, Congress can, within constitutional limits, legislate on these subjects as a means toward the exercise of its enumerated powers. The Clean Air Act and the Civil Rights Act represent congressional action based on the commerce clause.

Article II.   The framers needed sixty ballots to determine the method of electing a president, and the holder of that office was made commander-in-chief of the armed forces, as well as chief executive officer. They had no real model for this office and no way to anticipate the problems an executive would encounter, so the definition of presidential powers was purposefully left open and flexible. Religious tests for the executive, and for all other federal offices as well, were forbidden.

Article III.   A Supreme Court was created, with the proviso that judicial appointments would be held as long as appointees exercised "good behavior." Jurisdiction of this Court extended to all cases arising under the Constitution, laws, and treaties of the United States. It was to have original jurisdiction in any case in which a state became a party (plaintiff) or in any case involving ambassadors, other public ministers, or consuls of foreign nations. In all other cases it was to have appellate jurisdiction, as specified by Congress, over a system of lower courts that Congress was authorized to create.

Article IV.   The *full faith and credit clause*, sometimes spoken of as the union-making clause, is embodied in Article IV. It means that judgments rendered in one state by a court with proper jurisdiction will be enforced without a new trial in other states. This article also contains a *privileges and immunities clause* (the Fourteenth Amendment contains one as well), which provides that a state cannot unreasonably discriminate against citizens of another state.[1] For example, a state college or university can charge a higher tuition for nonresidents than it does for residents, but this difference must be grounded on some reasonable basis.

Article V. The British constitution, by which we mean those organic substantive acts of Parliament or the Crown dating back to the Magna Carta, 1215, has been amended by each more recent official act. The evolution of this constitution continues today through succeeding acts of Parliament. The framers of the U.S. Constitution could have gone that route themselves and, perhaps, after gaining familiarity with the procedure, taken it to be the "proper" way of doing things. But they did not.

The process they chose stipulates that amendments may be proposed by a two-thirds vote of each house of Congress or by a Constitutional Convention supported by two-thirds of the states. The United States has never used this latter alternative, perhaps for fear that such a convention would "go too far." Once amendments have been proposed, they must be ratified in three-fourths of the states, either by their legislatures or special conventions.

Article VI. All federal and state executive, legislative, and judicial officers are bound to affirm support of the Constitution; religious tests for U.S. officers are plainly forbidden. Further, Article VI embodies a *supremacy clause*: The supreme law of the land shall consist of the Constitution, laws of the United States made in pursuance thereof, and treaties made under the authority of the United States; state constitutions and laws, and state judges as well, are bound by this provision.

Article VII. The final article provided that ratification by a minimum of nine states through conventions called for that purpose would be sufficient to bind the ratifying states. New Hampshire was the ninth state; and on June 21, 1788, the Constitution of the United States of America was ratified.

THE BILL OF RIGHTS

The first ten amendments to the Constitution are collectively known as the Bill of Rights, though only the first eight contain substantive, fundamental protections. The remaining two amendments are not grants of specific rights at all, but rather are reservations of rights and of powers. For example, the Ninth Amendment dispels the notion that delegation or enumeration of rights in the Constitution can be taken to mean that the people have surrendered or given up other rights. This amendment is the core of what people speak of today as the right of privacy. The Tenth Amendment speaks in a similar voice, but it speaks of powers, not of rights. Sovereign powers originally held by the states under the Articles of Confederation, powers not delegated to the United States or prohibited to the states by the Constitution, are reserved to the states or to the people.

These ten amendments, ratified by a sufficient number of states by 1791, were in a sense "demanded" by many of the state conventions that were called to debate the original document. Although certain rights were woven into the original body of the Constitution, they were perceived to be inadequate for the protection of the most important individual interests. Article I, Section 9, for example, prohibited Congress from suspending the writ of habeas corpus except in time of rebellion or invasion and from passing bills of attainder and ex post facto laws. Further, Article I, Section 10 denied states the right to pass bills of attainder and ex post facto laws as well and prohibited them from impairing the obligation of contracts. Congress could impair contracts through its Article I, Section 8 power to enact uniform laws of bankruptcy.

James Madison, a member of the House of Representatives from Virginia, led the move for a Bill of Rights when Congress first met in 1789. The list of proposed amendments was pared to twelve, but one proposal that would have fixed the size of the House of Representatives and another that would have prohibited changes in the compensation of members of Congress from taking effect until after the next election did not gain sufficient support for passage. By December 1791, ten of these proposals were ratified by the states. Surprisingly, Massachusetts, which had been insistent on a Bill of Rights, was the tardiest. It ratified them in 1941.

DUE PROCESS OF LAW

PROCEDURAL DUE PROCESS

As the phrase suggests, *due process* literally means "due procedure" or "fair procedure." By *procedure* is meant the steps in a civil or criminal case that move the parties from pretrial all the way through the court of final resort, perhaps the U.S. Supreme Court.

A more difficult question concerns the meaning of the words *due* and *fair*. Although one might compile a string of synonyms that roughly mean "appropriate or deserving under the circumstances," it is probably better as a practical matter to pursue the historical record. The phrase *due process* has long been linked with the Magna Carta ("law of the land"), the noble document coerced from a reluctant King John by rebellious barons in 1215.

> No freeman shall be taken, or imprisoned, or disseized of his freehold, or liberties, or free customs, or be outlawed, or exiled, or any other wise destroyed, nor will we not pass upon him, nor condemn him, but by lawful judgement of his peers, or by the law of the land.

Today, due process or fair procedure is taken to mean *"at a minimum notice"* of proceedings against the defendant and an opportunity for a hearing before an impartial tribunal.[2] In common law trials—for example, trials that stem from judge-made laws like contracts, torts, and agency—the Seventh Amendment preserves the right to a jury if the amount in controversy exceeds twenty dollars. The framers clearly did not write in an escalation clause for inflation. One of the parties must request a jury, or else the judge alone will weigh the evidence in a "bench trial."

For those legal rights created by the legislature—statutory causes of action—there is no right to a jury trial unless the statute so provides. This means that, in most noncriminal matters (e.g., civil rights, social security, antitrust, securities), the judge alone will weigh the evidence and apply the law.

Procedural due process requires "some kind of hearing," according to *Wolff* v. *McDonnell*.[3] The requirement does not necessarily mean that the full panoply of legal protections and procedures are necessarily appropriate in every type of hearing. A court will determine this matter on a "contextual" basis—that is, on grounds of what is fitting under the circumstances to ensure that the injured party is treated fairly. Criminal trials and civil litigation guarantee the widest range of due process protections, but at least the basic protections must be available, for example, when a student is dismissed from school, when a person is deprived of a driver's license, and when government-owned services or government entitlements are terminated.

SUBSTANTIVE DUE PROCESS

Substantive due process is a difficult concept. The phrase *due process* brings to mind procedural safeguards, such as reasonable notice and a hearing before an impartial tribunal. But due procedure alone cannot ensure a just result if the substance of the law itself—the rights and duties embodied in a statute—is somehow inadequate, unreasonable, arbitrary, or defective.

A historic case illustrates this point. In 1854, Chief Justice Roger B. Taney, a Jackson appointee and former chief justice of the Maryland Supreme Court, wrote the leading opinion (there were eight others, including two dissents) in *Dred Scott* v. *Sanford*.[4] In this case, the Court was called on to decide whether Dred Scott was a free man and a citizen of the United States (thus entitled to invoke the jurisdiction of a federal court) by virtue of an act of Congress—the Missouri Compromise of 1820—that prohibited slavery in certain U.S. territories. Dred Scott, a slave to a U.S. Army surgeon, had moved with the surgeon and had lived in free territory and then in the free state of Illinois. On returning to Missouri, he brought this action in a U.S. district court, seeking official vindication of his freedom in a test case guided and financed by antislavery supporters. Dred Scott lost his case, and for the second time in U.S. history, the Supreme Court declared an act of Congress unconstitutional. The Chief Justice wrote:

> In the opinion of the court the legislation and histories of the times, and the language used in the Declaration of Independence, show, that neither the class of persons who had been imported as slaves, not their descendants, whether they had become free or not, were then acknowledged as a part of the people, nor intended to be included in the general words used in that memorable instrument. . . .
>
> They had for more than a century before been regarded as beings of an inferior order, and altogether unfit to associate with the white race, either in social or political relations; and so far inferior, that they had no rights which the white man was bound to respect; and that the negro might justly and lawfully be reduced to slavery for his benefit. . . . 60 U.S. at 407.

★ ★ ★

. . . And an act of Congress which deprives a citizen of the United States of his liberty or property, merely because he came himself or brought his property into a particular Territory of the United States, and who had committed no offence against the laws, could hardly be dignified with the name of due process of law. 60 U.S. at 450.

In the final analysis, Chief Justice Taney converted the Fifth Amendment's due process clause into a staunch defense of private property. Any federal act and, in years following the Fourteenth Amendment, any state act that infringed on liberty (freedom of contract) or property (private ownership) was in jeopardy of being declared null and void on the basis of due process.

This interpretation gave the clause a new direction. It allowed judges to selectively invalidate federal and state statutes that intruded on the basic institutions of free enterprise. The Constitution, of course, does not "adopt" the free enterprise economic system, nor does it even refer to Adam Smith's theory or any other. The Constitution is receptive to all economic ideas that are compatible with the commitment to freedom and individual liberties. Nevertheless, beginning with *Dred Scott*, and for the next eighty years or so, the Court used *substantive* due process to strike down minimum wage laws, maximum hour laws, and comparable reform measures that, in the justices' opinion, interfered with the operation of a free and competitive economy. In this manner, the Supreme Court read into the Constitution its own view of what the U.S. economic system should be.

Justice Oliver Wendell Holmes realized how such an application of substantive due process intruded on the sovereignty of the states, the separation of powers principle, and the policy-making function of the legislature. His vigorous dissent to the Court's invalidation of a New York statute limiting to ten the number of hours bakers could work each day is excerpted below.

Lochner v. *New York*
198 U.S. 45 (1905)

JUSTICE HOLMES, DISSENTING

This case is decided upon an economic theory which a large part of the country does not entertain. If it were a question whether I agreed with that theory, I should desire to study it further and long before making up my mind. But I do not conceive that to be my duty, because I strongly believe that my agreement or disagreement has nothing to do with the right of a majority to embody their opinions in law. It is settled by various decisions of this court that state Constitutions and state laws may regulate life in many ways which we as legislators might think as injudicious, or if you like as tyrannical as this, and which, equally with this, interfere with the liberty to contract. Sunday laws and usury laws are ancient examples. A more modern one is the prohibition of lotteries. The liberty of the citizen to do as he likes so long as he does not interfere with the liberty of others to do the same, which has been a shibboleth for some well-known writers, is interfered with by school laws, by the post office, by every state or municipal institution which takes his money for purposes thought desirable, whether he likes it or not.

The fourteenth amendment does not enact Mr. Herbert Spencer's Social Statics. . . . United States and state statutes and decisions cutting down the liberty to contract by way of combination are familiar to this court. . . . Two years ago we upheld the prohibition of sales of stock on margins, or for future delivery, in the Constitution of California. . . . The decision sustaining an eight-hour law for miners is still recent. . . . Some of these laws embody convictions or prejudices which judges are likely to share. Some may not. But a Constitution is not intended to embody a particular economic theory, whether of paternalism and the organic relation of the citizen to the state or of laissez faire. It is made for people of fundamentally differing views, and the accident of our finding certain opinions natural and familiar, or novel, and even shocking, ought not to conclude our judgment upon the question whether statutes embodying them conflict with the Constitution of the United States.

General propositions do not decide concrete cases. The decision will depend on a judgment or intuition more subtle than any articulate major premise. But I think that the proposition just stated, if it is accepted, will carry us far toward the end. Every opinion tends to become a law. I think that the word "liberty," in the fourteenth amendment, is perverted when it is held to prevent the natural outcome of a dominant opinion, unless it can be said that a rational and fair man necessarily would admit that the statute proposed would infringe fundamental principles as they have been understood by the traditions of our people and our law. It does not need research to show that no such sweeping condemnation can be passed upon the statute before us. A reasonable man might think it a proper measure on the score of health. Men whom I certainly could not pronounce unreasonable would uphold it as a first installment of a general regulation of the hours of work. Whether in the latter aspect it would be open to the charge of inequality I think it unnecessary to discuss. (198 U.S. at 75-76.)

Today, the judiciary is not in the practice of imposing economic doctrine when defining and applying substantive due process. The Court's substantive due process inquiry currently is limited to two questions. First, is the legislature pursuing a legitimate objective or exercising an acknowledged power? Recall that state sovereign powers consist of everything that was not carved out and delegated to the federal government, whereas congressional powers are those specifically enumerated in Article I, Section 8. Second, is the legislature—state or federal—pursuing these objectives or exercising these powers through means and measures that plainly and rationally advance its constitutional powers? For example, the federal government, to facilitate interstate commerce and conditions for safe travel, and your state government, in exercising its reserved Tenth Amendment powers to promote safety, have established speed limit laws. If you are fined for a speeding violation, you could not successfully challenge that conviction on the basis of due process. The governing body was exercising an acknowledged power, and the method it chose was reasonable and plainly adapted to achieve the legitimate end.

The following case illustrates the difficulty parties face in putting forth claims that they have been denied substantive due process.

TXO Production Corp. v. Alliance Resources
113 S.Ct. 2711 (1993)

[*Authors' note:* In its dealings with Alliance Resources, TXO Production Corporation advanced a claim that Alliance's title to oil and gas development rights was flawed. TXO sued Alliance for slander of title, alleging that Alliance knew its aspersion on title was spurious, because it was clearly based on a worthless quitclaim deed. TXO asserted that Alliance challenged TXO's title solely to gain coercive leverage in renegotiating existing royalty arrangements. The jury found TXO liable for slander of title and awarded $19,000 actual damages and $10 million punitive damages. On appeal, TXO challenged the punitive damages award as excessive and in violation of due process under the Fourteenth Amendment. The jury award was upheld unanimously by the state supreme court of appeals. The jury award of $10 million in punitive damages is evaluated by the United States Supreme Court in the decision that follows.]

TXO first argues that a $10 million punitive damages award—an award 526 times greater than the actual damages awarded by the jury—is so excessive that it must be deemed an arbitrary deprivation of property without due process of law.

TXO correctly points out that several of our opinions have stated that the Due Process Clause of the Fourteenth Amendment imposes substantive limits "beyond which penalties may not go." Moreover, in *Southwestern Telegraph & Telephone Co.* v. *Danaher*, the Court actually set aside a penalty imposed on a telephone company on the ground that it as so "plainly arbitrary and oppressive" as to violate the Due Process Clause. In an earlier case the Court had stated that it would not review state action fixing the penalties for unlawful conduct unless "the fines imposed are so grossly excessive as to amount to a deprivation of property without due process of law."

While respondents "unabashedly" denigrate those cases as "Lochner-era precedents," they overlook the fact that the Justices who had dissented in the Lochner case itself joined those opinions. More importantly, respondent do not dispute the proposition that the Fourteenth Amendment imposes a substantive limit on the amount of a punitive damages award. They contend, however, that the standard of review should be the same standard of rational basis scrutiny that is appropriate for reviewing state economic legislation.

TXO, on the other hand, argues that punitive damages awards should be scrutinized more strictly than legislative penalties because they are typically assessed without any legislative guidance expressing the considered judgment of the elected representatives of the community. TXO urges that we apply a form of heightened scrutiny, the first step of which is to apply certain "objective" criteria to determine whether a punitive award presumptively violates those notions of "fundamental fairness" inherent in the concept of due process of law. Relying heavily on the plurality opinion in *Schad* v. *Arizona*, petitioner argues that "'history and widely shared practices [are] concrete indicators of what fundamental fairness and rationality require,'" and that therefore we should examine, as "objective criteria of fairness, (1) awards of punitive damages upheld against other defendants in the same jurisdiction, (2) awards upheld for similar conduct in other jurisdictions, (3) legislative penalty decisions with respect to similar conduct, and (4) the relationship of prior punitive awards to the associated compensatory awards. Under petitioner's proposed framework, when this inquiry demonstrates that an award "exceeds the bounds of contemporary and historical practice by orders of magnitude," that award must be struck down as arbitrary and excessive unless there is a "compelling and particularized justification" for an award of such size.

The parties' desire to formulate a "test" for determining whether a particular punitive award is "grossly excessive" is understandable. Nonetheless we find neither formulation satisfactory. Under respondents' rational basis standard, apparently any award that would serve the legitimate state interest in deterring or punishing wrongful conduct, no matter how large, would be acceptable. On the other hand, we reject the premise underlying TXO's invocation of heightened scrutiny. The review of a jury's award for arbitrariness and the review of legislation surely are significantly different. Still, it is not correct to assume that the safeguards in the legislative process have no counterpart in the judicial process. The members of the jury were determined to be impartial before they were allowed to sit, their assessment of damages was the product of collective deliberation based on evidence and the arguments of adversaries, their award was reviewed and upheld by the trial judge who also heard the testimony, and it was affirmed by a unanimous decision of the State Supreme Court of Appeals. Assuming that fair procedures were followed, a judgment that is a product of that process is entitled to a strong presumption of validity.

Nor are we persuaded that reliance on petitioner's "objective" criteria is the proper course to follow. We have, of course, relied on history and "widely shared practice" as a guide to determining whether a particular state practice so departs from an accepted norm as to be presumptively violative of due process, and whether a term of imprisonment under certain circumstances is cruel and unusual punishment. We question, however, the utility of such a comparative approach as a test for assessing whether a particular punitive award is presumptively unconstitutional.

It is a relatively straightforward task to draw intrajurisdictional and interjurisdic-tional comparisons on such matters as the definition of first-degree murder (Schad) or the penalty imposed on nonviolent repeat offenders (Solem). The same cannot be said of the task of drawing such comparisons with regard to punitive damages awards by juries. Such awards are the product of numerous, and sometimes intangible, factors; a jury imposing a punitive damages award must make a qualitative assessment based on a host of facts and circumstances unique to the particular case before it. Because no two cases are truly identical, meaningful comparisons of such awards are difficult to make. Such analysis might be useful in considering whether a state practice of permitting juries to rely on a particular factor, such as the defendant's out-of-state status, would violate due process. As an analytical approach to assessing a particular award, however, we are skeptical. Thus, while we do not rule out the possibility that the fact that an award is significantly larger than those in apparently sim-ilar circumstances might, in a given case, be one of many relevant considerations, we are not prepared to enshrine petitioner's compar-ative approach in a "test" for assessing the constitutionality of punitive damages awards.

In the end, then, in determining whether a particular award is so "grossly excessive" as to violate the Due Process Clause of the Fourteenth Amendment, Waters-Pierce Oil Co., we return to what we said two Terms ago in Haslip: "We need not, and indeed we cannot, draw a mathematical bright line between the constitutionally acceptable and the constitutionally unacceptable that would fit every case. We can say, however, that [a] general concern of reasonableness . . . properly enters into the constitutional calculus." And, to echo Haslip once again, it is with this concern for reasonableness in mind that we turn to petitioner's argument that the punitive award in this case was so "grossly excessive" as to violate the substantive component of the Due Process Clause.

In support of its submission that this award is "grossly excessive," TXO places its primary emphasis on the fact that it is over 526 times as large as the actual damages award. TXO correctly notes that state courts have long held that "exemplary damages allowed should bear some proportion to the real damage sustained." Moreover, in our recent decision in Haslip, supra, in which we upheld a punitive damages award of four times the amount of compensatory damages, we noted that award "may be close to the line" of constitutional permissibility. Following that decision, the West Virginia Supreme Court of Appeals had also observed that as "a matter of fundamental fairness, punitive damages should bear a reasonable relationship to compensatory damages."

That relationship, however, was only one of the several factors that the State Court mentioned in its Garnes opinion. Earlier in its opinion it gave this example:

> "For instance, a man wildly fires a gun into a crowd. By sheer chance, no one is injured and the only damage is to a $10 pair of glasses. A jury reasonably could find only $10 in compensatory damages, but thousands of dollars in punitive damages to teach a duty of care. We would allow a jury to impose substantial punitive damages in order too discourage future bad acts."

When the Court identified the several factors that should be mentioned in instructions to the jury, the first one that it mentioned reflected that example. It said:

> "Punitive damages should bear a reasonable relationship to the harm that is likely to occur from the defendant's conduct as well as to the harm that actually has occurred. If the defendant's actions caused or would likely cause in a similar situation only slight harm, the damages should be relatively small. If the harm is grievous, the damages should be much greater."

Taking account of the potential harm that might result from the defendant's conduct in calculating punitive damages was consistent with the views we expressed in Haslip, supra. In that case we endorsed the standards that the Alabama Supreme Court had previously announced, one of which was "whether there is a reasonable relationship between the punitive damages award and the harm likely to result from the defendant's conduct as well as the harm that actually has occurred."

We agree with TXO that the emphasis [in the instructions to the jury] on the wealth of the wrongdoer increased the risk that the award may have been influenced by prejudice against large corporations, a risk that is of special concern when the defendant is a nonresident. We note, however, that in Haslip we referred to the "financial position" of the defendant as one factor that could be taken into account in assessing punitive damages. We also note that TXO did not squarely argue in the West Virginia Supreme Court of Appeals that these aspects of the jury instruction violated the Due Process Clause, possibly because many States permit the jury to take account of the defendant's wealth. Because TXO's constitutional attack on the jury instructions was not properly presented to the highest court of the State, we do not pass on it.

The judgment of the West Virginia Supreme Court of Appeals is affirmed.

CASE FOLLOW-UP

This case is significant for several reasons. From a pragmatic standpoint, it represents a significant setback for business interests that have asserted in recent years that jury awards against corporations are excessive and crippling, in some part because of an ostensible antipathy toward and prejudice against big business. As tort reform proponents seek to place limits on the magnitude of jury awards through state legislation, this case suggests that other states declining to curb jury awards will not be easily inhibited by constitutional limitations. From a legal standpoint, this case suggests that substantive due process will continue to play a limited role in protecting businesses from extremely large punitive damages awards.

EQUAL PROTECTION

The equal protection clause of the federal Constitution is contained in the Fourteenth Amendment. It says that no state shall "deny to any person within its jurisdiction the equal protection of the laws." Under ordinary circumstances, laws that discriminate against certain kinds of businesses will be upheld under equal protection analysis, provided there is a "rational basis" for the distinction made. As you will see later in this chapter, certain forms of invidious discrimination—such as on the basis of race—must meet the higher standard of promoting a "compelling state interest." In other words, two standards are used for determining whether differential treatment by statute is constitutional.

In the following case, in which only economic values are at stake, the Court is guided in its equal protection analysis by the *rational basis test*. This test requires a plausible or arguable basis for the legislative classification—a classification that differentiates in its treatment of apparently equal entities. For example, large businesses may be treated differently from small ones, retail stores may be treated differently from wholesale outlets, and metal products may be treated differently from plastic ones. These classifications do not violate the equal protection clause if they are supported on sound and reasonable grounds.

Following *Minnesota* v. *Clover Leaf Creamery*, a case that deals with a state ban on the retail sale of milk in nonreturnable and nonrefillable plastic containers, you will be introduced to situations dealing with fundamental constitutional rights and suspect classifications. In those cases, the Court is not nearly so casual in its analysis of the legislative classification as it is in cases involving economic considerations only.

Minnesota v. Clover Leaf Creamery Company

449 U.S. 456 (1981)

BRENNAN, JUSTICE

The parties agree that the standard of review applicable to this case under the Equal Protection Clause is the familiar "rational basis" test. Moreover, they agree that the purposes of the Act cited by the legislature—promoting resource conservation, easing solid waste disposal problems, and conserving energy—are legitimate state purposes. Thus, the controversy in this case centers on the narrow issue whether the legislative classification between plastic and nonplastic nonreturnable milk containers is rationally related to achievement of the statutory purposes.

Respondents apparently have not challenged the *theoretical* connection between a ban on plastic nonreturnables and the purposes articulated by the legislature; instead, they have argued that there is no *empirical* connection between the two. They produced impressive supporting evidence at trial to prove that the probable consequences of the ban on plastic nonreturnable milk containers will be to deplete natural resources, exacerbate solid waste disposal problems, and waste energy, because consumers unable to purchase milk in plastic containers will turn to paperboard milk cartons, allegedly a more environmentally harmful product.

But States are not required to convince the courts of the correctness of their legislative judgments. Rather, "those challenging the legislative judgment must convince the court that the legislative facts on which the classification is apparently based could not reasonably be conceived to be true by the governmental decision-maker."

Although parties challenging legislation under the Equal Protection Clause may introduce evidence supporting their claim that it is irrational, they cannot prevail so long as "it is evident from all the considerations presented to [the legislature], and those of which we may take judicial notice, that the question is at least debatable." Where there was evidence before the legislature reasonably supporting the classification, litigants may not procure invalidation of the legislation merely by tendering evidence in court that the legislature was mistaken. . . .

The State identifies four reasons why the classification between plastic and nonplastic nonreturnables is rationally related to the articulated statutory purposes. If any one of the four substantiated the State's claim, we must reverse the Minnesota Supreme Court and sustain the Act.

First, the State argues that elimination of the popular plastic milk jug will encourage the use of environmentally superior containers. . . .

. . . This Court has made clear that a legislature need not "strike at all evils at the same time or in the same way," and that a legislature "may implement [its] program step by step, . . . adopting regulations that only partially ameliorate a perceived evil and deferring complete elimination of the evil to future regulations." The Equal Protection Clause does not deny the State of Minnesota the authority to ban one type of milk container conceded to cause environmental problems, merely because another type, already established in the market, is permitted to continue in use. Whether *in fact* the Act will promote more environmentally desirable milk packaging is not the question: the

Equal Protection Clause is satisfied by our conclusion that the Minnesota Legislature could *rationally have decided* that its ban on plastic nonreturnable milk jugs might foster greater use of environmentally desirable alternatives.

Second, the State argues that its ban on plastic nonreturnable milk containers will reduce the economic dislocation foreseen from the movement toward greater use of environmentally superior containers. . . .

Moreover, the State explains, to ban both the plastic and the paperboard nonreturnable milk container at once would cause an enormous disruption in the milk industry because few dairies are now able to package their products in refillable bottles or plastic pouches. Thus, by banning the plastic container while continuing to permit the paperboard container, the State was able to prevent the industry from becoming reliant on the new container, while avoiding severe economic dislocation.

★ ★ ★

Third, the State argues that the Act will help to conserve energy. It points out that plastic milk jugs are made from plastic resin, an oil and natural gas derivative, whereas paperboard milk cartons are primarily composed of pulpwood, which is a renewable source. . . .

The Minnesota Supreme Court may be correct that the Act is not a sensible means of conserving energy. But we reiterate that "it is up to legislatures, not courts, to decide on the wisdom and utility of legislation." Since in view of the evidence before the legislature, the question clearly is "at least debatable," the Minnesota Supreme Court erred in substituting its judgment for that of the legislature.

Fourth, the State argues that the Act will ease the State's solid waste disposal problem. . . .

The Minnesota Supreme Court found that plastic milk jugs in fact take up less space in landfills and present fewer solid waste disposal problems than do paperboard containers. But its ruling on this point must be rejected for the same reason we rejected its ruling concerning energy conservation: it is not the function of the courts to substitute their evaluation of legislative facts for that of the legislature.

The Supreme Court of Minnesota is reversed.

CASE FOLLOW-UP

The Court has preserved an immense amount of discretion and latitude for the legislature in its dealing with matters that would cost some business firms a lot of money. This case addressed a state statute, and it gave this legislature a wide range to choose from alternative ways of dealing with environmental problems. That is expected. State legislators are, after all, sworn to uphold the Constitution. Their choices are entitled to as much dignity and respect as those made by Congress. The fact that a legislature may have made a misjudgment or may have got its facts wrong does not affect the Supreme Court's decision. A state legislature, operating under the Tenth Amendment, or Congress, operating under Article I, Section 8, may pass wise or foolish laws, practical or impractical laws, but if there is some rational, plausible, or arguable basis for the classifications made by these laws, they do not violate the equal protection clause.

The most recent case law suggests that businesses will have an increasingly difficult time challenging forms of economic discrimination in the future using equal protection arguments. In *FCC* v. *Beach Communications, Inc.*,[5] the Supreme Court upheld provisions of the Cable Act of 1984, which exempted from regulation cable systems for multiple-unit dwellings under common ownership or management but denied exemption to multiple-unit dwellings under separate ownership or management. Neither the Cable Act of 1984 nor its legislative history suggested even a rational basis for this distinction in regulatory coverage; nonetheless, the Court noted that a statute must be upheld if there is "any reasonably conceivable state of facts that could provide a rational basis for the classification." From this holding, one can infer that the Supreme Court confers tremendous discretion to state and federal legislators to fashion distinctions in treatment of various groups under the "rational basis" standard.

EQUAL PROTECTION AND RACIAL DISCRIMINATION

Brown v. *Board of Education*[6] is perhaps the most notable and far-reaching equal protection case of this century. It has touched practically every aspect of society in its wake. *Brown* ended the 105-year-old constitutional career of "separate but equal" facilities, a policy that dates back at least to *Roberts* v. *City of Boston* (1849).[7] Following the Civil War, the separate-but-equal approach to race relations was extended from Boston's racially segregated educational system to many other areas of the nation's political and social life.

Plessy v. *Ferguson*[8] dignified Louisiana's requirement of racial segregation in the transportation industry with constitutional sanction despite the resounding dissent of a lone voice, that of Justice John Marshall Harlan:

> [I]n view of the constitution, in the eye of the law, there is in this country no superior, dominant, ruling class of citizens. There is no caste here. Our constitution is color-blind, and neither knows nor tolerates classes among citizens. In respect of civil rights, all citizens are equal before the law. The humblest is the peer of the most powerful. The law regards man as man, and takes no account of his surroundings, or of his color when his civil rights as guaranteed by the supreme law of the land are involved. . . . In my opinion, the judgment this day rendered will, in time, prove to be quite as pernicious as the decision made by this tribunal in the Dred Scott case.

★ ★ ★

> We boast of the freedom enjoyed by our people above all other peoples. But it is difficult to reconcile that boast with a state of law which, practically, puts the brand of servitude and degradation upon a large class of our fellow citizens—our equals before the law. The thin disguise of "equal accommodations" for passengers in railroad coaches will not mislead any one, nor atone for the wrong this day done . . . 163 U.S. at 559, 562.

Brown also posed a confrontation between two of this country's outstanding attorneys: Thurgood Marshall, general counsel of the NAACP's Legal Defense and Education Fund and, years later, a President Lyndon B. Johnson appointee to the Supreme Court; and Wall Street lawyer John W. Davis, Democratic presidential nominee in 1924, whose 140 oral arguments before the Supreme Court included a victory in *Youngstown Sheet and Tube Co.* v. *Sawyer.*[9] Marshall's weakest point seemed to be that the same Congress that proposed the Fourteenth Amendment also segregated the schools in the District of Columbia. Davis's theme was that, although segregation might inflict harm in a sociological sense, reversal of a century-old policy would be nevertheless unfair. In oral argument, he urged: "Somewhere, sometime, to every principle comes a moment of repose when it has been so often announced, so confidently relied upon, so long continued, that it passes the limits of judicial discretion and disturbance." As events proved, such was not to be the case with "separate but equal."

Brown v. *Board of Education*
347 U.S. 483 (1954)

WARREN, CHIEF JUSTICE

[*Authors' note*: Cases from the state of Kansas, South Carolina, Virginia, and Delaware were consolidated for argument.]

The plaintiffs contend that segregated public schools are not "equal" and cannot be made "equal," and that hence they are deprived of the equal protection of the laws. Because of the obvious importance of the question presented, the Court took jurisdiction. Argument . . . and reargument . . . [were] largely devoted to the circumstance surrounding the adoption of the Fourteenth Amendment in 1868. It covered exhaustively consideration of the Amendment in Congress, ratification by the states, then existing practices in racial segregation, and the views of proponents and opponents of the Amendment. This discussion and our own investigation convince us that, although these sources cast some light, it is not enough to resolve the problem with which we are faced. At best, they are inconclusive.

In the first cases in this Court construing the Fourteenth Amendment, decided shortly after its adoption, the Court interpreted it as proscribing all state-imposed discriminations against the Negro race. The doctrine of "separate but equal" did not

make its appearance in this Court until 1896 in the case of *Plessy* v. *Ferguson* involving not education but transportation. American courts have since labored with the doctrine for over half a century.

★ ★ ★

We come then to the question presented: Does segregation of children in public schools solely on the basis of race, even though the physical facilities and other "tangible" factors may be equal, deprive the children of the minority group of equal educational opportunities? We believe that it does.

In *Sweatt* v. *Painter*, on finding that a segregated law school for Negroes could not provide them equal educational opportunities, this Court relied in large part on "those qualities which are incapable of objective measurement but which make for greatness in a law school." In *McLaurin* v. *Oklahoma State Regents*, the Court, in requiring that a Negro admitted to a white graduate school be treated like all other students, again resorted to intangible considerations: . . . his ability to study, to engage in discussions and exchange views with other students, and, in general, to learn his profession." Such considerations apply with added force to children in grade and high schools. To separate them from others of similar age and qualifications solely because of their race generates a feeling of inferiority as to their status in the community that may affect their hearts and minds in a way unlikely ever to be undone. The effect of this separation on their educational opportunities was well stated by a finding in the Kansas case by a court which nevertheless felt compelled to rule against the Negro plaintiffs:

> Segregation of white and colored children in public schools has a detrimental effect upon the colored children. The impact is greater when it has the sanction of the law; for the policy of separating the races is usually interpreted as denoting the inferiority of the Negro group. A sense of inferiority affects the motivation of a child to learn. Segregation with the sanction of law, therefore, has a tendency to [retard] the educational and mental

development of Negro children and to deprive them of some of the benefits they would receive in a racial[ly] integrated school system.

Whatever may have been the extent of psychological knowledge at the time of *Plessy* v. *Ferguson*, this finding is amply supported by modern authority. Any language in *Plessy* v. *Ferguson* contrary to this finding is rejected.

We conclude that in the field of public education the doctrine of "separate but equal" has no place. Separate educational facilities are inherently unequal. Therefore, we hold that the plaintiffs and others similarly situated for whom the actions have been brought are, by reason of the segregation complained of, deprived of the equal protection of the laws guaranteed by the Fourteenth Amendment. This disposition makes unnecessary any discussion whether such segregation also violates the Due Process Clause of the Fourteenth Amendment.

CASE FOLLOW-UP

Brown does not stand for the proposition that there can be no discrimination in the public school system. It simply demands a *reasonable* or *rational basis* for such discrimination. For example, in a classroom situation the teacher may divide the class into groups that include slow learners, average students, and high achievers for the purpose of facilitating special attention, for providing appropriate learning materials, or for other aca-

demically sound purposes. But these are legitimate classifications based on demonstrated learning abilities and are not arbitrarily chosen.

The Court restored *Brown* to its docket for the purpose of hearing argument on the appropriate form of relief to be granted. Subsequently, it concluded that desegregation was to proceed "with all deliberate speed."

STRICT EQUAL PROTECTION: FUNDAMENTAL RIGHTS AND SUSPECT CRITERIA

Since *Brown*, the Court has begun a careful scrutiny of governmental policies that classify or discriminate on the basis of *fundamental rights* (rights explicitly or implicitly guaranteed by the Constitution, such as voting and freedom of speech, as-

PART ONE · Introduction to the Study of the American Legal Environment

sociation, and privacy) or *suspect criteria* (criteria determined by accident of birth, such as race, gender, religion, national origin, alienage). When these matters are at stake, the statutory classification must, as always, be supported by some rational justification, but beyond that the classification must be shown to be *necessary to promote some compelling state interest* and *narrowly drawn to protect that state interest through the least burdensome alternative*.[10]

For example, the right to travel freely among the states is a constitutionally protected "fundamental" right. Hence, a state residency classification of one year in order to qualify for a basic necessity of life, such as free medical care for the indigent, was found to be in violation of the Court's strict scrutiny doctrine. Economizing on the cost of such programs was not found to be a sufficiently compelling reason.[11]

In addition to the right of interstate travel, other fundamental rights that merit strict scrutiny are voting rights, the right to procreate, and the right to basic procedural guarantees in criminal trials.

Among the suspect criteria, discrimination against blacks and other racial minorities receives the strictest scrutiny. Programs designed to benefit these groups have received a more limited or lenient evaluation even though they have the effect of imposing "reverse discrimination" on members of the majority group (these measures are discussed further in Chapter 15, "Labor and Employment Law").

State and federal laws that discriminate on the basis of gender, alienage, and illegitimacy receive something less than full, strict scrutiny. Although it must sound like playing with words, the Court has applied a kind of "intermediate scrutiny" by saying that such discrimination must be *substantially related* to advancing an *important governmental interest*. This refinement has had the practical effect of upholding a federal statute requiring men but not women to register for the draft and of striking down a Louisiana law that prohibited illegitimate children, but not legitimate children, from receiving certain benefits on the death of their parents.

THE COMMERCE POWER

One chief factor leading to the Constitutional Convention of 1787 was the inclination of each state to exploit its trade advantages at the expense of others. States with natural harbors wanted to tax goods destined for other parts of the country, and each state faced the temptation to tax out-of-state goods that competed with homegrown industries. The framers recognized such rivalry to be counterproductive to the well-being of the nation.

Thus, Article I, Section 8 conferred on Congress the commerce power, along with taxing, money, war, and other powers. The necessary and proper clause, which concluded Section 8, further authorized Congress to act in ways not specifically enumerated. The framers evidently intended to give Congress a certain amount of latitude in choosing among alternative means of achieving its enumerated powers.

McCULLOCH v. MARYLAND

Nowhere in the Constitution was Congress authorized to charter a bank, yet in 1791 it created one with a twenty-year charter. Five years after that charter expired, Congress established a second bank, and when a state attempted to tax the U.S. bank notes, the stage was set for a great constitutional showdown—*McCulloch* v. *Maryland*.[17]

The first issue was whether Congress acted within its powers; the second issue, if Congress had such powers, was whether Maryland could levy a tax on a federal bank's operations. In opposition to Maryland's argument that the necessary and proper clause conveyed only powers that were absolutely necessary and essential—powers consistent with the notions of John Locke and Thomas Jefferson that governments should be strictly limited—Daniel Webster convinced the Court that the framers intended Congress to have ample flexibility and discretion. After all, the clause was in the section of the Constitution that grants congressional powers, not limitations of these powers as in Article I, Section 9. Furthermore, where the framers intended that actions be "absolutely necessary," the Constitution stated that intention specifically, as in the Article I, Section 10 limitations on state taxation of imports or exports. Such taxes are permitted only to the extent that they are "absolutely necessary for executing its inspection laws."

John Marshall ended all debate on the matter with a famous pronouncement in support of broad congressional powers.

> Let the end be legitimate, let it be within the scope of the Constitution and all means which are appropriate, which are plainly adapted to that end, which are not prohibited, but consist with the letter and spirit of the Constitution, are constitutional. 4 Wheaton at 420.

From the conclusion that Congress had the power to create such a bank, it logically followed that the bank should be free of state intrusions. After all, "the power to tax involves the power to destroy." If Maryland were allowed to tax the federal bank, so could all the other states, and that would simply be intolerable.

GIBBONS v. OGDEN

Writing for the Court in *Gibbons* v. *Ogden*,[13] Chief Justice Marshall explained that commerce means commercial intercourse and that this includes navigation. The commerce that Congress may regulate is "among the several states." This means the power does not "stop at the external boundary line of each state, but may be introduced into the interior." Interstate commerce is not completely internal; it must "concern more states than one." In addition, Marshall continued, commerce-clause power is a complete, plenary power. It is a power that "may be exercised to its utmost extent," without limitations other than those expressly proscribed by the Constitution. The test of whether Congress has validly exercised its commerce-clause power, extrapolated from *Gibbons,* is whether the subject "affects interstate commerce."

The Chief Justice crystallized his thoughts as follows:

The genius and character of the whole government seems to be, that its action is to be applied to all the external concerns of the nation, and to those internal concerns which affect the states generally; but not to those which are completely within a particular state, which do not affect other states, and with which it is not necessary to interfere, for the purpose of executing some of the general powers of the government. The completely internal commerce of a state, then, may be considered as reserved to the state itself. . . . 9 Wheaton at 195.

THE BALANCING ACT: COMMERCE CLAUSE PROBLEMS WHEN CONGRESS HAS NOT ACTED

When Congress has *not* enacted legislation in a particular area, courts are sometimes confronted with the issue of how much latitude to allow states in restraining or influencing the free flow of interstate commerce. If the intrusion on interstate commerce by a state is blatant and discriminatory (e.g., if for economic reasons Texas prohibits the sale within its border of out-of-state citrus products), then a court will find it unconstitutional. But how should courts go about deciding cases in which the state is advancing a legitimate, local, Tenth Amendment issue—that is, the health, safety, or welfare of its citizens—but in which the statute has some sort of ripple effect on interstate commerce? Is it merely a matter of degree? And if it is, how does a court go about balancing safety and health of human beings against expense and inconvenience to interstate commerce?

SOUTHERN PACIFIC RAILROAD v. ARIZONA

In *Southern Pacific Railroad* v. *Arizona*,[14] the Court declared unconstitutional a state safety law that limited freight trains to seventy cars and passenger trains to fourteen in place of the standard industry practice allowing much longer trains. Chief Justice Stone "second-guessed" the Arizona legislature as follows:

Here we conclude that the state does go too far. Its regulation of train lengths, admittedly obstructive to interstate train operation, and having a seriously adverse effect on transportation efficiency and economy, passes beyond what is plainly essential for safety since it does not appear that it will lessen rather than increase the danger of accident. 325 U.S. at 765.

One has to wonder how appropriate it is for the court to set aside a state policy that might save human life and injury in order to promote transportation efficiency and economy. This is admittedly a difficult question. By way of guidance, the Court further observed:

. . . Although the commerce clause conferred on the national government power to regulate commerce, its possession of the power does not exclude all state power of regulation. It has been recognized that, in the absence of conflicting legislation by Congress, there is a residuum of power in the state to make laws governing matters of local concern which nevertheless in some measure affect interstate commerce or even, to some extent, regulate it. . . . Thus the states may regulate matters which, because of their number and diversity, may never be adequately dealt with by Congress.

But ever since *Gibbons* v. *Ogden* . . . the states have not been deemed to have authority to impede substantially the free flow of commerce from state to state, or to regulate those phases of the national commerce which, because of the need of national uniformity, demand that their regulation, if any, be prescribed by a single authority. . . . 325 U.S. at 761.

HURON PORTLAND CEMENT CO. v. *DETROIT*

Fifteen years later, and while still purporting to be guided by the principles in *Southern Pacific*, the court upheld a local health ordinance (the Smoke Abatement Code) that operated against an interstate carrier. The principle points of Portland Cement's argument in *Huron Portland Cement Co.* v. *Detroit*[15] were as follows:

- A comprehensive system of federal inspection, regulation, and licensing of Great Lakes shipping preempted the ordinance.

- The Smoke Abatement Code materially affected interstate commerce in matters for which *national uniformity is necessary* (the intrusion is comparable to that of the Arizona Train Limit Law).

Speaking for the Court, Justice Stewart rejected the plaintiff's argument and wrote

. . . Evenhanded local regulation to effectuate a legitimate local public interest is valid unless preempted by federal action . . . or unduly burdensome on maritime activities or interstate commerce. . . .

In determining whether state regulation has been pre-empted by federal action, "the intent to supersede the exercise by the state of its police power as to matters not covered by the Federal legislation is not to be inferred from the mere fact that Congress has seen fit to circumscribe its regulation and to occupy a limited field. In other words, such intent is not to be implied unless the act of Congress, fairly interpreted, is in actual conflict with the law of the state. . . ."

In determining whether the state has imposed an undue burden on interstate commerce, it must be borne in mind that the Constitution when "conferring upon Congress the regulation of commerce . . . never intended to cut the states off from legislating on all subjects relating to the health, life, and safety of their citizens, though the legislation might indirectly affect the commerce of the country. . . . But a state may not impose a burden which materially affects intestate commerce in an area where uniformity of regulation is necessary. . . .

★ ★ ★

TAXING AND SPENDING POWERS

Constitutional law is filled with instances of balancing various interests. The taxing power, like the power to legislate under the commerce clause, is another important example.

FEDERAL TAXATION

Article 1, Section 8 enumerates federal taxing and spending powers: "The Congress shall have Power to lay and collect Taxes . . . to pay the Debts and provide for the common Defense and general Welfare." For lack of a taxing power, the Confederation almost collapsed, so the framers made certain that defect was corrected. Taxation is the principal means of raising revenue, but the same section further conferred on Congress the power to borrow and coin money and to regulate its value. Borrowing money by issuing Treasury bills or Federal Reserve notes, for example, is a way of raising money to pay debts and to provide for defense and welfare. The fact that this borrowing may also have an inflationary impact on the economy is a matter of public policy for national lawmakers to determine. Its constitutional basis is a sound one, however.

Although Congress can tax and spend to promote the public well-being or welfare, it is not empowered to legislate *generally* for that purpose. The federal government is a government of enumerated or limited powers, and if it could legislate on any topic whatsoever, this limitation would be lost. States and their subdivisions—counties (or parishes) and municipalities—can legislate broadly for the general welfare under the Tenth Amendment.

Congress can use its taxing power to regulate a socially harmful activity and, in a sense, legislate for the general welfare. In *United States* v. *Doremus*,[16] the Court upheld as a constitutional revenue-raising measure a $1 per year tax on any person selling narcotics unless he or she used an official IRS order form (physicians treating patients were not covered). To the defendant's argument that this tax hardly raised sufficient revenue to finance its own enforcement, the Court replied that "the fact that other motives may impel the exercise of Federal taxing power does not authorize the courts to inquire into the subject. If the legislation enacted has some reasonable relation to the exercise of the taxing authority conferred by the Constitution, it cannot be invalidated because of the supposed motives which induced it." 249 U.S. at 93.

STATE TAXATION

Under the Tenth Amendment, states retain, among other powers, the power to tax. When these taxes fall on the instrumentalities of interstate commerce, however, conflicts can arise. For example, many firms in the United States are large enough to have operations in each of the fifty states. Multiple or duplicative state income or property taxation could easily bankrupt a firm. Interstate commerce could thus be unreasonably burdened, or states could use the taxing process to discriminate against out-of-state firms while promoting their local industries.

Multiple taxation, or taxation whereby each state levies on the nationwide sales, revenues, income, or property of a firm, will be unduly burdensome and hence unconstitutional. But if these state laws are fairly apportioned—that is, limited to the sales, revenues, income, payroll, or property generated or located within the state—the constitutional hurdle can be overcome. After all, interstate commerce should be expected to pay its own way, so if a plausible connection can be made between the state and the business activity, the tax will pass constitutional muster.

The case of *Commonwealth Edison Company* v. *Montana* deals with some of these relationships in the context of a mineral severance tax. The case involves a state's ability to tax and thereby regulate products (minerals) originating within the state and then shipped to other parts of the country. The plaintiff's argument was that the tax discriminated against interstate commerce.

Commonwealth Edison Company v. Montana
453 U.S. 690 (1981)

MARSHALL, JUSTICE

[*Authors' Note*: Montana imposed a severance tax on the extraction of its low-sulfur coal. The rate of tax varied according to value, energy content, and method of extraction; maximum rate allowed was 30 percent of the contract price. Four coal companies and eleven out-of-state coal buyers filed suit, alleging that the severance tax was unconstitutional. The trial court upheld the tax, and the Supreme Court of Montana affirmed.]

Montana, like many other States, imposes a severance tax on mineral production in the State. In this appeal, we consider whether the tax Montana levies on each ton of coal mined in the State . . . violates the Commerce and Supremacy Clauses of the United States Constitution. . . .

. . . We agree with appellants that the Montana tax must be evaluated under *Complete Auto Transit's* four-part test. Under that test, a state tax does not offend the Commerce Clause if it "is applied to an activity with a substantial nexus with the taxing State, is fairly apportioned, does not discriminate against interstate commerce, and is fairly related to services provided by the State."

Appellants do not dispute that the Montana tax satisfies the first two prongs of *Complete Auto Transit* test. . . . Appellants do

contend, however, that the Montana tax is invalid under the third and fourth prongs of the *Complete Auto Transit* test.

Appellants assert that the Montana tax "discriminate[s] against interstate commerce" because 90% of Montana coal is shipped to other States under contracts that shift the tax burden primarily to non-Montana utility companies and thus to citizens of other States. But the Montana tax is computed at the same rate regardless of the final destination of the coal, and there is no suggestion here that the tax is administered in a manner that departs from this even-handed formula. We are not, therefore, confronted here with the type of differential tax treatment of interstate and intrastate commerce that the Court has found in other "discrimination" cases. . . .

. . . Rather, appellants assume that the Commerce Clause gives residents of one State a right of access at "reasonable" prices to resources located in another State that is richly endowed with such resources, without regard to whether and on what terms residents of the resource-rich State have access to the resources. We are not convinced that the Commerce Clause, of its own force, gives the residents of one State the right to control in this fashion the terms of resource development and depletion in a sister State. . . .

In any event, appellants' discrimination theory ultimately collapses into their claim that the Montana tax is invalid under the fourth prong of the *Complete Auto Transit* test: that the tax is not "fairly related to the services provided by the State." . . . Because appellants concede that Montana may impose *some* severance tax on coal mined in the State, the only remaining foundation for their discrimination theory is a claim that the tax burden borne by the out-of-state consumers of Montana coal is excessive. . . .

. . . Thus, appellant's objection is to the *rate* of the Montana tax, and even then, their only complaint is that the *amount* the State receives in taxes far exceeds the *value* of the services provided to the coal mining industry. . . .

This Court has indicated that States have considerable latitude in imposing general revenue taxes. . . .

. . . [T]here can be no question that Montana may constitutionally raise general revenue by imposing a severance tax on coal mined in the State. The entire value of the coal, before transportation, originates in the State, and mining of the coal depletes the resource base and wealth of the State, thereby diminishing a future source of taxes and economic activity. . . .

Against this background, we have little difficulty concluding that the Montana tax satisfies the fourth prong of the *Complete Auto Transit test.* . . .

. . . *Consequently, the judgment of the Supreme Court of Montana is affirmed.*

CASE FOLLOW-UP

On the basis of *Complete Auto Transit, Inc.* v. *Brady*,[17] the activity taxed must have a substantial *nexus*, or connection, with the taxing state. This simply means that Montana could impose a severance tax on its own coal but certainly not on the coal mined in Wyoming, for example. *Fair apportionment* means the tax must be computed by a formula that does not allow multiple or overlapping levies by other taxing authorities. The test is met here because severance of minerals is an event that occurs in one state only. *Discrimination* against interstate commerce for the purpose of protecting a home industry and giving it an unfair competitive advantage is not a viable issue here. Montana is taxing "home" goods, not those involved in interstate commerce. Besides, the same rate is charged to intrastate as to interstate purchases. If the intrastate rate was half that of the interstate rate, discrimination could be proven. Finally, the argument that the tax is simply too high (exorbitant, con-

fiscatory) in relation to services provided by the state fails because the Court gives states great leeway in imposing general revenue taxes. After all, if a strict dollar-of-state-service per dollar-of-tax were a constitutional requirement, the state would not be able to raise any surplus revenue for the future. It would merely break even.

Due process does not impose an automatic ceiling or limitation on the tax rate. It simply demands that the *means* chosen by Montana be reasonably related to a legitimate Tenth Amendment *goal*, which is raising revenue. That relationship was fulfilled.

This case had to do with taxing an activity—the severance of minerals—that was wholly within the state of Montana. If the state had tried to impose a tax burden on an interstate activity (e.g., a state tax on interstate goods for the privilege of passing through Montana), that tax would not stand the test of constitutionality. Nor would the tax survive if it were a disguised attempt to inhibit or bar the sale of out-of-state goods to promote a home-grown industry. For example, Kansas can not constitutionally levy a tax on Nebraska or South Dakota wheat to promote the economic well-being of its own farmers. In *Bacchus Imports, Ltd.* v. *Dias*,[18] the Supreme Court found that Hawaii's excise tax of 20 percent on the sales of liquor at wholesale was discriminatory because it exempted certain locally produced alcoholic beverages for the purpose of encouraging the development of a Hawaiian liquor industry.

THE FIRST AMENDMENT

> Congress shall make no law respecting an establishment of religion, or prohibiting the free exercise thereof; or abridging the freedom of speech, or of the press; or the right of the people peaceably to assemble, and to petition the Government for a redress of grievances.

First Amendment guarantees—religion, speech, press, peaceable assembly, and petition—are written in absolute terms. On the face or literal language of the amendment, neither Congress nor the states can in any way intrude on or interfere with these guarantees. The states are included in this prohibition because the Supreme Court has interpreted the due process clause of the Fourteenth Amendment in such a way that it protects individuals from any state intrusions on the rights embodied in the First Amendment.

This literal, word-for-word understanding could be described as an *absolutist* position, one that admits of no exception. This position has never fully gained the support of the Supreme Court, although, to give one example, it had a remarkable spokesman in Justice Hugo Black. Justice Black's view, quite simply, was that *no law* means *no law*, and that a simple acknowledgment of the plain meaning of the amendment's language was sufficient to resolve all questions in favor of no governmental interference at all.

Most members of the Supreme Court, however, have never adopted such an absolutist position. In general, they support an effort to balance the interests people have in protecting First Amendment rights against the interests the people have in protecting other important values. For example, in *Engle* v. *Vitale*,[19] the Court found "school prayer" to be unconstitutional, yet the Court itself opens each session with prayerful language. Congress does the same thing, and the motto *In God We Trust* is inscribed on U.S. coins and the phrase *"one nation under God"* is in the Pledge of Allegiance.

In a later section, we discuss a balancing approach to speech. For now, consider the following illustration. If your reputation is slandered or libeled through oral or written speech, your lawsuit will seek a state or federal court damage judgment against the defendant speaker. Such court action is an intrusion on the defendant's right to speak freely. Do you agree with the Court that such defamation suits are constitutional? Is such a balance appropriate in your view? Because English and Colonial courts recognized defamation suits before the American Revolution, it is possible that the framers of the First Amendment did not intend for their words to be taken literally.

FREEDOM OF RELIGION

What is an establishment of religion? The earliest official though nonjudicial interpretation came from the author of the [First A]mendment. In 1811 a Baptist meetinghouse stood on public lands in Mississippi Territory. Congress, in confirming certain land grants, provided in the bill that five acres "be reserved for the use of the Baptist Church, at said meetinghouse." Nobody objected to the gift, worth about $10.00. But President Madison vetoed the measure, informing the House that he did so "because the bill, in reserving a certain parcel of land of the United States for the use of said Baptist Church, comprises a principle and precedent, for the appropriation of funds of the United States, for the use and support of religious societies; contrary to the article of the Constitution which declares that Congress shall make no law respecting a religious establishment."[20]

The prohibition against state-established religions is only part of the story. Interference with the free exercise of religion is forbidden as well. However, the Court found in the First Amendment nothing to prevent Congress from outlawing the Mormon practice of polygamy in the Utah Territory. In *Reynolds* v. *United States,*[21] the Mormon exercise of religious freedom was analogized by the Court to the immolation of widows on a funeral pyre; polygamy was no more tolerable than suicide or murder. Chief Justice Waite, writing for the Court, deferred to the authority of Thomas Jefferson on these matters by citing Jefferson's "wall of separation between church and state" letter to the Danbury Baptist Association. The Chief Justice then related that Virginia's charter of religious freedom, also authored by Jefferson, concluded with the note that government interference in religion was permissible if ill tendencies "break out into overt acts against peace and good order."

In a 1952 case, *Zorach* v. *Clauson,*[22] the Supreme Court upheld New York's modified "release time" program that coordinated class schedules with off-campus religious instruction services and permitted voluntary student attendance. Dissenting from the majority opinion written by Justice Douglas, Justice Black made clear his view that instead of treating the church-state issue as one in need of constant reinterpretation, the Court should simply acknowledge that the framers of the First Amendment intended to prevent church groups from linking the advancement of religious ideals and practices to legislative action.

In considering whether a state has entered this forbidden field, the question is not whether it has entered too far but whether it has entered at all. New York is manipulating its compulsory education laws to help religious sects get pupils. This is not separation but combination of Church and State. 343 U.S. at 318.

Justice Jackson, reacting to the suggestion that opposition to the New York plan was antireligious, atheistic, or agnostic, was more ascerbic. "The day that this country ceases to be free for irreligion it will cease to be free for religion—except for the sect that can win political power." 343 U.S. at 325.

Engle v. *Vitale* (370 U.S. 421 [1962]) is the most widely noted and most highly criticized Supreme Court decision involving religious freedom in this century. Justice Black wrote the opinion for an 8–1 majority, with Justice Potter Stewart dissenting. The New York State Board of Regents, a constitutional agency empowered by the legislature to exercise supervisory, executive, and legislative powers over public schools, prescribed a nonsectarian prayer to be recited at the beginning of each school day: "Almighty God, we acknowledge our dependence upon Thee, and we beg Thy blessings upon us, our parents, our teachers and our Country." Students could remain silent or be excused during the prayer if they chose.

The parents of ten school children challenged this practice as an infringement of the First Amendment's establishment clause—"Congress shall make no law respecting an establishment of religion . . ."—made applicable to the states through the due process clause of the Fourteenth Amendment. The courts of New York upheld the constitutionality of the regents' prayer; the U.S. Supreme Court reversed.

> There can be no doubt that New York's state prayer program officially established the religious beliefs embodied in the Regents' prayer. The respondents' argument to the contrary, which is largely based upon the contention that the Regents' prayer is "non-denominational" and the fact that the program, as modified and approved by state courts, does not require all pupils to recite the prayer but permits those who wish to do so to remain silent or be excused from the room, ignores the essential nature of the program's constitutional defects. Neither the fact that the prayer may be denominationally neutral nor the fact that its observance on the part of the students is voluntary can serve to free it from the limitations of the Establishment Clause, as it might from the Free Exercise Clause of the First Amendment, both of which are operative against the States by virtue of the Fourteenth Amendment. Although these two clauses may in certain instances overlap, they forbid two quite different kinds of governmental encroachment upon religious freedom. The Establishment Clause, unlike the Free Exercise Clause, does not depend upon any showing of direct governmental compulsion and is violated by the enactment of laws which establish an official religion whether those laws operate directly to coerce nonobserving individuals or not. . . . When the power, prestige and financial support of government is placed behind a particular religious belief, the indirect coercive pressure upon religious minorities to conform to the prevailing officially approved religion is plain. But the purposes underlying the Establishment Clause go much further than that. Its first and most immediate purpose rested on the belief that a union of government and religion tends to destroy government and to degrade religion.

In 1963, one year after *Engle* v. *Vitale*, the Court held that Bible reading and recitation of the Lord's Prayer as part of the daily activity of students required by state law to attend school also violated the establishment clause of the First Amendment.[23]

What is religion in the Court's view? Cases involving conscientious objection under the Selective Service Act have held that a religious belief is more than a mere sociological, philosophical, economic, or political view, but that it does not require belief in any particular dogma or in a Supreme Being. The belief must be sincere and meaningfully held, however, and occupy a place in one's life that is comparable to an orthodox belief in God in the life of a person regarded as religious.[24] If a belief is sincerely held, its reasonableness cannot be questioned. "Men may believe what they cannot prove."[25]

In *Lemon* v. *Kurtzman*,[26] the Supreme Court created a three-part test to determine when policies of the federal, state, or local government do not violate the establishment clause of the First Amendment.

> First the [governmental policy] must have a secular purpose; second, its principal or primary effect must be one that neither advances nor inhibits religion . . . ; finally, the [policy] must not foster "an excessive governmental entanglement with religion." 403 U.S. at 612–613.

In the case you are about to examine, Donald Thornton, a manager of one of the Caldor Incorporated's retail stores, told his employer he would no longer work on Sunday. He refused a transfer to another of Caldor's stores that did close on Sunday and was later demoted. Thornton resigned and filed a grievance with the appropriate state board, citing a Connecticut statute that gave Sabbath observers an absolute right to refuse Sunday work. The Connecticut Supreme Court upheld the board's decision in Thornton's favor, and the U.S. Supreme Court granted Caldor's petition for certiorari. The issue was whether the state statute violated the First Amendment establishment clause, and in an opinion authored by Chief Justice Burger, the Supreme Court decided that it did.

Thornton v. *Caldor*
105 S.Ct. 2914 (1985)

BURGER, CHIEF JUSTICE

Under the Religion Clauses, government must guard against activity that impinges on religious freedom, and must take pains not to compel people to act in the name of any religion. In setting the appropriate boundaries in Establishment Clause cases, the Court has frequently relied on our holding in *Lemon* [v. *Kurtzman*, 403 U.S. 692 (1971)], for guidance and we do so here. To pass constitutional muster under *Lemon* a statute must not only have a secular purpose and not foster excessive entanglement of government with religion, its primary effect must not advance or inhibit religion.

The Connecticut statute challenged here guarantees every employee, who "states that a particular day of the week is observed as his Sabbath," the right not to work on his chosen day. The State has thus decreed that those who observe a Sabbath any day of the week as a matter of religious conviction must be relieved of the duty to work on that day, no matter what burden or inconvenience this imposes on the employer or fellow worker. The state arms Sabbath observers with an absolute and unqualified right not to work on whatever day they designate as their Sabbath.

In essence, the Connecticut statute imposes on employers and employees an absolute duty to conform their business practices to the particular religious practices of the employee by enforcing observance of the Sabbath the employee unilaterally designates. The State thus commands that Sabbath religious concerns automatically control over all secular interest at the workplace; the statute takes no account of the convenience or interests of the employer or those of other employees who do not observe a Sabbath. The employer and others must adjust their affairs to the command of the State whenever the statute is invoked by an employee.

There is no exception under the statute for special circumstances, such as the Friday Sabbath observer employed in an occupation with a Monday through Friday Schedule—a school teacher, for example; the statute provides for no special consideration if a high percentage of an employer's workforce assert rights to the same Sabbath. Moreover, there is no exception when honoring the dictates of Sabbath observers would cause the employer substantial economic burdens or when the employer's compliance would require the imposition of significant burdens on other employees required to work in place of the Sabbath observers. Finally, the statute allows for no consideration as to whether the employer has made reasonable accommodation proposals.

This unyielding weight in favor of Sabbath observers over all other interests contravenes a fundamental principle of the Religion Clauses. . . . As such, the statute goes beyond having an incidental or remote effect of advancing religion. The state has a primary effect that impermissibly advances a particular religious practice.

FREEDOM OF SPEECH, PRESS, AND ASSOCIATION

Is freedom of speech an absolute right subject to no limitation, or is it relative and to be balanced against other important rights? We have already mentioned that Justice Black argued over a number of years that the prohibition against Congress—*no law* means *no law*—was intended to be literal and that this protection applied to state infringements through the Fourteenth Amendment's due process clause. The issue of any "balancing" to be done among competing or mutually incompatible constitutional rights had already been settled by those who wrote and ratified the amendment. Black argued there is simply no room for judges to maneuver within the legitimate confines of the plainly worded prohibition of the First Amendment. If flexibility and discretion can be read into such straightforward language, he urged, freedom is in serious jeopardy.

Since *Gitlow* v. *New York*,[27] protection of this right from state intrusion has become the law of the land, but the Court has never fully endorsed Justice Black's absolutist position. Instead, it has been guided by Justice Holmes's "clear and present danger" test, a formulation first advanced in *Schenck* v. *United States*.[28] Schenck, a socialist, was tried and convicted under the 1918 Espionage Act for distributing leaflets critical of the Draft Act (involuntary servitude) and of the U.S. role in bailing England (more specifically, English and Wall Street "plutocrats") out of World War I. In affirming the conviction, Holmes wrote:

> The most stringent protection of free speech would not protect a man in falsely shouting fire in a theater and causing a panic. It does not even protect a man from an injunction against uttering words that may have all the effect of force. . . . The question in ev-

ery case is whether the words used are used in such circumstances and are of such a nature as to create a clear and present danger that they will bring about the substantive evils that Congress has a right to prevent. It is a question of proximity and degree. 249 U.S. at 52.

The question in every case is whether the evil that the legislature has the right to prevent (e.g., overthrow of the U.S. government by force and violence) is sufficiently clear, present, and imminent to support the conviction or to uphold the statute. Again, in every case, the "evil" must be discounted by the likelihood or probability of being achieved. This means that the prohibition against abridging speech is relaxed to the extent necessary to prevent some real and imminent danger. Rather than being accorded an absolute status in line with the language of the First Amendment—"Congress shall make no law . . . ,"—it becomes relative or contextual; it must be balanced against other rights and, depending on the court's assessment, advanced or diminished as the situation requires.

CORPORATE SPEECH AND THE FIRST AMENDMENT

The First Amendment applies to all phases of people's lives, but within recent years courts have begun to focus on its application to business. The main question in this area has been whether business organizations, such as corporations, have the same First Amendment rights as individuals, or "natural persons."

Supporters of free speech, thought, and expression quite obviously had the rights of natural persons in mind when they advanced the First Amendment, and for good reason. Only natural persons had the capacity to speak, worship, petition, and assemble. Artificial persons (e.g., legal entities such as business corporations) played hardly any formative or constructive role in the thoughts of our forebears or in the settlement or early development of the United States. The concept of corporation was not new, but its historical origin was linked to church-related organizations, municipalities, guilds, and universities[29]—institutions that are not capable of *speech* in the normal sense of the word. One English jurist observed that these legal fictions (*persona ficta*) had "no pants to kick or soul to damn . . . and, by God, [they] ought to have both."[30]

Although corporations were capable of engaging in publication—hence, freedom of the press—the possibility was more potential than real in the late eighteenth century. Presses at that stage of the nation's history were distinctly one-person operations—one natural person, that is.

How have things changed since that time? Corporations are the predominant force in broadcast and print media today, as well as in other aspects of American economic life. Corporate presses have become the norm, rather than the exception to the rule. Broadcast journalism—radio, television, film—has assumed a role not even imagined by the framers of the First Amendment. Has this situation improved the quality of public discussion and political debate? Or has it only raised the noise level? Is this the climate of free thought and expression the framers were trying to bring about? If it is not, is anything about these developments inherently "bad"?

Before pursuing these questions further, we examine *First National Bank of Boston* v. *Bellotti, Attorney General of Massachusetts*. Analyzing this case will help clarify the constitutional grounds on which business as well as publishing corporations have First Amendment rights. By way of background, for constitutional purposes corporations have been treated as persons since the Supreme Court's 1819 *Dartmouth College* case[31] and these artificial persons have been accorded due process and equal protection coverage since 1886.[32]

First National Bank of Boston v. Bellotti, Attorney General of Massachusetts
435 U.S. 765 (1978)

POWELL, JUSTICE

The statute at issue ["§ 8"] prohibits appellants, two national banking associations and three business corporations, from making contributions or expenditures "for the purpose of . . . influencing or affecting the vote on any question submitted to the voters, other than one "materially affecting any of the property, business or assets of the corporation." The statute further specifies that "[n]o question submitted to the voters solely concerning the taxation of the income, property or transactions of individuals shall be deemed materially to affect the property, business or assets of the corporation. . . ."

The court below framed the principal question in this case as whether and to what extent corporations have First Amendment rights. We believe that the court posed the wrong question. The Constitution often protects interests broader than those of the party seeking their vindication. The First Amendment, in particular, serves significant social interests. The proper question therefore is not whether corporations "have" First Amendment rights and, if so, whether they are coextensive with those of natural persons. Instead, the question must be whether § 8 abridges expression that the First Amendment was meant to protect. We hold that it does. . . .

"[T]here is partially universal agreement that a major purpose of [the First] Amendment was to protect the free discussion of governmental affairs." If the speakers here were not corporations, no one would suggest that the State could silence their proposed speech. It is the type of speech indispensable to decision-making in a democracy, and this is no less true because the speech comes from a corporation rather than an individual. The inherent worth of the speech in terms of its capacity for informing the public does not depend upon the identity of its source, whether corporation, association, union, or individual.

. . . The question in this case, simply put, is whether the corporate identity of the speaker deprives this proposed speech of what otherwise would be its clear entitlement to protection. . . .

Freedom of speech and the other freedoms encompassed by the First Amendment always have been viewed as fundamental components of the liberty safeguarded by the Due Process Clause, and the Court has not identified a separate source for the right when it has been asserted by corporations.

* * *

[T]he First Amendment goes beyond protection of the press and the self-expression of individuals to prohibit government from limiting the stock of information from which members of the public may draw. A commercial advertisement is constitutionally protected not so much because it pertains to the seller's business as because it furthers the societal interest in the "free flow of commercial information."

We thus find no support in the First or Fourteenth Amendments, or in the decisions of this Court, for the proposition that speech that otherwise would be within the protection of the First Amendment loses that protection simply because its source is a corporation that cannot prove, to the satisfaction of a court, a material effect on its business or property. The "materially affecting" requirement is not an identification of the boundaries of corporate speech etched by the Constitution itself. Rather, it amounts to an impermissible legislative prohibition of speech based on the identity of the interests that spokesmen may represent in public debate over controversial issues and requirement that the speaker have a sufficiently great interest in the subject to justify communication. . . .

In the realm of protected speech, the legislature is constitutionally disqualified from dictating the subjects about which a person may speak and the speakers who may address a public issue. If a legislature may direct business corporations to "stick to business," it also may limit other corporations—religious, charitable, or civic—to their respective "business" when addressing the public. Such power in government to channel the expression of views is unacceptable under the First Amendment. Especially where, as here, the legislature's suppression of speech suggests an attempt to give one side of a debatable public question an advantage in expressing its views to the people, the First Amendment is plainly offended. Yet the State contends that its action is necessitated by governmental interests of the highest order. . . .

The constitutionality of § 8's prohibition of the "exposition of ideas" by corporations turns on whether it can survive the exacting scrutiny necessitated by a state-imposed restriction of freedom of speech. Especially where, as here, a prohibition is directed at speech itself, and the speech is intimately related to the process of governing, "the State may prevail only upon showing a subordinating interest which is compelling," and "the burden is on the government to show the existence of such an interest." Even then, the State must employ means "closely drawn to avoid unnecessary abridgement. . . ."

★ ★ ★

Judgment for the First National Bank of Boston.

CASE FOLLOW-UP

The Attorney General of Massachusetts, Bellotti, advanced two "compelling reasons" why the state should be permitted to limit corporate speech: (1) the state's interest in sustaining the active role of the individual citizen in the electoral process and (2) the state's interest in protecting shareholders whose views differ from those of management. Justice Powell responded by saying (1) no records, legislative hearings, or other evidence indicated that corporate speech was having any negative effect on the electoral process and (2) the state would have prohibited corporate speech even if the shareholders unanimously agreed with management.

Justice Rehnquist (now Chief Justice) dissented on the grounds that corporations were creatures of state law and that state law could expand, limit, or otherwise modify the privileges granted to corporations in their charter to conduct business in the state.

COMMERCIAL SPEECH

Speech that promotes the economic interests of a business firm, such as radio and newspaper advertisements and television commercials, is commonplace and of immense importance to producers and consumers alike. Although such commercial speech is not protected to the same extent as speech directed to political and social issues, some protections do exist. The more information available regarding the merits of a product or service, the more likely a consumer's rational choice will lead to maximum satisfaction with the purchase.

Commercial speech must be truthful and accurate and relate to some lawful commercial transaction. For example, the legislature can forbid deceptive advertising and prohibit advertising of banned products, such as illegal substances.

Beyond these basic requirements, any state or federal statute or administrative ruling regarding commercial speech must directly advance a substantial public purpose or goal, and the restriction must be *narrowly* written. In other words, because commercial speech is so important, any limitation placed on it must directly and closely focus on achieving an important governmental objective. For example, energy conservation is a significant enough public issue for the government to be concerned with. If the government prohibited all advertising of products that consumed energy, including *energy-efficient products,* that ban would be too broad to achieve its purpose, and the prohibition would be unconstitutional. That, in essence, was the issue faced by the Supreme Court in *Central Hudson Gas & Electric Corporation* v. *Public Service Commission.*[33]

Even if a commercial speech restriction is not overly broad, a good nexus must exist between the restriction and any legitimate ends it seeks to support. A restriction that discriminates against only commercial interests in the furtherance of public policy may violate the First Amendment. For example, in *City of Cincinnati* v. *Discovery Network Inc.,*[34] the Supreme Court prohibited the city of Cincinnati from enforcing an ordinance banning the distribution of commercial handbills in newsracks. The city claimed legitimate interests in safety and aesthetics in support of the ordinance. The Court determined "reasonable fit" between these ends and the means chosen. Because the ordinance called for the removal of only 62 newsracks (only those distributing commercial handbills) out of a total of 1,500 to 2,000 newsracks citywide, the effectiveness of the ordinance in achieving its ostensible safety and aesthetic goals was negligible. Furthermore, the discrimination against distributors of commercial handbills, compared with distributors of other items such as newspapers, created an impermissible denial of commercial speech rights under the First Amendment.

LIMITATIONS ON FEDERAL AND STATE GOVERNMENT

DUE PROCESS

With regard to federal action, the Fifth Amendment due process clause is supplemented by the other basic protections embodied in the Bill of Rights. If read in succession, practically every one of the first eight amendments makes it increasingly more difficult to convict a person of a crime. This in itself reflects that the framers of these amendments respected the integrity of individuals, even those accused of committing crimes, and intended to erect a fortress of protections to shield the accused from an improper conviction.

The due process clause of the Fourteenth Amendment is called on for double duty. It provides the same coverage as its companion in the Fifth Amendment, but by the process of judicial interpretation, it extends those protections in the Bill of Rights that are of the very essence of liberties as limitations on state action. The Fourteenth Amendment is addressed to the states, and through the process of interpretation it imposes on the states restraints comparable to those the Bill of Rights imposes on the federal government. The effect of this clause is to prohibit state governments from invading those principles of justice "so rooted in the traditions and conscience of our people as to be ranked as fundamental."[48]

THE FOURTH AMENDMENT AND ADMINISTRATIVE SEARCHES

The Fourth Amendment was intended to protect persons from unreasonable searches and seizures: "The right of the people to be secure in their persons, houses, papers, and effects, against unreasonable searches and seizures, shall not be violated, and no Warrants shall issue, but upon probable cause, supported by Oath or affirmation, and particularly describing the place to be searched, and the persons or things to be seized." In its application, the Fourth Amendment has been divided into two parts: the "reasonableness" clause and the "warrants" clause. Some kinds of searches may be made without a warrant so long as they are reasonable. Other kinds of searches require a warrant.

By far, most of the law of the Fourth Amendment involves the government's investigation of ordinary criminal conduct (e.g., assault, battery, murder, arson, illegal selling of drugs). In this context, the Supreme Court has recognized that some searches and seizures are constitutionally permissible if they are "reasonable." For example, if a suspect is about to destroy evidence or commit a crime, he or she may be searched or evidence may be seized without a warrant. However, the classification of "reasonable" events that constitute a legal search or seizure without a warrant is very limited. *The overwhelming preference is to require the use of the warrants clause.* The reason for the preference is that obtaining a warrant gives a judge the opportunity to review the facts to determine whether a search or seizure is justified. More specifically, the warrants clause has been interpreted to require law enforcement authorities to go before a judge or magistrate and personally swear to the existence of certain facts; these facts must lead the judge or magistrate to believe that a crime has been committed or is about to be committed. If the facts show this, the judge or magistrate issues the warrant giving the officer the authority to search and seize a particular person, place, or thing, but the search must not be broader than necessary.

At the heart of the Fourth Amendment and the warrants clause is the meaning of "probable cause." As we just pointed out, an officer must state facts, and not opinions, that lead him or her to believe a crime has been or will be committed.

This statement of facts is the probable cause of the issuance of the warrant. That is, on the basis of stated facts, the power of the state is brought to bear on individuals and a search and seizure permitted under the authority of a warrant.

If administrative agencies must have solid evidence of a violation before they inspect a property, however, this requirement would significantly hamper their activities. A definition of probable cause was needed that was not as strict as that required for criminal law enforcement. The decision in *Marshall* v. *Barlow's Inc.* defines administrative probable cause and is the leading case today on administrative searches. Notice what the decision has to say about when the "reasonableness" clause may be used in certain types of administrative searches. The case came before the Supreme Court because Ferrol Barlow refused to allow a warrantless search of his electrical and plumbing installation business.

Marshall v. *Barlow's Inc.*
436 U.S. 307 (1978)

WHITE, JUSTICE

Section 8(a) of the Occupational Safety and Health Act of 1970 (OSHA or Act) empowers agents of the Secretary of Labor (Secretary) to search the work area of any employment facility within the Act's jurisdiction. The purpose of the search is to inspect for safety hazards and violations of OSHA regulations. No search warrant or other process is expressly required under the Act.

On the morning of September 11, 1975, an OSHA inspector entered the customer service area of Barlow's Inc., an electrical and plumbing installation business located in Pocatello, Idaho. The president and general manager, Ferrol G. "Bill" Barlow, was on hand; and the OSHA inspector, after showing his credentials, informed Mr. Barlow that he wished to conduct a search of the working areas of the business. Mr. Barlow inquired whether any complaint had been received about his company. The inspector answered no, but that Barlow's Inc., had simply turned up in the agency's selection process. The inspector again asked to enter the nonpublic area of the business; Mr.

Barlow's response was to inquire whether the inspector had a search warrant. The inspector had none. Thereupon, Mr. Barlow refused the inspector admission to the employee area of his business. He said he was relying on his rights as guaranteed by the Fourth Amendment of the United States Constitution.

[A lower federal court] ruled in Mr. Barlow's favor.... Concluding that *Camara* v. *Municipal Court* . . . and *See* v. *Seattle* . . . controlled this case, the court held that the Fourth Amendment required a warrant for the type of search involved here and that the statutory authorization for warrantless inspections was unconstitutional.

The Secretary urges that warrantless inspections to enforce OSHA are reasonable within the meaning of the Fourth Amendment. Among other things, he relies on § 8(a) of the Act, . . . which authorizes inspection of business premises without a warrant. . . .

The Warrant Clause of the Fourth Amendment protects commercial buildings as well as private homes. To hold otherwise would belie the origin of that Amendment, and the American colonial experience. An important forerunner of the first 10 Amendments to the United States Constitution, the Virginia Bill of Rights, specifically opposed "general warrants, whereby an officer or messenger may be commanded to search suspected places without evidence of a fact committed." The general warrant was a recurring point of contention in the Colonies immediately preceding the Revolution. The particular offensiveness it engendered was acutely felt by the merchants and businessmen whose premises and products were inspected for compliance with the several parliamentary revenue measures that most irritated the colonists. "[T]he Fourth Amendment's commands grew in large measure out of the colonists' experience with the writs of assistance . . . [that] granted sweeping power to customs officials and other agents of the King to search at large for smuggled goods."

* * *

Against this background, it is untenable that the ban on warrantless searches was not intended to shield places of business as well as of residence.

* * *

. . . The reason is found in the "basic purpose of this Amendment . . . [which] is to safeguard the privacy and security of individuals against arbitrary invasions by governmental officials." . . . If the government intrudes on a person's property, the privacy interest suffers whether the government's motivation is to investigate violations of criminal laws or breaches of other statutory [provisions]. . . .

The Secretary urges that an exception from the search warrant requirement has been recognized for "pervasively regulated business[es]," *United States* v. *Biswell,* . . .

and for "closely regulated" industries "long subject to close supervision and inspection." *Colonnade Catering Corp.* v. *United States.* . . . These cases are indeed exceptions, but they represent responses to relatively unique circumstances. Certain industries have such a history of governmental oversight that no reasonable expectation of privacy, . . . could exist for a proprietor over the stock of such an enterprise. Liquor (*Colonnade*) and firearms (*Biswell*) are industries of this type; when an entrepreneur embarks upon such a business, he has voluntarily chosen to subject himself to a full arsenal of governmental regulation.

. . . The element that distinguishes these enterprises from ordinary businesses is a long tradition of close governmental supervision, of which any person who chooses to enter such a business must already be aware. "A central difference between those cases [*Colonnade* and *Biswell*] and this one is that businessmen engaged in such federally licensed and regulated enterprises accept the burdens as well as the benefits of their trade, whereas the petitioner here was not engaged in any regulated or licensed business. The businessman in a regulated industry in effect consents to the restrictions placed upon him."

* * *

We are unconvinced . . . that requiring warrants to inspect will impose serious burdens on the inspection system or the courts, will prevent inspections necessary to enforce the statute, or will make them less effective. In the first place, the great majority of businessman can be expected in normal course to consent to inspection without warrant; the Secretary has not brought to this Court's attention any widespread pattern of refusal.

* * *

Whether the Secretary proceeds to secure a warrant or other process, with or without prior notice, his entitlement to inspect will not depend on his demonstrating probable cause to believe that conditions in violation of OSHA exist on the premises. Probable cause in the criminal law sense is not required. For purposes of an administrative search such as this, probable cause justifying the issuance of a warrant may be based not only on specific evidence of an existing violation but also on a showing that "reasonable legislative or administrative standards for conducting an . . . inspection are satisfied with respect to a particular [establishment]." . . . A warrant showing that a specific business has been chosen for an OSHA search on the basis of a general administrative plan for the enforcement of the Act derived from neutral sources such as, for example, disper-

sion of employees in various types of industries across a given area, and the desired frequency of searches in any of the lesser divisions of the area, would protect an employer's Fourth Amendment rights. We doubt that the consumption of enforcement energies in the obtaining of such warrants will exceed manageable proportions.

★ ★ ★

We hold that Barlow's was entitled to a declaratory judgment that the Act is unconstitutional insofar as it purports to authorize inspections without warrant or its equivalent and to an injunction enjoining the Act's enforcement to that extent.

The judgment of the District Court is therefore affirmed.

CASE FOLLOW-UP

In this case, the Court refers to a very important circumstance. If a person properly authorized to do so gives consent to enter on and search the property, then the Fourth Amendment right is waived. A person may waive any of his or her constitutional rights, but

the waiver must be accomplished with the knowledge of what is being waived; that is, the person must understand that he or she has a constitutional right and what duties this places on the state (e.g., to get a warrant) before a proper waiver of the right will exist.

Since the *Barlow's* decision, one significant Supreme Court decision has refined the law in this area. In *Donovan* v. *Dewey,*[36] the Court held that the exceptions to the warrant clause requirement announced in the *Colonnade* and *Biswell* cases (mentioned in *Barlow's*) extended to a search of a quarry owned by the Waukesha Lime and Stone Company. The warrantless search was made pursuant to the Federal Mine Safety and Health Act of 1977. This act provided for *warrantless inspections but did limit the discretion of inspectors by defining the frequency of inspection, by stating specific standards of compliance, and by prohibiting forced entry.* The act required that the government initiate a civil action against a mine owner who refused entry to an inspector. These requirements were deemed to limit inspectors sufficiently so that arbitrary searches could be avoided. This case seems to expand the exceptions to the requirement of a warrant by focusing on the statutory limitations of the inspector's discretion.

In *Dow Chemical Company* v. *U.S.*,[37] the Supreme Court upheld the EPA's aerial surveillance and photography of Dow's industrial complex after Dow denied EPA's request for an on-site inspection. Dow argued that the EPA violated its Fourth Amendment protection against illegal search because the inspectors could have sought an administrative warrant. Chief Justice Warren Burger wrote:

> It may well be, as the Government concedes, that surveillance of private property by using highly sophisticated surveillance equipment not generally available to the public, such as satellite technology, might be constitutionally proscribed absent a warrant. But the photographs here are not so revealing of intimate details as to raise constitutional concerns. Although they undoubtedly give EPA more detailed information than naked-eye views, they remain limited to an outline of the facility's buildings and equipment. The mere fact that human vision is enhanced somewhat, at least to the degree here, does not give rise to constitutional problems. An electronic device to penetrate walls or windows so as to hear and record confidential discussions of chemical formulae or other trade secrets would raise very different and far more serious questions.

ZONING AND EMINENT DOMAIN

State and federal governments can regulate business and private property and can zone real estate without being required to compensate the owners for any losses that might ensue. If the government "takes" private property for a public purpose, however, a fair compensation must be paid. The Fifth Amendment requires this of the federal government, and the Fourteenth Amendment requires it of the states.

Beyond these general observations, the law in this area quickly blurs. What constitutes a taking? As Justice Brennan wrote in *Penn Central Transportation Co.* v. *New York*,[38]

> . . . The question of what constitutes a "taking" for purposes of the Fifth Amendment has proved to be a problem of considerable difficulty. While this Court has recognized that the "Fifth Amendment guarantee [is] designed to bar Government from forcing some people alone to bear public burdens which, in all fairness and justice, should be borne by the public as a whole," this Court, quite simply, has been unable to develop any "set formula" for determining when "justice and fairness" require that economic injuries caused by public action be compensated by the Government, rather than remain disproportionately concentrated on a few persons. Indeed, we have frequently observed that whether a particular restriction will be rendered invalid by the Government's failure to pay for any losses proximately caused by it depends largely "upon the particular circumstances [in that] case." 438 U.S. at 123-124.

A mere reduction in the value of property is not sufficient to make the government intrusion a taking. After all, taxes on property reduces its value beyond what it would have in the absence of taxes, and no one would argue that the government should reconvey to property owners the amount it extracts in taxes. For a taking to exist, such that the Constitution requires the government to make compensation to the property owner, a court must ordinarily determine that the government action has deprived the owner of any economically viable use of the land. As we observe in the following case, land-use regulation can comprise a taking for which compensation must be made, provided that the taking eliminates such viable use.

David H. Lucas v. South Carolina Coastal Council
112 S.Ct. 2886 (1992)

SCALIA, JUSTICE

In 1986, petitioner David H. Lucas paid $975,000 for two residential lots on the Isle of Palms in Charleston County, South Carolina, on which he intended to build single-family homes. In 1988, however, the South Carolina Legislature enacted the Beachfront Management Act, which had the direct effect of barring petitioner from erecting any permanent habitable structures on his two parcels. A state trial court found that this prohibition rendered Lucas's parcels "valueless." This case requires us to decide whether the Act's dramatic effect on the economic value of Lucas's lots accomplished a taking of private property under the Fifth and Fourteenth Amendments requiring the payment of "just compensation."

In the late 1970's, Lucas and others began extensive residential development of the Isle of Palms, a barrier island situated eastward of the city of Charleston. The Beachfront Management Act brought Lucas's plans to an abrupt end.

Lucas promptly filed suit in the South Carolina Court of Common Pleas, contending that the Beachfront Management Act's construction bar effected a taking of his property without just compensation. Lucas did not take issue with the validity of the Act as a lawful exercise of South Carolina's police power, but contended that the Act's complete extinguishment of his property's value entitled him to compensation regardless of whether the legislature had acted in furtherance of legitimate police power objectives. Following a bench trial, the court agreed. Among its factual determinations was the finding that "at the time Lucas purchased the two lots, both were zoned for single-family residential construction and . . .

there were no restrictions imposed upon such use of the property by either the state of South Carolina, the County of Charleston, or the Town of the Isle of Palms." The trial court further found that the Beachfront Management Act decreed a permanent ban on construction insofar as Lucas's lots were concerned, and that this prohibition "deprived Lucas of any reasonable economic use of the lots, . . . eliminated the unrestricted right of use, and rendered them valueless." The court thus concluded that Lucas's properties had been "taken" by operation of the Act, and it ordered respondent to pay "just compensation" in the amount of $1,232,387.50.

The Supreme Court of South Carolina reversed. It found dispositive what it described as Lucas's concession "that the Beachfront Management Act [was] properly and validly designed to preserve . . . South Carolina's beaches." Failing an attack on the validity of the statute as such, the court believed itself bound to accept the "uncontested . . . findings" of the South Carolina legislature that new construction in the coastal zone—such as petitioner intended—threatened this public resource. The Court ruled that when a regulation respecting the use of property is designed "to prevent serious public harm," no compensation is owing under the Takings Clause regardless of the regulation's effect on the property's value.

Where the State seeks to sustain regulation that deprives land of all economically beneficial use, we think it may resist compensation only if the logically antecedent inquiry into the nature of the owner's estate shows that the proscribed use interests were not part of his title to begin with. This accords, we think, with our "takings" jurisprudence, which has traditionally been guided by the understandings of our citizens regarding the content of, and the State's power over, the "bundle of rights" that they acquire when they obtain title to property. . . . In the case of land, however, we think the notion pressed by the Council that title is somehow held subject to the "implied limitation" that the State may subsequently eliminate all economically valuable use is inconsistent with the historical compact recorded in the Takings Clause that has become part of our constitutional culture.

The "total taking" inquiry we require today will ordinarily entail (as the application of state nuisance law ordinarily entails) analysis of, among other things, the degree of harm to public lands and resources, or adjacent private property, posed by the claimant's proposed activities, the social value of the claimant's activities and their suitability to the locality in question, and the relative ease with which the alleged harm can be avoided through measures taken by the claimant and the government (or adjacent private landowners) alike. The fact that a particular use has long been engaged in by similarly situated owners ordinarily imports a lack of any common-law prohibition. So also does the fact that other landowners, similarly situated, are permitted to continue the use denied to the claimant.

It seems unlikely that common-law principles would have prevented the erection of any habitable or productive improvements on petitioner's land; they rarely support prohibition of the "essential use" of land. The question, however, is one of state law to be dealt with on remand. We emphasize that to win its case South Carolina must do more than proffer the legislature's declaration that the uses Lucas desires are inconsistent with the public interest. As we have said, a "State, by ipse dixit, may not transform private property into public property without compensation . . ." Instead, as it would be required to do if it sought to restrain Lucas in a common-law action for public nuisance, South Carolina must identify background principles of nuisance and property law that prohibit the uses he now intends in the circumstances in which the property is presently found. Only on this showing can the State fairly claim that, in proscribing all such beneficial uses, the Beachfront Management Act is taking nothing.

The judgment is reversed and the case remanded for proceedings not inconsistent with this opinion.

CASE FOLLOW-UP

On remand, the Supreme Court of South Carolina reversed itself. Because antidevelopment regulation deprived Lucas of the economically viable use of his land, a taking was held to exist, and compensation was ordered. The Beachfront Management Act was not a mere exercise of a law in existence at the time Lucas bought the land; rather, it was a novel infringement upon the "bundle of rights" obtained by Lucas when he gained title to the land. As such, in accordance with the decision, Lucas was entitled to just compensation.

Notice that the standard that requires complete deprivation of economic use is not read in an extremely literal way. The owner of beachfront property, for example, might be able to rent the property without improvements for daily recreation of tourists. The difference between the revenues that would be generated by such use and the revenues that potentially would be generated by land development is so substantial as to comprise a virtually complete taking. Obviously, if courts were extremely punctilious in eliminating any minute use of regulated land before finding a taking, the concept of takings would be rendered meaningless.

CONCLUSION

A thorough study of the cases and discussions in this chapter will not make you a constitutional lawyer, but it will sharpen your insights into the most significant of the nation's great state papers. The commerce power has played an enormous role in binding the nation into a formidable economic unit. The country has prospered as a union of states with no artificial trade barriers between commercial centers and has grown into the greatest economic force in the world. Not all of this is due simply to the commerce clause, but the U.S. barrier-free marketplace has been the model for the European Common Market and comparable economic pacts throughout the world.

The commercial success of the nation is not the full measure of its greatness. It has experienced material success without losing sight of such important values as freedom of religion, speech, press, peaceable assembly, and petition. Skirmishes occur along the border of these remarkable rights, and each time the Supreme Court resolves these disputes, one point of view gains a bit at the expense of another. But the First Amendment seems to have a staying power that far outstrips the endurance of individuals and groups that want it amended or limited in some way. The reason for this staying power may be that the First Amendment has served the United States well for 200 years and has become very much a part of the national character.

REVIEW QUESTIONS AND PROBLEMS

1. When federal or state legislation focuses on categories or classifications that touch "fundamental rights" or the legislation utilizes "suspect criteria," courts exercise *strict equal protection*. What are these fundamental rights? What are suspect criteria? In what way does equal protection analysis become more strict?

2. Suppose a city zoning ordinance prohibits more than two people unrelated by blood or marriage from qualifying as a family unit living together in a household, hence no "hippie" communes, fraternity houses, or boarding houses within the city limits. Further, suppose the city proceeded to evict three elderly, retired people who were unrelated by blood or marriage but who lived together for mutual assistance and for economic reasons. Is the ordinance constitutional? *Village of Belle* v. *Boraas*, 416 U.S. 1 (1974).

3. The Supreme Court concluded in *Rostker* v. *Godberg*, 448 U.S. 1306 (1981), that the Military Selection Service Act, which required all males between the ages of eighteen and twenty-six to register, did not violate the Fifth Amendment's due process clause prohibition of gender-based discrimination. What arguments do you suppose were made for and against this act?

4. When the concept of due process focused exclusively on *procedural* matters, what was its meaning? Turn your attention now to *substantive* due process. What is the essence of this concept today?

5. The First Amendment relates that Congress shall make no law abridging freedom of speech and press, among other things, while the Fourth Amendment secures persons against unreasonable searches and seizures. Over the years, some people have taken the view that the framers of the amendments intended that *absolutely no law* (as opposed to reasonable laws) should limit speech or press. If that had not been their intention, then the framers would have qualified the speech and press protections, somewhat like the search and seizure protection, and would have expressly stipulated that reasonable restraints could be placed on speech and press. Since no such qualification on speech and press was expressly written into the First Amendment, this argument runs, the Supreme Court should not infer such a qualification. What do you think about this?

6. The First Amendment forbids Congress from establishing a religion and from interfering with the free exercise thereof. This protection has been applied to the states through the Fourteenth Amendment due process clause. The Supreme Court, however, has upheld Sunday Closing Laws and, more recently, nativity scenes sponsored by a municipality. The common thread of these cases is that while Sunday and Christmas have religious origins and significance, they have over time become secularized to the point that state recognition, sponsorship, or support does not amount to a prohibited "establishment." The contrary view, of course, is that these have not become secularized to the point of losing religious significance and that it is precisely that religious significance that inspires Sunday Closing Laws and nativity scenes to begin with.

First, in the role of a judge, ask yourself whether either of these practices is an establishment in the sense of a governmental sanction or positive reinforcement of a religious concept, belief, or practice. Second, in the role of a legislator, ask yourself whether such laws, though constitutional, make good sense in view of modern and historical examples to the contrary.

7. Assuming that zoning and other land-use regulations harm property owners (e.g., lessens the land value), why is no compensation required? Is this true when the same land is condemned for public purpose? Why?

8. Differentiate between the principles controlling speech on political matters and matters of public policy and those controlling commercial speech. Are these two sets of principles equally applicable to natural persons and to corporations?

ENDNOTES

1. In *Hicklin* v. *Orbeck,* 437 U.S. 518 (1978), the Court held unconstitutional an Alaska statute that discriminated against nonresident job seekers by granting Alaskans job preference. The state could demonstrate neither an overriding or compelling state interest (it could not show that the nonresidents were a "peculiar source of evil") nor that the statute was drawn narrowly enough to advance a legitimate purpose—jobs for unemployed Alaskans—without unreasonably trampling on the rights of others.

2. *Gross* v. *Lopez,* 419 U.S. 565 (1975).
3. 418 U.S. 539, 557—558 (1974).
4. 60 U.S. 393 (1856).
5. 113 S. Ct. 2096 (1933).
6. 347 U.S. 483 (1954).
7. 5 Cushing 198 (Mass. 1849).
8. 163 U.S. 537 (1896)
9. 343 U.S. 579 (1952).
10. *Shapiro* v. *Thompson,* 394 U.S. 618 (1969); *Speiser* v. *Randall,* 357 U.S. 531 (1958).
11. *Memorial Hospital* v. *Maricopa County,* 415 U.S. 250 (1974).

12. 4 Wheaton 316 (1819).

13. 9 Wheaton 1 (1824).

14. 325 U.S. 761 (1945).

15. 362 U.S. 440 (1960).

16. 249 U.S. 86 (1919).

17. 430 U.S. 274 (1977).

18. 468 U.S. 263 (1984).

19. 370 U.S. 421 (1962).

20. Brant, *The Bill of Rights; Its Origin and Meaning* 400 (1965).

21. 98 U.S. 148 (1878).

22. 343 U.S. 306 (1952).

23. *School District* v. *Schempp*, 374 U.S. 203 (1963).

24. *United States* v. *Seeger*, 380 U.S. 163 (1965).

25. *United States* v. *Ballard*, 322 U.S. 78 (1943).

26. 403 U.S. 602 (1971).

27. 268 U.S. 652 (1925).

28. 249 U.S. 47 (1919).

29. In *Trustees of Dartmouth College* v. *Woodward*, 4 Wheaton 518 (1819), Chief Justice Marshall defined a corporation as "an artificial being, invisible, intangible, and existing only in contemplation of law." The charter that established the institution was a contract, and the New Hampshire act that altered the charter was found to be in violation of Article I, Section 10, which prohibits states from "impairing the obligation of contracts."

30. Mencken, *A New Dictionary of Quotations on Historical Principles from Ancient and Modern Sources* 223 (1992).

31. 4 Wheaton 518 (1819).

32. *Santa Clara County* v. *Southern Pacific Railroad*, 118 U.S. 394 (1886). Responding to an imaginative but essentially vacuous argument of railroad attorney Roscoe Conkling, Chief Justice Waite related, "The Court does not wish to hear argument on the question whether the provision in the Fourteenth Amendment . . . applies to these corporations. We are all of the opinion that it does." Author Irving Brant asserts in *The Bill of Rights: Its Origin and Meaning* 351 (1965): "But for Conkling's contention there was not one word of support in the debates on the Fourteenth Amendment."

33. 447 U.S. 557 (1980).

34. 113 S. Ct. 1505 (1973).

35. *Snyder* v. *Massachusetts*, 291 U.S. 97 (1934).

36. 452 U.S. 594 (1981).

37. 476 U.S. 227 (1986).

38. 438 U.S. 104 (1978).

PART TWO

Commercial Law: Traditional and Emerging Concepts

Commercial law is alive; it is a massive organic being, and as such is as subject to change as American business itself. Any growth, any change, however, has its roots in the past. Thus, in Part Two we present text, cases and material on both the traditional views of commercial law as well as those categories of law that are developing and certainly will become much more important as we approach the year 2000.

Earlier in this century, the focus of the study of commercial law courses was on the law of contracts—those legally enforceable duties created by the exchange of promises between two autonomous persons or businesses. This focus made sense because in the nineteenth and early twentieth centuries people in business most likely thought of themselves as serving a local market no larger than their own community or state. In this area of individual business transactions, therefore, contract law was the most important feature of our commercial law system and evolved as the center of study of law in American law schools and colleges of business. Over the past few decades, however, the amount of time devoted to the study of contract law has steadily dwindled as other areas of law have become more prominent. You will find a discussion of contract law in this part, but we have placed it as the final chapter indicating that it is still important, but it has been supplanted by other areas of law study that demand attention.

It is our belief that as the large business corporation has gravitated toward center stage in the American political economy, it has attracted the attention that any lead player receives. Certainly the most important area of law, to either an individual or a business corporation, is that area of legal duties, the breach of which may result in the deprivation of one's freedom. Therefore, we begin the part on Commercial Law with an overview of the criminal law principles that apply in a business context. Because of its size, and the reach of its activities, the probability that a large business corporation may severely injure an individual or tear the social fabric of a community is becoming more substantial. There are both traditional and emerging concepts of criminal law that must be understood by those in business.

The very foundations of our economy are based on the concept of private property. The law plays a major role in protecting, enhancing, and changing concepts of private property. The ability to create, to manipulate, to transfer, and to destroy individual, corporate, and community property is the very essence of social power. In this chapter we look at the history of the concept of private property and this concept's recent changes and developments.

Tort law and contract law round out our presentation of the traditional concepts that define commercial law. Tort law defines many of the civil-law duties that any actor owes to individuals and to the community. Tort law embodies the very definition of "reasonableness"—that standard of care that society imposes on any actor in its midst. Toward the latter part of this chapter, you will read how two items in our economy—cigarettes and handguns called "Saturday Night Specials"—pose special challenges for any conception of commercial law based both on ideas of freedom for each actor and the ideas that this freedom does have limits—that no actor may place unreasonable risks on others in the economy.

Contract law is still vital to any economy based on the creation and transfer of private property. It is through the idea of a promise that any actor works its will in this economy. Most promises are for activities which are to take place in the future. To assure our common future, the law must provide a set of remedies that values this future action. Valuing future action is just one of the challenges of the legal system that is found in this final chapter in this part.

CHAPTER 5

Business Crimes

INTRODUCTION

Businesses have been subject to criminal laws for centuries. Until recently, most business crimes were fairly uncontroversial because they related primarily to some form of direct and universally condemned property conversion. Crimes such as larceny, theft of services, robbery, burglary, embezzlement, false pretenses, and extortion were the most common sources of criminal liability of businesses. In the late 20th century, computer crime has been added to this list. Although computer crime can be a complicated area because of the complex nature of technology, the essential theft of information that underlies most computer crime is widely denounced by society. All of these direct property conversion crimes are still common business crimes, and each is discussed in this chapter.

In recent years, business wrongdoing has come under substantial media scrutiny. In response to perceptions that business misbehavior is on the rise, state and federal governments enact increasing numbers of more controversial criminal laws that apply specifically to businesses. Criminal statutes prohibiting activities such as securities fraud, bribery, corrupt practices, tax abuse, and racketeering have been enacted during the twentieth century. These recent statutes are more controversial than their predecessors, in part because they reflect the discretionary adoption of public policies rather than some common moral voice of the people. Although virtually all agree that embezzlement of funds from one's employer is wrong, people in general and legal scholars in particular disagree about the moral status of insider trading. Likewise, although all can stand by laws that prohibit direct theft of property, critics of the more recent public policy crimes note that bribery is accepted practice in other cultures or that it may be unethical to pay taxes to support government activities one believes to be immoral.

As greater numbers of laws prohibit behaviors that may not be universally or even widely condemned by society, the application of criminal laws to business abuses becomes increasingly suspect. Traditionally, criminalization is intended to serve four essential functions: *punishment, deterrence, protection of society*, and *rehabilitation*.[1] To the extent that these effects are operative, they can become increasingly misguided as the behavior covered by the crime becomes increasingly debatable. Traders using inside information may contend that their behavior is economically rational and socially desirable, and they can cite highly respected scholarship from the literature of law or finance to support these views. If their contentions are correct, or at least feasible in an environment of wide disagreement, then application of the four functions of criminalization may be absurd: It can be argued that the criminal defendant should be rewarded, rather than punished, and that the goals of deterrence and social protection are meaningless, should the evil involved turn out to be a public good.

Both traditional business crimes and more recent public policy crimes are also subject to a second level of critical analysis: Even if the underlying behavior is clearly undesirable, how does one know that the four functions of criminalizaton are effective? Much has been written, particularly in regard to the role of deterrence, to suggest that criminalization may be less effective than people believe. The following article appeared in the *Boston Sunday Globe*. It questions the desirability of greater criminalization in light of dubious evidence of effectiveness and increasing costs associated with the development and maintenance of prison facilities.

CHRIS REIDY[2]

Crime and Punsihment

Boston has recently opened two modern new jails. Gov. Weld wants to add 2,500 cells to the state prison system. Congress, meanwhile, considers converting Fort Devens into a hospital for federal inmates. The business of crime and punishment appears to be booming in Massachusetts, but some other places are less fortunate. In California and South Carolina, new jails go unoccupied—not because huge numbers of criminals have suddenly seen the light, but because there is no money to pay the guards.

"California has invested enormous amounts in new prisons to the point we're facing bankruptcy," says Gerald Uelmen, dean of the Santa Clara University School of Law. "We can't open all the prisons we've built because we can't afford to staff them. For years, people have been saying that alternatives to incarceration would be more cost effective. It's ironic that we've finally come to that point as a result of a financial crisis rather than a rational discussion of the issues."

For the last two decades, the United States has been imprisoning criminals at record rates. Under both Republican and Democratic administrations, at the federal, state and county level, harsh sentencing legislation and law-and-order rhetoric have been the order of the day.

But now, some criminal justice scholars say, a policy of incarcerating criminals en masse is no longer affordable or effective. Forget about fine theories of deterrence and rehabilitation. Forget about the fact that the crime rate has remained about the same even as the US prison population has more than quadrupled. In a time of budget constraints, more and more local governments are being forced to deal with criminals on the cheap. As they seek to comply with court orders to relieve prison overcrowding, more and more are facing a dilemma. When voters are reluctant to approve tax increases of any sort, should scarce dollars go to schools and social programs or to building new prisons? And where, many ask, is the return on society's massive investment in prisons?

"We're locking more people up at the same time we're cutting teachers and school budgets, and all with no apparent effect on the crime rate," says Richard Jones, a sociologist who studies criminal justice issues at Marquette University.

"The upsurge in incarceration is absolutely extraordinary and unprecedented," says Elliott Currie, author of "Reckoning: Drugs, the Cities and the American Future" and a lecturer in law at the University of California at Berkeley. "It's one of the most massive social experiments in our history: spending $30 billion a year to put people behind bars. It's a disastrously failed policy."

That's an appraisal the Weld administration vehemently disputes. If Weld can win legislative approval of a $565 million construction program, Massachusetts would expand its state and county prison system by 4,000 cells. Others may talk of deterrence and rehabilitation, but "concern about public safety is our dominant theme," says Robert Cordy, who as the governor's chief legal counsel helps formulate the commonwealth's criminal justice policies.

Some academics argue that a steady crime rate is proof that the prison-expansion approach isn't working. If more prisons are the answer, they ask, why aren't crime rates declining? Cordy dismisses such claims. If officials had continued to practice the wrongheaded "tolerant" policies that were fashionable during the 1960s, crime rates would have risen exponentially, he argues.

"The notion that the get-tough policies of the last two decades have failed is flat-out wrong," Cordy says. "Who you're hearing from are the academic professionals who want us to return to the soft-headed policies of the '60s, and those are the policies that got us into trouble in the first place."

Weld may soon find himself in a minority, however.

"Your governor's views don't represent the mainstream of professional thinking," says Todd Clear of Rutgers University, the author of the upcoming book, " Punishment in America."

At this point, a bit of history may be in order. According to Clear, the lock-'em-up movement began with President Nixon. It continued under succeeding administrations, including President Carter's, and reached a peak during President Bush's so-called "War on Drugs." In other eras, it was thought tough prison terms could reduce recidivism. It also was thought prison could help rehabilitate some of those who had gone wrong. Those became lower priorities during the get-tough movement. Since the 1970s, prisons have been largely warehouses of punishment.

Many factors have led to overcrowded prisons. An increasingly violent society, more broken families, the widespread availability of drugs and handguns, a widening gap between rich and poor, a decline of the cities—all are cited as reasons. Some of these conditions can be found in other Western countries, but only the United States has responded by jailing such a large number of its citizens. It's not just the numbers of prisoners that have changed, observers say, but the type of prisoners has changed as well.

"Its not just the serious dudes who are in jail," Currie notes. Many of today's inmates are "small-time drug offenders" and people who commit repeated misdemeanors. As social services have been cut, "jail has become the social service agency of first resort," especially for young minority males.

According to Jerome Miller, the drug war was "an assault on the black community." A Massachusetts youth services commissioner during the Sargent administration, Miller directs the National Center on Institutions and Alternatives, a Virginia research group.

"No one is arguing about locking up murderers, rapists and muggers," says Miller, who is writing a book titled "Search and Destroy: The Plight of the African American in the Criminal Justice System." "But these aren't the ones peopling the local jails. Who's going in the front door? It's a large number of first-time offenders, people with bad legal representation."

Reserve prison for the truly dangerous and devise other punishments for the non-violent, Miller argues. By most estimates, about 20 percent of today's inmates suffer from mental illness, he says. Many have drug or alcohol problems. Some are homeless. Some are street people. Many are functionally illiterate. By Sheriff Bob Rufo's count, 70 percent of the Suffolk County inmates he supervises can neither read nor write.

Says Miller: "Most people are not in for anything serious. They're there for the want of 500 bucks. Most jails could safely lower their populations by a third to a half if prisoners had 500 bucks and a bail bondsman."

He adds, "In our society today, the social safety net has been replaced by a dragnet."

Dwight Eisenhower spoke of a military-industrial complex. Miller speaks of a "Correctional-industrial complex." Prisons are big business, he says. Jails are a source of political patronage for local officials. When you hear of officials "yakking about the need for a bigger jail" he says, it invariably "means they're running for higher office."

Today's economics may force a change in business as usual. According to most experts, it costs about $25,000 a year to imprison a criminal. Provide nonviolent offenders with drug-treatment programs instead. Teach inmates how to read and equip them with minimal job skills, and costs can be reduced by as much as 75 percent, Currie says.

"If you're going to make society safer and better, you have to attack the problem differently," says Wayne Budd, a former associate US attorney general and a senior partner at Goodwin, Procter & Hoar.

Some criminals "richly deserve" incarceration, Budd says, but others need a "level playing field." Poor people who turn to crime out of desperation need better housing, education and employment opportunities. "Building prisons alone, by any stretch of the imagination, will never reduce crime in this country," Budd says.

Such thinking may be gaining new converts, though Massachusetts continues to practice its get-tough approach. "First send them to jail, then help them" is how Cordy summarizes the Weld view toward criminals.

Out of economic necessity, other states explore other options. If nothing else, the United States has proved over the last two decades that "you can't punish your way out of a crime problem," says Clear of Rutgers. ". . . My sense is that the political winds are shifting."

At UC Berkeley, Currie makes a similar point. When it comes to a lock-'em-up approach toward criminals, Currie says, "There is definitely a sea change in attitudes."

ARTICLE FOLLOW-UP

The author of the preceding article quotes a sociologist who suggests that there may be a relationship between school budget cuts and crime rates. This observation raises an intriguing question: would increased emphasis on business ethics in higher education have any positive effect on white collar crime rates? Some students believe that morals are determined early in one's development, so that higher education of ethics would have little impact on business crime. Others believe that moral development is a lifelong process, and that adults can therefore refine their ethical decision-making capabilities. Which perspective seems more persuasive to you? Why?

Regardless of the degree of effectiveness of the criminal law system, increased criminal accountability of businesses is a reality in the United States today. In this chapter, we examine both traditional business crimes and some recent "public policy crimes" that are most likely to apply to businesses or in a business context. The chapter includes as well a discussion of the nature of criminal law compared with civil law, criminal procedures, constitutional criminal protections, and the extent to which individuals and business entities can be held liable for business-related crimes.

CRIMINAL LAW VERSUS CIVIL LAW

Both criminal and civil laws provide protection against the wrongful acts of businesses. Criminal prosecution is initiated by the state, seeking penalties in the form of fines or incarceration. Civil suits in tort or contract are private actions brought by the aggrieved party, who seeks compensation for the losses incurred from the wrongful act.

Occasionally, the functions of criminal and civil law may overlap, as when punitive damages are awarded to the plaintiff in a civil suit. Under ordinary conditions, however, the common law has traditionally separated the functions of civil and criminal law. The former is generally limited to the role of compensation; the latter performs the functions of deterrence and punishment. This clean distinction between civil and criminal functions, however, is increasingly blurred. Because the state and federal enforcement systems are heavily burdened by constraints of time and money, statutes are more likely than ever to provide severe civil sanctions, such as treble damages, intended to punish and deter wrongful action. Federal statutes that prohibit racketeering and insider trading, for example, provide strong civil remedies that encourage private individuals to seek personal compensation in the form of treble damages. This civil-remedy incentive encourages private individuals to be vigilant in recognizing abuses and to pursue the punitive private compensation in order to fill the enforcement gap that may be left by inadequate public policing resources.

In comparing and contrasting traditional criminal and civil sanctions, it is helpful to remember the following information:

- Separate claims may be made under both civil and criminal law, providing there is an appropriate cause of action. For example, mail fraud may constitute both a crime and the tort of conversion of property.

- The standard of proof is different for civil and criminal trials. The plaintiff in a civil suit must prove the elements of his or her cause of action by a preponderance of evidence; the prosecution must prove criminal culpability beyond a reasonable doubt.

- Criminal and civil trials are separate, and the findings of neither are technically binding on the other. Nonetheless, civil courts are very strongly persuaded by criminal court findings against a defendant's actions because the criminal finding, based on a burden of proof beyond a reasonable doubt, surpasses the relatively lax preponderance of evidence required to support a civil suit decision. Conversely, criminal courts cannot accept private suit determinations of wrongdoing as dispositive because those determinations are made under a burden of proof that is unacceptably weak for criminal liability.

- Although the doctrine of *res judicata* prohibits more than one civil hearing for one cause of action by a plaintiff against a defendant, it does not preclude subsequent criminal prosecution. Likewise, although the constitutional doctrine against double jeopardy prohibits retrying an acquitted defendant in criminal court, it does not dispose of a civil cause of action.

CLASSIFICATION OF CRIMES

Crimes are classified as major crimes (felonies) or minor crimes (misdemeanors). The distinction is important because the procedures applied to felonies and misdemeanors vary in most jurisdictions. Moreover, constitutional challenges rendered by criminal defenses may be affected by these procedural differences. For example, some form of hearing is guaranteed by the due process Clause of the Fifth and Fourteenth Amendments to the Constitution in connection with any deprivation of life, liberty or property. How elaborate that hearing must be to meet due process standards is a function, in part, of the severity of the crime and the related penalty. This means that the due process standards for a felony hearing may require greater procedural safeguards than the standards for a misdemeanor hearing.

MISDEMEANORS

Some jurisdictions define misdemeanor offenses as those punishable by one year's imprisonment or less. Other jurisdictions define misdemeanor offenses as those punishable by imprisonment in a jail, rather than a penitentiary. Ordinarily, the defendant charged with a misdemeanor is not entitled to a preliminary hearing or a grand jury review. In addition, some states provide smaller juries for trials of misdemeanors than for trials of felonies.

FELONIES

Like misdemeanors, felonies are generally defined by either length or locality of incarceration. In states that make the determination based on length of time, crimes punishable by more than one year's imprisonment are generally considered to be felonies. In states where the type of prison facility in which the crime is punishable determines the nature of the crime, a felony is considered to be a crime punishable in a penitentiary, rather than in a jail. Because felonies are more serious crimes associated with more severe penalties, procedural protections tend to be broad, including preliminary hearing, grand jury review, and larger juries at trial.

CRIMINAL INTENT

Both state and federal statutes often explicitly stipulate the mental state necessary for the commission of a particular crime. Murder, for example, traditionally requires "malice aforethought." In the area of business crimes, the requisite state of mind is usually "intent." Although the intent requirement is often expressly stated in statutory language, intent will also be inferred by courts even when not spelled out by the legislature. This inference is based on an interpretative presumption according to which criminal statutes are construed in favor of leniency, given the severity of criminal sanctions relative to civil sanctions.

Whereas tort liability may be founded on intent, on mere negligence, or even on strict liability regardless of intent under limited circumstances, the severity of criminal conviction has generally been held to require a culpable state of mind. In *Morissette* v. *United States*, Justice Jackson noted, "[T]he contention that an injury can amount to a crime only when inflicted by intention is no provincial or transient notion. It is as universal and persistent in mature systems of law as belief in freedom of the human will and a consequent ability and duty of the normal individual to choose between good and evil."[3]

Under tort analysis, the law presumes that a person intended the ordinary, natural consequences of his or her actions. It is therefore not uncommon in tort analysis for a court to presume that a defendant intended both immediate act and ordinarily foreseeable consequences. Unlike the law of tort, intent cannot ordinarily be presumed under criminal law. Rather, actual culpable state of mind must be proved "beyond a reasonable doubt." In some instances, intent to commit an infraction may be presumed for civil liability purposes but must be independently proven for criminal liability.

For example, civil liability for antitrust violations may be imposed simply because the defendant's actions had an anticompetitive effect. For criminal antitrust liability, proof of pernicious effect is not sufficient. In one criminal antitrust prosecution, the Supreme Court observed, "a defendant's state of mind or intent is an element of a criminal antitrust offense which must be established by evidence and inferences drawn therefrom and cannot be taken from the trier of fact through reliance on a legal presumption of wrongful intent from proof of an effect on prices."[4] The general rule that criminal liability requires criminal intent has been eroded as courts have interpreted some criminal statutes to impose liability on the basis of social expectations of reasonable preventive care. Accordingly, a statute may establish criminal liability of individuals who are unaware of corporate wrongdoings, provided they have the responsibility and authority to deal with and prevent such wrongdoings.[5]

CRIMINAL PROCEDURES

Criminal procedures are complex and may appear in some instances to be redundant. The procedures are elaborate because they serve two important functions. First, like civil procedure, criminal procedure provides a system of rules and regulations that the parties to a suit must follow in order to expedite the fair and orderly administration of justice. Second, because the stakes are so high, criminal procedures (and civil procedures, to a lesser extent) help ensure that the defendant's rights are protected and that loss of life, liberty, or property occur only when accompanied by due process. Because so many constitutional protections are at risk in the process of criminal prosecution, the multi-tiered approach requiring several seemingly repetitive steps is considered justified. Although procedures vary among different state courts and the federal courts, criminal prosecution usually includes some or all of the following processes.

INVESTIGATION

Prior to making an arrest, police officers generally investigate a crime by observation; interview of suspects, informants, and witnesses; and examination of the locality of the crime. Even at this early stage, constitutional issues may arise. For example, searches are lawful only if they are reasonable. Under ordinary circumstances, this test requires the use of a search warrant.

ARREST

The process of arresting a criminal suspect occurs when the police take the suspect into custody under charge of commission of a crime. To make an arrest, an officer must have probable cause to believe that the person charged has committed a crime. Briefer forms of detention short of arrest, called *stops*, may be allowed on less than probable cause, as when the police stop a party for purposes of inquiry on the basis of a reasonable suspicion of illegal activity. The legality of a stop ordinarily depends on its reasonableness, which is determined by balancing the state's law enforcement interests against the individual's autonomy, dignity, and freedom from harassment.[6]

DISCRETIONARY DECISION ANALYSIS

The police and state prosecutors are endowed under the law with a degree of prosecutorial discretion. Given limited resources, as well as varying probabilities of successful prosecution from one case to another, a decision against prosecuting may be made at any of a number of levels: The police report is reviewed first by higher-level police officials, and then by prosecuting attorneys to evaluate the quality of the evidence against the suspect and the importance of the case relative to other cases. In exercising their prerogative to evaluate cases and to establish prosecutorial priorities, law enforcement officials must discriminate on the basis of acceptable standards. For example, pursuit and prosecution of cases that provide the most promising quality of evidence is legitimate, whereas selection of cases on the basis of suspect classifications, such as race, ethnicity or gender, is not legitimate. Nonetheless, defendants' challenges of state decisions to prosecute, grounded in claims of discrimination and denial of equal protection, are seldom successful.

PRELIMINARY HEARINGS

If both the police and prosecuting attorneys file a complaint against the suspect, a preliminary hearing is held before a neutral magistrate to assess probable cause. The magistrate serves both as a screen to filter out cases relatively inexpensively before sending them to grand juries and as a level of protection to secure the public against possible prosecutory abuses.

GRAND JURY INDICTMENT

The purpose of the grand jury is to determine, during a process called *indictment*, whether the evidence compiled by the police is sufficient to warrant engaging in the process of a trial. Although it replicates the function of the preliminary hearing in this regard, it is an ex parte process, in which only the prosecution is allowed to present evidence. The defendant does not have the right to present countervailing evidence at this time. Some jurisdictions require a simple majority to approve the indictment; other jurisdictions require a greater percentage.

ARRAIGNMENT

If the grand jury labels the indictment a *true bill*, thereby approving the rendering of charges against the defendant, the defendant is asked to make a plea during the process called *arraignment*. If the defendant pleads guilty, there is no need to proceed to trial. If the defendant does not plead guilty immediately, the process of *plea bargaining* may occur. Plea bargaining permits the defendant to admit to a crime lesser than the one charged in the indictment in exchange for acceptance of this reduced plea by the prosecution.

Defenders of plea bargaining contend the process reduces the number of cases that eventually proceed to the trial stage, so that the limited resources of the judicial machinery thus are stretched to achieve greater speed and efficiency. Detractors suggest that plea bargaining turns justice into a sham, either by condoning compromised convictions of guilty criminals or by encouraging the innocent to compromise their innocence under thinly veiled prosecutorial threats. As prosecuting attorneys are encouraged to engage in plea bargaining by factors such as the degree of jail crowding at a particular time, the trade-off between criminal justice and resource utilization concerns is disturbing, at best.

TRIAL

If the defendant consistently pleads not guilty, refusing to participate in any existing process of plea bargaining, he or she has a right to trial by jury for felony charges and for misdemeanor charges punishable by more than six months' imprisonment. Unlike the grand jury hearing, the trial includes testimony and evidence provided by both the defense and the prosecution. As in the case of civil trials, criminal trials ordinarily provide the parties their only opportunity to question witnesses and to present evidence. Any appeals that follow are based exclusively on the trial record and are argued by appeals attorneys in the form of legal briefs and oral argument. Because factual evidence for both trial and all subsequent appeals is derived solely during the trial process, lawyers' legal and logistical strategies during this stage can be the determining factors that influence the ultimate disposition of a case.

SENTENCING

The processes of trial and sentencing are separated in the criminal justice system. Although the jury determines guilt or innocence at trial, assuming the right to jury trial has not been waived, the judge is responsible for sentencing. Within statutory guidelines restricting the judge's sentence, there is often considerable room for discretion. Some states apply indeterminate sentences, in which the court sets outer limits of incarceration, subject to parole board alterations. Other states limit judicial sentencing discretion, particularly through the use of *presumptive sentencing*. This process provides minimum, presumptive, and maximum sentences. The presumptive sentence is usually an average of the minimum and maximum sentences. In the absence of unusual circumstances, judges are required to apply the presumptive sentence. Under mitigating circumstances, judges are permitted to go below the presumptive sentence; under aggravating circumstances, they are permitted to exceed the presumptive sentence. In either case, they are bound, of course, by the minimum and maximum sentence limitations.

APPEAL

Defendants convicted of crimes have the right to appeal their convictions as a part of the due process guarantees of the Constitution, which ensure a fair hearing. Appeals are made on the record, to review the legitimacy of admission of evidence, the Constitutional claims made by the defendant, and the accuracy of the analysis of law rendered by the trial court.

CONSTITUTIONAL CRIMINAL PROTECTIONS

The Constitution provides safeguards that protect the rights of those brought into the criminal justice system. Police departments and other enforcement agencies, such as the FBI and the SEC, are large institutions supported by the power of the state. Although this power can be used to ensure justice, it can also be abused in ways that deprive criminal defendants of fundamental fairness or basic rights.

Because the disparity of power between individuals and the state is dramatic, some constitutional protections are clearly necessary to protect individuals who are confronted by the mechanisms of criminal law. Businesses come in a wide variety of shapes and sizes, from sole proprietorships to Fortune 500 firms, and all are protected by the general classes of constitutional doctrines discussed in this chapter.

THE FIFTH AND FOURTEENTH AMENDMENTS AND DUE PROCESS

The due process clauses of the Constitution prohibit the federal and state governments from depriving any person of life, liberty, or property without due process of law. The Fifth Amendment applies to federal prosecutions; the Fourteenth Amendment applies to state prosecutions. Due process is a flexible concept that requires "fundamental fairness," which includes the right to notice of the laws and notice of the charges and the right to a fair hearing when accused of violating those laws. If people know in advance the rules that constrain them and if they are given a fair hearing for their alleged violations, then criminal sanctions such as imprisonment or confiscation of property meet the constitutional requirements of due process.

Denials of due process may take many forms, and some are more likely to apply to businesses than others. For example, the right of indigent defendants to receive appointed counsel is a component of due process because access to adequate representation is considered necessary to a fair trial. (The right to counsel is also directly guaranteed in the Sixth Amendment, which grants the accused the right "to have the Assistance of Counsel for his defense.") Because court-appointed counsel is guaranteed under constitutional interpretation only to the indigent, this aspect of due process is not directly relevant to most business crime prosecutions.

Components of due process more likely to affect businesses directly include the following.

Due Process and Statutory Vagueness. Under both civil and criminal law, courts will declare a statute invalid if it is unreasonably vague. Unreasonably vague statutes abridge a person's right to due process because they fail to give adequate notice of what the law requires.

Courts apply different standards of clarity and specificity to civil and criminal statutes challenged for vagueness. Economic regulations that impose only civil penalties do not challenge the fundamental individual right of personal freedom and are therefore examined by using a "relaxed" due process standard. For example, a regulation that imposes cease and desist orders as a remedy for violations is non criminal in nature and will not require the degree of statutory specificity demanded of a law when it bears criminal sanctions. Regulations or laws that provide for criminal fines or incarceration of violators will be held to a stricter standard of clarity under the due process clause. Although due process always requires "reasonable certainty" regarding the scope and coverage of a statute, the standard for what is reasonable will generally be higher when there are criminal penalties than when there are civil penalties.

Due Process and Entrapment.   Under due process analysis, entrapment may serve as a defense to criminal responsibility. *Entrapment* defenses frequently hinge on police activities such as cajoling, badgering, and importuning. Entrapment is both a statutory violation in some states and a constitutional issue under the due process clause. Generally, statutory requirements for entrapment are less stringent than federal constitutional ones.

The definition offered in a California decision is typical of state statutes: Entrapment exists when police behavior is "likely to induce a normally law-abiding person to commit the offense."[7] For entrapment to be considered a constitutional violation of due process, it must reach the level of outrageous police overinvolvement. Needless to say, given this high standard, police sting operations have a fairly wide trap-setting berth before their activities will result in dismissal for denial of due process.

Statutory and constitutional challenges of entrapment are frequently made by defendants in several business contexts. For example, federal agents have set traps to identify business persons engaged in bribery, smuggling operations, and illegal kickback schemes. Although there is substantial legal doctrine on the subject, police operations will ordinarily pass constitutional challenge, provided they reflect real-world situations and pressures. Police activity that comprises a relentless series of temptations, however, such that the temptation is not modeled on reality, is most likely to comprise a denial of due process.

PROTECTION AGAINST UNREASONABLE SEARCHES AND SEIZURES

The Fourth Amendment of the Constitution states, "The right of the people to be secure in their persons, houses, papers, and effects, against unreasonable searches and seizures, shall not be violated, and no Warrants shall issue, but upon probable cause, supported by Oath or affirmation, and particularly describing the place to be searched, and the persons or things to be seized."

Courts, including the U.S. Supreme Court, have rendered hundreds of decisions interpreting this text. From these decisions arise several important observations.

The Fourth Amendment Does Not Require Warrants for All Searches.   The language of the Fourth Amendment simply prohibits "unreasonable searches" and states that warrants can only be issued when there is probable cause to believe that a crime has been committed. The courts have read this language literally, refusing to infer from the mention of warrants that their use is a basic component of any reasonable search. As it has been interpreted, then, the text of the Fourth Amendment does not require warrants for all lawful searches.

Instead, all searches must be reasonable, and this *usually* requires that the official engaging in a search against the will of the party searched first obtain a warrant stating with particularity the item(s) to be searched for and seized. To get a warrant, a police officer must appear before a neutral magistrate and demonstrate that he or she has probable cause to believe that a crime has been committed and that evidence of that crime is secreted in a private, protected area. The purpose of the warrant is to interpose a neutral agent between the party being searched and the law enforcement agent executing the search. Because the adversarial system of law enforcement discourages police neutrality, this buffer is viewed as an element essential to the protection of individual rights.

Warrantless Searches May Be Executed If They Are Deemed Reasonable. The Fourth Amendment exists to protect privacy against unwarranted intrusions. Varieties of warrantless searches and seizures of property are permitted because they provide useful criminal evidence with little or no cost to individual privacy. For example, an officer does not need a warrant when he or she detects evidence of a crime in "plain view," or even in "plain smell." Customs officers who detect the smell of marijuana, such that they develop probable cause to believe that vehicles contain contraband, have been permitted to search packages within those vehicles without obtaining a warrant. Likewise, officers are permitted to search, without warrant, areas within the "immediate control" of a person being lawfully arrested. This privilege is viewed as necessary to the physical protection and safety of law enforcement officers. An officer may search a partially open drawer or even a purse on a bed if these are within the reach of the person being arrested. Although the purpose of this license is to protect the officer against physical retaliation, any criminal evidence found in the process is admissible in court despite the lack of a search warrant.

The Fourth Amendment Provides Protection to Premises Other than Homes. Although the Fourth Amendment literally addresses only "homes," it has been interpreted to protect business premises as well, such as offices and stores. Because the Fourth Amendment is meant to protect privacy rights, however, the scope of what is considered reasonable, warrantless search and seizure behavior expands as the "expectation of privacy" regarding types of premises diminishes. From a practical standpoint, this means some searches and seizures that would be unconstitutional in the context of a home residence may be considered reasonable when they occur on business premises. For example, an owner of a home has a very substantial expectation of privacy, whereas the owner of a department store has a very diminished expectation of privacy because department stores are open to the public. As a result, police who search for evidence of a crime in the areas of a department store that are openly accessible to the public would ordinarily need no warrant. Obviously, reasonable expectations of privacy regarding the private areas of a department store, such as employee-only offices, are greater than the privacy expectations regarding open-access areas. To search private areas, the police must ordinarily obtain a search warrant.

Courts have also distinguished among heavily regulated, less regulated, and nonregulated businesses. Because the state interest in the control of heavily regulated industries is relatively high and because the history of regulatory practices effectively reduces the reasonable expectation of privacy, warrantless administrative searches are more likely to be condoned by the courts in the context of regulated industries.

For warrantless administrative searches to be permissible under Fourth Amendment scrutiny, the statutory terms that authorize such searches must be specific, clear, and certain, to preserve the private interests ordinarily protected by the warrant requirement. Generally, the statute must meet a substantial state interest and must define the scope of administrative searches with sufficient clarity to ameliorate the potential for arbitrariness or discrimination in the execution of searches. For example, the Supreme Court has permitted unannounced, warrantless administrative searches of junkyards and other spare parts businesses. The Court reasoned that the state has a substantial interest in controlling the resale of stolen goods that have been stripped down to spare parts. A statute authorizing warrantless searches is therefore reasonable, provided it establishes certainty and regularity guidelines that sufficiently limit the executory discretion of inspectors and thereby provide a reasonably protective warrant substitute.[8]

Evidence Obtained by Illegal Searches and Seizures Is Inadmissible in Court. The penalty imposed against the police for engaging in an illegal search and seizure of evidence is severe: Under the exclusionary rule, the evidence is disqualified from admission against the criminal defendant. The exclusionary rule is highly controversial and has been subject to severe criticism. Those who protest the rule claim that it needlessly banishes otherwise relevant and persuasive evidence potentially necessary for the conviction of a criminal and the protection of society. They contend that other sanctions, such as job-related penalties and fines assessed against law enforcement officers, would deter illegal searches without loss of evidence that may be necessary to convict a criminal. Those who support the exclusionary rule echo the Supreme Court in the classic cases of *Weeks* v. *United States*[9] and *Mapp* v. *Ohio*,[10] and suggest that exclusion of unlawfully gleaned evidence is the only sanction that will be effective to ensure the important privacy interests the Fourth Amendment was intended to protect. Because the exclusionary rule removes the only incentive to engage in unreasonable searches, it should prove highly effective in reducing the frequency of their occurrence.

CRIMINAL LIABILITY OF MANAGERS, SUBORDINATES, AND CORPORATIONS

The ability of criminal laws to punish and deter egregious behaviors depends on the threat of imprisonment. Because a company cannot be imprisoned, the weight of criminal law depends on its ability to locate people who can be held accountable and incarcerated for business crimes. Public policy demands that the agents of businesses be held accountable, under appropriate circumstances and conditions of individual culpability, for crimes committed in the name of private companies.

Business entities, such as partnerships and corporations, act through the behavior of their agents, including directors, officers, managers, and employees. When these agents engage in criminal activity, they expose the organization and themselves to liability. In this section, we address the question, Who can be held liable for the criminal activities of individuals within business entities and under what circumstances? Specifically, can company managers be held liable for the criminal acts of their subordinates? Can subordinates be held criminally liable for unlawful acts they commit under the orders of their superiors? And can a corporation be held criminally liable for the acts of individual employees?

COMPANY MANAGERS

Company managers may be held liable for the criminal acts of their subordinates. A manager will be held liable for the criminal actions he or she instructs subordinates to undertake or for those actions in which he or she is "personally concerned." Managers may also be held criminally liable for the activities of subordinates that fall within their sphere of managerial responsibility, even if the managers are unaware of the particular infractions. Such liability requires only that the defendant (a) was in a position of responsibility in relationship to the situation and (b) by virtue of that position was authorized and responsible to deal with the particular situation. In other words, managers must remain vigilant regarding the activities of subordinates within their scope of responsibility and authority.

Officers who promote a scheme may be held liable for aiding and abetting that scheme despite their lack of actual complicity in criminal activity. And some statutes, such as the Clayton Act, create liability for authorization or ordering of acts in violation of the law. Especially in industries where employee or public safety is an issue, failure to supervise employees adequately can establish managerial liability for the wrongful acts of subordinates. The ignorance that may result from failure to oversee the activities in this sphere may not be a viable defense against individual criminal liability. The following case illustrates the potential liability of management for the activities of employees.

United States v. *Park*
421 U.S. 658 (1975)

BURGER, CHIEF JUSTICE

Acme Markets, Inc., is a national retail food chain with approximately 36,000 employees, 874 retail outlets, 12 general warehouses, and four special warehouses. Its headquarters, including the office of the president, respondent Park, who is chief executive officer of the corporation, are located in Philadelphia, Pennsylvania. In a five-count information filed in the United States District Court for the District of Maryland, the Government charged Acme and respondent with violations of the Federal Food, Drug, and Cosmetic Act. Each count of the information alleged that the defendants had received food that had been shipped in interstate commerce and that, while the food was being held for sale in Acme's Baltimore warehouse following shipment in interstate commerce, they caused it to be held in a building accessible to rodents and to be exposed to contamination by rodents. These acts were alleged to have resulted in the food being adulterated. . . .

Acme pleaded guilty to each count of the information. Respondent [Park] pleaded not guilty. The evidence at trial demonstrated that in April 1970 the Food and Drug Administration (FDA) advised respondent by letter of unsanitary conditions in Acme's Philadelphia warehouse. In 1971 FDA found that similar conditions existed in the firm's Baltimore warehouse. An FDA consumer Safety officer testified concerning evidence of rodent infestation and other unsanitary conditions discovered during a 12-day inspection of the Baltimore warehouse in November and December 1971. He also related that a second inspection of the warehouse had been conducted in March 1972. On that occasion the inspectors found that there had been improvement in the sanitary conditions, but that, "there was still evidence of rodent activity in the building and in the warehouse and we found some rodent-contaminated lots of food items."

The Government also presented testimony by the Chief of Compliance of FDA's Baltimore office, who informed respondent by letter of the conditions at the Baltimore warehouse after the first inspection. There was testimony by Acme's Baltimore division vice president, who had responded to the letter on behalf of Acme and respondent and who described the steps taken to remedy the unsanitary conditions discovered by both inspections. The Government's final witness, Acme's vice president for legal affairs and assistant secretary, identified respondent as the president and chief executive officer of the company and read a bylaw prescribing the duties of the chief executive officer. He testified that respondent functioned by delegating "normal operating duties," including sanitation, but that he retained "certain things, which are the big, broad principles of the operation of the company," and had "the responsibility of seeing that they all work together."

* * *

Respondent was the only defense witness. He testified that, although all of Acme's employees were in a sense under his general direction, the company had an "organizational structure for responsibilities for certain functions" according to which different phases of its operation were "assigned to individuals who, in turn, have staff and departments under them." He identified those individuals responsible for sanitation and related that upon receipt of the January 1972 FDA letter, he had conferred with the vice president for legal affairs, who informed him that the Baltimore division vice president "was investigating the situation immediately and would be taking corrective action and would be preparing a summary of the corrective action to reply to the letter." Respondent stated that he did not "believe there was anything [he] could have done more constructively than what [he] found was being done."

On cross-examination, respondent conceded that providing sanitary conditions for food offered for sale to the public was something that he was "responsible for in the entire operation of the company," and he stated that it was one of many phases of the company that he assigned to "dependable subordinates." Respondent was asked about and, over the objections of his counsel, admitted receiving, the April 1970 letter addressed to him from FDA regarding unsanitary conditions at Acme's Philadelphia warehouse. . . .

At the close of the evidence, respondent's renewed motion for judgment of acquittal was denied. . . . Respondent's counsel objected to the [jury] instructions on the ground that they failed to reflect our decision in *United States* v. *Dotterweich*, 320 U.S. 277, and to define "'responsible relationship.'" The trial judge overruled the objection. The jury found respondent guilty on all counts of the information, and he was subsequently sentenced to pay a fine of $50 on each count.

The Court of Appeals reversed the conviction and remanded for a new trial. . . .

We granted certiorari because of an apparent conflict among the courts of appeals with respect to the standard of liability of corporate officers under the Federal Food, Drug, and Cosmetic Act as construed in *United States* v. *Dotterweich, supra,* and because of the importance of the question to the Government's enforcement program. We reverse.

The question presented by the Government's petition for certiorari in *United States* v. *Dotterweich, supra,* and the focus of this Court's opinion, was whether "the manager of a corporation, as well as the corporation itself, may be prosecuted under the Federal Food, Drug and Cosmetic Act of 1938 for the introduction of misbranded and adulterated articles into interstate commerce. . . ."

In reversing the judgment of the Court of Appeals and reinstating Dotterweich's conviction, this Court looked to the purposes of the Act and noted that they "touch phases of the lives and health of people which, in the circumstances of modern industrialism,

are largely beyond self-protection." It observed that the Act is of "a now familiar type" which "dispenses with the conventional requirement for criminal conduct—awareness of some wrongdoing. In the interest of the larger good it puts the burden of acting at hazard upon a person otherwise innocent but standing in responsible relation to a public danger."

Central to the Court's conclusion that individuals other than proprietors are subject to the criminal provisions of the act was the reality that "the only way in which a corporation can act is through the individuals who act on its behalf. . . ."

At the same time, however, the Court was aware of the concern which was the motivating factor in the Court of Appeals' decision, that literal enforcement "might operate too harshly by sweeping within its condemnation any person however remotely entangled in the prescribed shipment." A limiting principle, in the form of "settled doctrines of criminal law" defining those who "are responsible for the commission of a misdemeanor," was available. In this context, the Court concluded, those doctrines dictated that the offense was committed "by all who have . . . a responsible share in the furtherance of the transaction which the statute outlaws."

* * *

The rule that corporate employees who have "a responsible share in the furtherance of the transaction which the statute outlaws" are subject to the criminal provision of the Act was not formulated in a vacuum. Cases under the Federal Food and Drugs Act of 1906 reflected the view both that knowledge or intent were not required to be proved in prosecutions under its criminal provision, and that responsible corporate agents could be subjected to the liability thereby imposed. Moreover, the principle had been recognized that a corporate agent, through whose act, default, or omission the corporation committed a crime, was himself guilty individually of that crime. The principle had been applied whether or not the crime required "consciousness of wrongdoing," and it has been applied not only to those corporate agents who themselves committed the criminal act, but also to those who by virtue of their managerial positions or other similar relations to the act could be deemed responsible for its commission.

In the latter class of cases, the liability of managerial officers did not depend on their knowledge of, or personal participation in, the act made criminal by the statute. Rather, where the statute under which they were prosecuted dispensed with "consciousness of wrongdoing," an omission or failure to act was deemed a sufficient bases for a responsible corporate agent's liability. It was enough in such cases that, by virtue of the relationship he bore to the corporation, the agent had the power to have prevented the act complained of. . . .

★ ★ ★

"The accused, if he does not will the violation, usually is in a position to prevent it with no more care than society might reasonably expect and no more exertion than it might reasonably exact from one who assumed his responsibilities." Similarly, in cases decided after *Dotterweich*, the courts of appeals have recognized that those corporate agents vested with the responsibility, and power commensurate with that responsibility, to devise whatever measures are necessary to ensure compliance with the Act bear a "responsible relationship" to, or have a "responsible share" in, violations.

The Act does not, as we observed in *Dotterweich*, make criminal liability turn on "awareness of some wrongdoing" or "conscious fraud." The duty imposed by Congress on responsible corporate agents is, we emphasize, one that requires the highest standard of foresight and vigilance, but the Act, in its criminal aspect, does not require that which is objectively impossible. The theory upon which responsible corporate agents are held criminally accountable for "causing" violations of the Act permits a claim that a defendant was "powerless" to prevent or correct the violation to "be raised defensively at a trial on the merits." If such a claim is made, the defendant has the burden of coming forward with evidence, but this does not alter the Government's ultimate burden of proving beyond a reasonable doubt the defendant's guilt, including his power, in light of the duty imposed by the Act, to prevent or correct the prohibited condition. Congress has seen fit to enforce the accountability of responsible corporate agents dealing with products which may affect the health of consumers by penal sanctions cast in rigorous terms, and the obligation of the courts is to give them effect so long as they do not violate the Constitution. . . . Reading the entire charge satisfied us that the jury's attention was adequately focused on the issue of respondent's authority with respect to the conditions that formed the basis of the alleged violations. Viewed as a whole, the charge did not permit the jury to find guilt solely on the basis of respondent's position in the corporation; rather, it fairly advised the jury that to find guilt it must find respondent "had a responsible relation to the situation" and "by virtue of his position . . . had authority and responsibility" to deal with the situation.

★ ★ ★

We conclude that, viewed as a whole and in the context of the trial, the charge was not misleading and contained an adequate statement of the law to guide the jury's determination. . . .

The criminal conviction of Park was affirmed.

CASE FOLLOW-UP

1. Do you believe that the individual defendant, Park, had the intent to either contaminate or allow the contamination of the food? Did he have any criminal intent at all?

2. Because the Court dispenses with the element of intent in this criminal case, what item of proof or what element of the crime did it put in the place of intent? That is, what must the prosecutor prove (beyond a reasonable doubt) to find the defendant guilty?

3. According to the Court, what defenses are there to this element of the crime?

The decision of the U.S. Supreme Court recognized that a new element of proof was necessary in the legal environment to replace the traditional element of intent in criminal cases. Be careful not to read this case too broadly. Today, this case and its announced new element of proof is limited to situations in which the public is protected by statute (such as the FDA statute) from potentially extremely dangerous situations. Obviously, rat-infested food cannot be tolerated in a society that is dependent on food processing and shipment.

Although the Court in *Park* did not expressly address the point, it recognized that much commercial activity is carried out by corporations and that some statutes intended to protect the public could be subverted if the corporation alone was found guilty. After all, the penalty assessed was only $250. This penalty would not be felt by the large corporate defendant. Nor, really, would it be felt by the individual defendant, Park. If the individual defendant was found guilty of a crime, however, the notoriety following the conviction might serve as an example to others who had the same responsibilities as Park. This, more than the fine or penalty, promotes the objectives of the statute.

SUBORDINATES

Subordinates can be held criminally liable for the unlawful acts they commit under the orders of their supervisors. In other words, an individual is not exonerated from personal responsibility for crimes committed on command and in the name of the company. This stand reflects a departure from the principal-agency tenets of the civil law: Although authorized agents are not personally liable for the contracts they enter as representatives of others, they are liable for crimes they commit on behalf of their employers. In this regard, criminal law does not allow employees to detach themselves from responsibility for their efforts as agents of the firms they work for. The defense "But I did it for the company, not for myself" will not relieve an agent from responsibility for his or her crimes.

A defendant who follows orders, like any criminal defendant, can be convicted only if the prosecution can prove that the act was committed with the culpable mental state, or *mens rea*, required by the relevant statute. In *United States* v. *Gold*,[11] the Court of Appeals for the Eleventh Circuit observed, "[F]ollowing orders' can. . . . be a defense where a defendant had no idea that his conduct is criminal. . . . If [the defendant] was aware of the illegality of his conduct, the fact that it was authorized by a superior clearly cannot insulate him from criminal liability."

Because employees cannot defend criminal activities by evoking a "following orders" defense, legal protection of whistle-blowers is especially important. Strong protection of whistle-blowers against retaliatory firing may help employees make difficult decisions with diminished fear of losing their jobs as a result. Even with the protection of such laws, it is easy to imagine the difficulty workers often face when they refuse to follow the orders of their employers. To the extent that whistle-blower protection laws are incapable of providing complete security to those trying to "do the right thing," workers must rely on a combination of ethical rectitude and prospective criminal liability as incentives.

CORPORATIONS

Corporations can be held criminally liable for the acts of individual employees. At common law, a corporation, as a fictitious person, was viewed as incapable of committing a crime. As a result, punishment through the imposition of fines was considered inappropriate as applied to corporate entities. This perspective was abandoned by most courts during the early part of the twentieth century, and corporations are now often subject to criminal sanctions. Although a corporation cannot be arrested or imprisoned, criminal punishment in the form of property confiscation is not uncommon. Many statutes aimed at reducing business wrong-doing specify an intention to provide corporate as well as individual accountability. Courts generally justify the imposition of entity liability in terms of public policy. Corporate liability is viewed as an incentive for managers to oversee with care the acts of employees; such supervision should result in a reduction of illegal activity.

The development of corporate liability has followed the approach of corporate tort liability, which is based on principal-agent theory. Today, the corporation can be held liable as principal for both the torts and the crimes committed by employees "in the course of employment." If a statute provides for corporate liability regardless of criminal intent, the corporate employer may be held liable even for crimes it has not authorized and of which it has no knowledge, provided the acts were in furtherance of corporate objectives. This approach follows the "strict imputation" theory of agency, under which the agent's acts are strictly attributed to the principal corporation.

When statutes require proof of criminal intent, traditional or conservative judges have been reluctant to impose criminal corporate liability for acts of agents unauthorized by or outside the knowledge of executive superiors. Nonetheless, as the law moves toward greater corporate accountability, more and more courts have imputed strict liability to entities for intentional crimes committed by employees. This liability is based upon one of two forms of reasoning: (1) that the employees' intent can be attributed to the employer under principal-agent theory or (2) that the employer's failure to monitor the employees' actions establishes constructive intent in that the employer "should have known" of the activity.

EFFECT OF FEDERAL SENTENCING GUIDELINES ON CORPORATE CRIMINAL LIABILITY

During the 1980s, Congress began the process of sentencing reform. Pursuant to the Sentencing Reform Act of 1984,[12] Congress authorized the creation of new sentencing guidelines in 1987. A key feature of the guidelines is the provision of formulas for calculating corporate fines. The formulas are sensitive to a number of culpability factors, including the implementation of effective prevention programs, the prevention and detection of violations, and self-reporting of violations. Although different sets of guidelines have been adopted for different areas of federal criminal law, the antitrust example that follows illustrates how federal sentencing guidelines operate.

On November 1, 1991, the United States Sentencing Commission adopted Sentencing Guidelines for Antitrust Offenses. The theory behind the guidelines is that severity of fines should be related to the corporation's culpability. Culpability is assessed in terms of "the steps taken by the organization prior to the offense to prevent and detect criminal conduct, the level and extent of involvement in or tolerance of the offense by certain personnel, and the organization's actions after an offense has been committed." Using these criteria, the court can tally a base fine by using a company's culpability score. This score is translated, by using "minimum and maximum fine multipliers" into a "fine range" from which the corporation's punishment is chosen. The base fine amounts vary dramatically according to culpability scores—from thousands of dollars to many millions of dollars. If the pecuniary loss caused by the organization or the pecuniary gain received by the organization exceeds the base fine as calculated above, then that loss or gain will be used as the base fine figure.

Culpability scores, and therefore potential fine ranges, can be lowered by a number of precautionary measures, including the following:

1. Individuals in supervisory positions should not participate, condone, or remain willfully ignorant of criminal offenses.

2. Tolerance for criminal activities should not be pervasive throughout either the organization or the relevant organizational unit.

3. Corporations should develop effective programs to prevent and detect violations of law.

4. Corporate authorities should voluntarily report offenses without delay, cooperate with investigations, and accept responsibility for corporate criminal conduct.

These activities not only decrease the likelihood of an incident of corporate crime but also serve to reduce culpability scores under the specific scoring criteria contained in the guidelines. Under the federal sentencing guidelines, companies are increasingly engaged in legal and ethical training of employees and officers to avert criminal behavior whenever possible and to reduce fine levels if employees do break the law.

CRIMES UNDER STATE LAW

Although both common law and statute have been sources of state crimes, those crimes that originated in common law have been either embodied in statutes during the past century or expunged from the law. Although prohibited practices vary somewhat from one state to the next, the activities covered in this section are considered criminal acts in most states. Most business crimes fall under the general heading of theft, including larceny and theft of services, robbery, burglary, computer crimes, embezzlement, false pretenses, and extortion. Because it is often confusing to distinguish among these crimes, they are treated and defined individually in this text.

LARCENY AND THEFT OF SERVICES

Larceny is the intentional stealing, taking, or carrying away of the property of another with intent to convert it or to deprive the owner of its possession. Under the common law, larceny covered only the conversion of tangible goods, but statutes often extend this coverage to include theft of money or other intangibles. Larceny does not include the unlawful stealing of services, but many states have enacted legislation creating a crime called *theft of services*. Individuals convicted of theft of services typically gain access to those services by stealth and are then caught using them. For example, a person who enters a health club without paying the entry fees and uses the club's equipment may be held criminally liable. Likewise, a person who uses the computer facilities or proprietary databases of another without authorization can be convicted under state theft of services statutes.

ROBBERY

Robbery is the felonious taking of personal property from another, against the victim's will and in his or her immediate presence, through the use of force or fear. A conviction for robbery generally requires establishment of all the elements of larceny, plus "presence" of the victim, such that an act was required to sever the victim's control over and possession of the property. Because robbery entails the additional element of struggle for possession and the possibility of physical violence, it is generally considered a more serious crime than larceny and may be accompanied by more stringent prescribed statutory penalties or sentences.

BURGLARY

Burglary is the intentional breaking and entering onto the premises of another with intent to commit a felony. Under the common law, burglary was limited to unlawful entries into "dwelling places," as opposed to offices, and could occur only in the nighttime. In recent years, these archaic distinctions have been dropped in many states, so breaking and entering of workplaces with felonious intentions is considered burglary regardless of the time of day or night. The crime of burglary is often, but not always, related to intentions to convert property. Burglary may also occur when a person breaks and enters, for example, to commit felonious acts of vandalism or property damage, to commit felonious acts of violence, to learn trade secrets, or to gain access to confidential information. Charges of burglary may be especially useful when the defendant is caught entering business premises unlawfully, but before the intended felony has been committed. For example, an illegal entry that is thwarted by the police prior to the intended conversion of proprietary information or documents may not support a larceny conviction but will ordinarily qualify as burglary.

COMPUTER CRIMES

Many of the generic crimes of theft in this section can relate to the use of computers. Larceny, embezzlement, bribery, and extortion schemes have all been perpetrated with the help of computers. The power generated by computer usage and expedited information flows has caused criminal justice agencies and officials particular concern. The Department of Justice's Bureau of Justice Statistics has addressed computer crimes as a special issue in its Criminal Justice Manual.

The Manual defines a computer-related crime broadly as "any illegal act for which knowledge of computer technology is essential for successful prosecution." According to these guidelines, theft of a computer would not be a computer-related crime. Because stealing the computer itself requires no more knowledge of computer technology than stealing a washing machine, the act is not computer-related. Some common techniques for executing computer-related crimes include data manipulation and illegal electronic transfer of bank funds. Some perpetrators have engaged in "salami" scams, rounding thousands of customer bank accounts down to the nearest dollar and converting the accumulated cents into large sums.

Because computer-related crime has increased society's vulnerability to business wrongdoing, many states have passed statutes that address computer crimes specifically. If damages exceed a usually nominal amount ($300 in some states), the computer crime is a felony. In other states, all computer crimes are considered felonious, regardless of the amount of damages. Most of these statutes are more stringent than the laws covering non-computer-related thefts; this reflects the hope that especially tough criminal laws may help curb the use of computers to facilitate the commission of crimes.

The possibilities for creative high-technology criminal activity seem endless. The following article from the *Wall Street Journal* explains how voice-mail espionage has become a form of high-tech abuse. As the author indicates, vigilant voice-mail security may be the 1990s version of locking one's file cabinet to protect privacy interests in important documents.

WILLIAM M. BULKELEY[13]

Voice Mail May Let Competitors Dial 'E' for Espionage

BOSTON - When Joseph Corlese called Standard Duplicating Machines Inc. last month to ask about buying a $100,000 collating-machine, he reached the voice-mail system. So he left a message.

First thing next morning, Mr. Cortese, who buys equipment for the New England Journal of Medicine, received a call from a salesman offering attractive terms on collating equipment. Oddly enough, the salesman worked for Standard's chief competitor.

Standard, a family-owned, Andover, Mass., distributor of collators and other printing industry equipment, has charged in a lawsuit that the call was no coincidence. It says that its rival, the U.S. unit of Japan's Duplo Manufacturing Corp., engaged in a "prolonged and surreptitious campaign of business espionage" by stealing voice-mail messages to steal business.

Duplo officials didn't return calls to the U.S. unit's headquarters in Santa Ana, Calif. The U.S. unit hasn't responded yet in court to the suit, which was filed last week.

A Growing Security Problem

The case, in federal court in Boston, is the latest example of growing problems with voice-mail security. Companies like Spinnaker Software and International Data Group, a magazine publisher, have found their phone systems shut down by voice-mail vandals who clogged the systems so nothing more could fit. Hackers sometimes occupy a vacant corporate voice-mail box and use it to post messages to other hackers. In some cases phone thieves have even managed to go from voice-mail boxes into outbound calling, racking up thousands of dollars in international calls.

Voice-mail spying hasn't received much publicity before, but security experts say the Standard-Duplo case is a reminder of the risks companies run by leaving important messages on voice mail. "People don't realize that their voice-mail system is a computer that stores lots of valuable information, and computers are at risk," says Fred Cotton, a manager at Search, a Sacramento, Calif., organization that trains state investigators to chase high-tech criminals.

In its suit, Standard is seeking unspecified damages under trade-secret laws, and the Racketeer Influenced and Corrupt Organizations statutes. Standard explains how it ran a sting operation by asking loyal customers, such as the New England Journal, to place bogus orders in voice-mail boxes, only to find Duplo salespeople calling the customers a day or two later. It says it lost "numerous" sales of $100,000 collating units as a result of the espionage.

Standard's attorney, Thane Scott of Palmer & Dodge in Boston, says Standard began to suspect foul play when it "began to lose sales in inexplicable ways." Standard had long sold Duplo collators as a distributor, but last year Duplo set up its own direct sales operation, Mr. Scott said.

Tip From a Supplier

The suit says that on Aug. 30, a supplier called Standard's president, L. Guy Reny, and told him a competitor he wouldn't identify was stealing business leads from the voice-mail system. In the next two weeks, according to the suit, Standard arranged for six callers, including the New England Journal, to leave voice-mail messages. Some callers used unlisted phone numbers or gave fake names, but they still got calls from Duplo salespeople and dealers.

The lawsuit zeroes in on John Hebel, who Standard said it had "terminated" as a sales manager in September 1992. Last November, Duplo hired Mr. Hebel as its Midwest sales manager. Standard says Mr. Hebel was familiar with Standard's voice-mail system, which is made by American Telephone & Telegraph Co., and that he knew some of the passwords.

Standard says that it pinpointed Mr. Hebel by examining calls to its toll-free 800 number. A number of calls—all after Standard's 4:30 p.m. closing time—were from Duplo and Mr. Hebel's home. Mr. Hebel, who was among the Duplo salespeople named in the suit, didn't return phone calls.

Kevin Hanley, a telecommunications security expert at AT&T, says that one key to eliminating voice-mail espionage is for companies to force employees to change passwords regularly. He says he recommends changing passwords after every trip where access codes might have been viewed by "shoulder surfers" looking for calling-card numbers at Pay Phones, and at least once a quarter. "People lock their file cabinets at night. You have to treat information in a voice-processing system as securely as you would if it were on a piece of paper," he says.

ARTICLE FOLLOW-UP

In the computer age, business people must be careful to remember that paper documents are the traditional, but not the only, form of embodying information. As less and less trade secret and other confidential information becomes committed to hard copy, it becomes vital to develop security systems that protect electronic security. Finally, given the discussion of the nature of computer crimes that precedes this article, does voice mail espionage qualify as a computer crime? Does it also qualify as any of the more traditional property conversion crimes discussed earlier in this chapter?

EMBEZZLEMENT

Embezzlement is a form of theft involving breach of trust or fiduciary duty. Often, an individual or a business entity entrusts the control of property to an employee, trustee, or agent. If any of these actors appropriates that property for his or her own use, that actor has violated an embezzlement statute in virtually all states.

Many employees who face personal financial difficulties and who have access to company funds have been tempted to "borrow" money from their employers, sometimes with good-faith intentions of replacing any funds they take. Likewise, business executives holding funds on behalf of clients in some form of escrow account have sometimes transferred those funds to meet their own business's financial exigencies, anticipating the replenishment of the funds at some future date. When such individuals succumb to these temptations, courts generally refuse to admit into evidence either the employees' intent or the employees' ability to repay the converted monies. Because the funds have been appropriated without contractual arrangement, such behavior comprises embezzlement, notwithstanding the relatively innocent intentions or the ultimate good faith of the converter. The embezzlement occurs simply by virtue of appropriating assets to which the perpetrator has no rightful claim, even if the appropriation includes a bona fide desire or intention to replace the funds at a later date. The difference between one who embezzles and one who borrows legally rests in the knowledge and consent of the party whose funds are being used.

FALSE PRETENSES

It is a crime to make false statements regarding existing or past fact with fraudulent design to obtain money or merchandise. The elements of the crime are intent to defraud, actual fraud, false pretense, and resulting transfer of title to property.

False pretenses is a mechanism by which fraudulent acts, which serve under civil law to render contracts voidable by the defrauded party, may also be considered a crime. Although statutes prohibit the passing of "bad checks," the practice was also illegal under the common law as a form of false pretense—that is, the tacit representation that funds existed in the account sufficient to cover the amount of the check.

False pretenses is similar to "confidence game" crimes, in which a swindler uses tricks or devices that take advantage of the confidence the swindled party places in the swindler. It may be helpful here to distinguish false pretenses from two other crimes with which it is sometimes confused—larceny and forgery. Larceny entails the forced and involuntary relinquishment of property; false pretenses results in the voluntary transfer of property via fraudulent persuasion. Although false pretenses and forgery may overlap, there is a distinction. Whereas transfer of property is a required element of false pretenses, such transfer is not an essential element of forgery, which simply requires the false making, alteration, or publication of a written instrument.

EXTORTION

A party who employs unlawful threats to coerce another into transferring possession of or title to property is guilty of extortion. The law is careful to distinguish between unlawful and lawful threats so that only the former class can be the basis for an extortion conviction. Unlawful threats are those that have no reasonable and lawful bargaining relationship to the concession being sought. For example, threats to injure a party or the party's friends or family, to expose a party's private sexual acts to a spouse, or to provide harmful information to a party's employer unless payment is made constitute extortion. These are viewed as unreasonable and unlawful bargains that fall outside the realm of acceptable business practice.

Extortion may be related to incidents of contractual duress. Although extortion and duress can exist by virtue of the same single act, they are distinct and separate legal concepts. Extortion is a crime; duress is a civil defense that may be claimed against the enforcement of a contract. Suppose a supplier threatens to reveal to a buyer's spouse photographs of the buyer engaging in acts of promiscuity unless the buyer enters into a contract to purchase supplies at excessive rates. The supplier may be held criminally liable for extortion of the excessive profits. In addition, the supplier's efforts to enforce the contract against the buyer will be subject to the defense of duress. If the buyer can prove that he entered the contract in submission to the supplier's threats, the contract will be considered voidable for duress, at the buyer's option.

FEDERAL STATUTORY CRIMES

An increasing number of business-related crimes have been created under federal statute. Although the states have traditionally monitored the greater portion of criminal activities under their residual constitutional police powers, the federal government also has broad latitude in the enactment of criminal statutes, typically under the authority of the Constitution's commerce clause. Because a wide variety of activities are construed to affect commerce, the potential role of the federal government in regulating crimes is substantial. The federal statutory crimes discussed in this section are among those most commonly evoked by federal prosecutors.

MAIL FRAUD AND WIRE FRAUD

Federal law prohibits the use of United States mail to execute a "scheme" or "artifice" for the following purposes: to defraud; to obtain money or property through false or fraudulent pretenses, representations, or promises; or to "sell, dispose of, loan, exchange, alter, give away, distribute, supply, or furnish or procure for unlawful use" counterfeit articles of any kind. A similar federal statute prohibits wire fraud, which typically involves deceptive practices over telephone, telegraph, television, or radio. In many instances, mail and wire fraud cases involve false advertising campaigns or confidence schemes.

The mail and wire fraud statutes were enacted to protect the integrity of the U.S. mail and telecommunication conduits by prohibiting their use as instruments of crime. Both mail and wire communications and solicitations can descend unwanted on persons in the privacy of their homes. Because this susceptibility to federally regulated media channels renders private citizens potential captive audiences, some degree of federal protection has been deemed appropriate. The mail and wire fraud statutes thus also serve to strengthen federal jurisdiction over what might otherwise be exclusively state-law crimes.

The statutes have been interpreted to cover an expansive scope of activities in which the mail or wires are used. The mail fraud statute applies, for example, even when the fraud itself does not directly rely on or use the U.S. mail. It is not necessary that the mail be an essential component of the fraudulent act or scheme; rather, mail fraud may occur even when the use of the mail is incidental to the scheme. From a pragmatic standpoint, this means that the federal government can effectively prosecute fraudulent activities that are normally considered state rather than federal crimes under the wide variety of circumstances in which the mail is used to run a business. Needless to say, some incidental use of the U.S. mail in the operations of a business, legitimate or otherwise, is virtually ubiquitous.

BRIBERY AND CORRUPT PRACTICES

In the 1970s, the Securities and Exchange Commission investigated allegations that significant numbers of American companies were making questionable payments in their foreign business operations. As a result of these findings, Congress passed the Foreign Corrupt Practices Act of 1977 (amended in 1988), or FCPA, which prohibits agents of U.S. companies from paying bribes to foreign officials to gain or retain business.

The FCPA has proved extremely controversial among both business practitioners and scholars, many of whom vehemently disagree about the value of the Act. The FCPA has been attacked by business advocates as being unrealistic, ethnocentric, and harmful to the U.S. economy. Critics contend that bribery is a fact of doing business throughout much of the global marketplace and that Americans should be reluctant to impose their values on the business practices of other nations. They argue as well that the stringency of the FCPA, relative to the range of acceptable practices among other nations, in effect prohibits U.S. companies from lawfully vying for substantial segments of international business. As companies in countries unrestrained by such laws bid in a relatively open field to receive business through bribery, U.S. companies lose opportunities by default. Opponents of the FCPA also suggest that the United States cannot afford to be squeamish about bribery, given the realities of economic recession and the growing trade deficit.

In defense of the FCPA, supporters counter that bribery is morally wrong, as well as detrimental to the efficient functioning of the world economy. They contend that model market transactions should be entered on the basis of legitimate sales characteristics, such as quality, price, and service. The payment of bribery detracts from marketplace efficiency by focusing microtransactional decisions on characteristics unrelated to the quality and value of the goods or services received. For these reasons, FCPA supporters contend that bribery must be proscribed on the basis of principle regardless of the cost to Americans doing business abroad.

FEDERAL BANKING ACTS

With the rapid development of technology and the ever-increasing complexity of financial markets, opportunities for banking crimes have increased dramatically in recent years. As noted earlier, some banking crimes are facilitated by computer technology and fall within the scope of computer-related criminal laws. In addition, a number of federal statutes have been enacted during the past decade to protect financial institutions from theft, fraud, and corrupt practices.

The Federal Bank Fraud Statute.[14]   As a form of generic fraud, bank-related fraud was actionable under state common law before it became the subject of federal statute. Like mail and wire fraud statutes, the bank fraud statute brings causes of action traditionally reserved to the states under federal law. Federal authority is ordinarily justified by the relationship between banking and interstate commerce. Far from being simply redundant, the enactment of federal criminal laws serves both to strengthen enforcement and to improve consistency of expectations in an industry that is truly national and international in scope. The statute broadly prohibits the defrauding of financial institutions and has been applied to such activities as embezzlement, forgery, systematic overdrafting of customer accounts, and the alteration of the payee or the face value of a negotiable instrument.

The Money Laundering Control Act.[15]   *Money laundering* refers to efforts aimed at concealing or disguising the illegal source of money. Money laundering is often accomplished by a series of deposits, withdrawals, transfers, and exchanges of funds that occurs until the tainted derivation of the money can no longer be traced. Although money laundering has been illegal for many years, the Act provides a set of severe civil and criminal penalties meant to increase the deterrence of laundering activity. Penalties include up to twenty years' incarceration, disgorgement of gross receipts attributable to the infraction, and private civil causes of action for treble damages available to persons injured by money laundering activity.

The Bank Secrecy Act.[16]   The Bank Secrecy Act was passed to help the federal government control illegal activity by tracking large cash flows. Accordingly, financial institutions are required to file cash transaction reports (CTRs) for payments, receipts, or transfers in excess of $10,000. This reporting process enables the government to monitor the movement of funds and improves its ability to unveil money laundering activities, as well as the illegal activities that lead to money laundering, such as illegal drug traffic. Beginning in the mid-1980s, the federal government began auditing banks to determine compliance with the reporting requirements of the Bank Secrecy Act and imposing substantial fines on institutions guilty of knowingly and willfully neglecting to report cash transactions covered by the Act.

THE RACKETEER INFLUENCED AND CORRUPT ORGANIZATIONS ACT (RICO)

Congress passed RICO to strengthen federal enforcement and prosecution powers applied to the fight against organized crime and corruption. The statute applies to "enterprises." This requirement has been broadly interpreted by courts to include legitimate as well as illegitimate businesses. Some critics contend that this interpretation surpasses Congress's actual intent and argue that RICO was meant to cover only corrupt organizations whose core businesses are illegal, such as illegal drug operations. RICO prosecution requires a "pattern of racketeering activity," which has been loosely defined by courts as two or more criminal acts within a ten-year period. Federal authorities often decide to prosecute under RICO, in addition to or in lieu of the individual criminal laws that prohibit the predicate activities, because RICO is extremely tough on defendants, both procedurally and in its penalties. The following excerpts address both how RICO operates and some of the controversies that arise under the statute.

LAURA GINGER[17]

Language and Breadth of the RICO Statute

Few areas of the law have caused as much recent controversy as the application of the Racketeer Influenced and Corrupt Organizations Act (RICO). Hailed by some as an effective tool for enforcing ethical business practices while being condemned by others as an overbroad, incomprehensible nightmare that has needlessly tainted business reputations, RICO has generated numerous civil cases in the last several years.

RICO was enacted because Congress was alarmed by the "infiltration of organized crime and racketeering into legitimate organizations operating in interstate commerce." To cope with this perceived infiltration, Congress added the Racketeer Influenced and Corrupt Organizations Act (RICO) to the Organized Crime Control Act of 1970. In doing so, Congress stated that the purpose of RICO was "to seek the eradication of organized crime in the United States . . . by providing enhanced sanctions and new remedies. . . ."

One means by which Congress sought to provide new and powerful sanctions and remedies was the creation of a private right of action in favor of those who were injured in their "business or property by reason of a violation of section 1962," the criminal provision of the Act. This private civil remedy, found in section 1964(c), is generally referred to as "civil RICO," while the prohib-

ited activities listed in section 1962 of the Act are generally referred to as "criminal RICO."

Thus, civil RICO is based upon activities listed in criminal RICO, because only persons injured "by reason of a violation of section 1962" are able to sue under civil RICO.

Section 1962 makes it unlawful to use or invest any income derived from a "pattern of racketeering activity" to acquire, establish, or operate an "enterprise" in interstate commerce. In addition, section 1962 prohibits acquiring or maintaining an interest in such an enterprise through a pattern of racketeering activity or conducting or participating in such an enterprise's activities through a pattern of racketeering activity. Finally, section 1962 makes it unlawful to conspire to do any of those acts.

The statute defines an "enterprise" as "any individual, partnership, or corporation, association, or other legal entity, and any union or group of individuals associated in fact although not a legal entity." This provision has been interpreted by the United States Supreme Court as including legitimate "associations in fact" as well as illegitimate groups. This definition has been liberally construed by the courts to include foreign and domestic corporations, labor organizations, and governmental entities such as police departments, prosecutor's offices, judicial districts, and state and federal agencies.

The requirement of "racketeering activity" does not mandate conduct that fits within any accepted definition of the term. The Act defines racketeering activity in very broad terms as acts involving certain specifically enumerated state and federal criminal offenses, often referred to as "predicate acts." State crimes that give rise to RICO charges are those normally associated with racketeering, including any act or threat chargeable and punishable by imprisonment for more than one year under state laws relating to murder, kidnapping, gambling, arson, robbery, bribery, extortion, and drug dealing. Federal crimes that serve as predicate acts of racketeering are listed specifically by code and section number, and include both racketeering-type and nonracketeering-type crimes, such as mail fraud, wire fraud, fraud in the sale of securities, bankruptcy fraud. extortion, interference by violence or threats of violence with interstate commerce, embezzlement from pension, welfare, and other union funds, and interstate transportation of stolen property.

A "pattern of racketeering activity" is defined merely as two or more acts of racketeering activity committed within ten years of each other, as long as one of the acts occurred after the effective date of the Act.

Violations of RICO are punishable by maximum criminal penalties of a $25,000 fine, a twenty-year prison term, and criminal forfeiture of property; by equitable remedies available to the United States government; and by a cause of action for private civil litigants for treble damages and attorney's fees.

The structural and definitional features of RICO give it a potentially vast scope. Nearly any group of persons can be alleged to be an "enterprise," and private treble-damages suits can be brought by "any person injured in his business or property" by conduct punishable as a crime under the enumerated state and federal laws. On its face, then, civil RICO prohibits officials of government agencies, corporations, or other loose-knit "associations in fact" from running their agencies, businesses, or confederations through the commission of certain illegal acts; prohibits the investment of ill-gotten funds to acquire indirectly other "enterprises"; and forbids "any person employed or associated with" any enterprise which affects interstate commerce to participate in such acts "directly or indirectly."

Federal civil statutes and traditional state tort law also provide remedies for some of the acts prohibited by RICO. However, only RICO makes possible a *civil* cause of action for criminal violations committed in specified circumstances. The broad reach of civil RICO is based upon the expansive definition of the criminal "predicate acts."

The inclusion of mail fraud and securities fraud as racketeering activities vastly expands the potential scope of RICO civil actions. Mail fraud is a particularly broad offense "consisting in essence of a deceitful thought accompanied by the mailing of a letter." Ultimately, RICO civil remedies, which attach to anyone "injured in his business or property by reason of" a criminal RICO violation, could be applied to almost any commercial transaction.

Thus, RICO's broad provisions have been interpreted as encompassing many consumer protection, commercial fraud, bribery, official corruption, and securities violations which have no connection with organized crime; transforming criminal statutes into federal torts; and converting many commercial torts into the basis for federal treble-damage actions.

RICO FOLLOW-UP

RICO is a prosecutor's dream but, by any objective measure, a devil's brew. In the name of combatting organized crime, it permits, under certain circumstances, a pretrial seizure of a criminal defendant's assets even to the extent of a restraint that will intrude upon the defendant's ability to hire a defense counsel of choice.

Responding to a constitutional attack on this provision of RICO, Justice White, writing for the majority in *Caplin & Drysdale* v. *United States*,[18] and in *United States* v. *Monsanto*,[19] disposed of the issue summarily: (1) if the defendant has uncontested assets, he may hire an attorney of choice without fear of forfeiture; (2) if a defendant has no uncontested assets, he may accept appointed counsel and will receive effective assistance, and (3) if appointed counsel renders ineffective assistance, the defendant may later challenge the fairness of the prosecution.

Justices Blackmun, Brennan, Marshall, and Stevens dissented on grounds that RICO deprives criminal defendants of a fair trial guaranteed by the due process clause of the Fifth Amendment and further deprives defendants of the right of counsel guaranteed by the Sixth Amendment.

There are other reservations one might entertain about this act that relate to its wisdom if not its constitutionality. Although Congress has not given any recent evidence of an inclination to amend RICO, several provisions, in our opinion, would benefit by close congressional attention: (1) the government's power to seize assets that are not proven to have any connection with a criminal activity, (2) the timeliness and uniformity of post-seizure hearings, and (3) the protection of the property rights of innocent third parties who may be subject to restraining orders that essentially "freeze" their assets and destroy their ongoing business operations. Currently, these parties must wait until the end of the RICO trial to seek relief.

OTHER FEDERAL STATUTORY CRIMES

A number of other criminal business activities, covered in other chapters in this book, bear brief mention here. Insider trading is subject to both civil and criminal sanctions. Likewise, violations of Sections 1 and 2 of the Sherman Act have resulted in criminal convictions under charges of conspiracy to restrain trade, of monopolization, and of conspiracy to monopolize. The following case examines the scope of another federal statute—the National Stolen Property Act.

United States v. *Dowling*
473 U.S. 207 (S. Ct. 1985)

Justice Blackmun

... The National Stolen Property Act provides for the imposition of criminal penalties upon any person who "transports in interstate or foreign commerce any goods, wares, mechandise, securities or money, of the value of $5,000 or more, knowing the same to have been stolen converted or taken by fraud." 18 U.S.C. §2314. In this case, we must determine whether the statute reaches the interstate transportation of "bootleg" phonorecords, "stolen, converted or taken by fraud" only in the sense that they were manufactured and distributed without the consent of the copyright owners of the musical compositions performed on the records. . . .

The evidence demonstrated that sometime around 1976, Dowling, to that time an avid collector of Presley recordings, began in conjunction with codefendant William Samuel Theaker to manufacture phonorecords of unreleased Presley recordings. They used material from a variety of sources, including studio outtakes, acetates, soundtracks from Presley motion pictures, and tapes of Presley concerts and television appearances.[3]

The eight §2314 counts on which Dowling was convicted arose out of six shipments of bootleg phonorecords from Los Angeles to Baltimore and two shipment from Los Angeles to Miami. The evidence established that each shipment included thousands of albums, that each album contained performances of copyrighted musical compositions for the use of which no licenses had been obtained nor royalties paid, and that the value of each shipment attributable to copyrighted material exceeded the statutory minimum. . . .

Federal crimes, of course, "are solely creatures of statute." *Biparota* v. *United States,* 471 U.S. 419, 424 (1985), citing *United States* v. *Hudson,* 7 Cranch 32 (1812). Accordingly, when assessing the reach of a federal criminal statute, we must pay close heed to language, legislative history, and purpose in order strictly to determine the scope of the conduct the enactment forbids. Due respect for the prerogatives of Congress in defining federal crimes prompts restraint in this area, where we typically find a "narrow interpretation" appropriate. See *Williams* v. *United States,* 458 U. S. 279, 290 (1982). . . .

Applying that prudent rule of construction here, we examine at the outset the statutory language. Section 2314 requires, first, that the defendant have transported "goods, wares, (or) merchandise" in interstate or foreign commerce; second, that those goods have a value of "$5,000 or more;" and, third, that the defendant "know the same to have been stolen, converted or taken by fraud." Dowling does not contest that he caused the shipment of goods in interstate commerce, or that the shipments had sufficient value to meet the monetary requirement. He argues, instead, that the goods shipped were not "stolen, converted or taken by fraud." In response, the Government does not suggest that Dowling wrongfully came by the phonorecords actually shipped or the physical materials from which they were made; nor does it contend that the objects that Dowling caused to be shipped, the bootleg phono-records, were "the same" as the copyrights in the musical compositions that he infringed by unauthorized distribution of Presley performances of those compositions. The Government argues, however, that the shipments come within the reach of §2314 because the phonorecords physically embodied performances of musical compositions that Dowling had no legal right to distribute. According to the Government, the unauthorized use of the musical compositions rendered the phonorecords "stolen, converted or taken by fraud" within the meaning of the statute. We must determine, therefore, whether phonorecords that include the performance of copyrighted musical compositions for the use of which no authorization has been sought nor royalties paid are consequently "stolen, converted or taken by fraud" for purposes of §2314. We conclude that they are not. . . .

[I]nterference with copyright does not easily equate with theft, conversion, or fraud. The Copyright Act even employs a separate term of art to define one who misappropriates a copyright:

" 'Anyone who violates any of the exclusive rights of the copyright owner, that is, anyone who trespasses into his exclusive domain by using or authorizing the use of the copyrighted work in one of the five ways set forth in the statute, is an infringer of the copyright.' . . . There is no dispute in this case that Dowling's unauthorized inclusion on his bootleg albums of performances of copyrighted compositions constituted infringement of those copyrights. It is less clear, however, that the taking that occurs when an infringer arrogates the use of another's protected work comfortably fits the terms associated with physical removal employed by §2314. The infringer invades a statutorily defined province guaranteed to the copyright holder alone. But he does not assume physical control over the copyright; nor does he wholly deprive its owner of its use. While one may colloquially link infringement with some general notion of wrongful appropriation, infringement plainly implicates a more complex set of property interests than does run-of-the-mill theft, conversion, or fraud. As a result, it fits but awkwardly with the language Congress chose—"stolen, converted or taken by fraud"—to describe the sorts of goods whose interstate shipment §2314 makes criminal. . . .

[T]he deliberation with which Congress over the last decade has addressed the problem of copyright infringement for profit, as well as the precision with which it has chosen to apply criminal penalties in this area, demonstrates anew the wisdom of leaving it to the legislature to define crime and prescribe penalties. Here, the language of §2314 does not "plainly and unmistakably" cover petitioner Dowling's conduct. . . . In sum, Congress has not spoken with the requisite clarity. Invoking the "time-honored interpretive guideline" that "ambiguity concerning the ambit of criminal statutes should be resolved in favor of lenity," we reverse the judgment of the Court of Appeals.

It is so ordered.

CASE FOLLOW-UP

In his dissent, Justice Powell argues that the language of Section 2314 "fairly covers the interstate transportation of goods containing unauthorized use of copyrighted material."[21] Powell suggests that the majority opinion reflects the Court's unjustifiable difficulty in viewing the evils of intangible copyright infringement with a degree of condemnation equal to its view of more tangible forms of thievery. He suggests that Dowling's "unauthorized duplication and commercial exploitation of the copyrighted performances were intended to gain for himself the rights and benefits lawfully reserved to the copyright owner. . . . [H]is acts should be viewed as the theft of these performances."[22] Do you agree with the majority opinion or the dissent?

ACCOUNTING-RELATED CRIMINAL STATUTES

Because of the role they play in state and federal auditing, reporting, and taxation processes, accountants must be very careful to comply with both laws and standards of professional responsibility. Accounting crimes are generally established by statute or regulation, and the federal government has become increasingly active in monitoring and controlling the professional activities of accountants in recent years. The areas of potential liability covered in this section are those most frequently encountered in the profession.

Registration of Securities.   Under Section 24 of the Securities Act of 1933, accountants, as well as lawyers and promoters, can be held criminally liable for wrongful acts associated with the issuance of new securities. In particular, it is a federal crime (1) to sell unregistered securities or (2) to make willful misrepresentations or omissions of required material fact in the filed registration statement.[23] In *United States* v. *Benjamin*,[24] the Court of Appeals of the Second Circuit noted that the prosecution's burden in Section 24 criminal prosecutions is to prove "that a defendant deliberately closed his eyes to facts he had a duty to see," or "recklessly stated as facts things of which he was ignorant."[25] This standard suggests that gross negligence can be the foundation for accountants' criminal liability.

The Securities Exchange Act of 1934 created similar liability for misrepresentations contained in registration and disclosure statements required of publicly traded securities and large-scale over-the-counter securities. Section 32(a) sets criminal sanctions for false and misleading statements made in applications, reports, or documents filed under the 1934 Act.[26] Finally, Section 1001 of the Federal False Statements Statutes prohibits fraud relating not only to SEC statements but also to any other statements that fall within federal jurisdiction. The statutory language of Section 1001 covers falsification, concealment, fraud, and false writings.[27] In the following case, the defendants are charged with violations of Sections 32 and 1001, as well as applicable mail fraud statutes.

Evidentiary Effect of GAAP.   Both generally accepted accounting principles (GAAP) and expert testimony regarding usual professional practices are persuasive but not dispositive evidence in criminal prosecutions of accountants. Critics of this approach suggest a number of problems: accountants may be placed in the precarious position of having to second-guess the soundness of their professional standards. This possibility may discourage people from entering the profession, as the risk of criminal prosecution for seemingly appropriate behaviors is increased. Moreover, it may undermine the utility of GAAP, as accountants substitute the profession's cohesive standards with idiosyncratic judgments of their own.

On the other hand, accountants are expected to exercise professional judgment regularly in the course of their business. Moreover, the standards set by the profession can never be entirely comprehensive or inclusive of all contingencies. If technical compliance with GAAP were to be viewed as conclusive evidence of legality, accountants might be able to create liability loopholes to avoid responsibility for engaging in unacceptable business practices.

Criminal Tax Liability.   The Internal Revenue Code creates numerous categories of tax-related crimes that can be applied to both taxpayers and tax practitioners, provided the requisite criminal intent can be established. Business persons and accountants can be fined and/or incarcerated for the following classes of federal tax crimes: attempting to evade or defeat a tax; willfully failing to file a return, to supply information, or to pay taxes; making false or fraudulent statements; filing fraudulent returns, statements, or other documents; failing to obey a summons, attempting to interfere with the administration of Internal Revenue laws, and unlawfully using information obtained in the process of preparing returns.

CONCLUSION

The scope of criminal sanctions for various business practices continues to expand as legislators broaden the embodiment of public policy decisions within the criminal law. Readers of this chapter have probably developed their own opinions regarding the wisdom of criminalizing the many behaviors addressed in the various sections. As the subject of business crimes becomes increasingly controversial, the responsibilities of business persons become more complex. Business persons must be aware of the kinds of behaviors that can result in criminal liability, and they must continue to educate themselves in regard to the changes that continually occur in this area of the law. Moreover, as both business persons and citizens, readers have a responsibility to hold themselves personally responsible for acting in accordance with the highest ethical standards. To the degree that business practitioners accept personal and voluntary responsibility for their own behavior, the need for legislated accountability will be diminished. Furthermore, students of the law must continue to assess and debate the value of criminal laws as they exist on the books and as they are proposed during the political process for future enactment. The need for laws prohibiting truly unacceptable and pernicious behavior must be balanced against the need to respect autonomy and freedom in instances when personal differences in ideology might suggest that criminalization may become an unacceptably coercive imposition of controversial public policies.

REVIEW QUESTIONS AND PROBLEMS

1. A defendant is convicted under a New Jersey statute for "being a gangster." The penalty is a fine of up to $10,000 and/or up to twenty years in prison. The defendant claims that the wording of the statute was vague. Under the Fourteenth Amendment, should the defendant's conviction be upheld or overturned? Why? (*Lanzetta* v. *New Jersey*, 306 U.S. 451, 59 S.Ct. 618, 83 L.Ed. 888 [1939]).

2. Olivo was found guilty of petit larceny and appealed. He had been in the hardware section of a department store when a security guard noticed him. The guard watched Olivo look around cautiously and then crouch down to take a set of wrenches off the shelf and hide it under his outer clothes. The defendant then checked the surrounding area, proceeded past some cash registers, and headed for the exit. At this point, the guard stopped the defendant several feet before the exit doors. The defendant denied that he had the wrench set, yet on the way to the security office, he repositioned the set under his jacket. He claimed at trial that he was waiting to pay for the tools when the

guard stopped him. Has Olivo committed a crime? (*People* v. *Olivo* 52 N.Y. 2d 309, 438 N.Y. S.2d 242, 420 N.E.2d 40 (Ct. App. 1981)).

3. Janet Beaudry was the legal agent and co-owner (with her husband Wallace) of the Village Green Tavern. Wallace, acting on authorization from Janet, hired Mark Witkowski as tavern manager.

   Wallace informed Witkowski of the manager's duty to operate the tavern in accordance with all state liquor laws. Witkowski was never authorized to break those laws, throw private parties for friends, or allow friends to drink for free.

   Nonetheless, a deputy sheriff discovered Witkowski serving drinks to and drinking with two friends at the tavern one morning at 3:45 A.M. The front door was locked, and neither Beaudry was present. The next day, Witkowski told Wallace of the incident. Two days later, Wallace fired Witkowski.

   Three weeks after the incident, Janet was charged with unlawfully remaining open for business after 1:00 A.M. Witkowski was not charged. Given that none of the facts were disputed in trial by either party, what issues under vicarious liability come into play? Should the court enter judgment against the defendant? Why? (*State* v. *Beaudry*, 123 Wis.2d 40, 365 N.W.2d 593 [1985]).

4. Koczwara, a tavern owner, was arrested because his bartender violated the liquor laws of the state. The bartender acted without Koczwara's permission or knowledge, and Koczwara was not present at the time of illegal activity.

   Koczwara faces a mandatory fine of $500 and three months in jail because he is a second offender. Should the defendant receive the mandatory punishment? How is this case different from *State* v. *Beaudry*? (*Commonwealth* v. *Koczwara*, 397 PA 575, 155 A.2d 825 (1959).

5. A government informer meets with defendants Twigg and Neville to propose a drug manufacturing operation. The defendants agree to raise the necessary capital and coordinate the drug distribution network. The informer agrees to supply the materials to produce the drug ("speed"), the laboratory site, and all necessary equipment for production. The informer would oversee the lab operation, because neither defendant had the expertise to produce the drugs. Should the defendants be convicted of conspiracy to manufacture narcotics? (*United States* v. *Twigg*, 588 F.2d 373 [3d Cir. 1978]).

6. Each of several defendants agreed to commit individual and seemingly unrelated crimes: arson, obstruction of justice, selling of narcotics, and theft of goods from interstate commerce. The court applied RICO to "create a substantive offense which ties together these diverse parties and crimes." In effect, this interpretation allows separate, unrelated crimes—committed by different people—to constitute a conspiracy to further the affairs of a common "enterprise." Do you agree or disagree with the court's interpretation? Discuss. (*United States* v. *Elliott*, 571 F.2d 880 [5th Cir. 1978]).

7. Defendant Lund was a Ph.D. candidate in statistics at Virginia Polytechnic Institute and State University (V.P.I.). His dissertation required use of the campus computer center. Prior authorization is required by the university to charge use of computer time to a student's account. Lund used the V.P.I. computer facilities without authorization and charged the time to the accounts of other individuals or departments. Lund's dissertation advisor testified that Lund would have been entitled to assignment of his own computer time had he properly applied for it. The Commonwealth of Virginia sued Lund for larceny and computer crimes. What argument should be made by each side? Who should win, and why? (*Lund* v. *Commonwealth of Virginia*, 232 S.E. 2d 745 [Va. 1977]).

8. LeRoy, as Vice President of a union, engaged in two suspect activities: He received kickbacks from contractors who hired his union's workers, and he received union reimbursement for expenses the union had paid for as though he had laid out the

money himself. According to Section 1962(c) of RICO, it is unlawful "for any person employed by or associated with any enterprise engaged in, or activities which affect, interstate or foreign commerce, to conduct or participate, directly or indirectly, in conduct of such enterprise's affairs through a pattern of racketeering activity." When Leroy was prosecuted under RICO, he contended that a union is not an "enterprise" as required for RICO liability. He also contended that because he did not conduct the criminal acts in furtherance of the union, but rather on his own behalf, RICO does not apply. Is Leroy liable under RICO? (*United States* v. *LeRoy*, 687 F.2d 610 [2d Cir. 1982]).

9. A number of aspects of business crime law have been identified in this chapter as highly controversial. From a public policy standpoint, address the issues that arise in the following controversies. How do you believe each of these controversies should be resolved?

   a. Should criminalization of controversial business practices, such as insider trading and payment of bribes, be expanded in scope?

   b. Is criminalization of undesirable business practices an effective mechanism for deterring such behaviors? If so, is increased criminalization an efficient, cost-effective means of achieving deterrence? If so, is it the most efficient and cost-effective means of achieving deterrence?

   c. Is RICO an effective mechanism for reducing organized crime, including drug-related crimes? Is RICO overly broad in its coverage of "legitimate" business organizations engaged in crime, or is it a justifiably potent tool?

   d. Should U.S. law take the ethical "high road" in prohibiting the payment of bribes in international transactions, particularly when transacting with nations in which bribery is a common and accepted practice? Or is such prohibition an unnecessary and unjustifiable impediment to U.S. competitiveness in a global marketplace?

ENDNOTES

1. First, *Business Crime: Cases and Materials* 14 (1989).
2. Reidy, *Boston Sunday Globe*, June 27, 1993, p. 67.
3. 342 U.S. 246, 250-51 (1952).
4. *United States* v. *United States Gypsum Company*, 438 U.S. 411 (1978).
5. *United States* v. *Park*, 421 U.S. 658 (1975). An edited version of this case appears later in this chapter.
6. *Terry* v. *Ohio*, 392 U.S. 1 (1968).
7. *People* v. *Barraza*, 591 P. 2d 947 (Cal. 1979).
8. *New York* v. *Burger*, 107 S. Ct. 2636 (1987).
9. 232 U.S. 383 (1914).
10. 367 U.S. 643 (1961).
11. 473 F.2d 800 (11th Cir. 1984).
12. 18 U.S.C. § 3551 *et. seq.*
13. Bulkeley, Voice Mail May Let Competitors Dial "E" for Espionage, *Wall Street Journal*, September 28, 1993 p. B1.
14. 18 U.S.C.A. § 1344.
15. 18 U.S.C.A. § 1956(a)(1) (Supp., 1986).
16. 31 U.S.C.A. § 5313 (1970).
17. Portions of this article (originally titled "RICO Liability") and all footnotes have been deleted. The complete article with references can be found in 24 *American Business Law Journal*, 179, 181-84 (1986). Reprinted with permission.
18. 109 S. Ct. 2646 (1989).
19. 109 S. Ct. 2657 (1989).
20. 473 U.S. 207, 229 (1985).
21. *Id.* at 232-32 (1985).
22. 15 U.S.C. § 77x (1992).
23. 328 F.2d 854 (2d Cir. 1964).
24. *Id.* at 862.
25. 15 U.S.C. § 78ff(a) (1992).
26. 18 U.S.C. § 1001 (1992).

CHAPTER 6

Private Property, Law, and the Control of Economic Power

INTRODUCTION

No subject is more boring for the student in law school than "property"; yet, no subject is more important to understanding the legal system than the concept of private property and how the law has shaped and controlled this idea. Many areas of law and of legal conflict, no matter how abstract or technical they seem, grew from one of the five basic areas of law study: constitutional law, property law, contract law, tort law, and criminal law. A large part of contract law, tort law, and criminal law focuses on the meaning of property, how it is traded, how an owner is compensated when it is damaged, and the penalties one must suffer when one interferes with another's property. So, an overview of the idea of private property and its modern ramifications is a necessary starting point for the study of private law. *Private law* is that law concerned with individual, nongovernmental exchange transactions, duties, remedies, and related rights.

In this chapter, we begin with the history of private property and then discuss some traditional legal ideas that have grown out of that history. Next we examine intellectual property, a concept almost as important to the everyday functioning of the U.S. economy as land and physical goods. We close the chapter with a speculative exploration into economic and social power—power based on property, among other things, and the question of whether the law can control property and power in the public interest.

THE HISTORY OF PRIVATE PROPERTY

Property has been a chief source of wealth since ancient times. History reveals a fundamental conflict between those who possess and control property and those who do not possess it. Mediating this tension is the role of government.

Today, Americans seek to divide and control governmental power over them and their property by insisting that the government be divided into three branches of rule making power. The fear of such abuse, however, by those in charge of rule making, has been handled much differently by other civilizations.

GREEK AND ROMAN CONCEPTIONS OF PROPERTY

Plato (427–347 B.C.) realized the connection between property ownership and political power. Therefore, he suggested that those who ruled society not be allowed to own property. Politicians were forbidden to own gold or silver or land. In Plato's ideal state, private property would be owned by merchants, farmers, and artisans.[1] Those who made the rules that governed both people and property would live in barracks, their food and clothes provided by the property-owning classes.

Aristotle, writing about forty years after Plato, suggested that half of the land available for production should be owned in common by all citizens and worked by publicly owned slaves. The produce of the land would be used to supply common meals for those citizens who needed it and for the rulers of the society. The other half of the land could be owned by private individual citizens and could be worked by privately owned slaves.

Reflect for a moment on the ideas here. To the ancient Greeks, the objective of individual life was to seek virtue, truth, and wisdom; the objective of the state was to provide justice. The best way to ensure that the rulers would make just laws was to separate them from private property ownership. Would Americans be better off today if members of the state and federal legislatures, governors of states, the president, and all judges were forbidden to own property, forced to live in dorms and supported with meals and clothes provided by taxes?

Yet, the idea of justice for the Greeks did not pertain, certainly, to the slaves. To the Greeks, slaves were those born to "work like animals," whereas "citizens" were born to pursue leisure for themselves.[2] There is this paradox: In the ancient world, in the name of justice, property ownership was forbidden to those who made the laws, yet slavery was promoted; in the modern world, Americans abolished slavery in the name of justice, but allow all government officials to own private property, thus creating, at all levels of government, the potential for conflict because rulers can make laws to benefit themselves in their pursuit of private property and wealth. Actual records of property ownership in the time of Plato and Aristotle and how land was held and worked have not survived. What was left are writings about the ideal, not the real.

The next chapter in the history of private property was written by the Romans. Cicero (106–43 B.C.) developed the idea of natural law. True law, he wrote, is right reason in agreement with nature. Natural law referred to a set of intuitive ideas that existed in individuals and that allowed them to judge written laws as good or bad. In nature, all people were equal. This idea was a profound break with the Greek tradition that recognized some humans as more worthy than others.

Seneca, writing about A.D. 50–65, recognized two kinds of law—natural law, which existed beyond individuals and was therefore in nature and the mind of

God, and civil law, which was a product of the human mind and an everyday necessity. The idea of property ownership came to be associated with this latter kind of law. At the dawning of the Middle Ages, then, were two views of law (and property). Natural law was God's law, and it defined a perfect universe in which ideas of property would not be needed. In real life, however, laws about who owned what were needed. These views were carried into the lore of the early Christian Church and institutionalized.

St. Augustine (A.D. 354-430) acknowledged the conventional view of the Church, which saw a realm of divine rights created by God and not attainable, and a realm of human endeavor where imperfections were to be worked out by rulers. God created the earth but then left it up to the rulers to sort out the conflicts of everyday life. St. Augustine wrote:

> Whence does each possess what he does possess? . . . (B)y divine right, 'the earth is the Lord's and the fullness thereof: poor and rich are supported by one and the same earth.' But it is (by) human right he saith, 'this estate is mine, this house is mine. . . .' By human right, that is, by right of emperors. How so? Because it is through the emperors and princes of this world that God hath distributed human rights to mankind.[3]

The world at this time was visualized as a three-layer affair with God and perfection (and no laws) on top, then divinely inspired humans such as popes and rulers, and finally the lower level of ordinary people. St. Augustine may have been one of the first modern writers to assert that it is the province of the state or of rulers to create and enforce property rights. Within the areas of influence of the Catholic Church, private property came to mean that individuals could possess land and other things to the exclusion of others so long as one could trace their authority to possess the property to the Roman emperors.

At the fringes of the Roman empire, in Russia and areas of Northern Europe today, a different conception of property emerged. In these areas, no individual could own property to the complete exclusion of others. Property belonged only to a family or clan; individuals owned limited rights, such as the right to graze one's animals on a piece of land where others also had rights or the right to water their stock.[4]

As the Middle Ages drew to a close, the Roman view of direct and absolute ownership from a sovereign had combined with some aspects of property found in Northern Europe. So, one owned property through a grant from the sovereign, but one could then subdivide parts of it. At the same time, one could sell off a right to possess land for certain limited purposes and keep an overall possessory right for other purposes. The historian Richard Schlatter summarized the prevailing view of private property then this way:

> The theory developed that everything had moved from someone, was held of someone, had at some time been granted by someone. And it continued to be held by him. His interest in the thing granted did not cease with the grant. If he had granted land as lord to a vassal, his rights over the land remained, except for the particular interest he had parted with. The result was that no one could be said to own the land; every one from the king down through tenants and sub-tenants to the peasant who tilled it had

certain dominion over it, but no one had absolute lordship over it. The essence of the theory . . . is a hierarchy of rights and powers all existing in or exercisable over the same object or persons, and the fundamental relationship of one power to another in this hierarchy is the superiority of the higher to the lower.[5]

Thus, buried somewhere in the later Middle Ages and the waning of the influence of the early Christian Church in the Northern reaches of Europe (about one thousand years ago), is the emergence of one of the chief characteristics of property today: Ownership of property means that the owner may create types of subowners. He or she may separate out certain uses of property and deal them out separately to others. *For each piece of property, whether land or things that moved, an original owner may grant one person the right to possess it, another the right to pass over it or to use it in certain nonpossessory ways, yet another the right to take minerals from it, yet another the right to take water from it, and so on.*

Law schools today teach that the best way to think about the ownership of property is to view it as a bundle of sticks. Each stick represents one legal interest in the property—one represents possession for some purposes, and under some conditions (e.g., the right to lease a house so long as rent is paid and it is cared for in a reasonable way), another stick represents a certain use of the land, such as the right to mine coal from it.

NORMAN ENGLAND AND FEUDALISM

The basic ideas of property ownership begun in Northern Europe were carried to England and institutionalized following the Norman conquest in 1066. These ideas—the very hallmark of feudalism—took two forms. The first, the *doctrine of tenure,* was that all property ownership now originated with the sovereign. Even today, when a lawyer or an employee of a land title company searches title to land, it is traced back to some sort of original grant from the sovereign (the government).

The second, connected to the idea of tenure, is the *doctrine of estates.* This doctrine established the basic structure of society in feudal times. The doctrine of estates emerged because King William from Normandy (the conqueror of England in 1066) needed a way of consolidating his gains as he marched through England. The idea of an estate was essentially that William granted title to land to his followers in exchange for duties to be performed for the king in the future. Typically, the king would grant a few hundred acres to a dependable, favorite knight in exchange for the knight's promise to give to the king both his own service as a knight and the service of those to whom he choose to give land. This amounted to a sort of conditional grant of land—a knight or subordinate was granted the land so long as he performed whatever service was required.

If the tenant on the land did not perform the service, then his or her right to enjoy the land could be removed by a court convened by the lord to whom the service was owed. This method of land ownership spread throughout England and encompassed all classes of persons. This diffusion had two consequences. First, it stratified all of England into social classes based on land holdings; second, in the words of the legal historian A. W. B. Simpson, the law of the tribunals that could remove a person from land became not only the law of the knightly, aristocratic class, but also applied to all classes within the realm: "It became the common law of England."[6]

Not long after the Norman conquest, the duties held by the lesser possessors of land changed substantially. At first, the duties were to provide knights and armaments; then, as the countryside was settled, the duties expanded to include public projects, from building roads, to providing food to the manor house, to constructing public buildings. These duties became burdensome to some possessors of land, so they began to pay others to do these duties or would give a small parcel of land to peasants to perform the duty.

If the initial grant of property was large, then any number of rungs in the property ladder could be created to continue to supply the obligations. For example, the king would give one thousand acres to a favorite called a tenant-in-chief, the one who holds directly from the sovereign, in exchange for the service of one hundred knights, should they be needed. The tenant-in-chief could then either pay knights to perform this obligation or give fifty acres or so to a subordinate lord, who would be obligated to provide, say, fifteen knights, and so on.

In exchange for the service of the knights, the sovereign or superior lord provided protection and order and a court system to resolve conflicts.

This hierarchical system of property holding with duties running upward and protection flowing downward was called *subinfeudation,* and it provided the social, economic, and legal structures called feudalism. Virtually all services were provided in this way—some of them frivolous:

> In the reign of John we find that William, Earl Warren, granted lands in Stamford to be held for the service of finding annually a mad bull to divert his lordship, whilst there are several grants of land for the service of holding the seasick King's head on trips across the channel. Straw for the royal privy had to be found by one unfortunate landholder, and the tenant of lands in Suffolk, one Rolland, was obliged upon Christmas Day to make a leap, whistle and fart.[7]

This process as a means of consolidating a sovereign's power, however, contained the seeds of its own demise. Just a few decades after it was in place, the lords who owned directly from the king began to die off, and questions of who then owned the land emerged. The custom of inheritance by the eldest son (primogeniture) emerged and was protected by the courts so long as the son provided the services agreed on with his lord. But the eldest sons (or, in some cases, eldest daughters) of deceased loyal knights were not as loyal as their fathers.

The question of whether a possessor or estate holder could sell the land was, perhaps, more challenging to a sovereign's power. Could not a lord sell his interest in property so long as the new purchaser agreed to keep providing the service or paying others to do it? The Statute of Quia Emptores (1290) answered this question in the affirmative. This statute established the right of every landholder to sell his interest in the land he possessed subject to the right of the seller's lord to oust the seller should the service not be provided. The act followed by some seventy-five years the signing of the Magna Carta (1215), which acknowledged basic individual and property rights in the landholding class of England.

Some major ideas created during the feudal times in England are still features of land law today. The idea that if a person dies without heirs, the state is entitled to his or her land is called *escheat,* a feudal practice. The idea that if a person does not pay taxes, the sovereign (the state today) may take his or her property is also a feudal idea. The courts established by the various lords that decided property issues came to apply local custom, as well as the desires of the sovereign, to resolve disputes. English historian J. H. Baker writes, "The management of the manorial land was controlled in open court by decisions purporting to follow the 'custom of the manor.' These customs tied the lord's hand very considerably, and most lords probably submitted to the restraint."[8]

JOHN LOCKE AND THE BEGINNINGS OF THE MODERN ERA

Perhaps no writer is more important in the establishment of present-day conceptions of private property than the English philosopher John Locke (1632–1704). His most important contribution to Western thought and the development of ideas of private property are found in the *Two Treatises of Government*, which appeared for the first time (anonymously) in 1690 and was subsequently revised during his lifetime (only in his will did he admit to authorship).

The early writings about the nature of property were that, in an ideal state, no one would own anything because all was in nature or in God's kingdom. Locke sought to challenge this fundamental view by arguing that although property was found in nature, it could be owned by those individuals who used their own labor to change nature. In this pursuit, Locke did not write about God or a king or the state. It was possible, he argued, that persons could own property directly by imparting their own labor to nature.

Locke's influence on the founders of the American Republic—such men as Alexander Hamilton and Thomas Jefferson—was decisive. Here is one of his most famous passages.

JOHN LOCKE

Two Treatises on Civil Government[9]

Though the earth and all inferior creatures be common to all men, yet every man has a "property" in his "person." This nobody has any right to but himself. The "labor" of his body and the "work" of his hands, we may say, are properly his. Whatsoever, then, he removes out of the state that Nature hath provided and left it in, he hath mixed his labor with it, and joined to it something that is his own, and thereby makes it his property. It being by him removed from the common state Nature placed it in, it hath by this labor something annexed to it that excludes the common right of other men. For this "labor" being the unquestionable property of the laborer, no man but he can have a right to what that is once joined to, at least where there is enough, and as good left in common for others.

He that is nourished by the acorns he picked up under an oak, or the apples he gathered from the trees in the wood, has certainly appropriated them to himself. Nobody can deny but the nourishment is his. I ask, then, when did they begin to be his? When he digested? or when he ate? or when he boiled? or when he brought them home? or when he picked them up? And it is plain, if the first gathering made them not his, nothing else could. The labor put a distinction between them. . . . That added something to them more than Nature, the common mother of all, had done, and so they became his private right. And will any one say he had no right to those acorns or apples he thus appropriated because he had not the consent of all mankind to make them his? Was it a robbery thus to assume to himself what belonged to all in common? If such a consent as that was necessary, man had starved, not withstanding the plenty God had given him. We see part of what is common, and removing it out of the state Nature leaves it in, which begins the property, without which the common is of no use.

★ ★ ★

It will, perhaps, be objected to this, that if gathering the acorns or other fruits of the earth, . . . makes a right to them, then any one may engross as much as he will. To which I answer, Not so. The same law of Nature that does by this means give us property, does also bound that property too. "God has given us all things richly. . . . Is the voice of reason confirmed by inspiration? But how far has He given it to us—to enjoy?" As much as any one can make use of to any advantage of life before it spoils, so much he may his labor fix a property in. Whatever is beyond this is more than his share, and belongs to others. Nothing was made by God for man to spoil or destroy. . . .

Before the appropriation of land, he who gathered as much of the wild fruit, killed, caught, or tamed as many of the beasts as he could—he that so employed his pains about any of the spontaneous products of Nature as any way to alter them from the state Nature put them in, by placing any of his labor on them, did thereby acquire a propriety in them; but if they perished in his possession without their due use—if the fruits rotted or the venison putrefied before he could spend it, he offended against the common law of Nature, and was liable to be punished: he invaded his neighbor's share, for he had no right farther than his use called for any of them, and they might serve to afford his conveniences of life.

EXCERPT FOLLOW-UP

1. In Locke's view, what or where is the primary source of the right of private property?

2. Are there limits on this right or idea of private property?

Locke's writing freed the source of private property from religious or state-based foundations and put it squarely in one's own nature. "(E)very man has a 'property' in his 'person'," assumes Locke, thus what he transforms by his own hand from a state of nature becomes his. This right to transform nature has limits, however. Locke also carries forward the idea that nature's bounty is, at first, owned in a kind of common ownership. Although some property may be owned by imparting one's labor to it, if a man takes more than he needs, then he has invaded his neighbor's share because his "right" only extended no farther than his use called for.

THE EARLY AMERICAN EXPERIENCE

A combination of ideas was at work when the settlement of the American shores began. Because settlement of the first colonies was carried out under the auspices of the English sovereign, he, in theory, first owned all of the land "discovered" and could thus grant it to whomever he wished. His grantees took parcels of land, subject to the obligation to pay a form of annual rent either in money or in grain. Populating the early settlements was a first order of business, and many who held land grants from the king offered as much as fifty acres to any invited newcomer who would bring an additional person.[10]

Many first came to America bound by law to work for those who sponsored them. These workers, known as indentured servants, were bound by contract to work for their sponsors for a number of years, until the cost of passage or other debt was worked off.

Married women were thought to be in a state of suspended personhood. Early law viewed husband and wife as one person, but this person was almost wholly that of the husband. On marriage, the husband acquired a legal right to occupy the real estate of the wife and an absolute right to her personal property. Any property acquired during the marriage could also be occupied by the husband if it was land, and disposed of or otherwise controlled if it was personal property. The property of married women was not seen as separate until after the passage of married women's property acts, the first of which was passed in 1839. Not until about 1850 did most states recognize the right of married women to own property.

There is little doubt that the early (and darkest) chapters of the history of American property law concerned slavery. Some towns and states in the North outlawed slavery from the first days. Other states recognized it as a necessary evil and made attempts to outlaw it only late in the eighteenth century. As the eighteenth century gave way to the nineteenth, the institutions supporting slavery became more entrenched in the South. Historian Lawrence Friedman writes that as a matter of recorded history, "slavery grew more severe between the Revolution and the Civil War. The slave owning South dug in its heels (over time)."[11]

Slaves were first believed to be personal property, but as the influence of slavery deepened, their ownership was considered more of a capital asset, like land. The idea that one person could possess an ownership interest in another did not end in the United States until the Civil War, a time centuries after slavery died in Europe.

Another perplexing picture of property exploitation emerges as we focus on the Westward expansion in the late 1700s. If one applies the Lockean ideas of property ownership to the indigenous persons who inhabited North America at the time of the Westward expansion, then these native dwellers owned their land; the Europeans took it from them.

An undeclared and little-discussed principle of both political economy and property law, in its crudest form, is known as "might makes right." Waves of settlers rolled out of New England and through the mountains and across the plains of Ohio, Indiana, Illinois, and on. Theoretical niceties of natural ownership were assumed to apply to those who took from nature, and it seems indigenous inhabitants were part of nature, and not fellow owners.

Land law at the frontier was crude, if not chaotic. Some of the greatest early American trials involved the title to large tracts of land. The means of conveying land were still almost feudal. People marked the land as best they could, put themselves in possession of it, and when required, tried to register their ownership. This testimony is from a 1799 trial court in Kentucky involving the ownership of land. A man named Berry said he cut:

> (A) white ash or hickory to mark his claim, but which of them he can not be certain, and cut the two first letters of his name and blacked them with powder, and sat down at the foot of a small sugar tree and chopped a hole with his tomahawk in the root of it. (Where was the ash or hickory now?) Cut down, but the stump remained, in a very decayed state. The sugar tree was still standing, and identifiable; the tomahawk mark was still perceivable.[12]

This crude means of keeping track of America's greatest natural resource was wanting even to the very early American mind. In a congressional act of May 18, 1796, which applied to much of the land northwest of the Ohio River, the government provided for a federal office of the surveyor general and added that all public lands were to be surveyed into townships of six miles square. Half of the townships were to be further divided into sections of one mile square (640 acres), and these tracts were to be further divided into tracts of 160, 80, and 40 acres. All land in the West after about 1800 was to be surveyed before it was sold. Flying from Chicago to San Francisco today, one can see the result of this land policy—all of the tillable land is large squares and rectangles. Few of the land disputes that marked our early history exist today. Land is transferred by an owner-signed piece of paper called a *deed,* describing the exact location of the property and a copy of which has been on file with local county government.

SOME CLASSIC FORMS OF PROPERTY

Property comes in many forms. Below is an overview of some of the more classic forms of property or, more technically, types of property rights. You can see why legal scholars think of property ownership as a bundle of rights.

Fee simple absolute. is a technical term indicating that the one who has this property interest is the owner. The owner may have taken the property subject to others having the following interests in the land and improvements (the house), or the owner may convey these interests to others:

Mortgage. A property interest that allows the holder of it (usually a bank) to sell the property if an amount of money, usually that used to purchase the land, is not repaid to the original bank (lender) as promised. The holder of the mortgage may, in turn, sell this right to receive payments and to sell the land, on default, to others.

Lien. A property interest in those who benefit the property to secure payment for the value of the benefit; this is created usually by state law and is held by, for example, someone who puts on a new roof; a tax lien is a property interest in a governmental unit to secure payment of a tax; if no payment is made, the property interest "comes alive," and the roof provider or governmental unit may sell the property. Payment discharges the property interest.

Easement.   A property interest that enables a non-owner to use the property in a particular nonpossessory way. Usually, an easement is held by utility companies so they may come on to property to repair their underground pipes, wires, or machinery. Or, one landowner might have an easement across another's land to reach a stream to water livestock.

Licenses and invitees.   A license is a property interest, often created informally, to come onto property for a particular purpose. Usually, this purpose does not have any benefit for the owner. A neighbor who chases his or her cat onto your property may have a license to act reasonably to find and retrieve the cat. The holder of a license is a licensee; licensees are sometimes distinguished from "invitees," who also may have a small property interest. For example, a business with a sign that says "Restaurant" creates an informal property interest in potential customers to enter the building during business hours. Customers are invitees.

Lease.   A property interest created by contract or operation of law (a statute, usually) in which the holder is entitled to possession of the property for a certain term in exchange for the payment of rent.

Bailment.   A property interest in personal property (movables) that allows one to possess the property for a particular purpose. For example, a car repair shop has a property interest in a car delivered for repair.

MODERN FORMS OF PROPERTY

CONCURRENT OWNERSHIP

By no means can we attempt in this text to discuss or even outline all modern forms of property. We examine three forms of modern property—concurrent ownership, intangible property, and intellectual property—to emphasize the enormous impact of property on our lives. The first form is the idea and practice of concurrent ownership. This form of property may go by many names, each differing, technically, from the others. *Concurrent ownership* may be called a tenancy in common, or a joint tenancy, or a tenancy by the entirety, or a condominium or a cooperative. But the core idea, which is a unique form of property, is that each concurrent owner has an individual interest in the whole property. Husbands and wives, for example, often own their homes in a form of concurrent ownership. This means they both own all of the property and cannot be excluded from any part of it by the other.

Partners in a formal business partnership also are concurrent owners, and each has an equal right to possess all of the property for business purposes. Two modern forms of concurrent ownership of real property are the condominium and the cooperative apartment house. Usually, in both of these forms of property, owners have an individual fee simple absolute right to possess the interior living space but own the shared areas of hallways, walkways, yards, gardens, pools, and so forth in common. No owner can be excluded from these common areas.

INTANGIBLE PROPERTY—NAMES AND LIKENESSES

A second form of modern property—intangible property—is illustrated in the case below. In this case a group of Elvis Presley fans wanted to use his name, after his death, to form the Elvis Presley International Memorial Foundation. The foundation would support a new trauma center at the Memphis and Shelby County Hospital. Presley's heirs tried to block the use of his name without their permission.

Elvis Presley v. *Crowell*
733 S.W.2d 89 (Tenn. App., 1987)

Elvis Presley's career is without parallel in the entertainment industry. From his first hit record in 1954 until his death in 1977, he scaled the heights of fame and success that only a few have attained. His twenty-three year career as a recording star, concert entertainer and motion picture idol brought him international recognition and a devoted following in all parts of the nation and world.

Elvis Presley was aware of this recognition and sought to capitalize on it during his lifetime. He and his business advisors entered into agreements granting exclusive commercial licenses throughout the world to use his name and likeness in connection with the marketing and sale of numerous consumer items. As early as 1956, Elvis Presley's name and likeness could be found on bubble gum cards, clothing, jewelry and numerous other items. The sale of Elvis Presley memorabilia has been described as the greatest barrage of merchandise ever aimed at the teenage set. It earned millions of dollars for Elvis Presley, his licensees and business associates.

Elvis Presley's death on August 16, 1977 did not decrease his popularity. If anything it preserved it. Now Elvis Presley is an enter-tainment legend, somewhat larger than life, whose memory is carefully preserved by his fans, the media and his estate.

The demand for Elvis Presley merchandise was likewise not diminished by his death. The older memorabilia are now collectors items. New consumer items have been authorized and are now being sold. Elvis Presley Enterprises, Inc., a corporation formed by the Presley estate, has licensed seventy-six products bearing his name and likeness and still controls numerous trademark registrations and copyrights. Graceland, Elvis Presley's home in Memphis, is now a museum that attracts approximately 500,000 paying visitors a year. Elvis Presley Enterprises, Inc. also sells the right to use portions of Elvis Presley's filmed or televised performances. These marketing activities presently bring in approximately fifty million dollars each year and provide the Presley estate with approximately $4.6 million in annual revenue. The commercial exploitation of Elvis Presley's name and likeness continues to be a profitable enterprise. It is against this backdrop that this dispute between these two corporations arose.

★ ★ ★

Elvis Presley's Right of Publicity

We are dealing in this case with an individual's right to capitalize upon the commercial exploitation of his name and likeness and to prevent others from doing so without his consent. This right, now commonly referred to as the right of publicity, is still evolving and is only now beginning to step out of the shadow of its more well known cousin, the right of privacy.

The confusion between the right of privacy and the right of publicity has caused one court to characterize the state of the law as a "haystack in a hurricane." . . . This confusion will not retard our recognition of the right of publicity because Tennessee's common law tradition, far from being static, continues to grow and to accommodate the emerging needs of modern society. . . .

* * *

The concept of the right of property is multi-faceted. It has been described as a bundle of rights or legally protected interests. These rights or interests include: (1) the right of possession, enjoyment and use; (2) the unrestricted right of disposition; and (3) the power of testimonial disposition.

In its broadest sense, property includes all rights that have value. . . . It embodies all the interests a person has in land and chattels that are capable of being possessed and controlled to the exclusion of others. . . . Chattels include intangible personal property such as choices in action or other enforceable rights of possession. . . .

Our courts have recognized that a person's "business," a corporate name, a trade name and the good will of a business are species of intangible personal property. . . .

Tennessee's common law thus embodies an expansive view of property. Unquestionably, a celebrity's right of publicity has value. It can be possessed and used. It can be assigned, and it can be the subject of a con-

tract. Thus, there is ample basis for this Court to conclude that it is a species of intangible personal property.

Today there is little dispute that a celebrity's right of publicity has economic value. Courts now agree that while a celebrity is alive, the right of publicity takes on many of the attributes of personal property. It can be possessed and controlled to the exclusion of others. Its economic benefits can be realized and enjoyed. It can also be the subject of a contract and can be assigned to others.

What remains to be decided by the courts in Tennessee is whether a celebrity's right of publicity is descendible at death under Tennessee law. Only the law of this State controls this question. . . .

We have . . . concluded that recognizing that the right of publicity as descendible promotes several important policies that are deeply ingrained in Tennessee's jurisprudence. First, it is consistent with our recognition that an individual's right of testamentary distribution is an essential right. If a celebrity's right of publicity is treated as an intangible property right in life, it is no less a property right at death. . . .

Second, it recognizes one of the basic principles of Anglo-American jurisprudence that "one may not reap where another has sown nor gather where another has strewn. . . ."

This unjust enrichment principle argues against granting a windfall to an advertiser who has no colorable claim to a celebrity's interest in the right of publicity.

Third, recognizing that the right of publicity is descendible is consistent with a celebrity's expectation that he is creating a valuable capital asset that will benefit his heirs and assigns after his death.

* * *

Fourth, concluding that the right of publicity is descendible recognizes the value of the contract rights of persons who have acquired the right to use a celebrity's name and likeness. The value of his interest stems from its duration and its exclusivity. If a celebrity's name and likeness were to enter the public domain at death, the value of any existing contract made while the celebrity was alive would be greatly diminished. . . .

Fifth, recognizing that the right of publicity can be descendible will further the public's interest in being free from deception with regard to the sponsorship, approval or certification of goods and services. Falsely claiming that a living celebrity endorses a product or service violates Tenn. Code. . . . It should likewise be discouraged after a celebrity has died.

Finally, recognizing that the right of publicity can be descendible is consistent with the policy against unfair competition through the use of deceptively similar corporate names. . . .

The legal literature has consistently argued that the right of publicity should be descendible. A majority of the courts considering this question agree. . . .

We find this authority convincing and consistent with Tennessee's common law and, therefore, conclude that Elvis Presley's right of publicity survived his death and remains enforceable by his estate and those holding licenses from the estate.

CASE FOLLOW-UP

1. The opinion recognizes the "right of publicity" and awards a remedy which is a hallmark of property law. This is the court order to exclude others from the property. The court enters an injunction against those who would use Presley's name. How long, in your judgment, should such an injunction last? Forever?

2. What interests are promoted by holding that one's name and one's likeness continue to be private property after one's death? What interests would be promoted by holding that one's name and likeness become part of the public domain upon death? The estates of George Washington, Thomas Jefferson, and others have no such right of publicity. Why? Should they have?

This case makes plain at least two important ideas. First, one's name and likeness are a form of property called *intangible personal property*. Some of the basic classifications of property are tangible property (things that can be touched) such as real property (land and things permanently attached to it), and

personal property (movables); and intangible property (abstract ideas and things, such as a name, a reputation, an image, or likeness and other things not tangible).

Second, at death one's property passes into one's "estate" and then from the estate, following probate of the estate, to various heirs according to a will that is left or, if there is no will, then according to a state statute. In some cases, a will may establish something called a *trust*, which is a legal entity created by law to hold and administer property. Trusts may last as long as the instrument establishing them says they exist or until the objective of the trust is accomplished.

One justification for granting property rights after death is that it is assumed to affect the motivation of living persons who can know their efforts will contribute to the well-being of their heirs. Does this give heirs an undue head start over others who, by accident of birth, do not have parents who can leave an estate? What would life be like if, beyond a token amount of property left by one's ancestors, each generation had to start from scratch?

INTELLECTUAL PROPERTY

Intellectual property is, like land law, of fairly ancient origin in character, yet it involves some of the most modern conceptions of property and property law.

Intellectual property usually refers to the legal rights in the product of the mind and has been traditionally divided into the three areas of patents, trademarks, and copyrights. Intellectual property law is largely statutory in nature, which provides a convenient starting point for its study, yet by the very character of intellectual property, it is hopelessly tied to many other legal areas such as tort and contract law, and is affected mightily by antitrust law and other forms of governmental regulation. This is not the sort of subject the average practitioner of law handles. It is a highly specialized form of legal practice in which the law overlaps not only with other categories of law but also with the latest developments in science, the arts, and the humanities.

The essence of the law in this area is that the legal system affords protection to the originator of a practical idea, usually in the form of a machine or process of some sort or a work of art, to the exclusion of others. In more economic terms, the idea of intellectual property is the award of a monopoly to a person or firm; this monopoly will be enforced by the appropriate state or federal court or agency by enjoining others from using the idea or work of art, and such agency may award damages for the use of such an idea or work of art against those who risk exploiting others' creativity.

PATENTS

The history and practice of patent law is one of constant tension between protecting those persons (and firms) who (in the words of the current patent statute) invent or discover any "new and useful process, machine, manufacture or composition of matter" and, at the same time, protecting the public because the award of any monopoly is subject to widespread abuse at the expense of the public.

In the Middle Ages, parts of European commercial society became centralized into guilds. Each guild—for example, those in leather working, glassmaking, iron working, and the like—took to itself the ability to admit or exclude crafters from the manufacture of the item, subject to the guild. In the name of protecting the quality of the good produced and of training artisans to continue the trade, these guilds consciously attempted to corner and control the market in the good. Guilds were the historic model for today's professions. In the name of preserving quality (thus, protecting the public) and in the name of training new members, both the legal profession and the medical profession control admission to the profession and regulate their respective members.

By the end of the Middle Ages, the sovereign had usurped the right to control these increasingly specialized markets and would grant a royal privilege to be a guild member. These privileges were called *patent monopolies*. As commerce became more important in the daily lives of Europeans, the monarch would give a privilege to practice a particular manufacturing process or art to a foreigner who agreed to bring new skills into the kingdom. These were called *importation patents*. This patentee was then also required to train citizens in the new skill. This grant was always limited to a period of years.

In the sixteenth century, as the Middle Ages gave way to a new mercantile economy, tension heightened between the holders of these patents and those desiring more competition in these markets. At first, in England, the growing power of the common law courts recognized that it was unlawful to abuse this royal privilege. Thus were born the first ideas of unfair competition. A piecemeal, court-based approach was not satisfactory, so a legislative solution was tried. In 1623, the Statute of Monopolies, passed by Parliament, was intended to regulate the abuses of the patent privilege.

In the colonies, a more strident voice was raised against the idea of royal monopolies (then in England), though it was recognized that the importation patent was a useful way to encourage economic development. By the time of the Revolution, all of the colonies provided for patents. State-by-state recognition of patents was burdensome to the one seeking this protection, so at the time of the Constitutional Convention in 1787, support was widespread for a federal and even a constitutional right to patent protection.

Thus, Article 1, Section 8 of the Constitution sets out what are called the expressed powers of the federal government, and it provides that Congress shall have power "To promote the Progress of Science and useful Arts, by securing for limited Times to Authors and Inventors the exclusive Right to their respective Writings and Discoveries" (Clause 8). The first patent statute elaborating on this constitutional right was passed by Congress in 1790, and few major revisions of this act have been made since then.

The core idea in the modern statute is that the person (or firm) who wants a patent must demonstrate to the Patent Office (established in 1836) of the federal government that the process or product is *new, useful, and nonobvious*. Of course, a tremendous amount of case law defines these words and others in the patent statute. At one extreme, the Supreme Court said in 1850, in rejecting a patent for a porcelain doorknob (the only novelty was the use of the porcelain), that the recipient of a patent must demonstrate more ingenuity than that of an *ordinary mechanic acquainted with the business*; at the other extreme, the Supreme Court has said that an idea patented must amount to something akin to a *flash of thought*.[13] Ordinary or simple advances in technology or processes are not awarded the privilege of patent protection. Of course, every applicant for a patent believes his or her invention is a substantial leap forward.

Well into this century, large firms that already held many patents attempted to exploit all variations of a patent or to extend the length of the patent by all possible means. Lawrence Friedman reported,

> Large companies learned how to stretch out their monopoly by manipulating patents. Bell Telephone bought a German patent, vital for the technology of long-distance telephoning. It waited until its telephone patent had almost expired, then pressed ahead

with the German device. This gave it control of the telephone industry even after its first basic patent had passed into the public domain. Under the umbrella of the patent monopoly, companies divided up markets, licensed out the nation in segments, and chained whole counties or states to particular vendors of a patented good.[14]

Today, the basics of patent application involve, first, the filing of a patent application with the Patent Office. This office researches past patents and all of the relevant technical literature and decides whether the object of the patent is new, useful and nonobvious. If so, it grants a patent for the statutory period, which at present is seventeen years. Exceptions may extend this period by five years. At the end of the statutory period, the patent expires and the object of the patent passes into the public domain and may be used.

During the life of the patent, the holder may grant a property right, usually called a *license,* to others for a fee to use the patented object. The patent may be sold outright, or it may not be developed or used. The owner has the exclusive right to do with the patent whatever he or she wishes. Quite often, a patent owner must sue to keep others from using the patented object without authorization. The limits of a patent grant are never absolutely precise, and litigation is quite common. A nonauthorized use may show that the Patent Office erroneously granted the patent or that it was procured through fraud or misrepresentation. More often than not, courts have found that the patent challenged was not valid.

Recently, the case law has centered around just what can be patented in an age of mushrooming technology. In 1980, a patent application for an oil-eating bacterium was granted and upheld by the federal courts. In 1988, Harvard University was granted an animal patent for an "oncomouse," a small creature engineered for the study of cancer. Also in that year, the U.S. Senate became interested in the ethics of patenting life forms.

The ethical argument on this topic is twofold: (1) that humans do not have the "right" to bring into existence life forms to either experiment with or inflict pain on, and (2) that allowing patents on life forms is an example of technology run amok because one can never predict exactly what influence laboratory-bred animals will have on the natural environment should they escape the lab. The book and film *Jurassic Park* expanded on this point. Researchers at the University of Wisconsin have reported creating a genetically "perfect cow" whose genes can be cloned an infinite number of times.[15]

Proponents of patenting animals argue that patenting is no different from owning animals—animals are property and may be bought and sold, killed and bred, as the owner deems appropriate. Moreover, patents of life forms are needed to protect large investments in research. If Americans don't do it, so the argument goes, the Japanese or the Europeans will.

Are patents or state-sponsored monopolies needed? The answers are mixed. On the one hand, major inventions such as the printing press, early explosives, and one of the most basic inventions of all, the wheel—were not patented. The atom bomb, Einstein's formulations of basic forces, and the creative work of Benjamin

Franklin and Thomas Jefferson were brought to life without a thought to their patentability.

On the other hand, who can argue with success? The plethora of materialistic goods and technological wonders available today is some evidence that the protection of this form of intellectual property encourages such advances.

The case below, although a copyright case technically, discusses patent law and how federal patent law overlaps with state common law and state statutory law that defines unfair and deceptive trade practices. Actually, patent law is a subset of the legal principles that define unfair and deceptive trade practices. Patent law removes from competitive forces in the market the development and sale of goods that are new, useful, and nonobvious. But, what of the developments that do not qualify for patent protection. It would be unfair, would it not, to allow large competitors to "rip off" or copy almost exactly the commercial developments of someone who may just be starting off? The following case, when discussing the *Sears* v. *Stiffel* and the *Compco* v. *Day-Bright* cases, gives an astounding answer to this question.

Capitol Records, Inc. v. *Erickson*

Court of Appeals of California
2 Cal.App.3d 526, 82 Cal.Rptr.798 (1969), cert. denied,
398 U.S. 969 (1970)

WOOD, P. J.

For the purposes of the preliminary injunction, there is no dispute as to the facts. Phoenix (Defendant) is admittedly in the business of selling prerecorded stereophonic tape cartridges, which it produces as follows: Phoenix purchases on the open market records and tapes of musical performances which have been produced, recorded, and sold by Capitol. Phoenix then makes "master" recordings from the records and tapes which it purchased and uses the master recordings to produce tape cartridges which it sells to the general public. On the front of each cartridge package Phoenix affixes a label which bears the title of the recorded performance and the names of the performing artists; and, on the back of the cartridge package, it affixes a label bearing the following words: "No relationship of any kind exists between Phoenix and the original recording company nor between this recording and the original recording artist. This tape is not produced under a license of any kind from the original company nor the recording artist(s) and neither the original recording company nor artist(s) receives a fee or royalty of any kind from Phoenix. Permission to produce this tape has not been sought nor obtained from any party whatsoever."

Appellant (Phoenix) contends that the court erred in granting the preliminary injunction. It argues in effect that its conduct in duplicating recordings produced by Capitol, without permission of Capitol or the recording artists, and then selling the duplicated recordings in competition with Capitol, is condoned by the decision in *Sears, Roebuck & Co.* v. *Stiffel Co.*, 376 U.S. 225 and *Compco Corp.* v. *Day-Brite Lighting, Inc.*, 376 U.S. 234; and that a state court cannot, on the theory of unfair competition or otherwise, enjoin such conduct.

In the *Sears* case, Sears manufactured a pole lamp which was "a substantially exact copy" of a pole lamp manufactured by Stiffel, and Sears sold its pole lamps at a price lower than the price for which the Stiffel lamps were sold. Stiffel's lamp was not patentable under federal law. The trial court found that there was some confusion by the public as to the source of the lamps, and found that Sears was guilty of unfair competition. (To establish a case of unfair competition under Illinois law, it was necessary to prove that there was "palming off"— "likelihood of confusion as to the source of the products.") The Supreme Court has stated . . . that "the patent system is one in which uniform federal standards are carefully used to promote invention while at the same time preserving free competition," and that a state "could not extend . . . the life of a patent beyond its expiration date or give a patent on an article which lacked the level of invention required for federal patents." It was also said . . . "An unpatentable article, like an article on which the patent has expired, is in the public domain and may be made and sold by whoever chooses to do so. What Sears did was to copy Stiffel's design and to sell lamps almost identical to those sold by Stiffel. This it had every right to do under the federal patent laws. That Stiffel originated the pole lamp and made it popular is immaterial. 'Sharing in the goodwill of an article unprotected by patent or trademark is the exercise of a right possessed by all—and in the free exercise of which the consuming public is deeply interested.' To allow a State by use of its law of unfair competition to prevent the copying of an article which represents too slight an advance to be patented would be to permit the State to block off from the public something which that while federal law grants only 14 to 17 years' protection to genuine inventions, States could allow perpetual protection to

articles too lacking in novelty to merit any patent at all under encroachment on the federal patent system to be tolerated." The judgment (restraining Sears from selling its lamps) was reversed.

In the *Compco* case (decided on the same day as the *Sears* case), Compco manufactured a fluorescent lighting fixture which was substantially identical to a fixture manufactured by Day-Brite. Day-Brite's fixture was not patentable under federal law. The trial court found that there was confusion as to the source of the fixtures (Illinois law) and that Compco was guilty of unfair competition. The Supreme Court held that the order (restraining Compco from selling its fixtures, etc.) was "in conflict with the federal patent laws." It was also said "As we have said in Sears, while the federal patent laws prevent a State from prohibiting the copying and selling of unpatented articles, they do not stand in the way of state law, statutory or decisional, which requires those who make and sell copies to take precautions to identify their products as their own. A State of course has power to impose liability upon those who, knowing that the public is relying upon an original manufacturer's reputation for quality and integrity, deceive the public by palming off their copies as the original."

★ ★ ★

After the decisions in the *Sears* and *Compco* cases, several courts (state and federal) granted injunctive relief on the ground that misappropriation of unpatentable or uncopyrightable property by a competitor constituted unfair competition. . . . Specifically, lower court decisions have read the cases as prohibiting state injunctions against copying but not against appropriations—the distinction being between the duplication of one's work by another—copying—and "the use of the identical product for the profits of another"— misappropriation. Thus, for example, where the defendant, without authority, dubbed the plaintiff's recorded performance, the fact that the copying of a phonograph record was involved was deemed immaterial; after referring to *Sears* and *Compco*, the court concluded that the only issue presented hereon is whether defendants may appropriate the performance contained on plaintiff's phonograph records. In another post-Sears and Compco case, which involved the unauthorized recording of an announcer's newscast, the court, after determining that a "broadcaster's voice and style of talking is, to all intents and purposes, his . . . property," held that "What was here done was not the copying of some article or goods made and sold by another but rather the appropriation of the very product itself, taking in effect the original and incorporating it in the record."

★ ★ ★

Actually, what was here done was not the copying of some article or goods made and sold by another but rather the appropriation of the very product itself . . . (emphasis added)."

★ ★ ★

In California, section 3369, subdivision 3, of the Civil Code provides that unfair competition "shall mean and include unlawful, unfair or fraudulent business practice and unfair, untrue or misleading advertising any act denounced by Business and Professions Code Sections 17500 to 17535, inclusive."

It is to be noted further that in 1968 the California Legislature enacted section 653h of the Penal Code, which provides in part as follows: "(a) Every person is guilty of a misdemeanor who: (1) Knowingly and willfully transfers or causes to be transferred any sounds recorded on a phonograph record, disc, wire, tape, film or other article on which sounds are recorded, with intent to sell or cause to be sold, or to use or cause to be used for profit through public performance, such article

on which such sounds are so transferred, without the consent of the owner." Thus, the Legislature has in effect provided that "record piracy" is a misdemeanor.

In the present case, as above shown, Capitol expends substantial effort, skill and money in selecting performing artists and obtaining the exclusive right to record their performances, in mechanically reproducing their performances on discs and tapes of the highest quality, and in promoting the sale of the tapes and discs. Phoenix acquires the finished tapes and cartridges at little cost, labels the cartridges with the same title and the same name of the performing artists as appears on the Capitol recordings, and sells the cartridges in competition with, and at a substantially lower price than, the discs and tapes sold by Capitol. It is obvious that Phoenix is able to sell cartridges at such lower price, and still gain substantial profit, because Phoenix circumvents the necessity of expending skill and money in acquiring the artists and recording their performances. Thus, Phoenix unfairly appropriates artistic performances produced by Capitol's efforts, and Phoenix profits thereby to the disadvantage of Capitol. . . .

Phoenix's argument that the state court cannot restrain such unfair competition is not sustainable. Under some of the above-cited cases, state law, statutory or decisional, may in some circumstances grant relief where deceptive or fraudulent competitive practices are conducted, such as circumstances where one palms off his products as those of his competitor, or where he unfairly appropriates to his profit the valuable efforts of his competitor. . . . Phoenix has not merely copied or imitated discs or tapes produced by Capitol, rather, Phoenix has appropriated the product itself—performances embodied on the records. In addition, Phoenix has appropriated the titles of the performances [citations omitted] and has appropriated the name of the recording artists [citations omitted]. It is reasonable to conclude that permitting such appropriation would discourage invention and free competition—and that those engaged in the recording industry would be inclined not to utilize their skill and efforts, and expend large amounts of money, in producing unique recordings, but would wait for a recording to be produced, and then duplicate it and sell it, at maximum profit and with minimum effort and expense. The trial court herein did not err in granting the preliminary injunction.

The order (granting preliminary injunction) is affirmed.
LILLIE, J., and THOMPSON, J., concurred.

CASE FOLLOW-UP

1. How did this court decide the issue of the potential conflict between federal patent law and state unfair competition law?

2. What interests in society are served by deciding for Sears against Stiffel and Compco against Day-Brite?

3. Given the decision in this case, do you think it would be legally permissible to allow a remote country singer to copy the arrangement of Willie Nelson's rendition of one of his songs and not pay Nelson's recording company for it?

4. Does this case represent a form of governmental regulation? After all, an agency of the state (the court system) is ordering a business not to do something. When business leaders claim that government should get off their backs, do they have this kind of case in mind? What do they have in mind? That is, what kind of regulation do they favor?

5. Can businesses regulate themselves, or is government needed to set the boundaries of competitive markets by developing and applying concepts of unfair competition?

In the final analysis, we must ask, what is the substantive difference between what Phoenix did in copying tapes of Capitol and what Sears did in manufacturing a "substantially exact copy" of Stiffel's pole lamp, and what Compco did in manufacturing a "substantially identical" light of Day-Brite? The court writes about the differences between copying (which is allowable) and appropriating, which is the use of an identical product for the purpose of gaining profit (which is illegal). We confess it is very difficult to see that Phoenix may have produced an exact copy, whereas the others were substantially identical to the lamp and lights copied. Granted, the investment of Capitol was threatened, but what of the investment of Stiffel and Day-Brite?

These objections aside, the California statute quoted seems to resolve the issues between Phoenix and Capitol. The purpose of the case here is to illustrate that even if one fails to have an invention patented, both a state-based common law and statutory law might protect an inventor from deceptive and unfair practices of making exact copies.

COMPUTERS AND PATENT LAW

Before we go on and explore the other categories of intellectual property, we must note the tremendous impact that the computer has had on our legal environment of business in this area. So far we have explained that the U.S. Constitution and our current patent laws protect new, useful and nonobvious processes, machines and the like. On the other hand, the well-being of our economy is enhanced if ideas, concepts, laws of nature, mathematical formulae and the like are free for all to use. Between these two policy preferences, where do computer-related claims fall? The answer is not a clear one. Generally, protection for computer-related developments can come from both the patent and patent-related laws, and copyright and copyright-related laws.

The first major case was a 1972 U.S. Supreme Court decision (*Gottschalk* v. *Benson*, 409 U.S. 63) which held that a process for converting binary-coded decimal numerals into pure binary numerals could not be patented. The court held that a procedure for solving a given type of mathematical problem (referred to as an algorithm) is not patentable because it is like a form of logic or a law of nature.

In a 1981 decision (*Diamond* v. *Diehr*, 450 U.S. 175) the U.S. Supreme Court held that patentability of a computer program often depends on the end product produced by the program. In this case a process to cure synthetic rubber that involved a computer program was patentable. The court concluded that the process admittedly employed a well-known mathematical equation, but the petitioners did not seek to patent the equation. They sought, said the Court, only to foreclose from others the use of that equation in conjunction with all of the other steps in the process. These include installing rubber in a press, closing the mold, constantly recalculating the appropriate cure time through the use of the formula and a digital computer, and automatically opening the press at the proper time.

Thus, if a computer can be used to transform and reduce an article from one state to a different state or thing, the process (although it involves a computer program) may be patentable. We will have more to say about computers and intellectual property when we discuss copyrights.

TRADEMARKS

The word *trademark* is almost perfectly descriptive of the items to which it refers. A trademark is any work, name, symbol, device or combination of these used by one in trade to identify its product and to distinguish the product from those of competitors. Modern interpretations of these devices include colors, pictures, labels, package designs, slogans, sounds, arrangements of numbers and/or letters, and shapes of goods to identify and distinguish goods and services.

Trademarks had their origins before the Middle Ages in the Mid- and Far East, where archaeologists have unearthed artifacts with such symbols on them. During the Middle Ages, most guilds developed identifying marks for their goods. The purpose of such marks then was to indicate to the purchaser that the product bought was of the highest quality—the best the guild was capable of producing.

This idea is incorporated into the most recent federal trademark statute, the Lanham Act (1946), which protects the owners of federally registered trademarks against others using it if confusion would result. Trademark law evolved slightly differently than patent law. Patent law was to encourage innovation; trademark law, primarily, was to prevent unfair competition in the various markets for goods and services by prohibiting unscrupulous competitors from causing confusion between their inferior goods and those of a quality producer.

In 1988, the Lanham Act was amended to reduce protection for a registered trademark from twenty to ten years, but renewals for additional ten-year periods were possible. A trademark may be lost by a successful challenge from a competitor alleging that the trademark is confusing, or through abandonment of the trademark (failure to use it), or through the trademark acquiring a generic meaning by taking on a meaning that identifies a large class of similar products or services. Aspirin, cellophane, and in the years to come (in all probability), xerox are examples of such generic names.

COPYRIGHTS

Copyright law, like patent law, finds its American roots in the Constitution because Article I, Section, 8, quoted above, refers to securing exclusive rights to *authors* and *inventors*. Trademark law, however, is not rooted in the Constitution, but rather in the common law and, today this common law has been usurped by federal statute.

The idea of copyright protection, however, came to the United States from Europe and probably started with the invention of the printing press. The owners of the first printing presses in England sought protection of their investment in the creation of books, and the sovereigns and courts gladly helped out. Publishers soon gained the upper hand, and authors and the public protested. The Statute of Anne (1710) was the first statutory attempt to adjust the competing interests of publishers on the one hand and authors and the public on the other.

Authors in this period felt abused because although the law recognized their rights in written work before publication, the publisher held the legal right to the copyright after publication. Publishers often retained much more of the royalties than originators of the work thought they should. Even to this day, allegations of abuse and "sharp dealing" arise when an author negotiates with a publisher to publish creative work. The same may be said of almost any creative work. Where would publishers be without authors, or movie studios be without actors and writers, or record companies be without song writers and singers, or art galleries be without artists? Of course, the opposite—where would authors be without publishers, and so on—may also be worthy of mention. A system seems to have evolved in which the creative work is developed by one group of persons and the commercial exploitation of it is developed by others.

Copyright law today applies to creative expressions found in books, periodicals, dramatic and musical compositions, works of art, motion pictures, sound recordings, lectures, computer programs, and architectural plans. For creative works published in 1978 and thereafter, the date of the latest federal statute on copyrights, the copyrights usually last for the life of the author plus fifty years. This statute provides for registration and notice to the public of the owner of the copyright.

A major characteristic of this type of intellectual property is that federal law allows fair use of copyrighted material. The case below is an example of an assertion of the "fair use" defense to an allegation that one has infringed a copyright.

Basic Books, Inc. v. *Kinko's Graphics Corporation*
785 F. Supp. 1522 (U.S. Dist. Ct., S.D.N.Y.)

Background

Kinko's is a chain of duplication stores that was in the business of preparing course packets as part of its "Professor Publishing" program for its some 200 shops around the country located near colleges or universities. The program allowed teachers and professors to select excerpts from works that they wished to assign for the semester. Kinko's would then copy and bind the excerpts, often entire chapters or essays, in preparation for the course.

The major publishing houses of New York (Harper & Row, John Wiley & Sons, McGraw-Hill, Penguin books, Prentice-Hall, Richard D. Irwin, and William Morrow & Co.) sued alleging copyright infringement. Kinko's conceded that they indeed copied the excerpts in suit without obtaining permissions, compiled them, and sold them to students. However, they asserted a number of defenses: The fair use doctrine and others.

★ ★ ★

Opinion

I. Fair Use.

Coined as an "equitable rule of reason," the fair use doctrine has existed for as long as the copyright law. It was codified in § 107 of the Copyright Act of 1976. . . .

The codification was intended to "restate the present judicial doctrine of fair use, not to change, narrow or enlarge it in any way. . . ."

For almost 300 years, American law has protected intellectual property rights through the copyright law. . . . [In 1841], Justice Story set forth the meaning of fair use to which we adhere today. "In short, we must often . . . look to the nature and objects of the selections made, the quantity and the value of the materials used, and the degree in which the use may prejudice the sale, or diminish the profits, or supersede the objects of the original work. . . ."

Fair use more currently has been defined as the "privilege in others than the owner of a copyright to use the copyrighted material in a reasonable manner without his consent, notwithstanding the monopoly granted to the owner. . . ." The copyright law, through the fair use doctrine, has promoted the goal of encouraging creative expression and integrity by ensuring that those who produce intellectual works may benefit from them. . . .

A. The 4 Factors of Fair Use.

1. Purpose and Character of Use

Transformative use

It has been argued that the essence of "character and purpose" is the transformative value, that is, productive use, of the secondary work compared to the original. . . . Kinko's work cannot be categorized as anything other than a mere repackaging.

Most contested instances of copyright infringement are those in which the infringer has copied small portions, quotations or excerpts of works and represents them in another form, for example, a biography, criticism, new article or other commentary. . . . In this case, there was absolutely no literary effort made by Kinko's to expand upon or contextualize the materials copied. . . . The excerpts in suit were merely copied, bound into a new form, and sold. The plaintiffs refer to this process as "anthologizing." The copying in suit had productive value only to the extent that it put an entire semester's resources in one bound volume for students. It required the judgment of the professors to compile it, though none of Kinko's.

Commercial use

The use of the Kinko's packets, in the hands of the students, was no doubt educational. However, the use in the hands of Kinko's employees is commercial. Kinko's claims that its copying was educational and, therefore, qualifies as a fair use. Kinko's fails to persuade us of this distinction.

. . . Its Professor Publishing promotional materials clearly indicate that Kinko's recognized and sought a segment of a profitable market, admitting that "tremendous sales and profit potential arise from this program. . . ."

The extent of [Kinko's] insistence that theirs are educational concerns and not profit making ones boggles the mind.

Kinko's has periodically asserted that it acted at the instruction of the educational institution, that is, as the agent of the colleges and is without responsibility. Yet, Kinko's promotional materials belied this contention particularly because Kinko's takes responsibility for obtaining copyright permission while touting the expertise of its copyright permissions staff. . . .

★ ★ ★

While financial gain "will not preclude [the] use from being a fair use" . . . consideration of the commercial use is an important one.

2.   The Nature of the Copyrighted Work

The second factor concerns the nature of the copyrighted work. Courts generally hold that "the scope of fair use is greater with respect to factual than non-factual works. . . ." Factual works, such as biographies, reviews,

criticism and commentary, are believed to have a greater public value and therefore, uses of them may be better tolerated by the copyright law. . . . Fictional works, on the other hand, are often based closely on the author's subjective impressions and, therefore, require more protection. These are general rules of thumb. The books infringed in suit were factual in nature. This factor weighs in favor of defendant.

3.   The Amount and Substantiality of the Portion Used

. . . [The] third factor considers not only the percentage of the original used but also the "substantiality" of that portion to the whole of the work; that is, courts must evaluate the qualitative aspects as well as the quantity of material copied. . . . A short piece which is "the heart of" a work may not be fair use and a longer piece which is pedestrian in nature may be fair use. The balancing of the four factors must be complete, relying solely upon no one factor. the purpose of the use may be balanced against the amount and substantiality of the use. . . .

Additionally, "reference to a work's availability is appropriate." Therefore, longer portions copied from an out-of-print book may be fair use because the book is no longer available. . . .

This court finds and concludes that the portions copied were critical parts of the books copied, since that is the likely reason the college professors used them in their classes. . . .

This factor, amount and substantiality of the portions appropriated, weighs against defendant. . . . In one case Kinko's copied 110 pages of someone's work and sold it to 132 students. Even for an out-of-print book, this amount is grossly out of line with accepted fair use principles.

★ ★ ★

4.   The Effect of the Use on Potential Markets for or Value of the Copyrighted Work

The fourth factor, market effect, also fails the defendant. This factor has been held to be "undoubtedly the single most important element of fair use. . . ."

Kinko's confirms that it has 200 stores nationwide, servicing hundreds of colleges and universities which enroll thousands of students. The potential for widespread copyright infringement by defendant and other commercial copiers is great. . . . While it is possible that reading the packets whets the appetite of students for more information from the authors, it is more likely that purchase of the packets obviates purchase of the full texts. This court has found that plaintiffs derive a significant part of their income from textbook sales and permissions. This court further finds that Kinko's copying unfavorably impacts upon plaintiffs' sales of their books and collections of permissions fees. This impact is more powerfully felt by authors and copyright owners of the out-of-print books, for whom permissions fees constitute a significant source of income. This factor weighs heavily against defendant.

5. Other Factors

In this case an important additional factor is the fact that defendant has effectively created a new nationwide business allied to the publishing industry by usurping plaintiffs' copyrights and profits. This cannot be sustained by this court as its result is complete frustration of the intent of the copyright law which has been the protection of intellectual property and, more importantly, the encouragement of creative expression. . . .

★ ★ ★

Kinko's claims that "the evidence shows that course packets are of tremendous importance to teaching and learning, and are the subject of widespread and extensive use in schools throughout the country" and that "injunction against the educational photocopying at issue would pose a threat to teaching and the welfare of education. . . ." This appears to be a "fair use by reason of necessity" argument. Kinko's has failed to prove this central contention which is that enjoining them from pirating plaintiffs' copyrights would halt the educational process.

Kinko's did not produce any professor to testify that he or she uses course packets and would be disabled from teaching effectively if Kinko's could not copy without paying permissions fees.

★ ★ ★

Conclusion

This court finds the excerpts copied by defendant Kinko's are not a fair use of plaintiffs' copyrights and, therefore, constitute infringement. Plaintiff is granted statutory damages, injunctive relief and attorneys' fees and costs. . . .

So Ordered.

CASE FOLLOW-UP

1. Why was this lawsuit necessary? Why couldn't or didn't the publishers and Kinko's sit down and work out some arrangement in which Kinko's would agree to pay some amount for the fair use of the materials copied? Such an arrangement has now been worked out, in all probability. Why did it take this lawsuit to bring this out?

2. Does this case go too far to vindicate a principle of law? The payment plan worked out probably amounts to a paltry sum, compared with the grosses of publishing giants like these plaintiffs.

3. Is it fair to make any generalizations about the fact that, in the case above, the established interests in the form of the nation's largest publishing houses won, and in the

case before the one above, the established interests like Sears won? That is, what is the difference between the copying of Kinko's, which was enjoined (ordered stopped by the court), and the copying of Sears and Compco, which the court allowed? Shouldn't the copying of Kinko's be as valuable to society as that of Sears?

Given the cases above, it may seem that intellectual property law is the law of the "biggies." We have not accumulated or read all of the appellate cases in this area, but our general reading leads us to conclude that this is a reasonable conclusion concerning the law in this area.

PROPERTY, POWER, AND THE LAW: CHALLENGES FOR THE FUTURE

Much of property law involves a balancing of interests, but some generalizations can be made. The first is that the more property one has, the more one is likely to view the law (and government) as a positive force. Law protects property; it guides the uses of property and allows the accumulation of property.

As one moves up the property scale, one also moves up the power scale; law loses its strictly prohibitive character, and some of its facilitative aspects surface. Law enhances one's property; it sanctions valuable contracts and coordinates the transferring of valuable property. The property system of the United States provides for vast accumulations of property in the form of multinational corporations and also provides for the ownership of these aggregations of property by millions of persons. Understandably, people who have benefitted from this system extol its virtues, its permanence, and its immutability. Those on the outside looking in rarely experience this brighter side of law, in part, because they have no property to begin with.

The second generalization is that beliefs about property are some of the most important reasons to form governments. At the heart of the economic system called capitalism are beliefs about property and private ownership and about profit as a "just" return to private property.

Beliefs about property define cultures and civilizations. In the cosmology of the American Indian, the ownership of land was unthinkable. In modern times, beliefs about property ownership are a key to understanding national and world economies. Corporations—artificial persons created by law—own land anywhere in the world and on which the *owners* of the corporation need never set foot. Indeed, shareholders of corporations, although they are the owners, cannot possess corporate property—the property is possessed by the managers—those in control—who are not the owners.

The third generalization is that not all beliefs about property are consistent or seem logical. Some beliefs about property and the social institutions these beliefs have spawned can be quite complex and even convoluted or inconsistent.

Most contemporary Americans believe that private ownership of property with minimum outside intervention from the state is the best possible property arrangement. Textbooks from law and elsewhere affirm this belief. Yet, a close reading of U.S. governmental regulation of the past thirty years reveals an expansive role for government, especially in the areas of the protection of the environment and the extent to which one might use business-related property to discriminate on the basis of race, religion, gender, age, and national origin. It's fair to say that, over the past few decades, some uses of property have been increasingly restricted by government despite a popular nationwide political rhetoric that opposed such intervention. Presidents Reagan and Bush spent twelve years in office supported by the call to "get government office off our backs" and "out of our lives."

On the global scene, belief systems regarding property have been shifting at, it seems, the speed of light. The old Eastern Bloc countries have dumped their old property system and are moving toward a new one based on beliefs that they once rejected as grossly unjust. Only yesterday, in those same countries, universal principles seem to have led irrefutably toward public, rather than private, ownership of critical property and the means of production. For these countries, yesterday's truths are no longer self-evident.

The cold war between the United States and the Soviet Union was a battle over how property should be held and by whom, which manifested itself as a confrontation of nuclear weapons and a struggle for political influence. Students of property need to examine whether historically unique forms of property holding—for example, state-held property or individually held property—are today justified and otherwise squared with their universal principles.

Generalizations aside for a while, let's examine just one case in which the claims of the U.S. public conflict with those of individual landholders. The Bill of Rights to the U.S. Constitution deals prominently with property. The Fourth Amendment prohibits the state from interfering with both a person's freedom and his or her property unless the state acts reasonably and has a good reason; this reason, in law, is called *probable cause*. Both the Fifth Amendment and the Fourteenth Amendments prohibit the state from taking private property without just compensation. The very words of the Fifth Amendment are ". . . nor shall private property be taken for public use, without just compensation."

The power of the local, state, or federal governments to take private property is called the *power of eminent domain*. This power comes from historical Western notions of sovereignty. This means that inherent in the very idea of a government is the power of such government to take property to protect and promote the public health, safety, and welfare.

The key to understanding the ideas in the Fifth Amendment—(which apply to the federal government and to state and local governments) is the idea of a "taking." How far can the state go to regulate private property before it amounts to a taking which requires full compensation?

The most concrete idea here is that if a governmental unit *occupies* private land, then this is a taking. At the other extreme, a simple zoning ordinance that controls *just some of the uses* of land is not a physical occupation of the land and is not a taking, so no compensation is required. The following case (first presented in Chapter 4) is the latest word on this subject, but the test that it uses to trigger compensation (the test of a taking) is not all that clear, as we will explain.

Lucas v. *South Carolina Coastal Council*

60 U.S.L.W. 4842
Supreme Court Of The United States
Decided June 29, 1992

Background

In 1986, David H. Lucas paid $975,000 for two residential lots on the Isle of Palms in South Carolina, on which he intended to build single-family homes. At the time of the purchase, Lucas's lots were not subject to the state's coastal zone building permit requirements. In 1988, however, the state legislature enacted the Beachfront Management Act, which effectively prohibited Lucas from erecting any permanent habitable structures on the property. Lucas sued, claiming that even though the Act may have been a lawful exercise of the State's police power, the ban on construction deprived him of all "economically viable use" of his property and therefore effected a "taking" under the Fifth and Fourteenth Amendments entitling him to just compensation. The state trial court agreed, finding that the ban rendered Lucas's parcels "valueless" and entered an award exceeding $1.2 million. The State Supreme Court reversed, holding that when a regulation is designed to prevent "harmful or noxious uses" of property akin to public nuisances, no compensation is owing under the Takings Clause regardless of the regulation's effect on the property's value.

★ ★ ★

SCALIA, JUSTICE
Where the State seeks to sustain regulation that deprives land of all economically beneficial use, we think it may resist compensation only if the . . . inquiry into the nature of the owner's estate shows that the proscribed use interests were not part of his title to begin with.

This accords, we think, with our "takings" jurisprudence, which has traditionally been guided by the understandings of our citizens regarding the content of, and the State's power over, the "bundle of rights" that they acquire when they obtain title to property. . . .

Where "permanent physical occupation" of land is concerned, we have refused to allow the government to decree it anew (without compensation), no matter how weighty the asserted "public interest" involved . . . —though we assuredly would permit the government to assert a permanent easement that was a pre-existing limitation upon the landowner's title. . . . We believe similar treatment must be accorded confiscatory regulations, i.e., regulations that prohibit all economically beneficial use of land: Any limitation so severe cannot be newly legislated or decreed (without compensation), but must inhere in the title itself, in the restrictions that background principles of the State's law of property and nuisance already place upon land ownership. A law or decree with such an effect must, in other words, do no more than duplicate the result that could have been achieved in the courts—by adjacent landowners (or other uniquely affected persons) under the State's law of private nuisance, or by the State under its complementary power to abate nuisances that affect the public generally, or otherwise.

On this analysis, the owner of the lake bed, for example, would not be entitled to compensation when he is denied the requisite permit to engage in a land filling operation that would have the effect of flooding others' land. Nor the corporate owner of a nuclear generating plant, when it is directed to remove all improvements from its land upon discovery that the plant sits astride an earthquake fault. Such regulatory action may well have the effect of eliminating the land's only economically productive use, but it does not proscribe a productive use that was previously permissible under relevant property and nuisance principles. . . . When, however, a regulation that declares "off-limits" all economically productive or beneficial uses of land goes beyond what the relevant background principles would dictate, compensation must be paid to sustain it.

The "total taking" inquiry we require today will ordinarily entail (as the application of state nuisance law ordinarily entails) analysis of, among other things, the degree of harm to public lands and resources, or adjacent private property, posed by the claimant's proposed activities, . . . the social value of the claimant's activities and their suitability to the locality in question, . . . and the relative ease with which the alleged harm can be avoided through measures taken by the claimant and the government (or adjacent private landowners) alike. . . . The fact that a particular use has long been engaged in by similarly situated owners ordinarily imports a lack of any common-law prohibition (though changed circumstance or new knowledge may make what was previously permissible no longer so). So also does the fact that other landowners, similarly situated, are permitted to continue the use denied to the claimant.

It seems unlikely that common-law principles would have prevented the erection of any habitable or productive improvements on petitioner's land; they rarely support prohibitation of the "essential use" of land. . . . The question, however, is one of state law to be dealt with on remand. We emphasize that to win its case South Carolina must do more than proffer the legislature's declaration that the uses Lucas desires are inconsistent with the public interest. . . . Instead, as it would be required to do if it sought to restrain Lucas in a common-law action for public nuisance, South Carolina must identify background principles of nuisance and property law that prohibit the uses he now intends in the circumstances in which the property is presently found. Only on this showing can the State fairly claim that, in proscribing all such beneficial uses, the Beachfront Management Act is taking nothing.

The judgement is reversed and the cause remanded for proceedings not inconsistent with this opinion.

So ordered

CASE FOLLOW-UP

1. Justice Scalia writes of a bundle of rights that owners of property have. How do you word the pertinent property right that David Lucas, the owner in the case above, has following this case?

2. When, then, must a state or local government compensate an owner for a "taking" of private property?

The facts of this case do not make it easy to apply the ruling of the majority. The ruling or holding of the majority is that a state must compensate an owner of private property where a state regulation deprives land of all economically beneficial use unless an inquiry into the nature of the owner's estate shows that the prohibited use was not part of the title to begin with. So, what if the prohibited use was one that was not possible or was of questionable value to begin with? Then, one might argue that such a use was not part of the title to begin with and that any governmental regulation of that use does not require compensation.

In his dissent to this case, Justice Blackmun writes that Lucas was a contractor, manager, and part owner of a land development firm in the area of the property in question. He had lived there since 1978. The property purchased was "notoriously" unstable. In about half of the last forty years, all or part of Lucas's property was part of the beach and flooded twice a day by the ebb and flow of the tide. From 1957 to 1963, the property was under water. From 1963 to 1973, the shoreline was 100 to 150 feet onto Lucas's land, and in 1973, the first line of stable vegetation was about halfway through the property. From 1981 to 1983, the local government issued twelve emergency orders for sandbagging to protect property in the development where the land was located. This authority determined that the local habitable structures were in imminent danger of collapse and thus issued permits for two rock revetments to protect condominium developments near the property in question; one of the revetments extended more than halfway onto one of Lucas's lots.

How do you think a court will find on a retrial of this case? Was Lucas's property "taken" so that compensation was required?

The typical case revealing the state's power of eminent domain involves the construction of a highway through, for example, a series of farms in the countryside. The state surveys the land, notifies the owners that it is "taking" the land for public use, and offers to compensate the owners for the land taken. Just how much is taken is often subject to debate and may be decided in a court case instituted by the owner to protest the amount and value of the land taken. There is little question, however, that the state may take the land.

In a few cases, it has been held that the government may not have to occupy the land or to render it completely valueless. In the classic case of *United States* v. *Causby*,[16] the petitioner's land was rendered useless for purposes of raising chickens by the overflight of Navy aircraft. The Supreme Court got caught up in a flurry of technical words, declaring that the Navy had imposed a "navigational servitude by inverse condemnation," which essentially meant that the Navy was required to pay for the value of the land as a chicken farm even though they did not occupy the land.

More recently, the Supreme Court held in *Loretto* v. *Teleprompter Manhattan CATV Corporation*[17] that a statute authorizing private cable TV companies to install cables in apartment buildings over the landlord's objection is a physical invasion and a taking.

It may seem like splitting hairs, but assume that a builder buys a piece of commercial property near an airport with the intent to build a thirty-story building on it. Before the building is built, the local government passes a zoning restriction limiting all buildings near the airport to twenty stories. Most courts would view this as a legitimate use of the government's police power to regulate property, and it would not, in all probability, be viewed as a taking requiring compensation.

By and large, the productive property in the United States is to be held by nongovernmental entities. This is called *private property* and if the government occupies it or renders it valueless, then it must pay for it; it can take this property only so long as the taking is reasonably related to some "legitimate" state purpose of protecting the health, safety, and welfare of the residents. Lesser interventions with private property, such as zoning ordinances that merely restrict some uses, do not require payment to the owners.

THE TWENTIETH CENTURY PROPERTY REVOLUTION— SHARE OWNERSHIP

The dispute over the rights to intangibles, such as the name of Elvis Presley, marks the deep transformation of the nature of U.S. property and wealth that has been occurring in this century. More than one hundred years ago, the United States was a nation of small farmers, crafts people, and petty merchants. Back then, property was, well, you know—property: land and things you could touch. Historian Harry Braverman writes that the household was the center of production until the turn of the twentieth century and later.

> On the United States farm, for example, much of the construction work . . . was accomplished without recourse to the market, as was a good deal of house furnishing. Food production, including the raising of crops and livestock and the processing of these products for table use was of course the daily activity of the farm family, and so also was the home production of clothing. The farmer and his wife and their children divided among them such tasks as making brooms, mattresses and soap, carpentry and small smith work, tanning, brewing and distilling, harness making, churning and cheese making, processing and boiling sorghum for molasses, cutting posts and splitting rails for fencing, baking, preserving, and sometimes even spinning and weaving. Many of these farm activities continued as the natural mode of life of the family even after the beginnings of urbanization and the transfer of employment to the factory or other city job.[18]

The passage of the Sherman Antitrust Act of 1890 attests to the public concern about the growing loss of control of enterprises on which sustenance increasingly depended. The creation of business trusts controlling beef, sugar, tobacco, oil, railroads, and other essentials meant that the average American had become more economically vulnerable than ever before.

The career of John D. Rockefeller provides a handy measure of the transformation of American enterprise and property from the small, the local, and the tangible to the very large, the national, and the intangible. Rockefeller began as a clerk and eventually became a partner in a small commodity trading firm in Cleveland. The Civil War proved a boom to such companies and gave the firm capital for expansion into oil refining, which was in its infancy after the discovery of oil in Pennsylvania. The oil business outgrew the partnership form, and Rockefeller used the corporate form as the business grew. The corporate form, because of a rule of law that then limited corporate activity to one state, was itself too limiting, and the business trust was created to enable Rockefeller-controlled corporations to function as a national company. Finally, the state of New Jersey allowed business holding companies, obviating the need for the use of the business trust.

One of the most important revolutions of this century was the emergence of new forms of property that today dominate the economic and legal landscape. It is quite easy to say that the emergence of the modern, very large business corporation in this century (e.g., Rockefeller's Standard Oil) brought a revolution in how we think of property and wealth, but it is much more difficult to assess the impact of this revolution. One significant product of this revolution was the creation of what the noted corporation- law scholar Adolph Berle called *passive property*.

In 1932, Adolph Berle and Gardiner Means, both of Columbia University, published their seminal work, *The Modern Corporation and Private Property*. They argued that a primary impact of the large American business corporation at the beginning of this century was to create a new form of property. In the past, it was assumed that an owner of property controlled the property. Indeed, control was a key element in what was meant by ownership. A shareholder in a modern business corporation owned (almost in a technical sense) the corporation through ownership of common stock but did not *control* the corporation. The day-to-day control of the large business corporation was in those who possessed the corporation, *the managers*.

The authors built their argument by using the arcane language of the lawyer (Berle) and the economist (Means). In general, they said the separation of ownership from control came about because the shareholders in most large business corporations were so numerous and so dispersed that they could not vote as a block to elect the board of directors, those who are legally responsible for the management of the corporation. Moreover, the shareholders had even less influence on the hiring of the officers of the corporation, those who in practice controlled the corporation. The officers (managers), the authors maintained, set the agenda to be voted on at the shareholders' meetings as well as nominated those who would stand for election to the board. Berle and Means concluded that share ownership of the large modern business corporation had brought a revolution of unknown proportion to U.S. society:

> The translation of perhaps two-thirds of the industrial wealth of the country from individual ownership to ownership by the large, publicly financed corporations vitally changes the lives of property owners, the lives of workers, and the methods of property tenure. The divorce of ownership from control consequent on that process almost necessarily involves a new form of economic organization of society.[19]

In a 1965 scholarly article in the *Columbia Law Review*, Berle updated his work of thirty years earlier. Below is an excerpt from this article.

ADOLPH A. BERLE

Property, Production and Revolution

[*Author's note:* This article[20] has been edited and footnotes eliminated.]

The property system as applied to productive assets breaks down (as of the end of 1963) as follows: 525 billion dollars of shares of corporate stock; 210 billion dollars in fixed income financial assets (federal, state and local government securities, corporate and foreign bonds, life insurance values, etc.); and 360 billion dollars in liquid assets, chiefly cash in banks. These figures mean that, far and away, the largest item of personally owned "Property" representing productive assets and enterprise is in the form of stock of corporations.

. . . "Individually-owned" enterprise is thus steadily disappearing. Increasingly, the American owns his home, his car, and his household appliances; these are for his consumption. . . .

In crude summation, most "owners" own stock, insurance, savings and pension claims and the like, and do not manage; most managers (corporate administrators) do not own. The corporate collective holds legal title to the tangible productive wealth of the country—for the benefit of others.

★ ★ ★

The Corporation becomes the legal "owner" of the capital . . . collected and has complete decision-making power over it; the corporation runs on its own economic steam. On the other hand, its stockholders, by now grandsons or great-grandsons of the original "investors" or (far more often) transferees of their transferrees at thousands of removes, have and expect to have through their stock the "beneficial ownership" of the assets and profits thus accumu-

lated and realized, after taxes, by the corporate enterprise. Management thus becomes, in an odd sort of way, the uncontrolled administrator of a kind of trust having the privilege of perpetual accumulation. The stockholder is the passive beneficiary not only of the original "trust," but of the compounded annual accretions to it.

. . . These [ownership] shares nevertheless have become so desirable that they are now the dominant form of personal wealth-holding because, through the device of stock exchanges, they have acquired "liquidity"—that is, the capability of being sold for ready cash within days or hours. The stockholder, though no longer the sole . . . [passive beneficiary] of all profits, is the . . . [passive beneficiary] of about half of them, and that is the vast stake. Sophisticated estimates indicate that dividends better than eight percent per annum during the generation past. The package of passive property rights and expectations has proved sufficiently satisfactory to have induced an increasing number of Americans to place their savings in this form of property. . . . The aggregate market value of personally-owned shares now approximates ten to fifteen percent more than the annual personally-received income in the United States. . . .

Yet this is only the "top level" of passive property-holding. A very large number of shares are not held by individuals. One of the two largest groups of such intermediary institutions is that of the pension trust funds maintained by corporations or groups of corporations for the benefit of employees; these collect savings in regular installments from employers to be held in trust for their employees and subsequently paid to them as old age or other similar benefits. The second is the relatively smaller group of institutions known as mutual funds; these buy a portfolio of assorted stocks and sell participation in the portfolio to individuals desiring to hold an interest in diversified groups of stock instead of directly holding shares in one or more companies. . . .

The significance of [these] intermediate institutions is twofold. First, they vastly increase the number of citizens who, to some degree, rely on the stockholding form of wealth. Second, they remove the individual still further from connection with or impact on the management and administration of the productive corporations themselves.

* * *

Dr. Paul Harbrecht, at Columbia and now at Georgetown University, has been elaborating a theory that we have evolved a new wealth-holding and wealth-circulating system whose liquidity is maintained through the exchanges but is only psychologically connected with the capital gathering and capital application system on which productive industry and enterprise actually depend. (P. Harbrecht, *Pension Funds and Economic Power*, 1959). If this is the fact, one effect of the corporate system has been to set up a parallel, circulating "property-wealth" system, in which the wealth flows from passive wealth-holder, to passive wealth holder without significantly furthering the functions of capital formation, capital application, capital use or risk bearing. Yet these functions were the heart of the nineteenth

century "capitalist" system. Both wealth and wealth-holders are divorced from the productive—that is, the commercial—process though, at long last, the estimate of this wealth turns on an estimate of the productiveness, the character and effectiveness of the corporation who shares are its vehicles.

Now clearly, this wealth cannot be justified by the old economic maxims, despite passionate and sentimental arguments of neoclassic economists who would have us believe the old system has not changed. The purchaser of stock does not contribute savings to an enterprise, thus enabling it to increase its plant or operations. He does not take the "risk" of a new or increased economic operation; he merely estimates the change of the corporation's shares increasing in value. The contribution his purchase makes to anyone other than himself is the maintenance of liquidity for other shareholders who may wish to convert their holdings into cash. Clearly he can not and does not intend to contribute managerial or entrepreneurial effort or service.

This raises a problem of social ethics that is bound to push its way into the legal scene in the next generation. Why have stockholders? What contribution do they make, entitling them to heirship of half the profits of the industrial system, receivable partly in the form of dividends, and partly in the form of increased market values resulting from undistributed corporate gains? Stockholders toil not, neither do they spin, to earn that reward. They are beneficiaries by position only. Justification for their inheritance must be sought outside classic economic reasoning.

ARTICLE FOLLOW-UP

1. Is Berle's argument that the old logic of property—that owners should be entitled to the fruits of their property put at risk in the competitive market place—

should not apply to share ownership of passive wealth holders?

The latest figures from the U.S. government reveal that Berle's idea of a revolution has continued, if not accelerated, since the 1960s. Although an elaboration on the current value of all forms of property is beyond the scope of this book, we note the enormous increase in intangible "private" property as a source of wealth, as compared with the more classic forms of property, such as land, and personal property, such as vehicles.

2. If you are a business student, have you run into this idea before? Why not, do you think?

FIGURE 6-1 *Private Domestic Nonfinancial Institutions,—In Billions of Dollars*

Type of Financial Instrument	Dollar Value (Billions)
Checks, currency	1,975
Time and savings accounts	2,832
Pension fund reserves	3,473
Mutual fund shares	852
Other corporate equities	4,367
Credit market instruments	14,182
U.S. Treasury securities	2,758
Federal agency securities	1,589
Mortgages	4,049
Consumer credit	1,793
Bank loans	1,796
Proprietors equity	2,568

Source: Statistical Abstract of the United States 1992, page 491, Chart No. 765, Flow of Funds Accounts-Financial Assets and Liabilities of Financial and Nonfinancial Institutions, by Sector and Type of Instrument, 1991 (112th Edition).

The total value of U.S. financial instruments in 1991, such as those listed in Figure 6.1 (and many more), is $35.203 trillion. The total gross assessed value of real property in the United States was about $6.013 trillion. Property represented by financial instruments as diverse as checking accounts, stocks and bonds, claims on pension funds, and savings in all of the financial forms and other financially related claims exceeds the value of land by a factor of five. Certainly, we can conclude that this century has bred a new form of property—the financial claim. Thus, were we to write an up-to-date book on property law, we would have to cover the law of checks and all of the state and federal laws and regulations relating to banking and securities and much more.

We conclude this section, however, by just noting that modern life has brought a tremendous expansion of the kinds of property. This expansion, generally, has been from the solid, living soil of the land to the intangible legal claim on a checking account or corporate profits or hundreds of other financial conceptions represented by a piece of paper most usually called a *share of stock*.

THOUGHTS ON LAW, SOCIAL STRUCTURE, AND PROPERTY

This chapter is still introductory. It is the first of many chapters on substantive law—basic rights and duties that form property law. There may be no more fundamental substantive law to the U.S. economy and the American way of life than property law. Property law creates, protects, shapes, and destroys property. As the next century approaches, however, we must ask: Which fundamentals of U.S. social and legal policy of yesterday will serve the interests of tomorrow? Is the commitment Americans have shown to the pursuit of property a belief that will last?

Is the playwright and Czech politician Vaclav Havel correct when he says we are coming to the end of an age of the "proud belief that man, as the pinnacle of everything that exists, is capable of objectively describing, explaining and controlling everything that exists, and of possessing the one and only truth about the world?" A dominant truth of this century has been, the more property the better. Those who have it are somebodies; those who have none are nobodies. The key question for any regime built on property is not, what is property, but who should get it and what is to be done with those who have none?

The law in this area has grown by leaps and bounds, and entirely new forms of property have shaped the expectations and the very working environments of Americans. The drive for property (and technology) are the two beliefs that have shaped development in this century and that have been accepted as desirable commitments by almost everyone. It is time to take a moment and reflect on the pursuit of property.

We close this chapter with two readings, both challenging and speculative. Retired Harvard economist John Kenneth Galbraith needs almost no introduction. He certainly is one of the most noted and controversial economists of his age. The following first appeared in 1958, and revisions of it have been published in every decade since.

JOHN KENNETH GALBRAITH

The Dependence Effect[21]

[*Author's note:* Footnotes herein are Galbraith's]

. . . A leading modern theorist of consumer behavior, Professor Duesenberry, has stated explicitly that "ours is a society in which one of the principal social goals is a higher standard of living. . . . [This] has great significance for the theory of consumption . . . the desire to get superior goods takes on a life of its own. It provides a drive to higher expenditure which may even be stronger than that arising out of the needs which are supposed to be satisfied by that expenditure."[22] The implications of this view are impressive. The notion of independently established need now sinks into the background. Because the society sets great store by ability to produce a high living standard, it evaluates people by the products they possess. The urge to consume is fathered by the value system which emphasizes the ability of the society to produce. The more that is produced, the more that must be owned in order to maintain the appropriate prestige. The latter is an important point, for without going as far as Duesenberry in reducing goods to the role of symbols of prestige in the affluent society, it is plain that his argument fully implies that the production of goods creates the wants that the goods are presumed to satisfy.[23]

The even more direct link between production and wants is provided by the institutions of modern advertising and salesmanship. These cannot be reconciled with the notion of independently determined desires, for their central function is to create desires—to bring into being wants that previously did not exist.[24] This is accomplished by the producer of the goods or at his behest. A broad empirical relationship exists between what is spent on production of consumer goods and what is spent in synthesizing the desires for that production. A new consumer product must be introduced with a suitable advertising campaign to arouse an interest in it. The path for an expansion of output must be paved by a suitable expansion in the advertising budget. Outlays for the manufacturing of a product are not more important in the strategy of modern business enterprise than outlays for the manufacturing of demand for the product. None of this is novel. . . . The cost of this want formation is formidable. In 1974, total advertising expenditure—though, as noted, not all of it may be assigned to the synthesis of wants—amounted to approximately twenty-five billion dollars. The increase in previous years was by about a billion dollars a year. Obviously, such outlays must be integrated with the theory of consumer demand. They are too big to be ignored.

But such integration means recognizing that wants are dependent on production. It accords to the producer the function both of making the goods and of making the desires for them. It recognizes that production, not only passively through emulation, but actively through advertising and related activities, creates the wants it seeks to satisfy.

★ ★ ★

Is a new breakfast cereal or detergent so much wanted if so much must be spent to compel in the consumer the sense of want? But there has been little tendency to go on to examine the implications of this for the theory of consumer demand and even less for the importance of production and productive efficiency. These have remained sacrosanct. More often, the uneasiness has been manifested in a general disapproval of advertising and advertising men, leading to the occasional suggestion that they shouldn't exist. Such suggestions have usually been ill received in the advertising business.

And so the notion of independently determined wants still survives. In the face of all the forces of modern salesmanship, it still rules, almost undefiled, in the textbooks. And it still remains the economist's mission—and on few matters is the pedagogy so firm—to seek unquestioningly the means for filling these wants. This being so, production remains of prime urgency. We have here, perhaps, the ultimate triumph of the conventional wisdom in its resistance to the evidence of the eyes. To equal it, one must imagine a humanitarian who was long ago persuaded of the grievous shortage of hospital facilities in the town. He continues to importune the passersby for money for more beds and refuses to notice that the town doctor is deftly knocking over pedestrians with his car to keep up the occupancy.

And in unraveling the complex, we should always be careful not to overlook the obvious. The fact that wants can be synthesized by advertising, catalyzed by salesmanship, and shaped by the discreet manipulations of the persuaders shows that they are not very urgent. A man who is hungry need never be told of his need for food. . . . [Advertising agencies] are effective only with those who are so far removed from physical want that they do not already know what they want. In this state alone, men are open to persuasion.

The general conclusion of these pages is of such importance for this essay that it had perhaps best be put with some formality. As a society becomes increasingly affluent, wants are increasingly created by the process by which they are satisfied. This may operate passively. Increases in consumption, the counterpart of increases in production, act by suggestion or emulation to create wants. Expectation rises with attainment. Or producers may proceed actively to create wants through advertising and salesmanship. Wants thus come to depend on output. In technical terms, it can no longer be assumed that welfare is greater at an all-round higher level of production than at a lower one. It may be the same. The higher level of production has, merely, a higher level of want creation necessitating a higher level of want satisfaction. There will be frequent occasion to refer to the way wants depend on the process by which they are satisfied. It will be convenient to call it the Dependency Effect.

We may now contemplate briefly the conclusions to which this analysis has brought us.

Plainly, the theory of consumer demand is a peculiarly treacherous friend of the present goals of economics. At first glance, it seems to defend the continuing urgency of production and our preoccupation with it as a goal. The economist does not enter into the dubious moral arguments about the importance or virtue of the wants to be satisfied. He doesn't pretend to compare mental states of the same or different people at different times and to suggest that one is less urgent than another. The desire is there. That for him is sufficient. He sets about in a

workmanlike way to satisfy desire, and accordingly, he sets the proper store by the production that does. Like woman's his work is never done.

But this rationalization, handsomely though it seems to serve, turns destructively on those who advance it once it is conceded that wants are themselves both passively and deliberately the fruits of the process by which they are satisfied. Then the production of goods satisfies the wants that the consumption of these goods creates or that the producers of goods synthesize. Production induces more wants and the need for more production. So far, in a major tour de force, the implications have been ignored. But this obviously is a perilous solution. It cannot long survive discussion.

Among the many models of the good society, no one has urged the squirrel wheel. Moreover, as we shall see presently, the wheel is not one that revolves with perfect smoothness. Aside from its dubious cultural charm, there are serious structural weaknesses which may one day embarrass us. For the moment, however, it is sufficient to reflect on the difficult terrain which we are traversing. [We can see] how deeply we were committed to production for reasons of economic security. Not the goods but the employment provided by their production was the thing by which we set ultimate store. Now we find our concern for goods further undermined. It does not arise in spontaneous consumer need. Rather, the dependence effect means that it grows out of the process of production itself. If production is to increase, the wants must be effectively contrived. In the absence of the contrivance, the increase would not occur. This is not true of all goods, but that it is true of a substantial part is sufficient. . . . Clearly the attitudes and values which make production the central achievement of our society have some exceptionally twisted roots.

Perhaps the thing most evident of all is how new and varied become the problems we must ponder when we break the nexus with the work of Ricardo and face the economics of affluence of the world in which we live. It is easy to see why the conventional wisdom resists so stoutly such change. It is far, far better and much safer to have a firm anchor in nonsense than to put out on the troubled seas of thought.

ARTICLE FOLLOW-UP

Galbraith refers several times to the "conventional wisdom." This term (developed earlier in this classic work) has since passed into common usage. *Conventional wisdom* refers to traditional patterns of thought that become the fundamental beliefs that guide a society. Conventional wisdom associates what is desirable in a social policy sense with what is acceptable and familiar. American notions about what is economically and legally desirable are organized around and based on what the community as a whole finds acceptable and convenient. The dominant set of beliefs that cluster around the notion of capitalism have this economic system premised on the idea that large corporations exist to satisfy consumer demand for property.

And Galbraith warns that "in unraveling the complex, we should always be careful not to overlook the obvious." He seems to think it is obvious that the production process itself, the engine on which the economy is built, is today the creator of consumer demand.

Is he right? Consider this: The annual advertising budgets of the beer and soft drink producers in this country exceed $500 million. Why, one asks, when they are all essentially liquids, with minor taste differences? Moreover, is there a real difference between Budweiser and Miller or between Coke and Pepsi? The point is not whether Galbraith is right or wrong, but whether he accurately highlights some of the very powerful elements that structure people's lives. We believe him correct in this. In his notion of the dependence effect, he has laid bare how organizations spend hundreds of millions of dollars to shape people's preferences, which, ultimately, serve the ends of the productive portions of the economy.

This process is portrayed in the popular press and in most business schools as natural. Yet, Galbraith hints that there is an artificiality about it all. We are led to believe that business organizations fill demand, yet they may do the opposite; they may *create* demand. Our knowledge, therefore, if it is based on the first proposition, is not accurate.

Galbraith suggests that what we have been lead to believe about the entire nature of the economic environment—that businesses merely meet market demand, they simply fill a perceived (legitimate) human need—might be misguided. Galbraith argues that this elaborate economic structure created for the production of property is in place to serve its own primary interests—it creates and feeds on the need for ever more property. In this view, Americans may have ended up with something that, in the long run, does not serve their interests.

In the following piece of short, short fiction, Marilyn Krysl makes the point that we might all be riding on a train, being served something we seemed to have ordered, but did not really want once it arrives. The results, she suggests, may be disastrous.

MARILYN KRYSL[25]

The Artichoke

[*Author's note:* "The Artichoke" is part short story, part essay, part poetry. Some of the sentences do not read as ordinary prose.]

It will happen on a train to Banff, both of us think we're on a vacation. We'll be in the dining car, smoking and discussing Baudelaire or discussing Gulf Oil or discussing inflation, while we wait for the waiter. While we wait for the waiter, in no hurry, and not really very hungry. And in the discussion we'll use the expressions GNP and *market value* and *idea of evil*. And it will be you and I talking, not somebody else somewhere else, and not some fake couple got up for fiction.

The waiter comes to take our order. He's black, in a white jacket. He'll be black because that's how waiters on trains to Banff are, it's the decision of the railroad to conduct its business in this way. We'll wish he weren't our waiter, but there you are. And there we will be while the waiter waits as he's paid just enough but not too much to do, until I've made my point about Baudelaire and we break off this discussion to order.

The tablecloth will be starched white linen. Not because we want starched white linen, but because if you take a train to Banff you get a white linen tablecloth. And we're taking this train through these mountains. The mountains won't be there for us, of course, but they'll be there.

And we'll order an artichoke. Because we like them. We like them, and there they are on the menu.

We know we can change some things but not others, and we know which ones we can change, when you kick a rock you break your toe, and now we're hungry. By this time we've dispensed with the waiter's blackness, the starch in the linen, the mountainous mountains, we've adjusted our feelings about them to this fact. We're also bored with these feelings that insist on hanging around like tedious children who have nothing to do, but mostly we're hungry. And everyone of course gets hungry, we can gather together around this point as around a table. Right now I could easily dispense with high-toned moral phrases and sit down with the Chairman of the Board of Gulf, as long as each of us had an artichoke.

Here comes the waiter with a white platter. I see the artichoke's rows of spiked leaves, leaves shaped like feathers, and closer now, rounded to a point like feathers, much closer, and are those feathers coming closer, those are really feathers—and now my hunger backs all the way up from my belly into my mouth, a heart that wants to fly out and away—it's feathers, it's a feathered headdress, it's a head—and the waiter sets before me the purple head of Quetzalcoatl on a tray.

I want to say *No*, you've mixed up my order with someone else's, I'm not the one who asked for this, take it away. *But Madame*, he says, *you ordered it*. And I want to say "Don't call me Madame!" But there is Quetzalcoatl's head on my tray.

What we ordered isn't what we want, you'd think any fool could see that. We've always assumed our gentle intentions excuse our imperial way of life. But we still haven't got used to a waiter bringing Quetzalcoatl's head on a platter, whose head we'd forgotten we were supposed to ask for, having gone on this vacation through mountains forested, rugged, amazing though no longer virgin, leaving the kids in school studying how to manage the Corporation, whose managers we'd comfortably managed to forget we are.

ARTICLE FOLLOW-UP

This story is more like a poem than a story or a work of fiction. It is dense with meaning, and the author cannot come right out and say what she means because she is after a feeling and not trying to impart information. What feeling is she after? It seems to us that she writes of a feeling of frustration. She writes, "What we ordered isn't what we want, you'd think any fool could see that. We've always assumed our gentle intentions excuse our imperial way of life." Often, what we do is not what we want to do, yet we all know that we each mean well. Each American probably believes he or she is a decent human being, even somewhat of a humanitarian— yet we, a mere 5 percent of the planet's population, consume over 40 percent of the world's resources. *This is power.* How did it come to be? Much of it came to be through organization, and organization created the social structure that promotes a lifestyle that makes this reality seem acceptable, even somewhat moral; yet it is imperial, is it not? Moreover, the law seems to be a woefully inadequate social instrument to bring about change.

The symbolism represented by being served Quetzalcoatl's head is complex, and we can only guess at it. (Quetzalcoatl is the mythical god in the Aztec religion who symbolizes civilization and learning.) Krysl might be suggesting that unless people become more conscious about their lifestyle and their daily routines, they run the risk that they may be destroying civilization without intending to do so or without being aware that they are doing so.

U.S. history has emphasized property, its acquisition, its embellishment, and its transfer for still other property. Property helps define who people believe they are, and where people believe they stand in the pecking order of society. Marshall McLuhan retells the story of Tzu-Gung, to remind people that they become what they do:

> As Tzu-Gung was traveling through the regions north of the river Han, he saw an old man working in his vegetable garden. He had dug an irrigation ditch. The man would descend into a well, fetch up a vessel of water in his arms and pour it out into the ditch. While his efforts were tremendous, the results appeared to be very meager.
>
> Tzu-Gung said, "There is a way whereby you can irrigate a hundred ditches in one day, and whereby you can do much with little effort. Would you not like to hear of it?"
>
> Then the gardener stood up, looked at him and said, "And what would that be?"
>
> Tzu-Gung replied, "You take a wooden lever, weighted at the back and light in the front. In this way you can bring up water so quickly that it just gushes out. This is called a draw-well."
>
> Then anger rose up in the man's face, and he said, "I have heard my teacher say that whoever uses machines does all his work like a machine. He who does his work like a machine grows a heart like a machine, and he who carries the heart of a machine in his breast loses his simplicity. He who has lost his simplicity becomes unsure of the striving of

his soul. Uncertainty in the striving of the soul is something that does not agree with honest sense. It is not that I do not know of such things; I am ashamed to use them."[26]

If people are preoccupied with the acquisition of property, they may become the property they acquire. This philosophizing notwithstanding, none of us seem to be ready to give away blue-chip stocks, and until that time, property and property law will be somewhere near center stage.

Yes! Ideas of property permeate U.S. culture, a culture defined in a major way by the kind of property it keeps and doesn't keep. In the modern industrial-electronic era of multinational corporations, immense property systems predominate; hundreds of billions of dollars of assets spread over the entire world do not overwhelm the modern imagination. Are we each in danger of becoming just a cog in the wheel of this elaborate scheme of property shuffling? Is the tomorrow for each of us to become an account number in some corporate planner's program indicating how much property we own and what property we believe we need?

CONCLUSION

Property is a big subject, perhaps too big. This chapter had a humble purpose: to provide some familiarity with the history, a modicum of legal vocabulary, the legal frame of reference, and some of the policy considerations for use when thinking about property, while at the same time not obscuring the general movements and social impacts of property law by burying you in detail.

Returning to the beginning, we see that ideas of property originated before the civilizations in Greece and Rome and how the Middle Ages and especially the feudal period in England shaped the present property-based culture.

Property law provides a mechanism for holding and controlling wealth and channeling income. Some people win from the arrangement and some lose, and one must ask whether such gains and losses are an inevitable part of life everywhere and for all times, or whether they are open to human intervention and beneficial change through law or other forms of social action. Perhaps most fundamentally, property law intimately affects the national goal of maximizing equality, and one always needs to keep an eye on this objective and be aware of where one stands in this quest.

Questions worth keeping in mind would seem to include the following: What ought to be open to private ownership, and what ought never to be privatized? What is the relationship between private property and the evolution of economic organization—ought there be limits on the amount of property that can be directly or indirectly owned? John Locke was in favor of such limitations.

Another question, addressed this time by Plato and one especially vital for this or any age is, What is the relationship of property ownership to getting and keeping social, economic, and political power? And can the law do the job that will be necessary in the next century? Perhaps no question is more important for the year 2000 than, Are the traditional historical and legal arrangements that define who and how one gets and keeps property sufficient for the next century? As you read the material that follows in this text, keep this question in mind.

REVIEW QUESTIONS AND PROBLEMS

1. Reflect for a few moments on Plato's idea that those who make the rules in a society should not own property because of the enormous potential for a conflict of interest. Would the United States have better government if legislators, senior executive-branch administrators, and judges could not own private property?

2. Given the core ideas in this chapter, which features of American property law are ancient—over, say, 500 years old, and which are modern—those developed in this century?

3. Reread the *Lucas* v. *South Carolina Coastal Council* case. In your judgment and in light of the facts there presented, is this a good case? Is the legal "test" to determine a compensable taking one that is clearly applicable? If this test is not to your liking, try to develop one that is clearer and/or fairer.

4. What rational is there for allowing Elvis Presley's estate to just keep on growing and growing and for his heirs to receive ever larger checks from the public's appreciation for his talent?

5. What public policy reasons are there for the permissible use of reverse engineering to create competing products or expressions of artistic achievement?

6. Is Galbraith right, or is he off target? Is the purpose of most producers in the U.S. economy to fill the natural demand of consumers in rather organized markets for products and services, or do producers have a substantial hand in the creation of the "wants" that they create? Is this question, itself, an inconsequential one? That is, what difference does it make whether Galbraith is right or wrong?

7. What might be Marlyn Krysl's answer to the last question, above? What does she mean when she says that our gentle intentions excuse our imperial way of life? That is, who cares if Americans are 5 percent or so of the world's population, yet consume about 40 percent of the world's resources (property)?

ENDNOTES

[*Author's note:* Some of the ideas and some of the material and arrangement of topics in this chapter parallels that found in, *Understanding the Law: Principles, Problems and Potentials of the American Legal System*, Chapter 6, (1995), West Publishing Co., which was written by the same author (Wolfe).]

1. Schlatter, *Private Property: The History of An Idea*, 12 (1951).
2. *Id.* at 19.
3. *Id.* at 37-38.
4. *Id.* at 63.
5. *Id.* at 64
6. Simpson, *A History of The Land Law*, 3 (2d ed. 1986).
7. *Id.* at 6.
8. Baker, *An Introduction to Legal History*, 199 (2d ed. 1979).
9. Locke, *Two Treatises of Goverment* (Routledge ed, Book II, SS) 27, 28, 31 (2d ed. 1887).
10. L.M. Friedman, *A History of American Law*, 62 (2d Ed. 1985).
11. *Id.* at 219.
12. Quoted at *Id.* 243.
13. *Id.* 436-437.
14. *Id.*
15. *Chicago Tribune*, April 10, 1990, p. 1, 2.
16. 238 U.S. 256 (1946).
17. 458 U.S. 419 (1982).
18. Braverman, *Labor and Monopoly Capital*, 272-73 (1974).
19. Berle and Means, *The Modern Corporation and Private Property*, 1 (1932).
20. Berle, Property, Production and Revolution 65 *Col. L. Rev.* 1 (1965).
21. Excerpts from *The Affluent Society*, 4th edition, by John Kenneth Galbraith, pp 128-133. Copyright © 1958, 1969, 1976, 1984 by John Kenneth Galbraith. Reprinted by permission of Houghton Mifflin Co.
22. James S. Duesenberry, *Income, Saving and the Theory of Consumer Behavior* (Cambridge, Mass.: Harvard University Press, 1949), p. 28.
23. A more recent and definitive study of consumer demand has added even more support. Professors Houthakker and Taylor, in a statistical study of the determinants of demand, found that for most products, price and income, the accepted determinants, were less important than past consumption of the product. This "psychological stock," as they call it, concedes the weakness of traditional theory; current demand cannot be explained without recourse to past consumption. Such demand nurtures the need for its own increase. H.S. Houthakker and L.D. Taylor, *Consumer Demand in the United States*, 2nd ed., enlarged (Cambridge, Mass.: Harvard University Press, 1970).
24. Advertising is not a simple phenomenon. It is also important in competitive strategy and want creation is, ordinarily, a complementary result of efforts to shift the demand curve of the individual firm at the expense of others or (less importantly, I think) to change its shape by increasing the degree of product differentiation. Some of the failure of economists to identify advertising with want creation may be attributed to the undue asttention that its use in purely competitive strategy has attracted. It should be noted, however, that the competitive manipulation of consumer desire is only possible, at least on any appreciable scale, when such need is not strongly felt.
25. Krysl, M. The Artichoke, *Sudden Fiction*, American Short, Short Stories, R. Shapard and J. Thomas, eds., Gibbs M. Smith Inc., 1986. Reprinted by permission of the author.
26. McLuhan, *Understanding Media* 69 (1964).

CHAPTER 7

Torts and Liability for Defective Products

INTRODUCTION

The word *tort* is derived from the Latin *tortus*, which means "twisted." It is still a perfectly appropriate definition for this type of civil law. A tort is behavior that is crooked, not straight, and that gives the injured person a legal claim against the person causing the twisted or wrongful behavior.

Another approach is to define a tort by listing the types of legal claims it is *not*. It is not a crime or a breach of contract, nor is it necessarily concerned with governmental standards. Torts are the legally recognized claims left over. Tort law provides the bridges or links among contract law, governmental regulations, and criminal law. It fills the gaps between other areas of civil law and pushes into new areas of social conduct.

Sometimes a single act may be both a crime and a tort. For example, claims based on behavior so negligent and reckless that it causes death may give rise to both a criminal prosecution (often called manslaughter), and a case based on the torts of negligence or wrongful death. Tort law also overlaps with contract law, as in this chapter's cases regarding compensation for injury caused by defective products. In short, let's settle on a common definition of a tort, which sounds deceptively simple. A tort is a civil wrong, other than breach of contract, for which the law provides a remedy in the form of an action for damages.

CHARACTERISTICS OF THE COMMON LAW OF TORTS

TORT LAW IS JUDGE-MADE LAW

The chief characteristic of tort law is that it is *made by judges* at the *state* level. Juries find the facts of a case after a presentation of the evidence by opposing attorneys. Then the judge instructs the jury to apply legal principles of tort law to the facts. In this process of fact finding and applying principles to the facts, the jury makes law. Thus, this area of law grows almost organically as society demands, according to its changing perceptions of what is reasonable and what is fair. New torts are being established all the time. Some of the newest torts are the intentional infliction of mental suffering, the invasion of the right of privacy, the infliction of prenatal injuries, and the obstruction of the right of the plaintiff to go where he or she likes. Thus, tort law is dynamic, which makes it frustrating for businesspeople. In addition, because tort law is state based, it is irregular in its growth; behavior that is a tort in California may not be a tort in Ohio.

TORT LAW FOCUSES ON INJURY

The emphasis in tort law is not on conceptual uniformity from tort to tort or state to state, but rather on injury. The main purpose of tort law is *to compensate the plaintiff by providing a remedy (usually money damages) for an injury.* Tort law is invoked when one private person or business association sues another for the breach of a commonly recognized duty that causes injury. The government is rarely involved other than to provide a forum for the resolution of whether the law will compensate the plaintiff.

Generally, torts are defined by what most people recognize as *socially unreasonable activity.* For example, a common tort arises when a person drives a car down a country road and fails to give a bicyclist enough room on the edge of the road and strikes her. This act may be the common tort of negligence, which is committed when anyone fails to act as a reasonable person would under the circumstances and causes injury.

TORT LAW MAKES PUBLIC POLICY

Although the litigation in tort law appears to involve just two private parties, the judge and the jury must consider the interests of the public in deciding the case. For example, in the first case in this chapter, the court had to consider the impact of a decision for the plaintiffs on all businesses that might pollute the groundwater of a community. That is, if a court recognized a tort of negligence, for example, in the pollution of groundwater and thus found the defendant liable for damage to the surrounding community, it could jeopardize the well-being of all firms that discharged water into the environment. Thus, the interest of the public inevitably finds its way into tort law.

Courts engage in social engineering when they consider the impact of their decisions on the public. In this process, the judge, and perhaps the jury as well, makes public policy. In some crude form, courts must balance the greatest good for the greatest number against the justice of finding for the plaintiff. This is really the essence of tort law. The judgment rendered in the groundwater case would certainly have closed the plant of the defendant (it already had been closed by governmental action at the time of the court judgment). Judgments such as this one and those involving cigarettes and small powerful handguns called Saturday night specials, explained later in this chapter, have an impact on entire industries and, ultimately, on everyone's way of life.

FACTORS AFFECT LIABILITY

A decision in most tort cases involves a consideration of several factors:

1. *The need for compensation.* How badly was the plaintiff injured? Is it fair to order the plaintiff to pay the full loss suffered, or should the defendant pay part?

2. *The law of prior cases.* How similar is the nature of the defendant's intentional or unreasonable or dangerous conduct to conduct in past cases? If it is very similar, liability is almost certain to follow; if there are no prior cases like it, the plaintiff has an uphill battle.

3. *The convenience of administration.* Is the plaintiff asking for a money judgment or that the court close a local manufacturing plant? Courts are more comfortable making awards for money damages than overseeing the closing of a plant.

The following two factors, that affect liability are more speculative and subject to debate.

4. *The moral aspect of the defendant's conduct.* Is there a community consensus about blame and fault in this case? Do reason and experience tell the jury that the defendant should have acted other than he or she did? If so, liability is probable. If not, liability may be hard to establish.

5. *The extent to which a judgment will serve to prevent such conduct in the future.* Many commentators say that such a consideration is irrelevant; the court and the jury should focus on the two parties before the court and not on the impact of a decision on others. Many opinions, however, do indicate that tort law is to serve as a warning to others not to act as the defendant has acted.

OVERVIEW OF COMMON TORTS

Torts are classified according to general notions of how courts assess fault. The first classification includes torts based on the defendant's intent (called intentional torts). The second involves the defendant's unreasonable or careless conduct (called negligence). The third involves extremely dangerous or ultrahazardous activities that impose unreasonable risks on the public (called absolute or strict liability).

INTENTIONAL TORTS

Intentional torts require that the plaintiff prove the defendant intended the activity causing the damage or was so reckless that a fair-minded person could say the defendant acted as if he or she intended it. We are concerned, not with detailed definitions of these torts, but rather with a general kind of knowledge about them. A partial listing includes

1. Intentional interference with a person's body: battery (an intentional, unprivileged physical contact with another); assault (intentional threat of physical harm); false imprisonment (intended, unprivileged restraint of a person against his or her will); and infliction of mental distress (intentionally causing another to fear the loss of reputation or something dear to him or her).

2. Intentional interference with a person's reputation: libel (written, published false statements that injure one's reputation) and slander (speaking false and malicious words that injure another's reputation); together, libel and slander make up the general tort of defamation.

3. Intentional interference with property: trespass (wrongful entry onto another's property) and conversion (any act that deprives an owner of personal property without just cause).

4. Fraud: intentional misrepresentation of a fact that a person reasonably relies on, causing damage to the person.

NEGLIGENCE

Negligence is probably the most often discussed and most frequently occurring tort. *Negligence is an activity that creates an unreasonable risk of harm to a person or society with resulting injury.* When you exceed the speed limit in your car, you are creating an unreasonable risk to society; if you injure someone with your car while speeding, you have committed the tort of negligence. The elements of negligence are as follows:

1. A *duty* recognized by law requiring a person to conform to a certain standard of care for the protection of others. This duty usually is found by consulting previous cases in which negligence was found. The duty is based on the trial court's conclusion that the behavior of the defendant was unreasonable under the circumstances.

2. *Failure on a defendant's part* to conform to the standard of reasonable care under the circumstances. This is a breach of social duty.

3. *A reasonably close causal connection between the conduct and the resulting injury* (commonly known as legal cause or proximate cause). Some courts hold that the injury must have been reasonably foreseeable, given the breach of duty; fewer courts hold that proximate cause means the injury would not have happened but for the breach of duty.

4. *Actual loss* or *damage* resulting to another.

FIGURE 7.1 *Elements of the Tort of Negligence*

Element	Example
Social Duty Usually found by consulting previous, similar cases	To act reasonably under the circumstances: give bicyclists room on the highway
Breach of Duty Found in the facts of the case	Bicyclist on side of the road hit by auto
Legal Causation Facts of case show it was reasonably foreseeable that bicyclist would be injured if insufficient room given	Injury to bicyclist because of failure to give her room
Injury in Fact Injury is valued, and called damages	Bicyclist (plaintiff) suffered injury (damages) from the breach of duty—hospital bills, loss of bicycle

The plaintiff in a negligence case need not prove intent, only unreasonable or careless activity. When one is negligent, one does not desire to bring about the consequences that follow, nor does one know they are substantially certain to follow. Negligence is the creation of a risk sufficiently great to lead a reasonable person in the position of the defendant to anticipate it and then guard against it.

NUISANCE

A "nuisance" is a tort that seems to be very much like negligence. It is an unreasonable disturbance of the enjoyment of a person's property. *Sterling* v. *Velsicol Chemical Corp.*, reproduced in a later section, is a good example of action that is negligent, a nuisance, and a trespass.

ABSOLUTE OR STRICT LIABILITY

The terms *absolute liability* and *strict liability* are often used interchangeably by commentators on the law and courts. Both terms refer to a category of torts in which liability is imposed *without regard to intention or the reasonableness of the defendant's conduct*. In general, liability is imposed because the activity of the defendant is so dangerous that, in all fairness, the defendant should pay for any damage caused without regard to how careful the defendant is.

More specifically, *absolute liability* is a tort asserted by a plaintiff when seeking compensation for an injury to his or her person or land caused by an abnormally dangerous activity of the defendant. The first instance of this kind of tort was asserted in *Rylands* v. *Fletcher*, an 1868 case in which the defendant was sued because of injury caused when water he had dammed escaped and flooded out his neighbors. The damming of the water was such a risk to the community that, regardless of the care taken, the one responsible should pay any damage caused. We see this tort in *Sterling* v. *Velsicol Chemical Corp.*

Strict liability is usually used to designate a tort involving a defective and unreasonably dangerous *product* that has caused injury. We discuss this tort in greater detail in the part of this chapter on products liability.

DAMAGES

Tort damages usually consist of money awards paid to the plaintiff by the defendant or the defendant's insurance company to compensate the plaintiff for the loss caused by the defendant's misconduct. They are called *compensatory damages* and may include all out-of-pocket losses, such as medical bills, lost wages, and damages to property. Many courts today allow the jury to award an amount for pain and suffering. Few courts allow damages for pain and suffering when a person has suffered no physical damage.

Punitive damages are amounts of money paid to the plaintiff by the defendant when the judge and the jury think the defendant's conduct is so outrageous that the defendant should be punished. These damages may not be awarded arbitrarily; they must bear some relation to the wrong of the defendant. In the 1981 decision in *Grimshaw* v. *Ford Motor Co.*, for example, the jury originally allowed an award of punitive damages of $125 million, which was an approximation of the amount of money saved by Ford when it refused to redesign the position of the gas tank in its Pinto automobiles. (The gas tanks had a tendency to rupture in rear-end collisions, and the resulting fires quickly spread into the passenger compartments. Grimshaw, severely burned, had survived such a fire begun by a rear-end collision.) Years before, Ford had calculated that the approximately 360 serious burn cases resulting from the placement of the gas tank would cost the company $49.5 million in court judgments, but to rectify the design for 11 million cars and 1.5 million light trucks would cost $137 million. The *Grimshaw* jury was so struck by Ford's conscious decision to weigh the cost to itself to pay future plaintiffs against the savings of $137 million that it returned to Grimshaw some of the money Ford saved by its decision not to change the design. An appellate court later reduced the award of punitive damages to $3.5 million.

The case that follows contains many of the ideas discussed in the preceding sections. The case essentially involves groundwater pollution and the individual damages it caused. Although the defendant might have been liable for violating state and federal laws on groundwater pollution, such violations are not relevant to this suit. Moreover, state and federal environmental laws would not compensate the plaintiffs, so the plaintiffs sought compensation through the legal system by suing for the common-law torts of strict liability, negligence, trespass, and nuisance, seeking compensatory damages and punitive damages. Why so many torts? A plaintiff never knows exactly what the evidence will show when it unfolds and is examined at trial. Therefore, most plaintiffs allege as many claims as they think the evidence will fairly show. There is no inconsistency in this practice. The court and the jury should recognize as many torts in the case as the evidence shows. The damage recovery, however, is limited to the amount the plaintiffs can prove they lost. They do not recover three times the amount lost, for example, if they should prove three torts.

Sterling v. *Velsicol Chemical Corp.*
647 F.Supp. 303 (W.D. Tenn. 1986)

HORTON, DISTRICT JUDGE

The substance of plaintiffs' claims is that they have suffered physical injury, bodily harm, mental and emotional anguish, property damage, and loss and destruction of an entire community and a way of life, all proximately resulting from Velsicol's grossly negligent selection, implementation, operation and burial of more than 300,000 fifty-five gallon drums filled with ultrahazardous chemical waste, and hundreds of boxes of ultrahazardous dry chemical waste on its burial site which adjoined plaintiffs' homes and property. Plaintiffs contend Velsicol was grossly negligent in the selection and implementation of its chemical waste burial site, in the manner in which it containerized chemical waste, in its burial operations, and in allowing ultrahazardous and highly toxic chemical waste to escape from the burial site, infiltrate into and contaminate their underground well water.

Plaintiffs contend that as a result of their drinking, bathing, cooking, canning, cleaning, breathing steam from hot water, and otherwise using their home well water contaminated by hazardous chemicals from Velsicol's burial site, over a period of years—from on or about August 24, 1964 until June 1, 1973—they have suffered severe and permanent physical injuries, mental and emotional anguish, and damage to and loss of their property. . . .

Plaintiffs predicate this lawsuit and their right to recover damages from Velsicol upon the following legal theories:

1. strict liability

2. common law negligence

3. trespass

4. nuisance

Plaintiffs claim they are entitled to both compensatory and punitive damages from Velsicol. . . .

Plaintiffs claim the drums were often leaking chemical contaminants when they were hauled from Velsicol's Memphis Plant to the burial site and, that drums and boxes of waste were recklessly dumped into trenches and were often battered and ripped open while being buried and covered with dirt by a bulldozer. Finally, plaintiffs contend Velsicol was grossly negligent in its failure to monitor the chemical waste burial site for a long time after the burial site was in operation.

Plaintiffs charge Velsicol supplied the State of Tennessee with false information about its chemical waste dumping activities. Plaintiffs contend Velsicol informed officials of the State of Tennessee that it was dumping solid and semi-solid waste when, in fact, it was dumping liquid waste as well. Plaintiffs contend Velsicol informed the state it was using corrosion resistant containers when, in fact, it was not. Plaintiffs contend Velsicol did not inform the State of Tennessee what chemicals were being dumped into the site.

Plaintiffs claim Velsicol did not provide the Environmental Protection Agency (EPA) with a true and exact listing of chemicals buried on the site. Plaintiffs contend that when Velsicol actually knew or should have known that chemical waste was leaking and/or leaching from the site, Velsicol continued expanding its burial operations on the site. . . .

Strict Liability

Plaintiffs in this action argue Velsicol should be held responsible for damages, without regard to fault, on the theory of strict liability. The genesis of that theory stems from the "non-natural uses of lands" principle set forth in the landmark English case, *Rylands* v. *Fletcher* (1868). [In that case, Judge Blackburn wrote:]

> It appears from the statement in the case, that the plaintiff was damaged by his property being flooded by water which, without any fault on his part, broke out of a reservoir constructed on the defendants' land by the defendants' orders, and maintained by the defendants.

We think that the true rule of law is that the person who for his own purposes brings on his lands and collects and keeps there anything likely to do mischief if it escapes, must keep it in at his peril, and if he does not do so, is . . . answerable for all the damage which is the natural consequence of its escape. . . .

. . . In summary, the rule of law from *Rylands* v. *Fletcher* allows for the imposition of liability for damages proximately caused by the defendant's dangerous, unnatural use of land regardless of the standard of care defendant utilized in conducting that activity. Generally, modern courts have applied this strict or absolute liability to activities "variously characterized as 'perilous,' 'ultra or extra-hazardous,' or 'abnormally dangerous.'" The judicial rationalization seems to be that one who conducts a highly dangerous activity should prepare in advance to bear the financial burden of harm proximately caused to others by such an activity.

Common Law Negligence

The Court concludes the doctrine of common law negligence applies to this case and Velsicol is clearly guilty of negligence in this case for the following reasons:

1. The Court concludes that there was a duty, a standard of conduct, imposed by law on Velsicol to protect others from unreasonable harm arising from the dumping of the chemicals on its farm; and

2. The Court further concludes that defendant breached that duty by its failure to do the following:

    a. Defendant failed to investigate the geological makeup or strata under the dumpsite prior to its purchase or operation;

    b. Defendant failed to investigate the hydrological, or water bearing zones under the dumpsite prior to its purchase or operation;

    ★ ★ ★

    d. Defendant failed to install proper monitoring procedures in and around the dumpsite prior to commencing dumping operations at the dumpsite;

    ★ ★ ★

    m. Defendant failed to monitor the dumpsite at all from June of 1973 to the forced monitoring imposed on them by the State of Tennessee in 1980;

    n. Defendant failed to operate said dumpsite according to the state of the art methods to protect the plaintiffs by their failure to cover their wastes daily thereby allowing an increase in the infiltration rate;

* * *

q. Defendant failed to timely, completely and correctly respond to the requests of governmental agencies as to what was put into the dumpsite; . . . .

* * *

Trespass

A number of the plaintiffs in this class action are attempting to hold Velsicol liable for damages to their real property . . . and person under various legal theories; one of those is trespass. Plaintiffs state "[t]he tort of trespass is defined as intentional invasion and interference with an individual's exclusive right to possession of his property." "Trespass is an intentional harm, and where there is no intentional act, in the sense of an act voluntarily done, there is no trespass."

* * *

"Every entry upon another's soil without lawful authority is a trespass; and it matters not that there is no actual force for the law in such cases implies force." "An action of trespass presumes a wrongdoer's active agency in causing the injury complained of and doing of an act wantonly or in total disregard of others' rights . . . ."

Actual trespass is not an issue in this case. Velsicol admits the movement of certain chemicals from its dumpsite through the local aquifer and "onto property owned by various plaintiffs and into the sphere of influence of various wells constitutes a trespass under Tennessee law."

Nuisance

The doctrine of nuisance applies to this case. The Court finds Velsicol has interfered with plaintiffs' right to the use and enjoyment of their property—whether owned or leased— by the creation of a nuisance. This fact of nuisance is admitted by Velsicol.

Occasionally, a nuisance proceeds from a malicious desire to do harm, but usually a nuisance is intentional in the sense that the defendant has created or continued the condition causing the nuisance with full knowledge that the harm to the plaintiffs' interest is substantially bound to follow therefrom. A nuisance may also result from conduct which is merely negligence, to-wit: a failure to take precautions against a risk apparent to a reasonable man. Finally, a nuisance may occur when a defendant carries on in an inappropriate place an abnormally dangerous or hazardous activity. The Court finds that the Velsicol chemical dump meets all of the above requirements which are basic . . . nuisance elements. . . .

* * *

Compensatory Damages

Plaintiffs contend that as a result of the wrongful conduct of Velsicol, they suffered immense damage. The record is replete with evidence of such physical and mental damage. Moreover, the law recognizes that a plaintiff who is awarded a verdict is entitled to damages for the inconvenience and disruption of his or her life and normal activities as a result of the wrongful conduct of defendant.

The elements which are to be considered in determining damages are . . . :

1. Extent of injury and disability and whether such is permanent.

2. Pain and suffering, physical and emotional.

3. Impairment of enjoyment of life.

4. Impairment of earning capacity.

5. Expenses.

6. Punitive damages.

Velsicol's conduct caused chemical contaminants to come in contact with or invade each particular plaintiff's body, and impacted upon his or her body. Because those contaminants were of such a nature as to cause the reported symptoms and cellular damage, and adverse biological change, (however slight), the Court considers that this ingestion, inhalation or contact caused emotional distress in each plaintiff.

Moreover, plaintiffs are entitled to recover for fear, distress, or emotional injury because that fear or distress reasonably and naturally flowed or resulted from the disclosure of the nature and possible effects of those chemical contaminants.

* * *

Punitive Damages

The actions and/or inactions of Velsicol amounted, not only to negligence, but also to gross, willful and wanton negligence. As the evidence clearly showed, Velsicol's actions between 1964 and the trial of this case were controlled by the defendant's overriding concern for keeping its Memphis plant operating at the expense of human health and the environment. In this regard, the Court notes that . . . Velsicol admitted that it gave "no consideration as to the contamination which it was creating until it finally ceased dumping in June of 1972 under a direct order from the Tennessee Department of Health."

The general principles underlying the award of punitive damages [are based on] [e]vidence that the defendant's wrongful act was characterized by either willfulness, wantonness, maliciousness, gross negligence or recklessness, oppression, outrageous conduct, insult, indignity, or fraud. . . .

In the State of Tennessee, punitive damages are not recoverable as a matter of right but rest within the sound discretion of the trier of fact. The theory of punitive damages is not to compensate an injured plaintiff for personal injury or property damages but to punish a defendant, to deter him from com-

mitting acts of a similar nature and to make a public example of him.

The Court concludes that Velsicol's actions in creating, maintaining and operating its chemical waste burial site, with superior knowledge of the highly toxic and harmful nature of the chemical contaminants it disposed of therein, and specifically its failure to immediately cease dumping said toxic chemicals after being warned by several state and federal agencies several years prior to the final cessation of such abnormally hazardous and harmful activity, constituted gross, willful and wanton disregard for the health and well-being of the plaintiffs, and therefore is supportive of an award of punitive and exemplary damages.

The Court further concludes that Velsicol's attempts to allege that the plaintiffs were guilty of assuming the risk, or were guilty of contributory negligence is without factual basis and so outrageous as to subject the defendant to punitive damages.

In addition the Court further finds that Velsicol has also attempted to shift the liability and causation for the psychological disorders suffered by the plaintiffs to the local, state and federal authorities, claiming that the defendant cooperated with them in their attempts to monitor the situation and persuade Velsicol to limit its activities. They contend that news coverage of this case specifically caused the post-traumatic stress disorders. The Court concludes that these attempts by Velsicol are also so outrageous that punitive damages should be imposed.

If there has ever been a civil action filed in this Court that justifies the levy of punitive damages, it is the case at bar. All of the elements necessary to an award of punitive damages are present in this lawsuit. In fact, failure to award punitive damages in this case would, in itself, be an act of injustice.

[*The Court affirmed an award of $7.5 million in punitive damages.*]

CASE FOLLOW-UP

In this case, a firm with a plant in Memphis poured its toxic waste into containers that were dumped into large holes in the ground. Little regard was given for the consequences of its actions. The thrust of the case, though, is about compensation for those who suffered. The plaintiffs were compensated through the use of tort law, and this case shows that the court recognizes several types of torts for the damage caused. Strict liability is used when an owner of land engages in ultrahazardous activity and creates risks to neighbors. Placing containers of toxic chemicals in the ground is similar enough to the *Fletcher* case to cause liability here too. In other cases, courts have held that using poisons on one's property, blasting or using explosives, or keeping wild animals will also create liability, and no amount of care will protect the owner. Strict or absolute liability means that even if a property owner were as careful as possible (which was not true in the Velsicol case) by using government-approved drums and design standards for a dump pit, if injury results, there will be liability.

Note that when the court discusses the intentional tort of trespass it does not require actual intent to enter on the land of another. In many cases, intent may be inferred. If you pour large quantities of a liquid in the ground and the liquid finds its way onto others' property, the court will infer the intent because such is the natural and probable consequence of your action.

The negligence cause of action in *Velsicol* merits further discussion. Where do courts and juries get their ideas of what is reasonable? The court states that the defendant breached the duty (to be reasonable and careful) by failing to "investigate the geological makeup or strata under the dumpsite prior to its purchase or operation." What makes the failure to do this unreasonable? The answer is that notions of reasonableness come from general community standards or, if they are not appropriate, from common experience. In this case, part of the proof was probably that other firms across the country who disposed of similar wastes certainly investigated the geological makeup of the strata under their dumpsites. In addition, in defining what is reasonable, governmental standards may be used. If the activity was such that there was no prior community standard, the jury's common experience would create the standard of reasonableness.

We note that on appeal (855 Fed. Rep. 2d 1188, 1888) this case was reversed in part, affirmed in part and remanded for a recalculation of damages. The part of the case that was reversed did not alter the application of the tort theories; rather it involved the enormously complicated matter of calculating damages for individual plaintiffs in a class action law suit. After the case was filed, some of the original plaintiffs settled their claims, and others were added. The trial court then picked five plaintiffs to represent the class of about 130 remaining who went to trial. The appellate court allowed general damages for each of the plaintiffs, but those who asserted that they were entitled to more damages had to prove that each had their individual diseases (such as cancer of the kidney) caused "to a reasonable medical ucertainty" by ingesting the drinking water. This means that each had to prove by a preponderance of the evidence (over fifty percent of the evidence) that the torts committed caused specific diseases alleged. In some of these cases there was testimony by expert witnesses that the ground water "might have" caused the disease. This was held to be less than a reasonable medical certainty, thus the award should be recalculated. The matter was further complicated by the fact that at least three of these five plaintiffs were heavy smokers, plus, one expert witness testified that no one knows for sure what causes cancer of the kidney.

The point here is that the damage part of a tort case is often the most troublesome. Tort law is far from a perfect remedy in cases such as the this one. In addition, consider these issues: We are left with the impression that the toxic materials may still be in the ground. How are they to be cleaned up? From whom are future occupants of the land to seek compensation if defendant Velsicol goes out of business or declares bankruptcy? Will the amount of money recovered in such a case ever be sufficient to compensate adequately the injured plaintiffs? How much money is adequate compensation for an increased probability of contracting cancer in one's life or of passing on to one's child the increased risk of serious or fatal disease? These questions have no clear answers. The law provides some measure of compensation but leaves the matter far from a final resolution.

DEFENSES TO TORTS

Legal defenses to tort claims may take several forms. We examine the three major forms.

PROCEDURAL DEFENSES

Procedural defenses, usually based on state statute, can always defeat a tort claim. The most prominent is the existence of a state statute that limits the time in which tort claims (and contract and other claims) may be heard by a court. These state laws are called *statutes of limitations*. Generally, they provide that an injured party has three years from the time the injury was discovered to file the claim. This time limit varies from state to state but is usually shorter than the statute of limitations for contract claims, which is usually five years. More state laws may be used as a form of procedural defense, and we survey them in the section on products liability.

AFFIRMATIVE DEFENSES

A second kind of defense is called an affirmative defense and must be asserted at the beginning of the pleading stage, or else the right to argue the defense is lost. The most prominent forms of affirmative defenses are those that apply to negligence cases, and raise the issue of the plaintiff's contributory fault.

Contributory Negligence.   The first is called contributory negligence. When the plaintiff asserts that the defendant is negligent and has damaged her, the defendant may assert that the plaintiff has failed to exercise reasonable care for her own safety and was thus also at fault.

Take the example of the plaintiff's riding a bike on a country road. Assume the plaintiff asserts that she was riding on the side when the defendant's car passed so close by that she was brushed off the road, down an embankment, and into a river. That is the plaintiff's version of the facts. The defendant may answer that the plaintiff was *contributorily negligent* in that she was not on the side of the road, but toward the center, blocking the road on the defendant's side. Traffic was oncoming, the plaintiff was not watching either in front of her or behind because she was looking at the river, and as a consequence she wandered into the center of the road, thus helping to cause her own injury.

The assertion of the defense of contributory negligence (of the plaintiff) raises a number of related issues and brings out the fact that states do differ substantially in the definition and development of their tort law. In some states, for example, if a jury finds that the negligence of the plaintiff was a "substantial" factor, then this is an absolute defense. Other states allow a jury to compute a damage award based on comparative negligence. They allow the jury to weigh the negligence of the plaintiff against that of the defendant. If the jury finds, for example, that the plaintiff suffered $100,000 of damage but was 20% at fault, then it deducts 20% of the award ($20,000) and asks the judge to enter judgment against the defendant for the balance of $80,000.

Some states allow even further computation by allowing the plaintiff to rebut the assertion of contributory negligence with the legal doctrine of *last clear chance*. In this case, the biker asserts negligence, the driver defends by saying the biker was contributorily negligent, but to lessen the severe impact of the contributory negligence defense, some states allow the plaintiff to prove that the driver had the last clear chance to avoid the contact.

Assumption of Risk.   Another affirmative defense to negligence is assumption of risk. The idea in this defense is that the plaintiff has voluntarily placed him- or herself in an area of known danger and thus opened him- or herself to the risk that took place. Again, assume that the biker chose to ride on a very narrow road that had no shoulder and was intended only for cars and that a bike path was down closer to the river. This biker has voluntarily assumed some risks by choosing to ride on the road. Other instances of the assumption of a known risk occur when you take a drive with a person known to be intoxicated or engage in a friendly game of ice hockey on the township pond. If you are injured by the driver's negligent operation of the auto or are hit in the face by the hockey puck, your chances of recovering are diminished substantially because you voluntarily assumed the natural and probable consequences of the perceived risk of the ride or the game.

DISPROVING THE ELEMENTS OF THE TORT

A major method of defeating the plaintiff's case is to offer evidence and argue against the assertion of the elements of a tort. In a negligence case, for example, the defendant would argue one or more of the following: that there was no duty, no breach, no causation, and if applicable, no damages.

Modern tort litigation as exemplified by the "toxic tort," *Velsicol* case, is characterized by these kinds of arguments. For example, the defendant may admit that it dumped the drums of chemicals into the ground but that the evidence was insufficient to show the chemicals spilled out of the drums and into the ground, then flowed into the groundwater, then into the drinking systems of the plaintiffs, and into the plaintiff's bodies and their nervous systems. In short, the defense would be that the breach of the duty did not directly cause plaintiffs' injuries.

Even if the plaintiff can prove that the chemicals in the drums are in the drinking water and have been consumed for years, the plaintiff's case may be defeated in some states unless there is *physical evidence* of damage to the bodies of the plaintiffs. A few states, however, now allow recovery even without present physical proof of damage. This issue in the legal environment of business is bound to grow in importance in the years to come.

For example, in *Brafford* v. *Susquehanna Corp.*,[1] an appellate court allowed the issue of the existence of a tort to go to the jury when there was no physical evidence of damage to the five plaintiffs, all members of a single household. They alleged that uranium ore waste removed from a nearby uranium mining facility had been poured around the foundations of their home. Specifically, the plaintiffs asserted only that their experts would testify to a reasonable degree of medical probability that they had suffered present, permanent, irreparable, but undetectable genetic and chromosomal damage as a result of exposure to the radiation emitted from the mill tailings.

The defendant argued that the chromosomal changes cannot be considered a present injury as a matter of law because the changes are nothing more than a subcellular occurrence of an increased risk caused by the defendant expressed not as fact, but as a probability. The court concluded that the defense of no detectable physical injury would not bar the claim and that the parties should proceed to trial because, according to experts, the damage had most probably been done and the "trigger of cancer had been cocked."

A NOTE ON MALPRACTICE

Malpractice is a word used to designate negligence in one's profession. It is commonly used in the legal environment of business. Usually, those offering a service to the public, such as medical doctors, accountants, lawyers, insurance agents, bankers, hair stylists, and designers, may be liable for injury caused to another when they are negligent in providing their services. The standard of reasonableness applied is the standard of reasonableness in the profession. When doctors or lawyers are sued for malpractice, the case is proved by showing that the general community of doctors or lawyers would have done the particular injuring act in a different way, so the way the defendant did it breaches the generally accepted conduct in the profession.

Many commentators identify a "structural" problem with this approach. What if the generally accepted way a profession has done a procedure causes injury regularly? How will negligence ever be proved? The answer is that, under the current conception of negligence, it cannot be proved. For example, if the way doctors do a particular operation results in fifteen deaths per one hundred operations and the deceased died during the operation, a good defense would be to say that the operation was done according to the generally accepted method and that the plaintiff (deceased) was, unfortunately, one of the fifteen foreseeable deaths.

If an auto company was sued for designing an auto with, for example, a front-end gas tank and if other manufacturers also designed cars with front-end gas tanks, there is, by definition, no negligence. People depend heavily on professions to operate in the public good and to set standards of care in the operation of their profession that protect people from harm. They are, however, human institutions and not perfect.

LIABILITY OF ACCOUNTANTS AND ACCOUNTING FIRMS FOR MALPRACTICE

One of the most prominent areas of malpractice in the legal environment of business involves the liability for malpractice (negligence) in the accounting profession. The accounting profession regulates itself through professional licensing and the issuance of standards for public accounting developed by the American Institute of Certified Public Accountants (AICPA). These standards, like any rule of human behavior, can never be stated or applied with absolute clarity, so there is always room for interpretation. When a person or firm relies on financial statements prepared by a public accountant or public accounting firm, it may suffer damage if the figures are misleading.

Take a typical example of a malpractice suit involving the alleged malpractice of an accounting firm. Assume that C Co. wants to buy D Co. and contracts with A Accounting Firm to assess the value of D Co. Further, assume that C was asking B Bank for a loan to buy D Co. Assume that A was negligent (e.g., it failed to discover large debts of D) and made public its statement that D was worth so much, so B financed the purchase and C bought D Co. After taking over, D fails and so does C. B is left with the debt of a failed company. What is B's remedy?

A Accounting Firm is still a going entity, and it may be sued. Figure 7.2 reveals that several approaches may be taken. If A was guilty of gross negligence or intentionally misleading C, then criminal prosecution by the federal or state governments is a possibility. Also, a claim may be based on breach of contract and negligence.

FIGURE 7.2 *Liability of Accounting Firm for Malpractice (Accounting firm—omission or misrepresentation in the conduct of an audit causing damage; liability may depend on who was damaged and the nature of the legal theory used)*

Possible Claims		
Negligence	Contract	Crimes
Liable in some states to those who were in a class of persons who could be foreseen to suffer injury should there be negligence	Liable to parties who signed contract with accounting firm or were known by firm to rely on figures provided	Violation of S.E.C. or state rules for fraud in valuing securities—liable to federal or state governments

We introduce the idea of a contract claim here because, in the area of products liability, discussed next, as in the area of malpractice, claims for a single injury or item of damage may be based both on the implied promise found in contract law to do "good, professional-like work" and the social duty to act reasonably. That is, when one contracts to do professional work, there is a *contract duty* running to the client to not make mistakes, and there always is a more general social (tort) duty to act with care.

In our case of the accounting firm, an additional problem is unique to the accounting, engineering, and architectural professions: To whom should the accountants be liable?

Consider for a moment that public accountants render a valuable service—they assess and report on the value of living, going firms and make public their statements as to this value. If they operate in good faith but make a mistake, to whom should they be liable? If they should be liable to all who are damaged, they may be put out of business as a profession. Therefore, early cases in the areas of both contract and tort liability narrowly defined the class of persons who could recover.

Today, because states have differing contract and tort common law, our example has four possible outcomes:

1. *Traditional view.* The injured party must have been in contract with the accounting firm to recover; some states require that the relationship created by an exchange of promises—called privity—exists between the injured party and the accountant-defendant; negligence is not allowed.

2. *Foreseeable party view.* Some states hold that if the accounting firm knew about or could reasonably foresee that *B* Bank would rely on the financial data, then it may maintain both contract and tort claims.

3. *Foreseeable class view.* This view developed in the 1980s and holds that if the accounting firm knew about the general class of plaintiffs and that it might rely on the data provided, then an injured member of the class (usually limited to credit institutions, investors, and the like) may maintain both contract and negligence suits.

4. *Modern view.* The latest view followed by a few states requires that the injured party have a reasonably close connection to the auditor's negligence and its own harm.

In our example, a bank that was financing the transaction would fit within the second, third, or fourth view, and so could, in all probability, maintain both of its claims.

In the section that follows, we take a more expansive look at the liability of the producer of goods to one who is injured by a product.

LIABILITY FOR DEFECTIVE PRODUCTS

Today, there is no more dynamic, complex, or troublesome area of commercial law than the study of firms' liability for defective products. Many people call this *consumer law.* This area poses problems for the consumer, the manufacturer or seller, and the legal system.

HISTORY OF PRODUCTS LIABILITY LAW

Liability for defective products in the mid to late 1800s was almost unknown. The few cases that did provide a remedy for an injured consumer were based on contract. The appellate cases from this period held that an injured plaintiff could not bring an action against a producer or seller unless the defective good had been bought by the plaintiff from the manufacturer-defendant. The requirement that the plaintiff be a contracting party with the defendant is called the *requirement of privity*. Family members, friends, and bystanders were all unable to recover for a product-related injury in the nineteenth century because they lacked this special relationship created between contracting parties.

The notion that privity was needed to maintain an action served the industrial interests of the period and most probably eliminated numerous suits. Under an exception to the general rule requiring privity, however, one could recover in the absence of privity if the goods causing the injury were negligently made and were "inherently dangerous." In the mid to late 1800s and early 1900s, this class of goods included mislabeled poison, a defective scaffold ninety feet high, and a defective bottle of aerated water.

The restriction imposed by the requirement of privity was lessened shortly after the turn of the century, when the highest court in New York State held that, regardless of privity, a manufacturer was under an obligation to make a product carefully if it would become dangerous to a user if negligently made.[2] In this case, an injured plaintiff recovered against a corporate manufacturer with whom the plaintiff had not contracted. The court allowed recovery when a wheel on a Buick was classified as inherently dangerous because of the injury that could be caused if it was not properly made. In a later portion of this chapter, we discuss how the classification of inherently dangerous goods grew into a significant element of strict liability, one of the major theories of products liability today.

In addition to the requirement of privity, another reason for the relatively slow development of products liability law in the late 1800s and early 1900s was the doctrine of *caveat emptor*, or buyer beware. This notion, less precise than privity, arose from the social and economic climate of the times. Caveat emptor denotes a general policy of courts, rather than a precise legal principle. At a time when manufactured goods were relatively simple, it was judged best to let the consumer choose the appropriate product—even try it out—and if a purchase of a product were made, the consumer should be stuck with it and any resulting injury, even if the product were defectively made. This was good policy, some people believed, because in an economic system that encouraged the presence of numerous sellers in the market of goods, the producer of faulty products would go out of business as word spread about the quality of its product. With the increasing complexity of goods and with the trend toward concentration (fewer producers) in many major industrial markets, the doctrines of privity and caveat emptor were perceived as increasingly unjust.

The response of the law has been literally explosive. Today, in most jurisdictions, privity is no longer relied on to defeat many consumer claims. Indeed, many legal scholars would characterize products liability law as based on the premise of "seller beware."

TORT THEORIES OF PRODUCTS LIABILITY

The remedies available to an injured consumer today may come from one of three general areas: (1) the *common law of torts* (here, the two chief remedies are based on negligence and strict liability), (2) *federal and state statutory provisions* creating liability for sellers who sell defective products or who deceive consumers, and (3) the warranties provided for in Article 2 of the Uniform Commercial Code (UCC), a set of commercial rules that apply to most transactions required in the production of complex goods (discussed in Chapter 8).

Negligence and strict liability, two independent legal theories discussed in the first part of this chapter, are civil law theories on which an injured plaintiff may base his or her products liability claim. They may be alleged and proved in the same case in which a breach of warranty theory is argued, or they may serve as the sole basis for liability.

An important advantage of tort theories of liability over contract and warranty-based theories is that the statute of limitations favors torts. In most jurisdictions, the statute of limitations for a tort is three years, and for breach of contract usually four years. The statute of limitations for a tort, however, usually begins to run from the *date of injury* and not from the date of delivery of the good to the original purchaser. The latter date applies to warranty-based claims.

A disadvantage of tort theories is that most courts will not permit recovery for economic loss alone (e.g., damage to the goods or lost profits). To recover for economic loss, the plaintiff must also allege and prove personal injury. The chief purpose of tort law in products liability cases is to provide a remedy in the form of money damages to one who has suffered *personal* injury.

Below we discuss each of the five theories in general use which are used to establish a products liability claim.

1. NEGLIGENCE

To establish negligence in a products liability case, the plaintiff must prove that the defendant's conduct in manufacturing, designing, or inspecting goods produced a risk of harm greater than society is willing to accept in light of the benefits to be derived from that activity. Simply put, the risk of harm must be unreasonable under the circumstances. This idea is usually put in the form of an instruction to the jury: "You must find the defendant liable if it failed to meet the standard of care expected of an average, reasonable person under the circumstances." In almost all negligence cases, the issue of the "reasonableness" of the defendant's conduct is an issue for the jury to decide; that is, most of these cases present problems of proof, rather than issues of substantive law.

The legal issues that constitute negligent manufacture and design are numerous and diverse. We discuss two. The first is the legal device of *res ipsa loquitur;* the second, an issue of increasing importance, involves design defects.

Res Ipsa Loquitur. Proving that goods were negligently manufactured or designed is no easy task, and it is much more difficult if the goods are damaged or destroyed as a result of an alleged defect. In view of this difficulty, the law sometimes applies the legal device of *res ipsa loquitur,* which literally translated means "the thing speaks for itself." This device is properly used where a gap exists in the plaintiff's proof of negligence caused by missing items such as the product that caused the injury. If the plaintiff can show that (1) the injury complained of does not normally happen in the absence of negligence and (2) the defendant had exclusive control of the thing causing the injury at the time of the alleged negligent act—the time of the manufacture of the goods, not necessarily the time of injury—the application of *res ipsa loquitur* will cause the judge to state that the plaintiff has filled the gap in its evidence and that an inference of negligence will be created. It is then up to the defendant to rebut that inference.

The case of *Escola* v. *Coca-Cola Bottling Co. of Fresno* is a products liability classic. The majority opinion was composed of two opinions, the first of which expresses and applies the principle of *res ipsa loquitur.* The second opinion, concurring with the majority, would have applied strict liability.

Escola v. *Coca-Cola Bottling Co. of Fresno*
150 P.2d 436 (Cal. 1944)

GIBSON, CHIEF JUSTICE

Plaintiff, a waitress in a restaurant, was injured when a bottle of Coca Cola broke in her hand. She alleged that defendant company, which had bottled and delivered the alleged defective bottle to her employer, was negligent in selling "bottles containing said beverage which on account of excessive pressure of gas or by reason of some defect in the bottle was dangerous . . . and likely to explode." This appeal is from a judgment upon a jury verdict in favor of plaintiff.

Defendant's driver delivered several cases of Coca Cola to the restaurant, placing them on the floor, one on top of the other, under and behind the counter, where they remained at least thirty-six hours. Immediately before the accident, plaintiff picked up the top case and set it upon a nearby ice cream cabinet in front of and about three feet from the refrigerator. She then proceeded to take the bottles from the case with her right hand, one at a time, and put them into the refrigerator. Plaintiff testified that after she had placed three bottles in the refrigerator and had moved the fourth bottle about 18 inches from the case "it exploded in my hand." The bottle broke into two jagged pieces and inflicted a deep five-inch cut, severing blood vessels, nerves and muscles of the thumb and palm of the hand. . . .

The top portion of the bottle, with the cap, remained in the plaintiff's hand, and the lower portion fell to the floor but did not break. The broken bottle was not produced at the trial, the pieces having been thrown away by an employee of the restaurant shortly after the accident. Plaintiff, however, described the broken pieces, and a diagram of the bottle was made showing the location of the "fracture line" where the bottle broke in two.

One of the defendant's drivers, called as a witness by plaintiff, testified that he had seen other bottles of Coca Cola in the past explode and had found broken bottles in the warehouse when he took the cases out, but that he did not know what made them blow up.

Plaintiff then rested her case, having announced to the court that being unable to show any specific acts of negligence she relied completely on the doctrine of res ipsa loquitur.

Defendant contends that the doctrine of res ipsa loquitur does not apply in this case, and that the evidence is insufficient to support the judgment.

★ ★ ★

Res ipsa loquitur does not apply unless (1) defendant had exclusive control of the thing causing the injury and (2) the accident is of such a nature that it ordinarily would not occur in the absence of negligence by the defendant. . . .

★ ★ ★

Upon an examination of the record, the evidence appears sufficient to support a reasonable inference that the bottle here involved was not damaged by any extraneous force after delivery to the restaurant by defendant. It follows, therefore, that the bottle was in some manner defective at the time defendant relinquished control, because sound and properly prepared bottles of carbonated liquids do not ordinarily explode when carefully handled.

The next question, then, is whether plaintiff may rely upon the doctrine of res ipsa loquitur to supply an inference that defendant's negligence was responsible for the defective condition of the bottle at the time it was delivered to the restaurant. Under the general rules pertaining to the doctrine, as set forth above, it must appear that bottles of carbonated liquid are not ordinarily defective without negligence by the bottling company. . . .

★ ★ ★

The bottle was admittedly charged with gas under pressure, and the charging of the bottle was within the exclusive control of defendant. As it is a matter of common knowledge that an overcharge would not ordinarily result without negligence, it follows under the doctrine of res ipsa loquitur that if the bottle was in fact excessively charged an inference of defendant's negligence would arise. If the explosion resulted from a defective bottle containing a safe pressure, the defendant would be liable if it negligently failed to discover such flaw. If the defect were visible, an inference of negligence would arise from the failure of defendant to discover it. Where defects are discoverable it may be assumed that they will not ordinarily escape detection if a reasonable inspection is made, and if such a defect is overlooked an inference arises that a proper inspection was not made. . . .

A chemical engineer for the Owens-Illinois Glass Company and its Pacific Coast subsidiary, maker of Coca Cola bottles, explained how glass is manufactured and the methods used in testing and inspecting bottles. He testified that his company is the largest manufacturer of glass containers in the United States, and that it uses the standard methods for testing bottles recommended by the glass containers association. A pressure test is made by taking a sample from each mold every three hours—approximately one out of every 600 bottles—and subjecting the sample to an internal pressure of 450 pounds per square inch, which is sustained for one minute. (The normal pressure in Coca Cola bottles is less than 50 pounds per square inch.) The sample bottles are also subjected to the standard thermal shock test. The witness stated that these tests are "pretty near" infallible.

★ ★ ★

Although it is not clear in this case whether the explosion was caused by an excessive charge or a defect in the glass there is sufficient showing that neither cause would ordinarily have been present if due care had been used. Further, defendant had exclusive control over both the charging and inspection of the bottles. Accordingly, all the requirements necessary to entitle plaintiff to rely on the doctrine of res ipsa loquitur to supply an inference of negligence are present.

It is true that defendant presented evidence tending to show that it exercised considerable precaution by carefully regulating and checking the pressure in the bottles and by making visual inspections for defects in the glass at several stages during the bottling process. It is well settled, however, that when a defendant produces evidence to rebut the inference of negligence which arises upon application of the doctrine of res ipsa loquitur, it is ordinarily a question of fact for the jury to determine whether the inference has been dispelled. . . .

The judgement is affirmed.

CASE FOLLOW-UP

The *Escola* case represents an early approach by courts to search for and apply legal principles from the common law of negligence to provide remedies for injured consumers. It could be classified as a "negligence in manufacturing" or "manufacturing flaw" case. Generally, in these cases, the process of affixing liability is one of comparing the product with others that were the result of the process of manufacturing. The focus is on the defendant's mechanical techniques of production. If Coca-Cola could prove that its manufacturing process for making the bottles and filling them with liquid met the industry standards, there could be no finding of negligence because no industry standard of carefulness was breached. That is why one of the judges, Justice Traynor, preferred a finding of strict liability. His reasoning is given in the following section on strict liability.

Process and Design Defects. Recently, plaintiffs and courts have been changing their focus from the manufacturing *process* to the *design* of the product. Defective product design cases may be analyzed or explained as either negligence cases or strict liability cases. That is, if a product is alleged to have been improperly designed, a plaintiff or the court may characterize the case as one of negligent or defective design or may characterize the allegation as one of strict liability (explained in the next section), with the improper design argument being a major item of proof for this tort.

Generally, plaintiffs should prefer the application of strict liability because, in a negligence case, the defendant may meet the plaintiff's case with proof that its conduct is not unreasonable because it conforms to the generally accepted standards of performance. For example, Coca-Cola attempted to counter the plaintiff's case in *Escola* by introducing evidence that the industry standard of taking a sample bottle every three hours from the manufacturing mold (approximately one of every six hundred bottles) and subjecting it to an internal pressure of 450 pounds per square inch, sustained for one minute, is "pretty near" infallible in guarding against defective bottles.

2. STRICT LIABILITY

Strict liability as a tort theory used in products liability cases is of recent and increasing significance. Section 402A of the *Restatement of Tort* says that a manufacturer may be strictly liable when it

> [S]ells any product in a defective condition unreasonably dangerous to the user or consumer or to his property and is subject to liability for physical harm thereby caused to the ultimate user or consumer, or to his property, if
>
> **(a)** the seller is engaged in the business of selling such a product and
>
> **(b)** it is expected to and does reach the user or consumer without substantial change in the condition in which it is sold[3]

The basic reason for the increasing use of this theory is that there are fewer well-established legal defenses to such claims. For the reasons already stated, negligence theory still permits the successful assertion of defenses when a plaintiff may be injured by a product through no fault of the plaintiff. Strict liability is based on the notion that, as between an innocent injured plaintiff and a merchant, the latter should pay for an injury caused by a defect because it is in a better position to prevent the loss and can spread this loss over the life of its product.

The *Escola* case was so close on the negligence issue that Judge Traynor, a famous California jurist, would have applied the theory of strict liability in that case. In a concurring opinion, he wrote what has become the classic statement of the reasons for the application of this tort theory to products liability.

Escola v. *Coca-Cola Bottling Co. of Fresno*
150 P.2d 436 at p. 440 (Cal. 1944)
Concurring Opinion

TRAYNOR, JUSTICE

I concur in the judgment, but I believe that manufacturer's negligence should no longer be singled out as the basis of a plaintiff's right to recover in cases like the present one. In my opinion it should now be recognized that a manufacturer incurs [a strict] liability when an article that he has placed on the market, knowing that it is to be used without inspection, proves to have a defect that causes injury to human beings. . . . Even if there is no negligence, however, public policy demands that responsibility be fixed wherever it will most effectively reduce the hazards to life and health inherent in defec-tive products that reach the market. It is evident that the manufacturer can anticipate some hazards and guard against the recurrence of others, as the public cannot. Those who suffer injury from defective products are unprepared to meet its consequences. The cost of an injury and the loss of time or health may be an overwhelming misfortune to the person injured, and a needless one, for the risk of injury can be insured by the manufacturer and distributed among the public as a cost of doing business. It is to the public interest to discourage the marketing of products having defects that are a menace to the public. If such products nevertheless find their way into the market it is to the public interest to place the responsibility for whatever injury they may cause upon the manufacturer, who, even if he is not negligent in the manufacture of the product, is responsible for its reaching the market. However intermittently such injuries may occur and however haphazardly they may strike, the risk of their occurrence is a constant risk and a general one. Against such a risk there should be general and constant protection and the manufacturer is best situated to afford such protection. . . . It is needlessly circuitous to make negligence the basis of recovery and impose what is in reality liability without negligence. If public policy demands that a manufacturer of goods be responsible for their quality regardless of negligence there is no reason not to fix that responsibility openly.

* * *

As handicrafts have been replaced by mass production with its great markets and transportation facilities, the close relationship between the producer and consumer of a product has been altered. Manufacturing processes, frequently valuable secrets, are ordinarily either inaccessible to or beyond the ken of the general public. The consumer no longer has means or skill enough to investigate for himself the soundness of a product, even when it is not contained in a sealed package, and his erstwhile vigilance has been lulled by the steady efforts of manufacturers to build up confidence by advertising and marketing devices such as trademarks. . . . Consumers no longer approach products warily but accept them on faith, relying on the reputation of the manufacturer or the trademark. . . . Manufacturers have sought to justify that faith by increasingly high standards of inspection and a readiness to make good on defective products by way of replacements and refunds. . . . The manufacturer's obligation to the consumer must keep pace with the changing relationship between them; it cannot be escaped because the marketing of a product has become so complicated as to require one or more intermediaries. Certainly there is greater reason to impose liability on the manufacturer than on the retailer who is but a conduit of a product that he is not himself able to test. . . .

The manufacturer's liability should, of course, be defined in terms of the safety of the product in normal and proper use, and should not extend to injuries that cannot be traced to the product as it reached the market.

CASE FOLLOW-UP

In a fairly simple products liability case involving an exploding Coke bottle, the noted California jurist would impose strict liability on the manufacturer/bottler to compensate the injured plaintiff. He would do away with negligence in a case like this one because, as he puts it, public policy demands another theory. Exactly what does he mean? As he states it, the reasons for strict liability are as follows:

1. The manufacturer puts the product on the market, knowing that a consumer probably will not inspect it and is, therefore, more responsible for the product than the consumer. Also, the manufacturer creates a general expectation of reliability in the product through advertising.

2. By placing liability on the manufacturer, the law will, as a matter of policy, be placing the loss on the one that can most surely guard against such a loss by designing safer products.

3. The consumer is less financially prepared for this kind of injury than the producer of the product.

4. The manufacturer is in a better position to absorb the loss through buying insurance or increasing the cost of the product to cover such anticipated losses. It is fairer for the producer to absorb and spread the loss over all units of the product than for the consumer to absorb it alone.

Thus, public policy, expressed in these reasons, should be that, between an innocent user of a product and a fairly innocent manufacturer, the latter should suffer the loss caused by a defect in a product.

DEFECTIVE AND UNREASONABLY DANGEROUS PRODUCTS

Section 402A of the *Restatement of Torts*, which defines strict liability in tort for products, mentions that "any product in a defective condition unreasonably dangerous to the user or consumer" creates strict liability for the seller if it causes damages. The keys to understanding strict liability in tort are the words defect and unreasonably dangerous.

At first glance it would seem that a product must be both defective and unreasonably dangerous for a plaintiff to recover for injury. Most courts, however, lump them together and say that a product is unreasonably dangerous if it is defective. In the text that follows, we use these elements of a case in strict liability interchangeably.

There are today at least three generally accepted situations in which a product can be defective. These situations cluster in or around the following parts of the manufacturing process and are referred to as (1) design defects, (2) production defects, and (3) defective warnings or inspections. Within these situations are several definitions of *defect*. The best way to understand these definitions is to imagine a judge giving an instruction to a jury after all of the evidence is in. The judge may instruct the jury to apply one of the following three definitions of a defect:

1. The product sold was dangerous to an extent beyond what would be contemplated by the ordinary consumer who purchases it, with ordinary knowledge common to the community as to its characteristics (the consumer expectation test).

2. The product sold created such a risk that an ordinarily prudent company engaged in the manufacture of such products, being fully aware of the risk, would not have put it on the market (the prudent manufacturer test).

3. The product sold creates such a risk of serious injury that the "cost" to make it safe would outweigh the benefits from it to society (the risk/utility test).

These three definitions are all in use in various states, although it is not possible to say how many states use the first, how many use the second, and so on. All we can say is that, in products liability law, states generally use one of three tests to determine whether a product is defective or unreasonably dangerous.

These definitions do produce different results. Let's consider a straightforward example.

THE CASE OF THE DEFECTIVE UNDERWEAR

A four-year-old child, Richard, severely burned himself when he played with matches and his T-shirt caught fire. His father brought a lawsuit against the manufacturer, Union Underwear Co., alleging that the shirt was defective in that it was more flammable than it should have been. The plaintiff-father argued that the defendant-manufacturer should be strictly liable in tort for the injuries caused by the burning shirt.[4]

Notice that the T-shirt was not obviously defective in that it was not torn, unraveled, or otherwise noticeably of not fair or average quality. The father was alleging that it was defective because it caught fire when it should not have. Many cases are similarly problematic. Plaintiffs allege, for example, that a car was defective because it did not stop quickly enough or that an electric saw was defective because it did not have a guard around the blade. Defect in this sense does not mean the brakes were broken or the saw flew apart. The product operated correctly for most uses, but it failed (was defective) in the particular use that caused the injury of the plaintiff.

If the jurisdiction is one in which the first definition (the consumer expectation test) is used, the plaintiff will have to show that most consumers could not have foreseen the type of injury suffered. The focus of this definition is on the mind of the average consumer. The plaintiff must show through testimony of other consumers that they would not have known of the risk of the shirt flaming up. If the jury thinks most consumers would not have foreseen that a shirt of the kind worn by the child could have flamed up when a match was touched to it, it will have to find the product defective and return a verdict for the plaintiff.

If the second definition is used, the focus of the evidence will be on what other manufacturers know about the shirts they make. If most other manufacturers of T-shirts make their shirts of different material or use a different weave because they recognize the risk of children using matches close to the shirt, this is strong evidence of a defect in the shirt.

If the third definition (the risk/utility test) is used, the jury, after it views the evidence, will be called on to weigh whether the existence of such shirts on the market (designed the way they were) created such a risk that the risk outweighed the utility of the shirt. A further example here might be helpful. Ordinary kitchen knives are dangerous products that cause many injuries every year. In a jurisdiction recognizing this third definition of defect, could a plaintiff successfully maintain a products liability suit against a producer of such knives for a severe cut? Probably not. The utility of such knives outweighs their risk, so the plaintiff would not recover.

(THEORIES 3, 4, AND 5) THE WARRANTIES OF ARTICLE 2 OF THE UCC

A *warranty* is an expressed or implied promise or assurance that certain facts exist or that a product will perform in a certain way. Because warranties are essentially based on contract law, it has long been held that the parties to a sales transaction may bargain away, waive, disclaim, or modify warranties. The questions arising from whether a warranty was so changed by the "bargaining" of the parties present the chief defense or challenge to a warranty claim. If it is established that a warranty was so waived or modified as to affect the plaintiff's case, then in appropriate circumstances the plaintiff may counter the modification by arguing that the waiver or modification was unconscionable. *Unconscionability* refers to a contractual provision that is so unfair it would result in an injustice to enforce it. The issue of whether an "agreement" was unconscionable usually is litigated in this circumstance.

Three classifications of warranties are made by sellers or merchants: (1) express warranties, (2) implied warranties, and (3) warranties of title and against infringement of patent or copyright. Express and implied warranties are much more significant for our purposes of explaining products liability law than warranties of title and against infringements, so we concentrate on them.

3.   EXPRESS WARRANTIES

A seller makes express warranties by

1. Any affirmation of fact or promise made . . . to the buyer which relates to the goods and becomes part of the basis of the bargain. . . .

2. Any description of the goods which is made part of the basis of the bargain. . . .

3. Any sample or model which is made part of the basis of the bargain. . . .[5]

Simply put, this warranty must be expressed in writing or spoken by the seller or the seller's agent as an affirmation of fact or promise; or it may be created by a description, model, or sample provided by the seller or the seller's promise regarding future performance. It is not necessary that the words *warranty* or *guarantee* be used or that the seller have an intention to make a warranty.

The expression that the seller must make may be found in the sales agreement, in advertising, in plans or instructions furnished with the goods, or in packaging, or it may be made orally. This expression, however, must be more than a statement of opinion. The statement that "this car is tuned like an orchestra and will provide good service and will get thirty-two miles per gallon when driven at fifty miles-per-hour" contains just one expressed warranty—the mileage-per-gallon phrase.

Sometimes, however, the distinction is hard to make. Consider these assertions made by a merchant in an actual case: (1) The parts are of high quality; (2) experiences and testing have shown that the frequency of repairs was very low and would remain so; (3) the purchase of machines by the buyer and leasing of them to customers would return a substantial profit to the buyer; (4) replacement parts are readily available; and (5) the goods sold will not cause fires, and the machines have been tested and are ready. The court held that only the fourth and fifth assertions were statements of fact.[6]

4. IMPLIED WARRANTY OF MERCHANTABILITY

Implied warranties are imposed on a sales transaction by statute or court decision. The UCC, Article 2, provides that a seller who is a merchant (one who usually sells goods of the kind sold) has made implied warranties whether the merchant intended them or not. No discussion occurs between the parties about such warranties. They exist simply by virtue of the fact that a sale has been made.

An *implied warranty of merchantability,* imposed on all merchants, implies a promise by the selling merchant that the goods are fit for the ordinary purposes for which such goods are used.[7] A merchant is a person who sells goods or presents herself as having special knowledge or skill peculiar to the goods sold. This warranty made by merchants may be excluded or modified by agreement.

If a consumer buys a television set, a camera, a washing machine, or an automobile from a merchant, imposed on the sales transaction, unless waived or modified, is a warranty that the goods are of a quality comparable to that generally acceptable in that line of trade. Certainly, the goods must perform for the purposes for which they were intended. A television set must show a picture, a camera must take a picture, and so forth.

There are no "technical" requirements to prove the existence of this warranty other than evidence that the seller is a merchant with respect to goods of the kind sold. So, for example, a clothing merchant is not a merchant when she sells her used car. The sale of food items not to be consumed on the premises (e.g., from a grocery store) has traditionally been thought of as a sale of goods and therefore subject to the imposition of implied warranties.

5. IMPLIED WARRANTY OF FITNESS FOR A PARTICULAR PURPOSE

Section 2–315 of Article 2 of the UCC states,

> Where the seller at the time of contracting has reason to know any particular purpose for which the goods are required and that the buyer is relying on the seller's skill or judgment to select or furnish suitable goods, there is unless excluded or modified . . . an implied warranty that the goods shall be fit for such purpose.

This implied warranty is imposed on any seller (not just merchants) and requires two elements of proof: (1) that the seller knew the particular purpose for which the goods were bought and (2) that the buyer relied on the seller to select the goods. Actual knowledge of the particular purpose is not required as long as the circumstances of the purchase are such that the seller should have reason to know the purpose. This implied warranty usually arises when a consumer asks a merchant seller to provide goods for a specific task that is beyond the consumer's general knowledge. For example, a consumer may hire a heating and cooling firm to air-condition his or her home to seventy degrees during the summer months. If the equipment fails to cool the home as provided in the contract, this warranty is breached. The air-conditioning system installed may work properly and therefore be "merchantable," but it does not fulfill the particular purpose for which it was purchased.

A factual pattern or circumstance will illustrate the materials we have discussed thus far. If a buyer informs a seller of a purpose for the purchased goods and relies on the seller to select those goods, and if the seller goes on to say, "These goods will fit your needs," or similar language, the statement will be an express warranty. If the intended use of the goods was an ordinary use and if the product failed to operate for this use, both the express warranty and the warranty of merchantability may have been breached. Finally, if the conditions for the creation of a warranty of fitness are present, it may exist in addition to express warranties and warranties of merchantability.

It is obvious to most merchants that it is in their self-interest to make as few of the express and fitness warranties as prudent. Article 2 of the UCC aids merchants and manufacturers by allowing them to modify or exclude the warranties made.

EXCLUSION OR MODIFICATION OF WARRANTIES AND LIMITATION OF DAMAGES FOR BREACH OF WARRANTY

Perhaps the most fundamental notion in American contract law is "freedom of contract." Generally, this means that the parties to a contract should be free to work out the terms of their agreement and that courts should not interfere with the bargaining process or the terms of the contract. The function of courts should be to enforce the parties' contractual intent. If the parties intend, as evidenced by their written agreement or otherwise, to waive warranties implied by Article 2, then courts should enforce this intent unless the waiver is unconscionable or violates federal law. One place we find this freedom-of-contract notion in Article 2 is in Section 2–316, which permits the parties to exclude or modify the warranties just explained.

Although merchants often exclude or modify warranties when they deal with one another, legislatures and courts have tried to protect consumers when merchants try to exclude or modify the warranties made to consumers. For example, Section 2–719(3) provides that it is prima facie unconscionable (unenforceable) for a merchant to limit or exclude common damages to one's person (physical injury) caused to consumers by consumer products. Courts have had to police the merchant-consumer transaction because of the tendency of merchants to draft sales agreements in their own favor. Long ago, Karl Llewellyn, a noted legal scholar and chief drafter of Article 2, pointed out a practice among business lawyers to do what no intelligent engineer would think of doing. Business lawyers, he said, tend to draft to the edge of the possible, not to within *the margin of safety*[8] intelligent engineers would. Engineers allow for a margin of safety. This difference is explained by the fact that lawyers are advocates and are trained to push for their clients' interests to the absolute limit. Generally, courts use the doctrine of unconscionability to enforce a measure of fairness in the merchant-consumer sales transaction.

As a short summary we present Figure 7.3, which is an overview of the major legal principles argued in a products liability case.

Overview of Five Legal Principles Asserted in a Modern Products Liability Case Against Producers of Products

Tort Theories
1. Negligence
    Negligent Design
    Negligent Failure to warn of danger
    Negligent Manufacture

2. Strict Liability
    Liability based on idea of a *defect* or that good was *unreasonably dangerous*

Contract Theories
3. Expressed Warranty
4. Implied Warranty of Merchantability
5. Implied Warranty of Fitness for a Particular Purpose

Injured plaintiff may assert 1 and 2 if not a purchaser; may assert 3, 4, and 5 in addition to 1 and 2 if a plaintiff is a purchaser or member of the household of plaintiff

DEFENSES TO PRODUCTS LIABILITY CLAIMS

PLAINTIFF'S MISUSE OF THE PRODUCT

A significant category of defenses comprises what may be called the plaintiff's misbehavior in using the product. These defenses (similar to defenses to all tort claims) include contributory negligence of the plaintiff, assumption of a known risk, misuse, hypersensitivity, and lack of proximate causation. They are available to a manufacturer or seller in cases of a breach of warranty, negligence, or in a few states, strict liability. The use and application of these defenses vary so widely from state to state that generalization about them is almost impossible. Some states, for example, have adopted the position that contributory negligence is not a defense to a claim for damages based on a breach of warranty theory, whereas other state supreme courts have held that it is an absolute defense.[9]

Apparently, some courts confuse contract-based claims with negligence-based claims and allow a manufacturer to defend a breach of warranty case by proving the plaintiff's negligent use of the product. Moreover, some states might hold that if a woman uses a hair dye even though she knows she experiences severe skin reactions to hair dyes, a vague doctrine of hypersensitivity would preclude her recovery for damage. Some courts might hold that similar misconduct tended to prove a lack of proximate causation because the plaintiff's own acts, not the product, were the primary cause.

In a related, emerging defense involving auto injuries, failure to wear a seat belt may be considered contributory negligence. This is especially true in states that have passed mandatory seat belt use statutes.[10]

In short, where an injured plaintiff voluntarily and unreasonably proceeds to encounter a known danger or a danger that would be known to a reasonable person, or where the plaintiff uses a product in a manner that was not intended, the plaintiff will most probably encounter some form of defense. The reasonableness of the plaintiff's conduct ultimately will be decided by the jury.

THE STATE-OF-THE-ART DEFENSE

Is it a good defense for the manufacturer to plead that it used the most advanced knowledge and technology in designing and marketing the product? This is called the *state-of-the-art defense*. At this writing, most states do allow testimony about the state of technology available when the good was produced to show that no warning to users was necessary.

LAW, DANGEROUS PRODUCTS, AND PUBLIC POLICY

In the remaining part of this chapter, we expand our focus from an explanation of the technical, legal rules in products liability law to examine the contours of one of the most significant public policy debates in the legal environment of business. The general question now is this: In commercial society, how should people adjust the interests they have in a safe and healthful environment (and being compensated for injuries caused by products) and those interests people have in letting businesses develop products and practices they believe best for the markets in which they sell? First, let's examine the nature of the problem.

THE NATURE OF THE PROBLEM

People have created both production processes and products that are extremely dangerous to life. We present here an overview of some products and practices of commercial life that have occupied a tremendous amount of attention in the legal system in the past twenty-five years.

Asbestos.   Asbestos is a very thin, fiber-like mineral used in the construction industry since the 1940s. It was linked to lung cancer and related life threatening diseases in the 1950s, but the evidence of causation was not certain until the 1970s. The use of asbestos was pervasive. It was used in many household products, and in home, school, and public and private institutions to insulate steam pipes and the like. Perhaps millions of Americans were exposed to this product daily.

The largest seller of asbestos in the United States was the Manville Corporation, which used to be a prosperous construction and forest-products firm. As the evidence mounted that death and sickness were caused by this product, the law suits began to compensate those damaged. Many of these lawsuits were based on the legal principle of strict liability.

On August 26, 1982, Manville filed for bankruptcy. The reason was not that it was poorly managed or had suffered business reverses, but that it could not possibly hope to pay the 16,500 claims against it or the 500 new ones being filed each month. Experts estimated that the total number of lawsuits could reach 52,000 and that the total cost might reach $2 billion.

Manville argued that it certainly would not have produced the product had it known that asbestos was carcinogenic. The product was already a large presence in people's daily lives when it was proved to be dangerous. Today, tens of thousands of persons are sick and dying from a cancer caused by exposure to asbestos. Asbestos is now a regulated substance, and most people are aware of its danger to life, but this does not help those still suffering.[11]

Cigarettes.   The litigation seeking compensation for disease caused by cigarettes is just beginning to appear on the scene. The case of Rose Cipollone was heard by the U.S. Supreme Court in the Spring of 1993. Mrs. Cipollone's estate brought suit against Liggett (the tobacco company that manufactured Chesterfield cigarettes) in the mid-1980s. The complaint argued that she was induced to begin smoking in the early 1940s and that, by the end of 1943, she was smoking a pack a day. She relied on advertisements that made smoking appear cool, glamorous and grown- up. Beautiful and liberated women, the complaint alleged, created role models she wished to emulate. Moreover, she believed that the tobacco companies would never do anything that was really going to kill a person. She read and paid attention to statements from the industry that indicated there was no specific proof that smoking caused cancer.

At trial, attorneys presented testimony that $250,000 is spent per hour, twenty-four hours a day, seven days a week, 365 days a year on cigarette advertising. The industry created a magazine entitled *Tobacco and Health (Research)* and mailed it free to practically every doctor in the country. This was a "blatant and biased account of the smoking 'controversy'" that had as its only purpose to convince doctors that the claimed risks were unfounded.[12]

In 1981, Mrs. Cipollone was diagnosed with lung cancer. In 1982, she had a lung removed; she eventually died of cancer on October 21, 1984. In one of the earlier decisions in her lawsuit, her estate was awarded a judgment of $400,000. The chief legal argument was that the tobacco company had made affirmations of fact within the meaning of the Uniform Commercial Code concerning the health risks of smoking. An appellate court reversed this decision, ruling that companies could not be a sued by people who smoked after warning labels were placed on cigarettes.[13]

In 1993, the Supreme Court held that plaintiffs such as Mrs. Cipollone could sue cigarette companies for fraud and would make out a good case if they could prove the defendants covered up information that smoking was harmful.[14] Law suits against cigarette companies are few in number, but many people say the writing is on the wall. Defendants in these cases argue (like beer, wine, and alcohol companies) that they make their product available, warn the user of the dangers, and if a purchaser wants to use the product, the risks are theirs. Yet, figures indicate that cigarettes are directly linked to about 400,000 American deaths each year. Moreover, in spring of 1993, the U.S. Environmental Protection Agency reported conclusive evidence that environmental tobacco smoke increases the risk of lung cancer to nonsmokers.

It is too early to judge the outcome of lawsuits in this area of second-hand smoke, but two are noteworthy. A nonsmoking owner of a barbershop for thirty years has sued thirteen tobacco companies for $125 million for his lung cancer, and a class action lawsuit on behalf of 60,000 flight attendants asking for $5 billion in compensation has been filed.[15] If just a fraction of the anticipated lawsuits are successful, cigarettes will either disappear from the scene or become extremely expensive.

Prescription Drugs. Prescription drugs can be dangerous for consumers, and depending on one's genetic makeup, they can be very dangerous and even fatal for a small percentage of the population. Consider the facts of yet another products liability lawsuit that was the subject of great controversy in the 1980s.

Judith Sindell brought a lawsuit against eleven drug companies on behalf of herself and other women similarly situated. She alleged that, between 1941 and 1971, the defendant drug companies manufactured, promoted, and sold the drug diethylstilbestrol (DES), which was prescribed during pregnancy to prevent miscarriages.[16] After the drug was on the market for a number of years, studies revealed that it caused vaginal and cervical cancer in the daughters of women who took it. The form of cancer caused by this drug manifests itself after a minimum latent period of ten to twelve years. It is fast-spreading and deadly, and radical surgery is required to prevent it from spreading. The number of women who took the drug during pregnancy ranges from 1.5 million to 3 million.

A particularly difficult legal problem was presented in the *Sindell* case. Because the plaintiffs had inherited the genetic defect that allowed the cancer (caused by the drug their mothers took), how were the plaintiffs to identify the particular defendant drug company that sold the drug to their mothers twenty or so years ago? In this case, the California court of appeals created a new legal principle, called *market share liability,* that helped the plaintiff make her case.

Market share liability allows a plaintiff to sue all of the producers of a drug in a market at a certain time for injury when the plaintiff proves that (1) identification of the manufacturer is impossible through no fault of the plaintiff; (2) the product is exactly like every other products made by all the defendants; and (3) the plaintiffs have joined enough defendants so that a substantial percentage of the market for that product is represented. After this has been done, the recovery against a particular drug company will be measured by the sales of this company measured as a percentage of the total market. For example, if one drug company had 15 percent of the market for the drug twenty years ago, it pays 15 percent of the judgment.

Handguns.   Current estimates are that more than 22,000 men, women, and children are killed each year because of the ready availability of handguns and military-style assault weapons. Another 100,000 suffer painful and crippling injuries each year. In 1991, sales of just American-made Saturday night specials topped 400,000; some of these guns sold for as little as $35.[17]

Political movements are being made at the federal, state and local levels to regulate handguns. In fall of 1993, Congress passed the Brady Bill, which attempts to regulate the sale of handguns. There are, it seems, executive, legislative, and judicial approaches to this perplexing problem. The judicial approach is just beginning.

In recent years, persons injured by handguns have been suing the manufacturers of the handguns and a few have recovered damages. These injured persons allege that the handgun is, in a legal, not a mechanical sense, a defective product. *Kelley* v. *R. G. Industries, Inc.*[18] may be typical of a large number of cases to come. In this case, the plaintiff, Olen J. Kelley, was injured when an unknown assailant shot him in the chest during an armed robbery of the grocery store in which he was employed.

Kelley alleged, among other things, that the manufacturer of the gun should be strictly liable for his injuries caused by the shooting. The court was careful to note that not all handguns would be "defective" under the various definitions of strict liability but did allow the plaintiff to argue strict liability as applied to a subgroup of handguns called Saturday night specials. These guns have short barrels and are light in weight, easily concealed, low in cost, and particularly attractive for criminal use. In addition, they are virtually useless for the legitimate uses of law enforcement, sport, and target practice. The court, deciding for the plaintiff, reasoned that the manufacture and marketing of such a product by sellers who are well aware of its intended use would make such sellers strictly liable to injured, innocent bystanders.

THE IMMEDIATE FUTURE

Garbage.   The incidence of cancer in Americans is increasing. Why? Many say that ground water and air pollution may be the culprits. Who is at fault, and what is to be done? The answers to these questions are not clear. Consider just one case: A garbage dump outside New York City, called "Fresh Kills," in the late 1980s was accepting up to twenty-four thousand tons of garbage each day. The state of New York estimated that, in 1989, about "2 million gallons of contaminated gunk" leached into the groundwater each day.[19] By the year 2000, Americans will have increased their garbage disposed of (per person) by 100 percent since 1960. Americans toss out 160 million tons each year—"enough to spread 30 stories high over 1,000 football fields, enough to fill a bumper-to-bumper convoy of garbage trucks half way to the moon."[20]

If this garbage is incinerated, it adds to the air pollution; if it is deposited in the ocean or the Great Lakes, it substantially pollutes the water; if it stays on the land, it leaches into the drinking water of those close to disposal sites. Moreover, there is no consensus now on whether garbage is a significant problem. "What's the problem?" Some say, "put it in the ground and it will all decompose." Some scientists say that practically nothing decomposes in a landfill. One excavator of a dumpsite found recognizable hot dogs, corncobs, and grapes that had been buried for twenty-five years, and a readable newspaper that was more than thirty-five years old.[21]

Electric Utilities.   In 1992, researchers from Sweden's prestigious Karolinska Institute reported finding a nearly fourfold higher leukemia rate among Swedish children living near power lines.[22] So far, no scientific evidence has been offered to conclusively tie electromagnetic radiation (a form of radiation caused by the magnetic field produced by electric current) to cancer. But, the thought that it will soon be shown has sent shock waves through utilities industries. Some researchers say it could be another ten years before any answers are found to questions about cancer causation by electromagnetic fields. If a link is established, however, the major utilities could pay out billions of dollars in claims. What was once cheap electricity will become, almost overnight, very expensive electricity. To date, the case law in this area is sparse, but it was reported that IBM has paid more than $500,000 to settle a lawsuit filed by a former employee who claimed that his leukemia was caused by exposure to on-the-job electromagnetic radiation.[23]

OUTLINES OF THE PUBLIC POLICY DEBATE OVER PRODUCTS LIABILITY LAW

PRODUCTS LIABILITY LAW IS OUT OF CONTROL

Manufacturers of products claim that American products liability law is out of control and is placing what amounts to a tort tax on American manufacturers that substantially damages their competitive position in the world economy. The outlines of this argument are something like this:

1. *Cost. Forbes* magazine has reported that the tort system's direct costs to American manufacturers for defective products amounts to about $80 billion a year. This figure represents lawyers' fees, payouts to claimants, and insurers' administrative costs.[24] Some say this figure is low, and one study published in 1984 estimated that tort claims cost the United States about $117 billion. This number projected to 1992 would be about $184 billion, which is almost equal to the U.S. net private domestic investment.

2. *Who is Compensated?* Some allege that injured claimants end up with about half the judgments paid out. The other half is split about equally between lawyers' costs for the trial and fees for their services, and the administrative costs for insurance companies. The tort tax, in short, goes to support a large administrative apparatus that shackles American business and that does not fully compensate injured claimants.

3. *American competitiveness.* The amount of judgments paid out, according to one study, amount to about 2.5 percent of the GNP and impose a burden on U.S. companies that is five times that in England and almost seven times the level of such judgments in Japan.[25]

PRODUCTS LIABILITY LAW IS NOT OUT OF CONTROL

1. Products liability figures have only been kept in a formal way since 1991, and the best estimates are that the annual cost to the economy of tort judgments is, according to the RAND Corporation's respected Institute for Civil Justice, about $30 billion.[26]

2. Of the 250 million people in the United States in 1991, fewer than 56,000 per year, on average, over the past decade collected products liability claims—an average of 1,100 per state each year.[27] This is not a large number.

3. Products liability plaintiffs lost about 56 percent of the time; for every 100 people who were paid something on claims between 1982 and 1992, 128 people who filed received nothing.[28]

4. The average claim paid for product injuries from 1982 to 1992 was $8,577;[29] for each claim brought during this period, the average plaintiff's attorney received an estimated $1,256, whereas the typical defense attorney got about $2,028 for each claim handled.[30]

5. Many products liability lawsuits are dependent on scientific studies that show some relation between a corporation's product or a production process and an injury or disease but do not show scientific causation. Thus, it is a tactic of the parties, either plaintiff or defendant, who are betting on the outcome of these studies to drag out the trial process for years and years until the causation issue is settled. These tactics, argue some, are what drive up the costs of products liability litigation.[31]

SOLUTIONS TO THE PUBLIC POLICY DEBATE ON PRODUCTS LIABILITY LAW

The legal system's method of compensating those injured by the products and process of the industrial age is, perhaps, best characterized as crude. Yes, some lawyers get rich off others' misery, some firms go into bankruptcy and do not pay those injured by their products, products liability lawsuits do take years to reach resolution, and the productive portions of the economy do seem to be at a competitive disadvantage in the world economy. So, what should be done? Solutions are being proposed in several areas. We can do no more than trace out developments in these areas and wait to see which provides the most promise for all parties concerned.

STATE LEGISLATION

Many states—under the influence, no doubt, of the manufacturing sectors of their economies—have tried to limit and control the severity of products liability law judgments by enacting legislation that limits or denies recovery when

1. The product has been altered or modified.

2. The period of the "useful life" of the product has expired.

3. The manufacturer complied with the state-of-the-art of manufacture or design at the time of the sale of the product

4. The manufacturer complied with relevant professional, state, or federal guidelines for the design and manufacture of the product.

5. A time limit of, say, ten years, established in what are called statutes of repose, expires.

6. Warnings on the packaging or other materials included with the product were not followed

7. Evidence suggests contributory negligence.

8. Many states have set up specialty statutes to deal with unique problems, such as those created by asbestos claims and other products that threaten the public safety and welfare.

In addition, states have passed legislation that may limit the dollar value of a products liability recovery and that may limit the recovery of punitive damages. The Georgia Tort Reform Act, for example, attempted to allow only one punitive damage award against a manufacturer and stated that the state was to receive 75 percent of any products liability punitive award. This particular punitive damage limitation was declared unconstitutional in 1990.[32]

Non-lawyers have discussed eliminating the contingency fee arrangement that seems unique to the American legal system. This contingency fee arrangement allows lawyers to take a percentage of the judgment (usually about a third), but the client puts up no funds to cover costs of the litigation. The risks of the law suit are on the attorney, who may lose out-of-pocket trial costs and payment for the time put in if the case is not successful.

Reformers in this area push for what is called the English Rule, in which the loser of a tort suit pays all court costs and the costs of the winners. It is believed that this rule discourages speculative or less than meritorious suits, but those with a good claim but little resources are not represented quite as well as in the American system based on the contingency fee.

PROPOSED FEDERAL LEGISLATION

A tremendous amount of federal legislation has already been enacted to deal with the problems presented by unsafe products. The creation of the Consumer Product Safety Commission and the National Highway Traffic Safety Administration are just two such examples. We examine the operation of some of these agencies in the chapter on governmental regulation.

The idea we address here is the call for a type of federal products liability law. To date, no such comprehensive federal legislation has passed. Those who favor federal legislation are opposed to the haphazard, uncontrolled, and ambiguous changes in state-based products liability law. Specifically, they make the following points:[33]

ARGUMENTS FOR FEDERAL LEGISLATION

1. The uncertainties in the law flowing from numerous concepts of liability put all parties, including the plaintiffs, defendants, and insurance companies, at a disadvantage and increase the price of products generally.

2. The multiple causes of action and the differing interpretations of the meaning of the word *defect* create uncertainty in the business environment and keep some products off the market.

3. Further state legislation in this area will make a bad situation worse by overlaying more rules with yet more interpretations.

4. Some insurance companies have gone out of business because of unexpected, large recoveries by plaintiffs. From 1971 to 1976, a 280-percent average increase occurred in premiums paid per thousand dollars for all firms and a 385-percent increase occurred for small firms for certain products.[34] The use of federal law in federal courts would tend to establish standards for recovery that are lower than in state courts. Some commentators think juries at the state level are more easily swayed by local lawyers representing local plaintiffs. Therefore, state court judgments are higher than federal court judgments would be.

5. American competitiveness has been harmed because safety features not demanded by the legal environments in other countries must be built in, making U.S. products cost more relative to foreign products in foreign markets.

6. Some American firms have gone out of business because of large judgments by plaintiffs injured by defective products. A system of federally administered legal principles would be less likely to award excessive judgments because federal juries are often not as emotional as local juries.

ARGUMENTS AGAINST FEDERAL LEGISLATION

1. Any federal action is an unnecessary interference with states' rights in matters that have been traditionally within state jurisdiction (specifically, their own tort and contract law).

2. Federal preemption would destroy the multitude of ideas and concepts that could be developed with as many as fifty different sovereigns considering the problem; rigidity would be added and flexibility would be lost if federal law controlled.

3. Federal legislation in this area has never passed and probably never will because the present system benefits one very strong lobbying interest in Congress: attorneys.

4. Federal legislation would overburden an already strained federal judiciary when claims are brought in federal courts.

5. The promise of uniformity and certainty is illusive because federal courts sit in the various states; hence, a complete severance from state law is not possible (differences will still remain).

6. Product liability costs are a true cost of doing business, and business firms in a capitalist economy ought to be held accountable to cover these costs. If these costs drive them out of business, so be it.

The legal and public policy issues raised in this chapter are the most significant ones raised in this book because they deal very directly with individual and collective health and well-being. We said at the beginning of this chapter that tort law fills the gaps among the more established areas of law like contract law, property law, and agency law. We hope we have shown you how tort law does fill the gaps and, in doing so, provides the dynamic quality a growing society full of life demands. These gaps are growing so rapidly, however, that they demand the attention of all branches of the government. Many of the issues raised in products liability lawsuits today affect tens of thousands of people; they are on the forefront of science and technology and are claiming such a vast amount of resources that they may bring fundamental change in the legal system.

No longer does the typical products liability lawsuit involve issues such as those in the *Escola* case, wherein, a waitress sued because a Coca-Cola bottle exploded and cut her hand. Today's cases are more like the one filed in Texas, where 2,729 Lone Star Steel employees sued 372 separate defendants in a single action.[35] Attorneys for the plaintiffs allege that chemicals at the Lone Star plant combined to create a toxic cloud that infected workers with a form of chemical AIDS. They allege that from a quarter to a third of the workforce suffers serious work-related injuries from this toxic assault and that many others will develop work-related diseases in the near future.

At this point, about 150 law firms are involved. After a period of five years, only 79 of the 2,729 plaintiffs have been interviewed by attorneys for the defendants. At this rate, the pretrial part of the lawsuit will take thirty-eight years. Although the trial date is uncertain, some plaintiffs have already died; in addition, the court system is overwhelmed by the thirty-nine thousand documents filed thus far (a hearing on one motion was so crowded by attorneys that it had to be moved from the courthouse to the highschool gym), and many of the defendants (including such giants as Exxon and Union Carbide) say they have no idea why they have been joined as defendants.[36]

This case and others like it raise substantial questions about whether the current array of legal theories and the trial method of resolving disputes in this area of tort law will endure. It seems reasonable to expect substantial change in this area of law in the near future.

CONCLUSION

Tort law and its applications establishing liability for defective products is, without doubt, a more dynamic area of law than agency law, contract law, or sales law. It is expanding in many directions at once. The concept of negligence is a cornerstone of tort law and is vital in establishing in public policy the community standards of "reasonable" action. Toxic torts (e.g., the *Velsicol* case), which are nothing more than recent applications of negligence and related torts to the modern problems of groundwater contamination, have resulted in creating new avenues of compensation for those injured by unreasonable conduct.

Absolute and strict liability, however, are now the concepts of the future. This "liability without fault" came after decades of policy arguments by injured consumers (and others) who asserted that, in all fairness, those who put defective products (those that injure unsuspecting consumers) into the stream of commerce should pay for any damage caused to users. The U.S. system of common law jurisprudence is finally responsive and can grow and develop to recognize the danger inherent in such products as cigarettes and Saturday night specials. In the creation and applications of these new common law principles, one can see how the law adjusts interests between injured individuals and firms that proclaim they have a "right" to produce any product they wish. The law seems to be saying, go ahead and develop whatever product you wish, but if your product poses significant risks to the public, you must pay.

REVIEW QUESTIONS AND PROBLEMS

1. Define each of the following and then explain the difference between them; include a statement of the circumstances in which each may be excluded or modified:
   a. Express warranty
   b. Implied warranty of merchantability
   c. Implied warranty of fitness for a particular purpose
2. John wanted to buy a new electric drill. He saw an advertisement in the local newspaper saying that Sears was having a special sale on "½-inch electric drills, reduced 20% to $65." John went to Sears to buy the drill but was very interested in whether or not the drill was double-insulated. This meant the drill had special wiring so that if a short developed, the drill would not shock the user. John was interested in this feature because he often worked in his basement, where the floor was damp as the result of leaky plumbing, and a risk of electrocution was substantial. John asked the saleswoman at Sears, "Do you have double-insulated drills?" The saleswoman replied, "We have just what you want," and got for John one of the drills on sale. She said, "This drill is double-insulated." John then said, "Fine, I'll take it," and handed her his Sears credit card. The saleswoman made out the appropriate sales slip, and John left with the drill.

Answer the following questions in a series of short sentences, explaining briefly.

a. Did Sears make an express warranty?

b. Did Sears make an implied warranty of merchantability?

c. Did Sears make an implied warranty of fitness for a particular purpose?

d. Did Sears make any other warranties?

3. In Question 2 above, assume that John took the drill home and one day his daughter was using it in the basement and was injured because the drill was not double-insulated. If Sears were sued for the injuries on the basis of a warranty theory, what might Sears argue? Would Sears be successful? Assume that John, before using the drill, had sold it to a friend visiting from another state and the friend was injured in his (the friend's) home because the drill was not double-insulated. What would Sears argue in response to a claim for injury on the basis of warranty theories? Would Sears be successful this time?

4. In Questions 2 and 3 above, the packaging for the drill that John purchased and the instructions said in plain and conspicuous language:

> For one year from the date of purchase, Sears will repair or replace this drill free of charge if defective in material or workmanship.

And, in larger type, it added:

> Sears will not be liable for loss or damage to property or any incidental or consequential loss or expense from property damage due directly to defects in the drill.

Assume that all of the information in Question 2 is true and that, after John purchased the drill, he was severely injured when using the drill in his basement, which at the time was dry. Also assume that the drill was not properly double-insulated. As a result of this defect, the drill exploded and caused John's basement to catch fire; the result was $50,000 damage to the basement and personal injury to John. Does the above language on the packaging and directions limit John's measure of recovery to the value of the drill? What additional circumstances might help John's case?

5. Two of the most dangerous consumer products—cigarettes and handguns—are the least regulated. Why?

6. After years of marketing research, the Chevy division of GM decides that it will design, produce, and market the "muscle car" of the nineties. The result is the Corvette XRS, which can go from 0 to 60 mph in 4.5 seconds and has a top speed in excess of 170 mph; some experts in the automotive press say it may top 180 mph. Sarah, a recent MBA graduate, takes her first paycheck and orders an XRS. Sarah has always wanted to own the fastest car on the road, and now her expectations are about to be fulfilled. After the car is delivered, she takes great care to break it in. She has never driven such a powerful car before. One Friday afternoon, after a tough week of work, she is traveling the back roads of Michigan on her way to a small fishing village to visit a friend. She decides to "open up" the car. The country road is straight and has no traffic light. As she hits 180, she quivers with the excitement of this dream come true.

Just then, the road curves, and she loses control and slides into three small children walking home from school. All die in this tragic accident. Sarah leaves no estate. The parents of the children sue GM, alleging that the Corvette was negligently designed and is defective and unreasonably dangerous. Carefully state these arguments in greater detail, citing all appropriate law, and discuss whether you believe a court will hold that the plaintiffs can state a good case against GM so that the issues will be submitted to a jury.

7. Reread Question 6. GM must know that if it designs and markets a car capable of speeds in excess of 170 mph, innocent people will be killed as a result of a driver unable to handle the speed of the vehicle. What "policy" arguments favor GM's liability for these deaths? What arguments favor no liability? Which do you believe in and why?

8. Three Northeastern states—New Jersey, New York, and Pennsylvania—export about eight million tons of garbage per year to other states, much of it to the Midwestern states of Michigan, Ohio, Indiana, and Illinois, where land is cheaper and dump sites exist away from major population centers. The *Chicago Tribune* (November 5, 1989) reported in a page-one story that this export trade has spawned trash brokers, landfill speculators, rogue truckers, garbage pirates, and a flood of speeding trucks on the nation's highways. The rogue truckers, for example, take meat and produce in refrigerated vans to the East Coast and haul maggot-infested garbage to the Midwest on the return trip. These activities, reports the *Tribune,* are a sharp break from an earlier American tradition in which solid waste was considered a local matter.

Assume that the groundwater around your farm in Indiana becomes contaminated with toxic materials from a private dump site two miles upstream from you. You, your family, and your neighbors suffer severe physical and psychological damage. What remedies do you have? From whom would you seek compensation? Should you be entitled to compensation?

ENDNOTES

1. 586 F. Supp. 14 (1984).
2. *MacPherson v. Buick Motor Co.,* 111 N.E. 1050 (N.Y. 1916).
3. *Restatement (Second) of Torts,* Sec. 402A (1965).
4. See *Nichols* v. *Union Underwear Co.,* 602 S.W. 2d 429 (Ky. 1980).
5. UCC Sec. 2-313 (1) (a), (b) & (c).
6. *Royal Business Machines* v. *Lorraine Corp.,* 633 F2d 34, 41–42 (1980).
7. UCC Sec. 2–314(2)(c).
8. See New York Law Revision Commission Hearings on the Uniform Commercial Code (1954).
9. White and Summers, *Uniform Commercial Code* 336 (1972).
10. *Lowe, by Gazley* v. *Estate Motors, Ltd.,* 382 N.W. 811 (Mich. 1986).
11. See *Borel* v. *Fibreboard Paper Products,* 493 F 2d 1076 (1973).
12. *Cipollone* v. *Liggett Group, Inc.,* 893 F 2d 541 (1988).
13. *Id.*
14. *Cipollone* v. *Liggett Group, Inc.,* CCH Products Liability Reports, Par. 13,199, June 24, 1992.
15. *National Law Journal,* March 1, 1993, p. 1.
16. *Sindell* v. *Abbott Laboratories,* 607 p. 2d 924 (Cal. 1980).
17. *Wall Street Journal,* February 28, 1992, p. 1, col. 6.
18. 497 A.2d 1143 (1985).
19. *Newsweek,* November 27, 1992, at 27.
20. *Id.*
21. *Id.* at 70.
22. *Wall Street Journal,* February 5, 1993, p. 1, col 6.
23. *Id.*
24. *Forbes,* February 17, 1992, at 40.
25. *Id.*
26. *Id.*
27. *Id.*
28. *Public Citizen,* November/December, 1992, at 20.
29. *Id.*
30. *Id.* at 21.
31. *Wall Street Journal,* February 6, 1992, p. 1, col. 6.
32. *McBride* v. *General Motors Corp.,* 737 F. Supp. 1563 (1990).
33. See Reed and Watkins, Product Liability Tort Reform: The Case for Federal Action, 46 *Neb. L. Re.* 389 (1984).
34. *Id.* at 435.
35. *Wall Street Journal,* February 6, 1992, p. 1, col. 6.
36. *Id.*

CHAPTER 8

Contract Law

INTRODUCTION

Contract law is a body of legal principles used to create certainty in commercial transactions. The subject of a contract is often property one wishes to have or sell for business or personal use. Although property is often exchanged in a contract, the contract is not so much the property as it is the promise to either buy or sell the property for a price. The best definition of a contract focuses on this idea of the promise: A *contract* is the promise or set of reasonable promises for the breach of which the law will provide a remedy.

THE PROMISE IN HISTORY

The U.S. economy relies heavily on the fact that courts will enforce the exchange of promises. Adam Smith wrote forcefully about the place of exchange and the role of contract law in a capitalist society. At the most basic level in a capitalist society, he wrote, is the idea of working one's will through mutual exchanges: "Give me that which I want, and you shall have this which you want." We thus obtain what we need from others, he continued, by addressing ourselves "not to their humanity but to their self-love, and never talk to them of our own necessities but of their advantages."[1]

The idea that a promise itself may give rise to a legal duty to perform or pay damages was an achievement of the Roman law, although not until the close of the sixteenth century in England had courts sufficiently established their independence from the monarchy to be able to assert that these enforceable promises were free of both the Church and the sovereign and could be applied to the average person in commerce. Earlier, about the middle of the fourteenth century, promises to be performed had been accompanied by a wax seal affixed to a written declaration of the promise.[2] In the United States, the seal disappeared around the turn of the nineteenth century as a prerequisite for enforcing a promise.

THE KEY IDEA IN CONTRACT LAW

Today, perhaps the most prominent feature of contract law is that the exchange of promises creates the enforceable legal claim. A major function of contract law is to shift and allocate various business risks between the parties. The performance of the contract itself (e.g., the delivery of the good) almost always takes place in the future.

For example, in fall 1973, cotton farmers made contracts to sell their crops in the spring for what was then believed to be the market price in the spring, thirty cents per pound. By the time the cotton was ready for delivery, however, the market price had risen to almost three times the contract amount, or about eighty cents per pound, because of poor weather conditions and large purchases by the Chinese government. Many farmers did not ship to the buyers to whom they had promised their crop for thirty cents per pound; instead, they sold at the market rate in the spring. In the numerous lawsuits that followed, the farmers argued that, in the fall, they had no way of knowing about the future sales to China or the damage that would be caused by heavy rains. Each court that heard these cases approached them in the same way: The very idea of the contract was to cover such risks as occurred. You must, the courts ordered, convey your crops at thirty cents per pound or pay damages that would put the purchasers in the same position they would have been in had the selling farmers conveyed the crop.[3]

The common law of contracts is not as old as some tort and property concepts, but it has been around long enough to attract an enormous amount of scholarly and judicial attention. Many writers see contract law as the foundation of the capitalist economy and a major reason for its apparent success. Because of a large amount of both case law and scholarly writing about contract law, we must be very selective about the portions of it covered in a one-chapter presentation.

Businesspeople want to know when, in the process of negotiation, they become legally bound.[4] They also want to learn what kinds of enforceable promises must be documented in writing. Therefore, we limit most of our presentation of the substantive rules of contract law to the areas of offer, acceptance, and consideration (an exchange of value), which address the first area of interest, and to the statute of frauds, which responds to the second. We also include text and cases on areas of contract law we believe will become more prominent in the near future, the doctrines of equitable estoppel and unconscionability in contract law.

COMMON LAW OFFER AND ACCEPTANCE: THE CLASSICAL APPROACH

INTRODUCTORY NOTE ON THE COMMON LAW OF CONTRACTS

A central problem that the common law of contracts addressed was this: Among all the promises one makes and the expectations created in others, which of these promises and expectations are intended to be enforceable through the court system? Today, this question is answered by analyzing the intent of the offeror (the party making the promise). Did the offeror intend to enter into a bargain that could be enforced by the state-based court system?

The well-recognized common law approach is that enforceable bargains must contain (1) an offer, (2) an acceptance, and (3) an exchange of value (consideration); the parties must be (4) competent; and (5) the subject matter must be legal. The first three elements are evidence of the intent to contract. We examine the common law notions of offer and acceptance here, and in the next section briefly discuss the idea of an exchange of value or, as the common law called it, consideration for enforcing the promises. We do not cover competency of the parties or the legality of the subject in detail because they are determined by state statute and vary widely from state to state.

The typical business-related enforceable promise is based on the mutual intent of the parties. How is this intent ascertained? Intent is found by locating a clear expression from the initiator of the transaction, called either the offeror or the promisor, that he or she intends to be bound. An *offer* is a statement of a present willingness to enter into a bargain made in such a way that a person receiving the offer (the offeree or the promisee) could reasonably believe that the bargain could be concluded by accepting the offer.

Common law offers typically have three essential elements: (1) a manifestation of a *present contractual intent*, (2) *certainty and definiteness of the terms offered*, and (3) this intent *communicated* to another.

THE OBJECTIVE THEORY OF CONTRACT FORMATION

Because the element of intent is so crucial in finding both an offer and an acceptance, courts have adopted the objective theory of contracts to determine whether the parties did intend what they said or did. The objective theory does not focus on the true intent in the minds of the offeror and the offeree. Rather, courts tell juries to ask themselves *what a reasonable person in the position of each of the respective parties would be led to believe by the words or conduct of the other party.* This means that, for both offers and acceptances, the actions are interpreted, not according to what the actor subjectively meant or what the person to whom the words or conduct were addressed subjectively understood them to mean, but what a reasonable person would understand them to mean.

HOW LONG ARE OFFERS OPEN?

The legal significance of making an offer is that this action (words or conduct) creates a power of acceptance in the offeree. How long does this power exist? Or under what circumstances does the offer terminate? Unaccepted offers may be terminated by lapse of a reasonable time with no response. What constitutes a reasonable time depends on the circumstances, such as the subject matter of the offer, business customs, and the medium through which the offer is made. When the parties bargain face-to-face or by telephone, the time for acceptance usually does not extend beyond the end of the conversation unless the contrary intention is shown.

An offer may also be terminated by the offeror's receipt of a rejection or counteroffer from the offeree. A *rejection* is a statement or action by the offeree that he or she has no intent to accept. A *counteroffer* is a little more difficult to determine. It embodies two elements: a rejection and a new offer. For example, if the offeror says, "I will pay you $500 to repair my boat," and the offeree says, "Does your offer include the use of your materials or mine?" Then this is an inquiry. If the offeree replies, "I won't do it for $500, but I will do it for $600," then this is a counteroffer.

Inquiries do not terminate offers, but counteroffers do. When is a counteroffer or a rejection effective? The majority of courts have held that it is effective when it is communicated to the offeror.

COMMON LAW ACCEPTANCES

In a series of negotiations, once an offer is found, the traditional approach has been to search for an acceptance. This second step involves identifying who has the power to accept, whether the type of acceptance was proper and whether the acceptance was timely. An *acceptance* is an action by the offeree revealing an intention to exercise the power conferred by the offeror to create an enforceable promise. Unlike offers, counteroffers, and rejections, an acceptance may be effective when sent, and a contract may be formed even though the acceptance is never received.

An offer made to the public at large may be accepted by anyone so long as the means of acceptance is set out with clarity by the offeror. An offer made to a specific person may be accepted only by that person. In any case, if the acceptance reflects exactly what the offer required (this is often called the mirror image approach of the common law), a contract is formed when such a communication is sent to the offeror. According to the classical mailbox rule, when use of the mail or telegrams or the like is a reasonable method of communicating an acceptance, it is normally effective when dispatched. This rule does not require that the offeror actually receive an acceptance, but only that the offeree exercise reasonable diligence to communicate the acceptance.

CONSIDERATION

Consideration refers to the quality of the exchange of either promises or performances that must exist for there to be a contract. If X says to Y, "I promise to give you $100 this Friday at 2:00 P.M.," and Y says, "I accept," an offer and acceptance have been made, but no contract. Why? *To have an enforceable promise, an exchange of some sort must take place.* In our example, nothing is exchanged. A promise is made to make a gift. The required exchange may be defined very broadly to mean something more than just money or land. It may be any form of legally recognized benefit received by the offeror/promisor or a detriment surrendered or relinquished by the offeree/promisee. For example, if an uncle says to his twenty-two-year-old nephew, "I will give you $500 if you give up drinking beer for a year," a contract exists if the nephew gives up drinking beer (something he is legally entitled to do) for the year.

Under the traditional view of contract formation, the consideration was the heart of the bargain. A *bargain* is an exchange in which each party understands his or her performance as the price of the other's promise or requested performance. Viewed from the perspective of the reasonable person in the place of the offeree and offeror, it must appear that one thing (maybe a promise) was exchanged for another (maybe just a return promise). This idea has often been expressed in the following way: For an enforceable exchange of promises, there must be a quid pro quo, which literally translated means "what for what" (a better translation is "this for that"). This exchange of promises is, after all, mutually inspired. Whatever goes "out of the pocket" of one party by way of detriment—money, land, houses—is a benefit to the other party, and vice versa.

An important corollary to this central concept is that if courts believe a bargained-for exchange took place, they will not look into the "real value" of the exchange to verify that it is precisely equal. The traditional statement of this rule is that the adequacy of the consideration will not be reviewed. To do so would put the courts in the position of assessing how good or bad a bargain the parties made. This general rule, however, is subject to several categories of exceptions.

In the first category, courts may examine the adequacy of the consideration if one of the parties alleges that fraud or misrepresentation was committed in the making of the contract. This is also true when one of the parties alleges the bargain was fundamentally unfair or unconscionable. (We explain the doctrine of unconscionability later in this chapter.)

The second category involves a promise to do something one is already contractually bound to do or by law should do. For example, if *A* is contractually bound to deliver goods to *B* for $100 but *A* finds that it will cost more money than he first believed to make the delivery, a new promise to deliver the goods (even if assented to by *B*) for an additional $25 is not enforceable. A court would say there is no consideration for the second promise for $25 because *A* was already bound to make the delivery.

Courts will also delve into the agreed exchange of value if they believe that one or both of the promises are illusory. If one party makes an illusory promise in exchange for the other party's real promise, courts usually hold that neither party is bound. Mutuality of obligation must exist, which means that both parties must be bound or neither is. A simple example is a promise by an offeror that "I will do business with you if I want to." Obviously, the offeror is not bound to do anything if she promises to do business if she wants to.

At the real heart of common law contracts are the elements we have just outlined: offer, acceptance, and consideration. Although we have presented these ideas as three distinct elements they really are not so distinct.

REAL LIFE CLASSICAL COMMON LAW CONTRACTS

Discussing these elements of a contract makes contract formation appear overly technical. In general, when a dispute over the nature of a promise of the kind that is normally enforced in courts develops, courts often look at the entire transaction to determine, first, an intent to be bound. If this intent can be found in the words and actions of the parties, the court is likely to find that a contract exists and will then fashion a remedy for the party damaged by a breach of the promise. Searching for elements of a contract is just a generalization about the kinds of things the courts will look for in determining whether to allow the plaintiff to recover.

EXPRESS AND IMPLIED CONTRACTS

Almost every contract of a fairly complex nature will have expressed and implied portions. The *expressed contract* portions are those parts of the agreement stated and agreed on. *Implied contracts* or promises are those promises reasonably necessary to accomplish the expressed portions of the agreement but are left unstated. The case below illustrates that a court will "fill in the gaps" of the understanding of the parties once it finds a general intent to be bound. This gap filling requires certain implied promises.

QUASI-CONTRACTS

A quasi-contract is an idea used in contract law to provide a remedy to a person who has benefited another. The difference between implied contracts and quasi-contracts is that no basic promise is made to pay for the benefit to begin with when a quasi-contract remedy is sought. For example, a quasi-contract remedy would be awarded to a doctor (*D*) who sees a pedestrian (*P*) lying in the street unconscious and provides emergency medical services. *P* recovers and *D* sends him a bill. If *P* refuses to pay, *D* may successfully assert a remedy for the reasonable value of the benefit conferred on *P*, asserting the duty to pay created by quasi-contract.

Consider the case below. It is not filled with discussions of technical elements, but the court—correctly, we believe—concludes there is an exchange of promises for the breach of which it will provide a remedy.

Rockwell & Bond v. *Flying Dutchman, Inc.*
253 NW 2D 368 (Mich. 1977)

[I]n January or February of 1972, John VanAlstyne, president of defendant corporation, (Flying Dutchman Restaurant) decided to remodel the interior of the restaurant, the subject matter of this dispute. . . . Preliminary drawings were prepared and the project was put out for estimates. Plaintiff submitted an estimate of $55,000 to $60,000 based on these drawings and was chosen as the contractor for the job. Defendant secured a loan to cover this estimate. This estimate did not include mechanical and electrical costs. No written contract was ever drafted between plaintiff and defendant. . . .

The restaurant was closed during the period of . . . the construction. . . . Construction continued with additional drawings being prepared on a day-by-day and week-by-week basis to reflect the working decisions as they were made. VanAlstyne was present almost daily taking an active role in the project. Numerous changes, revisions and decisions were made as the job progressed.

Plaintiff billed defendant a total of $100,156.20 for labor and material. Defendant paid $54,337.72. Upon the failure of defendant to pay the remainder of the bill, plaintiff ceased work. Defendant has since expended additional funds for the completion of some of the unfinished work.

The trial court found a contract implied in fact and concluded that plaintiff should be paid for services rendered on a "time and materials" basis. The court then awarded plaintiff its requested damages.

* * *

A contract implied in fact has been defined as one that:

"arises under circumstances which according to the ordinary course of dealing and common understanding, . . . show a mutual intention to contract. . . . A contract is implied in fact where the intention as to it is not manifested by direct or explicit words between the parties, but is to be gathered by implication or proper deduction from the conduct of the parties, language used or things done by them, or other pertinent circumstances attending the transaction."

John Rockwell, president of plaintiff corporation, testified that it was his understanding that payments would be made on a "time and materials" basis. He also stated that his company would never have given a firm estimate based on drawings as incomplete as the ones initially submitted to him. The mechanical and electrical specifications were not determined until the equipment was already in place. This work was done by subcontractors on a "time and materials" basis and not by plaintiff itself. The types of materials and fixtures to be installed were determined on a daily basis as new drawings were prepared. Although VanAlstyne testified that he was unaware that the estimate was based on preliminary drawings, Hofland testified that he was fully aware of that fact and further stated that he advised VanAlstyne to hire kitchen and bar consultants for the purpose of determining the needed specifications. Defendant's own expert stated that any estimate based on the preliminary drawings would actually be a "guesstimate" because the materials used would greatly determine the cost.

The trial judge found no express agreement between the parties as to the price terms of the construction contract. He analyzed the conduct of the parties including, but not limited to, VanAlstyne's constant presence at the job site and the need to make day-to-day determinations of desired materials due to the absence of necessary specifications in the initial drawings submitted to plaintiff and concluded that the implied contract was on a "time and materials" basis. We find no mistake in his conclusion and find ample support in the evidence.

Decision of trial court is affirmed.

CASE FOLLOW-UP

Surely, given the facts of the case, one can say within reason that there is an intent to be bound to some form of agreement. There was an offer (the invitation to submit bids was a preliminary solicitation to do business; the submitting of the bid by the plaintiff was the offer), and acceptance of the offer (the award of the job to the plaintiff and the start of business), and consideration (the exchange of promises that contained value). The problem in this case, as in many contract cases, is not whether a contract exists, but rather, given a general intent to be bound, what was agreed on. This court is saying that if you agree to work with a contractor or supplier and accept their work and their materials, then you will be bound to pay the reasonable value for them even though no "technical" agreement was made about what is to be provided.

AMERICAN INDIVIDUALISM AND CONTRACT LAW

Contract law is one of the best expressions of American individualism and freedom. Everyone in the American economy, with the exception of people who lack the legal capacity to contract (usually, those under eighteen years of age, the insane, and some others), has the right, though perhaps not the means, to secure desired goods and services through contracts. This right means that the state, through its court system, will provide a remedy if a breach of promise occurs.

When you think of a "contract," do not think of it merely as a signed piece of paper. The paper is only a manifestation or evidence of the contract. The contract is really an intangible thing; it is the promises the courts will enforce. If the papers that are evidence of the contract burn, the contract still exists; it is just more difficult to prove.

THE COMMON LAW OF CONTRACTS AND THE UNIFORM COMMERCIAL CODE

The industrial revolution in the United States has provided masses of goods, things that move from state to state. Goods such as a car or a computer may be made from parts manufactured in many states. If each state had its own different set of commercial rules applicable to the sale of goods within its borders, the hundreds of exchanges required to produce an automobile would be governed by at least fifty sets of state rules. Such a situation is neither practical nor efficient. The numerous transactions required to produce complex goods demand that only one set of commercial rules apply to most of the transactions (see Figure 8.1). Such a single set of commercial rules has been formulated in the Uniform Commercial Code (UCC). The UCC has been adopted by all states except Louisiana, which has adopted only parts of it. It is statutory in character and applies to all transactions in goods.

FIGURE 8.1   ***American Business Exchange Transactions***
▬▬▬▬▬   *(those that will be enforced by a court)*

Exchanges involving money for goods or goods for
goods are governed by the UCC,
Article 2. This is a comprehensive (statutory)
code adopted in all states.

Exchanges involving the purchase of both goods
and services (e.g., having your car repaired)
are governed by Article 2 only if the sale of goods
predominates. If providing a service predominates (e.g., a business audit)
the common law applies.

Exchanges involving land or money for services
(e.g., the purchase of a lawyer's, accountant's, or doctor's services
or an insurance contract) are governed by the common law of contracts.

The part of the UCC applicable to the financing and exchange of goods has nine substantive articles. Generally, these articles apply to the following types of transactions:

- *Article 1* General Provisions. Contains primarily definitions used in the UCC.

- *Article 2* Sales. Applies to transactions in goods.

- *Article 3* Commercial Paper. Applies to negotiable instruments (checks), drafts, certificates of deposit, and notes.

- *Article 4* Bank Deposits and Collections. Applies to the process of collecting payment on negotiable instruments through banks.

- *Article 5* Letters of Credit. Deals with some but not all of the rules and concepts of letters of credit, which may be used to finance imported goods, among other things.

- *Article 6* Bulk Transfers. Applies when a seller sells a substantial part of the inventory not in the ordinary course of business; designed to prevent credit suppliers of the seller-retailer from being defrauded.

- *Article 7* Warehouse Receipts, Bills of Lading, and Other Documents of Title. Applies to various kinds of paper used to facilitate the exchange of goods.

- *Article 8* Investment Securities. Applies to the negotiation and transfer of certain investment securities, such as the stock of corporations.

- *Article 9* Secured Transactions. Applies to a transaction of goods in which a security interest is created (e.g., when goods are sold on credit the seller may retain an interest in the goods until the debt is fully paid).

Article 2, which provides the contract principles for the sale of goods, is the most important part of the UCC for our purposes. This article lifts some of the basic notions from that body of judge-made principles (the common law of contracts) and codifies them. So, we emphasize that *contract law is really two sets of principles: (1) Those governing land and services still are common law principles, and (2) Those governing the sale of goods are codified in the UCC.* We present basic rules from each area. Before we proceed with an explanation of these rules, we examine the nature and history of the UCC, which may be the single most important set of rules in commercial law.

THE CONCEPT OF A CODE

A distinct difference distinguishes a code from other statutory enactments. A *code* is a comprehensive, systematic collection of statutes in a particular legal area. The UCC contains and governs much of the law applicable to ordinary commercial transactions involving goods. A code, because of its comprehensive and integrated character, is its own best reference for interpretation. Noncode enactments are often fragmentary, and interpretation of them varies widely.

The purposes of the UCC are set out in one of its initial passages (UCC 1-102(2)). These purposes are

1. to simplify, clarify, and modernize the law governing commercial transactions;

2. to permit the continued expansion of commercial practices through custom, usage, and agreement of the parties; [and]

3. to make uniform the law among the various jurisdictions.

In short, the basic philosophy of the UCC is to facilitate commercial transactions through the twin objectives of simplicity and uniformity while allowing for reasonable growth and change in commercial practices.

THE PHILOSOPHICAL PERSPECTIVE OF THE UCC

Perhaps the single most influential person in the drafting of the UCC was its chief reporter, Karl Llewellyn, a law professor at the University of Chicago Law School. Llewellyn was the principal drafter of Articles 1 and 2. Much of the language of Articles 1 and 2 reflects notions he held as a result of his commitment to legal realism. *Legal realism* is a phrase used to designate a school of jurisprudential thought that maintains that the "law" is embedded fundamentally in situations or the everyday transactions of life. That is, rules should be stated to reflect what is socially desirable. No rule should be made for its own sake or merely because it is a logical extension of another rule. When one applies this notion to the development of a commercial code for the sale of goods as Llewellyn did, one should appreciate the fact that the rules are an attempt to *state simply* and *make uniform* much of the changing *current* commercial practices. Llewellyn believed that commercial law should reflect the most desirable practices of businesspeople.[5]

In this study of Article 2, be mindful of the fact that the words of these articles are but a starting point for study. In many key instances, the words direct us to current commercial practice to establish the standards for a transaction. No better example of this manifestation of Llewellyn's legal philosophy can be found than Section 1–204(2), which provides: "What is a reasonable time for taking any action depends on the nature, purpose and circumstances of such action." In addition, the official comments to Section 2–302 on *unconscionable contracts*, one of the most important sections of Article 2, provides in part: "The basic test is whether, *in the light of the general commercial background and the commercial needs of the particular trade or case* [emphasis added], the clauses involved are so one-sided as to be unconscionable under the circumstances."

The genius of this approach to law accommodates the seemingly inconsistent needs of commercial society. On the one hand, commercial society demands consistency, regularity, and stability in its rules. On the other hand, because commercial society is very dynamic, change and development of the rules must be provided for. The required measure of stability is provided by the fact that so many state legislatures have adopted the UCC and the fact that these state legislatures are discouraged from amending the UCC. A means for growth is provided, however, by the fact that in interpreting and applying the words of the UCC, especially Articles 1 and 2, attorneys and courts are directed to current commercial standards of performance that can be read into the language of the code. The words "reasonable" and "unreasonable" appear at least 97 times in Article 2.[6] As the standards change, so do the meanings of some of the key words of the sales article.

INTRODUCTION TO ARTICLE 2

Article 2 applies to "transactions" in goods, usually interpreted to mean a sale of goods, and not merely transactions in which only a security interest is transferred or a gift or lease of goods is involved.

A difficult distinction to make is whether Article 2 applies to transactions involving the sale of both goods and services or labor. In a case often cited for articulating the "test" for this kind of transaction, the court held that the deciding factor is not whether the contract for goods involves a service too, but granting that it does "whether the predominant factor, the thrust, the purpose, reasonably stated, is the rendition of services with goods incidentally involved (e.g., contract with artist for a painting . . .) or is a transaction of sale with labor incidentally involved (e.g., installation of water heater)."[7] By applying the predominance test to other cases, courts have held that an operation requiring the transfusion of blood and a beauty parlor treatment requiring the sale of hair dye are not predominantly a sale of goods.

In the material that follows, we separate the common law of contract principles from the UCC principles. Although Figure 8.1 would lead you to believe sharp divisions are found between Article 2 and the common law of contracts, no such division exists. The common law of contracts supplements Article 2 when Article 2 is ambiguous.

ARTICLE 2 OF THE UCC

It is natural for you to think of yourself as the "actor" when reading this material on contract law. Contracting is something everyone does. However, we suggest you use another image as you read this section on Article 2. The kinds of transactions in the private economy may be divided into three types: merchant-merchant, merchant-consumer, and consumer-consumer. Many provisions of Article 2 will make more sense to you if you imagine the first kind of transaction. The UCC applies to all three kinds of transactions, but the transactions between merchants are the most complex, as are the Article 2 provisions that apply to them. A merchant deals, in the ordinary course of business, in goods of the kind in question. Article 2 frequently applies more stringent standards to merchants than it does to consumers.

A GENERAL PATTERN OF COMMERCIAL CONDUCT IN THE 1990S

Today, dealings between merchants, especially the large corporate merchants, are often conducted by employees at a low level in the corporate organization who use standardized forms provided by their legal departments or management. These employees do not think of themselves as contracting, but they do realize that they place and receive orders or confirmations by using order forms, quotation forms, or any of a series of forms intended for such use.

Very often, a supplier will provide a catalogue with prices and descriptions of goods, and the first response from a merchant purchaser may be by telephone, asking for clarifications of price or credit terms. If the response is satisfactory, the purchaser's employee will take a form from a drawer or print out one on a computer while taking the order by phone. The employee will write or type the price, description of the goods, quantity, delivery time and means of transportation, and credit terms on the form. When the seller receives the form, an employee will usually transfer the crucial information from the filled-in blanks (after perhaps varying some terms) to his or her company's confirmation form and send it back to the purchaser. If the contract is a complex one, as for the construction of a large machine or the sale of complex goods over a period of years, it is likely that the exchange of forms was preceded by negotiations at several levels within the two corporate organizations.

Moreover, after the exchange of forms, numerous further changes or modifications may occur as the economic, technological, or political environment changes.

In addition to the forms, telephone calls, letters, resolutions from the board of directors, intracorporate communications, and other similar pieces of evidence may be made, all of which reflect the understanding of the parties.

If one were to attempt to apply the common law contract rules of offer and acceptance to this typical situation, a court would have to apply the mirror image rule and would be compelled to hold that no contract existed because a few terms in the acceptance varied. Given the common actual pattern of commercial activity as sketched here, this result would be absurd, especially when one considers that it was the terms, and not the general intent, that had been varied. The authors of the UCC recognized this commercial reality and drafted Article 2 to reflect it.

CONTRACT FORMATION UNDER ARTICLE 2

Article 2 substantially changes the common law doctrines of contract formation. It provides that a contract for the sale of goods may be made in any manner sufficient to show agreement by the parties. Agreement includes conduct by both parties that recognizes the existence of a contract. Moreover, it states that a contract for the sale of goods may be found to exist even though the moment of its making is undetermined or one or more terms are left open, so long as a court could find the general *intent to contract* and a reasonably certain basis exists for giving an appropriate remedy for its breach. The official comments to Section 2–204 add that commercial standards on the degree of indefiniteness should be applied and that, generally, the more terms the parties leave open, the less likely it is they have intended to be bound. Where parties' actions show agreement but some terms are uncertain, however, courts may conclude that a contract for sale exists.

For example, when Admiral Plastics Corporation, a leading manufacturer and supplier of plastic containers, could not meet the demand for its products, it contacted Trueblood, Inc., about manufacturing injection blow-mold machines to be used by Admiral to make plastic containers. An agent of Admiral visited Trueblood's plant and described the features of the machine it wanted. A firm price of $39,750 per machine was agreed on. Later, Admiral ordered three machines over the telephone. Admiral sent specifications for the machines, but Trueblood said they needed revising. The revisions were not adequate, and engineering drawings could not be made. Communications between the two companies became strained, and finally Admiral asked Trueblood to return its down payment of $29,812. Trueblood replied that it was keeping the down payment to cover expenses.

After the matter proceeded to court, the judge first had to decide whether a contract existed. Using the common law principles (finding an offer and an exact reply agreeing to the offer), the court would have found that no contract existed because the parties never agreed exactly on what was to be built. Instead, the court had to use Article 2 of the UCC, Section 2–204, which states:

(A) A contract for sale of goods may be made in any manner sufficient to show agreement, including conduct by both parties which recognizes the existence of such a contract.

(B) An agreement sufficient to constitute a contract for sale may be found even though the moment of its making is undetermined.

(C) Even though one or more terms are left open a contract for sale does not fail for indefiniteness if the parties have intended to make a contract and there is a reasonably certain basis for giving an appropriate remedy.

Applying this principle, the court held that a contract existed.[8] The agreement, the court explained, was for the manufacture of machines that neither company had seen before. Therefore, it was understandable that certain terms were left unspecified and were to be worked out. The court found that although a contract existed, both parties exhibited a lack of good faith in carrying it out. Both parties breached the contract, and the court ordered the return of the down payment.

ARTICLE 2: PERFORMANCE AS ACCEPTANCE

Article 2 protects the offeror by adding that where the beginning of a requested performance is a reasonable mode of acceptance, the offeree must notify the offeror that performance has begun.[9] If the offeror is not notified within a reasonable time, the offeror may treat the offer as having lapsed before acceptance. This section of the Code recognizes a basic fact of commercial life: Both buyers and sellers are looking forward to performance, and usually the sooner the better. If an offer form or order form requests prompt shipment, then to protect the offeree, an acceptance occurs when the requested performance begins so long as some notification is sent to the offeror. This notice must be sent within a reasonable time or the offeror may treat the offer as having lapsed. What is a reasonable time? When a merchant makes such an offer, it is usually to some other merchant from whom goods have been received in the past. Past conduct or, in the absence of this conduct, current commercial practice that will establish whether the notice of the beginning of performance was sent within a reasonable time. In addition, the nature of the goods (e.g., perishable fruit) or the purpose of the contract (e.g., greeting cards for an upcoming holiday season) may help define the reasonable time period.

MODERN CONTRACTING

One major feature of Article 2 is that it recognizes and deals with a significant portion of commercial reality that had, in a way, outgrown the principles of the common law of contracts. One such area that continues to this day is the widespread use of business forms or form contracts to make binding agreements. The common law of contracts was built on the image of two people or firms negotiating, bargaining, and then freely agreeing on terms that became enforceable contracts. But reality today is quite different.

Think of how you contract today with many merchants. When you buy gasoline for your car, pay for electricity you use, buy goods from Sears or L. L. Bean, or purchase an airline ticket, chances are you do not negotiate with the seller. You buy what is sold on the seller's terms and conditions or not at all. When one party cannot vary the terms of the contract, yet agrees to all the terms offered, the contract is one-sided in favor of the party that dictates the terms. The result is called a *contract of adhesion*, which means that the buyer has to stick to all the terms of the seller. The transition from an era of relative freedom of contact to an era of contracts of adhesion is noted by the following classic law review article first printed in 1943.

FRIEDRICH KESSLER

Contracts of Adhesion: Some Thoughts About Freedom of Contract[10]

The development of large scale enterprise with its mass production and mass distribution made a new type of contract inevitable—the standardized mass contract. A standardized contract, once its contents have been formulated by a business firm, is used in every bargain dealing with the same product or service. The individuality of the parties which so frequently gave color to the old type contract has disappeared. The stereotyped contract of today reflects the impersonality of the market. . . . Once the usefulness of these contracts was discovered and perfected in the transportation, insurance, and banking business, their use spread into all other fields of large scale enterprise, into international as well as national trade, and into labor relations.

★ ★ ★

. . . Standard contracts are typically used by enterprises with strong bargaining power. The weaker party, in need of the goods or services, is frequently not in a position to shop around for better terms, either because the author of the standard contract has a monopoly (natural or artificial) or because all competitors use the same clauses. His contractual intention is but a subjection more or less voluntary to terms dictated by the stronger party, terms whose consequences

are often understood only in a vague way, if at all. Thus, standardized contracts are frequently contracts of adhesion. . . .

★ ★ ★

The task of adjusting in each individual case the common law of contracts to contracts of adhesion has to be faced squarely and not indirectly. This is possible only if courts become fully aware of their emotional attitude with regard to freedom of contract. Here lies the main obstacle to progress, particularly since courts have an understandable tendency to avoid this crucial issue by way of rationalizations. They prefer to convince themselves and the community that legal certainty and "sound principles" of contract law should not be sacrificed to dictates of justice or social desirability. Such discussions are hardly profitable.

★ ★ ★

The individualism of our rules of contract law, of which freedom of contract is the most powerful symbol, is closely tied up with the ethics of free enterprise capitalism and the ideals of justice of a mobile society of small enterprisers, individual merchants and independent craftsmen. This society believed that individual and cooperative action left unrestrained in family, church and market would not lessen the freedom and dignity of man but would secure the highest possible social justice. It was firmly convinced of a natural law according to which the individual serving his own interest was also serving the interest of the community. Profits can be earned only by supplying consumable commodities. Freedom of competition will prevent profits from rising unduly. The play of the market if left to itself must therefore maximize net satisfactions. Justice within this framework has a very definite meaning. It means freedom of property and of contract, of profit making and of trade. Freedom of contract thus receives its moral justification. . . .

With the decline of the free enterprise system due to the innate trend of competitive capitalism towards monopoly, the meaning of contract has changed radically. Society, when granting freedom of contract, does not guarantee that all members of the community will be able to make use of it to the same extent. On the contrary, the law . . . does nothing to prevent freedom of contract from becoming a one-sided privilege. Society, by proclaiming freedom of contract, guarantees that it will not interfere with the exercise of power by contract. Freedom of contract enables enterprisers to legislate by contract and, what is even more important, to legislate in a substantially authoritarian manner with out using the appearance of authoritarian forms.

ARTICLE FOLLOW-UP

Kessler's article brings out a point that we emphasize throughout this text: Today, the world is dominated by large business and governmental institutions, yet people's ideas, language, and means of communicating about their social environment are often cast in terms that have come from a very individualistically oriented environment of the eighteenth and nineteenth centuries. The United States is no longer a nation of farmers and rural dwellers, each trying to make a living in his or her backyard. This is a nation of large business corporations in which much of people's existence is acted out in the form of a role defined pretty much by the business corporation.

The mass-produced, form contract is a social fact and has supplanted the means of contracting that is still written about so often: each person is an autonomous, freely willed consumer acting in a free market. Is there not some truth to the assertion that when people buy goods today, they take what the market has to offer, on its terms, or they do not act at all?

The response of the law to contracts of adhesion has proceeded along at least two lines of development. With regard to the consumer-merchant transaction, judges have claimed that they can police the use of form contracts by declaring them unconscionable or fundamentally unfair and thus unenforceable if the merchant form appears to take unreasonable advantage of the consumer.

In a second line of development with regard to the merchant-merchant transaction, UCC Article 2 addresses what it calls the battle of the forms.

THE BATTLE OF THE FORMS AND SECTION 2–207

Recall now the general pattern of commercial conduct we suggested involving merchants. Assume we have an exchange of forms with varying terms. What is the contract? Before we begin our analysis of the contract, you should read section 2–

207 of Article 2. It is one of the most complex sections used to determine the understanding of the parties.

(1) A definite and seasonable expression of acceptance or a written confirmation which is sent within a reasonable time operates as an acceptance even though it states terms additional to or different from those offered or agreed upon, unless acceptance is expressly made conditional on assent to the additional or different terms.

(2) The additional terms are to be construed as proposals for addition to the contract. Between merchants such terms become part of the contract unless:

(a) the offer expressly limits acceptance to the terms of the offer;

(b) they materially alter it; or

(c) notification of the objection to them has already been given or is given within a reasonable time after notice of them is received.

(3) Conduct by both parties which recognizes the existence of a contract is sufficient to establish a contract for sale although the writings of the parties do not otherwise establish a contract. In such case the terms of the particular contract consist of those terms on which the writings of the parties agree, together with any supplementary terms incorporated under any other provisions of this Act.

It should be obvious from the first paragraph that Section 2–207 shatters the mirror image requirements of an acceptance that prevailed at common law, so long as the acceptance is definite and timely and is not made expressly conditional on assent to the additional terms. The Code's approach here is to ask: Is there a bargain between the parties; do their forms substantially agree? If an objective intent to form an agreement exists, then a contract exists. The Code says: Speak up clearly to indicate your intent, for if you do not do so, this is how the UCC will interpret your expression or silence or conduct to determine your intent and its legal effect.

In the battle of forms context, then, the starting point is that the contract consists of the terms on which the forms agree, unless it is expressly stated in the acceptance that the acceptance is a counteroffer.

With regard to terms in the forms that vary, Section 2 provides two lines for analysis depending on the character of the parties. *If one or both of the parties are not merchants,* then the additional terms are to be construed as *proposals for additions to the contract.* This means they are not part of the contract unless the offeror agrees to them. This provision protects the offeror by allowing courts to find that a contract exists but essentially on the offeror's terms. The offeree, however, is also not without protection. If the *offeree* intends to be bound *only* if *all* of its conditions are met, then it must conspicuously state this, in which case the offeree's form will not appear as a definite and seasonable expression of acceptance. It will be a *counteroffer,* or, in the language of the Code, a "conditional acceptance," and no contract will result until the offeror accepts the offeree's terms.

Section 2–207 contemplates our given factual pattern involving merchants and provides a second and more significant line of analysis. *If both parties are mer-*

chants and if the acceptance does *not* expressly state it is *a counteroffer*, then the added or different terms of the offeree in the acceptance *become part of the contract* unless (1) the offer form expressly limits acceptance to *its* terms, or (2) the different terms materially alter the offeror's form, or (3) notification of objection to them is given within a reasonable time after notice of them is received.

Section 2–207 seems to favor the merchant offeror by making his or her document controlling if it limits acceptance to its terms only. If the offering form does not so limit acceptance, then the offeree's additions become part of the contract (again, on the assumption that the acceptance cannot be termed a counteroffer) unless the offeror objects to them within a reasonable time after notice of them is received or they materially alter the offeror's form. It is very important to both parties to read and understand the other's form.

What is a material alteration? The comments to Section 2–207 state that a *material alteration* is one that would result in unreasonable surprise or hardship to the other party. Comment 4 gives (in part) the following general examples of additions that would materially alter an offer:

1. "a clause negating . . . standard warranties"

2. "a clause reserving to the seller the power to cancel upon the buyer's failure to meet any invoice when due."

Another example is a clause requiring one of the parties to meet a much higher standard of performance than is accepted in the trade generally.

Comment 5 suggests alterations that would not materially alter an offer. They are (in part)

1. "a clause setting forth and perhaps enlarging slightly upon the seller's exemption [from liability] due to supervening causes beyond his control"

2. "a clause fixing a reasonable time for complaints within customary limits"

3. "a clause providing for interest on overdue invoices . . . where they are within the range of trade practice."

By comparing the above suggestions on defining materiality, one may discern the central policy of this section. It is, stated briefly: *Where either of the parties attempts to vary standard or accepted commercial usage, he or she should bring this to the attention of the other party and make it a subject of negotiation.* If such a variation is not negotiated, then a court may find that such a provision is not part of the contract.

A simple approach to the complexities created by doing business through standardized forms is to provide large spaces for the parties either to write or type in all key features of the understanding. Where trade usage is being varied (not merely clarified), this variation should be typed or written in and the offeror's approval of it should be sought. The UCC provides that, where express terms in a contract conflict with a course of performance or usage of trade, the express terms will control.

The following case is an example of the application of Section 2–207.

CBS, Inc. v. *Auburn Plastics, Inc.*
413 N.Y.S.2d 50 (Sup. Ct. 1979)

CARDAMONE, JUSTICE

In September, 1973 defendant submitted price quotations to plaintiff for the manufacture of eight cavity molds to be used in making parts for plaintiff's toys. The quotations were apparently based on drawings or samples which plaintiff had previously submitted to defendant.

The face of each price quotation was headed by the word "PROPOSAL" and specified the mold and tool charge, the number of cavities per mold, and the material to be used. The quotations further specified as to when sample parts could be submitted, when shipment could commence, and stated that "[u]nless accepted within 15 days from date, the proposal is not binding except at our option." Also imprinted on the face of each quotation was the following underlined sentence: "Please note that the conditions on the reverse side are made a part of this proposal and all subsequent orders." On the reverse side condition 8 stated, in part, that: "In consideration of the engineering services necessary in the designing of molds and tools, the customer hereby agrees to pay Auburn Plastics, Inc., an additional charge of thirty per cent above the quoted price of sale molds and tools when and if the customer demands delivery thereof."

Thereafter, in December, 1973 and January, 1974 plaintiff sent detailed purchase orders to defendant for the eight molds. The orders recited on their face that "[a]cceptance of this purchase order by the Vendor means that the Vendor understands and accepts all stipulations noted above." One such stipulation provided that plaintiff reserved the right to remove the molds from the defendant at any time without a withdrawal charge. The reverse side of the purchase orders similarly recited that the molds will be subject to removal without additional cost to the buyer, and also that no modification of the conditions of the contract shall be binding upon the buyer unless made in writing and signed by the buyer's representative.

In response to the purchase orders, defendant sent acknowledgments which described the molds, the price and the terms of payment and delivery essentially as contained in the purchase orders. However, the acknowledgment also stated that "[t]his sale subject to the terms and conditions of our quotation pertinent to this sale."

Thereafter plaintiff paid for the molds and ordered toy parts from the defendant which were fabricated from the molds. In May, 1978, however, as a result of the defendant's announcement of a price increase, plaintiff requested delivery of the molds. Defendant refused to do so on the ground that it was entitled to a 30% engineering charge. Plaintiff obtained an order directing the sheriff to seize the molds. Defendant moved to quash that order and appeals from the denial of its motion

The earliest communications between the parties shown in this record are defendant's price quotations. While it appears that the quotations were sufficiently detailed and specific so as to constitute offers, plaintiff did not respond to them until months after 15 days had passed. Thus the purchase orders submitted by plaintiff did not create enforceable contracts since they had no binding effect upon defendant.

In our view then, plaintiff's purchase orders constituted offers to buy the molds, and defendant's acknowledgment of those orders represented its acceptance of the offers. While the acknowledgment incorporate the conditions contained in the price quotations and therefore conflict with the terms of the offers with respect to the mold acquisition charge, the acknowledgments are nonetheless operable as acceptances since they are not expressly made conditional on plaintiff's assent to the different terms.

Whether the condition in defendant's acknowledgments calling for an additional 30% charge became a part of the contracts requires the application of subdivision 2 of section 2-207. The parties are clearly merchants, and, therefore, since the purchase orders expressly limited acceptance to their terms (Uniform Commercial Code, § 2-207, subd. 2, par. [a]) and also because notification of objection to a withdrawal charge was implicitly given by plaintiff, the provision for such a charge did not become a part of the contracts.

Order unanimously affirmed, with costs.

CASE FOLLOW-UP

This case is a fairly complicated one. The plaintiff sells toys and is the one ordering the molds and toys made by the defendant. The dispute is about who has a right to the molds after some toys were made and sent. When you look at "the contract" of the parties it seems their forms conflict about the right to possess the molds. The court decides that the defendant's form does not determine the issues here because the form itself said that it would not be binding unless accepted within fifteen days, and the plaintiff did not respond within fifteen days. Therefore, the plaintiff's form controls. This form allowed the plaintiff to get the molds. The lesson from this case is clear: Read and understand the form contracts you use in business.

In the remaining portion of the chapter we discuss general principles of contract law that *apply to both* common law contracts (land, services, etc.) and to Article 2 contracts (goods).

WHEN IS A WRITING REQUIRED (THE STATUTE OF FRAUDS)

Statutes of frauds require certain types of contracts to be proved by written evidence to be enforceable. The first statute of frauds was passed by the English Parliament in 1677. Its purpose was to prevent fraud and perjury (lying under oath) concerning the formation and terms of a contract. In the United States, many states have adopted a provision similar to the English statute. Like the law of offer and acceptance, the statute of frauds passed by the state legislatures is applicable to the common law contracts; Article 2 of the UCC has a section requiring a writing under some circumstances that applies to sales of goods. In this section, we integrate the two provisions.

There are two important things to remember when discussing the exchange of oral promises. First, *oral promises are enforceable unless the statute of frauds requires a kind of writing.* Substantial problems may occur in proving that an oral promise was made, but, if this can be done, then the promise may be enforced. Second, most statutes of frauds do not require that the contract be in writing. These statutes and Article 2 both require that *some written evidence of the promise and that it be signed by the party being charged with the making of the promise.*

Most state statutes of frauds identify five major categories of promises that must be evidenced by a writing.

1. Contracts for the sale of an interest in land

2. Contracts not to be performed within one year

3. Contacts of suretyship (promises of one person to pay for the debts of another)

4. Contracts in consideration of marriage

5. Certain kins of contracts for the sale of goods (now covered by Article 2).

Promises for the exchange of an interest in land must be evidenced by a writing and signed by the party to be charged. An interest in land is defined more precisely by the property law of each state. In most states, it covers leases, easements, licenses, and certainly the conveyance of the ownership of the land. Some state statutes provide that leases for less than one year need not be evidenced by a writing.

Both state statutes and common law also provide that the statute of frauds does not apply if the purchaser has partially performed the promise. In the past, this exception to the statute of frauds was applicable only if the seller had given consent to the purchaser to make valuable improvements to the property or if the purchaser took possession of the property and paid part of the purchase price. Also, the doctrine of estoppel (a legal bar to alleging or denying a fact because of one's own previous actions or words to the contrary) may apply to enforce an oral promise if sufficient evidence suggests that the seller did make a clear promise to the purchaser and that the purchaser did rely in a reasonable manner on the promise to the purchaser's detriment.

Most state statutes also require written evidence of promises that cannot, by their terms, possibly be performed within one year from the making. Such a promise might be "I will pay you $20,000 per year if you work for me for two years." The one-year period begins at the date of the contract, not when the performance is promised.

Contracts to answer for or discharge the debt of another if that person does not pay must be evidenced by a writing. A surety or a contract for suretyship is one in which the promisor becomes secondarily liable. These contracts have to be written because it is quite unusual to be held responsible for someone else's debt. If a bank expects to hold *B* liable if *A* does not repay a loan, *B*'s promise must be evidenced by a writing and signed by *B*.

Promises that must be evidenced in writing and that are made in consideration of marriage are part of prenuptial contracts that include financial provisions and do not apply to simple mutual promises to marry.

Article 2, Section 2–201 provides that a contract for the sale of goods for the price of $500 or more is not enforceable unless some writing recognizes the contract, states the quantity of goods involved, and is signed by the party against whom enforcement is sought. A distinction is made between saying *the contract must be in writing* and saying the promises must *be evidenced* by a writing. Article 2 requires only the latter. For example, suppose S orally agrees to sell his car to P for $1,000, and S then refers to this fact in his letter to Q, P's sister. In the event of a lawsuit, S may not assert the statute of frauds as a defense if P should sue for breach of the promise because the letter, if signed by S, is sufficient evidence of the promise to sell. This would be true even if the letter incorrectly stated one of the terms, but the promise would not be enforceable beyond the quantity of the goods referred to in the letter. Office memos, minutes of a board of directors' meeting, and other similar documents may be used in addition to letters.

Because the requirement for written evidence is a technical one and has nothing to do with whether the parties actually made a contract, many exceptions to the writing requirement have been created. The purpose of all of the provisions in the statute of frauds is to protect an innocent party against others who might *fraudulently* assert that the innocent party had promised to perform. The opportunity for fraud is minimized when some evidence suggests that a party who made an oral promise has begun to perform. Article 2 recognizes this and provides that an *oral promise is enforceable without a writing* when goods are to be specially manufactured for the buyer, *and* they are not suitable for sale to others in the ordinary course of the seller's business, *and* the seller has made either a substantial beginning of their manufacture or commitments for their procurement. Article 2 adds two other circumstances in which no writing is needed: (1) when the party being charged admits in pleadings or testimony in court that a contract was made and (2) when the party being charged has either paid for the goods in question or accepted the goods. It should be obvious that, in these three circumstances, the *actions* of the party being charged speak about the existence of a contract and that the technicality of a writing should not be held against one.

Finally, Article 2's version of the statute of frauds recognizes a different standard of performance for merchants and in so doing substantially changes the older common law interpretations. It provides that if a written confirmation of the contract is sent by one *merchant* to another merchant within a reasonable time of the exchange of oral promises and if the receiver has reason to know its contents, the writing requirement is satisfied for both the sender *and* the receiver. This holds true even though the writing is not signed by the receiver, unless the receiver objects in writing to its contents within ten days of receipt. This provision again reflects the perceptions of Llewellyn, who recognized that much of today's business is conducted by one merchant's merely filling in a few blanks on a form and sending it off to another merchant. This section of the Code puts a duty on merchants to read their mail! If the merchant receiving the form or confirmation has no intent to contract with the sending merchant and has reason to know the contents of the form, then the receiving merchant must reject the form within ten days. Otherwise, he or she cannot successfully defend a suit on the grounds that he or she has not signed a written order.

In general, Article 2 is fairly liberal in allowing evidence of an oral contract. The Code comments to the statute of frauds section make it clear that, when a writing is required, it need not state the price, time, or place of payment or delivery, or the general quality of the goods. Businesspeople frequently base their agreement as to price on a price list or catalogue known to both of them. Therefore, the only three essential ingredients of the required writing are that (1) it must refer to a contract for the *sale of goods* between the parties, (2) it must specify the *quantity* of goods, and (3) it must be *signed by the party* to be charged.

A diagram of Article 2's statute of frauds (2–201) might appear as in Figure 8.2.

FIGURE 8.2 *Diagram of UCC 2-201—Statute of Frauds*

Exchange of Oral Promises for the Sale of Goods Between:	A	B	C
Non-merchants	No written evidence of promises required if: (1) goods are to be specially manufactured and are not suitable for sale to others in the ordinary course of the seller's business, and there has been a substantial beginning on their manufacture or a commitment for their procurement; or (2) party against whom enforcement is sought admits in court that the contract was made; or (3) payment for or receipt of goods exists.	If transaction does not qualify in A and price of goods is $500 or over, then →	Written evidence of the promises is required and must be signed by the party to be charged and must state quantity of goods sold.
Merchants	No written evidence of promises signed by party to be charged if within a reasonable time of the exchange of oral promises the other merchant sends a written confirmation stating the quantity of the goods and the receiver has reason to know its contents and does not object in writing within 10 days of its receipt.	If transaction does not qualify in A and price of gods is $500 or over, then →	Written evidence of the promises is required and must be signed by the party to be charged and must state the quantity of the goods sold.

If a court decides that the requirements of the statute of frauds are met, or that an exception exists, or that the statute of frauds does not apply, the plaintiff must proceed with proof of the contents of the contract, its breach, and loss. Because the defense of the statute of frauds is overcome, do not assume that the plaintiff has won. Substantial problems of proof may remain. The plaintiff must still prove there were an offer and acceptance, consideration, breach, and damages.

THE UNCONSCIONABLE CONTRACT OR CLAUSE

Should courts allow the parties to argue that the promises embodied in an otherwise enforceable contract should not be enforced because the exchange of promises or the bargain subsequently turned out to be unwise or unprofitable? The answer, considering most circumstances, is a resounding No! Commercial undertakings inevitably involve risks. Indeed, all of commercial contract law may be viewed as a societal process giving structure to and enforcing the outcome of such risks. *When parties knowingly assume certain risks, they should be bound even if it means a possible great loss of money and even bankruptcy.* There is always, however, the exceptional case. The basic unfairness of an exchange of promises is usually raised by asserting that the exchange was unconscionable. The UCC embodies the common law of unconscionability, providing in Section 2–302 as follows:

> If the court as a matter of law finds the contract or any clause of the contract to have been unconscionable at the time it was made the court may refuse to enforce the contract, or it may enforce the remainder of the contract without the unconscionable clause, or it may so limit the application of any unconscionable clause as to avoid any unconscionable result.

This section gives the judge, not the jury, the right to "police" sales contracts for fundamental fairness. According to one legal scholar, what Llewellyn had in mind when he first drafted Section 2–302 was the development of an open and direct attack on one-sided, unbargained-for, small-print clauses in standardized form contract.[11] The official comments state that the basic test or definition is whether "in the light if the general commercial background and the commercial needs of the particular trade or case, the clauses involved are so one-sided as to be unconscionable under the circumstances existing at the time of making of the contract."

The notion of unconscionability is best understood by considering two kinds of transactions. When a merchant or knowledgeable businessperson deals with another merchant or knowledgeable businessperson, the courts are very reluctant to allow either party to argue unconscionability. Almost all instances of a successful assertion at the appellate level that a contract or clause of a contract is unconscionable involve consumers contracting with merchants.[12] Although a more precise definition of unconscionability is difficult and the definition may vary some from state to state, courts usually consider the following factors in holding that a contract or clause is unconscionable:

1. the background of the party asserting unconscionability—such facts as age, education, economic status

2. the "hidden" or complex nature of the language used

3. the degree of inequality in bargaining position

4. the number of "meaningful choices" available to the party asserting unconscionability

5. whether there was any meaningful opportunity to negotiate over contract terms took place

PROMISSORY ESTOPPEL

We have discussed how Article 2 of the UCC allows for flexibility in commercial transactions. In Chapter 2, we wrote of a body of law (equity law) that also was intended to add flexibility to the law. Equity law or equitable rules are becoming more important in contract law because the circumstances of the commercial environment are very dynamic and thus demand flexible rules. Promissory estoppel is one of the most flexible and important equitable rules in contract law.

Promissory estoppel is a principle of law that has wide applicability to both common law and Article 2 contracts. It is derived from the use of a court's equity powers and may be found in agency law, partnership law, contract law, and other generally recognized areas of law study. A court will use promissory estoppel to create a contract when representations by one party are relied on by another party to his or her detriment. Usually, the reliance must be reasonable and must result in some out-of-pocket loss. When a promise or representation is reasonably relied on to one's detriment, the courts will estop (stop) the one making the promise from denying the existence of a contract.

The case that follows is a recent, significant use of promissory estoppel in contract law.

Ypsilanti v. *General Motors Corporation*
506 N.W. 2d 556 (Mich. App., 1993)

[*Author's note:* The following is a published *trial court* opinion.]

The township (Ypsilanti-plaintiff) alleged that General Motors had entered into agreements with the township to obtain twelve year tax abatements on property in the Willow Run plant in 1984 and 1988 and that the closing of the plant prior to the expiration of those abatement periods would violate the agreements and representations General Motors had made to obtain those abatements. . . .

* * *

Michigan, like over thirty other states, permits municipalities to offer property tax abatements to industries as a supposed means of retaining and adding employment opportunities. The statutory framework for such abatements was established in Act 198 of 1974. . . . The intent of the statute, as codified in section 9(2)(e), is to provide tax abatements for industrial facilities which "will . . . have the reasonable likelihood to create employment, retain employment, prevent a loss of employment, or produce energy in the community in which the facility is located". . . .

* * *

For many years, General Motors has operated two adjacent plants in Ypsilanti Township, referred to as Hydra-Matic and Willow Run Assembly. Hydra-Matic employs approximately 9,000 persons and Willow Run employs approximately 4,500 persons. Within 90 days of the signing of Act 198, General Motors formed a group within the Hydra-Matic plant to seek a tax abatement. General Motors approached the State Department of Commerce and local Ypsilanti Chamber of Commerce officials to pursue such an abatement.

From 1975 through 1990, General Motors requested and received tax abatements on facilities investments in those two plants of over $1.3 billion, with eight of the abatements in the Hydra-Matic plant and three in the Willow Run plant. State-wide, General Motors has been one of the most frequent recipients of Act 198 subsidies, having received 122 such abatements on its various Michigan facilities.

* * *

General Motors Vice President Joseph Spielman made the decision following a short two week process which involved getting "proposals" from each of the plants and the affected communities. He recommended, and the corporation announced in February of 1992 that the work being done on the one shift at Willow Run (MICH.) would be transferred to the Arlington (TEXAS) plant, which would go on three shifts per day. . . .

[The court next analyzed the state statutory framework for such tax abatements and concluded that the legislature did not intend to create any contractual rights in the parties by passing the statute].

* * *

The rigid and technical rules of conventional contract law are designed to provide the framework for a Court to adjudicate the rights of parties in a contractual dispute. As with other generalized legal principles, these rigid rules sometimes fail us in our attempt to wring justice from a specific dispute between people whose expectations of each other are not fulfilled. Fortunately, our common law has also evolved concepts of equity which are designed to allow a Court the flexibility, which is the true hallmark of fairness, to do justice in such situations.

One such equitable concept in the law of contracts is the notion of promissory, or equitable, estoppel. As the Court of Appeals aptly described it:

> Application of the doctrine of promissory estoppel is based on the particular factual circumstances; as an equitable remedy, it is employed to alleviate an unjust result of strict adherence to established legal principles.

* * *

The elements of promissory estoppel have been clearly identified:

> In order for a promise to be enforceable under the concept of promissory estoppel, there must be a (1) promise that the promisor should reasonably have expected to induce action of a definite and substantial character on the part of the promisee, (2) which in fact produced reliance or forbearance of that nature, (3) in circumstances such that the promise must be enforced if injustice is to be avoided.

The plaintiffs in this case contend that, regardless whether the statute and application form created a contract by their own terms, General Motors, by its statements and conduct in connection with those and other applications, represented that it would provide continuous employment at the Willow Run plant if the government continued to provide tax abatement subsidies. The issue, in promissory estoppel terms, is whether those representations indeed constitute a promise and whether it is the type of promise that should be enforced by this Court to prevent an injustice.

For almost fifteen years before the 1988 abatement hearing, General Motors has established a repeated pattern of inducing the township to recommend approval of its tax abatement applications on both the Willow Run and Hydra-Matic plants. Each time General Motors wanted to substantially change the product line at one of the plants, it would "sell" the idea of a tax subsidy to the township with a ritual of "education" sessions and lunches. Every time, the inducement to the township was the same—jobs will be created or preserved at the plant—and it should have been, for that was the ostensible purpose of the abatement. And, to the credit of General Motors, each time it delivered and jobs were created or preserved at the plant, at least for the duration of that product line.

★ ★ ★

General Motors did not make any offhand or casual statements to the Board at the public hearing on the abatement application. In the context of this background, when the plant manager, in the prepared statement on behalf of General Motors, stated that, subject to "favorable market demand," General Motors would "continue production and maintain continuous employment" at the Willow Run plant, it was a promise. The promise was clearly that if the township granted the abatement, General Motors would make the Caprice at Willow Run and not just transfer that work somewhere else. Our courts have accepted the follow definition of a legal promise:

The fundamental element of promise seems to be an expression of intention by the promisor that his future conduct shall be in accordance with his present expression, irrespective of what his will may be when the time for performance arrives.

A statement that the granting of the abatement would enable General Motors to provide continuous employment at the plant was a *quid pro quo* type of statement that is associated in its common sense meaning with a promise.

In the context of the abatement application hearing the statement was also a promise that General Motors "should reasonably have expected to induce action of a definite and substantial character on the part of" the township. General Motors clearly made the statement to induce the township to cut its property taxes on the $75 million project in half. Most importantly, the promise was needed because the township otherwise had no incentive to approve the application. General Motors could not simply promise that it would make the investment in the plant *if* it was granted the abatement because it had already publicly committed to make the investment without any mention of an abatement. The only logical reason the township would have to give up half of the taxes on the project is that General Motors represented, as it had done in the past, that as long as it made those cars it was to make them in Willow Run.

General Motors asserts that the promise was conditioned upon "favorable market demand" and therefore a totally illusory one that the township could not reasonably have relied upon. The author of the prepared statement testified at trial that when he used the phrase "favorable market demand" he meant enough Caprice and station wagon sales orders to keep both the Willow Run and Arlington plants operating at a level of two shifts each per, 235 days a year. Such testimony is not credible. In the context of the corporate decision to transfer the Willow Run work to Arlington and the resulting trial almost five years later, this revelation of alleged intent is suspect. As indicated earlier, the intent of the parties is to be judged objectively by looking to the expressed, not unexpressed, words of the parties. There was no mention of Arlington anywhere in the public hearing and no testimony that work levels at the Arlington plant had ever been discussed with the township officials, must less stated to be a condition of Willow Run's work level.

★ ★ ★

The second element of promissory estoppel is that the promise produced "reliance of forbearance" of a definite and substantial character. If nothing else, and there is considerable else, the evidence that the township has given up over $2 million in local government taxes from 1988-92 for the 1988 abatement alone is sufficient to satisfy this element.

The final element is that the circumstances be such that General Motors' promise must be enforced "if injustice is to be avoided." The court is mindful of the fact that two federal courts have refused to apply the promissory estoppel doctrine to prevent plant closings. Neither of those situations involved specific representations or representations which were made as an inducement for a local government to approve a tax abatement. More important, in each of those situations, the corporation was simply closing a plant because it was economically necessary to close it and the courts concluded that the company never promised to operate a plant when there was no demand for its product. . . .

★ ★ ★

Aside from these distinctions in the facts of those cases, this court, perhaps unlike the judges there, simply finds that the failure to act in this case would result in a terrible injustice and that the doctrine of promissory estoppel should be applied. . . .

★ ★ ★

There would be a gross inequity and patent unfairness if General Motors, having lulled the people of the Ypsilanti area into giving up millions of tax dollars which they so desperately need to educate their children and provide basic governmental services, is allowed to simply decide that it will desert 4500 workers and their families because it thinks it can make these same cars a little cheaper somewhere else. Perhaps another judge in another court would not feel moved by that injustice and would labor to find a legal rationalization to allow such conduct. But in this Court it is my responsibility to make that decision. My conscience will not allow this injustice to happen.

Order: General Motors is hereby enjoined from transferring the production of its Caprice sedan, and Buick and Cadillac station wagons, from the Willow Run plant to any other facility.
Donald E. Shelton
Circuit Judge

CASE FOLLOW-UP

The opinion is a specially written trial court opinion. Usually, trial courts do not publish and make available to the public their opinions. Judge Shelton did so in this case because of the wide impact of his ruling and, we guess, because of the application of promissory estoppel in a case like this. Of course, this opinion was appealed by General Motors, and some six months later the opinion was reversed by the Michigan Court of

Appeals. The Michigan Court of Appeals (among other things) reasoned that:

1. The mere fact that a corporation solicits a tax abatement and persuades a municipality with assurance of jobs cannot be evidence of a promise;

2. The fact that a manufacturer used hyperbole and puffery in seeking an advantage or concession does not necessarily create a promise;

3. Almost all of the statements made to secure the abatement were expressions of General Motors hopes and expectations, not promises;

4. The actions of General Motors relied on by the trial court were the type that one would naturally expect a company to make in order to secure an abatement;

5. Even if the finding of a promise could be sustained, reliance on it by the city and the state would not be reasonable under the circumstances; (201 Mich. App. 128 (1993).

Following this decision, there was an outcry from the residents of Ypsilanti. The city promised a vigorous appeal to the state supreme court. On April 14, 1994, General Motors and the city announced that they had settled the matter. General Motors agreed to create 500 more jobs at its other facilities in the town, and spend $84 million to clean up the Willow Run site so the city could use the site for an industrial complex. The city dropped the lawsuit, let go of 4,000 jobs, and granted General Motors a twelve-year tax abatement on certain investments in the city.[13]

In this case we see a court-enforced, private solution to a dispute that has wide public policy implications. Should GM, the state legislature, the governor's office, some branch of the federal government, or a state court decide such issues as these? More specifically, should GM management alone have the power to make decisions that affect the lives of thousands and, in some cases, the economies of whole states? The answer it seems, is far from clear and is being fashioned as you read this book.

In conclusion, the equitable doctrine of promissory estoppel is properly argued in any case that has a promise by one party, reasonable reliance by another party, and out-of-pocket loss as a result of the breach of promise. The doctrine is properly used when the elements of a formal contract may not exist or their presence may be in dispute. The doctrine is used to avoid a manifest unfairness caused by failure to enforce the promises made.

CONTRACT LAW AND REMEDIES FOR BREACH

It has been said that the best measure of the value of contract law to a commercial society is in the remedies given to damaged parties as a result of breach. *If contract law is to protect the value of the promises exchanged, it must give to the nonbreaching party the value of the promise lost as a result of the breach.* That is, the law must attempt to compensate the nonbreaching party so that it is put as close as possible to the position it would have been in had there been performance. Courts, as a general guide to awarding remedies, recognize three basic principles that are usually phrased in terms of the nonbreaching party's interests in the transaction. They are, in order of importance, expectation, reliance, and restitution interests.

EXPECTATION INTEREST

No single legal principle provides a guide for action in every situation involving a breaching party. Given the general objective of compensation, however, the best principle to emphasize is that courts should give the nonbreaching party what was expected from the other party's performance. In some cases, this objective can be met by an award of money damages, and in others by an order of specific performance to the seller to convey certain property. The fundamental notion, though, is to give the damaged party the gain it had expected. When such a gain is given to the nonbreaching party, a court is protecting the expectation interest of that party.

For example, suppose a pro tennis shop (*P*) ordered 1,200 cans of tennis balls for $1,200 and paid $600 down when the order was placed with the Seller (*S*). If *S* breaches by providing defective tennis balls that are worthless, *P* may recover the difference between what it agreed to pay for the balls ($1,200) and the price it hoped to receive for the balls when they were sold, if *S* knew the balls were for resale. If the cans of balls were to sell for $2 each, for a total of $2,400, *P* could recover a total of $1,200 (its profits) plus its down payment of $600. Note that the $1200 puts *P* in the same position it would have been in had there been full performance—$1,200 ahead. In this case, just returning the down payment of $600 would not be sufficient to compensate *P*. The proper measure of damages gives *P* the full value of its bargain.

RELIANCE INTEREST

In some circumstances, a party may have incurred expenses in reliance on the expected performance that exceed the gain from the particular breached performance. For example, a manufacturer of small steel products may have spent $1,000 for concrete footings and supporting structures for a large steel stamping machine it ordered from the seller. Assume that the seller repudiated the contract and that the buyer found it could purchase a similar machine for the same price it was to pay the first seller. The new machine, however, required *new* concrete footings, which cost another $1000, and it cost $500 to remove the old ones. This buyer incurred expenses of $1,500 in *reliance* on the first seller's promise and should be able to recover that amount.

RESTITUTION INTEREST

In a few cases, the anticipated gain may be too speculative to measure and no amounts may be expended by the nonbreaching party in reliance on the breached promise, but the breaching party may have experienced a gain as a result of the transaction. In this case, the courts will measure the amount of loss to the nonbreaching party by allowing it to recover the breaching party's gain. Courts are protecting the restitution interest of the party in this instance. The best example of this measure of damage is a case in which the buyer pays $3,000 down on a $5,000 contract and there is a breach by the seller. Assume the buyer is unable to prove its gain had there been performance and cannot show damage caused by reliance on the breached promise (e.g., if a ski resort had ordered a large snowmaking machine the fall before a winter in which record snowfalls occurred). Courts would order the return of the $3,000.

We conclude this chapter with a case that is sure to become a modern classic. In this case, the jury awarded compensatory damages of $7.53 billion and punitive damages of $3 billion to Pennzoil Co. In subsequent litigation, the punitive damage award was reduced to $1 billion, but the judgment was still sufficient to put one of this country's most prestigious business corporations, Texaco, the defendant in the case, into bankruptcy.

We include this case here for three reasons. First, the court used older ideas of the common law of contracts to resolve a major issue: Was there sufficient evidence of intent to be bound by the exchange of promises so that a jury could properly conclude that a contract was formed? Although Article 2 of the UCC is modern commercial law, in appropriate cases involving services and the sale of intangibles, the older common law principles still apply.

Second, this case involves both contract law and tort law. The basic wrong sued on here, one not discussed in the following edited court opinion, was the tort of the intentional interference with contractual relations. This tort is well defined by its name. Also, notice that contract law and tort law often seem to overlap.

Third, the amount of compensatory damages awarded in this case appear astronomical but still had to follow accepted legal principles. Because this was essentially a tort case, the damage award should have reflected the amount of damages suffered by the plaintiff. Although damages were difficult to prove in this case, the appellate court could find no error of law in the jury's determination of damages and let the judgment stand.

The lesson of the case is that people in business should be very careful when there is a chance their own business activities may seem to interfere with the contractual relationships of other parties.

Texaco, Inc. v. Pennzoil Co.
729 S.W. 2d 768 (Tex. Ct. App. 1987)

[*Author's note:* The facts in this case are very complicated and, of course, disputed by the parties. An overview of the important events begins on December 28, 1983, when Pennzoil announced a public offer for sixteen million shares of Getty Oil at $100 each. Gordon Getty was a director of Getty Oil and as trustee controlled 40.2 percent of the 79.1 million outstanding shares of Getty Oil. On January 2, 1984, the board of Getty Oil, which had to approve any such sale of stock, rejected the $100-per-share offer and countered with a price of $110 per share plus a $10 debenture. On January 3, the Getty board received a revised Pennzoil offer of $110 per share plus a $3 per share bonus (referred to as a "stub") that was to be paid after the sale of a Getty Oil subsidiary. After discussion, the board voted 15 to 1 to accept Pennzoil's proposal if the stub price was raised to $5. At this same meeting, the Getty board voted themselves and Getty's officers and advisors indemnity for any liability arising from the events of the past few months. The board also authorized its executive compensation committee to give "golden parachutes" (generous termination benefits) to the top executives whose positions were likely to be affected by any change in management.

Pennzoil accepted the $110-per-share price with a $5 stub later the same day, January 3. Getty's lawyers and public relations staff drafted a press release announcing an agreement in principle based on the terms of a Memorandum of Agreement accepted by both parties. The release was made public by both parties on January 4. On January 6, the *Wall Street Journal* reported that an agreement had been reached based on the memorandum.

A core problem here was that an investment banker hired by Getty, Geoffrey Boisi, continued to let other companies know that Getty stock was available through January 3. On January 4, the day of the Getty-Pennzoil announcement, he contacted Texaco, whose officers indicated interest. The board of Texaco met on January 5 and authorized an offer of $125 per share for all of Getty's outstanding stock. This offer was communicated to the various Getty parties, and on January 6, the Getty board voted to "withdraw" its previous understanding with Pennzoil and to accept Texaco's offer. Pennzoil then sued Texaco for the intentional interference with contractual relations.

A significant preliminary issue was whether a contract existed between Pennzoil and Getty. A Memorandum of Agreement had been signed by parties representing a majority of the shares of Getty Oil and, we must assume, agreed to by Pennzoil. This memorandum, however, referred to many other provisions that had to be worked out in the future.]

WARREN, JUSTICE

Texaco contends that there was insufficient evidence to support the jury's finding that at the end of the Getty Oil board meeting on January 3, the Getty entities intended to bind themselves to an agreement with Pennzoil. Pennzoil contends that the evidence showed that the parties intended to be bound to the terms in the Memorandum of Agreement plus a price term of $110 plus a $5 stub, even though the parties may have contemplated a later, more formal document to memorialize the agreement already reached.

If parties do not intend to be bound to an agreement until it is reduced to writing and signed by both parties, then there is no contract until that event occurs. If there is no understanding that a signed writing is necessary before the parties will be bound, and the parties have agreed upon all substantial terms, then an informal agreement can be binding, even though the parties contemplated evidencing their agreement in a formal document later. It is the parties' expressed intent that controls which rule of contract formation applies. Only the outward expressions of intent are considered— secret or subjective intent is immaterial to the question of whether the parties were bound.

Several factors have been articulated to help determine whether the parties intended to be bound only by a formal, signed writing: (1) whether a party expressly reserved the right to be bound only when a written agreement is signed; (2) whether there was any partial performance by one party that the party disclaiming the contract accepted; (3) whether all essential terms of the alleged contract had been agreed upon; and (4) whether the complexity or magnitude of the transaction was such that a formal, executed writing would normally be expected.

Any intent of the parties not to be bound before signing a formal document is not so clearly expressed in the press release to establish, as a matter of law, that there was no contract at that time. The press release does refer to an agreement "in principle" and states that the "transaction" is subject to execution of a definitive merger agreement. But the release as a whole is worded in indicative terms, not in subjunctive or hypothetical ones. The press release describes what shareholders *will* receive, what Pennzoil *will* contribute, that Pennzoil *will* be granted an option, etc.

★ ★ ★

There was sufficient evidence for the jury to conclude that the parties had reached agreement on all essential terms of the transaction with only the mechanics and details left to be supplied by the parties' attorneys. Although there may have been many specific terms relating to the . . . draft that had yet to be put in final form, there is sufficient evidence to support a conclusion by the jury that the parties did not consider . . . "open items" significant obstacles precluding an intent to be bound.

Although the magnitude of the transaction here was such that normally a signed writing would be expected, there was sufficient evidence to support an inference by the jury that that expectation was satisfied here initially by the Memorandum of Agreement, signed by a majority of shareholders of Getty Oil and approved by the board. . . .

Judgment for Pennzoil affirmed.

CASE FOLLOW-UP

What can be learned from this case? The legal principles applied by the jury seem to be simple enough. If an informal memorandum reveals, within reason, that the parties intended a permanent exchange of promises, then those promises will be enforced in court and a remedy given.

In addition, consider what this case reveals about the legal system. Who were the winners and who were the losers in this lawsuit? The big losers were the shareholders and employees of Texaco, who most probably had no say in this transaction at all. The big winners, from what we can tell from the case, were the senior managers of Getty, who floated to earth after this event in their golden parachutes, and the shareholders of Getty. Yet, was it not the very large shareholders and management of Getty who were

as blameworthy as any other person or group? Getty's agent, Geoffrey Boisi, it seems, was as responsible as any person for Texaco's belief that Getty shares might still be available on January 4. In addition, Pennzoil appears to have come out fairly well, but it probably had to pay huge sums in legal fees and so is not as well off as if Texaco had never acted.

Was justice achieved in this case? Chances are the decision makers all landed on their feet while others who had no chance to participate in the decision did not do as well. As to Boisi, we have no knowledge of his fate. The law acts only on breaches of a duty or a promise. If he was not held accountable by Getty, to whom his duties as a professional ran, then he came out of the situation much better than the employees of Texaco did.

CONCLUSION

The American law of contracts is one of the most cherished portions of civil law. Many people believe this law promotes basic notions of freedom by permitting any person or institution to contract for services or property and then, in the case of breach, by providing a remedy that reflects the value of the promises exchanged. That is, each person in the commercial environment is free to realize his or her own expectations through contracting. This process of contracting is how people transfer their property, their talents, and their wealth; it is how people formalize the risks they are willing to take. It is, some commentators say, the foundation of a capitalist economy.

This assessment of the value of contract law seems particularly appropriate to the early part of this century, but the circumstances in the legal environment of business have changed substantially. Merchants now contract by exchanging forms. Moreover, as a consumer you do not bargain in the traditional sense with a merchant when you buy something; you take what the merchant offers you on his or her terms. The meaning of the idea of bargaining has changed. What this all means for the institution of contract law is unclear. Some evidence suggests that noncontract-related sanctions are as important in enforcing agreements as the remedies for a breach of contract. In addition, many merchants do business informally on a handshake or in response to a verbal order over the telephone. The formalities of the contract law are not used.

Contract law is so pervasive and vast, however, that any changes will come slowly. In this area of the law, it is most important that rules provide confidence and stability. Radical change would certainly serve as an impetus for slowed commercial activity. Nevertheless, over time, some rules become obsolete and change does creep in. We see change now in the increased use of equity principles, such as equitable estoppel and the doctrine of unconscionability. These ideas introduce a measure of flexibility in contract law. The application of equitable estoppel may result in a court creating a contractual obligation when none was intended (but equity required that one be created). Unconscionability may excuse a party from an agreement. In the use of these two equity-based rules of law, we can see the ever-present tension between what may be efficient (the creation of contract liability when there is offer, acceptance, and consideration) and what may be fair under a certain set of facts.

REVIEW QUESTIONS AND PROBLEMS

1. Assume that General Foods, a large producer of soups, has the following provision in its contracts that farmers sign: General will pay $800 per ton for certain tomatoes that only it uses if the tomatoes are acceptable to General Foods when delivered to it at its processing plant in Homestead, Florida. *F*, a farmer, signs General's contract and then grows some of these tomatoes but then decides to sell them to Special Foods, a new competitor of General. General sues *F* for breach of the contract *F* had signed. Will General recover? What could *F* argue?

2. Article 2 of the UCC changes the common law of contracts in the area of contract formation. How does it change the common law of offer and acceptance?

3. Roto-Lith, Ltd. is a corporation engaged in manufacturing cellophane bags for packaging vegetables. It ordered a drum of N–132–C emulsion from F. P. Bartlett & Co. on October 23, 1969, for the stated purpose of making wet-pack spinach bags. In response to Roto-Lith's order form, the seller sent its "acknowledgment" form and the goods were shipped. The acknowledgment form and the invoice accompanying the goods both stated in conspicuous language, "all goods sold without warranties, express or implied. . . ." Further, on the back of the acknowledgment was this statement: "If these terms are not acceptable, buyer must so notify seller at once."

   Roto-Lith did not protest the waiver of the warranties; it received, paid for, and used the emulsion. The emulsion was defective, and Roto-Lith sued F. P. Bartlett for breach of contract (warranties). Article 2 states that, in every contract for the sale of goods, the seller makes a warranty that the goods sold were fit for the use for which the goods were sold. These "implied" warranties exist unless *the contract* between the parties waives these warranties. What was the contractual understanding between these parties with regard to the warranties? [*Roto-Lith Ltd.* v. *F. P. Bartlett & Co.*, 297 F.2d 497 (1972)]

4. *P* purchased life insurance from *I*, an insurance company, on the representation of *I*'s agent that the policy would cover war and aviation risks. *P* relied on the representation and canceled his existing insurance coverage, which did cover such risks. In fact, the new policy said in plain language that it did not cover such risks. *P* did not read the policy, and *P* was killed in a helicopter crash in Vietnam. What arguments do the representatives of *P*'s estate have against *I*? In short, was there a contract of insurance on *P*'s life?

5. Dan Cohen, an active Republican associated with *W*'s campaign for governor of Minnesota, approached reporters from the *St. Paul Pioneer Press Dispatch* and the *Minneapolis Star and Tribune* and offered to provide documents relating to another candidate. He made clear to the reporters that he would provide the information only if he was given a promise of confidentiality. Reporters from both papers promised to keep Cohen's identity a secret, and he turned over copies of two public court records showing arrest records of the other candidate. Both newspapers disclosed Cohen's name and affiliation when they disclosed the content of the arrest records.

   Cohen was fired from his job as campaign consultant and claims that his career has been ruined by the breach of promise. He sued the newspapers for breach of contract. Was a contract in force here? What would be Cohen's best argument? What should the measure of damages be?

   The newspapers assert their First Amendment rights to publish such information as the name of the person who tendered the documents to them. Would this be a good defense? When two very fundamental sets of principles such as those in the contract law (the value of the exchange of one promise for another, or, as in this case, an act for a promise) conflict with such a basic idea as freedom of the press, which set of principles should prevail?

ENDNOTES

1. Farnsworth, *Contracts* (1982) Quoting Adam Smith at p.7. Some of the material in this chapter, and the arrangement of ideas and cases parallels that found in, *Understanding the Law: Principles, Problems and Potentials of the American Legal System*, Chapter 7, (West, 1995) because both were written by the same author (Wolfe).

2. *Id.* at 14.

3. *Id.* at 5.

4. Donnell, The Businessman and the Business Law Curriculum, 6 *Am. Bus. L.J.* 451 (1968); Elliot and Wolfe, The Need for Legal Education by Persons in Business, 19 *Am. Bus. L.J.* 153 (1981).

5. See Danzig, A Comment on the Jurisprudence of the Uniform Commercial Code, 27 *Stan. L. Rev.* 621–635 (1975).

6. See Bonsignore, Existentialism: The Rule of Law and Article 2 of the Uniform Commercial Code, 8 *Am. Bus. L.J.* 133 at 147 (1970).

7. *Bonebrake* v. *Cox*, 499 F.2d 951 (1974).

8. *Admiral Plastics Carp.* v. *Trueblood, Inc.*, 436 F.2d 1335 (6th cir. 1971).

9. Nordstrom, *Handbook of the Law of Sales* 86 (1970).

10. From 43 *Columbia L. Rev.* 629–642 (1943). This article has been edited, and footnotes have been deleted.

11. Zelermyer, The Unconscionable Contact, unpublished paper presented at the American Business Law Association Annual Meeting, College Park Md., Aug. 18, 1978.

12. White and Summers, *Uniform Commercial Code* 114 (1972).

13. *Detroit News*, April 14, 1994. p.1.

PART THREE

Legal and Social Control of the Large Business Corporation

We have suggested several times that the most prominent actor today in our business society is the large business corporation. Over half of the material in this text, and four out of five chapters in this part are devoted to an explanation of the law that applies to these massive aggregations of economic and social power.

We begin this part with an exploration of the state-based common law that defines the duties between any employer and its employees. This field of study is known as agency law, and is applicable to all proprietorships, partnerships, and business corporations. We end this chapter with an exploration of the inevitable tension between employers and employees in the special context where the employer demands action by the employee that may offend the latter's conscience. Quite often, the only choice of the employee is to engage in what is called "blowing the whistle" when the employer will not conform to social duties as employees see them. In the latter half of this chapter we examine both the law and public policy implications of this phenomenon.

The law that creates business corporations and that governs the structure of the corporation and many of the duties of the agents of the corporation, is state-based. In Chapter 10, we see that although business corporations are the creation of state law, their size and the wide range of their activities that stretch beyond state boundaries, and beyond the boundaries of this country, have necessitated the passage of federal law that, at the very least, will present the large modern business corporation with uniform conceptions of law that govern their activities.

We begin our exploration of the applicability of federal law to the legal environment of business by devoting one whole chapter to the history, methods and the very idea of government regulation. In Chapter 11, there is an added focus on the federal governmental regulation of product safety which is carried out largely through the Consumer Product Safety Commission.

In the following chapter, we see that our law is often guided by the practicalities of everyday power politics. The Justice Department, an arm of the Attorney General's Office of the federal government, is controlled both by the political party of the President in power, and by the traditions of past law enforcement. Although antitrust law enforcement by the federal government is not as active as it once was, this body of legal principles that define fair competition is still sufficiently prominent to merit its own chapter. No business manager can afford to engage in business practices that violate the basic principles of fair competition which we discuss.

Finally, perhaps the single most important area of federal law creating liability for the management of the large business corporation comes from court interpretations and SEC enforcement of the federal securities laws. Many of the cases in recent years involving such things as insider trading and corporate self-dealing will be found in Chapter 13.

If there is a major difference between the law in the chapters of this part, and the next, it is that principles discussed in this part are older, more settled, and, thus, less subject to change. The newer conceptions of law found in the federal law of employment discrimination and environmental law, two of the subjects of the following part, are less settled, and perhaps, more subject to the winds of political change, so they vary, it seems, every year or so.

CHAPTER 9

The Law of Agency, Partnerships, and Related Business Associations

INTRODUCTION

Americans pride themselves on their hard work, their freedom, and their ability to invent and innovate. Apply these notions to the law of business associations, and it means numerous forms of business enterprise—almost as many as can be thought of. Moreover, because of a tradition that is suspicious of governmental planning for business, the government does not provide an overall comprehensive or integrated legal theory about business associations. One can know the basics, however, and this chapter is about those basics.

The forms a business enterprise may take are found in state-based statutory and common law, so they vary from state to state. The only safe generalization is that the form and structure of business associations set by law are established in response to the most creative ideas entrepreneurs can dream up. In this chapter we provide an overview of the law of agency, partnerships, and related forms of business associations. The law applicable to the modern business corporation merits a separate chapter (Chapter 10).

Agency law legally binds a business (or anyone) to those with whom it contracts through an agent and those the agent injures in the course of business. Thus, in a major way, agency law forces a business association to be responsive to its business and social environment. Twenty to thirty years ago, the major areas of agency law study were the principles of apparent authority and respondeat superior, the primary legal principles that injured persons use to gain a remedy against a business association. Because these principles are still fundamental to an understanding of how the legal environment of business functions, we discuss them first.

Next, we explain the law of partnerships and related forms of business enterprises, such as the joint venture and the franchise. In the final portion of the chapter, we present the subjects within business association law that are most prominent today. These subjects, though technically involving agency law, apply to any partnership, business association, corporation, or employer-employee relationship. They are the legal and moral principles that outline the duties of a principal or employer to an agent and vice versa.

More specifically, we explore the legal and moral principles used to define a proper response when an employee's individual conscience conflicts with the collective conscience of others in the workplace. Most people in management work without an employment contract; they are called at-will employees because they work at the complete discretion of the employer. A vital question in the American workplace today is: under what circumstances may an employer fairly discharge an at-will employee?

Finally, we discuss the related issue of whistle-blowing. Under what circumstances may an employee go public with an insider's knowledge of alleged wrongdoing in the workplace? Issues in this area are both legal and moral in nature.

AGENCY LAW

An agency exists whenever one person voluntarily consents to act on behalf of another or under another's control. It is by far the most pervasive form of voluntary business organization and may exist for profit or nonprofit purposes. A student who leaves a dorm party to buy a keg of beer for the guests is an agent for the group sponsoring the party. When a properly authorized employee of IBM signs a contract to lease or sell a computer to a customer, the employee is an agent. When an authorized representative of the federal government signs a contract to purchase a ship for the U.S. Navy, the representative is an agent.

Agency law answers such questions as whether a third party can look to the dorm association for payment, whether IBM is required to make good on a warranty made by its agent to the customer, and whether the government is responsible for damages incurred in an automobile accident caused by its agent on the way to inspect the ship the Navy ordered.

Agency law applies to all types of business organizations and creates essentially two categories of legal duties. First, it defines the duties between the employer (or principal) and the employee (or agent). Second, it defines the relationship between the business organization, the employer, or the principal on the one hand and a third party, not a member of the organization or associated with the employer or principal, on the other. These duties of agency law are depicted in Figure 9.1, other duties may be defined by the laws creating the form of business organization such as corporation or partnership law.

Agency law is a large part of the total legal framework governing the employer-employee relationship. This law, created primarily by state judicial decisions, remains one of the most important bodies of law still based almost entirely on the common law. Because the common law varies from state to state, studies of agency law can be confusing. We have attempted to simplify the presentation of the most important agency rules by focusing on one widely recognized reference work, *The Restatement of Agency, 2nd*, referred to hereafter as the "Restatement."

FIGURE 9.1   *Agency Law as a Category of Employer-Employee Relationships*

Agency law defines
duties between all
these parties

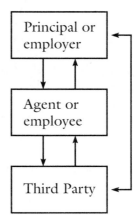

The Restatement was written by the legal practitioners, jurists, and scholars who comprise the American Law Institute (an organization founded in 1923 to promote the clarification and simplification of the law).

DEFINITION AND CREATION OF AN AGENCY RELATIONSHIP

Harvard Law Professor, Warren A. Seavey, provids a clear definition of agency. He stated: "Agency is a consensual relation between two persons, created by law by which one, the principal, has a right to control the conduct of the agent, and the agent has the power to affect the legal relations of the principal."[1] An agency relationship is a fiduciary one, which means it is based on a special trust that requires the agent to act in the best interests of the principal.

CREATION OF AGENCY BY CONTRACT

Most, but not all, agency relationships are created by contract. The best example of such a creation is one in which one person gives another a formal written document called a *power of attorney*. This document is given by the principal to the agent and confers on the agent the authority to perform certain specified kinds of acts for the principal. The primary purpose of a power of attorney is not so much to define the relationship between the principal and the agent, but rather to evidence the authority of the agent to third parties.

In addition to these formal contracts creating an agent relationship, in many circumstances courts will create or impose an agency relationship to protect the reasonable expectations of a third party who has relied on the agent. These circumstances are referred to as creation of an agency relationship by *ratification, by estoppel, or by operation of law.*

CREATION OF AGENCY BY RATIFICATION

Ratification is action by a principal that affirms a prior unauthorized act by an agent that did not bind the principal (when the act was done) but that was done for the purpose of advancing the principal's business. This action of ratification by the principal relates back to the unauthorized act so that the unauthorized act is then given effect as if originally authorized. For example, assume that Paul authorizes Angela to sell his car for him at an auction. Angela also takes along Paul's stereo, which she wrongly believes Paul would like to sell. Angela is not able to sell the car, but she does sell the stereo for less than it is worth. Paul is disappointed when he learns of the sale but accepts the money. Accepting the money is an act of ratification that relates back to the unauthorized sale and, for purposes of determining the liabilities of all the parties, authorizes it. Technically, if Paul wanted to, he could refuse the money and ask Angela for the full fair value of the stereo.

CREATION OF AGENCY BY ESTOPPEL

Estoppel is a doctrine we discussed in Chapter 8, on contract law. As applied to agency law, it creates an agency relationship between a principal and an agent when the principal intentionally or carelessly causes a third party to rely on representations by an agent that the agent is authorized to do a specific act. Or, stated a little differently, if a principal allows another to act on his or her behalf and a third party changes position (e.g., expends money or incurs a debt) relying on the act and on the belief that the act is authorized, then the principal cannot deny the consequences of the action. The principal is *estopped* from denying the consequences of his or her action.

One may be estopped because of a failure to act. For example, if Paul and Angela decide to go to an auction to sell Paul's stereo and if Paul is standing beside Angela when Angela tells Bob Buyer that she is authorized to sell it for $200, the law places a duty on Paul to speak up. If Angela is unauthorized to say that or if the sale price is $250, Paul must tell Bob. If he does not tell Bob and if Bob reasonably believes what he is told, then Paul will be estopped from denying the agency relationship.

An agency by estoppel cannot be created by an act of the agent alone. The principal must do something or place the agent in a position in which it reasonably appears the agent is acting in the principal's interest.

LIABILITY OF A PRINCIPAL TO A THIRD PARTY BECAUSE OF AN AGENT'S CONTRACTS

Another element of agency, in addition to the consent of the principal and agent, is the notion that the agent acts on behalf of the principal and is subject to this person's control. All partnerships, corporations, governmental units, and other business or nonbusiness organizations viewed as separate legal entities (separate from those who own or control them) must employ agents. Their function is to conduct business, which usually means making contracts. The central focus of this section is on the circumstances in which the agent can bind his or her principal to a third party with whom the agent purports to contract.

When an injured plaintiff alleges a breach of a contract entered into by an agent on behalf of the principal, courts seek to discern the authority that the principal gave to the agent. *The dominant rule is that courts will impose contract liability on a principal for the promises or representations made by an agent to a third party when the court finds the principal authorized the agent to make a promise.*

In most situations in which authority is an issue, the contract has been breached by either the third party or the principal and the legal issues are thus between these two parties. The agent usually drops out of the picture.

ACTUAL AUTHORITY—EXPRESS OR IMPLIED

Courts have defined two broad types of authority: actual authority (either express or implied) and circumstantial or apparent authority. *Express authority* is defined as that authority the principal gives either in writing or by spoken word to the agent when instructing the agent when and how to act on the principal's behalf. Express authority may take the form of a formal document, such as a *power of attorney*, which is a sworn statement in writing that another is to act for the principal on particular matters, or it may be manifested in less formal ways, such as a board of directors' resolution or a mere statement in an employment contract that the employee (agent) is to "sell the goods of the employer."

In a commercial transaction of any complexity at all, however, it is impossible for the principal to express all of the kinds of authority that may be needed by the agent to complete the transaction. Therefore, the law recognizes *implied authority*, which is that authority reasonably necessary to accomplish the act for which the express authority was given. Implied authority is found by examining the facts of the particular case, defining the express authority, and then asking whether a reasonable person familiar with the customs and ways of dealings of agents in the particular line of business could believe that the agent had the authority to act. The key difference between implied authority and the kinds of circumstantial authority described below is that the implied authority flows from the grant of express authority and must be reasonably necessary to accomplish the purpose of the express authority. If there is no express authority, there can be no implied authority, yet there may be circumstantial authority.

CIRCUMSTANTIAL OR APPARENT AUTHORITY

Circumstantial authority is authority that courts recognize and impose on an agency relationship even though there is no express or implied authority. Courts do this because the circumstances of the third party's dealing with the agent could reasonably lead a third party to believe that the agent was authorized. A key difference between actual and circumstantial authority is that the actual authority is defined by asking what measure of authority was really given to the agent by the principal, whereas circumstantial authority is defined by asking what measure of authority a third party could reasonably believe the agent to have under the circumstances.

The most comprehensive type of circumstantial authority is called *apparent authority*. Generally, a court must find two factual elements in order to conclude that the agent was apparently authorized. First, it must find that the principal, not the agent, created some of the circumstances leading the third party to believe the agent was authorized. Second, it must find that the third party reasonably relied on these circumstances. It makes no difference whether the principal has expressly forbidden the agent to act or has otherwise secretly placed restrictions on the agent's authority. If the court or jury can find these two basic factual elements, it is permitted to find that the agent's promise or conduct was apparently authorized.

Arkansas Poultry Federation Insurance Trust v. *Lawrence*
(805 S.W.2d 653, 1991)

RODGERS, JUDGE.

The insured, appellee Larry Lawrence, underwent a heart transplant on March 3, 1986. In 1978, Lawrence began working as a truck driver for Caldwell Milling Company . . . an egg production, grading and distribution operation. As a full-time employee, Lawrence was eligible for coverage, and was covered, under a group health insurance plan with appellant Arkansas Poultry Federation Insurance Trust (hereinafter "Trust"). In June of 1979, Lawrence stopped working for Caldwell Milling on a full-time basis, and resumed being an independent producer for the company as he had been before his employment. As a producer, Lawrence remained eligible for health insurance coverage with the Trust under a different plan, but his coverage was never formally converted. Nevertheless, Lawrence continued to pay premiums, and claims were submitted and accepted by the Trust on his behalf.

* * *

First, the Trust argues that the trial court erred in awarding judgment when Lawrence was not an eligible, covered employee pursuant to its written eligibility and termination provisions. Under the Trust's plan for employees, only full-time employees, those who work thirty hours a week, are eligible for coverage, and by its terms coverage terminates when this eligibility requirement is no longer met. Thus, the Trust argues that its coverage effectively terminated when Lawrence ceased full-time employment with Caldwell Milling in June of 1979. . . .

At trial, Lawrence testified that when he quit working for Caldwell Milling, he had a discussion with Reta Caldwell, the company bookkeeper, about continuing his coverage with the Trust. He said that it was his understanding that his coverage would remain in effect. He testified that the premiums for the insurance were deducted from the payments made to him by Caldwell Milling as a producer, and that he continued to submit claims to the Trust. There is documentation in the record reflecting the submission and payment of numerous claims on behalf of Lawrence and his family from 1981 through 1985.

Reta Caldwell testified that in her conversations with Lawrence, he indicated that he wanted to maintain the insurance by switching over to the producer plan without a gap in coverage. She called this a "unique" situation, as she had never done a change-over before. She said that normally, a producer requesting coverage would fill out a form proving insurability, but that she felt that this form would not apply since Lawrence was already insured. She stated that because she was unsure as to how to proceed, she called Fewell & Associates for instruction. She said that in this conversation she advised that Lawrence was no longer an employee, but that he wanted to continue coverage as a producer. Ms. Caldwell testified that the woman she spoke to on the phone told her to "leave it as it is for the time being." She said that she did what she was told, and had Lawrence fill out a form authorizing the company to withhold premiums from his earnings. She further testified that she never heard anything more from Fewell & Associates about the matter.

* * *

The trial court made the following written findings on this issue:

> The only real dispute as to any essential facts is whether or not Ms. Caldwell advised Arkansas Poultry Federation Insurance Trust of Mr. Lawrence's leaving Caldwell's employment at his request to continue his insurance coverage. The Court is of the conviction that the evidence preponderates the accuracy of her testimony on that fact. That testimony is supported by these facts: (1) Mr. Lawrence paid the entire premiums required for the following several years; (2) The claims paid subsequent to that notice are consistent with his family's continuing need for medical insurance coverage; . . .

* * *

[T]he Trust argues that Fewell & Associates, the third-party administrator, had no authority to bind it or to extend or modify the terms of the plan. In this respect the Trust contends that there was no direct communication between it and Lawrence, as principals, and that it cannot be bound by the actions and representations of Fewell & Associates. We disagree. A general agent is one who has authority to transact all business of the company of a particular kind and whose powers are coextensive to the business entrusted to its care. . . . Apparent authority in an agent is such authority as the principal knowingly permits the agent to assume or which he holds the agent out as possessing. It is such authority as he appears to have by reason of the actual authority which he has and such authority as a reasonably prudent man, using diligence and discretion, in view of the principal's conduct, would naturally suppose the agent to possess. . . . As stated in Appleman, *Insurance Law and Practice* §7230 (1981):

> Where an agent is furnished with indicia of authority by the insurer, it may be bound by his acts. Certainly such authority would seem to be present where the agent issues and delivers policies of the company. Where the evidence shows a holding out or apparent authority, the company is bound, if, in fact, he is an agent of the company.

Our law is well-settled that an agent acting within the apparent scope of his authority, even though in violation of actual authority, may bind his principal if the one with whom he deals does not have notice of these restrictions. . . . The record reflects that Fewell & Associates is entirely responsible for administering the Trust's plan. It drafts policies, accepts premiums, and furnishes claims forms, among other things, and the brochure directs all inquiries to it regarding claims and coverage. Although there is a procedure for appeal to the Trust, Fewell & Associates makes decisions concerning the denial and payment of claims. Furthermore, Ms. Caldwell testified that whenever she had questions about claims and procedures, she contacted Fewell & Associates for advice. It has been held that the employer is the employee's agent in connection with a group insurance policy. . . . The record as a whole suggests that Fewell & Associates is the general agent of the Trust, and has been clothed with either actual or

apparent authority in dealing with matters of the kind involved here. And, the knowledge of an agent of the insurer, obtained while performing the duties of his agency, is imputed to the insurer.

Affirmed in part, Reversed in part.

CASE FOLLOW-UP

We can be fairly sure that Larry Lawrence did not know much about agency law when he asked the bookkeeper for Caldwell Milling, Reta Caldwell, about continuing his insurance coverage. Yet, agency law is the legal vehicle that provides Lawrence with substantial help in this case. Many people do business through agents every day and are not aware of it.

The issue of whether Lawrence was covered by insurance is determined by the legal principle of authority. The judge asked, was Fewell & Associates authorized to make the insurance contract with Lawrence? The Trust argued that it was their expressed (written or otherwise stated) understanding with their agent (Fewell) that only full-time

employees who work thirty hours per week are eligible for coverage. Lawrence was not a full-time employee, so there was no expressed authority to make the insurance contract with him. But the circumstances of the case indicate that the Trust did put Fewell in the position to make it appear that Fewell was doing business for the Trust and that Lawrence reasonably relied on this. According to the court, above, Fewell was informed that Lawrence was not a full-time employee yet continued to accept premiums. Thus, the court held that Fewell's knowledge and the acceptance of the premiums bound the Trust. In short, Fewell had apparent authority to bind the principal.

CONTRACT LIABILITY OF THE AGENT

Regarding the liability of the agent, *the general rule is that if the existence of the principal is known to the third party at the time of the contract, the agent is not liable as a party to the contract.* This is true even though the agent signed the contract. The agent is liable on a contract with a third party if the agent made a personal promise to perform, signed a negotiable instrument without designating a principal, or misrepresented his or her authority. If the principal is undisclosed (not known) to the third party, the law assumes that the agent has personally promised to perform and therefore is liable for breach of the contract.

For example, if the Exxon Corporation hires Elena Ristov to negotiate and purchase a large tract of land for a new headquarters and the seller does not know of the Exxon-Ristov agency relationship, the seller may sue the agent, Ristov, if

Exxon breaches the agreement. Once the seller finds out about Exxon, it may sue either Ristov or Exxon. (And if the seller breaches, either Exxon or Ristov may sue the seller.)

TORT LIABILITY OF A PRINCIPAL AND AGENT TO THIRD PARTIES

In this part of the chapter, we explain the circumstances in which the principal will be liable for a tort (usually the tort of negligence) committed by the agent that injures a third party. As an introduction, we point out three rather simple propositions.

The first is that a person is always liable for his or her own torts. Thus, when an agent commits a tort and injures a third party, the agent can almost always be held liable.

The second is that principals are usually wealthier than agents, so it is advisable for the injured party to sue the principal. The chances of collecting the judgment are better than in a suit against the agent. If a third party injured by an agent recovers from the principal, the principal may seek reimbursement from the agent (but principals do this infrequently).

The third is that a principal may be liable to the third party if the principal was negligent in hiring someone who was not trained properly or was incompetent or if the principal entrusted tools to an agent who was unable to use them properly. Similarly, the principal will be liable for an agent's torts if the principal authorized the tort. Obviously, if a principal instructs an agent to engage in the torts of misrepresentation, fraud, or negligence, the principal is liable.

VICARIOUS LIABILITY OF PRINCIPALS

Vicarious liability is imposed on a person for the acts of another. The word *vicarious* means that which is experienced or endured for another. In agency law, vicarious liability of the principal for the acts of an agent (primarily acts involving a tort) is based on the doctrine of *respondeat superior*. These words mean "let the master answer." This is one of the most significant principles in all of agency law, and an understanding of it is crucial to knowing the legal environment of business.

Respondeat superior is applied under circumstances in which the principal is acting as a "master" and the agent is acting as a "servant." Although the origin of these terms dates from centuries past, they are still used in agency law and describe a set of circumstances in which the principal-master has the right to control the physical conduct of the agent-servant. The Restatement (Section 2) defines a master-servant relationship as a subclassification of the principal-agent relationship. More specifically, it provides these definitions:

1. A master is a principal who employees an agent to perform service in his or her affairs and who controls or has the right to control the physical conduct of the other in the performance of the service.

2. A servant is an agent employed by a master to perform service in his or her affairs whose physical conduct in the performance of the service is controlled or is subject to the right to control by the master.

The doctrine of respondeat superior creates vicarious liability of a principal by requiring that a master be liable for the torts of a servant committed while acting in the scope of employment. This doctrine does not relieve a servant of his or her liability because of the tortious conduct; rather, it makes the principal-master, as well as the agent-servant, liable.

Respondeat superior may initially seem to impose an unfair burden on the master. There are several reasons for the doctrine that may make it seem more fair, however. We will mention briefly six of these reasons.

1. If masters are held liable for the torts of their servants, they will be more apt to take precautions to prevent the circumstances that cause injury; they can change the patterns of commercial conduct or the sales routines or whatever set of circumstances may contribute to the tort.

2. In a similar way, because masters are held liable, they will be more careful in selecting servants to accomplish difficult and risky tasks.

3. Without this doctrine, the only way to prove a master liable is to prove the master's own negligence in hiring or training the servant. The task of proving such negligence places a difficult burden on an injured plaintiff, who must rely on the testimony of other servants of the master to prove the case; that is, accurate testimony in such cases is difficult to obtain from the other members of the master's organization.

4. A reason not frequently acknowledged by the courts is the "deep pockets" approach to justice: The master should pay because the master is probably wealthier than the servant, and the objective is to compensate the injured party.

5. A distinct but related idea is that the master seeks a profit through the servant's activities. Therefore, vicarious liability is simply another entrepreneurial risk that must be dealt with in the master's business plans.

6. A final reason applies most frequently today when a corporation or other business organization is a defendant. A corporation, as a practical matter, cannot operate unless it is through agents. The law recognizes the corporation as a legal entity apart from the owners and managers. The corporation is the principal; the employees who are authorized to deal with the public are its agents. It seems reasonable that because corporate owners and managers are given the privilege of doing business by using the corporation form, this form (which technically owns the assets) should pay for the tortious damage caused by its agents.

In the traditional application of respondeat superior, *courts focus on the central elements of control that the alleged master exercised over the servant.* The case of *Massey* v. *Tube Art Display, Inc.* is a modern illustration of this traditional application. If the required element of control is lacking, the employee or agent is termed an *independent contractor* by the law. The torts of independent contractors do not create vicarious liability for the principal.

Massey v. *Tube Art Display, Inc.*
551 P.2d 1387 (Wash. 1976)

SWANSON, JUSTICE

Tube Art Display, Inc. (Tube Art) appeals from a judgment entered on a jury verdict awarding $143,000 in damages to John Massey, doing business as Olympic Research & Design Associates (Massey).

The facts leading to the initiation of this action are not in substantial dispute. A recently opened branch office of McPherson's Realty Company desired to move a reader board sign from its previous location to a site adjacent to its new quarters in a combination commercial apartment building. An agreement was reached with Tube Art, the owner of the sign, to transport and reinstall it on the northwest corner of the building's parking lot. . . . Later, a Tube Art employee laid out the exact size and location for the excavation by marking a 4 by 4 foot square on the asphalt surface with yellow paint. The dimensions of the hole, including its depth of 6 feet, were indicated with spray paint inside the square. After the layout was painted on the asphalt, Tube Art engaged a backhoe operator, defendant Richard F. Redford, to dig the hole. In response to Tube Art's desire that the job be completed on the 16th of February, 1972, Redford began digging in the early evening hours at the location designated by Tube Art. At approximately 9:30 p.m. the bucket of Redford's backhoe struck a small natural gas pipeline. After examining the pipe and finding no indication of a break or leak, he concluded that the line was not in use and left the site. Shortly before 2 a.m. on the following morning, an explosion and fire occurred in the building serviced by that gas pipeline. As a result, two people in the building were killed and most of its contents were destroyed.

* * *

Traditionally, servants and non-servant agents have been looked upon as persons employed to perform services in the affairs of others under an express or implied agreement, and who, with respect to physical conduct in the performance of those services, is subject to the other's control or right of control.

An independent contractor, on the other hand, is generally defined as one who contracts to perform services for another, but who is not controlled by the other nor subject to the other's right to control with respect to his physical conduct in performing the services. In determining whether one acting for another is a servant or independent contractor, several factors must be taken into consideration. These are listed in Restatement (Second) of *Agency* § 220(2) (1958), as follows:

a. The extent of control which, by the agreement, the master may exercise over the details of the work;

b. whether or not the one employed is engaged in a distinct occupation or business;

c. the kind of occupation, with reference to whether, in the locality, the work is usually done under the direction of the employer or by a specialist without supervision;

d. the skill required in the particular occupation;

e. whether the employer or the workman supplies the instrumentalities, tools, and the place of work for the person doing the work;

f. the length of time for which the person is employed;

g. the method of payment, whether by the time or by the job;

h. whether or not the work is a part of the regular business of the employer;

i. whether or not the parties believe they are creating the relation of master and servant; and

j. whether the principal is or is not in business.

All of these factors are of varying importance in determining the type of relationship involved and, with the exception of the element of control, not all the elements need be present. It is the right to control another's physical conduct that is the essential and often times decisive factor in establishing vicarious liability whether the person controlled is a servant or a nonservant agent.

In discussing the actual extent to which the element of control must be exercised, we pointed out in *Jackson* v. *Standard Oil Co.,* 8 Wash. App. 83, 505 P.2d 139 (1972), that the plaintiff need not show that the principal controlled or had the right to control every aspect of the agent's operation in order to incur vicarious liability. Rather,

> [i]t should be sufficient that plaintiff present substantial evidence of . . . control or right of control over those activities from whence the actionable negligence flowed. . . .
>
> In this regard, it may be emphasized that it is not de facto control nor actual exercise of a right to interfere with or direct the work which constitutes the test, but rather, the *right to control* the negligent actor's physical condition in the performance of the service.

In making his ruling that Tube Art was responsible as a matter of law for Redford's actions the trail judge stated,

> I think that under the undisputed evidence in this case they not only had the right to control but they did control. They controlled the location of the spot to dig. They controlled the dimensions. They controlled the excavation and they got the building permits. They did all the discretionary work that was necessary before he started to operate. They knew that the method of excavation was going to be by use of a backhoe rather than a pick and shovel which might

have made a little difference on the exposure in this situation. They in effect created the whole atmosphere in which he worked. And the tact that even though he did not work for them all the time and they paid him on a piecework basis or the individual job didn't impress me particularly when they used him the number of times they did. Most of the time they used him for this type of work. So I am holding as a matter of law that Redford's activities are the responsibility of Tube Art.

Our review of the evidence supports the trial court's evaluation of both the right and exercise of control even though Redford had been essentially self-employed for about 5 years at the time of trial, was free to work for other contractors, selected the time of day to perform the work assigned, paid his own income and business taxes and did not participate in any of Tube Art's employee programs. The testimony advanced at trial, which we find determinative, established that during the previous 3 years Redford had worked exclusively for sign companies and 90 percent of his time for Tube Art. He had no employees, was not registered as a contractor or subcontractor, was not bonded, did not himself obtain permits or licenses for his jobs, and dug the holes at locations and in dimensions in exact accordance with the instructions of his employer. In fact, Redford was left no discretion with regard to the placement of the excavations that he dug. Rather, it was his skill in digging holes pursuant to the exact dimensions prescribed that caused him to be preferred over other backhoe operators. We therefore find no disputed evidence of the essential factor—the right to control, nor is there any dispute that control was exercised over the most significant decisions—the size and location of the hole. Consequently, only one conclusion could reasonably be drawn from the facts presented. In such a circumstance, the nature of the relationship becomes a question of law. We find no error.

CASE FOLLOW-UP

Why did the plaintiff want to sue Tube Art? Of course, the plaintiff could sue the servant-agent, Redford, who caused the damage because one is always liable for the tort damage one causes. But in this case, the master-employer was also sued because, the chances are, the master has more resources than the agent. If you recover a judgment against a person or corporation that has no resources, then you will never be paid. You have what is called an *uncollectible judgment*.

A judgment is usually paid in cash. As a plaintiff, you will always search for the most prosperous likely defendant. Agency law, through the use of the doctrine of respondeat superior, makes employers legally liable for the negligent acts of their servant-employees.

Independent Contractors. In *Massey v. Tube Art Display, Inc.*, the court uses the words *independent contractor*. An independent contractor is defined by the Restatement (Section 2) as a person who contracts with another to do something but who is not controlled by the other or subject to the other's right to control with respect for the physical conduct of the undertaking. For example, assume you wanted to plant a large tree in your front yard and called a person who advertised in the yellow pages under Excavation. You learned that this person had a backhoe and that he would plant your tree. If, when he arrived, you told him to plant the tree about in the middle of the front yard but exerted no control over him except to give him very general directions, then this backhoe operator would be an independent contractor. The same would be true if you called a plumber and said, "Fix my water heater." *Independent contractors do not create vicarious liability for their principals when they commit a tort in the operation of the task for which they were hired.*

In our explanation of the vicarious liability of principals, so far we have two categories of relationships: (1) If the right to control the agent is substantial, the relationship may be classified as a master-servant relationship and the torts of the servant that injure another do create liability for the master and (2) If there is no control, the torts of an independent contractor do not create liability. Between these two extremes is a third category of principal-agent relationship recognized by the Restatement: a principal-nonservant agent.

Nonservant Agents. Today's increasingly service-oriented economy has many nonservant agents. An accounting firm, for example, is usually owned and controlled by partners. Much of the work is done by employees/agents who, when they conduct an audit, for example, travel to a client's business. Using a car or some other form of transportation is necessary to the performance of the job, but in the operation of their cars the agents are not controlled by the partnership and therefore are not servants. They do conduct audits however, and in some instances these audits may be done negligently, and damage to third parties may result. Should an accounting firm be liable for the negligent performance of an audit done by one of the firm's employees? The law answers yes and achieves this result by classifying such an agent as a *nonservant agent*. A nonservant agent is hired to achieve a type of nonphysical result, such as accounting, selling insurance, and contracting for other services. The general rule applicable to this category of agency is that *nonservant agents create tort liability for their principals when they commit a tort within the area of endeavor for which they were hired*. Stated more simply, *a nonservant agent creates tort liability for a principal when the tort was committed within the inherent scope of the employment*.

The torts usually committed by nonservant agents are negligent performance of a specific task, misrepresentation, fraud, and deceit. The commission of these torts must be closely related to the work of the nonservant agent. The difference in the liability created by this type of agent and a servant is that the latter may create liability for an action that is only incidentally related to the work. A closely supervised trainee at a construction site, for example, will create liability for the principal if he or she negligently starts a fire while cooking his or her lunch at the site.

SUMMARY OF THE VICARIOUS LIABILITY OF PRINCIPALS

The classifications of master-servant, independent contractor, and nonservant agent are conceptual generalities, and sometimes the application of these generally stated principles can be difficult. Do not think of the term *servant* as denoting an agent who does only menial or manual work. Many servants perform work requiring brains, rather than brawn. Corporate officers, highly skilled engineers, interns in hospitals, and most other employees who are employed to achieve a physical result and to give their time, rather than their product, to their employers may be servants. Moreover, it may be possible for one person to be an independent contractor for some tasks and a servant for others.

To resolve complex issues in this area, first look for a precise definition of the conduct of work being performed for the principal at the time of the tortious conduct. Second, confine your focus to this circumstance and ask, What was the purpose of the agency, and what degree of control was exercised or capable of being exercised by the principal over the physical conduct of the agent? If the purpose of the agency was to achieve a physical result and if there was a high degree of control over the physical conduct of the agent, a master-servant relationship might exist. Adopting an ironclad rule in this matter is impossible. Definitions of the scope of the agency relationship and matters of control are presented in terms of degrees. An agency relationship and a principal's control are dynamic, always changing. It might be best to think of control on a scale on which the legal result varies as the control varies (see Figure 9.2).

AGENCY TERMINATION

The agency relationship may be terminated by consent or renunciation by either the principal or the agent, or termination may be inferred from events. When we

FIGURE 9.2 *Types of Agents and Liability of Principals*

Types of Agents		
Independent Contractor	*Nonservant*	*Servant*
Independent contractor (I/C) works for another using own skill and judgment	Nonservant agent works for employer doing nonphysical work; for example, an abstract or legal result is contemplated (e.g., salesperson, accountant, insurance agent, stock broker)	Servant is one whose physical conduct is controlled by or whose physical conduct may be controlled by an employer-master
Legal Results		
No right of control over physical conduct—employer not liable for torts of I/C	May be minimum right of control over physical conduct. Principal not liable for torts of nonservant agent unless tort was within inherent scope of employment	Master has the right of full control over the physical conduct of the servant; principal-master is liable for torts of servant within the inherent scope of the agency and those activities incidental to it

_____ *Increasing Right to Control the Agent's Physical Conduct* ⟶

use the term *termination*, we are speaking of an end to the agency relationship, which usually involves two phases. The first is the end of the legal relationship between the principal and agent. The second is the end of the agent's authority as perceived by others—third parties and potential third parties. A former agent may be cloaked with apparent authority even after the agency has ended in the eyes of the principal.

TERMINATION BY CONSENT

The mutual legal duties between the principal and the agent may be terminated by mutual consent at any time or in accordance with the terms of their agreement (which may include the completion of the authorized task). If no specific task is identified or if no time limit is set, the relationship ends when the agent should know that the principal no longer desires action.

An agency relationship may end by the expression of either party before the date set in a contract, but this expression might not relieve the parties of contractual liability. For example, a board of directors may contract with *A* for service as president of the corporation for a period of three years. State statutes usually provide that corporate officers may be removed at will by the board. The board then may discharge *A* as president at any time, but may be required to pay damages for the breach of the three year contract.

TERMINATION OF EVENTS

Generally, any event that would cause the agent to reasonably believe the principal would no longer wish the agent to act will cause a termination of the agency. Some common events are loss of capacity of the principal, impossibility of performance, death of either party, destruction of the subject matter, and declarations of bankruptcy or illegality.

Capacity as used here refers to the legal capacity to conduct business transactions or contracts. Capacity is defined by state statute, and usually all persons of sound mind and over eighteen years of age have the capacity to contract. A formal declaration of either insanity or death terminates the principal's capacity to contract, thus terminating the agent's capacity to act for the principal.

TERMINATION OF THE AGENT'S AUTHORITY AS PERCEIVED BY THIRD PARTIES

Apparent authority was created by the common law to protect the reasonable expectations of those dealing with agents. This authority is generally not terminated when the formal actual authority between principal and agent is terminated. *The general rule is that the agent's apparent authority continues until the third party knows or has reason to know of the termination.* The Restatement (Section 134) takes the position that death or incapacity of the principal and declared illegality of the agency relationship are events of such notoriety that it will be inferred that all third parties have notice of the event. Thus, if the death or incapacity of a principal terminates the agency relationship and the agent subsequently contracts with a third party for the benefit of the principal and if neither the agent nor the third party has actual knowledge of the death or incapacity, the contract cannot be enforced against the principal.

If the agency is not terminated by death, incapacity, or illegality, the principal is required to notify third parties of the termination of the agent's authority in order to be relieved of liability for an agent's action. In this case, the principal must proceed to give notice in one of two ways.

A third party who has contracted with or begun to contract with an agent on the basis of the agent's apparent authority must be given actual notice of termination of the agent's authority. This is notice given to the third party personally or mailed to the party's business or posted in a place where, in view of the business customs between the parties, the third party could reasonably be expected to look for such a notice.

With respect to those persons with whom the agent has not dealt prior to the termination of authority, notice of the agent's termination of apparent authority may be given by advertising the fact in a newspaper of general circulation in the place where the agency operates or by some other manner reasonably calculated to give notice to such third parties.

If a third party who has dealt with an agent on the basis of apparent authority does not receive actual notice of the agency termination and enters into a contract with the agent for the apparent benefit of the principal after the actual authority is terminated, the principal is bound to the third party.

PROPRIETORSHIPS

A *proprietorship* is a business organization controlled by one individual who owns all or most of the business property and who may hire employees to act as agents. The advantage of this form is its simplicity. There are about ten times as many proprietorships as partnerships and about five times as many proprietorships as corporations, although proprietorships account for only about one-tenth of the volume of business of all corporations. Figure 9.3 is a summary of the differences among the three dominant types of business enterprises in the United States. The laws of proprietorships and partnerships are discussed in this chapter; the law of corporations is discussed in Chapter 10.

The business liability of the proprietor cannot be separated from his or her other types of personal liability. The business assets and liabilities of the proprietorship are one and the same with the proprietor's nonbusiness or personal assets and liabilities.

One disadvantage of this form of organization is that the ability to raise capital is limited to the reputation and net worth of the proprietor. In some cases, especially when one is beginning a business, this may be a substantial limiting factor.

The proprietorship as a form of organization suffers the same fate as the owner. It stops or is incapacitated (legally) if the proprietor dies or suffers incapacity.

PARTNERSHIPS

A *partnership* is an organization of two or more persons to carry on as co-owners a business for profit. Individuals form partnerships when they wish to share the management, profits, and ownership of an enterprise for profit. In some instances where these aspects of co-ownership are intended but the partnership form was not specifically contemplated, courts will nevertheless impose the partnership form on individuals.

Partnerships are created by the contractual understanding, expressed or implied, of the partners. The usual process involves the drafting of written "articles of partnership" agreed to by all partners, although a partnership can be created without a written contract.

Although some authorities disagree on whether a partnership is a separate legal entity apart from the owners, we believe the best view is that it is separate for some purposes. A partnership contracts in its own name, holds the title to assets in its own name, can be sued in its own name, and files with the IRS in its own name. The Uniform Partnership Act (UPA), adopted by most states, does not expressly state that a partnership is a separate legal entity but treats it as one for special circumstances.

CHARACTERISTICS OF PARTNERSHIPS

A key distinction between a proprietorship and a partnership is that, under usual circumstances, every partner has an equal say in how the business is run. This

FIGURE 9.3   *Comparative Legal Aspects of Business Organizations*

	Proprietorship	Partnership	Corporation
Legal basis	Common law	Express contract of owners consistent with UPA or contract implied in law by courts	State statute
Legal entity	Not separate from owner	Separate from owner for some purposes	Separate legal person
Owner's liability	Owner liable for all debts	General partner(s) liable for all debts; limited partner liable for amounts contributed	Owners liable only to the extent of paid-in capital
Length of life	Same as owner	Agreed to by partners (usually life of any partner)	Perpetual
Management control	By owner directly	By majority vote of partners—owners manage	By vote of board of directors elected by owners—owners do not manage
Capital	Limited to what the single owner can raise	Limited to what partners can raise—may necessitate a new partner, thus a new partnership	Sale of more ownership shares
Federal income taxes	Profits taxed to owner as individual	Profits taxed proportionately to each owner as agreed in contract, or all share equally	Profits of corporation taxed to corporation—owners pay income tax on dividends
Complexity of creation/operation	Simplest; no agreement with other individuals or filings with state required unless doing business under a name other than owner's name	Should have partnership agreement and must file partnership name if name is other than those of partners	Numerous filings required, and formalities of organization imposed by state stature must be followed

shared control of the firm is accomplished without regard to how the profits are to be divided. For example, the partnership agreement may provide that *A* is to contribute 75 percent of the capital and receive 75 percent of the profits, whereas *B*'s share of both is 25 percent. But each will have an equal say in the management of the firm unless the partners expressly agree otherwise.

In a partnership, each partner is liable personally for any and all debts of the partnership acting as a business entity. That is, for the purposes of paying off those who obtain a court judgment against the partnership, the owner-partner cannot separate his or her own individual assets from those of the partnership. The partner cannot limit liability for partnership obligations to partnership assets alone. This liability is a chief distinction between corporations and partnerships; owners of corporations are able to limit their liability. This means that judgment creditors of the corporation must be paid from the corporation's assets, not from the owner's assets.

Another contrast between the partnership and the corporation is the limited life of a partnership and the perpetual life of the corporation. Any time a partner dies, is incapacitated, or voluntarily leaves the partnership, the old partnership is dissolved. Any time a new partner joins, the old partnership is dissolved and a new partnership is created unless the partnership agreement provides for the continuation of the business. Also, the ability and opportunities to raise capital are not as diverse as in a corporation because, in a partnership, this ability rests solely on the financial resources of the partners.

The advantages of a partnership are its simplicity in creation and the democratic methods it offers in operation. It allows, for example, one partner to contribute cash, one to contribute technical know-how, and another to contribute manual work, and then all three to share equally their profits and management of the partnership. Also a partner's income is taxed only once; the dividends of owners of corporations are taxed twice.

ADDITIONAL FEATURES OF A PARTNERSHIP

Partnerships and Agency Law. Partnership law, like corporation law, is specialized. We emphasize here some of the very basic and general rules. A fundamental of partnership law is that all partners are agents of the partnership for purposes of its business. The action of a partner that carries on business in the usual way binds the partnership. This means that all of the agency principles you learned about in the first part of this chapter apply to a partnership. In most cases, the partnership is the principal and the partner or other employee is the agent. If, for example, a partner is authorized to contract for a partnership (*authorized* in this context means the presence of either actual or apparent authority) and if the partner signs a contract with a third party, the partnership is bound by it.

The tort liability of a partnership is a bit more complicated to explain than its contract liability. *The general rule is that a partnership is liable for the torts of a partner (or agent) committed within the ordinary course of partnership business.* The ideas found in the agency concept of respondeat superior are applied in determining the liability of the partnership. If there is close control over the physical activity of a partner, then torts of the partner will create liability for the partnership.

In many cases of tort liability of a partnership, the partner committing the tort will probably be seen as a nonservant agent of the partnership. Thus, the negligent partner would create tort liability for the partnership only when he or she was negligent within the inherent scope of the partnership business. For example, negligence on the part of a partner in a CPA firm in the operation of his or her auto on the way to work would not create partnership liability, whereas the negligent conduct of an audit would. The one injured by the tort of a partner may elect to sue the partner who caused the tort, the partnership, or both. Consider the following case.

Meyer v. *Park South Associates*
552 N.Y.S.2d 614 (A.D. 1 Dept. 1990)

This action arises from a long-standing landlord-tenant dispute between the parties. The plaintiffs and their family are residents of five apartments at 100 Central Park South, a building owned by defendant Park South Associates. The individual defendant, Donald Trump, is a general partner of Park South, which is a limited partnership of Park South. The . . . complaint asserts four causes of action against both defendants. The first cause of action seeks injunctive relief to stay termination of the lease. The second cause of action alleges a breach of the warranty of habitability. The third cause of action seeks money damages for a long-term campaign of harassment and the last cause of action . . . seeks attorneys fees. The individual defendant, Trump, moved to dismiss the complaint against him on the ground that the partnership is the sole landlord of the building and, therefore, no action in this landlord-tenant dispute lies against him individually merely because he is a partner. The . . . Court (below) denied the motion in its entirety, finding that the complaint contained legally sufficient allegations that Trump's individual actions caused plaintiffs' emotional distress and constituted the harassment alleged in the complaint.

We find that the . . . Court (below) correctly determined that the complaint alleges sufficient acts by the individual defendant to sustain the charges against him. However,

these allegations pertain only to the third cause of action alleging "harassment," or intentional infliction of emotional distress, and not to the remaining causes of action in the complaint. No cause of action lies against an individual partner for violation of a lease by the partnership, absent an allegation that the partnership is insolvent or otherwise unable to pay its obligations. Here, the first cause of action seeks injunctive relief regarding a dispute concerning the lease, the second cause of action alleges a breach of the warranty of habitability by the landlord and the (last) cause of action seeks attorneys fees predicated on the contractual provisions in the lease regarding payment of attorneys fees. Since all of these causes of action arise out of the lease and the business activities of the partnership-landlord, they cannot lie against a partner individually and they should be dismissed as to defendant Trump. In distinction, the third cause of action alleges tortious conduct by the defendant (Trump) reciting a litany of charges of abuse, and sufficiently pleads a cause of action in tort for intentional infliction of emotional distress. . . . An individual partner is liable for a tortious action committed by the partnership, and an action may be brought against him in his individual capacity. Accordingly, the third cause of action should stand as against the individual defendant Trump.

CASE FOLLOW-UP

The tort alleged against Trump in this case requires that the element of intent be proved. Usually, intentional torts and crimes of partners do not create liability for the partnership (but, of course, do create liability for the partner who caused the injury). In a few cases, though, the partnership may be liable. In these cases, the tort is closely related to the conduct of the business. In this case, the court did not decide this issue but held that Trump could be sued for his own tortious conduct.

This case does have some complicating factors, however. The partnership here is a limited partnership. This means that some of the partners will have their liability limited to the amount of money they have paid into the partnership.

When a tort is committed within the ordinary course of partnership business, then an injured party may sue the partnership. If the judgment is against the partnership and payment is made, then the partner who caused the tort may be liable to the partnership for the amount of the judgment. As in this case,

the roundabout means of collecting from the partner who caused the injury may be shortened by just suing the partner who is liable. In many cases, an injured third party sues both the general partnership and appropriate general partners as individuals.

A related proposition is that a partner is a fiduciary of the partnership and to the other partners. This situation places on the partners the same duties placed on an agent to act at all times in the best interests of the partnership.

A major difference between agency law and partnership law is that much of the law applicable to partnerships is statutory law. The Uniform Partnership Act (UPA), a product of the National Conference of Commissioners on Uniform State Laws, has been adopted by most states. This organization is a body of well-known lawyers, judges, and law professors who meet yearly to draft and make available for adoption by the various state legislatures uniform laws covering a wide variety of topics. In some areas of the law, such as partnership law, uniformity in law among the states is desirable.

Partnership Property and a Partner's Interest in the Partnership. Once the partnership has been formed, a partner has certain rights in the partnership and its property that are unique features of a partnership. The manner in which the UPA characterizes a partner's rights in specific partnership property may be new to you. Generally, a partner has no "individual" right to specific partnership property. A partner has only an equal right shared with other partners to possess such property for the purpose of carrying out the partnership business. That is, once the partner's capital has been committed to the enterprise, the right to repossess or control it to the exclusion of others is lost unless the partner wishes to dissolve the partnership.

This form of ownership is not unique; it exists whenever persons jointly own property. Perhaps your home is jointly owned by you and your spouse, or perhaps your parents jointly own a home. The owners have an equal right to possess all of the property; no specific portion may be appropriated by any one of the owners. The same is true of partnership property. This duty to share partnership property and the right to possess partnership property for partnership purposes cannot be sold or given to someone else without the consent of all other partners, nor may an individual creditor of a partner seize this "right."

A Partner's Interest in the Partnership. Another classification of partnership rights is a partner's interest in the partnership. A partner's interest in the partnership is his or her share of the profits. This right to an interest in profits is a property right that can be assigned (sold or given to someone else) by the partner and is subject to a court order directing the partner to pay it to an individual judgment creditor.

A Partner's Right to Manage. A partner also has the right to participate in the management of the partnership. Some items of management may be delegated in the partnership agreement to specific partners. If not, and if differences arise as to the ordinary matters connected with the partnership business, the matter will be settled by a majority vote of the partners. Any act in violation of the partnership agreement, however, must have the consent of all partners. This right to vote is given to a partner regardless of the type or amount of the capital contribution to the partnership.

DISSOLUTION OF THE PARTNERSHIP

Because a partnership is a voluntary business association, it is dissolved (in a technical sense) when any partner wishes to withdraw or when a partner is incapacitated or dies. The other partners may elect to continue if the partnership agreement provides for them to do so, or they may form what amounts to a new partnership. The one leaving the partnership has his or her interest in the partnership valued and is paid the appropriate amount. Valuing a partner's interest on dissolution is a very important matter; a process for this valuation should be agreed on when the partnership is formed. If it is not agreed on, the UPA provides a method that can be used.

PROFESSIONAL PARTNERSHIPS—LIMITATION OF PARTNER LIABILITY

The past ten to fifteen years have seen a great increase in the judgments for negligence (or malpractice) against professional partnerships of accountants, lawyers, architects, and doctors. In 1991, the total damage awards against accountants and attorneys was close to $1 billion; and in May 1992, the prestigious accounting firm of Price Waterhouse was ordered to pay a record $338 million negligence award. If the judgment stands, it may put the accounting firm and many of its 950 partners into bankruptcy. It is estimated that there are about three thousand suits currently against accounting firms, alleging malpractice damage totaling about $10 billion.[2]

This increase has prompted three responses. First, many partnerships have been seeking insurance to cover malpractice, and many judgments are paid by insurance companies. Thus, professional malpractice insurance premiums have increased enormously. Second, many partnerships have been much more careful about the kinds of clients they accept and the types of professional advice they give. Third, a legislative limitation of damage awards has been sought.

If malpractice is proved, the partner who is negligent may be sued, and so may the partnership. If a judgment is made against the partnership, then partnership assets may be used first to satisfy the judgment. If the judgment is larger in amount than the value of partnership assets, then individual partners must pay out of their own pockets to satisfy the judgments. Professional partnerships are now arguing that it is unfair for partners who have no knowledge of the malpractice to go broke, personally, to pay a judgment caused by another partner. The reaction, so far, in state legislatures is mixed. Thirteen states, including Florida, Virginia, and Texas, have adopted legislation limiting the liability of partners in some cases for the malpractice of other partners.[3]

JOINT VENTURES

A joint venture, or joint adventure as it is sometimes called, is usually a form of partnership. It differs from general partnerships in that it has a narrower purpose. Usually, a joint venture is formed for a single undertaking or a series of related undertakings of fairly short duration that might not involve the complete attention of the members.

It is common for large corporations to explore new markets or ideas by forming joint ventures with other organizations that may provide expertise, capital, access to markets, or similar advantages. Such a venture may be accomplished by forming a jointly owned subsidiary that is incorporated. If the venture is risky, this method has the advantage of limiting the liability of the co-venturers to the amount of capital contributed to the subsidiary.

This method has the disadvantage of creating the potential for a breach of the fiduciary relationship that exists between co-venturers. The same fiduciary duties that apply to partnerships also apply to co-venturers, including the duty to render true and full information. If the co-venturers are engaged in similar business activities, first, the potential exists for an antitrust violation (Section 1 of the Sherman Act prohibits combinations and conspiracies—by competitors—that could be restraints of trade). Second, the nature of the joint venture would probably cause the co-venturers to have to choose between breaching the duty to disclose or disclosing trade secrets or related information in order to achieve the purposes of the joint enterprise. The matter of disclosure of information should be raised to the level of explicit understanding in the joint venture agreement.

For example, General Motors, Ford, and Chrysler all have joint venture agreements with various foreign automobile manufacturers, and it is reported that General Motors is teaming with Chrysler to manufacture car and truck transmissions. This reported joint venture will consolidate 4,100 GM and Chrysler employees in a Chrysler plant in Syracuse. Because these firms are major competitors, they should be very explicit about the kinds of information they share. One risk is that the information they share in this venture might damage their competitive positions. A second risk is that if Ford, for example, believes the GM–Chrysler joint venture is illegal, Ford may sue under an appropriate provision of the anti-trust laws. Despite these risks, corporations continue to form large joint ventures at a brisk pace.

LIMITED PARTNERSHIPS

A limited partnership, in contrast to a joint venture and partnership, is a distinctly different form of organization. The chief distinguishing features are in the formation and the nature of the liability of the limited partner. Limited partnerships, like corporations, can exist only where state legislatures have passed statutes providing for their formation. For this purpose, the National Conference of Commissioners on Uniform State Laws drafted the Revised Uniform Limited Partnership Act (RULPA), which states that a limited partnership must have at least one general partner (who controls the business) and one or more limited partners. It also states that a limited partner shall not be liable to firm creditors, as is a general partner, unless the limited partner takes part in the control of the business. That is, a limited partner is not liable beyond the amount of the contribution or the amount promised to the firm. The "limited" aspect of the partnership applies to the liability and participation of the limited partner.

This idea of limited liability is so important that we consider a few examples. Assume that four people (*A*, *B*, *C*, and *D*) wish to do business together and that they want to co-own the assets and share the profits. Assume that they form the *ABCD* general partnership. Further assume that, on behalf of this partnership, *A* signs a contract with *X*. The partnership has $20,000 in assets. *ABCD* breaches its contract with *X*, and *X* obtains a judgment of $35,000 against the partnership for damages suffered as a result of the breach. Issues of insurance and a possible bankruptcy filing aside, partnership law would require *ABCD* to pay the value of the assets ($20,000), and the remaining $15,000 would have to be paid by the partners. *General partners do not have limited liability for firm debts.*

However, *A*, *B*, *C*, and *D* could form a limited partnership with, for example, *A* as the general partner and *B*, *C*, and *D* as the limited partners, but *B*, *C*, and *D* would have to give up control in the partnership and become mere investors. In this instance, the liability of *B*, *C*, and *D* on a $35,000 judgment would be limited to the amounts they had contributed or promised to contribute to the firm. *A* would have no such limited liability and would have to pay the judgment to the extent that the firm assets would not cover it.

LIMITED PARTNERSHIPS WITH CORPORATE GENERAL PARTNERS

It is possible to combine the various forms of business organizations. One popular form of business organization used by entrepreneurs for medium-sized, rather risky ventures is the limited partnership form with a corporation as a general partner. In our example discussed above, *A*, *B*, *C*, and *D* could form a limited partnership—*Z Ltd.*,—with *Z* Corporation as the general partner. *A*, *B*, *C*, and *D*, would incorporate *Z*, sit on its board of directors, and be its various officers. *A*, *B*, *C*, and *D*, through *Z*, could control the limited partnership of *Z Ltd.* (see Figure 9.4). If a liability in excess of the net worth of *Z Ltd.* were to occur, the corporation would be liable as the general partner. Those involved with a corporate general partner may limit their liability. The liability of the shareholders of a corporation is limited to the amount they have paid into the corporation or have promised to pay in. In many states, it is possible to incorporate and begin business with as little as $1,000 paid in capital. So, the liability of *A*, *B*, *C*, and *D* would be limited to whatever they had paid into the limited partnership plus what they had paid into the corporation.

The advantages of this relatively new form of business organization are that the individual liability of the members of the corporate general partners is limited and that the double taxation of corporations (tax on corporate income and on dividends paid to the shareholders) is avoided. The disadvantage of this form is that the control exercised by *A*, *B*, *C*, and *D* through *Z* may violate the intent of the RULPA and its revisions. This is because, as individuals, *A*, *B*, *C*, and *D* are limited partners, but as shareholders and officers in *Z*, they can exercise some management control. State courts have viewed this new form in very different ways, and it is difficult to generalize about whether the form of business association will protect all investors. Some states allow the judgment creditors of *Z Ltd.* to sue limited partners if they have used a corporate general partner in very risky ventures.

FIGURE 9.4 *Corporate General Partner in a Limited Partnership*

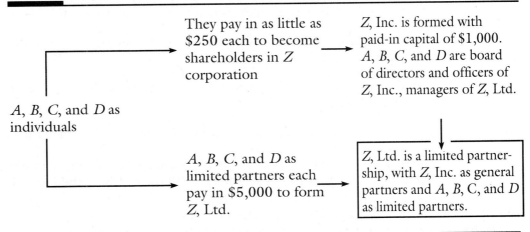

COOPERATIVES

The cooperative form of organization combines the democratic management aspects of a partnership with some advantages of a corporation. Cooperatives are being popularized at both ends of the economic spectrum. Large land developers are concentrating much of their resources into the construction of cooperative apartment buildings (and the related legal form, the condominium), and smaller organizations are forming food and consumer cooperatives. These enterprises have at least two things in common that cause them to be classified as cooperatives. First, they are organized primarily to provide the members (not the public) with an economic benefit or service; second, each member, usually an individual, has one vote in the management of the enterprise, which results in substantial equality of ownership.

In addition to these two general characteristics, a cooperative may make a profit, but that is not its primary purpose. The members usually expect no monetary return for putting their money into a cooperative. What they expect is to enjoy whatever nonmonetary but economically useful benefits the organization provides. The emphasis on *economically useful* benefits for members distinguishes the cooperative from charitable, religious, educational, or political organizations.

Generalizations about this form of organization should be attempted with caution, but the following have been suggested as some characteristics of a cooperative.[4]

1. Control and ownership are democratic. Each member has one vote.

2. Members are limited to those who avail themselves of the services furnished by the cooperative.

3. Transfer of membership is prohibited or limited.

4. Capital investment receives either no return or a limited return.

5. Economic benefits pass to members on a substantially equal basis.

6. Members are not personally liable for obligations of the organization unless they agree to such liability.

7. Death, bankruptcy, or withdrawal of one or more of the members does not terminate the organization.

8. Services of the organization are furnished primarily for the use of the members.

Cooperatives are not a new form of organization. Rural communities have been served by cooperatives since the early 1900s, with first the formation of marketing cooperatives to sell farmers' produce and later, the development of rural electrification cooperatives to furnish electricity.

Cooperatives may be either incorporated or unincorporated organizations. With the exception of labor unions (which have generally remained unincorporated because they prefer no regulation from the state), most cooperatives do incorporate. Because the management of the cooperative is conducted by a vote of the members and not by a board of directors, the enterprise is not managed like the typical corporation. This difference in management is allowed in almost all states by the existence of special cooperative statutes that provide for the incorporation and operation of cooperatives.

FRANCHISES

A franchise is a popular business organization device that may exist as a corporation, a partnership, or a proprietorship. It is like a cooperative in that it is a form of organization that exists on top of an underlying corporate or partnership form.

Individuals who drive down the street in an automobile purchased from a General Motors dealer, fill their cars' gasoline tanks at the corner Texaco station, have lunch at McDonalds, work at a Pepsi-Cola bottling plant, live in a home purchased through a Century 21 real estate broker, and sleep in a Holiday Inn while vacationing have dealt extensively with franchises.

The franchisor develops a concept or a product, the use of which is licensed to the franchisee. The franchisor protects that concept or product by contractual agreement with the franchisee or through the patent, copyright, or trademark law. The franchisee acquires the right to exploit the franchisor's idea by signing a franchise agreement. The franchisee is a legally separate entity from the franchisor. Each party is free to choose the form of business enterprise under which he or she wishes to operate each respective entity.

Most franchises are regulated by a Federal Trade Commission rule or state statute or both. The basic thrust of these rules is to require the franchisor to make full and fair disclosure concerning the terms of the franchising agreement. Violations may result in the imposition of fines or damage suits or both.

To protect their reputations, most franchisors exert tight control over the activities of their franchisees. A franchisor who spends substantial advertising dollars wants to ensure that the public will recognize the franchise in both physical appearance and the quality of the products offered. Restrictions placed on the franchisee in this regard will raise antitrust problems unless it can be shown that the restrictions are reasonable and related to quality control. For example, the requirement that a franchisee of a fast-food chicken outlet purchase its cooking equipment and supplies only from the franchisor is illegal.[5] It is not illegal for the franchisor to require the franchisee to purchase supplies from either the franchisor or franchisor-approved suppliers so long as the franchisor does not unreasonably withhold approval from outside suppliers.

This concludes our discussion of the law of business associations (except for corporate law, which is discussed in Chapter 10). We now turn to the agency law and a discussion of some of the general moral duties that apply to circumstances in which one person works for another.

EMPLOYER-EMPLOYEE RELATIONSHIPS AND THE DUTIES OF LOYALTY, DUE CARE, AND GOOD FAITH

One dynamic area of employment law involves the relationship between the principal and the agent. Because agency law is widely applicable to all types of business associations, we can say that agency law helps define the very nature of the relationship between the larger classification of an employee, a partner, or a business associate and the firm, partnership, or corporation for which he or she works. What is this relationship?

The starting point for our explanation must be the expressed contractual understandings between the parties. For example, employer-employee relationships in most federal, state, or local governments are defined by the applicable civil service laws. These laws, usually administered by a federal or state civil service commission, set out the terms of employment and have the force of a contract between the employer and employee. A central idea explicit in these contracts is that an employee may not be fired except for "cause" or "just cause." About 20 percent of the U.S. workforce is covered by these laws.[6] Similarly, for many nongovernmental employees, the terms and conditions of employment are established by a contract negotiated on their behalf by a labor union. Disputes involving the terms and conditions of employment are settled by negotiations between the employee's union and the employer. It is estimated that less than 25 percent of the nonagricultural labor force is represented by and through labor unions and the collective bargaining process. This process also includes standards for mutual fair dealing, including the requirement that an employee be discharged only for cause. Thus, for close to half of the nonagricultural workforce, the employer-employee relationship is fairly clearly established in publicized standards administered by a neutral body or authority.

In addition, membership in certain protected classes allows some employees to evoke application of a variety of laws if they face job discrimination on the basis of race, gender, age, or physical handicap or if an employer is alleged to have violated one of the federal statutes on the environment, worker safety and health, or retirement benefit plans.

This still leaves about seventy million employees in the nonagricultural work force who must negotiate individually with employers. What is this relationship like? Is it symmetrical (two-sided and fair) or asymmetrical (one-sided and presumably marked by unfairness) in the power that can be brought to negotiations? Are these negotiations fair, and what can be done if they are not? It is estimated that from one million to two million of this type of worker are fired each year for a variety of reasons as diverse as corporate downsizing, restructuring, and alleged insubordination.[7] Many of these workers are low- and mid-level managers in medium- and large-sized corporations.

In the remaining part of this section, we examine the law and moral duties that principals and employers owe or should owe to their agents and employees. The common law that applies to agents/employees not protected by civil service or the collective bargaining process seems straightforward. The Restatement states that an agent is a fiduciary and therefore owes the following duties:

1. To act with the utmost loyalty.

2. To act with due care and diligence.

3. To render complete and accurate information.

4. To account for all receipts and profits.

5. To follow directions.

In addition, the common law protects the trade secrets of the employer, and statutory law gives the employer certain rights in protecting inventions developed by employees as long as these inventions are patented. It is no exaggeration to say that, until very recently, the common law and statutory law exhibited a pronounced bias in favor of the employer. After all, if the duties of the employee/agent were to act with "utmost loyalty," "due care," and "diligence," who really defined these rather vague terms? It was the employer, and the employer enforced its interpretation by exercising the power of firing employees if they did not agree.

Moreover, the common law solidified the employer's power by emphasizing the idea that unless a written contract defined the terms of employment, an employee served at the will of the employer and could be discharged at any time without a justification or statement of cause. Most commentators attribute the common law rule of at-will employment to H. G. Wood, an early writer in agency law who gathered the nineteenth-century American cases on master and servant. He wrote that any general or indefinite hiring is a hiring at will and that the burden is on the employee to show that his or her employment was not at will if he or she was discharged.[8]

Wood's opinion found ready acceptance in the rapidly industrializing America of the late nineteenth and early twentieth centuries. This employment-at-will legal doctrine helped shape the environment in which the enormous hierarchies that have become large business corporations flourished. Middle-level managers, especially, were always subject to the threat, often spoken of in subtle terms, that unless they performed consistently with corporate goals in mind, they could be discharged. When Lee Iacocca turned Chrysler around, tens of thousands of white-collar workers were laid off indefinitely or fired—and the law did not require that individual reasons be given. The job is "gone," and it is as simple as that. As late as the 1970s, courts in most states were still enforcing the at-will doctrine.

For example, the prominent Court of Appeals for the Eighth Circuit held in 1976 that the head of General Motors Mechanical Development Department, a Mr. Percival, could be fired with no cause given, despite the fact that he had worked for GM for twenty-six years. Percival alleged in his complaint that he was discharged because he had complained about certain deceptive practices of GM in filing reports with the government and had undertaken to correct the misrepresentations.[9] The court held that whether an employee has performed satisfactorily is to be determined by the employer, not by the courts. The court accepted Percival's allegations as true and still dismissed his case for the alleged tort of "wrongful termination." The court articulated the conventional wisdom and reasoned that a large corporate employer such as GM must be accorded wide latitude in determining whom it will employ in managerial positions.

The Restatement (Section 385(1)) states that, unless otherwise agreed, an agent must obey all reasonable directions in regard to the manner of performing a service for the principal and that, in determining whether the orders of the principal are reasonable, courts are to consider the customs of business with regard to business and professional ethics and the effect on the business. In a comment on these words, the Restatement further provides that in no event would it be implied that an agent has a duty to perform acts that are illegal or unethical. The definition of *unethical* is not given. Even if it were, the Restatement is saying that an employee or an agent cannot be forced to perform an unethical act but the employer may fire an employee if he or she refuses to do something that would violate the employee's own ethical standards. Moreover, the Restatement is not the law, but rather is merely advisory. Acting on one's conscience against the employer is usually very costly to the employee and almost never a rewarding experience.

For example, in one of the more thoughtful articles in this area of law, the former dean of the University of Connecticut Law School, Phillip I. Blumberg, cites an example in which Eastern Air Lines flight procedures required pilots to jettison into the atmosphere excess fuel from holding tanks where it was stored after a previous landing. A senior pilot of thirty years' experience had repeatedly asked that the excess fuel be drained into tanks on the ground because of the impact of the discharge on the quality of the air around airports. Eastern management refused. The senior pilot then made arrangements for the fuel to be drained by a mechanic while on the ground. The pilot was fired. Eastern's logic was that an airline with 3,700 pilots cannot operate if each pilot begins to make his or her own rules.[10] After considerable adverse publicity, the pilot was rehired, but his experience was probably like that of many who act on their conscience: unhappy and costly. Furthermore, he probably returned to a hostile work environment because he had not been a team player. Under the law of the Restatement, the pilot should not have been forced to act against his own ethical standards, but he was, and when he exercised those standards, he was fired.

An avalanche of scholarly opinion has been written in favor of abolishing the at-will doctrine. The courts and legislatures of most states have responded by creating exceptions to this doctrine. We explain some of these exceptions here but will hold judgment about whether the law has responded sufficiently to counter the immense power of employers.

THE CHALLENGE TO THE EMPLOYMENT-AT-WILL DOCTRINE

The most widely recognized limitation on the at-will doctrine is the public policy exception. Examples of successful claims by employees who assert the public policy exception to the employment-at-will doctrine include dismissals caused by employees' refusal to commit unlawful acts, such as antitrust violations and perjury, and cases in which employees are fired because they have performed an important public function, such as serving on a jury, being subpoenaed to testify in governmental investigations, or reporting violations of law involving the employer—sometimes called blowing the whistle. Other cases include instances in which an employee has been fired for exercising a lawful right, such as filing a workers' compensation claim, joining a labor union, or refusing to take an illegal lie-detector test.[11]

Other courts have implied a contract-like obligation of the employer to discharge only for cause or good cause. This implied obligation may come from company employment manuals or corporate bylaws, which might state, for example, "We have enthusiastically accepted our responsibility to provide you with good working conditions, good wages, good benefits, fair treatment, and the personal respect that is rightfully yours."

Courts in California, Massachusetts, New Hampshire, and Montana have recognized a covenant of fair dealing. The following case is a good example of how some state courts are finding exceptions to the employment-at-will doctrine.

Pugh v. *See's Candies, Inc.*
116 Cal.App. 3d 311 (1981)

GORDIN, JUSTICE

Pugh began working for See's at its Bay Area plant (then in San Francisco) in January 1941 washing pots and pans. From there he was promoted to candy maker, and held that position until the early part of 1942, when he entered the Air Corps. Upon his discharge in 1946 he returned to See's and his former position. After a year he was promoted to the position of production manager in charge of personnel, ordering raw materials, and supervising the production of candy. When, in 1950, See's moved into a larger plant in San Francisco, Pugh had responsibility for laying out the design of the plant, making bids, and assisting in the construction. While working at this plant, Pugh sought to increase his value to the company by taking three years of night classes in plant layout, economics and business law. When See's moved its San Francisco plant to its present location in South San Francisco in 1957, Pugh was given responsibilities for the new location similar to those which he undertook in 1950. By this time See's business and its number of production employees had increased substantially, and a new position of assistant production manager was created under Pugh's supervision.

In 1971 Pugh was again promoted, this time as vice president in charge of production and was placed upon the board of directors of See's northern California subsidiary, in recognition of his accomplishments.

In 1972 he received a gold watch from See's "in appreciation of 31 years of loyal service."

In May 1973 Pugh travelled with Charles Huggins, then president of See's, and their respective families to Europe on a business trip to visit candy manufacturers and to inspect new equipment. . . .

★ ★ ★

Upon Pugh's return from Europe on Sunday, June 25, 1973, he received a message directing him to fly to Los Angeles the next day and meet with Mr. Huggins.

Pugh went to Los Angeles expecting to be told of another promotion. The preceding Christmas season had been the most successful in See's history, the Valentine's Day holiday of 1973 set a new sales record for See's, and the March 1973 edition of See's Newsletter, containing two pictures of Pugh, carried congratulations on the increased production.

Instead, upon Pugh's arrival at Mr. Huggins's office, the latter said, "Wayne, come in and sit down. We might as well get right to the point. I have decided your services are no longer required by See's Candies. Read this and sign it." Huggins handed him a letter confirming his termination and directing him to remove that day "only personal papers and possessions from your office," but "absolutely no records, formulas or other material"; and to turn in and account for "all keys, credit cards, et cetera." The letter advised that Pugh would receive unpaid salary, bonuses and accrued vacation through that date, and the full amount of his profit sharing account, but "No severance pay will be granted." Finally, Pugh was directed "not to visit or contact Production Department employees while they are on the job."

The letter contained no reason for Pugh's termination. When Pugh asked Huggins for a reason, he was told only that he should "look deep within [him]self" to find the answer, that "Things were said by people in the trade that have come back to us." Pugh's termination was subsequently announced to the industry in a letter which, again, stated no reasons.

During the entire period of his employment, there had been no formal or written criticism of Pugh's work. No complaints were ever raised at the annual meetings which preceded each holiday season, and he was never denied a raise or bonus. He received no notice that there was a problem which needed correction, nor any warning that any disciplinary action was being contemplated.

The 1971 [labor] agreement expired in 1973. In April of that year, Huggins asked Pugh to be part of the negotiating team for the new union contract. Pugh responded that he would like to, but he was bothered by the possibility that See's had a "sweetheart contract" with the union. In response, someone banged on the table and said, "You don't know what the hell you are talking about." Pugh said, "Well, I think I know what I am talking about. I don't know whether you have a sweetheart contract, but I am telling you if you do, I don't want to be involved because they are immoral, illegal and not in the best interests of my employees."

At the trial, Pugh explained that to him a "sweetheart contract" was "a contract whereby one employer would get an unfair competitive advantage over a competitor by getting a lower wage rate from the union." He also felt, he testified, that "if they in fact had a sweetheart contract that it wouldn't be fair to my female employees to be getting less money than someone would get working in the same industry under the same manager.

The union's alleged participation in Pugh's termination was in the form of a statement attributed to Mr. Button (the individual who succeeded Pugh as production manager) at a negotiating meeting between the company and the union in June 1973. According to one witness, Mr. Button stated at the commencement of the meeting, "Now we've taken care of Mr. Pugh. What are you going to do for us."

Historical Background. The law of the employment relationship has been, and perhaps still is, in the process of continuing evolution. The old law of master and servant, which held sway through the 18th century and to some extent beyond, viewed the relationship as primarily one of status rather than of contract. While agreement gave rise to the relationship and might establish certain of its terms, it was "custom and public policy, not the will of the parties, [which] defined the implicit framework of mutual rights and obligations."

The essence of the relationship as so defined drew its contours from the model of the household—in which, typically, the servant worked, the master had general authority to discipline the servant, and it was the servant's duty to obey. At the same time, the master had certain responsibilities for the servant's general welfare. The relationship was thus in a sense paternalistic. And it was not terminable at will; rather, there existed a presumption (in the absence of contrary agreement) that employment was for a period of one year.

With the industrial revolution in the 19th century the law of master and servant underwent a gradual remodeling, primarily at the hands of the judiciary. Primary emphasis came to be placed, through contract doctrine, upon the freedom of the parties to define their own relationship. The emphasis shifted from obligation to freedom of choice. The terms of the contract were to be sought in voluntary agreement, express or implied, the employee being presumed to have assented to the rules and working conditions established by the employer.

In light of the generally superior bargaining power of the employer, "the employment contract became [by the end of the nineteenth century] a very special sort of contract—in large part a device for guaranteeing to management unilateral power to make rules and exercise discretion." And management's unilateral power extended, generally, to the term of the relationship as well. The new emphasis brought with it a gradual weakening of the traditional presumption that a general hiring (i.e., one without a specific term) was for a year, and its replacement by the converse presumption that "a general or indefinite hiring is *prima facie* a hiring at will." In California, this presumption is reflected in Labor Code section 2922, which provides: "An employment, having no specified term, may be terminated at the will of either party on notice to the other. Employment for a specified term means an employment for a period greater than one month."

The recognized inequality in bargaining power between employer and individual employee undergirded the rise of the labor unions and the institutionalization of collective bargaining. And through collective bargaining, unions have placed limitations on the employer's unilateral right of termination. Under most union contracts, employees can only be dismissed for "just cause," and disputes over what constitutes cause for dismissal are typically decided by arbitrators

chosen by the parties. Collective bargaining agreements, however, cover only a small fraction of the nation's work force, and employees who either do not or (as in the case of managerial employees such as Mr. Pugh) cannot form unions are left without that protection.

★ ★ ★

. . . The employer's right to terminate employees is not absolute. "The mere fact that a contract is terminable at will does not give the employer the absolute right to terminate it in all cases." Two relevant limiting principles have developed, one of them based upon public policy and the other upon traditional contract doctrine. The first limitation precludes dismissal "when an employer's discharge of an employee violates fundamental principles of public policy," the second when the discharge is contrary to the terms of the agreement, express or implied. Appellant relies upon both these principles in contesting his termination here.

Public Policy Limitation. Appellant contends that his evidence established a prima facie case of retaliatory termination for reasons which offend public policy in three respects. First, he contends that the evidence tended to show he was terminated because he refused to participate in negotiations for a union contract which would have violated state and federal public policy against restraint of trade; second, that he was terminated because he refused to participate in negotiations for a union contract which violated declared public policy against discrimination based on sex; and third, that he was terminated for reasons which violate the state's policy favoring the exercise of a company director's duty of inquiry.

The presumption that an employment contract is intended to be terminable at will is subject, like any presumption, to contrary evidence. This may take the form of an agreement, express or implied, that the relationship will continue for some fixed period of time. . . .

* * *

In determining whether there exists an implied-in-fact promise for some form of continued employment courts have considered a variety of factors. . . . These have included, for example, the personnel policies or practices of the employer, the employee's longevity of service, actions or communications by the employer reflecting assurances of continued employment, and the practices of the industry in which the employee is engaged.

A related doctrinal development exists in the application to the employment relationship of the "implied-in-law covenant of good faith and fair dealing inherent in every contract.". . .

* * *

Recently one Court of Appeal has had occasion to confront the applicability of that doctrine more directly. In *Cleary* v. *American Airlines, Inc.*, 111 Cal.App.3d 443, an employee who had been dismissed for alleged theft after 18 years of allegedly satisfactory service brought suit claiming, among other things, that his dismissal was in violation of published company policy requiring a fair, impartial and objective hearing" in such matters, and in breach of the covenant of good faith and fair dealing. Holding that the complaint stated a cause of action on these grounds, the court reasoned: "Two factors are of paramount importance in reaching our result. . . . One is the longevity of service by plaintiff—18 years of apparently satisfactory performance. Termination of employment without legal cause after such a period of time offends the implied-in-law covenant of good faith and fair dealing contained in all contracts, in-

cluding employment contracts. . . . The second factor of considerable significance is the expressed policy of the employer . . . set forth in the regulation [referred to in the pleadings]. This policy involves the adoption of specific procedures for adjudicating employee disputes such as this one. While the contents of the regulation are not before us, its existence compels the conclusion that this employer had recognized its responsibility to engage in good faith and fair dealing rather than in arbitrary conduct with respect to all of its employees. In the case at bench, we hold that the longevity of the employee's service, together with the expressed policy of the employer, operate as a form of estoppel, precluding any discharge of such an employee by the employer without good cause."

If "[t]ermination of employment without legal cause [after 18 years of service] offends the implied-in-law covenant of good faith and fair dealing contained in all contracts, including employment contracts," as the court said in the above-quoted portion of *Cleary*, then a fortiori that covenant would provide protection to Pugh, whose employment is nearly twice that duration. Indeed, it seems difficult to defend termination of such a long-time employee arbitrarily, i.e., without *some* legitimate reason, as comparable with either good faith or fair dealing.

We need not go that far, however. In *Cleary* the court did not base its holding upon the covenant of good faith and fair dealing alone. Its decision rested also upon the employer's acceptance of responsibility for refraining from arbitrary conduct, as evidenced by its adoption of specific procedures for adjudicating employer grievances. While the court characterized the employer's conduct as constituting "[recognition of] its responsibility to engage in good faith and fair dealing," the result is equally explicable in traditional contract terms: the employer's conduct gave rise to an implied promise that it would not act arbitrarily in dealing with its employees.

Here, similarly, there were facts in evidence from which the jury could determine the existence of such an implied promise: the duration of appellant's employment, the commendations and promotions he received, the apparent lack of any direct criticism of his work, the assurances he was given, and the employer's acknowledged policies. While oblique language will not, standing alone, be sufficient to establish agreement, it is appropriate to consider the totality of the parties' relationship: Agreement may be "shown by the acts and conduct of the parties, interpreted in the light of the subject matter and of the surrounding circumstances." We therefore conclude that it was error to grant respondents' motions for nonsuit as to See's.

Since this litigation may proceed toward yet uncharted waters, we consider it appropriate to provide some guidance as to the questions which the trial court may confront on remand. We have held that appellant has demonstrated a prima facie case of wrongful termination in violation of his contract of employment. The burden of coming forward with evidence as to the reason for appellant's termination now shifts to the employer. Appellant may attack the employer's offered explanation, either on the ground that it is pretextual (and that the real reason is prohibited by contract or public policy), or on the ground that it is insufficient to meet the employer's obligations under contract. . . .

★ ★ ★

We therefore conclude that the judgment of nonsuit was erroneously granted with respect to the union as well.

Reversed.

CASE FOLLOW-UP

As we wrote before this case, the courts or legislatures of most states have now recognized some zones of protection for a discharged employee who had no employment contract. Three such zones of protection involve (1) instances in which the employer violated public policy in the discharge, or (2) instances in which the employer violated an implied contract-like obligation to discharge only for good cause, or (3) a few court-created covenants of fair dealing requiring employers to act fairly. In addition, employees may use libel and slander laws to gain compensation for injury to one's reputation caused by any untrue statement made by a past employer. For example, an employee dismissed from a high-paying job as an insurance broker because he was "a Jekyll and Hyde person, and a classic sociopath" (said the former employer to a prospective new employer) recovered $605,000 for lost wages and $1.3 million in punitive damages. [12]

One respected scholar of this area of law has said the decisions in this area are so chaotic and inconsistent that they make little sense. Moreover, in general, the case law seems to protect upper management or those who have the resources and inclination to hire an attorney to sue a former employer. Most mid-level employees still must do what they are told or risk being fired.[13]

Recently, an attempt has been made to bring some clarity to this area of law. In August 1991, the National Conference of Commissioners on Uniform State Laws made available for discussion a draft Uniform Employment-Termination Act.[14] In short, this Act would be a legislative replacement for common law (court-made) legal rights in this area. This Act requires employers with five or more employees to terminate protected workers for good cause only. The application and definition of good cause would be subject to arbitration. An employer and employee may waive the good cause standard, however, by any written agreement.

It is too early to tell whether this proposed uniform state law will be adopted by many, a few, or any of the states. All we can state by way of conclusion is that the legal principles defining the relationship between employer and employee and between principal and agent are in great flux. This is also true of the issues raised by whistle-blowing, the subject of the next section.

WHISTLE-BLOWING—WHEN MORAL OBLIGATIONS OF AGENTS AND EMPLOYEES CONFLICT WITH THOSE OF A PRINCIPAL OR EMPLOYER

A *whistle-blower* is an agent or employee who seeks to go beyond established lines of authority to report or make public illegal or morally troubling conduct of a principal or an employer. Whistleblowing may occur at three levels. If an employee seeks to report conduct within an organization and goes around his or her boss to a higher authority (still within the organization), this is internal whistle-blowing. If Jones, for example, believes that his superior, Smith, has asked Jones to do something that is either illegal or morally questionable and reports this incident to Smith's superior or to another with authority over Smith, the matter also is internal whistle-blowing.

Reporting or appealing what a superior has directed, again assuming that it is illegal or immoral, to a governmental agency that has authority over the kind of activity involved is external whistle-blowing. A third level of whistle-blowing involves reporting the alleged illegal or immoral activity to the press or to a popular media institution. Whistle-blowing of any kind poses enormous risks to one going against the established lines of authority.

One primary value holding institutions together is the value of loyalty. Indeed, the primary duty of the agent to the principal is one of loyalty—an agent must act, in almost all cases, in the best interests, for and on behalf of the principal. Whenever an agent does blow the whistle, it appears that such a person is pointing a finger at his or her superiors and saying they are either stupid, immoral, or acting in an illegal manner. Thus, from the perspective of the principal/employer, the whistle-blower is usually seen as a threat to the established order of the organization.

However, business and professional society has an interest in rectifying mistakes whenever they are made, whether the mistakes involve overcharging the government on a contract, dangerously designing a product, or publishing an accounting calculation that is wrong. That is to say, everyone may benefit when the conscience of a lone individual compels actions by the individual. Therefore, it has been the policy of the law, especially in the past fifteen years, to protect and encourage whistle-blowing.

As two scholars put it recently, the whistle-blower protection bandwagon is crowded these days.[15] We have already seen that courts in about a third of the states have created a public policy exception to the employment-at-will doctrine to protect those employees who report illegal behavior. In addition, about two-thirds of the states have enacted legislation in the past fifteen years specifically to protect and encourage whistle-blowers. Perhaps most important, more than twenty federal statutes have provisions intended to offer protection to whistle-blowers.

FEDERAL WHISTLE-BLOWER LEGISLATION

Generally, federal legislation in this area can be divided into two categories. The first category is a statutory provision that is part of a larger legislative enactment intended to protect an employee's job should he or she report a violation of that act. For example, the Water Pollution Control Act is intended to control water purity, but it also seeks to protect employees from retaliatory job-related actions if they file any claim under the act or testify in any proceeding under the Act.[16] The remedy under this Act, as in many other federal Acts, is reinstatement plus lost compensation if one has been fired.

The second category is exemplified by a revision of the federal False Claims Act.[17] This Act is designed to provide recovery of amounts falsely claimed by governmental contractors. Those who provide names of violators of the Act may keep up to 30 percent of the total damage award. Damage awards themselves are calculated by taking the proved damages times three (this is called a treble damage award, as is common for violations of some federal statutes such as the antitrust laws). The Insider Trading Sanctions Act also authorizes the Securities and Exchange Commission to offer rewards for information leading to civil insider-trading penalties. As much as 10 percent of the penalty assessed may be recovered.[18]

STATE STATUTES PROTECTING WHISTLE-BLOWING

About two-thirds of the states address the issue of whistle-blowing. Michigan was one of the first, and its legislature stated that,

> Sec. 2. An employer shall not discharge, threaten, or otherwise discriminate against an employee regarding the employee's compensation, terms, conditions, location, or privileges of employment because the employee, or a person acting on behalf of the employee, reports or is about to report, verbally or in writing, a violation or a suspected violation of a law or regulation or rule promulgated pursuant to law of this state, a political subdivision of this state, or the United States to a public body, unless the employee knows that the report is false, or because an employee is requested by a public body to participate in an investigation, hearing, or inquiry held by that public body, or a court action.[19]

If a court finds a violation of this act, it may order reinstatement with back wages and fringe benefits plus actual damages, if any.

Some studies of whistle-blowing suggest that both state and federal statutes that try to protect whistle-blowers or to offer compensation to encourage this activity are not having their intended impact. One study concludes:

> Our examination of state whistleblowing statutes indicates that the statutes are not having their desired effect. They do not seem to be encouraging whistleblowing. They are not being interpreted in a way that offers maximum protection to whistleblowers, and they are not drafted in a manner best designed to protect whistleblowers and to encourage them to report misconduct. Consequently, it seems foolish for legislatures to spend the time and effort to craft statutes that will have an appreciable effect, the more so if whistleblowing is not an activity amenable to statutory influence. The most positive thing the statutes may be doing is to influence some companies to change their policies.[20]

It may be that legislative responses and development of common law principles in this area to adjust the interests of agents, principals, and society are too crude to be of much value. It appears that no one comes out a winner when one blows the whistle. One of the first whistle-blowers, A. Ernest Fitzgerald, an Air Force analyst, was fired after testifying in 1969 about massive cost overruns on a Lockheed cargo plane. It took him thirteen years to win reinstatement. He said that if he had it to do over again, he would not blow the whistle. It was too costly on him personally.[21]

Karen Silkwood, the worker who charged that the large construction firm Kerr-McGee was responsible for flawed safety procedures at the nuclear plant where she worked was harassed day and night and some say, driven to a premature death because of her involvement in whistle-blowing. Acting on one's conscience, it seems, can be very costly.

From the perspective of the employer, whistle-blowing is a far from perfect solution. In some cases, no doubt, the information made public is not accurate, and thus employers suffer needlessly. Also, from the perspective of the public, whistleblowing seems enormously inefficient. The best solution, it seems, is a nonlegal one. Authors of one study conclude that the best solution is for organizations of all types to adopt measures to encourage internal whistle-blowing. Employees and agents, managers and executives need to be trained to manage, monitor and even encourage ethical behavior of all members of the organization.[22] Rigid lines of authority in large corporate hierarchies need to be softened, and questioning of decisions needs to be supported.

CONCLUSION

Agency law is the most fundamental body of law that applies to business associations. Numerous state and federal rules and regulations stipulate how an association is to be structured and how it is to behave, but the basis for its business activity, the ability to enforce and be bound by contracts, and the ability to sue and be sued for tort damage are created by agency law. In short, agency law relates the business association to its business environment. In the first part of this chapter, we explained the importance of the major concepts of authority, which bind third parties to the business association and vice versa. We also explained the law of respondeat superior, which focuses on the factual element of control and creates liability for the business association to those persons injured by its agents.

Partnership law and the law of joint ventures, franchises, and cooperatives are built on agency law. Partnership law, however, presented a new concept in our discussion of law (the concept that the property of the business association is separate for some purposes from that of the owners of the business). The business association stands on its own as a separate legal entity. Agency law, however, relates the employees or partners to the partnership and to one another.

The final portion of the chapter presented an in-depth explanation of duties owed by employees to employers and vice versa. We presented issues that transcend the law and reside in the arena of moral choice. We raised, but did not answer, the issue of what should be appropriate conduct when one's own conscience dictates action that puts one at odds with one's fellow workers. The position of the law in this area is changing. It is becoming more sensitive to providing remedies for employees fired unfairly after many years of loyal service, but the law provides no easy answers to the problems created when one chooses to go public with information that will damage the employer.

Review Questions and Problems

1. *A* falsely purports to be authorized by *P* to transfer some of *P*'s personal property. *T*, a prospective purchaser, calls *P* on the telephone and mentions that *A* has contacted her about the sale. *P* neither admits nor denies that *A* was authorized to act for *P*. *T* pays *A* for the property, and *A* gives *T* what is purported to be a "title" to the property. Between *T* and *P*, who is entitled to the property?

2. Luanne was on the audit staff of a large certified public accounting firm. She had been with the firm for six years and was at the level of supervisor. This position was crucial in the firm because the supervisor conducted the audit (through subordinates) and was, in general, responsible for its accuracy, although a partner in the firm was the one ultimately responsible to the partnership and to the public for it. When the audit on Darth Corporation, a client, was completed, Luanne was called into the partner's office. It was explained to her that a few of her qualifying notes would have to be changed. Although her notes were thorough and accurate and changing them was not illegal, the change did not represent what she thought was a fair presentation of the client's business operation. Is she under a duty to change the audit report? Can she be sued by her firm if she refuses to change it? Can she be fired if she refuses to change it? In general, what are the rights and obligations of Luanne and her partnership?

3. *P* made storefronts and other additions to commercial buildings and employed *A* to call on contractors and older commercial enterprises to promote the sales of *P*. *A* was specifically forbidden to collect payment for the erection of the storefronts and other improvements. *T* went to *P*'s place of business, inquiring about a new front for his store and was directed to *A*'s office. *A* negotiated a contract and signed on behalf of *P*, and *P*'s crew began work. *P* did not keep very good account of his workers or accounts receivable. *A* pocketed the payments made by *T* to *A* and absconded. When *P* discovered this, because *A* was unavailable, he sued *T* to recover the payments owed to him for the work done. Can he collect?

4. *P* employs *A* as the general manager of her manufacturing plant, instructing *A* to pur-

chase certain materials from specifically named suppliers and no others. *A*, realizing that some materials supplied by the designated suppliers are inferior and without consultation with *P*, contracts with other suppliers for better materials at a more reasonable price. The contracts with the new suppliers are written on plain paper (no letterhead), and *A* signs the contracts at *P*'s headquarters in the presence of the new suppliers, as follows: "*A*, general manager for *P*." Will *P* be bound by these contracts? Why?

5. The following was taken from a local newspaper:

> A local insurance man who has provided health insurance coverage for city employees for the past six years, admitted today that he misused premiums paid to him by the city.
>
> Michael Daher of M. Daher and Associates, Lakeshore Bank Building, made the admission to a newsman after Mayor Randall Miller said in a news release this morning that the city had been informed by the Golden Rule Insurance Co. that claims filed by city employees during June, July, and August of this year would not be honored by the company.
>
> The mayor said that the city was informed of the company's decision last week. He said at that time the company informed city officials that insurance premiums for those three months had not been remitted to the company by Daher.
>
> The mayor said that the city had paid the premiums in good faith to Daher, and Daher agreed that the city was not at fault. He said, "The mayor is correct, the premiums were remitted to me. The city did act in good faith." Daher went on, "I admit I have misused the funds."
>
> The mayor said today that, during conversations with company officials, the city had been informed that the company would be willing to honor the claims if the premiums ($17,000 per month) are paid. He said the city has contacted the office of the State Insurance Commis-

sioner . . . and that the office is sending an investigator to examine the situation. The mayor said that because the premiums have been paid to Daher, the company has a duty to honor the claims.

> He said, "If they continue to refuse to pay the claims, we will vigorously pursue any and every course of action to ensure the payment of claims to our employees, including legal action against Golden Rule Insurance Co., and Mr. Daher as their agent."

Assume you are the investigator sent by the state to examine the situation. Clearly state the legal rules under which the Golden Rule Co. could be held liable.

6. What kinds of evidence will you look for to substantiate your proper use of the listed legal rules in your answer to Question 5?

7. Clearly state whether Mr. Daher could be liable to either the Golden Rule Insurance Co. or the city for the premiums taken. Why?

8. Parker Drilling Company drilled for oil and employed a number of people on a full- or part-time basis to keep its equipment in good shape. Crouch was one of the people employed by Parker to do welding on the drilling equipment. Crouch owned his own truck and welding equipment; supplied his own welding materials, such as rods and an arc; and maintained his own insurance, submitting invoices to Parker for work done. He was not on the payroll and could take other jobs, but he worked steadily for Parker. Parker did supply drawings indicating the type of welding it wanted done and also supplied the steel when needed. One oil-drilling derrick that Crouch welded collapsed, killing a bystander. The estate of the bystander sued Parker. State the elements of the case the estate will have to prove. Do you believe the estate will be successful?

9. The following was taken from a newspaper:

> A structural engineer hired to study the effects of a possible earthquake on the Energy Department's nuclear-weapons plant at Oak Ridge, Tenn., was fired after he re-

ported that the walls would fall down. Other engineers rewrote the study to say that they would not.

The engineer, Paul Nestel, reported on Sept. 25 that the unreinforced clay tile walls of the main building of Oak Ridge's Y–12 nuclear plant would give way if struck by an earthquake with a lateral force of .12 percent of gravity.

That figure is well below the .19 percent used nationwide as a "design basis" for quake vulnerability studies.

By Oct. 30, after a series of meetings at which his conclusions were discussed, engineers from Lockwood Greene Inc. of Oak Ridge, Nestel's employer, and Martin Marietta Energy Systems Inc., which operates the Oak Ridge plant for the Energy Department, reported that the walls "have the capacity to withstand the design basis earthquake."

Nestel, a structural engineer from California, was recruited by Lockwood Greene in July to conduct the study. He was fired Nov. 3. A notation on his personnel record says he was "unsuitable for job position."

Nestel gave copies of the documents to The Washington Post. He accused the contractors of "burying unfavorable reports," in violation of orders from Energy Secretary James Watkins to put safety considerations ahead of production demands at all plants in the nuclear weapons complex. . . .

Lockwood Greene was a subcontractor to Martin Marietta for a "natural phenomena evaluation" of Oak Ridge's Building 9212, the major building of the Y–12 complex, which produces components and subassemblies for nuclear weapons. Oak Ridge and the Energy Department's Savannah River, S.C., complex have been cited as vulnerable to earthquakes, and new buildings are built to stronger specifications.

But Y–12 began operating in 1944 when, Nestel said, "nobody other than California paid any attention to this."

He said a fault known as New Madrid, 120 miles from Oak Ridge, "altered the course of the Mississippi River the last time it slipped, in the 19th century. If it slipped again, it would certainly destroy those walls."[23]

Would you hire Mr. Nestel to work for you? Why or why not?

10. The corporate employment office manager has been notified that federal Equal Employment Opportunity officers (EEO) will be conducting an EEO compliance review at the corporate headquarters facility. Part of the review will involve scrutiny of employment records to determine whether the corporation has made a "good faith" effort in recruiting and hiring minority candidates as stated in the corporation's affirmative action plan. The employment manager has been informed that the federal compliance officers will want to review the application forms of all minority candidates who were not employed during the past twelve months.

Although the corporation's minority hiring record is generally "acceptable," the employment manager is concerned that the interviewers' comments on some of these application forms may imply a less than enthusiastic commitment to minority hiring on the part of some managers—a situation he has kept to himself up to this point. The employment manager is particularly concerned about this situation because the company is about to conclude a $100 million contract with the federal government that could be canceled if the compliance review is unsatisfactory.

Faced with this situation, would you as the employment manager

a. Let things "ride" and take your chances during the compliance review?

b. Withhold those few employment applications that would pose a problem if reviewed by the compliance officers?

c. "Blow the whistle" on the "offending" managers during the review?

d. Risk your own job by finally informing management that this situation exists before the review takes place?

Evaluate each of these alternatives from the moral point of view (see Chapter 1). Then, ask yourself how well, if at all, this firm has internalized or institutionalized the moral point of view when it leaves so many loose ends for the employment manager to cope with. Would you prefer to work for this firm or for one with a clearly defined policy statement or code of ethics backed up by the corporate board of directors? (This situation is drawn from a classroom handout and personal communication with Don Jones, Drew University, used with permission.)

ENDNOTES

1. Seavey, *Law of Agency* 3 (1964).
2. *The Wall Street Journal*, June 10, 1992 p. 1, col. 6.
3. *Id.* at A6.
4. Packel, *The Organization and Operation of Cooperatives* 4–5 (1970).
5. See *Siegel* v. *Chicken Delight*, 448 F.2d 43 (1971).
6. Student Note, Protecting Employees at Will Against Wrongful Discharge: The Public Policy Exception, 96 *Harv. L. Rev.* 1931 (1983).
7. *Id.* at 1935.
8. Wood, *A Treatise on the Law of Master and Servant* Sec. 134 (1886).
9. *Percival* v. *General Motors Group*, 539 F.2d 1126 (8th Cir. 1976).
10. See Blumberg, Corporate Responsibility and the Employee's Duty of Loyalty and Obedience: A Preliminary Inquiry, 24 *Okla. L. Rev.* 279 (1971).
11. Phillips, Toward a Middle Way in the Polarized Debate Over Employment at Will, 30 *Am. Bus. L.J.* 441 (1992).
12. *Newsweek*, Feb. 16, 1987 p. 46.
13. Student Note, *supra* note 6, at 1932–1933.
14. Draft Uniform Employment-Termination Act, *Lab. Rel. Rep.* (BNA) (Aug. 2–9, 1991).
15. Dworkin and Callahan, Internal Whistle-blowing: Protecting the Interests of the Employee, the Organization, and Society, 29 *Am. Bus. L.J.* 267 (1991).
16. 33 U.S.C. 1367a (1988).
17. 31 U.S.C. Sec. 3730a (1988).
18. 15 U.S.C. Sec 78 u–i (1988).
19. Michigan Public Acts, No. 469, Sec. 15.362, Sec.2 (March 31, 1981).
20. Dworkin and Near, Whistleblowing Statutes: Are They Working? 25 *Am. Bus. L.J.* 241 (1987).
21. *New York Times*, November 19,1986 p. 32, col. 2.
22. Miceli and Near, *Blowing the Whistle* 283–287 (1992).
23. The article, by Thomas W. Lippman, appeared in the *Austin American Statesman* (Dec. 9, 1989, p. A22) and is reprinted by permission of the *Washington Post*.

CHAPTER 10

Corporations and Corporation Law

INTRODUCTION

Thinking about and studying American business corporations is a difficult task for three major reasons. The first reason is the tremendous size of the modern corporation. Many textbooks on corporation law fail to distinguish in importance between the very small or family-owned corporation and megacorporations (a word we use to describe the 200 largest corporations). We lament this failure. Treating all corporations as similar entities substantially undervalues the place of the megacorporation in American society. These very large American corporations are a dominating force in the nation's and the world's economies. Indeed, together with laws creating and protecting property rights, they are a major tool of capitalism and deserve to be treated as one of the most significant legal innovations in the development of the Western political economy. More than sixty years ago, one of the most distinguished legal scholars ever to study and write about large American business corporations said:

> The corporation has, in fact, become both a method of property tenure and a means of organizing economic life. Grown to tremendous proportions, there may be said to have evolved a "corporate system"—as there once was a feudal system—which has attracted to itself a combination of attributes and powers and has attained a degree of prominence entering it to be dealt with as a major social institution.[1]

The most recent data available on U.S. business associations shows that as of 1990, there were 20.054 million businesses for profit; of this number, 14.783 million were nonfarm proprietorships, 1.554 million were partnerships, and 3.717 million were business corporations.[2] Thus, proprietorships far outnumber both partnerships and corporations. This statistic is not very meaningful, however. Much more telling is the fact that the largest 500 business corporations are enormously influential in U.S. social and economic life: In 1992, they had a combined $2.365 trillion in sales, $2.565 trillion in assets (up 44 percent since 1987), and about $55 billion in profits.[3]

In years past, the ten largest New York Stock Exchange corporations (NYSE) had annual sales that exceeded the combined gross national products of Austria, Denmark, Finland, Greece, Ireland, Norway, Portugal, and Turkey.[4]

What does all this mean? *Of the 20 million business organizations, the 200 megacorporations are by far the most significant form of business organization.* Yet, the law does not recognize much of a difference between megacorporations and small family-owned corporations. In fact, the law often sees megacorporations as individual persons. This conceptual error (we believe) is what makes studying corporation law so difficult.

The second reason corporations are difficult to study is that they engage in every conceivable type of legal profit-making and even governmental activity. Towns and villages, churches, schools, YMCAs, and organizations such as the Girl Scouts may be incorporated. This diversity in size and function makes any discussion of corporations necessarily very general and subject to numerous exceptions.

The third reason is the lack of tradition of systematic inquiry, analysis, and evaluation of megacorporations as the significant and powerful actors they are. Unlike other power centers in U. S. society (e.g., government, organized religion), no formalized study of megacorporations themselves exists. By *formalized study*, we mean a systematic course of instruction in high schools and universities from which one can gain knowledge and understanding about these institutions.

Our purpose in pointing out the importance of megacorporations is merely to express our discomfort for a body of state-based legal principles that are supposed to apply equally to small, one- and two-person corporations and megacorporations. As we explain in the next section, corporation law began (and still resides primarily) at the state level. But, for a variety of reasons, not the least of which is the sheer growth in economic power of corporations, the states gradually lost the ability to control, in a substantial way, the behavior of corporations. The result has been the explosive growth of federal law to control primarily megacorporate behavior (e.g., the federal laws regarding trading in securities, employment discrimination, employer safety and health, and environmental pollution). This federal law is the subject of much of this book.

THE NATURE OF CORPORATION LAW

Corporation law refers to the state-level, mostly statutory, law that is, in essence, the structural or constitutional law of corporate existence. Corporation law prescribes how the shareholders relate to one another, to the directors, and to the corporation. It governs shareholder and board meetings and defines how power is to be distributed or circumscribed in corporations. Individuals who start corporations choose a state in which to file the papers creating the corporation. The law of this state then structures the corporation thus created. The larger the corporation, however, the greater the likelihood that federal law (primarily the federal securities laws) will govern primarily the rights of shareholders. For a thorough understanding of corporation law today, a brief look at its history is enormously helpful.

STATE-BASED CORPORATION LAW: A HISTORICAL NOTE

Prior to the middle of the nineteenth century, corporate existence was created by a specific state legislative act. The key features of corporate existence—limited liability of the owners, unlimited length of life (perpetual existence), and share ownership—were thought to be privileges and were bestowed when the recipients could convince the legislature that, in exchange for these privileges, a public purpose would be served. Thus, many early corporations were toll road companies, canal companies, and a few manufacturing companies. Banks and insurance companies were more severely limited in the grant of these privileges. Often, the life of banks was limited to twelve to twenty-five years, and their purposes were limited strictly to receiving deposits, lending money, discounting bills of exchange, and issuing drafts. Manufacturing companies and public utilities were encouraged, in some cases, by the award of a corporate charter with an unlimited life. Indeed, a primary legislative activity of the state legislatures until the middle of the nineteenth century was the granting of these corporate charters.

Granting corporate charters by specific act has several disadvantages. Foremost was the complaint that some of these grants also carried with them the award of a monopoly. Another was that those who received a corporate charter were usually politically powerful.

By the time of the election of Andrew Jackson (1829), the political debate about corporate charters focused on whether corporations would be abolished altogether or would be freely available to everyone. This debate was resolved in favor of general incorporation laws, which set out basic requirements that, if met, granted to any individual a corporate charter. These general laws were adopted first on the East Coast and spread to the Midwest by the 1850s. So, the first historical phase of corporation law was a movement from the creation of business corporations by individual state legislative act to general incorporation laws.

As manufacturing grew in importance, especially in Massachusetts, New York, and New Jersey, a second phase of the history of corporation law began. As corporations began doing business in states other than the state in which they were chartered, managers and entrepreneurs realized that some states would treat them more favorably than others. They began to shop around for the most convenient state in which to incorporate.

New Jersey was the first state to officially notice that corporations could be attracted by enacting favorable corporation laws. In the early 1890s, New Jersey was experiencing a severe financial crisis and officially went into the chartering business by first repealing its antitrust law, and in 1896, passing the General Revision Act, which contained the essential elements of most twentieth-century state corporation statutes. Today, these elements do not seem overly attractive, but against a historical background of suspicion and extreme legislative caution in chartering corporations, these revisions were radical.

The New Jersey approach had three themes:[5] The first was to allow unlimited corporate size and life, and it added that anyone could incorporate for any lawful purpose. The second was a revision of the capitalization requirements, which allowed undervalued or watered stock. This permitted one company to purchase another company by payment in its own stock; the value of the stock received was to be established by the directors of the acquired company. Thus, putative monopolists could gain control of competing corporations without paying a cent. They merely offered the owners of the acquired corporation quantities of stock at irresistible prices. The third theme was the evisceration of the notion of shareholder control by permitting stockholders to be classified as preferred (preferred over other shareholders with regard to payment of dividends but having no vote) or common. This enabled the organizers of a corporation to sell large quantities of nonvoting stock to the public while retaining all of the voting stock. This act also gave directors the right to amend bylaws without the consent of the shareholders.

New Jersey's approach worked. During the early twentieth century, competition erupted between the industrial states of the East for this apparently available industrial base; the winner was Delaware. As one scholar put it, "What began as a tragedy in New Jersey was institutionalized as a farce in Delaware."[6] Delaware retained the most attractive features of the New Jersey laws but expanded and liberalized those laws permitting economic concentration through stock pyramiding. This feature allowed a financier to have control of a subsidiary corporation through a parent and to reduce personal investment in the controlling stock to a small amount by selling off most of the parent's equity in nonvoting stock. This activity could be repeated at several levels, so multi million-dollar combinations resulted with control by persons who had less than 1 percent of the total ownership value.

From time to time, other states have tried to "out-Delaware" Delaware but have not succeeded. Delaware corporation law is so favorable to management, (usually at the expense of the shareholders and the public) that it has chartered about one half of the 1,000 largest American corporations—including 52 of the largest 100 and 251 of the largest 500.[7]

A more balanced corporation law has been proposed by a committee of the American Bar Association (ABA). The ABA first published a Model Business Corporation Act (MBCA) for consideration and adoption by the states in 1950. The MBCA has been very influential in the development of state incorporation statutes in the almost fifty years since then. Recently the ABA completed a comprehensive revision of this model act, now called the Revised Model Business Corporation Act (RMBCA).

It is not a central objective of this text to lay these legislative schemes side by side and compare them, but essentially two models are available to state legislatures when they choose to change or modify their state business corporation statutes. Generally, the Delaware model still favors the managers of corporations, and the RMBCA appears to be more neutral in the inevitable tension among the interests of the shareholders, management, and creditors of the corporation.

To round out our presentation of the history of state corporation law, we note two developments involving business corporations at both ends of the corporate size spectrum. At one extreme are the small corporations with relatively few shareholders (usually less than fifteen), which are called *closely held corporations.* These corporations are often operated as partnerships with one or two principals or owners and the others as employees. About a dozen states have supplemented their general corporation statutes to provide relaxed rules for these closely held corporations. In addition, the RMBCA has a supplement that applies to these small entities. The thrust of the legislation in this area is to protect the interests of the minority shareholders. Often, if a corporation has only seven shareholders, for example, they will all work for the corporation. Four of the seven may vote to fire the other three, and because there is no established market for the shares, the three will be substantially disadvantaged unless special legislation protects them by giving them a voice in management or special remedies enabling them to value their stock and then have the four remaining shareholders buy them out.

At the other extreme, is the dwindling of individual, human shareholders and the ascendancy of institutional owners. It is estimated that in excess of 40 percent of the outstanding shares of New York Stock Exchange listed companies are owned by institutions such as insurance companies, pension funds, investment companies, and bank trust departments. The impact of these institutional investors is not yet determined. Some scholars believe they may have an interest in exercising control over some corporations; others believe the only interest institutions have is to gain an economic return and will sell their shares rather than attempt to exercise control if they disagree with management.

In addition to this history of state corporation law, a brief look at how constitutional law has developed will be instructive in understanding the corporation in the legal environment.

CORPORATIONS AS LEGAL PERSONS UNDER THE CONSTITUTION

Primarily, this section is about how corporations are created, managed, and controlled through state corporation law. But underpinning this layer of law is the constitutional law applicable to corporations. To what extent do notions of fundamental fairness implied and explicit in the due process and equal protection clauses of the Fourteenth Amendment (applicable to state governments) and the Fifth Amendment (applicable to the federal government) apply to corporations? In the eyes of the law, is a corporation entitled to the same constitutional protections as a human being? The answer to this question is generally yes, but there are some exceptions.

The most fundamental proposition is that corporations are persons for purposes of the due process and equal protection clauses of both the Fourteenth and Fifth amendments to the Constitution. This means that most of the basic American rights and privileges are extended to corporations. The application of these rights and privileges to corporations was accomplished without much debate and discussion, as shown in the following excerpts from *Wheeling Steel Corp.* v. *Glander.* The case also reveals some judicial discomfort about this lack of thoughtful discussion in treating corporations almost equally with natural persons.

Wheeling Steel Corp. v. *Glander*

337 U.S. 562 at 574 (1949)

[*Author's note:* Mr. Justice Jackson wrote the opinion for the majority of the Court. Nowhere in the opinion did he explain why he believed the Fourteenth Amendment was applicable to corporations. He assumed it to be applicable. Two dissenting justices, however, chided Justice Jackson for this assumption. Apparently, Justice Jackson felt compelled to respond and, in an unusual move, wrote a personal vote that followed his opinion for the majority. Below are excerpts from this exchange between the dissenters and Justice Jackson.]

JUSTICE JACKSON

The writer of the Court's opinion deems it necessary to complete the record by pointing out why, in writing by assignment for the Court, he assumed without discussion that the protections of the Fourteenth Amendment are available to a corporation. It was not questioned by the state in this case, nor was it considered by the courts below. It has consistently been held by this Court that the Fourteenth Amendment assures corporations equal protection of the laws, at least since 1886, *Santa Clara County* v. *Southern Pacific R. Co.*, 118 U.S. 394, 396, and that it entitles them to due process of law, at least since 1889, *Minneapolis & St. L. R. Co.* v. *Beckwith*, 129 U.S. 26, 28.

It is true that this proposition was once challenged by one Justice. . . . But the challenge did not commend itself, even to such consistent liberals as Mr. Justice Brandeis and Mr. Justice Stone, and I had supposed it was no longer pressed. . . .

Without pretending to a complete analysis, I find that in at least two cases during this current term the same question was appropriate for consideration as here. In *Railway Express Agency* v. *New York*, . . . a corpora-tion claimed to be deprived of both due process and equal protection of the law. and in *Ott* v. *Mississippi Barge Line*, . . . a corporation claimed to be denied due process of law. At prior terms, in many cases the question was also inherent, for corporations made similar claims under the Fourteenth Amendment. . . . Although the author of the present dissent was the writer of each of the cited Court's opinions. It was not intimated therein that there was even doubt whether the corporations . . . were entitled to protection of the Amendment. Instead, in each case the author, as I have done in this case, proceeded to discuss and dispose of the corporations contentions on their merits. . . .

MR. JUSTICE DOUGLAS, *with whom* Mr. Justice Black *concurs, dissenting*.

It has been implicit in all of our decisions since 1886 that a corporation is a "person" within the meaning of the Equal Protection Clause of the Fourteenth Amendment. *Santa Clara County* v. *Southern Pac. R Co.*, 118 U.S. 394, 396, so held. The Court was cryptic in its decision. It was so sure of its ground that it wrote no opinion on the point, Chief Justice Waite announcing from the bench:

> The court does not wish to hear argument on the question whether the provision in the Fourteenth Amendment to the Constitution, which forbids a State to deny to any person within its jurisdiction the equal protection of the laws, applies to these corporations. We are all of opinion that it does.

There was no history, logic, or reason given to support that view. Nor was the result so obvious that exposition was unnecessary.

The Fourteenth Amendment became a part of the Constitution in 1868. In 1871 a corporation claimed that Louisiana had imposed on it a tax that violated the Equal Protection Clause of the new Amendment. Mr. Justice Woods (then Circuit Judge) held that "person" as there used did not include a corporation and added, "This construction of the section is strengthened by the history of the submission by congress, and the adoption by the states of the 14th amendment, so fresh in all minds as to need no rehearsal." *Insurance Co.* v. *New Orleans,* 1 Woods 85, 88.

What was obvious to Mr. Justice Woods in 1871 was still plain to the Court in 1873. Mr. Justice Miller in the *Slaughter-House Cases,* 16 Wall. 36, 71, adverted to events "almost too recent to be called history" to show that the purpose of the Amendment was to protect human rights—primarily the rights of a race which had just won its freedom. And as respects the Equal Protection Clause he stated, "The existence of laws in the States where the newly emancipated negroes resided, which discriminated with gross injustice and hardship against them as a class, was the evil to be remedied by this clause, and by it such laws are forbidden."

Moreover what was clear to these earlier judges was apparently plain to the people who voted to make the Fourteenth Amendment a part of our Constitution. For as Mr. Justice Black pointed out in his dissent in *Connecticut General Co.* v. *Johnson,* 303 U.S. 77, 87, the submission of the Amendment to the people was on the basis that it protected human beings. There was no suggestion in its submission that it was designed to put negroes and corporations into one class and so dilute the police power of the States over corporate affairs. Arthur Twining Hadley once wrote that "The Fourteenth Amendment was framed to protect the negroes from oppression by the whites, not to protect corporations from oppression by the legislature. It is doubtful whether a single one of the members of Congress who voted for it had any idea that it would touch the question of corporate regulation at all."[8]

Both Mr. Justice Woods in *Insurance Co.* v. *New Orleans,* and Mr. Justice Black in his dissent in *Connecticut General Co.* v. *Johnson,* have shown how strained a construction it is of the Fourteenth Amendment so to hold.

★ ★ ★

. . . As to the matter of construction, the sense seems to me to be with Mr. Justice Woods in *Insurance Co.* v. *New Orleans,* where he said, "The plain and evident meaning of the section is, that the persons to whom the equal protection of the law is secured are persons born or naturalized or endowed with life and liberty, and consequently natural and not artificial persons."

History has gone the other way. Since 1886 the Court has repeatedly struck down state legislation as applied to corporations on the ground that it violated the Equal Protection Clause. Every one of our decisions upholding legislation as applied to corporations over the objection that it violated the Equal Protection Clause has assumed that they are entitled to the constitutional protection. But in those cases it was not necessary to meet the issue since the state law was not found to contain the elements of discrimination which the Equal Protection Clause condemns. But now that the question is squarely presented I can only conclude that the *Santa Clara* case was wrong and should be overruled.

One hesitates to overrule cases even in the constitutional field that are of an old vintage. But that has never been a deterrent heretofore and should not be now.

We are dealing with a question of vital concern to the people of the nation. It may be most desirable to give corporations this protection from the operation of the legislative process. But that question is not for us. It is for the people. If they want corporations to be treated as humans are treated, if they want to grant corporations this large degree of emancipation from state regulation, they should say so. The Constitution provides a method by which they may do so. We should not do it for them through the guise of interpretation.

CASE FOLLOW-UP

Perhaps the most significant limitation on state governments in controlling both persons and business organizations is interpretations of the Fourteenth Amendment's due process and equal protection clauses. These clauses define, in essence, what is fair procedure when state governments act. Some commentators believe, like Justice Douglas above, that equating persons and corporations unduly restricts state governments in their treatment of business organizations within their state boundaries. It could be that in some fundamental sense, corporations are not just like persons; perhaps the difference is categorical. Assessing the costs and benefits or just the impact of equating persons and corporations is difficult, if not impossible. Realizing that this is what the law does, however, is helpful in understanding the nature of corporate law and how the states must view corporations.

Theories of Corporate Existence

Two theories (and many lesser ones) about corporate existence are prominent today. These theories help in understanding the place and role of megacorporations in society. The first is the traditional view expressed in the *Wheeling* case—that business corporations are fictional, legal persons who can contract with real persons, the state, or other corporations and whose property will be protected by the law much as a human's property would be. Corporations, like persons, have rights that must be honored.

One of the earliest prominent Supreme Court decisions establishing this view was *Dartmouth College* v. *Woodward*,[9] which held that a corporate charter granted to Dartmouth College was a contract between the corporation and the state and that the state could not change it. For over a century, this decision meant that once a state granted a charter to a corporation, it could not alter the fundamental structure of the corporation or the understandings about corporate purpose or function as set out in its charter. Today, because the state reserves the right to change corporate charters when it grants them, this case is not of great significance. It does point out, however, that this fictional, legal entity, once created, had real legal muscle and could not be regulated through changing its charter.

A more modern view is linked to the Chicago school of law and economics. This view sees the large business corporation as a structure that embodies a web of contractual relationships among various individuals and entities, such as the shareholders (the owners), labor, material suppliers, bankers, and consumers of the products or services of the corporation. This view is often referred to as the *nexus of contracts view*. True, proponents of this view say the corporation is a fictional, legal entity, but it is more properly understood as a large economic structure in which multitudes of self-driven interests exchange money for ownership, labor for money, money for goods, and so on. People should, proponents say, be most concerned with the efficiency of this economic and legal structure. Everyone would be better off if these machinelike structures operated with as little cost as possible. Cost, in this sense, is like friction—it should be reduced for the sake of efficiency. Cost is measured by the resources that those who own the corporation (primarily the shareholders) have to devote to monitor those in charge— namely, management.

Thus, Chicago school proponents see external audits of the corporation and outside members of the board as costs to shareholders and banks and further believe that these costs should be reduced by any scheme that would tend to align management with the maximization of value to the shareholders. Thus, they favor stock option plans and bonuses tied to performance and do not value outside or public directors or other schemes to keep a watch on management.

PROFESSIONS AND THE USE OF THE CORPORATE FORM

Until recently, corporations were prevented from engaging in a learned profession, such as law or medicine. Licenses to practice such professions are granted to individual human beings. A corporation could not qualify for such a license. The corporation was also barred from practicing such a profession through its shareholders or employees who were properly licensed. To permit such activity was viewed as being inappropriate, unethical, and against public policy primarily because the professionals would be able to avoid liability (the corporate entity, not the professional employee, would be liable). State legislatures simply believed it unwise to allow professionals to shield themselves from personal liability by incorporating. Thus, members of the medical and legal professions were forced to be solo practitioners or to form a partnership. This limitation put them at a disadvantage for some income tax purposes. After a great deal of lobbying by the various professions, many states enacted special incorporation statutes that permit members of a profession to incorporate and to engage in their profession through that corporation. These are called *professional corporations*. In many states, you may see a law firm called "Smith & Jones, P.C." for example. The initials indicate the form of the business organization is a professional corporation. This form of business allows professionals to enjoy the tax benefits of corporations—primarily the benefit of deferring income in years of large earnings to years of less earnings. At the same time, the statutes are designed to protect the interests of the public that deal with these professions. Protection of the public is accomplished by not allowing the professionals who incorporate under these statutes to limit their liability for their acts or for the tortious acts of fellow associates.

ESSENTIAL FEATURES OF CORPORATIONS

The corporate form of business organization can be distinguished from proprietorships and partnerships in three significant ways.

SHARE OWNERSHIP

First, a corporation is owned by shareholders who possess shares of stock. A stock is a certificate of ownership and may be sold at any time. Thus, unlike the other forms of business organizations, the ownership can change without a significant alteration of the corporation's business. This, of course, depends on the size of the corporation. In small corporations, the ownership and management of the corporation are usually vested in the same person or in a small number of persons so that a change in ownership does produce a significant change in the business.

The 1970s and 1980s saw the share ownership of very large corporations concentrated increasingly in large financial institutions. It is estimated that, in 1991, institutional investors (e.g., banks, pension funds, insurance companies) controlled 45 to 50 percent of the stock market in the United States, and could control about 48 percent of the largest 1,000 corporations; moreover, the largest single identifiable group of share owners represented by these institutional investors were public and private pension funds of American workers, which comprise about 43 percent of the capital of these large pension funds.[10] What this means, according to some analysts, is that the American worker is coming to own indirectly an increasingly large share of corporate America.

It is estimated that by the year 2000, over 25 percent of the companies traded on the New York Stock Exchange, the American Stock Exchange, and over-the-counter markets will be more than 15 percent owned by their employees; most corporations will be more than 25 percent owned by pension institutional investors as a whole.[11]

Here is a brief list of the most prominent ways employees of large companies are gaining ownership shares:

1. Company pension funds are using their cash reserves to buy up and hold their own stock.

2. Corporate management is encouraging employees to contribute part of their salaries to 401K plans and to invest it in company stock; we discuss Section 401(k) of the Internal Revenue Code, later in this chapter.

3. Companies are giving profit-sharing payments to employees in the form of share ownership.

4. Employees are buying stock directly through corporate-employee-share purchase plans, and the company may offer a discount and pay all brokerage fees.

5. Employees are being asked or required to take a proportion of their salaries and benefits in company stock or to trade wage and benefit concessions for stock.

6. Employees are purchasing their firms' stock directly on the stock market.[12]

7. Employees may share in a number of other kinds of plans, perhaps the most prominent being an Employee Share Ownership Plan (ESOP). It is the intent of this plan to turn over most of the share ownership to employees. It is also a way out of dire financial difficulty. In brief, a company sets up a trust fund for employees, the fund secures a large loan from a bank, the proceeds are used to buy either newly issued shares or outstanding shares, which are put into the trust fund. The revenues of the corporation are then used to pay the bank, and after a period of years, the employees own enough shares to control the corporation.[13]

One primary reason employees are owning more shares of the corporations they work for is that the federal government encourages corporations to provide for their employees' retirement. Corporate contributions to employee retirement plans are deductible from corporate income up to some limit, usually 15 percent of the W–2 wages of participating employees. Some of the largest U. S. corporations and their percentages of employee ownership are shown in Figure 10.1.

FIGURE 10.1 *Corporations and Their Percentages of Employee Ownership*

Company	Fortune Rank	Percent of Employee Ownership
Ford	2	11.30
Exxon	3	9.35
Texaco	10	10.00
Chevron	11	16.00
Proctor & Gamble	14	24.50
Xerox	21	11.11
McDonnell Douglas	25	32.60

Source: J.R. Blase & D.L. Kruse, The New Owner, 14, Table 5 (1991)

What do you make of this? Experts are, it seems, of two minds. The first is that it does not mean all that much. Employees almost never exercise as a class the share voting power they have; management is still in control of the business and, in reality, the employee shares held by various pension funds, financial institutions, and the like are held in trust for the employees. The apparent changes are touted by those who have always been in control (management), and they want to make it seem that the shareholders and employees are really the big beneficiaries of their management skills.

The other view asserts that the emerging information on employee ownership may bring about an entirely new era in corporate ownership and control. If employees begin to vote their ownership shares in corporations as a class, they will bring about a new form of capitalism in which the corporations are operated for the primary benefit of the workers.

PERPETUAL LIFE

The second way corporations can be distinguished from proprietorships and partnerships is that corporations may have perpetual life. The owners and the managers may come and go, but the legal entity lives on. Technically, a partnership is dissolved when one of the partners dies (though the remaining partners may elect to carry on the business), and a proprietorship ends when the owner dies or is incapacitated.

LIMITED LIABILITY OF OWNERS

In the corporate form of business organization, the liability of the owners (the shareholders) for the corporation's debts is limited to the amount paid into the corporation or promised to it in exchange for the shares. Consider a simple example. *A, B,* and *C* decide to incorporate, and each contributes $5,000 to the enterprise in exchange for shares of stock. The corporation is properly chartered as the *ABC* Corporation. In the first month of its existence, an agent of *ABC* Corporation is negligent and injures *D. D* sues *ABC* and recovers a judgment of $25,000. The judgment (which can be for more than the corporation is worth because it reflects the extent of the injury) will be limited in a practical way to the value of the corporation ($15,000). That is, the judgment may be for $25,000, but only $15,000 of it will be collectible. The other assets of the shareholder-owners cannot be attached or otherwise affected. You may think this result is unfair to the injured party, and this view is indeed held by some commentators on the law. But the fact that most corporations have insurance that might cover the full judgment lessens the impact of limited liability. In addition, some exceptions to this important rule fall under the principle of "disregarding the corporate entity" or "piercing the corporate veil."

DISREGARDING THE CORPORATE ENTITY OR PIERCING THE CORPORATE VEIL

Under certain circumstances, a court will "disregard the corporate entity" or "pierce the corporate veil" and hold the owner or owners liable for the actions of the corporation. The power to pierce the corporate veil is created by courts and their equitable powers and is designed to prevent the evasion of corporate law statutes, the perpetration of frauds, or any other activity that is against public policy.

The typical case of piercing involves suits by corporate creditors against shareholders for debts not paid by the corporation. On a very general level, courts will talk about allowing piercing to "prevent fraud or injustice." What they require as proof is either that the corporate entity was used as a mere appendage or "alter ego" of the shareholders and was not in fact separate or that the corporation was undercapitalized at the time the debt was incurred. The classic case of *Consolidated Sun Ray, Inc.* v. *Oppenstein et al.* is illustrative of the first approach.

Consolidated Sun Ray, Inc. v. Oppenstein et al.
335 F.2d. 801 (8th Cir. 1964)

VOGEL, CIRCUIT JUDGE

This suit . . . sought . . . judgment by Michael Oppenstein against appellant Consolidated Sun Ray, Inc. (Consolidated), and Berkson Brothers, Inc. (Berkson), with respect to a lease entered into on December 4, 1939, by Oppenstein. . . Oppenstein asked judgment declaring Consolidated liable under the lease on the theory that Berkson was the wholly owned subsidiary of Consolidated, under its complete domination and control beginning in June 1955 and continuing thereafter, and was accordingly the alter ego of Consolidated and as a result thereof Consolidated was liable on the lease as though it were in fact a named lessee. . . .

On April 5, 1963, the court made its . . . judgment holding Consolidated liable on the lease. Such judgment was entered [for $112,674] against both Berkson and Consolidated.

* * *

Appellant Consolidated bases this appeal upon the following grounds.

1. The District Court erred in holding that the separate corporate entity of Berkson should be disregarded and that Berkson was the alter ego of Consolidated.

The District Court, in its Findings of Fact, . . . found that all of the stock of Berkson was owned by Consolidated; that on December 4, 1939, Oppenstein leased certain property to Berkson for a term of 26 years and 11 months ending June 30, 1967; . . . that after June or July 1955 Consolidated made certain changes in its dealings with its wholly-owned subsidiary Berkson, such as (a) eliminated Berkson's control of money received from its retail store which was operated at the leased premises and reserved to Consolidated alone the right to issue checks on the bank account deposited in the Commerce Trust Company in Kansas City; (b) in 1959 closed the bank account, opening a new one in Consolidated's name so that thereafter Berkson operated without an account in its own name; (c) pledged Berkson's accounts receivable as security for a loan Consolidated negotiated for itself; . . . (g) arranged so that the directors and officers of Berkson were persons employed by Consolidated and were the same persons who were directors or officers of Consolidated, and no director or officer of Berkson lived in the Kansas City, Missouri trade area, and the local store manager was not a director or officer of Berkson; . . . (k) many of the corporate minutes of Berkson were printed forms apparently used by Consolidated for all of its subsidiaries, with the name "Berkson's" typed in; (l) all correspondence pertaining to the business of the lessee under the lease, whether written to the lessor, to third parties or to agent of Consolidated was on Consolidated's letterhead and was for the most part signed "Consolidated Retail Stores by;" . . . (o) Consolidated operated Berkson the same as if it were one of the division stores of Consolidated rather than a wholly-owned subsidiary; (p) Consolidated did maintain substantially all the legal formalities required of Berkson as a separate corporation, such as filing necessary papers, reports and corporate tax returns.

The court also found there was a default in the payment of rent beginning November 1961 with notices, etc. From these findings the District Court made its Conclusions of Law.

* * *

4. That Consolidated should be held liable for the actions and obligations of Berkson, the same as though they were the acts and obligations of Consolidated . . . .

From the evidence in this case there can be no reasonable doubt but that Consolidated did completely control and use Berkson as a mere conduit, instrumentality or adjunct of Consolidated itself. The ultimate fact question for determination, then, was Consolidated's purpose in so doing. If that purpose was unlawful or improper or for some illegitimate purpose which might result in damage to Oppenstein, then the court has the power to look behind Berkson, the alter ego, and hold Consolidated liable for Berkson's obligations. This necessitates a determination by the trier of the facts. Here the court . . . found against Consolidated on that issue. The law of Missouri is that, where the subsidiary is a mere conduit, instrumentality, or adjunct through which the parent corporation achieves some improper end, its own corporate entity will be disregarded. . . .

We hold here that Consolidated's complete and absolute control over Berkson, making Berkson a supplemental part of Consolidated's economic unit, and operating Berkson without sufficient funds to meet its obligations to its creditors, constituted circumstantial evidence from which the advisory jury and the court, as the finders of the facts, could reasonably draw the inference that Consolidated's purpose was improper and was detrimental to Oppenstein. Such inference is sustained by substantial evidence. It may not be disturbed here on appeal. . . .

As to the first issue wherein the court and jury held Consolidated liable, this case is affirmed. . . .

CASE FOLLOW-UP

This case shows that if a corporation is the alter ego of another person or corporation, then courts will pierce the corporate veil and consider them as one unit. Another major group of elements of proof that will result in the piercing of the corporate veil involves evidence of undercapitalization. Undercapitalization usually means that the amount of money (the capital) paid into the corporation is too small in relation to the nature of the business and the risks the business necessarily entails. In some states, undercapitalization is just one element of proof tending to show fraud, misrepresentation, or an abuse of the state's statutory scheme; in other states, such as California,[14] the single fact of undercapitalization may be sufficient to pierce the corporate veil.

Reliance on any one test or one set of facts to pierce the corporate veil and hold shareholders liable for the debts of the corporation is not wise. Each case must be viewed on its own facts. Some facts that a court would consider when urged to pierce would be that the corporation was formed to (1) conceal misrepresentation, fraud, insider deals, or other illegality; (2) aid in the working of an injustice; (3) provide a mere conduit, instrumentality, or alter ego of dominant shareholders—whether other corporations or humans; (4) present a potential for harm to creditors or the public because of undercapitalization or the indiscriminate commingling of assets; or (5) do any other acts that aid in the accomplishment of an injustice to those who relied on the corporate form.[15]

BUSINESS CORPORATIONS AND THE INTERNAL REVENUE CODE

Although corporation law is appropriately thought of as either state legislative or judicial law, the Internal Revenue Code of the federal government does affect corporate structure in increasingly important ways. This is not a technical text on corporations and tax law, so the following are generalizations, but they are necessary to understanding the world of corporate form and structure.

SUBCHAPTER S CORPORATIONS

Subchapter S of Sections 1371–1377 (as amended from time to time) of the federal Internal Revenue Code creates a special form of corporation called either a subchapter S corporation or just an S corporation. The idea here is that the owners of some small businesses would like the tax advantages of a partnership in which the losses of the partnership can be set against incomes of the individual partners to determine tax liability. So, Congress allows some small corporations to be treated as partnerships for purposes of tax liability. The owners of the corporation still enjoy the limited liability of the corporate form.

Specifically, if the number of shareholders does not exceed thirty-five, there is but one class of stock, all shareholders consent to the election of the S form, plus a few other qualifications, and then shareholders may elect to be individually taxed as partners. These owners are taxed on their shares of the corporation's income or may deduct (from other items of income they have) their proportionate share of the corporation's losses. The corporation itself pays no corporate income tax. This feature relieves the owners from the normal double taxation on their corporate income—first, the corporation pays income tax on its income, and then when dividends are paid out, the shareholder who receives them is taxed again.

Section 401(k) of the Internal Revenue Code also is becoming increasingly influential in the area of corporation law. This section creates a form of employee ownership of corporate shares by providing that employee savings (which are deducted from their salaries), plus the corporation's matching contributions and bonuses, may be used to purchase company stock for the employees.

Also, Section 4975 allows for ESOPS, in which employees may borrow money to purchase company stock for themselves and then pay back the loan from ongoing operating profits

CORPORATIONS AND AGENCY LAW

Corporations must do business with the public through agents. When corporations make a contract with a third party, the law of agency, together with contract law, will probably provide the legal principles used to resolve any legal conflicts between the parties. Corporations as principals are bound by contracts made by their agents if the agents were properly authorized to make the contracts. In determining whether an agent was properly authorized, a court will focus on the various legal definitions of authority used in agency law. For expressed authority, the court may consider resolutions or minutes from the meetings of the board of directors, job descriptions, employment contracts, and the like. In cases in which expressed authority is not present, courts may attempt to apply the principles of circumstantial authority, such as apparent authority. Respondeat superior may also be used to hold a corporation (as either a principal or a master) liable for the torts of its employees (as either servants or nonservant agents).

THE POWERS OF SHAREHOLDERS

Generally, the powers, rights, and duties of the shareholders of a business corporation are found somewhere within the *shareholder contract*. This general term refers to all five of the legal documents that could possibly define shareholder rights and duties:

1. The state constitution

2. The state business corporation statute

3. The articles of incorporation issued to the incorporators (founders) of the corporation when it is properly registered with the state

4. The bylaws of the corporation

5. Any contractual agreements between the corporation and the shareholders found written on the shares themselves or in separate contracts that pertain to shareholders

In this hierarchy of sets of rules (also used to define the rights, duties, and powers of the directors and officers of the corporation), the state constitution is the most important and contractual agreements are the least important. Whenever a dispute develops, the controlling document is the state constitution, which usually has only a few provisions that apply to business corporations; the state business corporation statute is considered next, then the articles, and so on. Thus, any corporate bylaw that conflicts with the wording or intent of the state business corporation statute is not valid.

The conventional wisdom is that shareholders exercise ultimate control of the corporation. This control takes place through the shareholders' election of the board of directors. This board, as provided by state law, is to manage the corporation. So, the orthodox theory holds, the shareholders can at least influence corporate policy by their legal right to vote for those responsible for the management of the enterprise. This conventional view may hold true for the millions of corporations with ten shareholders or fewer.[16]

For the roughly 1,500 corporations with more than 3,000 shareholders, this conventional view was challenged more than sixty years ago by Adolph Berle and Gardiner Means in their classic work on corporation law and economics, *The*

Modern Corporation and Private Property. The authors pointed out that because the shareholders were so many and so scattered and because management had access to all the vital corporate records and information, it could perpetuate itself in office.

In megacorporations, shareholders, most of whom cannot attend annual meetings, elect the board by using written ballots that technically authorize *proxies*— usually management personnel—to cast votes. Management (the board of directors) can and does influence the entire voting process by nominating the people who stand for election to the board. Berle and Means argued that because management is in a position to perpetuate itself in control, a separation of ownership (by the shareholders) and control (by management) exists in the large American corporation.

Just how much power or influence does a shareholder have today? The answer depends on the size of corporation involved. If the corporation is very small or closely held, shareholder democracy is alive and working. If the corporation is a megacorporation, shareholder influence is minimal unless, of course, the shareholder is a similarly large institution, such as a bank or insurance company.

Most state statutes provide that the shareholders have the following powers:

1. To elect and remove directors

2. To approve or disapprove amendments to the articles

3. To approve or disapprove of fundamental changes not in the ordinary course of business, such as proposals for mergers, stock exchanges with other corporations, and a disposition of substantially all of the corporate assets

One of the oldest and most highly regarded rights of a shareholder is the access to corporate records and books. Today, corporate charters mandated by state statutory law and, before that, the common law, granted to a shareholder the right to inspect the corporate books and records for a legitimate purpose. The requirement of a legitimate purpose is designed to protect the corporation and its other shareholders from harassment or other abuses. For example, an officer of a chemical manufacturer who is also a shareholder of a competing enterprise could not see the competitor's books to learn trade secrets or to obtain customer lists. A dissident shareholder, however, could obtain a list of shareholders in order to solicit their votes for an attempt to remove current management. Such an effort constitutes a proper purpose, as does an inspection of the records to discover relevant evidence for a lawsuit against the directors and officers. Other legitimate purposes include a determination of the corporation's financial position or its ability to pay dividends and the investigation of possible mismanagement.

A "legitimate purpose" for obtaining corporate books and records is nowhere defined with great precision. The case of *State ex rel. Pillsbury* v. *Honeywell, Inc.* is a good example of a court's struggling with this definition.

State ex rel. Pillsbury v. Honeywell, Inc.
191 N.W. 2d 406 (S. Ct. Minn. 1971)

KELLEY, JUSTICE

Petitioner attended a meeting on July 3, 1969, of a group involved in what was known as the "Honeywell Project." Participants in the project believed that American involvement in Vietnam was wrong, that a substantial portion of Honeywell's production consisted of munitions used in that war, and that Honeywell should stop this production of munitions. Petitioner had long opposed the Vietnam war, but it was at the July 3rd meeting that he first learned of Honeywell's involvement. He was shocked at the knowledge that Honeywell had a large government contract to produce antipersonnel fragmentation bombs. Upset because of knowledge that such bombs were produced in his own community by a company which he had known and respected, petitioner determined to stop Honeywell's munitions production.

On July 14, 1969, petitioner ordered his fiscal agent to purchase 100 shares of Honeywell. He admits that the sole purpose of the purchase was to give himself a voice in Honeywell's affairs so he could persuade Honeywell to cease producing munitions. . . .

Prior to the instigation of this suit, petitioner submitted two formal demands to Honeywell requesting that it produce its original shareholder ledger, current shareholder ledger, and all corporate records dealing with weapons and munitions manufacture. Honeywell refused.

On November 24, 1969, a petition was filed for writs . . . ordering Honeywell to produce the above mentioned records.

In a deposition petitioner outlined his beliefs concerning the Vietnam war and his purpose for his involvement with Honeywell. He expressed his desire to communicate with other shareholders in the hope of altering Honeywell's board of directors and thereby changing its policy. To this end, he testified, business records are necessary to insure accuracy. . . .

A hearing was held on January 8, 1970, during which Honeywell . . . conceded all material facts stated therein, and argued that petitioner was not entitled to any relief as a matter of law. . . . On April 8, 1970, the final court dismissed the petition, holding that the relief requested was for an improper and indefinite purpose. Petitioner contends in this appeal that the dismissal was in error.

Honeywell is a Delaware corporation doing business in Minnesota. . . . The trial court, applying Delaware law, determined that the outcome of the case rested upon whether or not petitioner has a proper purpose germane to his interest as a shareholder. . . . [*Author's note:* It is a well-settled principle of law that a state where an action is brought (here, Minnesota) will resolve questions of law concerning corporations by looking at the law of the state where the corporation was created (here, Delaware). As we related earlier, Delaware corporation law is favorable to management, rather than to shareholder rights.]

Under the Delaware statute the shareholder must prove a proper purpose to inspect corporate records other than shareholder lists. . . .

★ ★ ★

The trial court ordered judgment for Honeywell, ruling that petitioner had not demonstrated a proper purpose germane to his interest as a stockholder. Petitioner contends that a stockholder who disagrees with management has an absolute right to inspect corporate records for purposes of soliciting proxies. He would have this court rule that such solicitation is per se a "proper purpose." Honeywell argues that a "proper purpose" contemplates concern with investment return. We agree with Honeywell.

This court has had several occasions to rule on the propriety of shareholders' demands for inspection of corporate books and records. . . . While inspection will not be permitted for purposes of curiosity, speculation, or vexation, adverseness to management and a desire to gain control of the corporation for economic benefit does not indicate an improper purpose.

Several courts agree with petitioner's contention that a mere desire to communicate with other shareholders is, per se, a proper purpose. . . . We believe that a better rule would allow inspections only if the shareholder has a proper purpose for such communication.

★ ★ ★

The act of inspecting a corporation's shareholder ledger and business records must be viewed in its proper perspective. In terms of the corporate norm, inspection is merely the act of the concerned owner checking on what is in part his property. In the context of the large firm, inspection can be more akin to a weapon in corporate warfare.

★ ★ ★

That one must have proper standing to demand inspection has been recognized by statutes in several jurisdictions. Courts have also balked at compelling inspection by a shareholder holding an insignificant amount of stock in the corporation.

Petitioner's standing as a shareholder is quite tenuous. . . . He had previously ordered his agent to buy 100 shares, but there is no showing of investment intent.

★ ★ ★

Petitioner had utterly no interest in the affairs of Honeywell before he learned of Honeywell's production of fragmentation bombs. Immediately after obtaining this knowledge, he purchased stock in Honeywell for the sole purpose of asserting ownership privileges in an effort to force Honeywell to cease such production.

★ ★ ★

But for his opposition to Honeywell's policy, petitioner probably would not have bought Honeywell stock, would not be interested in Honeywell's profits and would not desire to communicate with Honeywell's shareholders. His avowed purpose in buying Honeywell stock was to place himself in a position to try to impress his opinions favoring a reordering of priorities upon Honeywell management and its other shareholders. Such a motivation can hardly be deemed a proper purpose germane to his economic interest as a shareholder.

★ ★ ★

We do not mean to imply that a shareholder with a bona fide investment interest could not bring this suit if motivated by concern with the long- or short-term economic effects on Honeywell resulting from the production of war munitions. Similarly, this suit might be appropriate when a shareholder has a bona fide concern about the adverse effects of abstention from profitable war contracts on his investment in Honeywell.

In the instant case, however, the trial court, in effect, has found from all the facts that petitioner was not interested in even the long-term well-being of Honeywell or the enhancement of the value of his shares. His sole purpose was to persuade the company to adopt his social and political concerns, irrespective of any economic benefit to himself or Honeywell. This purpose on the part of one buying into the corporation does not entitle the petitioner to inspect Honeywell's books and records.

The order of the trial court . . . is affirmed.

CASE FOLLOW-UP

In this case, we can see the clash of many interests and values. On the one hand is the legally created property right of a shareholder to secure corporate records for a proper purpose. Probably the most important information to the petitioner was the list of current shareholders and their addresses. The court acknowledges that some states hold that a mere desire to communicate is, by itself, a proper purpose. It seems that if shareholder democracy is to mean anything, shareholders should be accorded the right to communicate with one another. The shareholders are, after all, the owners. The conventional view of ownership is that an owner should have the right to at least be heard with regard to the ownership interest. This case represents a rather severe limitation on a shareholder's property rights.

On the other hand we can see that the court is guarding the corporate form from possible abuse by someone who would misuse the information sought. But consider further the kind of possible abuse. How could a shareholder abuse the right to the names and addresses of shareholders? Perhaps management could have a good reason not to disclose corporate financial records dealing with weapons and munitions. But is not this type of information different from the names and addresses of shareholders? Do you agree with this court that a proper purpose for gaining access to these records should be a concern with investment return?

In conclusion, the powers of shareholders over corporate business matters is greater in smaller corporations. In very large corporations, shareholders may act (by voting) only in a properly called meeting of the shareholders at which management controls the agenda.

THE POWERS OF DIRECTORS AND OFFICERS

The RMBCA, the Delaware statute, and almost all other state business corporation statutes provide that the corporation shall be managed by the board of directors. This means that, unless altered by special agreement, the board of directors has the authority and may make all decisions in the regular course of business. In most cases, members of the board are not paid much more than expenses. Usually, most members of the board are also officers or employees and receive compensation as a salary from the corporation. Large corporations may have members of the board who are not employed by the corporation; they are called *outside directors*. Outside directors serve because of the prestige they receive and the business and social connections they make or because of expertise they may add to that of management.

The board of directors hires the officers of the corporation who usually make the day-to-day business decisions. Traditional corporation statutes require every corporation to have certain designated officers, such as a president, a secretary, and a treasurer. The RMBCA and the Delaware statute both have eliminated all mandatory titled officers and provide that each corporation shall have the officers described in its bylaws or appointed by the board.

The powers of the directors and officers of a corporation are to be found in the same hierarchy of documents that define the shareholder contract: First consult the state constitution (it is unlikely you will find provisions here on the powers of directors and shareholders), then the state corporation statute, the articles of incorporation, the bylaws, and any shareholder agreements (including any understandings about powers that may be present in resolutions of the board). When we speak of powers here, we mean the expressed authority to make decisions with regard to business matters and implied authority, which is needed to carry out the expressed authority.

The powers of directors and officers are limited by various laws covered in this text (especially the federal and state securities and antitrust laws) and the more general notions of what is called the *duty of care* and the *duty of loyalty*.

CIVIL LIABILITY OF MANAGEMENT

Management designates those members of the corporation who have the authority to decide matters relating to the corporate purpose. Management is usually composed of members of the board of directors and the officers of the corporation. The legal liability of management is established by criminal and civil laws. The criminal liability of management is created by a particular state or federal statute. The federal securities laws and antitrust laws, for example, impose criminal liability for some actions. In this section, we examine only the civil liability of the individual members of management. This liability makes clear management's duty of care.

Civil liability of management is of two general types. First, corporation law statutes in most states provide for civil liability for the violation of specific standards. For example, in most states, management may be liable to creditors of the corporation if they declare a dividend or authorize distribution of assets to shareholders while the corporation is insolvent. Second, and much more general, the board of directors owes a general duty of care to the shareholders and the corporation. The duty of care that is found in many state corporation statutes is well stated in the RMBCA (Section 8.30), which provides that directors' duties must be discharged

1. In good faith

2. With the care an ordinary, prudent person in a similar position would exercise under similar circumstances

3. In a manner one reasonably believes to be in the best interests of the corporation

BUSINESS JUDGMENT RULE

These standards create the often-cited business judgment rule. This rule "*immunizes directors and other members of management* from liability where the transaction is within the powers of the corporation and the authority of management, and involves the exercise of due care."[17] That is, if management makes a decision that appears, through hindsight, to be negligent or to breach a standard of care, management will not be liable so long as the decision was made in good faith, was within the corporation's powers and management's authority, and was the result of independent discretion and judgment.

Every day, large and small corporations lose money, and some file bankruptcy as a result of bad business decisions. The policy position of the law is that management should be given tremendous freedom to make these judgments. Only in rare cases will a court attempt to interfere with the internal management of a corporation and substitute its judgment for that of management.

The breach of the duty of care involves the concept of negligent management or mismanagement. This concept is so amorphous it almost lacks meaning. The idea of negligence and negligent acts of *individuals* is much clearer. In these cases, such as throwing a baseball through a window or crossing the center line in an automobile and hitting someone, good faith is not an excuse. What appears to be a negligent business decision, however, creates no liability so long as it was done in good faith. The next case demonstrates an expression of this rule.

SHAREHOLDER'S DERIVATIVE ACTION

An additional point needs to be made before you read this case. If management is negligent, who or what suffers the damages? In corporation law, the answer is that usually the corporation suffers the damage incurred by negligent management. If the corporation is damaged as a result of management's action, is it reasonable to assume that those in control of the corporation (management) will authorize the corporation to bring a claim against themselves? Of course not, so state laws recognize a *shareholder's derivative action*. These actions are initiated by shareholders on behalf of the corporation against management or against some other entity that management has refused to sue. *Gall* v. *Exxon Corp.* is illustrative of both the shareholder's derivative action and the business judgment rule.

Gall v. *Exxon Corp.*
418 F.Supp. 508 (D. Ct. N.Y. 1976)

CARTER, DISTRICT JUDGE

Plaintiff's complaint arises out of the alleged payment by Exxon Corporation of some $59 million in corporate funds as bribes or political payments, which were improperly contributed to Italian political parties and others during the period 1963-1974, in order to secure special political favors as well as other allegedly illegal commitments.

★ ★ ★

The complaint demands that the individual defendants be held jointly and severally liable for damages, including loss of goodwill, allegedly suffered by Exxon. It further demands, among other things, the commencement of an investigation through independent auditors in conjunction with plaintiff's counsel, the immediate election of four new members of the Board of Directors proposed by plaintiff and, within 12 months, the election of a new Chairman of the Board and President, and reconstituting the composition of the membership of the Board of Directors and Executive Committee, such that at least 55% of the Board and the Executive Committee be made up of independent outside directors.

On September 24, 1975, Exxon's Board of Directors unanimously resolved . . . to establish a Special Committee on Litigation, . . . and refer to the Special Committee for the determination of Exxon's action the matters raised in this and several other pending actions, relating to the Italian expenditures. With respect to the matters within its mandate, the Special Committee acts as the Boards of Directors of Exxon.

★ ★ ★

On January 23, 1976, after an investigation of approximately four months, . . . an 82-page document summarizing the Committee's findings and recommendations [was published].

★ ★ ★

The investigation . . . revealed that political contributions by Esso Italiana to various Italian political parties during the nine-year period form 1963 through 1971 totalled $27.9 million. . . . Of this amount, $13.5 million were recycled into one or more of the 40 secret bank accounts. All political contributions by Esso Italiana were ended in 1972.

It is clear that several of the Exxon directors named as defendants in this suit were aware of the existence of the political payments in Italy prior to their termination in 1972.

★ ★ ★

After careful review, analysis and investigation, and with the advice and concurrence of Special Counsel, the Special Committee unanimously determined on January 23, 1976,

that it would be contrary to the interests of Exxon and its shareholders for Exxon, or anyone on its behalf, to institute or maintain a legal action against any present or former Exxon director or officer. The Committee further resolved to direct and authorize the proper officers of Exxon and its General Counsel to oppose and seek dismissal of all shareholders derivative actions relating to payments made by or on behalf of Esso Italiano S.p.A. . . .

There is no question that the rights sought to be vindicated in this lawsuit are those of Exxon and not those of the plaintiff suing derivatively on the corporation's behalf. . . . Since it is the interests of the corporation which are at stake, it is the responsibility of the directors of the corporation to determine, in the first instance, whether an action should be brought on the corporation's behalf. It follows that the decision of corporate directors whether or not to assert a cause of action held by the corporation rests within the sound business judgment of the management. . . .

This principle, which has come to be known as the business judgment rule, was articulated by Mr. Justice Brandeis speaking for the unanimous Court in *United Copper Securities Co.* v. *Amalgamated Copper Co.,* . . . 244 U.S. at 263–64. 37 S.Ct. at 510. In that case the directors of a corporation chose not to bring an antitrust action against a third party. Mr. Justice Brandeis said:

> Whether or not a corporation shall seek to enforce in the courts a cause of action for damages is, like other business questions, ordinarily a matter of internal management, and is left to the discretion of the directors, in the absence of instruction by vote of the stockholders. Courts interfere seldom to control such discretion . . . except where the directors are guilty of misconduct equivalent to a breach of trust, or where they stand in a dual relation which prevents an unprejudiced exercise of judgment. . . .

* * *

It is clear that absent allegations of fraud, collusion, self-interest, dishonesty or other misconduct of a breach of trust nature, and absent allegations that the business judgment exercised was grossly unsound, the court should not at the instigation of a single shareholder interfere with the judgment of the corporate officers. . . .

The question remains as to the requisite showing of good faith on the part of the corporate directors sufficient to warrant a dismissal based on the business judgment rule defense.

* * *

In this regard, plaintiff challenges the independence of the Special Committee's judgment, arguing that the decision of the Special Committee was, in effect, a decision by those accused of the wrongdoing or by a body under the control of those accused of the wrongdoing. . . .

* * *

This argument clearly misses the mark. The focus of the business judgment rule inquiry is on those who actually wield the decision-making authority, not on those who might have possessed such authority at different times and under different circumstances. In no sense was the decision of the Special Committee not to sue merely an advisory one. Indeed, in carrying out its investigation and in reaching its conclusions, the Special Committee exercised the full powers of the Board.

Plaintiff next argues that the challenged political payments were illegal and that such illegality removes this case from the operation of the business judgment rule.

[E]ven assuming that the political payments in Italy were illegal where made, the business judgment rule is nonetheless applicable. The decision not to bring suit with regard to past conduct which may have been illegal is not itself a violation of law and does not result in the continuation of the alleged violation of law. Rather, it is a decision by the directors of the corporation that pursuit of a cause of action based on acts already consummated is not in the best interest of the corporation. Such a determination, like any other business decision, must be made by the corporate directors in the exercise of their sound business judgment. . . .

Moreover, this conclusion is all the more appropriate in view of the fact that there is not a scintilla of evidence on the record before me that the political payments in issue here were illegal either under the laws of the United States or of Italy. On the contrary, the Special Committee on the basis of its intensive investigation, and with the concurrence of its Special Counsel, determined that there was no basis for concluding that the Italian payments were in any way illegal.

* * *

Again, to quote Mr. Justice Brandeis,

Mere belief that corporate action, taken or contemplated, is illegal gives the stockholder no greater right to interfere than is possessed by any other citizen. Stockholders are not guardians of the public. The function of guarding the public against the acts deemed illegal rests with the public officials. . . .

* * *

. . . I am constrained to conclude that it is premature at this stage of the lawsuit to grant summary judgment. Plaintiff must be given an opportunity to test the bona fides and independence of the Special Committee through discovery and, if necessary, at a plenary hearing. . . . Issues of intent, motivation, and good faith are particularly inappropriate for summary disposition. . . .

Accordingly, defendants' motion for summary judgment is hereby denied without prejudice to its renewal after plaintiff has conducted relevant discovery. Plaintiff will be given 60 days from the date of entry of this order to conduct discovery, and if neces-sary to request a hearing, in order to put be-fore the court significant probative evidence tending to support its position. . . .

So ordered.

CASE FOLLOW-UP

The question remains, If the persons who made the payments for Exxon or authorized them or set them up did not think the pay-ments were illegal, why was $13.5 million recycled into one or more of the forty secret bank accounts? In your judgment, would the standard of conduct for directors be too high or too severe if the directors should be held liable for the improper payments? As the court indicates, making payments for political favors in foreign countries did not violate American law in the years in which they were made (1963–1971). The Foreign Cor-rupt Practices Act, discussed in another part of this book, does declare such payments to be illegal, but it was not passed until 1977.

In your estimation, is it good policy to have a legal principle that exempts manage-ment from liability (such as in this case) if the breach of the duty of care was done in good faith? If good faith were shown, Exxon's management would be exempted from liability. We could locate no record that indicates whether this case ever came to trial.

The duty of care of managers is a vague notion. It certainly is not as precise as the duty of care of *individuals* expressed in our ideas about common negligence. Tied to the expression of this corporate duty of care is the *business judgment rule,* or "doctrine" as some commentators call it. This rule and the preceding case hold that directors are granted broad discretion with respect to the management of the corporation and that the exercise of that discretion is not subject to judicial re-view unless there is "bad faith" action. *Bad faith action* usually implies some form of self-dealing at the expense of others or action so negligent that it appears to be intentional. For example, if managers attempted to loot the corporation by paying themselves exorbitant salaries, they would breach the duty of care.

BOARD LIABILITY FOR THE SALE OF CONTROL

This standard of recognizing a breach of the duty of care when management acts in bad faith may be changing. In the Delaware state court decision of *Smith* v. *Van Gorkom,*[18] the court held a board of directors liable when it failed to exercise its own independent and informed judgment on the value of a controlling interest that was sold. In this case, the owner of a substantial block of shares (also CEO of the corporation) single-handedly negotiated the price for the sale of controlling interest. The board relied on his assertions as to the value of the shares sold. Ap-parently, the shares could have been sold for more, or other shareholders should have been given the opportunity to sell their shares as well. The other shareholders were damaged. The court held that the board's inattention to this matter was a breach of care. Members of the board were held individually liable for the difference between the price at which the shares sold and their fair market value. This case suggests that the sale of a controlling interest may be a special instance in which the courts will exercise stricter scrutiny of board actions.

How can directors protect themselves from liability for not acting "reasonably"? They must take an active role in informing themselves about corporate matters. In making board decisions, each director must act on the basis of his or her own judgment. Directors should not accept passively such vitally important suggestions as the sale of control without some active inquiry as to what is best for the remaining shareholders.

The *Van Gorkom* case and a few others like it have caused most directors and officers to seek insurance ("directors and officers" or "D & O" insurance) to cover court judgments against them for the breach of the duty of care. In many states, a few large recoveries by shareholders against directors have caused the cost of D & O insurance to rise dramatically.

In some states, the directors of large corporations have asked legislatures to pass statutes that permit limiting directors' liability through corporate bylaws. A survey of 3,120 Delaware corporations revealed that 75 percent of them would ask their shareholders to approve bylaws that would limit director liability.[19] Presumably, these bylaws would either bind the shareholders to amounts for which they could sue or in some way limit their suits through contract law. Courts would read the bylaws as a contract between the shareholders and the corporation limiting such suits, or the bylaws could provide for reimbursement for any director loss due to a shareholder suit.

MANAGEMENT LIABILITY FOR TORTS

The tort liability of management (as individuals) may be created when management authorizes or knows of tortious actions by an agent of the corporation.

Attorney General v. *Acme Disposal Co.*
473 N.W.2d 824 (Mich. App. 1991)

SHEPHERD, JUDGE

Defendants and others were alleged by plaintiff to have violated the Solid Waste Management Act, . . . the Environmental Protection Act, . . . and administrative rules promulgated under those acts, by virtue of their involvement in the operation of a landfill located in Oceana County. Plaintiff also alleged public nuisance against the various defendants. The landfill, located on property owned by the Heggs and leased to Circle Leasing Company in 1977, was operated by Acme Disposal Company from 1978 to April 1985, when the landfill was closed by court order. Acme had an operating license only for the year 1978.

★ ★ ★

The crux of plaintiff's claim against Charles Leonard is that because he was the manager of the landfill during the time it allegedly discharged leachate into the ground water and operated without a license, he is liable for the damages caused thereby as well as for cleanup costs. We disagree and hold that the trial court properly found no cause of action against Leonard.

First, with respect to the claim that Leonard is liable under a public nuisance theory, we agree with plaintiff that employees of a corporation can, under certain circumstances, be held. However, liability for damage caused by a nuisance turns upon whether the defendant was in control. . . . The evidence at trial showed that Mr. Leonard, while holding the title of manager, had no authority or control over the operation of the landfill. He was subject to the direction of Dennis Forst, his employer, reporting to him at least daily. Leonard had no authority to hire or fire employees, had no access to Acme funds or accounts other than to make deposits, had no access to the corporate books, and made no decisions regarding management of the landfill. . . .

The element of a control, we believe, is equally crucial to a finding of liability for violation of the acts. The legislature, in enacting the various antipollution provisions, intended not to target mere employees who, despite knowledge of their employers' violations, can do nothing about them, but rather those who, within the corporate structure, have the power and authority to correct the conditions which are deemed deleterious to the environment or people of this state. . . .

We likewise affirm the judgment entered in favor of the Heggs. Plaintiff asserted a claim of public nuisance against the Heggs, alleging that they sanctioned the creation and maintenance of a public nuisance at the landfill by failing to terminate their lease with Circle Leasing and evict Acme Disposal. Liability on the part of the Heggs for the alleged damage-causing conduct of their lessee turns upon whether the Heggs sanctioned Acme's conduct. . . . The evidence adduced at trial did not support such a finding. Rather, the evidence showed that while Mr. Hegg may have suspected there might be problems at the landfill, neither he nor Mrs. Hegg had knowledge of the alleged violations or even that the landfill was operating without a license. The evidence indicates that such information about the operation of the landfill was kept from the Heggs by Forst.

However, we cannot reach the same conclusion with regard to the trial court's dismissal of the nuisance claim against H. Roy Valkema. Valkema, who had a trash-hauling business and was familiar with solid waste collection and disposal, owned fifty-one percent of Acme stock. While he claimed to have no knowledge of Acme's unlawful activities at the landfill, he possessed control over the company's finances and purchasing, and acted as president, from 1982 to 1983, during the time Acme is alleged to have pumped leachate into the ground water. A director or officer of a corporation may be held liable for a nuisance created or maintained by that corporation if he had knowledge of the existence or continuance of the nuisance, or if he should have known of it by exercising ordinary diligence.

. . . Likewise, where a party, by virtue of his position or ownership interest, is vested with the power to control corporate activities, he may also be held responsible for a nuisance created or maintained by the corporation. . . . Thus, Valkema's denial of active participation in the activities in question here is not determinative. There was ample evidence that he was in a position of authority within the corporation and that he should have known, through the exercise of ordinary diligence, of Acme's activities at the landfill, particularly while he was acting as president. The trial court erroneously focused only on the issue whether Valkema actively participated or sanctioned Acme's illegal activities and further found that Valkema had a right to rely on what may have been misinformation supplied to him by Forst. The court did not, however, consider whether Valkema should have known of the conditions which the court found constituted a nuisance or whether he was in a position to abate the nuisance. Consequently, we find that the judgment in Valkema's favor must be vacated and the matter remanded with regard to the issue of his personal liability.

* * *

CASE FOLLOW-UP

The law of this case seems simple: A director or officer of a corporation is liable for a tort created by an agent of the corporation if he or she had knowledge of the tort or authorized it or if he or she should have known of it by exercising ordinary diligence. What of the management of Exxon in the case before this one? Were they not involved in the tort of conversion which is the intentional deprivation of another's (shareholders') property, or the tort of negligence? After all, they were aware of the large payments of money to secure political favors. The only explanation we can think of is that nuisance is a typical, almost common tort and that there was real damage to others' interests. In the Exxon case, no real damage was done to a traditionally protected interest of another. Moreover, the business judgment rule applied because the payments were not then illegal and because management supposedly did use their discretion and exercised "good faith."

SHAREHOLDER SUITS AGAINST MANAGEMENT

Litigation brought by shareholders may be divided into two categories. The first, a *direct suit,* involves the alleged breach of a contractual claim between the corporation and the shareholder. A common example is a suit to recover a dividend when a shareholder owns shares that clearly entitle the holder to dividends. The second, a *derivative suit,* exemplified in the *Gall* case, is an action by one or more shareholders to prevent or remedy a wrong that belongs to the corporation but that the directors will not pursue because they may be involved in the decision that is at the heart of the complaint. Would the directors of Exxon have authorized a suit against themselves when a few of their number caused Exxon to pay what appear to be bribes to Italian officials? Of course not.

The dispute about the value of these suits continues. Some policy commentators claim that because so many attorneys in this country will accept clients on a fee-based-on-recovery basis and because corporations have a tradition of settling shareholder suits to avoid adverse publicity, many of these suits are not meritorious. They are brought merely to make a few shareholders and their attorneys well-off. Others respond that the shareholder's derivative suit is one of the only meaningful checks on the discretion of management. In many jurisdictions, the right to bring a shareholder's derivative suit is conditioned on (1) the shareholder's good faith effort to resolve the conflict or to convince the board to bring the suit, (2) refusal of the board to respond to this demand, (3) shareholder ownership of shares when the cause of action arose, and (4) deposit by the shareholder of a bond or other form of security that would cover reasonable expenses, including attorneys' fees if the court hearing the case determines the defendant is entitled to expenses. These conditions seem to keep the number of shareholder derivative suits to a minimum.

If the shareholder does recover, the sum is usually paid to the corporation because the shareholder was vindicating the corporation's rights in the first place.

Managers of corporations have a duty not to compete with the corporation in any way and to act in the best interests of the corporation. Cases in this area usually center on one of four circumstances:

1. Transactions between a director and the corporation (e.g., when the corporation sells its management retreat house on the shores of Lake Michigan to a director)

2. Transactions between corporations that have common directors

3. Transactions made by directors taking advantage of business opportunities they know about because of their position with the corporation

4. Competition between the director and the corporation

Many state corporation statutes allow directors and officers to contract with their corporations to receive loans, sell property, and receive other benefits. *The general rule is that no breach of the duty of loyalty exists as long as the transaction is fair to the corporation (whatever was sold was priced at prevailing market prices) and no evidence suggests fraud, overreaching, or possible looting.* In questionable cases, courts have affirmed the transaction when it was voted on by the shareholders.

MERGERS AND ACQUISITIONS UNDER STATE CORPORATE LAW

One of the most dynamic areas of corporate law on the state level involves attempts by one corporation to gain control of another. Sometimes such transactions are friendly. For example, a local corporation may have lost senior management to death or retirement, and a controlling group of shareholders may actually seek out another corporation to buy their shares. An interested party may have the shares valued by an appraiser (usually an accounting firm), and the purchase of the shares for a fair price is made. If the purchasing firm decides to completely take over the sold firm, with the purchasing firm as the survivor, the firms are said to be *merged*. In some instances, both the purchasing firm and the purchased firm disappear and a new corporation appears; this is referred to as a *consolidation*.

Sometimes the purchase of control of another corporation is against the wishes of management. Such an attempted takeover is called *hostile*. Why would management oppose a purchase of outstanding voting shares that would change the control of the corporation? The answer is simple: Management jobs are on the line. If a hostile takeover is successful, many top-level managers almost certainly would be fired and replaced by new management.

The reasons for corporate takeovers and mergers are many. Usually, an outside person who has access to considerable amounts of cash believes he or she can do a better job of managing a target firm and so sets out to buy shares. We proceed here on the assumption that a hostile takeover is in the making and current management wants to oppose it. What is the position of the law in this circumstance?

The law applicable here is multilayered. If stock manipulation or insider trading is done by management, federal securities laws apply; if the resulting (merged) firm may present anticompetitive forces in the relevant marketplaces, antitrust laws may be applicable; or, as we discuss here, management may use several devices that involve state corporation law.

Before we proceed with a fuller explanation of this state law, we define some legal and popular terms found in the business press. *Corporate raiders* usually refers to a group of people who have begun to buy up outstanding shares of a corporation that is ripe for a takeover because its shares may be temporarily undervalued. Corporate raiders become known if they announce a tender offer in the *Wall Street Journal* or other popular financial press. A *tender offer* is a public invitation to shareholders of the target corporation to sell their shares to the raiders for 15 to 25 percent above market prices.

Federal law (the Williams Act of 1968) requires such raiders to disclose the purpose for which the offer is made, the plans the raiders may have if successful, and the sources of funds used in the offer. This disclosure is triggered when more than 5 percent of the outstanding shares of any class of a corporation registered with the SEC are purchased. So, if raiders want control (usually about 8 to 15 percent of outstanding shares of a megacorporation), they must disclose their intent before they reach their goal. In addition, to alert competitors and others interested in the target firm, the Hart-Scott-Rodino Antitrust Improvement Act of 1976 requires public disclosure of a plan to acquire voting shares or assets when one firm has assets or annual net sales of $100 million or more and the acquiring firm gives 15 percent or more of another's stock. A few other conditions must also be met.

The management of the target corporation now swing into action. They have many alternatives, depending on the powers given them by their bylaws, the articles of the corporation, and the state corporation statute. Incumbent management may search for a "white knight," a more friendly corporation that will come riding to the rescue and buy control before the raiders do. Management will have worked out some arrangement with the white knight by which most of their jobs are protected. Another alternative is for management to buy another corporation that competes with the raiders, thus raising antitrust problems. The Justice Department looks very carefully when one competitor (the raiders) buys up another (the expanded target with the addition of the competitor). Or management may offer to pay the raiders more than the raiders paid for the outstanding shares they purchased. Such sums paid to raiders are called *Green Mail*. Or a corporation may purchase its own outstanding shares or may use its influence with the trustees of the employees' retirement system to purchase outstanding shares so that a takeover might be defeated. Or management may offer a generous dividend that will drive up the price of the shares and make the purchase of control more expensive. Or management may present a "poison pill" to the raider by creating new classes of stock in which the rights of all shareholders increase if any person acquires more than a specified percentage of outstanding shares.

In many instances involving raiders or friendly takeovers, the source of funds used by the buyers has been the subject of much public comment. Many cash tender offers involve the use of capital raised through the issuance of bonds subordinate to all other of the debt securities of the issuer. These "junk bonds" are very speculative because they are secured by few, if any, assets. The idea is to pay off the bonds quickly by selling a division of the target corporation. Thus, the real value of the bonds, the proceeds of which are used to buy the target, depends on how profitably the new management sells parts of the target. It is not much of an exaggeration to say that the raiders feed off the target corporation in raising the funds needed to pay off the junk bonds they used to buy control.

Perhaps by now it is obvious why management usually opposes any attempt to oust them through a tender offer. A final defensive move by management is to use their influence to change the state corporation law to protect themselves in a takeover attempt. Local politicians usually support such changes in legislation because they also view new management as somewhat hostile to local interests such as local employees and vendors. The problem with using state law to thwart the movement of capital across state lines to buy control of corporations is that it may run afoul of the free flow of commerce standard protected by the Constitution.

Both federal law (the Williams Act) and other statutes and state law have become increasingly concerned with takeover attempts in order to protect uninvolved shareholders so that the value of their shares will not be unfairly dispersed. The Williams Act and most state schemes require public disclosure and attempt to buy time in takeover circumstances so that shareholders may evaluate any offer given.

In attempting to regulate the recent wave of takeovers, new federal and state laws sometimes conflict. The following U.S. Supreme Court case attempts to adjust the balance between federal and state interests and to give an impetus to state-level control and the primary protection of shareholders.

CTS Corp. v. Dynamics Corp. of America
481 U.S. 69 (1986)

POWELL, JUSTICE

A

On March 4, 1986, the Governor of Indiana signed a revised Indiana Business Corporation Law. Ind. Code 523-1-17-1 *et seq.* (Supp. 1986). That law included the Control Share Acquisitions Chapter (Indiana Act or Act). Beginning on August 1, 1987, the Act will apply to any corporation incorporated in Indiana, unless the corporation amends its articles of incorporation or bylaws to opt out of the Act. Before that date, any Indiana corporation can opt into the Act by resolution of its board of directors. . . .

The Act focuses on the acquisition of "control shares" in an issuing public corporation. Under the Act, an entity acquires "control shares" whenever it acquires shares that, but for the operation of the Act, would bring its voting power in the corporation to or above any of three thresholds: 20%, 33-1/3% or 50%. An entity that acquires control shares does not necessarily acquire voting rights. Rather, it gains those rights only "to the extent granted by resolution approved by the shareholders of the issuing public corporation." Section 23–1 12-9(b) requires a majority vote of all disinterested shareholders holding each class of stock for passage of such a resolution. The practical effect of this requirement is to condition acquisition of control of a corporation on approval of a majority of the pre-existing disinterested shareholders.

★ ★ ★

B

On March 10, 1986, appellee Dynamics Corporation of America (Dynamics) owned 9.6% of the common stock of appellant CTS Corporation, an Indiana corporation. On that day, six days after the Act went into effect, Dynamics announced a tender offer for another million shares in CTS; purchase of those shares would have brought Dynamics' ownership interest in CTS to 27.5%. . . . On March 27, the board of directors of CTS, an Indiana corporation, elected to be governed by the provisions of the Act.

II

The first question in these cases is whether the Williams Act pre-empts the In-diana Act. As we have stated frequently, absent an explicit indication by Congress of an intent to pre-empt state law, a state statute is preempted only

> "where compliance with both federal and state regulations is a physical impossibility. . . or where the state law stands as an obstacle to the accomplishment and execution of the full purposes and objectives of Congress."

Because it is entirely possible for entities to comply with both the Williams Act and the Indiana Act, the state statute can be pre-empted only if it frustrates the purpose of the federal law.

★ ★ ★

The longstanding prevalence of state regulation in this area suggests that, if Congress had intended to pre-empt all state laws that delay the acquisition of voting control following a tender offer, it would have said so explicitly. The regulatory conditions that the Act places on tender offers are consistent with the text and the purposes of the Williams Act. Accordingly, we hold that the Williams Act does not pre-empt the Indiana Act.

III

As an alternative basis for its decision, the Court of Appeals held that the Act violates the Commerce Clause of the Federal Constitution. We now address this holding. On its face, the Commerce Clause is nothing more than a grant to Congress of the power "[t]o regulate Commerce . . . among the several States. . . ." But it has been settled for more than a century that the Clause prohibits States from taking certain actions respecting interstate commerce even absent congressional action. Rather, as the volume and complexity of commerce and regulation have grown in this country, the Court has articulated a variety of tests in an attempt to describe the difference between those regulations that the Commerce Clause permits and those regulations that it prohibits.

A

The principal objects of dormant Commerce Clause scrutiny are statutes that discriminate against interstate commerce. The Indiana Act is not such a statute. It has the same effects on tender offers whether or not the offeror is a domiciliary or resident of Indiana. Thus, it "visits its effects equally upon both interstate and local business."

This Court's recent Commerce Clause cases also have invalidated statutes that adversely may affect interstate commerce by subjecting activities to inconsistent regulations. . . . The Indiana Act poses no such problem. So long as each State regulates voting rights only in the corporations it has created, each corporation will be subject to the law of only one State. No principle of corporation law and practice is more firmly established than a State's authority to regulate domestic corporations, including the authority to define the voting rights of shareholders. Accordingly, we conclude that the Indiana Act does not create an impermissible risk of inconsistent regulation by different States.

We think the Court of Appeals failed to appreciate the significance for Commerce Clause analysis of the fact that state regulation of corporate governance is regulation of entities whose very existence and attributes are a product of state law. As Chief Justice Marshall explained:

> A corporation is an artificial being, invisible, intangible, and existing only in contemplation of law. Being the mere creature of law, it possesses only those properties which the charter of its creation confers upon it, either expressly, or as incidental to its very existence. These are such as are supposed best calculated to effect the object for which it was created.

Every State in this country has enacted laws regulating corporate governance. By prohibiting certain transactions, and regulating others, such laws necessarily affect certain aspects of interstate commerce. This necessarily is true with respect to corporations with shareholders in States other than the State of incorporation. Large corporations that are listed on national exchanges, or even regional exchanges, will have shareholders in many States and shares that are traded frequently. The markets that facilitate this national and international participation in ownership of corporations are essential for providing capital not only for new enterprises but also for established companies that need to expand their businesses. This beneficial free market system depends at its core upon the fact that a corporation—except in the rarest situations—is organized under, and governed by, the law of a single jurisdiction, traditionally the corporate law of the State of its incorporation.

These regulatory laws may affect directly a variety of corporate transactions. Mergers are a typical example. In view of the substantial effect that a merger may have on the shareholders' interests in a corporation, many States require supermajority votes to approve mergers. By requiring a greater vote for mergers than is required for other transactions, these laws make it more difficult for corporations to merge. State laws also may provide for "dissenters' rights" under which minority shareholders who disagree with corporate decisions to take particular actions are entitled to sell their shares to the corporation at fair market value. By requiring the corporation to purchase the shares of dissenting shareholders, these laws may inhibit a corporation from engaging in the specified transactions.

It thus is an accepted part of the business landscape in this country for States to create corporations, to prescribe their powers, and to define the rights that are acquired by purchasing their shares. A State has an interest in promoting stable relationships among parties involved in the corporations it charters, as well as in ensuring that investors in such corporations have an effective voice in corporate affairs.

There can be no doubt that the Act reflects these concerns. The primary purpose of the Act is to protect the shareholders of Indiana corporations. It does this by affording shareholders, when a takeover offer is made, an opportunity to decide collectively whether the resulting change in voting control of the corporation, as they perceive it, would be desirable. A change of management may have important effects on the shareholders' interests; it is well within the State's role as overseer of corporate governance to offer this opportunity. The autonomy provided·by allowing shareholders collectively to determine whether the takeover is advantageous to their interests may be especially beneficial where a hostile tender offer may coerce shareholders into tendering their shares.

Appellee Dynamics responds to this concern by arguing that the prospect of coercive tender offers is illusory, and that tender offers generally should be favored because they reallocate corporate assets into the hands of management who can use them most effectively. . . . Indiana's concern with tender offers is not groundless. Indeed, the poten-

tially coercive aspects of tender offers have been recognized by the SEC and by a number of scholarly commentators. The Constitution does not require the States to subscribe to any particular economic theory. We are not inclined "to second-guess the empirical judgments of lawmakers concerning the utility of legislation." In our view, the possibility of coercion in some takeover bids offers additional justification for Indiana's decision to promote the autonomy of independent shareholders.

* * *

IV

On its face, the Indiana Control Share Acquisitions Chapter evenhandedly determines the voting rights of shares of Indiana corporations. The Act does not conflict with the provisions or purposes of the Williams Act. To the limited extent that the Act affects interstate commerce, this is justified by the State's interests in defining the attributes of shares in its corporations and in protecting shareholders. Congress has never questioned the need for state regulation of these matters. Nor do we think such regulation offends the Constitution. Accordingly, we reverse the judgment of the Court of Appeals [that declared the Indiana statute unconstitutional].

It is so ordered.

CASE FOLLOW-UP

About fifteen states have enacted some form of control share acquisition (CSA) legislation. Generally, these statutes, like the Indiana statute in the *CTS Corp.* case, seek to protect local management, employees, and others living off the corporation. Also protected by these statutes are shareholders who may

know their shares are selling at a depressed price but who do not want new management. These statutes allow the shareholders to vote in a properly called shareholders meeting on whether to give the potential new management (the raiders) the control they seek.

CONCLUSION

The legal environment of business is comprised of rules that attempt to guide and direct the behaviors of business organizations. Many of these rules are created by the federal government and are a major source of material for this book. This book's chapters on administrative law, environmental law, and international law, just to name a few, are based on federal action. With few exceptions, these categories of law attempt to direct and control the behavior, not the structure, of business organizations. In this chapter, we have examined some state-based laws that govern business structure, as well as some behaviors. This state law is older than the federal law and changes very slowly.

Several times, we alluded to the fact that the larger the business organization, the less its management seems to worry about state control of organizational structure. No doubt, megacorporations must comply with this state law; it is just that their directors are generally more concerned about other types of law (e.g., the federal securities laws). We explained how this came about, and it appears to us that little change can be expected. Nevertheless, if you plan to start your own corporation, you should be very concerned with state-level corporation law!

The cases we selected for this chapter represent to us the major areas of importance in corporation law. We must recognize that corporations were analogized with humans more than one hundred years ago by a U.S. Supreme Court that gave the issue almost no thought. Were corporations not given almost the same rights as people, we may have evolved a different type of control for them.

The rights that shareholders have to obtain corporate books and to sue management for negligence and improper activities are substantially limited. The cases we examined help in explaining why the management of megacorporations concerns itself, in all probability, little with shareholder preferences other than to earn as much money as possible. Shareholders are removed from the scene, and so management is more sensitive to pressures from, for example, competition and the federal government.

If Berle and Means were correct when they acknowledged more than sixty years ago that our American civilization is characterized by a "corporate system," then an exploration of the state law basics is important. Should the purpose of these legal structures go beyond the pursuit of profit? This is an open but very significant question. The issues and questions are not even outlined with clarity, so we should not expect clear answers. At this point, we just raise the question and suggest that if you are interested in pursuing this topic further, you read Chapter 3 on corporate social responsibility. There we explore the relationship of law and morality and the place of the modern business corporation in this relationship.

Review Questions and Problems

1. Assume you and a friend want to start a retail business selling discount merchandise, which would be ordered through catalogues available in your store. You would carry some inventory, but the main intent of the business would be to provide the customer with catalogue information and guidance in ordering, reasonable prices, and delivery service. Besides a small store, you plan to lease warehouse space and either buy or lease a delivery truck. For the present time, you do not plan to hire any employees because you and your friend can do all of the required work. You and your friend plan to furnish $2,500 each to the enterprise, and you are hoping to borrow another $2,500 from a bank. Assume you have decided to call your business the Quality Discount Service. Which type of business organization would you choose and why? The material in Chapter 9 is also relevant to the answer of this question.

2. The plaintiff has been run down and injured by a negligently operated taxicab. The cab is owned by Seon Cab Corporation. Seon has only two cabs and carries only the legally required minimum automobile liability insurance ($10,000) on each cab. The defendant, Carlton, is a stockholder in ten corporations, including Seon. Each corporation has only two cabs and carries the minimum amount of insurance. The plaintiff alleges that the stockholders are personally liable for damages because the multiple corporate structure constitutes an unlawful attempt to defraud members of the general public who might be injured by the cabs. The defendant argues that the law permits taxi owner-operators to form such corporations and that corporations are designed to permit the owners to escape personal liability. Furthermore, he points out that he has complied with the legislative branch's insurance mandates. What decision? [*Walkovszky* v. *Carlton*, 223 N.E.2d 6 (N.Y. Ct. App. 1966)]

3. The plaintiff is injured by the negligent operation of a taxicab. It is owned and operated by one of four corporations affiliated with Terminal. Terminal is not a stockholder in any of the four operating corporations. For the most part, the individuals who own Terminal also own the four corporations. Terminal actually serviced, inspected, repaired, and dispatched all the cabs of the four corporations. The Terminal name was conspicuously displayed on the sides of all the cabs used in the enterprise. Should the veil of the operating company, whose cab injured the plaintiff, be pierced to hold Terminal liable? [*Magnum* v. *Terminal Transp. Sytem*, 286 N.Y.S. 666, 1936]

4. Should the results in the above two cases differ because in one an attempt is made to hold an individual liable, whereas in the other the plaintiff seeks to hold liable another corporation?

5. Assume that you were a shareholder of AT&T and you found out that, in 1968, the Democratic National Committee (DNC) did not pay $1.5 million owed to AT&T for communication services provided at the 1968 Democratic National Convention. Assume further that, by 1972, the management had not instituted any action to collect the amount owed by the DNC. Describe your legal remedy, if any, if you wanted to force management to collect its legal debts. Who would be the defendants, and what response would you expect from them? Would it make a difference in your statement of a claim that corporations were forbidden by federal law from making contributions to political parties? [*Miller* v. *AT&T*, 507 F.2d 759 (3rd Cir. 1974)]

6. The *Legal Times* for the week of March 12, 1990 (at p. 21) reported that the directors of General Motors sought and obtained shareholder approval to amend the articles of incorporation to provide that the directors should no longer be liable to share-

holders for "lapses of their duty to act carefully, even if they are grossly negligent." Under such a provision, Delaware law provides that directors may still be liable for intentional wrongdoing or self-dealing. Whose interests are served, and whose are not served by such a provision?

7. *A, B,* and *C* incorporated a furniture-moving business known as Texas Transfer *(TT)*. Each owned one-third of the shares. The business was soon so successful that *B* formed his own corporation called Elite Moving *(E)* to compete with *TT. C* found out about *E* and threatened to sue for part ownership of *E. A* and *B* agreed that *C* should be bought out of *TT,* and *C* exchanged his shares of *TT* for a $42,000 promissory note of *TT.* At the time of this transaction, *TT* had a net income of $65,479; net income fell to $2,814 in the next year, and it lost over $16,000 the next year. In this year in which *TT* lost heavily, *E* made $195,765. *C* was paid only $1,000 of the $42,000 promised by *TT.* What are *C's* remedies?

ENDNOTES

1. Berle and Means, *The Modern Corporation and Private Property* 1 (1932).
2. *Statistical Abstract of the United States* 539 (1994).
3. *Id.* at 551.
4. Blumberg, *The Megacorporation in American Society* 31 (1975).
5. Nader, Green, and Seligman, *Taming the Giant Corporation* 45 (1976).
6. *Id.* at 50.
7. *Id.* at 57.
8. The Constitutional Position of Property in America, 64 *Independent* 834, 836 (1908). He went on to say that the Dartmouth College case (4 Wheat. 518) and the construction given the Fourteenth Amendment in the Santa Clara case "have had the effect of placing the modern industrial corporation in an almost impregnable constitutional position." *Id.* at 836. As to whether the framers of the Amendment may have had such an undisclosed purpose, see Graham, The "Conspiracy Theory" of the Fourteenth Amendment, 47 *Yale L. J.* 371.
9. 4 Wheaton 518 (1819).
10. Blasi and Kruse, *The New Owners* 2 (1992).
11. *Id.* at 3.
12. *Id.*
13. *Id* at 23.
14. See, for example, *Gordon* v. *Aztec Brewing,* 33 Cal.2d 514 (1949).
15. See Ashe, Lifting the Corporate Veil: Corporate Equity in the Modern Day Court, 768 *Commercial Law Journal* 121 (1973).
16. See Eisenberg, *The Structure of the Corporation* 42 (1976).
17. Henn, *Law of Corporations* 482 (1970).
18. 488 A.2d 858 (1985).
19. Shaw, Statutory Limits on Director Liability, *Business Horizons* 43 (July-August), 1989.

CHAPTER 11

Governmental Regulation: The Policies and Politics of Consumer Protection

INTRODUCTION

In this chapter, we examine two separate but related parts of the legal environment of business. The first is the process of governmental regulation. How is governing done in the United States? We present our view of how the policies of government are made in Congress and the administrative agencies of the executive branch through the use of power politics and compromise.

We also present some substantive issues and law specifically involving the regulation of product safety. We show how the nationwide concern for product safety not only is manifest in the court system but also is the subject of many approaches in the state and federal legislatures and administrative agencies. We examine closely the work of the Consumer Product Safety Commission (CPSC) and the role of the Federal Trade Commission (FTC) in the regulation of product warranties, advertising, and the use and abuse of consumer credit.

ORIGINS OF THE ADVERSARIAL RELATIONSHIP: BUSINESS VERSUS GOVERNMENT

The popular perception of governmental regulation in the United States is markedly different from the perception of the place of government in the economies of virtually all other economically advanced countries. In Europe and Japan, for example, the common perception is that the role of government is to promote and encourage the development of business. People in the United States tend to believe that governmental regulation inevitably restrains and interferes with the development of business. The relationship between business and government is basically antagonistic.

Businesspeople in Europe and Asia look to their governments for guidance and even help. Harvard business historian Thomas McCraw observed, "Few European or Japanese businessmen took it for granted that they could make important investment decisions without consulting the state. American businessmen, by contrast, thought it outrageous when the U.S. government first did claim such a role."[1] Today, this American view, argue such scholars as McCraw, does not serve Americans' best interests. Why, then, does this adversarial relationship persist? It persists because its origins are deep. Generations of business leaders and government policy makers have been conditioned by history.

The United States was created in the absence of any established institutions, such as a dominating church, a formidable standing army, and an entrenched aristocracy. Moreover, the founders consciously created a government of divided sovereignty—between the state and federal governments and among the judicial, legislative, and executive branches. Until this century, U. S. society was expanding to fill the land between the two coasts, and the scramble for wealth and power was not disruptive because the energetic and the dissident could always move on when conflicts arose. The society was open, rough, and individualistic.

A dominant American belief even into this century was that of individualism. A person was responsible for the quality of his or her own existence, and happiness was achieved through a lonely struggle with nature and, if need be, with fellow human beings. Success was to have one's own self created piece of the great American pie and to live on one's own property with family, who would also engage in the struggle to find meaning and enjoyment from life. The deep suspicion of centralized power, carried over from Europe, took hold of the collective conscience of those on the American frontier and became the dominant belief that shaped public life. The function of both law and government was believed to be the protection of the property each person could accumulate. Otherwise, the legal institutions should stand clear so that individuals could achieve their own destiny.

A substantial contribution to this century's popular beliefs about the proper conception of government came from the 1913 publication of historian Charles A. Beard's book, *An Economic Interpretation of the Constitution.* Beard argued that even the founders, who were much involved with government, stood to profit personally from the adoption of the Constitution. This book stimulated a view of American history called the *Progressive School,* which soon dominated the teaching of history, political science, and related disciplines in the United States.[2] The central message of this school of thought was that people in government were not to be trusted to act in the public interest.

In addition to the forces of American individualism and Beard's book was the growth of the large American business corporation in the latter part of the nineteenth century. Management allied itself and its corporation expressly with the rhetoric of the American frontier. The proper role of the government, argued management, was to allow large business corporations, such as Rockefeller's Standard Oil Company, the United States Steel Corporation, and others, to guide and negotiate the future of American enterprise.

The American public was not entirely blinded by this rhetoric. The growing perception at the turn of the century was that large business corporations could be a menace and, in fact, represented the very kind of centralized power against which the founders had fought a revolution. Calls went out for the government to do something. But what could the government do? It had no history of regulation of business, and the public was still in conflict about whether to trust the government.

Historian McCraw points out that, in America alone of all major market economies, the rise of big business preceded the rise of big government. "In Britain, France, Germany, and Japan, a substantial civil bureaucracy was embedded in the culture long before the appearance of big business."[3] American big business took for its own the historically significant rhetoric of individualism, which cast the government as a benign form of evil. Many Americans still identify with this rhetoric. Presidents Reagan, Bush, and Clinton all included the promise of "less government" in their election campaigns.

The forces of individualism and mistrust of government explain why people in big business and government often see themselves as adversaries when it comes to regulation. Examine your own feelings about governmental regulation. Chances are you do not believe, as Europeans and the Japanese do, that government should enjoy a kind of presumptive legitimacy. Many Americans still believe that every time the government tries to do something, it will be inefficient at best and corrupt at worst. Despite the historical prejudices against it, governmental regulation is a reality. Since the turn of the century, the American public gradually has perceived the necessity of governmental regulation.

The only way to fully understand the relationship of business and government today is to realize that the forces of history have cast these two major institutions as adversaries. Sometimes big business wins out and regulation is retracted or forestalled. Examples are the deregulation of the airlines in the late 1970s and a measure of deregulation of banks during the same period. Yet, the U. S. government remains responsive to the practical, perceived need for regulation of business in many areas. We now turn to an overview of the more specific reasons for governmental regulation in the American economy.

REASONS FOR GOVERNMENTAL REGULATION IN THE AMERICAN ECONOMY

There are many reasons for governmental regulation in the U. S. economy. In the following discussion, we summarize some of these basic reasons. Any one circumstance involving governmental regulation usually has a variety of reasons, so more than one of these reasons is usually given.

1. *Natural monopoly.* A common reason for governmental regulation in certain markets is that one firm can most efficiently supply all of the good or service. An example is the market for natural gas and electricity. In these markets, having more than one system of distribution, such as parallel electric lines, would be wasteful. State governments usually establish a public utility commission that determines both price and quality of the service. This is a form of very direct regulation.

2. *Destructive competition.* In some markets for goods and services, if firms were allowed to compete without any governmental oversight protecting the public interest, the long term results from the competition might produce socially undesirable consequences. The regulation of banking and insurance companies is an example of this. Without governmental regulation of banks (e.g., setting accounting standards and methods), open and fierce competition would surely result in bank failures. Although a few bank failures are inevitable under any scheme of regulation, widespread bank failure would be destructive to the kind of public confidence needed to support these institutions.

3. *Production externalities.* Economists call unintended effects of the production process either *external diseconomies* or simply *externalities.* These unintended effects on persons or things outside the production process may be either positive or negative. The government has an interest in the negative externalities especially. For example, a company that discharges its used toxic chemicals by dumping them into the local sewer system is externalizing a part of its production costs. The same may be said of a purchaser of a new car that has no pollution control devices on it. The new owner does not incur the full costs or consequences of ownership. Without governmental regulation to impose the costs of these externalities on those who cause them, producers and owners do not pay the full amount. They derive a benefit at the expense of the public and the environment.

   Moreover, producers and owners under the U. S. system of capitalism are not in a position to impose these costs on themselves. It is unlikely that a firm in competition with others will voluntarily increase its costs 10 percent to pay for externalities unless it is assured that its competitors will do likewise.

4. *Other market imperfections.* In many instances, a quick look at the circumstances of the production of a good or service will reveal that governmental regulation is the most practical way of dealing with problems that may arise. Consider these examples:

   a. If the government did not regulate the frequencies available for public broadcast on radio, television, and other types of wireless transmission, there would be chaos. Some authority should decide which frequencies are available for police and other public uses, for emergency messages, for national defense, and for organizations putting out messages intended to make a profit.

   b. The regulation of natural resource extraction and consumption is usually justified on the basis of the protection of the national interest and defense of the country. The government regulates the extraction of crude oil, for example, on the theory that if it were not regulated, drillers would extract all American oil first (because, presumably, it would be cheaper than imported oil). Without regulation, the United States would be more dependent on foreign sources for this vital natural resource than it is now.

    c. A significant portion of governmental regulation is justified on the ground that the competitors in the market will not provide sufficient information about their goods and services to consumers. In some markets, the nature of the good or service is so complex that consumers may be incapable of making important decisions without government compelled disclosure. The Magnuson-Moss Warranty Act, which requires disclosure of certain consumer warranty information, and the requirement that some corporations file a registration statement with the SEC are examples of this kind of regulation.

5. *Social regulation.* Governmental regulation has been used as a tool to achieve several broad social policy objectives. These include (among many others):

    a. Redistribution of income: To a certain extent, most forms of taxation are governmental regulation. The inheritance tax especially was intended to redistribute some wealth; social security schemes, unemployment compensation, and welfare programs also tend to redistribute income.

    b. Objectives of equity and fairness, such as governmental regulation to prevent employment discrimination.

    c. Protection of those who provide essential goods and services to society (e.g., special legislation protecting prices for agricultural products, fish, and tobacco).

    d. Protection to preserve the environment for future generations.

    e. Protection of employees from unsafe and unhealthful work environments.

    f. Protection of consumers when the forces in the market for a product are not sufficient to create a safe or healthful environment. The CPSC can ban certain products, and the FDA approves, regulates, and bans certain types of drugs and potentially dangerous substances.

In some cases, the initial reasons for the governmental regulation disappear, but the regulation continues because of political pressure from either those regulated or those who benefit from regulation.

The U. S. economy depends very heavily on the idea of competitive markets for goods and services. In this sense, a *market* is any generally recognized place, institution, or means of exchanging goods and services. It is believed that if the government promotes and preserves the competitive forces (by encouraging more than just a few buyers and sellers), the public interest will be served. But any system predicated on competition necessarily implies both winners and losers and some rules enforced by some authority for governing the competition.

As the rough edges of market competition are perceived, government is called on to either fill the gaps or smooth out the roughness. It seems obvious today that the unregulated marketplace does not deal adequately with most circumstances that generated the governmental regulation of the past two decades (employment discrimination, environmental pollution, product safety, and worker health).

ADMINISTRATIVE PROCESS OF GOVERNMENTAL REGULATION

Governmental regulation of business is accomplished through the administrative process, which usually takes place within the executive branches of the federal and state governments. We focus on the federal level, but *all states have governmental regulation and an administrative process* usually patterned on the federal model. Generalizing about a regulatory process at the federal level, which involves about 128,000 permanent, full time employees who work in over one hundred agencies with a combined budget amounting to an estimated $14.3 billion[4] and which affects almost every business, is difficult and subject to exception, but necessary.

Three central bodies of legal principles control the administrative process:

1. *The enabling legislation.* This is the major legislative enactment by Congress that usually establishes the regulatory agency and the broad outlines of the agency's powers and functions.

2. *The Administrative Procedures Act.* This federal act (referred to as the APA) was passed in 1946 and sets out the procedures that regulatory agencies are to follow in legislating, adjudicating, and conducting agency business. This Act should be read with the enabling legislation of an agency because either may call for procedures not contained in the other.

3. *The United States Constitution.* Constitutional law pervades all governmental activity. Any time a provision of enabling legislation (or agency action pursuant to such legislation) conflicts with the U.S. Constitution, this provision is unconstitutional and cannot be enforced. Also, constitutional law may add to, explain, or change the APA.

In this book, discussions of the enabling legislation for specific agencies, such as the Environmental Protection Agency (EPA), the Securities and Exchange Commission (SEC), and the Consumer Product Safety Commission (CPSC) will be found in the specific chapters devoted to this type of regulation. *The legal process of regulating business conduct under these enabling statutes we call the regulatory process.*

An overview of each governmental agency's power and procedures is set by the legislature when the basic bill that creates the agency passes. This legislation is the result of numerous forces at work in the political process. The traditional textbook view of this process does not emphasize the crucial role of staffers in the creation of much major legislation. The following article is a short comment on the legislative process by a former professional staffperson.

MARK BISNOW[5]

Congress: An Insider's Look at the Mess on Capitol Hill

... Together, about two dozen of us—staff representatives from the Senate Finance Committee—assembled earlier this year around a long conference table in room 211 of the Dirksen Senate Office Building and week after week set about drafting the Omnibus Trade and Tariff Act of 1987.

Most of our bosses—the 20 senators on the committee—had little idea what we were doing. But no matter: we freely interjected personal points of view, dickered loudly over provisions that might save or ruin entire industries and blithely cut deals that could cost consumers billions of dollars—all in the cause of facilitating the legislative process. The result? A 1,100 page bill of numbing detail, questionable merit and next to no chance of enactment as law.

Big Increase

The 535 members of the U.S. Congress accomplished very little this year, and it took 20,000 staffers to help them do it. Over the last 15 years the size of the congressional staff has increased threefold. At the same time, the institution has grown so unruly and unproductive that this year Congress failed to pass a single appropriations bill, much less cure the trade deficit or solve the budget crisis. My own experience as a staffer for three senators, three congressmen and three different committees over the past 13 years tells me this is not a coincidence. Able as staffers are, and noble though their mission, they have unwittingly become agents of conflict and impasse.

★ ★ ★

I came to learn there are all sorts of ways congressional staffers serve themselves or their bosses but not always the national interest. Like hyperactive stockbrokers who buy and sell for quick commissions regardless of the long term profit to their clients, congressional staffers become adept at the art of churning. The result is ever more friction among members, factions, parties and branches of government.

Congress has no less than 150 subcommittees, and each one has its own staff that must justify its existence. Writing long, duplicative and largely unread reports is one

time honored way. Summoning cabinet members to testify before congressional committees is another obvious resort, since it is bound to lure television cameras even if the testimony has been given many times before. I recall seeing William French Smith in a crowded Capitol Hill elevator shortly after he became attorney general in 1981. Somewhat dazed, he was trying to remember which congressional committee he was scheduled to appear before next. Earlier this year the Senate Finance Committee summoned a parade of present and former senior government officials and CEO's to testify on how to restore America's competitive edge. No one bothered to tell these busy executives that the trade bill had already been written by the committee staff; the hearings were merely to build a record. In fact, the testimony actually contradicted central portions of the bill. That bill, at least, was a serious effort. Many staffers draft bills just to raise a congressman's profile—and attract contributions from special interest groups. Many of these bills have absolutely no chance of passing and in fact, of the 6,504 bills introduced this year, a mere 197 passed.

A Crutch

But aren't staffers essential to helping congressmen comprehend the increasingly complex and broad ranging issues that they face? One might guess so but actually lawmakers use staffers as a crutch. Why should a congressman master a subject if an aide can do it for him? Just watch senators step out of the elevator on their way into the chamber for a vote. Many will quickly glance to the side where aides stand compressing into a single gesture the sum of information their bosses need: thumbs up or thumbs down. Huge staffs have also helped spawn the vast schools of lobbyists swimming about Capitol Hill. If an influence peddler can't get in to see a congressman, there's always an aide available to listen to his pitch. I was happy to oblige, since lobbyists generally prefer to do business by taking you to lunch or furnishing some other perk. My favorite special pleaders were the chocolate manufacturers who sought help in reducing Japanese tariffs on their products. Candy lobbyists plied congressional offices with unending supplies of one pound bags of M&M's to sweeten our task, and Congress gratefully drafted a

resolution calling on the Japanese to reduce their chocolate tariffs. So threatening were we that when Prime Minister Nakasone visited the Hill earlier this year, he made a point of announcing that his country had taken important steps to resolve the chocolate crisis. Some of the congressmen and senators looked a little puzzled. I just nodded—and reached for the M&M's.

ARTICLE FOLLOW-UP

Mark Bisnow revealed one of the reasons that Americans' experience with (and attitude toward) governmental regulation is the way it is. It seems that many Americans both inside and outside government have not seen governmental activity as something to

value. In short, we leave it to others.

The law applicable to the process of an administrative agency is called *administrative law*. We now turn our attention to this largely overlooked and unstudied form of law for insight into the regulatory process.

ADMINISTRATIVE LAW

Administrative law is at the heart of the administrative process. At first, it may seem that studying it is overly technical and of little practical value, but this perception is far from the truth. Administrative law reveals, more than any other legal topic, how the government works. One noted scholar at the University of Michigan Law School has characterized this law and the study of it this way.

> Much of the writing on administrative law, mired as it is in disputation over the details of administrative procedure, lacks dash ... but the tedium (of administrative procedures) is deceptive. Procedures are power. . . .
>
> Once the relationship between procedure and power is appreciated, the political content of even the most apparent boring administration law scholarship becomes manifest. Preferences for one type of decision maker or process over another are at base political preferences, which regularly escape the bounds of technical legalistic argumentation and become the subject of explicit ideological conflict. . . . Presidents Carter and Reagan. . .both brought administrative procedural reform to the level of presidential politics.
>
> Administrative law and procedure are thus unabashedly associated with politics and government, which helps to account for their awkward posture within a legal system that finds it generally useful to camouflage the relationship between law and political authority. In administrative law, political ideas are on the surface of, as well as at the heart of, the law. In this regard, administrative law is kin to constitutional law, a simi-

larly politicized subject. In fact, *administrative law can best be thought of as the collection of principles of which the idea of government under law, an idea older and more basic than the written American constitution itself, is effectuated in practice.*[6] (Emphasis added.)

In the administrative process today in the United States, two models of rule- or policy-making procedure are used. We begin with a discussion of the legislative model. This model depends on the Administrative Procedures Act (APA) for guidance and is the more widely used model. Next, we explain the adjudicative model, which depends on the APA, as well as court interpretations of the Constitution and past agency practice.

LEGISLATIVE RULE MAKING BY REGULATORY AGENCIES

The Legislative Model.   The APA was passed in 1946, the product of a struggle between interests that supported the programs of the regulatory-prone New Deal and those that were afraid or suspicious of the power given those agencies. A major objective of the APA was the establishment of minimum procedural requirements applicable to many types of agency proceedings.[7] Section 553 of the APA sets out the minimum procedural elements for the creation of regulatory agency rules. This process is called *Informal Notice and Comment Rulemaking.* Section 553 provides the following:

1. A notice of proposed rule making must be published in the *Federal Register* that includes a statement of the time, place, and nature of the public rule-making proceedings; a reference to the legal authority under which the rule is proposed; and either the terms or a description of the subjects and issues to be addressed by the proposed rule.

2. Interested persons must be given an opportunity to submit written data, views, or arguments on the proposal, with or without opportunity for oral presentation.

3. A concise general statement of the basis and purpose must accompany the final rule.

4. Subject to certain exceptions, publication of the final rule must take place not less than 30 days before its effective date.

These procedures apply to the creation of agency rules. For example, the Internal Revenue Service (IRS) makes thousands of rules by using this procedure. These rules carry out the intent of Congress when it passes tax legislation. All regulatory agencies make such rules because Congress is not specialized enough to have the knowledge it takes to operate an administrative agency.

The crux of Section 553 is the requirement of publication of potential agency action in the *Federal Register* with an opportunity for those affected to present their views on the regulation. Because agency decision makers are not elected and are not susceptible to the ordinary democratic processes, the notice and comment procedures allow those affected by a rule to air their views.

The Federal Register and Rule Making.   The *Federal Register* is a form of legal newspaper published daily by the Executive Department, Office of the *Federal Register*. Most major corporations (and medium-sized corporations, if they are prudent and can afford it) have staff that receive and analyze the *Federal Register*. These people alert departments within the corporation of proposed and final rules affecting them. They also respond in the corporation's interest by preparing written statements in response to proposed rules.

The *Federal Register* gives notice of the rule-making process. After the rules become final, they are printed in the Code of Federal Regulations (C.F.R). Federal agency law is also found in a separate set of books called the United States Codes (U.S.C.), which contains all of the laws passed by Congress and signed by the president. Many of these U.S.C. statutes are the enabling legislation for the federal-level regulatory agencies. So, a complete listing of documents that contain the law of federal governmental regulation would be the U.S.C., the *Federal Register*, the C.F.R, and the various U.S. Supreme Court and federal court interpretations of enabling legislation and rules and regulations.

ADJUDICATORY POLICY MAKING AND THE RIGHT TO BE HEARD

The Adjudicatory Model.   Because it is an American tradition to value individual freedom, dignity, and rights, a second regulatory model has evolved. This model in its operation looks much like a typical civil trial. To understand the circumstances in which the adjudication model should be used, as opposed to the legislative model, consider two hypothetical examples.

Assume that the Federal Aviation Administration (FAA), which is a separate agency within the executive branch and under the control of the Secretary of Transportation, learns that the seat coverings on commercial U. S. aircraft could be made safer by requiring that they be sprayed with a fire retardant. Because the FAA is one of the agencies charged with maintaining air safety, it issues a rule requiring that all commercial aircraft be equipped with seat fabric sprayed with the retardant and that seats be sprayed each year after their production and initial inspection.

The second example also involves information coming to the attention of the FAA. This information reveals that the human reaction time of pilots begins to decrease at age sixty. Because of this decrease in reaction time, pilots over the age of sixty could pose a safety threat to their passengers. Because the FAA is also charged with the training and certification of all professional air personnel, it issues a rule requiring the forfeiture of one's commercial pilot's license at age sixty.

Let's analyze these two examples with a view to explaining the reason for the two regulatory models. First, we must recognize a central feature of almost all governmental regulation and apparent in both of our examples: *Governmental regulation almost always costs someone money or property.* In almost all cases, the fact that a regulation or rule would cost the one regulated a lot of time, expense, or property is of little or no legal significance. The reply to this possible objection is that the rule will fall with equal weight on all those in the market similarly situated.

Second, governmental regulation may affect large and small business organizations, as well as individuals. But here is the difference. For some reason, we believe that the pilot license rule will have a more severe impact on the pilots than the seat cover regulation will have on aircraft producers and airlines. How is this basic belief recognized by the law? *When individuals or businesses are exceptionally affected on individual grounds, they may force the government to provide an adjudicatory hearing for the creation or imposition of a rule.* Thus, an entirely different type of regulatory model is used for the pilot's license example. The pilots are more individually affected than aircraft producers.

Elements of an Adjudicatory Hearing.

An adjudicatory hearing is not defined in the APA with great precision. Moreover, from time to time, courts have varied the requirements for such a hearing. From various court opinions, however, we can glean what the ideal or "full" adjudicatory hearing would look like. It would resemble a civil trial (without a jury) and would include these elements:

1. *Notice.* Timely and adequate notice of the proposed governmental action must be given.

2. *Time and manner.* The hearing must be conducted at a time and in a manner meaningful to those concerned; this means it should not be held at an unreasonable hour or day and should not unreasonably inconvenience the participants.

3. *Confrontation of witnesses.* The person affected by agency action must be afforded an opportunity to confront any adverse witnesses and to present his or her own arguments and evidence; written submissions of evidence are not considered a substitute for the confrontation in person of adverse witnesses; however, a trial-type cross-examination with formal rules of evidence may not be permitted.

4. *Right to counsel.* The affected party has the right to be represented by counsel, but so far the Supreme Court has not required the government to provide counsel at its expense.

5. *Statement of reasons.* The decision maker must state the reasons for the final decision, and the decision must be based only on the evidence presented at the hearing.

6. *Unbiased hearing officer.* The decision maker who presides at the hearing should not have participated in the agency action that is the subject of the hearing.

A reasonable presumption in the law is that an adjudication hearing affords more protection to individuals and is therefore more desirable from that perspective. This presumption arises primarily from the so-called right to cross-examine those proposing the governmental action. This cross-examination, together with the other elements of the adjudicatory process, helps in building a record that can be used to appeal an adverse decision to the court system. Under the legislative model (notice and comment rule making), there is no *individual* record of how a party's interests are affected. Therefore, it is difficult for those affected to appeal an undesirable decision of the government.

The government, however, recognizes that adjudicatory hearings are inefficient: They are very time consuming events. So, the *government usually prefers the legislative model* to create rules.

In our example of the airline pilots, should the rule affecting them be generated and applied in an adjudicatory hearing? In this case, the agency would most probably announce the rule and then allow persons wanting exceptions to appear before a hearing officer; most probably, the hearing would be adjudicatory in nature.

INFORMAL ADMINISTRATIVE ACTIVITY AND THE EXERCISE OF DISCRETION

Respected authorities on the administrative process have estimated that between 80 and 90 percent of the government's work is conducted outside the procedural safeguards of the APA or the scrutiny of the court.[8] Moreover, the work of most agencies goes beyond the two rather formal activities of legislation and adjudication. Most agencies combine in their daily activities the general process of all the other branches of government. For example, agencies can generate rules, investigate business conduct under those rules, prosecute violators, adjudicate where there is a violation, and conduct appeals of its decisions.

Informal administrative action should be understood broadly enough to include such governmental activity as granting a driver's license, issuing a traffic ticket, accepting applicants to graduate school (at a state institution), and operating city, county, or state hospitals. All of the following informal activities are examples of governmental regulation that affects everyday life.[9]

1. *Tests and inspections.* Most agencies collect data of various sorts and then use these data for more formal rule creation. A major part of this process is conducting tests and inspections. Activities in this category include administering and grading tests for a driver's license; inspecting all public transportation vehicles, such as railroads, buses, and airplanes; and administering tests and procedures to prevent the distribution of unsafe plants, food, and drugs and to control various kinds of products and substances.

2. *Supervision.* The federal and state governments regulate banks, insurance companies, utilities, and other auxiliary services. The SEC supervises the dissemination of information from large corporations that are governed by its rules; the FCC supervises the use of the airwaves; and the ICC supervises much of the public transportation network.

3. *Applications and claims.* The FCC receives and disposes of half a million applications for transmitters, and agencies such as the Social Security Administration and the Veterans Administration process millions of applications and claims for governmental benefits.

4. *Negotiation and settlement.* Many agencies negotiate between competing claims and then make awards. The National Labor Relations Board (NLRB) functions in this process; in addition, the FCC awards broadcast frequencies on a competitive basis, the Justice Department gives advice on mergers and acquisitions (a form of negotiation), and the Pentagon (Defense Department) negotiates on behalf of the federal government large defense contracts and claims.

5. *Informal sanctions, publicity.* Many administrative agencies have the power to publicize events and circumstances affecting the interests of businesses and persons. This is perhaps the most powerful remedy that some agencies have. For example, in late fall 1959, the secretary of health, education, and welfare announced at a press conference that some cranberries had been contaminated by a cancer-causing agent. This publicity virtually destroyed the entire cranberry market for that year. Later, it appeared that the secretary was in error, and Congress made amends to the growers by providing compensation for funds for the lost 1959 crop. Not all businesses, however, have the political clout to force such compensation for the abuse of this power.

6. *Informal advice, advisory opinions, and declaratory opinions.* Almost all governmental agencies have staff trained and paid to give informal advice and opinions to individuals and businesses. At the most common but most significant level, this involves merely answering telephone and letter requests for advice. The IRS issues tens of thousands of informal rulings each year. These do not have the force of laws, but it is rare that an agency will go back on its word and engage in activity it said it would avoid. The SEC issues about 5,000 letters of advice yearly, and the FTC issues about 5200 opinions per year. Also, the Justice Department will answer inquiries about anticompetitive behavior and about its intent to prosecute. These activities give you some idea of the informal activities of most administrative agencies. But how do they operate?

THE WORK OF TWO ADMINISTRATIVE AGENCIES

The administrative process creates governmental rules and orders, and these operate on many activities of the business firm. They are a large part of the legal environment of business. In this part of the text, we examine the work of the Consumer Product Safety Commission (CPSC) and the Federal Trade Commission (FTC). In other parts of the text, we explain the work of such agencies as the Securities Exchange Commission (SEC), the Equal Employment Opportunities Commission (EEOC), the Environmental Protection Agency (EPA), and others.

CONSUMER PRODUCT SAFETY LEGISLATION

Despite the rapidly developing concepts in the common law that provide remedies for injuries caused by defective products, commercial society remains filled with dangerous products, and consumer injuries still abound. In the early 1970s, 20 million Americans were hospitalized each year as a result of incidents associated with consumer products, 110,000 were permanently disabled, and 30,000 were killed (consumer products "do not include autos, drugs or firearms which are regulated by other agencies which specialize in these products"). The cost of these consumer-product related injuries was about $5.5 billion annually.[10]

In 1992, a federal agency, the Consumer Product Safety Commission (CPSC) reported that there were 28.5 million injuries and 21,600 deaths associated with the 15,000 different types of consumer products regulated by the CPSC.[11] The types of some of the consumer products that caused the most serious injuries as of 1992, are shown in Figure 11.1

FIGURE 11.1   *Estimates of Hospital Emergency Room Treated Injuries Associated with the use of Certain Consumer Products, October 1, 1991—September 30, 1992* (**Source:** **National Electronic Injury Surveillance System (NEISS).** **Note:** **NEISS data indicates that a product was associated with an injury but not necessarily that the product caused the injury.**)

Product Group	Age Group				
	Total	Under 5	5-24	25-64	65 & over
Child Nursery Equipment and Supplies	118,179	97,9221	9,543	7,185	3,512
Toys	175,208	84,052	67,685	21,829	1,642
Sports and Recreational Activities and Equipment	4,497,768	217,598	3,170,671	1,055,546	52,5322
Home Communication, Entertainment and Hobby Equipment	132,176	33,294	42,477	39,003	17,403
Personal Use Items	531,144	164,067	195,478	137,477	34,044
Packaging and Containers for Household Products	335,911	51,830	122,784	138,468	22,646
Yard and Garden Equipment	280,302	14,153	71,832	156,699	37,582
Home Workshop Apparatus, Tools and Attachments	374,186	16,928	94,735	226,729	35,794
Home and Family Maintenance Products	133,095	36,607	30,821	55,840	9,767
General Household Appliances	161,556	37,294	39,495	69,893	14,874

Source: U.S. Consumer Product Safety Commission, 1992 Annual Report, Appendix A p. A-5.

A crucial question is whether the traditional legal theories of breach of warranty, negligence, and strict liability, together with the forces that economic theory assumes to be at work in the retail marketplace, provide society with reasonably safe products. If we consider the activity of both federal and state governments in the area of consumer product safety, the answer to this question must be NO! Why?

The answer, very simply, is that competition and voluntary actions of businessmen do not always suffice to safeguard the public interest. Competition does not inevitably take the form of a rivalry to produce the safest product. Indeed, the competitive struggle may sometimes lead to a "shaving" of the costs of manufacture involving some sacrifice of safety. Nor does competition always reward, in the form of greater volume and higher profits, the manufacturer who tries to sell "safety" as a feature of his products.[12]

Recoveries in court for injuries caused by defective products do not necessarily mean safer products will be designed and produced. It is difficult to draw meaningful conclusions about product safety from related lawsuits. First, consider that an injured consumer must be aware of his or her legal right to sue the sellers and producers of a defective product. Second, he or she must have sustained sufficient damage so that an attorney will find the promise of an adequate fee in the case. Probably the most serious limitation on recovery of damages to consumers is the cost of litigation. Some experts say it hardly pays to go to trial for less than $5,000 to $10,000. Moreover, at the trial, the plaintiff usually runs a substantial risk that one of the defenses available to the seller or manufacturer may be successfully asserted. Even in the best of circumstances, the evidence shows that a products liability case is a financially bruising, onerous undertaking for the plaintiff.

Only the most serious products liability cases ordinarily are litigated. A survey of 276 persons in Denver and Boston who had reported injuries to the FDA showed that only 4 percent contacted an attorney to investigate the possibility of initiating a claim for injury.[13] Another study revealed that some manufactures do not even respond to letters claiming compensation because they know that over two-thirds will never pursue their claims further.[14] As for those cases that are litigated, let's assume that a plaintiff does recover a substantial judgment for injury owing to, for example, a defective power saw. How does the manufacturer respond? More likely than not, the manufacturer will increase the price of the product just a bit to amortize the cost of the judgment. Even where there is a monetary recovery, no coherent or organized effort is made to publicize the name of a manufacturer held liable so that consumers could in the future select safer products over those produced by firms with bad safety records. In short, litigation compensates people for injuries caused by defective products, but is not very successful in preventing injuries in the first place, nor is litigation a successful way to bring about design changes.

THE CONSUMER PRODUCT SAFETY ACT OF 1972

The Consumer Product Safety Act of 1972[15] created the Consumer Product Safety Commission (CPSC), which was activated as an independent federal regulatory agency on May 14, 1973. The CPSC has jurisdiction over every consumer product *except* automobiles, food, and a few other items regulated by older federal agencies (e.g., liquor and firearms).

The commission operates under a mandate to collect and disseminate information relating to injuries and to conduct investigations and tests on consumer products and their use. When a consumer product creates a hazard of injury or illness, the CPSC may develop consumer product safety standards. These standards must be set forth in performance requirements. If the CPSC finds that an unreasonable risk exists and that no standard will provide protection, it may ban a product. It has banned such products as garments containing asbestos, some baby cribs, some drain cleaners, assorted types of fireworks, furniture painted with lead paint, some kinds of lawn darts, and pressurized products containing vinyl chloride. In late 1988, the CPSC banned the sale of motorized tricycles known as all-terrain vehicles, or ATVs, after they had been involved in more than 900 deaths since their introduction (from Japan) in the early 1980s. Most recently (Sept., 1995) the CPSC demanded that some scarves that burned faster than a sheet of paper be withdrawn from the market.[16]

One of the most important activities of the CPSC is to develop data banks on consumer injuries. To find out what products are involved in accidents, the commission has established a network of hospital emergency rooms that report daily to Washington headquarters. National estimates can be derived from these reports. More than 2 million accident reports have been logged since 1973. In addition, the commission has conducted more than 40,000 in-depth accident investigations to collect more detailed information about the involvement of consumer products in accidents and injuries.

The CPSC also involves consumers in another way. When the commission is seeking to develop a standard for a particular product, an announcement is made in the *Federal Register*. Consumers or consumer organizations may respond by offering to develop a proposed mandatory standard. In this way, consumer groups have developed or assisted in the development of several standards in the past.

In summary, the basic idea of the CPSC is to collect and disseminate information about product safety and to attempt to reduce hazards through rule making and enforcement. Accidents and injury would have increased more sharply if it were not for the work of the commission.

The 1992 Annual Report of the CSPC estimated that its emphasis on the preventions of electrocutions, poisonings, power mower injuries, and fire safety alone saved Americans $2.5 billion in that year. In one decade alone, the report concludes, from 1977 to 1986, deaths associated with consumer products decreased by 13 percent; and, the average rate of death per 100,00 consumers decreased by 23 percent.

The case of *Southland Mower Company* v. *Consumer Product Safety Commission* was selected to let you read about and understand the standard setting mechanisms of the CPSC. Judge for yourself the value of this agency and whether you think it contributes to the objective of producing safer consumer products.

This case is also an example of the judicial review of administrative rule making. Courts do not second-guess administrative agencies, but they may review administrative action if it is alleged that such action is arbitrary, capricious, or based on inadequate evidence in the administrative hearings.

Southland Mower Company v. *Consumer Product Safety Commission*
619 F.2d 499 (5th Cir. 1980)

GEE, CIRCUIT JUDGE

Approximately 77,000 people are injured each year in the United States by contacting the blades of walk-behind power mowers. Of these injures, an estimated 9,900 involve the amputation of at least one finger or toe, 11,400 involve fractures, 2,400 involve avulsions (the tearing of flesh or a body part), 2,300 involve contusions, and 51,400 involve lacerations. The annual economic cost inflicted by the 77,000 yearly blade contact injures has been estimated to be about $253 million. This figure does not include monetary compensation for pain and suffering or for the lost use of amputated fingers and toes.

To reduce these blade-contact injuries, the Consumer Product Safety Commission ("CPSC" or "the Commission") promulgated a Safety Standard for Walk-Behind Power Lawn Mowers ... pursuant to section 7 of the Consumer Product Safety Act ("CPSA" or "the Act"). ... In the present case we consider petitions by the Outdoor Power Equipment Institute ("OPEI"), manufacturers of power lawn mowers and an interested consumer to review the Safety Standard for Walk-Behind Power Lawn Mowers.

The standard consists of three principal provisions: a requirement that rotary walk-behind power mowers pass a foot-probe test, ... a requirement that rotary machines have a blade-control system that will stop the mower blade within three seconds after the operator's hands leave their normal operating position, ... and a requirement applicable to both rotary and reel-type mowers, that the product have a label of specified design to warn of the danger of blade contact. ...

... OPEI argues that substantial evidence on the record as a whole does not support the Commission's determination that the foot-probe and shielding requirements "are reasonably necessary to reduce or eliminate an unreasonable risk of injury" associated with walk-behind power lawn mowers. ...

* * *

[A] key element of the standard requires a blade-control system that (1) will prevent the blade from rotating unless the operator activates a control, (2) allows the blade to be driven only if the operator remains in continuous contact with the "deadman's" control, and (3) causes the blade to stop moving within three seconds after the deadman's control is released. ...

The blade-control system is intended to protect the operator against blade-contact injuries to both hands and feet by stopping the blade before the operator can contact it after he or she leaves the normal operating position and thus releases the deadman's control. The Commission estimates that the blade-control provisions will eliminate approximately 46,500 operator blade-contact injures a year. This figure represents approximately 60 percent of all blade-contact injures and nearly 80 percent of all injuries claimed to be reduced by the standard. As OPEI acknowledges, the blade-contact requirements thus are the "centerpiece" of the Commission's strategy for reducing blade-control injuries.

... OPEI asserts that the blade-control system provision is expressed as a design requirement, rather than as a performance requirement, in violation of the Act. It argues that a number of alternative requirements are available that are less design restrictive and more performance oriented than the blade-stop criterion and that the Commission therefore erred in adopting the blade-stop approach. . . .

The CPSA directs that a safety standard's provisions "shall, whenever feasible, be expressed in terms of performance requirements." . . . The statutory preference for performance requirements is rooted in the belief that this mode of regulation stimulates product innovation, promotes the search for cost-effective means of compliance, and fosters competition by offering consumers a range of choices in the marketplace, while design-restrictive rules tend to freeze technology, stifle research aimed at better and cheaper compliance measures, and deprive consumers of the opportunity to choose among competing designs. . . .

Although only a limited number of designs can satisfy the blade-stop provision, we find this part of the standard is nonetheless a performance requirement. While the standard mandates that mower blades stop within a specified time period, it does not dictate a specific means of fulfilling this condition. Manufacturers are neither formally nor practically restricted to employing a particular design, since two existing mechanisms, a blade-disengagement system employing a brake-clutch device and an engine-stop system, are capable of passing the blade-stop test.

We turn now to the issue of whether substantial evidence supports the selection of three seconds as the time limit within which blades must stop. The Commission based the three-second blade-stop time limit primarily upon four time-motion studies of operator blade access time. These experiments were designed to measure the interval between the moment the operator released the deadman's control and the instant he or she reached the mower blade. . . .

In setting the blade-stop time, the Commission considered not only the time in which an operator could reach the blade af-

ter releasing the deadman's control but also the incremental cost of successively faster blade-stop times. The record contains substantial evidence that the cost of blade-stop mechanisms varies inversely with the length of time in which the device stops the blade so that a three-second blade-stop requirement will be cheaper to implement than a one- or two-second time limit.

We find that the three-second blade-stop requirement is not too lax, contrary to petitioner Hayward's claim. The three-second measure will protect consumers against many, although certainly not all, blade-contact injures. While the Commission may not rely upon mere "common sense" or speculation to establish the *existence* of an *unreasonable risk* of injury it may exercise considerable discretion in determining an appropriate *remedy*. The Commission was entitled to consider the incremental cost of requiring a shorter blade-spot time in rejecting a one- or two-second blade-stop solution. The standard need not guarantee protection for all consumers; it is sufficient that it promises greater safety for consumers and is reasonably necessary to *reduce* the risk of blade-contact injuries.

Correspondingly, we find no merit in OPEI's contention that the requirement of a three-second stopping time is unreasonably demanding. OPEI strenuously urges that the empirical studies cannot support a three-second blade-stop limit because they unrealistically fail to account for such psychological factors as a person's fear of a noisily operating machine and resulting reluctance to approach it. . . .

★ ★ ★

We are also unpersuaded by OPEI's contention that current technology is inadequate safely to achieve a three-second blade-stop time. . . .

★ ★ ★

Most convincing proof that safe and reliable three-second blade-stop mowers are currently feasible is the fact that, at the time the standard was issued, at least two mower manufacturers were currently producing and marketing mowers that had a brake clutch mechanism complying with the standard. As one of these manufacturers declared, that such mowers are offered for sale demonstrates their manufacturer's belief in the safety and reliability of this type of brake-clutch mechanism. . . .

This evidence provides substantial support for the Commission's judgment that technology is available to design, produce, and assemble brake-clutch power lawn mowers that are unlikely to fail in an unsafe manner. . . .

★ ★ ★

We have carefully scrutinized the record and find that substantial evidence supports the conclusion that the safety benefits expected from the standard bear a reasonable relationship to its costs and make the standard reasonably necessary and in the public interest. . . . The Commission estimated that the regulations would raise the retail price of a complying lawn mower $35, costing the consumer $4.40 per year over the projected eight-year life of the mower. Total yearly compliance costs were believed to be $189 million for 5.4 million mower units (1978 production estimate). Blade-contact injuries were calculated to cost $253 million annually, exclusive of pain and suffering. Since, as we have noted, there are approximately 77,000 blade-contact injures from walk-behind power mowers each year, each injury costs about $3,300, without counting the cost of pain and suffering. Currently there are some 40 million mowers in use by consumers, so that a consumer has about one chance in 500 . . . of incurring an injury costing $3,300, exclusive of pain and suffering. The standard's injury cost associated with each mower without the safety features is thus $6.35 per year. The Commission anticipated that implementation of the standard would reduce this injury cost by 83 percent, for an annual savings of $5.30 per mower, exclusive of the savings of pain and suffering costs. Because the standard would result in a net benefit of $.90, a mower meeting the standard's safety requirements would represent a worthwhile investment for the consumer, and the standard's implementation is in the best interests of society.

★ ★ ★

In summary, the standard's scope and its requirements that mowers pass a rearfoot-probe test, shield-strength and obstruction tests, satisfy a three-secondblade-stop criterion, and carry a prescribed warning label are upheld. The Commission's conclusion that the standard is reasonably necessary and in the public interest is also valid. . . .

Affirmed in part.

CASE FOLLOW-UP

As of this writing, the future function and direction of the CPSC are uncertain. Business people view the CPSC as an unnecessary intrusion into the process of product development and production. Yet, it seems that, especially in light of the evidence of injury presented in the *Southland Mower* case, the free market forces so heavily depended on by business people have failed at times to produce consumer products that are "reasonably" safe.

THE FEDERAL TRADE COMMISSION

The Federal Trade Commission (FTC) was created in 1914. The wording of the enabling legislation was intentionally vague, giving the commission potential jurisdiction over a wide range of activities. Section 5 of the Federal Trade Commission Act (as amended) states simply, "Unfair methods of competition . . . and unfair or deceptive acts or practices in or affecting commerce are declared unlawful."[17]

To promote and police the competitive practices of the economy, the FTC

- Protects the public from false and deceptive advertising, particularly that involving food, drugs, cosmetics, and therapeutic devices
- Prevents practices that tend to lessen competition or lead to monopoly
- Prohibits interlocking directorates that lessen competition
- Requires accurate labels on fur and textile products
- Regulates the packaging and labeling of consumer products to prevent deception
- Supervises the operations of associations of American exporters

The FTC accomplishes its regulation of unfair and deceptive trade practices in several ways. The most important and effective regulatory power of the FTC is the authority to issue trade regulation rules. These rules can apply to an entire industry and have the force of law. The following early trade regulation rule controlled the practice of a supermarket advertising a product at one price and then either not having the product on hand when a consumer arrives or attempting to divert the consumer to another good by failing to reduce the price on the product to reflect the advertised price. If this practice (often called "bait and switch") were not covered by such a regulatory rule, very few consumers would use the common law remedies available through the torts of deception and fraudulent misrepresentation.

**Trade Regulation Rule Concerning Retail Food
Store Advertising and Marketing Practices
16 C.F.R. Part 424 (1972)**

§424.1 The Rule

(a) The Commission, . . . hereby promulgates as a trade regulation rule its determination that:

(b) In connection with sale or offering for sale by retail food stores of food and grocery products or other merchandise, . . . it is an unfair method of competition and an unfair or deceptive act or practice to:

(1)(i) Offer any such products for sale at a stated price, by means of any advertisement disseminated in an area served by any of its stores which are covered by the advertisement which do not have such products in stock, and readily available to customers during the effective period of the advertisement. (If not readily available, clear and adequate notice shall be provided that the items are in stock and may be obtained upon request.)

(ii) Provided, however, that it shall constitute a defense to a charge under subdivision (i) of this subparagraph if the retailer maintains records sufficient to show that the advertised products were ordered in adequate time for delivery and delivered to the stores in quantities sufficient to meet reasonably anticipated demands.

(2) Fail to make the advertised items conspicuously and readily available for sale at or below the advertised prices.

Another major method of regulation available to the FTC is the initiation of an adjudicatory proceeding. These are filed against particular companies (respondents) because of an alleged unfair or deceptive trade practice. This allegation may be based on a complaint filed with the FTC by the public, Congress, other regulatory agencies, and consumer or business groups. The FTC then conducts an investigation and issues a formal complaint to which the respondent has thirty days to answer. Often, the respondent does not wish to reply to the charges, fearing, perhaps, the reaction by the public to the adverse publicity of a hearing. In this case, a settlement is finalized in the consent order, in which the respondent does not admit the alleged wrongdoing but agrees to stop the activity and, in some cases, gives restitution to damaged parties.

If a party does not agree with the petition and wishes to challenge its truthfulness and the legal conclusion asserted—that the activity complained of is unfair and deceptive—then the respondent so replies to the complaint, and a hearing before an administrative law judge (ALJ) is scheduled. At this hearing, witnesses for both sides are examined and cross-examined. The ALJ makes findings of fact and draws conclusions of law and eventually issues a decision. This decision becomes an order of the FTC after thirty days if neither party files for an appeal within ten days of the decision. An appeal can be taken, under appropriate circumstances, to the U.S. Court of Appeals.

Once an order becomes final, if a respondent fails to comply with it or if a party is found in violation of a trade regulation rule, the FTC may seek a court order demanding compliance. If a party still fails to comply, a penalty of $10,000 per day for each day a party knowingly violates the order may be assessed.

UNFAIR AND DECEPTIVE TRADE PRACTICES

The definition of the term *unfair and deceptive trade practice* is unusually broad. It must be so because it was intended as a principle for application to the entire range of commercial practices. Some general principles have been recognized, however, and help us in defining this term. These principles are usually applied to advertising. The advertising may be on television or radio, in newspapers, magazines, or other print media, or on the box or package of the product. The general principles developed by the FTC and the courts are the following:

1. The FTC may act when there is a tendency to deceive; proof of an actual deception is not necessary.

2. The merchant or advertiser need not have knowledge of the untruthfulness of a claim. The basic purpose of the FTC is to protect consumers; its focus is therefore on the impression created in the mind of the consumer. Knowledge of the untruthfulness (falsity) of the claim and even the interest of the advertiser are immaterial.

3. Sometimes it is an insufficient defense to plead and prove literal truthfulness. Even though almost every sentence of an advertisement considered separately

is true, the FTC considers the advertisement's impact as a whole, which may be deceptive because of factors omitted from the message. Thus an unfair or deceptive trade practice is judged by considering the overall impact of a statement on the ordinary consumer.[18]

These general principles are applied in the following case of *Warner-Lambert Co. v. FTC*. This case is presented for its discussion of two key issues: (1) the quantity of evidence needed to sustain an FTC order and (2) a discussion of the FTC's power to remedy decades of false advertising.

Warner-Lambert Co. v. FTC
562 F.2d 749 (D. C. Cir. 1977)

J. Skelly Wright, Circuit Judge

The Warner-Lambert Company petitions for review of an order of the Federal Trade Commission requiring it to cease and desist from advertising that its product, Listerine Antiseptic mouthwash, prevents, cures, or alleviates the common cold. The FTC order further requires Warner-Lambert to disclose in future Listerine advertisements that: "Contrary to prior advertising, Listerine will not help prevent colds or sore throats or lessen their severity." We affirm but modify the order to delete from the required disclosure the phrase "Contrary to prior advertising."

I. Background

The order under review represents the culmination of a proceeding begun in 1972, when the FTC issued a complaint charging petitioner with violation of Section 5(a)(1) of the Federal Trade Commission Act by misrepresenting the efficacy of Listerine against the common cold.

Listerine has been on the market since 1879. Its formula has never changed. Ever since its introduction it has been represented as being beneficial in certain respects for colds, cold symptoms, and sore throats. Direct advertising to the consumer, including the cold claims as well as others, began in 1921.

Following the 1972 complaint, hearings were held before an administrative law judge (ALJ). The hearings consumed over four months and produced an evidentiary record consisting of approximately 4,000 pages of documentary exhibits and the testimony of 46 witnesses. In 1974 the ALJ issued an initial decision sustaining the allegations of the complaint. Petitioner appealed this decision to the Commission. On December 9, 1975 the Commission issued its decision essentially affirming the ALJ's findings. It concluded that petitioner had made the challenged representations that Listerine will ameliorate, prevent, and cure colds and sore throats, and that these representations were false. . . .

* * *

II. Substantial Evidence

The first issue on appeal is whether the Commission's conclusion that Listerine is not beneficial for colds or sore throats is supported by the evidence. The Commission's findings must be sustained if they are supported by substantial evidence on the record viewed as a whole. We conclude that they are.

Both the ALJ and the Commission carefully analyzed the evidence. They gave full consideration to the studies submitted by petitioner. The ultimate conclusion that Listerine is not an effective cold remedy was based on six specific findings of fact.

First, the Commission found that the ingredients of Listerine are not present in sufficient quantities to have any therapeutic effect. . . .

Second, the Commission found that in the process of gargling it is impossible for Listerine to reach the critical areas of the body in medically significant concentration. . . .

Third, the Commission found that even if significant quantities of the active ingredients of Listerine were to reach the critical sites where cold viruses enter and infect the body, they could not interfere with the activities of the virus because they could not penetrate the tissue cells.

Fourth, the Commission discounted the results of a clinical study conducted by petitioner on which petitioner heavily relies. Petitioner contends that in a four-year study schoolchildren who gargled with Listerine had fewer colds and cold symptoms than those who did not gargle with Listerine. The Commission found that the design and execution of the "St. Barnabas study" made its results unreliable. . . .

Fifth, the Commission found that the ability of Listerine to kill germs by millions on contact is of no medical significance in the treatment of colds or sore throats. Expert testimony showed that bacteria in the oral cavity, the "germs" which Listerine purports to kill, do not cause colds and play no role in cold symptoms. Colds are caused by viruses. Further, "while Listerine kills millions of bacteria in the mouth, it also leaves millions. It is impossible to sterilize any area of the mouth, let alone the entire mouth."

Sixth, the Commission found that Listerine has no significant beneficial effect on the symptoms of sore throat. . . .

* * *

III. *The Commission's Power*

Petitioner contends that even if its advertising claims in the past were false, the portion of the Commission's order requiring "corrective advertising" exceeds the Commission's statutory power. The argument is based upon a literal reading of Section 5 of the Federal Trade Commission Act, which authorizes the Commission to issue "cease and desist" orders against violators and does not expressly mention any other remedies. The Commission's position, on the other hand, is that the affirmative disclosure that Listerine will not prevent colds or lessen their severity is absolutely necessary to give effect to the prospective cease and desist order; a hundred years of false cold claims have built up a large reservoir of erroneous consumer belief which would persist, unless corrected long after petitioner ceased making the claims.

The need for the corrective advertising remedy and its appropriateness in this case are important issues which we will explore. . . . But the threshold question is whether the Commission has the authority to issue such an order. We hold that it does.

* * *

We have concluded that part 3 of the order should be modified to delete the phrase "Contrary to prior advertising." With that modification, we approve the order.

Our role in reviewing the remedy is limited. The Supreme Court has set forth the standard:

> The Commission is the expert body to determine what remedy is necessary to eliminate the unfair or deceptive trade practices which have been disclosed. It has wide latitude for judgment and the courts will not interfere except where the remedy selected has no reasonable relation to the unlawful practices found to exist.

The Commission has adopted the following standard for the imposition of corrective advertising:

> [I]f a deceptive advertisement has played a substantial role in creating or reinforcing in the public's mind a false and material belief which lives on after the false advertising ceases, there is clear and continuing injury to competition and to the consuming public as consumers continue to make purchasing decisions based on the false belief. Since this injury cannot be averted by merely requiring respondent to cease disseminating the advertisement, we may appropriately order respondent to take affirmative action designed to terminate the otherwise continuing ill effects of the advertisement.

We think this standard is entirely reasonable. It dictates two factual inquiries: (1) did Listerine's advertisements play a substantial role in creating or reinforcing in the public's mind a false belief about the products? and (2) would this belief linger on after the false advertising ceases? It strikes us that if the answer to both questions is not yes, companies everywhere may be wasting their massive advertising budgets. Indeed, it is more than a little peculiar to hear petitioner assert that its commercials really have no effect on consumer belief.

★ ★ ★

We turn next to the specific disclosure required: "Contrary to prior advertising, Listerine will not help prevent colds or sore throats or lessen their severity." Petitioner is ordered to include this statement in every future advertisement for Listerine for a defined period. In printed advertisements it must be displayed in type size at least as large as that in which the principal portion of the text of the advertisement appears and it must be separated from the text so that it can be readily noticed. In television commercials the disclosure must be presented si-

multaneously in both audio and visual portions. During the audio portion of the disclosure in television and radio advertisements, no other sounds, including music, may occur.

These specifications are well calculated to assure that the disclosure will reach the public. It will necessarily attract the notice of readers, viewers, and listeners, and be plainly conveyed. Given these safeguards, we believe the preamble "Contrary to prior advertising" is not necessary. It can serve only two purposes: either to attract attention that a correction follows or to humiliate the advertiser. The Commission claims only the first purpose for it, and this we think is obviated by the other terms of the order. The second purpose, if it were intended, might be called for in an egregious case of deliberate deception, but this is not one. While we do not decide whether petitioner proffered its cold claims in good faith or bad, the record compiled could support a finding of good faith. On these facts, the confessional preamble to the disclosure is not warranted.

Finally, petitioner challenges the duration of the disclosure requirement. By its terms it continues until respondent has expended on Listerine advertising a sum equal to the average annual Listerine advertising budget for the period April 1962 to March 1972. That is approximately ten million dollars. Thus if petitioner continues to advertise normally the corrective advertising will be required for about one year. We cannot say that is an unreasonably long time in which to correct a hundred years of cold claims. But, to petitioner's distress, the requirement will not expire by mere passage of time. If petitioner cuts back its Listerine advertising, or ceases it altogether, it can only postpone the duty to disclose. The Commission concluded that correction was required and that a duration of a fixed period of time might not accomplish that task, since petitioner could evade the order by choosing not to advertise at all. The formula settled upon by the Commission is reasonable related to the violation it found.

Accordingly, the order, as modified, is

Affirmed.

CASE FOLLOW-UP

This case reveals the power of the FTC in the days of its greatest prominence. The passage of the Magnuson-Moss Warranty-Federal Trade Commission Improvement Act in 1975 (discussed in the next section) and the election of President Carter in 1976 brought added strength to the FTC. Michael Pertschuk, Carter's appointee to the chairmanship of the FTC, had a pronounced consumer point of view. During 1977, the FTC was more aggressive in confronting powerful corporate and trade association interests than at any other time in its history. However, the powerful interests affected by the FTC began to organize and to exercise their strength in Congress. The late 1970s saw a successful movement to (1) give Congress the power to veto any and all FTC regulations, (2) eliminate or cut funding for groups paid with federal funds to present testimony that would not otherwise be given at agency hearings, and (3) stop the FTC from proceeding with investigations, rule makings, and lawsuits against specific business interests.

In 1979 and the early 1980s, trade and professional associations, such as the American Medical Association, the organized bar associations of lawyers and the insurance, television, automobile, and drug industries, all joined in the attempt to sharply curtail FTC powers. In 1980, the House refused to approve any further funding until the executive branch, still under Carter, agreed to let Congress have veto power of FTC rules. Carter argued that this would make the executive branch subservient to Congress. Congress did withhold funding, and for one day the FTC ceased to exist as a regulatory agency. A quick compromise was reached, that resulted in Congress winning the veto issue. Much of the FTC's power was lost because its rule-making authority was subject to the same assertions of power politics that one finds in Congress.

To round out our discussion of the FTC and its work on consumer affairs, we now turn to a discussion of the Magnuson-Moss Act, which addresses warranty abuse by merchants and which is administrated by the FTC.

THE MAGNUSON-MOSS WARRANTY-FEDERAL TRADE COMMISSION IMPROVEMENT ACT

The Magnuson-Moss Warranty-Federal Trade Commission Improvement Act (also called the Consumer Product Warranty and Federal Trade Commission Improvement Act) became law on July 4, 1975, and was prompted, in part, by consumers' dissatisfaction with the protection afforded by the UCC warranties. Warranty abuse was a phenomenon substantiated in 1974 when a congressional sub-committee reviewed 200 warranties from 51 major companies and found only one that offered a warranty free of ambiguous phrases, exemptions, and disclaimers.[19]

This Act seeks to make warranty enforcement a reality by providing to the consumer the information needed to pursue a claim for a breach. The Act does not alter the warranties of merchantability or fitness for a particular purpose. Also, the Act does not compel a merchant to make a warranty. The general provisions of the Act apply when a written warranty is made and the cost of the item purchased exceeds fifteen dollars. This requirement, as well as many other standards and procedures under this Act, is established by FTC regulation. The one who makes a warranty (called a warrantor) is required by the act to fully and conspicuously disclose the terms and limitations of the warranty to the consumer before the sale. Some of the items that warrantors should disclose are

1. The names and addresses of the warrantors

2. The product or parts covered

3. A statement of what the warrantor will do on breach of the warranty, at whose expense the work will be done, and the period of time the warranty will last

4. The step-by-step procedure consumers must take to obtain performance of any obligation under the warranty

5. A brief summary of the legal remedies available to the consumer on breach

The Act requires that, when a warranty is made, it be conspicuously designated as either a *full* (statement of duration) *warranty* (e.g. "full one-year warranty") or a *limited warranty*. If a warranty is labeled a *full warranty*, the warrantor, unless exempted from the requirements by FTC rules, must meet these standards (among others):

1. A warrantor must remedy a defective consumer product within a reasonable time and without charge.

2. A warrantor may not exclude or limit consequential damages for breach of an implied warranty unless the exclusion or limitation conspicuously appears on the face of the warranty.

3. If the product (or a part of it) contains a defect or malfunction after a reasonable number of attempts by the warrantor to remedy the defect, a warrantor must permit the consumer to elect either a refund or replacement of the product at no charge.[20]

Finally, this Act creates a private cause of action for an injured consumer and provides that the consumer may sue for a sum equal to the aggregate amount of cost and expenses (including attorney's fees) determined by the court to have been reasonably incurred by the consumer.[21] In other words, subject to some qualifications, damaged consumers may sue for both attorney's fees and court costs (to be awarded to the attorney) plus an amount of damage as determined generally by the breadth of warranty.

Evidence of the impact of the Magnuson-Moss Act on warranties and consumers is difficult to assess. In stores today, signs are posted proclaiming a full or, more often, a limited warranty. When a limited warranty is given, the warrantor may still limit recovery for consequential damages if done in conspicuous language, and the duration of implied warranties is allowed if reasonable. The substance of implied warranties cannot be disclaimed or modified, however, if a supplier makes any written warranty or provides a service contract at the time of sale or ninety days thereafter.

Some legal scholars have argued that the period of warranty abuse is at an end and that warranties are of value to a commercial society because they help in optimizing the productive services of the economy.[22] Warranties accomplish this by allocating between manufacturer and consumer the responsibility for investments to prolong the useful life of the products. To the extent that the Magnuson-Moss Act clarifies the obligations of the parties with regard to breaches of warranty, this conclusion may be justified.

In another study of the Act, however, one author seems to contradict this conclusion by declaring that warranties are no easier to read and understand than before the Act and that no dramatic shift in the amount of warranty protection was detected.[23] In addition, according to the study, the Act does not appear to have stimulated warranty competition, but the Act does improve the disclosure of information to consumers about understanding how to enforce warranty rights.

As a final word about the FTC, the FTC administers and enforces other trade regulation statutes, some of which may be administered jointly with other agencies. For example, under the Fair Packaging and Labeling Act, passed in 1966 and often called the Truth-in-Packaging Act, the FTC and the FDA establish standards regarding contents information to be shown on packages and to encourage the voluntary development of standards for package sizes.

STATE LEGISLATION ON UNFAIR AND DECEPTIVE TRADE PRACTICES

The FTC cannot police every merchant; some of this burden must be assumed by the states. More than thirty-nine states have legislation to provide remedies to consumers damaged by the more unscrupulous merchants. This legislation, plus the fact that many states allow consumer-related complaints to be filed without an attorney's help in small claims courts, provides remedies within the reach of many consumers. For example, Michigan law provides that "unfair, unconscionable or deceptive methods, acts or practices in the conduct of trade or commerce are unlawful." The legislation defines twenty-nine unlawful acts, among which are the following:

- Making false or misleading statements of fact concerning the reasons for, existence of, or amounts of price reductions.

- Representing that a part replacement, or repair service is needed when it is not.

- Causing a probability of confusion or of misunderstanding as to the legal rights, obligations, or remedies of a party to a transaction.

- Causing a probability of confusion or of misunderstanding as to the terms or conditions of credit if credit is extended in a transaction.

- Representing that a consumer will receive goods or services "free," "without charge," or in words of similar import without clearly and conspicuously disclosing with equal prominence in immediate conjunction with the use of those words the conditions, terms, or prerequisites to the use or retention of the goods or services advertised.

- Failing to reveal a material fact, the omission of which tends to mislead or deceive the consumer, and which fact could not reasonably be known to the consumer.

- Making a representation of fact or statement of fact material to the transaction such that a person reasonably believes the represented or suggested state of affairs to be other than it actually is.

- Failing to reveal facts which are material to the transaction in light of representations of fact made in a positive manner.[24]

This Michigan Consumer Protection Statute also provides that a person who suffers loss as a result of a violation of one of the unfair or deceptive practices may bring an action to recover actual damages or $250, whichever is greater. The legislation does not provide a remedy for the recovery of amounts for personal injury as a result of a defective product but does allow recovery for deception. For example, a student at Michigan State University showed, in a local small claims court, he was told by a merchant that his defective stereo speaker was covered by warranty and would be repaired without charge. When he went to pick up the speaker from the merchant, he was told it would cost him $60. He paid the amount under protest and then filed his claim. The court awarded him $250.

FEDERAL AND STATE CONSUMER PROTECTION LEGISLATION—CREDIT

A substantial amount of consumer protection legislation involves the regulation of credit transactions. Closely related to the actual sale of goods (or real property) is the manner in which the buyer pays. Quite often, the buyer pays a small portion of the purchase price and then promises to pay the balance plus interest on this outstanding balance until the full amount is paid. When a seller relies on a buyer's promise to pay in the future, it is extending credit to the buyer.

Often, it is difficult for a consumer to assess the exact amount that will be paid for goods when credit is involved, and just as difficult is the computation of the cost of credit itself. Both Congress and state legislatures have passed statutes to provide the consumer with knowledge about his or her credit transactions.

THE CONSUMER CREDIT PROTECTION ACT

The Consumer Credit Protection Act[25] (also called the Truth-in-Lending Act) is administered by the Federal Reserve System and has been in force since 1969. The Act and its rules reach all extensions of credit for personal, family, household, and agricultural purposes. The applicability of the Act is suspended if state legislation covers similar transactions and the requirements for disclosure are substantially similar to those imposed by the Act.

Under the Act, the lender must furnish to the borrower, before the credit is extended, a written disclosure statement that sets forth (1) the cash price, (2) the down payment, (3) the total amount financed, (4) the dollar amount the loan will cost, (5) the approximate amount of the true annual interest rate, and (6) an explanation of the delinquency and default charges. The Act does not set any ceiling on finance charges or interest rates, nor does it affect state laws setting a maximum amount that may be charged as interest.

A violator of the Act may incur both civil and criminal liability. If a creditor fails to disclose the required information, the debtor can bring a civil action and seek to recover double the amount of the finance charge. Under an amendment to the Act, giving false or inaccurate information is a criminal offense punishable by a fine up to $5,000 or a year in jail or both.

The act is enforced by a number of federal agencies, such as the Director of the Bureau of Federal Credit Unions, the Federal Home Loan Bank Board, and a few others. The coverage of the Act has been extended by enactment of the Fair Credit Reporting Act of 1970,[26] which covers credit card transactions. This amendment limits the liability of new credit-card holders to $50 if this liability is incurred by someone using the owner's lost or stolen credit card.

THE FAIR CREDIT REPORTING ACT

The Fair Credit Reporting Act became law in 1970.[27] Its purpose is to provide to consumers requesting credit the information relied on by the merchant or the one extending the credit. This is done so that the consumer may verify the accuracy of this information. The Act covers credit information supplied to potential creditors, insurers, and employers of that person. A less important goal is to help protect consumers against the discharge of such confidential information to persons who may have no legitimate use for it.

The Act focuses on the disclosure by the merchant to the consumer of the name and address of the credit reporting agency or credit bureau that made the report. If the consumer asks, the user of the information must disclose free of charge the information in the report. The consumer may require the credit reporting agency to delete any inaccurate or obsolete information from the file. If a dispute develops, the consumer may give his or her version of the dispute to the credit agency, and the agency must put it in the file.

The consumer can require that a credit report be withheld from anyone who, under the law, does not have a legitimate business need for the information. The users of this information generally are businesses extending credit or employing the consumer. If a violation of the Act occurs, the consumer may sue for damages plus punitive damages and attorney's fees.

THE EQUAL CREDIT OPPORTUNITY ACT

The Equal Credit Opportunity Act (ECOA)[28] was passed in 1977 to help in preventing discrimination against any credit applicant on the basis of race, color, religion, national origin, gender, or marital status. One of the strongest provisions of this Act requires the party extending credit to provide each applicant who is denied credit or whose account is terminated the reasons for such action if the applicant requests. The Act applies to banks, finance companies, retail stores, credit card issuers, and other firms that usually extend credit. The Act does not guarantee credit to any applicant. The creditors may still set the standards, but the standards may not discriminate against one of the classes mentioned above.

CONSUMER PROTECTION AGAINST CREDIT ABUSES AT THE STATE LEVEL

Banks and credit agencies are regulated on the local level by the various state governments. Any deceptive practice should be reported to the proper state regulatory agency. Only one fairly comprehensive state-based regulatory scheme transcends state boundaries. It is the Uniform Consumer Credit Code (UCCC). Like the Uniform Commercial Code, the UCCC was drafted by the National Conference of Commissioners on Uniform State Laws and was published in 1968 for adoption by the states. This legislation has been quite controversial: By 1974, it had undergone six redrafts, and only a few states had adopted it.

As in the Truth-in-Lending Act, the annual percentage rate for the credit and the difference between the cash price and the credit price must be disclosed in every transaction involving retail installment sales, consumer credit, or small loans.

This ends our discussion of some formal rules, orders, and regulations in the legal environment of business. We end this chapter with a discussion of some ethical considerations and observations about general policies of governmental regulations.

ETHICS, GOVERNMENTAL REGULATION, AND THE COST OF HUMAN LIFE

The idea that governmental regulation must be measured to provide a check on efficiency became prominent during the Reagan presidency. One of President Reagan's first official acts was to sign an executive order providing that regulatory action not be undertaken unless the potential benefits to society for the regulation outweighed the potential costs to society. The idea was to make it appear that the government had a concrete formula for determining whether a regulation was a "good deal" for society. For example, suppose the appropriate governmental agency wants to require new, safer car seats. It is estimated that this regulation would cost auto companies $90 million. (Much of this cost, of course, would be passed on to the purchasers of cars.) Is the regulation worth it? If we assume that it will save eighty lives per year, the regulation may not be worth it if the value of the lives saved is less than the cost to consumers. Implied in this calculation of efficiency is a dollar value for human life. If, for example, each life is valued at $1 million, our regulation brings a "savings" of $80 million (the benefit) and, because this amount is $10 million less than the regulation cost, the regulation should be scrapped.

In this example, as in much of governmental regulation, we can discern a certain asymmetry in the measurement process. Companies and the government have been keeping cost figures for decades on various alternative procedures, products, and methods of doing business. These are readily measurable. But how does one measure the perceived benefit? It is almost always in lives saved, in injuries prevented, in a society somehow strengthened by less discrimination, or in a cleaner environment. The natural advantage in this process seems to be in favor of the side with the most concrete data—the cost.

Moreover, consider the other side of the equation. A fundamental assumption is that life and limb, or a meaningful job, or the value of a clean river can be measured. One recent survey pointed out that the Occupational Safety and Health Administration (OSHA) valued a life at between $2 million and $5 million; the CPSC, $2 million; the EPA, $475,000 to $8.3 million; and both the Department of Transportation (DOT) and the Federal Aviation Administration (FAA), about $1 million.[29] In many of these calculations, the value of a life is dependent on one's earning potential in the money economy. Thus, the life of a bank vice president who earns $400,000 annually is valued more than the life of a teenager whose father is a laborer and more than a woman who has pursued no career but rather opts to stay home to raise her children instead.

These figures are used to make subjective and value-laden political judgments seem objective and apolitical. Moreover, the value of a life is manipulated to achieve various results. For example, in 1985, the FAA wanted airplane manufacturers to design and install safer seats, which the FAA estimated would save between ten and fifty lives over the next ten years. When cost-benefit analysis showed the regulation was not beneficial enough and when those in the government still wanted the regulation, they simply raised the value of a life to $1 million and the regulation went forward.[30]

Others have criticized the use of cost-benefit analysis for the following reasons:

- Cost-benefit analysis by itself will never determine which policies should be followed in the first place; it is effective only for choosing between alternatives. That is, cost-benefit analysis could not indicate that it is a good idea to clean up the environment. Once people have decided to do it, however, cost-benefit analysis may be used to help in choosing between alternative ways of achieving this objective.

- No single scale exists against which many types of choices can be measured. People often try to weigh the benefits of health derived from a cleaner environment against a decreased income for everyone. Here, we are comparing health to income. It is a crude form of measurement at best.

- Almost every definition of a cost and a benefit includes substantial subjective judgments. What are sugar-laden desserts, for example? To young, active persons with a sweet tooth, they are a major source of joy, a benefit; to an overweight, middle-aged executive they are a cost, perhaps a life-threatening cost. Cost and benefit often depend on who one is.

- Comparing costs and benefits implies certain notions of cause and effect. If pollution control devices are installed on factories, the air will be cleaner and the quality of lives will be enhanced. Although this result seems desirable, no positive results are *assured*. If required pollution control devices are cut back, firms will have more money to spend creating jobs. This is not *assured* either. In short, no one is ever quite fully assured of an action's consequences.

- Making a decision today on the basis of cost-benefit analysis devalues the future. Any decision made today is made on the information available today. It might appear today that the sugar substitute found in almost all sugar-free soft drinks is safe. Suppose that next year, significant quantities of young people develop cancer because of overconsumption of this chemical; the calculation would then change drastically.

In short, the rhetoric of cost-benefit analysis was a facade to hide essentially political decisions to drastically cut the budgets and the output of administrative agencies during the late 1970s and 1980s. Cost-benefit analysis would be legitimate if the costs could be measured accurately over time, if the costs and benefits accrued to the same body of people, and if all subjective elements were minimized. But these conditions are rare. Such measurement is often a subjective, political judgment, not a scientific one.

Moreover, what is called governmental regulation of one sort or another will not go away. In fact, the presence of government is everywhere, but people do not seem to notice it, as the following story indicates. The story (told here by Jonathan Yates in *Newsweek*) is one used by Ernest F. Hollings to sum up the American view of government regulation:

A veteran returning from Korea went to college on the GI Bill; bought his house with an FHA loan; saw his kids born in a VA hospital; started a business with an SBA loan; got electricity from TVA and, then, water from a project funded by the EPA. His kids participated in the school-lunch program and made it through college courtesy of government-guaranteed student loans. His parents retired to a farm on their social security, getting electricity from the REA and the soil tested by the USDA. When the father became ill, his life was saved with a drug developed through NIH; the family was saved from financial ruin by Medicare. Our veteran drove to work on the interstate; moored his boat in a channel dredged by Army engineers; and when floods hit, took Amtrak to

Washington to apply for disaster relief. He also spent some of his time there enjoying the exhibits in the Smithsonian museums.

Then one day he wrote his congressman an angry letter complaining about paying taxes for all those programs created for ungrateful people. In effect, he said, the government should get off his back.[31]

Government regulation is never a static phenomenon; it is constantly changing. The proper balance between the presence of government and the freedom of those in the markets is subject to constant debate. As new failures in market structure and the performance of those in it are exposed, both old and new regulatory techniques are tried. The proper balance often seems as if it is just around the corner, so people try to fine-tune the rules just one more time.

In addition, governmental regulation is almost always portrayed as being very expensive and intrusive on some sort of "natural" functioning of a social system or a market. As this third edition is being written, the great public debate is on whether medical care should be moved from the private sector to the public sector. There is also debate on whether much of the nations schooling should move the other way—from the public to the private sector. The debate never ends.

CONCLUSION

Governmental regulation comes despite a strong tradition against such activity in the marketplace. The results, therefore, are mixed. After all, many politicians are elected on promises that they will reduce the presence of government in the business environment. The CPSC and the FTC exist to fill a vital need in the economy, but they exist with little or no public support. If you believe that governmental regulation does not work in the U. S. economy and if you want an explanation of why, ask yourself how many of your fellow students have expressed a desire to work for a governmental agency. If you are a business student, the answer is probably none. When we ask our MBA classes, "How many of you plan to work for the government when you graduate?" Only one or two hands in a class of seventy go up. Perhaps this, more than anything, is the best indication of why government is thought not to succeed in the U. S. economy: The talent goes into the private sector.

Many believe that the FTC and a few other agencies are on the verge of extinction. But, as almost all other advanced economies in the world show, regulation and perceived efficiency need not be exclusive. The United States can have both, and the economy will be stronger if the public would only believe this were so.

The permanent and perfect solution for the products liability crisis and for the protection of consumers in general has not been found. Indeed, it appears that the law has trailed behind and is not catching up with this substantial problem. Americans can be proud, though, that their legal system is flexible enough to develop many legal theories, approaches, laws, agencies, and rules to address this problem. Out of these numerous attempts at a solution will emerge one or several that, we hope, will become satisfactory.

REVIEW QUESTIONS AND PROBLEMS

1. How would you explain the fact that the United States has more types of governmental regulation of business today than ever before despite a substantial ideological and historical bias against governmental interference with private business activity?

2. In a short paragraph, describe the most often used method for creating governmental regulation through rules (legislative model) and then contrast it with the trial type (adjudicatory) model.

3. On August 7, 1964, the Civil Aeronautics Board (CAB) issued a regulation providing that only all-cargo air carriers could provide blocked space service. This blocked space service referred to reserved space of a specified amount for cargo usually established by agreement. In essence, the regulation forbade passenger carriers, such as American Airlines, TWA, and United, from providing blocked space for freight. It was issued following the notice and comment procedure usually used by the CAB for making rules that would not substantially modify a carrier's certificate from the CAB. The Federal Aviation Act provided that a CAB certificate could be modified only after a full adjudicatory hearing.

   The passenger carriers argued that this new rule would change them from combination passenger freight carriers into just passenger carriers. This change would put them at a competitive disadvantage, compared with freight carriers and, they alleged, would substantially affect not only their certificate but also their business revenues.

   Develop all of the arguments to entitle the passenger carriers to an adjudicatory hearing. *American Airlines, Inc.* v. *Civil Aeronautics Board*, 359 F.2d 624 (D.C. Cir. 1965)

4. Several high school students in Columbus, Ohio, were suspended from school for ten days. They were not provided with a hearing, nor were they given effective notice or a statement of reasons (before the suspension) for the temporary expulsion. Do you believe that such a state action (expulsion from high school for ten days) is part of the administrative process? In this case, do you believe that the affected students should be given an adjudicatory type hearing before the temporary expulsion? Why or why not? *Goss* v. *Lopez*, 419 U.S. 565 (1975)

5. The following statement is a concise suggestion for ways that people should think about remedies for the informal exercise of discretion by administrative agencies. In what ways might you amend this statement? It is from K. C. Davis, *Administrative Law* 460 (1977).

   [R]eviewing courts should require that administrators must as far as feasible reduce their discretion in individual cases by the use of various tools that either eliminate or control discretion, including rigid rules, flexible rules or rules with escape clauses, rules containing standards to guide the exercise of discretion, and systems of writing reasoned opinions and following precedents unless precedents are distinguished or a reasoned analysis explains why precedents are overruled; but these tools should not be used beyond the point where they cut into such individualizing as is necessary to do justice, and in minor action the use of these tools may appropriately yield to considerations of economy and convenience.

6. Some medical studies show that childhood consumption of large quantities of sugar helps create hypertension and other related life-long diseases and tends to cause tooth decay and overweight. Saturday morning television is filled with commercials advertising cereals that have comparatively large quantities of sugar in them. In your judgment, should the FTC or some other governmental agency attempt to regulate the advertising that is not in the best interests of children's health? What arguments are there against such regulation?

7. STP, an automotive oil additive, is advertised as a product that makes car engines

run smoothly. The ads illustrate this by showing a race car driver who is unable to hold a screwdriver shaft that has been dipped into STP. Certainly, this shows that STP made the screwdriver shaft slippery. Do you believe that such an ad should be regulated by the federal government? Why or why not?

8. From the public perspective, what real difference does it make whether the government through administrative agencies enforces strict safety (and other) regulations or, on the other hand, avoids safety issues and simply allows an injured consumer to collect money damages in a lawsuit? Isn't the latter approach about as effective as the former?

9. The Consumer Product Safety Act specifies that safety standards be supported by "substantial evidence." Indeed, in most cases when a governmental agency acts to set some standard of conduct, it must meet this burden. What is substantial evidence?

10. In *Southland Mower Co.* v. *Consumer Product Safety Commission*, what arguments did the petitioners (OPEI) use to attack the safety standards of the Commission? In your opinion, is regulation of power mower safety worthwhile

11. The number of deaths each year caused by automobiles is still very significant. A large percentage of these could have been prevented if the occupants were wearing their seat belts or if the auto had been equipped with a passive restraint device. What arguments are there for and against government regulation in this area?

12. In the late 1970s, the federal government sponsored studies on automobile safety intended to reveal possible design improvements. One test suggested that a third brake light installed in the center of the rear window of autos at the height of a person's eyes seated in another car might prevent up to 50 percent of the rear-end collisions. It was estimated that this would save consumers about $434 million in property damage and eliminate up to 40,000 injures per year. The cost of the light would be between $4 and $7 per car. NHTSA promulgated a regulation that required such a light, and it became effective for all cars built after the 1985 model year. If the results of this study are accurate, why did not "the forces" at work in the marketplace result in such an improvement in safety design before 1985? If you do not favor government regulation of business in any sense, what arguments do you advance against this form of regulation?

13. A consumer was attracted into a gas station by a large sign that said, "Free Wash With Fill Up." She filled her car with gas from the self-service pumps, and asked for the free wash when she paid. The gas station employee told her that the sign advertising a free wash applied only to full service pumps despite the fact that this condition was not on the sign. She paid the $2 charge for the car wash, washed her car, and drove off. In the absence of an applicable state or federal statute, what are her remedies? Under Michigan law (and some other states) describe her remedy.

ENDNOTES

1. McCraw, Business and Government: The Origins of the Adversary Relationship, 26 *Calif. Mgt. Rev.* 2, 33 (1984).
2. *Id.* at 40.
3. *Id.* at 42.
4. *Congressional Quarterly, Federal Regulatory Directory* 7th ed., (1994) p. 15.
5. Mark Bisnow is a former aide to Sen. Bob Dole. Excerpted from Bisnow, M., "Congress: An Insider's Look at the Mess on Capitol Hill," *Newsweek*, Jan. 4, 1988, p. 24. Reprinted with permission.
6. Payton, Administrative Law: What Is It, and What Is It Doing in Our Law School? 28 *Law Quadrangle Notes* 1, 30 (University of Michigan Law School, Fall 1983).
7. Administrative Conference of the United States, *A Guide to Federal Agencies Rulemaking* 1 (1983).
8. Gardner, The Procedures by Which Informal Action Is Taken, 24 *Admin. L. Rev.* 155 (1972).
9. Gelhorn, *Administrative Law and Process* 108–112 (1972).
10. *Final Report of the National Commission on Product Safety* 74 (June 1970).
11. *1992 Annual Report, U.S. Consumer Product Safety Commission*, p. iii (Introduction).
12. Davis, *Administrative Law* 9 (1977).
13. *Final Report, supra* note 10.
14. *Id.*
15. 15 U.S.C.A. Sec. 2051 *et seq.*
16. *USA Today*, Sec. D, p. 10 (September 7, 1995).
17. 15 U.S.C.A. Sec. 45 (A)(6).
18. Kintner, *A Primer on the Law of Deceptive Practices* 30–31 (1971).
19. Haemmel, George, and Bliss, *Consumer Law* 285 (1975).
20. 15 U.S.C.A. Sec. 2304.
21. 15 U.S.C.A. Sec. 2310.
22. *See* Priest, A Theory of Consumer Product Warranty, 90 *Yale L. J.* 1297 (1981).
23. Student Note, An empirical study of the Magnuson-Moss Warranty Act, 31 *Stan. L. Rev* 1117 at 1144–1145 (1979).
24. 14 Mich. Stat. Ann. Sec. 19, 418(3) *et seq.*
25. 15 U.S.C.A. Sec. 1601 *et seq.*
26. 15 U.S.C.A. Sec. 1642–1644.
27. 15 U.S.C.A. Sec. 1681 *et seq.*
28. 15 U.S.C.A. Sec. 1691 *et seq.*
29. *Newsweek,* January 11, 1988, p. 40.
30. *Id*
31. *Newsweek,* November 28, 1988, p. 12.

CHAPTER 12

Antitrust Law and Policy

INTRODUCTION

Beginning with the second edition of our textbook, we reduced the antitrust coverage. Now, we emphasize policy as much as law. This change reflects what we believe to be a pronounced shift of emphasis in the legal environment of business. The Reagan and Bush administrations quelled the activism that had long characterized the Antitrust Division of the Justice Department and the Federal Trade Commission and brought a distinct reduction to the intensity of antitrust enforcement. It remains to be seen whether that approach will characterize the Clinton administration.

Some well-known scholars—for example, Lester Thurow, dean of the Management School at MIT,—have urged a repeal of certain antitrust laws. In their view, the market—if left to operate without undue intrusions by the government—is capable of handling most issues labeled as problems. These issues would turn out to be nonproblems if the market was simply permitted to respond to them in its inexorably efficient manner.

Why the decrease in the interest in antitrust law? The answer lies largely in a shift in ideology or beliefs about how to achieve a productive society. Many commentators believe the U.S. economy is facing the severest challenge since the Great Depression. Studies show an alarming challenge by foreign corporations to both the technology and the efficiency of the industries that have established the U.S. economic base. Foreign competition in steel production, automobiles, consumer goods (especially electronics), and most recently computers has caused politicians and scholars to argue that the only way to meet this challenge is to relax the antitrust laws, which have prohibited monopolies, so that large U.S. corporations can combine energies, talents, and expertise. Will this work? Do large aggregations of economic power necessarily breed efficiencies of scale? Is it worthwhile to sacrifice the small businesses and farms that will be lost to make way for "bigness" in economic institutions? We may not have the answer to this question in our lifetimes.

A few scholars argue against the mainstream of thought. They say the only way to survive the current challenge is to vigorously enforce the antitrust laws. They believe U.S. corporations should be smaller, more able to adapt and respond, and more sensitive to market pressures and the subtle shifts in demand. Their view presents a profound policy debate: What should the United States do about increasing its ability to compete in international markets? Is competitiveness achieved by encouraging firms to become larger, more complex hierarchies or by cutting them down in size? We explore both approaches in our discussion.

We divide the antitrust material into two sections. The first section presents an overview of the antitrust laws and then focuses on the Sherman Act. The next section emphasizes the Clayton Act and the law and policy of mergers in the legal environment.

We deal with at least four dimensions of the mergers of large corporations in this textbook. First, mergers may involve potential violations of the federal securities laws, and so you will find in that material discussions of the merger process. Second, mergers also involve the application of state-based corporation law, and you will find discussions there of the merger process. Mergers also inevitably involve lay-offs of white-collar managers, many with decades of service. At the same time, many workers may be recently hired to help achieve some notion of affirmative action. Thus, third, mergers also involve issues of business ethics: Just how should loyal employees and agents be treated? You will find discussions of ethics issues in the agency material and, in general, throughout this book. Fourth, mergers frequently result in larger aggregations of economic power, so they may violate traditional notions of competitive fair play that serve as the basis for some antitrust laws. This last dimension is the focus of our attention in this section.

We include a rather long, comprehensive treatment of America's antitrust merger policy in the form of a law review article. This article is intended to raise questions about the current drift of antitrust policy. The article raises and then answers many complex questions in the area of antitrust enforcement. We follow it with an explanation of some issues of antitrust law that are important to an understanding of the legal environment of business but that are not central to Sherman Act or Clayton Act violations.

A HISTORY OF COMMON LAW CONTRACTS IN RESTRAINT OF TRADE

As early as 1414, a contract in which a craftsman promised his guild master[1] that he would not compete with his master in a lawful trade, that of a dyer, was found to be void per se.[2] The phrase *void per se* means that this agreement was illegal in itself (or "automatically") because it was so contrary to public policy and so devoid of redeeming merit—enforcement would leave a skilled tradesman without a means of providing for himself and his family—that the judges would not become involved in an extensive evaluation of evidence supporting the contract. From the eighteenth century to the present, common law courts have not enforced contracts intended to create or preserve a monopoly or to advance some other economically oppressive objective.

Antitrust law in the United States has its origin in a paradox or contradiction. Following the Civil War, the business practices of certain aggressive firms gave evidence that the rough-and-tumble version of free enterprise that characterized the economy—the unbridled and unregulated pursuit of profit—threatened to destroy the system. By "hook or crook," these aggressive firms would force others out of business and take over their market share. One tactic used with some success was that of *predatory pricing*—that is, setting prices so low that competitors would be driven to insolvency. On other occasions, aggressive firms would try to absorb their competitors through *merger*, or purchasing competitors' stock or assets, or they would neutralize and control competitors through a legal device known as a *trust*.

A trust conferred majority voting control of a firm in one person or a small group while stock ownership and the right to receive dividends would remain unchanged. In this manner, the firms in a particular industry could be centrally coordinated to the advantage of the *conspirators*, those in collusion with one another. Other firms would be forced to cooperate with the trust or would be run out of business. This practice was successfully manipulated by Rockefeller in the oil industry, but it spread to industries such as sugar, steel, coal, and textiles. It threatened to stifle and extinguish the norm—a kind of balanced competition among businesses of roughly equal strength—and replace it with a dominant and controlling firm or group. This practice became so threatening and unpopular that the public demanded it be abolished. Congress responded with a law that made it unlawful to form a trust for purposes of damaging competition. Hence, the word *antitrust* in the 1890 Sherman Antitrust Act.

Although the particular business practice that the Sherman Antitrust Act was designed to remedy is now a thing of the past, the phrase *antitrust law* has remained in the legal vocabulary to designate those statutes Congress has passed to preserve and promote competition and, toward this end, to regulate interstate business structures and practices. States generally have undertaken comparable legislation, the applicability of which, of course, is limited to intrastate operations, or operations within state borders.

ANTITRUST OBJECTIVES

The series of antitrust laws that now exist in the United States have three central objectives. The first objective is to promote competition by outlawing monopolization. Any unchecked, centralized power will probably not perform in the public interest, so the best policy is to encourage many producers of goods and services in the hopes that these producers will check each other. This policy is Adam Smith's invisible hand in action: each producer pursuing its own self-interest will promote the common good by competing with other producers. The desirable image here is a market with many sellers. The undesirable image is a market with only one seller. One seller in a market for a particular good or service is called a *monopoly*. The economic problem a monopoly involves for society is that the monopolist's insulation from competition will normally lead to a restriction in supply, which in turn will lead to higher prices and higher profits than would exist under conditions of competition.

The concepts represented in Figures 12.1 and 12.2 may be familiar to you from an introductory economics course. Figure 12.1 represents a perfectly competitive industry in which the entire quantity produced can be sold at the market price, illustrated by the intersection of the supply and demand curves. In contrast, Figure 12.2 illustrates that self-interested monopolists will restrict the output of goods (from Q_1 to Q_2) to increase their price (from P_1 to P_2) while the consuming public picks up the tab. Monopoly profits consist of the cross-hatched rectangle in Figure 12.2, where wealth is transferred from the general public to the monopolist. The solid triangle represents the social welfare loss of consumers who purchase less desirable substitutes because the preferred item is not produced and available at the lower competitive price.

FIGURE 12.1 *Competitive Gizmo Industry*

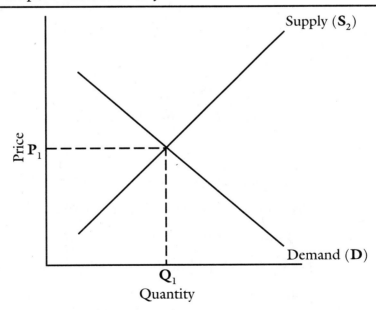

FIGURE 12.2 *Monopolized Gizmo Industry*

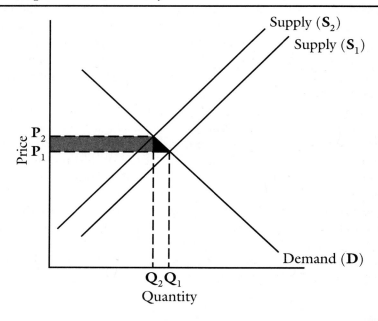

The characteristics of a monopoly market are as follows:

1. A single seller occupies the entire market.

2. The product it sells is unique.

3. Substantial barriers bar entry by other firms into the industry.

4. Knowledge of price, quality, and sale terms in the industry is imperfect.

The characteristics of a perfectly competitive market are as follows:

1. Many buyers and many sellers trade in the market.

2. All buyers and sellers can freely enter or leave the market.

3. No buyer or seller has a substantial share of the market.

4. The commodities of each seller are so similar that buyers do not care from which seller they buy; there is perfect information about commodities.

5. All costs of production have been paid by each seller.

6. Prices are free to rise or fall without interference from government.

Antitrust laws seek to discourage the first type of market structure and encourage the second.

The United States subscribes to the concept of a free economy, as opposed to one that is centrally planned and controlled. The ideals of freedom, free enterprise, and perfect competition live in the law and affect the moral tone of society.

The social objectives advanced under conditions of perfect competition are

1. Maximization of public welfare or utility, enhanced by efficient methods of production (Bentham's concept of "the greatest good for the greatest number")

2. Individual freedom (Locke's theory of natural rights that links the protection and enhancement of personal liberties to the institution of private property)

3. Happiness (Aristotle's notion that the highest good—happiness—consists of human flourishing or fulfillment in a community of like-minded individuals).

Not everyone will endorse these ideals. Yet, in a significant way, utilitarian, personal freedom, and virtue ethics concepts provide the philosophical underpinnings for a competitive free-market system.

The second central objective of the antitrust laws is to achieve desirable economic results. Here, the objective is more than efficiency (the production of goods and services at the lowest cost), although efficiency is a prominent objective. Other economic objectives are to encourage progress, or growth of total output per person, to provide a stable business environment in which businesspeople can plan, and to provide an equitable distribution of income.

Finally, the third central objective is to promote fair conduct. The name of the competitive game is Win market share, but it must be done fairly. For example, some firms are so large they could probably set the prices for their products so low that they could drive competitors out of business.

In Figure 12.3 are listed all of the major provisions of the antitrust laws and a summary of the anticompetitive behavior or structure that is the focus of the various provisions.

FIGURE 12.3 *Selected Anititrust Statures*

The Sherman Act	
Agreements Restraining Trade Illegal	*Section 1.* Contracts, combinations, conspiracies in restraint of interstate commerce are declared illegal. Criminal (felony) and civil sanctions are administered, but a violation requires the involvement of two or more parties.[1]
Single Party Conduct Prohibited	*Section 2.* Monopolization and attempts and conspiracies to monopolize are prohibited (one party may violate this section by monopolizing or attempting to do so).

The Clayton Act

Price Differences and Other Discriminatory Conduct that Injures Competition	*Section 2.* Amended in 1936 by the Robinson-Patman Act, this section principally addresses price discrimination where the effect may be to injure competition with the buyer, the seller, or customers of either. Discrimination in the provision of services to various customers, in the payment of brokerage fees, and in allowances for advertising and promotion are also covered if they have the prohibited effect.
Vertical (Supplier-Dealer) Arrangements that *May* Have a Harmful Effect	*Section 3.* Tie-in and exclusive dealing arrangements in commerce are made illegal—specifically the sale or lease of commodities made on the condition that the recipient will not deal in goods of a competitor if the effect may substantially lessen competition or tend to create a monopoly.
Private Enforcement Treble Damages and *Parens Patriae* Proceedings	*Section 4.* Any person who is injured by anything forbidden in the antitrust laws may recover treble damages and reasonable attorney fees. State attorney generals may sue in the name of the state on behalf of natural persons residing in such who have sustained injury by reason of Sherman Act violations (*parens patriae*).
Utilization in Private Actions of Final Antitrust Judgments Obtained by United States	*Section 5.* A final judgement in a civil or criminal proceeding brought by the United States to the effect that defendant has violated the antitrust laws is prima facia evidence (evidence that the defendant must disprove) of a violation in a private treble damage action brought by an injured plaintiff, i.e., a business competitor.
Mergers with Certain Effects Prohibited	*Section 7.* Mergers and acquisitions through stock or asset purchases are prohibited if the effect may be to substantially lessen competition or tend to create a monopoly. Advance notice of large mergers must be given to the Justice Department and FTC.[2]
Interlocks May Be Prohibited	*Section 8.* No person shall at the same time be a director in tow or more corporations where either one has capital, surplus, or undivided profits aggregating more that $1 million if elimination of competition among them would violate any of the antitrust laws.

The Federal Trade Commission Act

Catch All	*Section 5.* Unfair methods of competition and unfair or deceptive acts or practices in or affecting commerce are unlawful.

[1]A business corporation cannot conspire or combine illegally with a wholly owned subsidiary corporation. *Copperweld Corp.* v. *Independence Tube Corp.*, 52 U.S.L.W. 4821 (1984).

[2]Title II of the Hart-Scott-Rodino Antitrust Improvement Act of 1976 added Section 7A to the Clayton Act. It required disclosure by any person (the word *person* was used to cover noncorporate as well as corporate associations) of a plan to acquire voting securities or assets of another firm where (1) one firm has assets or net annual sales of $100 million or more and the other $10 million in assets or net annual sales, and (2) the acquiring firm gains 15 percent or more of the other's stock or assets or $15 million in stock or assets.

BASIC ANTITRUST CONCEPTS

INTERSTATE COMMERCE

The antitrust laws we discuss in this section are federal laws that obviously affect business. The power of the federal government to legislate in areas that affect business is limited by the Constitution to activity that is interstate in character. The basic test is stated this way: Does the activity that is in violation of federal law "affect interstate commerce"? The commerce affected may move only within one state (intrastate), but if the impact of the alleged violation is on interstate activity, the federal government has the power to act.

THE ROLE OF THE COURTS

The role of the federal judiciary and the U.S. Supreme Court is very important in antitrust law. When Congress passed the various antitrust rules, it was quite conscious of the difficulty in describing just what kind of business behavior should be illegal. For example, just what does it mean to "monopolize" a market? Many commentators have said that Congress intended to have the federal courts, using general guidelines set by Congress, develop a common law of antitrust. Federal courts take the general ideas set out by Congress in the statutory scheme set out in Figures 12.3 and have added to it the following major ideas.

Per Se Illegality. Through case interpretation over the past century, courts have developed the concept that some behaviors are "in themselves" (*per se*) violations of the antitrust laws. Per se violations apply in such a way that all the federal government or an injured competitor need to prove is the existence of a particular behavior. The behavior is deemed to be so anticompetitive that no justification will be allowed. For example, there are no defenses to a charge of price fixing that is proved in court.

Over the decades, courts have held that the following behaviors are per se violation of the antitrust laws. (We first describe the behavior and then the rule it violates.)

1. *Price fixing.* Competitors in the same market agree to set or "fix" the prices of goods or services. In the early cases, the defendants argued that agreement about prices of competing goods was really good for the market and for consumers because it eliminated the ups and downs of the market and provided stability. In some later cases, defendants argued that setting prices actually kept some competitors in business who would have failed otherwise. In all of these cases, the courts have taken the position that no agreement, whether written or unwritten, to set the price of competing goods or services is legal under Section 1 of the Sherman Act. Such a setting of prices is the kind of conspiracy outlawed in the Act.

2. *Market division.* Competitors in the same line of commerce agree to divide geographical markets. For example, suppose Miller Brewing agreed with Anheuser Busch that Miller would sell west of the Mississippi and Anheuser

Busch would sell east of the Mississippi and that neither would interfere with the other's territory. This is also a Section 1, Sherman Act, violation.

3. *Vertical price restraints.* Vertical price fixing occurs when a producer tells a wholesaler or retailer the price at which to sell. If a court believes an attempt has been made by a producer to impose either maximum prices or minimum prices at the retail level, it holds that this is a per se violation of Section 1 of the Sherman Act. For example, in a classic case, Seagram & Sons entered into agreements with wholesalers not to charge more than certain prices on its products. Seagram would not sell to some wholesalers unless they agreed to sell at the same prices as the wholesalers who had already agreed to the plan. This price setting was held to be illegal.

4. *Group boycotts.* Situations in which a group of competitors agrees not to deal with a person or firm outside the group or to deal only on certain terms is a per se violation of Section 1 of the Sherman Act. For example a National Football League rule, agreed to by all teams, requiring that teams signing a free agent (a player whose contract had ended and who was free to negotiate with other teams) compensate the player's former team was held a per se violation. The compensation rule made it very difficult for players to offer their talents to the highest bidder because a player's new salary plus compensation to the player's old team had to be paid.

5. *Tying agreements.* If a company with a legal monopoly in one product (perhaps because of a patent) attempts to expand sales in another product by "tying" the second product to a purchase of the first product, this action is a per se violation of Section 3 of the Clayton Act. For example, International Salt Company was found guilty of violating Section 3 when it leased salt machines (for dissolving rock salt into brine for use in industrial processes) covered by a patent it held and required as a condition of the lease that the party leasing it buy all its salt from International. This action foreclosed competition in the market for the sale of salt.

The Rule of Reason Approach.   The per se violations of the antitrust laws represent a fairly small number of the cases litigated, but they do give a glimpse of the kinds of behaviors that are obviously illegal under U.S. antitrust laws. They are illegal because their anticompetitive effects so far outweigh any offsetting desirable results that they are simply not permitted.

More difficult are the cases arguing that although a restraint of trade exists in the activity alleged, the restraint is outweighed by other factors that may enhance the common good. Most antitrust cases involve such a balancing. When a court weighs the negative or anticompetitive effects of business behavior or a proposed structural change against projected positive effects of the same behavior, the court applies a standard of "reasonableness" to determine whether the behavior is against the law. This process of weighing the many factors in an antitrust lawsuit, some of which restrain trade, is called applying the *rule of reason.*

In a now famous passage, Justice Brandeis wrote in 1918:

> The legality of an agreement or regulation cannot be determined by so simple a test as whether it restrains competition. Every agreement concerning trade, every regulation of trade, restrains. To bind, to restrain, is of their very essence. The true test of legality is whether the restraint imposed is such as merely regulates and perhaps thereby pro-

motes competition or whether it is such as may suppress or even destroy competition. To determine that question the court must ordinarily consider the facts peculiar to the business to which the restraint is applied; its condition before and after the restraint was imposed; the nature of the restraint and its effect, actual or probable. The history of the restraint, the evil believed to exist, the reason for adopting the particular remedy, the purpose or end sought to be attained, are all relevant facts. This is not because a good intention will save an otherwise objectionable regulation or the reverse; but because knowledge of intent may help the court to interpret facts and to predict consequences.[3]

So far in our analysis, antitrust law either falls within per se restrictions or is subject to a balancing test wherein the reasonableness of the restraint is the guiding standard. The cases, however, especially some of the recent ones, are not that simple. Some cases that involve an agreement on prices, especially those involving a service such as fees for lawyers or doctors, may not be obvious per se violations and, until recently, were viewed as involving the rule of reason approach.

In the following excerpt from a U.S. Supreme Court case, a professional engineering society sought to justify its rules against competitive bidding on the ground that competition itself in the award of a contract for engineering services was not in the public interest. If competitive bidding were instituted, they argued, engineers might cut corners and public safety would be jeopardized.

National Society of Professional Engineers v. *United States*
435 U.S. 679 (1978)

STEVENS, JUSTICE

. . . Petitioner's ban on competitive bidding prevents all customers from making price comparisons in the initial selection of an engineer, and imposes the Society's views of the costs and benefits of competition on the entire market place. It is this restraint that must be justified under the Rule of Reason, and petitioner's attempt to do so on the basis of the potential threat that competition poses to the public safety and the ethics of its profession is nothing less than a frontal assault on the basic policy of the Sherman Act.

The Sherman Act reflects a legislative judgment that ultimately competition will not only produce lower prices, but also better goods and services. The heart of our national economic policy long has been faith in the value of competition. The assumption that competition is the best method of allocating resources in a free market recognizes that all elements of a bargain—quality, service, safety, and durability—and not just immediate cost, are favorably affected by the free opportunity to select among alternative offers. Even assuming occasional exceptions to the presumed consequences of competition, the statutory policy precludes inquiry into the question whether competition is good or bad.

. . . We are faced with a contention that a total ban on competitive bidding is necessary because otherwise engineers will be tempted to submit deceptively low bids. Certainly, the problem of professional deception is a proper subject of an ethical canon. But once again, the equation of competition with deception, like the similar equation with safety hazards, is simply too broad; we may assume that competition is not entirely conducive to ethical behavior, but that is not a reason, cognizable under the Sherman Act, for doing away with competition.

In sum, the Rule of Reason does not support a defense based on the assumption that competition itself is unreasonable. . . .

CASE FOLLOW-UP

The per se approach is used to declare illegal any agreements on prices between competitors who sell goods or basic raw materials. Agreements between organizations that sell a service are subject to a rule of reason (weighing) approach. In 1989, the Department of Justice announced that it was beginning an investigation of Ivy League colleges concerning their long-standing practice of exchanging information about entering students' qualifications, financial aid offered to minorities, and graduate students and tuition. The Justice Department also asked for information on whether data on professors' salaries have been exchanged. Because these modern cases involve setting prices for services, the rule of reason approach is used, rather than the per se approach found in the older, product-oriented cases.

All of the colleges except MIT settled in 1991 by agreeing not to exchange financial aid information. MIT went to court in 1992, lost, and had the judgment reversed by a three-judge appellate court panel in September 1993. At the end of that year, the Justice Department dropped the charges and entered a settlement that allowed colleges to exchange limited information regarding the award of student financial aid.

A scholar who has followed the case and written about it observed that the settlement comes close to overturning Supreme Court rulings by allowing a defendant to justify price fixing with evidence that one's conduct improves social welfare. Georgetown University law professor Steven Salop said that it raises questions whether nonprofit hospitals or insurers like Blue Cross could agree to fix prices if they made a commitment to subsidize the uninsured.

ENFORCEMENT OF THE ANTITRUST LAWS

Antitrust laws may be enforced by four entities.

1. *The Antitrust Division of the Justice Department of the executive branch of the federal government.*

2. *The Federal Trade Commission.* The division of work between these two executive branch agencies may change from administration to administration. Recently, the Antitrust Division has handled cases involving the banking, computer, newspaper, and steel industries and the professions; the FTC has handled food, textiles, and product distribution.

3. *Private litigants.* The antitrust laws provide that both the federal govern-

ment and an injured competitor may sue to seek redress for an antitrust violation. Usually, the federal government seeks a fine, or an order from a court to break up a large corporation, or an order to stop certain alleged violations. An injured competitor seeks damages for the injury resulting from the violation. Because private litigants may sue or be sued by the government or by nongovernmental businesses, many large corporations have staffs of lawyers who do nothing but antitrust work. It is estimated that most informal antitrust enforcement takes place when these legal staffs educate management about antitrust law.

4. *State regulations.* Most states have antitrust laws, and the attorney general of each state may seek a fine or imprisonment or compensation on behalf of the public when it is injured by anticompetitive behavior.

ANTITRUST REMEDIES

Remedies for an antitrust violation are both criminal and civil. If the government sues, it may seek a fine, imprisonment, or both. For violation of the Sherman Act, for example, corporate defendants may have to pay up to $1 million for each violation, and individuals may have to pay $250,000. Individuals may also be subject to a felony conviction and may be sentenced to three years in jail.

If an injured competitor sues, the real damages are ascertained by regular methods of proof (the plaintiff must prove it is more probable than not that it suffered the damages it is seeking to prove), and then they are multiplied by three. These treble damages are provided for by Section 4 of the Clayton Act. Treble damages are provided because it is very difficult to prove damages that result from anticompetitive behavior. In addition, private antitrust trials are very long, complex, and costly. Congress put into the antitrust laws this provision for treble damages so that injured competitors will be encouraged to sue and thus relieve the government of constantly watching over the economy to protect competition.

In addition to these remedies, the plaintiff may ask the court to issue an injunction to stop anticompetitive behavior or to use its equity powers to fashion other kinds of remedies that will provide a measure of justice under the circumstances.

A unique feature of the antitrust laws provides that a firm that violates these laws may be sued by both the federal government and injured competitors. Quite often, injured competitors will either urge the government to sue or wait to see whether the government will bring any type of action when it receives notice of an alleged violation. The damaged competitor may then wait until after the government's trial to see what evidence unfolds. This evidence (of an antitrust violation) may then be used by the injured competitor in its trial. Because of the threat of subsequent civil cases by injured competitors, firms sued by the federal government often plead *nolo contendere* to a government charge. That is, the defendant firm neither admits nor denies guilt but says to the government, in effect, "go ahead and impose a remedy, we will not contest it, and we will not introduce any of our evidence against or in favor of guilt." In such a case, an injured competitor must use its own evidence of a violation in a subsequent case.

COMMON SHERMAN ACT VIOLATIONS

SECTION 1 OF THE SHERMAN ACT

Section 1 of the Sherman Act declares illegal any contracts, combinations, and conspiracies in restraint of interstate commerce. The contemplated illegal activity involves two or more firms or members of a profession that, in some form, agree to mutual action that would have an anticompetitive impact on interstate trade. We have already discussed the core ideas of section 1. Most of the per se violations are Section 1 violations: agreements about pricing between competitors, division of markets, group boycotts, and so on.

If the agreements do not involve pricing or market division and, especially, if a service is involved (as opposed to the sale of a good or product), courts use the rule of reason approach to balance the anticompetitive effects of any agreement with the desirable effects.

SECTION 2 OF THE SHERMAN ACT

Section 2 of the Sherman Act declares that monopolization or attempts to monopolize are illegal. Nowhere in the Act is a monopoly defined, so courts have been left to their own system of precedents and their own logic and knowledge of economics to guide them in developing an American law of monopolization. Anticompetitive business activity does not neatly break down into Section 1 and Section 2 violations, and often lawsuits by the government or injured competitors allege violations of both sections. If only one firm is involved in anticompetitive behavior, such as cutting its prices to drive out a competitor in a local market, this is a Section 2 violation (monopolization). When more than one firm is involved, Sections 1 and 2 may both be used. In the following classic antitrust case, the government alleged and proved that both Section 1 (agreements and combinations that restrain trade) and Section 2 (attempts to monopolize) violations were present.

United States v. *National City Lines, Inc.*
186 F.2d 562 (1951)

LINDLEY, CIRCUIT JUDGE

[*Author's note*: This case was a criminal prosecution against corporate officers and corporations themselves. In the part of the case reproduced here, there are two sets of corporate defendants. One set includes National City Lines, Inc., Pacific City Lines, and other corporations that operated city bus lines in many U.S. cities; they are here designated by the court as the "City Lines defendants." The other set of defendants is a group of prominent business corporations: Firestone Tire and Rubber Co., General Motors, Standard Oil of California, Mack Manufacturing Corp., and others that supplied buses and related equipment and fuel to the City Lines defendants. They are called the "supplier defendants."]

On April 9, 1947, nine corporations and seven individuals, constituting officers and directors, were indicted on two counts, the second of which charged them with conspiring to monopolize certain portions of interstate commerce, in violation of Section 2 of the (Sherman) Antitrust Act. . . . (The defendants) contend . . . that the evidence is insufficient to support the verdict. . . . The jury . . . having found them guilty . . . we are concerned only with the legality of the judgment entered upon that verdict.

It is undisputed that on April 1, 1939, defendant National City Lines, Inc., had grown from a humble beginning in 1920, consisting of the ownership and operation of two second-hand busses in Minnesota, to ownership or control of 29 local operating transportation companies located in 27 different cities in 10 states. At the time the indictment was returned, the City Lines defendants had expanded their ownership or control to 46 transportation systems located in 45 cities in 16 states. The supplier defendants are manufacturers and marketers of busses, tires, tubes and petroleum products necessarily used by the local operating companies of the City Lines defendants and others.

★ ★ ★

In 1938, National conceived the idea of purchasing [existing street car] transportation systems . . . and supplanting [them] with passenger busses. Its capital was limited and its earlier experience in public financing convinced it that it could not successfully finance the purchase of an increasing number of operating companies in various parts of the United States by such means. Accordingly it devised the plan of procuring funds from manufacturing companies whose products its operating companies were using con-

stantly in their business. National approached General Motors, which manufactures busses and delivers them to the various sections of the United States. It approached Firestone, whose business of manufacturing and supplying tires extends likewise throughout the nation. . . . Pacific undertook the procurement of funds from General Motors and Firestone and also from Standard Oil of California which operates on the Pacific coast. Mack Truck Company was also solicited. Eventually each of the suppliers entered into a contract with City Lines companies [in which the City Lines] agreed that they would buy their exclusive requirements from the contracting supplier and from no one else.

[*Author's note*: The case reveals that the supplier defendants bought large amounts of preferred stocks from the City Lines defendants at prices in excess of the market price. This gave the City Lines defendants surplus funds, which they used to buy controlling interests in the various transportation systems that used electric streetcars. The City Lines defendants then scrapped the streetcars and replaced them with busses and vehicles made by the supplier defendants.]

★ ★ ★

The indictment charges a concerted conspiracy by the City Lines defendants and supplier defendants to monopolize that part of interstate commerce which consists of all the busses, all the tires and tubes and all the gas, oil, and grease, used by the public transportation systems of some 45 cities owned or controlled by the City Lines companies. . . . We conclude that, on the face of the indictment, there is a charge of elimination of competition, or monopolization as to a substantial segment of interstate commerce, within the language of the Act. . . .

★ ★ ★

Defendants maintain that, even though we hold that Count 2 of the indictment sufficiently charges them with an offense against the United States, their conviction must be set aside for the reason that the evidence does not support the verdict. It is their contention that the evidence fails to establish (1) that there was a conspiracy, (2) that the defendants . . . acted with an unlawful specific intent, . . . but that it discloses only activities lawful in all respects. The government, on the other hand, asserts that the evidence establishes the existence of all elements essential to a finding of guilt and that, consequently the verdict may not be disturbed by this court of review. This difference presents the difficult crucial question of this appeal.

* * *

The first evidentiary question presented is whether the evidence was sufficient to support a finding that defendants acted in concert, with a common design or purpose. The government's evidence, much of it in documentary form, is that, during the period preceding the execution of the contracts under consideration, representatives of the City Lines defendants on several occasions met and conferred with one or more of the supplier defendants; that each of the latter knew that other supplier defendants had executed or were about to execute investment and requirements contracts with one or more of the City Line defendants, and that these conferences and proposed contracts were the subject of no inconsiderable amount of correspondence among the several defendants. . . .

* * *

Although defendants insist that each supplier merely obtained business from the City Lines defendants through separate negotiations, the documentary evidence referred to above and other circumstances in evidence seem to us clearly sufficient to justify the jury finding that the contrary was true. It is clear that representatives of two or more supplier defendants were in attendance in Chicago and New York at meetings and conferences, out of which grew the investment and requirements contract. And the fact that copies of a memorandum, of discussions held between one of the supplier defendants and one of the City Lines defendants, as well as copies of many of the letters which passed between the contracting parties prior to the execution of the contracts, were sent to representatives of other supplier defendants . . . is hardly reconcilable with defendants' contention that their several contracts were negotiated independently of one another but is, rather, convincing that each of the contracts was regarded by the parties as but a part of a "larger deal" or "proposition," to use the words of certain of the defendants, in which all of the supplier defendants were involved. At least the evidence submitted to the jury in this respect was clearly adequate to support its verdict.

* * *

Of course, it may well be that defendants did not intend affirmatively to violate the law, but it seems quite evident that they did intend, by making their mutually concerted investments in City Lines' stock conditional on the execution of exclusive requirements contracts in their favor, to join forces in making investments in consideration of the several exclusive contracts and thus, by their united and concerted action, to exclude their competitors from a market composed of the City Lines defendants and their operating subsidiaries, . . . and, thus, that they intentionally performed acts which inevitably led to violation of Section 2 of the Statute.

* * *

We believe that what we have said sufficiently disposes of all contentions of defendants. . . . Inasmuch as the charge was sufficient at law, the evidence substantial and adequate and the trial without error, as a court of review, we may not properly interfere.

The judgment is affirmed.

CASE FOLLOW-UP

What is monopolization? It is the elimination of competition by means other than skill, hard work, innovation, and more general notions of fair play; it is the attempt to overcome or manipulate the forces of supply and demand in the various markets. As Walter Adams and James Brock said in their widely respected study of "bigness" in the American economy:

> As the nation's dominant producer of buses as well as automobiles, General Motors understood at an early date that if urban railways could be eliminated as a viable competitive option, the sales of its buses could be vastly expanded. And if transit systems using buses could subsequently be made to decline or fail, a huge market would open up for additional sales of private automobiles. Anything that reduced the attractiveness of urban mass transportation—its speed, cleanliness, or reliability—would be perceived as a desirable trend from GM's private perspective, adverse public consequences for urban congestion to the contrary notwithstanding.[4]

The commercial environment is not always the result of accident or due solely to the autonomous play of free market forces innocently responding to the commands of consumer preference. This case is evidence for the assertion that large corporations consciously desire to shape the environment to suit their perceived objectives. In the name of profit and expanding market share, some of the largest and most respected business corporations executed a plan to bring about the demise of U.S. urban electric railways. As one concerned writer concluded:

> Thirty-five years ago Los Angeles was a beautiful city of lush palm trees, fragrant orange groves and ocean-clean air. It was served then by the world's largest electric railway network. In the late 1930's General Motors and allied highway interests acquired the local transit companies, scrapped their pollution-free electric trains, tore down their power transmission lines, ripped up their tracks, and placed GM buses on already congested Los Angeles streets. The noisy, foul-smelling buses turned earlier portions of the high-speed rail system away from public transit and, in effect, sold millions of private automobiles. Largely as a result, this city is today an ecological wasteland: the palm trees are dying of petrochemical smog; the orange groves have been paved over by 300 miles of freeways; the air is a septic tank into which 4 million cars, half of them built by General Motors, pump 13,000 tons of pollutants daily.[5]

Americans have always been suspicious of monopolies; this case is evidence that the suspicions are well founded. As a result of this prosecution, a few managers of the defendant corporations spent a few months in prison.

What should be the remedies for antitrust violations? Many commentators have taken the position that the remedies are not severe enough. The fines paid by corporations (or the months spent in prison for a few individual offenders) do not often offset the competitive advantage gained by the antitrust offense.

Antitrust violations can be divided into anticompetitive *behaviors*, on the one hand, and, on the other, situations in which certain behaviors lead to economic and social *structures* that favor monopolistic forces. This case is an example of the latter. Once the contracts were in place and operating, they changed the structure of public transportation in large cities to the advantage of the City Lines participants. Courts and commentators have been aware of these structural impairments for decades, but it is difficult to dismantle them once they are created. Section 2 of the Sherman Act and Section 7 of the Clayton Act (prohibiting certain kinds of mergers that substantially lessen competition) are both thought of as structurally oriented antitrust weapons.

Monopoly Power in a Relevant Market

Two antitrust concepts demand explanation for an understanding of Sherman Act basics. The first is that monopoly power must be found to exist in a certain, identifiable market for a product or service. The second, discussed in the next section, is the matter of the intent to exercise monopoly power in a relevant market. The antitrust laws do not condemn size alone. The plaintiff must show an attempt to use monopoly power once that power is established.

Defining the relevant market is a key to understanding some Section 2, Sherman Act, cases and some merger cases. To help define the relevant market, economists have used the process of determining the *cross elasticity of demand*, a measure of how readily consumers of a product will switch to another product, given a slight rise in the price of one product. This indicator really measures which products are interchangeable or readily substitutable. If products are readily interchangeable (given a little price rise in one, consumers will switch to another), both products must be included in the relevant product market, and the cross elasticity of demand is high.

For example, if the price of a mainframe computer goes up, will a consumer of data processing equipment switch to a personal computer? Probably not. Thus, these products are not readily substitutable and are not in the same relevant product market. The definition of a relevant market often determines the outcome of a case.

The Intent to Monopolize

Over the years, the element of intent in the trial of a Section 2 case on monopolization has been very troublesome. For a successful Section 2 case, courts require that the government or an injured competitor must prove monopoly power in a relevant product and geographical market and show that the defendant formulated a purpose or intent to seize or use that monopoly power. If the defendant can be shown to (1) control prices, (2) exclude competitors from the market (usually by lowering the price just when it looks like a new competitor is about to enter the market), or (3) control the market structure to its advantage by manipulating patents or trade secrets, intent is shown.

Perhaps the most famous Section 2 case on monopolization is *United States* v. *Alcoa*, decided in 1945 by Judge Learned Hand. In this case, the court first had some problems defining the relevant market because Alcoa dealt in the new (virgin) ingot market for aluminum (in which it had 90 percent of the sales), the secondary market for "used" scrap, or reconstituted aluminum (which, if added to the virgin market, gave Alcoa sales of about 64 percent of the combined market), and imported aluminum (which, if added to the first two markets, gave Alcoa about 33 percent of the total sales). Which market is the relevant market for antitrust purposes? It makes a difference because, as the court said, 90 percent of sales is a monopoly, but 33 percent of the sales in a market is hardly a monopoly. The court found that the relevant market was the virgin market, where Alcoa could exert monopoly power. The crucial question, then, was whether Alcoa had the required intent to exercise this power.

Judge Hand found that, during its half-century of existence, Alcoa's profits on capital invested after payment of income taxes had been only about 10 percent, which is low for an alleged monopolist. Still, a monopolist need not extract unfair profits. Congress, Judge Hand said, did not condemn bad monopolists and condone good ones. It forbade all monopolies. "It is possible," he said, "because of its indirect social or moral effect, to prefer a system of small producers, each dependent for his success upon his own skill and character, to one in which the great mass of those engaged must accept the direction of a few."[6]

In deciding that Alcoa did manifest intent to use its monopoly power, Judge Hand relied on evidence that showed Alcoa effectively anticipated and forestalled all competition. It both stimulated demand and then stood ready to meet that demand with an already expanded plant capacity. He said:

> In order to fall within Section 2, the monopolist must have both the power to monopolize, and the intent to monopolize. To read the passage as demanding any "specific" intent, makes nonsense of it, for no monopolist monopolizes unconscious of what he is doing. So here, "Alcoa" meant to keep, and did keep, that complete and exclusive hold upon the ingot market with which it started. That was to "monopolize" that marker, however innocently it otherwise proceeded.[7]

The case that follows is a private, treble-damage action by one allegedly injured competitor, Berkey Photo, against an alleged monopolist, Kodak. Kodak's economic power derives from its many patents on the production and processing of photographic film. A monopoly position resting on a patent not only is allowed by law, but also is encouraged. The right to secure a patent and to seek governmental protection of it is found in the Constitution. Kodak, however, did not have a monopoly over the processing of film. There were about six hundred film processors in the United States, and it was possible for any person to process black-and-white photos by buying the proper equipment.

The issue in this case was whether Kodak sought to extend its legal monopoly in film production to film processing by introducing cameras that required a Kodak-created cartridge. In 1963, Kodak first marketed the 126 Instamatic instant-loading camera, and in 1972 it came out with the much smaller 110 Pocket Instamatic. The ease of loading the film into these cameras and the ease with which they can be used caused a dramatic leap in Kodak's sales of cameras and film and a similar dramatic leap in the film that Kodak itself processed. Was this the move of a monopolist?

Berkey Photo, Inc. v. Eastman Kodak Company
603 F.2d 263 (2nd Cir. 1979)

KAUFMAN, CHIEF JUDGE

. . . Indeed, there is little argument over the principle that existence of monopoly power—"the power to control prices or exclude competition"—is "the primary requisite to a finding of monopolization." The Supreme Court has informed us that "monopoly power, whether lawfully or unlawfully acquired, may itself constitute an evil and stand condemned under §2 even though it remains unexercised."

This tenet is well grounded in economic analysis. There is little disagreement that a profit-maximizing monopolist will maintain his prices higher and his output lower [than] the socially optimal levels that would prevail in a purely competitive market. The price excess represents not a reasonable return on investment but the spoils of the monopolist's power. It is not a defense to liability under §2 that monopoly power has not been used to charge more than a competitive price or extract greater than a reasonable profit. Learned Hand stated that rationale in the *Alcoa* case. He said in his incisive manner that the Sherman Act is based on the belief "that possession of unchallenged economic power deadens initiative, discourages thrift and depresses energy; that immunity from competition is a narcotic, and rivalry is a stimulant, to industrial progress; that the spur of constant stress is necessary to counteract an inevitable disposition to let well enough alone."

If a finding of monopoly power were all that were necessary to complete a violation of §2, our task in this case would be considerably lightened. Kodak's control of the film and color paper markets clearly reached the level of a monopoly. And, while the issue is a much closer one, it appears that the evidence was sufficient for the jury to find that Kodak possessed such power in the camera market as well. But our inquiry into Kodak's liability cannot end there.

★ ★ ★

[A]fter possession of monopoly power is found, the second element of the §2 offense is "the willful acquisition or maintenance of that power as distinguished from growth or development as a consequence of a superior product, business acumen, or historic accident." . . .

In sum, although the principles announced by the §2 cases often appear to conflict, this much is clear. The mere possession of monopoly power does not *ipso facto* condemn a market participant. But, to avoid the proscriptions of §2, the firm must refrain at all times from conduct directed at smothering competition. This doctrine has two branches. Unlawfully acquired power remains anathema even when kept dormant.

And it is no less true that a firm with a legitimately achieved monopoly may not wield the resulting power to tighten its hold on the market.

Kodak, in the period relevant to this suit, was never close to gaining control of the markets for photofinishing equipment or services and could not be held to have attempted to monopolize them. Berkey nevertheless contends that Kodak illicitly gained an advantage in these areas by leveraging its power over film and cameras. Accordingly, we must determine whether a firm violates §2 by using its monopoly power in one market to gain a competitive advantage in another, albeit without an attempt to monopolize the second market. We hold, as did the lower court, that it does.

[The] use of monopoly power attained in one market to gain a competitive advantage in another is a violation of §2, even if there has not been an attempt to monopolize the second market. It is the use of economic power that creates the liability. But, as we have indicated, a large firm does not violate §2 simply by reaping the competitive rewards attributable to its efficient size, nor does an integrated business offend the Sherman Act whenever one of its departments benefits from association with a division possessing a monopoly in its own market. So long as we allow a firm to compete in several fields, we must expect it to seek the competitive advantages of its broad-based activity—more efficient production, greater ability to develop complementary products, reduced transaction costs, and so forth. These are gains that accrue to any integrated firm, regardless of its market share, and they cannot by themselves be considered uses of monopoly power.

We shall now apply to the case at bar the principles we have set forth above. . . .

Because a monopolist is permitted, and indeed encouraged, by §2 to compete aggressively on the merits, any success that it may achieve through "the process of invention and innovation" is clearly tolerated by the antitrust laws.

The verdict [against Kodak], therefore, cannot stand.

CASE FOLLOW-UP

A fair reading of this case is that the court said the use of monopoly power attained in one market to gain a competitive advantage in another is a violation of Section 2. Although Kodak faced competition in the photo-finishing market, and although it had a monopoly in the film production market, its development of the Instamatic camera with a cartridge in it that could best be developed by Kodak only was not an attempt to monopolize the competitive market in which Berkey operated.

Some commentators believe Kodak was merely being efficient and using good business judgment by bringing out new cameras and film packages; others take the side of Berkey and point out that smaller film processors probably went out of business (to Kodak's advantage) because of Kodak's practice. In short, there was no monopolization here. It seems fair to conclude that the definition of intent for a Section 2 case has changed from the days of Learned Hand and the *Alcoa* case.

Intent is an intangible, intellectual thing. Because a court cannot look inside the mind of an alleged monopolist, it will make judgments based on what is said and done. In *Aspen Skiing Co.* v. *Aspen Highlands Skiing Corp.*[8] Aspen Skiing Company (SkiCo), the defendant in this private treble-damage action, discontinued its participation in an All Aspen Ski Ticket, which had previously allowed skiers to choose from any of its three mountains or from Aspen Highlands' mountain. The effect of this move was to drop Aspen Highlands (A-H) from 20 percent of the market in 1976–77 to 11 percent by 1980–81.

A-H argued that SkiCo had monopolized the market in violation of the Sherman Act, Section 2, and that its refusal to deal was evidence of its intent. The U.S. Supreme Court affirmed the jury award of $2.5 million (which was trebled to $7.5 million). The most significant evidence against SkiCo, the Court related, was its failure to convince the jury that its refusal to deal was justified by any normal business conduct. The jury had sufficient evidence before it to conclude that SkiCo elected to forgo short-term profits because it was more interested in reducing competition in the Aspen market over the long term by harming competition.

ATTEMPTS AND CONSPIRACIES TO MONOPOLIZE

ATTEMPTS TO MONOPOLIZE

Attempts to monopolize require both an intent and a "dangerous possibility" that the attempt will succeed.[9] Intent may be proved by evidence of a "refusal to deal," as in the *SkiCo* case above, or by evidence of predatory pricing. Predatory pricing may consist of sales below cost, but sometimes sales below cost are made for a good, legitimate, competitive reason, such as breaking down a barrier to entry and trying to gain a toehold in a new market. How can a court tell the difference, then, between (1) legitimate sales below cost, sales that will clearly benefit consumers, and (2) intent to monopolize through a strategy of predatory pricing? In *A.A. Poultry Farms, Inc.* v. *Rose Acre Farms*,[10] Judge Frank Easterbrook looked at

> "the back end, the 'high price later' part of the predatory sequence." Predatory prices are an investment in a future monopoly, a sacrifice of today's profits for tomorrow's. The investment must be recouped. If a monopoly price is impossible later, then the sequence is unprofitable and we may infer that the low price was not predatory.

In evaluating the structure of the egg market, Judge Easterbrook affirmed the trial court judge's decision in favor of defendant Rose. Persistent entry into the market by other firms and expansion by old ones made recoupment impossible. The most plausible explanation for Rose's success, the judge observed, was that it simply beat its rivals to the punch by automating its processes and by using its lower costs to take away their business.

What about the "dangerous possibility of success" component of this formula? Judge Richard A. Posner dealt with that issue in *American Academic Suppliers,*

Inc. v. *Beckley-Cardy, Inc.*[11] and concluded, "The smaller the defendant is in his market and the less time and money it takes for a new firm to enter that market, the less plausible is an inference that the defendant has monopoly power." In this case, the defendant had hundreds of competitors and held no more than 3 percent of a nationwide market that had virtually no barriers to entry. Under these circumstances, Beckley-Cardy's price cuts, steep as they were, were no more than a normal response to American Academic's strategy of recruiting so many of B-C's key salespeople. Given these market realities, there was simply no dangerous possibility that Beckley-Cardy could establish a monopoly.

CONSPIRACIES TO MONOPOLIZE

A conspiracy to monopolize consists of (1) the intent implicit in planned collective action and (2) the commitment of some (at least one) overt act in furtherance of the plan. In the case that follows, two U.S. corporations that manufacture consumer electronic products (CEPs—mainly television sets) sued twenty one Japanese firms for engaging in the practice of fixing and maintaining artificially low prices in the United States over a twenty-year period and offsetting those prices by fixing and maintaining artificially high prices in Japan over the same time span. The Supreme Court reinstated the trial court's grant of a summary judgment dismissing the complaint of the U.S. firms.

Matsushita Electric Industrial Co. v. *Zenith Radio Corporation*
106 S.Ct. 1348 (1986)

POWELL, JUSTICE

. . . Respondents cannot recover antitrust damages based solely on an alleged cartelization of the Japanese market, because American antitrust laws do not regulate the competitive conditions of other nations' economies.

The thrust of respondents' argument is that petitioners used their monopoly profits from the Japanese market to fund a concerted campaign to price predatorily and thereby drive respondents and other American manufacturers of CEPs out of business. Once successful, according to respondents, petitioners would cartelize the American CEP market, restricting output and raising prices above the level that fair competition would produce. The resulting monopoly profits, respondents contend, would more than compensate petitioners for the losses they incurred through years of pricing below market level.

A predatory pricing conspiracy is by nature speculative. Any agreement to price below the competitive level requires the conspirators to forego profits that free competition would offer them. The foregone profits may be considered an investment in the future. For the investment to be rational, the conspirators must have a reasonable expectation of recovering, in the form of later monopoly profits, more than the losses suffered. The success of any predatory scheme depends on *maintaining* monopoly power for long enough both to recoup the predator's losses and to harvest some additional gain. Absent some assurance that the hoped-for monopoly will materialize, *and* that it can be sustained for a significant period of time, "[t]he predator must make a substantial investment with no assurance that it will pay off." For this reason, there is a consensus among commentators that predatory pricing schemes are rarely tried, and even more rarely successful.

Finally, if predatory pricing conspiracies are generally unlikely to occur, they are especially so where, as here, the prospects of attaining monopoly power seem slight. In order to recoup their losses, petitioners must obtain enough market power to set higher than competitive prices, and then must sustain those prices long enough to earn in excess profits what they earlier gave up in below-cost prices. Two decades after their conspiracy is alleged to have commenced, petitioners appear to be far from achieving this goal: the two largest shares of the retail market in television sets are held by RCA and respondent Zenith, not by any of the petitioners. The alleged conspiracy's failure to achieve its ends in the two decades of its asserted operation is strong evidence that the conspiracy does not in fact exist.

As our discussion shows, petitioners had no motive to enter into the alleged conspiracy. To the contrary, as presumably rational businesses, petitioners had every incentive not to engage in the conduct with which they are charged, for its likely effect would be to generate losses for petitioners with no corresponding gains. The Court of Appeals did not take account of the absence of a plausible motive to enter into the alleged predatory pricing conspiracy.

[T]he predatory pricing scheme that this conduct is said to prove is one that makes no practical sense: it calls for petitioners to destroy companies larger and better established than themselves, a goal that remains far distant more than two decades after the conspiracy's birth. Even had they succeeded in obtaining their monopoly, there is nothing in the record to suggest that they could recover the losses they would need to sustain along the way. In sum, in light of the absence of any rational motive to conspire, neither petitioners' pricing practices, nor their conduct in the Japanese market, nor their agreements respecting prices and distribution in the American market, suffice to create a "genuine issue for trial."

The decision of the Court of Appeals is reversed, and the case is remanded for further proceedings consistent with this opinion.

CASE FOLLOW-UP

Matsushita, A.A. Poultry Farms, and *American Academic* are all good illustrations of the impact the Chicago school of antitrust analysis has had on antitrust jurisprudence. In *Matsushita,* Justice Powell interprets the conduct of the defendants in accordance with the Chicago view that cartels (in this case, the agreement among the Japanese firms to fix prices and so forth) are notoriously difficult to maintain. "Cheaters" would normally be expected to break out of the agreement when, or if, they could do so profitably. This is clearly consistent with the view that everyone, from every culture and at all times, is a rational profit (or preference) maximizer. Further, to imagine that a group like this could hold the line and abide by the terms of the cartel for twenty years would be totally unreal.

A second component of the Chicago thesis relates to the near impossibility of being able to subsidize low prices in the United

States with high prices in Japan. Further, the argument that the U.S. market could be cartelized once the U.S. firms had been driven out of business seemed highly improbable to the Court. Because the Japanese firms would have no reasonable assurance that they could hold a monopoly on the U.S. market or not be able to hold it long enough to recoup the profits they had lost by pricing below the competitive level, they would have no motive to undertake such a venture. "For this reason," Justice Powell concluded, "there is a consensus among commentators that predatory pricing schemes are rarely tried and even more rarely successful." He might as well have added that the consensus was among those who take this mode of economic analysis as near-scriptural.

In essence, the Court is saying that every firm, and every person, always seeks a competitive advantage, and further that it is only rational to do that. Because rational firms always seek their advantage and because, according to Chicago antitrust theory, the alleged cartel of Japanese firms could not succeed in executing such a plan profitably, it must not have hatched such a plan in the first place. No allowance is made here for cultural differences (everyone fits into this mold), and no allowance is made for those who are willing to take risks beyond the limits that these economists prescribe as rational limits. In other words, the Chicago theory is all-encompassing. Those who are willing to bet that Chicago economic theory is too narrow and limiting and who are motivated to take risks on the basis of some other economic theory are not taken very seriously or those motives are quickly discounted. In summary, if the conduct of the antitrust defendant(s) does not measure up to the expectations or the prescription of Chicago antitrust theory, there can be no antitrust violation.

Some evidence that the Chicago view may be in eclipse could be squeezed from *Eastman Kodak* v. *Image Technical Service*,[12] but this observation amounts to speculation, rather than prediction. The relevant facts of the case are as follows: Seven years before the case reached the Court, Kodak discontinued selling replacement parts for its equipment to its customers unless they agreed not to use independent repair firms. Further, Kodak quit selling parts to those independent repair firms.

Behavior such as this is essentially a tying arrangement, which may be a per se antitrust violation. Tying agreements are per se illegal (1) if the defendant has sufficient power in the market for the tying product to (2) substantially restrain competition in the market for the tied product. By way of qualifying or softening this per se treatment, the defendant may introduce evidence to show that it had no other reasonable, less harmful alterative(s) that would protect its legitimate business objectives. Tying agreements may be attacked as contracts in restraint of trade under Section 1 of the Sherman Act and/or as evidence of monopolization under Section 2. Beyond that, such contracts are specifically prohibited by Section 3 of the Clayton Act.

In line with Chicago antitrust economics, Kodak argued that it could not raise prices of service and parts above a competitive level because any increase in profits from aftermarket sales would be counterbalanced by a loss in equipment sales. Employing the concept of cross elasticity of demand, Kodak theorized that losses in equipment sales would increase as customers switched to suppliers with more attractive service prices.

The district court granted a summary judgment for Kodak. The Court of Appeals of the Ninth Circuit reversed. Affirming the Court of Appeals, the Supreme Court remanded for trial.

> Legal presumptions that rest on formalistic distinctions rather than actual market realities are generally disfavored. . . . The Court's requirement in *Matsushita* that the plaintiffs' claims make economic sense did not introduce a special burden on plaintiffs facing summary judgment. . . . The Court did not hold that if the moving party enunciates any economic theory supporting its behavior, regardless of its accuracy in reflecting the actual market, it is entitled to a summary judgment. *Matsushita* demands only that the nonmoving party's inferences be reasonable in order to reach the jury, a requirement that was not invented, but merely articulated, in that decision. If the plaintiff's theory is economically senseless, no reasonable jury could find in its favor, and summary judgment should be granted.

In counterpoint to our statement above that *Eastman Kodak* may signal that Chicago antitrust economics is in retreat, some compelling evidence that it is alive and well is found in *Liggett Group* v. *Brown & Williamson Tobacco Corp.*[13] The Court held not enough evidence was presented at the trial to support a judgment that a cigarette manufacturer illegally waged a price war against a competitor. Addressing the argument that the defendant's predatory pricing strategy had inflicted $150 million in damages on the defendant, Justice Kennedy wrote that "the anticompetitive scheme . . . when judged against the realities of the market, does not provide an adequate basis for . . . liability." No reasonable jury, he concluded could find that the defendant's pricing tactics had a reasonable possibility of harming competition.

VERTICAL RESTRAINTS ON COMPETITION AND THE SHERMAN ACT

Vertical restraints occur in the various levels of production and distribution for a good. The three basic levels are (1) the manufacture of the good, (2) its shipping to a wholesaler or distributor, and (3) the movement of the good to a resale outlet. Essentially, vertical restraints involve the extent to which a manufacturer may control the good once it has left its plant and the title to the good passed along to a firm in the next level. The control of the movement of goods in the chain of distribution may violate Sections 1 and 2 of the Sherman Act, as well as Section 3 of the Clayton Act. For our rather nontechnical purposes of providing an overview of the law in this area, we confine ourselves to the Sherman Act.

The older view is that once a manufacturer has sold the good to a distributor or to a retailer, the manufacturer cannot dictate or force the distributor or retailer to resell the good at a particular price. To do so was a per se violation of Section 1 of the Sherman Act. Such attempts to control the price through sales agreements were referred to as *resale price maintenance agreements.* A violation occurred, it was thought, because at each level of distribution the entity that held title to the good and that was subject to the market forces at that level should have the freedom to respond by setting prices.

This older view has been challenged by changing circumstances. Once the per se rule was announced by the Court in 1911 in the case of *Dr. Miles Medical Co.* v. *John D. Park & Sons.,*[14] manufacturers began to control the price of distributed goods by regulating the distribution of the goods in nonprice ways. In 1967, the Supreme Court held in *United States* v. *Arnold Schwinn & Co.*[15] that it was a per se violation of the Sherman Act for a manufacturer to let title for the goods pass and yet attempt to control to whom and where the goods were to be sold. In this case, the largest U.S. seller of bicycles created the Schwinn Plan, in which distributors could sell only to retailers within their exclusive territories. Retailers who also received Schwinn shipments from the factory could sell only to ultimate consumers and not to other unfranchised retailers. This plan would be legal only if title to the goods had not passed. In this case, a manufacturer could control the goods because it was still the owner. Following this case, manufacturers developed various technical types of consignments in which the title did not pass so that power over distributors and retailers could be exercised.

This case spawned wide criticism because of its technical requirement that the outcome of the case should turn on who had title and, some commentators thought, a misunderstanding about the anticompetitive effects of vertical restrictions. To make a long story short, the Supreme Court overruled the per se approach of Schwinn in the 1977 decision *Continental TV, Inc.* v. *GTE Sylvania, Inc.*[16] Today, the law of restraints is as follows: If a manufacturing firm with a dominant position in a relevant market (it is the largest or second-largest seller) attempts to dictate (through the contracts it makes with its distributors) the resale price of a good to other firms in the chain of distribution, this action probably violates Section 1 of the Sherman Act. Most other vertical restraints, however, are subject to a rule of reason approach, in which the court is to weigh the anticompetitive effects of the restraint against the interest that a manufacturer has in attempting to protect the quality of its goods by dictating terms to its distributors.

The law of vertical restraints applies most prominently today to franchise arrangements. When, for example, a person buys a McDonald's franchise, he or she should have the right to vary the price of the food to meet local conditions, such as a sale by a Wendy's across the street. The owner of the trademark, McDonald's, however, certainly has an interest in many nonprice conditions of the sale of both the franchise and the food, including the design of the restaurant, how the food is packaged, and perhaps most important, how the food is cooked. Although the franchise and the food have been sold, the seller retains some power to determine how the food should be presented and sold. There is no other way to adjust the interests of the two parties in a franchise dispute than to decide alleged anticompetitive actions on a case-by-case basis by using the rule of reason.

MERGERS AND ACQUISITIONS

Section 7 of the Clayton Act prohibits mergers and acquisitions if the effect may be to lessen competition or may tend to create a monopoly. The original Clayton Act passed in 1914 was so weak that entrepreneurs quickly found a way around its key provisions. After World War II, Congress, concerned about increases in business concentration, passed the Celler-Kefauver Amendment to Section 7. This amendment made it clear that any attempts to merge, whether by stock acquisition or purchase of assets, would be opposed by the government if the result was to lessen competition in any relevant product and geographical market. The concepts of the relevant product market and the relevant geographical market are applicable to Section 7 cases, as well as section 2 (Sherman Act) cases. In merger cases that the government wishes to oppose, it seeks a court order either blocking the merger or allowing it if certain conditions are met.

Since the 1950s and until the 1970s, the courts approached each type of merger differently. The following paragraphs give common definitions of mergers and brief explanations of how the federal government and courts responded to them.

1. *Horizontal mergers.* A horizontal merger is a merger in which a firm purchases control of another that is in the same or a closely related product line. For example, until the past few years, it was a safe bet to say that the government would oppose any attempt by NBC to buy ABC or by Ford to buy Chrysler. The result of such a merger is obvious: Where there were once two competitors, there is now one. Clearly, this would result in a substantial lessening of competition. A change has occurred in the approach to horizontal mergers. It is difficult to say with certainty which mergers, if any, will be challenged today. The Justice Department has been allowing competitors to combine in various forms if the result might be to increase productive efficiency in international markets.

2. *Vertical mergers.* A vertical merger is a merger between a manufacturer or producer and one of its wholesalers or retailers or a merger between two firms, one that supplies the other with raw materials. DuPont, a large producer of plastics and materials that sold vast quantities of glass, paint, plastic, and material for car seats, could not purchase a controlling interest in General Motors. Again, this is the older way of thinking about Section 7; today, such associations are not as sure as they were twenty years ago.

3. *Conglomerate mergers.* A conglomerate merger is a combination between firms that do not compete or buy large quantities of goods from one another. Although some attempts were made to build a body of principles that would find these kinds of mergers anticompetitive, today that case law is simply not used. It is safe to say that if firms do not compete or sell to one another in a major way, an attempted merger will not be challenged by the federal government. In fact, many commentators believe conglomerate mergers are good for the economy because they allow firms to diversify.

Other commentators, however, see any merger between large firms as anticompetitive. The recent furious merger activity has produced no new plants or productive assets, but rather has produced more centralized economic power that has economic and other consequences. Perhaps the noneconomic consequences are as important as the economic ones, but meaningful ways to measure noneconomic aggregations of power have not been developed.

4. *Local control of business.* A major reason that prompted passage and then amendment of Section 7 was Congress's concern about local control over business, as well as industrial concentrations resulting from the disappearance through merger of many small business establishments. C. Wright Mills, while teaching sociology at the University of Texas, documented a social phenomenon that gave credence to these concerns in a study that compared three cities characterized by local businesses with three others dominated by absentee ownership. Local business cities ranked higher in public facilities, social services, and civic participation. His conclusion was that more incentive for community participation and improvement exists for locally based owners. Absentee firms tend to hire, promote, and transfer their employees with little attention to participation in local civic affairs.[17]

It is difficult to grasp some aspects of antitrust law enforcement without an actual case in front of you. The case that follows is a classic in antitrust law. By reading and understanding it, you will appreciate the complexities of an antitrust trial, as well as understand the anticompetitive and social issues involved.

In the *Brown Shoe* case, both Brown and Kinney engaged in manufacturing and retailing. Their contemplated merger involved a possible violation with regard to the *vertical aspect* of competition: Brown's manufacturing plants would find retail outlets in Kinney's retail chain (and vice versa) to the exclusion of other suppliers. Further, with regard to the *horizontal aspects*, both firms competed in manufacturing and retailing, so the merger posed at least the possibility of a violation there as well. As you study the case, notice that Chief Justice Warren first reviews the facts and then turns to a review of the act and its legislative intent. Next, both the vertical and horizontal components are analyzed: (1) The product and geographical markets are delineated, and (2) a judgment is made regarding the probable impact of the merger on these markets.

Brown Shoe Company, Inc. v. *United States*
370 U.S. 294 (1952)

WARREN, CHIEF JUSTICE

This suit was initiated . . . when the Government filed a civil action . . . alleging that a contemplated merger . . . would violate §7 of the Clayton Act.

A motion by the Government for a preliminary injunction . . . was denied, and the companies were permitted to merge provided, however, that their businesses be operated separately and that their assets be kept separately identifiable.

★ ★ ★

[*The Industry.*] The District Court found a "definite trend" among shoe manufacturers to acquire retail outlets. And once the manufacturers acquired retail outlets, the

District Court found there was a "definite trend" for the parent-manufacturers to supply an ever increasing percentage of the retail outlets' needs, thereby foreclosing other manufacturers from effectively competing for the retail accounts. Manufacturer dominated stores were found to be "drying up" the available outlets for independent producers.

Another "definite trend" found to exist in the shoe industry was a decrease in the number of plants . . . [and] . . . in the number of firms manufacturing shoes.

[*Brown Shoe.*] Brown Shoe was found not only to have been a participant, but also a moving factor, in these industry trends.

[*Kinney Shoe.*] Kinney is principally engaged in operating the largest family-style shoe store chain in the United States. At the time of trial, Kinney was found to be operating over 400 such stores in more than 270 cities. These stores were found to make about 1.2% of all national retail shoe sales by dollar volume.

In addition to this extensive retail activity, Kinney owned and operated four plants which manufactured men's, women's, and children's shoes and whose combined output was 0.5% of the national shoe production in 1955, making Kinney the twelfth largest shoe manufacturer in the United States.

★ ★ ★

[*Vertical Aspects of the Merger.*] Economic arrangements between companies standing in a supplier-customer relationship are characterized as "vertical." The primary vice of a vertical merger or other arrangement tying a customer to a supplier is that, by foreclosing the competitors of either party from a segment of the market otherwise open to them, the arrangement may act as a "clog on competition". . . which "deprive[s] . . . rivals of a fair opportunity to compete." . . . However,

the Clayton Act does not render unlawful all such vertical arrangements, but forbids only those whose effect "may be substantially to lessen competition, or to tend to create a monopoly" "in any line of commerce in any section of the country." Thus, as we have previously noted, "[d]etermination of the relevant market is a necessary predicate to a finding of a violation of the Clayton Act because the threatened monopoly must be one which will substantially lessen competition 'within the area of effective competition.' Substantiality can be determined only in terms of the market affected." The "area of effective competition" must be determined by reference to a product market (the "line of commerce") and a geographic market (the "section of the country").

★ ★ ★

[*Product Market.*] The outer boundaries of a product market are determined by the reasonable interchange ability of use or the cross-elasticity of demand between the product itself and substitutes for it. However, within this broad market, well-defined submarkets may exist which, in themselves, constitute product markets for antitrust purposes. The boundaries of such a submarket may be determined by examining such practical indicia as industry or public recognition of the submarket as a separate economic entity, the product's peculiar characteristics and uses, unique production facilities, distinct customers, distinct prices, sensitivity price changes, and specialized vendors. . . .

Applying these considerations to the present case, we conclude that the record supports the District Court's finding that the relevant lines of commerce are men's, women's, and children's shoes. These product lines are recognized by the public; each line is manufactured in separate plants; each has characteristics peculiar to itself rendering it generally noncompetitive with the others;

and each is, of course, directed toward a distinct class of customers.

Appellant, however, contends that the District Court's definitions fail to recognize sufficiently "price-quality" and "age-sex" distinctions in shoes. Brown argues that the predominantly medium-priced shoes which it manufactures occupy a product market different from the predominantly low-priced shoes which Kinney sells. But agreement with that argument would be equivalent to holding that medium-priced shoes do not compete with low-priced shoes. We think the District Court properly found the facts to be otherwise. It would be unrealistic to accept Brown's contention that, for example, men's shoes selling below $8.99 are in a different product market from those selling above $9.00.

[*Geographic Market.*] We agree with the parties and the District Court that insofar as the vertical aspect of this merger is concerned, the relevant geographic market is the entire Nation. . . .

★ ★ ★

[*Probable Effects of Vertical Merger.*] Since the diminution of the vigor of competition which may stem from a vertical arrangement results primarily from a foreclosure of a share of the market otherwise open to competitors, an important consideration in determining whether the effect of a vertical arrangement "may be substantially to lessen competition, or to tend to create a monopoly" is the size of the share of the market foreclosed. . . .

[Another] . . . important such factor to examine is the very nature and purpose of the arrangement. . . .

★ ★ ★

. . . In 1955, the date of this merger, Brown was the fourth largest manufacturer in the shoe industry while Kinney . . . owned and operated the largest independent chain of family shoe stores in the Nation. Thus, in this industry no merger between a manufacturer and an independent retailer could involve a larger potential market foreclosure. Moreover, it is apparent both from past behavior of Brown and from the testimony of Brown's President, that Brown would use its ownership of Kinney to force Brown shoes into Kinney stores. . . .

Another important factor to consider is the trend toward concentration in the industry. . . .

The existence of a trend toward vertical integration, which the District Court found, is well substantiated by the record. Moreover, the court found a tendency of the acquiring manufacturers to become increasingly important sources of supply for their acquired outlets.

The necessary corollary of these trends is the foreclosure of independent manufacturers from markets otherwise open to them. . . .

★ ★ ★

The District Court's findings, and the record facts . . . convince us that the shoe industry is being subjected to just such a cumulative series of vertical mergers which, if left unchecked, will be likely "substantially to lessen competition."

[*Horizontal Aspects of the Merger.*] An economic arrangement between companies performing similar functions in the production or sale of comparable goods or services is characterized as "Horizontal." . . .

. . . [Brown and Kinney] contest the District Court's finding that the merger of the companies' retail outlets may tend substantially to lessen competition, [but the court resolved the horizontal combination at the manufacturing level in favor of Brown-Kinney].

[*Product Market.*] Shoes are sold in the United States in retail shoe stores and in shoe departments of general stores. These outlets sell: (1) men's shoes, (2) women's shoes, (3) women's or children's shoes, or (4) men's, women's or children's shoes. Prior to the merger, both Brown and Kinney sold their shoes in competition with one another through the enumerated kinds of outlets characteristic of the industry.

[*Geographic Market.*] The criteria to be used in determining the appropriate geographic market are essentially similar to those used to determine the relevant product market. Congress prescribed a pragmatic, factual approach to the definition of the relevant market and not a formal, legalistic one. The geographic market selected must, therefore, both "correspond to the commercial realities" of the industry and be economically significant. Thus, although the geographic market in some instances may encompass the entire Nation, under other circumstances it may be as small as a single metropolitan area. The fact that two merging firms have competed directly on the horizontal level in but a fraction of the geographic markets in which either has operated, does not, in itself, place their merger outside the scope of §7. That section speaks of "any . . . section of the country," and if anticompetitive effects of a merger are probable in "any" significant market, the merger-at least to that extent-is proscribed.

★ ★ ★

[*Probable Effects of Horizontal Merger.*] The market share which companies may control by merging is one of the most important factors to be considered when determining the probable effects of the combination on effective competition in the relevant market. In an industry as fragmented as shoe retailing, the control of substantial shares of the trade in a city may have important effects on competition. If a merger achieving 5% control were now approved, we might be required to approve future merger efforts by Brown's competitors seeking similar market shares. The oligopoly Congress sought to avoid would then be furthered and it would be difficult to dissolve the combinations previously approved.

A significant aspect of this merger is that it creates a large national chain which is integrated with a manufacturing operation. Of course, some of the results of large integrated or chain operations are beneficial to consumers. Their expansion is not rendered unlawful by the mere fact that small independent stores may be adversely affected. It is competition, not competitors, which the Act protects. But we cannot fail to recognize Congress' desire to promote competition through the protection of viable, small, locally owned businesses. Congress appreciated that occasional higher costs and prices might result from the maintenance of fragmented industries and markets. It resolved these competing considerations in favor of decentralization. We must give effect to that decision. In the light of the trends in this industry we agree with the Government and the court below that this is an appropriate place at which to call a halt. We hold that the District Court was correct in concluding that this merger may tend to lessen competition substantially in the retail sale of men's, women's, and children's shoes in the overwhelming majority of those cities and their environs in which both Brown and Kinney sell through owned or controlled outlets.

The judgment is affirmed.

CASE FOLLOW-UP

Brown Shoe is a classic, but it is a classic that has fallen into disfavor. To understand this turn of events more fully, it would be valuable to you now to examine the appendix to this chapter, "The Chicago and Harvard Schools of Antitrust Analysis: A Study in Contrasts." Whether you do that or not, keep in mind that *economics*—a word cryptically plural, like *ethics* and *mathematics*—provides you with a wide array of choices. Even if you exclude Marxism, socialism, and other rival concepts, you still have to deal with a perplexing variety of theories within the capitalist supermarket. The current theory of choice and, evidently, the only theory available to those who hope to be candidates for the Nobel Prize is price theory as advanced by the Chicago school.

Price theory supposes that every rational economic unit (that's you and we) will expend its purchasing power on choices that maximize its market basket mix of utilities. In the Chicago mind-set, the meaning of the word rational is limited to folks who do that. Hence, in this circular economic logic, it is virtually impossible to act irrationally because, defined in this way, rational behavior includes all manner of bizarre behavior. This makes it virtually impossible to characterize anyone's behavior as irrational. For example, it cannot be said that a person acted irrationally by purchasing beer and cigarettes with his or her last few bucks because the very fact that beer and cigarettes were purchased is proof that the buyer preferred the utility or pleasure-production or that market basket mix to any other—food for the baby, for example.

What does this example have to do with antitrust and with *Brown Shoe*? Rational people simply do not worry about the trivial mergers that characterized the jurisprudence of the Warren era. Mergers like the one in *Brown Shoe* are such tiny blips on the megascale of global economics. They do not rise to a level of economic significance because they are not big enough to affect price or quantity.

Although the horizontal aspects of large mergers and other horizontal conduct, such as price fixing, do concern Chicago school antitrust economists, *Brown Shoe*-types do not. Even greater abuse is heaped on another such Warren-era case, *United States* v. *Von's Grocery*.[18] Both of these cases are relevant for learning purposes, but until "what goes around, comes around," they are out of step with prevailing economic wisdom.

The tide began to turn against the *Brown Shoe-Von's Grocery* mode of analysis with *United States* v. *General Dynamics*.[19] The Court put aside the historical production figures of the merged coal companies, as well as their imposing market share and the industry trend toward concentration, and looked to factors that would affect the firms' viability for years to come. The same arguments that, a few years earlier, would have made these firms prime targets for the government's efforts to gain a divestiture fell on deaf ears in 1974. *United States* v. *General Dynamics* and *Continental TV, Inc.* v. *GTE Sylvania, Inc.* marked the first important victories of the Chicago school. *Sylvania* applied rule of reason, rather than per se analysis, to sanction Sylvania's restriction of a franchisee, Continental TV, to a particular location.

As this chapter develops, we pursue the repercussions of Chicago's ascendancy through the Justice Department's merger guidelines and its recent antitrust policies. Then we examine the position of certain critics in an extended excerpt from the *California Law Review* and close the chapter with the most anti-Chicago of all antitrust statutes—the Robinson-Patman Act.

No one will deny that the Robinson-Patman Act was explicitly designed to protect the existence of small, inefficient competitors—"Mom and Pop operations"—at the expense of an efficient, competitive market. This Act, with all of its exasperating detail, stands in stark contrast to the presumed credo of Chicago antitrust analysis, which is to advance consumer welfare through an efficient, competitive marketplace.

Ironically, the Chicago credo is borrowed from the much disparaged *Brown Shoe* case. *Brown Shoe*, as you will see in the following passage, gave only "one cheer" for efficiency:

"It is competition, not competitors, which the [Clayton] Act protects. But we cannot fail to recognize Congress' desire to promote competition through the protection of viable, small, locally owned businesses." The Chicago response is simply, "You can't have it both ways" or "You can't fix an omelet without cracking some eggs." In other words, to have an efficient, well-functioning economy, inefficient firms are necessarily going to go belly up, but that's the way the capitalist system is supposed to function. Money tied up in those inefficient firms is then available for more efficient ones, and the consumer benefits in the long run.

MERGER GUIDELINES

In an effort to reduce uncertainty regarding enforcement policy, the Department of Justice issued antitrust guidelines in 1982[20] and revised them in 1984. These guidelines substantially depart from those of 1968. The primary objective of the new guidelines is to prevent the exercise of market power, the ability of a firm or a collusive group of firms to profitably maintain prices above competitive levels for a significant period of time. The FTC related that it would give these guidelines considerable weight as well.

The guidelines reflects a strong influence of the Chicago school of antitrust thought discussed in greater detail in the appendix to this chapter. Political and social values—for example, concern for local control and the protection of small competitors—are supplanted by economic theory. Vertical and conglomerate mergers are deemed important only in their horizontal effects. The guidelines address the product market by establishing first a hypothetical market including the products of the merging firms and good substitutes. The department will then project a 5 percent price increase in the products of the merging firms and ask how many buyers would shift out of the provisional market within *one year*. This market will be successively expanded until there is no "substantial" shifting.

This methodology is simply a formalized effort to measure cross-elasticity of demand. If, for example, two manufacturers of plastic drinking cups sought to merge, the Justice Department would try to determine what would happen if the price of these drinking cups was increased by 5 percent. Would consumers switch to substitute or interchangeable products (paper or glass cups) within one year? A substantial amount of shifting would identify other products in the drinking cup industry and indicate that the two firms, if allowed to merge, could not profitably maintain prices above competitive levels. If there was little or no shifting, the firms could maintain prices above competitive levels. Such a merger would be subject to closer scrutiny, and perhaps it would be challenged.

Product: Supply Side. Firms included in this product market are not merely firms that currently produce the product or good substitutes. The market also consists of foreign and domestic firms that will likely begin production and sale of the product within one year of the 5 percent increase.[21] Also included are firms that recycle or recondition comparable products, as well as vertically integrated firms that consume the product internally. For example, firms that recycle aluminum cans would be considered within the aluminum market, as well as those firms that manufactured such cans for their own product.

Geographical Market. The next step in this methodology is to determine the relevant geographical market. Thus, the guidelines advocate beginning with a hypothetical market that is coextensive with shipment patterns of the merging firms and their closest competitors (not all the firms included in the product market) and then projecting a 5 percent price increase and expanding the geographical boundaries of the market to include the location of firms that would make significant sales to former customers of the merging firms within one year.

The effect of this expansion of the relevant product and geographical market is to reduce the share that each firm will control. The market then will not appear to be as concentrated as it was initially.

Herfindahl-Hirshman Index. Given this extensive market, the guidelines then apply the Herfindahl-Hirshman Index (HHI), which is calculated by summing the squares of the individual market shares of all the firms within the relevant market. A monopolist (100 percent of the market) would have an HHI number of 10,000. If four firms had market shares of 40 percent, 30 percent, 20 percent, and 10 percent, the industry HHI would be 3,000 ($40^2 + 30^2 + 20^2 + 10^2$). A merger between the two smallest firms would increase the industry HHI by 400 points to 3,400 ($40^2 + 30^2 + 30^2$).

Concentration Categories. The guidelines characterize markets below HHI 1,000 as unconcentrated, those between 1,000 and 1,800 as moderately concentrated, and those over 1,800 as concentrated. Except in extraordinary circumstances, the Justice Department will not challenge a merger if the postmerger index is below 1,000. If the postmerger HHI is between 1,000 and 1,800, a challenge is unlikely if the increase is less than 100 points and likely if 100 points or greater. With a postmerger index substantially above 1,800, the Justice Department will challenge the merger in all but extraordinary cases if the HHI increases more than 100 points. Again, for mergers resulting in a postmerger index greater than 1,800, the Justice Department is unlikely to challenge if the HHI increase is less than 50. A challenge is likely if the HHI increase is between 50 and 100 points. This is what the guidelines provide. In the past fifteen years, the federal government itself has paid little attention to them.

RECENT ANTITRUST POLICY

Ronald Reagan was elected president with a clear mandate to "get the government off the back" of business. This he did in grand style. During the eight years of the Reagan presidency, the size of the Department of Justice's Antitrust Division shrank by 50 percent and its appropriation declined by 33 percent (in terms of 1980 dollars). As a result, between 1979 and 1988, the number of cases filed by the Antitrust Division decreased by 65 percent.[22] Perhaps the largest decline in antitrust enforcement by the federal government was in the area of mergers. Between 1982 and 1987, for example, 11,547 premerger notifications were received by the Antitrust Division; only 33 of these were challenged. This is an average of just 4 per year.[23]

The decline in attention given by the federal government to mergers in the 1980s brought about the most massive merger wave in U.S. history. The largest eighteen mergers in U.S. history occurred during the past fifteen years. Until 1987, each year saw a new record for the number of large mergers (those over $100 million in size): In 1981, 113; in 1983, a 20 percent increase to 137; and in 1984, 200. In 1985, 268, a 137 percent increase over 1981.[24]

In this section, we present two views of American antitrust laws that outline the sharp disagreement about enforcement of the antitrust laws. We begin with a summary of the *Report of the Task Force of the American Bar Association's Section of Antitrust Law*, published July 19, 1989. It recommends:

1. Increases in the budget and professional staff of the Antitrust Division. Enforcement requires more resources. The serious morale problems facing the Division must be reversed;

2. The 1984 Merger Guidelines should be retained with less emphasis on departures from their written provisions. In this vein, some sort of generic public reporting of the Division's merger enforcement decisions should be developed. To ease budgeting restraints, greater cooperation between the Division and the states' attorneys general should be developed in this area;

3. The Division's criminal enforcement should become more efficient. More resources should be devoted to investigations of a greater variety of industries. Cooperation with other federal and state agencies should be pursued as a means to accommodate problems and maximize efficiency;

4. The viability of Section 2 Sherman Act cases should be reassessed, particularly in industries in which deregulation has not fostered competitive conditions. Other areas ripe for Section 2 investigation include industries that have "market imperfections" resulting from industry structure or from government regulation, as well as those that are protected by trade law proceedings;

5. The Division should end its "highly visible" opposition to private civil cases and efforts by states in the vertical area. Vertical cases should simply not be a Division priority. The Division's Vertical Guidelines should also be withdrawn;

6. Rhetoric should be toned down. The Division should become an advocate for competition and de-emphasize its nonenforcement pronouncements;

7. The Division's relationships with the FTC, Congress and the states' attorneys general should be strengthened. This will serve to promote a "national antitrust policy" pursued with maximum efficiency and public support.[25]

At this point, we make an exception to the general format of this text. Usually, we present longer law review articles and opinion pieces in a chapter appendix so that professors may assign this material or not, as they deem appropriate. In the case of antitrust enforcement, however, the issues are so complex and so contentious that we believe it worthwhile to reproduce within the regular chapter what we believe is some of the best writing in the area of antitrust policy. The following law review article by professors Walter Adams and James W. Brock defines four key arguments against antitrust enforcement today (especially in the areas of mergers) and then answers each.

WALTER ADAMS AND JAMES W. BROCK[26]

The "New Learning" and the Euthanasia of Antitrust

. . . Stripped to its essentials, the current attack on antitrust, and the "foreign competition" garb in which it is clothed, can be reduced to four major assertions.

First, as portrayed by the antitrust critics, foreign competition is an all-encompassing, overpowering, and—most importantly—a self-sustaining and self-sufficient force for controlling corporate behavior, for neutralizing market power, and for compelling good economic performance in the public interest. . . . As [Economist Lester] Thurow puts it,

> I don't care whether General Motors is the only American car manufacturing company. It's still in a competitive fight for its life with the Japanese and the Germans. And it doesn't make sense to hamstring General Motors or anybody else with antitrust laws since they must operate in an international competitive environment, whether or not there are other domestic producers.

Foreign competition is pictured as an immutable fixture of the universe—immune to subversion, either from within the global market, or from without. Therefore, government efforts to maintain competition are redundant and unnecessary.

Second, according to the critics, the antitrust statutes have been so rigidly and oppressively enforced as to hobble American companies and cripple their international competitive capacity. . . . The critics contend, "our antitrust laws have straitjacketed U.S. manufacturers in international trade."

Third, the critics conceive corporate giantism to be the touchstone for production efficiency, technological advance, and international competitiveness in the modern era. Bigness, especially when induced by mergers and acquisitions, marks the path to world-class economic performance. It promotes efficiency and economies of scale in production. It fosters technological invention and innovation. According to the President's Council of Economic Advisers, mergers, takeovers, and the generalized "market for corporate control" discipline errant managements, transfer resources to higher-valued uses, and substitute good management for bad. . . . Above all, the current attack on antitrust proceeds from a root premise that . . . Robert H. Bork calls an "obvious point"—that "larger size shows greater efficiency." . . .

Fourth, according to the critics, the concentration of power resulting from mergers and acquisitions poses neither economic nor political problems for society. The competitive global market, they implicitly posit, neutralizes problems in the political economy of power and renders them obsolete. The press of foreign competition will force corporate giants to perform in the public interest according to the rules of the competitive market. The competitive global market, they implicitly assume, will guard against any abuse of power, both in the political arena and in the economic realm.

★ ★ ★

In the following pages, this Article will evaluate the empirical validity of these propositions. . . .

I

The Fragility of Global Competition

One important premise of current attacks on antitrust is that foreign competition negates the need for an antitrust policy. The relevant market, the critics contend, is not domestic, but global in scope. It comprises a multitude of rivals from a myriad of locations around the world. The steel industry, they would say, is not composed of American firms alone; instead, it encompasses competitors from Europe, Great Britain, Japan, South Korea, and South American nations. They reason that this global competition more than compensates for noncompetitive industry structure in the domestic market. Hence, domestic industry structure is irrelevant, and the maintenance of domestic competition unnecessary.

★ ★ ★

. . . [The] argument is flawed in a fundamental respect. It mistakenly presumes global competition to be an automatic, self-sustaining, and self-regulating mechanism—a natural phenomenon, immune to subversion and control, to which international rivals passively submit. The argument fails to recognize that, in reality, global markets, like domestic markets, are susceptible to control. International rivals do not submissively subject themselves to the discipline of global competition for long. Instead, they come to recognize that collusion and cooperation, not competition, are most conducive to their mutual profitability, group security, and collective stability. They strive to elude the rigors of global competition and to control the international marketplace through a variety of devices, including international cartels, joint ventures and other cooperative arrangements as well as through mergers and acquisitions. They may attain global control privately through their own efforts. Or, as is frequently the case, they may manipulate governments to aid them in achieving their anticompetitive ends.

★ ★ ★

Those who today counsel an abandonment of antitrust on the grounds that foreign competition provides adequate safeguards betray a collective amnesia. They seem unaware of the extensively documented record of international cartels forged by world producers to control global markets and ignore the corollary anticompetitive role of transnational joint ventures and mergers. A review of the evidence is enlightening.

★ ★ ★

1. The Petroleum Industry. The world's major petroleum companies are not autonomous centers of initiative who passively submit to the discipline of the global marketplace. Instead, they have long striven to spin a complex web of carteloid controls in order to eliminate the threat of global competition. Joint ventures encompassing every major stage of production in the industry and extending around the globe are a traditional manifestation of the symbiotic interrelationship between the world's largest oil companies. Joint ventures establish—and sustain—an intimate community of interest among the "Seven Sisters." They have been a key instrument in the worldwide control of oil.

★ ★ ★

II

The Myth of Oppressive Antitrust Enforcement

First, the mega-merger mania engulfing the nation since the 1970s hardly suggests burdensome antitrust interference. In 1984 *alone*, mergers and acquisitions totalled 2,543. The total value of all acquisitions in the United States reached a record $82.6 billion in 1981, and new records of $122.2 billion in 1984 and $179.8 billion in 1985; since 1970, more than a half *trillion* dollars has been expended on mergers and acquisitions. Combinations of firms valued at $100 million (or more) have increased steadily—from ninety-four in 1980, to 200 in 1984.

In fact, the 200 largest industrial corporations in the country have been in the forefront of the mega-merger movement and the consolidation of American industry. They not only have bought "small" and "medium-sized" companies, but—increasingly—they have merged with one another. In recent years, DuPont (fifteenth largest industrial firm in the nation) has acquired Conoco (fourteenth largest in the nation at the time of the acquisition); United States Steel (nineteenth largest) has acquired Marathon Oil (thirty-ninth largest); Occidental Petroleum (twentieth largest) has acquired Iowa Beef Processors (eighty-first largest); Allied Corporation (fifty-fifth largest) has acquired Bendix (eighty-sixth largest) and Signal Companies (sixty-first largest); Standard Brands (128th largest) and Nabisco (152nd largest) merged, and the resulting firm, Nabisco Brands (fifty-fourth largest) was merged into R J. Reynolds (twenty-third largest); Philip Morris (thirty-second largest) and General Foods (thirty-ninth largest) have merged; and General Electric (ninth largest) has acquired RCA (second largest diversified service company).

Particularly dramatic—and virtually untrammelled—has been the merger spree in the petroleum industry. . . . Recent mega-mergers in oil have featured consolidations between Occidental Petroleum and Cities Service, Texaco and Getty Oil, Standard Oil of California (Chevron) and Gulf; these represent combinations between the industry's twelfth and nineteenth, third and thirteenth, and fifth and sixth largest firms, respectively. Also notable have been the merger in 1984 between Mobil, the second largest integrated oil company, and Superior, the nation's largest independent explorer and producer of oil and natural gas, and Occidental Petroleum's announced intention to acquire Midcon Corporation, one of the nation's largest natural gas pipeline companies. All told, the top twenty oil companies spent $26.6 billion on mergers and acquisitions in the short period 1978-81; for the years 1981-83, members of the oil and gas industry spent an additional $44.2 billion on mergers and acquisitions.

Overall, according to one count, the Justice Department has challenged only twenty-six of the 10,000 merger applications it has received in the 1980s, while, at the same time, Justice has approved most of the largest mergers in American history—hardly a record of oppressive government intervention.

III

The Mythology of Bigness

. . . [T]he weight of the available evidence shows that bigness and industrial concentration are neither guarantors of, nor prerequisites for, production efficiency and technological progress. The evidence shows that, more often than not, mergers and corporate giantism undermine the kind of economic performance necessary to reindustrialize the American economy and compete on a world-class basis.

A. Bigness and Reality in Operating Efficiency. Countless studies and analyses, for specific industries as well as for manufacturing generally, for specialized firms as well as for conglomerates, have demonstrated that mergers, giant firm size, and high industry concentration are not conducive to greater operating efficiency and production at lowest cost.

1. *Mergers and Acquisitions.* An impressive body of evidence shows that mergers and acquisitions are *not* the magical elixir for efficiency proclaimed by the apostles of bigness.

On the conglomerate merger front, for example, diversified giantism has not streamlined American industry into a sleek machine of operating efficiency. Instead, conglomerate mega-mergers and diversified giantism have enmeshed American industry in a snare of organizational disorder and ill-fitted bureaucracy. "Our major corporations have blossomed into multiproduct, multidivisional, multi-locational hydras," *Business Week* recently reported in an issue devoted to the reindustrialization of America.

> They became far too diverse for any one corporate leader to embrace. So one formerly monolithic company after another decentralized into such things as profit centers, strategic business units, and the like. Every profit center had to have a general manager or a divisional president. Corporate headquarters had to have new staff people to whom the divisional people would report. Layer upon layer of management jobs were added to the structure.

★ ★ ★

2. *Corporate Giantism Generally.* The belief that corporate giantism, however attained, is a vehicle for operating efficiency is equally mythological.

In steel, for example, elephantine mass has hardly signified superior efficiency in production. Over fifty years ago, a management consulting firm retained by U.S. Steel reported the nation's largest steel maker to be

> a big sprawling inert giant, whose production operations were improperly coordinated; suffering from a lack of a long-run planning agency; relying on an antiquated system of cost accounting; with an inadequate knowledge of the costs or of the relative profitability of the many thousands of items it sold; with production and cost standards generally below those considered everyday practice in other industries; with inadequate knowledge of its domestic markets and no clear appreciation of its opportunities in foreign markets; with less efficient production facilities than its rivals had. . . .

Today, more than a half-century later, U.S. Steel has been described as "one of corporate America's most hierarchical, bureaucratic managements . . . an inbred, centralized, autocratic bureaucracy that stifle[s] change."

★ ★ ★

In automobiles, no disinterested observer would have the temerity to suggest that Brobdingnagian size and high industry concentration have unleashed efficiency gains. Instead, the operating disabilities of bigness in autos, as in steel, have long been in evidence. In 1925, Alfred Sloan, General Motors' legendary board chairman, confided:

> In practically all our activities we seem to suffer from the inertia resulting from our great size. It seems to be hard for us to get action when it comes to a matter of putting our ideas across. There are so many people involved and it requires such a tremendous effort to put something new into effect that a new idea is likely to be considered insignificant in comparison with the effort that it takes to put it across.

I can't help but feel that General Motors has missed a lot by reason of this inertia. You have no idea how many things come up for consideration in the technical committee and elsewhere that are discussed and agreed upon as to principle well in advance, but too frequently we fail to put the ideas into effect. . . .

Decades later, GM president Elliott M. Estes was reported to have observed: "Chevrolet is such a big monster that you twist its tail and nothing happens at the other end for months and months. It is so gigantic that there isn't any way to really run it."

★ ★ ★

. . . Bigness and noncompetitive industry structures are *not* instruments for inducing technical experimentation and advance.

First, contrary to the presuppositions of received orthodoxy, the independent inventor is *not* an anachronism, nor has he or she been displaced by the mammoth, bureaucratic corporate organization as a superior source of technical invention. Rather, independent inventors—garage mechanics and backyard tinkerers, toiling on their own, with limited funds and simple equipment—are responsible for a surprisingly large share of major modern inventions. For example, one landmark study found independent inventors to be primarily responsible for more than one-half of the seventy inventions considered by experts to be among the most important of the twentieth century. Conversely, the record is replete with large companies that "frequently missed or overlooked important new departures or remained unconvinced of the merits of an invention which, it might have been thought, would have appealed strongly to them."

Second, small firms are superior to giant corporations in their capacity to generate technological innovations. In iron and steel, bituminous coal, petroleum, and pharmaceuticals, for example, "the largest few firms did *not* do the most innovating (relative to their size)." For the chemical industry in particular, "there is no evidence that the biggest chemical firms did any more innovating (or developing) [of new manufacturing techniques], relative to their size, than somewhat smaller firms."

Third, smaller firms exert greater inventive and innovative "effort" by spending a proportionately larger share of their revenues on research and development—a phenomenon that, in turn, may partly explain why small companies are so much more prolific inventors.

★ ★ ★

Fourth, smaller companies conceive and commercialize inventions at substantially lower cost than do corporate giants.

★ ★ ★

Fifth, the available evidence refutes the belief that oligopolistic giantism is a blueprint for technical progress.

★ ★ ★

Thus, contrary to mythology, we find that in technical innovation, as in operating efficiency, bigness *undermines* good economic performance. . . . [R]eality is overtaking dogma as corporate leaders—increasingly attuned to the inventive infirmities of giantism—are launching small, organizationally distinct "startup" subsidiaries which, they anticipate, will be more inventive and entrepreneurial in spirit.

IV

Bigness and the Political Economy of Power

★ ★ ★

The apostles of bigness seem oblivious to the fact that economic concentration and disproportionate size inevitably have political consequences—that in the real world, politics and economic organization are not hermetically sealed spheres. They seem incognizant of the fundamental principle of political economy, articulated long ago by Richard T. Ely, that it is "a necessary outcome of human nature that those persons who are to be controlled should enter politics in order that they may either escape the control, or shape it to their own ends." They do not recognize the important corollary to this principle—that the giant corporation is inevitably as much a political institution as it is an economic organization.

Contrary to current apologetics, bigness does not meekly submit to the rules of the global competitive game when confronted with the consequences of delinquent economic performance. Instead, giant corporations—often in concert with allied interest groups—reach out to manipulate the state in order to change the rules of the game, to avoid the competitive market's sanctions for poor performance, and to shift them onto society. In reality, bigness mobilizes the vast political resources at its command—funds, employees, executives, labor unions, subcontractors, suppliers, governors and mayors, senators and representatives, Republicans and Democrats—to neutralize global competition through government-imposed import quotas, tariffs, "voluntary" export restraints, "orderly" marketing agreements, and the like.

The labor-industrial complex in automobiles is a case in point. Confronted with a deluge of innovative, fuel-efficient foreign cars induced by a deplorable postwar performance record, the auto giants joined with the United Auto Workers to mobilize an all-out assault on government—the International Trade Commission, the Congress, the President—in order to restrain foreign competition and restrict imports. These coalescing power blocs seized on the calculus of catastrophe that had earlier succeeded in obtaining a government bailout for Chrysler. They threatened that the nation's economic health was inextricably bound up with the health of the Big Three auto companies. Their not-so-subtle efforts at economic extortion succeeded: "voluntary" Japanese export quotas [went into effect in] 1981—at an exorbitant cost to American consumers. The story in steel is similar.

★ ★ ★

The implications of our findings for public policy are fourfold.

First, public policy must be guided by an explicit recognition that competitiveness, not bigness, is the key to the reindustrialization of the American economy. Corporate giantism per se does not guarantee success in the world marketplace. . . .

Second, the guideposts for public policy must be shaped with a recognition that merger mania is a costly, economically wasteful, and, ultimately, futile exercise—a diversion of entrepreneurial energy the nation can no longer afford. Merger madness has provided a new vocabulary of white knights, poison pills, pac-man strategies, and golden parachutes. It generates millions of dollars in new fees for Wall Street law offices and investment banking houses. But it does not contribute to resolving the crucial challenges confronting the nation: the development and investment in new production techniques, new plants and equipment, new products. Nor is merger madness merely benign. It diverts management and investor attention from the critical tasks at hand, and dissipates scarce talents and resources in an economically barren paper chase. Rather than tolerating or encouraging mega-mergers, shapers of public policy would be well advised to arrest the trend. . . .

Third, public policy must be guided by an appreciation for the positive role that antitrust must play in promoting world-class competitiveness for American industry. It must be grounded in the reality that antitrust, particularly in its orientation toward maintaining competitive industry structure, is as relevant today as ever. It must be informed by a recognition that economic performance can be enhanced by arresting helter-skelter consolidations, and that limitations on "paper entrepreneurialism" promote genuine entrepreneurship productive of the kind of economic performance tailored to an era of global competition.

* * *

[Fourth,] above all else, public policy must be congruent with the facts. If efficiency, innovation, and world-class competitiveness are the goals, then the time has come at last, not for a euthanasia of antitrust, but for its revitalization to combat the backwardness of bigness.

ARTICLE FOLLOW-UP

You will have no difficulty placing Adams and Brock at the opposite end of the spectrum from those economists who adhere to the Chicago theory of antitrust analysis. How do you know who's right?

To begin with, this matter is too important to have someone decide for you. In pursuing your own answer, you have to back up and ask questions about antitrust objectives. What is to be achieved by having antitrust laws in the first place?

A review of U.S. history will probably remind you that this was once a nation of small farmers, shopkeepers, and artisans who mainly expected the government to defend the borders, build roads and schools, and keep the courtroom doors open to settle criminal and civil actions fairly. Although that's an overgeneralization, test it out and see if it isn't basically true. Add to that historical mix the notion that our counterparts two hundred years ago "hated" monopoly, privilege, and concentrations of wealth. Why? Probably, in part, because they didn't have any, but also because such things intruded on their pocketbooks and, generally, on their way of life. From the close of the Civil War to the end of the nineteenth century, resentment began to focus on trusts which were legal devices that allowed beneficial ownership to remain with the stockholder while control (e.g., coordination of production, pricing, marketing) passed into the hands of a few powerful men. The Sherman Act was supposed to correct this, but the Act was so vaguely drawn that it took twenty one years, until the *United States* v. *Standard Oil* case, to decide that it imposed a rule of reason.

The concept of reasonableness—specifically, the rule of reason—dominates any inquiry into the objectives of antitrust policy. One can say, with Adams, Brock, and the Harvard school (see this chapter's appendix), that antitrust objectives are multiple (progress in the long-term advancement of real personal income; stable, full employment of all resources; an equitable distribution of income), or one can say with the Chicago school that the antitrust objective is singular (economic efficiency). We certainly cannot say that these positions have no basis in reason.

If you choose the first, you are asking judges to balance a lot of factors in making each of their decisions. The latter asks these judges to focus on one factor only (the efficient allocation of resources), and to leave it to Congress to address other concerns, such as a fair distribution of resources. Deciding who is right, then, is not a matter of adding up a column of figures. It is the far more momentous task of deciding what kind of society (economically, culturally, ideologically) you want the United States to be and then advancing an antitrust policy that is best calculated to get it there.

OTHER ISSUES IN ANTITRUST POLICY

THE FEDERAL TRADE COMMISSION ACT

Section 5 of the Federal Trade Commission Act, passed in 1914, prohibits unfair methods of competition and unfair or deceptive acts or practices affecting commerce. It was conceived as something like a third line of defense against oppressive business conduct following the Sherman and Clayton Acts. FTC power under Section 5 is far reaching. It overlaps and includes Sherman Act violations and also deals with practices, unheard of in 1914, that are not full-blown violations of either the Sherman Act or the Clayton Act.

In a second *Brown Shoe* case, *Federal Trade Commission* v. *Brown Shoe, Inc.*,[27] the FTC argued that Brown's franchise program involving more than 650 stores amounted to an unfair method of competition and ordered Brown to cease and desist. The program prohibited any of its franchisees from purchasing shoes from any of Brown's competitors. This program foreclosed a substantial number of retail shoe outlets from Brown's competitors at the manufacturing level.

Brown contended that the FTC had no power to declare the franchise program unfair without proof that its effect "may be to substantially lessen competition or tend to produce a monopoly." Justice Hugo Black, who wrote for the Court, conceded that would be true if the commission were proceeding under section 3 of the Clayton Act. When the commission proceeds under Section 5 of the FTC Act, however, it has the power to stop trade restraints in their incipiency without proof of an outright violation of any other provision of the antitrust laws.

The FTC's powers are by no means limited to antitrust activities. The FTC challenges many unfair or deceptive trade practices on behalf of consumers in the areas of health care, food labeling, housing practices, and especially general advertising claims made as a significant part of the competitive process. (We discuss the FTC's major role in protecting consumers in Chapter 8.) We now wind up our examination of the major antitrust laws with an overview of the Robinson-Patman Act, which amended the Clayton Act.

THE ROBINSON-PATMAN ACT

The price discrimination prohibitions of the Clayton Act, Section 2, were reshaped in 1936 by Senate Majority Leader Joe Robinson (Dem., Ark.) and Representative Wright Patman (Dem., Tex.).[28] The moving force behind the 1936 amendment was to protect small retailers (e.g., "Mom and Pop" stores like the corner grocery that once thrived in your grandparents' neighborhood) from the buying power of large chain stores that could get quantity discounts from their suppliers. These discounts allowed the large chains to sell their products to the consuming public at prices lower than small stores charged; this practice tended to run small stores out of business. Lower consumer prices charged by the chain stores may not sound like a bad idea to you, so it is understandable to ask, Why pass such a law? The reason is that Congress wanted to protect a "way of life" (small, family-owned businesses were spoken of as the backbone of the U.S. economy). Congress also feared that these lower consumer prices would be a short-term phenomenon only. Once the small stores were driven out of business, prices would in all likelihood go back up.

To prove a Robinson-Patman Act violation, the government, or an injured party seeking treble damages, must prove a competitive injury—that is, an ongoing, systematic, or permanent injury, rather than a single instance or an isolated injury.

Primary Line Competitive Injury.   Primary line competitive injury was prohibited by section 2 of the original Clayton Act and continues to be the law today. It is addressed to the seller-level of competition (see Figure 12.4).

On the assumption that S_1 has induced away a portion of S_2's market share (represented in the illustration by B_2) by charging discriminatory prices—that is, by selling to B_2 at \$4 per unit while continuing to charge B_1 \$5 per unit—we have primary line price discrimination. If S_1's sales to B_2 are also below seller's cost, displaying an intention to attract S_2's customers despite the loss, they may be described as being predatory, as well as discriminatory.

FIGURE 12.4   ***Primary Line Competitive Injury***

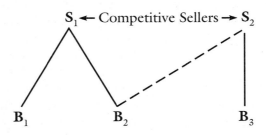

Secondary Line Competitive Injury.   The 1936 Robinson-Patman amendments to Section 2 of the original Clayton Act created secondary line prohibitions. Competitive injury inflicted in this manner results when one buyer (R_1) receives a price discount from a seller (S) but R_1's competitor (R_2) does not. This is illustrated by hypothesizing a large chain store versus small store context to emphasize the effect of price discrimination, but the Act literally applies to all purchasers of S (see Figure 12.5).

If the seller charges R_1 \$4.00 per unit while R_2 pays \$5.00 per unit, it is clear that R_1 will have a competitive advantage over R_2. R_1 can attract R_2's customers by passing along its discount to consumers. Even if R_1 passes along only part of its discount (or none of it), R_2 will still be at a competitive disadvantage because the discriminatory prices will allow R_1 to experience a larger margin of profit.

There have been few Robinson-Patman cases in the past decade. Many commentators believe that this attempt to save the "Mom and Pop" stores, for example, is pretty much a lost cause.

FIGURE 12.5   *Secondary Line Competitive Injury*

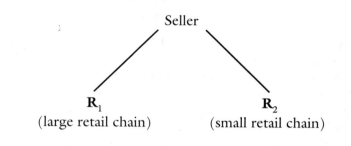

RECIPROCITY

"You scratch my back and I'll scratch yours." This type of agreement, a violation of Section 3 of the Clayton Act, is the essence of reciprocity, which comes about when a firm uses its power or leverage in the *buying* market to "persuade" (or coerce) its supplier to purchase some of the goods that it produces in return. For example, Breakfast Bits, a cereal firm, may purchase grain from a conglomerate that operates an agricorp and a chain of cafeterias. The use of its clout as a purchaser of grain from the agricorp to force the sale of its finished product to the cafeteria is reciprocity. Because Clayton Act, Section 3, applies only to leases and sales of goods, the practice will be condemned by the Sherman Act, Section 1, if Breakfast Bits has substantial buying power and the dollar volume is large in relation to the market. Like Robinson-Patman Act violations, there are few examples of reciprocity dealing prosecuted today.

PATENTS AND ANTITRUST LAW

Contrasting sharply with public policy favoring free enterprise, the U.S. Constitution, Article I, Section 8, establishes exclusive seventeen-year monopoly rights for inventors of new and useful processes, machines, and the like, plus comparable rights for improvements on those inventions. The framers of the Constitution evidently thought that the profit incentive for inventors (and their financial backers) more than offset the irony of free enterprise coexisting with monopoly. The genius of this approach is that, at the end of the patent period, the invention, which may not have been made except for the patent protection, passes into the public domain and is available to everyone.

The Patent Act implemented this constitutional provision by establishing the Patent Office. Applications for patents are reviewed there to determine whether the invention is

- *New*—Was it known or used by others in the United States or described in a publication or patented in any country prior to the date of invention?

- *Useful*—Is the invention developed to the degree that specific benefits exist in its currently available form?

- *Not Obvious*—Could one having ordinary skill in that area of knowledge create the process or machine (e.g., the U.S. Supreme Court said that a porcelain doorknob, modeled on wooden and metal ones, was not patentable)?

If the patent is granted by the Patent Office or through the appeals process, the inventor (patentee) is entitled to a seventeen-year right to exclude others from making, using, or selling the invention in the United States. The inventor or patentee can license the patent to a licensee, but any other person who uses or sells the patented item is subject to an injunction against further infringement and to a damage suit for losses that were previously inflicted.

Keep in mind the possibility of an antitrust violation—monopolization under Sherman Act, Section 2—if one pursues the practice of acquiring all available patents in a particular area. Moreover, although patents can be licensed to others, charging discriminatory royalty rates is an antitrust violation. Further, a patentee will not be permitted to engage in tying arrangements whereby the desirable patented item will not be sold or leased unless the buyer also takes a less desirable unpatented item.

EXEMPTIONS FROM ANTITRUST LAW

For reasons of public policy—either the businesses or industries are regulated by other agencies or they require special protection—Congress has created certain express exemptions or the courts have inferred them from Congress's regulatory structure.

The following examples illustrate express statutory exemptions:

1. Common carriers (motor, rail, ship) regulated by the Interstate Commerce Commission are exempt, as are water carriers regulated by the Federal Maritime Commission.

2. Agricultural or horticultural stock companies and cooperatives, and fishing cooperatives under the Capper-Volstead Act, are exempt.

3. Export trade associations formed solely for this purpose are exempted by the Webb-Pomerene Act.

4. Labor unions are exempt.

5. Professional baseball is exempt.

Conclusion

A fundamental idea that shapes the law and public policy and has profound moral overtones is the idea that the commercial society is best served by promoting competition in the marketplace for goods and services. Some behaviors are so anticompetitive that no defense or excuse will be permitted when they are known to exist. These behaviors are referred to as the per se violations and are dealt with in Section 1 of the Sherman Act. Other behaviors are mixed, in the sense that they have some pro-competitive and some anti-competitive effects. The rule of reason will be applied in these cases.

Section 2 of the Sherman Act outlaws monopolization, but defining a monopoly is much more difficult than one imagines at first. The plaintiff, whether the federal government or an injured competitor, must prove that monopoly power exists in a relevant product and geographical market and that this power was used so that an intent to establish a monopoly or to monopolize existed. In addition, the Sherman Act's rule of reason is used today to resolve complaints alleging anticompetitive behavior involving the distribution of goods (referred to as vertical restraints).

This explanation of antitrust law merely scratches the surface of a multidimensional area of inquiry. Perhaps more so than any other area of federal law, the enforcement of antitrust provisions is subject to the political winds that blow through Washington and the varying perceived insights of those who speak in the name of economics. In fact, we will go so far as to state that antitrust law cannot be understood fully unless one has an appreciation of just how political many antitrust issues are.

We suggest that you read the appendix to this chapter. It provides an overview of the Chicago school of law and economics as applied to antitrust enforcement. This school has provided the dominant set of beliefs that have guided policy administrators for the past thirteen to fifteen years. The Chicago school of thought supplanted the Harvard school of thought, which had dominated antitrust policy since the late 1930s. In discussions of antitrust policy today, you will find both of these schools of thought still contending for prominence.

In the past twenty years or so, a major influence on the U.S. economic and legal environment has been competition from firms located around the Pacific Rim and in Europe. This competition will intensify. The key question that explains the arrangement of the material in this chapter is, What should be the American response to this foreign competition?

The article by Adams and Brock answers the four major objections by scholars and public policy commentators who would have the United States scrap its antitrust laws as a response to this foreign competition. Adams and Brock write that those who argue for such scrapping base their arguments on myths—in particular, the myth that large firms will necessarily be more competitive than smaller ones. Many, if not most, of the issues about the American response to foreign competition do revolve around the set of beliefs one holds about firm size. Is bigger better? What is the evidence for and against this proposition?

A fundamental belief that supports almost all of the federal antitrust laws is that the public interest is served by an economy in which almost all markets for goods and services have many competitors. When many competitors are in a market, the market will tend to regulate and police itself because if one competitor attempts to gain unfairly high or monopoly profits, consumers will shift their buying habits to other producers. In addition, the law should not promote or condone barriers to entering a market that tend to keep other producers out. Freedom to enter (and leave) a market is a key to competitiveness.

In the past fifteen years, the federal government's role in antitrust has diminished significantly. At the very least, this shift means that, in almost all major industrial markets, mergers have not been challenged and firms have dropped out for one reason or another so that almost all of these markets are more concentrated today (there are fewer firms) than they were just a few years ago. The idea that the United States should keep barriers to entering a market low or nonexistent has almost disappeared. As a result, the few firms in major U.S. markets are all more powerful in the classic sense of the word: They are more able to work their will on people, institutions, and events.

REVIEW QUESTIONS AND PROBLEMS

1. Why, do you suppose, didn't Congress spell out more clearly what it meant by such phrases as *contracts in restraint of trade, substantially lessen competition,* and *unfair methods of competition*?

2. Representatives of two roofing firms in Kansas City, Kansas (Suntar and Ronan), met to discuss and, ultimately, agree on an allocation or division of the market. Subsequently, they were brought to trial on criminal charges for their conduct. The jury found them guilty, and their appeal was based on the argument that the trial court judge erred in regard to the jury instructions. The instructions were to the effect that customer allocation schemes are per se violations of Section 1, Sherman Act. Would evidence of the reasonableness of this arrangement be relevant? Was the trial court judge in error for excluding such evidence?

3. Since Congress repealed the fair trade law (Miller-Tydings) in 1975, vertical, as well as horizontal, price-fixing is per se illegal under Section one of the Sherman Act. Suppliers then moved to "recommended" or "suggested" resale prices. If these prices are ad-

hered to, retailers in the trade area will not have to worry about price cutting by other retailers of the same brand item and can concentrate their competitive efforts on other brands.

In Houston, Business Electronics (BE) made a regular practice of selling Sharp calculators below the suggested price. Other authorized Sharp retailers in the Houston trade area complained to the corporate headquarters of Sharp, and Sharp terminated BE's dealership. Was this action by Sharp per se illegal as a contract in restraint of trade under Section 1, Sherman Act?

4. Pure monopoly power does not really exist because some products on the market can be substituted (though with less satisfaction to the consumer) for the monopolist's product. In theory, however, a monopolist will always produce fewer units and charge a higher price than would be the case in a competitive industry. This is presumably true as well for sophisticated oligopolists. Why?

5. The Superior Court Trial Lawyers Association (SCTLA), a professional association composed of court-appointed attorneys who regularly represent indigent defendants

in Washington, D.C., "went on strike" for higher fees. Their strike (for purposes of this case, a "group boycott") severely disrupted the district's criminal justice system. After higher fees were agreed on, members of the association returned to work, but the FTC charged the officers of SCTLA with a per se illegal group boycott. Is this a legitimate per se offense, or should the defendants be permitted to put on evidence of justification? By way of justification, the association could argue that higher fees attracted more competent defense attorneys and that the collective work stoppage actually strengthened the bar representing indigent defendants.

6. Brunswick acquired several bowling alleys when the proprietors could not meet the installment provisions of their credit agreements. A private treble-damage action was instituted by owners of competing alleys, alleging that Brunswick's deep pockets contributed to a substantial lessening of competition. Will the private petitioners succeed in this action?

7. Consider the structure of the steel industry as shown in the table following these questions. Evaluate the logic of the court in forbidding the merger of Bethlehem and Youngstown on the reasoning that if these firms were permitted to merge to compete more effectively with U.S. Steel, other firms would be entitled to the same opportunity and the industry would become even more concentrated.

8. In *United States* v. *Continental Can Company,* 378 U.S. 441 (1964), the Court enjoined the merger of Continental Can, the second-largest metal container manufacturer, and Hazel-Atlas, the third-largest glass container manufacturer.

American Can	26.8%
Continental Can	22.0%
Owens-Illinois Glass	11.2%
Anchor-Hocking Glass	3.8%
National Can	3.3%
Hazel-Atlas Glass	3.0%
Total	70.1%

Compute the HHI for a Continental Can and Hazel-Atlas merger. Would this merger likely be challenged under today's guidelines? How would the Court use the concept of cross elasticity?

9. In *Brown Shoe Company. Inc.* v. *United States* involving Brown's efforts to merge with Kinney, both the manufacturing and retailing sectors were structured competitively. Entry barriers, such as economies of scale and capital formation, were relatively insignificant. Another entry barrier, product differentiation, was not a large one. Competitors were quick to copy style changes, and in the Brown-Kinney market, most customers were concerned with price. Both sectors had large numbers of buyers and sellers, and profits were low. The shoe retailing industry remained competitive during the premerger, merger, and postmerger periods Firms simply entered during periods of high profitability and during periods of low profitability. The impact of *Brown Shoe* was practically nil on this competitive structure.

Why was this suit initiated? What was the effect of the merger on the level of effective competition? Should the Justice Department have found a more concentrated industry to focus on?

10. If the antitrust laws were declared null and void, who or what would represent the interests of the typical consumer against large aggregations of economic power?

Market Structure in the Bethlehem Youngstown Case

Premerger Rank	Name	Percent Ingot Capacity	Premerger Absolute Concentration	Premerger Relative Size	Postmerger Relative Size
1	U.S. Steel	29.7	29.7%	100	100
2	Bethlehem	15.4	45.1%	52	—
	(Beth-Youngstown)	(20.1)	—	—	68
3	Republic	8.3	53.4%	28	28
4	Jones & Laughlin	4.9	58.3%	17	17
5	Youngstown	4.7	63.0%	16	—
6	National	4.6	67.6%	15	15
7	Armco	4.5	72.1%	15	15
8	Inland	4.1	76.2%	14	14
9–24	16 other integrated producers	13.8			
	Total	90.0			

U.S. Steel's ingot capacity in 1957 of 29.7 percent of the steel industry equals 100.

ENDNOTES

1. Guilds were associations of merchants and skilled craftsmen. Their function was to foster the economic well-being of their members. A master carpenter, for example, would teach his craft to a young apprentice and thereby prepare the younger man with job skills while at the same time benefiting from the young man's labor at little or no expense to the master.

2. Dyer's Case, Y. B. Pasch., 2 Hen. V, f.5, pl. 26 (1414).

3. *Chicago Board of Trade* v. *United States*, 246 U.S. 231 at 236 (1918).

4. Adams and Brock, *The Bigness Complex* 68 (1986).

5. *Id.*, quoting Bradford Snell at 69.

6. *United States* v. *Aluminum Company of America (Alcoa)*, 148 F.2d 416 at 422 (2d Cir. 1945).

7. *Id.* at 430.

8. 472 U.S. 585 (1985).

9. *Spectrum Sports* v. *McQuillan.* 61 U.S.L.W. 4123 (1993) (reversing a decision by the Court of Appeals for the Ninth Circuit that allowed a jury to infer specific intent and dangerous probability of success in monopolizing a relevant market from proof of predatory conduct but without proof of relevant market or of dangerous probability).

10. 881 F.2d 1396 (7th Cir. 1991).

11. 992 F.2d 1317 (7th Cir. 1991).

12. 112 S.Ct. 2072 (1972).

13. 61 U.S.L.W. 4699 (1993).

14. 220 U.S. 373 (1911).

15. 338 U.S. 365 (1967).

16. 443 U.S. 36 (1977).

17. Mills, Small Business and Civic Welfare, in Broom and Selernick Sociology (1955).

18. 384 U.S. 270 (1966) (ordering Von's to divest itself of Shopping Bag, the sixth ranked chain of grocery stores in the Los Angeles market; together Von's and Shopping Bag commanded only 7.5% of the retail grocery sales in that market).

19. 415 U.S. 486 (1974).

20. Merger Guidelines Sections I-V (U.S. Dept. of Justice, June 14, 1982).

21. This concept is supported by Chicago school scholar and U.S. Circuit Court of Appeals Judge Richard A. Posner in *Economic Analysis and the Law* 222 (1977).

22. *National Law Journal*, October 16, 1989, p. 13.

23. *Id.* at 14.

24. Speech by Senator Metzenbaum, Chairman of the Antitrust Subcommittee of the U.S. Senate on the Judiciary, January 8, 1987; *Tr. Reg. Rptr.* ¶s 50,004.

25. The report contains a "fair consensus" of the fifteen members of the Task Force, although there were some dissents by Task Force members concerning portions of the report. The Council of the Section on Antitrust Law, House of Delegates and the Board of Governors of the American Bar Association have not reviewed or approved this report. Therefore, the views expressed should not be construed as representing the positions of the Antitrust Section or the ABA. Copyright 1989 by the American Bar Association.

26. Walter Adams is a distinguished university professor and past president, Michigan State University, and erstwhile member of Attorney General Brownell's National Committee to Study the Antitrust Laws. James W. Brock is associate professor of economics, Miami University (Ohio). Professors Adams and Brock are co-authors of the book, *The Bigness Com-plex*. We apologize to Professors Adams and Brook and the authors of sources they cite for severely editing this material and for eliminating the footnotes. The full text, complete with footnotes, may be found in 74 *Calif. L. Rev.* 1540 (October 1986) pp. 1515–1566. This article is reproduced here with permission of the *California Law Review* and the authors.

27. 384 U.S. 316 (1966).

28. Clayton Act, 38 Stat. 730 (1914), *as amended* by the Robinson-Patman Act, 49 Stat. 1526, 25 U.S.C.A. Section 13 (1936). By way of a summary, Robinson-Patman Section 2(a) stipulates the basic elements of a prim facie case of price discrimination and the cost justification defense; Section 2(b) contains the "good faith in meeting competition" defense; Section 2(c) prohibits phony brokerage; Sections 2(d) and 2(e) forbid a seller from furnishing promotional payments, allowances, or services to a buyer unless made to all buyers on proportionally equal terms; Section 2(f) makes it unlawful for a buyer knowingly to induce or receive a prohibited price discrimination.

The Chicago and Harvard Schools of Antitrust Analysis: A Study in Contrasts

It may not be apparent to many people beyond attorneys and economists who deal with antitrust matters on a daily basis, but for several decades an ideological war regarding the goals and objectives of antitrust law, and the appropriate strategies for implementing these goals, has been under way. We survey these opposing views to convey an understanding of some forces within this struggle and to illustrate the way this struggle affects the economic life of the United States.

An entry point for this discussion is the way economic and legal scholars, some associated with what we describe as the Chicago school of antitrust analysis and others with the Harvard school, view economic policy. The Chicago school approach[1] generally is to allow economic efficiency to be the principal criterion and to apply antitrust law in a way that enhances productivity, profitability, and growth. Governmental intervention by antitrust officials would be rare, or at least limited to the worst offenses, such as price fixing. By contrast, the Harvard school tends to be more activist, more inclined to intervene in, adjust, or finely tune the machinery of the U.S. economic system in a way that makes antitrust policy serve broader objectives than efficiency. Harvard school proponents would use antitrust policy to advance full employment and equity in income distribution as well.

Examine the following pages with a view toward making up your own mind regarding which of these approaches is more compatible with a sound antitrust policy. The ideas contained in the edited passages that follow represent alternative worldviews. The scholars who wrote them are like medical doctors with different diagnoses who prescribe different medicines. What if they're all wrong?

The Chicago School

Former Solicitor General Robert Bork, of Washington, D.C., told the luncheon audience that "an intellectual revolution in the understanding of antitrust laws" has been taking place during the last 20 years. The outcome of this debate, he commented, is the understanding that antitrust "can't pursue goals other than economic efficiency."

He said that it is clear that the current Supreme Court has "jettisoned" the Warren Court doctrines in certain areas. These Warren Court decisions, Bork said, rested on two ideas—(1) that antitrust law has social and political objectives and that economic considerations are not dispositive, and (2) that efficiency is not a defense to antitrust cases. The current Supreme Court is clearly right in rejecting these New Deal-derived ideas, Bork declared, because they are "intellectually mushy."

While the Supreme Court has changed, the Justices "have no program" for systematically reexamining the antitrust laws, Bork said. In fact, they do not seem "eager to take antitrust cases with fundamental issues."

Bork also defended Deputy Attorney General Baxter for antitrust enforcement and other Republican officials accused of not enforcing the antitrust laws when certain cases seem to apply. "Antitrust enforcement today does not flout any directive of Congress," Bork declared. The law that is being referred to was not made by Congress, but by the courts, and it is not at all clear "that it is the law today," Bork added.[2]

Robert H. Bork's distinguished colleague Richard A. Posner, a U.S. Court of Appeals appointee, regards Bork's book *The Antitrust Paradox* as "the most complete and most orthodox statement of the Chicago position."[3]

Regarding Bork's critique of the Warren Court, which was strongly identified with the Harvard school of antitrust analysis, notice that he focused on two principal issues: (1) the goals or values that antitrust law may legitimately implement and (2) the role of economic reality, (efficiency) in antitrust law. The paradox he found in the midst of this confusion is that certain antitrust doctrines "preserve competition, while others suppress it, resulting in a policy at war with it self."[4]

Neither Bork nor Posner lay claim to the role of founder of the Chicago school, which, by the way, is not so tightly knit as the phrase implies.[5] Both of these men single out Aaron Director and his work in the early 1950s.[6] Director was influenced heavily by the insights that price theory brings to economic analysis. He explained business behavior in a way that made it consistent with basic economic theory and particularly with the assumption that business firms are guided by the concept of rational profit maximization.

Harvard school lawyers and economists, according to Posner,[7] observe the same behavior but interpret it, not in accordance with sound theory—rationality, profit maximization, downward-sloping demand curves—but with colorful concepts of their own—cutthroat competition, leverage, administered prices. In brief, Harvard school theorists believe that economic theory should be subordinate to or balanced against other social goals, such as income distribution and full employment. Its view of the place and role of the federal government contrasts sharply with that of Chicago. The Harvard school is identified with active antitrust surveillance and intervention; the Chicago school favors much less involvement in antitrust enforcement.

In what you must regard as a mere summary attempt to capture the fundamental Chicago concepts, consider the following examples:

A. Tying Arrangements. Section 3 of the Clayton Act prohibits tying arrangements wherein the effect may be to lessen competition or to create a monopoly. Tying arrangements are agreements in which manufacturer *A*, supplier of a desirable product (Blazes), will sell or lease only on the condition that a less desirable one (Blahs) will be taken as well. Chicago analysts scoff at this method of doing business as contrary to the principle of rational profit maximization. The market itself, they maintain, tends to penalize and eliminate the practice. Supplier-manufacturer *A*, perhaps a legal monopolist with a grip on Market #1 (Blazes), will not rationally use its power or leverage to seek monopoly profits in Market #2 (Blahs). Why? Price theory teaches that the customer who must pay the combined package price will simply reduce the number of purchases. Sales will then fall below the optimum level for monopoly profits and firm *A* will realize that this practice is self-destructive.

B. Vertical Merger. Vertical integration—for example, a manufacturer-retailer merger—is basically congenial to Chicago analysts. This is so because, given equal access to capital or money markets, rival firms will experience no barriers to enter competition with the newly merged firms. Thus, Chicago proponents assume that rivals can integrate as easily as, or with no more difficulty than, the merging firms. In essence, "Anyone can do it," so why punish those firms with the initiative to integrate vertically?

C. Predatory Pricing. Predatory pricing, or sales below cost, can be viewed as evidence of monopolization prohibited by the Sherman Act, Section 2. Such sales may also be a violation of the price discrimination provision of the Robinson-Patman Act, Section 2, if higher prices are charged to some customers than are charged to preferred or favored customers. Bork maintains that such conduct is irrational because if firm *A* is successful in driving out competitors and gaining a monopoly, other firms, attracted by monopoly profits, will inevitably enter the market.[9] Antitrust enforcement should not concern itself with such matters, he concludes.

These selected illustrations of the Chicago position on antitrust law lead one back to the introductory remarks of Robert Bork—economic efficiency is the name of the game. In his view, it should shape the course of judicial interpretation and legislative reform as well. The major thrust of antitrust enforcement should be focused on cartelization (agreements among competitors) and large horizontal mergers-to-monopoly.

The Harvard School

Harvard school theorists are unconvinced that the single-faceted criterion of economic efficiency best serves the public interests. In line with the widely acclaimed tenet that the basic task of economics is to provide an efficient distribution of scarce resources, they are not unmindful that the productive efficiency of a single firm or group of firms promotes the allocative efficiency of the economy generally. These lawyers and economists by and large share the view that price theory, as advanced by Aaron Director and his adherents, is simply not the ultimate in economic wisdom, that market imperfections prevent operation in the textbook fashion that Chicagoans suppose, that too much emphasis is placed on short-run rather than long-run efficiency, and that other national goals may legitimately call for the sacrifice of economic efficiency.

To acquaint you with the main outlines of this contrasting approach and to provide you with a useful framework for further analysis, the work of Edward S. Mason[10] can be used to counter that of Aaron Director. Rather than exalting productive allocative efficiency alone, he advanced three other goals of good industrial performance:

1. The use of progress in science and technology to advance long-term, real personal income
2. Stable, full employment of all resources, particularly human resources
3. An equitable distribution of income

It should not be assumed that Chicago adherents are opposed to these goals; they simply think it is unrealistic to push one's expectations for antitrust laws beyond a contribution to efficiency. Instead of allowing efficiency to be the principal criterion, the Harvard school seeks a balance among each of these three objectives.

Finally, you will detect the Harvard theme in the inaugural remarks of University of California-Berkeley's Lawrence A. Sullivan following his appointment as the Earl Warren Professor of Public Law.

Antitrust was once different. It was more eclectic. . . .

The Warren Court was the custodian of a multi-valued antitrust tradition. To that Court, the idea of competition included political and social objectives. Among these were easing market access, protecting dealer independence, promoting good faith in transactions, and correcting extreme disparities in bargaining power. The Warren Court also was interested in assuring, on grounds of equity and fairness, and regardless of supposed impact on resource allocation, that prices be closely related to cost. It sought each of these goals as an end in itself. Competition could foster all of them.[11]

It is easy to detect here a sense of pride in achievement, but there is something akin to nostalgia and alarm as well. Chicago is gaining and may sweep the day.

Ascendancy of the Chicago School

Illustrative of the emergence of the Chicago mode of analysis is *Berkey Photo, Inc.* v. *Eastman Kodak Company*.[12] Berkey alleged that Kodak used its power or leverage in the camera, film, and photofinishing equipment market to monopolize or gain a competitive advantage in the film development industry in violation of the Sherman Act, Section 2. Berkey's trial court judgment for more than $4.5 million—the jury trebled Berkey's actual damages in this private action under Section 4 of the Clayton Act—was reversed on appeal to the Second Circuit. The Court of Appeals concluded that because a monopolist is encouraged to compete aggressively, any success through invention and innovation is obviously tolerated by the antitrust laws.

This is clearly the Chicago position. Its proponents would argue that if a monopoly develops, rivals will enter the market until monopoly prices and profits are forced down to competitive levels. Sullivan, however, laments the fact that opportunities for smaller

firms or possible entrants are diminished in the name of short-run efficiencies. In his view, these efficiencies will be more than offset by long-run losses.[13] Given Berkey's fate, the new entrants envisioned by Chicago proponents are more likely to be fictitious than real. Even if they do emerge in the future, much harm can be done in the interim

A Concluding Note

Perhaps the chief criticism of the Chicago school generally is that its proponents are simply naive in thinking that the market operates as smoothly as they suggest. Many variables affect the outcome of antitrust strategies, and a step in the direction of short-term price competition is no guarantee that the economy generally is moving toward greater consumer welfare. Because other markets are less than competitive and because of the distortions or imperfections in resource allocation (e.g., taxes and externalities), we really cannot assume that Chicago's highly touted efficiency criterion, employed successfully in *Berkey*, is making anyone better off. People may be worse off, or their position may remain the same. In the view of Harvard school adherents, there are simply too many imponderables to be corralled by the single standard of economic efficiency. And beyond that, the standard itself is dynamic.

Any judicial dream of gaining certainty through contemporary economics will inevitably be shattered because economics itself evolves. As courts realize this, they may realize too that economic theories are not simply means for analyzing problems. In choosing among theories, courts are not selecting tools from a kit, but making important social judgments that should be made with full awareness. Courts should refuse to surrender to any group of theorists the basic value judgments that should be made by Congress and, with deliberation, by the courts themselves.[14]

Endnotes

1. The Reagan administration adopted the set of beliefs designated the Chicago school of law and economics, which supplanted a set of beliefs predominant since the Roosevelt years. This article is a brief explanation of these contrasting schools of thought.

2. News & Comment, *The Bureau of National Affairs* 3 (November 19, 1981).

3. Posner, The Chicago School of Antitrust Analysis, 127 *U. Pa. L. Rev.* 925, n.2 (1979). Posner's views resemble, but are not identical to, those of Bork. See generally Posner, *Antitrust Law: An Economic Perspective* (1975).

4. Bork, *The Antitrust Paradox* 7 (1978).

5. Without attempting an exhaustive listing, one might place the following in the Chicago camp: Bowman, Tying Arrangements and the Leverage Problem, 67 *Yale L. J.* 19 (1957); McGee, Predatory Price Cutting: The Standard Oil (N.J.) Case, 1 *J.L. & Econ.* 137 (1958); Telser, Why Should Manufacturers Want Fair Trade? 3 *J. L. & Econ.* 86 (1960). Nobel recipients Milton Friedman and George Stigler head the list of economists who have been instrumental in bringing the Chicago school to the forefront.

6. Director and Levi, Law and the Future: Trade Regulation 51 *Nw. U.L. Rev.* 281 (1956).

7. Posner, *Antitrust Law, An Economic Perspective* 132 (1975).

8. For the opposing view, see Turner, The Validity of Tying Arrangements Under the Antitrust Laws 72 *Harv. L. Rev.* 50 (1958).

9. Bork, *supra* note 4, at 144–155.

10. Price and Production Policies of Large Scale Enterprise, *Am. Econ. Rev.,* Supplement 29, 61–74 (March 1939); The Current State of the Monopoly Problem in the United States 62 *Harv. L. Rev.* 1265 (1949).

11. Sullivan, Antitrust, Microeconomics, and Politics: Reflections on Some Recent Relationships, 68 *Cal. L. R.* 1, 4 (1980).

12. 603 F.2d 263 (2nd Cir. 1979).

13. Sullivan, *supra* note 11, at 3.

14. *Id.* at 12.

CHAPTER 13

Securities Regulation

INTRODUCTION

A *security*, as we use the term in this chapter, is a unique kind of property. Securities have no inherent worth; they are pieces of paper that represent rights in something else. A security, however, is something more. It does represent value, and this value depends on the profitability or future prospects of profitability of the corporation or other entity that issued it. As the prospects for profit of a corporation go up, its outstanding securities (especially common stock) become worth more; the opposite is true for a decline in the prospects for profit. Thus, an inextricable and significant link exists between a corporation's prospects for profit and the value of its securities.

Because a corporation's profit, esteem, and popular worth are reflected in the value of its securities (determined by the demand for and supply of its securities), it is in the corporation's best interest to see that only favorable information gets to the securities marketplace, where securities are bought and sold. It is in the best interests of the securities traders and the public in general (and ultimately the corporation involved), however, that the information provided be as accurate as possible. It is the central purpose of federal securities regulation to ensure that the flow of information from the corporations covered by the statutes to the securities market is as accurate and timely as possible. This chapter focuses on why and how this regulation of information takes place. The only major "right" as such that we examine is the right of both prospective buyers and sellers of securities to accurate information. This often-assumed right ultimately determines the value of the security that is bought or sold.

The study of securities law is much more complicated than one might at first imagine. This complexity is created by at least three unique features of securities. First, because (1) agents, directors, officers, and employees of the corporation often hold stock in the corporation, (2) it is in their own personal best interests as well as the interest of the corporation to have a strong stock, and (3) they are in control of much of the information that goes to securities markets, these people are susceptible to manipulative and deceptive practices. Tremendous amounts of money—indeed, whole fortunes—can be made or lost in a single strategic, or not so strategic, transaction. Often, seemingly innocent people are damaged by their association with such a transaction.

When to trade a security is dependent on the type of information the trader has; if this trader is an insider (a member of management), certain statutes, rules, and regulations apply. These laws are the subject of a major portion of this chapter.

Second, securities are unique in that they are created by a corporation in unlimited amounts and without significant cost. They are not "produced" as so many commodities are. This facet of a security also gives rise to regulation by statute. In this chapter, we examine the issuance (creation) of securities.

Third, securities are not consumed or used by purchasers. They become a kind of currency, a kind of very liquid investment that can be readily sold.[1] The stock of most major corporations (certainly, this applies to the more than 1,500 corporations listed on the New York Stock Exchange) can be converted to cash at a moment's notice. Very well organized markets exist for the selling and buying of securities. Regulation of the technical aspects of the trading in these markets is split between the federal government and the markets or stock exchanges themselves. We examine some of this regulation here.

The general topics of federal regulation of issuance of securities and liability for insider trading are presented after discussions of the forces that brought about the perceived need for securities regulation. Then, we examine state regulation of securities, the necessary explanations of the definition of a security for purposes of the Securities Act of 1933, exemptions from the 1933 Act registration, and the operation of the Securities and Exchange Commission (SEC) created by the Securities Exchange Act of 1934. We conclude this overview of federal securities laws with an explanation of the remedies available to injured investors and an evaluation of both the SEC and the problems of insider trading.

These materials are presented in a chapter that is separate from those on the financial structure of corporations (regulated to some extent by state law), from the rights of shareholders, and from the vaguer issues of control of corporations through share ownership. Also separate is the discussion of control of both corporations and market structure by an application of the antitrust laws. Even though these discussions of the law are separate, they are related. For example, a single transaction, such as a merger between two large corporations, may present substantial legal problems in all of the areas just mentioned. The separation that we suggest here is done for instructional purposes.

STATE SECURITIES LAWS

Every state has some type of securities regulation. In most cases, this regulation applies to transactions not covered by the federal laws. The transactions covered by the state and federal laws, however, are not entirely separate. Indeed, a single issuance of stock, for example, may have to comply with applicable federal laws and one or more state laws.

Most state regulation of securities takes place at the time of the original distribution of securities. State statutes that regulate the original distribution of securities are called *blue sky laws*. This phrase became common usage after a judge's decision referred to the purpose of state securities laws as the prevention of "speculative schemes which have no more basis than so many feet of blue sky."[2]

WHY REGULATE THE DISTRIBUTION OF SECURITIES?

Why is regulation in the issuance and distribution of securities needed? Suppose that *F Corporation* has been owned by the *F* family for a few generations. The top management are all related to the *F*'s or are friends of the family. Management sees an opportunity to expand substantially but needs capital to do so. Essentially, they have two alternatives. First, they may borrow the money either by getting a commercial loan from a bank or by issuing bonds to themselves or to the public. Second, they may take in new owners by issuing some form of common or preferred stock. Usually, the common stock carries with it the right to vote and thus the right to participate in the election of the board of directors. No matter which source of funds is relied on—the bank for a loan or the public for debt or equity financing—it is crucial that the source of funds have accurate information about the past and present earnings and the future earning potential of *F Corporation*.

In the case of a lending bank, it has its own staff of experts to rely on to assess the value and potential of *F Corporation*. But on whom can the public rely? The investing public must rely on the management of *F Corporation* to provide it with accurate information about the performance and potential of *F Corporation*. That is, the public must rely on *F*'s assertions about its own operations. The general proposition that the investing public should rely on the unregulated assertion of management about its own worth places too great a burden on management to be objective and accurate and too great a risk on the public. Therefore, both state and federal laws regulate the original issuance and distribution of securities with a view to ensuring, to the extent practical, that a firm's assertions are accurate.

THE UNIFORM SECURITIES ACT

The Commissioners on Uniform State Laws drafted a Uniform Securities Act that has been adopted, in part, by about thirty of the states.[3] This Act is divided into four sections: broker-dealer registration, registration of new securities offerings, fraud in general, and remedy provisions. Recently, the commissioners drafted a Revised Uniform Securities Act (RUSA), which may be adopted to replace the original version at the option of individual states. Generally, the focus of much state regulation is on the same areas of securities activity as the federal laws. So, having offered these brief comments about state regulation, we refocus our attention on the federal level.

The Theory of Securities Regulation: Who Is Protected and Why

The essence of all of this regulation is to ensure the accuracy of information that flows to the investing public. If this information is not accurate, either buyers or sellers of securities may be defrauded. These laws exist for their protection. A simple example will make this clearer. Suppose that the board of directors of *X Corporation*, a nationally prominent manufacturing corporation, has just decided to double its quarterly dividend. This decision reflects a very profitable past quarter and creates expectations for the same or even increased earnings in future quarters. Suppose further that, at this time, the corporation's common shares are selling for $20, but on disclosure of the new dividend, the price would likely be closer to $24. *M,* a member of the board, owns ten thousand shares of *X* common; immediately after the board meeting and before disclosure of the dividend declaration, *M* orders a broker to buy one hundred shares from you, who are selling your shares at the market price. Commissions and various taxes aside, assume you sell for $2,000. The next day, you see the value of what you had sold go from $2,000 to $2,400 because the market reflected the increased value of the stock owing to the new dividend disclosure. That is, had the market known of the dividend declaration, what you owned and then sold would have been worth $400 more. Have you not sold something to *M* for less than its worth because of *M*'s failure to tell you (and the market) of the dividend? Have you not been defrauded of $400? The answer, according to the application of the federal securities laws, is yes.

You may change the example above in many ways to understand who may be injured by deception in the securities market and to understand whom the securities laws protect. For example, suppose the dividend went down and the price of a share might then be $16, but suppose you bought 100 shares from *M* at $20. You paid $400 more than they were worth.

This example highlights a different phase of securities transactions. When a corporation sells a class of securities to the investing public, this is a sale to or in a primary market and is called *primary distribution*. When a private owner of securities, such as you or I, sells to another private purchaser, this is a *secondary distribution* or sale. The principles that apply to these markets are the same. Unless both sides of the transaction, the buyer and the seller, have access to the same relevant or *material* information, the potential for fraud exists. The faith that the investing public has in the stockmarket is directly dependent on equal access to past information about a corporation's prospects for earnings.

DEFINITION OF A SECURITY

The 1933 Act and the 1934 Act, as well as the activities of the SEC, apply only to securities. A *security* is defined in the 1933 Act as "any note, stock, treasury stock, bond, debenture, evidence of indebtedness, certificate of interest or participation in any profit-sharing agreement, . . . investment contract, . . . certificate of deposit for security, factional undivided interest in oil, gas, or other mineral rights, or, in general, any interest or instrument commonly known as a 'security.' . . ."⁴ Chances are that anything you understand to be a security, such as all forms of stocks and bonds, is a security for purposes of the 1933 and 1934 Acts.

In addition, investment contracts are also securities. These were defined in the now classic Supreme Court case of *SEC v. Howey Co.*⁵ In this case, Howey-in-the-Hills Service, Inc., a Florida corporation, offered for sale a land contract and a service contract for acreage of a large Florida orange grove. Purchasers were encouraged to sign the service contract if they also signed the land contract. On full payment of the purchase price, the portion of the orange grove (in units of an acre that supported forty-eight orange trees) was conveyed by warranty deed to the purchaser. The service contract was of ten years' duration and gave Howey the full and complete possession of the acreage. Howey planted and pruned the trees and harvested and marketed the oranges. The owner had no right of entry onto the land purchased nor a right to any specific tree or fruit. The owner did have a right to share in the net profit based on a check made at the time of picking. In holding that the land contracts and service contracts and even the warranty deeds were investment contracts and thus securities, the Supreme Court reasoned that Congress intended an investment contract to mean any contract or profit-making scheme whereby a person invests money in a common enterprise and expects to make a profit solely from the efforts of a third party who is responsible for management. This definition has been expanded to apply to schemes in which one expects to derive a profit *predominantly* from the efforts of another. The word *solely* has been read out of the definition.

The following case concerns the status of promissory notes as potential securities, governed by the Securities Exchange Act of 1934. The Supreme Court adopts a family resemblance approach: If it looks like a security and smells like a security, it is a security.

Reves v. *Ernst & Young*
110 S. Ct. 945 (1990)

JUSTICE MARSHALL delivered the opinion of the Court. This case presents the question whether certain demand notes issued by the Farmers Cooperative of Arkansas and Oklahoma (Co-Op) are "securities" within the meaning of § 3(a)(10) of the Securities Exchange Act of 1934. We conclude that they are.

The Co-Op is an agricultural cooperative that, at the time relevant here, had approximately 23,000 members. In order to raise money to support its general business operations, the Co-Op sold promissory notes payable on demand by the holder. Although the notes were uncollateralized and uninsured, they paid a variable rate of interest that was adjusted monthly to keep it higher than the rate paid by local financial institutions. The Co-Op offered the notes to both members and non-members, marketing the scheme as an "Investment Program." Advertisements for the notes, which appeared in each Co-Op newsletter, read in part: "YOUR CO-OP has more than $11,000,000 in assets to stand behind your investments. The Investment is not Federal [sic] insured but it is . . . Safe . . . Secure . . . and available when you need it." Despite these assurances, the Co-Op filed for bankruptcy in 1984. At the time of the filing, over 1,600 people held notes worth a total of $10 million.

After the Co-Op filed for bankruptcy, petitioners, a class of holders of the notes, filed suit against Arthur Young & Co., the firm that had audited the Co-Op's financial statements (and the predecessor to respondent Ernst & Young). Petitioners alleged, inter alia, that Arthur Young had intentionally failed to follow generally accepted accounting principles in its audit, specifically with respect to the valuation of one of the Co-Op's major assets, a gasohol plant. Petitioners claimed that Arthur Young violated these principles in an effort to inflate the assets and net worth of the Co-Op. Petitioners maintained that, had Arthur Young properly treated the plant in its audits, they would not have purchased demand notes because the Co-Op's insolvency would have been apparent. On the basis of these allegations, petitioners claimed that Arthur Young had violated the antifraud provisions of the 1934 Act as well as Arkansas' securities laws.

Petitioners prevailed at trial on both their federal and state claims, receiving a $6.1 million judgment. Arthur Young appealed, claiming that the demand notes were not "securities" under either the 1934 Act or Arkansas law, and that the statutes' antifraud provisions therefore did not apply. A panel of the Eighth Circuit, agreeing with Arthur Young on both the state and federal issues, reversed.

In *Landreth Timber Co.* v. *Landreth*, 471 U.S. 681 (1985), we held that an instrument bearing the name "stock" that, among other things, is negotiable, offers the possibility of capital appreciation, and carries the right to dividends contingent on the profits of a business enterprise is plainly within the class of instruments Congress intended the securities laws to cover.

While common stock is the quintessence of a security, and investors therefore justifiably assume that a sale of stock is covered by the Securities Acts, the same simply cannot be said of notes, which are used in a variety of settings, not all of which involve investment.

Because the Landreth Timber formula cannot sensibly be applied to notes, some other principle must be developed to define the term "note." A majority of the Courts of Appeals that have considered the issue have adopted, in varying forms, "investment versus commercial" approaches that distinguish, on the basis of all of the circumstances surrounding the transactions, notes issued in an investment context (which are "securities") from notes issued in a commercial or consumer context (which are not).

The Second Circuit's "family resemblance" approach begins with a presumption that any note with a term of more than nine months is a "security." Recognizing that not all notes are securities, however, the Second Circuit has also devised a list of notes that it has decided are obviously not securities. Accordingly, the "family resemblance" test permits an issuer to rebut the presumption that a note is a security if it can show that the note in question "bear[s] a strong family resemblance" to an item on the judicially crafted list of exceptions, or convinces the court to add a new instrument to the list.

To determine whether a note is a security, we examine the transaction to assess the motivations that would prompt a reasonable seller and buyer to enter into it. If the seller's purpose is to raise money for the general use of a business enterprise or to finance substantial investments and the buyer is interested primarily in the profit the note is expected to generate, the instrument is likely to be a "security." If the note is exchanged to facilitate the purchase and sale of a minor asset or consumer good, to correct for the seller's cash-flow difficulties, or to advance some other commercial or consumer purpose, on the other hand, the note is less sensibly described as a "security." Second, we examine the "plan of distribution" of the instrument, to determine whether it is an instrument in which there is "common trading" for speculation or investment. Third, we examine the reasonable expectations of the investing public: The Court will consider instruments to be "securities" on the basis of such public expectations, even where an economic analysis of the circumstances of the particular transaction might suggest that the instruments are not "securities" as used in that transaction.

Finally, we examine whether some factor such as the existence of another regulatory scheme significantly reduces the risk of the instrument, thereby rendering application of the Securities Acts unnecessary. We conclude, then, that in determining whether an instrument denominated a "note" is a "security," courts are to apply the version of the "family resemblance" test that we have articulated here: A note is presumed to be a "security," and that presumption may be rebutted only by a showing that the note bears a strong resemblance (in terms of the four factors we have identified) to one of the enumerated categories of instrument. If an instrument is not sufficiently similar to an item on the list, the decision whether another category should be added is to be made by examining the same factors.

Applying the family resemblance approach to this case, we have little difficulty in concluding that the notes at issue here are "securities." Ernst & Young admits that "a demand note does not closely resemble any of the Second Circuit's family resemblance examples." Nor does an examination of the four factors we have identified as being rel-evant to our inquiry suggest that the demand notes here are not "securities" despite their lack of similarity to any of the enumerated categories. The Co-Op sold the notes in an effort to raise capital for its general business operations, and purchasers bought them in order to earn a profit in the form of interest. Indeed, one of the primary inducements offered purchasers was an interest rate constantly revised to keep it slightly above the rate paid by local banks and savings and loans. From both sides, then, the transaction is most naturally conceived as an investment in a business enterprise rather than as a purely commercial or consumer transaction.

As to the plan of distribution, the Co-Op offered the notes over an extended period to its 23,000 members, as well as to nonmembers, and more than 1,600 people held notes when the Co-Op filed for bankruptcy. To be sure, the notes were not traded on an exchange. They were, however, offered and sold to a broad segment of the public, and that is all we have held to be necessary to establish the requisite "common trading" in an instrument.

The third factor—the public's reasonable perceptions—also supports a finding that the notes in this case are "securities." We have consistently identified the fundamental essence of a "security" to be its character as an "investment." The advertisements for the notes here characterized them as "investments," and there were no countervailing factors that would have led a reasonable person to question this characterization. In these circumstances, it would be reasonable for a prospective purchaser to take the Co-Op at its word.

Finally, we find no risk-reducing factor to suggest that these instruments are not in fact securities. The notes are uncollateralized and uninsured. Moreover, the notes here would escape federal regulation entirely if the Acts were held not to apply.

For the foregoing reasons, we conclude that the demand notes at issue here fall under the "note" category of instruments that are "securities" under the 1933 and 1934 Act. Accordingly, we reverse the judgment of the Court of Appeals and remand the case for further proceedings consistent with this opinion.

CASE FOLLOW-UP

In a case like *Reves* v. *Ernst & Young*, plaintiffs may have a cause of action even if the promissory notes at issue are found not to comprise securities. Claims in such instances must typically be brought under the common law prohibition of fraud that exists in all states. If, as in the case you just read, the notes do qualify as securities, the antifraud provisions of both state and federal securities laws apply as well. A number of advantages may obtain from the ability to resort to such securities statutes. For example, the application of additional causes of action with somewhat different requirements increases the likelihood that plaintiffs will receive satisfaction without undue interference of legal technicality. Moreover, resort to federal courts may provide procedural, substantive, or strategic advantages. Finally, some state and federal securities statutes provide for enhanced damages, including treble damages or punitive damages. For all of these reasons, plaintiffs in cases like *Reves* often take pains to ensure that the instruments under which they are suing qualify as securities.

WHY IS THE DEFINITION OF A SECURITY IMPORTANT?

Why should a person in business care about the definition of a security? First, if a business deal involves an investment scheme that may involve an investment contract, registration may be required (if the transaction is not exempt), and failure to register may subject one to penalties. Second, from the viewpoint of the investor, if a scheme results in the perception that one has been defrauded or dealt with unfairly, an appeal to the SEC to halt the scheme may be successful. Entire schemes and large transactions may be stopped or significantly altered by the SEC's injunctive power. Also, if a security is involved, the SEC may prosecute, or at least investigate, and the threat of such an investigation may make recalcitrant promoters more accommodating in any discussions regarding the scheme. Finally, of no small significance is the reality that those who believe they have been the victim of a fraud may use the securities laws to seek a remedy. These laws are more developed than the common law notions of fraud. Therefore, it is a distinct advantage to the investor to argue successfully that an investment contract or other scheme is a security.

THE SECURITIES AND EXCHANGE COMMISSION

The SEC was created by the Securities Exchange Act of 1934, but we place the discussion of it before both the 1933 Act and the 1934 Act because its work is so important to the application of these Acts. The SEC is an independent regulatory agency headed by five commissioners, not more than three of whom may be members of the same political party. The agency is independent in that the commissioners are nominated by the president and confirmed by the Senate for five-year terms.

In the literature on governmental regulation, the SEC is almost always singled out as one of the best of the regulatory agencies.[6] It seems to be efficient and fair, and it responds relatively quickly to changes in the securities markets. This reputation can probably be traced to the strong and effective leadership of the first three SEC chairmen—Joseph P. Kennedy, James M. Landis, and William O. Douglas. Douglas, who was chairman from 1937 until he joined the U.S. Supreme Court in 1939, was particularly effective in forcing the reorganization of the New York Stock Exchange (NYSE). By threatening to forcefully impose the provisions of the 1934 Act, Douglas was able to change the NYSE from a private men's club to a respected public institution.[7]

Between 1935 and 1940, there was a flurry of securities regulation. In 1935, Congress substantially expanded the jurisdiction of the SEC by passing the Public Utility Holding Company Act of 1935. In 1939, more power was given to the SEC by the passage of the Trust Indenture Act and in 1940 by the Investment Company Act and the Investment Advisers Act. From 1940 until 1960, little new action took place in the field of securities regulation.

The 1960s was a significant decade for both the SEC and securities law. Early in the decade, the SEC issued a three-thousand-page report on the status of the securities industry. This report was the source for most of the ideas in the Securities Act Amendments of 1964.[8] Generally, these amendments extended SEC jurisdiction to markets not as formally organized as the NYSE, called *over-the-counter markets*. They also required dealers in over-the-counter issues either to join the National Association of Securities Dealers (NASD), a group that had been self-regulated, or to accept SEC supervision. Later in the decade, the SEC turned its attention to the regulation of mutual funds and finally to the growing importance of stock investments by institutions such as pension funds, insurance companies, banks, and other organizations that managed portfolios. Institutional investing accounted for most of the rising stock market activity during the 1960s.

Issues confronting the SEC in the 1970s involved the movement toward a national system of securities exchange and making brokers for securities more competitive in their services. In 1975 the SEC published an order abolishing fixed brokerage commissions to increase competition.

In 1990, Congress passed the Securities Enforcement and Penny Stock Reform Act, in order to provide specifically for protection of investors in speculative, low-cost stocks commonly called *penny stocks*. The Act contains disclosure requirements for brokers dealing in penny stocks, mandating information regarding (1) price spreads, (2) market liquidity of the securities being sold, (3) risk of investment, (4) broker duties, (5) remedies available to purchasers, and (6) amount of broker compensation.

Today, the SEC has the following major responsibilities:

1. Through the application of the 1933 and 1934 Acts, it issues rules and investigates, enforces, and prosecutes those who violate the public disclosure requirements for material facts that concern public offerings and other transactions in securities.

2. It regulates the disclosure requirements in the process of the solicitation of proxies for meetings of shareholders of companies listed on the exchanges, public utilities, holding companies, and investment companies.

3. It regulates the trading in securities on numerous national securities exchanges and in the over-the-counter markets.

4. It regulates certain activities of securities brokers, dealers, and investment advisors.

5. It advises federal courts in corporate reorganization proceedings under Chapter X of the Bankruptcy Act and recommends administrative sanctions, injunctive remedies, and criminal prosecutions against those who violate the securities laws.

6. It engages in other activity that would make the exchange of securities more efficient and fair.

Although the SEC is a well-respected agency with the potential to bring to bear significant legal and political power, it has a history of not regulating unless necessary. Self-regulation still plays an important role in securities law. Like the remedy provisions of the antitrust laws, many securities laws may be privately enforced.

Finally, the various stock exchanges and the NASD as well as the entire public accounting profession are expected to regulate their own activity in the securities markets.

THE SECURITIES ACT OF 1933

THE NECESSARY JURISDICTIONAL REQUIREMENTS

The 1933 Act, the 1934 Act, and the other federal acts discussed in this chapter all require that the transaction in securities or any transportation or communication relating to securities be among "the several states."[9] This language triggers the requirement that the matter involved affect interstate commerce.

The definition of *interstate commerce* as a jurisdictional requirement for the 1933 and 1934 Acts is one of the broadest definitions in all of federal regulation. This definition is so broad it is safe to conclude that if Congress or the SEC wants to regulate the issuance or trading of securities or fraud involving a security, it probably can do so. In an early case defining interstate commerce for purposes of the federal securities laws, a federal court held that when fraud was alleged in the sale of stock of a closed corporation (a corporation owned by a very few—usually fewer than one hundred—shareholders) and where the only interstate instrumentality used was the telephone, this was sufficient interstate commerce to give rise to the application of the federal securities laws. This was true even though the telephone was used to make an intrastate call involving the sale of the securities.[10] Other cases have affirmed federal jurisdiction where the U.S. mail was used to accomplish any part of the securities transaction.[11]

The 1933 Act is intended to regulate the original distribution of the securities of an issuer. The primary means of doing so is to require issuers to file a formal document called a *registration statement*. Section 5 of the 1933 Act requires registration for any sale by any person of any security unless specifically exempted from registration by the Act itself. The exemptions from registration are a very important part of securities regulation. Before we proceed with the formal requirements for registration, we outline these exemptions.

EXEMPTIONS BASED ON THE TYPE OF SECURITY OFFERED

The easiest exemption from registration are those based on the type of security offered. The types of exempt securities include the following:

- Bank and government securities

- Notes, drafts, and some other negotiable paper if the maturity date does not exceed nine months

- Securities issued by charitable organizations

- Savings and loan association securities if the corporations are regulated by federal or state authorities

- Securities of common carriers regulated by federal law

- Securities issued by a receiver or trustee in bankruptcy with the approval of the bankruptcy court

- Insurance, endowment, or annuity policies issued by companies supervised by state agencies

EXEMPTIONS BASED ON THE NATURE OF THE TRANSACTION

Probably the most important exemption for the average corporate issuer desiring to raise money through registration is the *private-placement exemption*. Approximately 25 percent of the securities offered for cash are sold through private placement.[12] The basic reason for the exempt status of most offerings is that the securities are being sold to purchasers or in circumstances for which the requirements of registration would serve no useful purpose. The purchasers of such an issue, for example, are usually in a position to ask for information about the issuer or can afford a staff to find the information. The majority of the private placement offerings go to institutional investors, such as large insurance companies or pension funds, or to key employees of the issuer or are issued in exchange offers to acquire the stock of closely held companies.

The circumstance creating the most problems has been the use of the private-placement exemption for promotional offerings to a limited number of people. In 1974, the SEC adopted Rule 146 to provide objective standards for the determination of a private offering.

The application of Rule 146 was complex and technical and generated many complaints that the elements of proof to meet its standards were burdensome on small businesses.

Rule 146 was therefore replaced with Regulation D and a series of rules. In very general terms, Regulation D, together with these rules, exempts securities from registration when

1. An issuer sells an aggregate of $1,000,000 of securities in any twelve-month period to any number of purchasers (Rule 504)

2. An issuer sells up to $5 million in securities in any twelve-month period to any number of accredited investors (defined as, generally, knowledgeable investors, such as banks or persons with a net worth of more than $1 million) and up to thirty-five other purchasers (Rule 505)

3. An issuer sells an unlimited amount of securities to any number of accredited investors and up to thirty-five other purchasers if the issuer reasonably believes that each nonaccredited purchaser has such experience that he or she is capable of evaluating the risk of the investment (Rule 506)

Rules 504 and 505 also provide for exemption from registration when the offering is small (as of 1987, under $5 million) or when the offering is to persons within a single state (the intrastate-offering exemption). Whether a security offering is exempt from registration is a technical legal matter and should be determined by a securities lawyer. The general rule is that registration is required unless the offering of securities is exempt, and exemptions are provided for when the reasons requiring registration are not present.

THE REGISTRATION STATEMENT

The process of registration with the SEC was purportedly simplified in March 1982, when a new system integrating the requirements of the 1933 Act and 1934 Act took effect. Basically, the 1933 Act requires registration and complete disclosure of all material information on the original issuance of shares, and the 1934 Act requires a continuous updating of that information in the form of an annual report filed as Form 10K. *Material information*, a key phrase used in securities law, refers to information that is so valuable to an investment decision that reasonable investors might act (trade) if they knew it.

The heart of the registration process is the filing of a registration statement. The SEC exercises broad discretion in deciding what information should be disclosed. It does not have (in theory) the power to approve or disapprove of the merits of a security and certainly does not protect the investor from risk. Generally, the SEC requires the following information in the registration statement:

1. A thorough picture of the financial status of the issuer. This includes a balance sheet dated not more than ninety days before filing and a profit-and-loss statement for at least five years past, both of which should be certified by independent auditors who attest that the information presented complies with generally accepted accounting principles.

2. Other material facts that might affect the price or value of the securities:

   a. The difference between the book value (the excess of assets over all liabilities, or net assets) of the corporation's presently issued shares and the offering price of the new shares

   b. Any substantial disparity between the public offering price and the cost of shares owned by management (officers, directors, and/or promoters)

   c. The elements used to compute the offering price of the securities if the issuer is a new company and other related financial information

   d. Any facts making the securities a high risk (e.g., no operating history or no history of earnings, the competitive nature of the industry, impending major lawsuits or governmental action against the issuer)

   e. Facts regarding the financial status of the management of the issuer (e.g., substantial loans by the issuer to management, pledges of the issuer's stock by management to secure loans to management, any information revealing financial difficulty of key members of management)

A key figure in the construction of the registration statement and in the distribution and sale of the securities is the underwriter.

DEFINITION AND FUNCTION OF AN UNDERWRITER

An *underwriter* is defined in the 1933 Act as a person who purchases securities from the issuer with a view toward public distribution, a person who offers or sells securities for an issuer, or a person who participates in the offering. Underwriters and other dealers are regulated by the 1933 Act and most of the other securities laws because their marketing expertise makes the selling of securities possible. An issuer does not usually have the expertise or financial ability to market its own securities, so underwriters are inextricably involved in any new securities issue.

One of the first things an issuer of securities does (after the decision to issue) is to make an agreement with an underwriter. The underwriter will buy the securities outright (for resale) or will take the responsibility for their sale on some other basis. The role of underwriters was contemplated by the drafters of the 1933 Act. The general pattern of a registration is as follows:[13]

Securities Movement

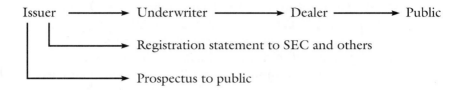

In the normal pattern, the underwriter, for a fee, agrees to advise the issuers in the preparation of the registration statement and promises to buy all or a large portion of the securities from the issuer and to resell them to dealers for resale to the public.

A registration statement often runs fifty to one hundred pages and is too technical for the average investor to understand, so issuers publish a *prospectus,* a glossy, positive document that outlines the best features of the issuer. Certainly, the prospectus must not contain any false or misleading statements, but it does present the information about the issuer in the best possible light.

CIVIL LIABILITY UNDER THE 1933 ACT

Section 11 of the 1933 Act provides, in part, that if a registration statement contains an untrue statement of a material fact or omits to state a material fact necessary to make the statement not misleading, a person who acquired any security covered by the registration can sue those required to sign the registration statement. The amount sued for shall be the difference between the price paid for the security (but not more than the public offering) and the price at which he or she disposed of it or, if it is still owned, its value at the time of suit.

This measure of liability—indeed, liability itself—was considered such a Draconian measure at the time of its enactment that some people thought it would eclipse underwriting activity and that "grass would grow in Wall Street."[14] These fears were unfounded, however, because the first fully litigated decision interpreting the civil liability provisions of Section 11 did not come until some thirty-five years later. By the time of the 1968 *BarChris* decision, more than twenty-seven thousand registration statements (covering offerings to the public of more than $384 billion in securities) had been filed.[15]

The *BarChris* case is enormously instructive for students of the legal environment of business. A brief overview of the facts shows that BarChris wanted working capital and thus sought to sell debentures to the public. An underwriter was consulted, a registration statement was filed, and a prospectus was issued. These documents were in error. The 1960 earnings were calculated on reported sales of $9.1 million, whereas the correct figure was $8.5 million; similarly, operating income was overstated by $245,605. The prospectus balance sheet reported an overstatement of $609,689 for current assets, and current liabilities were understated by $325,000, with contingent liabilities understated by $618,853. On the basis of these and similar crucial overstatements of earnings potential and gross understatements of liabilities, the public bought the debenture (bond) issue. Notwithstanding this infusion of capital, BarChris filed for bankruptcy under Chapter XI on October 29, 1962. As a result, a number of innocent parties were damaged. The investing public had been misled if not defrauded. Are those responsible for this transaction individually liable? Should they be liable? The court reasoned that the answer should be yes in both cases. The basis of the liability was signing the registration statement that purported to be a fair and accurate reflection of the financial condition of BarChris.

Escott v. BarChris Construction Corporation
283 F.Supp. 643 (1968)

McLEAN, DISTRICT JUDGE

This is an action by purchasers of $5\frac{1}{2}$ per cent convertible subordinated fifteen year debentures of BarChris Construction Corporation (BarChris). Plaintiffs purport to sue on their own behalf and "on behalf of all other and present and former holders" of the debentures. . . .

The action is brought under Section 11 of the Securities Act of 1933. Plaintiffs allege that the registration statement with respect to these debentures filed with the Securities and Exchange Commission, which became effective on May 16, 1961, contained material false statements and material omissions.

Defendants fall into three categories: (1) the persons who signed the registration statement; (2) the underwriters, consisting of eight investment banking firms, led by Drexel & Co. (Drexel); and (3) BarChris's auditors, Peat, Marwick, Mitchell & Co. (Peat, Marwick).

★ ★ ★

Liability Issues

. . . On the main issue of liability, the questions to be decided are (1) did the registration statement contain false statements of fact, or did it omit to state facts which

should have been stated in order to prevent it from being misleading; (2) if so, were the facts which were falsely stated or omitted "material" within the meaning of the Act; (3) if so, have defendants established their affirmative defenses?

Before discussing these questions, some background facts should be mentioned. At the time relevant here, BarChris was engaged primarily in the construction of bowling alleys. . . .

★ ★ ★

In general, BarChris's method of operation was to enter into a contract with a customer, receive from him at that time a comparatively small down payment on the purchase price, and proceed to construct and equip the bowling alley. When the work was finished and the building delivered, the customer paid the balance of the contract price in notes, payable in installments over a period of years. BarChris discounted these notes with a factor and received part of their face amount in cash. The factor held back part as a reserve.

★ ★ ★

By early 1961, BarChris needed additional working capital. The proceeds of the sale of the debentures involved in this action were to be devoted, in part at least, to fill that need.

★ ★ ★

By that time BarChris was experiencing difficulties in collecting amounts due from some of its customers. Some of them were in arrears in payments due to factors on their discounted notes. As time went on those difficulties increased. . . .

. . . In October 1962 BarChris came to the end of the road. On October 29, 1962, it filed in this court a petition for an arrangement under Chapter XI of the Bankruptcy Act. BarChris defaulted in the payment of the interest due on November 1, 1962, on the debentures.

★ ★ ★

Peat, Marwick, BarChris's auditors, who had previously audited BarChris's annual balance sheet and earnings figures for 1958 and 1959, did the same for 1960. These figures were set forth in the registration statement. In addition, Peat, Marwick undertook a so-called "S-1 review," the proper scope of which is one of the matters debated here.

The registration statement in its final form contained a prospectus as well as other information. Plaintiff's claims of falsities and omissions pertain solely to the prospectus, not to the additional data.

The prospectus contained, among other things, a description of BarChris's business, a description of its real property, some material pertaining to certain of its subsidiaries, and remarks about various other aspects of its affairs. It also contained financial information. It included a consolidated balance sheet as of December 31, 1960, with elaborate explanatory notes. These figures had been audited by Peat, Marwick. . . .

Plaintiffs challenge the accuracy of a number of these figures. They also charge that the text of the prospectus, apart from the figures, was false in a number of respects, and that material information was omitted. . . .

False Statements/Misleading Omissions

1960 Net Sales, Net Operating Income and Earnings per Share. The earnings figure set forth at page 4 of the prospectus shows net sales for the calendar year 1960 of $9,165,320. Plaintiffs claim that this figure was overstated by $2,525,350. . . .

★ ★ ★

. . . I find that the 1960 sales figure of $9,165,320, as stated in page 4 of the prospectus, was inaccurate. . . . The total figure, instead of $9,165,320, should have been $8,511,420.

It necessarily follows that the figure for net operating income for 1960 appearing on page 4 of the prospectus was also incorrect. . . .

★ ★ ★

Contingent Liabilities as of December 31, 1960

★ ★ ★

. . . [I]nstead of $750,000, the contingent liability figure under the alternative method of financing should have been $1,125,795. Capitol [an alley owned and operated by BarChris] should have been shown as a direct liability in the amount of $325,000.

★ ★ ★

Net Sales, Gross Profit and Net Earnings
Plaintiffs correctly contend that the net sales of $2,138,455 for the three months ended March 31, 1961 were overstated.

★ ★ ★

Materiality

It is a prerequisite to liability under Section 11 of the Act that the fact which is falsely stated in a registration statement, or the fact that is omitted when it should have been stated to avoid misleading, be "material." The regulations of the Securities and Exchange Commission pertaining to the registration of securities define the word as follows.

> The term 'material,' when used to qualify a requirement for the furnishing of information as to any subject, limits the information required to those matters as to which an average prudent investor ought reasonably to be informed before purchasing the security registered.

What are "matters as to which an average prudent investor ought reasonably to be informed"? It seems obvious that they are matters which such an investor needs to know before he can make an intelligent, informed decision whether or not to buy the security.

★ ★ ★

Judged by this test, there is no doubt that many of the misstatements and omissions in this prospectus were material. . . .

Affirmative Defense/Due Diligence

Peat, Marwick. Section 11(b) provides:

> Notwithstanding the provisions of subsection (a) no person . . . shall be liable as provided therein who shall sustain the burden of proof—

★ ★ ★

> (3) that . . . (B) as regards any part of the registration statement purporting to be made upon his authority as an expert . . . (i) he had, after reasonable investigation, reasonable ground to believe and did believe, at the time such part of the registration statement became effective, that the statements therein were true and that there was no omission to state a material fact required to be stated therein or necessary to make the statements therein not misleading. . . .

This defines the due diligence defense for an expert. Peat, Marwick has pleaded it.

★ ★ ★

The 1960 Audit. Peat, Marwick's work was in general charge of a member of the firm, Cummings, and more immediately in charge of Peat, Marwick's manager, Logan. Most of the actual work was performed by a senior accountant, Berardi, who had junior assistants, one of whom was Kennedy.

Berardi was then about thirty years old. He was not yet a C.P.A. He had had no previous experience with the bowling industry. This was his first job as a senior accountant. He could hardly have been given a more difficult assignment.

★ ★ ★

Capitol Lanes. First and foremost is Berardi's failure to discover that Capitol Lanes had not been sold. This error affected both the sales figure and the liability side of the balance sheet. Fundamentally, the error stemmed from the fact that Berardi never realized that Heavenly Lanes and Capitol were two different names for the same alley.

★ ★ ★

. . . The vital question is whether he failed to make a reasonable investigation which, if he had made it, would have revealed the truth.

★ ★ ★

The burden of proof on the issue is on Peat, Marwick. Although the question is a rather close one, I find that Peat, Marwick has not sustained that burden. Peat, Marwick has not proved that Berardi made a reasonable investigation as far as Capitol Lanes was concerned and that his ignorance of the true facts was justified.

★ ★ ★

Contingent Liabilities. Berardi erred in computing the contingent liability on Type B leaseback transactions at 25 per cent. He testified that he was shown an agreement with Talcott which fixed the contingent liability at that amount. In this testimony he was mistaken. No such document is contained in Peat, Marwick's work papers. The evidence indicates that it never existed. Berardi did not examine the documents which are in evidence which establish that BarChris's contingent liability on this type of transaction was in fact 100 per cent. Berardi did not make a reasonable investigation in this instance. . . .

The S-1 Review. The purpose of reviewing events subsequent to the date of a certified balance sheet (referred to as an S-1 review when made with reference to a registration statement) is to ascertain whether any material change has occurred in the company's financial position which should be disclosed in order to prevent the balance sheet figures from being misleading. The scope of such a review, under generally accepted auditing standards, is limited. It does not amount to a complete audit.

Peat, Marwick prepared written program for such a review. I find that this program conformed to generally accepted auditing standards. . . .

Berardi made the S-1 review in May 1961. He devoted a little over two days to it, a total of 20 hours. He did not discover any of the errors or omissions pertaining to the state of affairs in 1961 which I have previously discussed at length, all of which were material. The question is whether, despite his failure to find out anything, his investigation was reasonable within the meaning of the statute.

What Berardi did was to look at a consolidating trial balance as of March 31, 1961 which had been prepared by BarChris, compare it with the audited December 31, 1960 figures, discuss . . . certain unfavorable developments which the comparison disclosed, and read certain minutes. He did not examine any "important financial records" other than the trial balance. . . .

. . . He asked questions, he got answers which he considered satisfactory, and he did nothing to verify them. . . .

★ ★ ★

Berardi had no conception of how tight the cash position was. He did not discover that BarChris was holding up checks in substantial amounts because there was no money in the bank to cover them. . . .

★ ★ ★

There had been a material change for the worse in BarChris's financial position. That change was sufficiently serious so that the failure to disclose it made 1960 figures misleading. Berardi did not discover it. As far as the results were concerned, his S-1 review was useless.

Accountants should not be held to a standard higher than that recognized in their profession. I do not do so here. Berardi's review did not come up to that standard. He did not take some of the steps which Peat, Marwick's written program prescribed. He did not spend an adequate amount of time on a task of this magnitude. Most important of all, he was too easily satisfied with glib answers to his inquiries.

This is not to say that he should have made a complete audit. But there were enough danger signals in the materials which he did examine to require some further investigation on his part. Generally accepted accounting standards required such further investigation under these circumstances. It is not always sufficient merely to ask questions.

Here again, the burden of proof is on Peat, Marwick. I find that the burden has not been satisfied. I conclude that Peat, Marwick has not established its due diligence defense.

CASE FOLLOW-UP

This case is one of the classics in federal securities law enforcement. It is important because of what the court said about the obligations of persons who signed the registration statement but who were not "inside" members of the board of directors or members of top management. Reconsider the general circumstances of this case. BarChris issued some securities to investors. In all probability, these investors relied on the value of the company as asserted in the registration statement and the prospectus. These documents contained material omissions and misstatements of fact. After the issuance of the securities, the firm failed. It is not accurate in these matters to say that the material omissions caused the failure, but the reality is that the investors are left with securities worth a fraction of the amount they paid for them. It should be obvious that no one intended the failure of BarChris. But failures do occur. In essence, all involved in the enterprise lost money and prestige. Who is to blame?

The law takes the side of the investor and focuses on the registration statement and its materially misleading statements about the value and potential of BarChris. Consider the cases of BarChris's officers. Some of these people were new to the enterprise. They may have operated in good faith. Nevertheless, once they signed the registration statement and thus attested to the value of BarChris, they were held liable.

Also, consider the cases of the lawyer, the underwriter, and the accounting firm. It seems each tried to blame the others. The court held that they all had duties to independently inquire into and to verify the assertions made in the registration statement. In general terms, this case holds that you cannot rely on the representations made in what appears to be a friendly and chummy atmosphere. Each person who signs a registration statement must make a reasonable effort to ascertain the accuracy of the data in the registration statement.

The Securities Exchange Act of 1934

REGISTRATION

The 1934 Act—unlike the 1933 Act, which focuses on a single transaction—contains provisions that regulate a number of different securities transactions. The 1934 Act provides for the creation of the SEC, the regulation of trading markets, and the registration and regulation of some publicly held companies. This Act requires that companies whose securities are traded on a national securities exchange *or* companies having assets of $5 million or more *and* a class of equity security held by five hundred or more persons must register with the SEC.

The process of registration, although required by the 1934 Act, supplements and extends the requirements of the 1933 Act. A central purpose of the 1934 Act is to create a system of continuing disclosure of all material information from registered companies to the various securities agents and markets. As of early 1982 about nine thousand companies were subject to the 1934 Act's disclosure requirements; about three thousand of these had securities listed on various organized and established exchanges; and about six thousand had securities traded only in the less formal over-the-counter market.[16]

Section 12 of the 1934 Act requires all companies that register to supply the SEC with information similar to that contained in a registration statement. *The difference between the 1933 Act and 1934 Act registration requirements is largely one of timing.* Whenever a firm issues a new class of securities, or goes public for the first time, 1933 Act registration is required unless an exemption applies. Technically, under the 1934 Act, a corporation registers only once, but periodic updates are required. Moreover, if a corporation has registered under the 1934 Act and then desires to issue a new class of securities, 1933 Act registration is required.

PERIODIC REPORTING OF MATERIAL INFORMATION

Under the provisions of the 1934 Act, Section 13 requires such basic reports as an annual report on Form 10-K, a quarterly report on Form 10-Q, and a report on Form 8-K for any month in which certain listed events occur. Recently, the SEC adopted new procedures and forms to simplify this periodic reporting and to reconcile any major differences between the 1933 Act and 1934 Act registering requirements. Also, in 1980–1981, the SEC adopted a controversial requirement that the corporate annual report Form 10-K be signed not only by the corporate issuer but also by its principal executive, financial, and accounting officers and by at least a majority of its board of directors. The SEC's formal explanation for this individual assertion of corporate record accuracy was to refocus the attention of management toward the 1934 Act filings—to make certain that no one took this obligation lightly—and not to effect new legal liabilities.[17] Under Section 18, however, any person who makes or causes to be made a false or misleading statement in any report or other document filed under the 1934 Act can be held liable in damages to any person who buys or sells securities in reliance on such statement.

In addition to regulating the flow of information from the corporation to the public and the securities markets, the SEC, under the authority of the 1934 Act, regulates the proxy process and the related process of tender offers. Understanding these processes is of vital importance to an appreciation of the legal environment of large enterprises.

REGULATION OF PROXY SOLICITATIONS

Section 14 of the 1934 Act regulates the proxy process. A *proxy* is a power of attorney to vote shares owned by someone else. It is usual for management to solicit proxies from shareholders who may not desire to attend a shareholders' meeting. The proxy rules require that anyone soliciting proxies must submit the material used in the solicitation to the SEC in advance of their use. Essentially, disclosure is required of all material facts regarding matters to be voted on by shareholders.

THE PROXY PROCESS AND UNDERSTANDING CORPORATE CONTROL

The use of proxies by management and the regulation of the proxy process by the SEC are important to understanding the legal control of corporations. In theory, the shareholders of a corporation are supposed to be the ultimate location of power. They elect the board of directors, who are legally responsible for the management of the corporation. However, this theory holds true more for small corporations than for large ones. In the very large corporations, management is the de facto controller of the corporation. There are three central reasons for this. The first, identified by Adolph Berle and Gardiner Means in 1932 in *The Modern Corporation and Private Property*, is that very large corporations have so many shareholders that, chances are, no single identifiable group of them is unified enough to vote as a block to elect members to the board. In reality, the unifying force is management, and they control the election process, as we explain below.

A second reason is that shareholders are primarily interested in a return on their investment by way of higher dividends or an increase in the value of the stock. A third reason, and one closely related to the first, is that management controls the proxy process by which votes for the members of the board are cast and accumulated. These three reasons help explain why, in a 1974 survey of shareholder annual meetings in Delaware, it was reported that "Cities Service Company, the 77th largest industrial corporation with some 135,000 shareholders, had 25 attend the meeting; El Paso Natural Gas with 125,000 shareholders had 50 shareholders and Coca-Cola, the 69th largest corporation with 70,000 shareholders had 25."[18] In the most publicized shareholder challenge to this system of corporate control, labeled "Campaign GM," no more than 3,000 of General Motors 1.4 million shareholders (about .2 percent) attended the shareholder meeting.[19]

Shareholders do have a right to vote, but this right is usually given to management in the form of a proxy. Directors of corporations are responsible for sending out the proxies. These proxies almost always contain nominations by management for the election or reelection of one of their members. It is true that many boards of directors contain "outside" directors (by definition, these people are not members of management), but these outsiders nominated by management are usually members of a management team from another large corporation, large law firm, accounting firm, or like business. In 1974, of the 6,744 corporations registered with the SEC, management retained control of the corporation in 99.9 percent of the shareholders' elections.[20] In 1973, a study found that, in the 500 largest industrial corporations the United States, no incumbent management was even challenged.[21]

The Proxy Statement.   When corporation management desires to solicit proxies, it must file a preliminary copy of the proxy statement (the statement of issues or persons to be voted on) with the SEC. In sensitive elections where the issues presented are contested, the SEC may comment on the preliminary statement. Generally, the content of the preliminary and definitive (final) proxy statements must include several kinds of information.

1. The statement must identify for whom the solicitation is being made, who bears the cost, the amount already spent, and an estimate of the total amount to be spent.

2. If directors are to be elected, the statement must name and give detailed information about the nominees of the party that is soliciting the proxy, other directors whose terms of office continue beyond the meeting, and the present officers of the issuer.

3. Other detailed information relating to the specific matter for which the proxy is being solicited, such as a detailed statement about a shareholder proposal, must be included.

The Costs of Proxy Solicitations. Who bears the costs of proxy solicitations is crucial to understanding a major reason for the lack of challenge to incumbent management. Generally speaking, if a challenge to management control is made by outsiders—often referred to as *insurgents*—and if this challenge is based on corporate policy (as opposed to a personal power contest), the corporation bears the costs for management's solicitation of proxies and the insurgents must bear their own costs. These costs can exceed $100,000. In the very rare case in which an insurgent is successful in challenging management, the insurgents may ask the shareholders to authorize the corporation to reimburse them.

The SEC-sanctioned proxy statement and a proxy card, which may be signed and returned to the corporate office, are mailed to shareholders. This material must be accompanied by an annual report of the issuer when directors are to be elected. Typically, the vast number of shareholders do not bother to return these cards, so they represent no threat to the status quo. Institutional investors, however, such as the trust departments at major banks, will give these proxy matters close attention. With few exceptions, they vote with management because their interests are represented on the board by an agent of theirs or someone from a comparable institution.

Prior to the early 1990s, the SEC held individual shareholders to the same kind of proxy solicitation filing standards as corporate management. In 1992, the SEC modified these requirements, reducing the regulatory control over shareholder proxy solicitations. Shareholders are now provided with a "safe harbor," which permits them to communicate with other shareholders, and effectively persuade those shareholders to favor either the incumbents or a particular group of insurgents. Although the safe harbor does not permit direct proxy solicitation, it does allow between-shareholder lobbying regarding the desirability of the existing proxy solicitations of those who have filed SEC proxy statements.

Shareholders' Proposals. To what extent can shareholders, by their vote, influence corporate management? Generally, management sets the agenda and the matters to be voted on at a shareholders' meeting.

Recently, however, interest has been increasing in the types of issues that may be put to a shareholder vote. Under SEC Rule 14a–8, if a security holder of a registered company gives timely notice to management of an intention to present a proposal for action, management must include the proposal in the proxy statement and give security holders the opportunity to vote for or against it in the proxy itself. However, Rule 14a–8(c) permits management to exclude the proposal if, among other things, it

1. Is, under the governing state law, not a proper subject for action by security holders
2. Relates to a personal claim or grievance
3. Is not significantly related to the company's business or is beyond the company's power to effectuate (e.g., general political and moral concerns)
4. Relates to the conduct of the company's ordinary business operations
5. Relates to elections to office (security holders may not use the rule to nominate candidates for the board of directors) or
6. Is substantially similar to a proposal previously submitted during the past five years, which received affirmative votes from less than a specified percentage of the shares voted.

Proxy Contests, Tender Offers, Mergers, and the SEC.   The image of a wealthy and powerful individual buying shares of a relatively large corporation on the open market and then electing himself or herself to the board and exerting influence is unrealistic. The much more common occurrence is for one relatively large corporation to begin buying the shares of another relatively large corporation with a view toward merger, a relatively cooperative (though, perhaps, unwelcomed) process, or a *takeover,* an actively opposed effort. One reason for such a merger of business activities is often a desire by management of one corporation to put some of its resources into another market to spread business risks. Another reason is that, in some cases, it may be cheaper to buy the shares and then merge with another company that has larger cash and liquid reserves than it would be to issue more ownership securities to get the same cash and liquid reserves. Or, management may be motivated by the desire to become more powerful by controlling another corporation.

In the event of a takeover, management of the target corporation will not be receptive. In many cases, once a corporation has enough shares (between 5 percent and 10 percent of the outstanding voting shares) to elect a controlling number of the board of directors (this number varies from case to case, but it could be less than one-half), it can be expected to fire some or all of the top management of the acquired firm. Thus, in many mergers the attempt is opposed by the management of the acquired firm.

In 1968, Congress, in the wake of almost a decade of rampant merger activity, added Sections 14(d), (e), and (f) to the 1934 Act. These sections, together with Section 13(d), regulate the process of proxy contests and tender offers. A *tender offer* is an offer by one corporation (the tendering corporation) to purchase the securities of another corporation (the tendered corporation). Such an offer is made directly to the shareholders of the latter and may be in the form of cash or of stock of the tendering corporation; it may be made with or without the knowledge or cooperation of the management of the tendered corporation.

The SEC rules and the applicable section of the 1934 Act attempt to regulate tender offers through disclosure. Generally, they provide as follows:

1. Any party acquiring 5 percent or more of an equity security registered under Section 12 of the 1934 Act must report such acquisition and its intentions with respect to the tendered corporation (Section 13(d)).

2. Any party intending to make a tender offer must disclose this intention prior to commencing the offering (Section 14(d)).

3. Any party making an untrue statement of a material fact or engaging in a deceptive or manipulative act in connection with a tender offer is guilty of a fraud (Section 14(e)).

The following case demonstrates how the Supreme Court has interpreted the concept of manipulative acts in Section 14(e).

Schreiber v. *Burlington Northern, Inc.*
105 S. Ct. 2438 (1985)

BURGER, JUSTICE

On December 21, 1982, Burlington Northern, Inc., made a hostile tender offer for El Paso Gas Co. Through a wholly owned subsidiary, Burlington proposed to purchase 25.1 million El Paso shares at $24 per share. Burlington reserved the right to terminate the offer if any of several specified events occurred. El Paso management initially opposed the takeover, but its shareholders responded favorably, fully subscribing the offer by the December 30, 1982, deadline.

Burlington did not accept those tendered shares; instead, after negotiations with El Paso management, Burlington announced on January 10, 1983, the terms of a new and friendly takeover agreement. Pursuant to the new agreement, Burlington undertook, inter alia, to (1) rescind the December tender offer, (2) purchase 4,166,667 shares from El Paso at $24 per share, (3) substitute a new tender offer for only 21 million shares at $24 per share, (4) provide procedural protections against a squeeze-out merger of the remaining El Paso shareholders, and (5) recognize "golden parachute" contracts between El Paso and four of its senior officers. By February 8, more than 40 million shares were tendered in response to Burlington's January offer, and the takeover was completed.

The rescission of the first tender offer caused a diminished payment to those shareholders who had tendered during the first offer. The January offer was greatly oversubscribed and consequently those shareholders who retendered were subject to substantial proration. Petitioner Barbara Schreiber filed suit on behalf of herself and similarly situated shareholders, alleging that Burlington, El Paso, and members of El Paso's board of directors violated § 14(e)'s prohibition of "fraudulent, deceptive, or manipulative acts or practices . . . in connection with any tender offer." She claimed that Burlington's withdrawal of the December tender offer coupled with the substitution of the January tender offer was a "manipulative" distortion of the market for El Paso stock. Schreiber also alleged that Burlington violated § 14(e) by failing in the January offer to disclose the "golden parachutes" offered to four of El Paso's managers. She claims that this January nondisclosure was a deceptive act forbidden by § 14(e).

The District Court dismissed the suit for failure to state a claim. The District Court reasoned that the alleged manipulation did not involve a misrepresentation, and so did not violate § 14(e). The District Court relied on the fact that in cases involving alleged violations of § 10(b) of the Securities Exchange Act, this Court has required misrepresentation for there to be a "manipulative" violation of the section. 568 F. Supp., at 202. The Court of Appeals for the Third Circuit affirmed.

Petitioner relies on a construction of the phrase, "fraudulent, deceptive, or manipulative acts or practices." Petitioner reads the phrase "fraudulent, deceptive, or manipulative acts or practices" to include acts which, although fully disclosed, "artificially" affect the price of the takeover target's stock. Petitioner's interpretation relies on the belief that § 14(e) is directed at purposes broader than providing full and true information to investors.

Petitioner's reading of the term "manipulative" conflicts with the normal meaning of the term. We have held in the context of an alleged violation of § 10(b) of the Securities Exchange Act:

> "Use of the word 'manipulative' is especially significant. It is and was virtually a term of art when used in connection with the securities markets. It connotes intentional or willful conduct designed to deceive or defraud investors by controlling or artificially affecting the price of securities." *Ernst & Ernst* v. *Hochfelder*, 425 U.S. 185, 199 (1976) (emphasis added).

Petitioner argues, however, that the term "manipulative" takes on a meaning in § 14(e) that is different from the meaning it has in § 10(b). Petitioner claims that the use of the disjunctive "or" in § 14(e) implies that acts need not be deceptive or fraudulent to be manipulative. But Congress used the phrase "manipulative or deceptive" in § 10(b) as well, and we have interpreted "manipulative" in that context to require misrepresentation. Moreover, it is a "'familiar principle of statutory construction that words grouped in a list should be given related meaning."

We hold that the term "manipulative" as used in § 14(e) requires misrepresentation or nondisclosure. It connotes "conduct designed to deceive or defraud investors by controlling or artificially affecting the price of securities." Without misrepresentation or nondisclosure, § 14(e) has not been violated.

Applying that definition to this case, we hold that the actions of respondents were not manipulative. The amended complaint fails to allege that the cancellation of the first tender offer was accompanied by any misrepresentation, nondisclosure, or deception. The District Court correctly found: "All activity of the defendants that could have conceivably affected the price of El Paso shares was done openly."

Petitioner also alleges that El Paso management and Burlington entered into certain undisclosed and deceptive agreements during the making of the second tender offer. The substance of the allegations is that, in return for certain undisclosed benefits, El Paso managers agreed to support the second tender offer. But both courts noted that petitioner's complaint seeks only redress for injuries related to the cancellation of the first tender offer. Since the deceptive and misleading acts alleged by petitioner all occurred with reference to the making of the second tender offer—when the injuries suffered by petitioner had already been sustained—these acts bear no possible causal relationship to petitioner's alleged injuries. The Court of Appeals dealt correctly with this claim.

The judgment of the Court of Appeals is affirmed

CASE FOLLOW-UP

The *Schreiber* case is illustrative of judicial restraint in the interpretation of securities regulations during the 1980s. The Supreme Court, in recent years, has tended to read statutory and regulatory language as literally as possible, in contrast with many earlier federal trial and appellate courts, including the Supreme Court. Prior to the 1980s, courts were more likely to extend literal statutory and regulatory meanings to analogous situations that were viewed as being in the spirit of the literal meaning of the words at issue. This shift may reflect a concomitant shift in the general political climate toward greater conservatism during the Reagan and Bush administrations. Do you think that courts should interpret statutory and regulatory edicts as narrowly and literally as possible or that they should extend literal meanings in efforts to faithfully execute drafters' intentions?

The federal government, operating through the SEC, plays a leading role in regulating the national securities markets. It does this to ensure their continued fairness and integrity. In the next case, *Revlon* v. *MacAndrews & Forbes Holdings*, you may assume no fraudulent stock manipulations nor any misleading proxy statements. It is litigated on a backdrop of regularity in the securities market. The issue is the integrity of target management. Under the business judgment rule, corporate management is supposed to operate the firm in the best interest of the owners; that is, management must exhibit the legal and moral qualities of loyalty and due care. If managers put their own self-interest before that of the owners, they are clearly involved in a conflict of interest and can be held legally and morally accountable. Follow closely the *Revlon* court's evaluation of the performance of target management.

Revlon, Inc. v. *MacAndrews & Forbes Holdings, Inc.*
506 A.2d 173 (1986)

MOORE, JUSTICE

In this battle for corporate control of Revlon, Inc. (Revlon), the Court of Chancery enjoined certain transactions designed to thwart the efforts of Pantry Pride, Inc. (Pantry Pride) to acquire Revlon. The defendants are Revlon, its board of directors, and [Forstmann]. The injunction barred consummation of an option granted Forstmann to purchase certain Revlon assets (the lock-up option), a promise by Revlon to deal exclusively with Forstmann in the face of a takeover (the no-shop provision), and the payment of a $25 million cancellation fee to Forstmann if the transaction was aborted. The Court of Chancery found that the Revlon directors had breached their duty of care by entering into the foregoing transactions and effectively ending an active auction for the company. The trial court ruled that such arrangements are not illegal *per se* under Delaware law, but that their use under the circumstances here was impermissible. We agree.

In our view, lock-ups and related agreements are permitted under Delaware law where their adoption is untainted by director interest or other breaches of fiduciary duty. The actions taken by the Revlon directors, however, did not meet this standard. Moreover, while concern for various corporate constituencies is proper when addressing a takeover threat, that principle is limited by the requirement that there be some rationally related benefit accruing to the stockholders. We find no such benefit here.

Thus, under all the circumstances we must agree with the Court of Chancery that the enjoined Revlon defensive measures were inconsistent with the directors' duties to the stockholders. Accordingly, we affirm.

[*Author's note*: In mid-1985, Pantry Pride undertook a negotiated takeover of Revlon at $40 to $50 per share. Revlon rejected these efforts on ground that the price was inadequate and adopted two defensive measures: (1) repurchase of up to five million of thirty million outstanding shares, and (2) a poison pill (the "Rights") authorizing shareholders to receive a $65 note at 12 percent effective if a hostile bidder acquired 20 percent of Revlon shares. The Rights would not be available to Pantry Pride, and prior to the 20 percent trigger, the Rights could be redeemed at ten cents per share.

On August 23, 1985, Pantry Pride made its first hostile offer—a cash tender for all shares of Revlon at $47.50 common, $26.67 preferred. Revlon countered with an offer to purchase up to ten million shares in exchange for Notes (the "Notes") that limited its ability to incur additional debt, sell assets, or pay dividends unless approved by "outside" board members.

Revlon's board authorized management to find other parties interested in acquiring the company on September 24. Within two weeks of that meeting, Pantry Pride bid up to $56.25 per share.

Meeting October 3 and October 12, the Revlon board authorized a leveraged buyout by Forstmann at $57.25, conditioned on a lock-up option on valuable Revlon divisions at $100 to $175 million below estimated value if another firm acquired 40 percent of Revlon's stock. The conditions also included a no-shop provision forbidding Revlon from negotiating with another "white knight," the deposit in escrow of a $25 million cancellation fee to be paid if the agreement was terminated or if Pantry Pride acquired 19.9 percent of the stock, and redemption of the Rights by Revlon. Further, Revlon was to waive the Note covenants and sell its cosmetics division. Waiver of the note covenants caused these securities to drop 12.5 points. Litigation was threatened by so many note holders that Forstmann agreed to support the notes at par.

This was the status of the case at the time the Delaware Supreme Court sustained a lower court's injunction issued at Pantry Pride's request.]

★ ★ ★

The ultimate responsibility for managing the business and affairs of a corporation falls on its board of directors. In discharging this function the directors owe fiduciary duties of care and loyalty to the corporation and its shareholders. *Aronson* v. *Lewis* (1984). These principles apply with equal force when a board approves a corporate merger pursuant to *Smith* v. *Van Gorkom* (1985); and of course they are the bedrock of our law regarding corporate takeover issues. *Unocal Corp.* v. *Mesa Petroleum Co.* (1985). While the business judgment rule may be applicable to the actions of corporate directors responding to takeover threats, the principles upon which it is founded—care, loyalty, and independence—must first be satisfied.

If the business judgment rule applies, there is a "presumption that in making a business decision the directors of a corporation acted on an informed basis, in good faith and in the honest belief that the action taken was in the best interests of the company." However, when a board implements anti-takeover measures there arises "the omnipresent specter that a board may be acting primarily in its own interests, rather than those of the corporation and its shareholders...." *Unocal Corp.* v. *Mesa Petroleum Co.* This potential for conflict places upon the directors the burden of proving that they had reasonable grounds for believing there was a danger to corporate policy and effectiveness, a burden satisfied by a showing of good faith and reasonable investigation. In addition, the directors must analyze the nature of the takeover and its effect on the corporation in order to ensure balance—that the responsive action taken is reasonable in relation to the threat posed.

★ ★ ★

The first relevant defensive measure adopted by the Revlon board was the Rights Plan, which would be considered a "poison pill" in the current language of corporate takeovers—a plan by which shareholders receive the right to be bought out by the corporation at a substantial premium on the occurrence of a stated triggering event.... Thus, the focus becomes one of reasonableness and purpose.

The Revlon board approved the Rights Plan in the face of an impending hostile takeover bid by Pantry Pride at $45 per share, a price which Revlon reasonably concluded was grossly inadequate.... In adopting the Plan, the board protected the shareholders from a hostile takeover at a price below the company's intrinsic value, while retaining sufficient flexibility to address any proposal deemed to be in the stockholders' best interests.

To that extent the board acted in good faith and upon reasonable investigation. Under the circumstances it cannot be said that the Rights Plan as employed was unreasonable, considering the threat posed. Indeed, the Plan was a factor in causing Pantry Pride to raise its bid from a low of $42 to an eventual high of $58. At the time of its adoption the Rights Plan afforded a measure of protection consistent with the directors' fiduciary duty in facing a takeover threat perceived as detrimental to corporate interests. *Unocal.*

Although we consider adoption of the Plan to have been valid under the circumstances, its continued usefulness was rendered moot by the directors actions on October 3 and October 12 [when the Rights—that is, the "poison pill"—were redeemed by the Revlon board].

★ ★ ★

The second defensive measure adopted by Revlon to thwart a Pantry Pride takeover was the company's own exchange offer for 10 million of its shares.

★ ★ ★

The Revlon directors concluded that Pantry Pride's $47.50 offer was grossly inadequate. In that regard the board acted in good faith, and on an informed basis, with reasonable grounds to believe that there existed a harmful threat to the corporate enterprise. The adoption of a defensive measure, reasonable in relation to the threat posed, was proper and fully accorded with the powers, duties, and responsibilities conferred upon directors under our law. *Unocal.*

★ ★ ★

However, when Pantry Pride increased its offer to $50 per share, and then to $53, it became apparent to all that the break-up of the company was inevitable. The Revlon board's authorization permitting management to negotiate a merger or buyout with a third party was a recognition that the company was for sale. The duty of the board had thus changed from the preservation of Revlon as a corporate entity to the maximization of the company's value at a sale for the stockholders' benefit. This significantly altered the board's responsibilities under the *Unocal* standards. It no longer faced threats to corporate policy and effectiveness, or to the stockholders' interests, from a grossly inadequate bid. The whole question of defensive measures became moot. The directors' role changed from defenders of the corporate bastion to auctioneers charged with getting the best price for the stockholders at a sale of the company.

★ ★ ★

This brings us to the lock-up with Forstmann and its emphasis on shoring up the sagging market value of the Notes in the face of threatened litigation by their holders. Such a focus was inconsistent with the changed concept of the directors' responsibilities at this stage of the developments. The impending waiver of the Notes covenants had caused the value of the Notes to fall, and the board was aware of the noteholders' ire as well as their subsequent threats of suit. The directors thus made support of the Notes an integral part of the company's dealings with Forstmann, even though their primary responsibility at this stage was to the equity owners.

The original threat posed by Pantry Pride—the break-up of the company—had become a reality which even the directors embraced. Selective dealing to fend off a hostile but determined bidder was no longer

a proper objective. Instead, obtaining the highest price for the benefit of the stockholders should have been the central theme guiding director action. Thus, the Revlon board could not make the requisite showing of good faith by preferring the noteholders and ignoring its duty of loyalty to the shareholders. The rights of the former already were fixed by contract. The noteholders required no further protection, and when the Revlon board entered into an auction-ending lock-up agreement with Forstmann on the basis of impermissible considerations at the expense of the shareholders, the directors breached their primary duty of loyalty.

The Revlon board argued that it acted in good faith in protecting the noteholders because *Unocal* permits consideration of other corporate constituencies. . . . However, such concern for non-stockholder interests is inappropriate when an auction among active bidders is in progress, and the object no longer is to protect or maintain the corporate enterprise but to sell it to the highest bidder.

A lock-up is not *per se* illegal under Delaware law. Its use has been approved in an earlier case. *Thompson* v. *Enstar Corp.*, Del. Ch. (1984). Such options can entice other bidders to enter a contest for control of the corporation, creating an auction for the company and maximizing shareholder profit. Current economic conditions in the takeover market are such that a "white knight" like Forstmann might only enter the bidding for the target company if it receives some form of compensation to cover the risks and costs involved. However, while those lock-ups which draw bidders into the battle benefit shareholders, similar measures which end an active auction and foreclose further bidding operate to the shareholders' detriment.

The Forstmann option has a similar destructive effect on the auction process. Forstmann had already been drawn into the contest on a preferred basis, so the result of the lock-up was not to foster bidding, but to destroy it. The board's stated reasons for approving the transactions were: (1) better financing, (2) noteholder protection, and (3) higher price. As the Court of Chancery found, and we agree, any distinctions between the rival bidders' methods of financing the proposal were nominal at best, and such a consideration has little or no significance in a cash offer for any and all shares. The principal object, contrary to the board's duty of care, appears to have been protection of the noteholders over the shareholders' interests.

. . . The principal benefit went to the directors, who avoided personal liability to a class of creditors to whom the board owed no further duty under the circumstances. Thus, when a board ends an intense bidding contest on an insubstantial basis, and where a significant by-product of that action is to protect the directors against a perceived threat of personal liability for consequences stemming from the adoption of previous defensive measures, the action cannot withstand the enhanced scrutiny which *Unocal* requires of director conduct.

In addition to the lock-up option, the Court of Chancery enjoined the no-shop provision as part of the attempt to foreclose further bidding by Pantry Pride. The no-shop provision, like the lock-up option, while not *per se* illegal, is impermissible under the *Unocal* standards when a board's primary duty becomes that of an auctioneer responsible for selling the company to the highest bidder. The agreement to negotiate only with Forstmann ended rather than intensified the board's involvement in the bidding contest.

The court below similarly enjoined the payment of the cancellation fee, pending a resolution of the merits, because the fee was part of the overall plan to thwart Pantry Pride's efforts. We find no abuse of discretion in that ruling.

★ ★ ★

In conclusion, the Revlon board was confronted with a situation not uncommon in the current wave of corporate takeovers. A hostile and determined bidder sought the company at a price the board was convinced was inadequate. The initial defensive tactics worked to the benefit of the shareholders, and thus the board was able to sustain its *Unocal* burdens in justifying those measures. However, in granting an asset option lock-up to Forstmann, we must conclude that under all the circumstances the directors allowed considerations other than the maximization of shareholder profit to affect their judgment, and followed a course that ended the auction for Revlon, absent court intervention, to the ultimate detriment of its shareholders. No such defensive measure can be sustained when it represents a breach of the directors' fundamental duty of care. See *Smith* v. *Van Gorkom*. In that context the board's action is not entitled to the deference accorded it by the business judgment rule. The measures were properly enjoined. The decision of the Court of Chancery, therefore, is

Affirmed.

CASE FOLLOW-UP

You probably noted the frequent reference to *Unocal Corporation* v. *Mesa Petroleum Co.*[22] in the *Revlon* opinion. That case involved an effort by T. Boone Pickens (Mesa) to take over Unocal with a two-tiered, front-loaded tender offer. The first tier would pay $54 per share cash for sixty-four million shares. That would bring Mesa's control to 51 percent. The second tier was for $54 per share for the remaining shares, but the financing of the second tier was with junk bonds combining both high risk and high yield.

The Unocal board considered this price to be inadequate and the bid structure to be coercive. It was coercive in the sense that it was designed to induce shareholders to accept the first tier for fear that the second tier, financed by junk bonds, would not really be worth $54.

Unocal responded with a self-tender for 49 percent of its stock at $72 per share financed by fully secured, unsubordinated Unocal bonds (1) if Mesa was successful in accumulating 51 percent but (2) excluding Mesa from the tender offer. On the basis of Mesa's petition alleging that the Unocal board violated its fiduciary responsibly to act in the best interest of all shareholders, the lower court issued an injunction against Unocal's self-tender. The Delaware Supreme Court vacated that injunction for the reasons that follow.

> We must bear in mind the inherent danger in the purchase of shares with corporate funds to remove a threat to corporate policy when a threat to control is involved. The directors are of necessity confronted with a conflict of interest, and an objective decision is difficult.
>
> In the face of this inherent conflict directors must show that they had reasonable grounds for believing that a danger to corporate policy and effectiveness existed because of another person's stock ownership. However, they satisfy that burden "by showing good faith and reasonable investigation. . . ." Furthermore, such proof is materially enhanced, as here, by the approval of a board comprised

of a majority of outside independent directors who have acted in accordance with the foregoing standards. . . .

A further aspect is the element of balance. If a defensive measure is to come within the gambit of the business judgment rule, it must be reasonable in relation to the threat posed. This entails an analysis by the directors of the nature of the takeover bid and its effect on the corporate enterprise.

Specifically, the Unocal directors had concluded that the value of Unocal was substantially above the $54 per share offered in cash at the front end. Furthermore, they determined that the subordinated securities to be exchanged in Mesa's announced squeeze out of the remaining shareholders in the "back-end" merger were "junk bonds" worth far less than $54. It is now well recognized that such offers are a classic coercive measure designed to stampede shareholders into tendering at the first tier, even if the price is inadequate, out of fear of what they will receive at the back end of the transaction. Wholly beyond the coercive aspect of an inadequate two-tier tender offer, the threat was posed by a corporate raider with a national reputation as a "green mailer."

In adopting the selective exchange offer, the board stated that its objective was either to defeat the inadequate Mesa offer or, should the offer still succeed, provide the 49% of its stockholders, who would otherwise be forced to accept "junk bonds," with $72 worth of senior debt. We find that both purposes are valid.

However, such efforts would have been thwarted by Mesa's participation in the exchange offer. First, if Mesa could tender its shares, Unocal would effectively be subsidizing the former's continuing effort to buy Unocal stock at $54 per share. Second, Mesa could not, by definition, fit within the class of shareholders being protected from its own coercive and inadequate tender offer. . . .

FRAUD IN THE SECURITIES MARKET

SECTION 10(b) OF THE 1934 ACT AND SEC RULE 10(b)–5

Rule 10b-5, issued by the SEC pursuant to its power under Section 10(b) of the 1934 Securities Exchange Act, is the basis for civil and criminal sanctions against fraud in the purchase and sale of securities. Rule 10b-5 is most widely recognized for its role in controlling inside trading, but, as you will see in *Levinson* v. *Basic*, that is not its sole function.

Rule 10b-5 provides as follows:

It shall be unlawful for any person, directly or indirectly, by the use of any means or instrumentality of interstate commerce, or of the mails, or of any facility of any national securities exchange,

1. To employ any device, scheme, or artifice to defraud,

2. To make any untrue statement of a material fact or to omit to state a material fact necessary in order to make the statements made, in the light of the circumstances under which they were made, not misleading, or

3. To engage in any act, practice, or course of business which operates or would operate as a fraud or deceit upon any person

in connection with the purchase or sale of any security.

Basic, Inc., was a publicly traded company engaged in the manufacture of chemical refractors for the steel industry. Beginning in 1976, Combustion Engineering, Inc. (CEI) initiated a series of meetings concerning the possibility of merger. These meetings continued through October 1977, and following a day of exceptionally high trading in Basic common stock, Basic's president announced that "Basic knew of no reason for the stock's activity," and that "no merger negotiations were under way."

Negotiations proceeded through 1978, and the price of Basic stock continued to rise. In July 1978 and again in September, officials of the NYSE approached Basic to inquire into the reasons for the activity in its stock. Both times Basic denied any undisclosed merger or acquisition plans or other significant corporate developments. In its November 1978 earnings statement to its stockholders, Basic repeated its denial of corporate developments that would account for the abnormally heavy trading in its stock: "With regard to stock market activity in the Company's shares we remain unaware of any present or pending developments that would account for the high volume of trading and price fluctuations in recent months."

Later in November 1978, CEI offered to pay $35 per share for Basic's outstanding shares; this offer was rejected by the Basic board of directors. In mid-December, CEI increased its offer to $46 per share. The next day, Friday, December 15, 1978, the price of Basic stock rose again, and, responding to a NYSE inquiry, Basic again denied knowledge of corporate developments that would explain the volume of shares traded.

On the following Monday, Basic asked the NYSE to suspend trading in its common shares because it had been approached concerning a merger. Basic announced its acceptance of CEI's merger terms, $46 per share, on Tuesday, December 19.

Levinson and other former Basic shareholders joined in a class action consisting of those who sold their stock between the time of Basic's first denial of significant corporate activity (October 1977) and the suspension of trading (December 1978). They claimed that Basic's false and misleading statements of material fact violated Rule 10b-5 and that this violation inflicted monetary losses on them because the misinformation reduced the market price of their common stock at the time they sold.

The class action was accepted by the courts because of common law and fact questions that linked all members of the class to Basic's conduct. The issues before the Supreme Court were (1) whether the misrepresentations were *material* and (2) whether there was *reliance* on those misrepresentations.

The second of these two points requires some appreciation of the *fraud-on-the-market* theory. Justice Blackmun explains this theory in his opinion, which follows. Essentially, it consists of the view, supported by some empirical evidence, that in efficient capital markets—for example, stock exchanges as you would recognize them in New York, London, and Tokyo—every scrap of information about a firm's performance and future prospects is fully, totally, and completely integrated into the market price quoted on a public exchange. If the information is good, such as the prospects for increased earnings (or, perhaps, for a merger), the share price would tend to increase. Bad information, such as the likelihood of a large products liability judgment or a pending antitrust action, would tend to depress stock price.

The position of the Levinson plaintiffs is that the misrepresentations made by Basic management tended to depress market price below the level they would have gone if the statements had been true. Further, the Levinson argument runs, even if members of the class did not hear or read Basic's false statements and did not explicitly rely on those statements, that information was nevertheless incorporated into the market price quoted for Basic stock, and they relied on the integrity of those market prices. Therefore, the argument concludes, they are entitled to recover an amount in damages that is the difference between the price at which they sold the stock and the price the stock would have reached if the information regarding corporate activity had been truthful.

Levinson v. Basic, Inc.
485 U.S. 224 (1988)

BLACKMUN, JUSTICE

The 1934 Act was designed to protect investors against manipulation of stock prices. Underlying the adoption of extensive disclosure requirements was a legislative philosophy: There cannot be honest markets without honest publicity. Manipulation and dishonest practices of the market place thrive upon mystery and secrecy.

The Court previously has explicitly defined a standard of materiality under the securities laws, concluding in the proxy-solicitation context that "[a]n omitted fact is material if there is a substantial likelihood that a reasonable shareholder would consider it important in deciding how to vote." *TSC Industries, Inc.* v. *Northway, Inc.* (1976). Acknowledging that certain information concerning corporate developments could well be of "dubious significance," the Court was careful not to set too low a standard of materiality; it was concerned that a minimal standard might bring an overabundance of information within its reach, and lead management "simply to bury the shareholders in an avalanche of trivial information—a result that is hardly conducive to informed decisionmaking." It further explained that to fulfill the materiality requirement "there must be a substantial likelihood that the disclosure of the omitted fact would have been viewed by the reasonable investor as having significantly altered the 'total mix' of information made available. . . ."

As we clarify today, materiality depends on the significance the reasonable investor would place on the withheld or misrepresented information. Because the standard of materiality we have adopted differs from that used by both courts below, we remand the case for reconsideration.

We turn to the question of reliance and the fraud-on-the-market theory. Succinctly put:

The fraud on the market theory is based on the hypothesis that, in an open and developed securities market, the price of a company's stock is determined by the available material information regarding the company and its business. . . . Misleading statements will therefore defraud purchasers of stock even if the purchasers do not directly rely on the misstatements. . . The causal connection between the defendants' fraud and the plaintiffs' purchase of stock in such a case is no less significant than in a case of direct reliance on misrepresentations.

Our task is to consider whether it was proper for the courts below to apply a rebut-

table presumption of reliance, supported in part by the fraud-on-the-market theory.

Basic complains that the fraud-on-the-market theory effectively eliminates the requirement that a plaintiff asserting a claim under Rule 10b-5 prove reliance. We agree that reliance is an element of a Rule 10b-5 cause of action. Reliance provides the requisite causal connection between a defendant's misrepresentation and a plaintiff's injury. There is, however, more than one way to demonstrate the causal connection. Indeed, we previously have dispensed with a requirement of positive proof of reliance, where a duty to disclose material information had been breached, concluding that the necessary nexus between the plaintiffs' injury and the defendant's wrongful conduct has been established. *Affiliated Ute Citizens* v. *United States* (1972).

The modem securities markets, literally involving millions of shares changing hands daily, differ from the face-to-face transactions contemplated by early fraud cases, and our understanding of Rule 10b-5's reliance requirement must encompass these differences.

In face-to-face transactions, the inquiry into an investor's reliance upon information is into the subjective pricing of that information by that investor. With the presence of a market, the market is interposed between seller and buyer and, ideally, transmits information to the investor in the processed form of a market price. Thus the market is performing a substantial part of the valuation process performed by the investor in a face-to-face transaction. The market is acting as the unpaid agent of the investor, informing him that given all the information available to it, the value of the stock is worth the market price.

Presumptions typically serve to assist courts in managing circumstances in which direct proof, for one reason or another, is rendered difficult. The courts below accepted a presumption, created by the fraud-on-the-market theory and subject to rebuttal by Basic, that persons who had traded Basic shares had done so in reliance on the integrity of the price set by the market, but because of Basic's material misrepresentations that price had been fraudulently depressed. Requiring a plaintiff to show a speculative state of facts, *i.e.*, how he would have acted if omitted material information had been disclosed, or if the misrepresentation had not been made, would place an unnecessarily unrealistic evidentiary burden on the Rule 10b-5 plaintiff who has traded on an impersonal market.

The presumption of reliance employed in this case is consistent with, and by facilitating Rule 10b-5 litigation, supports the congressional policy embodied in the 1934 Act. In drafting that Act, Congress expressly relied on the premise that securities markets are affected by information, and enacted legislation to facilitate an investor's reliance on the integrity of those markets. . . . The presumption is also supported by common sense and probability. Recent empirical studies have tended to confirm Congress' premise that the market price of shares traded on well-developed markets reflects all publicly available information, and hence, any material misrepresentations. It has been noted that "it is hard to imagine that there ever is a buyer or seller who does not rely on market integrity. Who would knowingly roll the dice in a crooked crap game?" An investor who buys or sells stock at the price set by the market does so in reliance on the integrity of that price. Because most publicly available information is reflected in market price, an investor's reliance on any public material misrepresentations, therefore, may be presumed for purposes of a Rule 10b-5 action.

The Court of Appeals found that Basic "made public, material misrepresentations and Levinson sold Basic stock in an impersonal, efficient market. Thus Levinson and the other shareholders have established the threshold facts for proving their loss." The court acknowledged that Basic may rebut proof of the elements giving rise to the presumption, or show that the misrepresentation in fact did not lead to a distortion of price or that a shareholder traded or would have traded despite his knowing the statement was false.

Any showing that severs the link between the alleged misrepresentation and either the price received (or paid) by the plaintiff, or his decision to trade at a fair market price, will be sufficient to rebut the presumption of reliance. For example, if Basic could show that "the market makers" were privy to the truth about the merger discussions here with Combustion, and thus that the market price would not have been affected by their misrepresentations, the causal connection could be broken: the basis for finding that the fraud had been transmitted through market price would be gone. Similarly, if, despite Basic's allegedly fraudulent attempt to manipulate market price, news of the merger discussions credibly entered the market and dissipated the effects of the misstatements, those who traded Basic shares after the corrective statements would have no direct or indirect connection with the fraud. Basic also could rebut the presumption of reliance as to shareholders who would have divested themselves of their Basic shares without relying on the integrity of the market. For example, a shareholder who believed that Basic's statements were false and that Basic was indeed engaged in merger discussions, and who consequently believed that Basic stock was artificially underpriced, but sold his shares nevertheless because of other unrelated concerns, *e.g.*, potential antitrust problems, or political pressures to divest from shares of certain businesses, could not be said to have relied on the integrity of a price he knew had been manipulated. . . .

Judgment vacated and remanded to the Court of Appeals.

CASE FOLLOW-UP

This case ought to make it clear that corporate directors may find themselves on the hot seat when they engage in merger negotiations. If they want the merger to be successful, they will keep negotiations totally confidential so that rumors will not increase the price of the stock. An increased price would be harmful to merger negotiations because (1) the price that CEI or some other firm was willing to pay might not look as good if the stock price of the target increased significantly, and (2) the price of the target stock could become so high that CEI could not afford the merger.

In other words, there can be sound business reasons for keeping the negotiations a total secret. Merger negotiations and the damage that may be done to those negotiations are good enough reasons to maintain confidentiality. The SEC and the stock exchanges try to encourage the flow of important information to the public, but the company is not compelled to make a public announcement about merger negotiations unless (1) it is specifically required by the reports it must file periodically, (2) the corporation is trading in its own stock, (3) corporate developments make previously true statements false, or (4) the corporation is responsible for the rumors that have leaked into the marketplace.

Roeder claims that a corporation has an affirmative duty to disclose all material information even if there is no insider trading, no statute or regulation requiring disclosure, and no inaccurate, incomplete, or misleading prior disclosures. The prevailing view, however, is that there is no such affirmative duty of disclosure. *Roeder* v. *Alpha Industries, Inc.,* 814 F.2d 22, 27 (1st Cir. 1987).

Even without an affirmative duty to disclose, if the firm makes any public statement other than "no comment," that statement must be complete and accurate with regard to all material facts.

INSIDER TRADING

It is not out of the question that insider trading accounts for some of the price run-up in the *Basic* case. That was not an issue in the civil action for damages against the firm, but insider trading probably goes undetected in many cases.

If inside traders had been identified, they could have been prosecuted criminally by the Justice Department. As we shall see in the cases that follow, the antifraud provisions of Rule 10b-5 are the main source from which a prohibition of insider trading has been inferred. In addition, two statutes were enacted during the 1980s to strengthen that prohibition. The Insider Trading Sanctions Act of 1984 (ITSA)[23] authorizes the SEC to seek civil penalties from those who have purchased or sold securities using material, nonpublic information or who have tipped others whose transactions occurred on a national securities exchange or through a broker or dealer. The Insider Trading and Securities Fraud Enforcement Act of 1988 (ITSFEA)[24] established tougher civil and criminal penalties for insider trading. The ITSFEA also established liability of "controlling persons"—

those who employed insiders and, through knowing and reckless misconduct, failed to adequately supervise the insider's activities. Finally, the ITSFEA established liability to contemporaneous traders. This means a buyer who purchased stocks in the market at the same time an insider sold shares of the same stock has a cause of action against that insider, even though no direct transaction between the two parties can be traced. Because transactions in stock markets occur anonymously, the ITSFEA eliminates any requirement that a plaintiff prove the stocks he or she purchased were the same stocks the defendant sold. Likewise, the ITSFEA permits the actions of plaintiff sellers against contemporaneous purchasing insiders without the need to establish actual transactional privity between the specific parties.

Contemporaneous traders—those who were trading in the market for the same security and within the same time frame as an insider or a misappropriator—can institute a civil action to recover an amount equivalent to the insider's or misappropriator's profit gained or loss avoided. Misappropriation is a special breed of insider trading that will be discussed in connection with *United States* v. *Carpenter* later in the chapter. The recovery in a civil action may be offset by the amount of profit disgorgement compelled by the SEC.

Bounty hunters—those who provide information leading to the recovery of a penalty by the SEC or the Justice Department—may recover up to 10 percent of the amount of the penalty.

With all the publicity about insider trading, one would probably expect the 1988 Act to define the forbidden conduct, but that is not the case. The framers of this measure feared that a definition would be too constricting and that clever insiders could find their way around it. The Act does address its penalties to those who purchase or sell securities while in possession of material, nonpublic information, but that does not tell the whole story.

The Efficient Capital Market Hypothesis.   Many hardworking investors and professional security analysts dig out material information about a firm's performance potential and legally trade on that information. In a sense, this information is not nonpublic; it is available to anyone who is bright and resourceful enough to put together the pieces in a puzzle. But at the same time, the information is obscure, partial, and conjectural. It is surely not public information in the sense of being headline news, but it is legally available to anyone smart enough to know what to look for and determined enough to find it.

People who engage in this effort provide an immensely valuable service to all other members of the public. Information sleuths in the securities markets are like bargain hunters, whose shrewd shopping and purchasing habits force competitors to reduce prices (which are then made available to all other members of the public). Their informed bargain hunt results in stock purchases and sales. These transactions communicate information to the securities market and result in a price adjustment that is available and beneficial to all.

In efficient capital markets, the price adjustment brought about by the infusion of this information promotes the optimum allocation of scarce capital resources. That, at least, is the efficient capital market hypothesis (ECMH), which states that positive information about innovative firms will make their stock prices increase. In addition, raising capital at minimum cost will become easier for them. That is exactly what is supposed to happen in capitalist economic systems.

If the information about a firm's prospects is negative, however, shareholders will want to sell out; this will send the market price of its stock down. That is what is supposed to happen, too. This firm will have difficulty raising capital, but from a strictly economic point of view, unproductive firms are wasting scarce resources anyway. These firms ought to be dissolved, or taken over, so that the capital they are tying up can be used more productively.

Again, we are talking hypothesis, and that is not necessarily the way of the real world. We cannot explore all arguments to the contrary, but countertheses suggest that the kind of efficiency noted in capital markets with regard to the quick adjustment of stock prices to informational inputs has speculator usefulness only. It says nothing at all about the real economic or productive value of the firms involved. For example, when stock prices "crashed" dramatically in fall 1987, the underlying productive value of those firms remained virtually the same as before.

Efficient Capital Markets and Insiders. Bargain hunters like those just described are much like Raymond L. Dirks, the principal figure in a case you will examine in this chapter. His main role as a securities analyst was to act as an investigative reporter—or a detective. The more he could find out about a firm's prospects, the better he could advise his clients to buy or sell that stock. His duty was to his clients, not to the stockholders of the firm he was investigating.

What the law attempts to do in this area is preserve and encourage the efforts of people like Dirks and other legitimate security analysts. We want to maintain such efforts because we have sufficient confidence in the ECMH to hang on to it until a better explanatory thesis comes along. At the same time, however, the law seeks to punish those who engage in fraud even at the expense of the additional degree of efficiency this fraudulent trading may bring into the market.

And so, the first thing you need to learn about the application of Rule 10b-5 to fraudulent insider trading is that the trader must owe a duty to the stockholders with whom he or she trades. This duty must be breached, and the breach must cause the victim to suffer monetary loss.

The Players. The following is a list of traders who merit the watchful eye of federal enforcers and traders who may be affected by Rule 10b-5 violations.

1. *True insiders.* Corporate employees who come into possession of corporate information (material, nonpublic information) by virtue of their status or position in the firm.

2. *Tipper.* A true insider, or anyone else on this list, who intentionally informs or tips another person regarding the material, nonpublic information.

3. *Tippees.* Recipients of material, nonpublic information. These may be friends, relatives, business associates, or anyone else in whom the tipper chooses to confide. *Raymond L. Dirks* v. *SEC* explores both tipper and tippee liability.

4. *Misappropriators or quasi insiders.* Employees of firms such as investment banking firms, law firms, accounting firms, or printing firms who, in the course of performing their jobs, come into possession of material, nonpublic information belonging to the corporation that employs their firm. For example, an attorney employed by a law firm representing a corporation (a "shark") that is trying to take over a target company might "misappropriate" that information and purchase stock in the target while prices remain relatively low. *United States* v. *Carpenter* explores the application of Rule 10b-5 to misappropriators.

In as concise a statement as we can make of the law pertaining to these parties, they must either disclose the material, nonpublic information in their possession or abstain from purchasing or selling stock of the company that owns that information. *Disclose* and *abstain* are the guts of Rule 10b-5's legal admonition.

In a 1961 SEC decision, *In re Cady, Roberts & Co.*,[25] Rule 10b-5 was found to prohibit a tip by a Curtiss-Wright director to the brokerage firm of which he was a partner. The subject matter of the tip was confidential information that corporate dividends were about to be reduced. At some advantage to itself, the brokerage firm dumped large blocks of Curtiss-Wright stock prior to public announcement of the bad news. As a result of this conduct, the director and his brokerage firm were subjected to SEC sanctions and penalties. Beyond that, the decision inaugurated a new mandate in securities fraud, a mandate applicable to exchange members and to laypeople alike: Disclose or abstain from trading. The SEC cited two important considerations as a basis for its judgment: (1) information intended for corporate purposes should not be treated as a personal emolument by an officer or director, and (2) a situation in which one party takes advantage of such information knowing it to be unavailable to those with whom he or is dealing is inherently unfair.

Hence, unauthorized gain became the first component of the SEC's rationale and inherent unfairness the other. Because the integrity of the securities market could be jeopardized by collaborators/tippees (friends, relatives, and associates on the receiving end of nonpublic market information), as well as by insiders, they were treated as equally culpable.

In applying the rule to cases in which the stock was sold to investors who prior to the purchase were not shareholders, there could be no breach of fiduciary duty. At the time of purchase, those investors were simply outsiders, essentially strangers, who had no special duty to disclose unfavorable news. The SEC evidently believed, however, that, on many other occasions, insiders would likely buy stock from shareholders prior to the announcement of good news and thereby profit from a fiduciary breach. So, for the sake of consistency and due regard for the language of Rule 10b-5 and because the prohibition of unauthorized gain and inherent unfairness were deemed to be adequate justifications in themselves, the commission announced a policy that applied to sales or purchases based on nonpublic, inside information.

A second illustration of fraudulent inside trading by true insiders stems from *SEC* v. *Texas Gulf Sulphur Co.*[26] This case involves purchases of company stock by corporate officers and employees who knew of the firm's discovery of some potentially rich mineral deposits in Canada. These purchases were made prior to publication of the nature and extent of the mineral discovery. In fact, some of the officers who made purchases of TGS stock took part in formulating false and misleading press releases and public announcements relating to the mineral find.

The information involved here is material, nonpublic corporate information, and the corporation had good reason for wanting that information to remain confidential. If news of the discovery had been announced immediately, the price of mineral leases would have skyrocketed. Farmers, ranchers, and other property owners would have held out for more money, and the value of the discovery to TGS would have been significantly diminished. After all, TGS had invested a lot of money in this mineral search, and not only TGS, but also society generally, has a lot to gain by encouraging mineral developers to undertake the risk involved in expending money on exploratory efforts. Such undertakings will not continue to happen unless firms like TGS can make a profit on them.

But, as shown in the *Basic* case, the law does not compel a firm to immediately announce all material, nonpublic information. The firm can remain absolutely silent about merger negotiations (as in *Basic*), or it can remain absolutely silent about mineral discoveries while it buys up as many mineral leases as it can afford. A "no comment" policy is a legal policy.

Two very important lessons from *In re Cady, Roberts & Co.* come immediately to mind, however: (1) If the firm chooses to speak, it cannot legally make a false or misleading statement (or omission) of material fact. (2) If the firm chooses not to speak, insiders must abstain from purchasing or selling company stock.

As important as the *Texas Gulf Sulphur* case was to the development of the law, it is no longer an accurate statement of the Supreme Court's position on Rule 10b-5. TGS proceeded on the assumption that the law compelled information parity, or that Rule 10b-5 was written to compel a level informational playing field. However, the Supreme Court is not guided by the level playing field paradigm. Some traders are always going to be better informed than others, betting that the stock is going up (or down) while the seller (or buyer) is betting just the opposite. The Supreme Court inquires, first, whether the insider owes a duty to the person on the other side of that transaction, and second, whether that transaction breaches the duty and causes a loss to be imposed on the victim.

In the TGS context, the company owed no duty to disclose the mineral discovery to property owners. That relationship was third party, or at arm's length, and the buyer is not expected to divulge the results of its very expensive mineral survey.

The relationship of TGS and its insiders to the shareholders, however, was a fiduciary relationship, a relationship that demanded trust, confidence, and loyalty. This relationship required full and accurate disclosure or abstention from trading in TGS stock by insiders.

In essence, Rule 10b-5 makes a federal crime of the common law of action of deceit, a species of intentional tort. The common law plaintiff-victim must prove that the defendant-wrongdoer was at fault (duty + breach of duty) and that the defendant's fault was the cause of the plaintiff-victim's loss. In the absence of a duty, there cannot possibly be a breach of duty, hence no fault.

The duty that is so important to establish is the fiduciary duty of trust and loyalty that the insider—board member, officer, or other corporate employee—owes to the stockholders. After all, the stockholders own the firm, and they have every reason to expect that the people who work for them will not violate the law in their stock transactions with the owners.

Prior to the 1934 Act, not only was insider trading not a federal crime, but it also was scarcely recognized as common law deceit. In the early decades of this century, most state courts proceeded on the notion that a corporate employee's duty was to the corporate entity and not to its far-flung shareholders individually. With no duty to the shareholders, there could be no breach, hence no tort.

A lot of people liked it this way and viewed inside trade profits as an emolument of office, a salary perk that provided an extra measure of reward for employees who were enterprising enough to create the information to trade on. Even today, some scholars advocate a return to the common law origins (see Henry Manne, *Insider Trading and the Stock Market*) to use insider trading as a means of rewarding risk-taking managers and of making capital markets more informationally efficient.

The first significant insider trading case after *Texas Gulf Sulphur* involved Vincent Chiarella, a mark-up man who worked for a financial printing firm in New York. Using the materials that he saw in his job, he could make a good guess at tender offer targets of major corporations. Because the stock of these targets usually goes up at the announcement of a tender offer, he would buy their stock before the information was public. After the announcement was public and the stock of the target company had leveled off a bit, he would sell. He made about $30,000 in a fourteen-month period. Chiarella was tried in a lower court and convicted of seventeen counts of securities fraud. The Supreme Court, however, held in *Chiarella* v. *United States*[27] that he did not commit securities fraud because

1. Failure to disclose material information before trading is a securities fraud only if there is a *duty to disclose arising from a relationship of trust and confidence between parties to a transaction.*

2. Chiarella was not a corporate insider and received no confidential information from the target companies, and therefore he had no duty to disclose *because mere possession of confidential information does not give rise to a duty to disclose.*

The decision in *Chiarella* was criticized by many legal scholars and other commentators, who suggested that unfair and economically inefficient transactions were being condoned by virtue of a loophole in the securities fraud provisions. Accordingly, the SEC issued Rule 14e-3, which precludes trading by anyone who uses nonpublic information regarding a forthcoming tender offer. Rule 14e-3 only applies to insider trading regarding tender offers and thus essentially creates a two-tiered system of liability. Although anyone who trades by using inside information regarding a prospective tender offer can be held liable under Rule 14e-3, only those who breach a fiduciary duty are liable under Rule 10b-5 for insider trading that uses other (nontender offer related) kinds of nonpublic information.

A more recent case involves Raymond L. Dirks, the securities analyst we spoke of earlier. His case relies on *Chiarella* and further refines the law in this area.

Raymond L. Dirks v. SEC

463 U.S. 646 (1983)

POWELL, JUSTICE

* * *

In 1973, Dirks was an officer of a New York broker-dealer firm who specialized in providing investment analysis of insurance company securities to institutional investors. On March 6, Dirks received information from Ronald Secrist, a former officer of Equity Funding of America. Secrist alleged that the assets of Equity Funding, a diversified corporation primarily engaged in selling life insurance and mutual funds, were vastly overstated as the result of fraudulent corporate practices. Secrist also stated that various regulatory agencies had failed to act on similar charges made by Equity Funding employees. He urged Dirks to verify the fraud and disclose it publicly.

Dirks decided to investigate the allegations. He visited Equity Funding's headquarters in Los Angeles and interviewed several officers and employees of the corporation. The senior management denied any wrongdoing, but certain corporation employees corroborated the charges of fraud. Neither Dirks nor his firm owned or traded any Equity Funding stock, but throughout his investigation he openly discussed the information he had obtained with a number of clients and investors. Some of these persons sold their holdings of Equity Funding securities, including five investment advisers who liquidated holdings of more than $16 million.

While Dirks was in Los Angeles, he was in touch regularly with William Blundell, *The Wall Street Journals* Los Angeles bureau chief. Dirks urged Blundell to write a story on the fraud allegations. Blundell did not believe, however, that such a massive fraud could go undetected and declined to write the story. He feared that publishing such damaging hearsay might be libelous.

During the two-week period in which Dirks pursued his investigation and spread word of Secrist's charges, the price of Equity Funding stock fell from $26 per share to less than $15 per share. This led the New York Stock Exchange to halt trading on March 27. Shortly thereafter, California insurance authorities impounded Equity Funding's records and uncovered evidence of the fraud. Only then did the Securities and Exchange Commission (SEC) file a complaint against Equity Funding and only then, on April 2, did the *Wall Street Journal* publish a front-page story based largely on information assembled by Dirks. Equity Funding immediately went into receivership.

The SEC began an investigation into Dirks' role in the exposure of the fraud. After a hearing by an administrative law judge, the SEC found that Dirks had aided and abetted violations of § 17(a) of the Securities Act of 1933, . . . §10(b) of the Securities Exchange Act of 1934 . . . and SEC Rule 10b-5 . . . by repeating the allegations of fraud to members of the investment community who later sold their Equity Funding stock. The SEC concluded: "Where 'tippees'—regardless of their motivation or occupation—come into possession of material 'information that they know is confidential and know or should know came from a corporate insider,' they must either publicly disclose that information or refrain from trading."

* * *

In view of the importance to the SEC and to the securities industry of the question presented by this case, we [decided to hear the case]. We now reverse.

In the seminal case of *In re Cady, Roberts & Co.*, 40 S.E.C. 907 (1961), the SEC recognized that the common law in some jurisdictions imposes on "corporate 'insiders,' particularly officers, directors, or controlling stockholders" an "affirmative duty of disclosure . . . when dealing in securities." The SEC found that not only did breach of this common-law duty also establish the elements of a Rule 10b-5 violation, but that individuals other than corporate insiders could be obligated either to disclose material nonpublic information before trading or to abstain from trading altogether. In *Chiarella*, we accepted the two elements set out in *Cady, Roberts* for establishing a Rule 10b-5 violation: "(i) the existence of a relationship affording access to inside information intended to be available only for a corporate purpose, and (ii) the unfairness of allowing a corporate insider to take advantage of that information by trading without disclosure." In examining whether Chiarella had an obligation to disclose or abstain, the Court found that there is no general duty to disclose before trading on material nonpublic information, and held that "a duty to disclose under §10(b) does not arise from the mere possession of nonpublic market information." Such a duty arises rather from the existence of a fiduciary relationship. We were explicit in *Chiarella* in saying that there can be no duty to disclose where the person who has traded on inside information "was not [the corporation's] agent . . . was not a fiduciary, [and] was not a person to whom the sellers [of the securities] had placed their trust and confidence." 445 U.S. at 232.

★ ★ ★

In effect, the SEC's theory of tippee liability in both cases appears rooted in the idea that the antifraud provisions require equal information among all traders. This conflicts with the principle set forth in *Chiarella* that only some persons, under some circumstances, will be barred from trading while in possession of material nonpublic information. Judge Wright correctly read our opinion in *Chiarella* as repudiating any notion that all traders must enjoy equal information before trading: "[T]he 'information' theory is rejected. Because the disclose-or-refrain duty is extraordinary, it attaches only when a party has legal obligations other than a mere duty to comply with the general antifraud proscriptions in the federal securities laws." We reaffirm today that "[a] duty [to disclose] arises from the relationship between parties . . . and not merely from one's ability to acquire information because of his position in the market. . . ."

Imposing a duty to disclose or abstain solely because a person knowingly receives material nonpublic information from an insider and trades on it could have an inhibiting influence on the role of market analysts, which the SEC itself recognizes is necessary to the preservation of a healthy market.

★ ★ ★

And for Rule 10b-5 purposes, the insider's disclosure is improper only where it would violate his *Cady, Roberts* duty. Thus, a tippee assumes a fiduciary duty to the shareholders of a corporation not to trade on material nonpublic information only when the insider has breached his fiduciary duty to the shareholders by disclosing the information to the tippee and the tippee knows or should have known that there has been a breach. . . .

★ ★ ★

In determining whether a tippee is under an obligation to disclose or abstain, it thus is necessary to determine whether the insider's "tip" constituted a breach of the insider's fiduciary duty. . . . Whether disclosure is a breach of duty therefore depends in large part on the purpose of the disclosure. This standard was identified by the SEC itself in *Cady, Roberts*: a purpose of the securities laws was to eliminate "use of inside information for personal advantage." Thus, the test is whether the insider personally will benefit, directly or indirectly, from his disclosure. Absent some personal gain, there has been no breach of duty to stockholders. And absent a breach by the insider, there is no derivative breach. . . .

Under the inside-trading and tipping rules set forth above, we find that there was no actionable violation by Dirks. It is undisputed that Dirks himself was a stranger to Equity Funding, with no pre-existing fiduciary duty to its shareholders. He took no action, directly or indirectly, that induced the shareholders or officers of Equity Funding to repose trust or confidence in him. There was no expectation by Dirks' sources that he would keep their information in confidence. Nor did Dirks misappropriate or illegally obtain the information about Equity Funding. Unless the insiders breached their *Cady, Roberts* duty to shareholders in disclosing the nonpublic information to Dirks, he breached no duty when he passed it on to investors as well as to the *Wall Street Journal*.

It is clear that neither Secrist nor the other Equity Funding employees violated their *Cady, Roberts* duty to the corporation's shareholders by providing information to Dirks. The tippers received no monetary or personal benefit for revealing Equity Funding's secrets, nor was their purpose to make a gift of valuable information to Dirks. As the facts of this case clearly indicate, the tippers were motivated by a desire to expose the fraud. In the absence of a breach of duty to shareholders by the insiders, there was no derivative breach by Dirks. Dirks therefore could not have been "a participant after the fact in [an] insider's breach of a fiduciary duty."

We conclude that Dirks, in the circumstances of this case, had no duty to abstain from use of the inside information that he obtained. The judgment of the Court of Appeals therefore is

Reversed.

Justice Blackmun, with whom Justice Brennan and Justice Marshall join, dissenting.

The Court today takes still another step to limit the protections provided investors by §10(b) of the Securities Exchange Act of 1934. . . . The device employed in this case engrafts a special motivational requirement on the fiduciary duty doctrine. This innovation excuses a knowing and intentional violation of an insider's duty to shareholders if the insider does not act from a motive of personal gain. Even on the extraordinary facts of this case, such an innovation is not justified.

CASE FOLLOW-UP

A major area of Supreme Court scrutiny in federal securities law has been tippee liability. The Supreme Court has narrowed its definition of this liability since the *Texas Gulf Sulphur* decision. *Tippee liability* exists when the tippee trades on material, nonpublic information in breach of the duty to disclose. The duty of the tippee is derived from the tipper's duty. Whether the tip violates a fiduciary duty to the shareholders depends on the purpose of the tip. The test, then, is whether the tipper will benefit directly or indirectly. If there is no personal gain, there is no breach of duty, hence no breach of a derivative duty by the tippee. However, if the tipper has breached a fiduciary duty in disclosing information to the tippee and if the tippee knows or has reason to know of the breach, the tippee falls within the disclose-or-abstain-from-trading rule.

Contrary to the prevailing view, *United States* v. *Carpenter* does not involve yuppies at all. Instead, it is a story about yippees—young indicted professionals. This case was expected to be a test of the misappropriation theory of inside trading. A misappropriator differs from a true insider in that the misappropriator does not breach a duty toward the shareholder with whom he or she trades. In fact, a misappropriator is not employed by the firm in which stock is traded and does not owe a duty to the shareholders of that firm. That was the basis for the outcome in *Chiarella* v. *United States*.

You will see a different result here for reasons that are important to explore. The misappropriator does breach a duty, but that breach is with, for example, Corporation *A*. On the basis of the material, nonpublic information gained (or stolen) there, the misappropriator trades in the stock of Corporation *B*. These stockholders bear the loss, but the question is whether they can recover their losses from the misappropriator because the misappropriator breached no duty to them.

In this case, you will read Justice White's opinion, but it says nothing of consequence because the Court split 4–4, which has the effect of affirming the court below. The real work, then, begins with your study of the appellate court opinion.

Carpenter v. *United States*
484 U.S. 19 (1987)

WHITE, JUSTICE

In 1981, Winans became a reporter for the *Wall Street Journal* (the Journal) and in the summer of 1982 became one of the two writers of a daily column, "Heard on the Street." That column discussed selected stocks or groups of stocks, giving positive and negative information about those stocks and taking "a point of view with respect to investment in the stocks that it reviews." Winans regularly interviewed corporate executives to put together interesting perspectives on the stocks that would be highlighted in upcoming columns, but, at least for the columns at issue here, none contained corporate inside information or any "hold for release" information. Because of the "Heard" column's perceived quality and integrity, it had the potential of affecting the price of the stocks which it examined. The District Court concluded on the basis of testimony presented at trial that the "Heard" column "does have an impact on the market, difficult though it may be to quantify in any particular case."

The official policy and practice at the Journal was that prior to publication, the contents of the column were the Journal's confidential information. Despite the rule, with which Winans was familiar, he entered into a scheme in October 1983 with Peter Brant and petitioner Felis, both connected with the Kidder Peabody brokerage firm in New York City, to give them advance information as to the timing and contents of the "Heard" column. This permitted Brant and Felis and another conspirator, David Clark, a client of Brant, to buy or sell based on the probable impact of the column on the market. Profits were to be shared. The conspirators agreed that the scheme would not affect the journalistic purity of the "Heard" column, and the District Court did not find that the contents of any of the articles were altered to further the profit potential of petitioners' stock-trading scheme. Over a four-month period, the brokers made prepublication trades on the basis of information given them by

Winans about the contents of some 27 "Heard" columns. The net profits from these trades were about $690,000.

In November 1983, correlations between the "Heard" articles and trading in the Clark and Felis accounts were noted at Kidder Peabody and inquiries began. Brant and Felis denied knowing anyone at the Journal and took steps to conceal the trades. Later, the Securities and Exchange Commission began an investigation. Questions were met by denials both by the brokers at Kidder Peabody and by Winans at the Journal. As the investigation progressed, the conspirators quarreled, and on March 29, 1984, Winans and Carpenter went to the SEC and revealed the entire scheme. This indictment and a bench trial followed. Brant, who had pled guilty under a plea agreement, was a witness for the Government.

The District Court found, and the Court of Appeals agreed, that Winans had knowingly breached a duty of confidentiality by misappropriating prepublication information regarding the timing and contents of the "Heard" columns, information that had been gained in the course of his employment under the understanding that it would not be revealed in advance of publication and that if it were, he would report it to his employer. It was this appropriation of confidential information that underlay both the securities laws and mail and wire fraud counts. With respect to the §10(b) charges, the courts below held that the deliberate breach of Winans' duty of confidentiality and concealment of the scheme was a fraud and deceit on the Journal. Although the victim of the fraud, the Journal, was not a buyer or seller of the stocks traded in or otherwise a market participant, the fraud was nevertheless considered to be "in connection with" a purchase or sale of securities within the meaning of the statute and the rule. The courts reasoned that the scheme's sole purpose was to buy and sell securities at a profit based on advance information of the column's contents. The courts below rejected petitioners' submission, which is one of the two questions presented here, that criminal liability could not be imposed on petitioners under Rule 10b-5 because "the newspaper is the only alleged victim of fraud and has no interest in the securities traded."

In affirming the mail and wire fraud convictions, the Court of Appeals ruled that Winans had fraudulently misappropriated "property" within the meaning of the mail and wire fraud statutes and that its revelation had harmed the Journal. It was held as well that the use of the mail and wire services had a sufficient nexus with the scheme to satisfy §§1341 and 1343. The petition for certiorari challenged these conclusions.

The Court is evenly divided with respect to the convictions under the securities laws and for that reason affirms the judgment below on those counts. For the reasons that follow, we also affirm the judgment with respect to the mail and wire fraud convictions.

United States v. Carpenter
791 F.2d 1024 (2d Cir. 1986)

PIERCE, CIRCUIT JUDGE
We do not say that merely using information not available or accessible to others gives rise to a violation of Rule 10b-5. That theory of 10b-5 liability has been rejected. See *Chiarella* (rejecting "parity of information" theory), (rejecting "access to information" theory). There are disparities in knowledge and the availability thereof at many levels of market

functioning that the law does not presume to address. However, the critical issue is found in the district judge's careful distinction between "information" and "conduct." . . . Obviously, one may gain a competitive advantage in the marketplace through conduct constituting skill, foresight, industry and the like. . . . But one may not gain such advantage by conduct constituting secreting, stealing, purloining or otherwise misappropriating material nonpublic information in breach of an employer-imposed fiduciary duty of confidentiality. Such conduct constitutes chicanery, not competition; foul play, not fair play. Indeed, underlying section 10(b) and the major securities laws generally is the fundamental promotion of " 'the highest ethical standards . . .' in every facet of the securities industry." . . .

. . . Winans "misappropriated—stole, to put it bluntly—valuable nonpublic information entrusted to him in the utmost confidence." *Chiarella* (Burger, C.J., dissenting). The information misappropriated here was the *Journal's* own confidential schedule of forthcoming publications. It was the advance knowledge of the timing and content of these publications, upon which appellants, acting secretively, reasonably expected to and did realize profits in securities transactions. Since section 10(b) has been found to proscribe fraudulent trading by insiders or outsiders, such conduct constituted fraud and deceit, as it would had Winans stolen material nonpublic information from traditional corporate insiders or quasi-insiders. Felis' liability as a tippee derives from Winans' liability given the district court's finding of the requisite scienter on Felis' part.

Nor is there any doubt that this "fraud and deceit" was perpetrated "upon a[ny] person" under section 10(b) and Rule 10b-5. It is sufficient that the fraud was committed upon Winans' employer. See *Materia* (printing press employee liable for fraud upon employer); *Newman* (investment banking employees liable principally for "sullying the reputations" of their employers); *Musella* (office manager liable for sullying reputation of law firm). Appellants Winans, and Felis and Carpenter by their complicity, perpetrated their fraud "upon" the *Wall Street Journal*, sullying its reputation and thereby defrauding it "as surely as if they took [its] money."

As to the "in connection with" standard, the use of the misappropriated information for the financial benefit of the defendants and to the financial detriment of those investors with whom appellants traded supports the conclusion that appellants' fraud was "in connection with" the purchase or sale of securities under section 10(b) and Rule 10b-5. We can deduce reasonably that those who purchased or sold securities without the misappropriated information would not have purchased or sold, at least at the transaction prices, had they had the benefit of that information. Certainly the protection of investors is the major purpose of section 10(b) and Rule 10b-5. Further, investors are endangered equally by fraud by non-inside misappropriators as by fraud by insiders.

Appellants correctly point out that "not every instance of financial unfairness constitutes fraudulent activity under Section 10(b)," that the "misappropriation theory" requires a nexus between the duty and the federal securities regulatory scheme. Here, however, the misappropriated information regarding the timing and content of certain *Journal* columns had "no value whatsoever [to appellants] except 'in connection with' [their] subsequent purchase[s] [and sales] of securities." The "sole purpose" of the scheme was to purchase and sell securities, and thereby virtually to "reap instant no-risk profits in the stock market." Indeed, given the breadth of the "in connection with" standard, appellants' argument to the contrary seems frivolous.

Appellants argue that it is anomalous to hold an employee liable for acts that his employer could lawfully commit. Admittedly, the employers in *Newman* were investment banks that would be barred by federal securities laws from trading in securities of their clients, while in the present case the *Wall Street Journal* or its parent, Dow Jones Company, might perhaps lawfully disregard its own confidentiality policy by trading in the stock of companies to be discussed in forthcoming articles. But a reputable newspaper, even if it could lawfully do so, would be unlikely to undermine its own valued asset, its reputation, which it surely would do by trading on the basis of its knowledge of forthcoming publications. Although the employer may perhaps lawfully destroy its own reputation, its employees should be and are barred from destroying their employer's reputation by misappropriating their employer's informational property. Appellants' argument that this distinction would be unfair to employees illogically casts the thief and the victim in the same shoes.... Here, appellants, constrained by the employer's confidentiality policy, could not lawfully trade by fraudulently violating that policy, even if the Journal, the employer imposing the policy, might not be said to defraud itself should it make its own trades.

Thus, because of his duty of confidentiality to the *Journal*, defendant Winans—and Felis and Carpenter, who knowingly participated with him—had a corollary duty, which they breached, under section 10(b) and Rule 10b-5, to abstain from trading in securities on the basis of the misappropriated information or to do so only upon making adequate disclosure to those with whom they traded.

The district court properly found that defendants had adequate notice of the illegality of their scheme.... They clearly treaded closely enough along proscribed lines for the district court to find that they had adequate notice of the illegality of their acts.

Finally, we do not agree with the position ... that the district court's decision portends First Amendment infringements. The confidentiality restrictions stem from the *Wall Street Journal* and Dow Jones company rules, not from any action by the government. Moreover, we cannot see how the convictions will chill free speech. If Winans had respected his employer's reasonable confidentiality policy, he would have had nothing to fear by publishing his "Heard" columns. Indeed, where a columnist uses his position to profit in transactions, at least one court has held that he may be compelled to disclose to his readers his potential financial stake in the impact of his columns.

CASE FOLLOW-UP

Why does it make a difference that the Supreme Court divided 4–4 on the misappropriation issue since it upheld the convictions on the mail and wire fraud charges? Stock traders cannot recover damages based on violation of the Mail and Wire Fraud Act, but they can recover damages based on 10b-5. If the Supreme Court had affirmed the 10b-5 conviction, that would have sent a clear message to lower courts that the misappropriation theory was a legitimate basis

of support for civil damage actions.

This point is essentially moot since the passage of the Insider Trading and Securities Fraud Enforcement Act of 1988. As we related earlier in our discussion of this Act, the right of action for contemporaneous traders is specifically intended to overturn court cases that have precluded recovery by plaintiffs where the defendants' violation is premised on the misappropriation theory.

The mail and wire fraud conviction that the Supreme Court upheld did not add a lot to the law on that subject. Basically, it stands for the proposition that property rights, such as publication dates and financial information that was misappropriated by the defendants from the *Wall Street Journal*, fall within the purview of the statute's definition of property. This part of the Supreme Court's opinion further concluded that the conduct of the defendants produced harm or injury and that this outcome was facilitated by the use of interstate mail and wire services.

RULE 10b-5 LIABILITY: ELEMENTS OF VIOLATION IN SUMMARY

1. *Transactions covered.* Rule 10b-5 applies to all securities transactions whether the securities are registered with the SEC, are traded on a national securities exchange or over-the-counter, or are private transactions. The only qualification is that the transaction involve interstate commerce, and this qualification is construed very broadly by the courts.

2. *Misrepresentation or deceptive omission of a fact.* If misrepresentations are made to a purchaser or seller of securities, they must be misrepresentations of fact, as opposed to opinions. If there is an omission, it must be one of fact.

3. *Materiality.* The misrepresented or undisclosed fact must be material to the purchaser's or seller's decision. The basic test of materiality is whether a reasonable person would attach importance to the fact in question in making a decision as to the securities in the transaction.

4. *Reliance.* If importance is attached to the fact, some courts have said that there must be actual reliance on the material fact by the investor. Whether reliance on the material fact is an independent element of the cause of action or whether it is assumed that reliance follows more or less automatically from material facts depends on the court applying the rule. With regard to omissions, reliance is presumed if the omission is material.

5. *Purchase and sale required.* The rule covers only deceptive transactions that occur in connection with the purchase or sale of a security by the plaintiff. The purpose of this requirement is to prevent bothersome litigation because plaintiffs might otherwise bring Rule 10b-5 actions simply to use the liberal federal discovery rules to disrupt a defendant's business.

6. *Scienter* (an intent to do wrong). Rule 10b-5 itself does not mention the word *intent*, but an element of common law fraud is *scienter*, or guilty knowledge or an intent to do wrong.

In 1976, the Supreme Court attempted an answer to the question of intent in *Ernst & Ernst* v. *Hochfelder*,[28] in which it seemed to say that some form of intent to deceive was required. In this case, the defendant accounting firm audited the books of a small securities firm. The president of the investment firm engaged in a massive fraud and invested some of the customers' money in his own "escrow accounts"; in reality, he embezzled the funds. To prevent detection of this fraud, the president had a firm rule that no mail addressed to him could be opened by any other person. No reports of the special escrow accounts ever showed up in the financial statements prepared by the defendant. After the fraudulent scheme was discovered, the injured clients of the securities firm sued the auditors, Ernst & Ernst. The plaintiff alleged that because the audit failed to disclose the fraudulent scheme, the auditors were guilty of aiding and abetting the fraud. The Supreme Court found the defendants not guilty on the basis that there would be no liability unless the plaintiff could show more than negligence; that is, mere negligence was not sufficient to state a cause of action under Rule 10b-5.

Perhaps the best interpretation of the *Hochfelder* decision is to say that, by the use of the term *scienter* in the opinion, the Court meant that 10b-5 liability cannot be predicated on a showing of mere negligence.[29] Some scholars have suggested that the imposition of 10b-5 liability should be based on a showing of reckless or knowing behavior. This standard is severer than negligence, yet not so strict as to require the allegation and proof of actual intent.

7. *Who is a proper defendant?* Rule 10b-5 was certainly adopted with a view to its application to corporate officers, directors, and other employees—true insiders. The rule has been extended now to cover tippees and misappropriators as well.

SECTION 16 AND LIABILITY FOR SHORT-SWING PROFITS ON INSIDER TRANSACTIONS

Section 16 of the 1934 Act explicitly creates liability for insiders who realize profits on the short-term purchase and sale of their corporation's securities. Section 16 applies to all companies whose equity securities are registered under Section 12 of the Act. Section 16(a) requires any person who beneficially owns 10 percent or more of a registered class of equity securities and every insider (defined as every officer or director of a covered corporation) to file a report with the SEC at the time of attaining the status of an insider and at the end of every month when securities of that corporation are purchased. Because a large number of insiders have failed to meet the filing requirements of 16(a) that are triggered by intermittent changes in status or insider acquisition or sale of securities, the SEC in 1991 began to require insiders to file an additional annual form in which any reporting omissions must be remedied. Because this new form, referred to as Form 5, must be submitted by insiders every year, both inadvertent and intentional failures to report occasional transactions in relevant securities are less likely to slip through bureaucratic cracks. Section 16(b) provides that any profit made by an insider by the (i) purchase and sale, or (ii) sale and purchase of an equity security within six months belongs to the corporation.

The section, in effect, creates a presumption that any purchase or sale by an insider within six months is made on the basis of inside information and should be prohibited. The statute does not give any guidance as to how a profit should be calculated. Courts often seem to arbitrarily match purchases and sales so as to achieve the maximum profit. Some courts have held that any loss incurred during the six-month period cannot be set off against the profit to reduce it. Consider the following situation:[30]

- Day 1 An insider owns one hundred shares of stock.
- Day 2 She purchases ten shares at $7 per share.
- Day 3 She sells ten shares at $5 per share.
- Day 4 She purchases ten shares at $3 per share.
- Day 5 She sells ten shares at $1 per share.

The result of these transactions is to leave her still owning one hundred shares of stock. But by matching two of the transactions—the purchase at $3 and the sale at $5—a profit was realized. It does not matter that she paid $100 for the additional stock and received $60 from her sales, thus appearing to suffer a loss of $40.

Section 16(b) is a strong statement of the law prohibiting insider trading on material information. The best way to balance the desire of management to trade in their corporation's stock with the strong policy statement in Section 16 is for the board to adopt stock compensation schemes that are filed with the SEC. Any purchase or sale by an insider as defined in the 1934 Act should be according to a regular plan. But for members of management not in the defined group of insiders, when can they trade? This question can best be answered by a close examination of the elements of a Rule 10b-5 violation.

REGULATION OF THE SECURITIES MARKETS AND BROKER-DEALERS

The 1934 Act provides that the SEC shall have the primary responsibility to regulate the securities markets and broker-dealers. There are three primary markets for the exchange of securities. The first is the market on the formal and established security exchanges, such as the NYSE and the regional stock exchanges. The second is the over-the-counter market. These are much less formal exchanges, but the prices of some of the securities sold in this market are reported to the Dow Jones financial news reporting service and are thus available to establish something of a national market. The third is the market established by the very large institutions that deal with one another in security exchanges.

The 1934 Act provides for the registration with the SEC of all broker-dealers who undertake to sell securities in interstate commerce. A *broker* is a person engaged in the business of effecting transactions in securities for the accounts of others. The regulation of broker-dealers and the regulation of securities markets are, in reality, a shared responsibility. The 1934 Act allows extensive self-regulation of security exchange members' activities and business practices. Thus, the NYSE and the NASD have a substantial amount of authority to regulate their members.

An important function of the 1934 Act is to compel stockbrokers to deal fairly with their clients. If a broker engages in fraudulent conduct toward a client, the Act permits a client to file suit against the broker to recover losses caused by the fraud. That was the situation the court faced in your next case.

The McMahons alleged that their Shearson broker violated Section 10(b) of the Act. Specifically, the McMahons argued that their broker had defrauded them by engaging in the practice of *churning*, or trading excessively in the stock of a client mainly for the purpose of creating brokerage commissions on the transactions. Other 10(b) allegations were made as well (false statements by the broker and the omission of material facts), and the McMahons expected that this kind of dispute would have to be resolved in a federal court.

Shearson/American Express made a motion in court to have the dispute arbitrated on the basis of customer agreements signed by the McMahons. They argued that even though they actually signed those agreements, the agreements were not enforceable under the 1934 Exchange Act because (1) that would be in plain violation of the policy of the Act expressed in Section 29(a), and (2) they should not be maneuvered by their broker into a position that would weaken their claim under the Act.

The trial court granted the defendant's motion to compel arbitration, and the court of appeals reversed. The Supreme Court reinstated the trial court order for reasons you are about to examine. In *Wilko* v. *Swan*, a 1953 case that the Court cites a number of times, the Court concluded that claims were not arbitrable under the 1933 Securities Act. See if you can understand why the Court changed its mind on this issue.

Shearson/American Express, Inc. v. McMahon
482 U.S. 220 (1987)

O'CONNER, JUSTICE

★ ★ ★

Between 1980 and 1982, respondents Eugene and Julia McMahon, individually and as trustees for various pension and profit-sharing plans, were customers of petitioner Shearson/American Express Inc. (Shearson), a brokerage firm registered with the Securities and Exchange Commission (SEC or Commission). Two customer agreements signed by Julia McMahon provided for arbitration of any controversy relating to the accounts the McMahons maintained with Shearson. . . .

In October 1984, the McMahons filed an amended complaint against Shearson and petitioner Mary Ann McNulty, the registered representative who handled their accounts, in the United States District Court for the Southern District of New York. The complaint alleged that McNulty, with Shearson's knowledge, had violated §10(b) of the [Securities] Exchange Act [of 1934] and Rule 10b-5 by engaging in fraudulent, excessive trading on respondents' accounts and by making false statements and omitting material facts from the advice given to respondents. . . .

Relying on the customer agreements, petitioners moved to compel arbitration of the McMahons' claims pursuant to §3 of the Federal Arbitration Act 9 U.S.C. §3. . . .

* * *

The Federal Arbitration Act provides the starting point for answering the questions raised in this case. The Act was intended to "revers[e] centuries of judicial hostility to arbitration agreements" by "plac[ing] arbitration agreements 'upon the same footing as other contracts.'" The Arbitration Act accomplishes this purpose by providing that arbitration agreements "shall be valid, irrevocable, and enforceable, save upon such grounds as exist at law or in equity for the revocation of any contract." . . .

* * *

The Arbitration Act, standing alone, therefore mandates enforcement of agreements to arbitrate statutory claims. . . .

* * *

When Congress enacted the Exchange Act in 1934, it did not specifically address the question of the arbitrability of §10(b) claims. The McMahons contend, however, that congressional intent to require a judicial forum for the resolution of §10(b) claims can be deduced from §29(a) of the Exchange Act, which declares void "[a]ny condition, stipulation, or provision binding any person to waive compliance with any provision of [the Act]."

First, we reject the McMahons' argument that §29(a) forbids waiver of §27 of the Exchange Act. Section 27 provides in relevant part:

The district courts of the United States . . . shall have exclusive jurisdiction of violations of

this title or the rules and regulations thereunder, and of all suits in equity and actions at law brought to enforce any liability or duty created by this title or the rules and regulations thereunder.

The McMahons contend that an agreement to waive this jurisdictional provision is unenforceable because §29(a) voids the waiver of "any provision" of the Exchange Act. The language of §29(a), however, does not reach so far. . . . By its terms, §29(a) only prohibits waiver of the substantive obligations imposed by the Exchange Act. Because §27 does not impose any statutory duties, its waiver does not constitute a waiver of "compliance with any provision" of the Exchange Act under §29(a).

We do not read *Wilko* v. *Swan* (1953), as compelling a different result. In *Wilko*, the Court held that a predispute agreement could not be enforced to compel arbitration of a claim arising under §12(2) of the Securities Act. The basis for the ruling was §14 of the Securities Act, which, like §29(a) of the Exchange Act, declares void any stipulation "to waive compliance with any provision" of the statute. . . . *Wilko* must be understood . . . as holding that the plaintiff's waiver of the "right to select the judicial forum" was unenforceable only because arbitration was judged inadequate to enforce the statutory rights created by §12(2).

* * *

The second argument offered by the McMahons is that the arbitration agreement effects an impermissible waiver of the substantive protections of the Exchange Act. . . . They reason, as do some commentators, that *Wilko* is premised on the belief "that arbitration clauses in securities sales agreements generally are not freely negotiated." According to this view, *Wilko* barred enforcement of predispute agreements because of this frequent inequality of bargaining power, reasoning that Congress intended for §14 generally to ensure that sellers did not "maneuver buyers into a position that might weaken their ability to recover under the Securities Act." The McMahons urge that we should interpret §29(s) in the same fashion.

We decline to give *Wilko* a reading so far at odds with the plain language of §14, or to adopt such an unlikely interpretation of §29(a). . . . Section 29(a) is concerned, not with whether brokers "maneuver[ed customers] into" an agreement, but with whether the agreement "weaken[s] their ability to recover under the [Exchange] Act." The former is grounds for revoking the contract under ordinary principles of contract law; the latter is grounds for voiding the agreement under §29(a).

The other reason advanced by the McMahons for finding a waiver of their §10(b) rights is that arbitration does "weaken their ability to recover under the [Exchange] Act." That is the heart of the Court's decision in *Wilko*, and respondents urge that we should follow its reasoning. *Wilko* listed several grounds why, in the Court's view, the "effectiveness [of the Act's provisions] in application is lessened in arbitration." First, the *Wilko* Court believed that arbitration proceedings were not suited to cases requiring "subjective findings on the purpose and knowledge of an alleged violator." *Wilko* also was concerned that arbitrators must make legal determinations "without judicial instruction on the law," and that

an arbitration award "may be made without explanation of [the arbitrator's] reasons and without a complete record of their proceedings." . . . *Wilko* concluded that in view of these drawbacks to arbitration, §12(2) claims "require[d] the exercise of judicial direction to fairly assure their effectiveness."

★ ★ ★

. . . [T]he mistrust of arbitration that formed the basis for the *Wilko* opinion in 1963 is difficult to square with the assessment of arbitration that has prevailed since that time. This is especially so in light of the intervening changes in the regulatory structure of the securities laws. Even if *Wilko's* assumptions regarding arbitration were valid at the time *Wilko* was decided, most certainly they do not hold true today for arbitration procedures subject to the SEC's oversight authority.

★ ★ ★

We conclude, therefore, that Congress did not intend for §29(a) to bar enforcement of all predispute arbitration agreements. In this case, where the SEC has sufficient statutory authority to ensure that arbitration is adequate to vindicate Exchange Act rights, enforcement does not effect a waiver of "compliance with any provision" of the Exchange Act under §29(a). Accordingly, we hold the McMahons' agreements to arbitrate Exchange Act claims "enforce[able] . . . in accord with the explicit provisions of the Arbitration Act."

CASE FOLLOW-UP

The waiver signed by the McMahons was not a waiver of their protection against a broker's fraud. It simply waived their right to have the broker's obligations to them examined in a federal court. If they can prove

their allegations against Shearson/American Express, they should get an award from the arbitration panel comparable to that which they would have received in court. If the McMahons win, they can enforce the award in court if it is not paid voluntarily by the brokerage firm.

This decision was influenced by *Mitsubishi Motors Corp.* v. *Soler Chrysler-Plymouth*,[31] which compelled the arbitration of antitrust claims arising in an international context. Ironically, the person who authored the *Mitsubishi* opinion, Justice Blackmun, dissented in *Shearson* because he believed that both the 1933 and the 1934 Acts were, in themselves, exceptions to the Federal Arbitration Act. He was concerned that public investors would be thrown into a forum controlled by the securities industry.

CONCLUSION

The federal securities acts are now both just over sixty years old. It wasn't until the late 1960s, however, that strong action was initiated by the SEC, followed by appellate court decisions that seemed to breathe an entirely new life into these laws. Major action affecting the legal environment of business under these laws is still emerging. The law in this area is far from settled, and continued change should be expected. Indeed, major policy makers in government, the academic community, and the private sector continue to make statements that indicate their belief that no government "interference" in the regulation of corporate securities is needed. Others assert that all corporate managers and agents of corporations should be forbidden from trading in the stock of their own corporations. What do you think?

The harm caused by securities fraud is often not directly perceivable by the wrongdoer. Traders in securities markets do not meet face-to-face. The transactions are usually completed through layers of agents and others, with the final trade itself being made by a computer. Many kinds of securities fraud damage traders' confidence in the system of securities markets; this damage may have long-term effects. We believe that law and accompanying moral restraint are vital to this area of the legal environment of business.

REVIEW QUESTIONS AND PROBLEMS

1. The federal securities laws apply, obviously, to certain circumstances involving securities. Define this term and give an example of an investment contract. Why are there securities laws in the legal environment of business? Who is protected by the federal securities laws?

2. A union contract called for an employer-sponsored pension plan and stated that the employer was to make all payments into the plan. To be eligible for a pension, an employee was required to have twenty years of continuous service. An employee who had more than twenty years of service was denied a pension on retirement because of a break in service. He brought suit in Federal District Court, alleging that the union had misrepresented and omitted to state material facts with respect to the value of covered employees' interest in the pension plan and

that such statements and omissions constituted a fraud in connection with the sale of a security in violation of the securities acts. Do you believe the pension plan as described above is a security for purposes of the federal securities acts? Why do you think this employee wanted the pension plan defined as a security? *(International Brotherhood of Teamsters v. Daniel, 99 S.Ct. 790 (1979))*

3. Purchasers of apartments in a cooperative housing project had to buy eighteen shares of stock, at $25 per share, for each room desired. An information bulletin for the project estimated average monthly costs of $23.02 per room. Increased costs during construction resulted in a room cost of $39.68. A group of purchasers seeks damages, reductions in rent, and other relief in federal court. They allege violations of the fraud provisions of the securities laws. The defendant argues that the purchase of the "stock" does not mean the apartment holders have purchased a "security" under the federal law. What result? *(United Housing v. Forman, 421 U.S. 837 (1975))*

4. Issuer, Inc., a New York corporation engaged in retail sales within New York City, was interested in raising $1.6 million in capital. In this connection, it approached through personal letters eighty-eight people in New York, New Jersey, and Connecticut, and then followed up with face-to-face negotiations where it seemed promising to do so. After extensive efforts in which Issuer disclosed all of the information these people requested, nineteen people from the areas purchased Issuer's securities. Issuer did not limit its offer to insiders, their relatives, or wealthy or sophisticated investors. Did this constitute an exempt offering?

5. Scotch whiskey warehouse receipts are being promoted for sale through direct mail and newspaper advertisements. A typical statement contained in such ads reads as follows: "Invest in Scotch Whiskey for Profit. Exceptional Capital Growth Is Possible When You Buy Scotch Whiskey Reserves by the Barrel. Insured Investment for Profit and Growth in Scotch Whiskey." In addition to the phrase "Insured Investment," some ads carried the phrase "insured no loss policy." If a potential investor read a brochure prepared by the promoters, he or she could learn that the investment was not being insured. Instead, the whiskey was insured against loss from fire and cask leakage. The SEC contends that the defendants are violating the 1933 Act by selling unregistered securities and the 1934 Act by using deceptive and fraudulent promotional advertisements. What do you think? *(SEC v. Lundy Associates, 362 F.Supp. 226 (1973))*

6. Whitworth has been charged by Bonanza Corporation with violating the Securities Exchange Act of 1934. Whitworth was formerly the president of Bonanza, but he was ousted as a result of a proxy battle. Bonanza seeks to recover from Whitworth any and all of his short-swing profits. Which of the following would be a valid defense to the charges?

   a. Whitworth is a New York resident, Bonanza was incorporated in New York, and the transactions were all made through the New York Stock Exchange; therefore, interstate commerce was not involved.

   b. Whitworth did not actually make use of any insider information in connection with the various stock transactions in question.

   c. All of the transactions alleged to be in violation of the 1934 Act were purchases made during February 1979, with the corresponding sales made in September 1979.

   d. Whitworth's motivation in selling the stock was solely a result of the likelihood that he would be outset as president of Bonanza.[32]

7. Owners of corporations may propose some issues for action by the other owners at a properly called shareholders' meeting, and these issues must be included in proxy statements that are sent. However, some matters SEC regulations define as inappropriate for shareholder vote. What are these, and why are they excluded?

8. What is a tender offer? How are such offers regulated and why?

9. Oreamuno and Gonzalez are directors of Management Assistants, Inc. With their wives, they own approximately 14 percent of the company's common stock. In August 1966, they learned that corporate earnings would be sharply reduced from earlier figures. This information did not become available to the other shareholders and the investing public until October 18, 1966. In September 1966, Oreamuno sold 28,500 shares of common stock and Gonzalez sold 28,000 shares. The selling price was $23.75 per share; after release of the earnings report, the stock fell to $11 per share. Diamond, another shareholder, now brings a stockholders' derivative suit to recover the difference between the two prices. Neither Diamond nor the corporation purchased any of the shares that were sold. The corporation sustained no loss. Should Diamond's lawsuit be dismissed? Can the purchasers of the stock also bring suit? Do you think this potential double liability is a wise policy? (*Diamond* v. *Oreamuno*, 248 N.E.2d 910 (1969))

ENDNOTES

1. Ratner, *Securities Regulations* 1–3 (1982).
2. See *Hall* v. *Geiger Jones & Co.*, 242 U.S. 539, 550 (1917).
3. Ratner, *supra* note 1, at 202–203.
4. Securities Act of 1933 Section 2(1), 15 U.S.C. Section 77b(1).
5. 328 U.S. 293 (1946).
6. Ratner, *supra* note 1, at 14.
7. *Federal Regulatory Directory*, 455 (1980–1981).
8. *Id.*
9. Securities Act of 1933, 15 U.S.C. Section 2(7).
10. See *Myzel* v. *Fields*, 386 F.2d 718 (8th Cir. 1967); see also *Dupuy* v. *Dupuy*, 5ll F.2d 641 (5th Cir. 1975).
11. *Franklin Savings Bank* v. *Levy*, 551 F.2d 521 (2nd Cir. 1977).
12. Ratner, *supra* note 1, at 54.
13. *Id.* at 44.
14. *Id.* at 80.
15. *Id.*
16. *Id.*
17. *Id.* at 100.
18. Nader, Green, and Seligman, *Taming the Giant Corporation* 80–81 (1976).
19. *Id.* at 81.
20. *Id.*
21. *Id.*
22. 493 A.2d 946 (1985).
23. Pub. L. No. 98–376, 98 Stat. 1264 (1984).
24. Pub. L. No. 100–704, 102 Stat. 4677 (1988).
25. 40 S.E.C. 907 (1961).
26. 401 F.2d 833 (2d Cir. 1968).
27. 445 U.S. 222 (1980).
28. 425 U.S. 986 (1976).
29. See Metzger and Heinty, Hochfelder's Progeny: Implications for Auditors, 63 *Minn. L. Rev.* 79, 86 (1978).
30. From Wolfe and Naffziger, *Legal Perspectives of American Business Associations* 486 (1977).
31. 473 U.S. 614 (1985).
32. Adapted from CPA Exam Law Problem #1, Questions #32 and #27 of the November 1979 exam. This material from Uniform CPA Examination Questions and Unofficial Answers, copyright 1979, by the American Institute of Certified Public Accountants, Inc. is reprinted with permission.

PART FOUR

Classic and Emerging Issues in the Legal Environment of Business

Some legal issues never go away. There are tensions in our society that never seem to be resolved completely. One of the classic issues of the legal environment of business is how an employer treats an employee. What kinds of matters within the corporaion are appropriate for the legal system, and what kinds are better left to management theory, scholars, and public opinion? Chapter 14, on employment law, has been expanded significantly since the second edition because law concerning employment discrimination has expanded so rapidly in the past few years. Chapter 15, on labor law, also presents new material on public sector employment collective bargaining.

Chapter 16, "Environmental Law," presents the federal law that attempts to protect and preserve our natural environment from the pollutants discharged (mostly) by our business corporations. This area of inquiry, however, demands more than just a presentation of the various laws that exist. We offer, therefore, several writings that are more subjective in character than most of the information in this book in order to raise the moral issue of how we should think about and act in our natural environment.

The final chapter presents an overview of some of the basic concepts of international law, but focuses more on business conduct in the international marketplace. Since international laws change continually, we provide discussion of classic and current issues to help the reader identify emerging issues and possible legal solutions.

CHAPTER 14

Employment Law—Discrimination and Equal Opportunity

INTRODUCTION

This chapter explores selected federal employment laws that address issues of fairness and equity in the distribution of social goods and ills, benefits and costs. If it were not for the requirements embodied in these statutes—the Civil Rights Act and the Equal Pay Act—business firms might arguably experience certain cost savings. Reduced expenditures would improve the firms' earning statements analogous to the repeal of pollution control laws. More money would be available for dividends, expansion, research, marketing, and other pursuits. In the short term at least, private-sector firms would show a marked improvement in the efficient or productive use of the shareholders' invested capital. From the private sector's perspective, the additional revenues generated from these savings would, in the long run, contribute to a bigger "pie" for everyone to share—more wealth, more jobs, and a higher material standard of living.

This point of view is not likely to be shared, however, by the beneficiaries of these statutes. Promises of pie-in-the-sky improvements in society's material standard of living are easier to make than they are to keep, and one supposes that many people would prefer a more equitable distribution of jobs and other social goods today even though that may mean reduced expectations for future generations.

These remarks set the stage for the material in this chapter, but you can see, in a larger sense, their application to government control generally. In rough cut, the private sector balances fairness and efficiency by seeking a reduction in regulation and taxation to a level compatible with the Lockean notion of a government limited to that which is necessary to preserve life, liberty, and property.[1] Others insist that employment and related laws should be used to structure a fairer society today, even at the cost of certain economic efficiencies.

An analysis of the text and cases that follow will assist you in making an informed judgment. Do U.S. employment laws go far enough, or do they go too far, in seeking a balance between fairness and efficiency?

Title VII of the 1964 Civil Rights Act[2] is the first major section; it deals comprehensively with the full range of employment problems: discrimination in recruitment, hiring, promotion, termination, and pay based on race, color, religion, national origin, and sex. The Equal Employment Opportunity Commission (EEOC), a five-person, presidentially appointed group, has interpretive, investigative, and enforcement powers under the 1964 Civil Rights Act.

EMPLOYMENT DISCRIMINATION: AN HISTORICAL CONTEXT

A plausible case can be made that the North won the Civil War, but the matter is not free from doubt. The Union was preserved, the Constitution was amended to incorporate the victories of that bitter conflict, and Congress moved to implement the amendments with appropriate legislation. Then a curious chapter in U.S. history began to unfold. In its effort to heal the nation's wounds, the North seems to have lost its energy or staying power and thus lost an opportunity to institutionalize the practice of racial equality.[3]

The year 1876 sealed the fate of Reconstruction. Following the most controversial U.S. presidential election, a Republican-dominated congressional commission confirmed Ohio governor Rutherford B. Hayes's one-vote electoral college margin over the popular vote winner, New York's Democratic governor, Samuel J. Tilden. Hayes then made good on the promise that gained him the White House. Within two months of his inauguration, the last federal troops were marched from Louisiana, and the South resumed a business-as-usual disenfranchisement and domination of blacks.

The U.S. Supreme Court contributed mightily to these efforts. The *Civil Rights Cases*[4] declared unconstitutional Sections 1 and 2 of the 1875 Civil Rights Act forbidding racial discrimination in private-sector facilities such as restaurants, theaters, business establishments, and railroads. A majority of the Court found that Congress was empowered by the Fourteenth Amendment to enact legislation appropriate to enforce its *prohibitory language* only. States were precluded from abridging privileges and immunities of U.S. citizens and were further barred from depriving any person of life, liberty, or property without due process or equal protection of the law. But, the Supreme Court continued, although Congress could legislate to prohibit such unwarranted state action, private citizens were free to discriminate on the basis of race if they chose to do so.

★ ★ ★

Who can say what might have happened in the realm of race relations and employment law had the Court moved differently. We only know that the Court, in fact, endorsed state policies disenfranchising and segregating blacks through literacy tests, poll taxes, Jim Crow laws, and other measures collectively known as the Black Codes. In *Plessy* v. *Ferguson*,[5] the Supreme Court endorsed Louisiana's requirement of "separate but equal" facilities in public transportation. The phrase, borrowed from a pre-Civil War case sanctioning racially segregated public schools in Boston,[6] spread throughout the South and permeated not only transportation facilities but also education and other areas of social and economic life. Again and again in vain, Justice Harlan railed against his brethren on the Court.

> [I]n view of the constitution, in the eye of the law, there is in this country no superior, dominant, ruling class of citizens. There is no caste here. Our constitution is color-blind, and neither knows nor tolerates classes among citizens. In respect of civil rights, all citizens are equal before the law. The humblest is the peer of the most powerful. The law regards man as man, and takes no account of his surroundings or of his color when his civil rights as guaranteed by the supreme law of the land are involved. It is therefore to be regretted that this high tribunal, the final expositor of the fundamental law of the land, has reached the conclusion that it is competent for a state to regulate the enjoyment by citizens of their civil rights solely upon the basis of race. (163 U.S. at 553)

For more than one hundred years, certain Civil War-era statutes lay dormant on the theory that their Fourteenth Amendment basis made them applicable against state action only and not against private action. That view has not endured. In *Jones* v. *Alfred H. Mayer Co.,*[7] the Supreme Court was asked to determine the scope and constitutionality of 42 U.S.C.A. Section 1982. In its original form, section 1982 was part of section 1 of the Civil Rights Act of 1866. The Court held that Section 1 and its derivative, Section 1982, prohibit "all racial discrimination, private as well as public, in the sale or rental of property. . . ." The constitutionality of Section 1982 was upheld on the basis of Congress' power to enact legislation to enforce the Thirteenth Amendment.

TITLE VII AND ITS ENFORCEMENT

This section of the chapter develops the main components of Title VII. Illustrative cases are used for a more complete understanding of the interpretation and implementation of the Act through the administrative and judicial processes. Before we get to an explanation of the substance of Title VII, we examine two important enforcement agencies.

The Equal Employment Opportunity Commission (EEOC), a five-person, presidentially appointed group, has the initial task of *interpreting* Title VII, *investigating* complaints, *settling* the complaints if possible through conference or conciliation, and *enforcing* decisions in the federal courts. Once a complaint has been filed, the commission has exclusive jurisdiction for 180 days. If the matter is not resolved by that time, the injured party may request from the EEOC a "right to sue" letter and then bring a private legal action in federal court.

TITLE VII: COVERAGE

Title VII prohibits employment discrimination based on criteria of race, color, religion, national origin, and sex in hiring, compensation, terms of employment, and discharge. Furthermore, these criteria may not be used to segregate or classify employees or prospects in a way that deprives them of employment opportunities. The Act extends to employers, corporations, partnerships, trusts, individuals, labor unions, and governments of fifteen or more employees engaged in an industry affecting commerce.

Religious organizations may hire on the basis of religion, but not on the basis of race, color, national origin, or sex. The racial policies of state and local governments are not covered by the Act. They are reached through Section 5 of the Fourteenth Amendment,[8] which authorizes Congress to enforce its provisions by appropriate legislation.

Labor unions are covered if they "affect commerce" by maintaining a hiring hall or by having fifteen or more members. Employment agencies, whether they have fifteen employees or not, are covered insofar as their referrals or placement activities are concerned. Colleges, through their placement services and newspaper help-wanted ads, are not, in the generally accepted sense of the term, in the business of procuring employment. If a college, a news organization, or a professional licensing authority, such as a bar or medical association, has fifteen or more employees, however, Title VII will apply to its internal employment relationships.

The following provisions of the 1964 Civil Rights Act, Title VII, have been selected to confirm the principal points we have discussed so far. Title VII is codified at 42 U.S.C. Section 2000e. It has become conventional to cite the less cumbersome section numbers, beginning at Section 701. That practice is followed here.

Discrimination Because of Race, Color, Religion, Sex, or National Origin

§703 (a) It shall be an unlawful employment practice for an employer—

1. to fail or refuse to hire or to discharge any individual, or otherwise to discriminate against any individual with respect to his compensation, terms, conditions, or privileges of employment, because of such individual's race, color, religion, sex, or national origin; or
2. to limit, segregate, or classify his employees or applicants for employment in any way which would deprive or tend to deprive any individual of employment opportunities or otherwise adversely affect his status as an employee, because of such individual's race, color, religion, sex, or national origin

Section 703(d) forbids training programs that discriminate against individuals on the basis of race, color, religion, sex, or national origin, and Section 703(j) relates that no employer shall be required to give any preferential treatment to individuals in protected groups.

THE CIVIL RIGHTS ACT OF 1991

During the 1980s, both case decisions interpreting Title VII and the implementation of civil rights policies led to some significant changes in the civil rights laws. A number of these changes were restrictive ones, in which the conservative administrations under Presidents Reagan and Bush, as well as increasingly conservative courts, attempted to curtail the application of civil rights doctrines that were viewed as either excessive or comprehensive, depending on the viewer's philosophy and political bent.

Largely in response to these incursions into Title VII, Congress passed the Civil Rights Act of 1991. Particular elements of the 1991 Act are discussed in this chapter because they are relevant to particular discussions throughout. As an overview, it may be helpful at this point to summarize its most crucial effects. The Civil Rights Act of 1991 is aimed at achieving the following ends:

1. To provide remedies for intentional discrimination and sexual harassment in the workplace.

2. To overrule the decision in *Wards Cove Packing Co.* v. *Atonio*[9] (as discussed on p. 601).

3. To provide guidelines for the adjudication of disparate impact discrimination suits (as discussed on p. 601).

4. To respond to a number of Supreme Court decisions that expanded statutory civil rights protections "in order to provide adequate protection to victims of discrimination."

TITLE VII: AFFIRMATIVE ACTION AND THE PROBLEM OF REVERSE DISCRIMINATION

Affirmative action programs are designed to overcome the effects of historical discrimination against women, minorities, and other disadvantaged groups. Basically, affirmative action permits firms to give an employment or promotion advantage to women or members of a minority group who meet the minimum requirements of the applicant pool. For example, if, on a relevant and credible performance test for a particular job, a minimally acceptable score is 25 out of 30, a woman or member of a minority who scores 25 may be given the job or promotion in preference to a white male who scores higher. This may initially have a negative impact on the efficiency of the firm's performance, but with thorough job training programs, that will not necessarily be the case in the long term.

Prior to an examination of our next case, *Johnson* v. *Santa Clara County*, it will be helpful to focus on the Supreme Court's analysis of a comparable affirmative action plan in *Steelworkers of America* v. *Weber*.[10] *Weber* is the first case to give rise to the phrase "reverse discrimination." In view of the statute's prohibition against racial discrimination, it gave voice to an apparent inconsistency: Supreme Court approval of a racially discriminatory employment training program—a collectively bargained program that discriminated against white laborers to help make up for years of discrimination against black laborers. In an effort to break down old patterns of racial segregation, Justice Brennan commented:

It would be ironic indeed if a law triggered by a Nation's concern over centuries of racial injustice and intended to improve the lot of those who had "been excluded from the American dream for so long" constituted the first legislative prohibition of all voluntary, private, race-conscious efforts to abolish traditional patterns of racial segregation and hierarchy. 443 U.S. at 204 (quoting remarks of Sen. Humphrey, 110 *Cong. Rec.* 6552 (1964).

Racial discrimination was definitely involved because jobs were allocated on the basis of race, yet no constitutional equal protection issue was implicated because the program was not officially governmentally compelled. The corporation involved was a private-sector firm, not a governmental body. Further, the labor-management affirmative action job training program was not in violation of Title VII, Section 703(j), which specifically prohibited any required preferential treatment. The reason there was no violation is that the collective bargaining agreement was voluntary and consented to by representatives of the union and the employer.

Do you agree that *Weber* is consistent with the letter and spirit of U.S. national policy prohibiting employment decisions from being made on a racial basis? Think about the problems involved when white workers are required to stand aside from job opportunities because their ancestors required black workers to do the same. Is it fair for one generation to pay for the errors of past generations? What of the possibility that the plaintiff in this case, a white worker by the name of Brian Weber, may have been more economically and socially disadvantaged in his lifetime than some of the black workers who were given a preference? That is the type of problem that must be confronted when a public policy is addressed to groups of people, because the people within these groups will not have been equally disadvantaged. Finally, where does it end? Will employers be expected to create and maintain a labor force that perfectly reflects the percentage of protected group members in the general population?

In an effort to allay misgivings that a number of people may have against preferential treatment plans, Justice Brennan established the following parameters in *Steelworkers of America* v. *Weber.* They play an important role in our next case, *Johnson* v. *Santa Clara County. Johnson,* however, involves gender-based discrimination. See if you think these criteria would be appropriate in a different context.

★ ★ ★

[T]he plan does not unnecessarily trammel the interests of the white employees. The plan does not require the discharge of white workers and their replacement with new black hires. Nor does the plan create an absolute bar to the advancement of white employees; half of those trained in the program will be white. Moreover, the plan is a temporary measure; it is not intended to maintain racial balance, but simply to eliminate a manifest racial imbalance. Preferential selection of craft trainees at the Gramercy plant will end as soon as the percentage of black skilled craft workers in the Gramercy plant approximates the percentage of blacks in the local labor force.

We conclude, therefore, that the adoption of the Kaiser-USWA plan for the Gramercy plant falls within the area of discretion left by Title VII to the private sector voluntarily to adopt affirmative action plans designed to eliminate conspicuous racial imbalance in traditionally segregated job categories. 443 U.S. 193 (1979).

Johnson v. *Santa Clara County*
480 U.S. 616 (1987)

BRENNAN, JUSTICE

Respondent, Transportation Agency of Santa Clara County, California, unilaterally promulgated an Affirmative Action Plan applicable to promotions of employees. In selecting applicants for the promotional position of road dispatcher, the Agency, pursuant to the Plan, passed over petitioner Paul Johnson, a male employee, and promoted a female employee applicant, Diane Joyce. The question for decision is whether in making the promotion the Agency impermissibly took into account the sex of the applicants in violation of Title VII of the Civil Rights Act of 1964, 42 U.S.C. §2000e *et seq.* The District Court for the Northern District of California, in an action filed by petitioner following receipt of a right-to-sue letter from the Equal Employment Opportunity Commission (EEOC), held that respondent had violated Title VII. The Court of Appeals for the Ninth Circuit reversed. We granted certiorari. We affirm.

★ ★ ★

In December 1978, the Santa Clara County Transit District Board of Supervisors adopted an Affirmative Action Plan (Plan) for the County Transportation Agency. The Plan implemented a County Affirmative Action Plan, which had been adopted, declared the County, because "mere prohibition of discriminatory practices is not enough to remedy the effects of past practices and to permit attainment of an equitable representation of minorities, women and handicapped persons." Relevant to this case, the Agency Plan provides that, in making promotions to positions within a traditionally segregated job classification in which women have been significantly underrepresented, the Agency is authorized to consider as one factor the sex of a qualified applicant.

In reviewing the composition of its work force, the Agency noted in its Plan that women were represented in numbers far less than their proportion of the county labor force in both the Agency as a whole and in five of seven job categories. Specifically, while women constituted 36.4% of the area labor market, they composed only 22.4% of Agency employees. Furthermore, women working at the agency were concentrated largely in EEOC job categories traditionally held by women: women made up 76% of Office and Clerical Workers, but only 7.1% of Agency Officials and Administrators, 8.6% of Professionals, 9.7% of Technicians, and 22% of Service and Maintenance workers. As for the job classification relevant to this case, none of the 238 Skilled Craft Worker positions was held by a woman. The Plan noted that this underrepresentation of women in part reflected the fact that women had not traditionally been employed in these positions, and that they had not been strongly motivated to seek training or employment in them "because of the limited opportunities that have existed in the past for them to work in such classifications."

★ ★ ★

[*Author's note:* The agency's benchmark was the long-term attainment of a workforce whose composition reflected the proportion of minorities and women in the area labor force. For the at-issue job of road dispatcher, about 36 percent of the positions would eventually be occupied by women. The plan set aside no specific number of jobs for women; it proceeded on the expectation that short-range goals would be established and adjusted annually to reflect the realities of the workforce.

When the position of road dispatcher came open, Paul Johnson and Diane Joyce were among the final seven applicants. Both qualified on the basis of their work experience and, following interviews by a two-person board, were certified as eligible by the appointing authority. Johnson was tied for second with a score of 75 on the interview; Joyce was next at 73. Joyce contacted the county's affirmative action office, which in turn contacted the county's affirmative action coordinator. The coordinator recommended to the director of the agency that Joyce be hired.

The director was authorized to choose any of the seven persons deemed eligible. He selected Diane Joyce. At the trial, he testified as follows: "I tried to look at the whole picture, the combination of her qualifications and Mr. Johnson's qualifications, their test scores, their expertise, their background, affirmative action matters, things like that. . . . I believe it was a combination of all those." He further related that he did not regard it as significant that Johnson scored 75 to Joyce's 73 on the interview.

Justice Brennan noted at the outset that the burden of establishing the invalidity of the plan was on petitioner Johnson. Johnson established his *prima facie* case by showing that sex had been taken into account in the employment decision. The burden then shifted to the agency to articulate, rather than prove, a nondiscriminatory basis for its action. When this defense or rationale is the existence of an affirmative action plan, the petitioner must prove that the plan is invalid or that it is being used as a mere pretext for an unjustified decision.

In keeping with the Court's *United Steelworkers* v. *Weber* analysis, the plan must be designed to "eliminate manifest racial imbalances in traditionally segregated job categories." Given this objective, the plan must observe certain limitations: (1) It must not unnecessarily trammel the interests of white employees by discharging them, (2) it must not create an absolute bar to the advancement of white employees, and (3) it must be a temporary measure designed to eliminate a manifest racial imbalance, rather than to maintain a racial balance.]

The first issue is therefore whether consideration of the sex of applicants for skilled craft jobs was justified by the existence of a "manifest imbalance" that reflected underrepresentation of women in "traditionally segregated job categories." In determining whether an imbalance exists that would justify taking sex or race into account, a comparison of the percentage of minorities or women in the employer's work force with the percentage in the area labor market or general population is appropriate in analyzing jobs that require no special expertise.

★ ★ ★

Where a job requires special training, however, the comparison should be with those in the labor force who possess the relevant qualifications. . . . The requirement that the "manifest imbalance" relate to a "traditionally segregated job category" provides assurance both that sex or race will be taken into account in a manner consistent with Title VII's purpose of eliminating the effects of employment discrimination, and that the interests of those employees not benefiting from the plan will not be unduly infringed.

★ ★ ★

It is clear that the decision to hire Joyce was made pursuant to an Agency plan that directed that sex or race be taken into account for the purpose of remedying underrepresentation.

★ ★ ★

As an initial matter, the Agency adopted as a benchmark for measuring progress in eliminating underrepresentation the long-term goal of a work force that mirrored in its major job classifications the percentage of women in the area labor market. Even as it did so, however, the Agency acknowledged that such a figure could not by itself necessarily justify taking into account the sex of applicants for positions in all job categories. For positions requiring specialized training and experience, the Plan observed that the number of minorities and women "who possess the qualifications required for entry into such job classifications is limited." The Plan therefore directed that annual short-term goals be formulated that would provide a more realistic indication of the degree to which sex should be taken into account in filling particular positions. The Plan stressed that such goals "should not be construed as 'quotas' that must be met," but as reasonable aspirations in correcting the imbalance in the Agency's work force. . . .

As the Agency Plan recognized, women were most egregiously underrepresented in the Skilled Craft job category, since none of the 238 positions was occupied by a woman.

★ ★ ★

In considering the candidates for the road dispatcher position in 1980, the Agency hardly needed to rely on a refined short-term goal to realize that it had a significant problem of underrepresentation that required attention. Given the obvious imbalance in the Skilled Craft category, and given the Agency's commitment to eliminating such imbalances, it was plainly not unreasonable for the Agency to determine that it was appropriate to consider as one factor the sex of Ms. Joyce in making its decision. The promotion of Joyce thus satisfies the first requirement enunciated in *Weber*, since it was undertaken to further an affirmative action plan designed to eliminate Agency work force imbalances in traditionally segregated job categories.

We next consider whether the Agency Plan unnecessarily trammeled the rights of male employees or created an absolute bar to their advancement. In contrast to the plan in *Weber*, which provided that 50% of the positions in the craft training program were exclusively for blacks, and to the consent decree upheld last term in *Firefighters* v. *Cleveland*, 478 U.S.—(1986), which required the promotion of specific numbers of minorities, the Plan sets aside no positions for women. The Plan expressly states that "[t]he 'goals' established for each Division should not be construed as 'quotas' that must be met." Rather, the Plan merely authorizes that consideration be given to affirmative action concerns when evaluating qualified applicants. As the Agency Director testified, the sex of Joyce was but one of numerous factors he took into account in arriving at his decision.

★ ★ ★

In addition, petitioner had no absolute entitlement to the road dispatcher position. Seven of the applicants were classified as qualified and eligible, and the Agency Director was authorized to promote any of the seven. Thus, denial of the promotion unsettled no legitimate firmly rooted expectation on the part of the petitioner. Furthermore, while the petitioner in this case was denied a promotion, he retained his employment with the Agency, at the same salary and with the same seniority, and remained eligible for other promotions.

Finally, the Agency's Plan was intended to attain a balanced work force, not to maintain one. The Plan contains ten references to the Agency's desire to "attain" such a balance, but no references whatsoever to a goal of maintaining it.

★ ★ ★

The Agency acknowledged the difficulties that it would confront in remedying the imbalance in its work force, and it anticipated only gradual increases in the representation of minorities and women. It is thus unsurprising that the Plan contains no explicit end date, for the Agency's flexible, case-by-case approach was not expected to yield success in a brief period of time. Express assurance that a program is only temporary may be necessary if the program actually sets aside positions according to specific numbers. . . . In this case, however, substantial evidence shows that the Agency has sought to take a moderate, gradual approach to eliminating the imbalance in its work force, one which establishes realistic guidance for employment decisions, and which visits minimal intrusion on the legitimate expectations of other employees. Given this fact, as well as the Agency's express commitment to "attain" a balanced work force, there is ample assurance that the Agency does not seek to use its Plan to maintain a permanent racial and sexual balance.

Affirmed.

STEVENS, O'CONNOR: Concurring.

JUSTICE SCALIA, with whom THE CHIEF JUSTICE joins, and with whom JUSTICE WHITE joins in Parts I and II, dissenting.

With a clarity which, had it not proven so unavailing, one might well recommend as a model of statutory draftsmanship, Title VII of the Civil Rights Act of 1964 declares:

"It shall be an unlawful employment practice for an employer [to discriminate on the basis of race, color, religion, sex or national origin]."

The Court today completes the process of converting this from a guarantee that race or sex will *not* be the basis for employment determinations, to a guarantee that it often *will*.

Several salient features of the plan should be noted. Most importantly, the plan's purpose was assuredly not to remedy prior sex discrimination by the Agency. It could not have been, because there was no prior sex discrimination to remedy. The majority, in cataloguing the Agency's alleged misdeeds, neglects to mention the District Court's finding that the Agency "has not discriminated in the past, and does not discriminate in the present against women in regard to employment opportunities in general and promotions in particular." This finding was not disturbed by the Ninth Circuit.

Not only was the plan not directed at the results of past sex discrimination by the Agency, but its objective was not to achieve the state of affairs that this Court has dubiously assumed would result from an absence of discrimination—an overall work force "more or less representative of the racial and ethnic composition of the population in the community." Rather, the oft-stated goal was to mirror the racial and sexual composition of the entire county labor force, not merely in the agency work force as a whole, but in each and every individual job category at the Agency. In a discrimination-free world, it would obviously be a statistical oddity for every job category to match the racial and sexual composition of even that portion of the county work force *qualified* for that job; it would be utterly miraculous for each of them to match, as the plan expected, the composition of the *entire* work force. Quite obviously, the plan did not seek to replicate what a lack of discrimination would produce, but rather imposed racial and sexual tailoring that would, in defiance of normal expectations and laws of probability, give each protected racial and sexual group a governmentally determined "proper" proportion of each job category.

★ ★ ★   ★ ★ ★

The most significant proposition of law established by today's decision is that racial or sexual discrimination is permitted under Title VII when it is intended to overcome the effect, not of the employer's own discrimination, but of societal attitudes that have limited the entry of certain races, or of a particular sex, into certain jobs. Even if the societal attitudes in question consisted exclusively of conscious discrimination by other employers, this holding would contradict a decision of this Court rendered only last Term. *Wygant* v. *Jackson Board of Education,* 476 U.S. 267 (1986), held that the objective of remedying societal discrimination cannot prevent remedial affirmative action from violating the Equal Protection Clause. . . . While Mr. Johnson does not advance a constitutional claim here, it is most unlikely that Title VI was intended to place a lesser restraint on discrimination by public actors than is established by the Constitution. The Court has already held that the prohibitions on discrimination in Title VII, 42 U.S.C. §2000d, are at least as stringent as those in the Constitution. [Citing *University of California* v. *Bakke;* Title VI applies to recipients of federal funds.]

In fact, however, today's decision goes well beyond merely allowing racial or sexual discrimination in order to eliminate the effects of prior *societal discrimination.* The majority opinion often uses the phrase "traditionally segregated job category" to describe the evil against which the plan is legitimately (according to the majority) directed. As originally used in *Steelworkers* v. *Weber,* that phrase described skilled jobs from which employers and unions had systematically and intentionally excluded black workers—traditionally segregated jobs, that is, in the sense of conscious, exclusionary discrimination. But that is assuredly not the sense in which the phrase is used here. It is absurd to think that the nationwide failure of road maintenance crews, for example, to achieve the Agency's ambition of 36.4% female representation is attributable primarily, if even substantially, to systematic exclusion of women eager to shoulder pick and shovel. It is a "traditionally segregated job category" *not* in the *Weber* sense, but in the sense that, because of long-standing social attitudes, it has not been regarded *by women themselves* as desirable work. . . . Given this meaning of the phrase, it is patently false to say that "[t]he requirement that the 'manifest imbalance' relate to a 'traditionally segregated job category' provides assurance that sex or race will be taken into account in a manner consistent with Title VII's purpose of eliminating the effects of employment discrimination." There are, of course, those who believe that the social attitudes which cause women themselves to avoid certain jobs and to favor others are as nefarious as conscious, exclusionary discrimination. Whether or not that is so (and there is assuredly no consensus on the point equivalent to our national consensus against intentional discrimination), the two phenomena are certainly distinct. And it is the alteration of social attitudes, rather than the elimination of discrimination, which today's decision approves as justification for state-enforced discrimination. This is an enormous expansion, undertaken without the slightest justification or analysis.

★ ★ ★

I have omitted from the foregoing discussion the most obvious respect in which today's decision o'erleaps, without analysis, a barrier that was thought still to be overcome. In *Weber,* this Court held that a private-sector affirmative-action training program that overtly discriminated against white applicants did not violate Title VII. However, although the majority does not advert to the fact, until today the applicability of *Weber* to public employers remained an open question. This Court has repeatedly emphasized that *Weber* involved only a private employer. . . . This distinction between public and private employers has several possible justifications. *Weber* rested in part on the assertion that the 88th Congress did not wish to intrude too deeply into private employment decisions. Whatever validity that assertion may have with respect to private employers (and I think it negligible), it has none with respect to public employers or to the 92d Congress that brought them within Title VII. Another reason for limiting *Weber* to private employers is that state agencies, unlike private actors, are subject to the Fourteenth Amendment. As noted earlier, it would be strange to construe Title VII to permit discrimination by public actors that the Constitution forbids.

★ ★ ★

In addition to complying with the commands of the statute, abandoning *Weber* would have the desirable side-effect of eliminating the requirement of willing suspension of disbelief that is currently a credential for reading our opinions in the affirmative action field—from *Weber* itself, which demanded belief that the corporate employer adopted the affirmative action program "voluntarily," rather than under practical compulsion from government contracting agencies.

CASE FOLLOW-UP

The views of Justices Brennan and Scalia have little in common. Brennan finds the *Weber* criteria to be just as compelling in a situation where the employer has not adhered to a policy of race or sex discrimination in the past (Santa Clara County) as they are when past discrimination is evident even if not acknowledged or proved (Kaiser-Gramercy plant).

Justice Brennan focuses on the plan's effort to overcome the gross underuse of qualified women in supervisory positions. Justice Scalia finds it to be totally beyond Title VII's objective to remedy gender-based discrimination that is the product of social and cultural patterns. He believes that remedial efforts should at least be reserved for situations in which the employment discrimination was conscious, intentional, and systematic.

You might also note that the Court did not apply the equal protection clause to the affirmative action plan. After all, Santa Clara County is an instrumentality of the state, and usually when states or state subdivisions engage in suspect classifications, at least racial ones, strict scrutiny is applied. If strict scrutiny were applied, the state body would have to articulate a compelling basis in support of its classification and advance that objective in a way that was narrowly tailored— that is, in a way that was least intrusive on the rights of the disfavored.

Because the discrimination complained of in this case was gender based, not racial, the Court would have been guided by the intermediate scrutiny test, rather than strict. It probably sounds like "phrase making" to you, but *intermediate scrutiny* is a more lenient evaluation. It is understood to mean that the discrimination or the classification must be substantially related to an important governmental purpose.

If the Court had shifted to an intermediate scrutiny analysis, Scalia would probably have reminded it of the rule announced one year earlier in *Wygant* v. *Jackson Board of Education*.[11] Cultural or societal discrimination, as opposed to discrimination by the governmental entity itself, was not deemed to be a sufficiently compelling basis for a county school board plan that discriminated on the basis of race. He would probably argue that if societal discrimination based on race was not a sufficient basis for an affirmative action plan in *Wygant,* societal discrimination based on gender would not be a sufficient basis, given the facts, in *Johnson* v. *Santa Clara County.*

Beyond that, however, *Wygant* was different in that the collective bargain/affirmative action plan was not narrowly tailored; it involved layoffs of white teachers with greater seniority than black teachers. *Santa Clara* involved the prospect of promotion only, and that is not considered to be quite as serious a matter as the loss of a job.

Despite these differences, Justice Scalia's dissent leads one to believe that a new coalition is emerging on the Court and that affirmative action plans will not receive the more or less cordial blessing they have in the past. That impression is strengthened by *City of Richmond* v. *J. A. Croson Company,* the next major case you will examine.

TITLE VII: SET-ASIDES FOR MINORITY BUSINESS ENTERPRISES

In *Fullilove* v. *Klutznick,*[12] the Supreme Court held that a congressional program requiring 10 percent of certain federal construction grants be awarded to minority business enterprises (MBEs) did not violate the equal protection component embodied in the due process clause of the Fifth Amendment. This federal program was established by the Public Works Employment Act of 1977. It authorized a $4 billion appropriation for federal grants to state and local governments. The primary objective of the Act was to give the national economy a quick boost during a recessionary period.

The *Fullilove* opinion, written by Chief Justice Burger, did not employ the strict scrutiny test or any other standard of equal protection clause review. The Chief Justice noted the great deference the Court has always shown a coequal branch of the federal government and further related that such deference was especially appropriate, given Congress' power "to provide for the . . . general welfare" and to enforce the equal protection guarantees of the Fourteenth Amendment.

On the issue of congressional power, the Court found that the commerce clause was broad enough to allow it to reach the practices of prime contractors on federally funded local construction projects. Congress could require state and local governments to comply under its Fourteenth Amendment enforcement powers.

State and local set-aside programs, basically patterned on *Fullilove,* presented different, and difficult, problems in lower levels of the federal courts. The Supreme Court noted probable jurisdiction in *City of Richmond* v. *J. A. Croson Company* and affirmed the court of appeals decision that struck down the MBE set-aside program.

City of Richmond v. J. A. Croson Company

448 U.S. 469 (1989)

O'CONNOR, JUSTICE

In this case, we confront once again the tension between the Fourteenth Amendment's guarantee of equal treatment to all citizens, and the use of race-based measures to ameliorate the effects of past discrimination on the opportunities enjoyed by members of minority groups in our society. . . .

★ ★ ★

On April 11, 1983, the Richmond City Council adopted the Minority Business Utilization Plan (the Plan). The Plan required prime contractors to whom the city awarded construction contracts to subcontract at least 30% of the dollar amount of the contract to one or more Minority Business Enterprises (MBEs). . . .

The Plan defined an MBE as "[a] business at least fifty-one (51) percent of which is owned and controlled . . . by minority group members." "Minority group members" were defined as "[c]itizens of the United States who are Blacks, Spanish-speaking, Orientals, Indians, Eskimos, or Aleuts." There was no geographic limit to the Plan; an otherwise qualified MBE from anywhere in the United States could avail itself of the 30% set-aside. The Plan declared that it was "remedial" in nature, and enacted "for the purpose of promoting wider participation by minority business enterprise in the construction of public projects." The Plan expired on June 30, 1988, and was in effect for approximately five years.

The Plan authorized the Director of the Department of General Services to promulgate rules which "shall allow waivers in those individual situations where a contractor can prove to the satisfaction of the director that the requirements herein cannot be achieved."

★ ★ ★

The Plan was adopted by the Richmond City Council after a public hearing. Seven members of the public spoke to the merits of the ordinance: five were in opposition, two in favor. Proponents of the set-aside provision relied on a study which indicated that, while the general population of Richmond was 50% black, only .67% of the city's prime construction contracts had been awarded to minority businesses in the 5-year period from 1978 to 1983. It was also established that a variety of contractors' associations, whose representatives appeared in opposition to the ordinance, had virtually no minority businesses within their membership.

★ ★ ★

There was no direct evidence of race discrimination on the part of the city in letting contracts or any evidence that the city's prime contractors had discriminated against minority-owned subcontractors. . . .

Opponents of the ordinance questioned both its wisdom and its legality. They argued that a disparity between minorities in the population of Richmond and the number of prime contracts awarded to MBEs had little probative value in establishing discrimination in the construction industry. Representatives of various contractors' associations questioned whether there were enough MBEs in the Richmond area to satisfy the 30% set-aside requirement. Only 4.7% of all construction firms in the United States were minority owned and . . . 41% of these were located in California, New York, Illinois, Florida, and Hawaii. . . . Councilperson Gillespie indicated his concern that many local labor jobs, held by both blacks and whites, would be lost because the ordinance put no geographic limit on the MBEs eligible for the 30% set-aside. . . .

[*Author's note:* J. A. Croson then sought a city contract. It made attempts to secure an MBE subcontractor, but to no avail. The city denied Croson's request for a waiver and informed Croson that it would rebid the project. Shortly thereafter, Croson brought this action (Croson I) to have the city ordinance declared unconstitutional.

The District Court upheld the plan in all respects. The U.S. Court of Appeals for the Fourth Circuit, by a divided panel, found to be reasonable the city council's conclusion that low MBE participation in public contracts resulted from past discrimination. It further found the 30-percent set-aside to be a reasonable remedy.

Croson then sought review of the Fourth Circuit opinion. The Supreme Court vacated it and remanded for reconsideration in light of *Wygant* v. *Jackson Board of Education.*

In *Croson II,* the Fourth Circuit, by a divided panel, struck down the Richmond plan. It applied the strict scrutiny test under the equal protection clause of the Fourteenth Amendment and concluded that the city failed to establish a compelling basis for the set-aside. On the authority of *Wygant,* the appeals court related that the city could establish a compelling basis only by showing "prior discrimination by the governmental unit involved." Broad-brush findings of "societal discrimination" were seen by the appellate court as insufficient for this purpose.

In closing, it held that even if the city had demonstrated a compelling basis, the 30 percent set-aside was not narrowly tailored to achieve a remedial purpose.]

[Distinguishing the present case from *Wygant,* Justice O'Connor observed:]

It would seem equally clear, however, that a state or local subdivision (if delegated the authority from the State) has the authority to eradicate the effects of private discrimination within its own legislative jurisdiction. . . . As a matter of state law, the city of Richmond has legislative authority over its procurement policies, and can use its spending powers to remedy private discrimination, if it identifies that discrimination with the particularity required by the Fourteenth Amendment. . . .

. . . It is beyond dispute that any public entity, state or federal, has a compelling interest in assuring that public dollars, drawn from the tax contributions of all citizens, do not serve to finance the evil of private prejudice.

★ ★ ★

The Equal Protection Clause of the Fourteenth Amendment provides that "[N]o State shall . . . deny to *any person* within its jurisdiction the equal protection of the laws" (emphasis added). As this Court has noted in the past, the "rights created by the first section of the Fourteenth Amendment are, by its terms, guaranteed to the individual. The rights established are personal rights." *Shelly* v. *Kraemer,* 334 U.S. 1, 22 (1948). The Richmond Plan denies certain citizens the opportunity to compete for a fixed percentage of public contracts based solely upon their race. To whatever racial group these citizens belong, their "personal rights" to be treated with equal dignity and respect are implicated by a rigid rule erecting race as the sole criterion in an aspect of public decisionmaking.

Absent searching judicial inquiry into the justification for such race-based measures, there is simply no way of determining what classifications are "benign" or "remedial" and what classifications are in fact motivated by illegitimate notions of racial inferiority or simple racial politics. Indeed, the purpose of strict scrutiny is to "smoke out" illegitimate uses of race by assuring that the legislative body is pursuing a goal important enough to warrant use of a highly suspect tool. The test also ensures that the means chosen "fit" this compelling goal so closely that there is little or no possibility that the motive for the classification was illegitimate racial prejudice or stereotype.

* * *

Even were we to accept a reading of the guarantee of equal protection under which the level of scrutiny varies according to the ability of different groups to defend their interests in the representative process, heightened scrutiny would still be appropriate in the circumstances of this case. One of the central arguments for applying a less exacting standard to "benign" racial classifications is that such measures essentially involve a choice made by dominant racial groups to disadvantage themselves. If one aspect of the judiciary's role under the Equal Protection Clause is to protect "discrete and insular minorities" from majoritarian prejudice or indifference, see *United States* v. *Carolene Products Co.,* 304 U.S. 144, 153, n. 4 (1938), some maintain that these concerns are not implicated when the "white majority" places burdens upon itself. See J. Ely, *Democracy and Distrust* 170 (1980).

In this case, blacks comprise approximately 50% of the population of the city of Richmond. Five of the nine seats on the City Council are held by blacks. The concern that a political majority will more easily act to the disadvantage of a minority based on unwarranted assumptions or incomplete facts would seem to militate for, not against, the application of heightened judicial scrutiny in this case.

* * *

While there is no doubt that the sorry history of both private and public discrimination in this country has contributed to a lack of opportunities for black entrepreneurs, this observation, standing alone, cannot justify a rigid racial quota in the awarding of public contracts in Richmond, Virginia. . . . [A]n amorphous claim that there has been past discrimination in a particular industry cannot justify the use of an unyielding racial quota.

[The Court then concluded that the city had not produced a sufficiently strong basis in evidence that remedial action was necessary. The 30 percent quota could not "in any realistic sense be tied to any injury suffered by anyone."]

* * *

In sum, none of the evidence presented by the city points to any identified discrimination in the Richmond construction industry. We, therefore, hold that the city has failed to demonstrate a compelling interest in apportioning public contracting opportunities on the basis of race. To accept Richmond's claim that past societal discrimination alone can serve as the basis for rigid racial preferences would be to open the door to competing claims for "remedial relief" for every disadvantaged group. . . .

The foregoing analysis applies only to the inclusion of blacks within the Richmond set-aside program. There is *absolutely no evidence* of past discrimination against Spanish-speaking, Oriental, Indian, Eskimo, or Aleut persons in any aspect of the Richmond construction industry. . . . It may well be that Richmond has never had an Aleut or Eskimo citizen. The random inclusion of racial groups that, as a practical matter, may never have suffered from discrimination in the construction industry in Richmond, suggests that perhaps the city's purpose was not in fact to remedy past discrimination.

* * *

As noted by the court below, it is almost impossible to assess whether the Richmond Plan is narrowly tailored to remedy prior discrimination since it is not linked to identified discrimination in any way. We limit ourselves to two observations in this regard.

First, there does not appear to have been any consideration of the use of race-neutral means to increase minority business participation in city contracting. . . . Many of the barriers to minority participation in the construction industry relied upon by the city to justify a racial classification appear to be race neutral. If MBEs disproportionately lack capital or cannot meet bonding requirements, a race-neutral program of city financing for small firms would, *a fortiori,* lead to greater minority participation. . . . There is no evidence in this record that the Richmond City Council has considered any alternatives to a race-based quota.

Second, the 30% quota cannot be said to be narrowly tailored to any goal, except perhaps outright racial balancing. It rests upon the "completely unrealistic" assumption that minorities will choose a particular trade in lockstep proportion to their representation in the local population.

* * *

Since the city must already consider bids and waivers on a case-by-case basis, it is difficult to see the need for a rigid numerical quota.

* * *

Given the existence of an individualized procedure, the city's only interest in maintaining a quota system rather than investigating the need for remedial action in particular cases would seem to be simple administrative convenience. But the interest in avoiding the bureaucratic effort necessary to tailor remedial relief to those who truly have suffered the effects of prior discrimination cannot justify a rigid line drawn on the basis of a suspect classification.

* * *

JUSTICE MARSHALL, with whom JUSTICE BRENNAN and JUSTICE BLACKMUN join, dissenting.

It is a welcome symbol of racial progress when the former capital of the Confederacy acts forthrightly to confront the effects of racial discrimination in its midst. In my view, nothing in the Constitution can be construed to prevent Richmond, Virginia, from allocating a portion of its contracting dollars for businesses owned or controlled by members of minority groups. Indeed, Richmond's set-aside program is indistinguishable in all meaningful respects from—and in fact was patterned upon—the federal set-aside plan which this Court upheld in *Fullilove* v. *Klutznick,* 448 U.S. 448 (1980).

A majority of this Court holds today, however, that the Equal Protection Clause of the Fourteenth Amendment blocks Richmond's initiative. The essence of the majority's position is that Richmond has failed to catalogue adequate findings to prove that past discrimination has impeded minorities from joining or participating fully in Richmond's construction contracting industry. I find deep irony in second-guessing Richmond's judgment on this point. As much as any municipality in the United States, Richmond knows what racial discrimination is; a century of decisions by this and other federal courts has richly documented the city's disgraceful history of public and private racial discrimination. In any event, the Richmond City Council *has* supported its determination that minorities have been wrongly excluded from local construction contracting. Its proof includes statistics showing that minority-owned businesses have received virtually no city contracting dollars and rarely if ever belonged to area trade associations; testimony by municipal officials that discrimination has been widespread in the local construction industry; and the same exhaustive and widely publicized federal studies relied on in *Fullilove* studies which showed that pervasive discrimination in the Nation's tight-knit construction industry had operated to exclude minorities from public contracting. These are precisely the types of statistical and testimonial evidence which, until today, this Court had credited in cases approving of race-conscious measures designed to remedy past discrimination.

More fundamentally, today's decision marks a deliberate and giant step backward in this Court's affirmative action jurisprudence. Cynical of one municipality's attempt to redress the effects of past racial discrimination in a particular industry, the majority launches a grapeshot attack on race-conscious remedies in general. The majority's unnecessary pronouncements will inevitably discourage or prevent governmental entities, particularly States and localities, from acting to rectify the scourge of past discrimination. This is the harsh reality of the majority's decision, but it is not the Constitution's command.

CASE FOLLOW-UP

Croson should be viewed as a writing-on-the-wall case for set-asides and a distinct cautionary signal for affirmative action as well. It is likely that the Court will sanction neither unless the entity adopting the plan has (1) identified (thoroughly documented) past or current discrimination by that entity or within that entity's sphere of influence or control and (2) exhausted all reasonable race-neutral alternatives.

SEX, SECTION 701(K) OF TITLE VII

(k) The terms "because of sex" or "on the basis of sex" include, but are not limited to, because of or on the basis of pregnancy, childbirth or related medical conditions; and women affected by pregnancy, childbirth, or related medical conditions shall be treated the same for all employment-related purposes, including receipt of benefits under fringe benefit programs, as other persons not so affected but similar in their ability or inability to work, and nothing in Section 703(h) of this title shall be interpreted to permit otherwise. This subsection shall not require an employer to pay for health insurance benefits for abortion, except where the life of the mother would be endangered if the fetus were carried to term, or except where medical complications have arisen from an abortion: Provided, That nothing herein shall preclude an employer from providing abortion benefits or otherwise effect bargaining agreements in regard to abortion.

Congress amended Title VII in 1978 by adding Section 701(k), which included *pregnancy* and *childbirth* in the definition of sex. It requires that pregnancy be treated the same as other medical conditions that relate to job performance. Employers are not required to adopt a health or disability benefit plan, but if they do, pregnancy must be treated just as other medical conditions are treated. To illustrate, discharging women who become pregnant or depriving them of seniority is a form of sex discrimination. It should be noted, however, that medical plans may exclude coverage of abortion unless an abortion is necessary to save the mother's life.

Sexual Harassment. Sexual harassment actions fall into two categories: (1) Category One, *quid pro quo* sexual harassment: exchange of sexual favors for special employment consideration, the promise of special job treatment (hiring, promotion, or other tangible benefit, status, or opportunity) by the employer or the employer's agent in return for sexual favors, provided that the employer's request for sexual favors was unwelcome; and (2) Category Two, hostile environment sexual harassment: (a) the employer or the employer's agent makes an unwelcome request for sexual favors, but the request, although creating an offensive or intimidating job environment, is not tied to special employment treatment, benefit, status, or opportunity; or (b) the employer knowingly tolerates a hostile or abusive work environment.

The following case, written for the Court by Chief Justice Rehnquist, illustrates a hostile work environment.

Meritor Savings Bank v. *Vinson*
477 U.S. 57 (1986)

REHNQUIST, JUSTICE

[*Author's note:* Michelle Vinson, a former employee of the Meritor Savings Bank, sued the bank for sexual harassment in federal district court under Title VII. She was fired for allegedly taking excessive sick leave. At trial, she testified that, during her four years with the bank, her supervisor, Sidney Taylor, made repeated demands on her for sexual favors and that she had sexual intercourse with him on forty to fifty separate occasions. She also contended that Taylor fondled her in front of other employees, that he fondled other female employees, and that he followed her into the women's restroom when she went there alone, exposed himself to her, and forcibly raped her on several occasions. Vinson asserted that she never reported this behavior to Taylor's superiors and never used the bank's employee grievance procedure because she was afraid of Taylor. Taylor denied all of Vinson's assertions about his sexual behavior. The bank argued that if Taylor had committed sexual harassment, this was without the bank's knowledge, consent, or approval. Finally, it was undisputed that Vinson had received three promotions during her four years with the bank and that her advancement was based solely on merit.

Without resolving this conflicting testimony, the district court held for the bank because it concluded that any relationship between Taylor and Vinson was a voluntary one that had nothing to do with her employment or advancement at the bank. Vinson appealed, and the court of appeals reversed the district court. The bank appealed to the U.S. Supreme Court.]

[W]hen a supervisor sexually harasses a subordinate because of the subordinate's sex, that supervisor "discriminates" on the basis of sex. The bank apparently does not challenge this proposition. It contends instead that in prohibiting discrimination with respect to "compensation, terms, conditions, or privileges" of employment, Congress was concerned with what petitioner describes as "tangible loss" of "an economic character," not "purely psychological aspects of the workplace environment." . . .

We reject [the bank's] view. First, the language of Title VII is not limited to "economic" or "tangible" discrimination. The phrase "terms, conditions, or privileges of employment" evinces a congressional intent "to strike at the entire spectrum of disparate treatment of men and women" in employment. . . . Second, in 1980 the EEOC issued guidelines specifying that "sexual harassment," as there defined, is a form of sex discrimination prohibited by Title VII. [*Author's note:* The EEOC's guidelines are influential but not controlling on the Court.]

In defining "sexual harassment," the guidelines first describe the kinds of workplace conduct that may be actionable under Title VII. These include "unwelcome sexual advances, requests for sexual favors, and other verbal or physical conduct of a sexual nature." Relevant to the charges at issue in this case, the guidelines provide that such sexual misconduct constitutes prohibited "sexual harassment," whether or not it is directly linked to the grant or denial of an economic *quid pro quo,* where "such conduct has the purpose or effect of unreasonably interfering with an individual's work performance or creating an intimidating, hostile, or offensive working environment."

. . . Since the guidelines were issued, courts have uniformly held, and we agree, that a plaintiff may establish a violation of Title VII by proving that discrimination based on sex has created a hostile or abusive work environment. . . .

. . . For sexual harassment to be actionable, it must be sufficiently severe or pervasive to alter the conditions of the victim's employment and create an abusive working environment. Vinson's allegations in this case . . . are plainly sufficient to state a claim for "hostile environment" sexual harassment. . . . Since it appears that the District Court made its findings without ever considering the "hostile environment" theory of

sexual harassment, the Court of Appeals' decision to remand was correct.

In addition, the District Court's conclusion that no actionable harassment occurred might have rested on its finding that "if respondent and Taylor did engage in an intimate or sexual relationship, . . . that relationship was a voluntary one." But the fact that sex-related conduct was "voluntary," in the sense that the complainant was not forced to participate against her will, is not a defense to a sexual harassment suit brought under Title VII. The basis of any sexual harassment claim is that the alleged sexual advances were "unwelcome." While the question whether particular conduct was indeed unwelcome presents difficult problems of proof and turns largely on credibility determinations by the trier of fact, the District Court in this case erroneously focused on the "voluntariness" of respondent's participation in the claimed sexual episodes. The correct inquiry is whether respondent by her conduct indicated that the alleged sexual advances were unwelcome, not whether her actual participation in sexual intercourse was voluntary. . . .

. . . The trier of fact must determine the existence of sexual harassment in light of the record as a whole [including evidence of Vinson's provocative speech and dress] and the totality of circumstances, such as the nature of the sexual advances and the context in which the alleged incidents occurred. . . .

Although the District Court concluded that respondent had not proved a violation of Title VII, it nevertheless went on to consider the question of the bank's liability. Finding that "the bank was without notice" of Taylor's alleged conduct, . . . the court concluded that the bank therefore could not be held liable for Taylor's alleged actions. The Court of Appeals took the opposite view, holding that an employer is strictly liable for a hostile environment created by a supervisor's sexual advances, even though the employer neither knew nor reasonably could have known of the alleged misconduct. . . .

. . . [W]e decline the parties' invitation to issue a definitive rule on employer liability [because the evidentiary record is incomplete], but we do agree with the EEOC that Congress wanted courts to look to agency principles for guidance in this area. While such common-law principles may not be transferable in all their particulars to Title VII, Congress's decision to define "employer" to include any "agent" of an employer surely evinces an intent to place some limits on the acts of employees for which employers under Title VII are to be held responsible. For this reason, we hold that the Court of Appeals erred in concluding that employers are always automatically liable for sexual harassment by their supervisors. For the same reason, absence of notice to an employer does not necessarily insulate that employer from liability.

Finally, we reject petitioner's view that the mere existence of a grievance procedure and a policy against discrimination, coupled with respondent's failure to invoke that procedure, must insulate petitioner from liability. While those facts are plainly relevant, the situation before us demonstrates why they are not necessarily dispositive. Petitioner's general nondiscrimination policy did not address sexual harassment in particular, and thus did not alert employees to their employer's interest in correcting that form of discrimination. Moreover, the bank's grievance procedure apparently required an employee to complain first to her supervisor, in this case Taylor. Since Taylor was the alleged perpetrator, it is not altogether surprising that respondent failed to invoke the procedure and report her grievance to him. . . .

. . . [T]he case is remanded for further proceedings consistent with this opinion.

CASE FOLLOW-UP

Following this case, the EEOC issued further guidelines that impose *strict liability* on the employer for Category One sexual harassment (exchange of sexual favors in return for special job treatment or *quid pro quo* sexual harassment). Common law agency principles are the basis for employer liability in Category Two (hostile environment) cases. *Meritor Savings Bank* v. *Vinson,* of course, is the model for the second category. Business firms would be well advised to pay close attention to these guidelines. They are not binding on the judiciary, but courts are respectful of the expertise and experience that goes into their formulation.

Prior to 1993, a number of federal circuit courts required a plaintiff employee to demonstrate serious impairment of or effect on psychological well-being to establish an "abusive work environment" in a hostile en-

vironment sexual harassment action. Other circuit courts rejected the psychological impairment requirement. This inconsistency in the conceptualization of hostile environment harassment was resolved by the Supreme Court in *Harris* v. *Forklift Systems, Inc.,*[13] in late 1993. In the opinion of the Court, Justice O'Connor held that Title VII does not require a showing of "concrete psychological harm." The decision emphasizes that the holding in *Meritor* "takes a middle path between making actionable any conduct that is merely offensive and requiring the conduct to cause a tangible psychological injury." In other words, an abusive environment, including impediments to job performance and advancement, can exist even when the effect on the plaintiff employee is not tantamount to psychological injury.

Harassment by lower-echelon employees who have no supervisory or other power over the person being sexually victimized falls under Category Two because the offenders would have no employment benefits to offer in exchange. The firm will probably be liable, however, if it has knowledge of this conduct and expressly or implicitly condones it.

What is the value of a company policy that forbids both categories of sexual harassment? On the assumption that most firms will have the good judgment to formulate such a policy, it will have maximum effectiveness both in foreclosing such conduct and, if necessary, in defending a lawsuit if it is (1) communicated to every employee in clear and specific language, (2) communicated in such a way as to educate the workforce that sexual harassment is a problem and that such conduct will not be tolerated, (3) internalized and integrated into company channels so that complaints will be acknowledged and processed, and (4) strictly enforced by procedures that respect the rights of the victim and of the accused.

Sex-Plus Discrimination.   Sex-plus discrimination involves one rule for women and another for men. In *Phillips* v. *Martin Marietta Corp.*,[14] the Supreme Court rejected an employment policy that screened out women, but not men, who were parents of preschool-age children. The court of appeals found that sex alone did not operate to a woman's detriment, because 75 percent of the firm's employees were female. It judged that the hiring standard, *sex plus a neutral factor* (preschool children), was not a violation. In a *per curium* reversal of the Court of Appeals, the Supreme Court said that Section 703(a) of Title VII required persons of like qualifications to be treated equally regardless of sex. It refused to permit one hiring policy for women and another for men.

An employer may refuse to employ married persons if it uniformly applies that rule to both sexes. It is a violation of Title VII to prohibit women from marrying[15] or to fire those who have children[16] while not applying the same rule to men.

Pension and Retirement Systems.   In *City of Los Angeles* v. *Manhart*,[17] the Court examined the legality of unequal contributions to pension funds. Women paid into the fund at higher rates than men because as a group, they live longer. The question before the Court was whether Title VII permitted such class- or gender-based generalizations even though the generalization was unquestionably true. In other words, was discrimination to be determined by comparison of class characteristics or individual characteristics?

Justice Stevens's opinion made it clear that the focus of Title VII was on the individual, rather than the group. Although as a group women do live longer than men, that is not a legitimate basis for discriminating against a particular woman who, despite gender-based averages, might not enjoy that life span.

Equalizing the contributions is what this case is all about. Once that is done, the employer (or the employee) may shop around on the annuity market and purchase the best bargain compatible with the employee's relevant health characteristics.

Sexual Orientation. Discrimination based on homosexual behavior or trans-sexualism is not a Title VII violation. Title VII relates exclusively to gender-based discrimination. *Holloway* v. *Arthur Anderson & Co.*,[18] cited with approval in *DeSantis* v. *Pacific Telephone & Telegraph Co.*,[19] relates as follows:

> Giving the statute its plain meaning, this court concludes that Congress had only the traditional notions of "sex" in mind. Later legislative activity makes this narrow definition even more evident. Several bills have been introduced to amend the Civil Rights Act to prohibit discrimination against "sexual preference." None have been enacted into law.
>
> Congress has not shown any intent other than to restrict the term "sex" to its traditional meaning. Therefore, this court will not expand Title VII's application in the absence of Congressional mandate. (566 F.2d at 665)

PROTECTED CLASSES—RELIGION, SECTION 701(J)

(j) The term "religion" includes all aspects of religious observance and practice, as well as belief, unless an employer demonstrates that it is unable to reasonably accommodate to an employee's or prospective employee's religious observance or practice without undue hardship on the conduct of the employer's business.

The definition of *religion* used by the courts and the EEOC is broad enough to include non-Judeo-Christian faiths and unorthodox cults. Atheism is protected as well.[20] Given the wide-ranging judicial interpretation of the word "religion," Title VII adds that it "includes all aspects of religious observance and practice, as well as belief." This aspect protects religious activities that are voluntarily assumed in good faith; it is not limited to those observances required by one's religion. Religious organizations and the educational institutions they operate are exempt from Title VII with regard to hiring individuals of that particular religion. Just as a Methodist church is entitled to give an employment preference to members of its faith, so might a Catholic church or Jewish synagogue.

An employer's duty not to discriminate on the basis of religion is a limited duty. Discrimination is permitted, however, if "an employer demonstrates that he is unable to reasonably accommodate to an employee's or prospective employee's religious observance or practice without undue hardship on the conduct of the employer's business." This point is illustrated effectively in *Trans World Airlines, Inc.* v. *Hardison*.[21] In this case, plaintiff Hardison's religion required that he refrain from work between sunset Friday and sunset Saturday, whereas Trans World's operations were around the clock, seven days a week. When Hardison's lack of seniority resulted in Saturday duty, and no voluntary replacement could be found, the union refused to ignore the seniority system and compel a senior person to pull the shift. Trans World refused to assign some other qualified person because of premium overtime pay or understaffing of another department.

The Court concluded that to require TWA to bear more than a *de minimis* cost in order to give Hardison Saturdays off was an undue hardship. Like abandonment of the seniority system, to require TWA to bear additional costs when no such costs were incurred to give other employees the days off that they want would involve unequal treatment of employees on the basis of their religion.

PROTECTED CLASSES—NATIONAL ORIGIN, SECTION 703

A person's *national origin* refers to the country in which he or she was born. If a person is legally or illegally in another country but is not a citizen of that country or a visitor, then that person is an alien.

In the United States, undocumented aliens can be deported, but they are entitled to the same constitutional protections as everyone else. *Espinoza* v. *Farah Mfg. Co.*[22] explores the intention of Congress: Did it intend to allow private employers to discriminate against noncitizens (legal aliens) despite the language in Title VII that prohibited discrimination on the basis of national origin?

In an opinion written by Justice Marshall, the Court concluded that Title VII did allow private employers to discriminate on the basis of alienage. First, the language of the Act does not forbid it. Second, the federal government, acting through the Civil Service Commission and in other ways, has a long record of discrimination against noncitizens. It would be ironic, Justice Marshall observed, if the government could bar aliens from federal employment but private employers could not do so in their own factories and plants.

Justice Marshall reaffirmed that Title VII protects all individuals, including aliens or noncitizens, from illegal discrimination. But for the discrimination against aliens to be legally relevant, the discrimination must be based on national origin. If Farah Mfg. Co. discriminated against aliens of German, French, or Mexican origin, that would be illegal. There was no evidence of such discrimination, however. In fact, Mrs. Espinoza, a legal alien and citizen of Mexico, was replaced by a U.S. citizen with a Spanish surname. Beyond that, more than 96 percent of the employees at Farah's San Antonio division were of Mexican ancestry.

In affirming the judgment for Farah, the Court closed with the observation that the language of the Act, its history, and the specific facts of the case failed to indicate that the employer engaged in unlawful discrimination based on national origin.

TITLE VII: PROOF OF CLAIMS

DISPARATE TREATMENT—PROOF OF DISCRIMINATION MOTIVATED BY PROHIBITED CONSIDERATIONS

Direct Proof; Intentional Conduct; Single Motive. The principle requirement of Title VII is that *job-relevant considerations only* be considered in hiring, training, promotion, compensation, and discharge decisions. The employer is free to evaluate applicants and employees on the basis of merit but is prohibited from considering race, color, religion, sex, or national origin. In fact, the employing firm is free to define merit however it chooses, but with the caveat that prohibited considerations cannot enter into the decision process.

A plaintiff in a discrimination suit is required to prove that an adverse employment decision was made "because of" race, sex, or one of the other prohibited considerations, but that does not mean *solely* because of that consideration. At the time the decision was made, if even one of several reasons for the decision was that the applicant or employee was a woman or a minority, a court would say the decision was made "because of" an illegal consideration.

A person (or business firm) is held to have intended a particular outcome or result if that person could reasonably foresee the probable consequences of the conduct. If a company, then, adopts and implements the employment policy "no women or minorities need apply," proof of that policy would be direct evidence of intentional, illegal behavior. The Title VII complainant would have to prove this intentional behavior by a preponderance of evidence; that is, the plaintiff would have to show that it is *more likely than not* that the employment decision consciously, deliberately considered sex or race in the hiring process. That would not be hard to do with the facts just described; they represent the kind of "smoking gun" evidence that litigants dream of. The pretrial discovery process could reveal such documents, the deposition of a company manager might elicit such an admission, or at the trial, one of the employer's officers might acknowledge the application of such a policy on cross-examination.

Behavior of this nature may be motivated by a hostility toward women and minorities or by a paternalistic or stereotypical belief that women and minorities are inherently incapable of doing the job. Whatever the motivations, they are plainly not relevant in the context of an employment decision.

It is sufficient in a Title VII case for the plaintiff to show that the employer intentionally, consciously, or deliberately took the prohibited factors into consideration in arriving at a decision. If the plaintiff can prove this, the plaintiff has carried the burden of persuasion—that the employment decision was made "because of" race, color, religion, sex, or national origin.

Direct Proof; Intentional Conduct; Mixed Motives.   What about situations in which the employer was motivated, in part, by prohibited considerations (race, color, religion, sex, or national origin) and, in part, by valid considerations (e.g., an employment history of poor performance, tardiness, absenteeism, lack of interpersonal skills, insubordination)? Such cases are frequently labeled *mixed-motives cases.* They are a common variation on the theme we have been considering.

In these mixed-motives cases, the plaintiff carries the burden of proving that the decision was made "because of" one of the prohibited motives by introducing direct evidence to that effect. It then becomes the task of the defendant/employer to make an affirmative defense; that is, the defendant, acting under the burden of proof that is usually placed on the plaintiff, is required to persuade the court that the "same decision" would have been made even if the prohibited motives had not entered into the decision process. Courts consider this to be the fairer way of distributing the burden of proof. After all, it was the defendant's use of an illegal motive that created this jumble in the first place. Because the employer has knowingly engaged in wrongdoing, courts have concluded that it would be unfair to put this burden on the victim.

Employment Discrimination and After-Acquired Evidence. A number of recent cases have raised an intriguing question about employee suits for unlawful discrimination. Suppose an employee is discharged and brings suit for unlawful discrimination. Prior to termination, the employee becomes fearful of being fired and purloins his personnel file from the office of his supervisor. Subsequent to the firing, in the course of litigation, the employer becomes aware that the employee has taken the personnel file without authority, an offense for which employees can be fired under company policy. Does the employee's taking of the file serve as a defense on which the employer can rely in the discrimination action, even though the employer was unaware of the prohibited activity at the time the employee was terminated? This issue raises the question of whether *after-acquired evidence* (evidence acquired subsequent to termination) can be used to cleanse an otherwise potentially illegal discriminatory firing.

The application of after-acquired evidence in such contexts is controversial, and courts in the past varied in their approach to the problem. Some courts held that after-acquired evidence was not a valid defense against a claim of unlawful discrimination. These courts reasoned that a discharge rendered prior to the receipt of the after-acquired evidence obviously cannot be explained or justified by that evidence, because, by definition, the employer lacked that information at the moment of firing. A growing number of courts, however, began admitting after-acquired evidence as a valid defense in discrimination cases. These courts reasoned that the firing was justified by the infraction regardless of whether the employer had knowledge of the infraction at the moment of firing. They contended that when there is justification to fire, known or unknown to the employer at the time of firing, the termination should not be viewed as unlawful.

In 1995, the Supreme Court resolved the question of admissibility of after-acquired evidence.

In *McKennon v. Nashville Banner Publishing Co.*, 115 S. Ct. 879 (1995), the Court held that after-acquired evidence of wrongdoing that could have resulted in legitimate discharge of an employee does not bar the employee from receiving relief for wrongful discharge. In other words, an employer who violates federal antidiscrimination statutes cannot whitewash such wrongful behavior simply because the employer fortuitously discovers bona fide grounds that would have justified the dismissal at the time of dismissal, had the employer known of the grounds at the time. The Court emphasized the role of antidiscrimination litigation as an "enforcement mechanism" and an incentive to employers to eliminate illegal discrimination. By failing to hold after-acquired evidence of grounds for legitimate termination to be a bar to recovery for the true discriminatory motives that existed at the time of discharge, the Court strengthened the force of antidiscrimination statutes.

Indirect Proof; Intentional Conduct. In the absence of direct proof, how does a plaintiff establish intentional discrimination based on a prohibited motive? These cases move in stages: (1) The plaintiff establishes a *prima facie* case (the defendant must come forward with some evidence, or else the plaintiff wins); (2) the defendant produces evidence that rebuts the plaintiff's case; and (3) the plaintiff then proves, or tries to prove, that the defendant's official reasons are not the real reasons, but rather are a mere pretext for hidden, illegal reasons.

Stage One: The Prima Facie *Case. McDonnell Douglas Corp.* v. *Green* [23] created a format for cases of this nature. Initially, the plaintiff must create a *prima facie* case by showing that

1. Complainant is an individual who falls within one of the protected groups (race, color, religion, sex, national origin).

2. Complainant applied and was qualified for a job for which the employer was seeking applicants.

3. Despite the qualifications, complainant was rejected.

4. After rejection, the position remained open and employer continued to seek applicants from persons with complainant's qualifications, or employer filled the position with a nonminority.

The genius of the *prima facie* case is that it removes certain legitimate reasons on which an employer might rely to reject an applicant. Ruling out these reasons is sufficient to create an inference or presumption that the decision was illegal.

If the complaint challenges an allegedly illegal discharge or firing, the plaintiff's case will be a slight variation on this format:

1. Complainant is an individual within a protected group.

2. Complainant was qualified and was performing the job satisfactorily.

3. Complainant was fired.

4. Complainant's job remained open or was given to a nonminority.

Stage Two: Defendant's Rebuttal. Once the plaintiff has established a *prima facie* case, the employer must articulate a legitimate, nondiscriminatory reason for the action. In other words, the defendant/employer must rebut the presumption of discrimination by producing (documenting or testifying to) some valid reason that explains why the plaintiff was not hired or was fired.

The burden of persuasion that the defendant acted intentionally is still on the plaintiff; it does not shift to the defendant. This point was established in *Texas Dept. of Community Affairs* v. *Burdine*.[24] The defendant/employer need only set forth the reasons for the plaintiff's rejection.

The reasons for not hiring a person or for firing one are too numerous to elaborate, but consider a few plausible ones. The person finally hired may have been better qualified. A firm may have refused to hire an applicant because the applicant's previous job history was unsatisfactory. Perhaps the qualifications were there, but letters of recommendation related that the applicant was always tardy, had excessive absences, had poor work habits, or could not get along with coworkers.

Once a qualified person has been employed, that employee may be discharged for theft, dishonesty, failing to get along with customers, insubordination, and a host of other performance-related reasons. A fired employee may have been only marginally qualified, and therefore replaced by a more skilled worker.

Bear in mind the important distinctions between a person's qualifications and performance. One may be qualified to do a job, yet if he or she has not performed well for a previous employer, that could be a good reason for failing to hire. When a qualified person is fired, that person may not have performed up to expectations or potential. The reason could be laziness, carelessness, family problems, debts, or legal problems. Some of these reasons may not be avoidable, but if they get in the way of performance, the employer has the right to discharge.

3. *Stage Three: Plaintiff Must Prove Pretext.* The plaintiff must now prove that the defendant's official reasons are not the real reasons at all. By ruling out the defendant/employer's asserted reasons, the plaintiff effectively proves that he or she was the victim of intentional discrimination.

This is the real battleground. Prior to this stage, it is relatively easy for the plaintiff to establish a *prima facie* case and for the defendant to advance some reason supporting its action. Now the plaintiff must reveal the cover-up; the pretextual reasons must be thrust aside and the real reasons—discrimination based on race, color, religion, sex, or national origin—exposed.

DISPARATE IMPACT—FAIR FORM/DISCRIMINATORY PRACTICE

Griggs v. *Duke Power Co.*, which you are about to examine, originated the concept of *disparate impact analysis.*

Griggs v. *Duke Power Co.*
401 U.S. 424 (1971)

BURGER, CHIEF JUSTICE

We granted the writ in this case to resolve the question whether an employer is prohibited by the Civil Rights Act of 1964, Title VII, from requiring a high school education or passing of [a] standardized general intelligence test as a condition of employment in or transfer to jobs when (a) neither standard is shown to be significantly related to successful job performance, (b) both requirements operate to disqualify Negroes at a substantially higher rate than white applicants, and (c) the jobs in question formerly had been filled only by white employees as part of a long-standing practice of giving preference to whites.

[*Author's note:* Prior to the effective date of the Civil Rights Act, July 2, 1965, the company openly discriminated on the basis of race. Blacks were employed only in the Labor Department, where the highest paying jobs paid less than the lowest paying jobs in other departments. Beginning in 1955, the company required a high school diploma for employment in any department except Labor; later, a high school education was required for transfer from Labor to any other department. In September 1965, the company began to permit employees without a high school education to transfer to better jobs by passing two tests: (1) a measure of general intelligence and (2) a measure of mechanical comprehension.]

* * *

. . . The Act proscribes not only overt discrimination but also practices that are fair in form, but discriminatory in operation. The touchstone is business necessity. If an employment practice which operates to exclude Negroes cannot be shown to be related to job performance, the practice is prohibited.

On the record before us, neither the high school completion requirement nor the general intelligence test is shown to bear a demonstrable relationship to successful performance of the jobs for which it was used. Both were adopted, as the Court of Appeals noted, without meaningful study of their relationship to job performance ability. Rather, a vice president of the Company testified, the requirements were instituted on the Company's judgment that they generally would improve the overall quality of the work force.

The evidence, however, shows that employees who have not completed high school or taken the tests have continued to perform satisfactorily and make progress in departments for which the high school and test criteria are now used. The promotion record of present employees who would not be able to meet the new criteria thus suggests the possibility that the requirements may not be needed even for the limited purpose of preserving the avowed policy of advancement within the Company. In the context of this case, it is unnecessary to reach the question whether testing requirements that take into account capability for the next succeeding position or related future promotion might be utilized upon a showing that such long-range requirements fulfill a genuine business need. In the present case the Company has made no such showing.

The Court of Appeals held that the Company had adopted the diploma and test requirements without any "intention to discriminate against Negro employees." We do not suggest that either the District Court or the Court of Appeals erred in examining the employer's intent; but good intent or absence of discriminatory intent does not redeem employment procedures or testing mechanisms that operate as "built-in headwinds" for minority groups and are unrelated to measuring job capability.

The Company's lack of discriminatory intent is suggested by special efforts to help the undereducated employees through Company financing of two-thirds of the cost of tuition for high school training. But Congress directed the thrust of the Act to the *consequences* of employment practices, not simply the motivation. More than that, Congress has placed on the employer the burden of showing that any given requirement must have a manifest relationship to the employment in question.

The facts of this case demonstrate the inadequacy of broad and general testing devices as well as the infirmity of using diplomas or degrees as fixed measures of capability. History is filled with examples of men and women who rendered highly effective performance without the conventional badges of accomplishment in terms of certificates, diplomas, or degrees. Diplomas and tests are useful servants, but Congress has mandated the commonsense proposition that they are not to become masters of reality.

CASE FOLLOW-UP

It is important to keep in mind that proof of disparate impact does not involve proof of wrongful intent. An employer honestly and in good faith could associate height/weight with strength (or test scores with job performance) and, on the basis of that unexamined assumption, use a test that had an illegal disparate impact.

Testing procedures must be job relevant; that is, they must test the applicant or employee for performance-related skills or potential rather than in the abstract. The fallacy of the Duke Power approach was the easy assumption that a high school diploma or a certain level of achievement on an IQ test was indicative of successful job performance. The employer had taken no steps to establish a strong, or any, correlation between test scores and work achievement.

Section 703(h) of Title VII authorizes the use of professionally developed ability tests if they are not *designed, intended, or used* to discriminate against protected groups. This is not a requirement that all such tests be validated, but tests and practices that are validated will have greater credence in defending a lawsuit, and they may be instrumental in avoiding one. *Validation* means that the test must be predictive of or significantly correlated with job-relevant behaviors for which the applicant is being evaluated. The EEOC has established guidelines for test validation based on American Psychological Association standards.

DISPARATE IMPACT AFTER *GRIGGS*

In *Wards Cove Packing Co.* v. *Atonio,* the Supreme Court attempted to raise the hurdles of plaintiffs seeking to prove disparate impact by using statistical data. These constraints were short-lived, as Congress passed the Civil Rights Act of 1991, which restores the civil rights protections to previous levels. In light of the 1991 Act, the law presently operates as follows:

A plaintiff initiating a Title VII claim who lacks direct evidence of discriminatory intent can begin by proving discriminatory impact. This requires a showing that an employment practice causes a disparate impact based on race, color, religion, sex, or national origin. By proving disparate impact, the employee makes a *prima facie* case, which shifts the burden of proof to the defendant employer. (The party with burden of proof must prove his or her claims or else lose the case. The party that has the burden of proof is therefore at a serious disadvantage because the "default" conclusion operates against that party.)

Shifting the burden of proof to the employer at this point makes sense, given the disparity in information between the two parties. The employee knows that his or her group is disproportionately harmed by the practice but does not have explicit access to the reasons behind the practice. Because the employer is best equipped to explain these reasons, the burden of proof shifts once the employee has made a *prima facie* case by simply demonstrating the impact. Once the burden has shifted, the employer has an opportunity to defend the contested practice. This requires that the employer demonstrate the practice is (a) job related and (b) consistent with a business necessity. Should the employer fail to make this showing, the employee wins the case. Should the employer successfully demonstrate a job-related business necessity, the employee has one last opportunity: If the employee can show that an alternative practice meets the business necessity without disparate impact and the employer refuses to adopt it, then the employee wins. If the employee cannot demonstrate such an alternative practice, then the employer wins by virtue of having proved a job-related business necessity.

Bona Fide Occupational Qualification. In addition to the defenses discussed in the section on disparate treatment—legitimate, nondiscriminatory reasons plus credible evidence—an employer will frequently advance a bona fide occupational qualification (BFOQ) as a defense to the charge of discriminatory practice. The BFOQ defense in a disparate treatment case is equivalent to a business necessity defense in a disparate impact case. This statutory defense is a limited one applicable only in rare situations; but if it is proved, this exception will allow an employer to discriminate on the basis of religion, sex, or national origin. It is not available in meeting allegations based on racial discrimination, and even when properly evoked it is restricted to cases involving *hiring* (by any employer) and *referrals* (by any employment agencies).

To use the BFOQ defense, the employer must successfully establish (a) a nexus or connection between the classification and job performance, (b) the necessity of a classification, and (c) that the classification and job performance are the essence of the business operation. The Act rejects romantic and paternalistic stereotypes, the traditional view of women in society, and unsupported assumptions about the ability of women to perform traditionally "male" jobs. If sex is not necessarily part of the job (as it would be for actresses or female models for women's clothing), the EEOC will challenge the BFOQ classification.

Customer preference does not automatically translate into a BFOQ necessity. For example, although many air travelers may prefer female to male flight attendants, the principal function of an airline is the safe transport of passengers from one place to another, and the employment of female flight attendants is not essential to the performance of that task.

The Supreme Court further restricted the nature of BFOQ in the landmark *Johnson Controls* case.[25] Defendant employer Johnson Controls had a policy that excluded women from jobs manufacturing batteries unless they could provide documentation showing sterility. Johnson Controls defended the policy by suggesting that exposure to lead in the manufacturing process exposed fetuses to danger of birth defects and that because of these risks, nonfertile female status was a BFOQ.

The Court rejected this argument, observing that a BFOQ must be a qualification that relates to the essence of the job or the central mission of the employee's business. Thus, an airline can lay off pregnant flight attendants if pregnancy impairs their ability to achieve the essence of their job. Because the foremost function of the flight attendant is the protection of passenger safety, advanced pregnancy that impedes the physical ability to protect passengers is a BFOQ. Compare the *Johnson Controls* scenario—sterility is certainly not even related to the ability to manufacture a battery. Therefore, under the Supreme Court's standard, status other than fertile female cannot be considered a BFOQ for battery manufacture positions.

Critics of the *Johnson Controls* case have suggested that the decision does not provide adequate consideration of fetus rights or of the liability posture of companies sued by persons damaged as fetuses during maternal exposure to such risks as lead. Although the majority opinion suggests that the *Johnson Controls* holding in itself should provide a defense to such liability claims, dissenting Justices disagreed.

ROLE OF SENIORITY SYSTEM IN TITLE VII

A *seniority system* is a system that prefers certain employees for promotions and benefits exclusively on the basis of time in the job. The most "senior" employee in the job is preferred. Discrimination against protected groups is not a Title VII violation if it results from a bona fide seniority system—that is, a system operated in good faith and not for the purpose of perpetuating discrimination. A problem arises, however, when the system does perpetuate a pattern of discrimination that stems from previous years in which intentional racial, ethnic, or gender-based segregation was practiced.

THE EQUAL PAY ACT

ENFORCEMENT AND COVERAGE

Effective July 1979, the Reorganization Plan of 1978 transferred interpretation and enforcement of the Equal Pay Act (EPA)[26] from the Secretary of Labor to the EEOC. Coverage extends to firms with as few as two employees[27] if those employees are engaged "in commerce" or "in the production of goods for commerce." Even if a firm has fewer than two employees, EPA coverage will be extended if annual sales or business reaches $362,500.

Labor unions are not covered, but they will be affected if they obstruct the Act's purposes. "No labor organization representing employees of an employer who has covered employees shall cause or attempt to cause such employer to discriminate against an employee in violation of the Act."[28] The Supreme Court has never determined whether the EPA constitutionally extends to state and local governments, but the weight of authority supports the Act's constitutionality.[29]

SELECTED PROVISIONS

The following passage is brief and sufficiently straightforward to convey to you the fundamentals of the Act.

> (d)(1) No employer having employees subject to any provisions of this section shall discriminate, within any establishment in which such employees are employed, between employees on the basis of sex by paying wages to employees in such establishment at a rate less than the rate at which he pays wages to employees of the opposite sex in such establishment for equal work on jobs the performance of which requires equal skill, effort, and responsibility, and which are performed under similar working conditions, except where such payment is made pursuant to (i) a seniority system; (ii) a merit system; (iii) a system which measures earnings by quantity or quality of production; or (iv) a differential based on any other factor other than sex: Provided, That an employer who is paying a wage rate differential in violation of this subsection shall not, in order to comply with the provisions of this subsection, reduce the wage rate of any employee.

★ ★ ★

(3) For purposes of administration and enforcement, any amounts owing to any employee which have been withheld in violation of this subsection shall be deemed to be unpaid minimum wages or unpaid overtime compensation under this Act.[30]

Equal work has not been taken to mean identical work.[31] The assignment of additional menial tasks to males, for example, in order to justify higher pay would frustrate the remedial purposes of the Act. The court will focus first on the primary duties of the jobs assigned to males and females. If they are similar or substantially equal, it will then determine whether any duties or differences of sufficient secondary importance justify the conclusion that the jobs are unequal. The work of male tailors and female seamstresses has been found to be substantially equal, as has that of male barbers and female beauticians and male and female flight attendants.

AFFIRMATIVE DEFENSES: FACTORS OTHER THAN SEX

The affirmative defenses of seniority, merit, and quantity or quality of production are chiefly illustrative of "factors other than sex." Used as an affirmative defense, a factor other than sex may be a business reason such as the profitability of a particular department; for example, the men's clothing department within a particular establishment may be more profitable than the women's clothing department. A "bona fide" training program for management or skill positions may be a factor other than sex, and the same is true for a *shift differential,* which provides higher pay for night work than for day work. These opportunities, of course, must be equally available to women and men.

Labor market realities, such as the availability of women in the workforce and their willingness to work for the lower prevailing wage, are not factors other than sex. To incorporate these considerations into the wage scale would be counterproductive. Because the EPA is remedial in nature, courts have declined to accept defenses that simply validate the status quo. They have expressed the same view toward stereotypical assumptions about the quality of female workers.

EQUAL PAY ACT REMEDIES

An employer found to be in violation of the EPA cannot eliminate the wage differential by reducing the pay of males to a lower level. The lower wage rate of female employees must be increased.

Unlike violations of the 1964 Civil Rights Act, Title VII, the injured employee can file suit without first resorting to administrative proceedings. A successful plaintiff is entitled to recover unpaid back wages and an equal amount as liquidated damages unless the court finds that the employer acted in good faith and with objective reasons to believe that past wages were lawful.

Statute of Limitations.   Each payday that an employer is in violation of the Act amounts to a separate cause of action. Back wages are recoverable for two years, and this limit will be extended to three years if the violation was willful or deliberate, rather than through negligence or oversight.

Whistle-Blowers.   Employees who file complaints, institute proceedings, testify, or otherwise cooperate in an investigation under EPA cannot be discharged or discriminated against by the employer for their whistle-blowing behavior.

COMPARABLE WORTH OR PAY EQUITY

To make the transition from the EPA to Title VII, first imagine a situation in which men and women employed by a business firm or governmental entity are receiving different rates of pay and working at different jobs—for example, secretaries and mechanics. The EPA would not cover this situation because the work is not equal or substantially equal, but the argument has been made by the EEOC and others that if the "unequal" work is comparable in worth or value to the employer, the pay should be the same.

The idea of comparable worth is intended to combat what some people call "structural discrimination." Suppose job categories, such as nurses or secretaries, have been the subject of historical sex discrimination. If the law equalized the pay of all sexes within these categories (there are a few male secretaries and nurses), this will not remedy the problem. The remedy is to inquire into the value of the services offered by the group. The work of nurses and secretaries must be valued by comparing it with the work of similar groups that have not been the subject of historical sex discrimination. In short, comparable worth or pay equity evaluates and balances the contribution to an employer of Group *A* that has been discriminated against with Group *B* that has not been discriminated against. Otherwise, Group *A* will be exploited. In effect, this group subsidizes or underwrites the firm to the extent that it is paid less than it contributes.

In 1976, the EEOC took the position that the logic of the situation compelled comparable worth compensation—i.e., compensation based on skill, effort, responsibility, and working conditions. After all, Title VII is designed to remedy discrimination regarding sex and other matters. Thus, even though the jobs of secretaries and mechanics are different and even though the labor market sets disparate wages, the employees should be compensated on factors that relate their contribution or worth to success of the business firm or governmental employer. If these factors indicate that secretaries and mechanics contribute equally, they should be paid the same even though market considerations (labor supply and demand) indicate that secretaries would be available at lower salaries than mechanics. As a practical matter, the Title VII career of comparable worth was ended in 1985 by *American Federation of State, County, and Municipal Employees* v. *State of Washington.*[32]

Variants of the comparable worth approach to pay equity have been adopted in several nations, most notably in Canada, where it has a significant impact on salaries and labor markets. The following case provides a look into the workings of comparable worth doctrine in Canada.

Syndicat des employes de production du Quebec
et de l'Acadie v. Canada
62 D.L.R. 4th 385; 17 A.C.W.S. (3d) 479 (1989)

[*Author's note:* Plaintiff Syndicat appealed a decision of the Canadian Human Rights Commission that defendant employer did not violate Section 11 of the Canadian Human Rights Act. The majority decision dismissed the appeal on procedural grounds. What follows is a part of the dissenting opinion. The dissenting Justice disagreed with the dismissal of the appeal and, in the excerpt that follows, examines the comparable worth questions that the majority justices declined to consider. Although this is a dissenting opinion, it is interesting as an explanation of the comparable worth laws of Canada as they apply to the facts of the case.]

L'HEUREUX-DUBE, J. (dissenting).

The complaint which gave rise to the present proceedings alleges that the employer maintains a difference in wages between male and female employees employed in the same establishment who are performing work of equal value, contrary to s. 11 of the Act. Specifically, the complaint focuses on the discrepancy in the wages paid to the predominantly female employees of the Section Costumes and those paid to the predominantly male employees of the Section Decors.

In appellant's submission, the organization of the workforce perpetuates a wage differential between "women's work" and "men's work" and such job segregation in and of itself constitutes prima facie evidence of wage discrimination under section 11 of the Act.

Section 11 states:

11(1) It is a discriminatory practice for an employer to establish or maintain differences in wages between male and female employees employed in the same establishment who are performing work of equal value.

(2) In assessing the value of the work performed by employees employed in the same establishment the criterion to be applied is the composite of the skill, effort and responsibility required in the performance of the work and the conditions under which the work is performed.

(3) Notwithstanding subsection (1), it is not a discriminatory practice to pay to male and female employees different wages if the difference is based on a factor prescribed by guidelines issued by the Canadian Human Rights Commission pursuant to subsection 22(2), to be a reasonable factor that justifies the difference.

(4) For greater certainty, sex does not constitute a reasonable factor justifying a difference in wages.

The evidence of professional segregation in the present case is considerable. Section Costumes employs 40 persons, close to three-quarters of whom are female (72.5%), while Section Decors employs 280 persons, nearly all of whom are male (99.65%). The work performed in the former section is subdivided into six jobs by the employer, while that performed on the latter is subdivided into over 20 jobs. The average salary paid in the Section Costumes is $19,782, while in the Section Decors that average is $21,715. This discrepancy of close to $2,000 is further reflected in the wage scales for jobs in each section. In the Section Costumes, the wages range from $15,559 to $23,367, while in the Section Decors, according to the appellant, the wages range from $15,559 to $25,579. In the appellant's submission, these wage discrepancies are especially serious in view of a principle of economics which posits an inversely proportional relationship between the degree of specialization of a task and the average salary of those who perform that task. Since the work performed in the Section Decors is considerably more subdivided than the work performed in the Section Costumes, on the basis of this principle, one would have expected a lower average salary in the former section. Appellant adds that the French job titles further indicate segregation, some job titles in Section Costumes being feminine ("habilleuse", "habilleuse en chef", "script assistante") while all those in Section Decors are masculine. This evidence, appellant contends, establishes that the organization of labour is segregated and that the lower wage scales in Section Costumes reflect an under-valuing of the work performed by its predominantly female employees. In its factum, appellant writes (translation):

> ... when, within the same bargaining unit, composed of a minority of women, these women fill, majoritarily, certain "female jobs" which are less well paid than the other "male jobs" in the unit, and where men and women work under similar working conditions and at jobs having the same objective, proof of job segregation establishes prima facie that the wage disparity is in part caused by sex discrimination.

This argument raises the legal definition of wage discrimination under s. 11 of the Act. A first step in this direction is this court's clear statement that intent is not a precondition to a finding of adverse discrimination under the Canadian Human Rights Act. As written by La Forest J. for the court in *Robichaud* v. *The Queen, supra,* at p. 581:

> Since the Act is essentially concerned with the removal of discrimination, as opposed to punishing anti-social behaviour, it follows that the motives or intention of those who discriminate are not central to its concerns. Rather, the Act is directed to redressing socially unde-sirable conditions quite apart from the reasons for their existence.

As intent is not a prerequisite element of adverse discrimination, a complainant may build his or her case under ss. 7 and 10 by presenting evidence of the type adduced by the complainant in the present case. Statistical evidence of professional segregation is a most precious tool in uncovering adverse discrimination. Section 11, however, differs from ss. 7 and 10. Its scope of protection is delineated by the concept of "equal value." That provision does not prevent the employer from remunerating differently jobs which are not "equal" in value. Wage discrimination, in the context of that specific provision, is premised on the equal worth of the work performed by men and women in the same establishment. Accordingly, to be successful, a claim brought under s. 11 must establish the equality of the work for which a discriminatory wage differential is alleged.

Section 11(2) defines in general terms the manner in which the value of work is to be assessed. The criterion to be applied, under that provision, is the composite of the skill, effort, and responsibility required in the performance of the work and the conditions under which the work is to be performed. At the time material to this appeal, s. 3 of the Equal Wages Guidelines defined this criterion in somewhat greater detail:

> 3. Subsections 11(1) and (2) of the Act apply in any case in such a manner that in assessing the value of work performed by employees employed in the same establishment to determine if they are performing work of equal value,
>
> (a) the skill required in the performance of the work of an employee shall be considered to include any type of intellectual or physical skill required in the performance of that work that has been acquired by the employee through experience, training, education or

natural ability, and the nature and extent of such skills of employees employed in the same establishment shall be compared without taking into consideration the means by which such skills were acquired by the employees;

(b) the effort required in the performance of the work of an employee shall be considered to include any intellectual or physical effort normally required in the performance of that work, and in comparing such efforts exerted by employees employed in the same establishment,

(i) such efforts may be found to be of equal value whether such efforts were exerted by the same or different means, and

(ii) the assessment of the effort required in the performance of the work of an employee shall not normally be affected by the occasional or sporadic performance by that employee of a task that requires additional effort;

(c) the responsibility required in the performance of the work of an employee shall be assessed by determining the extent to which the employer relies on the employee to perform the work having regard to the importance of the duties of the employee and the accountability of the employee to the employer for machines, finances and any other resources and for the work of other employees; and

(d) the conditions under which the work of an employee is performed shall be considered to include noise, heat, cold, isolation, physical danger, conditions hazardous to health, mental stress and any other conditions produced by the physical or psychological work environment, but shall not be considered to include a requirement to work overtime or on shifts where a premium is paid to the employee for such overtime or shift work.

The Aiken plan [i.e., the employer's plan for valuing jobs] which was ultimately communicated to the appellant shows the complexity of the evaluation and the many possibly different outcomes of the process. Under that plan, the factor of "skill" is broken down into "complexity-judgment," "education" and "experience"; "effort," into "initiative" and "physical and mental demands"; and "responsibilities," into "result of errors," "contacts" and "supervision (character and scope)." The factor of "working conditions" remains entire, and as a result there is a total of nine compensable factors. Each of these factors in the Commission's Aiken plan is allocated a range of possible scores. "Complexity-judgment" ranges from 10 to 150; "education," from 10 to 120; "experience," from 5 to 150; "initiative," from 10 to 90; "physical and mental demands," from 5 to 30: "result of errors," from 5 to 100; "contacts," from 5 to 100; "supervision," from 5 to 80 for "character," and from 5 to 50 for "scope"; and "working conditions," from 5 to 40. As can readily be seen, the relative weights of each of the factors prescribed by s. 11 of the Act are unequal, being far more important in the case of "skill" and "responsibilities" than they are in the case of "effort" and "working conditions."

[A]ppellant submitted that a number of true compensable characteristics were not caught by the subdivision of factors defined in the Commission's interpretation of that plan. For instance, the ability of employees in Section Costumes to adapt to a flexible allocation of work, the resourcefulness of these employees, as well as the dexterity and speed with which they are required to perform the work were said to have been overlooked by the Aiken plan. In addition, appellant contested the factor of "experience." This factor, according to the appellant, was biased against women. . . .

At no time was the appellant involved in the selection of compensable factors or the respective weighing of these factors. . . .

[A]ppellant should have been allowed to make informed submissions with respect to the legal standard of equal value under s. 11, and, if the Aiken method was chosen as that standard, then appellant should also have been heard on the selection and relative weight of the compensable factors as well. Any other aspect of the methodology proposed to be adopted by the Commission which the parties might have felt could unfairly prejudice the assessment of the value of the work could also be dealt at such a hearing. Such a hearing should have been granted either orally or in writing, so as to give the parties concerned an effective means of advancing their own interpretation of the applicable legal standard before the investigation could proceed.

For these reasons, I am of the view that the Commission failed to observe a principle of natural justice in proceeding without affording such an opportunity to the appellant and that its decision must accordingly be set aside.

On the whole, I would allow the appeal, quash the decision of the Federal Court of Appeal dismissing the application for judicial review. Exercising that court's powers under s. 28(1) of the Federal Court Act, I would set aside the decision of the Commission and remit the matter to it for further consideration.

CASE FOLLOW-UP

This case raises a number of interesting policy questions in regard to the alleviation of employment discrimination. Under U.S. employment law, we allow the marketplace to determine the value of an employee's services and confine antidiscrimination efforts to the statutory coverage of discriminatory intent and impact, as discussed earlier in this chapter. The Canadian approach discussed in this case reflects a far greater degree of regulatory intervention in the determination of value. Very generally, what are the strengths and weaknesses of the two approaches? More specifically, do you agree with Justice L'Heureux-Dube that motives or intent to discriminate should not be considered central to the concerns and application of antidiscrimination legislation? What are the strengths and weaknesses of the precise legal mandates in Sections 11(1)–11(4)? How would you assess the criteria adopted in the Aiken plan for job valuation?

CONCLUSION

In this chapter, we reviewed the history of modern civil rights legislation Next, we explored the bureaucracy of the 1964 Civil Rights Act, its scope, and its moral basis. The most controversial aspect of Title VII—affirmative action—was analyzed in two important cases, *Johnson* v. *Santa Clara County* and *City of Richmond* v. *J. A. Croson Company*. An informed observer would have to acknowledge that the majority of the Court responds unfavorably to this preferential measure because of its reverse discrimination or spillover effects. In addition, it seems clear that the Court will approve such programs only in cases involving the most egregious violations by private and public sector employers.

We then examined Title VII's protection against discrimination on the basis of sex, religion, and national origin. We took a detailed look at proof of claims by exploring, first, a *prima facie* case; second, the employer's rebuttal; and finally, the plaintiff's burden of persuasion in both disparate impact and disparate treatment cases.

Recent developments in this area of the law are found in the Supreme Court's restrictions on disparate impact analysis in *Wards Cove Packing Co* v. *Atonio*. The net effect of *Wards Cove* is to take a substantial amount of pressure off employers in defending such lawsuits. The diminution of this pressure will probably result in the adoption of fewer affirmative action plans.

REVIEW QUESTIONS AND PROBLEMS

1. What were the principal matters of contention between Justices Brennan and Scalia in their *Johnson* v. *Santa Clara County* opinions?

2. Enumerate the components of a minority business enterprise set-aside program that will meet the constitutional requirements of *City of Richmond* v. *J. A. Croson Company.*

3. Suppose you were asked by your employer to draft the sexual harassment prohibitions for the corporate code of ethics. What would be the main elements of your proposal?

4. What is the Title VII justification for allowing an employer to discriminate on the basis of alienage? Isn't that the same thing as discrimination on the basis of national origin?

5. With regard to indirect proof of causation under Title VII, summarize the *prima facie,* the rebuttal, and the pretextual stages of the litigation.

6. The state of Alabama had a long history of racial discrimination in the composition of its police force. To ameliorate this problem, a policy was adopted by which one black promotion was required for every white promotion. Provided the upper ranks of the police department had a smaller percentage of blacks than the lower ranks, is this policy enforceable? (*U.S.* v. *Paradise*, 107 S.Ct. 1053 (1987)).

7. Contrast disparate impact with disparate treatment cases under Title VII.

8. Memphis, Tennessee, adopted hiring and promotion goals for minorities to remedy a record of illegal discrimination. These goals were part of a "consent decree," i.e., a court-appointed settlement. The decree did not address the possibility of future layoffs. When the city was later faced with budgeting constraints, it applied the "last hired, first fired" rule of a seniority system it had adopted during the process of collective bargaining. As a result, a disproportionate number of minority employees were fired. Is this legal? (*Firefighters Local Union #1784* v. *Stotts*, 467 U.S. 561 (1984)).

ENDNOTES

1. Locke, *Two Treatises of Government* 398 (Laslett ed. 1963).
2. 42 U.S.C.A. §§2000e *et seq.* (1976).
3. Forrester, *Constitutional Law* 596 (1959). Forrester has described this era of U.S. history as the Second Civil War.
4. 109 U.S. 3 (1883).
5. 163 U.S. 537 (1896).
6. *Roberts* v. *City of Boston,* 59 Mass. (5 Cush.) 198 (1849).
7. 392 U.S. 409 (1968).
8. *Fitzpatrick* v. *Bitzer,* 427 U.S. 445 (1976).
9. 490 U.S. 642 (1989); 57 U.S.L.W. 4583 (June 6, 1989).
10. 443 U.S. 193 (1979).
11. 476 U.S. 267 (1986).
12. 448 U.S. 448 (1980).
13. 114 S.Ct. 367(1993).
14. 400 U.S. 542 (1971).
15. *Sprogis* v. *United Airlines, Inc.,* 444 F.2d 1194 (7th Cir. 1971).
16. *Airline Stewards and Stewardesses Association, Local 550* v. *American Airlines,* 573 F.2d 960 (7th Cir. 1978).
17. 435 U.S. 702 (1978).
18. 566 F.2d 659 (9th Cir. 1977).
19. 608 F.2d 327 (9th Cir. 1979).
20. *Young* v. *Southwestern Savings and Loan Association,* 509 F.2d 140 (5th Cir. 1975). The courts recently reinforced this point by striking down a Connecticut statute that gave an automatic priority to an employee's request to take the Sabbath day off. State and federal statutes that only provide for reasonable accommodation of an employee's request are not endangered, however, because they do not involve "excessive entanglement" and because they advance religion only incidentally or remotely.
21. 432 U.S. 63 (1977).
22. 414 U.S. 86 (1973).
23. 411 U.S. 792 (1973).
24. 450 U.S. 248 (1981).
25. *United Automobile Aerospace et al.* v. *Johnson Controls, Inc.,* 111 S.Ct. 1196 (1991).
26. Fair Labor Standards Act of 1938 §6(d), as amended, 29 U.S.C. §§201, 206(d) (1976). The Fair Labor Standards Act regulates minimum wages, overtime, and child labor. Coverage, exemption, and enforcement provisions of the Fair Labor Standards Act are applicable to the substance of the EPA.
27. Fifteen employees are required for coverage under the Civil Rights Act of 1964, §701(b), 42 U.S.C.A. §2000e(b) (1976).
28. 29 U.S.C.A. §206(d)(2).
29. *Marshall* v. *City of Sheboygan,* 577 F.2d 1 (7th Cir. 1978); *Usery* v. *Charlston County School District,* 558 F.2d 1169 (4th Cir. 1977); *Usery* v. *Allegheny County Institutional Dist.,* 544 F.2d 148 (3rd Cir. 1976); *National League of Cities* v. *Usery,* 426 U.S. 833 (1976).
30. 29 U.S.C.A. §206(d).
31. *Wirtz* v. *Wheaton Glass Co.,* 427 F.2d 259 (3rd Cir. 1970).
32. 770 F.2d 1401 (9th Cir. 1985).

CHAPTER 15

Labor and Employment Law

INTRODUCTION

The first labor laws in Western Europe were passed in response to labor shortages caused by the great plagues of the fourteenth century. As the number of peasants, artisans, crafters, and other workers were reduced by the Black Death, production slowed and inflation increased. As laborers realized that their value had increased, they demanded and received some concessions from their masters. Their success was short-lived, however, as the ruling classes reacted with legislation requiring them to work at the reduced wages of earlier years. These fourteenth-century lords were unrelenting in their use of the law to deal with labor problems. Labor laws continued to be used for the next two centuries, culminating with the Tudor Industrial Code of 1562.

As the feudal system in Europe declined in favor of mercantilism, manufacture for export became the focus of business society. Early manufacturers built factories to which workers were brought to improve productivity efficiency and to meet the export demand. Increased production led to greater wealth and an increased standard of living, but laboring people shared few of these gains. Under these new conditions (a centralized labor force), individual laborers could at least bargain with their employers to try to get a larger share of the new wealth.

Although the American version of the industrial revolution got a later start, development followed along similar lines. During the latter half of the nineteenth century, American capitalists began to build their empires, and such companies as Standard Oil and United States Steel came into existence. As factories became larger and employed more workers, the individual laborer's bargaining power was reduced. Given these conditions, it is easy to see why workers began to cooperate to achieve the common goal of greater equality in dealing with employers. The early attempts to collectively improve wages, however, were met with charges of criminal conspiracy.

Employers argued that it was an illegal conspiracy for employees to act together to improve working conditions. Because employers could not act together to improve their position, logical consistency implied that employees should be treated the same. As a result, the full force of the law was used to halt strikes.

In the *Philadelphia Cordwainers'* case of 1806,[1] employees stopped work and refused to continue unless they received a specified wage. They also attempted to prevent other employees from working. Management requested and received the aid of the public prosecutor, who then issued an indictment. Reflecting the views of the time, the court held that whether the laborers hoped to benefit themselves or to injure others, their purpose was illegal. The strike was declared unlawful, and state and local law enforcement officers were called out to enforce the court order.

This method of addressing the labor problem was used by management with varying results until public criticism made criminal prosecutions politically unpopular. In the 1842 *Commonwealth* v. *Hunt*[2] case, the Massachusetts court held that the mere fact that workers were acting in unison did not necessarily imply a criminal conspiracy unless the means used or the objective to be obtained was unlawful. The *Hunt* case struck a major blow against the use of criminal penalties when workers acted together to gain concessions from their employers.

Deprived of criminal action as a weapon to fight labor movements, employers returned to the courts in their own behalf with civil actions. Two approaches were used by management: (1) actions for the intentional infliction of economic harm and (2) actions seeking injunctive relief to prevent economic harm. Initially, these actions were begun in state courts and were not always decided in favor of management. But this changed after passage of the Sherman Antitrust Act.[3] Around the turn of the century, a growing number of employers sought injunctive relief in the federal courts. In the *Danbury Hatters* case,[4] the Supreme Court held that the "restraint of trade" prohibition in the Sherman Act, Section 1, applied to union-instigated boycotts. As a result, the union was subjected to the act's treble-damages provisions.

The injunction soon became the major tool to fight employee combinations for two reasons. First, an injunction was usually issued immediately on filing the action. The injunction would then be in force until a hearing could be scheduled. The subsequent hearing was the first time the union would be able to tell its side of the story, and this was usually too late to help because the strike had already been broken by the initial injunction. Second, it was often difficult to locate the union's assets, if they existed at all, and monetary damages rarely benefitted the employers.

In 1914, Congress acted in an apparent attempt to aid the labor unions with passage of the Clayton Act.[5] The Clayton Act contained definitions that removed a person's application of the Sherman Act's restraint of trade provisions from economic strikes by labor unions. Seven years later, however, in the *Duplex Printing* case,[6] the Supreme Court gave a narrow reading to the Clayton Act and circumvented the attempted protection. The case involved a secondary boycott[7] by nonemployees. On the basis of the wording in the statute, the Court held that the protection was accorded only to legitimate labor activities of employees and did not include secondary boycotts by nonemployees.

In 1932, Congress took a more direct approach to the problem with passage of the Norris-LaGuardia Act.[8] Through this law, Congress removed the court's jurisdiction to issue injunctions in labor disputes. This Act marked the beginning of a shift to legislation in support of the labor movement.

MODERN LEGISLATION

THE NATIONAL LABOR RELATIONS ACT

In 1935, Congress passed the single most important piece of pro-labor legislation—the National Labor Relations Act (NLRA), also known as the Wagner Act.[9] Congress not only showed support for unionism and collective bargaining but also set up the infrastructure for their continued and strong existence. Based on the commerce clause, the NLRA had three major purposes: First, it established a number of employees' rights, the most important of which was the right to act and bargain collectively. Second, it prohibited certain employer conduct as unfair labor practices; these practices had the effect of preventing or weakening labor organizations. Third, it created an administrative body, the National Labor Relations Board (NLRB) to administer and enforce the Act.

Section 7 of the Wagner Act lists and defines employee rights.

> Employees shall have the right to self-organization, to form, join or assist labor organizations, to bargain collectively through representatives of their own choosing, and to engage in concerted activities for the purpose of collective bargaining or other mutual aid or protection.

Exemptions from the Wagner Act.   The employee rights, however, do not extend to all workers in the United States. The Act itself is restricted to exclude employees of airlines or railroads, agricultural workers, domestic servants, related employees of a parent or spouse, governmental employees, and independent contractors. Moreover, the NLRB itself does not attempt to exercise jurisdiction over all employers theoretically covered by the Act. Budget, personnel, and other practical considerations simply preclude it. Finally, managers and supervisors are not covered. Employees who exercise independent decision-making authority and discretion are exempted to ensure their loyalty to the company and to prevent them from becoming involved in conflicts of interest between the employer and union representatives.

Employer Unfair Labor Practices.   A major contribution of the Wagner Act was to define *unfair labor practices*. Section 8 of the Act lists and defines the five unfair labor practices of employers.

1. Interference with employee efforts to form, join, or assist labor organizations or to engage in concerted activities for mutual aid or protection (Section 8(a)(1))

2. Domination of a labor organization or contribution of financial or other support to it (Section 8(a)(2))

3. Discrimination in hiring or tenure of employees for reasons of union affiliation (Section 8(a)(3))

4. Discrimination against employees for filing charges or giving testimony under the act (Section 8(a)(4))

5. Refusal to bargain collectively with a duly designated representative of the employees (Section 8(a)(5))

Congress prohibited these practices to ensure that the employee rights granted in Section 7 were not undermined. They are discussed more fully later in the chapter.

Employee Bargaining Agents.   Section 9 of the Act establishes the methods the employees and the NLRB are to follow in selecting the exclusive representative of the employees. To avoid numerous, separate employee groups attempting to bargain with management, the Act provides for an election whereby an exclusive bargaining agent is chosen by majority vote. Once the agent is selected, it is then an unfair labor practice for the employer not to bargain with him or her. This process is explained later in detail.

The National Labor Relations Board.   The act also created the NLRB to administer and enforce the Act. The five members of the board are appointed by the president with Senate approval. The board conducts and supervises the representation selection process and investigates and prosecutes unfair labor practice complaints. To separate the enforcement and adjudication functions, the Wagner Act was later amended by the Taft-Hartley Act to establish the office of General Counsel as the enforcement arm of the board.

Congress based the Wagner Act on the commerce clause in the stated belief that its provisions were necessary to ensure the free flow of trade. In light of the increased power given to the unions, it was predictable that the Act would be challenged by employers who thought Congress had trespassed into areas reserved for state regulation under the Tenth Amendment. The Supreme Court considered these arguments and held that the Act was constitutional in *NLRB* v. *Jones & Laughlin Steel Corporation*.[10]

THE TAFT-HARTLEY ACT AND THE LANDRUM-GRIFFIN ACT

After passage of the Wagner Act, unions enjoyed considerable growth under the protections it offered. Although the purpose of the Act had been to place laborers on an equal footing with employers, the power and growth of the unions soon shifted the balance in favor of labor. Just as the individual had little bargaining power with the employer, few companies had bargaining power with a union that represented labor for the entire industry.

In an effort to adjust this perceived imbalance, Congress passed the Taft-Hartley Act in 1947.[11] It amended Section 7 of the Wagner Act by adding an employee's right to refrain from joining the union activities of Section 7. In addition, Congress added Section 8(b) to the Wagner Act to provide for the following unfair labor practices on the part of unions:

1. Restraining or coercing an employee to join a union or an employer in selecting his or her representatives to bargain with the union (Section 8(b)(1))

2. Causing or attempting to cause an employer to discriminate against nonunion employees, unless a legal union-shop agreement is in effect (Section 8(b)(2))

3. Refusal to bargain with the employer by the NLRB-designated employee representative (Section 8(b)(3))

4. Striking, picketing, and engaging in secondary boycotts for illegal purposes (Section 8(b)(4))

5. Charging new members excessive or discriminatory initiation fees where there is a union-shop agreement (Section 8(b)(5))

6. Causing an employer to pay for work not performed (Section 8(b)(6))

Congress also acted to lessen the length and severity of strikes by providing for an eighty-day cooling-off period in national emergency situations and by creating the Federal Mediation and Conciliation Service, which works with the parties to resolve their differences during the eighty-day period. The Taft-Hartley Act equalized bargaining positions while still encouraging union activity free from employer influence.

Congress again amended the Wagner Act when it passed the Landrum-Griffin Act in 1959.[12] During the 1950s, congressional committee hearings concerning union corruption took place. In response, Congress passed this Act to provide for more internal control of union activities, to require financial disclosures by unions and employers, and to create penalties for misbehavior by union officials.[13] The Landrum-Griffin Act also added the following unfair labor practices to the Wagner Act:

1. Employers agreeing with a labor organization to engage in secondary and hot-cargo agreements (Section 8(e)). A *secondary agreement* of the type that this section prohibits would be one in which an employer (E_1) with which the union does *not* have a dispute agrees with a union to refrain from making purchases from an employer (E_2) with which the union does have a dispute. Such an agreement would obviously be an attempt to pressure E_2 into settling on terms favorable to the union. A *hot-cargo* contract is one in which an employer agrees with a union not to purchase or otherwise deal with the nonunion goods.

2. Union picketing to require an employer to recognize or bargain with a union that is not currently certified to represent its employees in certain cases (Section 8(b)(7)).

THE COLLECTIVE BARGAINING PROCESS

ELECTION OF AN EXCLUSIVE BARGAINING REPRESENTATIVE

The first step in the collective bargaining process is selection of the employees' exclusive representative. An employer, an employee, or a union can begin the process by filing a petition in an NLRB regional director's office. The petition may be filed to select an initial bargaining representative or to rescind certification of the existing representative. For either purpose, an employee or union filing for an election must allege support from a substantial (interpreted to mean 30 percent) number of employees. Employee support is usually indicated by signed authorization cards. An employer filing for an election of an initial bargaining representative, however, usually does so in response to union pressure and need not allege any support. When attempting to have certification rescinded, however, the employer must show that it doubts, in good faith, that the employees continue to support the union.

Unions seeking recognition as the exclusive bargaining unit fall into three categories. First, employees in a particular bargaining unit may form their own union and seek recognition. Second, interested employees may contract an existing union and then work with the union to seek election. Third, an outside union may make the initial contract with employees to get them to join and then work for election as the bargaining representative. The third category is most prevalent, whereas formation of a new union is the least likely to occur.

Once the petition is filed with the NLRB, the regional staff determines whether the board has jurisdiction. In cases involving an existing bargaining representative, little difficulty is encountered. When a petition requests recognition of an initial representative, however, the staff must determine whether the employees and the employer fall within the language of the Act. Next, it must decide whether the board's discretionary conditions are also met. The discretionary provisions concern total annual sales, purchases, and other business characteristics that demonstrate the effect on commerce. If the effect is not sufficiently substantial, the board does not exercise jurisdiction.

Prior to any election, the board must also determine the appropriate bargaining unit. Subject to certain minor exceptions, the bargaining unit could be the total employer unit (e.g., two or more plants owned by a single firm), or it could be a single factory or plant unit, craft unit, or any subdivision of these. How the board determines the unit plays a large part in the success or failure of the particular election because the number of votes needed for a simple majority is based on the size of this unit. In establishing the unit, the board attempts to include all employees having similar economic interest while excluding those with conflicting interests. The board looks to the plant organization, past history of collective bargaining, and the geographical location of employees; these and other factors are balanced in selecting the bargaining unit.

After the above steps are completed, the board directs an election. Failure by either the employer or the union to maintain these conditions may be considered an unfair labor practice and will result in a new election. The board's regional office certifies the election results. If a union receives majority support of the employees in the bargaining unit, it is certified as the exclusive bargaining representative for that employee unit. If no union receives majority support, that result is also certified. Once an election is completed and the union certified, no further elections may be held for a period of one year, if no unfair practices have taken place during the election. The one-year period is intended to give the chosen representative a chance to fulfill promises made during the election. Moreover, once a representative has entered into a collective agreement with an employer, no elections can be held during the term of the agreement. This provision represents a move toward stability for employers and employees alike.

COLLECTIVE BARGAINING

Once the bargaining representative is elected, the individual employees of the bargaining unit lose the right to negotiate separate employment contracts with the employer. Instead, the employer and representatives meet to set the terms and conditions of employment. Section 8(d) of the NLRA imposes a mutual obligation on employers and the employee representatives to "meet at reasonable times and confer in good faith with respect to wages, hours, and other terms and conditions of employment, or the negotiation of an agreement, or any question arising thereunder, and the execution of a written contract incorporating any agreement reached if requested by either party." The obligation, however, does not require either party to agree to a proposal or to make concessions.

Bargaining in Good Faith.   *Good faith* is one major element of the collective bargaining process. Bad faith bargaining is an unfair labor practice and is exemplified in two kinds of circumstances. First are actions considered per se violations of the good faith requirement—that is, violations for which there is no defense. Examples of this type of action include refusal to bargain at all, designation of individuals who have no bargaining authority as bargaining representatives, insistence on illegal terms in contracts, refusal to execute a written contract, union refusal to agree on a reasonable contract period, and unilateral employer actions in changing wages, hours, or working conditions. Second are actions that, viewed in relation to other factors and in consideration of all the circumstances, reveal a general disregard for the integrity of the process. These actions occur when a party is merely going through the motions of bargaining. The determination of whether the parties are bargaining in good faith requires an appraisal of people's states of mind. Understandably, this appraisal is difficult to undertake and involves considerable uncertainty.

A prime consideration in determination of good faith is whether the parties approach the table with an open mind and are willing to listen to the other side. When a party has come with a closed, "take-it-or-leave-it" proposal, the board and the courts have held that the party was not bargaining in good faith. General Electric (GE) once used such an approach, known as Boulwareism, named after

GE vice-president Lemuel R. Boulware. Prior to negotiations, GE studied all of the bargaining issues, developed a comprehensive employment package, and sold the package to the employees with extensive publicity. The company then entered into negotiations with a firm, take-it-or-leave-it stand on the package. The board held that Boulwareism was illegal because it allowed for no compromise. Although the employer does not have to make concessions to reach an agreement, it cannot enter the bargaining process with a firm intention of not budging from a position. The board's decision was later upheld by the Court of Appeals for Second Circuit in *NLRB* v. *General Electric Co.*[14]

Subject Matter of Collective Bargaining.   A second major element of the collective bargaining process is the subject of negotiations. Three classifications of subjects are involved in bargaining discussions: mandatory, permissive, and prohibited. The *mandatory* subjects are wages, hours, and other terms and conditions of employment. These subjects include wage rate, bonus plans, holiday and severance pay, working time, shifts, breaks, holidays, vacations, discharge and discipline provisions, as well as seniority, promotion, transfer, and layoff policies. Both parties must bargain on these matters. Refusal to do so is an unfair labor practice.

The *permissive* subjects are those that either party may refuse to bargain over without committing an unfair labor practice. Examples of permissive subjects include arbitration provisions and nonstrike clauses. Although failure to bargain over these subjects is not an unfair labor practice, insistence on bargaining as a condition to an agreement may be considered a refusal to bargain in good faith.

The subjects *prohibited* by the Act include closed-shop, hot-cargo, and secondary boycott provisions. *Hot-cargo agreements*, those in which an employer agrees not to handle nonunion goods, and *secondary boycotts*, those in which the union pressures a neutral firm to agree not to do business with the employer that the union has a dispute with, have already been discussed. *Closed shops*, outlawed by the Taft-Hartley Act, are those in which employers agree not to hire nonunion employees. *Union shops*, agreements that give a new employee thirty days to join a union, are legal, however. Except for the union shops, even if an agreement contains one of these provisions, neither the board nor the courts will enforce them.

Classification of an issue is also important because strikes and lockouts are legal only if a mandatory issue is at stake. Strikes or lockouts on permissive subjects result in payment by the offending party of any damages or back pay. For example, if the union went on strike for an arbitration provision, it would be liable to the company for damages.

The case that follows deals with the employer's duty to bargain over a partial shutdown of its operations.

First National Maintenance Corp. v. NLRB
452 U.S. 666 (1981)

BLACKMUN, JUSTICE

Must an employer, under its duty to bargain in good faith "with respect to wages, hours, and other terms and conditions of employment," Section 8(d) and 8(a)(5) of the National Labor Relations Act negotiate with the certified representative of its employees over its decision to close a part of its business? In this case, the National Labor Relations Board (Board) imposed such a duty on petitioner with respect to its decision to terminate a contract with a customer, and the United States Court of Appeals, although differing over the appropriate rationale, enforced its order.

Petitioner, First National Maintenance Corporation (FNM), is a New York corporation engaged in the business of providing housekeeping, cleaning maintenance, and related services for commercial customers in the New York City area. It contracts for and hires personnel separately for each customer, and it does not transfer employees between locations.

★ ★ ★

Petitioner's business relationship with Greenpark, seemingly, was not very remunerative or smooth. In March 1977, Greenpark gave petitioner the 30 days' written notice of cancellation specified by the contract, because of "lack of efficiency.". . .

While FNM was experiencing these difficulties, District 1199, National Union of Hospital and Health Care Employees, Retail, Wholesale and Department Store Union, AFL-CIO (Union), was conducting an organization campaign among petitioner's Greepark employees. On March 31, 1977, at a Board-conducted election, a majority of the employees selected the union as their bargaining agent. . . .

With nothing but perfunctory further discussion, petitioner on July 31 discontinued its Greenpark operation and discharged the employees.

The union filed an unfair labor practice charge against petitioner, alleging violations of the Act's Sections 8(a)(1) and (5). After a hearing held upon the Regional Director's complaint, the Administrative Law Judge made findings in the union's favor. . . . [H]e ruled that petitioner had failed to satisfy its duty to bargain concerning both the decision to terminate the Greenpark contract and the effect of that change upon the unit employees.

★ ★ ★

The National Labor Relations Board adopted the Administrative Law Judge's findings without further analysis. . . .

The United States Court of Appeals for the Second Circuit, with one judge dissenting in part, enforced the Board's order.

The Court of Appeals' decision in this case appears to be at odds with decisions of other Courts of Appeals, some of which decline to require bargaining over any management decision involving "a major commitment of capital investment" of a "basic operational change" in the scope or direction of an enterprise, and some of which indicate that bargaining is not mandated unless a violation of Section 8(a)(3) (a partial closing motivated by antiunion animus) is involved. The Board itself has not been fully consistent in its rulings applicable to this type of management decision.

Although parties are free to bargain about any *legal* subject, Congress has limited the *mandate* or duty to bargain to matters of "wages, hours, and other terms and conditions of employment." Congress deliberately left the words "wages, hours, and other terms and conditions of employment". . . [vague].

Nonetheless, in establishing what issues must be submitted to the process of bargaining, Congress had no expectation that the elected union representative would become an equal partner in the running of the business enterprise in which the union's members are employed.

Some management decisions, such as a choice of advertising and promotion, product type and design, and financing arrangements, have only an indirect and attenuated impact on the employment relationship. Other management decisions, such as the order of succession of layoffs and recalls, production quotas, and work rules, are almost exclusively "an aspect of the relationship" between employer and employee. The present case concerns a third type of management decision, one that had a direct impact on employment, since jobs were inexorably eliminated by the termination, but had as its focus only the economic profitability of the contract with Greenpark, a concern under these facts wholly apart from the employment relationship. This decision, involving a change in the scope and direction of the enterprise is akin to the decision whether to be in business at all. . . . At the same time, this decision touches on a matter of central and pressing concern to the union and its member employees: the possibility of continued employment and the retention of the employees' very jobs.

Petitioner contends it had no duty to bargain about its decision to terminate its operations at Greenpark. This contention requires that we determine whether the decision itself should be considered part of petitioner's retained freedom to manage its affairs unrelated to employment. The aim of labeling a matter a mandatory subject of bargaining, rather than simply permitting, but not requiring, bargaining, is to "promote the fundamental purpose of the Act by bringing a problem of vital concern to labor and management within the framework established by Congress as most conducive to industrial peace." The concept of mandatory bargaining is premised on the belief that collective discussions backed by the parties' economic weapons will result in decisions that are better for both management and labor and for society as a whole. This will be true, however, only if the subject proposed for discussion is amenable to resolution through the bargaining process. Management must be free from the constraints of the bargaining process to the extent essential for the running of a profitable business. It also must have some degree of certainty beforehand as to when it may proceed to reach decisions without fear of later evaluations labeling its conduct an unfair labor practice. Congress did not explicitly state what issues of mutual concern to union and management it intended to exclude from mandatory bargaining. Nonetheless, in view of an employer's need for unencumbered decisionmaking, bargaining over management decisions that have a substantial impact on the continued availability of employment should be required only if the benefit, for labor-management relations and the collective-bargaining process, outweighs the burden placed on the conduct of the business.

★ ★ ★

A union's interest in participating in the decision to close a particular facility or part of an employer's operations springs from its legitimate concern over job security. The Court has observed: "The words of [Section 8(d)]. . . plainly cover termination of employment which . . . necessarily results" from closing an operation. . . .

Moreover, the union's legitimate interest in fair dealing is protected by Section 8(a)(3), which prohibits partial closings motivated by antiunion animus, when done to gain an unfair advantage.

★ ★ ★

Management's interest in whether it should discuss a decision of this kind is much more complex and varies with the particular circumstances. If labor costs are an important factor in a failing operation and the decision to close, management will have an incentive to confer voluntarily with the union to seek concessions that may make continuing the business profitable. At other times, management may have great need for speed, flexibility, and secrecy in meeting business opportunities and exigencies. It may face significant tax or securities consequences that hinge on confidentiality, the

timing of a plant closing, or a reorganization of the corporate structure. . . .

There is an important difference, also, between permitted bargaining and mandated bargaining. Labeling this type of decision mandatory could afford a union a powerful tool for achieving delay, a power that might be used to thwart management's intentions in a manner unrelated to any feasible solution the union might propose.

★ ★ ★

We conclude that the harm likely to be done to an employer's need to operate freely in deciding whether to shut down part of its business purely for economic reasons outweighs the incremental benefit what might be gained through the union's participation in making the decision, and we hold that the decision itself is not part of Section 8(d)'s "terms and conditions," over which Congress has mandated bargaining. . . .

CASE FOLLOW-UP

Illinois Coil Spring Co., citing the loss of a major customer and other economic problems at its Milwaukee division, sought contract concessions from the union and further proposed that the Milwaukee operations be relocated at McHenry, a nonunion facility. When the union rejected these proposals, Illinois unilaterally announced its decision to relocate at McHenry. The union then challenged the move in a petition before the NLRB (268 NLRB No. 87 (1984)).

The board concluded that management cannot unilaterally change or modify a term or clause contained in the collective bargaining agreement. In this case, however, no "work preservation clause" was in the contract, so management did not fail in its good faith obligations nor did it engage in an unfair practice.

Although such clauses are not uncommon, the absence of one here opened the door to relocation at the McHenry facility.

The board thought this outcome would have the positive effect of forewarning the union of what it might expect in the absence of a work preservation clause and that, henceforth, unions would have a better idea of the concessions they could afford to make to keep open marginally productive sites. As you will recall from *First National Maintenance Corp.*, "[I]n establishing what issues must be submitted to the process of bargaining, Congress had no expectation that the elected union representative would become an equal partner in the running of the business enterprise. . . .'"

The final elements of the collective bargaining process are the economic measures used to secure favorable collective bargaining agreements. Employees use pickets, strikes, or threats of strike to secure concessions on the part of the employer. The employers' weapon is the lockout (or threatened lockout), in which employees are not permitted to work and therefore are not paid. Occasionally, with a multiemployer bargaining group, the employees may strike against some members of the group yet continue to work for the others—a *whip saw strike*. In *NLRB* v. *Truck Drivers Local 449,*[15] the Supreme Court held that a lockout by all members of the employer group was a legal response to such a strike.

NATIONAL EMERGENCY COOLING-OFF PROVISION

Strikes and lockouts involve work stoppages. In some cases, these measures may have severe consequences to the economy or national defense. In writing the NLRA, Congress was sensitive to these possible effects and provided measures for avoiding them. The Taft-Hartley Act authorized the president to start the procedure for an eighty-day cooling-off period when a strike or threatened strike imperils the national health, economy, or defense. When these cooling-off periods have been necessary in the past, the disputes have often been settled with the assistance of the Federal Mediation and Conciliation Service.

The collective bargaining agreement is the ultimate goal of the process, but even after that is worked out, later disputes may arise as to interpretation of the terms. Again, the parties are to bargain in good faith to resolve the disputes. Often, the agreements themselves provide for arbitration as a means of settling interpretation problems. Under this method, both sides present evidence and arguments to an independent arbitrator, who then decides the issues. The courts have adopted a policy of not interfering with the arbitrator's decisions.

Unfair Labor Practices

Employers wield a great deal of power through control of their employees' livelihoods. To prevent employers from using this power to deny employee rights enumerated in the Wagner Act, Congress prohibited certain employer unfair labor practices. As unions grew after passage of the NLRA, the Taft-Hartley Act defined as unfair certain union practices to prevent the unions from misusing their power. Commission of these prohibited practices may result in damages being awarded to the injured party. Thus, unfair practices form the basis of much litigation.

EMPLOYER PRACTICES

When Congress made employer interference with unionization an unfair labor practice, it empowered the NLRB and the federal courts to distinguish between wrongful interference and proper management activities. The difficulty Congress created is that not all activities that deter union organization are properly considered to be interference. The board and appellate courts must balance the organizational rights of employees with the property and constitutional rights of employers.

An example of the conflict occurs when companies have rules prohibiting solicitation and distribution of literature on company property. For union organizers, the workplace is the most effective location for reaching employees, especially where the organizers are not themselves employees. Organizational efforts are frustrated if the employers prohibit solicitation at the workplace. In balancing the conflicting rights, the board has allowed employer rules consistent with valid workplace purposes, such as efficiency, safety, and discipline. The board and the courts have also upheld prohibitions that limit organizational efforts at the workplace during hours of employment. A total ban of such efforts, however, is likely to be considered an unfair labor practice. In *NLRB* v. *Babcock and Wilcox*,[16] the Supreme Court ruled that an employer's property may be opened up to nonemployee organizers if no other effective alternatives are available.

Another means of interference that is prohibited as an unfair labor practice is the employer's action of granting additional benefits. In *NLRB* v. *Exchange Parts Co.*,[17] the Supreme Court upheld the board's finding of an unfair practice a situation in which the employer granted additional employee benefits during union organizational efforts. The Court pointed to the coercive effects of such well-timed increases as being similar to the "fist inside a velvet glove." According to the Court, such tactics by the employer lead to the inference among employees that such benefits may be denied in the future if the union is elected. If an employer grants such benefits regularly, however, the changes do not have to be postponed beyond the time when they are scheduled just because an election is pending.

A further conflict of rights is involved when employers exercise the privilege of speaking to employees. The board and courts have held that the employer has the right to express its opinion, but must not abuse the right by threatening or coercing employees.

American Spring Wire Co.
237 N.L.R.B. No. 185 (N.L.R.B., 1978)

Respondent (American Spring Wire) is engaged in the manufacture of spring wire at its Bedford Heights, Ohio, plant. In October 1974 and October 1976, Board-conducted elections were held at the Bedford Heights plant in which a majority of Respondent's employees voted not to be represented by the union. . . .

On May 27, 1977, Respondent held a meeting with its employees to explain certain operational changes that it intended to implement. Approximately 95 of Respondent's 149 employees attended, and all of the employees who attended that meeting received 2 hours' pay at their straight-time hourly rate. L. O. Selhorst, Respondent's president, conducted the meeting and spoke from a prepared text. Selhorst informed the employees that, based on recommendations from a private consulting firm, Respondent was going to implement a number of changes in job descriptions and pay rates. Under the new system, all of the employees were to receive a pay raise. Selhorst told the employees that the pay raise would make them among the best paid workers in the Nation. Selhorst also reviewed the history of the Company and its recent rapid expansion and thanked the employees for their part in helping Respondent to grow. He then told the employees that management would continue to attempt to create the "best place to work in America" and that the employees' cooperation and teamwork was needed for continued growth and improvement. Selhorst then stated that he had:

> One additional important thought. We have beaten the Union on two occasions in this plant by overwhelming majorities and I know the majority of us are tired of such activity. The majority of us do not deserve such continuing harassment. We have set up in this Company all the means of communication possible, and to those of you who still think you can win more with the Union than you have with us in the past 9 years, well—you are dead wrong—leave us alone—get the hell out of our plant. . . .
>
> I want to say something to you as clearly as I possibly can. Whether or not ASW has a union is really not significant to the Corporation's future, or to myself, Dave Carruthers, or other major employees of this Company. As far as I am concerned those of us who are loyal to each other as a group can make valve spring wire, music wire, alloy wire, in Moline, Illinois; Saskatchewan, Canada; Puerto Rico; or Hawaii. We don't need Cleveland, Ohio, or all this beautiful property. Remember, nine years ago we had nothing. Today our Company has developed a certain amount of wealth and goodwill at the banks, a

fantastic organization of people and many friends who supply us goods, and above all a long and growing list of customers. These people do business with us, not with this building or this land. We do not intend to have this statement appear as a threat because it is not. It is a statement of fact. Facts are that our real concern regarding a union is with the majority of you who have opposed it in the past, and who would be locked into it should it come to this plant.

> With that in mind, I want to tell you that those of us in management do not wish to become involved in another election. We need the time to do the things that will continue to promote our Company, ourselves, and hopefully, you. I am asking you as your friend not to sign union cards, as we don't have the patience to put up with it again. This next battle is yours, not ours. It is up to each one of you who is against the union to stop the card signing before it gets started. I don't care how you do it. Organize yourselves and get it done.

Based on the above speech, the General Counsel issued a complaint alleging that Respondent violated Sections 8(a)(1) and (3) of the Act by: (a) threatening its employees with unspecified reprisals by telling them that, if they thought they could gain more benefits from Respondent with the Union, they could "get the hell out of our plant"; (b) threatening its employees with plant closure in order to discourage their union activity; and (c) soliciting its employees to stop employees from signing authorization cards on behalf of the Union by any means necessary. . . .

Section 8(a)(1) of the Act prohibits an employer from interfering with, threatening, or coercing employees in the exercise of their Section 7 rights to support or oppose a labor organization, or to engage in or refrain from engaging in concerted activity. The issue, simply, is whether Respondent's statements complained of by the General Counsel are views or opinions, or are threatening and coercive.

We note that the first portion of the speech emphasized Respondent's commitment to its work force and the importance of employee cooperation to Respondent's growth and employee job security. The employees were also informed that they were receiving pay increases and that in the future Respondent would continue to try to improve working conditions and pay. However, immediately thereafter Selhorst changed the tone of the speech abruptly as he invited the union supporters to "get the hell our of our plant." In this context of union animus, Respondent's statement that it could produce its product elsewhere and that it did not need its Cleveland, Ohio plant was a clear and unambiguous threat of plant closure.

In light of the threat of plant closure, Respondent's statement to union supporters to "get the hell out of our plant" and Respondent's exhortation to the assembled employees to stop the card singing by any means also were coercive and threatening. Although the major portion of Selhorst's speech was devoted to explaining legitimate business changes, conferring increased benefits, and promising further improvements in the future, we find that the speech also had an underlying message that a continuation of these benefits was conditioned on a continuation of a nonunion plant. Thus, the speech represents a classic example of "the suggestion of a fist inside the velvet glove [as] employees are not likely to miss the inference that the source of benefits now conferred is also the source from which future benefits must flow and which may dry up if it is no obliged." *NLRB* v. *Exchange Parts Co.* . . .

In view of the above, we find no merit to Respondent's claim that Selhorst's statements were not threatening or coercive because they did not occur within the context of a union campaign. This Board has never found that threatening or coercive conduct, such as a threat of plant closure, is unlawful only in the context of a union campaign. Moreover, we note that the Union had filed two petitions within the last 3 years and less than 6 months remained before the union could file a new petition under Section 9(c)(3) of the Act. Thus, Respondent's unlawful statements were made in the context of recent union campaigns and possible latent or preliminary union activity.

So ordered.

CASE FOLLOW-UP

Adair Standish Corp. v. *NLRB*,[18] is a more recent case addressing unlawful employer practices in connection with unionization campaigns. When Congress made employer interference with unionization an unfair practice, it empowered the NLRB and the federal courts to distinguish between (1) wrongful interference by management and (2) proper management activities. Not all activities that deter union organization are properly considered to be interference. The board and appellate courts must balance the organizational rights of employees with the property and constitutional rights of employers.

Adair Standish Corporation was a printing firm that operated from two plants—Dexter and Standish. New presses were targeted for installation at the Standish plant, but when management heard of efforts to unionize that site, employees were told that the firm might scuttle those plans. After a successful union election at the Standish plant, the firm encouraged employees to revoke their authorization cards and published notices that, henceforth, tardiness rules would be strictly enforced. Subsequently, two employees were disciplined for tardiness and the firm scheduled its new presses for the Dexter plant, rather than the one at Standish.

The NLRB found these actions to be unfair and ordered the firm to cease and desist this conduct, to reinstate and award back pay to the two disciplined employees, and to install the new press at Standish.

The Court of Appeals for the Sixth Circuit concluded that statements *prior* to the union election regarding cancellation of the new presses scheduled for the Standish plant were unfair because employees could reasonably infer that such statements were directed toward their decision to join the union.

Conduct *after* the election—posting notice of union members' right to revoke authorization cards, posting notice of the tardiness policy, and disciplining of two employees—was found to be unlawful interference with the employees rights to organize (Section 8(a)(1)), and discrimination for reasons of union affiliation (Section 8(a)(3)).

The issue of the new printing presses was remanded to the NLRB to determine whether or not that decision was within the legitimate discretion of management.

DOMINATION BY MANAGEMENT

The Wagner Act (1935) also made it an unfair labor practice for a company to dominate a labor union. Prior to 1935, many companies formed and dominated labor unions to head off outside organizers, to ease employee pressure for collective bargaining, and to ensure that the union was aligned with management. Congress prohibited this practice to ensure that the employees, not management, were being represented. Under the Act, employers may not contribute financial or other support to a union. In addition, employers must be neutral in controversies or elections involving two unions. This prohibition, however, does not mean that unions and employers may not cooperate with each other, so long as the union remains independent. In *NLRB* v. *Post Publishing Company,*[19] the Court of Appeals for the Seventh Circuit distinguished between "support" and "cooperation" and stated that the latter was the "end result . . . sought by the underlying philosophy motivating the National Labor Relations Act."

In dealing with domination allegations, the board distinguishes between domination and interference by the employer. In the case of employer domination, the board will order that the organization be dissolved as an employee representative. If employer actions indicate something less than domination, the board will order the employer to cease the interfering practices.

Discharge and Discipline. Another unfair employer practice is discrimination between employees on the basis of union membership. Under Section 8(a)(3) of the NLRA, an employer cannot treat employees differently in either hire or tenure policies for the purposes of encouraging or discouraging union membership. Included within the prohibition is discrimination in the terms of employment, such as hours, wages, holidays, and work assignments. This prohibition does not prevent the employer from discharging or disciplining employees for valid reasons. If the workers discharged or disciplined are disproportionately union members, however, the board is likely to review the practice carefully, and it will be judged unfair if the reason for the action is union participation or support. One exception to the discrimination prohibition is the collective bargaining agreement calling for a union shop. Employers subject to those provisions require newly hired employees to join the union within thirty days. Union shops are allowed under the NLRA unless they conflict with a state's *right-to-work law* (a state law that forbids union shops). Some states pass such laws to encourage firms to build new plants there and to keep established firms from relocating out of state.

Whistle-blowing. Section 8(a)(4) of the Act protects employees who have defended their rights or provided testimony under the Act from any reprisals by an employer. The primary purpose of this provision is to ensure that employers do not threaten or intimidate employees into foregoing the NLRA protections. Companies must present evidence that their actions were based on other motives if they are accused of this violation.

Secondary Practices. Unlike the other unfair practices we have discussed, this employer unfair labor practice involves cooperation between a company and a union. Section 8(e) was added to the Act and prohibits an employer from agreeing to engage in secondary practices, including secondary boycotts. A secondary boycott is an indirect economic weapon. It is discussed more fully in the cases in the next section, but you may find the following illustration helpful. If a union has a legitimate dispute with employer *A*, it is an unfair practice for the union to induce *employees* of a supplier or a customer of *A* to strike or refuse to handle *A*'s goods in order to pressure *A* into meeting union demands. The Landrum-Griffin Act further strengthened this provision by outlawing "hot-cargo" agreements, whereby customers or suppliers of employer *A* committed themselves through an agreement with a union not to deal with *A*'s goods.

UNION PRACTICES

The Wagner Act recognized an employee right to organize free from fear of employer reprisals. The 1947 Taft-Hartley amendments to the Wagner Act protected those employees who did not want to organize and prohibited the union from coercing or intimidating employees. Section 8(b)(1) of the amended Act makes it an unfair labor practice for unions to restrain or coerce employees in the exercise of their collective bargaining rights. This violation is frequently alleged during representation elections. It involves threats by union organizers of lost jobs or physical violence toward employees who do not support the union. This section also forbids a union to coerce or restrain an employer in the selection of its negotiating representatives.

The Taft-Hartley Act further prohibits a union from forcing an employer to discriminate against employees who are at odds with the union. Examples of violations are union pressure forcing the employer to fire or to refuse to hire employees not acceptable to the union. One exception to the prohibition allows the union to require dismissal of employees who fail to pay "periodic dues and initiation fees" where a valid union shop agreement is in effect.

Section 8(b)(4) allows a union to use "publicity, other than picketing, for the purpose of truthfully advising the public" that another employer—that is, a neutral, secondary party with whom the union has no dispute—is handling products of the primary employer. Publicity, such as handbills, that simply informs the public and requests its support in refusing to purchase the primary employer's product from the secondary employer is legal. This principle was established in *NLRB* v. *Fruit and Vegetable Packers,*[20] (the Tree Fruits case). The following case illustrates the application of the *Tree Fruits* principle in a somewhat different context.

NLRB v. *Retail Store Employees Union, Local 1001, Retail Clerks International Ass'n*
477 U.S. 607 (1980)

POWELL, JUSTICE

Safeco Title Insurance Co. underwrites real estate title insurance in the State of Washington. It maintains close business relationships with five local title companies. The companies search land titles, perform escrow services, and sell title insurance. Over 90 percent of their gross incomes derives from the sale of Safeco insurance. Safeco has substantial stockholdings in each title company, and at least one Safeco officer serves on each company's board of directors. Safeco, however, has no control over the companies' daily operations. It does not direct their personnel policies, and it never exchanges employees with them.

Local 1001 of the Retail Store Employees Union became the certified bargaining representative for certain Safeco employees in 1974. When contract negotiations between Safeco and the Union reached an impasse, the employees went on strike. The Union did not confine picketing to Safeco's office in Seattle. The Union also picketed each of the five local title companies. The pickets carried signs declaring that Safeco had no contract with the Union, and they distributed handbills asking consumers to support the strike by canceling their Safeco policies. . . .

Section 8(b)(4)(ii)(B) of the National Labor Relations Act makes it "an unfair labor practice for a labor organization . . . to threaten, coerce, or restrain" a person not party to a labor dispute "where . . . an object thereof is . . . forcing or requiring [him] to cease using, selling, handling, transporting, or otherwise dealing in the products of any other producer . . . or to cease doing business with any other person. . . ."

In *Tree Fruits,* the Court held that Section 8(b)(4)(ii)(B) does not prohibit all peaceful picketing at secondary sites. There, a union striking certain Washington fruit packers picketed large supermarkets in order to persuade consumers not to buy Washington apples. Concerned that a broad ban against such picketing might run afoul of the First Amendment, the Court found the statute directed to an "isolated evil." The evil was use of a secondary picketing "to persuade the customers of the secondary employer to cease trading with him in order to force him to cease dealing with, or to put pressure upon, the primary employer." Congress intended to protect secondary parties from pressures that might embroil them in the labor disputes of others, but not to shield them from business losses caused by a campaign that successfully persuades consumers "to boycott the primary employer's goods." Thus, the Court drew a distinction between picketing "to shut off all trade with the secondary employer unless he aids the union in its dispute with the primary employer" and picketing that "only persuades his customers not to buy the struck product." The picketing in the case which "merely follow[ed] the struck product," did not "threaten, coerce, or restrain" the secondary party within the meaning of Section 8(b)(4)(ii)(B).

Although *Tree Fruits* suggested that secondary picketing against a struck product and secondary picketing against a neutral party were "poles apart," the courts soon discovered that product picketing could have the same effect as an illegal secondary boycott. In *Hoffman ex rel. NLRB* v. *Cement Masons Local 337*, for example, a union embroiled with a general contractor picketed the housing subdivision that he had constructed for a real estate developer. Pickets sought to persuade prospective purchasers not to buy the contractor's houses. The picketing was held illegal because purchasers "could reasonably expect that they were being asked not to transact any business whatsoever" with the neutral developer. "[W]hen a union's interest in picketing a primary employer at a 'one product' site [directly conflicts] with the need to protect . . . neutral employers from the labor disputes of others," Congress has determined that the neutrals' interests should prevail.

Cement Masons highlights the critical difference between the picketing in this case, and the picketing at issue in *Tree Fruits* is but one item among the many that made up the retailer's trade.

If the appeal against such a product succeeds, the Court observed, it simply induces the neutral retailer to reduce his orders for the product or "to drop the item as a poor seller." The decline in sales attributable to consumer rejection of the struck product puts pressure upon the primary employer, and the marginal injury to the neutral retailer is purely incidental to the product boycott. The neutral therefore has little reason to become involved in the labor dispute. In this case, on the other hand, the title companies sell only the primary employer's product and perform the services associated with it. Secondary picketing against consumption of the primary product leaves responsive consumers no realistic option other than to boycott the title companies altogether. If the appeal succeeds, each company "stops buying the struck product, not because of a falling demand, but in response to pressure designed to inflict injury on [its] business generally." Thus, "the union does more than merely follow the struck product; it creates a separate dispute with the secondary employer." Such an expansion of labor discord was one of the evils that Congress intended Section 8(b)(4)(ii)(B) to prevent.

As long as secondary picketing only discourages consumption of a struck product, incidental injury to the neutral is a natural consequence of an effective primary boycott.

But the Union's secondary appeal against the central product sold by the title companies in this case is "reasonably calculated to induce customers not to patronize the neutral parties at all." The resulting injury to their businesses is distinctly different from the injury that the Court considered in *Tree Fruits*. Product picketing that reasonably can be expected to threaten neutral parties with ruin or substantial loss simply does not square with the language or the purpose of Section 8(b)(4)(ii)(B). Since successful secondary picketing would put the title companies to a choice between their survival and the severance of their ties with Safeco, the picketing plainly violates the statutory ban on the coercion of neutrals with the object of "forcing or requiring [them] to cease . . . dealing in the [primary] produc[t]

. . . or to cease doing business with" the primary employer.

★ ★ ★

Accordingly, the judgment of the Court of Appeals is reversed, and the case is remanded with directions to enforce the National Labor Relations Board's order.

So ordered.

CASE FOLLOW-UP

Safeco limited informational picketing at the secondary site to situations in which the product of the primary employer accounts for less than a substantial portion of the secondary or neutral employer's business. If the product of the primary employer is merged with that of a secondary or neutral employer (e.g., the plastics of primary employer *A* are used to manufacture a line of toys by secondary or neutral employer *B*), the informational picketing of *Safeco* would not be permitted because it would totally shut down the operations of *B*.

First Amendment considerations are uppermost in the deliberations of the Court when a complaint challenges a union's informational activities. In *Safeco*, the Court was confronted with secondary picketing that "threaten[ed] neutral parties with ruin or substantial loss." First Amendment protection simply does not extend to such coercive measures, nor are such measures consistent with the language or purpose of the NLRA. In *Tree Fruits*, union picketing at the secondary site affected a single product only and did not seriously jeopardize the operations or the economic success of the supermarket.

In a more recent case, *DeBartolo* v. *Florida Gulf Coast Building and Construction Trades Council*,[21] the Supreme Court crafted an outcome (some would say a fairly awkward one) consistent with the language of *Safeco* and *Tree Fruits*. It did so principally on the ground that the case involved handbills rather than picketing. Handbills are considered to be less threatening and less coercive than picketing. The dispute arose because a construction company that was building a department store for a tenant at DeBartolo's shopping mall was paying substandard wages and benefits. The union distributed handbills urging shoppers not to patronize *any* of the mall's stores until DeBartolo promised that the wage/benefit matter would be corrected.

DeBartolo filed an unfair labor practice complaint with the NLRB. The complaint was dismissed, appealed, and remanded to the Board. *DeBartolo* v. *NLRB*, 463 U.S. 147 (1983). On remand, the board upheld the complaint as coercive of and threatening to neutral, secondary parties. It did not consider the First Amendment aspects of the case, however, and for that reason the Court of Appeals for the Eleventh Circuit denied enforcement of the board's order. *Trades Council* v. *NLRB,* 796 F.2d 1328 (1986). Both the Court of Appeals and the Supreme Court gave controlling force to *NLRB* v. *Catholic Bishop of Chicago.* [22] Although the Board's NLRA interpretations are normally entitled to deference, where an otherwise acceptable construction of the Act (an interpretation prohibiting handbills that harmed the operations of secondary or neutral parties) would raise serious constitutional problems, the *Catholic Bishop* rule requires the courts to construe the statute to avoid such problems unless such construction is plainly contrary to Congress's intent. Implicit in *DeBartolo* is the view that the shopping mall developer and tenants just have to put up with some secondary activity and that perhaps marginally diminished business is the "price" for constitutionally protected speech or informational activities.

Congress has further prohibited, as an unfair labor practice by unions, the changing of an excessive or discriminatory initiation fee or dues and requiring employers to pay for work not done. In the former case, the board and the courts are required to make determination of what is reasonable so that employees who are compelled to join because of a union-shop agreement will not be penalized by payments disproportionately higher than those normally charged. That latter practice is known as *featherbedding.* This prohibition has limited application because the courts have only required that *some* work be performed in exchange for wages. The prohibition does not extend to make-work clauses in contracts. So long as some services are performed, the practice is not illegal even though the services are not really necessary.

PUBLIC SECTOR EMPLOYMENT

All governmental employees, unlike those in the private sector, benefit from constitutional safeguards such as the right of free speech and privacy, protection against unreasonable searches and seizures and self-incrimination, and due process and equal protection guarantees. The federal Civil Service Act, in place since 1883, has been expanded to permit employees to organize and present their views on terms and conditions of employment. The Civil Service Reform Act of 1978 included the Federal Service Labor-Management Relations Act (FSLMRA). It was modeled on the NLRA and created a Federal Labor Relations Authority, which for all practical purposes operates in the federal sector. Exempt from FSLMRA coverage are the FBI, CIA, National Security Agency, TVA, military services, and postal workers.

The FSLMRA determines the appropriateness of representation units, supervises representation elections, and requires that agencies and union representatives bargain in good faith. Because governmental employment is essential to the public interest and because disruptions could jeopardize the public welfare, there is a general prohibition against strikes, slowdowns, stoppages, or picketing that interferes with agency operations (*Professional Air Traffic Controllers (PATCO)* v. *FLRA*).[23] Some states authorize governmental employees to strike if the jobs involved would not endanger public safety or welfare.

The scope of collective bargaining in the public sector is more restrictive than in the private sector. An attempt to bargain about "wages, hours, and other terms and conditions of employment" would, in reality, be an attempt to modify or amend federal law, a matter committed by the Constitution to the legislative branch. A "delegation of powers" problem would arise if Congress or a state legislature turned collective bargaining over to representatives of the governmental agencies and governmental employee unions.

Some states have passed right-to-work laws that apply to both public and private sector employment and that prohibit union security agreements, such as union shops (collectively bargained agreements that require newly hired employees to join the union within thirty days) and agency shops (comparable agreements that do not require union membership but do require dues payment in an amount approximating union dues). The following case involves public employment in a state that did not have a right-to-work law. The bargaining agreement, however, contained agency-shop provisions and required nonunion public school teachers to pay dues equivalent to 95 percent of the union dues. This requirement was to protect the union against "free riders" who would otherwise benefit from the union contract without contributing funds to support the collective bargaining effort. It was also designed to protect the nonunion members from being compelled to support the political activities of the union.

Payroll deductions were made automatically, and a procedure was established to hear the objections of nonmembers who believed that the money was being spent on projects unrelated to collective bargaining or who had other reasons for protesting the deduction. This case was initiated to challenge the deduction procedure as a violation of the teachers' First Amendment and Fourteenth Amendment rights.

Chicago Teachers Union v. Hudson
475 U.S. 292 (1986)

STEVENS, JUSTICE

★ ★ ★

In *Abood* v. *Detroit Board of Education*, 431 U.S. 209 (1977), we recognized that requiring nonunion employees to support their collective-bargaining representative "has an impact upon their First Amendment interests," and may well "interfere in some way with an employee's freedom to associate for the advancement of ideas, or to refrain from doing so, as he sees fit.". . . We nevertheless rejected the claim that it was unconstitutional for a public employer to designate a union as the exclusive collective-bargaining representative of its employees, and to require nonunion employees, as a condition of employment, to pay a fair share of the union's cost of negotiating and administering a collective-bargaining agreement. We also held, however, that nonunion employees do have a constitutional right to "prevent the Union's spending a part of their required service fees to contribute to political candidates and to express political views unrelated to its duties as exclusive bargaining representative."

The question presented in this case is whether the procedure used by the Chicago Teachers Union and approved by the Chicago Board of Education adequately protects the basic distinction drawn in *Abood*. "[T]he objective must be to devise a way of preventing compulsory subsidization of ideological activity by employees who object thereto without restricting the Union's ability to require every employee to contribute to the cost of collective-bargaining activities."

Procedural safeguards are necessary to achieve this objective for two reasons. First, although the government interest in labor peace is strong enough to support an "agency shop" notwithstanding its limited infringement on nonunion employees' constitutional rights, the fact that those rights are protected by the First Amendment requires that the procedure be carefully tailored to minimize the infringement. Second, the nonunion employee—the individual whose First Amendment rights are being affected—must have a fair opportunity to identify the impact of the governmental action on his interests and to assert a meritorious First Amendment claim.

* * *

In this case, we must determine whether the challenged Chicago Teachers Union procedure survives First Amendment scrutiny, either because the procedure upheld by the District Court was constitutionally sufficient, or because the subsequent adoption of an escrow arrangement cured any constitutional defect. We consider these questions in turn.

The procedure that was initially adopted by the Union and considered by the District Court contained three fundamental flaws. First, . . . a remedy which merely offers dissenters the possibility of a rebate does not avoid the risk that dissenters' funds may be used temporarily for an improper purpose. "[T]he Union should not be permitted to exact a service fee from nonmembers without first establishing a procedure which will avoid the risk that their funds will be used, even temporarily, to finance ideological activities unrelated to collective bargaining." The amount at stake for each individual dissenter does not diminish this concern. For, whatever the amount, the quality of respondents' interest in not being compelled to subsidize the propagation of political or ideological views that they oppose is clear. In *Abood*, we emphasized this point by quoting the comments of Thomas Jefferson and James Madison about the tyrannical character of forcing an individual to contribute even "three pence" for the "propagation of opinions which he disbelieves." A forced exaction followed by a rebate equal to the amount improperly expended is thus not a permissible response to the nonunion employees' objections.

Second, the "advance reduction of dues" was inadequate because it provided nonmembers with inadequate information about the basis for the proportionate share. In *Abood*, we reiterated that the nonunion employee has the burden of raising an objection, but that the union retains the burden of proof: "Since the unions possess the facts and records from which the proportion of political to total union expenditures can reasonably be calculated, basic considerations of fairness compel that they, not the individual employees, bear the burden of proving such proportion." Basic considerations of fairness, as well as concern for the First Amendment rights at stake, also dictate that the potential objectors be given sufficient information to gage the propriety of the union's fee. Leaving the nonunion employees in the dark about the source of the figure for the agency fee—and requiring them to object in order to receive information—does not adequately protect the careful distinctions drawn in *Abood*.

In this case, the original information given to the nonunion employees was inadequate. Instead of identifying the expenditures for collective bargaining and contract administration that had been provided for the benefit of nonmembers as well as members—and for which nonmembers as well as members can fairly be charged a fee—the Union identified the amount that it admittedly had expended for purposes that did not benefit dissenting nonmembers. An acknowledgment that nonmembers would not be required to pay any part of 5 percent of the Union's total annual expenditures was not an adequate disclosure of the reasons why they were required to pay their share of 95 percent.

Finally, the original Union procedure was also defective because it did not provide for a reasonably prompt decision by an impartial decision maker. Although we have not so specified in the past, we now conclude that such a requirement is necessary. The nonunion employee, whose First Amendment rights are affected by the agency shop itself and who bears the burden of objecting, is entitled to have his objections addressed in an expeditious, fair, and objective manner.

The Union's procedure does not meet this requirement. As the Seventh Circuit observed, the "most conspicuous feature of the procedure is that from start to finish it is entirely controlled by the union, which is an interested party, since it is the recipient of the agency fees paid by the dissenting employees." The initial consideration of the agency fee is made by Union officials, and the first two steps of the review procedure (the Union Executive Committee and Executive Board) consist of Union officials. The third step—review by a Union-selected arbitrator—is also inadequate because the selection represents the Union's unrestricted choice from the state list. . . .

We hold today that the constitutional requirements for the Union's collection of agency fees include an adequate explanation of the basis for the fee, a reasonably prompt opportunity to challenge the amount of the fee before an impartial decisionmaker, and an escrow for the amounts reasonably in dispute while such challenges are pending.

The determination of the appropriate remedy in this case is a matter that should be addressed in the first instance by the District Court. The Court of Appeals correctly revised the District Court's original judgment and remanded the case for further proceedings. That judgment of reversal is affirmed, and those further proceedings should be consistent with this opinion.

It is so ordered.

CASE FOLLOW-UP

The FSLMRA Act authorizes automatic deduction of union dues or agency fees only if the employee permits. Employee authorization is good for one year only, cannot be revoked prior to that time, and may be resubscribed on an annual basis.

Age Discrimination in Employment Act of 1967

The Age Discrimination in Employment Act (ADEA)[24] is modeled on Title VII and enforced by EEOC. In effect, it places those between the ages of forty and seventy into a protected class of persons comparable to that of women and minorities.

Employers in industries affecting interstate commerce that have twenty or more employees are regulated by the ADEA. This protection extends to state and local governments and to U.S. military and executive branch personnel. Labor unions in industries affecting interstate commerce are included as well. The commerce requirement is met if the union maintains a hiring hall that supplies an above-defined employer, has at least twenty-five members, and is certified or represents or seeks to represent employees of a defined employer. Employment agencies, insofar as their advertising and referral services are concerned, are within the scope of the Act if they seek prospects for a defined employer. To be covered with regard to their own internal operations, the agencies must employ twenty or more persons.

Statutory defenses to a charge of age discrimination consist of the bona fide occupational qualification (BFOQ), bona fide seniority systems and employee benefit plans, and reasonable factors other than age such as discharge for good cause. The *victim* must be within the protected class; the age of the preferred person is irrelevant. A twenty-year-old or a seven-year-old could be discriminated against in favor of someone in the forty-to-seventy bracket without violation of the ADEA, but it would be illegal if the forty-year-old was preferred to the seventy-year-old or vice versa because of age alone.

Victims of illegal age discrimination are entitled to back wages. The employer cannot escape liability by reducing the pay of the favored employees. Damages equal to the amount of back pay are recoverable if the plaintiff can prove that the defendant acted "willfully"—that is, with the purpose of achieving a particular result. Interest on back pay is recoverable in the event that liquidated damages are denied. Attorney' fees are available to a successful plaintiff, but authority is divided on whether compensatory and punitive damages are available.

Rehabilitation Act of 1973

Persons with disabilities—those who have a physical or mental impairment that substantially limits one or more of such persons' major life activities—are within the coverage of the Rehabilitation Act of 1973,[25] designed to aid them in their rehabilitation and employment efforts. Federal agencies must initiate affirmative action programs for hiring, placement, and advancement of persons with disabilities. The substance of this program is modeled on Title VII and enforced by the EEOC. Not only must federal agencies undertake affirmative action plans, but also, along with those administering programs that receive federal financial assistance, these agencies must not engage in discrimination against people with disabilities. The Department of Education oversees these efforts.

With regard to procurement contracts between federal agencies and private firms exceeding $2,500, the Department of Labor has been given a mandate by Congress to require the insertion of a clause in all such contracts that prohibits discrimination and requires the firm to take affirmative action. Within the Department of Labor, the Office of Federal Contract Compliance Programs is in charge of enforcement. Virtually the same terms and enforcement procedures are stipulated by the Vietnam Era Veterans Readjustment Assistance Act, but the private sector—federal government contracts must be $10,000 or more, instead of $2,500.

EMPLOYEE RETIREMENT INCOME SECURITY ACT OF 1974

Private pension plans (retirement income) and welfare plans (health, accident, unemployment protection) initially arose as a means of rewarding valuable employees and attracting others. The first of these plans was initiated voluntarily by employers, and the beneficiaries were usually managerial personnel, whereas the impetus for widespread coverage of laboring people came from unions. Today, for qualified plans, employer contributions are tax exempt, and income tax on the employees' portion is deferred until after retirement when, presumably, a lower income tax rate will be applied. Because of the improper management of some of these plans, the insolvency of some firms offering them, and the technical requirements that could defeat an employee's rights to coverage at retirement, Congress passed the Employment Retirement Income Security Act (ERISA).[26]

The law does not require that a corporation have a pension plan. For those that do, however, the following requirements apply. First, the plan must cover all employees who are at least twenty-five years old and have one year of service. If the employee is to have an immediate vested right in the retirement benefits on payment to the fund, three years of service may be required. Second, employers may choose one of three ways to let employees gain vested or guaranteed rights in the fund, which become payable at the retirement age provided in the plan or at age sixty-five. The first way is to provide that rights in the pension plan become nonforfeitable after ten years of service, even if the employee quits. A second way is to provide that a participant be entitled to 25 percent of the accrued benefits after five years of service; this percentage would increase to 50 percent after ten years and 100 percent after fifteen years. A third way is to adopt the "rule of 45," which provides half of a participant's benefits when the age of the worker and years of service total forty-five (but a minimum of five years of service is required). For younger participants, the rule provides for full vesting after fifteen years of service. These three methods provide a measure of protection for the employee against discharge or circumstances compelling one to quit.

Another objective of the ERISA is to protect employees' benefits when the corporation fails. A study by the Labor and Treasury departments reveals that 1,227 pension plans terminated in 1972 and thus resulted in almost $50 million of lost benefits to approximately twenty thousand participants. The Act creates a new Public Pension Benefit Guaranty Corporation that guarantees workers through a scheme of insurance, that they will receive the benefits they are entitled to if the company fails. The premiums for this insurance are about $1 per worker per year or 50¢ each for workers under more comprehensive multiemployer plans. The insurance will provide maximum benefits to the lesser of $750 per month or 100 percent of the employees' average wages for the best-paid five consecutive years of employment. This corporation could also seek to recover from the employer up to 30 percent of the collapsed firm's net worth if pension fund assets were insufficient to pay benefits.

Some of the Act's major provisions concern the standards to be observed by the fiduciaries administering the plan. Such fiduciaries are barred from engaging in such transactions as buying for the pension fund any property they own personally. Pension funds holding stock and real property of the employer must reduce such holdings to 10 percent of the fund's total assets over the next ten years.

To ensure compliance with the terms of the Act, extensive reporting requirements must be met. Reports to employees, the Labor and Treasury Departments, and the Pension Benefit Guaranty Corporation are necessary. This reporting is designed to provide detailed information to the government, as well as to participants in the plan.

OCCUPATIONAL SAFETY AND HEALTH ACT

Every standard treatise on the Occupational Safety and Health Act[27] begins with a litany of horror stories of the criminal and near-criminal treatment of American working women and men and then turns an obligatory focus on the sheer muddle-headedness, bungling, and incompetence of early administrators of the Occupational Safety and Health Administration (OSHA). For example, simpleminded rules and regulations were issued on ladder safety ("one step at a time," "don't climb broken ladders"), farmwork ("don't slip on cow dung"), and lifting ("bend at the knees," "keep the back straight"). While American men and women were dying in the work place and being subjected to high risks of crippling and incapacitating accidents and diseases, OSHA was more than incompetent. An era of high expectations was met by such timidity and failure of leadership that the nation was shocked, and the agency was both ridiculed and resented.[28]

Given perspective, however, the performance of OSHA can be viewed in a somewhat clearer light. Could anyone expect more when the task that Congress mandated was overwhelming, the funding and expertise paltry, and the spirit of cooperativeness and compliance by American firms nonexistent? In a real sense, the administrators were forced into a strategy of starting slowly while gearing up for the more difficult road ahead.

In any event, no more time or space will be spent lamenting a bad situation. The following segment of the chapter surveys the organizational structure of OSHA and then gives an inside look into the complexities of a particular health standard.

OSHA: AN OVERVIEW

The Occupational Safety and Health Act is based on the commerce clause. Consequently, the Act provides that a firm engaged in business affecting commerce is covered if it has at least one employee.

The Act places two major duties on employers. First, employers must furnish to employees a place of employment that is free from recognized hazards likely to cause death or serious physical harm. This statement is referred to as the general duty clause of the Act, but it applies only where no specific safety standard promulgated under the Act is applicable. A second and related duty is for the employer to comply with all appropriate standards for safety. The Department of Labor and OSHA have promulgated literally thousands of safety standards that apply to employers. Most were developed from the earlier "national consensus standards" designed by nationally recognized organizations such as the American National Standards Institute and the National Fire Protection Association. These very specific safety regulations cover such subjects as the proper construction and maintenance of equipment, machine guarding, and fire and injury prevention procedures. They also specify the type of personal protection equipment worn by employees and training requirements necessary to ensure safe work practices.

In addition to complying with the two major duties above, employers with more than ten employees must also keep substantial records and make reports on all work-related injuries and deaths. The act does not provide for compensation for injuries, nor does it affect workmen's compensation. It is not compensatory in concept. It is preventive.

Three entities are established by the OSHA within the Department of Labor: the administration, the National Institute of Occupational Safety and Health (NIOSH), and the Occupational Safety and Health Review Commission (OSHRC). With the scientific guidance of NIOSH, the administration must establish standards[29] as authorized by Congress. With regard to toxic materials and harmful physical agents, Congress has provided as follows:

> The Secretary, in promulgating standards dealing with toxic materials or harmful physical agents . . . shall set the standard which most adequately assures, *to the extent feasible,* on the basis of the best available evidence, that *no employee* will suffer material impairment of health or functional capacity even if such employee has regular exposure to the hazard dealt with by such standard for the period of his working life. Development of standards under this subsection shall be based upon research, demonstrations, experiments, and such other information as may be appropriate. In addition to the attainment of the *highest degree* of health and safety protection for the employee, other considerations shall be the latest available scientific data in the field, the feasibility of the standards, and experience gained under this and other health and safety laws.[30]

With these instructions and the scientific expertise of NIOSH, the administration may publish a rule stipulating, for example, a one part per million (ppm) standard for cotton dust. Benzene, asbestos, vinyl chloride, and coke oven emissions are illustrative of other toxins for which standards have been published. In each situation, OSHA gives notice of proposed rule making, holds public hearings on the soundness of the proposed rule, and receives oral and written evidence from public interest groups, professional associations, industry, unions, and interested individuals. The testimony and other input received through these hearings affect OSHA's final rule that is published in the Code of Federal Regulations (C.F.R.).

When a rule goes into operation, OSHA inspectors, acting on a complaint or on their own initiative, may detect a violation. Violations that threaten job safety will be pursued by a citation that describes the offense and gives the employer an opportunity to abate or correct the defect. It must be issued within six months of the alleged violation. Searches and seizures for these purposes may be undertaken through the use of administrative warrants.[31] This area of the law is covered by the Fourth Amendment.

Penalties, should they be appropriate, range from a high of $1,000 for nonserious and serious unwillful offenses; to $10,000 for serious, willful offenses; and to $20,000 plus a one-year jail term for repeated serious, willful offenses. Serious violations are those involving an employer who knew or should have known that the hazard was likely to result in death or serious bodily injury. *Willful* denotes deliberateness or intent.

If the firm decides to challenge the citation, it must do so within fifteen days after service of the citation. A hearing will be set before an administrative law judge, who will decide the matter without a jury. Either side can appeal to the Review Commission, and beyond the final judgment of the commission is a limit of thirty days to file for review with the United States Circuit Court of Appeals.

WHISTLE-BLOWERS

The Act forbids retaliation against employees who make use of its provisions. This policy, parallel to that found in the Equal Pay Act and Title VII, is exactly what one would expect in view of Congress's determination that employers not undermine the integrity of the Act.

COST-BENEFIT ANALYSIS

It would be helpful at this point for you to review the portion of Chapter 1 that introduces *utilitarianism*, as well as other ethical concepts. Cost-benefit analysis, familiar to most business students from accounting, finance, and economics courses, is a spin-off from utilitarianism. It is a decision-making tool that aids management in choosing the optimum course of action by evaluating the positive and negative features of each alternative.

At least one adjustment is notable, however. When business executives engage in cost-benefit analysis, they are particularly interested in benefits and costs to the firm itself, not to society as a whole. The narrow perspective of this unique variety of utilitarianism, known also as *egoism*, may result in the selection of a course of action that maximizes private-sector (firm) benefits at the expense of social benefits. For example, social benefits might be maximized if a firm voluntarily went beyond the minimum legal demands of OSHA or Title VII. Such a course of action, however, would cost money that might otherwise be devoted to product research, expansion, dividends, or executive salaries. In effect, unless a firm puts social conscience ahead of competitive or productive efficiency, it may choose an alternative that is suboptimum from society's point of view.

Writers such as Ralph Nader[32] and Christopher Stone[33] argue that improved social performance should be brought about by legally restructuring large, publicly held firms. For example, members of the public, consumer groups, and other interest groups could be named to the board of directors to give the firm a wider spectrum of concerns. Milton Friedman,[34] however, relates that these firms are pursuing the most socially responsible course when they are left alone to produce goods and services efficiently and within the bounds of the law and ethical custom. With regard to cost-benefit analysis, each of these writers sees it as a valuable decision-making tool. Nader and Stone, however, believe that the law should institutionalize their brand of social responsibility; Friedman supports a firm-dominated approach with a minimum of legal intrusions.

The thoughtful application of utilitarianism and cost-benefit analysis has contributed immensely to the well-being of society. Yet, it cannot be said that these concepts are synonymous or co-extensive with the rational process. One point of view says that benefits should be maximized over costs, but another—one that exalts individual rights and a just distribution of social goods and bads—insists that those who bear the costs or burdens should not be exploited even in the process of maximizing public welfare. For example, the employment of young workers might contribute more to productivity than the employment of older workers; but a society concerned with the rights of senior men and women could choose to sacrifice a certain amount of this productivity so that the preferred group (the older workforce) could remain employed.

Kant teaches that individuals should not be sacrificed as mere means to an end. To give an example, the economic benefits to a firm may be maximized by skimping on safety and health measures, but that approach exploits or impoverishes individual workers and society as a whole. It externalizes, or passes along to society, responsibility for the real cost of production just as polluting factories pass along their wastes and garbage for someone else to clean up. The danger is that utilitarianism or cost-benefit may become the only frame of reference consulted. Valuable as it is, it is not a perfect model, and it needs to be adjusted in light of other important considerations, such as individual rights and the distribution of social goods.

People concerned that the cost-benefit view might become the dominant mode of thought (that it might be mistaken for the high mark of the rational process) point to the following executive order:

> By the authority vested in me as President by the Constitution and laws of the United States of America, and in order to reduce the burdens of existing and future regulations ... and [to] insure well-reasoned regulations, it is hereby ordered as follows:

★ ★ ★

Sec. 2. General Requirements. In promulgating new regulations, reviewing existing regulations, and developing legislative proposals concerning regulation, all agencies, to the extent permitted by law, shall adhere to the following requirements:

★ ★ ★

(b) Regulatory action shall not be undertaken unless the potential benefits to society for the regulation outweigh the potential costs to society; . . . .

(c) Regulatory objectives shall be chosen to maximize the net benefits to society;

(d) Among alternative approaches to any given regulatory objective, the alternative involving the least net cost to society shall be chosen. . . . [35]

Certainly, nothing is unconstitutional, nor even surprising, in a president's order to officials in the executive department to follow his policy. Problems arise, however, when Congress is vague about the decision-making methodology that should be used by governmental agencies. For example, most environmental legislation commands that the EPA and related agencies use cost-benefit analysis in their rules and regulations. The Occupational Safety and Health Act, however, as well as the legislation creating the Consumer Product Safety Commission, is not so explicit. Can a president or an agency impose on the enabling legislation the requirement that governmental regulations be justified by proving that the benefits exceed the costs? The *American Textile Manufacturers* case addresses this point.

American Textile Manufacturers Institute, Inc. v. *Donovan*
452 U.S. 490 (1981)

BRENNAN, JUSTICE

Congress enacted the Occupational Safety and Health Act of 1970 (Act) "to assure so far as possible every working man and woman in the Nation safe and healthful working conditions. . . ." In 1978, the Secretary, acting through the Occupational Safety and Health Administration (OSHA), promulgated a standard limiting occupational exposure to cotton dust, an airborne particle byproduct of the preparation and manufacture of cotton products, exposure to which induces a "constellation of respiratory effects" known as "byssinosis."

Petitioners in these consolidated cases, representing the interests of the cotton industry, challenged the validity of the "Cotton Dust Standard" in the Court of Appeals for the District of Columbia Circuit pursuant to § 6(f) of the Act. . . . They contend in this Court, as they did below, that the Act requires OSHA to demonstrate that its Standard reflects a reasonable relationship between the costs and benefits associated with the standard. Respondents, the Secretary of Labor and two labor organizations, counter that Congress balanced the costs and benefits in the Act itself, and that the Act should therefore be construed not to require OSHA to do so. They interpret the Act as mandating that OSHA enact the most protective standard possible to eliminate significant risk of material health impairment, subject to the constraints of economic and technological feasibility. The Court of Appeals held that the Act did not require OSHA to compare costs and benefits.

We granted certiorari to resolve this important question. . . .

* * *

The principal question presented in these cases is whether the Occupational Safety and Health Act requires the Secretary, in promulgating a standard pursuant to § 6(b)(5) of the Act, . . . to determine that the costs of the standard bear a reasonable relationship to its benefits.

* * *

The starting point of our analysis is the language of the statute itself. Section 6(b)(5) of the Act, . . . (emphasis added), provides:

> The Secretary, in promulgating standards dealing with toxic materials or harmful physical agents under this subsection, shall set the standard which most adequately assures, *to the extent feasible,* on the basis of the best available evidence, that no employee w ill suffer material impairment of health or functional capacity even if such employee has regular exposure to the hazard dealt with by such standard for the period of his working life.

Although their interpretations differ, all parties agree that the phrase "to the extent feasible" contains the critical language in § 6(b)(5) for purposes of these cases.

The plain meaning of the word "feasible" supports respondents' interpretation of the statute. According to Webster's Third New International Dictionary of the English Language 831 (1976), "feasible" means "capable of being done, executed, or effected." Accord, The Oxford English Dictionary 116 (1933) ("Capable of being done, accom-

plished or carried out"); Funk & Wagnalls New "Standard" Dictionary of the English Language 903 (1957) ("That may be done, performed or effected"). Thus, § 6(b)(5) directs the Secretary to issue the standard that "most adequately assures . . . that no employee will suffer material impairment of health," limited only by the extent to which this is "capable of being done." In effect then, as the Court of Appeals held, Congress itself defined the basic relationship between costs and benefits, by placing the "benefit" of worker health above all other considerations save those making attainment of this "benefit" unachievable. Any standard based on a balancing of costs and benefits by the Secretary that strikes a different balance than that struck by Congress would be inconsistent with the command set forth in § 6(b)(5). Thus, cost-benefit analysis by OSHA is not required by the statute because feasibility analysis is.

When Congress has intended that an agency engage in cost-benefit analysis, it has clearly indicated such intent on the face of the statute.

[*Author's note:* At this stage of its opinion, the Court enumerated the following acts as illustrative of a disclosure of congressional intent when cost-benefit analysis is intended: Flood Control Act of 1936; Outer Continental Shelf Lands Act Amendments of 1978; Energy Policy and Conservation Act of 1975; Federal Water Pollution Control Act Amendments of 1972; and Clean Air Act of 1977.]

We therefore reject the argument that Congress required cost-benefit analysis in § 6(b)(5).

Even though the plain language of § 6(b)(5) supports this construction, we must still decide whether § 3(8), the general definition of an occupational safety and health standard, either alone or in tandem with § 6(b)(5), incorporates a cost-benefit requirement for standards dealing with toxic materials or harmful physical agents. Section 3(8) of the Act (emphasis added) provides:

> The term "occupational safety and health standard" means a standard which requires conditions, or the adoption or use of one or more practices, means, methods, operations, or processes, *reasonably necessary or appropriate* to provide safe or healthful employment and places of employment.

Taken alone, the phrase "reasonably necessary or appropriate" might be construed to contemplate some balancing of the costs and benefits of a standard. Petitioners urge that, so construed, § 3(8) engrafts a cost-benefit analysis requirement on the issuance of § 6(b)(5) standards, even if §6(b)(5) itself does not authorize such analysis. We need not decide whether § 3(8), standing alone, would contemplate some form of cost-benefit analysis. For even if it does, Congress specifically chose in § 6(b)(5) to impose separate and additional requirements for issuance of a subcategory of occupational safety and health standards dealing with toxic materials and harmful physical agents; it required that those standards be issued to prevent material impairment of health *to the extent feasible*. Congress could reasonably have concluded that *health* standards should be subject to different criteria than *safety* standards because of the special problems presented in regulating them.

CASE FOLLOW-UP

Feasibility analysis does not pave the way for a risk-free workplace, it does however, elevate Congress's concern for the health of U.S. workers above that of the cost of protecting them from toxic materials. With regard to these impacts on health, OSHA is not permitted to perform any cost-benefit analysis. Congress specified this when it passed the Act.

The Supreme Court did not foreclose the possibility of OSHA's use of cost-benefit analysis for safety.

CONCLUSION

In this chapter, we followed the development of labor law from the early application of conspiracy law to the present-day enforcement of the 1935 National Labor Relations Act, or Wagner Act. This commerce clause-based Act guarantees laborers the right to bargain collectively with management and, in its original form, prohibited certain unfair practices by employers. The Act also created an administrative and enforcement agency—the National Labor Relations Board—to guide these efforts toward the achievement of a major national policy objective: reducing industrial strife.

The NLRA gave such a boost to union power that Congress prohibited unfair union practices in the 1947 Taft-Hartley amendments. These amendments were followed in 1959 by the Landrum-Griffin Act, which further limited union power by defining as unfair certain union practices, as well as by mandating reporting and disclosure requirements for union officials. In sum, this chapter has surveyed the principal components of labor law in the United States today and illustrated it with text materials and cases that address these points.

The focus of the chapter then moved from private sector to public sector employment, and closed with an examination of federal statutes that prohibit discrimination on the basis of age or physical/mental impairment and protect employee pension plans and employee safety and health.

REVIEW QUESTIONS AND PROBLEMS

1. Helen Chizmar had supervised office staff of Salvatore Monte since 1963. Three of seven members of Salvatore's clerical staff were Helen's relatives. When the office staff designated a union bargaining representative, Salvatore became upset. Helen, a supervisor, was not unionized, and she did not explicitly engage in pro-union conduct. The NLRA does not protect supervisors who do engage in union activity. When Helen was fired "on the spot," she and the others filed an unfair labor practice complaint with the NLRB. Salvatore was reported as saying to others that he could get someone else to do her job for "$20,000 less," that he planned to "get rid of the whole family," and that he "was not going to put up with any union bullshit." Even if this conduct by Salvatore is in violation of Section 8(a)(1)—interference with employee efforts to join a labor union—is Helen entitled to a remedy?

2. The collective bargaining agreement negotiated by the Communication Workers of America (CWA) for AT&T employees required nonunion workers to pay dues equivalent to those paid by union members. This was an effort to avoid the negative effect of free riders, but it did intrude on the freedom of those who chose not to become union members. Nonunion workers objected to this term, arguing that a portion of the dues they were required to pay was used by the union to support non-collective bargaining activities (social, charitable, and political events). The essence of their complaint was that they should not be required to pay more than the bare minimum necessary to finance the collective-bargaining and related activities of the union. Result?

3. Laidlaw Corporation hired replacement workers when the papermill workers went on strike for higher wages. Jobs are not protected during strikes for economic reasons, such as higher wages, as they are during strikes protesting unfair labor practices. After the strike ended and the strikers offered to return to work, Laidlaw hired a limited number of them to fill open positions but would not consider the others even when vacancies occurred. Did Laidlaw commit an unfair labor practice?

4. Prior to negotiations on a new collective bargaining agreement, *ABC* company made numerous studies of employees' potential demands. *ABC* then reviewed the results and formulated a comprehensive package. When the employees and *ABC* began bargaining, *ABC* placed the package on the table. Both sides negotiated on all aspects of the package, but no agreement was reached. Has *ABC* committed an unfair labor practice?

5. *XYZ* is involved in contract negotiations. *XYZ* unilaterally increases wages and certain benefits after an impasse is reached. Has *XYZ* committed an unfair labor practice?

6. The employees of *DEF* Company elect a collective bargaining representative. Four months after the election, 60 percent of the

employees become dissatisfied with the contract and vote to oust the union. What result?

7. *GHI* is a family company. After the employees unionize, *GHI* closes its entire business. *JKL* owns four factories. One factory unionizes and is closed down. Has either company committed an unfair practice?

8. The president of *MNO* Company spoke to employees during a union's organization drive. He reminded employees of an earlier strike that almost put the company out of business. He also stated that the company was on "thin ice" and that a strike was not the union's only "weapon." The president sent letters to employees, warning them that a strike would close the plant permanently. Is *MNO* guilty of an unfair labor practice?

9. A union representing local musicians required theater owners to hire a pit orchestra before allowing stage bands to play. The pit orchestra was to play overtures, intermissions, and "chasers." A local theater refused to hire the orchestra. As a result, the stage band refused to play. Is the union guilty of featherbedding?

ENDNOTES

1. *Commonwealth* v. *Pullis* (Philadelphia Mayor's Court, 1806).
2. 45 Mass. (4 Mat.) 111 (1842).
3. Sherman Act, 26 stat. 209, 15 U.S.C. Sections 1–7.
4. *Loewe* v. *Lawlor*, 208 U.S. 274 (1908).
5. Clayton Act, 38 Stat. 730, 15 U.S.C. Sections 12-27.
6. *Duplex Printing Press* v. *Deering*, 254 U.S. 443 (1921).
7. Secondary activities are directed by a union at the customers or suppliers of an employer, rather than directly against the employer. Boycotts are efforts to get these customers or suppliers to refuse to deal with the employer.
8. Norris-LaGuardia, 29 U.S.C. Sections 101 *et seq.*
9. Wagner Act, 49 Stat. 449, 29 U.S.C. Sections 151 *et seq.*
10. 301 U.S. 1 (1937).
11. Taft-Hartley Act, 61 Stat. 136, 29 U.S.C. Sections 141 *et seq.*
12. Landrum-Griffin Act, 73 Stat. 519, 29 U.S.C. Sections 153 *et seq.*
13. U.S. district courts are authorized to grant temporary injunctions sought by the NLRB against illegal secondary activities. The 1959 Landrum-Griffin Act authorized a private remedy for damages resulting from a prohibited secondary action.
14. 418 F.2d 736 (2nd Cir. 1959), *cert. denied,* 397 U.S. 965 (1970).
15. 353 U.S. 87 (1957).
16. 351 U.S. 105 (1956).
17. 375 U.S. 405 (1964).
18. 912 F.2d 854 (6th Cir. 1990).
19. 311 F.2d 565 (7th Cir. 1962).
20. 377 U.S. 58 (1964).
21. 485 U.S. 568 (1988).
22. 440 U.S. 490 (1979).
23. 685 F.2d 547 (D.C.C. 1982).
24. 29 U.S.C. Sections 621 *et seq.*
25. U.S.C. Sections 791 *et seq.*
26. 29 U.S.C. Sections 1001 *et seq.* (1974).
27. U.S.C. Sections 651–678 (1976 and Supp. IV 1980).
28. Within one year of the effective date of OSHA, members of Congress introduced one hundred bills to amend or repeal the law. Kelman, *Regulating America, Regulating Sweden* 205 (1981).
29. A health standard is one that "requires conditions, or the adoption or use of one or more practices, means, methods, operations or processes, reasonably necessary or appropriate to provide safe or healthful employment and places of employment." 20 U.S.C. Section 652(8).
30. 29 U.S.C. Section 655(b)(5).
31. In *Marshall* v. *Barlow's, Inc.,* 436 U.S. 307 (1978), the Supreme Court held unconstitutional that part of the Act authorizing warrantless searches. The Fourth Amendment forbids unreasonable searches and seizures; however, warrants can be issued "on the basis of a general administrative plan for the enforcement of the Act," for example, a plan that takes into consideration the nature of complaints, frequency of complaints, and the compliance record of the firm or industry.
32. Nader, *Taming the Giant Corporation* (1976).
33. Stone, *Where the Law Ends* (1975).
34. Friedman, *Capitalism and Freedom* (1962).
35. Executive Order No. 12291, 46 Fed. Reg. 13,193 (1981).

THOMAS L. CARSON
RICHARD E. WOKUTCH
KENT F. MURRAMAN

Bluffing in Labor Negotiations: Legal and Ethical Issues

[*Author's note:* The process of bargaining collectively in good faith is at the heart of national labor policy. Because it plays such a significant role in achieving the objective of reducing industrial strife, we are legitimately concerned that it have a sound footing. This concern is heightened when we hear stories or learn firsthand that union and management negotiators bluff one another in the process of bargaining about the terms and conditions of employment. Is it a good thing to have lying and deception among the tactics available to both parties represented at the bargaining table? Is bluffing a form of lying, and, if so, should it be permitted? The following essay[1] addresses this problem.]

The Legal Status of Bluffing

The National Labor Relations Act, as amended (1970), provides the legal framework within which the collective bargaining process in the private sector of our economy is carried out. Section 8(a)(5) and 8(b)(3) of the National Labor Relations Act provide that it shall be an unfair labor practice for a union or an employer in a properly constituted bargaining relationship to fail to bargain in good faith. The statute left it to the national Labor Relations Board and the courts to establish criteria for determining whether a party is bargaining in good faith. Over the years numerous such criteria have been established by the Board and the courts.

The Honest Claims Doctrine. Of particular interest with respect to the legal status of bluffing is the "honest claims" doctrine, established by the U.S. Supreme Court in its Truitt Mfg. Co. decision [*NLRB* v. *Truitt Mfg. Co.,* 351 U.S. 149 (1956)]. This states that "good faith necessarily requires that claims made by either party should be honest claims." The central issue in the Truitt Case was whether the employer would be required to substantiate its claim that it could not afford to pay a certain wage increase. In addition to enunciating its "honest claims" doctrine, the court declared that if an "inability to pay argument is important enough to present in the give and take of bargaining it is important enough to require some sort of proof of its accuracy" (*NLRB* v. *Truitt Mfg. Co.*, at p.152). This "honest claims" policy has been consistently upheld and applied in numerous court decisions to this day. Thus, it is clear that the law requires honesty in collective bargaining. However, the "honest claims" requirement applies only to those types of claims that pertain directly to issues subject to bargaining and the employer's ability to provide certain conditions of employment. Thus, the "honest claims" policy requires a union to refrain from presenting false information to management concerning the level of wages and fringe benefits provided by employers under other union contracts. Likewise, the employer must refrain from falsely claiming an inability to provide a certain benefit.

Bluffing and the Honest Claims Doctrine. How does the "honest claims" doctrine apply to the practice of bluffing? It is clear that bluffing that involves the presentation of false information about issues subject to bargaining (i.e., wages, hours, and conditions of employment) is a violation. However bluffing about objective issues not subject to negotiation such as one's ability to withstand a strike (e.g., the size of the union strike fund, or the union membership's vote on the question of whether or not to go out on strike) is allowable. Also, bluffing that is limited to representations of one's bargaining intentions or one's willingness to impose or endure costs in order to win a more favorable contract does not constitute a violation. Of course, this type of bluffing is more effective and more prevalent because it can not be as easily discredited through refer-

ence to objective information as can false statements about working conditions. In sum, though the Truitt decision requires honesty with regard to the making of claims concerning bargaining topics, it does not proscribe the more effective and important forms of bluffing commonly used in bargaining today.

Bluffing and the Concept of Lying

Suppose (example 1) that I am a management negotiator trying to reach a strike settlement with union negotiators. I need to settle the strike soon and have been instructed to settle for as much as a 12% increase in wages and benefits if that is the best agreement I can obtain. I say that the company's final offer is a 10% increase. Am I lying? Consider also whether any of the following examples constitute lying:

2. Management negotiators misstating the profitability of a subsidiary to convince the union negotiating with it that the subsidiary would go out of business if management acceded to union wage demands.

3. Union officials misreporting the size of the union strike fund to portray a greater ability to strike than is actually the case.

4. Management negotiators saying, "We can't afford this agreement," when it would not put the firm out of business but only reduce profits from somewhat above to somewhat below the industry average.

5. Union negotiators saying, "The union membership is adamant on this issue," when they know that while one half of the membership is adamant, the other half couldn't care less.

6. Union negotiators saying, "If you include this provision, we'll get member-

ship approval of the contract," when they know they'll have an uphill battle for approval even with the provision.

Defining Lying. What is lying? A lie must be a false statement, but not all false statements are lies. If I am a salesman and say that my product is the best on the market and *sincerely believe this to be the case*, my statement is not a lie, even if it is untrue. A false statement is not a lie unless it is somehow deliberate or intentional. Suppose that we define a lie as an intentional false statement. According to this definition, I am telling a lie when I say, "This aftershave will make you feel like a million bucks." This definition implies that we lie when we exaggerate, e.g., a negotiator representing union workers making $10/hour but seeking a substantial raise says, "These are slave wages you're paying us." When I greatly exaggerate or say something in jest, I know that it is very improbable that the other person(s) will believe what I say. The reason that these examples do not appear to be lies is that they do not involve the intent to deceive. This suggests the following definition of lying:

1. A lie is a deliberate false statement intended to deceive another person.

This definition is inadequate in cases in which a person is compelled to make false statements. For example, I may lie as a witness to a jury for fear of being killed by the accused. But it doesn't follow that I hope or intend to deceive them. I may hope that my statements don't deceive anyone. We might say that what makes my statements lies is that I realize or foresee that they are likely to deceive others. This then suggests the following definition of lying:

2. A lie is a deliberate false statement which is thought to be likely to deceive others by the person who makes it.

This definition is also lacking because a person can lie even if he or she has almost no hope of being believed. A criminal protesting his or her innocence in court is lying no matter how unlikely it is that he/she thinks the argument will be convincing to the judge or jury. The following definition is more plausible than either (1) of (2):

3. A lie is a deliberate false statement which is either intended to deceive others or foreseen to be likely to deceive others.

Implications for bluffing. It appears that this definition implies that the statements in our first three examples constitute lies. In examples (1) and (2) one is making deliberate false statements with the intent of deceiving others about matters relevant to the negotiations. In the first case I am making a deliberate false statement with the intent to deceive the other party into thinking that I am unwilling to offer more than 10%. One might object that this needn't be my intention in example (1). So one familiar with standard negotiating practices is likely to take at face value statements which a person makes about a "final offer." One might argue that in the two cases in question I intend and expect my statement that 10% is my best offer to be taken to mean my highest possible offer is something around 12%. If this is my intention and expectation, then my bluffing does not constitute a lie. To this we might add the observation that such intentions are quite uncommon in business negotiations. Even if I don't *expect* you to believe that 10% is my final position, I probably still *hope* or intend to deceive you into thinking that I am unwilling to offer as much as 12%. Examples (2) and (3) are clear instances of lying - they involve deliberate false statements intended to deceive others. It's not so clear, however, that examples (4), (5) and (6) constitute instances of lying. These cases do seem to involve the intent to deceive, but the statements involved are sufficiently ambiguous that it is not clear that they are untrue. We can still say that these are cases in which one affirms (or represents as true) statements which one allows to be dubious with the intent to deceive others. Morally speaking this may be just as bad or wrong as straightforward instances of lying.

An alternative definition of lying. Our proposed definition of lying implies that bluffing in standard negotiation settings constitutes lying. There is at least one other approach to defining the concept of lying which does not have this consequence and it would be well for us to consider it here. In his *Lectures on Ethics,* Immannuel Kant (1775–1780) holds that a deliberate false statement does not constitute a lie unless the speaker has "expressly given" the other(s) to believe that he/she intends to speak the truth.[2] According to Kant's original view, when I make a false statement to a thief about the location of my valuables, I am not lying because "the thief knows full well that I will not, if I can help it, tell him the truth and that he has no right to demand it of me" (1775–1780, p. 227). According to this view, false statements uttered in the course of business negotiations do not constitute lies except in the very unusual circumstances that one promises to tell the truth during the negotiations. Kant's definition is open to serious objections. It seems to rule out many common cases of lying. For example, suppose that a child standing in line to see an X-rated movie claims to be 18 when he or she is only 15. This is a lie in spite of the fact that no explicit promise to tell the truth was made to the ticket seller. There does seem to be one relevant difference between the two cases in question. The ticket taker has a right to be told the truth and a right to the information in question, the thief has no right to the information on one's valuables. This suggests the following

revision of Kant's definition:

4. A lie is a deliberate false statement which is (i) either intended to deceive others or foreseen to be likely to deceive others, and (ii) either the person who makes the statement has promised to be truthful or those to whom it is directed have a right to know the truth.

Many would take it to be a virtue of (4) that it implies that deliberate false statements made during the course of certain kinds of competitive activities do not constitute lies. Carr [Is Business Bluffing Ethical, 46 *Harv. Bus. Rev.* 143-153 (1968)] quoted the British statesman Henry Taylor who argued that "falsehood ceases to be falsehood when it is understood on all sides that the truth is not expected to be spoken" (p. 143). Carr argued that in poker, diplomacy, and business, individuals (through mutually implied consent) forfeit their rights to be told the truth. It seems at least plausible to say this with respect to standard cases of negotiation. However, it is surely not the case in situations in which one of the parties is unfamiliar with standard negotiating procedures (e.g. children, immigrant laborers, naive individuals or the mentally impaired), and who enters into the discussion assuming that all of the parties will be perfectly candid.

If (4) is a correct definition of lying, then it does seem plausible to say that bluffing typically does not amount to lying. So, in order to defend our earlier claim that bluffing usually involves lying we need to give reasons for thinking that (3) is preferable to (4). We are inclined to think that deliberate falsehoods uttered in the course of games and diplomacy as well as business do constitute lies, and are thus inclined to prefer (3) to (4). This is a case about which people have conflicting intuitions; it cannot be a decisive reason for preferring (3) to (4) or vice versa. A more decisive consideration in favor of (3) is the following case. Suppose that a management negotiator asks a union negotiator the size of the union strike fund. The union negotiator responds by saying it is three times its actual amount. Definition (4) implies that this statement is not a lie since the management negotiator didn't have a right to know the information in question and the union didn't explicitly promise to tell the truth about this. But surely this is a lie. The fact that management has no right to know the truth is just cause for withholding the information, but responding falsely is a lie nonetheless.

There is, to the best of our knowledge, no plausible definition of lying which allows us to say that typical instances of bluffing in labor and other sorts of business negotiations do not involve lying. We should stress that it is only bluffing which involves making false statements which constitutes lying. One is not lying if one bluffs another by making the true statement "We want a 30% pay increase." Similarly, it is not a lie if one bluffs without making any statements as in a game of poker or overpricing (on a price tag) a product where bargaining is expected (e.g. a used car lot or antique store).

The Concept of Deception. At this point is would be useful to consider the relationship between lying and the broader concept of deception. Deception may be defined as intentionally causing another person to have false beliefs. (It is not clear whether preventing someone from having true beliefs should count as deception.) As we have seen, lying always involves the intent to deceive others, or the expectation that they will be deceived as a result of what one says, or both. But one can lie without actually deceiving anyone. If you don't believe me when I lie and tell you that 10% is our final offer, then I haven't succeeded in deceiving you about anything. It is also possible to deceive another person without telling a lie. For example, I am not lying when I deceive a thief into thinking that I am at home by installing an automatic timer to have my lights turned on in the evening. Only deception which involves making false statements can be considered lying.

It seems that one can often avoid lying in the course of a business negotiation simply by phrasing one's statements very carefully. In negotiations, instead of lying and saying that 10% is the highest wage increase we will give, I could avoid lying by making the following true, but equally deceptive statement: "Our position is that 10% is our final offer" (without saying that this position is subject to change). It is questionable whether this is any less morally objectionable than lying. Most people prefer to deceive others by means of cleverly contrived true statements, rather than lies. Some who have strong scruples against lying see nothing wrong with such ruses. It is doubtful, however, whether lying is any worse than mere deception. Consider the following example. I want to deceive a potential thief into thinking that I will be at home in the late afternoon. I have the choice between (i) leaving my lights on, and (ii) leaving a note on my door which says "I will be home at 5 p.m." Surely this choice is morally indifferent. The fact that (ii) is an act of lying and (i) isn't, is not, itself, a reason for thinking that (i) is morally preferable to (ii).

4. *Moral Issues in Lying*

Common sense holds that lying is a matter of moral significance and that lying is *prima facie* wrong, or wrong everything else being equal. This can also be put by saying that there is a presumption against lying, and that lying requires some special justification in order to be considered permissible. Common sense also holds that lying is not always wrong, it can sometimes be justified [Ross,

The Right and the Good (1930)]. Almost no one would agree with Kant's (1797) later view in "On the Supposed Right to Tell Lies from Benevolent Motives," that it is wrong to lie even if doing so is necessary to protect the lives of innocent people. According to this view it would be wrong to lie to a potential murderer concerning the whereabouts of an intended victim. Common sense also seems to hold that there is a presumption against simple deception.

Assuming the correctness of this view about the morality of lying and deception, and assuming that we are correct in saying that bluffing involves lying, it follows that bluffing and other deceptive business practices require some sort of special justification in order to be considered permissible.

We will not attempt to determine whether there is any special justification for the kind of lying and deception which typically occurs in labor and other sorts of business negotiations. Bluffing and other sorts of deceptive strategies are standard practice in these negotiations and they are generally thought to be acceptable. Does the fact that these things are standard practice or "part of the game" show that they are justified? We think not. The mere fact that something is standard practice, legal, or generally accepted is not enough to justify it. Standard practice and popular opinion can be in error. Such things as slavery were once standard practice, legal and generally accepted. But they

are and *were* morally wrong. Bluffing constitutes an attempt to deceive others about the nature of one's intentions in a bargaining situation. The *prima facie* wrongness of bluffing is considerably *diminished* on account of the fact that the lying and deception involved typically concern matters about which the other parties have no particular right to know. The others have no particular right to know one's bargaining position—one's intentions. However, there is still some presumption against lying or deceiving other people, even when they have no right to the information in question. A stranger has no right to know how old I am. I have no obligation to provide him/her with this information. Other things being equal, however, it would still be wrong for me to lie to this stranger about my age.

In our view the main justification for bluffing consists in the fact that the moral presumption against lying to or deceiving someone holds only when the person or persons with whom you are dealing is/are not attempting to lie to or deceive you. Given this, there is no presumption against bluffing or deceiving someone who is attempting to bluff or deceive you on that occasion. The prevalence of bluffing in negotiations means that one is safe in presuming that one is justified in bluffing in the absence of any special reasons for thinking that one's negotiating partners are not bluffing (e.g., when one is dealing with an unusually naive or scrupulous person).

ARTICLE FOLLOW-UP

The authors of this essay conclude that the U.S. competitive system, which many people believe is flawed in that it encourages dishonesty and corrupts moral character, is not totally to be blamed for such outcomes. The principal alternatives to capitalism, socialism, and communism elicit unethical conduct as well. Economic systems that are less conducive to such behavior (feudalism, hunting and gathering) have such undesirable features that they do not provide practical, realistic models for adjusting the U.S. system.

Beyond that, however, an economic system alone does not shape the nature of moral goodness and moral virtues.

. . . The extent to which a person possesses the different moral virtues is a function of how that person is *disposed* to act in various actual and possible situations. My courage or cowardice is a function of my ability to master fear in dangerous situations. Suppose that I am drafted into the army and sent to serve in the front lines. If I desert my post at the first sign of the enemy we would not say that being drafted into the army has made me a more cowardly person. Rather we could say that it has uncovered and actualized cowardly dispositions which I had all along. Similarly, competitive economic arrangements do not usually *cause* people to become dishonest or treacherous, etc. However these arrangements often actualize dispositions to act dishonestly or treacherously which people had all along. This is not to deny that the economic institutions of our society can in some cases alter a person's basic behavioral dispositions and thereby also his/her character for the worse. For example, the activities of a negotiator may cause him/her to be less truthful and trusting in his/her personal relationships. Our claim is only that most of the "undesirable moral effects" attributed to our economic institutions involve actualizing preexisting dispositions, rather than causing any fundamental changes in character. (Carson et al., pp. 20-21)

The authors' main theme in this essay is that bluffing is lying, but that it may be justified in a collective bargaining context. The reason they give in support of this proposition is that the moral presumption against lying or deceiving only holds when the person one is dealing with is not attempting to lie or deceive in return. What do you think of this reason?

In her 1978 book *Lying,* Sissela Bok draws an analogy between lying, a tactic by which one manipulates other people, and violence, which is even worse. To put it another way, lying is the "lesser of two evils." It follows from this that, on those occasions when violence would be justified (e.g., self-defense), lying could be justified even more easily. What do you think? Is it consistent with the essay you have just studied? Does that justification make sense in a collective-bargaining context that is an effort to reduce industrial strife?

Endnotes

1. *Journal of Business Ethics* 1 (1982) 15-19. Copyright ©1982 by D. Reidel Publishing Co., Dordrecht, Holland and Boston, U.S.A. Reprinted by permission.
2. Kant's analysis of lying offered here differs from the one presented in Kant's later and more well-known work, "On the Supposed Right to Tell Lies from Benevolent Motives" (1797) in Barauch Brody (ed.). *Moral Rules and Particular Circumstances* (Prentice-Hall, 1970), pp.31-36. There he says that any intentional false statement is a lie (p.32). Kant also gives a different account of the morality of lying in these two works. His well-known absolute prohibition against lying is set forth only in the latter work.

CHAPTER 16

Environmental Law

INTRODUCTION

Appropriate for every occasion that confronts you with a dilemma—a tough choice that presents you with conflicting goals or objectives—is the cliche, "You can't have your cake and eat it too." People cannot have both an unspoiled environment *and* a robust economy that produces the goods and services needed for the material quality of life that they have been seeking for themselves and their families. It is within their reach, however, to modify their material values and to adjust them in light of environmental, conservational, aesthetic, and spiritual values so that wants and needs can be satisfied without exacting a heavy toll on the natural environment. Beyond this, means of production can be modified in such a way that they will be less destructive of the natural environment and less pollutive of the air and water, while at the same time still capable of producing the goods and services needed by the public.

This chapter deals with the ways the United States has tried to resolve the dilemma posed above. Through the National Environmental Policy Act (NEPA), environmental values have been elevated to a level equaling that of economic and technological values in many federal projects. The NEPA is by no means the perfect piece of legislation, but it is teaching that respect for the integrity of the environment is compatible with economic production and that at times the long-term best interests of the nation are served by reducing emphasis on production in the name of environmental protection.

The intent behind the NEPA is embodied in each of the other federal acts that we examine in this chapter: the Clean Air Act, the Clean Water Act, and other legislative acts that seek a reduction in the hazardous and sometimes toxic pollutants that the productive system of the United States is inflicting on its population and on future generations. Except in unusual situations in which the public health is imminently threatened, these laws do not halt or prohibit the production of goods and services. They merely regulate the means of production or the method by which these products are stored or disposed of in the environment.

The United States has confronted the dilemma of economic production versus environmental protection and has sought to resolve it with a compromise that gives a certain measure of both. No one claims that this outcome is ideal. But the American people do care about the environment and have insisted that its abuse come to an end.

The subject matter of this chapter, then, is a study of the ways the environmental conscience of the United States is put into practice.

THE WAY OF THE WORLD: LIVING AND POLLUTING

To live and breathe is to pollute. Living systems demand inputs of energy. Some of it is captured or harnessed for the time being in the human body; the nutrients are metabolized and the remainder is rejected in the form of waste. This is true of all forms of life. In a very real sense, it is the way of the world.

At one time, pollution in the form of natural wastes was no great problem because it was not excessive in relation to the natural assimilative or absorptive capacity of the environment. The acquisition of energy inputs—food and water, for example—was the greatest source of turmoil, and the chances are good that the human race will always be faced with a scarcity of energy (after all, how much is enough?). Only in recent years, however, has society begun to deal seriously with the problem, magnified by an increasing population and changing technologies, of managing the inevitable waste by-product in an environmentally sound manner.

SOCIAL COST OR EXTERNALITIES

Part of the difficulty seems to be that society's level of affluence and expectation is such that natural resources are being depleted and pollutants are being created at ever-increasing rates. When we turn on a light or an air conditioner, or fail to turn one off, we realize that this does something to our electricity bill. Given society's rational self-interest and a rate structure that penalizes excess, strides are already being made toward conservation. Beyond that, however, everyone must learn to appreciate the costs—social costs or externalities (polluted air or water)— over and above the amount paid for electricity consumption. The "exchange" price (the amount people pay on their monthly utility bills) does not cover the full cost of production.

Polluted air or water is evidence that an industrial source, for example, is using a public or common good to dispose of the waste product of its operations. It is as if you were to dump your garbage in the middle of Main Street for someone else to clean up, rather than pay a fee for its collection. Economists call a fee or charge imposed for preventing environmental pollution *internalizing the externality*. This approach to accountability affects the cost (supply) curve of business operations and, as a rule, these businesses will pass along as much of the cost to the consumer as the demand curve permits.

Notice in figure 16.1 that the increase in cost of pollution control (dashed line a-b) is greater than the increase in price (dashed line c-b or line P_1-P_2). This means that,

FIGURE 16.1 *Industry Schedule*

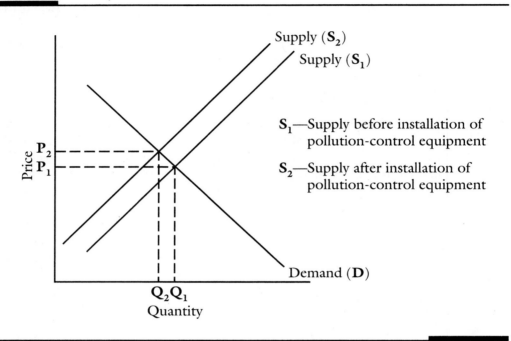

depending on the aggregate demand for the product reflected in the slope of the demand curve, some of the cost can be passed along (dashed line c-b), but part of it (dashed line a-c) will have to be absorbed by the firm. As a result, shareholders will receive a lower return on investment, a reduction will occur in employment or terms of employment and in product research/product quality, or in other ways the cost of the firm's new pollution-control equipment will be paid out of someone's pocket.

Suppose, however, that a firm within a competitive industry wanted to enhance its reputation for social responsibility and community leadership. It could voluntarily and unilaterally install pollution controls, but it would have to pay for the full cost of the equipment. If it tried to pass along these costs to its customers in the form of higher prices, these customers presumably would switch to comparable, substitute products manufactured by a polluting competitor that did not have to raise prices to cover any additional costs. This is why uniform, institutional measures are preferable to individual altruistic or self-sacrificing efforts in the ongoing fight for a cleaner environment.

DEALING WITH EXTERNALITIES

Most of the material in this chapter focuses on command-and-control type legislation that attempts to achieve a uniform, institutional approach to pollution problems. For example, in dealing with water pollution as an externality, the government will command a particular result (reduced pollution by a specified deadline) and control the methods of achieving that result (water pollution permits that require the installation of cleanup equipment). This command and control will compel the private-sector firm to be accountable for its water pollution and to spend money on equipment that will internalize the externality. Notice in figure 16.1 that if this is done uniformly throughout the industry, cost will increase (dashed line a-b, the vertical distance between S_1 and S_2) and quantity will decrease (Q_1 - Q_2). Pollution is then controlled in two ways: (1) The plant will not emit as much pollution, and (2) fewer pollution-producing goods will be manufactured. Reduced air and water pollution, however, will be brought about by trapping the waste in filters and other more sophisticated devices. Disposing of this solid waste in an environmentally sound manner adds another cost.

The problems of dealing with negative pollution externalities are explored in the following selections. The first is written by a biologist, the second by economists.

GARRETT HARDIN

The Tragedy of the Commons[1]

At the end of a thoughtful article on the future of nuclear war, Wiesner and York[2] concluded that: "Both sides in the arms race are . . . confronted by the dilemma of steadily increasing military power and steadily decreasing national security. *It is our considered professional judgment that this dilemma has no technical solution.* If the great powers continue to look for solutions in the area of science and technology only, the result will be to worsen the situation."

* * *

The class of "No technical solution problems" has members. My thesis is that the "population problem," as conventionally conceived, is a member of this class. . . .

What Shall We Maximize?

Population, as Malthus said, naturally tends to grow "geometrically," or, as we would now say, exponentially. In a finite world this means that the per capita share of the world's goods must steadily decrease. Is ours a finite world?

A fair defense can be put forward for the view that the world is infinite; or that we do not know that it is not. But, in terms of the practical problems that we must face in the next few generations with the foreseeable technology, it is clear that we will greatly increase human misery if we do not, during the immediate future, assume that the world available to the terrestrial human population is finite. "Space" is no escape.

A finite world can support only a finite population; therefore, population growth must eventually equal zero. (The case of perpetual wide fluctuations above and below zero is a trivial variant that need not be discussed.) When this condition is met, what will be the situation of mankind? Specifically, can Bentham's goal of "the greatest good for the greatest number" be realized?

No—for two reasons, each sufficient by itself. The first is a theoretical one. It is not mathematically possible to maximize for two (or more) variables at the same time. This was clearly stated by von Neumann and Morgenstern,[3] but the principle is implicit in the theory of partial differential equations, dating back at least to D'Alembert (1717–1783).

The second reason springs directly from biological facts. To live, any organism must have a source of energy (for example, food). This energy is utilized for two purposes: mere maintenance and work. For man, maintenance of life requires about 1600 kilo-calories a day ("maintenance calories"). Anything that he does over and above merely staying alive will be defined as work, and is supported by "work calories" which he takes in. Work calories are used not only for what we call work in common speech; they are also required for all forms of enjoyment, from swimming and automobile racing to playing music and writing poetry. If our goal is to maximize population it is obvious what we must do: We must make the work calories per person approach as close to zero as possible. No gourmet meals, no vacations, no sports, no music, or literature, no art. . . . I think that everyone will grant, without argument or proof, that maximizing population does not maximize goods. Bentham's goal is impossible.

In reaching this conclusion I have made the usual assumption that it is the acquisition of energy that is the problem. The appearance of atomic energy has led some to question this assumption. However, given an infinite source of energy, population growth still produces an inescapable problem. The problem of the acquisition of energy is replaced by the problem of its dissipation, as J. H. Fremlin has so wittily shown.[4] The arithmetic signs in the analysis are, as it were, reversed; but Bentham's goal is still unobtainable.

The optimum population is, then, less than the maximum. . . .

We can make little progress in working toward optimum population size until we explicitly exorcise the spirit of Adam Smith in the field of practical demography. In economic affairs, The Wealth of Nations (1776) popularized the "invisible hand," the idea that an individual who "intends only his own gain," is, as it were, "led by an invisible hand to promote . . . the public interest." Adam Smith did not assert that this was invariably true, and perhaps neither did any of his followers. But he contributed to a dominant tendency of thought that has ever since interfered with positive action based on rational analysis, namely the tendency to assume that decisions reached individually will, in fact, be the best decisions for an entire society. . . .

Tragedy of Freedom in a Commons

The rebuttal to the invisible hand in population control is to be found in a scenario first sketched in a little known pamphlet[5] in 1833 by a mathematical amateur named William Forster Lloyd (1798–1852). We may well call it "the tragedy of the commons," using the word "tragedy" as the philosopher Whitehead used it.[6] "The essence of dramatic tragedy is not unhappiness. It resides in the solemnity of the remorseless working of things." He then goes on to say, "This inevitableness of destiny can only be illustrated in terms of human life by incidents which in fact involve unhappiness. For it is only by them that the futility of escape can be made evident in the drama."

The tragedy of the commons develops in this way. Picture a pasture open to all. It is to be expected that each herdsman will try to keep as many cattle as possible on the commons. Such an arrangement may work reasonably satisfactorily for centuries because tribal wars, poaching, and disease keep the numbers of both man and beast well below the carrying capacity of the land. Finally, however, comes the day of reckoning, that is, the day when the long-desired goal of social stability becomes a reality. At this point, the inherent logic of the commons remorselessly generates tragedy.

As a rational being, each herdsman seeks to maximize his gain. Explicitly or implicitly, more or less consciously, he asks, "What is the utility *to me* of adding one more animal to my herd?" This utility has one negative and one positive component.

1. The positive component is a function of the increment of one animal. Since the herdsman receives all the proceeds from the sale of the additional animal, the positive utility is nearly +1.

2. The negative component is a function of the additional overgrazing created by

one more animal. Since, however, the effects of overgrazing are shared by all the herdsmen, the negative utility for any particular decision-making herdsman is only a fraction of −1.

Adding together the component partial utilities, the rational herdsman concludes that the only sensible course for him to pursue is to add another animal to his herd. And another; and another. . . . But this is the conclusion reached by each and every rational herdsman sharing a commons. Therein is the tragedy. Each man is locked into a system that compels him to increase his herd without limit—in a world that it limited. Ruin is the destination toward which all men rush, each pursuing his own best interest in a society that believes in the freedom of the commons. Freedom in a commons brings ruin to all.

Some would say that this is a platitude. Would that it were! In a sense, it was learned thousands of years ago, but natural selection favors the forces of psychological denial.[7] The individual benefits as an individual from his ability to deny the truth even though society as a whole, of which he is a part, suffers. Education can counteract the natural tendency to do the wrong thing, but the inexorable succession of generations requires that the basis for this knowledge be constantly refreshed.

ARTICLE FOLLOW-UP

It is clear that Garrett Hardin considers the global population problem to be within a category of those having "no technical solution." Given the finite supply of resources, he finds the "Adam Smith approach" that would allow total individual freedom in the choice of family size to be not merely unacceptable but disastrous and immoral. Although many people would probably regard the freedom to decide such matters as an inalienable right to be exercised in the privacy of one's own home, Hardin challenges this position: "The morality of an act is a function of the state of the system at the time it is performed." The freedom to breed, he insists, is intolerable because "the state of the system" is such that "irresponsible" exercise of freedom will bring social ruin. Hardin does not believe that a change in population policy means an end to freedom, however: "[W]hat does freedom mean? When men mutually agreed to pass laws against robbing, mankind became more free, not less so. Individuals locked into the logic of the commons are free only to bring on universal ruin; once they see the necessity of mutual coercion, they become free to pursue other goals. . . . Freedom is the recognition of necessity.'"

Hardin has written a provocative essay, one that we do not find to be fully convincing. You will have to give it your own tough examination, however, and come to a conclusion of your own regarding the magnitude of the population problem. Is it really the driving force behind environmental problems today? If so, is Hardin's solution an appropriate one? Paul Ehrlich, a Stanford professor and author of *The Population Bomb,* is a supporter of Hardin's position, but his arguments have been challenged by Barry Commoner, a Washington University

professor and author of *The Closing Circle.* (Their arguments are pursued in some detail in *Environment,* Vol. 14, p. 24 [1972].)

We do not regard ourselves as experts in this area. Nevertheless, we do see promising signs of population control that flow naturally from the process of industrialization, the movement of population from rural to urban centers, widespread public education, increased numbers of women in the workforce, the postponement of marriage and childbearing, reduced infant mortality, and the improved quality of child care. These trends are no guarantee against population and pollution problems, but they do indicate that coercive solutions may not be necessary. They further indicate that the important human values of freedom, privacy, and the choice of family size are voluntarily responsive to social necessity.

Agreement on issues as controversial as population control measures will probably never be reached. There is agreement, however, that the "tragedy of the commons"—the problems associated with the use of free or common goods like air and water to dispose of industrial wastes—must be resolved. The next selection focuses on economic measures that put a price on goods that heretofore were regarded as free.

ROBERT HEILBRONER
LESTER THUROW

Is Regulation Useful?[8]

Regulation can be a good or a bad way to control pollution. This depends on two things: the quality of the regulation itself and the efficiency with which it is carried out. For example, regulations may be poorly phrased in law, so that many loopholes exist for firms or individuals, or they may fail to discriminate among different cases of pollu-

tion. An antismoke regulation may be sensible in a city but foolish if applied to a plant in the country where air currents easily disperse the smoke.

So, too, regulations are good or bad depending on their ease of enforcement. Compare the effectiveness of speed limits, which attempt to lessen the externality of accidents, and of regulations against littering. It is difficult enough to enforce speed laws, but it is almost impossible to enforce anti-littering laws. On the other hand, regulation of the disposal of radioactive wastes is simpler to enforce because the polluters are few and easily supervised.

This in turn is largely a matter of cost. If we are prepared to have traffic policemen posted on every mile of highway or every city block, regulation could be just as effective for speed violations or littering as for radioactive disposal. But the cost would be horrendous, and so would most people's reaction to being overpoliced.

Taxation

A second way to cope with pollution is to tax it. When a government decides to tax pollution (often called effluent charges) it is essentially creating a price system for disposal processes. Ideally, the tax would be set high enough so that the city or state would have enough tax revenue to install the devices for cleaning up whatever pollution remains. If an individual company found that it could clean up its own pollutants more cheaply than paying the tax, it would do so, thereby avoiding the tax. If the company could not clean up its own pollutants more cheaply than the tax cost (which is often the case because of economies of scale in pollution control) it would pay the necessary tax and look to the state to clean up the environment.

The effluent charge looks like, but is not a "license to pollute." It is a license that allows you to give some of your pollutants to the state, for a price.

As a result of effluent charges, an activity that was formerly costless, is no longer so. Thus, in terms of their economic impacts these charges are just like government regulations. They raise the supply curve for the good in question, with all of the corresponding ramifications. The difference is that each producer can decide for himself whether it pays to install clean-up equipment and not pay the tax, or to pollute and pay whatever tax costs are imposed.

Antipollution Taxes vs. Regulations

Which is better, regulation or taxation? As we have seen, regulation affects all polluters alike, and this is both its strength and its weakness. Taxation enables each polluter to determine for himself what course of action is best. Some polluters will achieve low pollution targets more cheaply by installing antipollution equipment, thereby avoiding taxes on their effluents, while other polluters will find it more profitable to pay the tax.

Here practical considerations are likely to be all-important. For example, taxation of effluents discharged into streams is likely to be more practical than taxation on smoke coming from chimneys. The state can install a sewage treatment plant, but it cannot clean up air that is contaminated by producers who find it cheaper to pay a pollution tax than to install smoke-suppressing equipment. Moreover, to be effective, a pollution tax should vary with the amount of pollution—a paper mill or a utility plant paying more taxes if it increases its output of waste or smoke. One of the problems with taxation is that of installing monitoring equipment. It is difficult to make accurate measurements of pollution or to allow for differences in environmental harm caused by the same amount of smoke coming from two factories located in different areas.

Subsidies

The third way of dealing with pollution is to subsidize polluters to stop polluting; that is, the government pays polluters to install the necessary equipment to clean up their effluents.

As we might expect, subsidies have impacts quite different from those of regulation or taxation. Because the government pays the costs of the antipollution equipment, the private firm incurs no costs. Its supply curves do not shift. No fewer factors are employed. Prices to the consumer remain unchanged. One curious effect is that the total amount of resources devoted to pollution control will therefore be larger under subsidy than under taxation or regulation. The reason is obvious, there will be no reduction in output, as in the case of the other two techniques.

Are Subsidies Useful?

Economists typically object to subsidies because they camouflage the true economic costs of producing goods and services cleanly. When regulations or taxes increase the price of paper or steel, the individual or

firm becomes aware that the environment is not free and that there may be heavy costs in producing goods in a way that will not damage the environment. The increased price will lead him to demand less of these goods. But when he gets clean environment through subsidies, he has no "price signal" to show him the cost of pollution associated with particular commodities.

Nevertheless, there are cases when subsidies may be the easiest way to avoid pollution. For example, it might be more effective to pay homeowners to turn in old cans and bottles than to try to regulate their garbage disposal habits or to tax them for each bottle or can thrown away. Subsidies may therefore sometimes be expedient means of achieving a desired end, even if they may not be the most desirable means from other points of view.

ARTICLE FOLLOW-UP

Any approach to resolving pollution problems will involve some costs. Each system suggested here requires policing, so an eye will have to be kept on administrative costs. With that in mind, which of these approaches (taxation, regulation, or subsidies), or which mix, do you find to be most compatible with the social interest of promoting economic efficiency, conservation of resources, equitable distribution of goods, and consumer sovereignty?

NATIONAL ENVIRONMENTAL POLICY ACT

The acquisition and use of energy inputs trigger some environmental outputs or repercussions that are inevitable and some that are avoidable. The reason is that technology simply has not developed to the point that minerals and other raw materials can be extracted and processed without causing environmental problems. People can improve on the way things have been done in the past, but a price tag is attached. Only recently has this price tag become explicit. In previous years, it simply did not rise to the national consciousness, or at least not to the extent common today.

Perhaps more than any other single instrument, the National Environmental Policy Act (NEPA)[9] has democratized environmental issues by giving the public an early voice in the way federal projects are planned so that environmental impact can be minimized or avoided. Prior to the Act, the federal government could undertake a project, such as a highway or a dam, or license a private-sector person or firm to build, say, a nuclear plant while accounting for economic and technological factors only. Environmental considerations did not enter into the decision calculus. NEPA changed that.

Environmental protection is not the only goal however. The national policy has other important components, and Congress appears to be seeking flexibility and a harmonious balance.

Other parts of the Act—for example, Section 102—are more specific and concrete. It provides that *to the fullest extent possible* all federal agencies shall prepare early planning documents, environmental impact statements (EISs), for "every recommendation or report on proposals for legislation and other major Federal actions significantly affecting the quality of the human environment."[10]

THE COUNCIL ON ENVIRONMENTAL QUALITY

The Council on Environmental Quality (CEQ), created by NEPA, Title II, as a presidential advisory body, issued regulations to all federal agencies regarding implementation of the entire Act. Specifically, with regard to an EIS, the CEQ format[11] requires these agencies to incorporate the following statutory elements:

(i) The environmental impact of the proposed action,

(ii) Any adverse environmental effects which cannot be avoided should the proposal be implemented,

(iii) Alternative to the proposed action,

(iv) The relationship between local short-term uses of man's environment and the maintenance and enhancement of long-term productivity, and

(v) Any irreversible and irretrievable commitments of resources which would be involved in the proposed action should it be implemented.

THE ENVIRONMENTAL PROTECTION AGENCY

The Environmental Protection Agency (EPA) was established by a 1970 executive reorganization plan designed to consolidate federal environmental activities into a single agency. The objective was to structure a coordinated response to a broad range of pollutants—air, water, noise, solid wastes, toxic chemicals, pesticides, and radiation. Generally speaking, Congress has conferred on the EPA a twofold task: (1) creating national pollution standards and (2) enforcement of these standards (normally in conjunction with the states).

The problems are enormous, however. First, within each area, millions of dollars in research are needed to make way for enlightened regulation. Second, environmentally sound solutions often run into opposition from energy- and production-minded interests; for example, emission control limits on automobiles sometimes frustrate fuel economy and production schedules. Finally, progress in one area may provoke difficulties in another area. To illustrate, cleaner air and water require the removal of solid and chemical wastes. Disposal of these wastes create land-use problems that are not entirely within the jurisdiction of the EPA. The cooperative efforts of federal, state, regional, and local governmental agencies are frequently essential to progress toward an environmentally acceptable solution. Such problems are not respecters of political boundaries.

ENVIRONMENTAL IMPACT STATEMENTS AND APPROPRIATE CONSIDERATION

EISs, along with other procedures embodied in Section 102,[12] were to be the *means* or *procedure* whereby NEPA's *ends* or *goals* ("man and nature in productive harmony . . . fulfill[ing] the social, economic, and other requirements of present and future generations of Americans") were to be accomplished. While still speaking in its procedural voice, Section 102 further relates that to *the fullest extent possible* "presently unquantified environmental amenities and values . . . be given *appropriate* consideration. . . ." (Emphases added.)

The problems here are of measurement and quantification: How can one monetize the belief that endangered species or scenic vistas should be preserved? How much money is the snail darter or a view of the Tetons really worth? In a clumsy sort of way, these things are frequently priced, or valued, at the cost of protection measures or the cost that would have to be paid to restore the environment to its original condition. One hesitates to say "valued," though, because the real worth of one's conviction or belief can hardly be articulated in ordinary market terms.[13] NEPA and other federal acts have democratized or socialized such matters through public hearings. These hearings allow opposition views to be expressed, and in this way the sometimes arbitrary best guesses of cost-benefit analysis can be ameliorated.

Beyond that is some uncertainty with regard to how much consideration these federal agencies must give to environmental problems. *How much consideration is enough?*

NEPA does not give CEQ a veto over projects that, on balance, are environmentally harmful.[14] CEQ can recommend certain action to the president, and Congress controls project funding, but if the federal agency gives environmental issues a purely shallow and grudging consideration, the responsibility is on members of the public to challenge this in court. By invoking judicial review of administrative action, individuals and interest groups play an important role in making NEPA into more than a paper tiger.

For example, under the fairly lenient procedural rules regarding standing to sue,[15] you may seek a temporary injunction against a federal project or a federally licensed private project until an EIS is prepared or until an inadequate EIS is amended. Following this delay, however, you might anticipate that the project will be permitted to continue, perhaps modified by court-ordered mitigating features. Although this process involves delay, as well as public and private expense, it is designed to ensure that the completed project will be environmentally sound. Prior to NEPA, citizens had little opportunity to effectively challenge ecologically questionable (or even disastrous) federal projects.

NEPA: PROCEDURE OR SUBSTANCE?

In *Vermont Yankee Nuclear Power Corporation* v. *Natural Resources Defense Council*,[16] the Supreme Court overturned an appellate court decision that held that the Nuclear Regulatory Commission (NRC) acted *arbitrarily* and *capriciously* in violation of the Administrative Procedure Act.[17] The NRC permitted a utility company to construct a nuclear-fire electrical generating plant. The appellate court concluded that the NRC failed to explore the possibilities of energy conservation insofar as they related to the need or lack of need for another nuclear plant. A group of citizens that would be affected by the operation of the plant initiated this segment of the case and was trying to persuade the NRC to deny the utility company a construction permit. Perhaps for lack of funds, the citizens' group did not press its case actively. It evidently expected the NRC to exercise an affirmative duty to following up on its leads. After all, the *Calvert Cliffs* case had given federal agencies—specifically, NRC's predecessor, the Atomic Energy Commission—a stinging tongue-lashing for failing to exercise this affirmative duty. Citizens' groups should not be expected to do the job of a professionally staffed and funded federal agency.

When the NRC did not do this job to the satisfaction of the citizens' group, the group renewed its efforts and urged that the commission acted in an arbitrary and capricious manner. Specifically, it argued that the NRC failed to consider all relevant factors (energy conservation) and made a clear error of judgment (the NRC issued a construction permit for an "unnecessary" plant) in granting the permit.

The Supreme Court eventually affirmed the NRC's decision granting the permit. "NEPA does set forth significant substantive goals for the Nation, but its mandate to the agencies is *essentially procedural*," (emphasis added) the Court concluded.

Does this mean that federal agencies can comply simply by shuffling papers and observing formal procedures? That may be the new reality in environmental law, but in theory, observance of procedural requirements will bring environmental issues to the attention of the appropriate government official, who will then resolve the matter in an objective, conscientious, and professional way.

THE CLEAN AIR ACT

EARLY REGULATION

State and local governments and private citizens were the first to address the problems of air pollution. In the late nineteenth century, local governments adopted smoke codes aimed at the use of high-sulfur coal. Some legislatures also acted in an attempt to control particulate matter. In addition, citizens attempted to use the state courts to address the effects of pollution through private suits based on a variety of common law doctrines, such as nuisance, trespass, negligence, and strict liability. These early attempts to control air pollution suffered from uneven standards and inconsistent enforcement and failed to provide a broad solution to the problem.

Federal involvement in the regulation of ambient (surrounding) air quality developed slowly. In 1955, Congress passed the Air Pollution Control Act. This first act authorized the surgeon general to study air pollution and its control, but it failed to provide for regulation. In 1963, Congress passed the Clean Air Act[18] in an attempt to directly regulate polluters. Administered by the Department of Health, Education, and Welfare (HEW), the enforcement provisions proved too cumbersome to be effective.[19] The Act also failed to define pollution and required consideration of the practicability and feasibility of pollution control measures. These common-sense considerations were probably necessary to gain support for the Act, but they were later used as excuses for a do-nothing attitude. The Clean Air Act was amended in 1965 and again in 1967. The former amendments addressed the pollution problem of automobiles, trucks, and other mobile sources. The latter amendments authorized HEW to supervise the establishment of ambient air quality standards for district air quality control regions within state borders. States were also required to submit state implementation plans (SIPs) that would describe how they would achieve these standards. The Act still failed to define pollution, and it retained the practicability/feasibility provisions. Moreover, the states retained too much flexibility in setting standards and time limits for compliance. In sum, although the Clean Air Act as amended to 1967 provided a structure, it did not develop a workable solution to the pollution problem.

In 1970, Congress made its most dramatic advance by amending the act to greatly expand federal authority. The newly created EPA was given nine months to establish national uniform primary (health) standards and secondary (welfare) standards. States were required to submit SIPs within nine months of the establishment of these standards. Although states retained primary responsibility for pollution control, the EPA acted as an overseer to ensure due speed in compliance. The 1970 amendments also eliminated the practicability/feasibility loophole and provided a definition of air pollution. The amended Act has been transformed into a strict law requiring businesses to develop new methods to reduce pollution.

NATIONAL AMBIENT AIR QUALITY STANDARDS

Under the 1970 amendments, the EPA administrator was required to establish standards for the six major air pollutants: sulfur dioxide (SO_2), particulates, carbon monoxide (CO), ozone (photochemical oxidants or smog), hydrocarbons (HC) and nitrogen dioxide (NO_2). Lead was later added to the list. Although only seven pollutants are named, more elements are covered because hydrocarbons, ozone, and particulates are generic terms covering a variety of elements.

The administrator established primary standards to protect the public health with a reasonable margin of safety for especially susceptible people, such as infants, the elderly, and bronchial asthmatics.

The standards are uniform throughout the United States. In other words, they fix the maximum *allowable* concentrations of air pollutants anywhere in the nation. The margin of safety was to protect the public from known, as well as potential, but not yet identified, health hazards. Although the administrator was to consider the health of "particularly sensitive citizens" in setting primary standards, the secondary standards are even more restrictive. They attempt to protect forests, crops, visibility, climate, property, and personal comfort and well-being. Figure 16.2 shows a list of pollutants, their sources, and their environmental effects.

FIGURE 16.2 *Sources and Health Effects of Selected Pollutants*

Pollutant	Source	Environmental Effect
Sulfur dioxide (SO_2)	Power Plants and industrial sources burning sulfur-laden fuel (coal)	Causes and aggravates respiratory ailments; acid rain
Particulates	Power plants; oil and coal combustion; agricultural	Injury to lungs; throat and eye irritation
Carbon Monoxide (CO)	Automotive emissions	Decreases blood oxygen; impairs heart functions; impairs visual perception
Photochemical oxidants (ozone)	Refineries; petrochemical plants; automotive emissions	Aggravates respiratory ailments; causes eye irritation
Nitrogen dioxide (NO_2)	Power plants; oil and coal combustion	Combines with hydrocarbons to form photochemical oxidants (ozone)
Hydrocarbons	Petroleum products; refineries; automobiles	Combines with nitrogen oxides to form photochemical oxidants (ozone)
Lead	Automotive fuel; paint	Central nervous system damage

STATE IMPLEMENTATION PLANS

The states are responsible for reducing the level of pollutants below the national standards. SIPs were used to map out the steps necessary to achieve a reduction. Development of a SIP involved three steps. First, the state determined the current concentration of pollutants. This step necessarily involved measurement of each pollutant in the ambient air and determination of a regional average of air quality. Second, the state determined the degree to which the national standard was exceeded and the amount of reduction necessary to meet it. In industrialized states, the pollution level generally exceeded the NAAQS in every case.[20] Third, the state distributed the burden of reducing emissions among the industrial sources. The states were free to decide which firms were required to reduce emissions. One approach allocated the burden among those sources with the least cost of pollution reduction. This approach was subject to the criticism that it unfairly discriminated against firms with the lowest costs and thus forced them to shoulder the burden of firms with higher costs. Another approach, more widely used, allocated the required reduction among all sources. This approach, however, was subject to the argument that it was not economically efficient and resulted in poor allocation of resources. Moreover, this approach did not take into account the fact that some firms were technologically and economically incapable of reducing emissions to their quota. Strict enforcement of the equal allocation would require them to close until new technology was developed. Some states considered these claims in establishing their implementation plans and adjusted emissions limitations as appropriate.

Once the SIP was complete, the EPA had the nondiscretionary duty to accept or reject the plan, depending on its evaluation of the plan's effectiveness. If a plan was not accepted or if the state did not enforce the plan, the EPA was empowered to take over. In certain situations, a state's failure to enforce a plan could result in a complete freeze on all construction of major emission sources within the state.

MOBILE SOURCES OF AIR POLLUTION

SIPs cover only stationary sources of pollution, such as factories, utilities, and mills. The EPA is directly responsible for regulation of mobile sources of pollution within the states and has the authority to regulate emissions from aircraft and automobile engines. In addition, the EPA can regulate vehicle fuels because they affect emissions.

Under the 1990 amendments, new car exhaust emission standards were required to be phased in. By 1998, all new cars must reduce emissions of nitrogen oxide by 60 percent. Other emissions must be reduced by 35 percent, and pollution control equipment must be warranted for ten years or 100,000 miles. Firms that operate fleet vehicles must use alternative fuels by 1998. Gas stations in cities with carbon monoxide pollution problems were given until 1992 to make available gasoline with higher oxygen content. By 1995, all gasoline in the smoggiest U.S. cities were to have had 15 percent fewer hydrocarbons. The overall objective is to cut mobile source emissions by 3 percent annually.

ECONOMIC AND TECHNOLOGICAL INFEASIBILITY

The National Ambient Air Quality Standards (NAAQS) were based on public health and welfare considerations and without regard to available pollution control technology. A common complaint from businesses subject to the Clean Air

Act's provisions was that emissions limitations could not be met because of economic and/or technological infeasibility. These complaints were considered by the state, the EPA, and the courts in three specific instances. First, the state and the EPA could agree at the implementation plan stage that emissions limitations should be adjusted to reflect economic and technological concerns. The burden of reduction, however, was merely shifted to other firms of the state. The SIP was required to provide for reduction of pollution below national standards. Business firms could challenge EPA approval of SIPs at this phase. Second, the feasibility issue could be raised if a firm applied for a state or federal variance from the emissions limitations established by the SIP. Third, as the Supreme Court concluded in *Union Electric Co* v. *EPA*,[21] feasibility could be raised as a defense to an enforcement action.

ECONOMIC GROWTH UNDER THE CLEAN AIR ACT

Under the Clean Air Act, the EPA and the states were to reduce air pollution in dirty areas as quickly as possible and to protect and enhance the existing quality of air in clean areas. A strict interpretation of the Act would require the EPA to prohibit the construction of new emissions sources. Obviously, such an interpretation would have a disastrous effect on economic growth. To provide for growth, as well as for reduced pollution, the EPA distinguished between attainment (clean) and nonattainment (dirty) regions and promulgated construction review regulations for each area.

Clean Air Areas. Initially, the EPA imposed no requirements to control new emissions sources in clean air areas that were meeting the national standards (attainment areas). The EPA's concern in these clean air areas was that pollution in the region remained below the standards. Consequently, new plants constructed in these areas were free to pollute so long as the region remained below NAAQS. In *Sierra Club* v. *Ruckelshaus*,[22] the plaintiff sued to require the EPA to prevent deterioration of clean air areas.

As a result of the *Sierra Club* case, the EPA developed regulations to prevent degradation of clean air areas. Strictly interpreted, the Court's decision would require a complete ban on new emissions sources in clean air areas. In 1974, the EPA adopted "prevention of significant deterioration" (PSD) regulations, which protected clean air areas while still providing for economic growth.

Each state was divided into three regions. In Class I regions, which included national parks and wilderness areas, almost any change would be considered significant. In Class II regions, deterioration accompanying moderate, well-controlled growth was permitted. In Class III areas, air quality was allowed to be deteriorated as low as the NAAQS secondary standards.

In 1977, Congress dealt with PSD (clean air) areas in the amended Clean Air Act. Congress established mandatory Class I areas, which included international parks, large national parks, and wilderness areas. Class I areas may not be reclassified. Class II areas, by an elaborate process that requires state and federal participation, may be reclassified as Class III. The amendments also reduced the maximum allowable increase for Class III areas and expanded the number of plants that are required to submit to preconstruction review. As a result, all major facilities (plants with potential emissions of 100 tons per year of particulates or sulfur dioxides, or 250 tons per year of *any* pollutant) must use the best available control technology and show that maximum allowable increases will not be exceeded, regardless of the type of industry involved.

Nonattainment or Dirty Air Areas.   The 1977 amendment also approved the EPA's emissions offset policy, which had been adopted to provide for growth in nonattainment areas. Owners wanting to build or modify major facilities in dirty air regions are required to meet even more restrictive preconstruction requirements. Major emitting facilities—plants emitting or with the potential to emit one hundred tons of pollutants annually—must meet three requirements to obtain a permit for new construction or modification. First, the plant must use technology that will produce the lowest achievable emissions rate (LAER). Second, the owner or operator must demonstrate that all other major emitting facilities of the same owner within the state are complying with applicable emissions limitations. Third, the owner or operator must demonstrate that offsets or cutbacks for existing sources will result in a net reduction.

The third requirement is a primary means of achieving reasonable further progress toward the NAAQS. New plants are built or modified only if the net result is a reduction of pollution. Owners attempting to build or expand must obtain offsets by installing better pollution control devices, by closing their own plants, or by paying other firms to do the same. The requirement provides for the most efficient allocation of resources because the owner will presumably choose the method with the least cost. Society benefits from both the improved air quality and the lower costs reflected in prices. In addition, the emissions offset policy allows for economic growth and requires movement toward attaining national standards.

The Bubble Concept.   Beginning in 1981, the EPA approved the use of the alternative bubble concept for clean air regions. Under this concept, a firm's industrial complex (one or more plants at a single location, with each plant having numerous stacks, chimneys, and other outlets) is treated as a single emissions source. It is as if the entire complex were covered by an imaginary bubble with a single stack emitting pollutants. All emissions are measured in the aggregate from the single stack. Additions or modifications to the complex may be made as long as the net result is no increase in pollutants emitted from the imaginary stack. The bubble concept allows changes to be made without regulatory consequences. Owners have more freedom to develop a low-cost mix of controls. Most important, firms avoid the need for the expensive pollution control technology. Although the bubble concept allows owners more discretion, critics argue that it slows the rate of pollution reduction. By 1983, the EPA had approved the bubble for dirty as well as clean air regions. This approval was challenged in your next case.

Chevron, Inc. v. *Natural Resources Defense Council*
467 U.S. 837 (1984)

STEVENS, JUSTICE

When a court reviews an agency's construction of the statute which it administers, it is confronted with two questions. First, always, is the question whether Congress has directly spoken to the precise question at issue. If the intent of Congress is clear, that is the end of the matter; for the court, as well as the agency must give effect to the unambiguously expressed intent of Congress. If, however, the court determines Congress has not directly addressed the precise question at issue, the court does not simply impose its own construction on the statute, as would be necessary in the absence of an administrative interpretation. Rather, if the statute is silent or ambiguous with respect to the specific issue, the question for the court is whether the agency's answer is based on a permissible construction of the statute. . . .

* * *

. . . Based on the examination of the legislation and its history we agree with the Court of Appeals that Congress did not have a specific intention on the applicability of the bubble concept in these cases, and conclude that EPA's use of that concept here is a reasonable policy choice for the agency to make.

The 1977 Amendments contain no specific reference to the "bubble concept." Nor do they contain a specific definition of the term "stationary source." The legislative history of the portion of the 1977 Amendments dealing with nonattainment areas does not contain any specific comment on the "bubble concept" or the question whether a plantwide definition of a stationary source is permissible under the permit program. It does, however, plainly disclose that in the permit program Congress sought to accommodate the conflict between the economic interest in permitting capital improvements to continue and environmental interest in improving air quality.

[T]he EPA . . . noted that the definitional issue was not squarely addressed in either the statue or its legislative history and therefore that the issue involved an agency judgment as how to best carry out the Act. It then set forth several reasons for concluding that the plantwide definition was more appropriate. It pointed out that the dual definition "can act as a disincentive to new investment and modernization by discouraging modifications to existing facilities" and "can actually retard progress in air pollution control by discouraging replacement of older, dirtier processes or pieces of equipment with new, cleaner ones." . . . Finally, the agency explained that additional requirements that remained in place would accomplish the fundamental purposes of achieving attainment with NAAQS's as expeditiously as possible. These conclusions were expressed in a proposed rulemaking in August in 1981 that was formally promulgated in October.

When a challenge to an agency construction of a statutory provision, fairly conceptualized, really centers on the wisdom of the agency's policy, rather than whether it is a reasonable choice within a gap left open by Congress, the challenge must fail. In such a case, federal judges—who have no constituency—have a duty to respect legitimate policy choices made by those who do. The responsibilities for assessing the wisdom of such policy choices and resolving the struggle between competing views of the public interest are not judicial ones: "Our constitution vests such responsibilities in the political branches."

In this case, the Administrator's interpretation represents a reasonable accommodation of manifestly competing interests and is entitled to deference: the regulatory scheme is technical and complex, the agency considered the matter in a detailed and reasoned fashion, and the decision involves reconciling conflicting policies. . . .

We hold that the EPA's definition of the term "source" is a permissible construction of the statute which seeks to accommodate progress in reducing air pollution with economic growth.

CASE FOLLOW-UP

The Natural Resources Defense Council (NRDC) has been at bat for environmental protection many times over the years. In this case, it is challenging EPA approval of the bubble in dirty or nonattainment areas rather than clean or PSD areas. It is NRDC's position that not enough progress can be made quickly enough with the latter approach. The emissions offset policy, which is NRDC's choice, is more demanding because it requires, among other things, the use of technology that will produce the LAER.

The counterposition of EPA is simply that its policy is a fair judgment call, given the lack of specificity of Congress. The Supreme Court concluded that the EPA's judgment was entitled to deference.

1990 AMENDMENTS TO THE CLEAN AIR ACTS

Acid Rain.   Studies indicate that coal-fired power plants contribute to acid rain through excessive emissions of sulfur dioxide. Emission caps were expected to cut sulfur dioxide five million tons annually by 1995 and ten million tons annually by 2000. This will reduce by half the national annual sulfur dioxide emissions by 2000.

Under Phase I of the program, the 110 oldest and highest emitting coal-fired utility plants were given until the year 2000 to cut their emissions by 40 percent. Phase II, which is even tougher, begins 1 January 2000 and affects most other electric utilities. Nitrogen oxide, also a factor in acid rain, must be cut by two to four million tons annually, beginning in 1992, with additional controls scheduled for 1997.

Utilities were given sulfur dioxide "credits" or "allowances," which they can "bank" or save for use in the event of future expansion, or they can "trade" at a profit. In early 1993, the Chicago Board of Trade initiated a market in such credits. A firm that reduces its emissions below the level permitted by the amendments can create additional credits for itself and trade them in a nationwide market. This possibility creates some incentive for firms to install leading edge technology, reduce its costs, and finance this package of improvements, in part at least, through these credits. New plants (those starting up after the date of the Act, 15 November 1990) will not get any allowances. New plants must cover sulfur dioxide emissions with allowances purchased on the market.

Toxic Emissions. *Hazardous or toxic pollutants*—emissions that are likely to increase mortality or result in irreversible or incapacitating illnesses—must be limited by the application of the best available technology. If this does not result in a 90 percent reduction by the end of the decade, the EPA may initiate further measures to protect the public health.

Since 1970, the EPA has established standards for only seven such pollutants—asbestos, benzene, beryllium, cadmium, mercury, radiation, and vinyl chloride. Congress understood the complexity of addressing the problem of toxic emissions but eventually became dissatisfied with the EPA's snail pace. Hence, it named 189 pollutants to be controlled by industry under the EPA's cautious eye.

Ozone Depletion. Chlorofluorocarbons and carbon tetrachloride are being phased out by the 1990 amendments and will be totally prohibited by 2000.

ENFORCEMENT MEASURES

The Clean Air Act includes civil and criminal penalties, deprives businesses of the cost savings they would experience by noncompliance with the terms of the Act, includes citizen enforcement provisions, and protects whistle-blowers.

Civil and Criminal Penalties. Whenever the EPA administrator finds that a firm is in violation of a SIP, the polluting firm and the state air quality agency must be notified. If the violation continues beyond thirty days, the EPA may order compliance or begin a civil action for an injunction or a civil penalty not to exceed $25,000 per day. The EPA administrator may even seek both the injunction and the civil penalty. These same penalties apply when the administrator finds violations of the state plan so widespread, even after the state has been given a thirty-day notice, that EPA has to begin a period of federal enforcement.

If a person *knowingly* and *deliberately* violates a SIP, an EPA order, or provisions of the Clean Air Act, the penalty may be imprisonment of not more than one year in addition to the $25,000 per day fine. Beyond the first conviction, the penalty increases to $25,000 per day and/or imprisonment of up to two years. Any person who knowingly makes a false statement or representation on an application, plan, or other document required by the Act or who knowingly falsifies or tampers with monitoring devices shall, on conviction, be fined not more than $10,000, or be imprisoned for a maximum of six months, or both.

Noncompliance Penalty. To discourage businesspeople from failing to comply with the Act, the EPA, on direction by Congress, has developed a plan that deprives violators of the cost savings they would experience through noncompliance. This plan restores competitive fairness to the industry by closing off the incentive or advantage of cheating and thereby gaining an edge on one's business rivals.

Citizen Suit Provisions. Any person may bring an action against the United States or a federal agency regarding any of its facilities—for example, TVA—that is in violation of an emissions limitation or an EPA order. That "person" is normally an environmental group, such as the Sierra Club or the NRDC acting through one of its members, but it may be an individual like yourself or a neighborhood group. Such actions may further be pursued against the EPA for failing to carry out a nondiscretionary duty. When the act relates that the EPA *shall* do something, such as approve qualified SIPs, that duty is nondiscretionary (discretionary duties are designated *may*). These citizen suits may also be brought against firms that build or modify large facilities without air pollution permits or that violate their permits.

A sixty-day notice must be given by the citizen-plaintiff to the EPA, to the state in which the violation occurs, and to the alleged violator before a suit may be commenced. The sixty-day period is specified to give the targeted defendant an opportunity to voluntarily comply with the law. If the matter is pursued in court to a final order, the judge may award the citizen costs of litigation, including reasonable attorney and expert witness fees. No opportunity is provided here for a person to personally profit by bringing one of these suits. There is no such thing under the Clean Air Act as a bounty or treble damages, such as are available to an injured party under the Sherman Act.

Whistle-Blowers. No employer may discharge any employee or otherwise discriminate against the employee with respect to compensation or other terms, privileges, or conditions of employment because the employee has commenced a proceeding against the employer under this Act or has testified or otherwise participated in such a proceeding. An employee who believes that he or she has been treated in this manner may file a complaint with the secretary of labor and, on investigation of the complaint, may be entitled to reinstatement, back pay, and compensation for other expenses, including attorney and expert witness fees.

THE CLEAN WATER ACT

EARLY DEVELOPMENT

The regulation of water pollution developed slowly. Local and state governments were the first to address the problem, but they were unsuccessful. Early regulations required little more than filtering out solid particles. The first federal regulation, the Rivers and Harbor Act of 1899, required a permit before discharging pollutants into U.S. waters. It was applicable only to navigable waters and was intended to prevent the blockage of water transportation by regulating specific discharge sources.

The Water Pollution Control Act of 1948 was the first federal attempt to address the problem. The Act authorized the Surgeon General to study the nature of municipal and industrial wastes, to inform the states, and to encourage their development of water pollution controls. Primary responsibility for control remained with the states. The Water Pollution Control Act amendments of 1956 provided grants for municipal sewage plants and created an enforcement conference proceeding to be used whenever water pollution from one state endangered the health of citizens in another state.

In 1965, Congress enacted the Water Quality Act, which created the Federal Water Pollution Control Administration (later merged into the EPA) and required the states to establish water quality standards for their waterways. First, the state was to zone the waterway for a particular use, such as drinking, swimming, or industrial waste disposal. Then, the state was to set appropriate quality standards. Once these standards were in place, the water was to be tested to see how closely it matched the standard. If the quality was below standard, the state was to develop an implementation plan to reduce pollution. The Act provided penalties for firms that exceeded discharge limits set in the implementation plans.

In 1972, Congress passed the Federal Water Pollution Control Act, which gave the EPA primary responsibility for water pollution control. The Act set two goals: (1) swimmable, fishable waters by 1983 and (2) zero pollutant discharge by 1985. The Act authorized the EPA to establish industrial and municipal effluent standards and to specify the pollution control technology to be used at effluent sources. The Act's name was changed to the Clean Water Act in 1977 amendments.

THE CLEAN WATER ACT

The Clean Water Act[23] required the EPA to establish technology-based effluent limitations for *point sources,* which are discrete discharge points, such as pipes, ditches, and channels, as distinguished from the natural runoff of water from the countryside. The latter pollution source is to be addressed by a state water plan similar to a SIP under the Clean Air Act. Municipal and industrial sources are treated differently. Municipalities were required to meet secondary-treatment levels by 1977. These levels involved letting soil elements settle out and treating the remainder through a combination of bacterial and chemical means. By 1983, municipalities were to use the most practical treatment control technology.

Stricter standards were demanded of industrial sources. The EPA established permissible ranges of discharge for each of twenty-seven industrial groups, such as rubber, plastics, and forest products. Within each group, every firm is required to use the same pollution control technology. Phase I of the 1972 Act required the best practicable treatment control levels by 1977. Phase II required the "best available control technology economically achievable" by 1983. The 1977 amendments changed the Phase II requirements. The amendments established three broad categories of pollutants: conventional, nonconventional, and toxics.

The best conventional treatment control technology was to be in use by July 1, 1984, for *conventional* pollutants such as suspended soils and fecal coliform. The stricter, best available technological controls were to be in use by the same date for *toxics,* such as arsenic, cyanides, phenols, and pesticides, and for *nonconventional* pollutants, such as thermal pollution.

PERMITS: THE NATIONAL POLLUTANT DISCHARGE ELIMINATION SYSTEM

The Clean Water Act uses a permit system to translate water quality standards into specific effluent control requirements for plants. The Act provides that "the discharge of any pollutant is illegal" in the absence of a discharge permit. Even firms for which there are no established standards must apply for a discharge permit.

The National Pollutant Discharge Elimination System (NPDES) permits are issued by the EPA or by EPA-sanctioned state agencies. They specify the control technology required, the compliance dates, and the permissible amount of pollutants to be discharged. The permits also contain provisions for modifications in the event stricter standards are found to be necessary to achieve the Act's goals. The courts have upheld the EPA's authority to include modification provisions. Although they do inject some uncertainty into a firm's future (owing to the potential for stricter requirements after a plant has completed construction and begun operations), they also allow a firm to begin operations pending the establishment of standards for certain effluents.

Although the permits generally apply a national standard for pollutant limitations, the Act itself allows for more stringent standards if required by the state. Ordinarily, the state will apply more stringent standards for heavily polluted waterways where the national standards fail to achieve the desired water quality. The additional standards cannot be modified by the EPA and are not subject to its review.

One complaint leveled at the permit system is that it does not adequately provide for daily fluctuation in pollutant discharge (known as *excursions*) or for accidental fluctuations owing to special circumstances, such as human error, natural catastrophes, or equipment failures (known as *upsets*). Companies complain that upsets and excursions would require them to use more advanced technology than the permits require. To resolve their dilemma, some companies have asked the courts to require that permits include provisions that forgive the companies for violations beyond their control. Although the courts have given conflicting responses,[24] they are reluctant to penalize a firm for unintentional, uncontrollable violations.

In addition to upsets and excursions, some companies may exceed effluent standards when the EPA grants a variance as an alternative to shutting down the plant. Variances on nonconventional discharges may be granted on a showing of economic necessity. In addition, the EPA may grant a variance on a showing that a specific plant differs substantially from other firms covered by the industrywide standard. If the required technology is inappropriate for the specific firm, the EPA will substitute alternative requirements.

ENFORCEMENT MEASURES

Except for the absence of a noncompliance penalty, Clean Water Act provisions are comparable to those in the Clean Air Act. Specifically, the act provides for criminal sanctions and for civil suits instituted by private citizens, the EPA, or the responsible state authority. For criminal sanctions or governmental civil suits, the EPA first advises the state authority of discharge violations. If the state fails to act within thirty days, the EPA can begin enforcement proceedings. Private, civil actions (citizen suits) can be instituted at any time, whether the governmental authorities decide to act or not. Early enforcement often took the form of civil actions, but consider the *Frezzo Bros.* case as an example of the use of criminal sanctions as a means of enforcement.

United States v. *Frezzo Bros., Inc.*
602 F.2d 1123 (3rd Cir. 1979)

ROSENN, CIRCUIT JUDGE

Frezzo Brothers, Inc., is a Pennsylvania corporation engaged in the mushroom farming business near Avondale, Pennsylvania. The business is family-operated with Guido and James Frezzo serving as the principal corporate officers. As part of the mushroom farming business, Frezzo Brothers, Inc., produces compost to provide a growing base for the mushrooms. The compost is comprised mainly of hay and horse manure mixed with water and allowed to ferment outside on wharves.

The Frezzo's farm had a 114,000 gallon concrete holding tank designed to contain water run-off from the compost wharves and to recycle water back to them. The farm had a separate storm water run-off system that carried rain water through a pipe to a channel box located on an adjoining property owned by another mushroom farm. The channel box was connected by a pipe with an unnamed tributary of the East Branch of the White Clay Creek. The waters of the tributary flowed directly into the Creek.

[*Author's note:* A local health official collected samples of wastes flowing into the channel boxes on six days. Some samples were taken after rains; some were taken when there had been no rain. All samples showed high concentrations of pollutants characteristic of manure. The Frezzos were charged for six separate violations.]

The jury returned guilty verdicts on all six counts against the corporate defendant, Frezzo Brothers, Inc., and individual defendants, Guido and James Frezzo.

★ ★ ★

The Frezzos next contend that the indictment should have been dismissed because the EPA had not promulgated any effluent standards applicable to the compost manufacturing business. The Frezzos argue that before a violation of Section 1311(a) can occur, the defendants must be shown to have not complied with existing effluent limitations under the Act. . . .

The core provision of the Act is found in Section 1311(a) which reads:

Except as in compliance with [the Act] . . . the discharge of any pollutants by any person shall be unlawful.

The Government argues, however, . . . for the proposition that:

By 1972 Congress determined upon wholly a new approach. The basic concept of the Act [Section 1311(a)] we construe in this case is an ultimate flat prohibition upon all discharges of pollutants.

Indeed, the court specifically noted that "[t]his prohibition which is central to the entire Act is statutory and requires no promulgation."

. . . The Government contends in the instant case that the lack of effluent limitations is no defense to violation of Section 1311(a). It argues that when no effluent limitations have been established for a particular business, the proper procedure is for the business to apply for a permit to discharge pollutants, . . . which allows the Administrator to establish interim operating conditions pending approval. [Other courts have] . . . explicitly reflected this argument as placing too harsh a burden on the defendant because it viewed the Act as not allowing any discharge pending approval of the permit. The Government contends in the present case, however, that the absence of effluent limitations should not be allowed to nullify the flat prohibition on discharges under Section 1311(a). We agree.

. . . The basic policy of the Act is to halt uncontrolled discharges of pollutants into the waters of the United States. In fact, the Act sets forth "the national goal that the discharge of [all] pollutants into the navigable waters be eliminated by 1985." We see nothing impermissible with allowing the Government to enforce the Act by invoking Section 1311(1), even if no effluent limitations have been promulgated for the particular business charged with polluting. Without this flexibility, numerous industries not yet considered as serious threats to the environment may escape administrative, civil, or criminal sanctions merely because the EPA has not established effluent limitations. Thus, dangerous pollutants could be continually injected into the water solely because the administrative process has not yet had the opportunity to fix specific effluent limitations. Such a result would be inconsistent with the policy of the Act.

We do not believe . . . that the permit procedure urged by the Government is unduly burdensome on business. If no effluent limitations have yet been applied to an industry, a potential transgressor should apply for a permit to discharge pollutants. . . . The administrator may then set up operating conditions until permanent effluent limitations are promulgated by the EPA. The pendency of a permit application, in appropriate cases, should shield the applicant from liability for discharge in the absence of a permit. EPA cannot be expected to have anticipated every form of water pollution through the establishment of effluent limitations. The permit procedure, coupled with broad enforcement under Section 1311(a) may, in fact, allow EPA to discover new sources of pollution for which permanent effluent standards are appropriate.

In the present case, it is undisputed that there was no pending permit to discharge pollutants; nor had Frezzo Brothers, Inc., ever applied for one. This case, therefore, appears to be particularly compelling for broad enforcement. . . . The Frezzos, under their interpretation of the statute, could conceivably have continued polluting until EPA promulgated effluent limitations for the compost operation. The Government's intervention by way of criminal indictments brought to a halt potentially serious damage to the stream in question, and has no doubt alerted EPA to pollution problems posed by compost production. We therefore hold that the promulgation of effluent limitation standards is not a prerequisite to the maintenance of a criminal proceeding based on violation of . . . the Act.

The Frezzos next contend that there was insufficient evidence to convict them of the charges in the indictment. They virtually concede that the Government presented sufficient evidence to sustain Count five. However, defendants charge that the Government had failed to prove willful or negligent discharges of pollutants. We disagree because we are persuaded that substantial evidence in the record supports all six counts of the indictment.

The Government contended at trial that the discharges giving rise to Counts One through Four to the indictment were willful. To establish this claim, the Government relied on the samples collected on those four occasions, the absence of rain on the dates in question, and the elimination of other possible causes of the pollution. The Frezzos maintain that the Government on this evidence failed to establish a willful act. We disagree. The jury was entitled to infer from the totality of the circumstances surrounding the discharges that a willful act precipitated them. The Government did not have to present evidence of someone turning on a valve or diverting wastes in order to establish a willful violation of the Act.

The Government's theory on Counts five and Six was that the discharges were negligently caused by the inadequate capacity of the holding tank. Count five was amply supported by eyewitness testimony, samples of the pollutants, evidence of rainfall and expert hydrologic evidence of the holding tank's capacity. Count Six was similarly supported by evidence of rainfall, samples, expert testimony, and photographs of the holding tank three days before the incident, showing it to be near capacity. The jury could properly have concluded that the water pollution abatement facilities were negligently maintained by the Frezzos and were insufficient to prevent discharges of the waters. We therefore conclude that there was sufficient evidence to sustain the verdict on all six counts.

CASE FOLLOW-UP

This case is chiefly notable for its policy-making aspects. The court could have concluded that no statutory violation occurred because the EPA had not published effluent guidelines for the industry in which the firm operated. Other courts had decided similar cases on just such a basis. Given the immensity of the EPA's task, however, and the reality that it would take years for the EPA to complete that undertaking, the court adhered to the statutory prohibition against all discharges in the absence of a permit. What did the court consider to be some positive features of this approach? What are some of its negative features?

HAZARDOUS SUBSTANCES

Today's technological society continues to develop new products and new uses for products. This growth is paralleled by an increase in the number of hazardous products produced for use or as by-products of industrial or chemical manufacturing processes. The Love Canal chemical waste dump in New York and the Times

Beach, Missouri, PCB episodes illustrate problems posed by hazardous substances. This section discusses the Resource Conservation and Recovery Act (RCRA),[25] the Toxic Substances Control Act (TOSCA),[26] the Federal Insecticide, Fungicide, and Rodenticide Act (FIFRA),[27] and the Comprehensive Environmental Response, Compensation, and Liability Act (CERCLA) or Superfund Act[28] that Congress passed to address these problems.

RESOURCE CONSERVATION AND RECOVERY ACT

In 1965, Congress passed the Solid Waste Disposal Act in an attempt to regulate pollution caused by soil waste. As with the regulation of water and air pollution, primary responsibility was left with the states until 1976, when the Act was amended by RCRA. Amended again in 1984, RCRA gave the EPA primary responsibility for identifying and regulating hazardous wastes.

Hazardous wastes are defined as solid wastes that significantly contribute to an increase in mortality or serious illness or that pose a substantial hazard to the environment or human health if improperly handled. Solid wastes include "solid, liquid, semi-solid or contained gaseous materials." The EPA has used two methods of identifying hazardous wastes. First, it has specifically identified some substances as hazardous. Second, it has used four criteria in characterizing hazardous wastes: ignitability, corrosivity, reactivity, and toxicity.[29] The first three characteristics pose a threat of immediate harm; the fourth poses a threat of long-term harm. A substance with any of these characteristics is judged to be a hazardous waste and is subject to regulation.

RCRA authorizes the EPA to control hazardous substances from "the cradle to the grave." The EPA exercises this authority in two ways. First, it requires operators of treatment, storage, or disposal facilities (TSDFs) to apply for permits before disposing of hazardous wastes. The EPA or an authorized state agency ensures that permits are not issued unless the TSDF meets certain operating and performance standards covering proper treatment, storage, and disposal methods; the necessary record keeping; and the required monitoring and inspection methods.

Second, it tracks the wastes from the generation facilities to the TSDFs through the use of manifests or written permits. The generator of hazardous wastes must initiate this record, which travels with the wastes. The generator prepares the wastes for transportation, certifies the document, and has the initial transporter sign the manifest. The transporter must follow the delivery instructions on the manifest and must have it signed by the secondary transporter or the TSDF that receives the wastes. Each transporters retains a copy of the signed manifest. Ultimately, the operator of the TSDF receiving the wastes must sign the manifest and return a copy to the generator. The generator must report to the EPA any manifests not returned within forty-five days of shipment. The completed manifest contains a record of every individual who handled the wastes and may be used to determine responsibility for mishandling or accidents.

The EPA is charged with enforcing RCRA. It must first notify the state of violations. If the state fails to act, the EPA can seek civil or criminal sanctions.

TOXIC SUBSTANCES CONTROL ACT

The Toxic Substance Control Act (TOSCA) gave the EPA regulatory authority over *toxic chemicals,* substances that produce detrimental effects in living organisms. The EPA's first duty was to compile an inventory of all chemicals transported in interstate commerce. Following the inventory, the EPA's regulatory authority under TOSCA is exercised in three ways. First, the EPA uses a premanufacture notification program to review and ensure the safety of new chemicals before they are manufactured. Anyone intending to develop a new chemical substance, one not included in the initial inventory of chemicals, must notify the EPA and submit the chemical to a screening process. The manufacturer must provide such information as the new chemical's composition, intended uses, potential health hazards, and volume to be produced. The EPA reviews the data to determine whether the new substance poses an unreasonable risk to either health or the environment. After reviewing the data, the EPA must issue the least burdensome rules that will be effective to ensure the chemical's safe use. The rules can range from requiring warning notices to an absolute ban on production. The latter is available only if the EPA believes the chemical poses an unreasonable risk. The EPA may also restrict the uses of the chemicals or require additional testing.

Second, the EPA requires testing of existing chemicals. The Interagency Testing Committee (ITC) prepares, and each six months reviews and revises, a priority list of fifty chemicals to be tested. The EPA will either require the manufacturers to test the chemicals on the list or respond to the ITC with reasons for not testing the recommended chemicals. The EPA requires testing if it finds that a chemical may present significant risk; if the available data are insufficient to properly judge the risks; or if a chemical is produced in high volume, exposure is widespread, and test data are limited.

Third, the EPA has the authority to control existing chemicals. The EPA can establish rules for production, distribution, use, record keeping, testing, and reporting at all stages of the chemical's life. If available data show that a chemical poses an unreasonable risk, the EPA can prohibit production just as it can with new chemicals. As with RCRA, the EPA can enforce provisions of TOSCA through the use of civil and criminal sanctions.

FEDERAL INSECTICIDE, FUNGICIDE, AND RODENTICIDE ACT

Pesticides were the first toxic substances to be regulated. Early regulation required adequate labels and ensured that the pesticides were not adulterated. In 1972, the Act was amended to authorize the EPA to exert more regulatory control. Under these amendments, manufacturers are required to register pesticides with the EPA prior to their being sold in interstate commerce. *Pesticides* are defined as substances "intended for preventing, destroying, repelling, or mitigating any pest, (and substances) . . . intended for use as a plant regulator, defoliant, or desiccant." The registration process is to ensure that the pesticide's composition warrants proposed claims; that the labeling and warning requirements are met; that the pesticide will perform its intended function without unreasonable, adverse environmental effects; and that when used in accordance with widespread, common practice, it will not cause unreasonable, adverse environmental effect.

In addition, the EPA classifies pesticides as intended for general or restricted use. Pesticides classified as restricted must be applied by a certified applicator. Pesticides that pose a potential for unreasonable adverse effects on the environment, including injury to the applicator, receive the restricted classification. Violators of FIFRA may be subject to penalties that increase in severity for violations by certified applicators. The EPA may also cancel or suspend registration on a showing that a pesticide poses a potential for "unreasonable, adverse, environmental effects."

COMPREHENSIVE ENVIRONMENTAL RESPONSE, COMPENSATION, AND LIABILITY ACT: THE SUPERFUND

The three acts previously discussed are measures intended to prevent unnecessary exposure to hazardous substances in the future. To deal with hazardous wastes accidentally spilled or stored in abandoned dump sites, Congress passed CERCLA in 1980 to create the Superfund. The goals are to eliminate the threats from uncontrolled hazardous waste sites and to remove hazardous substance threats to public health and the environment in a cost-effective manner. The Act created a trust fund of $1.6 billion generated, in part, from taxes levied on the production of certain hazardous wastes.

The Act has four basic elements. First, owners of hazardous waste dump sites are required to notify the EPA of the type of wastes buried in their dumps. This notification process allows the EPA to identify the problem areas and abandoned dump sites. Second, the act authorizes the EPA to act to clean up hazardous waste spills or leaking dump sites for which it is not possible to locate the responsible party. Third, the Act authorizes the EPA to use the $1.6 billion Superfund to perform the necessary cleanup. Fourth, the Act imposes liability for remedial action on the generators and disposers of hazardous wastes. The party responsible for the release of the hazardous substance is liable for the costs of cleanup efforts and for damages. The responsible party may limit liability by assisting in cleanup efforts if the spill or leak was not the result of willful negligence or misconduct. The Act also requires businesses to carry liability insurance that covers the damages from release of hazardous substances. Because of the inadequacy of the amount in the fund, however, the Act is not intended to provide a remedy for private citizens injured by such release.

A 1986 amendment to CERCLA, the Superfund Amendment and Reauthorization Act (SARA), extended the original Act's provisions for five years and increased funding to $9 billion. It strengthened the 1980 standards for cleaning up abandoned sites, gave the EPA more authority in undertaking priority actions, and implemented tougher penalties against violators.

Violators are strictly liable—that is, liable without negligence or fault. They will also be met with "joint and several liability," which means that a single firm that may have contributed to the waste site along with numerous others may be held financially responsible for the full amount of the cleanup. The firm will then have to seek financial recovery against the others. Recovery will be in proportion to the degree or percentage the other firms contributed to the waste site.

CERCLA DEFENSES

CERCLA permits only three defenses. If an individual or a firm is found to be (1) the present owner or operator of a facility or the owner or operator at the time of disposal of the hazardous substances, (2) a person who arranged for treatment or disposal of the materials, or (3) a person who transported the materials to the site, that person or firm is potentially liable for the costs of cleanup. The defendant may escape liability by showing that release or threat of release was caused solely by (1) an act of God, (2) an act of war, or (3) the act or omission of a third party.

The third-party defense is not easily proved. The innocent landowner or property that is later subject to cleanup must show that a third party was solely responsible for the contamination and that the third party was not in a contractual relationship with the defendant. For example, if the landowner hired a third party to do work on the property and if, in the process, hazardous substances were released, the third-party defense would not be available to the landowner. In this case, the landowner would be required to reimburse the government for cleanup and then seek recovery from the third party.

If the defendant took title from the third party, the defendant must show that it did not know or have any reason to know of the presence of hazardous substances at the site and that it made all appropriate inquiries consistent with commercial or customary practices. As a practical matter, a prudent purchaser will undertake some sort of environmental audit of the property prior to purchase.

As a general rule, parent firms are not liable for the cleanup costs of their wholly owned subsidiaries,[30] but that will not hold true if the parent exercises substantial control over the activities of the subsidiary.[31] When two corporations merge, the prevailing view is that the acquiring or surviving corporation is liable for the pollution of the acquired firm even though that pollution occurred long before it was illegal to dump or abandon such hazardous substances.[32] Officers and shareholders who exercise substantial authority and control of corporate operations have been found personally liable for conduct in violation of CERCLA.[33]

THE EPA-FLEET FACTORS RULE

In a case that caused much controversy in the financial community, one court held that a secured creditor of a bankrupt printing firm was liable to the government for reimbursement of cleanup costs.[34] Fleet Factors Corporation advanced funds to Swainsboro Print Works and took an assignment of its accounts receivable. In connection with this advance, Fleet obtained a security interest in Swainsboro's plant, its equipment, inventory, and fixtures. After the printing firm was declared bankrupt, Fleet foreclosed on part of Swainsboro's inventory and equipment, had it auctioned off, and contracted with Nix to haul off everything that remained and to leave the premises "broom clean."

Later, the EPA spent $400,000 removing seven hundred fifty-five gallon drums of toxics and forty-four truckloads of materials containing asbestos from the facility. It then proceeded against the two principal officers and stockholders of Swainsboro and against Fleet. The trial court refused to dismiss Fleet on summary judgment.

In affirming the trial court's denial of Fleet's motion, the court of appeals concluded that a security holder that participated "in the financial management of [the bankrupt printing firm] to a degree indicating a capacity to influence the corporation's treatment of hazardous wastes" may be held liable as an operator. "It is not necessary," the court continued, "for the secured creditor actually to involve itself in the day-to-day operations of the facility. . . . Nor is it necessary for the secured creditor to participate in the management decisions relating to hazardous wastes. Rather, a secured creditor will be liable if its involvement with the management of the facility is sufficiently broad to support the inference that it could effect hazardous waste disposal decisions."

The uncertainty that *Fleet Factors* introduced into the law regarding the possible liability of security holders led to an EPA rule, effective April 29, 1992, on the Security Interest Exemption under CERCLA. The EPA rule, following the lead of *In re Bergose Metal Corp.*,[35] rather than *Fleet,* relates that participation in the management of a facility sufficient to render a security holder liable for cleanup costs means participation in the "management or operational affairs" of the facility, and *does not include the mere capacity to influence or ability to influence the operations.*

This rule has survived judicial challenge under the "arbitrary and capricious" test, and like other administrative rules that interpret legislation, it will be given substantial deference by the courts. It means that a security holder may exercise influence over the facility manager *but still not be liable for cleanup costs* if it has no power to direct or implement operational decisions.

Although this and each other act we have discussed, beginning with the Clean Air Act, are administered by the EPA, the following piece of legislation is enforced by the Interior Department.

SURFACE MINING CONTROL AND RECLAMATION ACT

In 1977, Congress passed the Surface Mining Control and Reclamation Act (SMCRA)[36] to regulate the environmental aspects of coal mining. The Act established the Office of Surface Mining Reclamation and Enforcement in the United States Interior Department to correct past abuses and to prevent future ones. SMCRA addresses the pollution problems caused by the exposure to heavy metals and by the runoff of silt during mining operations. The Act applies to surface strip mining and to effects on the surface of subsurface mining.

To correct past abuses, SMCRA provides for reclamation of abandoned surface mines. This involves replacing rock, gravel, and topsoil and reseeding the topsoil to restore the land to its approximate original condition prior to the mining. Reclamation is expensive and is funded by fees collected from coal-mining operations subject to SMCRA. One criticism of reclamation is that its costs are more than the land is worth after reclamation. This criticism, however, presumes to foresee the future with greater clarity than almost anyone can claim, and it does not take into account the loss of aesthetic value or other intangibles that cannot be readily monetized.

PERMITS AND STANDARDS

To prevent future abuses, the Act prohibits any surface mining in the absence of a permit. A reclamation plan and permit application must be submitted to the Surface Mining, Reclamation, and Control Office or to the authorized state regulatory agency. The Interior Department has primary enforcement responsibility, but this responsibility may be shifted to states that submit regulatory programs for the secretary of interior's approval. These regulatory programs must conform to the requirements of the Act and the secretary's regulations before they are approved. Permits may then be issued that require the operator to comply with certain standards, including

1. Restoration of the land to a condition capable of supporting the premining use or a higher or better use

2. Restoration of the "approximate original contour" of the land

3. Removal of topsoil as a separate layer and replacement on the backfilled area

4. Special provision for removal, storage, and replacement of soil for prime farmlands

5. Prevention of ground or surface water pollution from disposal of debris and toxic materials

6. Reclamation efforts carried out in an environmentally sound manner

7. Assumption of responsibility for successful revegetation for five years (ten years in areas of the country where average annual precipitation is twenty-six inches or less)

   In addition to the performance standards, the permit process also considers the surface owner's rights when the mineral rights have been severed. Mining operators seeking permits must also submit the surface owner's permission, the deed that clearly provides for surface mining, or a deed interpreted under state law as providing for surface mining of the mineral estate. The Act also provides for public notice and hearings on permit applications.

ENFORCEMENT MEASURES

Violations of the Act are punishable by civil and criminal sanctions. In addition, the act creates a private cause of action. Private citizens can sue either the violating operator or the Interior Department to compel compliance with the Act's provisions.

REVIEW QUESTIONS AND PROBLEMS

1. The Administrative Procedure Act has application to environmental law and to many other areas as well. For example, it prohibits administrative agencies from operating in an *arbitrary and capricious* manner. What does this phrase mean?

2. What is the common legislative plan or pattern to the regulation of air and water pollution?

3. How is the Clean Air Act "technology forcing"?

4. How does the bubble concept benefit firms?

5. If the Clean Air Act is "technology forcing," how might one characterize the Clean Water Act?

6. What does the Clean Water Act prohibit? What effect does the absence of standards for a particular industry have?

7. What are hazardous wastes? What is the extent of the EPA's regulatory authority of hazardous wastes under RCRA? How does the EPA exercise this authority?

8. What are the CERCLA defenses available to an owner or operator of a hazardous waste site in an action by the government to recover cleanup costs?

9. Following the *Fleet Factors* case, the EPA promulgated a rule that brought about changes in the liability of security holders regarding the activities they undertook to preserve their security interests. What were those changes?

10. What pollution problems are addressed by SMCRA? How does reclamation correct the problems?

ENDNOTES

1. From *Science* 162 (December 13, 1968) at 1243-1248. Used by permission. Copyright © 1968 by the American Association of the Advancement of Science.

2. J. B. Wiesner and H. F. York, Sci. Amer. 211 (No. 4), 27 (1964).

3. J. von Neumann and O. Morgenstern, Theory of Games and Economic Behavior (Princeton Univ. Press, N.J. 1947), p.11.

4. J. H. Fremlin, New Sci., No. 415 (1964), p.285.

5. W. F. Lloyd, Two Lectures on the Checks to Population (Oxford Univ. Press, Oxford, England, 1833), reprinted (in part) in Population, Evolution, and Birth Control, G. Hardin, Ed. (Freeman, San Francisco, 1964), p.37.

6. A. N. Whitehead, Science and the Modern World (Mentor, New York, 1948), p.17.

7. G. Hardin, Ed., Population, Evolution, and Birth Control (Freeman, San Francisco, 1964), p.56.

8. Robert L. Heilbroner and Lester C. Thurow, The Economic Problem, 4th Ed., © 1975, pp. 216-217. Reprinted by permission of Prentice-Hall., Inc., Englewood Cliffs, N.J.

9. 42 U.S.C. Sections 4321-4370a (1982 & Supp. 1987).

10. The phrase *human environment* has been given a regulatory content by 40 C.F.R. Section 1508.14, which relates that is shall be interpreted comprehensively to include the natural and physical environment and the relationship of people with that environment.

11. 40 C.F.R. Section 1502.10 reads as follows:

Recommended format

Agencies shall use a format for environmental impact statements which will encourage good analysis and clear presentation of the alternatives including the proposed action. The following standard format for environmental impact statements should be followed unless the agency determines there is a compelling reason to do otherwise:

(a) Cover sheet.
(b) Summary.
(c) Table of Contents.
(d) Purpose of and Need for Action.
(e) Alternatives Including Proposed Ac-

tion (sec. 102(2)(C)(iii) and 102(2)(E) of the Act).

(f) Affected Environment.

(g) Environmental Consequences (especially sections 102(2)(C)(i),(ii),(iv), and (v) of the Act).

(h) List of Preparers.

(i) List of Agencies, Organizations, and Persons to Whom Copies of the Statement Are Sent.

(j) Index.

(k) Appendices (if any).

12. For example, Section 102(2)(E) requires federal agencies to study, develop, and describe alternatives to projects involving unresolved environmental problems even if the project does not necessitate an EIS.

13. Sagoff, Economic Theory and Environmental Law, 79 *Mich. L. Rev.* 1393 (1981).

14. 40 C.F.R. Section 1505.2.

15. Plaintiff must, on this threshold issue, first allege injury-in-fact to some economic, conservational, recreational, aesthetic, or environmental interest and, second, further allege that this injury arguably falls within the zone or scope of some federally protected right, e.g., within the coverage of NEPA. *Association of Data Processing Service Organizations* v. *Camp,* 397 U.S. 150 (1970); *Barlow* v. *Collins,* 397 U.S. 159 (1970).

16. 435 U.S. 519 (1978).

17. U.S.C.A. Section 706(2)(A). In *Citizens to Preserve Overton Park* v. *Volpe,* 401 U.S. 402 (1972), the arbitrary and capricious standard, the standard whereby the judiciary reviews many types of administrative action, was taken to mean that the agency must consider all *relevant factors* and that it must not make a *clear error of judgment.* For example, if most environmental factors are considered but water quality is omitted, a court might say that the agency failed to evaluate all relevant factors. Further, if the decision was based on political factors rather than economic, technological, and environmental ones, a court might say that the agency made a clear error of judgment.

18. 42 U.S.C. Sections 7401-7642 (1982 & Supp. 1987), as amended by the Clean Air Act of 1990, Pub. L. 101-549, 104 Stat. 2399, 1990.

19. Only one action was ever taken to court. R. Meiners & A. Ringleb, *The Legal Environment of Business* 342 (1982).

20. *Id.* at 349.

21. 427 U.S. 246 (1976).

22. 344 F. Supp. 253 (D.D.C. 1972), *aff'd.* 412 U.S. 541 (1973).

23. 33 U.S.C. Sections 1251-1387 (1988).

24. Compare *FMC Corp.* v. *Train,* 539 F.2d 973 (1976) with *Marathon Oil* v. *EPA,* 564 F.2d 1253 (1977).

25. 42 U.S.C. Sections 6901-6991(i) (1982 & Supp. 1987).

26. 15 U.S.C. Sections 2601-2671 (1982 & Supp. 1987).

27. 7 U.S.C. Sections 136-136y (1982 & Supp. 1987).

28. 42 U.S.C. Sections 9601-9675 (1982 & Supp. 1987).

29. Council on Environmental Quality (12th Annual Report, 1981), at 96.

30. *Joslyn Manufacturing Co.* v. *T.L. James & Co.,* 893 F.2d 80 (5th Cir. 1990).

31. *U.S.* v. *Kayser-Roth Corp.,* 910 F.2d 24 (1st Cir. 1990).

32. *Anspec Co.* v. *Johnson Controls, Inc.,* 922 F.2d 1240 (6th Cir. 1991).

33. *New York* v. *Shore Realty Corp.,* 759 F.2d 1032 (2d Cir. 1985).

34. *U.S.* v. *Fleet Factors Corp.,* 901 F.2d 1550 (11th Cir. 1990).

35. 910 F.2d 668 (9th Cir. 1990).

36. 30 U.S.C. Sections 1201-1211, 1231-1328 (1982 & Supp. 1987).

VINCENT E. BARRY

Moral Issues In Business

Rich Epstein couldn't understand the problem. After all, his metal working firm was complying with all existing pollution controls laws. And yet somehow he'd incurred the wrath of a local environmental protection group that wanted him to stop polluting a river that passed through the center of town.

Epstein had informed the group that the pollution they referred to amounted to such an insignificant amount that any reasonable person, even a federal agency, would consider it a tolerable social cost for the benefits of doing business. But the committee didn't see it that way.

"Your obligations," one member told him, "extend beyond the letter of the law."

Another member indicated that federal regulations simply served as guidelines. The goal of the environmental movement was to stop all pollution, minor as well as major. As one member put it, "You should remember that all major pollution probably began as what you call an insignificant insult to the environment." In the same vein, another member pointed out that while Epstein's effluent discharge didn't amount to much in isolation, taken together with all other so-called tolerable amounts, it was contributing to a serious water-pollution problem.

In reply, Epstein asked the group if they realized how much pollution-control equipment would cost. He would have to pay about $70,000 for installation and over $20,000 annually for operating expenses. "Such an expense," he pleaded, "won't make a dime's worth of difference in my product." Then he added, "But I can tell you one thing: I'm going to have to change more than a dime more if I do what you're asking."

The committee deplored this economic reality but said that if that was the only way to erase pollution, then so be it.

"Easy for you to say," Epstein told them bitterly, "but I sell my product nationally. Do you have any idea of the competitive disadvantage you're imposing on me? Why, it wouldn't surprise me that, in addition to freezing salaries, your proposal would cause a production tailspin that would force me to lay off workers." Then Epstein asked them sharply: "Are you sure people would rather have cleaner water than a steady job?"

The committee remained adamant in its demands. It told Epstein that it would return in ten days to find out what Epstein intended to do to curb pollution of the river. Should he do nothing, they were prepared to take him to court.[1]

Now consider these specific questions:

1. Does an individual or a business firm have a moral obligation to go beyond what the law demands?
2. Since the law doesn't require Epstein to clean up all of his firm's pollution, shouldn't that political judgment be respected by others?
3. Enumerate, as best you can, the benefits and costs of cleaning up and not cleaning up the firm's wastes. Can you trace this cost-benefit approach to some ethical theory?
4. If you were Epstein, would you feel comfortable with the general rule that anyone, under comparable circumstances, could reasonably decline to install any additional pollution control equipment? Would you feel the same way if you lived down-stream from the plant?
5. If Epstein refuses to install the equipment, has he acted immorally?

Endnote

1. Source: *Moral Issues in Business,* by Vincent E. Barry. © 1979 by Wadsworth, Inc., used by permission.

RICHARD NELSON

Coming into Clearcut[1]

[*Author's note:* We are not attaching a sermon or undertaking to lecture you about forestry practices or anything like that. We have heard professional foresters and environmentalists face off on the issue of clearcutting, but the reality of the matter is that we know too little to undertake a blanket indictment of the practice.

The following piece of literature is too moving to omit from our coverage of environmental issues. We share the writer's quandary and his sense of outrage, desolation, and loss. We understand as well that we are implicated in this endeavor; we may be tiny "bit" players, perhaps, but players nevertheless.

You will have to write the Follow-Up to this selection. It is not out of the question that some very thoughtful responses will be shaped along lines of economic necessity, meeting payrolls, and staying solvent - considerations that are a very important part or our quality of life. But where does it end; where do you draw the line?]

After a long hike, taking the easy routes of deer trails, we move into a stand of shore pine that ends beside a half-overgrown logging road. This is the first sign of human activity since we left camp, and it indicates we're approaching the clearcut valley. The road follows a narrow band of muskeg that has all the delicate loveliness of a Japanese garden, with reflecting ponds and twisted lines in bonsai shapes. Farther on, it cuts through an alder thicket and runs up a steep, forested slope. A dense flock of birds sprays into the high trees, twittering like canaries, hundreds of them, agitated and nervous, moving so quickly they're difficult to hold for long in the binoculars.

After another half-mile, a slot appears in the road ahead. As we approach, it widens to a gateway out of the forest—a sudden, shorn edge where the trees and moss end and where the dark, dour sky slumps down against a barren hillside strewn with slash and decay. Oversize snowflakes blotch against my face and neck, and the breeze chills through me. I look ahead, then look back toward the trees, breathless and anxious, almost wishing I hadn't come.

The road angles into a wasteland of hoary trunks and twisted wooden shards, pitched together in convulsed disarray, with knots of shoulder-high brush pressing in along both sides. Fans of mud and ash splay across the roadway beneath rilled cutbanks. In one place, the lower side has slumped away and left ten feet of culvert hanging in midair, spewing brown water over the naked bank and into a runnel thirty feet below.

Thirty yards into it I realize that moving through a clearcut is unlike anything I've ever tried before. The ground is covered with a nearly impenetrable confusion of branches, roots, sticks, limbs, stumps, blocks, poles, and trunks, in every possible size, all gray and fibrous and rotting, thrown together in a chaotic mass and interwoven with a tangle of brittle bushes.

An astonishing amount of wood was left here to decay, including whole trees, hundreds of them in this one clearcut alone. Some flaw must have made them unusable even for pulp, but they were felled nonetheless, apparently so that the others would be easier to drag out. Not a single living tree above sapling size stands in the thirty or forty acres around me.

I creep over the slippery trunks and crawl beneath them, slip and stumble across gridworks of slash, and worm through close-growing salmonberry, menziesia, and huckleberry. In some places I walk along huge, bridging trunks, but they're slick and perilous, and I risk falling into a deadly skewer of wood below. By the time we near the top I am strained, sweating, sore, frustrated, and exhausted. It has taken almost an hour to cross a few hundred yards of this crippled land.

A large stump raised six feet above the ground on buttressed roots offers a good lookout. The man who felled this tree cut two deep notches on its base, which I use to clamber on top. It's about five feet in diameter and nearly flat, except for a straight ridge across the center where the cutter left hinge wood to direct the tree's fall. The surface is soggy and checked but still ridged with concentric growth rings. On hands and knees, nose almost touching the wood, using my knife blade as a pointer, I start to count. In a short while, I know the tree died in its 423rd year.

I stand to see the whole forest of stumps. It looks like an enormous graveyard, covered with weathered markers made from the remains of its own dead. Along the slope nearby is a straight line of four stumps lifted on convoluted roots, like severed hands still clasping a nearly vanished mother log. Many of the surrounding stumps are smaller than my platform, but others are as large or larger. A gathering of ancients once stood here. Now it reminds me of a prairie in the last century, strewn with the bleached bones of buffalo. Crowded around the clearcut's edges are tall trees that seem to press forward like curious, bewildered gawkers.

Two centuries ago it would have taken the native people who lived here several days to fell a tree like this one and weeks or months to wedge it into planks. Earlier in this century, the hand loggers could pull their huge crosscut saws through it in a couple of hours. But like the Native Americans before them, they selected only the best trees and left the others. Now I gaze into a valley miles deep, laid bare to its high slopes, with only patches of living timber left between the clearcut swaths.

Where I stand now a great tree once grew. The circles that mark the centuries of its life surround me, and I dream back through them. It's difficult to imagine the beginnings—perhaps a seed that fell from a flurry of crossbills like those I saw a while ago. More difficult still is the incomprehensible distance of time this tree crossed, as it grew from a limber switch on the forest floor to a tree perhaps 150 feet tall and weighing dozens of tons. The man who walked up beside it some twenty years ago would have seemed no more significant than a puff of air on a summer afternoon.

Perhaps thin shafts of light shone down onto the forest floor that day and danced on the velvet moss. I wonder what that man might have thought, as he looked into the tree's heights and prepared to bring it down. Perhaps he thought only about the job at hand, or his aching back, or how long it was until lunch. I would like to believe he gave some consideration to the tree itself, to its death and his responsibilities toward it, as he pulled the cord that set his chainsaw blaring.

The great, severed tree cut an arc across the sky and thundered down through its neighbors, sending a quake deep into the earth and a roar up against the valley walls. And while the tree was limbed and bucked, dozens of other men worked along the clearcut's advancing front, as a steady stream of trucks hauled the logs away.

The clearcut valley rumbled like an industrial city through a full decade of summers, as the island's living flesh was stripped away. Tugs pulled great rafts of logs from Deadfall Bay through tide-slick channels toward the mill, where they were ground into pulp and slurried aboard ships bound for Japan. Within a few months, the tree that took four centuries to grow was transformed into newspapers, read by commuters on afternoon trains, and then tossed away.

I think of the men who worked here, walking down this hill at the day's end, heading home to their families in the camp beside Deadfall Bay. I could judge them harshly indeed and think myself different; but that would be a mistake. The loggers were people just like me, not henchmen soldiers in a rebel army, their pockets filled with souvenirs. They probably loved working in the woods and found their greatest pleasures in the outdoors.

I once had a neighbor who was a logger all his life, worked in these very clearcuts, and lost most of his hearing to the chainsaw's roar. He was as fine a man as I could hope to meet. And he lived by the conscience of western culture—that the forest is here for taking, in whatever way humanity sees fit.

The decaying stump is now a witness stand, where I pass judgment on myself. I hold few convictions so deeply as my belief that a profound transgression was committed here, by devastating an entire forest rather than taking from it selectively and in moderation. Yet whatever judgment I might make against those who cut it down I must also make against myself. I belong to the same nation, speak the same language, vote in the same elections, share many of the same values, avail myself of the same technology, and owe much of my existence to the same vast system of global exchange. There is no refuge in blaming only the loggers or their industry or the government that consigned this forest to them. The entire society—one in which I take active membership—holds responsibility for laying this valley bare.

I try to take encouragement from the ten-foot hemlock and spruce saplings scattered across the hillside. Interestingly, no tender young have taken root atop the flat stumps and mossless trunks. Some of the fastgrowing alders are twenty feet tall, but in winter they add to the feeling of barrenness and death. Their thin, crooked branches scratch against the darkened clouds and rattle in the wind. The whole landscape is like a cooling corpse, with new life struggling up between its fingers. If I lived a long time, I might see this hillside covered with the beginnings of a new forest. Left alone for a few centuries, the trees would form a high canopy with scattered openings. Protected from the deep snows of open country, deer would again survive the pinch of winter by retreating into the forest. The whole community of dispossessed animals would return: red squirrel, marten, great horned own, hairy woodpecker, golden-crowned kinglet, pine siskin, blue grouse, and the seed-shedding crossbills. In streams cleared of sediment by moss-filtered runoff, swarms of salmon would spawn once more, hunted by brown bears who emerged from the cool woods.

There is comfort in knowing another giant tree could replace the one that stood here, even though it would take centuries of unfettered growth. I wish I could sink down into the earth and wait, listen for the bird voices to awaken me, rise from beneath the moss, and find myself sheltered by resplendent boughs. And in this world beyond imagination, such inordinate excesses toward nature will have become unthinkable.

Endnote

1. From *The Island Within,* copyright 1989 by Richard Nelson. Reprinted by permission of North Point Press.

CHAPTER 17

International Law and Business Transactions

INTRODUCTION

International law is a body of principles, customs, and rules recognized as effectively binding obligations by sovereign states and other international persons in their mutual relations.[1] Undertaking this subject matter in the space of one chapter is certainly no more intimidating than a comparable attempt at constitutional, environmental, or labor law. Each of these fields has an enormous substance, and we concentrate here on the most significant elements. International law evokes a kind of romance and intrigue that is not associated with many of the topics you have studied: The muffled throbs of ghost ships break on misty, nameless shores; a courier from Prague fails to keep her rendezvous in a West Bank cafe; the predawn roar of a bullet train conceals the sound of furtive men loading crates ("spare parts") with an icy, Volga destination. But international law is, in reality, none of these things. There is as large a gap between this stuff of B-movies and international law as there is between Istanbul and Buenos Aires. It can be as mundane as a city ordinance in Dallas or Stuttgart requiring a bond for street vendors and as hopeful as a treaty banning nuclear weapons. A comprehensive treatment would involve both of these topics and much in between. In this chapter, we principally emphasize international business transactions and the institutions that facilitate them. First, we examine the seven major kinds of governing principles that are called international law.[2] Then, we explain the most important areas of international law for the legal environment of today's students of business. We close the chapter with a focus on significant moral issues involved in doing business in foreign markets.

SEVEN CATEGORIES OF INTERNATIONAL LAW

1. CLASSICAL PUBLIC INTERNATIONAL LAW

Those rules by which intercourse between nations is conducted with an attempt to ensure world peace and harmony. This classical concept of international law is best exemplified by such world organizations as the United Nations and its organs (e.g., the International Court of Justice). Basically, public international law is of great interest to students of diplomacy, political science, and the like. It suffers in its business law importance for various reasons, not the least of which is the criticism that it is without effective sanctions. Because sanctions are often considered an essential element of any legal system, and often as the only effective deterrent to the harmful behaviors of business, public international law has limited effect on a businessperson's decision making.

2. CLASSICAL PRIVATE INTERNATIONAL LAW

The area of the law that deals with the conflicts between the laws of various jurisdictions. This category is most often applicable to situations in which citizens of two or more nations are involved in a controversy that must be decided by the application of the laws of one of those nations or of a third nation. How this is done is often called the study of the "conflict of laws." This category has often been criticized, however, as being neither truly a matter of international law nor actually related to conflict of laws, but rather more in the nature of a comparison of legal systems.

3. TRANSNATIONAL INTERNATIONAL LAW

Multinational legislation that binds its signatory members together in an attempt to pass uniform laws with sanctions. Transnational law attempts to facilitate world or regional commercial activity through the adoption of common legislation by multiple countries. This rather new law may be typified by the attempt at unification of the law governing international sales of goods. The United Nations Convention on the International Sale of Goods (CISG) is a good illustration of this type of international law. It is an interesting experiment that has been evident for some time, although it still suffers from growing pains. This type of legislation is of interest to the international businessperson because it allows one to simplify the educational process: Commonalities among laws limit the need to be familiar with the separate laws of each nation-state. It is in its infancy, however, and has not yet assumed great importance to the business person. By analogy, transnational law is at a stage comparable to that of an early phase in the development of the Uniform Commercial Code (UCC).

4. REGIONAL ECONOMIC INTERNATIONAL LAW

Those laws that govern the internal and external workings of economic trade areas. Regional economic international law is a rapidly growing area. Examples of regional economic pacts are the European Economic Community (EEC), the Andean Common Market (ANCOM), and the Caribbean Economic Community (CARICOM). This area is of importance to businesspeople who plan projects in any member country of a trade area. For example, a U.S. exporter of products that did not meet health standards in this country would necessarily want to know the position of the regional economic pact on such sales, as well as the position of the importing nation. Especially helpful is the general proliferation of printed materials and reports published by the central commissions of such communities. Further, as such organizations grow, they tend to increase the available body of unified law. Although each of these regional economic pacts has unique features and institutions that address its particular needs, in this chapter we use the EEC—the first and most widely recognized economic community—as illustrative of their role and function.

5. BILATERAL INTERNATIONAL LAW

Those laws embodied in mutual benefit pacts executed between two (or more) sovereign nations. This category of law is immense and covers virtually every conceivable matter that countries may agree on among themselves. Treaties and accords are the best-known examples of this category. These accords (e.g., U.S. bilateral tax treaties that allow U.S. firms income tax credits for taxes paid abroad) are of great importance to the businessperson dealing within that particular area. Such agreements are easily accessible and continue to be of considerable use in business.

6. UNILATERAL INTERNATIONAL LAW

Those laws of any sovereign nation or one of its subdivisions that are designed to affect the actions of those from outside that state or to affect those from within the state in their relationship with foreigners. From the U.S. perspective, examples of unilateral international law exist at both the federal and state levels. Federal statutes in this category include the Foreign Corrupt Practices Act and acts concerning immigration and naturalization. Illustrative state laws are those limiting foreign ownership of real estate. Often, this category is extremely important in the international business sphere because failure to comply may lead to an inability to engage in any activity at all.

7. DOMESTIC LEGISLATION WITH INTERNATIONAL SIGNIFICANCE

Those laws that are enacted without regard for international matters and that affect international business only in the instance where one attempting to do business finds such laws to be of significance. Of all the categories, this is the most difficult to deal with because of the lack of actual international content in these laws. This category includes virtually all legislation of any type without regard to whether it emanates from federal, state, or local level. For example, it may be quite important for a Brazilian firm to be informed of a city ordinance in Dallas or Stuttgart. In fact, often local ordinances become problematic for the international businessperson because local laws are generally difficult for the outsider to know. Further, this category of laws is often disregarded by international businesspeople, and by their specialized counsel as well, because of the mistaken view that the local nature of the laws makes them less important. We illustrate this point later in this chapter in the complex but realistic setting of *Sumitomo Shoji America, Inc.* v. *Avagliano.* This case involves treaty interpretation, as well as application of the 1964 Civil Rights Act, Title VII, to a New York corporation (Sumitomo) that is a wholly owned subsidiary of a Japanese firm.

OVERVIEW: DOING BUSINESS INTERNATIONALLY

Doing business with customers and suppliers in a foreign country does not necessarily involve a personal presence or an investment abroad. It can be as straightforward as doing business with another firm in the United States involving sales and financing provisions that are compatible with the UCC. You should not underestimate the problems that may arise from language, cultural, and legal differences, but these issues can be dealt with in a variety of ways and through alternative forms of doing business. Our purpose here is to acquaint you with some ways that international trade is conducted: export/import, licensing, direct investment and joint ventures. In getting down to business, however, there is no substitute for having counsel at home and abroad to smooth the hurdles that newcomers will encounter and to advise more experienced businesspeople of changes on the horizon.

EXPORT-IMPORT TRANSACTIONS

Direct sales and purchases abroad involve the least legal exposure for a firm entering the international marketplace. This does not mean, however, that it is the most appropriate method from an economic perspective. One thing a businessperson has to do is balance the probability and magnitude of potential legal tangles against the expected yield on a particular venture. Only the legal factors in that calculus are addressed here.

Direct transactions involve the time-consuming process of developing one's own contacts. That is just one more cost of doing business internationally. Dealing through agents and trade representatives reduces that cost but may involve the time, anxiety, and expense of litigating tax, labor, and principal-agent problems.

Letters of Credit. International irrevocable letters of credit are one way of taking some risk out of doing business with unfamiliar parties. The following description (which is capable of many variations) is from the perspective of a U.S. exporter.

The foreign buyer or importer of goods will usually allay the U.S. seller's fear of doing business with a commercial stranger by having its bank (buyer's bank) issue an irrevocable letter of credit for an amount sufficient to cover the price and all charges in U.S. dollars. The importer makes the necessary financial arrangements to secure its bank (now designated as the issuing bank) and, operating through international banking channels, to contract with the seller's bank to confirm this letter of credit.

There is no rigid format for who arranges what, but the most frequent pattern, and surely the most convenient one, is to find a confirming bank in the seller's locality that would agree to pay the sale price named in the letter. Such payment would be made on proof, via certain documents, that the contracted-for goods had been shipped. This would mean that once the seller delivered conforming goods to the carrier (air, sea, or rail) and received, as per prearrangement, a bill of lading, an invoice, an insurance policy, and other specified documents, the confirming bank would pay the seller the contract price and certain named charges. The confirming bank would then forward the documents to the issuing bank to be reimbursed. In turn, the issuing bank would be paid by its customer, the importer, according to the original agreement. These documents would then be released to the importer so that the goods could be picked up from the carrier.

An essential feature of this method of financing international business transactions is that bank obligations accrue independently of the underlying sales contract; that is, they mature and are discharged on presentation of the proper documents. In other words, the goods will be paid for prior to the time of a contractual dispute between seller and buyer, if any such dispute should arise. Contractual matters will be settled according to the terms of the contract and the dispute-resolving concepts discussed later in the chapter.

Convention on International Sale of Goods. One effort of the United Nations to deal with contract disputes is the Convention on International Sale of Goods (CISG). The United States, a signatory to this convention along with many of its trading partners, has followed the CISG provisions since they took effect in January 1988.

In many ways, the CISG is comparable to the UCC, and its provisions apply to contracts between parties from different signatory nations. It contains no statute of frauds, no consumer sales provisions, no provision covering passage of title, and no provision on product liability for death or personal injury. The CISG does not control the validity of the contract; instead, the conflict-of-laws rules of the forum determine which nation's law applies to the issue of validity. Finally, the CISG allows the parties to exclude the application of the convention in its entirety or to modify the effect of any of its provisions.

The CISG provides that an offer is sufficiently definite if it indicates the goods and makes provision for determining the quantity and the price. An offer may be revoked if the revocation reaches the offeree before an acceptance is sent. Contrary to UCC and common law practice, the acceptance is not effective to create a contract immediately on dispatch; such dispatch merely terminates the offeror's power to revoke. In a concession to civil law jurisdictions, the acceptance does not become effective until the indication of assent reaches the offeror. Also in the civil law tradition, if the offeree is to perform an act, the acceptance is effective at the moment the act is performed rather than when notice of performance is given to the offeror.

The CISG does not adopt the UCC "firm offer," but it does provide that "an offer cannot be revoked if it indicates, whether by stating a fixed time for acceptance or otherwise, that it is irrevocable." The convention does not have quite the "battle of forms" provision of UCC 2–207; it parallels the common law mirror image rule instead. If, under the CISG, an offeree's purported acceptance contains additional or changed terms, it amounts to a rejection and counteroffer. Although the original offeror can object to and defeat the inclusion of any additions or changes (even minor ones), only the major modifications (material alterations) are automatically screened out. Material alterations are terms relating to price, payment, quality, quantity, and place and time of delivery. Compared to the UCC, a change in any of these terms is far more likely to be considered a material alteration. The convention will recognize far fewer contracts resulting from the exchange of forms.

Even though the CISG does not contain a statute of frauds, any signatory nation may make a reservation to the effect that the statute of frauds of the nation of either contracting party will control. If this reservation is not made, the oral contract provisions of the convention will be left in effect. In that case, the parties to the contract may create their own "private" parol evidence rule as follows: Either the offeror or the offeree may stipulate, in writing, that the writings that do exist embody all the terms and conditions of the contract and that those terms and conditions cannot be modified orally.

LICENSING

Licensing agreements allow a firm to enter a foreign market by an investment of intellectual property, rather than by an investment of capital in the conventional sense. In return for an agreed-on royalty, a U.S. firm might license a foreign national to use a patent, copyright, trademark, or trade name. Franchise operations, such as those used by Coca-Cola, Pepsi, McDonald's, Kentucky Fried Chicken, Pizza Hut, and Hertz, are another frequent entry point. This approach "ups the ante" in comparison with importing/exporting. It involves greater risks and greater investment, but generally speaking, the potential return makes the risks worthwhile.

The Paris Union, more formally the International Union for the Protection of Industrial Property, has as its goal the protection of industrial property, including patents, industrial designs, trademarks, service marks, trade names, and the repression of unfair competition. The United States is a signatory, along with many other nations. Broadly speaking, these nations give registrants the same protection the registrant has in its home country. This proviso is subject to so many exceptions that it makes sense to be informed by experienced patent attorneys in the nations involved.

Technology licensing agreements may be with foreign governments, such as the Bank of Japan, rather than with foreign nationals. Such governmental entities may drive a harder bargain or may have in mind long-range plans that forego immediate returns in favor of "capturing" the technology after a limited period of time. These administrative units frequently require the training of a local workforce and the local purchase of materials and equipment.

By the time a firm becomes interested enough in foreign markets to consider franchising and the licensing of technology, it should consider a choice of language clause, a payment clause, and a *force majeure* clause. Other important matters, such as choice of forum, choice of law, and arbitration, are discussed subsequently.

1. *Language Clause.* If the parties do not share a common language, it is becoming commonplace to stipulate an official language for purposes of interpreting the terms of the agreement. This may result in an official language (German) and an authorized translation (French, English, Japanese).

2. *Payment Clause.* A payment clause is an effort to anticipate the caprices of fluctuating currencies and, with such forewarning, to minimize the negative impact of these movements by naming the currency that protects one's profit margin. For example, because dollars, pounds, marks, yen, and the like are traded on an international exchange market, the "currency of choice" today may not be worth as much (not have as much buying power) six months from now. The price of one currency in terms of another—*the foreign exchange rate*—is influenced by changes in inflation rates, balance of payments, interest rates, and central bank policies.

    These matters have to be taken into account in assessing credit terms, currency terms, and reinvestment opportunities. For example, if the relationship of dollars to pounds is 2 to 1 ($2U.S. will purchase £1 sterling), your Charleston, South Carolina, firm, which sold fabrics on January 1 to a British merchant with payment due July 1, would probably prefer payment in pounds sterling if (a) you had reinvestment or buying opportunities in Great Britain and (b) during the credit period, the dollar was expected to drop in relation to the pound on the foreign exchange market. Failure to make this stipulation would not affect your sales revenue in U.S. dollars, but it would reduce the number of pounds you had for reinvestment in Great Britain or for the purchase of British equipment.

    A $2,000 cash sale on January 1 would bring £1,000, but a $2,000 credit sale on January 1 due July 1 would bring only £500 if the exchange rate fell to 4 to 1. Notice that the number of dollars, $2,000, remains unchanged in either situation and that on the positive side, a dollar that is declining in relation to the pound will be likely to enhance your British exports.

3. *Force Majeure Clause.* The title of this clause refers to the power or authority of a higher source. If the parties so agree, this clause will relieve one or both from performance under "impossible" or "impracticable" circumstances. Acts of God (fire, earthquake, flood) and political upheaval, riot, war, and strikes are typically enumerated as reasons for nonperformance. Riot damage to business firms after the 1989 U.S. invasion of Panama was the basis on which many insurance companies denied reimbursement to their policyholders.

DIRECT INVESTMENT

Foreign subsidiaries, wholly owned by a U.S. parent corporation or joint ventures in which ownership and control is shared by the U.S. firm and a firm of the host country (or with the government of the host country), are the next rung on the investment ladder. This step may be undertaken to avoid tariff and other barriers, to tap into a reduced wage and tax structure, or to place a firm at a competitive advantage vis-à-vis a large and undeveloped market.

These matters should be given thoughtful consideration from the outset because, whatever the potential, the parent will experience a certain loss of managerial control of enterprises undertaken jointly. Furthermore, the inducements made to the parent firm may not materialize as expected, the parent may have difficulty repatriating its earnings, and capital recovery may be undertaken only at great loss. In other words, a firm had better be prepared for the long term before embarking on a direct investment in a foreign country.

JOINT VENTURES

The international joint venture is a rapidly developing form of business organization. As markets became increasingly global in the 1970s and 1980s and as artificial political barriers began to fall in the 1990s, transnational business activity has accelerated. With this process, collaborative arrangements among existing businesses have become popular, both domestically and internationally.

The increasing number of parent companies that develop international joint ventures tend to be motivated by one or more of a consistent set of goals. Some ventures are created to provide entry into a host country that restricts or once restricted direct investment. Countries moving toward more open economies are able to do so gradually and securely by restricting direct investment to situations in which the foreign corporation enters a joint venture with a domestic partner. Even in countries that do not require a degree of local ownership in foreign investments, the use of a joint venture may expedite entry into foreign markets because of opportunities to use a host country firm's existing labor, operations, and marketing structures. Transnational joint ventures are especially promising in countries, such as Mexico, that have negotiated treaties for more open trade with the United States. Likewise, joint venture activity in Europe is likely to increase in the future as EEC market efficiencies and open competition provide opportunities for U.S. companies whose domestic markets are saturated.

International joint ventures may facilitate geographical diversification in nonpolitical ways as well—for example, when foreign investors rely on the marketing expertise and established distribution networks of the domestic partner. Joint ventures may be formed across borders to promote the transfer of proprietary technologies and processes or to exploit synergies that exist by virtue of differentiated but complementary strengths of parent companies. Some international joint ventures are created to reduce risk, particularly in volatile industries such as biotechnology. Joint ventures can also provide U.S. partners with host-country managers who are motivated by an equity stake in the endeavor and who understand the local business environment.

Although all collaborative strategies bring an array of complex problems, the international joint venture is among the most demanding. Difficulties associated with cooperation can be magnified by legal, linguistic, and cultural differences. Managers contemplating joint venture activity across international borders should address these differences when they develop the contract that establishes and governs the joint venture. The contracting stage can be utilized as an opportunity for joint venture partners to engage in careful strategic planning. Several important planning issues should be considered during joint venture contracting:

- Division of managerial responsibility between joint venture parents
- Division of joint venture profits
- Scope of permissible joint venture business operations
- Ownership of and access to proprietary technologies developed by the joint venture
- Degree of flexibility the venture will be given in changing the orientation of its tasks in response to changing business conditions
- Choice of laws provisions establishing which country's law will apply in the event of disputes

INTERNATIONAL, REGIONAL, AND NATIONAL INSTITUTIONS AND STATUTES

THE INTERNATIONAL COURT OF JUSTICE

The United Nations, organized in 1945 and consisting of 184 sovereign states, has as its four main purposes the preservation of world peace and security, the establishment of justice among the nations of the world, cooperation in solving international problems, and service as an instrument to carry out these goals. The UN charter created a General Assembly in which all nations participate as equals, a Security Council for preserving peace, a Secretariat or executive chamber, an Economic and Social Council to advance human rights and promote material well-being, a Trusteeship Council to protect territories that are not self-governing, and an International Court of Justice (ICJ). Headquartered at The Hague, Netherlands, the ICJ has fifteen judges selected by the General Assembly and Security Council for nine-year terms. Operating within its mandate to decide cases in accordance with international law (Article 38 of the Court statute), the ICJ applies international conventions and customs, general principles of law, and the provisions of the statute.

Of great importance to foreign investors and multinational firms is the provision that violation of international law by a host country empowers the country of the investor or multinational to take the grievance before the ICJ. Individuals and firms have no standing in themselves to initiate such a suit. Only nations may be parties before the ICJ in these proceedings, and their governments have full discretion in deciding whether to pursue the claims of their residents. Judgments for money damages and injunctive relief, if necessary, may be referred to the Security Council for enforcement, but when the judgment is paid, the country of the investor or multinational need not distribute to the investor or firm any part of the money unless domestic law requires otherwise. In the United States, remittances are made through the Foreign Claims Settlement Commission.

THE WORLD BANK

The World Bank, or the International Bank for Reconstruction and Development, assists business firms of its member nations in making financial arrangements to promote "private foreign investment by means of guarantees or participation in loans and other investments made by private investors." It is also engaged in the facilitation of loans to Third World nations for long-term capital development.

THE INTERNATIONAL MONETARY FUND

The International Monetary Fund (IMF) was established for the purpose of assisting those nations with persistent balance-of-payment problems to stabilize their foreign exchange rates and to expand the growth of their international trade. This purpose is accomplished through special borrowing rights—that is, Special Drawing Rights (SDR) from the fund or from member nations—that will give its central bank the flexibility to expand or to restrict the supply of its currency in relation to the demand.

GENERAL AGREEMENT ON TARIFFS AND TRADE (GATT)

The General Agreement on Tariffs and Trade, or GATT, is known principally for its "most favored nation" clause. This document, which is really a composite of more than one hundred international agreements and has evolved from a series of "rounds" or trade negotiations, provides that each member nation will give to the products of every other member nation the same tariff treatment accorded to the products of the "most favored nation." The United States is one of GATT's eighty-eight signatory nations.

Elimination of discriminatory or projectionist import-export duties, quotas, licenses, and other barriers is clearly the long-term objective of GATT, but there are provisional exceptions for developing nations, for regional pacts, and for nations with serious balance-of-payment problems. In 1973, Congress passed the Trade Agreement Act, which authorizes "retaliatory" duties on products being "dumped" in the United States at prices below those that are charged for the product in the country of origin. Implementation of this Act requires a careful judgment by the International Trade Commission (ITC) and the Departments of

Commerce and Treasury that the goods are, in fact, being sold in the United States at less than fair value and that these sales materially injure, threaten, or retard domestic industry. The Act also implements the provision of GATT that authorizes a signatory nation to impose "countervailing" duties on products that receive governmental subsidization in the country of origin. Cooperative efforts of the ITC, Commerce, and Treasury limit these duties to the amount that will control for the nonmarket subsidy and, in the interest of fair competition, raise the price of the imported goods to a competitive level.

EXPORTS AND ANTITRUST: AT HOME AND ABROAD

The promotion of an export trade compatible with U.S. antitrust policy, along with the extraterritorial application of U.S. antitrust laws, has created many problems. The 1918 Webb-Pomerene Act and the 1982 Export Trading Company Act together grant limited antitrust immunity to U.S. firms for the purpose of organizing export trading companies. Today, the exports of these firms may involve consulting, communications, accounting, legal, insurance, and architectural services, as well as goods. The Export Administration Act imposes a licensing requirement on the export of sensitive goods, services, software, and technical assistance in the interest of military, diplomatic, and economic considerations. The qualified antitrust exemption does not authorize conduct resulting in a substantial lessening of competition or a restraint of trade within the United States or with a competitor. Neither may the activities of an export trading company unreasonably affect the price of the exported goods or services or impose unfair competition on a competitor.

U.S. firms have an alternative to proceeding under the Export Trading Company Act. If its antitrust exemptions appear too limited or too vague, the firm may "take its chances" under the Effects Doctrine, which is embodied in the Foreign Trade Antitrust Improvements Act of 1982. It applies the body of U.S. antitrust laws to the activities of all businesspersons and firms, including foreign firms and foreign governments, doing business extraterritorially. The activities of these persons violate U.S. antitrust laws if (a) they have a direct and substantial effect on U.S. commerce and (b) this effect on U.S. commerce was foreseeable. With regard to the activities of foreign governments and to persons acting under the compulsion of foreign governments, there are exceptions to these rules (discussed later in this chapter in the "Act of State Doctrine" section).

Japan's trade policy fosters the cooperative efforts of its exporters, and, in fact, its central bank administers an import program that is protectionist by many standards. The EEC administers an antitrust policy through its Commission that, generally speaking, prohibits the same kind of contracts and practices that U.S. antitrust law prohibits, and it treats these contracts and practices as void. Under Article 85 of the Treaty of Rome, however, these contracts and practices will be given clearance by the Commission if (a) the Commission is notified before the occurrence of the business conduct, (b) the contract or practice will produce economic benefits that would not otherwise be available in the member nations, and (c) these benefits can be produced without substantially eliminating competition. EEC Article 86 is comparable to U.S. prohibitions against monopolization, market dominance, and abuse of economic power. Questionable or "borderline" activities may be given a "negative clearance" by the Commission, which brings legal certainty to the conduct, although it may be limited as to duration, scope, and geographical area.

THE EUROPEAN ECONOMIC COMMUNITY

On January 1, 1958, the Treaty of Rome created the European Common Market. Today, this supranational community, with its own legislature, judiciary, and executive branches, is composed of fifteen member states: Austria, Belgium, Denmark, Finland, France, Germany, Greece, Ireland, Italy, Luxembourg, the Netherlands, Portugal, Spain, Sweden and the United Kingdom. Its principal objectives are as follows:

- Free movement of persons, goods, services, and capital

- Elimination of tariffs and quotas within the Community

- Common agricultural and transportation policies

- A system of free competition

The EEC is a political, economic, and legal community operated through the institutions discussed below. It illustrates the main features of economic pacts that circle the globe.

Structure and Operation of the EEC.   The *Commission* exercises both legislative and executive power. It is the main component of the EEC and has the mandate to carry out the treaty provisions. The Commission is independent of member states; thus, the commissioners do not represent their home countries.

The Commission initiates legislation that is subject to the opinion of the Assembly prior to being presented to the Council for adoption. It maintains relations with the United Nations and, as executive, enforces the observance of treaty provisions by individuals and member states.

The *Assembly*, whose members are elected from districts within member states, plays an important role in the EEC. It has supervisory powers over the Commission and the Council and has the right to be consulted and give advisory opinions on Community legislation.

The *Council of Ministers* coordinates economic policies of the member states. Each national government will be represented by ministers of finance, ministers of transportation, and so forth. The Council does not have authority to initiate legislation, but it may act on proposals submitted to it by the Commission. On important matters, the Council tries to act unanimously, although the treaty requires a majority vote only.

As you would imagine, the main function of the *Court of Justice* is to resolve disputes pertaining to interpretation and application of the Treaty of Rome. Although courts of member states are bound by community law, the Court of Justice operates as highest court of appeal. It functions independently of the Commission, the Assembly, and the Council.

The European Economic Community—1992.   The Single Europe Act of 1987 (SEA), principally authored by EEC President Jacques Delors, was designed to achieve the completion of a fully integrated Europe by 1992. Except for tax matters, all issues that relate to the internal functioning of the EEC are determined by a voting majority. Unanimity is still required on the community's value added tax (VAT). Parliament has veto power over the addition of new members and over the establishment of new trade agreements with non-EEC nations.

The delivery of goods across national boundaries to the Community's consumers is facilitated by a single administrative document instead of the two-pound stack of papers previously required. A European passport is already replacing those of its member states, and the same will soon be true of driver's licenses. The "ultimate," reports *Business Week*,[3] will be the ability to "plug personal computers into any wall socket and wire modems to any phone system in Europe."

Much remains to be done in harmonizing Community legislation with practices that are regarded as national and business prerogatives. For example, safety and environmental product standards are regarded by some as disguised protectionist measures; others characterize efforts by the community to require uniform standards across the board as "bureaucratic interference."

Uniform proficiency measures are also a matter of concern. National certification of skilled labor and professionals through vocational training, university degrees, and professional boards has been the tradition. Community licensing has met its greatest success in the health care sector, but negotiations on other fronts are dragging.

Banks, insurance companies, and other providers of financial services are expanding their outlets in every area of the Community. This movement has contributed to a wave of takeovers, hostile and friendly, to joint ventures and other cooperative efforts. National boundaries are falling in broadcasting as well. European satellites have hastened the demise of purely national channels. They have opened possibilities of communitywide advertising and raised alarm about appropriate standards for newfound audiences of children and of religious and ethnic groups.

In sum, much remains to be done to create a fully unified market, and at the time of this writing, it is too early to foresee the impact of events in Eastern Europe on these developments. The EEC is positioned now to wage an intense economic rivalry with the United States and Japan into the next century, and it gives every indication of a willingness to pursue that objective.

National Sovereignty and the Treaty of Rome.   It is important to understand that the Treaty of Rome is no mere multinational treaty. The EEC is built on the concept of sovereignty; that is, sovereign rights pertaining to executive, legislative, and judicial functions are transferred to the Community and, like a separate nation, it has the power and independence to make its own international treaties. The courts of member states must enforce Community law whenever it is properly invoked, and this includes EEC treaties and the laws that implement them.

The Commission and the Council act on the basis of regulations, directives, or decisions. A regulation has general application and creates rights and duties for member states and their citizens. A directive compels a member state to achieve a particular outcome, but the state retains discretion regarding the implementation. Decisions are binding on particular individuals and on legal entities or persons such as corporations.

Each of these bodies, the Commission and the Council, must give reasons for the action and document its legal basis. The Court of Justice may declare void any such act found to be an infringement of the treaty. In the event of a conflict between Community and national law, community law takes precedence.

NORTH AMERICAN FREE TRADE AGREEMENT (NAFTA)

A successful EEC may result in stronger and more efficient European markets as unified economic policies and laws become more responsive to global competitive realities and less encumbered by artificial impediments of national sovereignty. Because the logic behind a unified Europe applies as well among the Americas, the United States, Mexico, and Canada began negotiating a trade agreement called the North American Free Trade Agreement, or NAFTA, in early 1991. In late 1993, Congress approved the adoption of NAFTA. Presently, the specifics of the agreement are being fine-tuned among the three participating nations.

Although NAFTA proposals are presently in flux in response to the political process, its most salient feature is and always has been the reduction or elimination of trade barriers among the three nations. Tariffs and quotas will be immediately reduced in many industries, including automobiles, textiles, and agriculture. In some instances, tariff reductions are scheduled to be replaced by eventual tariff elimination. In addition, the agreement will facilitate private ownership of some electric utilities in Mexico.

NAFTA will also facilitate foreign investment. The agreement opens financial services markets, so U.S. banks can eventually develop wholly-owned subsidiaries in Mexico. Likewise, foreign investment in the insurance industry will be opened under NAFTA: Existing joint ventures were transformed to complete foreign ownership in 1996, and new endeavors will be allowed majority foreign ownership by 1998. By 2000, all restrictions regarding market share in the insurance industry will be lifted.

In addition, NAFTA contains sections that facilitate commercial transportation across borders. For example, U.S. truckers have historically been prohibited from carrying cargo into Mexico. Truckers have been required to switch their trailers to Mexican cabs, driven by Mexican drivers, at the border. NAFTA will eliminate these provisions and thus effectively open the roads within the three countries for commercial transportation purposes.

The controversy over NAFTA has focused on three central issues: economic efficiency, employment, and the environment. Proponents of the agreement argue against all artificial barriers to trade, suggesting that the reduction and elimination of tariffs and quotas can only render markets more efficient, as products and services compete on their merits, without impediment by protectionist forces. NAFTA's supporters also suggest that achievement of these efficiencies will be essential in competing against EEC members, who have a head start in developing and exploiting the advantages of a more unified market.

NAFTA's detractors suggest that these efficiency gains are illusory, arguing that the agreement is damaging to U.S. interests in ways that undermine its value. Labor unions in the United States have been among the most vehement opponents of NAFTA. They say that the agreement will cause massive job losses in the United States as low-wage positions are shifted to Mexico, where wages are even lower. The unions argue that the economic losses occasioned by this exodus of jobs will eliminate potential open-market advantages, and will devastate the U.S. economy.

Likewise, environmentalists argue that NAFTA fails to address environmental implications of free trade. In particular, they are concerned that NAFTA will allow and encourage U.S. companies to relocate in order to evade U.S. environmental laws. Because environmental pollution knows no sovereign boundaries, any increase in border pollution that might result from NAFTA could directly diminish the quality of air and water resources in the United States.

RESOLUTION OF INTERNATIONAL DISPUTES

Disputes between investors and persons in the host country may be settled by a court of the host country, of the investor's country, or of a third nation, depending on the circumstances of the case. Although a litigant may encounter problems in securing persons or documents as the procedures of the forum require, in taking evidence abroad, and in complying with forum rules regarding notice and proof of foreign law, these difficulties are not insurmountable.

In such cases there is no substitute for representation by an attorney experienced in these matters. It is simply a cost of doing business abroad that should be planned for ahead of time. Sumitomo, Inc., a New York corporation operating as a wholly owned subsidiary of a Japanese trading company, found belatedly that Title VII of the 1964 Civil Rights Act applied to its operations.

Sumitomo Shoji America, Inc. v. *Avagliano*
102 S.Ct. 2374 (1982)

BURGER, CHIEF JUSTICE

We granted certiorari to decide whether Article VIII(1) of the Friendship, Commerce and Navigation Treaty between the United States and Japan provides a defense to a Title VII employment discrimination suit against an American subsidiary of a Japanese company.

Petitioner, Sumitomo Shoji America, Inc., is a New York corporation and a wholly-owned subsidiary of Sumitomo Shoji Kabushiki Kaisha, a Japanese general trading company or *sogo shosha*.[4] Respondents are past and present female secretarial employees of Sumitomo. All but one of the respondents are United States citizens; that one exception is a Japanese citizen living in the United States. Respondents brought this suit as a class action claiming that Sumitomo's alleged practice of hiring only male Japanese citizens to fill executive, managerial and sales positions violated both 42 U.S.C. §1981 and Title VII of the Civil Rights Act of 1964, as amended, 42 U.S.C. §2000e *et seq.*[5] Respondents sought both injunctive relief and damages.

Without admitting the alleged discriminatory practice, Sumitomo moved to dismiss the complaint. Sumitomo's motion was based on two grounds: (1) discrimination on the basis of Japanese citizenship does not violate Title VII or §1981; and (2) Sumitomo's practices are protected under Article VIII(1) of the Friendship, Commerce and Navigation Treaty between the United States and Japan. The District Court dismissed the §1981 claim, holding that neither sex discrimination nor national origin discrimination is cognizable under that section. The court refused to dismiss the Title VII claims, however; it held that because Sumitomo is incorporated in the United States it is not covered by Article VIII(1) of the Treaty. The District Court then certified to the Court of Appeals under 28 U.S.C. §1292(b) the question of whether the terms of the Treaty exempted Sumitomo from the provisions of Title VII.

The Court of Appeals reversed in part. The court first examined the Treaty's language and its history and concluded that the Treaty parties intended Article VIII(1) to cover locally incorporated subsidiaries of foreign companies such as Sumitomo. The

court then held that the Treaty language does not insulate Sumitomo's executive employment practices from Title VII scrutiny. The court concluded that under certain conditions, Japanese citizenship could be a bona-fide occupational qualification for high-level employment with a Japanese-owned domestic corporation and that Sumitomo's practices might thus fit within a statutory exemption to Title VII. The court remanded for further proceedings.

We granted certiorari, — U.S. —, and we reverse.

★ ★ ★

Interpretation of the Friendship, Commerce and Navigation Treaty between Japan and the United States must, of course, begin with the language of the Treaty itself. The clear import of treaty language controls unless "application of the words of the treaty according to their obvious meaning effects a result inconsistent with the intent or expectations of its signatories." . . . Article VIII(1) of the Treaty provides in pertinent text:

> [C]ompanies of either Party shall be permitted to engage, within the territories of the other Party, accountants and other technical experts, executive personnel, attorneys, agents and other specialists of their choice. (Emphasis added.)

Clearly Article VIII(1) only applies to companies of one of the Treaty countries operating in the other country. Sumitomo contends that it is a company of Japan, and thus Article VIII(1) of the Treaty grants it very broad discretion to fill its executive, managerial and sales positions exclusively with male Japanese citizens.

Article VIII(1) does not define any of its terms; the definitional section of the Treaty is contained in Article XXII(3). Article XXII(3) provides:

As used in the present Treaty, the term "companies" means corporations, partnerships, companies, and other associations, whether or not with limited liability and whether or not for pecuniary profit. Companies constituted under the applicable laws and regulations within the territories of either Party *shall be deemed companies thereof* and shall have their juridical status recognized within the territories of the other Party. (Emphasis added.)

Sumitomo is "constituted under the applicable laws and regulations" of New York; based on Article XXII(3), it is a company of the United States, not a company of Japan. As a company of the United States operating in the United States, under the literal language of Article XXII(3) of the Treaty, Sumitomo cannot invoke the rights provided in Article VIII(I), which are available only to companies of Japan operating in the United States and to companies of the United States operating in Japan.

The Governments of Japan and the United States support this interpretation of the Treaty. Both the Ministry of Foreign Affairs of Japan and the United States Department of State agree that a United States corporation, even when wholly owned by a Japanese company is not a company of Japan under the Treaty and is therefore not covered by Article VIII(l). The Ministry of Foreign Affairs stated its position to the American Embassy in Tokyo with reference to this case:

> The Ministry of Foreign Affairs, as the Office of [the Government of Japan] responsible for the interpretation of the [Friendship, Commerce and Navigation] Treaty, reiterates its view concerning the application of Article 8, Paragraph 1 of the Treaty: For the purpose of the Treaty, companies constituted under the applicable laws . . . of either Party shall be deemed companies thereof and therefore, a subsidiary of a Japanese company incorporated under the laws of New York and is not covered by Article 8 Paragraph 1 when it operates in the United States.

The United States Department of State also maintains that Article VIII(1) rights do not apply to locally incorporated subsidiaries. Although not conclusive, the meaning attributed to Treaty provisions by the governmental agencies charged with their negotiation and enforcement is entitled to great weight.

Our role is limited to giving effect to the intent of the Treaty parties. When the parties to a treaty both agree as to the meaning of a treaty provision, and that interpretation follows from the clear treaty language, we must, absent extraordinarily strong contrary evidence, defer to that interpretation.

Sumitomo maintains that although the literal language of the Treaty supports the contrary interpretation, the intent of Japan and the United States was to cover subsidiaries regardless of their place of incorporation. We disagree.

Contrary to the view of the Court of Appeals and the claims of Sumitomo, adherence to the language of the Treaty would not "overlook the purpose of the Treaty." 638 F.2d, at 556. The Friendship, Commerce and Navigation Treaty between Japan and the United States is but one of a series of similar commercial agreements negotiated after World War II. The primary purpose of the corporation provisions of the Treaties was to give corporations of each signatory legal status in the territory of the other party, and to allow them to conduct business in the other country on a comparable basis with domestic firms. Although the United States negotiated commercial treaties as early as 1778, and thereafter throughout the 19th and 20th centuries, these early commercial treaties were primarily concerned with the trade and shipping rights of individuals. Until the 20th century, international commerce was much more an individual than a corporate affair.

As corporate involvement in international trade expanded in this century, old commercial treaties became outmoded. Because "corporation[s] can have no legal existence out of the boundaries of the sovereignty by which [they are] created," it became necessary to negotiate new treaties granting corporations legal status and the right to function abroad. A series of treaties negotiated before World War II gave corporations legal status and access to foreign courts, but it was not until the postwar Friendship, Commerce and Navigation Treaties that United States corporations gained the right to conduct business in other countries. The purpose of the treaties was not to give foreign corporations greater rights than domestic companies, but instead to assure them the right to conduct business on an equal basis without suffering discrimination based on their alienage.

The treaties accomplished their purpose by granting foreign corporations "national treatment" in most respects and by allowing foreign individuals and companies to form locally incorporated subsidiaries. These local subsidiaries are considered for purpose of the Treaty to be companies of the country in which they are incorporated; they are entitled to the rights, and subject to the responsibilities of other domestic corporations. By treating these subsidiaries as domestic companies, the purpose of the Treaty provisions—to assure that corporations of one treaty party have the right to conduct business within the territory of the other party without suffering discrimination as an alien entity—is fully met.

Nor can we agree with the Court of Appeals view that literal interpretation of the Treaty would create a "crazy-quilt pattern" in which the rights of branches of Japanese companies operating directly in the United States would be greatly superior to the right of locally incorporated subsidiaries of Japanese companies. The Court of Appeals maintained that if such subsidiaries were not considered companies of Japan under the Treaty, they, unlike branch offices of Japanese corporations, would be denied access to the legal system, would be left unprotected against unlawful entry and molestation, and would be unable to dispose of property, obtain patents, engage in importation and exportation, or make payments, remittances and transfers of funds. That this is not the case is obvious; the subsidiaries, as companies of the United States, would enjoy all of those rights and more. The only significant advantage branches may have over subsidiaries is that conferred by Article VIII(1).

We are persuaded, as both signatories agree, that under the literal language of Article XXII(3) of the Treaty, Sumitomo is a company of the United States; we discern no reason to depart from the plain meaning of the Treaty language. Accordingly, we hold that Sumitomo is not a company of Japan and is thus not covered by Article VIII(1) of the Treaty. The judgment of the Court of Appeals is reversed, and the case is remanded for further proceedings consistent with this opinion.

Reversed and remanded.

CASE FOLLOW-UP

You might review the material on section 1981 and Title VII in Chapter 15, but that is not the main purpose of inserting *Sumitomo* at this stage. U.S. investors are not the only ones confronted with unfamiliar legal codes in exotic and inscrutable lands.

In Chapter 3 of the text dealing with business ethics and corporate social responsibility, you encountered materials on ethical relativity, which is especially relevant for multinational corporations. Employment practices woven through the closely knit social fabric of Japan may not be appropriate for African, European, or American cultures, but are they morally wrong as, for example, murder and rape are wrong? What role do treaties play in the process of resolving such disputes?

EXHAUSTION OF LOCAL REMEDIES

In disputes between nations, the application of international laws and treaties is ordinarily unavoidable because the questions raised by the clash of sovereign interests are ineluctably international in scope. Business disputes, however, are not definitively international even when the companies involved in the dispute are domiciled in different countries. The doctrine of "exhaustion of local remedies," applied to private business relations, favors the application of local proceedings over international proceedings. The doctrine is typically adopted by countries through the ratification of a treaty requiring that companies exhaust local judicial remedies before seeking redress through international tribunals.

"Exhaustion doctrine" provides a means of balancing the local and international aspects of transnational business transactions. The philosophy behind the doctrine includes two main assumptions:

1. Disagreements between companies engaged in transnational business should be resolved by using local law, when the disagreement is essentially local in nature. For example, consider a U.S. company engaged in a manufacturing joint venture with a French company. If operations are located in France, legal issues related to manufacturing are essentially local issues rightfully covered by French law. For example, a contract dispute or a labor dispute arising from the manufacturing process will ordinarily be resolved under local laws without recourse to international tribunals.

2. When a dispute contains a genuine issue related to international laws, application of local laws will be inadequate, and the application of remedies from international law is appropriate. In other words, disputes between parties are not considered international in nature simply because the parties originate from differing sovereignties. Rather, international law applies when the controversy at issue has a fundamentally international dimension.

   For example, a labor dispute that includes questions of visa qualifications to work in the United States will ordinarily concern solely issues of U.S. immigration law. If, however, U.S. immigration policy toward workers from particular countries is circumscribed by international treaties with those countries, attempts to resolve a dispute by applying U.S. immigration law exclusively may be impossible. If application of the U.S. law is in conflict with enforcement of the international treaty, the dispute will be unresolvable when only local (U.S.) remedies are applied. The exhaustion doctrine recognizes that such conflicts are inherently international in scope and require the application of international laws.

CHOICE OF FORUM

Choice of forum (selection of the nation in which the court will be located) and choice of law (e.g., the law of France, Egypt, or Japan) are important clauses and thus are commonplace in international contracts. There is so much uncertainty regarding jurisdiction under conflict-of-law rules (classical private international law), and such divergent practices in selection of the applicable law, that all parties to an international business transaction will gain by specifying the forum and the law to be applied.

U.S. choice-of-forum policy was established in *The Bremen* v. *Zapata Off-Shore Co.*[6] A dispute arose when a U.S. corporation, Zapata, sued a German towing firm after a Louisiana-to-Italy voyage was cut short by storm damage to an oil rig in the Gulf of Mexico. The rig was towed back to Florida, and, ignoring the choice-of-forum clause requiring that any dispute be submitted to the High Court of Justice in London, Zapata sued in a U.S. district court. The Supreme Court vacated the refusal of the District Court and the Fifth Circuit Court of Appeals to enforce the clause.

As you peruse the next section, notice that the U.S. Supreme Court has built on *The Bremen* even to the extent of allowing the arbitration of antitrust issues in a Japanese forum. Some people might support the policy of allowing foreign tribunals to determine basic contract rights and duties because it involves a relatively straightforward interpretation of the terms that the parties have agreed on. But does that line of reasoning hold true for antitrust laws; securities law; and environmental, health, and safety laws? Give this some thought before you study *Mitsubishi Motors* v. *Soler Chrysler-Plymouth* in the next section.

INTERNATIONAL ARBITRATION

Arbitration is an alternative to judicial resolution of disputes. It makes possible greater speed and privacy, as well as reduced expense, compared with dispute resolution in the United States or another judicial system. A typical arbitration clause, this one suggested by the Japan Commonwealth Arbitration Association, would be constructed along the following lines:

> Arbitration: All disputes, controversies, or differences which may arise between seller and Buyer, out of or in relation to or in connection with this Contract, or for the breach thereof, shall be finally settled by arbitration in Osaka, Japan, in accordance with the Commercial Arbitration Rules of the Japan Commercial Arbitration Association. The award rendered by the arbitrator(s) shall be final and binding upon both parties. Governing Law: This Contract shall be governed in all respects by the laws of Japan.[7]

Such a clause played an important role in the case you are about to examine. Petitioner, a Japanese auto maker, entered a joint venture with Chrysler International, S.A. (CISA), a Swiss corporation. The aim of the joint venture was the distribution through Chrysler dealers outside the continental United States of vehicles manufactured by Mitsubishi. In 1979, Soler Chrysler-Plymouth, Inc., a Puerto Rican corporation, entered into a distributor agreement with CISA that provided for the sale by Soler of Mitsubishi-manufactured vehicles and into a sales procedure agreement with CISA and Mitsubishi providing for the direct sale of Mitsubishi products to Soler. Paragraph VI of the sales agreement provided for arbitration in Japan in accordance with the rules and regulations of the Japan Commercial Arbitration Association of disputes arising under the contract.

A dispute arose, and Mitsubishi sought a court order to compel arbitration. Soler counterclaimed against both Mitsubishi and CISA, alleging numerous breaches of the sales agreement as well as violations of the Sherman Act and several other laws. The district court ordered arbitration of the claims. On appeal, the court of appeals held the antitrust claim to be nonarbitrable because antitrust claims involve issues of important American public policy that should be decided by the courts. Mitsubishi appealed to the Supreme Court.

Mitsubishi Motors v. *Soler Chrysler-Plymouth*
473 U.S. 614 (1985)

BLACKMUN, JUSTICE

★ ★ ★

The first task of a court asked to compel arbitration of a dispute is to determine whether the parties agreed to arbitrate that dispute. The court is to make this determination by applying the "federal substantive law of arbitrability, applicable to any arbitration agreement within the coverage of the Act." And that body of law counsels

> that questions of arbitrability must be addressed with a healthy regard for the federal policy favoring arbitration. . . . The Arbitration Act establishes that, as a matter of federal law, any doubts concerning the scope of arbitrable issues should be resolved in favor of arbitration. . . .

That is not to say that all controversies implicating statutory rights are suitable for arbitration. . . . By agreeing to arbitrate a statutory claim, a party does not forego the substantive rights afforded by the statute; it only submits to their resolution in an arbitral, rather than a judicial, forum. It trades

the procedures and opportunity for review of the courtroom for the simplicity, informality, and expedition of arbitration. . . . Having made the bargain to arbitrate, the party should be held to it unless Congress itself has evinced an intention to preclude a waiver of judicial remedies for the statutory rights at issue. Nothing, in the meantime, prevents a party from excluding statutory claims from the scope of an agreement to arbitrate. . . .

We now turn to consider whether Soler's antitrust claims are nonarbitrable even though it has agreed to arbitrate them. . . . We conclude that concerns of international comity, respect for the capacities of foreign and transnational tribunals, and sensitivity to the need of the international commercial system for predictability in the resolution of disputes require that we enforce the parties' agreement, even assuming that a contrary result would be forthcoming in a domestic context.

. . . [T]his Court had recognized the utility of forum selection clauses in international transactions. In *The Bremen*, an American oil company, seeking to evade a contractual choice of an English forum and, by implication, English law, filed a suit in admiralty in a United States District Court against the German corporation which had contracted to tow its rig to a location in the Adriatic Sea. Notwithstanding the possibility that the English court would enforce provisions in the towage contract exculpating the German party which an American court would refuse to enforce, this Court gave effect to the choice-of-forum clause. It observed:

> The expansion of American business and industry will hardly be encouraged if, notwithstanding solemn contract, we insist on a parochial concept that all disputes must be resolved under our laws and in our courts. . . . We can-

not have trade and commerce in world markets and international waters exclusively on our terms, governed by our laws, and resolved in our courts. . . .

★ ★ ★

A parochial refusal by the courts of one country to enforce an international arbitration agreement would not only frustrate these purposes, but would invite unseemly and mutually destructive jockeying by the parties to secure tactical litigation advantages. . . . [It would] damage the fabric of international commerce and trade, and imperil the willingness and ability of businessmen to enter into intentional commercial agreements. . . .

The judgment [was for Mitsubishi]

CASE FOLLOW-UP

With regard to the concern expressed by some people that U.S. policy—antitrust, securities, environmental, health, or safety—should not be "abandoned" to foreign tribunals, the Court wrote as follows:

> [T]he national courts will have the opportunity at the award enforcement stage to ensure that the legitimate interest in the enforcement of the antitrust laws has been addressed. The Convention reserves to each signatory coun-

try the right to refuse enforcement of an award where the "recognition or enforcement of the award would be contrary to the public policy of that country."

This is an indication that national courts retain the power to examine such awards and make a determination whether or not they are in contravention of national policy. If an award does violate national policy, it would not be enforced in the United States.

CHOICE OF LAW

Where the parties to a transnational contract have stipulated a choice-of-law provision, the courts will usually enforce the agreement to apply the parties' chosen law. The rationale for such enforcement is the need for certainty so as to protect the expectations of the parties and for predictability of a certain result, no matter where the case is brought for litigation. The policy consideration reflected in this approach is that competent parties have a right to enter freely into contract in such a manner as would best promote their respective business interests, although obviously each state has a legitimate interest in regulating the conduct of business conducted within its borders or affecting its citizens. Thus, as a general rule, parties with capacity to contract are afforded wide latitude to determine the terms of their contract. Since lawyers would normally draft transnational contracts with the law of a particular jurisdiction in mind, it seems desirable to allow the parties to a transnational contract to specify in the contract the applicable law and to uphold the choice-of-law provisions in transnational contracts.[8]

The Uniform Commercial Code, adopted in almost all of the United States and governing the law of sales, provides, in Article 1, Section 105 (1), that "when a transaction bears a reasonable relation to this state and to another state or nation, the parties may agree that the law either of this state or of such other state or nation shall govern their rights and duties." For a sample choice-of-forum and choice-of-law clause, consider the following.

> This contract (is made and) shall be construed (interpreted) according to the laws of _(state)_, and any controversy arising under or in relation to this contract shall be settled . . . in _(place and state)_. The courts and authorities of _(state)_ shall have jurisdiction over all controversies that may arise under or in relation to this contract, especially with respect to the execution, interpretation, and compliance of this Agreement, the parties hereto waiving any other venue to which they might be entitled by virtue of domicile, habitual residence or otherwise.[9]

ENFORCEMENT OF FOREIGN JUDGMENTS

Obtaining a judgment in a foreign court is not the end of the matter. It must be enforced, and the successful litigant must anticipate that the validity of such a judgment may be questioned in another country where that litigant tries to seize the assets of the opposing party. In the United States at least, courts will presume foreign judgments are valid and give conclusive effect to them unless it is contrary to public policy. This presumption of validity is recognized by the policy of comity in American courts.

> "Comity," in the legal sense, is neither a matter of absolute obligation, on the one hand, nor of mere courtesy and good will, upon the other. But it is the recognition that one nation allows within its territory to the legislative, executive or judicial acts of another nation, having due regard both to international duty and convenience, and to the rights of its own citizens or of other persons who are under the protection of its laws. . . . Where there has been opportunity for a full and fair trial abroad before a court of competent jurisdiction, conducting the trial upon regular proceedings, after due citation or voluntary appearance of the defendant, and under a system of jurisprudence likely to secure an impartial administration of justice between the citizens of its own country and those of other countries, and there is nothing to show either prejudice in the court, or in the system of laws under which it was sitting, or fraud in procuring the judgment, or any other special reason why the comity of this nation should not allow it full effect, the merits of the case should not, in an action brought in this country upon the judgment, be tried afresh, as on a new trial or an appeal, upon the mere assertion of the party that the judgment was erroneous in law or in fact."[10]

NATIONALIZATION AND EXPROPRIATION

People in the United States are familiar with the concepts of "taking," "condemnation," and "eminent domain." Comparable action by the national governments of foreign countries resulting in the taking of U.S.-owned properties there or the properties of U.S. investors is spoken of as nationalization or expropriation.[11] A 1979 analysis by *Business International* evaluated the likelihood of such takeovers in fifty-seven countries and rated the United States fourteenth in being likely to expropriate foreign investments.

On the assumption that the host country is motivated by a legitimate public purpose and provides just compensation for the investor's loss, the taking or expropriation is in accord with international law. The absence of a legitimate public purpose and just compensation is a matter of "confiscation." Although the investor and the investor's nation may not be pleased with the development, Third World nations frequently espouse the Mexican position that the legality of public purpose is to be decided solely by the taking state.

A respected legal treatise, the Restatement (Second) of Foreign Relations Law of the U.S. (1965), defines *just compensation* as an adequate amount paid as soon as reasonable under the circumstances and, unless essential to the health and welfare of the taking nation, readily withdrawable from it in cash or convertible property according to principles of international law. Calculation of the investment's value does not always take place in the most cordial setting, but eventually it will (or should) proceed along lines of recognized accounting techniques: (a) depreciated book value, (b) sale value (this usually presupposes willing sellers and buyers, a condition not likely to be met in this context), (c) replacement value (favored by investors), and (d) going concern value. In the event that a U.S. national "accepts" less than fair value, the U.S. government reserves the right to pursue the remainder through appropriate international channels.

Beyond this, there are ways for U.S. citizens and business firms to protect against loss. Private insurance is one possibility. Another is the Overseas Private Investment Corporation. It provides a relatively inexpensive means of acquiring insurance against expropriation; inconvertibility of foreign earnings; and loss from war, revolution, and insurrection.

THE ACT OF STATE DOCTRINE

The act of state doctrine has its foundation in the respect that nations of the world have for the independence and integrity of other sovereign states. In accordance with this doctrine, courts of one nation will not question the legal validity of acts of a foreign government on its home soil. In the United States, this doctrine receives impetus from the constitutional concept of separation of powers.

> [The Act of State Doctrine] arises out of the basic relationships between branches of government in a system of separation of powers. It concerns the competency of dissimilar institutions to make and implement particular kinds of decisions in the area of international relations. The doctrine as formulated in past decisions expresses the strong

sense of the Judicial Branch that its engagement in the task of passing on the validity of foreign acts of state may hinder rather than further this country's pursuit of goals both for itself and for the community of nations as a whole in the international sphere.[12]

The act of state doctrine concerns itself with conduct or behavior of a sovereign (or a sovereign acting in conjunction with another person) within that sovereign's territory. In extending its protection to nonsovereigns acting with sovereigns, other nations simply regard judicial abstention based on the act of state doctrine as the wisest policy.

For example, in *Interamerican Refining Corp.* v. *Texaco Maracaibo*,[13] plaintiff alleged an antitrust violation on foreign soil. Specifically, Interamerican related that Texaco and others engaged in a boycott concocted to end its supply of Venezuelan crude oil. Defendant answered that it did not seek the boycott order, but that it was compelled to participate by Venezuelan authorities. The court concluded that a sovereign has the authority to regulate trade within its borders and that because businesses within that jurisdiction must obey such regulations, an antitrust suit cannot be based on acts directed by a foreign sovereign within that sovereign's territory.

If private firms are found to be merely "manipulating" instrumentalities of foreign governments, however, and this conduct is shown to be, for example, in restraint of foreign commerce of the United States, the act of state doctrine will not immunize that firm from judicial sanctions in this country. In *Timberlane Lumber Co.* v. *Bank of America*[14] the defendant was using specious claims in a Honduran court to foreclose plaintiff's entry into the timber exporting industry. Although the judicial process of a foreign nation is an act of state, abuse of that process by private litigants may result in the violation of U.S. law such as the Sherman Act. The Court of Appeals for the Ninth Circuit remanded the case to the district court. Even though the act of state doctrine was not an appropriate basis for dismissal, it instructed the lower court to make a determination whether federal jurisdiction existed over claims alleging illegal antitrust behavior in Honduras.

The test to be applied required a balance of three factors: (1) the effect or intended effect on the foreign commerce of the United States, (2) the type and magnitude of the alleged illegal behavior, and (3) the appropriateness of exercising extraterritorial jurisdiction in the light of considerations of international comity and fairness.

On a second dismissal of the complaint by the district court, Timberlane's appeal was unsuccessful for the following reasons:

> The potential for conflict with Honduran economic policy and commercial law is great. The effect on the foreign commerce of the United States is minimal. The evidence of intent to harm American commerce is altogether lacking. The foreseeability of the anticompetitive consequences of the allegedly illegal actions is slight. Most of the conduct that must be examined occurred abroad. The factors that favor jurisdiction are the citizenship of the parties and, to a slight extent, the enforcement effectiveness of United States law. We do not believe that this is enough to justify the exercise of federal jurisdiction over this case.
>
> In this case, we find no abuse of discretion in the district court's [dismissal of Timberlane's antitrust claims].[15]

However, when private parties "conspire" to influence the public policy of a foreign government so that discriminatory legislation or other action favorable to the conspirators is initiated, the nonsovereign parties will be shielded from condemnation in a U.S. court by the act of state doctrine.[16] In *Hunt* v. *Mobil Oil Corp.*,[17] the plaintiff alleged that the "Seven Sisters," the major oil companies in Libya, conspired to influence that government to nationalize Hunt's oil interests. The purpose, of course, was to protect the Libyan oil monopoly controlled by the conspirators. Hunt's claim was found to be nonjusticiable. The act of the sovereign state was presumed to be legal; therefore, the conduct of the Seven Sisters in encouraging, supporting, and influencing this legal act was immunized from judicial sanction in the United States.

SOVEREIGN IMMUNITY

Sovereign immunity and act of state are alike insofar as they shield certain conduct from judicial review in another land. When private-sector third parties (individuals and firms) are removed from the scene, the core concept emerges centerstage: "L'état, c'est moi." Historically, *sovereign immunity* stems from an age when nation-states were identified with their sovereigns; *act of state* is linked to separation of powers and comity or courtesy between nations. This picture changes substantially, however, as the sovereign leaves that lofty perch and "descends" into the marketplace. With regard to the trading or commercial activities of a nation, its claim to sovereign immunity is diminished or abandoned in the courts of other nations.

Chemical Natural Resources, Inc., a U.S. corporation, sued the Republic of Venezuela.[18] The plaintiffs had contracted with the Venezuelan government for the construction of power generation facilities, the power to be bought by the Venezuelan government. The latter canceled the contract and expropriated all installations involved. Efforts to obtain redress in Venezuelan courts failed. In autumn of 1963, a ship, the *S.S. Ciudad de Valencia*, operated by the Venezuelan government through a wholly owned company and engaged in commerce, arrived in Philadelphia. Chemical attempted, through a writ, to seize the vessel as part payment for damages claimed.

Venezuela challenged the jurisdiction of the Pennsylvania Court of Common Pleas, claiming that the vessel was not governmental property and that U.S. courts could not exercise jurisdiction. Venezuela also secured the intervention of the U.S. Department of State, which filed a "Suggestion of Immunity." The lower court denied that Venezuela was entitled to immunity. Venezuela then filed an appeal with the Pennsylvania Supreme Court to resolve the sovereign immunity issue.

The court pointed out that the established rule of law was that foreign sovereigns "duly recognized by the State Department, and their property" were not amenable without their consent to suit in the courts of the United States and that "a determination of Sovereign Immunity by the Executive branch . . . is . . . conclusive." Although the Department of State has abandoned the principle of absolute governmental immunity, it appears that the department has substituted a case-by-case foreign sovereign immunity policy. The Department of State will recognize or grant or suggest sovereign immunity in each case presented to it, depending on (a) the foreign and diplomatic relations that the United States has at that particular time with the other country and (b) the best interests of the United States at that particular time. In this case, the decision was for the Republic of Venezuela.

THE FOREIGN SOVEREIGN IMMUNITY ACT

In 1976, the United States adopted the Foreign Sovereign Immunities Act. Although limited in effectiveness by existing international agreements binding the United States at the time of the Act, it nevertheless advances two principal objectives:

1. Creation of a unitary rule for determining claims of sovereign immunity in the United States

2. Bringing the United States into conformity with the practice of virtually every other country

The Act codifies a rule of restrictive sovereign immunity; the immunity is lifted only insofar as the commercial activities of a foreign state are concerned. The reach of the term *foreign state* includes its political subdivisions, agencies, and instrumentalities as well. Commercial activity is taken to mean a regular course of conduct or a particular transaction. It is defined in reference to its nature or character, rather than to its purpose. For example, a foreign government may advance its national interest, prestige, or purpose through any of the following: purchase of arms; sale of a product or service; leasing, buying, constructing, or investing in buildings; and borrowing money to do so. But the purpose that motivates such conduct does not mask or disguise its essential commercial nature, so there would be no legal immunity from disputes arising out of any of these or other comparable transactions. The Act further provides that property of a foreign state used for commercial activity in the United States is not immune from attachment in aid of an execution of judgment of a state or federal court.

In the next case, the Supreme Court examines the conditions under which national activity may be considered commercial in nature and hence beyond the protection of sovereign immunity.

Republic of Argentina and Banco Central De La Republica Argentina, Petitioners, v. Weltover, Inc., et al.
112 S.Ct. 2160 (1992)

JUSTICE SCALIA DELIVERED THE OPINION OF THE COURT.
This case requires us to decide whether the Republic of Argentina's default on certain bonds issued as part of a plan to stabilize its currency was an act taken "in connection with a commercial activity" that had a "direct effect in the United States" so as to subject Argentina to suit in an American court under the Foreign Sovereign Immunities Act of 1976, 28 U.S.C. § 1602 *et seq.*

I

Since Argentina's currency is not one of the mediums of exchange accepted on the international market, Argentine businesses engaging in foreign transactions must pay in U.S. dollars or some other internationally accepted currency. In the recent past, it was difficult for Argentine borrowers to obtain such funds, principally because of the instability of the Argentine currency. To address these problems, petitioners, the Republic of Argentina and its central bank, Banco Central (collectively Argentina), in 1981 instituted a foreign exchange insurance contract program (FEIC), under which Argentina effectively agreed to assume the risk of currency depreciation in cross-border transactions involving Argentine borrowers. This was accomplished by Argentina's agreeing to sell to domestic borrowers, in exchange for a contractually predetermined amount of local currency, the necessary U.S. dollars to repay their foreign debts when they matured, irrespective of intervening devaluations.

Unfortunately, Argentina did not possess sufficient reserves of U.S. dollars to cover the FEIC contracts as they became due in 1982. The Argentine government thereupon adopted certain emergency measures, including refinancing of the FEIC-backed debts by issuing to the creditors government bonds. These bonds, called "Bonods," provide for payment of interest and principal in U.S. dollars; payment may be made through transfer on the London, Frankfurt, Zurich, or New York market, at the election of the creditor. Under this refinancing program, the foreign creditor had the option of either accepting the Bonods in satisfaction of the initial debt, thereby substituting the Argentine government for the private debtor, or maintaining the debtor/creditor relationship with the private borrower and accepting the Argentine government as guarantor.

When the Bonods began to mature in May 1986, Argentina concluded that it lacked sufficient foreign exchange to retire them. Pursuant to a Presidential Decree, Argentina unilaterally extended the time for payment, and offered bondholders substitute instruments as a means of rescheduling the debts. Respondents, two Panamanian corporations and a Swiss bank who hold, collectively, $1.3 million of Bonods, refused to accept the rescheduling, and insisted on full payment, specifying New York as the place where payment should be made. Argentina did not pay, and respondents then brought this breach of contract action in the United States District Court for the Southern District of New York, relying on the Foreign Sovereign Immunities Act of 1976 as the basis for jurisdiction. Petitioners moved to dismiss for lack of subject-matter jurisdiction, lack of personal jurisdiction, and forum non conveniens. The District Court denied these motions, 753 F.Supp. 1201 (S.D.N.Y. 1991), and the Court of Appeals affirmed, 941 F.2d 145 (CA2 1991). We granted Argentina's petition for certiorari, which challenged the Court of Appeals' determination that, under the Act, Argentina was not immune from the jurisdiction of the federal courts in this case. 502 U.S. —, 112 S.Ct. 858, 116 L.Ed.2d 766 (1992).

II

The Foreign Sovereign Immunities Act of 1976, 28 U.S.C. § 1602 *et seq.* (FSIA), establishes a comprehensive framework for determining whether a court in this country, state or federal, may exercise jurisdiction over a foreign state. Under the Act, a "foreign state shall be immune from the jurisdiction of the courts of the United States and of the States" unless one of several statutorily defined exceptions applies. §1604 (emphasis added). The FSIA thus provides the "sole basis" for obtaining jurisdiction over a foreign sovereign in the United States. See *Argentine Republic* v. *Amerada Hess Ship-*

ping Corp., 488 U.S. 428, 434-439, 109 S.Ct 683, 68S690, 102 LEd.2d 818 (1989). The most significant of the FSIA's exceptions—and the one at issue in this case—is the "commercial" exception of §1605(a)(2), which provides that a foreign state is not immune from suit in any case

> "in which the action is based upon a commercial activity carried on in the United States by the foreign state; or upon an act performed in the United States in connection with a commercial activity of the foreign state elsewhere; or upon an act outside the territory of the United States in connection with a commercial activity of the foreign state elsewhere and that act causes a direct effect in the United States." §1605(a)(2).

In the proceedings below, respondents relied only on the third clause of §1605(a)(2) to establish jurisdiction, 941 F.2d, at 149, and our analysis is therefore limited to considering whether this lawsuit is (1) "based . . . upon an act outside the territory of the United States"; (2) that was taken "in connection with a commercial activity" of Argentina outside this country; and (3) that "cause[d] a direct effect in the United States."[19]

* * *

Respondents and their *amicus,* the United States, contend that Argentina's issuance of, and continued liability under, the Bonods constitute a "commercial activity and that the extension of the payment schedules was taken in connection with" that activity. The latter point is obvious enough, and Argentina does not contest it; the key question is whether the activity is "commercial" under the FSIA.

The FSIA defines "commercial activity" to mean:

> "[E]ither a regular course of commercial conduct or a particular commercial transaction or act. The commercial character of an activity

shall be determined by reference to the nature of the course of conduct or particular transaction or act, rather than by reference to its purpose." 28 U.S.C. §1603(d).

This definition, however, leaves the critical term "commercial" largely undefined: The first sentence simply establishes that the commercial nature of an activity does not depend upon whether it is a single act or a regular course of conduct, and the second sentence merely specifies what element of the conduct determines commerciality (i.e., nature rather than purpose), but still without saying what "commercial" means. Fortunately, however, the FSIA was not written on a clean slate. As we have noted, see *Verlinden B.V.* v. *Central Bank of Nigeria,* 461 U.S. 480, 486-489, 103 S.Ct. 1962, 1967-1969, 76 L.Ed.2d 81 (1983), this Act (and the commercial exception in particular) largely codifies the so-called "restrictive" theory of foreign sovereign immunity first endorsed by the State Department in 1952. The meaning of "commercial" is the meaning generally attached to that term under the restrictive theory at the time the statute was enacted. . . .

This Court did not have occasion to discuss the scope or validity of the restrictive theory of sovereign immunity until our 1976 decision in *Alfred Dunhill of London, Inc.* v. *Republic of Cuba,* 425 U.S. 682, 96 S.Ct. 1854, 48 L.Ed.2d 301. Although the Court there was evenly divided on the question whether the "commercial" exception that applied in the foreign-sovereign-immunity context also limited the availability of an act-of-state defense, . . . there was little disagreement over the general scope of the exception. The plurality noted that, after the State Department endorsed the restrictive theory of foreign sovereign immunity in 1952, the lower courts consistently held that foreign sovereigns were not immune from the jurisdiction of American courts in cases "arising out of purely commercial transactions," . . . . The plurality further recognized that the distinction between state sovereign acts, on the one hand, and state commercial and private acts, on the other, was not entirely novel to American law. . . . The plurality stated that the restrictive theory of foreign sovereign immunity would not bar a suit based upon a foreign state's participation in the marketplace in the manner of a private citizen or corporation. . . . A foreign state engaging in "commercial" "activities do[es] not exercise powers peculiar to sovereigns"; rather, it "exercise[s] only those powers that can also be exercised by private citizens."

[W]hen a foreign government acts, not as regulator of a market, but in the manner of a private player within it, the foreign sovereign's actions are "commercial" within the meaning of the FSIA. Moreover, because the Act provides that the commercial character of an act is to be determined by reference to its "nature" rather than its "purpose," 28 U.S.C. §1603(d), the question is not whether the foreign government is acting with a profit motive or instead with the aim of fulfilling uniquely sovereign objectives. Rather, the issue is whether the particular actions that the foreign state performs (whatever the motive behind them) are the *type* of actions by which a private party engages in "trade and traffic or commerce," *Black's Law Dictionary* 270 (6th ed. 1990). Thus, a foreign government's issuance of regulations limiting foreign currency exchange is a sovereign activity, because such authoritative control of commerce cannot be exercised by a private party; whereas a contract to buy army boots or even bullets is a "commercial" activity, because private companies can similarly use sales contracts to acquire goods.

The commercial character of the Bonods is confirmed by the fact that they are in almost all respects garden-variety debt instruments: they may be held by private parties; they are negotiable and may be traded on the international market (except in Argentina); and they promise a future stream of cash income. We recognize that, prior to the enactment of the FSIA, there was authority suggesting that the issuance of public debt instruments did not constitute a commercial activity. *Victory Transport* 336 F.2d, at 360 (dicta). There is, however, nothing distinctive about the state's assumption of debt (other than perhaps its purpose) that would cause it always to be classified as *jure imperii*.

Because the FSIA has now clearly established that the "nature" governs, we perceive no basis for concluding that the issuance of debt should be treated as categorically different from other activities of foreign states.

Argentina points to the fact that the transactions in which the Bonods were issued did not have the ordinary commercial consequence of raising capital or financing acquisitions. Assuming for the sake of argument that this is not an example of judging the commerciality of a transaction by its purpose, the ready answer is that private parties regularly issue bonds, not just to raise capital or to finance purchases, but also to refinance debt. That is what Argentina did here: by virtue of the earlier FEIC contracts, Argentina was *already* obligated to supply the U.S. dollars needed to retire the FEIC-insured debts; the Bonods simply allowed Argentina to restructure its existing obligations. Argentina further asserts (without proof or even elaboration) that it "received consideration [for the Bonods] in no way commensurate with [their] value," Brief for Petitioners 22. Assuming that to be true, it makes no difference. Engaging in a commercial act does not require the receipt of fair value, or even compliance with the common-law requirements of consideration.

Argentina argues that the Bonods differ from ordinary debt instruments in that they "were created by the Argentine Government to fulfill its obligations under a foreign exchange program designed to address a domestic credit crisis, and as a component of a program designed to control that nation's critical shortage of foreign exchange." *Id.*, at 23–24. In this regard, Argentina relies heavily on *De Sanchez* v. *Banco Central de Nicaragua*, 770 F.2d 1385 (CA5 1985), in which the Fifth Circuit took the view that "[o]ften, the essence of an act is defined by its purpose"; that unless "we can inquire into the purposes of such acts, we cannot determine their nature"; and that, in light of its purpose to control its reserves of foreign currency, Nicaragua's refusal to honor a check it had issued to cover a private bank debt was a sovereign act entitled to immunity. *Id.*, at 1393. Indeed, Argentina asserts that the line between "nature" and "purpose" rests upon a "formalistic distinction [that] simply is neither useful nor warranted." Reply Brief for Petitioners 8. We think this line of argument is squarely fore-

closed by the language of the FSIA. However difficult it may be in some cases to separate "purpose" (i.e., the reason why the foreign state engages in the activity) from "nature" (i.e., the outward form of the conduct that the foreign state performs or agrees to perform), see *De Sanchez*, *supra*, at 1393, the statute unmistakably commands that to be done. 28 U.S.C. §1603(d). We agree with the Court of Appeals, see 941 F.2d, at 151, that it is irrelevant why Argentina participated in the bond market in the manner of a private actor; it matters only that it did so.

We conclude that Argentina's issuance of the Bonods was a "commercial activity" under the FSIA; that its rescheduling of the maturity dates on those instruments was taken in connection with that commercial activity and had a "direct effect" in the United States; and that the District Court therefore properly asserted jurisdiction, under the FSIA, over the breach-of-contract claim based on that rescheduling. Accordingly, the judgment of the Court of Appeal is

Affirmed.

CASE FOLLOW-UP

Weltover tells us that foreign sovereignties cannot hide behind the shield of sovereign immunity when they engage in activities that are essentially commercial in nature. This holding is particularly important to companies that do business in countries that have substantial or partial nationalization of industry. Even as some nations move towards increased privatization of industry, sovereignties continue to hold ownership interests in transitional joint ventures. Indeed, in a number of countries, foreign investment is limited to partnerships with nationalized host country co-venturers. This means that governmental ownership of industry is still a

reality throughout much of the world despite apparent movement toward increased private ownership. The FSIA's restrictive approach to immunity, as embodied in *Weltover*, increases the security of doing business with state-owned companies. To the extent that the activities of those companies are commercial in nature, they are considered under the FSIA to be as accountable under contract and tort law as any privately owned entity. Still, businesspersons considering doing business abroad must assess the risk that may be created by political climates and conditions of instability.

FOREIGN INVESTMENT CODES

Many nations have qualms about being "bought out" by investors from foreign countries. The reason, of course, is the possibility of being exploited as some mere client-colony that has its natural resources plundered for the advantage of others. Even the United States, with its not unblemished record in this regard, displayed some concern about a reversal of this process when oil sheiks began buying up large chunks of domestic firms and farmland.

Foreign investment is a two-way street, however. The investor will expect to receive as high a rate of return (or higher) as would be earned on reasonably available alternative investments, while the developing or underdeveloped nation is benefiting from an infusion of scarce resources—capital, technology, managerial expertise. The challenge for the developing nation, then, is to shape an investment policy that will offer inducements to foreign capital, ensure a degree of stability that will put to rest questions of confiscation, and at the same time make certain that its natural resources are not looted and that its businesses are not mere branches of foreign firms.

It is a common practice among nations of the world to adopt statutes that effectuate the objectives we have just mentioned. Not every nation labels such statutes the *foreign investment code*, but some of them do, and we are using the phrase simply to identify this concept. Because each nation will draft a code to meet its particular needs, there is no commonality in provisions of these numerous statutes. This fact simply underlines the importance of consulting attorneys in those nations who are experienced with such matters.

FOREIGN CORRUPT PRACTICES ACT OF 1977

In response to revelations of foreign corruption involving major U.S. corporations, Congress passed the Foreign Corrupt Practices Act of 1977, which imposed strict accounting standards and antibribery prohibitions on American businesses. The scandals caused embarrassment to the nation and jeopardized American foreign interests abroad, and the Act itself provoked much controversy. As an amendment to the Securities Exchange Act of 1934, the 1977 Act required issuers of stock—that is, publicly held corporations—to "make and keep books, records, and accounts, which, in reasonable detail, accurately and fairly reflect the transactions . . . of the issuer" and to "devise and maintain a system of internal accounting controls sufficient to provide reasonable assurances" of management control over the firm's assets. These accounting requirements established a "paper trail" that led to corporate accountability. In this sense, the accounting provisions serve as a mechanism for detecting illicit payments to foreign government officials, the other major focus of the Act. Under the antibribery provisions, the Act prohibited payment by an issuer or a domestic concern to any foreign official, except foreign employees "whose duties are essentially ministerial or clerical," for the purpose of obtaining or retaining business. Likewise, the Act proscribed such payments to a third party while "knowing or having reason to know" that the money would be used for the above purpose. Under the original Act, both civil and criminal sanctions attach to violations of the accounting and antibribery provisions.

THE 1988 AMENDMENTS

The 1988 amendments significantly modify the 1977 Act. Changes in the accounting provisions (a) limit criminal liability to knowing falsifications of accounting records, (b) define "reasonable detail" and "reasonable assurances" using a *prudent person standard*, and (c) require the U.S. firm to exercise good faith influence on its foreign subsidiary (one in which it owns 50 percent or less voting power) to ensure the subsidiary's compliance with the accounting provisions.

Amendments to the antibribery provisions replace the controversial "knowing or having reason to know" standard with the requirement that U.S. firms have actual knowledge that a third person may bribe a foreign official or consciously disregard circumstances that would alert a reasonable person to such a transaction. Further, these amendments (a) define prohibited payments as those used to induce a foreign official to violate legal duties, (b) clarify the types of "facilitating payments" that are allowed, and (c) give an affirmative defense for payments that are lawful in the foreign country and payments that constitute reasonable and bona fide expenditures directly related to business conducted in that country.

Under the 1988 Act, conviction of the company is no longer necessary before employees or agents who violate the Act may be prosecuted. Other changes include increased criminal and civil sanctions, new civil subpoena authority in the Department of Justice, and a procedure under which the attorney general may issue guidelines regarding conduct that may violate the Act. Finally, the amendments require the President to pursue an international agreement to ban bribery abroad.

CLARIFICATION OF THE ACCOUNTING PROVISIONS OF THE ACT

Criticism of the accounting provisions of the Foreign Corrupt Practices Act of 1977 revolved around the lack of clarity and lack of certainty caused by the standards. Under the provisions of that Act, liability for one inaccurate record was possible. For business managers, uncertainty as to the interpretation of the provisions resulted in a proliferation of documentation and increased accounting costs. In fact, concern over enforcement of technical and insignificant errors in records led to overcompliance without necessarily advancing the purposes of the statute.

To address these increasing costs, the 1988 amendments to the accounting standards of the Act are significant. The original Act required "reasonable detail" in record keeping and "reasonable assurances" from internal accounting controls, but legislators failed to delineate the level of precision required under these provisions. Businesspeople were then unable to discern what would be determined reasonable in the eye of the Securities and Exchange Commission (SEC). As a result, the new provisions define "reasonable detail" and "reasonable assurances" as such "level of detail and degree of assurances as would satisfy prudent officials in the conduct of their own affairs." Likewise, the 1988 amendments limit criminal liability to those who "knowingly" circumvent or fail to implement a system of internal accounting controls or "knowingly" falsify books or records.

CHANGE IN THE STANDARD OF CULPABILITY FOR THIRD-PARTY PAYMENTS

Like the accounting standards, the "reason to know" provision imposing liability for third-party payments caused considerable anxiety among business executives. The difficulty lies in assuring oneself that some employees or agents somewhere are not making illegal payments abroad. Under the 1977 Act, critics claim that U.S. firms are asked to determine with certainty that a third person will not engage in illicit conduct, risking criminal prosecution if their judgment about that person is wrong. Congress was strongly influenced by testimony that U.S. citizens should not be held strictly liable for the actions of foreign agents.

Perhaps the strongest criticism of the "reason to know" standard is that this standard is not a proper basis for criminal liability carrying serious felony penalties. The "reason to know" standard has no analogue in domestic bribery law, meaning that liability could exist under the 1977 Act on the basis of payments to foreign officials where no liability would exist if the payments were made to U.S. officials.

The 1988 amendments employed a knowledge standard in which knowledge includes a conscious purpose to avoid learning the truth about the payment, but they deleted the "reckless disregard" element. Because the knowledge standard usually includes the conscious disregard or "head in the sand" scenario, congressional concerns over this problem are largely alleviated by the standard adopted. The committee explained that the knowledge standard encompassed actual knowledge, as well as evidence of a conscious disregard or conscious ignorance of known circumstances that would alert a reasonable person to probable violations. For further clarity, the committee expressly stated that mere negligence is not a basis for liability.

CLARIFICATION OF "FACILITATING PAYMENTS" EXCEPTION

Under the original Act, payments to foreign employees whose duties were "ministerial or clerical" were not prohibited. American executives viewed these payments, often called "facilitating" or "grease" payments, as necessary to conduct business in a foreign country. Because one could not be certain whether a foreign official's duties are purely ministerial or clerical, this exception alleviated very little uncertainty in the enforcement of the Act. The 1977 Act nevertheless required a determination that the foreign official's duties were, in fact, ministerial. The U.S. firm risked criminal liability if the determination was erroneous.

To eliminate this ambiguity, changes to the Act shift the focus from the person to whom the payment was made to the purpose for which the payment was made. Specifically, the inquiry is whether the purpose of the payment falls within those permitted and whether such a payment is customary in that foreign country to facilitate or expedite performance. To accomplish this clarification, the amendments create an exception for "routine governmental action" as long as payments for this type of expediting activity are not prohibited. Under the new provisions, "routine governmental action" includes obtaining permits, processing government papers, providing police protection and mail pickup, providing utility service, loading and unloading cargo, and performing "actions of a similar nature." Still, the amendments clearly state that such routine action does not include any decision by a foreign official involving the rewarding of new business or the continuation of business.

CONCLUSION

In this chapter, we explored international law and business transactions emphasizing the principal concepts and institutions that give it structure. We examined the problems involved in choosing a forum and choosing the national law to be applied in that forum. These efforts raised other problems—for example, the enforcement of foreign judgments. Throughout these discussions, we suggested solutions, such as the utilization of international arbitration, an alternative that is quicker, more private, and less expensive than judicial resolution of disputes.

We discussed the act of state doctrine, a concept whereby the international community of nations will show respect and restraint toward the sovereign conduct of other nations while that conduct takes place on its own soil. We found, however, that sovereign immunity, a related concept that means a nation cannot be sued in foreign courts unless it grants permission, has been restricted. For commercial and trading purposes, sovereign immunity has been restricted to the point that nations may be treated just as business people and firms are treated.

One circumstance of commercial reality we cannot ignore is that large corporations conduct much of their business in foreign countries. When they do, they take with them their beliefs and their methods of operation. A conflict between the way things are done in U.S. society and in foreign societies is inevitable. Which belief or method is right or best? The answer is seldom clear. People can learn from past experience, however, and from disciplined reflection and discussion on the nature of this tension.

U.S. law has attempted to reach many firms doing business in foreign countries by compelling them to keep accurate records of all transactions and to disclose these transactions to the SEC and to the public. This solution arguably has a negative impact on the ability of U.S. firms to compete in the international marketplace. In 1988, the Foreign Corrupt Practices Act was amended to reduce many of these concerns.

In the final analysis, the reader is left with the challenge of trying to find a rational approach to the problems presented in this chapter. Discerning the difference between a conflict of interest and conflicting interests is a start. If you identify those values to which you are committed, values that would predominate in the case of conflict, at least you bring clarity to your own motives and send an unmistakable message to those with whom you do business: I advance some principles to be fundamentally, objectively true and not subject to negotiation.

REVIEW QUESTIONS AND PROBLEMS

1. Three of the four principal institutions of the European Economic Community are the Commission, the Council of Ministries, and the Court of Justice. What is the other institution, and what is its role in passing Community legislation?

2. How does the Treaty of Rome creating the European Common Market differ from most other treaties?

3. Both the U.S. government and the government of Japan interpreted the treaty to mean that Sumitomo was a corporation of the United States, not of Japan. What effect did the Court give to this interpretation, and why?

4. What is the difference between a "choice of forum" and a "choice of law" clause in an international business contract?

5. What reasons did the Supreme Court give for enforcing the "choice of forum" clause in *The Bremen* v. *Zapata*? In *Mitsubishi Motors* v. *Soler Chrysler-Plymouth*?

6. What is "comity," and what role does it play in the enforcement of foreign judgments?

7. What are some of the principal attributes of international arbitration as opposed to judicial resolution of disputes?

8. Under what conditions will nationalization or expropriation of a foreign investor's assets be legal according to international law?

ENDNOTES

1. Von Glahn, *Law Among Nations* 3 (1981).

2. We thank Mark Baker, associate professor of business law, University of Texas at Austin, for his contribution of this classification.

3. *Business Week*, Dec. 12, 1988, p. 48.

4. General trading companies have been a unique fixture of the Japanese economy since the Meiji era. These companies each market large numbers of Japanese products, typically those of smaller concerns, and also have a large role in the importation of raw materials and manufactured products to Japan. In addition, the trading companies play a large part in financing Japan's international trade. The largest trading companies—including Sumitomo's parent company—in a typical year account for over 50 percent of Japanese exports and over 60 percent of imports to Japan. See Krause & Sekiguchi, "Japan and the World Economy," in H. Patrick & H. Rosovsky, *Asia's New Giant: How the Japanese Economy Works* 383, 389-397 (1976).

5. Prior to bringing this suit, respondents each filed timely complaints with the Equal Employment Opportunity Commission. The EEOC issued "right to sue" letters to the respondents on October 27, 1977. This suit was filed on November 21, 1977, well within the statutory ninety-day period allowed for filing suits after receipt of an EEOC notice of right to sue. 42 USC, §2000e-5(f)(1).

6. 407 U.S. 1 (1972).

7. Wilson, *International Business Transactions* 344.

8. Nanda, *The Law of Transactional Business Transactions* 8–13 (1981).

9. *Id.* at 8–22.

10. *Hilton* v. *Guyot*, 159 U.S. 113 (1895).

11. Wilson, *supra* note 7, at 242–243.

12. *Banco Nacional de Cuba* v. *Sabbatino* 376 U.S. 398, 421, 423 (1964).

13. 30 F. Supp. 1291 (D. Del. 1970).

14. 549 F.2d 597 (9th Cir. 1976).

15. F.2d 1378 (9th Cir. 1984).

16. Judicial restraint comparable to this is embodied in domestic policy of the United States and finds its roots in the First Amendment right to "petition" or, within limits, to influence congressional policy. *Eastern Railroad Presidents Conference* v. *Noerr Motor Freight, Inc.*, 365 U.S. 127 (1961) .

17. 550 F.2d 68 (2nd Cir. 1977).

18. *Chemical Natural Resources, Inc.* v. *Republic of Venezuela*, 420 Pa. 134, cert. denied 87 S.Ct. 50 (1966).

19. It is indisputable that both the Republic of Argentina and Banco Central are "foreign states" within the mean of FSIA. See 28 U.S.C. §1603(a), (b) ("[F]oreign state" includes certain "agenc[ies] or instrument-alit[ies] of a foreign state").

The Constitution of the United States of America

We the People of the United States, in Order to form a more perfect Union, establish Justice, insure domestic Tranquility, provide for the common defence, promote the general Welfare, and secure the Blessings of Liberty to ourselves and our Posterity, do ordain and establish this Constitution for the United States of America.

Article I

Section 1. All legislative Powers herein granted shall be vested in a Congress of the United States, which shall consist of a Senate and House of Representatives.

Section 2. The House of Representatives shall be composed of Members chosen every second Year by the People of the several States, and the Electors in each State shall have the Qualifications requisite for Electors of the most numerous Branch of the State Legislature.

No Person shall be a Representative who shall not have attained to the Age of twenty five Years, and been seven Years a Citizen of the United States, and who shall not, when elected, be an Inhabitant of that State in which he shall be chosen.

Representatives and direct Taxes shall be apportioned among the several States which may be included within this Union, according to their respective Numbers, which shall be determined by adding to the whole Number of free Persons, including those bound to Service for a Term of Years, and excluding Indians not taxed, three fifths of all other Persons. The actual Enumeration shall be made within three Years after the first Meeting of the Congress of the United States, and within every subsequent Term of ten Years, in such Manner as they shall by Law direct. The Number of Representatives shall not exceed one for every thirty Thousand, but each State shall have at least one Representative; and until such enumeration shall be made, the State of New Hampshire shall be entitled to chuse three, Massachusetts eight, Rhode Island and Providence Plantations one, Connecticut five, New-York six, New Jersey four, Pennsylvania eight, Delaware one, Maryland six, Virginia ten, North Carolina five, South Carolina five, and Georgia three.

When vacancies happen in the Representation from any State, the Executive Authority thereof shall issue Writs of Election to fill such Vacancies.

The House of Representatives shall chuse their Speaker and other Officers; and shall have the sole Power of Impeachment.

Section 3. The Senate of the United States shall be composed of two Senators from each State, chosen by the Legislature thereof, for six Years; and each Senator shall have one Vote.

Immediately after they shall be assembled in Consequence of the first Election, they shall be divided as equally as may be into three Classes. The Seats of the Senators of the first Class shall be vacated at the Expiration of the second Year, of the second Class at the Expiration of the fourth Year, and of the third Class at the Expiration of the sixth Year, so that one third may be chosen every second Year; and if Vacancies happen by Resignation, or otherwise, during the Recess of the Legislature of any State, the Executive thereof may make temporary Appointments until the next Meeting of the Legislature, which shall then fill such Vacancies.

No Person shall be a Senator who shall not have attained to the Age of thirty Years, and been nine Years a Citizen of the United States, and who shall not, when elected, be an Inhabitant of that State for which he shall be chosen.

The Vice President of the United States shall be President of the Senate, but shall have no Vote, unless they be equally divided.

The Senate shall chuse their other Officers, and also a President pro tempore, in the Absence of the Vice President, or when he shall exercise the Office of President of the United States.

The Senate shall have the sole Power to try all Impeachments. When sitting for that Purpose, they shall be on Oath or Affirmation. When the President of the United States is tried the Chief Justice shall preside: And no Person shall be convicted without the Concurrence of two thirds of the Members present.

Judgment in Cases of Impeachment shall not extend further than to removal from Office, and disqualification to hold and enjoy any Office of honor, Trust or Profit under the United States: but the Party convicted shall nevertheless be liable and subject to Indictment, Trial, Judgment and Punishment, according to Law.

Section 4. The Times, Places and Manner of holding Elections for Senators and Representatives, shall be prescribed in each State by the Legislature thereof; but the Congress may at any time by law make or alter such Regulations, except as to the Places of chusing Senators.

The Congress shall assemble at least once in every Year, and such Meeting shall be on the first Monday in December, unless they shall by Law appoint a different Day.

Section 5. Each House shall be the Judge of the Elections, Returns and Qualifications of its own Members, and a Majority of each shall constitute a Quorum to do Business; but a smaller Number may adjourn from day to day and may be authorized to compel the Attendance of absent Members, in such Manner, and under such Penalties as each House may provide.

Each House may determine the Rules of its Proceedings, punish its Members for disorderly Behaviour, and, with the Concurrence of two thirds, expel a Member.

Each House shall keep a Journal of its Proceedings, and from time to time publish the same, excepting such Parts as may in their Judgment require Secrecy; and the Yeas and Nays of the Members of either House on any question shall, at the Desire of one fifth of those Present, be entered on the Journal.

Neither House, during the Session of

Congress, shall, without the Consent of the other, adjourn for more than three days, nor to any other Place than that in which the two Houses shall be sitting.

Section 6. The Senators and Representatives shall receive a Compensation for their Services, to be ascertained by Law, and paid out of the Treasury of the United States. They shall in all Cases, except Treason, Felony and Breach of the Peace, be privileged from Arrest during their Attendance at the Session of their respective Houses, and in going to and returning from the same; and for any Speech or Debate in either House, they shall not be questioned in any other Place.

No Senator or Representative shall, during the Time for which he was elected, be appointed to any civil Office under the Authority of the United States, which shall have been created, or the Emoluments whereof shall have been encreased during such time; and no Person holding any Office under the United States, shall be a Member of either House during his Continuance in Office.

Section 7. All Bills for raising Revenue shall originate in the House of Representatives; but the Senate may propose or concur with amendments as on other Bills.

Every Bill which shall have passed the House of Representatives and the Senate, shall, before it become a Law, be presented to the President of the United States; If he approve he shall sign it, but if not he shall return it, with his Objections to that House in which it shall have originated, who shall enter the Objections at large on their Journal, and proceed to reconsider it. If after such Reconsideration two thirds of that House shall agree to pass the Bill, it shall be sent, together with the Objections, to the other House, by which it shall likewise be reconsidered, and if approved by two thirds

of that House, it shall become a Law. But in all such Cases the Votes of both Houses shall be determined by Yeas and Nays, and the Names of the Persons voting for and against the Bill shall be entered on the Journal of each House respectively. If any Bill shall not be returned by the President within ten Days (Sunday excepted) after it shall have been presented to him, the Same shall be a Law, in like Manner as if he had signed it, unless the Congress by their Adjournment prevent its Return, in which Case it shall not be a Law.

Every Order, Resolution, or Vote to which the Concurrence of the Senate and House of Representatives may be necessary (except on a question of Adjournment) shall be presented to the President of the United States; and before the Same shall take Effect, shall be approved by him, or being disapproved by him, shall be repassed by two thirds of the Senate and House of Representatives, according to the Rules and Limitations prescribed in the Case of a Bill.

Section 8. The Congress shall have Power To lay and collect Taxes, Duties, Imposts and Excises, to pay the Debts and provide for the common Defence and general Welfare of the United States; but all Duties, Imposts and Excises shall be uniform throughout the United States;

To borrow Money on the credit of the United States;

To regulate Commerce with foreign Nations, and among the several States, and with the Indian Tribes;

To establish an uniform Rule of Naturalization, and uniform Laws on the subject of Bankruptcies throughout the United States;

To coin Money, regulate the Value thereof, and of foreign Coin, and fix the Standard of Weights and Measures;

To provide for the Punishment of counterfeiting the Securities and current Coin of the United States;

To establish Post Offices and post Roads;

To promote the Progress of Science and useful Arts, by securing for limited Times to Authors and Inventors the exclusive Right to their respective Writings and Discoveries;

To constitute Tribunals inferior to the supreme Court;

To define and punish Piracies and Felonies committed on the high Seas, and Offences against the Law of Nations;

To declare War, grant Letters of Marque and Reprisal, and make Rules concerning Captures on Land and Water;

To raise and support Armies, but no Appropriation of Money to that Use shall be for a longer Term than two Years;

To provide and maintain a Navy;

To make Rules for the Government and Regulation of the land and naval Forces;

To provide for calling forth the Militia to execute the Laws of the Union, suppress Insurrections and repel Invasions;

To provide for organizing, arming, and disciplining, the Militia, and for governing such Part of them as may be employed in the Service of the United States, reserving to the States respectively, the Appointment of the Officers, and the Authority of training the Militia according to the discipline prescribed by Congress;

To exercise exclusive Legislation in all Cases whatsoever, over such District (not exceeding ten Miles square) as may, by Cession of particular States, and the Acceptance of Congress, become the Seat of the Government of the United States, and to exercise like Authority over all Places purchased by the Consent of the Legislature of the State in which the Same shall be, for the Erection of Ports, Magazines, Arsenals, dock-Yards, and other needful Buildings;—And

To make all Laws which shall be necessary and proper for carrying into Execution the foregoing Powers, and all other Powers vested by this Constitution in the Government of the United States, or in any Department or Officer thereof.

Section 9. The Migration or Importation of such Persons as any of the States now existing shall think proper to admit, shall not be prohibited by the Congress prior to the Year one thousand eight hundred and eight, but a Tax or duty may be imposed on such Importation, not exceeding ten dollars for each person.

The Privilege of the Writ of Habeas Corpus shall not be suspended, unless when in Cases of Rebellion or Invasion the public Safety may require it.

No Bill of Attainder or ex post facto Law shall be passed.

No Capitation, or other direct, Tax shall be laid, unless in Proportion to the Census or Enumeration herein before directed to be taken.

No Tax or Duty shall be laid on Articles exported from any State.

No Preference shall be given by any Regulation of Commerce or Revenue to the Ports of one State over those of another; nor shall Vessels bound to, or from, one State, be obliged to enter, clear or pay Duties in another.

No Money shall be drawn from the Treasury, but in Consequence of Appropriations made by Law; and a regular Statement and Account of the Receipts and Expenditures of all public Money shall be published from time to time.

No Title of Nobility shall be granted by the United States: And no Person holding any Office of Profit or Trust under them, shall, without the Consent of the Congress, accept any present, Emolument, Office, or Title, of any kind whatever, from any King, Prince, or foreign State.

Section 10. No State shall enter into any Treaty, Alliance, or Confederation; grant

Letters of Marque and Reprisal; coin Money; emit Bills of Credit; make any Thing but gold and silver Coin a Tender in Payment of Debts; pass any Bill of Attainder, ex post facto Law, or Law impairing the Obligation of Contracts, or grant any Title of Nobility.

No State shall, without the Consent of the Congress, lay any Imposts or Duties in Imports or Exports, except what may be absolutely necessary for executing its inspection Laws: and the net-Produce of all Duties and Imposts, laid by any State on Imports or Exports, shall be for the Use of the Treasury of the United States; and all such Laws shall be subject to the Revision and Controul of the Congress.

No State shall, without the Consent of Congress, lay any Duty of Tonnage, keep Troops, or Ships of War in time of Peace, enter into any Agreement or Compact with another State, or with a foreign Power, or engage in War, unless actually invaded, or in such imminent Danger as will not admit of delay.

Article II

Section 1. The executive Power shall be vested in a President of the United States of America. He shall hold his Office during the Term of four Years, and, together with the Vice President, chosen for the same Term, be elected, as follows

Each State shall appoint, in such Manner as the Legislature thereof may direct, a Number of Electors, equal to the whole Number of Senators and Representatives to which the State may be entitled in the Congress: but no Senator or Representative, or Person holding an Office of Trust or Profit under the United States, shall be appointed an Elector.

The Electors shall meet in their respective States, and vote by Ballot for two Persons, of whom one at least shall not be an Inhabitant of the same State with themselves. And they shall make a List of all the Persons voted for, and of the Number of Votes for each; which List they shall sign and certify, and transmit sealed to the Seat of the Government of the United States, directed to the President of the Senate. The President of the Senate shall, in the Presence of the Senate and House of Representatives, open all the Certificates, and the Votes shall then be counted. The Person having the greatest Number of Votes shall be the President, if such Number be a Majority of the whole Number of Electors appointed; and if there be more than one who have such Majority, and have an equal Number of Votes, then the House of Representatives shall immediately chuse by Ballot one of them for President; and if no Person have a Majority, then from the five highest on the List the said House shall in like Manner chuse the President. But in chusing the President, the Votes shall be taken by States, the Representative from each State having one Vote; a quorum for this Purpose shall consist of a Member or Members from two thirds of the States, and a Majority of all the States shall be necessary to a Choice. In every Case, after the Choice of the President, the Person having the greatest Number of Votes of the Electors shall be the Vice President. But if there should remain two or more who have equal Votes, the Senate shall chuse from them by Ballot the Vice President.

The Congress may determine the Time of chusing the Electors, and the Day on which they shall give their Votes; which Day shall be the same throughout the United States.

No Person except a natural born Citizen, or a Citizen of the United States, at the time of the Adoption of this Constitution, shall be eligible to the Office of President; neither shall any Person be eligible to that Office who shall not have attained to the Age of thirty five Years, and been fourteen years a Resident within the United States.

In Case of the Removal of the President from Office, or of his Death, Resignation, or Inability to discharge the Powers and Duties of the said Office, the Same shall devolve on the Vice President, and the Congress may by Law provide for the Case of Removal, Death, Resignation or Inability, both of the President and Vice President, declaring what Officer shall then act as President, and such Officer shall act accordingly, until the Disability be removed, or a President shall be elected.

The President shall, at stated Times, receive for his Services, a Compensation, which shall neither be encreased nor diminished during the Period for which he shall have been elected, and he shall not receive within that Period any other Emolument from the United States, or any of them.

Before he enter on the Execution of his Office, he shall take the following Oath or Affirmation:—"I do solemnly swear (or affirm) that I will faithfully execute the Office of President of the United States, and will to the best of my Ability, preserve, protect and defend the Constitution of the United States."

Section 2. The President shall be Commander in Chief of the Army and Navy of the United States, and of the Militia of the several States, when called into the actual Service of the United States; he may require the Opinion, in writing, of the principal Officer in each of the executive Departments, upon any Subject relating to the Duties of their respective Offices, and he shall have Power to grant Reprieves and Pardons for Offences against the United States, except in Cases of Impeachment.

He shall have Power, by and with the Advice and Consent of the Senate, to make Treaties, provided two thirds of the Senators present concur; and he shall nominate, and by and with the Advice and Consent of the Senate, shall appoint Ambassadors, other public Ministers and Consuls, Judges of the supreme Court, and all other Officers of the United States, whose Appointments are not herein otherwise provided for, and which shall be established by Law: but the Congress may by Law vest the Appointment of such inferior Officers, as they think proper, in the President alone, in the Courts of Law, or in the Heads of Departments.

The President shall have Power to fill up all Vacancies that may happen during the Recess of the Senate, by granting Commissions which shall expire at the End of their next Session.

Section 3. He shall from time to time give to the Congress Information of the State of the Union, and recommend to their Consideration such Measures as he shall judge necessary and expedient; he may, on extraordinary Occasions, convene both Houses, or either of them, and in Case of Disagreement between them, with Respect to the Time of Adjournment, he may adjourn them to such Time as he shall think proper; he shall receive Ambassadors and other public Ministers; he shall take Care that the Laws be faithfully executed, and shall Commission all the Officers of the United States.

Section 4. The President, Vice President and all Civil Officers of the United States, shall be removed from Office on Impeachment for, and Conviction of, Treason, Bribery, or other high Crimes and Misdemeanors.

Article III

Section 1. The judicial Power of the United States, shall be vested in one supreme Court, and in such inferior Courts as the Congress may from time to time ordain and establish. The Judges, both of the supreme and inferior Courts, shall hold their Offices during good Behaviour, and shall, at stated Times, receive for their Services, a Compensation, which shall not be diminished during their Continuance in Office.

Section 2. The judicial Power shall extend to all Cases, in Law and Equity, arising under this Constitution, the Laws of the United States, and Treaties made, or which shall be made, under their Authority;—to all Cases affecting Ambassadors, other public Ministers and Consuls;—to all Cases of admiralty and maritime Jurisdiction;—to Controversies to which the United States shall be a Party;—to Controversies between two or more States;—between a State and Citizens of another State;—between Citizens of different States;—between Citizens of the same State claiming Lands under Grants of different States, and between a State, or the Citizens thereof, and foreign States, Citizens or Subjects.

In all Cases affecting Ambassadors, other public Ministers and Consuls, and those in which a State shall be Party, the Supreme Court shall have original Jurisdiction. In all the other Cases before mentioned, the supreme Court shall have appellate Jurisdiction, both as to Law and Pact, with such Exceptions, and under such Regulations as the Congress shall make.

The Trial of all Crimes, except in Cases of Impeachment, shall be by Jury; and such Trial shall be held in the State where the said Crimes shall have been committed; but when not committed within any State, the Trial shall be at such Place or Places as the Congress may by Law have directed.

Section 3. Treason against the United States, shall consist only in levying War against them, or in adhering to their Enemies, giving them Aid and Comfort. No Person shall be convicted of Treason unless on the Testimony of two Witnesses to the same overt Act, or on Confession in open Court.

The Congress shall have Power to declare the Punishment of Treason, but no Attainder of Treason shall work Corruption of Blood, or Forfeiture except during the Life of the Person attainted.

Article IV

Section 1. Full Faith and Credit shall be given in each State to the public Acts, Records, and judicial Proceedings of every other State. And the Congress may by general Laws prescribe the Manner in which such Acts, Records and Proceedings shall be proved, and the Effect thereof.

Section 2. The Citizens of each State shall be entitled to all Privileges and Immunities of Citizens in the several States.

A Person charged in any State with Treason, Felony, or other Crime, who shall flee from Justice, and be found in another State, shall on Demand of the executive Authority of the State from which he fled, be delivered up, to be removed to the State having Jurisdiction of the Crime.

No Person held to Service or Labour in one State, under the Laws thereof, escaping into another, shall, in Consequence of any Law or Regulation therein, be discharged from such Service or Labour, but shall be delivered up on Claim of the Party to whom such Service or Labour may be due.

Section 3. New States may be admitted by the Congress into this Union; but no new State shall be formed or erected within the Jurisdiction of any other State; nor any State be formed by the Junction of two or more States, or Parts of States, without the Consent of the Legislatures of the States concerned as well as of the Congress.

The Congress shall have Power to dispose of and make all needful Rules and Regulations respecting the Territory or other Property belonging to the United States; and nothing in this Constitution shall be so construed as to Prejudice any Claims of the United States, or of any particular State.

Section 4. The United States shall guarantee to every State in this Union a Republican Form of Government, and shall protect each of them against Invasion; and on Application of the Legislature, or of the Executive (when the Legislature cannot be convened) against domestic Violence.

Article V

The Congress, whenever two thirds of both Houses shall deem it necessary, shall propose Amendments to this Constitution, or, on the Application of the Legislature of two thirds of the several States, shall call a Convention for proposing Amendments, which, in either Case, shall be valid to all Intents and Purposes, as Part of this Constitution, when ratified by the Legislatures of three fourths of the several States, or by Conventions in three fourths thereof, as the one or the other Mode of Ratification may be proposed by the Congress; Provided that no Amendment which may be made prior to the Year One thousand eight hundred and eight shall in any Manner affect the first and fourth Clauses in the Ninth Section of the first Article; and that no State, without its Consent, shall be deprived of its equal Suffrage in the Senate.

Article VI

All Debts contracted and Engagements entered into, before the Adoption of this Constitution, shall be as valid against the United States under this Constitution, as under the Confederation.

This Constitution, and the Laws of the United States which shall be made in Pursuance thereof; and all Treaties made, or which shall be made, under the Authority of the United States, shall be the supreme Law of the Land; and the judges in every State shall be bound thereby, any Thing in the Constitution or Laws of any State to the Contrary notwithstanding.

The Senators and Representatives before mentioned, and the Members of the several State Legislatures, and all executive and judicial Officers, both of the United States and of the several States, shall be bound by Oath or Affirmation, to support this Constitution; but no religious Test shall ever be required as a Qualification to any Office or public Trust under the United States.

Article VII

The Ratification of the Conventions of nine States, shall be sufficient for the Establishment of this Constitution between the States so ratifying the Same.

Amendment I [1791]

Congress shall make no law respecting an establishment of religion, or prohibiting the free exercise thereof; or abridging the freedom of speech, or of the press; or the right of the people peaceably to assemble, and to petition the Government for a redress of grievances.

Amendment II [1791]

A well regulated Militia, being necessary to the security of a free State, the right of the people to keep and bear Arms, shall not be infringed.

Amendment III [1791]

No Soldier shall, in time of peace be quartered in any house, without the consent of the Owner, nor in time of war, but in a manner to be prescribed by law.

Amendment IV [1791]

The right of the people to be secure in their persons, houses, papers, and effects, against unreasonable searches and seizures, shall not be violated, and no Warrants shall issue, but upon probable cause, supported by Oath or affirmation, and particularly describing the place to be searched, and the persons or things to be seized.

Amendment V [1791]

No person shall be held to answer for a capital, or otherwise infamous crime, unless on a presentment or indictment of a Grand Jury, except in cases arising in the land or naval forces, or in the Militia, when in actual service in time of War or public danger; nor shall any person be subject for the same offence to be twice put in jeopardy of life or limb; nor shall be compelled in any criminal case to be a witness against himself, nor be deprived of life, liberty, or property, without due process of law; nor shall private property be taken for public use, without just compensation.

Amendment VI [1791]

In all criminal prosecutions, the accused shall enjoy the right to a speedy and public trial, by an impartial jury of the State and district wherein the crime shall have been committed, which district shall have been previously ascertained by law, and to be informed of the nature and cause of the accusation; to be confronted with the witnesses against him; to have compulsory process for obtaining Witnesses in his favor, and to have the Assistance of Counsel for his defence.

Amendment VII [1791]

In Suits at common law, where the value in controversy shall exceed twenty dollars, the right of trial by jury shall be preserved, and no fact tried by a jury, shall be otherwise re-examined in any Court of the United States, than according to the rules of the common law.

Amendment VIII [1791]

Excessive bail shall not be required nor excessive fines imposed, nor cruel and unusual punishments inflicted.

Amendment IX [1791]

The enumeration in the Constitution, of certain rights, shall not be construed to deny or disparage others retained by the people.

Amendment X [1791]

The powers not delegated to the United States by the Constitution, nor prohibited by it to the States, are reserved to the States respectively, or to the people.

Amendment XI [1798]

The Judicial power of the United States shall not be construed to extend to any suit in law or equity, commenced or prosecuted against one of the United States by Citizens of another State, or by Citizens or Subjects of any Foreign State.

Amendment XII [1804]

The Electors shall meet in their respective states and vote by ballot for President and Vice-President, one of whom, at least, shall not be an inhabitant of the same state with themselves; they shall name in their ballots the person voted for as President, and in distinct ballots the person voted for as Vice-President, and they shall make distinct lists of all persons voted for as President, and of all persons voted for as Vice-President, and of the number of votes for each, which lists they shall sign and certify, and transmit sealed to the seat of the government of the United States, directed to the President of the Senate;—The President of the Senate shall, in the presence of the Senate and House of Representatives, open all the certificates and the votes shall then be counted;—The person having the greatest number of votes for President, shall be the President, if such number be a majority of the whole number of Electors appointed; and if no person have such majority, then from the persons having the highest numbers not exceeding three on the list of those voted for as President, the House of Representatives shall choose immediately, by ballot, the President. But in choosing the President, the votes shall be taken by states, the representation from each state having one vote; a quorum for this purpose shall consist of a member or members from two thirds of the states, and a majority of all the states shall be necessary to a choice. And if the House of Representatives shall not choose a President whenever the right of choice shall devolve upon them, before the fourth day of March next following, then the Vice-President shall act as President, as in the case of the death or other constitutional disability of the President—The person having the greatest number of votes as Vice-President, shall be the Vice-President, if such number be a majority of the whole number of Electors appointed, and if no person have a majority, then from the two highest numbers on the list, the Senate shall choose the Vice President; a quorum for the purpose shall consist of two-thirds of the whole number of Senators, and a majority of the whole number shall be necessary to a choice. But no person constitutionally ineligible to the office of President shall be eligible to that of Vice President of the United States.

Amendment XIII [1865]

Section 1. Neither slavery nor involuntary servitude, except as a punishment for crime whereof the party shall have been duly convicted, shall exist within the United States, or any place subject to their jurisdiction.

Section 2. Congress shall have power to enforce this article by appropriate legislation.

Amendment XIV [1868]

Section 1. All persons born or naturalized in the United States and subject to the jurisdiction thereof, are citizens of the United States and of the State wherein they reside. No State shall make or enforce any law which shall abridge the privileges or immunities of citizens of the United States; nor shall any State deprive any person of life, liberty, or property, without due process of law; nor deny to any person within its jurisdiction the equal protection of the laws.

Section 2. Representatives shall be apportioned among the several States according to their respective numbers, counting the whole number of persons in each State, excluding Indians not taxed. But when the right to vote at any election for the choice of electors for President and Vice President of the United States, Representatives in Congress, the Executive and Judicial officers of a State, or the members of the Legislature thereof, is denied to any of the male inhabitants of such State, being twenty-one years of age, and citizens of the United States, or in any way abridged, except for participation in rebellion, or other crime, the basis of representation therein shall be reduced in the proportion which the number of such male citizens shall bear to the whole number of male citizens twenty-one years of age in such State.

Section 3. No person shall be a Senator or Representative in Congress, or elector of President and Vice President, or hold any office, civil or military, under the United States, or under any State, who, having previously taken an oath, as a member of Congress, or as an officer of the United States, or as a member of any State legislature, or as an executive or judicial officer of any State, to support the Constitution of the United States, shall have engaged in insurrection or rebellion against the same, or given aid or comfort to the enemies thereof. But Congress may by a vote of two-thirds of each House, remove such disability.

Section 4. The validity of the public debt of the United States, authorized by law, including debts incurred for payment of pensions and bounties for services in suppressing insurrection or rebellion, shall not be questioned. But neither the United States nor any State shall assume or pay any debt or obligation incurred in aid of insurrection or rebellion against the United States, or any claim for the loss or emancipation of any slave; but all such debts, obligations and claims shall be held illegal and void.

Section 5. The Congress shall have power to enforce, by appropriate legislation, the provisions of this article.

Amendment XV [1870]

Section 1. The right of citizens of the United States to vote shall not be denied or abridged by the United States or by any State on account of race, color, or previous condition of servitude.

Section 2. The Congress shall have power to enforce this article by appropriate legislation.

Amendment XVI [1913]

The Congress shall have power to lay and collect taxes on income, from whatever source derived, without apportionment among the several States, and without regard to any census or enumeration.

Amendment XVII [1913]

The Senate of the United States shall be composed of two Senators from each State, elected by the people thereof, for six years; and each Senator shall have one vote. The electors in each State shall have the qualifications requisite for electors of the most numerous branch of the State legislatures.

When vacancies happen in the representation of any State in the Senate, the executive authority of such State shall issue writs of election to fill such vacancies: *Provided,* That the legislature of any State may empower the executive thereof to make temporary appointments until the people fill the vacancies by election as the legislature may direct.

This amendment shall not be so construed as to affect the election or term of any Senator chosen before it becomes valid as part of the Constitution.

Amendment XVIII [1919]

Section 1. After one year from the ratification of this article the manufacture, sale, or transportation of intoxicating liquors within, the importation thereof into, or the exportation thereof from the United States and all territory subject to the jurisdiction thereof for beverage purposes is hereby prohibited.

Section 2. The Congress and the several States shall have concurrent power to enforce this article by appropriate legislation.

Section 3. This article shall be inoperative unless it shall have been ratified as an amendment to the Constitution by the legislatures of the several States, as provided in the Constitution, within seven years from the date of the submission hereof to the States by the Congress.

Amendment XIX [1920]

The right of citizens of the United States to vote shall not be denied or abridged by the United States or by any State on account of sex.

Congress shall have power to enforce this

article by appropriate legislation.

Amendment XX [1933]

Section 1. The terms of the President and Vice President shall end at noon on the 20th day of January, and the terms of Senators and Representatives at noon on the 3rd day of January, of the years in which such terms would have ended if this article had not been ratified; and the terms of their successors shall then begin.

Section 2. The Congress shall assemble at least once in every year, and such meeting shall begin at noon on the 3rd day of January, unless they shall by law appoint a different day.

Section 3. If, at the time fixed for the beginning of the term of the President, the President elect shall have died, the Vice President elect shall become President. If a President shall not have been chosen before the time fixed for the beginning of his term, or if the President elect shall have failed to qualify, then the Vice President elect shall act as President until a President shall have qualified; and the Congress may by law provide for the case wherein neither a President elect nor a Vice President elect shall have qualified, declaring who shall then act as President, or the manner in which one who is to act shall be selected, and such person shall act accordingly until a President or Vice President shall have qualified.

Section 4. The Congress may by law provide for the case of the death of any of the persons from whom the House of Representatives may choose a President whenever the right of choice shall have devolved upon them, and for the case of the death of any of the persons from whom the Senate may choose a Vice President whenever the right of choice shall have devolved upon them.

Section 5. Sections 1 and 2 shall take effect on the 15th day of October following the ratification of this article.

Section 6. This article shall be inoperative unless it shall have been ratified as an amendment to the Constitution by the legislatures of three-fourths of the several States within seven years from the date of its submission.

Amendment XXI [1933]

Section 1. The eighteenth article of amendment to the Constitution of the United States is hereby repealed.

Section 2. The transportation or importation into any State, Territory, or possession of the United States for delivery or use therein of intoxicating liquors, in violation of the laws thereof, is hereby prohibited.

Section 3. This article shall be inoperative unless it shall have been ratified as an amendment to the Constitution by conventions in the several States, as provided in the Constitution, within seven years from the date of the submission hereof to the States by the Congress.

Amendment XXII [1951]

Section 1. No person shall be elected to the office of the President more than twice, and no person who has held the office of President, or acted as President, for more than two years of a term to which some other person was elected President shall be elected to the office of the President more than once. But this Article shall not apply to any person holding the office of President when this Article was proposed by the Congress, and shall not prevent any person who may be holding the office of President, or acting as President, during the term within which this Article becomes operative from holding the office of President or acting as President during the remainder of such term.

Section 2. This article shall be inoperative unless it shall have been ratified as an amendment to the Constitution by the legislatures of three-fourths of the several States within seven years from the date of its submission to the States by the Congress.

Amendment XXIII [1961]

Section 1. The District constituting the seat of Government of the United States shall appoint in such manner as the Congress may direct:

A number of electors of President and Vice President equal to the whole number of Senators and Representatives in Congress to which the District would be entitled if it were a State, but in no event more than the least populous State; they shall be in addition to those appointed by the States, but they shall be considered, for the purposes of the election of President and Vice President, to be electors appointed by a State; and they shall meet in the District and perform such duties as provided by the twelfth article of amendment.

Section 2. The Congress shall have power to enforce this article by appropriate legislation.

Amendment XXIV [1964]

Section 1. The right of citizens of the United States to vote in any primary or other election for President or Vice President, for electors for President or Vice President, or for Senator or Representative in Congress, shall not be denied or abridged by the United States or any State by reason of failure to pay any poll tax or other.

Section 2. The Congress shall have power to enforce this article by appropriate legislation.

Amendment XXV [1967]

Section 1. In case of the removal of the President from office or of his death or resignation, the Vice President shall become President.

Section 2. Whenever there is a vacancy in the office of the Vice President, the President shall nominate a Vice President who shall take office upon confirmation by a majority vote of both Houses of Congress.

Section 3. Whenever the President transmits to the President pro tempore of the Senate and the Speaker of the House of Representatives his written declaration that he is unable to discharge the powers and duties of his office, and until he transmits to them a written declaration to the contrary, such powers and duties shall be discharged by the Vice President as Acting President.

Section 4. Whenever the Vice President and a majority of either the principal officers of the executive departments or of such other body as Congress may by law provide, transmit to the President pro tempore of the Senate and the Speaker of the House of Representatives their written declaration that the President is unable to discharge the powers and duties of his office, the Vice President shall immediately assume the powers and duties of the office as Acting President.

Thereafter, when the President transmits to the President pro tempore of the Senate and the Speaker of the House of Representatives his written declaration that no inability exists, he shall resume the powers and duties of his office unless the Vice President and a majority of either the principal officers of the executive department or of such other body as Congress may by law provide, transmit within four days to the President pro tempore of the Senate and the Speaker of the House of Representatives their written declaration that the President is unable to discharge the powers and duties of his office. Thereupon Congress shall decide the issue, assembling within forty-eight hours for that purpose if not in session. If the Congress, within twenty-one days after receipt of the latter written declaration, or, if Congress is not in session, within twenty-one days after Congress is required to assemble, determine by two thirds vote of both Houses that the President is unable to discharge the powers and duties of his office, the Vice President shall continue to discharge the same as Acting President; otherwise, the President shall resume the powers and duties of his office.

Amendment XXVI [1971]

Section 1. The right of citizens of the United States, who are eighteen years of age or older, to vote shall not be denied or abridged by the United States or by any State on account of age.

Section 2. The Congress shall have power to enforce this article by appropriate legislation.

The Sherman Act (Excerpts)

Section 1. Trusts, etc., in Restraint of Trade Illegal; Penalty

Every contract, combination in the form of trust or otherwise, or conspiracy, in restraint of trade or commerce among the several States, or with foreign nations, is declared to be illegal. Every person who shall make any contract or engage in any combination or conspiracy hereby declared to be illegal shall be deemed guilty of a felony, and, on conviction thereof, shall be punished by fine not exceeding one million dollars if a corporation, or, if any other person, one hundred thousand dollars or by imprisonment not exceeding three years, or by both said punishments, in the discretion of the court.

Section 2. Monopolizing Trade a Felony; Penalty

Every person who shall monopolize, or attempt to monopolize, or combine or conspire with any other person or persons, to monopolize any part of the trade or commerce among the several States, or with foreign nations, shall be deemed guilty of a felony, and, on conviction thereof, shall be punished by fine not exceeding one million dollars if a corporation, or, if any other person, one hundred thousand dollars or by imprisonment not exceeding three years, or by both said punishments, in the discretion of the court.

The Clayton Act (Excerpts)

Section 3. Lease, Sale, etc. on Condition Not To Use Competitor's Goods

It shall be unlawful for any person engaged in commerce, in the course of such commerce, to lease or make a sale or contract for sale of goods, wares, merchandise, machinery, supplies, or other commodities, whether patented or unpatented, for use, consumption, or resale within the United States or any Territory thereof or the District of Columbia or any insular possession or other place under the jurisdiction of the United States, or fix a price charged therefor, or discount from, or rebate upon, such price, on the condition, agreement, or understanding that the lessee or purchaser thereof shall not use or deal in the goods, wares, merchandise, machinery, supplies, or other commodities of a competitor or competitors of the lessor or seller, where the effect of such lease, sale, or contract for sale or such condition, agreement, or understanding may be to substantially lessen competition or tend to create a monopoly in any line of commerce.

Section 4. Suits by Persons Injured; Amount of Recovery; Prejudgment Interest

Any person who shall be injured in his business or property by reason of anything forbidden in the antitrust laws may sue therefor in any district court of the United States in the district in which the defendant resides or is found or has an agent, without respect to the amount in controversy, and shall recover threefold the damages by him sustained, and the cost of suit, including a reasonable attorney's fee. The court may award under this section, pursuant to a motion by such person promptly made, simple interest on actual damages for the period beginning on the date of service of such person's pleading setting forth a claim under the antitrust laws and ending on the date of judgment, or for any shorter period therein, if the court finds that the award of such interest for such period is just in the circumstances. In determining whether an award of interest under this section for any period is just in the circumstances, the court shall consider only—

(1) whether such person or the opposing party, or either party's representative, made motions or asserted claims or defenses so lacking in merit as to show that such party or representative acted intentionally for delay, or otherwise acted in bad faith;

(2) whether, in the course of the action involved, such person or the opposing party, or either party's representative, violated any

applicable rule, statute, or court order providing for sanctions for dilatory behavior or otherwise providing for expeditious proceedings; and

(3) whether such person or the opposing party, or either party's representative, engaged in conduct primarily for the purpose of delaying the litigation or increasing the cost thereof.

Section 4B. Limitation of Actions

Any action to enforce any cause of action under sections 4 or 4A (omitted) of this title shall be forever barred unless commenced within four years after the cause of action accrued. No cause of action barred under existing law on the effective date of this section and sections 15a and 16 of this title shall be revived by said sections.

Section 4C. Actions by State Attorneys General — Parens Patriae; Monetary Relief; Damages; Prejudgment Interest

(a)(1) Any attorney general of a State may bring a civil action in the name of such State, as parens patriae on behalf of natural persons residing in such State, in any district court of the United States having jurisdiction of the defendant, to secure monetary relief as provided in this section for injury sustained by such natural persons to their property by reason of any violation of Sections 1 to 7 of this title. The court shall exclude from the amount of monetary relief awarded in such action any amount of monetary relief (A) which duplicates amounts which have been awarded for the same injury, or (B) which is properly allocable to (i) natural persons who have excluded their claims pursuant to subsection (b)(2) of this section, and (ii) any business entity.

(2) The court shall award the State as monetary relief threefold the total damage sustained as described in paragraph (1) of this subsection, and the cost of suit, including a reasonable attorney's fee. The court may award under this paragraph, pursuant to motion by such State promptly made, simple interest on the total damage for the period beginning on the date of service of such State's pleading setting forth a claim under the antitrust laws and ending on the date of judgment, or for any shorter period therein, if the court finds that the award of such interest for such period is just in the circumstances. In determining whether an award of interest under this paragraph for any period is just in the circumstances, the court shall consider only—

(A) whether such State or the opposing party, or either party's representative, made motions or asserted claims or defenses so lacking in merit as to show that such party or representative acted intentionally for delay or otherwise acted in bad faith;

(B) whether, in the course of the action involved such State or the opposing party, or either party's representative, violated any applicable rule, statute, or court order providing for sanctions for dilatory behavior or otherwise providing for expeditious proceedings; and

(C) whether such State or the opposing party, or either party's representative, engaged in conduct primarily for the purpose of delaying the litigation or increasing the cost thereof.

Notice; Exclusion Election; Final Judgment. (b)(1) In any action brought under subsection (a)(1) of this section, the State attorney general shall, at such times, in such manner, and with such content as the court may direct, cause notice thereof to be given by publication. If the court finds that notice given solely by publication would deny due process of law to any person or persons, the court may direct further notice to such person or persons according to the circumstances of the case.

(2) Any person on whose behalf an action is brought under subsection (a)(1) of this section may elect to exclude from adjudication the portion of the State claim for monetary relief attributable to him by filing notice of such election with the court within such time as specified in the notice given pursuant to paragraph (1) of this subsection.

(3) The final judgment in an action under subsection (a)(1) of this section shall be res judicata as to any claim under section 5 of this title by any person on behalf of whom such action was brought and who fails to give such notice within the period specified in the notice given pursuant to paragraph (1) of this subsection.

Dismissal or Compromise of Action. (c) An action under subsection (a)(1) of this section shall not be dismissed or compromised without the approval of the court, and notice of any proposed dismissal or compromise shall be given in such manner as the court directs.

Attorney's Fees. (d) In any action under subsection (a) of this section—

1. the amount of the plaintiffs' attorney's fee, if any, shall be determined by the court; and
2. the court may, in its discretion, award a reasonable attorney's fee to a prevailing defendant upon a finding that the State attorney general has acted in bad faith, vexatiously, wantonly, or for oppressive reasons.

Section 5. Judgment in Favor of Government as Evidence; Suspension of Limitations

(a) A final judgment or decree heretofore or hereafter rendered in any civil or criminal proceeding brought by or on behalf of the United States under the antitrust laws to the effect that a defendant has violated said laws

shall be prima facie evidence against such defendant in any action or proceeding brought by any other party against such defendant under said laws or by the United States under section 15a of this title, as to all matters respecting which said judgment or decree would be an estoppel as between the parties thereto: *Provided,* That this section shall not apply to consent judgments or decrees entered before any testimony has been taken or to judgments or decrees entered in actions under section 15a of this title.

(b) Whenever any civil or criminal proceeding is instituted by the United States to prevent, restrain, or punish violations of any of the antitrust laws, but not including an action under section 15a of this title, the running of the statute of limitations in respect of every private right of action arising under said laws and based in whole or in part on any matter complained of in said proceeding shall be suspended during the pendency thereof and for one year thereafter: *Provided, however,* That whenever the running of the statute of limitations in respect of a cause of action arising under section 15 of this title is suspended hereunder, any action to enforce such cause of action shall be forever barred unless commenced either within the period of suspension or within four years after the cause of action accrued.

Section 6. Antitrust Laws Not Applicable to Labor Organizations

That the labor of a human being is not a commodity or article of commerce. Nothing contained in the antitrust laws shall be construed to forbid the existence and operation of labor, agricultural or horticultural organizations, instituted for the purposes of mutual help, and not having capital stock or conducted for profit, or to forbid or restrain individual members of such organizations from lawfully carrying out the legitimate objects thereof; nor shall such organizations, or the members thereof, be held or construed to be illegal combinations or conspiracies in restraint of trade, under the antitrust laws.

Section 7. Acquisition by One Corporation of Stock of Another

No corporation engaged in commerce shall acquire, directly or indirectly, the whole or any part of the stock or other share capital and no corporation subject: to the jurisdiction of the Federal Trade Commission shall acquire the whole or any part of the assets of another corporation in any section of the country, the effects of such acquisition may be substantially to lessen competition, or to tend to create a monopoly.

No corporation shall acquire, directly or indirectly, the whole or any part of the stock or other share capital and no corporation subject to the jurisdiction of the Federal Trade Commission shall acquire the whole or any part of the assets of one or more corporations engaged in commerce, where in any line of commerce in any section of the country, the effect of such acquisition, of such stocks or assets, or of the use of such stock by the voting or granting of proxies or otherwise, may be substantially to lessen competition, or to tend to create a monopoly.

This section shall not apply to corporations purchasing such stock solely for investment and not using the same by voting or otherwise to bring about, or in attempting to bring about, the substantial lessening of competition. Nor shall anything contained in this section prevent a corporation engaged in commerce from causing the formation of subsidiary corporations for the actual carrying on of their immediate lawful business, or the natural and legitimate branches or extensions thereof, or from owning and holding all or a part of the stock of such subsidiary corporations, when the effect of such formation is not to substantially lessen competition.

Nor shall anything herein contained be construed to prohibit any common carrier subject to the laws to regulate commerce from aiding in the construction of branches or short lines so located as to become feeders to the main line of the company so aiding in which construction or from acquiring or owning all or any part of the stock of such branch lines, nor to prevent any such common carrier from acquiring and owning all or any part of the stock of a branch or short line constructed by an independent company where there is no substantial competition between the company owning the branch line so constructed and the company owning the main line acquiring the property or an interest therein, nor to prevent such common carrier from extending any of its lines through the medium of the acquisition of stock or otherwise of any other common carrier where there is no substantial competition between the company extending its line and the company whose stock, property, or an interest therein is so acquired.

Nothing contained in this section shall be held to affect or impair any right heretofore legally acquired: *Provided,* That nothing in this section shall be held or construed to authorize or make lawful anything heretofore prohibited or made illegal by the antitrust laws, nor to exempt any person from the penal provisions thereof or the civil remedies therein provided.

Nothing contained in this section shall apply to transactions duly consummated pursuant to authority given by the Civil Aeronautics Board, Federal Communications Commission, Federal Power Commission, Interstate Commerce Commission, the Securities and Exchange Commission in the exercise of its jurisdiction under section 79j of this title, the United States Maritime Commission, or the Secretary of Agriculture under any statutory provision vesting such power in such Commission, Secretary, or Board.

Section 8. *Interlocking Directorates and Officers*

No private banker or director, officer, or employee of any member bank of the Federal Reserve System or any branch thereof shall be at the same time a director, officer, or employee of any other bank, banking association, savings bank, or trust company organized under the National Bank Act or organized under the laws of any State or of the District of Columbia, or any branch thereof, except that the Board of Governors of the Federal Reserve System may by regulation permit such service as a director, officer, or employee of not more than one other such institution or branch thereof; but the foregoing prohibition shall not apply in the case of any one or more of the following or any branch thereof:

1. A bank, banking association, savings bank, or trust company, more than 90 per centum of the stock of which is owned directly or indirectly by the United States or by any corporation of which the United States directly or indirectly owns more than 90 per centum of the stock.
2. A bank, banking association, savings bank, or trust company which has been placed formally in liquidation or which is in the hands of a receiver, conservator, or other official exercising similar functions.
3. A corporation, principally engaged in international or foreign banking or banking in a dependency or insular possession of the United States which has entered into an agreement with the Board of Governors of the Federal Reserve System pursuant to sections 601 to 604a of Title 12.
4. A bank, banking association, savings bank, or trust company, more than 50 per centum of the common stock of which is owned directly or indirectly by persons who own directly or indirectly more than 50 per centum of the common stock of such member bank.
5. A bank, banking association, savings bank, or trust company not located and having no branch in the same city, town, or village as that in which such member bank or any branch thereof is located, or in any city, town, or village contiguous or adjacent thereto.
6. A bank, banking association, savings bank, or trust company not engaged in a class or classes of business in which such member bank is engaged.
7. A mutual savings bank having no capital stock.

Until February 1, 1939, nothing in this section shall prohibit any director, officer, or employee of any member bank of the Federal Reserve System, or any branch thereof, who is lawfully serving at the same time as a private banker or as a director, officer, or employee of any other bank, banking association, savings bank, or trust company, or any branch thereof, on August 23, 1935, from continuing such service.

The Board of Governors of the Federal Reserve System is authorized and directed to enforce compliance with this section, and to prescribe such rules and regulations as it deems necessary for that purpose.

No person at the same time shall be a director in any two or more corporations, any one of which has capital, surplus, and undivided profits aggregating more than $1,000,000, engaged in whole or in part in commerce, other than banks, banking associations, trust companies, and common carriers subject to the Act to regulate commerce, approved February fourth, eighteen hundred and eighty-seven, if such corporations are or shall have been theretofore, by virtue of their business and location of operation, competitors, so that the elimination of competition by agreement between them would constitute a violation of any of the provisions of any of the antitrust laws. The eligibility of a director under the foregoing provision shall be determined by the aggregate amount of the capital, surplus, arid undivided profits, exclusive of dividends declared but not paid to stockholders, at the end of the fiscal year of said corporation next preceding the election of directors, and when a director has been elected in accordance with the provisions of this Act it shall be lawful for him to continue as such for one year thereafter.

When any person elected or chosen as a director or officer or selected as an employee of any bank or other corporation subject to the provisions of this Act is eligible at the time of his election or selection to act for such bank or other corporation in such capacity his eligibility to act in such capacity shall not be affected and he shall not become or be deemed amenable to any of the provisions hereof by reason of any change in the affairs of such bank or other corporation from whatsoever cause, whether specifically excepted by any of the provisions hereof or not, until the expiration of one year from the date of his election or employment.

The Federal Trade Commission Act (Excerpts)

Section 5. Unfair Methods of Competition Unlawful; Prevention by Commission — Declaration of Unlawfulness; Power to Prohibit Unfair Practices

(a)(1) Unfair methods of competition in or affecting commerce, and unfair or deceptive acts or practices in or affecting commerce, are declared unlawful.

Penalty for Violation of Order, Injunctions and Other Appropriate Equitable Relief. (1) Any person, partnership, or corporation who violates an order of the Commission after it has become final, and while such order is in effect, shall forfeit and pay to the United States a civil penalty of not more than $10,000 for each violation, which shall accrue to the United States and may be recovered in a civil action brought by the Attorney General of the United States. Each separate violation of such an order shall be a separate offense, except that in the case of a violation through continuing failure to obey or neglect to obey a final order of the Commission, each day of continuance of such failure or neglect shall be deemed a separate offense. In such actions, the United States district courts are empowered to grant mandatory injunctions and such other and further equitable relief as they deem appropriate in the enforcement of such final orders of the Commission.

The National Labor Relations Act (Excerpts)

National Labor Relations Board

Section 3. (a) The National Labor Relations Board (hereinafter called the "Board") created by this Act prior to its amendment by the Labor Management Relations Act 1947 is hereby continued as an agency of the United States, except that the Board shall consist of five instead of three members, appointed by the President by and with the advice and consent of the Senate. Of the two additional members so provided for, one shall be appointed for a term of five years and the other for a term of two years. Their successors, and the successors of the other members, shall be appointed for terms of five years each, excepting that any individual chosen to fill a vacancy shall be appointed only for the unexpired term of the member whom he shall succeed. The President shall designate one member to serve as Chairman of the Board. Any member of the Board may be removed by the President, upon notice and hearing, for neglect of duty or malfeasance in office, but for no other cause.

Section 6. The Board shall have authority from time to time to make, amend, and rescind, in the manner prescribed by the Administrative Procedure Act, such rules and regulations as may be necessary to carry out the provisions of this Act.

Rights of Employees

Section 7. Employees shall have the right to self organization, to form, join, or assist labor organizations, to bargain collectively through representatives of their own choosing, and to engage in other concerted activities for the purpose of collective bargaining or other mutual aid or protection, and shall also have the right to refrain from any or all of such activities except to the extent that such right may be affected by an agreement requiring membership in a labor organization as a condition of employment as authorized in section 8(a)(3).

Unfair Labor Practices

Section 8. (a) It shall be an unfair labor practice for an employer—

(1) to interfere with, restrain, or coerce employees in the exercise of the rights guaranteed in section 7;

(2) to dominate or interfere with the formation or administration of any labor orga-

nization or contribute financial or other support to it: Provided, That subject to rules and regulations made and published by the Board pursuant to section 6, an employer shall not be prohibited from permitting employees to confer with him during working hours without loss of time or pay;

(3) by discrimination in regard to hire or tenure of employment or any term or condition of employment to encourage or discourage membership in any labor organization: Provided, That nothing in this Act, or in any other statute of the United States, shall preclude an employer from making an agreement with a labor organization (not established, maintained, or assisted by any action defined in section 8(a) of this Act as an unfair labor practice) to require as a condition of employment membership therein on or after the thirtieth day following the beginning of such employment or the effective date of such agreement, whichever is the later, (i) if such labor organization is the representative of the employees as provided in section 9(a), in the appropriate collective-bargaining unit covered by such agreement when made, and (ii) unless following an election held as provided in section 9(e) within one year preceding the effective date of such agreement, the Board shall have certified that at least a majority of the employees eligible to vote in such election have voted to rescind the authority of such labor organization to make such an agreement: Provided further, That no employer shall justify any discrimination against an employee for nonmembership in a labor organization (A) if he has reasonable grounds for believing that such membership was not available to the employee on the same terms and conditions generally applicable to other members, or (B) if he has reasonable grounds for believing that membership was denied or terminated for reasons other than the failure of the employee to render the pe-

riodic dues and the initiation fee uniformly required as a condition of acquiring or retaining membership;

(4) to discharge or otherwise discriminate against an employee because he has filed charges or given testimony under this Act;

(5) to refuse to bargain collectively with the representatives of his employees, subject to the provisions of section 9(a).

(b) It shall be unfair labor practice for a labor organization or its agents—

(1) to restrain or coerce (A) employees in the exercise of the rights guaranteed in section 7: Provided, That this paragraph shall not impair the right of a labor organization to prescribe its own rules with respect to the acquisition or retention of membership therein; or (b) an employer in the selection of his representatives for the purposes of collective bargaining or the adjustment of grievances;

(2) to cause or attempt to cause an employer to discriminate against an employee in violation of subsection (a)(3) or to discriminate against an employee with respect to whom membership in such organization has been denied or terminated on some ground other than his failure to tender the periodic dues and the initiation fees uniformly required as a condition of acquiring or retaining membership;

(3) to refuse to bargain collectively with an employer, provided it is the representative of his employees subject to the provisions of section 9(a);

(4)(i) to engage in, or to induce or encourage any individual employed by any person engaged in commerce or in an industry affecting commerce to engage in, a strike or a refusal in the course of his employment to use, manufacture, process, transport, or otherwise handle or work on any goods, articles, materials, or commodities or to perform any services; or (ii) to threaten, coerce, or restrain any person engaged in commerce or in an industry affecting commerce, where in either case an object thereof is:

(A) forcing or requiring any employer or self-employed person to join any labor or employer organization or to enter into any agreement which is prohibited by section 8(e);

(B) forcing or requiring any person to cease using, selling, handling, transporting, or otherwise dealing in the product of any other producer, processor, or manufacturer, or to cease doing business with any other person, or forcing or requiring any other employer to recognize or bargain with a labor organization as the representative of his employees unless such labor organization has been certified as the representative of such employees under the provisions of section 9: Provided, That nothing contained in this clause (B) shall be construed to make unlawful, where not otherwise unlawful, any primary strike or primary picketing;

(C) forcing or requiring any employer to recognize or bargain with a particular labor organization as the representative of his employees if another labor organization has been certified as the representative of such employees under the provisions of section 9;

(D) forcing or requiring any employer to assign particular work to employees in a particular labor organization or in a particular trade, craft, or class rather than to employees in another labor organization or in another trade, craft, or class, unless such employer is failing to conform to an order or certification of the Board determining the bargaining representative for employees performing such work:

Provided, That nothing in this subsection (b) shall be construed to make unlawful a refusal by any person to enter upon the premises of any employer (other than his own employer), if the employees of such employer are engaged in a strike ratified or approved by a representative of such employees whom such employer is required to recognize under this Act: Provided further, That for the purposes of this paragraph (4) only, nothing contained in such paragraph shall be construed to prohibit publicity, other than picketing, for the purpose of truthfully advising the public, including consumers and members of a labor organization, that a product or products are produced by an employer with whom the labor organization has a primary dispute and are distributed by another employer, as long as such publicity does not have an effect of inducing any individual employed by any person other than the primary employer in the course of his employment to refuse to pick up, deliver, or transport any goods, or not to perform any services, at the establishment of the employer engaged in such distribution;

(5) to require of employees covered by an agreement authorized under subsection (a)(3) the payment, as a condition precedent to becoming a member of such organization, of a fee in an amount which the Board finds excessive or discriminatory under all the circumstances In making such a finding, the Board shall consider, among other relevant factors, the practices and customs of labor organizations in the particular industry, and the wages currently paid to the employees affected;

(6) to cause or attempt to cause an employee to pay or deliver or agree to pay or deliver any money or other thing of value, in the nature of an exaction, for services which are not performed or not to be performed; and

(7) to picket or cause to be picketed, or threaten to picket or cause to be picketed, any employer where an object thereof is forcing or requiring an employer to recognize or bargain with a labor organization as the representative of his employees, or forc-

ing or requiring the employees of an employer to accept or select such labor organization as their collective bargaining representative, unless such labor organization is currently certified as the representative of such employees:

(A) where the employer has lawfully recognized in accordance with this Act any other labor organization and a question concerning representation may not appropriately be raised under section 9(c) of this Act,

(B) where within the preceding twelve months a valid election under section 9(c) of this Act has been conducted, or

(C) where such picketing has been conducted without a petition under section 9(c) being filed within a reasonable period of time not to exceed thirty days from the commencement of such picketing; Provided, That when such a petition has been filed the Board shall forthwith, without regard to the provisions of section 9(c)(1) or the absence of a showing of a substantial interest on the part of the labor organization, direct an election in such unit as the Board finds to be appropriate and shall certify the results thereof: Provided further, That nothing in this subparagraph (C) shall be construed to prohibit any picketing or other publicity for the purpose of truthfully advising the public (including consumers) that an employer does not employ members of, or have a contract with, a labor organization, unless an effect of such picketing is to induce any individual employed by any other person in the course of his employment, not to pick up, deliver or transport any goods or not to perform any services.

Nothing in this paragraph (7) shall be construed to permit any act which would otherwise be an unfair labor practice under this section 8(b).

(c) The expressing of any views, argument, or opinion, or the dissemination thereof, whether in written, printed, graphic, or visual form, shall not constitute or be evidence of an unfair labor practice under any of the provisions of this Act; if such expression contains no threat of reprisal or force or promise of benefit.

(d) For the purposes of this section, to bargain collectively is the performance of the mutual obligation of the employer and the representative of the employees to meet at reasonable times and confer in good faith with respect to wages, hours, and other terms and conditions of employment, or the negotiation of an agreement, or any question arising thereunder, and the execution of a written contract incorporating any agreement reached if requested by either party, but such obligation does not compel either party to agree to a proposal or require the making of a concession: Provided, That where there is in effect a collective-bargaining contract covering employees in an industry affecting commerce, the duty to bargain collectively shall also mean that no party to such contract shall terminate or modify such contract, unless the party desiring such termination or modification—

(1) serves a written notice upon the other party to the contract of the proposed termination or modification sixty days prior to the expiration date thereof, or in the event such contract contains no expiration date, sixty days prior to the time it is proposed to make such termination or modification;

(2) offers to meet and confer with the other party for the purpose of negotiating a new contract or a contract containing the proposed modifications;

(3) notifies the Federal Mediation and Conciliation Service within thirty days after such notice of the existence of a dispute, and simultaneously therewith notifies any State or Territorial agency established to mediate and conciliate disputes within the State or Territory where the dispute occurred, pro-

vided no agreement has been reached by that time; and

(4) continues in full force and effect, without resorting to strike or lockout, all the terms and conditions of the existing contract for a period of sixty days after such notice is given or until the expiration date of such contract, whichever occurs later:

The duties imposed upon employers, employees, an labor organizations by paragraphs (2), (3), and (4) shall become inapplicable upon an intervening certification of the Board, under which the labor organization or individual, which is a party to the contract, has been superseded as or ceased to be the representative of the employees subject to the provisions of section 9(a), and the duties so imposed shall not be construed as requiring either party to discuss or agree to any modification of the terms and conditions contained in a contract for a fixed period, if such modification it to become effective before such terms and conditions can be reopened under the provisions of the contract. Any employee who engages in any strike within the appropriate period specified in subsection (g) of this section shall lose his status as an employee of the employer engaged in the particular labor dispute, for the purposes of sections 8, 9, and 10 of this Act, as amended, but such loss of status for such employee shall terminate if and when he is reemployed by such employer. Whenever the collective bargaining involves employees of a health care institution, the provisions of this section 8(d) shall be modified as follows:

(A) The notice of section 8(d)(1) shall be ninety days; the notice of section 8(d)(3) shall be sixty days; and the contract period of section 8(d)(4) shall be ninety days;

(B) Where the bargaining is for an initial agreement following certification or recognition, at least thirty days' notice of the existence of a dispute shall be given by the labor organization to the agencies set forth in section 8(d)(3).

(C) After notice is given to the Federal Mediation and Conciliation Service under ether clause (A) or (B) of this sentence, the Service shall promptly communicate with the parties and use its best efforts, by mediation and conciliation, to bring them to agreement. The parties shall participate fully and promptly in such meetings as may be undertaken by the Service for the purpose of aiding in a settlement of the dispute.

(e) It shall be an unfair labor practice for any labor organization and any employer to enter into any contract or agreement, express or implied, whereby such employer ceases or refrains or agrees to cease or refrain from handling, using, selling, transporting or otherwise dealing in any of the products of any other employer, or to cease doing business with any other person, and any contract or agreement entered into heretofore or hereafter containing such an agreement shall be to such extent unenforceable and void: Provided, That nothing in this subsection (e) shall apply to an agreement between a labor organization and an employer in the construction industry relating to the contracting or subcontracting of work to be done at the site of the construction, alteration, painting, or repair of a building, structure, or other work: Provided further, That for the purposes of this subsection (e) and section 8(b)(4)(B) the terms "any employer," "any person engaged in commerce or in industry affecting commerce," and "any person" when used in relation to the terms "any other producer, processor, or manufacturer," "any other employer," or "any other person" shall not include persons in the relation of a jobber, manufacturer, contractor, or subcontractor working on the goods or premises of the jobber or manufacturer or performing parts of an integrated process of production in the apparel and clothing industry: Provided further, That nothing in this Act shall prohibit the enforcement of any agreement which it within the foregoing exception.

(f) It shall not be an unfair labor practice under subsections (a) and (b) of this section for an employee engaged primarily in the building and construction industry to make an agreement covering employees engaged (or who, upon their employment, will be engaged) in the building and construction industry with a labor organization of which building and construction employees are members (not established, maintained, or assisted by any action defined in section 8(a) of this Act as an unfair labor practice) because (1) the majority status of such labor organization has not been established under the provisions of section 9 of this Act prior to the making of such agreement, or (2) such agreement requires at a condition of employment, membership in such labor organization after the seventh day following the beginning of which employment or the effective date of the agreement, whichever is later, or (3) such agreement requires the employer to notify which labor organization of opportunities for employment with such employer, or gives which labor organization

an opportunity to refer qualified applicants for such employment, or (4) such agreement specifies minimum training or experience qualifications for employment or provides for priority in opportunities for employment based upon length of service with such employer, in the industry or in the particular geographical area: Provided, That nothing in this subsection shall set aside the final proviso to section 8(a)(3) of this Act: Provided further, That any agreement which would be invalid, but for clause (1) of this subsection, shall not be a bar to a petition filed pursuant to section 9(c) or 9(3).

(g) A labor organization before engaging in any strike, picketing, or other concerted refusal to work at any health care institution shall, not less than ten days prior to such action, notify the institution in writing and the Federal Mediation and Conciliation Service of that intention, except that in the case of bargaining for an initial agreement following certification or recognition the notice required by this subsection shall not be given until the expiration of the period specified in clause (B) of the last sentence of section 8(d) of this Act. The notice shall state the date and time that such action will commence. The notice, once given, may be extended by the written agreement of both parties.

Index of Court Cases

---

*Indicates case is excerpted; all other cases are discussed in the body of the text.

Subject Index